For Our Teachers

THE JEWS
A History

JOHN EFRON
University of California, Berkeley

STEVEN WEITZMAN
Indiana University

MATTHIAS LEHMANN
Indiana University

JOSHUA HOLO
Hebrew Union College

PEARSON
Prentice
Hall

Upper Saddle River, New Jersey 07458

Library of Congress Cataloging-in-Publication Data

The Jew : a history / John Efron . . . [et al.].—1st ed.
    p. cm.
  Includes index.
  ISBN-13: 978-0-13-178687-5
  ISBN-10: 0-13-178687-3
  1. Jews—History. 2. Judaism—History. I. Efron, John M.
  DS117.J424 2009
  909'.04924—dc22

                    2008010849

VP/Publisher: Priscilla McGeehon
Executive Editor: Charles Cavaliere
Editorial Assistant: Lauren Aylward
Marketing Manager: Laura Lee Manley
Marketing Assistant: Athena Moore
Managing Editor (Production): Lisa Iarkowski
Project Manager: Marianne Peters-Riordan
Senior Operations Specialist: Mary Ann Gloriande
Cover Art Director: Jayne Conte
Cover Design: Bruce Kenselaar
Cover Photos: Andrian Andrusier/SA'AR YA'ACOV/© The National Museum of Bosnia and Herzegovina
AV Project Manager: Mirella Signoretto
Director, Image Resource Center: Melinda Patelli
Manager, Rights and Permissions: Zina Arabia
Manager, Visual Research: Beth Brenzel
Manager, Cover Visual Research & Permissions: Karen Sanatar
Image Permission Coordinator: Debbie Hewitson
Photo Researcher: Susan Kaprov
Composition/Full-Service Project Management: Aptara®, Inc./Puneet Lamba
Printer/Binder: Hamilton Printing Company
Cover Printer: Coral Graphics Services Inc.

Credits and acknowledgments borrowed from other sources and reproduced, with permission, in this textbook appear on appropriate page within text or on pages TC-1, PC-1, MC-1.

Pearson Education LTD., London
Pearson Education Singapore, Pte. Ltd
Pearson Education, Canada, Ltd
Pearson Education–Japan
Pearson Education Australia PTY, Limited

Pearson Education North Asia Ltd
Pearson Educación de Mexico, S.A. de C.V.
Pearson Education Malaysia, Pte. Ltd
Pearson Education, Upper Saddle River, New Jersey

10 9 8 7 6 5 4 3
ISBN-13: 978-0-13-178687-5
ISBN-10: 0-13-178687-3

Contents

Chapter 3   *Jews and Greeks*   49

Chapter 4   *Between Caesar and God*   70

Chapter 5   *Rabbinic Revelations*   92

Chapter 6   **Under the Crescent**   *116*

Chapter 7   **Under the Cross**   *147*

Chapter 13   *A World Upended*   334

Chapter 14   *The Holocaust*   374

Preface

The book you are about to read—a comprehensive history of the Jewish people—is itself the work of a specific historical era. The first attempt since antiquity to write a history of the Jews was that of the Frenchman Jacques Christian Basnage, whose five-volume *History of the Religion of the Jews Since Jesus Christ to the Present* appeared between 1706 and 1711. It would be three decades before a second effort would appear when, in 1742, the Danish author and playwright Ludvig Holberg published his sympathetic work entitled *Jewish History*. Both Basnage and Holberg were Christians. It would be an even longer wait for a historian to emerge from among the Jewish people. In 1820, Isaac Marcus Jost, a German Jew, published the first volume of his ten-volume *History of the Israelites from the Maccabean Period to Our Own Day*. Given the vast scope of his project and the critical methods that he employed, Jost is duly entitled to be called the first modern historian of the Jewish people. The present book, however different its twenty-first-century approach to its subject matter is from that of nineteenth-century predecessors, is at its core the work of the same historical consciousness and intellectual orientation that led scholars like Jost to believe it possible to understand Jewish history with the methods and kinds of evidence that scholars used to reconstruct the histories of other peoples.

What led historians, especially Jewish ones, to write a history of the Jews, and why did it take so long for them to do so? The answer is complex, but it boils down to this: Modern historiography is tied to the rise of nationalism in the nineteenth century, an instrument by which the French, the Germans, and other peoples defined and justified their emerging collective identity as sovereign political communities. Because Jews did not conform to the modern understanding of nationhood—they were a people

without a common territory and a common language—it was thought, even by many Jews, that there was no Jewish history to write. Indeed, to some, Jewish culture seemed entirely static, lacking the capacity to change and innovate, thus preserving in petrified form a religious life inherited from biblical times. As such, Jews seemed to exist outside of normative historical development. Change, the engine of history, did not seem to feature in Jewish life. Prominent philosophers such as Kant and Hegel, for example, referred to Judaism as a "fossil" religion. Over the course of the nineteenth century, however, Jews too began to see themselves in national terms, and with that perception came the idea that, like other peoples, they had a history—one worthy of being recorded.

The notion that the Jews are a group with a national identity was also tied to the increased secularization of European and Jewish culture, which seemed to undercut the idea that the Jews should only be defined as a community of faith. When, over the course of the nineteenth century, the Jews were considered by historians as a social group, they were seen to encompass a much broader spectrum of people—believers and nonbelievers; left-wingers, right-wingers, and centrists; capitalists and communists; rural Jews and urban ones; Jews from every country and, crucially, from every epoch. Modern attempts to write comprehensive histories of the Jews, have tried to account for the variety of Jewish identities and cultures, crossing political, religious, and linguistic boundaries. Indeed, Jewish historiography itself reflected this variety. General histories of the Jews have been written in German, French, Russian, Yiddish, Hebrew, English, and many other languages, and from a dizzying array of ideological perspectives ranging from orthodox Marxism to ultra-Orthodox Judaism. This book represents another link in the chain of this historiographical tradition. Our goal, like that of earlier attempts, has been to recount Jewish history from its ancient Israelite origins to the recent past in a way that captures the religious, cultural, social, and economic diversity of Jewish life.

But while our book ultimately derives from a nineteenth-century project, it also reflects more recent intellectual currents. After all, our knowledge of the past is always changing in light of new evidence and new approaches, and we have tried to take account of those changes in our narrative. New research—recent archaeological excavation in Israel and elsewhere, the discovery and publication of previously unknown texts from the ancient and medieval periods, feminist scholarship, the opening of archives in the former Soviet Union and its satellites, a new attentiveness to Jewish life in Muslim lands, revisions in Israeli historiography, and many other developments—have conspired to unsettle many established ideas about the Jewish past, challenging how historians have thought about and described it, and sometimes making it appear less accessible than it was thought to be in earlier generations.

While all these recent developments have made the writing of Jewish history more complicated than before, we also believe that they have both deepened and broadened our understanding of that history. For one thing, the reader will find throughout this book topics neglected or insufficiently covered in earlier accounts. Our narrative includes many familiar names: Moses, Jeremiah, Hillel, Rashi, Maimonides, Spinoza, Freud, Einstein, Sholem Aleichem, and Golda Meir, but in its pages will also be found a broader range of people: mothers, children, workers, students, artists, and radicals whose perspectives greatly expand our story. So too, while one will find here accounts of the Exodus, the Babylonian Exile, the Spanish Expulsion, the Holocaust, and other monumental events, we recognize that historical experience unfolds in many different registers and thus have tried to include in our account descriptions not just of transformative but the quotidian moments that make up everyday life as well.

To help those who are trying to learn Jewish history, or teach it, we have added a number of features that we hope make our subject more user friendly than it has been in other accounts. Each chapter contains supplemental boxes that discuss high-interest topics (Where does God come from? Did Someone Conspire to Cover up the Dead Sea Scrolls? The Koran and the Jews, Rebelling Against Jewish Suburbia); geographic and thematic maps; and questions for reflection. A timeline of Jewish history and three sets of color plates provide a visual record of Jewish history, and detailed captions accompany both color and black-and-white illustrations. A glossary of key terms is included for convenient reference.

Recent historiography often stresses the localized character of Jewish culture, the varied ways in which it has developed in specific settings. Indeed, some scholars now prefer to speak of Jewish cultures, in the plural, as a way of resisting generalizations about Jewish experience. We respect that position and have tried to register the localized nature of Jewish experience in our narrative, but we believe we would be missing something about Jewish culture if we did not also factor into our account the perception of many Jews that they were part of something larger than their local communities, a people or nation or religion defined by shared memories, texts, traditions, and destiny. It is ultimately this perception that justifies a single account of the Jewish people, as opposed to dozens of microhistories of more local Jewish communities, though they too are of great value.

This is not to suggest that Jewish history can be clearly distinguished from that of the other cultures with which it has interacted—ancient Near Eastern, Greek, Roman, Christian, Islamic, modern, and so forth. All these categories are but modern approximations of a much more complex historical reality, sometimes obscuring continuities between cultures. Some recent scholars have challenged boundaries like that between Judaism and Christianity, or stressed the degree of interaction between Jewish and non-Jewish culture; indeed, a case can be made that Jewishness is not so much a distinct culture but simply a position, a particular orientation, within much larger cultures. However, we do not see Jewish life as merely an echo of was happening around it, or Jews themselves as passive recipients of influences stemming from a larger majority culture. Without ignoring the porous boundaries and continuous traffic between Jewish and non-Jewish culture, we have tried to capture the agency of Jews *as Jews* within the larger cultural environments in which they lived and operated, not simply how they have adapted to or mirrored those environments but how they have maneuvered within them and enlisted elements drawn from the larger culture for their own religious, cultural, or social ends. We have also been mindful of the process whereby Jews have rejected elements of the larger culture and how creative tension has emerged at the intersecting point of acceptance and rejection of non-Jewish cultures.

We are all too aware that we inevitably distort and oversimplify reality by trying to distill Jewish historical experience into a single coherent and digestible narrative—

we doubt that even a multivolume narrative would have avoided these pitfalls—and therefore we have tried where possible to both problematize and ramify our account of the past, raising methodological issues, introducing historiographical debates, and following the distinct trajectories of different local communities. As mindful as we are of how quixotic it may be to attempt a history such as this, our effort is rooted in the conviction that Jewish history is knowable, tellable, and ultimately teachable, and we have shaped our account accordingly.

One problem that especially vexed us, however, was the question of where precisely to end our presentation. (A proper starting point was no simple matter either.) We have found that any of the historical developments of the last three decades by which we might close our account— the settlement of the West Bank and Gaza after the Six-Day War, the impact of Jewish feminism and the ordination of women as rabbis, the fall of the Soviet Union and the Jewish immigration it unleashed, the emergence of the Jewish Renewal movement in America, postmodernist Jewish thought, Palestinian uprisings in the territories, the Oslo peace process, the assassination of Yitzhak Rabin, the creation of a Jewish Internet culture, the recent resurgence of antisemitism in Europe and the Muslim world, the surprising revitalization of Jewish life in Germany, the debate over the inclusion of gays and lesbians in Jewish religious life, and so on—would likely convey to readers something about the meaning and direction of Jewish history that we do not intend to communicate. Not only do we lack the ability to forecast the future, the present moment seems very opaque to us as well—a confusing entanglement of different personalities, trends, and forces that we cannot fully unravel—and we therefore had a difficult time isolating out from the present what events or developments are most important for understanding the course of Jewish history from here on. We never did find a solution to this problem, but we have concluded that a lack of a definitive ending is not a bad problem to have since it reminds us that the Jews, whatever their present state and whatever their future, are not yet a thing of the past.

Acknowledgments

The authors have benefited enormously from the expertise and generosity of Zachary Baker, Amos Bitzan, Michael Brenner, Javier Castaño, Simeon Chavel, Chaya Halberstam, Shaun Halper, Paul Hamburg, Bert Harrill, Kathleeen Karcher, Puneet Lamba, Steven M. Lowenstein, Shaul Magid, Derek Penslar, Marianne Peters-Riordan, Aron Rodrigue, Heath Lynn Silberfeld, Yuri Slezkine, Brad Storin, Mira Wasserman, the students of Indiana University's "Introduction to Jewish History" course, and those participating in the graduate seminar, "Modern Jewish Historiography," at the University of California at Berkeley.

The authors would also like to thank David Myers, University of California, Los Angeles; Marsha Rozenblit, University of Maryland; Stephen G. Burnett, University of Nebraska, Lincoln; Glenn Dynner, Franklin and Marshall College; Howard Lupovitch, Colby College; Benjamin Sommer, Northwestern University; Ronald Hendel, University of California, Berkeley; Jeffrey Veidlinger, Indiana University; Saul M. Olyan, Brown University; Hindy Najman, University of Toronto; Olga Litvak, Clark University; David Graizbord, University of Arizona; Robert Chazen, New York University; ChaeRan Freeze, Brandeis University; Daniel Schroeter, University of California, Irvine; Elisheva Carlebach, Queens College; and Executive Editor at Pearson/Prentice Hall, the ever-gracious Charles Cavaliere.

List of Maps

List of Color Plates

Note on Spellings and Transliteration

The spellings of many place names that appear in the history of the Jews have multiple variants, reflecting the different languages spoken by the people who inhabited them. In cases such as Vilna/Wilno/Vilnius (the modern-day capital of Lithuania), we have chosen the name used by the place's Jewish inhabitants. Wherever possible, the authors have transliterated Hebrew terms using those forms most familiar to them and to lay readers.

These forms may occasionally vary from chapter to chapter because they originate with different authors. Yiddish words typically follow the YIVO system of transliteration. Hebrew expressions less familiar to non-specialists are transliterated to ensure accurate pronunciation of the words. We have followed a similar procedure for terms drawn from other languages, such as Greek and Arabic.

About the Authors

John Efron (chs. 10–15) holds the Koret Chair in Jewish History at the University of California, Berkeley, where he is a specialist in the cultural and social history of German Jewry. A native of Melbourne, Australia, he has a B.A. from Monash University in Melbourne, has studied at the Hebrew University in Jerusalem, took his M.A. at New York University, and earned a Ph.D. at Columbia University.

In addition to many articles, most recently dealing with Jewish popular culture, his books include *Medicine and the German Jews: A History* (Yale University Press, 2001); and *Defenders of the Race: Jewish Doctors and Race Science in Fin-de-Siècle Europe* (Yale University Press, 1994). He also co-edited the volume *Jewish History and Jewish Memory: Essays in Honor of Yosef Hayim Yerushalmi* (University Press of New England, 1998). He is now working on a monograph entitled *Orientalism and the German Jews in the Age of Emancipation*.

Steven Weitzman (chs. 1–5), the Irving M. Glazer Chair of Jewish Studies at Indiana University, is a scholar of the Hebrew Bible and early Jewish texts, such as the Dead Sea Scrolls. His first book, *Song and Story in Biblical Narrative*, was the winner of the Gustave O. Arlt Prize for Outstanding Scholar-ship in the Humanities. Other publications include *Surviving Sacrilege* (Harvard University Press, 2005) and *Religion and the Self in Antiquity*, edited with David Brakke and Michael Satlow (Indiana University Press, 2005).

Matthias B. Lehmann (chs. 8–9) is a historian of early modern and modern Jewish history, with a special interest in the history of the Spanish Jews and the Sephardi Diaspora in the Mediterranean world. After studying in Freiburg, Jerusalem, Berlin, and Madrid, he earned his Ph.D. from Freie Universität Berlin in 2002 and is an associate professor of history and Jewish studies at Indiana University. He is the author of *Ladino Rabbinic Literature and Ottoman Sephardic Culture* (Indiana University Press, 2005), runner-up for the National Jewish Book Award in 2006. His articles have appeared in *Jewish History, Jewish Social Studies, Sefarad,* and *Jewish Studies Quarterly.* He is currently working on a book entitled *Networks of Benevolence:* Philanthropy and Identity in the Sephardi Diaspora, which looks at rabbinic networks and networks of support for the Jewish communities of Palestine in the Sephardi Diaspora in the eighteenth and nineteenth centuries.

Joshua Holo (chs. 6–7) is Associate Professor of Jewish History and Director, Louchheim School of Judaic Studies at the Hebrew Union College–Jewish Institute of Religion in Los Angeles. He has published on the Jews in Byzantium, Italy, and Spain in the medieval period, including *The Jews of Byzantium in the Mediterranean Economy* (forthcoming from Cambridge University Press), and a number of articles ranging from Genizah studies to intellectual history. He curated an exhibition of Spanish Hebrew documents and inscriptions in Valencia, Spain, and edited the scholarly catalogue *Los judíos españoles según las Fuentes hebreas.* He is currently investigating the German-Jewish community of Venice and the founding of the first ghetto in the sixteenth century, while continuing his work on the Jews of Byzantium.

Chapter 1

Ancient Israel
and Other Ancestors

Before we can begin a history of the Jewish people, we must decide when exactly to begin it, and it is not easy to commit oneself to a particular starting point. Jews themselves have long believed their history begins with the patriarchs of Genesis and the Exodus from Egypt in the age described by the Hebrew Bible. The people described in much of the Bible are not Jews, however, but Israelites, whose culture differs from that of later Jews in many ways. For this reason, many scholars place the beginnings of Jewish history at the end of the period described by the Hebrew Bible, in the wake of the Babylonian exile in 586 BCE. Some place it later, after the conquests of Alexander the Great in the fourth century BCE, and some still later, in the age that produced Christianity and Islam. Depending on who one believes, Jewish history can span 4,000 or 3,000 or even fewer than 2,000 years, and the difference all comes down to where to start.

One reason it is difficult to fix a clear starting point for Jewish history is that it is not clear what *Jewish* means exactly and how it relates to or differs from overlapping terms used in the Bible, such as *Israelite* and *Hebrew.* The term *Jew* derives from the name "Judah" or *Yehuda,* but even in the Hebrew Bible that term has several possible meanings, referring to an Israelite tribe, to a territory in the southern part of Canaan, and also to the kingdom based in this territory and ruled by David and his descendants. After the end of the biblical period, the terms *Judean* and *Jewish* acquired still other connotations, coming to signify a particular way of life or adherence to particular beliefs. The term's ambiguity continues to this day, with *Jewish* signifying a religion for some, for others a cultural or ethnic identity that may not be religious in orientation, and for still others a national identity such as French, Turkish, or American. To fix a single starting point for "Jewish" history would commit us to a specific definition of Jewishness at the expense of other definitions that also have merit.

Still, we must begin somewhere, and this book has opted to begin where Jews themselves have long looked to understand their origins, with "history" as described in the Hebrew Bible. We put the word *history* in quotes here because it is not clear that the biblical account corresponds to what most of us mean by history: the past as it actually happened. Modern scholarship has expressed doubts about the Hebrew Bible's value as a historical document, questioning whether the people described in the Bible, such as Abraham and Moses, really existed and whether key events, such as the Exodus and the revelation at Mount Sinai, really occurred. Answers to these questions have outraged some Jews and Christians, coming into conflict with their belief in the Bible as an accurate account of how reality works, but some reasons for scholars' skepticism cannot be dismissed out of hand and constitute evidence we must reckon with in our pursuit of the Jewish people's origins. Mindful of this evidence, one of our goals in this chapter is to open the question of what really happened, to ask whether the Hebrew Bible's account of Israel's history—its stories of Abraham and his family, the exodus from Egypt, Joshua's conquest of the land of Canaan, the rule of King David, and so on—correspond to the past as reconstructed by modern historians and archaeologists.

Even as we question the biblical account, however, we will also try to provide a sense of how it tells the story of ancient Israel because, whether or not that description is historically accurate, it is crucial for understanding the development of Jewish culture. For one thing, Jewish culture did not suddenly appear one day; it evolved out of an earlier Israelite culture from which it inherited beliefs, practices, language(s), texts, and patterns of social organization. We have to be wary of what the historian

Marc Bloch calls the "idolatry of origins," of overestimating what we can learn about Jewish culture by going back to ancient Israel, but that does not mean we cannot learn many things. Why do Jews worship God? Why are Canaan and Jerusalem so central in Jewish culture? What are the origins of Jewish religious practices such as circumcision, the Sabbath rest, and keeping kosher? Why are today's Jews the descendants only of the tribe of Judah, and not of Reuben, Simeon, Gad, and other Israelite tribes mentioned in the Bible? These questions cannot be answered without referring to pre–Jewish Israelite culture, and biblical literature is our richest source for understanding that culture.

A second reason for beginning with the Bible is that the *perception* of the Bible as the starting point for Jewish history is a historical fact in its own right, and an important one for understanding Jewish identity. For the last 2,000 years at least, Jews have looked to the Hebrew Bible to understand who they are and how they are to behave. To this day, in fact, many Jews trace their lineage back to patriarchs such as Abraham and Jacob; during Passover, they recount the Exodus as if in Egypt themselves, and they celebrate Passover in the first place because they believe God commanded them to do so during the Exodus. Even if the Bible had no value whatsoever as a historical source (and the fact that what it says about history can be questioned does not mean that the Bible does not have great value for understanding Israelite history), it is important to know what it says about the past if only to better understand how Jews throughout the centuries have seen themselves.

Keeping both these points in mind, we have settled on not one but two starting points for Jewish history. The first is ancient Israelite history prior to the Babylonian exile in 586 BCE. Where did the Israelites come from, and what is the historical connection between them and later Jews? The present chapter will attempt to answer these questions by drawing on the Hebrew Bible, as well as other kinds of archaeological and literary evidence. Our review of Israelite history, a distillation of the insights and theories of modern biblical scholarship, will sometimes challenge what the Hebrew Bible says about the past and raise questions we cannot answer, but it will also mine the Bible for insights into ancient Israelite politics, religion, family life, and literary practice.

Our second starting point, and the focus of Chapter 2, is the emergence of the Hebrew Bible itself: Where does biblical literature come from, and how did it become so important to Jewish culture? It is no easier to answer these questions than it is to reconstruct ancient Israelite history, for there remains much uncertainty about who wrote the texts included in the Hebrew Bible, and when and why they were written. It is also unclear when these texts acquired the resonance and authority they would enjoy in later Jewish culture. Despite the many gaps in our knowledge, however, we can demonstrate that the emergence of the biblical canon marks a watershed moment in the transition from Israelite to Jewish culture; indeed, we will argue that the formation of Jewishness and the formation of the Hebrew Bible are inextricably intertwined.

Rethinking the Origins of the Ancient Israelites

For modern scholars who approach the Bible as a text composed by humans, nothing is sacred about the history it tells. Consider a story that may already be familiar to you: the Bible's account of how David defeated the Philistine Goliath:

> A champion came out of the Philistines' camp, Goliath was his name, from Gath, and his height was six cubits and a span. He had a helmut of bronze on his head, and was armed with a coat of mail; the weight of the coat was five thousand bronze shekels. He had greaves of bronze on his legs and a javelin of bronze slung between his shoulders. The shaft of his spear was like a weaver's beam, and his spear's head weighed six hundred shekels of iron.
>
> As the Philistine approached David, David ran quickly toward the battle line toward the Philistine. David put his hand in his bag, took from there a stone, slung it, and struck the Philistine on his forehead. The stone sank into his forehead, and he fell face down on the ground. So David triumphed over the Philistine with a sling and a stone, striking the Philistine and killing him. (1 Samuel 17:4–7, 48–50)

For thousands of years people have accepted this story as true, but is it historically accurate? Does it describe a battle that really happened or individuals who really lived? One reason for skepticism is the existence of a seemingly inconsistent reference to the defeat of Goliath tucked away in 2 Samuel:

> There was another battle with the Philistines at Gob; and Elhanan son of Jaareoregim, the Bethlehemite, struck Goliath the Gittite, the shaft of whose spear was like a weaver's beam. (2 Samuel 21:19)

Goliath is still the enemy here, described the same way as in the more famous version of the story (cf. 1 Samuel 17:7, "the shaft of his spear was like a weaver's beam"). The hero who slays Goliath is not the young shepherd David, however, but an otherwise obscure warrior named Elhanan. Interpreters have long tried to reconcile the discrepancy—maybe Elhanan was another name for David, some propose, ignoring the Bible's claim that he was David's servant, but another possibility has to be considered too: perhaps it is 2 Samuel 21 that records the name of the real slayer of Goliath, not David but the long forgotten Elhanan, and the more famous version of the story in 1 Samuel 16 is a later development, an attempt to boost King David's heroic image by giving him the credit for another man's victory.

Modern scholars raise such possibilities, not because they are hostile to God or to religion but because they are committed to a particular way of knowing reality that bases itself not on a passive acceptance of faith or tradition but on empirical evidence, unfettered questioning, and reasoned explanation. Like judges in a trial, the modern scholar wants to hear from multiple witnesses and to cross-examine them about how they know what they claim to know, before rendering a judgment about what happened.

From this perspective, what the Hebrew Bible says about reality becomes much more credible when other witnesses can back up its testimony, when other independent sources provide corroboration. Two possible sources of corroboration for ancient Israelite history are (1) written testimony composed independently of the Bible and (2) the discipline of archaeology, the retrieval and interpretation of physical evidence generated by the activities of earlier humans, such as pottery, the remnants of buildings, tools, weapons, jewelry, and so forth. The former includes inscriptions from Israel itself and texts from other ancient Near Eastern cultures that refer to Israel. Evidence from the latter sometimes confirms what the Bible says about history, but more frequently it challenges our sense of what really happened, or speaks to aspects of Israel's history, culture, or religion simply not reflected in biblical literature.

Partly because we know so little about ancient Israel, partly because we know so much, biblical scholarship today is marked by a lively and unresolved debate about what really happened in Israelite history. Some follow the biblical account more or less, but others have proposed alternative accounts of Israelite history that diverge from or even contradict the biblical account. These alternative reconstructions are invariably hypothetical, and you may not find them persuasive, but the most productive response in that instance is to develop another hypothesis that better accounts for the evidence.

Let us begin with the interrelated problems of *where* and *when* Israelite history begins. The Hebrew Bible acknowledges that people were living in **Canaan** well before the Israelites arrived there, and their existence has been confirmed by both literary and archaeological evidence (Canaan's settlement began long before the invention of writing, in fact, originating sometime in prehistory). From the Bible's perspective, though, these earlier pre-Israelite peoples, the **Canaanites,**

had lost their claim on the land when God transferred ownership to the Israelites. When did the Israelites themselves emerge? Did they come to inhabit the land in the way the Bible claims? What is their relationship to the earlier peoples and cultures known to have existed in Canaan prior to their arrival? (*See* Map 1-1.)

In our effort to answer these questions, we can latch on to at least one fairly solid fact: we can be virtually certain that the early Israelites were present in Canaan as early as the thirteenth century BCE because, in addition to the Hebrew Bible's testimony, a people known as Israel is mentioned in another source from this time, a victory hymn from the reign of the Egyptian king Merneptah (ca. 1213–1203 BCE) inscribed on a stela or stone slab. The relevant part of the inscription reads as follows:

> Plundered is the Canaan with every evil;
> Carried off is Ashkelon;
> Seized upon is Gezer;
> Yanoam is made as that which does not exist;
> *Israel is laid waste, his seed is not.*

The peoples listed here are various enemies defeated by Merneptah in the land of Canaan, including a people known as Israel, allegedly annihilated by the king (of course, had that claim been true, this book would have been a very short one). Beyond confirming that Israel lived in Canaan in the time of Merneptah, the inscription may also contain a clue about Israel's social organization. The Egyptians used special signs to indicate what kind of thing a word was, and the names "Ashkelon," "Gezer," and "Yanoam" in the inscription are all written with a sign that indicates they were city-states, whereas "Israel" is written with a sign used to signal a people or an ethnic group. The difference in signs may indicate that the early Israelites were a rural or nomadic people without the connection to a city that defines the other peoples listed in the hymn.

But who is this Israel, and from where did it come? No sources exist for Israel's history before Merneptah outside of the Hebrew Bible itself, and scholars debate the degree to which we can rely on the biblical account of Israel's origins. As the Bible depicts events, the Israelites did not begin as Canaanites but originated as outsiders to the land who migrated to Canaan from abroad. Genesis traces the Israelites' ancestry back to a single person named **Abraham** who is said to have traveled with his wife **Sarah** to Canaan at God's behest from a region between the Tigris and the Euphrates Rivers referred to by later Greek authors as **Mesopotamia** (from the Greek for "between the rivers"), a region located in present-day Iraq and Syria. Abraham and his family retain their sense of connection to Mesopotamia even after they settle in Canaan. When it

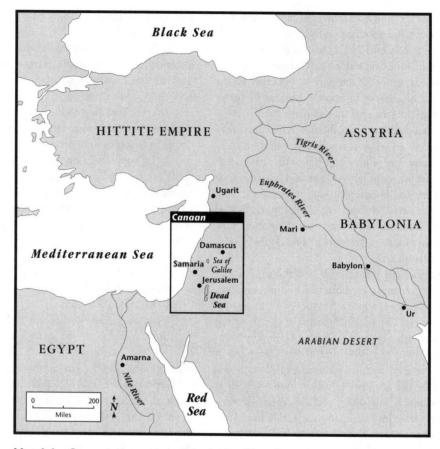

Map 1-1   Canaan in the context of the Ancient Near East.

comes time to find a wife for his son **Isaac,** for example, Abraham shuns the Canaanites and sends his servant back to Mesopotamia where the servant meets Rebecca, the woman who will marry Isaac. That is also where Abraham's grandson **Jacob,** or **Israel** as he would come to be known, finds his two wives, **Leah** and **Rachel.** According to the Bible, in other words, the Israelites are not Canaanites; they are immigrants from Mesopotamia who retain a sense of connection to their homeland long after they leave it.

If true, this would help us to integrate Israel's origins into ancient Near Eastern history. Mesopotamia was host to a succession of civilizations, including the Sumerians, one of the earliest civilizations in the world, and the Assyrians and Babylonians, who play a major role in later biblical history. Mesopotamia was home to some of the earliest cities of the Near East, including Ur, probably the very city mentioned in Genesis 12 as the birthplace of Abraham, and Babylon, the ill-fated Babel described in Genesis 11. It may also have been where writing was invented, and it is this invention that allows

us to know so much about Mesopotamian society, religion, and literature, including—as scholars first recognized in the nineteenth century—the ways in which these resemble Israelite society, religion, and literature. Among the Mesopotamian stories that have survived, for example, are versions of a flood story that are remarkably similar to the story of Noah's ark, one of dozens of parallels between the Bible and Mesopotamian mythology (*see box,* The Bible and Babylon).

Is there evidence to support a Mesopotamian origin for ancient Israel? Scholars have tried to establish the historical plausibility of Abraham and his family by connecting them to a Mesopotamian people known in ancient Near Eastern sources as the **Amorites.** As depicted in the Bible, Abraham and his descendants, often referred to collectively as "the Patriarchs," travel from Mesopotamia to Canaan, and then wander from camp to camp, never settling in a single place for long. The Patriarchs' nomadic lifestyle fits well with the alleged nomadism of the Amorites in the period between 2100 and 1800 BCE. Furthermore, while evidence of the Patriarchs

THE BIBLE AND BABYLON

One of the great intellectual accomplishments of the nineteenth century was the decipherment of cuneiform, the writing system developed in Mesopotamia. Scholars were able to understand texts that had not been read for millennia, and among what they discovered were some very precise similarities with a text people had been reading all along: the Bible. Especially astonishing was the narrative that has come to be known as the *Gilgamesh Epic,* which, as first announced to the world in 1872 by a scholar named George Smith, includes a flood story strikingly similar to that told in Genesis 6–9. Compare the following passages from the end of the two stories (the *Gilgamesh* flood story is told in the first person by the survivor of the flood, a figure named Utnapishtim):

1. The Dispatch of Birds At the end of forty days Noah opened the window of the ark that he had made and sent out the raven; and it went back and forth until the waters dried up from the earth. Then he sent the dove from him to see if the waters had subsided from the face of the ground; but the dove found no place to set its foot, and returned to him to the ark, for the waters were still on the face of all the earth, and he put out his hand and took it and brought it into the ark to him. He waited another seven days and again sent out the dove from the ark; and the dove came to him in the evening, and there in its mouth was a freshly plucked olive leaf, and Noah knew that the waters had subsided from the earth. (Genesis 8:6–11)

When the seventh day arrived, I sent forth and set free a dove. The dove went forth, but came back; since no resting place for it was visible, she turned around. Then I sent forth and set free a swallow. The swallow went forth, but came back; since no resting place for it was visible, she turned round. Then I sent forth and set free a raven. The raven went forth and, seeing that the waters had diminished, he eats, circles, caws, and turns not around. (*Gilgamesh Epic,* Tablet 11, line 150)

2. A Pleasing Odor Noah built an altar to the Lord and he took from every clean animal and from every clean bird and offered burnt offerings on the altar. The Lord smelled the pleasing odor. (Genesis 8:20–21)

Then I let out [all] to the four winds and offered a sacrifice. I poured out a libation on the top of the mountain. Seven and seven cult-vessels I set up, upon their potstands I heaped cane, cedarwood, and myrtle. The gods smelled the savor, the gods smelled the sweet savor. (*Gilgamesh Epic,* Tablet 11, line 160)

3. The Rainbow as Sign God said, "This is the sign of the covenant that I establish between Me and you. . . . my bow I have put in the clouds, and it will be a sign of the covenant between Me and the earth. When I bring clouds over the earth, and the bow appears in the clouds, I will remember my covenant." (Genesis 9:12–15)

When at length as the great goddess [Ishtar] arrived, she lifted up the great jewels which Anu had fashioned to her liking. "Ye gods here, as surely as the lapis upon my neck I shall not forget, I shall be mindful of these days, forgetting [them] never." [The goddess's jeweled necklace is probably to be understood as a rainbow.] (*Gilgamesh Epic,* Tablet 11, line 165)

There are many differences between the two stories, but the similarities leap into focus first. The Flood story proved to be one of many points of resemblance between biblical and Babylonian literature, though as other ancient sources came to light in the twentieth century, it became clear that the Bible shared much in common with other ancient Near Eastern cultures as well, especially the pre-Israelite culture of Canaan itself.

---

themselves cannot be found outside the Bible, evidence can be found that such figures *might* have existed. Names resembling Abram (Abraham's name before God changed it) and Jacob (Abraham's grandson) appear in Mesopotamian sources from the early or mid-second millennium BCE, and the description in Genesis of the Patriarchs' family life—Abraham's adoption of a servant as his heir, the details of how marriages are arranged, the importance of deathbed blessings—also seemed at first to fit the culture of this period as known from texts discovered at northern Mesopotamian sites such as the city of Nuzi. When these parallels came to light, they were seized on as evidence that Genesis, which is the first book of the Hebrew Bible, preserves to some degree an accurate memory of Israel's emergence from an earlier nomadic people with links to northern Mesopotamia.

A closer look at the evidence has called this conclusion into question, however. No specific event in Genesis can be corroborated, and even the effort to connect Abraham to the Amorites has proven unpersuasive in the end. Someone in this period may have been named Abraham—no evidence proves that Abraham *did not* exist—but such a figure could have as easily lived a thousand years later if he lived at all since his name, and the nomadic lifestyle he led, have parallels as well from later periods of Near Eastern history. In fact, indications can be found within Genesis itself that it was composed at a later time. According to Genesis 11, Abraham's family migrated from a place called "Ur of the Chaldeans." As we have noted, Ur is a well-known city in Mesopotamia, but the Chaldeans, a people from south Mesopotamia who are known only from sources dating to the ninth century BCE and later, could not have been living in Ur at the time of Abraham. Other details in Genesis—its reference to the Philistines, for example—also reflect realities that only emerge in Canaan after about 1200 BCE, complicating attempts to place a historical Abraham in the early centuries of the second millennium BCE. While it is still conceivable that Genesis preserves memories of real people and events, it seems those memories have been framed within a narrative from a later age that projects the circumstances of the author's day—sometime after 1200 BCE—onto Israel's past. To date, there is no agreed-upon way to distinguish between genuine historical experience and later invention in the book of Genesis, and the majority of scholars are skeptical of what can be learned about the Israelites' origins from the narrative.

The absence of any extrabiblical evidence for the Patriarchs' existence or their connection to Mesopotamia has led some scholars to suggest that **Egypt** is the best place to begin an account of Israel's history. Like Mesopotamia, Egyptian civilization was a river culture, forming on the banks of the Nile River. Its development is roughly parallel to that of Mesopotamia: a pictographic writing system (hieroglyphics, or their cursive equivalent: hieratic) developed there sometime in the fourth millennium BCE, as did the institution of the kingship, temples, and other attributes of early Near Eastern civilization. From an early period, even before the invention of writing, Egypt was in contact with Canaan. Egyptians came to Canaan as travelers, soldiers, traders, and—in periods when Egypt controlled Canaan—as administrators, while Canaanites traveled to Egypt as migrants, slaves, and traders (in fact, the word *Canaan* might originate from the word for "trader"). In 1482 BCE, the Egyptian king Thutmoses III won a major battle against his enemies at Megiddo in Canaan, the first of a series of military expeditions that established Egyptian control over Canaan for the next several centuries, until shortly after the reign of Merneptah at the end of the thirteenth century BCE.

Egypt's dominance in this early period loosely corresponds to the dominant role that it plays in the Bible's account of Israel's early history. The final chapters of Genesis, from Chapter 37 to the end, explain how Abraham's descendants ended up in Egypt, focusing on **Joseph,** Jacob's most beloved son. Joseph is hated by his brothers, who sell him into slavery in Egypt. Years pass, and Joseph's skills as a dream interpreter help him rise to the position of second in command in Egypt. When a famine besets Canaan, Joseph's brothers travel into Egypt to seek food, coming before Joseph without realizing who he is. Joseph tests his brothers to see if they have

changed, and when he is satisfied that they have, he reveals his identity and forgives them. Genesis concludes with what seems like a happy ending: a reconciled family of Jacob living in prosperity in Egypt. As the book of Exodus begins, however, the descendants of Jacob suffer a great reversal: a new king comes to power in Egypt and enslaves them, and the Israelites languish in servitude until God sends Moses to free them from Egypt and lead them back to Canaan.

The Bible itself attests examples of likely Egyptian influence. A segment of the biblical book of Proverbs is so similar in its content and organization to an Egyptian collection of wise sayings, a text called the *Teachings of Amenemope,* that it seems this material was essentially copied from there (one scholar even detects a reference to Amenemope's name in Proverbs 22:19). Some argue that Israel borrowed the idea of monotheism—its belief in one God—from Egypt since it was there that the first known experiment with monotheism was undertaken by **Amenhotep IV** (1352–1336 BCE). In a break from traditional Egyptian religion, Amenhotep declared the sun god Aten the only true god and renamed himself Akhnaten in his honor; given the connections between Egypt and Israel, it is possible that his reform is what first triggered the rise of Israelite monotheism. Even Moses' name is a possible Egyptian borrowing, conceivably deriving from the Egyptian verbal root *msy* ("born") that also appears in the Egyptian royal name *Rameses* ("the god Ra is born"). It was largely on the basis of this similarity that Sigmund Freud conjectured that Moses was really an Egyptian himself.

Of course, none of this amounts to evidence that the Exodus really happened, and the silence of sources outside the Bible lead some to conclude that it did not. While the Merneptah Stele refers to Israel, as we have noted, it is our *only* reference to Israel in ancient Egyptian literature, and the people to whom the hymn is referring already live in Canaan: there is no hint that they are former slaves. It is impossible even to determine the period of time to which the Bible refers. Some place the Exodus in the fifteenth century BCE, but others date it to the thirteenth century, and there is no way to decide the matter because what chronological information the Bible supplies fails to match up clearly or consistently with what we know from other sources about Egyptian history.

Another reason for doubting that the Exodus actually happened is that the biblical account seems to reflect the influence of ancient Near Eastern storytelling tradition. One of the Exodus story's best-known episodes tells of how Moses' mother saved her son from Pharaoh's lethal decree by putting the baby in a basket and sending him down the Nile River, where he was discovered by Pharaoh's daughter (see Exodus 2). The story is suspiciously similar to a legend told of other ancient Near Eastern leaders, such as Sargon I, founder of the first great Mesopotamian empire around 2300 BCE. Here is how Sargon describes his birth:

> Sargon, the mighty king, king of Agade, am I. . . . My mother, the high priestess, conceived me, in secret she bore me. She set me in a basket of rushes, with bitumen she sealed my lid. She cast me into the river which rose not [over] me. The river bore me up and carried me to Akki, the drawer of water. Akki, the drawer of water lifted me out as he dipped his e[w]er. Akki, the drawer of water, appointed me as his gardener.

Just as the portrait of David may have been filled out with material once associated with other heroes, so too Moses' image reflects a similar kind of mythological expansion. This does not rule out the possibility of a real Moses, but where to draw the line between fact and fiction in the Bible's account is unclear.

One event in Egyptian history does bear an intriguing resemblance to the Exodus: the expulsion from Egypt of a group known as the **Hyksos.** The Hyksos (a Greek transliteration of the Egyptian *heqaw khasut,* "rulers of foreign lands") were a line of Asiatic rulers, quite possibly from Canaan itself, who gained control over part of Egypt in the seventeenth century BCE. Some see Hyksos rule as the background for Genesis 37–50, for in this period it would be plausible for Joseph, an outsider from Canaan, to rise to a position of power in Egypt. Hyksos rule came to an end in the sixteenth century BCE, when the native Egyptians rebelled against their rule and chased them from Egypt, and their expulsion calls to mind Israel's flight from Egypt, a connection that had already occurred to Manetho, an Egyptian historian, more than two thousand years ago.

As tempting as it is to accept this connection, however, the Hyksos period was not the only time in Egyptian history when people from Canaan settled in Egypt. In fact, two-way traffic was frequent between Canaan and Egypt—including slaves imported to Egypt and people fleeing from Egypt into Canaan—all of which makes the idea of Israel's sojourn in Egypt and subsequent exodus plausible in a general sense but also gives one pause about connecting the Exodus to any specific event, such as the Hyksos expulsion. Egyptian texts from the period between 1500 and 1100 BCE also speak of another troublesome people: tribes of seminomads referred to as the **Shasu** from the area of Palestine—and they constitute a possible candidate for the role of proto-Israelite. Several such groups seem to have been in the area during the second millennium BCE, unruly peoples on the fringes of second-millennium urban society, who created problems for the authorities as they moved back and forth between a nomadic and settled existence (we will be meeting another such people

a bit later, the Habiru). While the Israelites may have originated as one of those groups, we lack the evidence that could clinch an identification with any particular people we know from other sources. Indeed, it is possible that the Hebrew Bible absorbs the memories of several such groups—the Amorites, the Hyksos, and the Shasu.

Unable to verify the biblical account of Israel's origins, many recent scholars have reached a radical conclusion about where Israel came from: Israel did not arrive in Canaan from the outside; it did not migrate there from Mesopotamia or escape there from Egypt. It originated from within Canaan as an offshoot of the indigenous culture that had existed there in preceding centuries. According to this hypothesis, the Bible's efforts to differentiate Israel from the Canaanites, to assign the Israelites an identity rooted somewhere else, conceal the true Canaanite pedigree of Israelite culture.

Several converging lines of evidence support this proposal, radical though it may seem. First is the lack of evidence for Israel entering the land of Canaan from the outside. According to the book of Joshua, Israel settled in the land after violently destroying walled cities such as Jericho and Ai and displacing their indigenous inhabitants. Archaeology does not support the occurrence of such a conquest, at least not on the scale described by the book of Joshua. A few Canaanite cities, such as Hazor, show evidence of destruction in this period, but no evidence exists to confirm that this destruction was wrought by the Israelites, and some cities allegedly destroyed at this time, according to the Bible, show no signs of violent destruction at all. Ai, for example, is described as being conquered in Joshua 8, but it does not seem to have even been inhabited in this period, much less destroyed. What of the famous story of the conquest of Jericho? Again, no evidence of destruction: Jericho in this period did not even have walls that could come tumbling down.

What archaeology has discovered is evidence of a rapidly growing settlement of Canaan's central highlands during the period associated with Joshua. Prior to this period, Canaan's central highlands, the mountain region between the coastal plain and the eastern desert, were—understandably—sparsely inhabited. The region was difficult to farm and water was hard to find. The area's new inhabitants found ways to address these problems, however. They cleared the slopes, shaping their steep sides into terraces that made them easier to farm, and they cut cisterns where they could store the water they needed. These settlers were certainly resourceful, but were they newcomers to the land? If they had just arrived from Egypt or the Sinai wilderness, one might expect their material culture—the houses they lived in, the pots they used—to differ from that of the indigenous population, but it is difficult to recognize such differences in the evidence.

In addition to this archaeological data, literary evidence connects Israelite culture to the indigenous culture of Canaan. Some of our best sources for Canaanite culture in the period prior to Israel's emergence are the hundreds of texts recovered from the ancient Syrian city-state of **Ugarit,** a kingdom that was especially prosperous in the fourteenth and thirteenth centuries BCE. The people of Ugarit were not Canaanites themselves, but their culture, religion, and mythology are closely related to those of Canaanites known from later sources. Ugaritic literature tells us much about the gods of Canaan and their misadventures—**El,** the supreme creator deity; **Asherah,** his consort and mother of the gods; and **Baal,** a warrior god associated with fertility—and their description parallels how God is described in the Bible. In fact, the biblical God is given some of the titles bestowed on El in Ugaritic literature, as in Genesis 14:19 where he is called "El Elyon," El the Most High.

Also consistent with the Canaanite origins theory is the language in which most of the Bible is written, now known as Hebrew but sometimes referred to in the Bible as *yehudit,* the language of Judah in southern Canaan (Israelites to the north

Statue of the god Baal in a striking pose, from the city of Ugarit around 1300 BCE.

appear to have spoken a slightly different dialect). Linguists classify this language as an offshoot of a western branch of the Semitic family of languages that also includes Arabic, Aramaic, and Ugaritic, and its closest relatives within this branch are other languages that were used in Canaan: Moabite, Ammonite, Edomite, and Phoenician. If Israel's ancestors had originated in Mesopotamia or Egypt, one might expect it to use the languages of those places or at least to bear a clearer imprint of their influence. Instead, they use the same language that all of Canaan's other indigenous inhabitants used.

The resemblance between Israelite and Canaanite culture becomes all the more striking when contrasted with another people that emerges in Canaan in the same period that the Israelites do: the **Philistines.** The Philistines came to the coast of Canaan in the early twelfth century BCE as part of a larger migration of peoples identified as the "Sea Peoples" in Egyptian, Ugaritic, and Akkadian sources. They came from the Aegean world of the Mycenaean age, the early Greek world described in Homer's *Iliad* and *Odyssey*, and their background is visible in the archaeological record. Philistine pottery is basically a variant of Mycenaean/Greek pottery; Philistine urban design, craftsmanship, and consumption habits (Philistines liked eating pork and drinking wine mixed with water) all point to the Aegean world as their place of origin. Even what little we know of Philistines' language supports this idea. The Philistine word *seren,* used in the Bible to describe Philistine rulers, is probably related to the Greek *tyrannos* or "tyrant." In other words, it is possible to see the Philistines' origins as outsiders to Canaan, the distinctness of their culture, clearly reflected in the archaeological and linguistic record. Not so with the Israelites, whose language, literature, and material culture all connect them to earlier Canaanite culture.

But if the Israelites came from within Canaan, where were they coming from and why would they suddenly take to the hills as it were, settling in relatively rugged areas that were so difficult to farm? And how do we explain the explosion of new settlements in this period? These are questions under investigation to this day, but scholarship now seems inclined to connect the changes happening within Canaan to larger changes in the Near East and Mediterranean. The transition from the Late Bronze Age to the early Iron Age in the thirteenth and twelfth centuries BCE is marked by political upheaval, decentralization, and large-scale migration. The New Kingdom of Egypt was in decline in this period, as was the Hittite Kingdom in Asia Minor; major urban centers such as Ugarit were destroyed, trade networks broke down, and as the Sea People illustrate, many felt they had to move to survive, displacing those who lived where they wanted to live or else settling whole new territory. Such changes seem mirrored in what was happening in Canaan at this time: the destruction

or decline of the cities that had dominated Canaan in the Late Bronze Age, the breakdown of ties with Egypt, the arrival of new peoples such as the Philistines, and the shift from an urban-based to a more rural economy. None of this precludes the possibility of an Exodus or of an Israelite conquest of Canaan, but one does not need to assume these events happened to understand what was happening in Canaan.

And yet, over the centuries, a distinctive Israelite culture would emerge in Canaan characterized by a new religious ideology, a distinctive diet and religious life, and a mythic tradition that celebrated Israel's difference from the other peoples of Canaan. How did these presumably Canaanite villagers come to think of themselves as non-Canaanites, and why did they emphasize their differences from the Canaanites in their ritual and sexual practices? Where did the stories of Genesis and Exodus come from if they do not reflect real events? These questions remain unsolved to this day, but what little we know about this period does allow for some educated guesses about how the transition from Canaanite culture to a distinct Israelite culture might have unfolded.

In the centuries prior to the Merneptah Stele, Canaan had been a colony of Egypt, as we have noted. Important information about what life in Canaan was like in this period comes from a collection of texts discovered in el-Amarna in Egypt in 1887, including a number of letters sent to the Egyptian King by the rulers of Canaanite city-states such as Tyre, Shechem, and Jerusalem. The **Amarna Letters** indicate that ruling Canaan was a challenge. The Egyptians were represented by a governor in Gaza, but for the most part they ruled through local kings based in Canaan's city-states, kings who were constantly at odds with one another. What is most important about these letters for our purposes is their references to a group known as the **Habiru** (or perhaps *Hapiru*). The term originally meant something like "dust maker," and although the significance of this label is not clear, it is often applied to people who occupy socially marginal positions in society as laborers, mercenaries, runaways, and rebels, as if the term connoted something like outcast or outlaw. The particular Habiru groups mentioned in the Amarna Letters, concentrated in parts of Canaan outside the control of its city-states, may have been brigands or fugitives, Canaanites alienated from or at odds with the city-states of Late Bronze Canaan.

The Habiru have long intrigued scholars because of the name's similarity to *Hebrew,* a word used in the Bible in reference to the Israelites. There are problems with that identification. The term *Hebrew* as used in the Bible always refers to Israel, whereas the Habiru is most likely a designation not of an ethnic group but of a kind of social class, not just in Canaan but elsewhere in the ancient Near East. Still, the linguistic similarity between *Hebrew* and *Habiru* is too striking

A CONFIRMABLE CHRONOLOGY OF BIBLICAL EVENTS

It is not easy to date the events mentioned in the Hebrew Bible because the chronological information it provides is vague, implausible (one biblical figure, Methuselah, is said to have lived for 969 years), or impossible to connect to events of a known date. However, a partial chronology can be constructed by correlating biblical chronology with information from extrabiblical sources.

1207 BCE. The people of Israel appear to live in Canaan by this point, as corroborated by the reference to Israel in the Merneptah Stele. Events that occurred before the Israelites' settlement of the land—such as Abraham's sojourn from Mesopotamia, the Exodus from Egypt—presumably occurred before this date, if they in fact occurred.

1150 BCE. Numerous sources document the arrival of the Sea Peoples on the southeast coast of the Mediterranean around 1180 CE, a movement that included the Philistines who arrived on the southern coast of Canaan at this time. The Philistines' presence is easy to discern archaeologically, and such evidence also shows them expanding into Canaan after the death of the Egyptian king Rameses III in 1153 BCE, the end of Egypt's control over Canaan. It was in this period of expansion, presumably, that the Philistines encountered the Israelites.

Ca. 925 BCE. King Shishak of Egypt invades Canaan. Mentioned in 1 Kings 14:26 as happening in the fifth year of Rehoboam, Shishak's invasion is the first event in the Bible confirmed by an extrabiblical source, an Egyptian text that describes the campaign. If the Bible's chronology is correct, King Solomon would have died five years earlier, in 930 BCE, placing the rise of a monarchy in Israel sometime around 1000 BCE.

The ninth century BCE. The kingdoms of Israel and Judah exist by this time, as corroborated by an inscription found at Tel Dan that refers to a king of Israel and a king of the House of David. According to a recent study, the two kingdoms are

---

to simply dismiss. Perhaps, some scholars hypothesize, the Israelites/Hebrews originated from a group of unruly Habiru who had taken refuge in the mountains of Canaan to elude the control of the Canaanite city-states, their emergence part of the same ruralization process at work in the proliferation of small settlements in this region a century or two after the Amarna Letters. With the breakdown of Egyptian control and the decline of Canaan's city-states, these Habiru were able to assert themselves, eventually becoming what the Bible refers to as the Hebrews. No direct evidence confirms this hypothesis, but in its favor is its effort to explain Israel's origins in light of what other sources reveal about Canaan in this period.

Taken all together, the evidence reviewed in this section—the problems with treating biblical books such as Genesis and Exodus as history, the different picture of Canaanite history that emerges from extrabiblical sources, and the connections between Israelite culture and Canaanite culture—at least raise the possibility that the Israelites originated in a manner that is completely different from what the Bible asserts. The story of the Patriarchs and the Exodus cast the Israelites as "a people living alone" (Numbers 23:9), originating outside Canaan and separated from its other inhabitants by distinctive religious beliefs and practices. In the alternative version of history reconstructed by modern scholars, the true origins of Israel lie not in Mesopotamia or Egypt but within Canaan itself, developing as

an offshoot of Canaanite culture. It would be wrong to view this reconstruction as certain fact: not enough data support it, and any existing data can be interpreted in more than one way. The resulting hypotheses are debatable, and the scholarly consensus, to the extent that there is one, is subject to continuous revision in the light of new evidence. What is certain is that we cannot take it for granted that we know the origins of ancient Israel (and by extension, the Jews).

Tracking the Historical Israel

Even though the biblical account of history can be challenged in many ways, that does not mean that it has no value as a historical source. On the contrary, it is possible in many cases to demonstrate the existence of specific persons and events featured in the Bible. We have already mentioned an Egyptian inscription that refers to Israel. Whether a kingdom of David and Solomon existed is a subject of debate, but we have plenty of evidence of monarchic activity: the building of fortifications and other public structures, royal inscriptions, and Assyrians and Babylonian sources that refer to the kings Ahab, Jehu, Jehoash, Menahem, Pekah, Hosea, Ahaz, Hezekiah, Manasseh, Jehoiachin, and Zedekiah (*see box,* A Confirmable Chronology of Biblical Events). We can likewise confirm the existence of also mentioned in another ninth-century inscription from Moab known as the Mesha Inscription (which also features the earliest datable reference to YHWH, the god of Israel).

853 BCE. Ahab, king of Israel, participates in a battle against the Assyrians. Ahab is known from the Bible but this particular battle is only reported by an extrabiblical source, a text from the Assyrian king Shalmaneser III. Assyrian and Babylonian sources also refer to subsequent kings of Israel and Judah from the ninth through the early sixth centuries—among them, Jehu, Hezekiah, and Jehoiachin, the last surviving king of Judah. This evidence lines up with how the Bible orders their reigns.

722–720 BCE. Assyria's conquest and destruction of the Northern Kingdom of Israel, reported in 2 Kings 17, are confirmed by Assyrian and Babylonian sources. Fragmentary commemorative inscriptions, Assyrian-style buildings, and imported Assyrian pottery confirm Assyria's rule of the former kingdom of Israel.

701 BCE. Assyria's conquest of most of Judah, reported in 2 Kings 18–19, is confirmed by Assyrian documentation, including highly detailed reliefs from a palace of Sennarcherib that depicts the Assyrian siege of Lachish, a Judahite city.

598/97 BCE. The Babylonian capture of Jerusalem, an event reported in 2 Kings 24, is confirmed by the following report in a Babylonian chronicle:

In the month of Kislev, the king of Babylon mobilized his troops and marched to the west. He encamped against the city of Judah (Jerusalem), and on the second of Adar, he captured the city and he seized [its] king. A king of his choice he appointed there; he to[ok] its heavy tribute and carried off to the Babylon.

From this same period, two seals have been published bearing the name of Baruch, probably the scribe by that name who wrote down the prophecies of Jeremiah, though at least one of these finds is now suspected to be a forgery. Inspiring more confidence is a Babylonian text that confirms the existence of Judahites in Babylonia and even refers to Jehoiachin—the captive king of Judah who was taken off into exile in 598 BCE.

many of the peoples mentioned in the Bible—the Egyptians, the Philistines, the Ammonites, the Moabites, the Edomites, and others—and the Bible's description of Canaan's terrain is also rooted in reality. While Israelite history and culture may have been very different from what is depicted in the Bible, its testimony has empirically demonstrable historical value.

What can we say for sure about Israelite history? The following account of Israelite history, based on the available textual and archaeological evidence, focuses on those events and experiences reported in the Bible that can be corroborated, at least in part, by extrabiblical sources. This approach yields a different historical picture than the one found in the Bible, beginning Israel's history not with Abraham or the Exodus but with events in Canaan after the thirteenth century BCE. It cannot fill all gaps, and it cannot answer all questions, but it can help fit Israel into what we know of the history of the region, offering insight into Israelite politics, social life, and religion along the way.

The End of Egyptian Domination and the Emergence of an Israelite Monarchy

As we have noted, a number of major changes occurred in the ancient Near East in the thirteenth and twelfth centuries BCE that help to illumine Israel's emergence as a distinct society.

One of the most important of these changes was the end of Egypt's control of Canaan in the twelfth century. An Egyptian tale composed in this period tells of how an Egyptian official named Wenamon traveled to the city of Byblos in what is now Lebanon to purchase timber, only to be told by the ruler there to go away. That a local king would dare show such disrespect to an Egyptian is a hint of the area's independence. So too— even without Moses, the ten plagues, or a miraculous flight from Egypt—something historical may lie behind the Bible's description of Egypt as an oppressor and the early Israelites as willing to break away from Egypt's control.

In fact, the breakdown of Egyptian rule allowed various peoples living in the region to assert themselves. Among those peoples were the Philistines, who arrived on the coast of Palestine (a name inspired by the Philistines) between 1180–1150 BCE as part of a larger migration of Sea Peoples. The story of David and Goliath—whoever it was who actually killed Goliath—may have it right when it describes the Philistines as an intimidating enemy. All around the eastern Mediterranean, the Sea Peoples had a highly disruptive effect. Many important cities, such as Ugarit, were destroyed in this period, and even powerful kingdoms like Egypt had a hard time fending off the Sea Peoples. The Philistines had a similarly disruptive effect on Canaan according to the Bible, and archaeology confirms that they not only established a secure foothold on the coast but also began to expand into Canaan's interior.

How were the Israelites able to fend off this threat? Here we only have the Bible for a source. As it depicts events, the Israelites were highly decentralized, a loose confederation of tribes prior to the Philistines' arrival. In theory they were united by a common ancestry; in practice they may have felt little allegiance to one another and sometimes came into violent conflict. The book of Judges, named for such temporary leaders, records several attempts to establish a more permanent form of leadership in this early period, a form of rule passed down from father to son, but these efforts fail. It is only during their conflict with the Philistines that the Israelites establish permanent, centralized rule: the first king, **Saul,** played a military role similar to that of the earlier judge, but as king was entitled to transmit his authority to his sons. Saul loses his claim to the kingship when he violates a command of God, and is replaced by **David,** who defeats the Philistines and secures Israel's boundaries. We cannot confirm any of these events, but what we know from other sources suggests it is not implausible that the same changes that allowed the Philistines to assert themselves in Canaan—the end of Egyptian domination, and the decline of the city-states that dominated Canaan during the Late Bronze Age—allowed Israelite society to develop into an independent kingdom.

According to the Bible, however, the Davidic dynasty was not able to hold its kingdom together for long. From its inception, we are told, the monarchy had been suspect—the prophet Samuel had tried to warn the Israelites of the dangers of monarchy when they first demanded a king—and what were perceived as royal abuses, especially **Solomon's** policy of extracting forced labor from his Israelite subjects to support his ambitious building projects, deepened those reservations among many Israelites. When Solomon's son **Rehoboam** came to power, a leader named **Jeroboam** led ten of the twelve tribes of Israel in a rebellion, leaving the Davidic dynasty a much reduced kingdom based in the territory of the tribe of Judah (hence, it is known as the kingdom of Judah). Jeroboam established a kingdom in the north known as Israel, and the two kingdoms existed side by side for two centuries until the northern kingdom was destroyed by Assyria, who exiled its inhabitants, the ten "lost tribes," to other parts of its empire.

Here at last we are beginning to move into a historical period reflected in extrabiblical sources, for there is confirmation for the kingdoms of Israel and Judah as early as the ninth century BCE. In fact, an inscription discovered in the early 1990s at Tel-Dan, the site of an important sanctuary in the northern kingdom of Israel, even refers to one of these kingdoms as the "House of David"—the earliest reference to this king outside the Bible and evidence that he may really have

existed. Whether there was ever a united kingdom of Israel, a state that united both Judah and Israel, is an open question, however, and some argue that there were two kingdoms from the very beginning: the northern kingdom of Israel developing first in the ninth century BCE, and the kingdom of Judah only coming into its own after the north's destruction at the end of the eighth century BCE. Since archaeologists make new discoveries every year, some new discovery may yet confirm an earlier period of unity between the two kingdoms, but for the moment it remains questionable whether a kingdom of David existed in the tenth century BCE.

Much clearer is the impact that the institution of the monarchy had on Israelite society after the tenth century BCE, both in Judah and the northern kingdom of Israel. The monarchy created, or tried to create, a political and religious center for Israelite culture, consolidating not just power and wealth but also the symbols of Israelite religion under royal control. In Judah, that center was **Jerusalem,** where the monarchy itself was situated, and where under Solomon, according to the Bible, it constructed a home for God—the Temple of Solomon. The importance of Jerusalem as the political and religious center of Judah is reflected in its growth. In the tenth century BCE, it was inhabited by only a few thousand people. By the seventh century BCE, it was many times larger, with an estimated population of 25,000 or more.

The northern kingdom of Israel underwent a similar process of royally initiated centralization, perhaps even earlier than the kingdom of Judah. In 1 Kings 12, it is reported that Jeroboam built two sanctuaries at the borders of his kingdom, one in the south at **Bethel,** not that far from Jerusalem, and the other in the north at **Dan.** Each housed a golden calf, identified with the god or gods who led Israel out of Egypt, and their purpose, claimed in 1 Kings, was to prevent the Israelites from shifting their allegiance back to Jerusalem and its king. The calves have not been discovered, but a momentous sanctuary has been unearthed at Dan, which includes a large platform area where the calves may have been displayed. It took longer for the kingdom of Israel to settle on a permanent site for its capital, but it eventually did so at Samaria, where a huge palace also has been excavated.

Even as the emergence of the monarchy centralized society, it also divided it in new ways, setting the stage for the development of two similar but distinct Israelite cultures. The kingdoms of Judah and Israel shared a language and a reverence for the same god, Yahweh, but according to the Bible they developed two separate forms of Israelite worship. Judah based its official cult in Jerusalem; the northern kingdom based its shrines at Dan and Bethel. North and south also had different political cultures. Judah continued to be ruled by the House of David, whereas the north was less stable,

Archaeologist Avraham Biran, posing with an inscription that he discovered in the ancient Israelite city of Dan. The inscription, dated to the ninth century BCE, refers to the "House of David," the earliest extrabiblical reference to the Davidic kingdom of Judah.

with shorter-lived dynasties and more assassinations and purges. The northern kingdom was the larger, wealthier, and less isolated of the two, but it was Judah's version of Israelite culture, with its allegiance to the House of David and the Temple in Jerusalem, that survived for a longer period.

Family Ties

The term *history* often calls to mind a sequence of dramatic events and changes—wars, migrations, the rise and fall of leaders, the conception and dissemination of new ideas—that affect large numbers of people. But for most people, life does not unfold on such a grand scale. Think about your own life. Is the most influential person in your personal history the president of the United States or the Pope, or is it a parent, a spouse, a sibling, or a friend? Events such as elections, wars, and epidemics certainly shape the world you live in, and may even impinge on your personal life in important ways, but so too do events that would not make it into the average history book: the birth of siblings, meeting a future spouse, losing a loved one. Experience on this more personal level is part of history too, though it may not be as well documented or dramatic as what usually gets recorded in history textbooks. Fortunately, apart from what the evidence reveals about large-scale events such as the end of Egyptian domination and the Philistine incursion, it also tells us something about Israelite life on this more personal scale.

The majority of Israelites lived in villages—one estimate places the figure at 66 percent in the period from 1000 to 500 BCE. The rest lived in larger towns or cities, but these were very small by current standards—Jerusalem in the tenth century BCE was probably home to about 1,000 to 2,000 people. The center of ancient Israelite/Judahite social life and economic activity was the house, presumably inhabited by the nuclear family, and it was in this setting that "history" unfolded for the majority of Israelites—birth, marriage, death, and the other events that defined their lives.

By synthesizing the Bible's testimony with archaeological evidence, scholars have reconstructed a picture of family life in ancient Israel. The most common house plan in ancient Israel is known as a four-roomed house (though it probably had more than four rooms), a house plan that probably predates the Israelites but became widespread in Canaan precisely in the period of Israelite settlement (around 1200 BCE). The family might have lived in the back rooms of the ground floor, but it is also possible that their quarters were on a second story reached by a ladder. Much of the first story was probably used for storage and as a manger for a family's animals, which not only kept the animals safe but warmed the house when it was cold outside. It is not clear where the

bathroom was located. People probably went outside and, in any case, rarely washed themselves.

Some houses shared a courtyard with other houses probably inhabited by members of the same extended family. Indeed, the members of one's village, and of neighboring villages, were likely distant kin. The Bible can help fill out what it meant to be part of such an extended kinship unit: families were united by a shared responsibility to protect their members. It was the responsibility of the next of kin, a brother or cousin, to avenge the murder of a family member, and according to the Bible, when a married man died without an heir, it was the duty of his next of kin to beget a child with his widow so as to preserve the deceased's inheritance, a practice known as *levirate marriage*. If the Bible is any indication, Israel's sense of itself as a community, the bond that tied its members to one another in relationships of obligation and support, was based on its idea of itself as a large family descended from a common ancestor.

Understanding this family structure is important for understanding Israelite society in general. Modern historians often describe Israel as a nation—a community united by a shared territory, language, and common history. The label fits, more or less, but it does not quite capture how Israelites perceived their own identity. Biblical texts such as the book of Genesis suggest that one's family was essential to this identity. Individual Israelites traced their family back at least five generations, and indeed, if Genesis is any indication, imagined themselves to be members of one superfamily descended from the twelve sons of Jacob (whose name was changed by God to Israel). Those who did not descend from this line were considered outsiders, non-Israelites, though groups that lived near the Israelites and shared certain customs with them and a language—the Edomites, the Moabites, and the Ammonites—were thought to be closer to Israel on the family tree than less culturally similar peoples, such as the Egyptians. What defined the Israelite community, as implied in the Hebrew Bible—what bound Israelites and Judahites together and distinguished them from other peoples—was the same ties of kinship that bound together parents, spouses, children, siblings, and cousins into a family.

The kinship-based structure of Israelite/Judahite society left many individuals on the edges of or outside this structure—widows, orphans, and non-Israelites living in Israel's midst—in a highly vulnerable position. In the Bible, God is identified as "the father of orphans and protector of widows" (Psalm 68), showing special concern for those who fell through the cracks of a kinship-based system. Like other ancient Mediterranean societies, Israel had a strong code of hospitality: one was supposed to be welcoming to strangers, offering them a meal if they came to your home. Even so, some Israelites were suspicious and sometimes abusive of strangers, a problem widespread enough that the Bible repeatedly addresses it: "You shall not oppress a resident alien, for you were aliens in the land of Egypt" (Exodus 22:21). Caring for those who fell through the safety net of the family, or stood outside of it, was an issue of great concern to biblical authors.

The most cherished possession that an Israelite family could own was its land, the source of the family's livelihood. When the Israelite king Ahab tried to buy a vineyard next to his palace, offering its owner, an Israelite named Naboth, another plot of land or the equivalent in money, Naboth staunchly refused:, "The Lord forbid that I give you my ancestral inheritance" (1 Kings 21:3). If one was fortunate enough to inherit land from one's ancestors, it was vital to keep it in the family. This is why one of the worst punishments the authors of the Hebrew Bible can imagine is exile: the alienation of Israel from its land.

The father, or grandfather, was the ultimate authority in the household, passing that authority to male heirs after his death (which is why the household was known in Hebrew as *bet av,* "house of the Father"). In such a system, a woman was usually under the control of men for the duration of her life. As a child, she was under the control of her father; at marriage (brokered between her fiancé and her father), she passed to the control of her husband. The household was a place of residence but also an important site of economic activity—the storage of agricultural produce, the stabling of animals, and the production of pottery and textiles—and the women of the house probably played an important role in all these activities, but their main role, also an economic role in a sense, was having and caring for children. For Genesis, the ultimate blessing that God bestows on Abraham and his descendants, apart from the land, is offspring, especially male offspring, and the women in his family—Sarah, Hagar, Rebecca—are of interest to the narrative only to the extent that they help realize this blessing (*see box,* Sex and Death in Ancient Israel).

Not everyone living in the Israelite household was a biological relative. Slaves and hired servants lived there as well. Slavery was a universally accepted institution in the ancient Near East, and ancient Israel was no exception. To be sure, the core experience in Israel's collective memory was its escape from slavery, an inspiration for modern-day abolitionists, but actually the Exodus story does not imply a rejection of slavery as an institution. The Bible implies that the Egyptians were wrong to enslave the Israelites not because slavery itself was wrong but because the Israelites did not deserve such treatment—they had not been purchased or captured in battle but were the descendents of an ancestor, Joseph, who had once done Egypt a great service and had settled in the land of Egypt along with his father and brothers with the permission of its king. The memory of the Exodus does elicit sympathy for Israelites who have

become the slaves of other Israelites, and the Bible limits their servitude and protects them in other ways, but slavery was woven into the fabric of Israelite society, as it was other ancient Near Eastern societies, and it never occurred to whoever wrote the Bible to abolish it.

Some biblical sources composed late in biblical history betray signs of a possible weakening of tribal bonds. In a society where an individual's destiny was bound up with that of one's family, it made sense to imagine God punishing children for the actions of their ancestors: "(God) visit[s] the iniquity of the parents upon the children and the children's children, to the third and fourth generation" (Exodus 34:7). By the sixth century BCE, however, at least some Judahites, such as the prophet Ezekiel, were questioning this idea:

> The word of the Lord came to me [Ezekiel]: "What are you doing reciting this proverb about the land of Israel, 'The parents eat sour grapes, and the children's teeth are set on edge [i.e., a person sins and their child suffers the consequences]?' As I live, declares the Lord God, you will no longer recite this proverb in Israel. All lives are mine; the life of the parent as well as the life of the child are mine: it is only the person who sins that shall die." (Ezekiel 18:1–4)

Reflected in this passage is the idea that a person's fate ought to be detached from that of his or her family, determined not by inheritance but by his or her own actions—evidence, some scholars have argued, of an emerging individualism in Judahite society at odds with the collective thinking of a tribal society. Already in the biblical period, in other words, the family structure of Israelite society may have begun evolving in a way that allowed other kinds of personal and group identity to emerge.

Still, tribal affiliation continued even after the Babylonian exile, or so it appears from the biblical account of this period in the books of Ezra and Nehemiah. Those who survived that experience identified as members of Israelite tribes—the majority from the tribe of Judah but some from the tribes of Levi and Benjamin—and continued to believe that they owned the territory allotted to their ancestors. Evidence from the New Testament and other sources shows that such tribal affiliation continued well into the first century. Today, the label *Jewish* (derived from the tribal name Judah) does not imply a specifically tribal identity in any practical sense—the term took on other geographic, cultural, and religious resonances in the postbiblical period—but even now, vestiges of tribal identity persist. Note, for example, how some Jews identify themselves as descendants of the Levites, the tribe charged in the Bible with special duties related to worship (an identity frequently reflected in a person's last name—"Levi," "Levine," and the like,

SEX AND DEATH IN ANCIENT ISRAEL

Both sex and death are rooted in human biology, but how people behave sexually and how they respond to death are also shaped by values and norms that can vary from society to society. Most of what we know about sexual behavior and the response to death in ancient Israel comes from the Bible. We cannot treat its testimony as some kind of survey that can tell us what the average Israelite thought about these topics, but it does reveal something of Israelite and Judahite attitudes, anxieties, and responses.

Sex in Ancient Israel

Many people assume that the Bible endorses a prudish attitude toward sex, forbidding it outside of heterosexual marriage. There is and isn't truth to that characterization. Something does seem incompatible between sexuality and sacredness in the Hebrew Bible. Before it can experience God's revelation at Mount Sinai, Israel must abstain from sexual activity (Exodus 19:15), and priests were subject to more sexual restrictions than other Israelites. In contrast to some other ancient Near Eastern deities, God himself never acts in a sexual way, and—so far as we know—his worship did not involve any kind of sexual activity. This does not mean that the Bible's authors were opposed to sexual expression in other contexts, however. One of the most erotic texts ever written is the Song of Songs, a collection of love songs attributed to King Solomon but probably written by someone else, perhaps for use in a wedding celebration or for some other erotically charged occasion. The song gives unforgettable expression to the feeling of sexual yearning, the lover's restless desire to be with the beloved:

> Upon my couch at night, I sought the one I love—I sought him but did not find him. I shall rise and go about the city, through the streets and through the squares; I will seek the one I love. I sought him but did not find him. The watchmen found me, the ones who patrol the town. "Have you seen the one I love?" Just a little after I passed them, I found the one I love; I grabbed him, and would not let him go until I brought him to my mother's house, to the room of the one who conceived me. (Song of Songs 3:1–4)

Nowhere in the song is this sexual longing condemned as wrong. To the contrary, it is celebrated as a mighty, irrepressible power: "vast floods cannot quench love, nor rivers drown it" (8:6–7). And we are not dealing here with some kind of spiritual love; the lovers in the song focus on the body of the beloved, described in arousing detail:

> Your rounded thighs are like jewels, the work of a craftsman's hands. Your navel is like a round goblet. Let mixed wine not be lacking. Your belly like a heap of wheat hedged about with lilies. Your two breasts are like two fawns, twins of a gazelle . . . your stature is like a palm, your breasts are like clusters. I say, "I shall climb the palm, I shall take hold of its branches and may your breasts be like grape clusters on a vine, the scent of your breath like apples." (7:2–9)

But the lovers of the song cannot fully realize their desire for one another. They seem to stand outside society, roaming among beautiful gardens, but scruples keep them apart—"if only it could be as with a brother," says the female lover, "then I could kiss you and no one would despise me" (8:1). The verse presupposes some kind of sanction against sexual intimacy in public; a woman in this society is permitted to kiss a brother in public but not a lover. The Song of Songs is a remarkably uninhibited celebration of desire, but it also acknowledges social constraints on the physical expression of that desire.

The Hebrew Bible does not treat sex as an inherently sinful activity. To the contrary, Genesis 1 casts sex as the fulfillment of God's first commandment to humanity to be fruitful and multiply. But it does recognize sexual behavior as a potentially destructive act not just for the individuals involved but for the entire community. As related in Leviticus 18, the land had expelled the earlier Canaanites largely because of their sexual behavior, their practice of incest, adultery, homosexuality, and bestiality, acts that confuse the ties that hold a family together, fail to produce children, or blur the boundary between divinely defined categories (male versus female; human versus animal). But lest one think that the Hebrew Bible's sexual ideal is the modern two-parent household, it is worth noting that it also allows for sexual behaviors at odds with contemporary ethical norms: polygamy (men marrying multiple wives, not women marrying multiple husbands) and married men having sex with concubines.

In Israelite culture, a woman's sexual activity was controlled by fathers and husbands, and female sexuality outside that control was considered shameful, even threatening. Seductive and sexually aggressive women were seen as a potentially mortal danger:

"do not stray onto her paths, for many are the slain she has struck down" (Proverbs 7:25–26). Biblical law regulates the sexual life of both men and women, but it imposes more restrictions on the latter. A man could have multiple sexual partners—wives, servants, even prostitutes—and divorce a woman to marry another. By contrast, biblical law does not allow women to engage in polygamy, nor does it sanction female sex before marriage or grant women the right to initiate a divorce. It never prohibits lesbianism—probably not because it endorsed it but because what women did among themselves, outside their interaction with men or children, was of little interest to the storytellers of the Bible.

What ancient Israelites actually did behind the (probably not so private) walls of their houses is unknown to us, but with the Hebrew Bible's help, one can imagine the darker possibilities. Consider as an example the sexual experience of Jacob's children: his daughter Dinah was raped by a man who subsequently offered to marry her (Genesis 34); his oldest son Reuben had sex with Jacob's concubine (Genesis 35:22); Judah, the ancestor of the Judahites, had sex with a woman he thought was a prostitute but was really his daughter-in-law Tamar in disguise (Genesis 38); and Joseph, Jacob's favorite, was propositioned by another man's wife (Genesis 39). Whether or not these incidents actually happened, the authors who report them recognize that sexual behavior often involved the exercise of violence and deceit, and beyond restricting sexual activity, biblical law also sought to protect Israelites from being victimized in these ways.

Death in Ancient Israel

In the pre-Israelite religion of Canaan, or at least in Ugaritic literature, death was imagined as a deity, Mot, not the object of worship in the way other gods were but a powerful, voracious being with an immense mouth and appetite, able not only to consume multitudes of humans but to overcome the gods. In one of the stories told of him in Ugaritic literature, Mot defeats Baal himself, the god of fertility, and sends him into the underworld. Mot is defeated in turn by the goddess Anat, and Baal is revived, but the victory is only temporary. The struggle against death seems to be an ongoing one.

Biblical literature may allude to the Mot myth, but death is not depicted there as a deity. The power of death is recognized (as in Song of Songs 8:6, "Love is as strong as Death"), but the Hebrew Bible contains no stories of combat between God and death, nor does it record any rituals for fending off death in the way that Ugaritic literature does. In the Bible, death goes the way of other Canaanite deities, such as Baal and Asherah, losing its status as an independent being with a will of its own.

In fact, the Hebrew Bible seems remarkably uninterested in the problem of death compared with other ancient Near Eastern literature. Much of the *Gilgamesh Epic* from Mesopotamia is a quest to find the secret of immortality. Ancient Egyptian culture seems to have been preoccupied with death. Some part of a person's identity was thought to survive death, going on to an afterlife that could either be very terrible or very pleasant, and various rituals and spells were developed to ensure a happy outcome. The Hebrew Bible does not reflect this kind of preoccupation with death. God does seem to have the power to spare certain special people from death—figures such as Enoch and Elijah—and even to resurrect the dead, as He does through the prophet Elisha in 2 Kings 4, but these are rare exceptions, and for the most part death is depicted as a divinely ordained part of experience. Those who die do go on to some kind of afterlife in a place called Sheol, but like the Homeric Hades, it seems to be a rather gloomy place, its inhabitants unable to speak: the dead are "cut off" from the Lord (Psalm 88), forsaken and forgotten about. The Israelites believed in ghosts—as shown by 1 Samuel 28, where the ghost of the prophet Samuel rises from the underworld—but the Bible forbids Israel from consulting the dead or making offerings to them. Death, and the dead, are marginalized in the Hebrew Bible.

None of this is intended to suggest that the death of a loved one was not a traumatic experience for ancient Israelites. Like other ancient Near Eastern peoples, the Israelites expressed their bereavement in an intense and dramatic way, tearing their clothes, putting dust on their head, beating their breasts, shaving their hair, wearing special mourning garments, and uttering lamentations in honor of the dead. The objects found in tombs—jewelry worn by the deceased and other personal items; possible evidence of food offerings, human- and animal-shaped figurines to protect, or provide company for, the dead; even miniaturized shrines possibly intended to give the dead access to the divine—give further witness to the concern that people had for their dead loved ones.

But in the Hebrew Bible at least, the distress caused by death does not motivate a yearning for immortality in the way that it does in the *Gilgamesh Epic*. Instead, what the Israelites of the Hebrew Bible seem to aspire to is a long, prosperous life and many children, the latter a kind of virtual immortality that sustained a person's memory after death. Abraham's death is the model of a good death: he reached an exceptionally old age (175, according to Genesis 25:8) and, by the time he died, he had many descendants. Finally, he was buried in a tomb with his wife Sarah on land that he owned. That kind of death—resting peacefully alongside one's family members in the tomb and a legacy of many children, and not personal immortality—is what the Hebrew Bible regards as a happy ending to life.

though secularized Jews with such names may not realize or care about their name's original significance). Passed down from father to son, Levitical identity is a lingering trace of how tribalism once shaped identity in ancient Israel, a person's position in Israel's family shaping his status and role in the community.

The remarkable resilience and elasticity of this kinship structure, seemingly persisting even when kin do not live in the same place or know each other in a personal way, may help to explain how Israelite culture was able to survive the Babylonian exile and proved much more durable than the other structures that held Israelite society together in the pre-exilic period: the monarchy and the temple. These other institutions did not survive Babylonian conquest in the sixth century BCE; Israel's kinship structure did, at least to some extent: exiles seems to have preserved their sense of family identity, continuing to trace their ancestry back to the twelve tribes of Israel, and using that identity to distinguish themselves as a people from other neighboring peoples with whom they shared customs, language and political interests, such as the Edomites and Moabites.

Surviving Mesopotamian Domination

The opening created by the end of Egyptian domination, during which time the Israelite and Judahite kingdoms developed, began to close in the ninth and eighth centuries BCE as the **Assyrian Empire** expanded westward from Mesopotamia into Syria and Canaan. As it did with other kingdoms that it encountered, Assyria forced the kings of Israel and Judah to submit to its rule and pay tribute. The northern kingdom of Israel, the larger of the two kingdoms, resisted this imposition and was destroyed when the Assyrian king Shalmaneser and his successor Sargon II smashed its rebellion in 722–720 BCE, an event corroborated by Assyrian sources. A people known as the **Samaritans** claim to this day to descend from the northern tribes of Ephraim and Manasseh (see Chapter 4), but from the vantage point of the Bible's authors and later Jews, the destruction of the northern kingdom marked the end of this part of the Israelite people. The Assyrians exiled the population of the northern kingdom to other parts of their empire, and what happened to these "ten lost tribes" remains a mystery to this day.

Panel from the black obelisk of King Shalmaneser III, from Nimrud, ca. 825 BCE, showing the tribute of King Jehu of Israel, who is on his knees at the feet of the Assyrian king.

The kingdom of Judah was also conquered by Assyria a few decades later, under the Assyrian ruler Sennacherib, and here too the Bible's account (2 Kings 18–19) can be corroborated, at least in part:

> In the fourteenth year of King **Hezekiah,** Sennacherib king of Assyria came up against all the fortified cities of Judah and captured them. Hezekiah King of Judah sent a message to the king of Assyria at Lachish saying, "I have sinned. Turn back from me and I will bear any penalty," so the king of Assyria imposed on Hezekiah a penalty of three hundred silver talents and thirty talents of gold. (2 Kings 18:13–14)

This is more or less consistent with how events are described by Sennacherib himself in his annals:

> As to Hezekiah, the Judahite, he did not submit to my yoke, I laid siege to 46 of his strong cities, walled forts and to the countless small villages in their vicinity and conquered [them]. . . . I drove out [of them] 200,150 people, young and old, male and female, horses, mules, donkeys, camels, big and small cattle beyond counting, and considered [them] booty. [Hezekiah] I made prisoner in Jerusalem, his royal residence, like a bird in the cage.

Sennacherib says that after destroying Judah's other cities and forts, he pinned King Hezekiah in Jerusalem "like a bird in a cage," but he does not destroy Jerusalem itself, as the Assyrians had done with Samaria, the capital of the northern kingdom of Israel—perhaps because Hezekiah was willing to pay a fine, as 2 Kings 18:14 reports. So far so good, but the biblical account goes on to describe a miraculous defeat of the Assyrian army:

> It happened that night [after Hezekiah prayed to the Lord for help against the Assyrians] that the angel of the Lord went out and struck down one hundred and eighty-five thousand in the camp of the Assyrians. When morning dawned—behold, they were all corpses. Then King Sennacherib of Assyria returned home and lived at Nineveh. (2 Kings 18:13; 19:35–36)

According to the Bible, in other words, what ultimately saved Jerusalem was not Hezekiah's submission but an act of divine intervention that destroyed the Assyrian army in Judah and sent Sennacherib packing. Nothing like this is mentioned in the Assyrian account, which depicts what happened as a typical Assyrian victory. We will not try to resolve the

discrepancy between the two accounts here, but we do note that each author had reasons for putting his own spin on what happened, with the biblical account serving to underscore the power of God, the Assyrian account underscoring Sennacherib's. Even in the rare cases when we have external corroboration for the biblical account, as this example illustrates, the extrabiblical evidence can generate more historical questions than it resolves.

Assyrian domination is well attested in the archaeological record, leaving behind not just a layer of destruction but inscriptions and the remains of buildings. It has left a similarly deep imprint on biblical literature. Much of the prophetic literature in the Bible—texts imputed to such prophets as Isaiah, Amos, and Micah—comes from the Assyrian period and records the fear, confusion, and resentment triggered by Assyrian conquest. Why would God allow his chosen people to be subjugated by a foreign people? Was God angry with the people of Judah, and if so, why? Would the enemy's dominance ever come to an end, and what would life be like then? Prophetic literature addresses these questions, interpreting Assyrian conquest as divine punishment but also holding out hope of God coming to the rescue. Here, for example, is one such note of prophetic consolation, a passage from the book of the prophet Isaiah, who lived in the time of Hezekiah and Sennacherib:

> Therefore thus says the Lord God of hosts: My people that dwell in Zion, don't be afraid of the Assyrians when they beat you with a rod and lift up their staff against you in the way of Egypt, for in a very little while my indignation will end, and my anger will be directed to their destruction. . . . On that day his burden will be lifted from your shoulder; his yoke [removed] from your neck and destroyed. (Isaiah 10:24–27)

The kingdom of Judah was able to survive Assyrian conquest because, for whatever reason, the Assyrians left the kingdom of Judah intact, if only as a rump state, destroying many cities and usurping much territory but never destroying Jerusalem itself. Babylonian conquest in the period between 598–586 BCE was a more devastating experience. To punish the Judahites for their rebelliousness, the Babylonian king **Nebuchadnezzar II** destroyed the kingdom of Judah in 586 BCE: he burned down the Temple, killed those members of the Davidic dynasty he did not take captive, and exiled a substantial portion of Judah's population to Babylonia. But Judahite culture survived this trauma too, and the Hebrew Bible tells us something of how it did so.

The book of Jeremiah, the second-longest book of biblical prophecy after Isaiah, suggests that here too prophecy helped Judahites to come to terms with traumatic social change. Many of the prophecies recorded in Jeremiah are set after Babylon's initial conquest of Jerusalem in 597 BCE, when part of Judah's population had already been exiled to Babylon. One of these prophecies, recorded in Jeremiah 29, is a letter that Jeremiah is said to have written to those exiles. The letter does not encourage the exiles to place their hope in the possibility of return but instead urges them to settle down:

> Build houses and live; plant gardens and eat their produce. Take wives and have sons and daughters; take women for your sons, and give your daughters to men, that they may bear sons and daughters; multiply there, and do not decrease. Seek the welfare of the city to where I have exiled you, and pray for it to the Lord, for in its welfare will be your welfare. (Jeremiah 29:5–7)

Faced with the complete devastation of his society, Jeremiah does not envision or seek an immediate restoration of what has been lost—the land of Canaan, Judah's independence, or the Temple—but instead urges his audience to adapt to their altered circumstances, to submit to foreign rule for the time being and make a life for themselves in exile, predicting a new relationship, a "new covenant," between God and Israel in the future.

The Babylonian documents known as the **Murashu archives,** the records of a banking firm compiled in the Mesopotamian city of Nippur, show that Judahites living in Mesopotamia in the fifth century BCE did indeed settle in Babylonia, for the archives include mention of some eighty names identified as Judahite, individuals seemingly integrated into Babylonian social and economic life. In fact, apart from their names, little distinguishes these individuals from the non-Judahites in the Murashu texts; some even gave their children Babylonian names that incorporated the names of Babylonian gods, such as Shamash (though Yahwistic names continued too). If these were the descendants of Judahite exiles, they seem very settled into their new home.

This does not mean, however, that the exiles lost their connection to their ancestral home. Even as the book of Jeremiah counsels its audience to settle down, it also urges them to sustain hope in the eventual restoration of Israel, envisioning a renewed relationship with God, a revitalized Davidic dynasty, even a newly reunified Israelite people. Such texts as Jeremiah are our best evidence for how it was that Judahite society was able to survive the devastating impact of Mesopotamian conquest despite losing so many central institutions, illustrating a process of creative adjustment that allowed the exiles to sustain their Judahite identity even as they adapted to life in exile under foreign rule.

Learning to adapt in this way proved crucial for the long-term survival of Judahite culture. After the biblical period, its descendants, the Jews, would find themselves ruled by other foreigners: Persians, Greeks, Romans, Muslims, and others. Biblical texts such as Jeremiah proved an important asset in coming to terms with foreign domination, endorsing the decision to submit to foreign rule as a religiously acceptable one and developing ways for Judah to continue its relationship with God outside of Canaan.

The Evolution of God

Both the Bible and extrabiblical evidence show that religious life in Israel and Judah, while it had some distinguishing features, resembled that of surrounding cultures. At the center of religious life in the Near East was one's relationship with the gods, beings who were like humans in many respects but were bigger, stronger, longer lived, and harder to see. Two major objectives of religious practice were (1) to discern the intentions of the gods by reading clues they left in nature, a practice known as divination, and (2) to secure the goodwill of the gods by praising them, tending to their needs, and giving them gifts (food and vegetable offerings). The challenge of sustaining such relationships was that the gods were not accessible—they lived at a distance, on remote mountaintops or in the heavens, or were simply too large or incomprehensible for humans to take in. Fortunately, the gods sometimes revealed themselves in certain natural settings—mountaintops, caves, trees, by the sides of rivers—or in special buildings constructed for their residence, such as temples. There, mortals could come into their presence, tend to their needs, and interact with them through prayer, sacrifice, and other rituals.

All this has a counterpart in Israelite religious life. Archaeologists have uncovered several sanctuaries in Israel and Judah—not the Jerusalem Temple (the one supposed relic of that temple, a small ivory pomegranate inscribed with the words "Belonging to the Temple of the Lord, a holy thing to the priests," was recently exposed as a probable forgery) but the sanctuary at Dan in the north, a temple at Arad in Judah, and other examples. Their design, indeed even the design of the Jerusalem Temple as described in the Bible, exhibit the conventional characteristics of temples in Syria–Palestine.

One supposedly distinctive characteristic of Israelite religion may not be unique, although it is often understood to be. The gods of the ancient Near Eastern cultures surrounding Israel and Judah often manifested themselves to humans in the form of anthropomorphic or zoomorphic statues. The Bible is opposed to the use of human and animal images to represent God, and indeed no statue of God has been discovered to date, but evidence does exist to show that the Israelites believed their

THE ARK AND MERCY SEAT.

Ark of the Covenant.

god was actually resident in the sanctuary, manifest in cult symbols that signaled its presence indirectly rather than representing it in a fully visible form. As described in the Bible, the **Ark of the Covenant,** a kind of footstool or chariot for God, served such a purpose in the Jerusalem Temple, signaling the divine presence but leaving God Himself unseen and mysterious. While other ancient Near Eastern and Mediterranean cultures often used human- or animal-like images to visualize their gods, some resembled the biblical cult in using nonrepresentational symbols to suggest rather than represent the deity's presence, probably reflecting a widespread belief that it was dangerous or difficult for mortals to see a god.

In other respects, the worship life of ancient Israel and Judah was very similar to that of surrounding cultures. Like other deities, God was attended in the sanctuary by a class of servants, or priests, who oversaw sacrifice and other cultic performances. The Bible condemns some of the divination techniques used in surrounding cultures to discern the will of the gods, but it allows for such others as dream interpretation and the casting of lots. The Bible's sacrificial terminology and the form and wording of certain biblical psalms have very close parallels in earlier Ugaritic literature. Other evidence from Syria—especially tablets discovered in the ancient city of Mari from the nineteenth and eighteenth centuries BCE—shows that biblical prophecy also had deep roots in the culture of the region. The tablets include letters from prophets with divine messages for the king.

What is most recognizably distinctive about Israelite worship is the deity to whom it was directed. Inscriptions from the period of the kingdoms of Israel and Judah mention the names of several Canaanite gods—Baal, Asherah, El— but the deity most frequently referred to is a god never mentioned in Ugaritic literature or other sources for Canaanite

The "holy of holies" or most sacred section of the temple at Arad. The altars in the picture are stationed before stone pillars that rendered manifest the divine beings worshipped in the temple.

religion: a god whose name is spelled **YHWH.** Apart from its appearance in the Bible, YHWH is mentioned in letters, prayers, blessings, and other texts known from inscriptions, and a shortened form, *yahu,* is incorporated into many personal names in Israel and Judah: Uri*yahu* ("YHWH is my light"), Netan*yahu* ("YHWH has given"), and so on.

YHWH (or *Yahweh,* as scholars spell the name) appears to be a new deity relative to other deities worshipped in Canaan. He does not appear in Ugaritic literature or in any other Canaanite source, though we know of a few place and personal names that sound similar. While Israel's name, which we know from the Merneptah Stele, goes back to at least the thirteenth century BCE and incorporates a divine name, it is the name "El," a god known from earlier Ugaritic/Canaanite sources, not a form of *Yahweh* as in later Israelite/Judahite names. *Yahweh* seems to come out of nowhere, appearing for the first time in a clearly datable context in the period of Israel's monarchy, and we can only make educated guesses about His origins prior to that (*see box,* Where Does God Come From?).

Still, Yahweh was not completely discontinuous with earlier Canaanite religion. Judaism as practiced today is monotheistic, acknowledging Yahweh as the only god. The origins of monotheism can certainly be traced back to the Bible, but the Bible also preserves glimpses of an earlier form of Israelite religion much closer to Canaanite polytheism, a religion that identified Yahweh with the Canaanite god El or Baal and allowed for the existence of less powerful deities alongside him. One such glimpse is preserved in Psalm 89:

Who among the heavenly beings is like the Lord, a God feared in the council of the holy ones, great and dreaded above all around him? Lord God of hosts, who is like

You? Your strength and faithfulness surround you. You rule the surge of the sea; when its waves rise, you quiet them. You crushed Rahab like a carcass; with your mighty arm, you scattered your foes. (Psalm 89:7–10)

The words *heavenly beings* here translate an expression that literally means "sons of els" and can be taken to mean "gods," and what we know of Canaanite religious tradition supports that interpretation. In Ugaritic literature, the gods, also known as "the holy ones," convene in special assemblies, such as one in which Baal meets with the gods before confronting a god called Yam, the Sea. The psalm seems to be describing a similar divine council, and Yahweh's subjugation of the sea parallels Baal's victory over Yam. Another divine battle story in Ugaritic literature pits Baal against a dragon, Lotan, a rough equivalent to the monster Rahab mentioned in this psalm and an even more precise parallel to another creature defeated by God—

WHERE DOES GOD COME FROM?

The early history of God—where and when He was first worshipped—remains a mystery. The earliest reference to God outside the Bible, or YHWH as his name is spelled, is in a ninth-century Moabite inscription known as the Mesha Stela in a context that associates him with Israel. Whether his history goes back any further is unknown, but scholars have tried to tease out his origins from clues found here and there in the Bible.

One such clue is God's name. The meaning of YHWH is unknown—it is not even clear how to pronounce it because its vowels have been long forgotten (in the postbiblical period, Jews began to avoid pronouncing God's name out of respect for its sanctity, at least outside the confines of the Temple, preferring more generic titles instead, and in this way, it seems, its vowels were forgotten. YHWH as it appears in Hebrew Bibles today can be written with vowels, but these are taken from the Hebrew word for "My Lord," *Adonay,* pronounced in lieu of God's name). For its part, though, the Bible suggests a connection to the Hebrew verb "to be." When Moses asks his name, God responds, "I am who I am" (Exodus 3:14)—an answer that puns on the similarity between the consonants of YHWH and the verbal form "I am" (*ehyeh*). While the root of "to be" may be the source of Yahweh's name, the story may misconstrue the precise connection, however, for some scholars think that it arose not from "I am" but from the causative form of "to be"—"The One who *causes* to be" or, in other words, "the Creator."

If this reconstruction is correct (and it may not be correct; other etymologies have been proposed), Yahweh's name derives from his role as a creator god. The god El plays this role in Canaanite mythology, and that and other connections to El (e.g., the fact that the Bible assigns Yahweh "El" names, *such as el-Elyon;* the incorporation of *El* in the name Israel; Yahweh's association with Asherah, El's consort) all support the idea that Yahweh originated from within the Canaanite pantheon as a version of the god El.

But other clues within the Bible suggest Yahweh originated *outside* Canaan, in the Sinai wilderness between Canaan and Egypt. A few biblical texts describe Yahweh as coming from the south (e.g., Deuteronomy 33:2, Judges 5:4, Habbakuk 3.3–7), and he is called "Yahweh of the South" in inscriptions from Kuntillet Ajrud in the Negev. "South" here seems to be the Sinai wilderness, a territory inhabited by a people known as the Midianites, and some scholars have hypothesized that Yahweh originated as a Midianite god, an idea known as the "Midianite Hypothesis." Mount Sinai, located in this territory, is where Moses first encounters Yahweh in the burning bush, and where the Israelites establish their covenant with him—stories that may reflect a vague memory of Yahweh as a deity first encountered in this region. How to reconcile Yahweh's Canaanite links with his possible Midianite origins is unclear, but several possibilities arise. Perhaps, for example, Israel adopted Yahweh from the Midianites and subsequently integrated him with more northern traditions connected to the Canaanite god El. Just as there were multiple Baals associated with different cities or regions (Baal of Lebanon, Baal of Sidon, etc.), more than one Yahweh may have existed originally—a Yahweh of Samaria *and* a Yahweh of the south—and perhaps the biblical God is a conflation of these different Yahwehs.

Leviathan, a variant of the name Lotan, who is alluded to in Psalm 74:13–14: "You divided the sea by your might; you broke the heads of the dragons in the waters. *You crushed the heads of Leviathan.*" The site of Baal's conflict with Yam, and the place where his home is and from which he issues decrees, is the mountain Zaphon in northern Syria, and its description in Ugaritic texts is similar to the Bible's description of the holy mountains of Sinai and even more so to **Zion,** the mountain where Yahweh's temple in Jerusalem was located. Indeed, the Bible transfers the name Zaphon to Zion in Psalm 48: "His holy mountain . . . Mount Zion, summit of Zaphon."

Extrabiblical evidence also ties Yahweh to indigenous Canaanite religion. At a site in the Negev known as Kuntillet Ajrud, Hebrew inscriptions were discovered that refer to "Yahweh of Samaria and His Asherah" or "Yahweh of the South and His Asherah." The inscription may be referring to Asherah herself or to some object associated with her worship. While the meaning of "his Asherah" in these inscriptions is debated, it may indicate that at some stage in Israelite religion, Yahweh, like El in Ugaritic mythology, had a mate.

All this has led to the theory that early Israelite religion was not that different from pre-Israelite Canaanite religion. Yahweh was another name for the god El, with a consort named Asherah, or else he was a variant of the god Baal, defeating the enemies that Baal defeats in Ugaritic myth and taking up residence on a sacred mountain. In this early form of Israelite religion, other less important deities seem to have existed, the holy ones alluded to in Psalm 89, though these were overshadowed by Yahweh's superior power. The fact that Yahweh seems to combine the traits of El and Baal may seem strange, but a similar consolidation of the Canaanite divine population has been observed in neighboring cultures in the first millennium, as cultures zeroed in on a single deity as the most important or fused attributes of various deities into a single god. In the second millennium BCE, the single city-state of Ugarit acknowledged the existence of more than two hundred gods. By contrast, the number of gods from any given Canaanite state in the first millennium BCE number ten or fewer. Moabite religion coalesced around the god Chemosh, the Edomites around the god Qaws, and the Ammonites around the god Milkom. Perhaps this same trend is reflected in Israelite/Judahite religion, with El and other Canaanite gods consolidated into Yahweh.

Monotheism, the worship of Yahweh as the only god, may in fact have emerged very late in Israelite history, in the period of Assyrian and Babylonian conquest. The Bible is full of passages that praise God as the most powerful or unique god, but such texts do not necessarily rule out the existence of other deities; similar statements are found in the divine praise of other Near Eastern cultures we know to be polythe-istic. Truly monotheistic statements—texts that assert God as the only god—are surprisingly rare in the Hebrew Bible, only surfacing in texts from the Assyrian–Babylonian–Persian period, such as Isaiah 44:6–8, where God declares, "I am the first and I am the last, *besides me there is no god.*" How then did Israelite religion evolve into a monotheistic religion?

Some scholars see the Egyptian religious reformer Akhnaten as the inspiration for monotheism, but as we have noted, the most unambiguously monotheistic statements appear in late biblical texts from the Assyrian or Babylonian period, leading many scholars to explain the emergence of Israelite monotheism within that later historical context. Perhaps Assyria or Babylonia were themselves the catalyst. Both were polytheistic cultures, but each flirted with quasi-monotheistic ideas. In one Assyrian text, for example, the body of the god Ninurta is described as a composite of all the other gods: "Lord your face is Shamash (the sun god) . . . your head is Adad (a storm god) . . . your neck is Marduk, judge of heaven"—as if all the gods were really only extensions of a single supreme god. The monotheism of such biblical texts as Isaiah 44—the insistence that Yahweh is the one and only god—may reflect the influence of such ideas. Alternatively, it might have arisen as a reaction *against* Mesopotamian religious dominance, resisting efforts to subordinate Yahweh to the conqueror's gods by denying their very existence.

However we understand the origins and history of Yahweh, the point we want to stress here is the importance of this deity in Judahite identity. As in other ancient Near Eastern cultures, a person's identity was defined in ancient Israel and Judah not just by kinship ties, birthplace, or political allegiance but also by a relationship with a deity, a relationship that expressed itself in ritual behavior, myths, and even a person's name. Several deities seem to have been venerated in Israel and Judah—Baal, Asherah, and others—but judging from the prevalence of Yahwistic names and references in the inscriptional record and the Bible, Yahweh was the most popular deity in Canaan of the first millennium, associated with the people of Israel and Judah in a way that the god Chemosh was associated with the Moabites and the god Qaws with the Edomites. How Yahweh was imagined changed in the wake of Assyrian and Babylonian conquest, but Judah's allegiance to him survived, becoming part of what it passed on to later Jewish culture.

From the Historical Israel to Biblical Israel

The historical picture we have reconstructed here is very different from the story of Israel that emerges out of the Bible. It is an account without such figures as Abraham, Moses, or King David, without such events as the Exodus or Joshua's conquest. Whereas the Bible sharply distinguishes the Israelites from the Canaanites, locating their origin outside Canaan, we have suggested that Israelite culture may have developed as an offshoot of Canaanite culture, and we have seen reason to identify the Israelites with various precursors in Syria–Palestine—the Amorites, the Hyksos, and the Habiru. We have even complicated God's history a bit, citing evidence that Israelite religion may not have been that different from the religion of neighboring Canaanite peoples.

Even as we challenge biblical history in this way, however, we also acknowledge that it is our single most valuable source for understanding the Israelite culture out of which Jewish culture evolved. Indeed, the Bible captures the beginnings of the process by which Israelite culture evolved into Jewish culture: the emergence of a distinctly Judahite variant of Israelite culture and its evolution under Assyrian and Babylonian conquest.

Still, our understanding of that trajectory is hardly complete. The changes imposed by Babylonian rule—the end of the Davidic dynasty, the destruction of the Temple, and the exile from Judah—play a critical role in the development of Jewish culture out of Judahite culture, but these events alone cannot account for the transformation. It turns out that the Hebrew Bible itself played a catalytic role. Judahites read the Bible, or the texts that would become the Bible, to retrieve the life they had lost through foreign conquest and exile, and through the act of doing so they created the beginnings of something new: a culture focused on and generated through the interpretation of sacred texts. To understand the rise of Jewish culture, therefore, we must learn more about the Bible itself—how it came to be, what it consists of, and the role that it came to play in Judahite culture as it developed after Babylonian conquest.

Questions for Reflection

1. Why begin a history of the Jews with the Hebrew Bible? What makes the Bible a difficult starting point for Jewish history?

2. The Bible draws a sharp distinction between the Israelites and the Canaanites. Why then do many recent scholars regard Israelite culture as an offshoot of Canaanite culture?

3. Decide in your judgment, which of the following events really happened: Abraham's journey from Canaan; the Exodus from Egypt; David's defeat of Goliath; the Assyrian conquest of Israel and Judah. If you believe an event to be historical, can you cite corroborating evidence? If you believe it did not happen, what is the reason for your skepticism? If you believe that the event in question involves some mixture of fact and fiction, can you tell what is historical and what is not, and if so, how?

4. How are the structure and daily life of an ancient Israelite family different from your own?

5. Try writing a history of God based on the evidence presented in this chapter. In what ways does the history of God seem to parallel the history of the Israelites?

For Further Reading

For a more detailed overview of Israelite/Judahite history than can be presented here, see M. Coogan, *The Oxford History of the Biblical World* (Oxford, England: Oxford University, 1998). On the ancient Near East, see Daniel Snell, *Life in the Ancient Near 3100–332 B.C.E.* (New Haven: Yale University Press, 1997). For an English translation of ancient Near Eastern texts, see J. B. Pritchard, *Ancient Near Eastern Texts Relating to the Old Testament* (Princeton, NJ: Princeton University Press, 1969), from which this book draws its translations of the Merneptah Stele and other ancient Near Eastern texts.

On family and daily life in Israel, see Philip King and Lawrence Stager, *Life in Biblical Israel* (Louisville, KY: Westminster John Knox Press, 2001). On Israelite women, see Carol Meyers, *Discovering Eve: Ancient Israelite Women in Context* (New York: Oxford University Press, 1998). On how God relates to Canaanite religion, see Mark Smith, *The Early History of God: Yahweh and Other Deities in Ancient Israel* (San Francisco: Harper-Collins 1990), and on ancient Israelite religion in general, see Susan Niditch, *Ancient Israelite Religion* (New York: Oxford University Press, 1997) and Patrick Miller, *The Religion of Ancient Israel* (London: SPCK/Louisville, KY: Westminster, 2000).

To find more information about other topics in Israelite history and culture, try the *Anchor Bible Dictionary* (ed. D. N. Freedman, New York: Doubleday, 1992).

Chapter 2

Becoming the People of the Book

At what point did ancient Judahite culture evolve into Jewish culture? One reason it is difficult to answer this question is that the precise difference between *Judahite* and *Jewish* is unclear. As used in the Bible, the Hebrew term *yehudi* refers to a person from the tribe of Judah or from the territory known by that name, but in the centuries after the Babylonian exile, the term evolved other meanings it did not have in the pre-exilic period. By the first century BCE, the term still associates the people that it labels with a particular place, Judah, but it can also signify a people defined by its way of life—what one text from this age calls "Judaism," an originally Greek word that refers to the distinctive laws and customs that distinguished the Jews from other peoples, such as the Greeks and Egyptians. By that point in time, *yehudi* can be justifiably translated as "Jewish" instead of "Judahite," but it is not clear when we should place the beginnings of this transition—in the first century BCE itself or in some earlier century.

An example will help to drive home why it is difficult to pinpoint the precise transition point between Judahite and Jewish culture. Over the course of the nineteenth century, a group of ancient documents came to light and revealed a Judahite (or is it Jewish?) community in the fifth century BCE in a very unexpected place: a small island known as **Elephantine** situated in the middle of the Nile River in what is now southern Egypt. Egypt at this point was controlled by the Persian Empire, and these people were stationed there as soldiers working on its behalf, settling on Elephantine with their families to help guard the frontier zone between southern Egypt and Nubia to the south. The Elephantine Papyri, written in **Aramaic** (another Semitic language widely used in the ancient Near East under the Persian Empire), provide a remarkable witness to the community that produced them, furnishing scholars with personal and official letters, legal and economic documents, and even a literary text about a scribe named Ahiqar.

The people reflected in these documents refer to themselves as *yehudiyin,* a term often translated as "Jews," and there is much to recommend that translation: they worshipped Yahweh (or Yaho as he is known in Elephantine texts), bore Yahwistic names, and celebrated such holy days as the Sabbath and the Passover, important in later Jewish culture. But they are also different from the Jews we know about from other sources: they did not regard Jerusalem as the only legitimate site of sacrifice—they offered sacrifice to Yaho at a temple situated at Elephantine itself, destroyed in 410 BCE—and they seemed to acknowledge other gods alongside Yaho. They might have learned something of biblical law through their contacts with religious authorities in Jerusalem, but the Elephantine Papyri do not include texts that cite or interpret the Bible, much less biblical manuscripts themselves. Their ancestors seem to have settled in Egypt well before the Babylonian exile, moving there when it was under Assyrian rule, so not even their collective memories were like those of Jews we know from other sources. If by "Jewish" we mean a person from the land of Judah or descended from Judahites, the Elephantine community can be labeled Jewish, but it would be a mistake to think its members were like the Jews we know from later sources, and it might be less anachronistic to describe them as another separate offshoot of pre-exilic Judahite culture.

Because the definition of the term *Jewish* is so fuzzy, we will not try to pinpoint a specific date when Judahite culture becomes Jewish culture. Instead, this chapter will focus on several events that appear *in retrospect* to have been crucial in the development of Jewish culture out of Judahite culture. We say "in retrospect" because it is not clear that the people involved in these transformative moments saw themselves as different from their ancestors. What we can gather from the few literary sources surviving from this period indicates that *continuity with the past* is a central value of the Judahite/Jewish culture that emerges after the Babylonian exile. The people depicted in these sources identify with the Israelites of the pre-exilic period and yearn to preserve or restore the cultural and religious traditions they had inherited from them. It is only from our much later vantage point, knowing as we do what Jewish culture would become in later periods, that we can recognize something new emerging among the Judahites who survived the destruction of the kingdom of Judah, a culture distinct enough from earlier Judahite culture to merit a new label. Moving from the term *Judahite* to *Jewish* is as good a way as any to signal the difference without completely obscuring the connection between these cultures.

The most important turning point from our perspective and the one to which we will devote the most attention in this chapter, is the rise of the Bible itself. In the last chapter, we focused on biblical literature as a historical source, sometimes rejecting its testimony, sometimes accepting it, but always focusing on what it does or does not tell us about the past as it actually happened. But whatever actually happened in ancient Israelite history was only one factor in the rise of Jewish culture; another was what early Jews *thought* happened, a perception of the past that both shaped and was shaped by biblical literature. To understand the development of Jewish culture, therefore, we have to focus on the composition and canonization of the Hebrew Bible as events in their own right, doing our best to understand the origins and impact of these processes with the help of the scant evidence that happens to survive from this period of Judahite/Jewish history.

Judahite Culture Under Foreign Rule

We begin with an event we have already introduced: Babylon's conquest of the kingdom of Judah in the early sixth century BCE. Although scholars question whether the Babylonian conquest was as disruptive as the Bible suggests, most continue to regard it as a watershed moment, and with good reason. With the end of the Davidic dynasty, Judah lost its independence, and the political destiny of its inhabitants would henceforth be shaped by foreign rule. The destruction of the Jerusalem Temple disrupted the core of Judahite religious life, forcing Judahites to find new ways to interact with God. Many people may have remained in place in Judah, but a significant portion of the population, including King Jehoiachin, was exiled to Babylon, where the exiles had to adapt their identity and traditions to a very different cultural and political environment.

Babylonian conquest had a highly destructive effect on Judahite culture, measurable by the archaeological evidence of Judah's destruction during this period, but it also stimulated a considerable amount of creativity, measurable by the literature from this period now preserved in the Hebrew Bible. As we noted in Chapter 1, prophetic texts such as Jeremiah, or at least substantial portions of them, were composed in this period, and these aimed to reimagine Judahite religious tradition in a way that would allow it to continue without the Davidic king and the Temple. It was also during this period that one of the great historical narratives in the Hebrew Bible, dubbed by modern scholars the **Deuteronomistic History,** was completed, a hypothetical work that includes the now distinct books of Deuteronomy, Joshua, Judges, 1–2 Samuel, and 1–2 Kings. Many of the stories that appear in this work probably predate the Babylonian exile, some going back to the very beginnings of Israelite history perhaps, but their integration into a single history was completed at this time—a dating that one infers from the fact that the last event in the narrative is Babylon's conquest of Jerusalem. One of the goals of the Deuteronomistic History, it seems, is to explain why God allowed this catastrophe to happen, and it places much of the blame on the kings of Israel and Judah for leading the people astray from God. The last verses of the narrative (2 Kings 25:27–30) note the release from prison of King Jehoiachin, an ending that makes one wonder whether the Deuteronomistic editor anticipated the imminent restoration of the Davidic dynasty, but what exactly his hopes were for the future are unknown.

This apparent outburst of religious and literary creativity, rooted in the impulse to sustain Israelite culture and religion in the face of traumatic change, is certainly an important stage in the transition from Judahite to Jewish culture, which is why many scholars date the beginning of Judaism to 587–586 BCE, the year that Nebuchadnezzar destroyed Jerusalem and its temple. Babylonian rule was relatively brief, however, ending in 539 BCE when the Neo-Babylonian Empire was itself defeated by the Persian king **Cyrus II,** founder of the **Achaemenid dynasty** that would dominate the Near East for the next two centuries. (*See* Map 2-1.) The Persians did not restore the Davidic monarchy as some Judahites might have hoped, but instead ruled Judah as a Persian province until they were conquered in turn by Alexander the Great. Persia's impact on Judahite culture is less obviously disruptive than that of the Babylonians—biblical sources depict Persian rule as an age of restoration, in fact—but this may very well be the age in which the transformation of *Judahite* culture into *Jewish* culture ought to be placed.

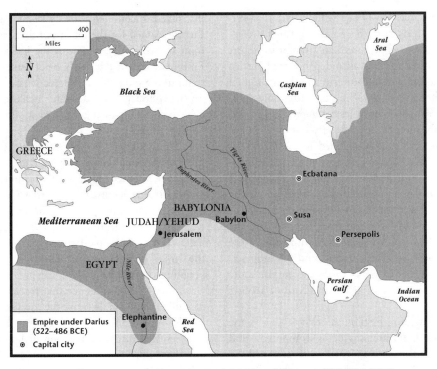

Map 2-1   The Persian Empire Ruled by the Achaemenid Dynasty (539–332 BCE).

Cyrus was a remarkably effective empire builder. First he conquered the Medes, a people settled in present-day Iran, and then moved on to Asia Minor (present-day Turkey), where by conquering the kingdom of Lydia he sowed the seeds of a long war with the Greeks famously described by the Greek historian Herodotus. In 539 BCE, Cyrus conquered Babylon, coming into control of all its territory, including what had been the kingdom of Judah, and it was at this point, according to the biblical book of Ezra, that he allowed the exiles to return home and restore their Temple. Chapters 40–55 of the book of Isaiah—known as **Deutero-Isaiah** (*deutero-* is Greek for "second") because this section seems to have been added to the original core of Isaiah by a later author or authors—celebrates Cyrus as a divinely appointed savior, commissioned by Yahweh to help restore what the Judahites had lost under Babylonian rule:

> I [the Lord] am the one who says to Cyrus, "my shepherd," and all my purpose he shall fulfill; and who says to Jerusalem, "It shall be rebuilt," and to the temple, "You shall be established." Thus says the Lord to his anointed, to Cyrus, whose right hand I have grasped. . . . I will go before you. (Isaiah 44:28–45:2)

Why do scholars date this part of Isaiah to the Persian period despite the fact that Isaiah himself was from the much earlier Assyrian period? This passage contains the answer: Deutero-Isaiah refers explicitly to Cyrus. As depicted here, Cyrus is an agent of Jerusalem's restoration; in fact, the text hints that he is much more than that by referring to him as "his anointed," a royal title that refers to the Israelite custom of anointing a person with oil to designate him king (the Hebrew for "anointed one" is the source of the English word *messiah*). For the post-exilic author of Deutero-Isaiah, it was as if the descendant of David himself had come back to repair the damage caused by Babylonian conquest, only God's "anointed one" was not a Judahite king but a foreign ruler.

Despite the Bible's efforts to depict this period as an age of restoration, the reality was in fact very different. The Judahites, both those returning home and those remaining in Babylon or living in Egypt, were now part of a large empire that expected their loyalty. They could return to their ancestral land, they were even permitted to rebuild their Temple, but they were not allowed to restore an independent state in Judah with a king of their own. Instead, this territory was now to be administered as a province known as *Yehud* (Aramaic for *Yehuda*), part of a still larger imperial administrative unit in the Persian Empire, a satrapy known as "Beyond the River" that encompassed the land of Canaan along with other territory west of the Euphrates River.

Not all Judahites may have been willing to accept Persian rule, and biblical texts from this period hint that a rebellion against Persia may have occurred, an attempt to restore the Davidic king or build the Temple independent of Persian control. Whatever effort such Judahites made to regain their independence failed, however, and Persian control only tightened with time. Cyrus's son **Cambyses** conquered Egypt, and that gave Persia all the more stake in the area linking Egypt to the rest of its empire, an area that included Yehud. Cambyses did not last long—he died before getting home from Egypt—but the person who emerged as his successor, **Darius I** (522–486 BCE), greatly consolidated the Persian Empire by restructuring imperial administration, expanding roadways, and even initiating a canal between the Red Sea and the Mediterranean. His decision to allow the completion of the Temple, initiated by Cyrus but halted under Cambyses, might have been part of this effort to tie the empire more closely together, a way of securing the goodwill of Yehud's inhabitants.

Persian rule falls within the biblical period—that is, the period when biblical literature was being composed—and the cultural effects of Persian domination are detectable in parts of the Hebrew Bible. In fact, the term *Hebrew Bible* is a slight misnomer because some of the Bible's content— portions of the books of Ezra, Nehemiah, and Daniel—are written in Aramaic, a language that became widespread among Judahites in the Persian period because of its use as an imperial administrative language. Hebrew was not abandoned— Jews would continue to write in it for many centuries—but Aramaic became so dominant at this time that it altered Hebrew grammar and vocabulary, and even changed the way its alphabet was written, displacing the script of pre-exilic Hebrew with the Aramaic script in which Hebrew is written to this day.

Beyond this linguistic change, Judahite integration into the Persian Empire is also detectable in the stories that the Bible tells about this period. Biblical literature from this time makes frequent reference to the kings of Persia, and as we have seen in the case of Deutero-Isaiah, they often appear as good guys, helping the Judahites to restore their culture. Even the biblical book of **Esther** (probably written in the fourth century BCE), which describes an attempt made during the reign of the Persian king **Ahasueres** to destroy the Judahites, assigns the blame not to the king himself but to his evil advisor **Haman,** who misleads King Ahasueres into believing that the Judahites are disloyal. Fortunately, the king happens to be married to a Judahite himself—a beautiful woman named Esther—and she uses her influence with the king to persuade Ahasueres to revoke his decree and punish Haman instead, a happy ending that the Judahites are

instructed to commemorate by keeping a holiday known as **Purim** (named for the lot or *pur* that Haman cast to determine on which day to destroy the Judahites). In the Persian Empire as described in the book of Esther, other subjects seek to harm the Judahites, but Persia itself is not a hostile power. To the contrary, what saves the Judahites in the end is their close connection to the king, exemplified by Esther's marriage to Ahasueres.

The book of Jeremiah records a debate between the prophet Jeremiah and a prophetic opponent named Hananiah over whether Judah should submit to Babylonian rule or not. It was Jeremiah's view that God wanted Judah to submit to Babylonian rule and he drove his point home by wearing a yoke around his neck. The prophet Hananiah believed otherwise, predicting that God would soon break the "yoke" of Babylonian rule—a point he drove home by breaking the yoke that Jeremiah was wearing. Hananiah's viewpoint—his confidence that foreign rule could be successfully challenged—was the one that prevailed, and Judah soon launched a revolt against Babylonia, a decision that resulted in the destruction of Jerusalem and its Temple. If a similar debate arose among Judahites about Persian rule, it has not been recorded in surviving sources; the Judahites of Esther, and of the Elephantine Papyri, all cooperate with and submit to Persian rule, a posture that may explain how Judahite culture was able to survive this period, for by aligning themselves with Persian rule, the people of Judah may have lost their political autonomy but were able to enlist Persian support for their efforts to return to the land of Judah, revive their Temple, and sustain their culture.

In opting to preserve their culture in this way, however, Judahites were also introducing a major change into that culture, giving up—at least for the time being—the idea of Judah as an independent kingdom. Accepting foreign rule meant that Judahites would have to find ways to preserve their indigenous traditions in political contexts ruled by other peoples, and in some cases that meant downplaying or reinterpreting their culture to avoid a confrontation. They would have to learn the languages of their rulers, along with other aspects of their rulers' culture, so as to successfully interact with them, and this, together with the new trade contacts opened up under foreign rule, inevitably exposed Judahites to new cultural influences. Their very identity was different now; beyond their sense of themselves as members of a particular family or kingdom, Judahites were now subjects in a vast, multicultural empire presided over by a ruler who was remote but also, through the mediation of an extensive administrative structure and royal propaganda, importantly present as well.

Relief sculpture of King Darius the Great.

All these changes are part of the story of how Judahite culture evolved into Jewish culture, but by themselves they are not enough to understand the transition. The Persian period is also the age in which Judahites first seem to turn to the Bible, or rather to the texts that would eventually become the Bible, to keep their ancestral culture alive. On the surface, this also seems to be a highly conservative move, a turn back to the past that had been disrupted by Babylonian conquest, but like the acceptance of foreign rule, it too represents a new phase in Judahite culture. Indeed, as we will explain, it is arguably the most important development in the Persian period for understanding how Judahite culture gave birth to Jewish culture.

Looking for a figure with whom to associate this change, historians often associate it with the scribe **Ezra,** an important leader of the Judahite community in the Persian period, but the changes we describe here—the parallel development of both the Bible and Jewish culture—are not the result of any single event or individual but an accumulation of changes that begin before the Babylonian exile. Like Israelite history in general, this history can only be partially retrieved and is probably far more complicated than we can surmise from the few sources we have available, but it is possible to reconstruct its main outlines, and to do so in ways that intersect with the history of Judah we have been following until now. Greatly simplifying this history to accommodate the brief confines of this chapter, we will divide this history into two stages. The first encompasses the actual composition of biblical literature—when and why the various texts that would become the Hebrew Bible were composed in the first place. The second is the emergence of this literature as a biblical canon, a sacred, authoritative collection of texts to which Judahites turned to understand their history and relationship with God. In reality, the two processes of composition and canonization cannot be distinguished so neatly—some parts of the Bible were only written after other parts were already regarded as sacred Scripture—but they are roughly sequential, and ordering them in this way will help us to see how the Jewish Bible took shape as Jewish culture itself was taking shape.

Stage 1: How the Texts Now in the Bible Came to Be

Sometime in the fourth millennium BCE, roughly 5,000 to 6,000 years ago, writing was invented in the ancient Near East, perhaps originating in Mesopotamia. Its invention is something we take for granted now, but it is a development that transformed the nature of human experience. Speech, communicating by word of mouth, allowed human beings to transmit information and ideas to one another, but its communicative potential was limited. A community without writing had to rely on memory, a fragile information storage system, to store its collective knowledge. Writing made it possible to store information for long periods of time and also to communicate across great distances.

It also made it possible to communicate with the gods in new ways. The gods sometimes revealed themselves to humans, directly or in the form of a dream, oracle, omen, or vision, but communicating across the human–divine divide was very difficult—the gods lived in faraway places or on mountaintops, and their vast size and radiance made it hard to perceive or interact with them. Writing created a way to

cross this barrier and started to play this role in the ancient Near East in the second millennium BCE. In Mesopotamia, for example, certain special texts were thought to come from the mouth of the god Ea, via human dictation, or recorded the experiences of those who had experienced divine revelation. People wrote to the gods, and sometimes the gods wrote back, sending written messages directly or revealing the techniques by which their messages, encrypted in the stars and other portents, could be decoded. The idea that writing could bridge the human and the divine realms would prove crucial for the formation of biblical literature, much of it a record of the two-way communication between Israel and Yahweh. The most famous example is found in the laws revealed to the Israelites at Mount Sinai: divine words inscribed on tablets and hand delivered by Moses.

Writing reached Canaan well before it did the ancient Israelites. In fact, it was probably in Canaan or its vicinity that the **alphabet** was invented sometime in the Middle Bronze Age (2000–1500 BCE). Using a small number of twenty to thirty signs to indicate the basic sounds in a language—twenty-two in Hebrew—the *alphabet* (a word derived from the first two letters of this writing system—*aleph* and *bet*) may have been easier to learn and quicker to write than the cumbersome writing systems that existed until that point, and its advantages help to explain both why it prevailed in Canaan and why it eventually spread to other places, such as Greece and Rome. Inscriptional evidence records various alphabetic experiments in ancient Canaan: it took a while for people to settle on how, and in what direction, to write their letters. By about 1050 BCE, however—not long before our first evidence of the kingdoms of Israel and Judah, coincidentally—the Canaanite alphabet had settled into a conventional form, eventually developing into the more localized Phoenician, Edomite, Moabite, Ammonite, and Hebrew scripts.

We know from later Hebrew inscriptions that writing was used for a variety of purposes in ancient Israel and Judah. Reading and writing were rare skills in antiquity, and as in other Near Eastern societies, there arose in Israel and Judah a class of professional scribes whose job it was to write and read official documents on behalf of the king or the Temple—records, letters, and so forth. But we also have examples of private writing, texts produced by individuals for their own benefit: pious graffiti, tomb inscriptions, even a petition for help by someone trying to reclaim a cloak that had been confiscated from him. One of the most remarkable of these inscriptions comes from a tomb at Ketef Hinnom, south of Jerusalem. Two small silver amulets are inscribed with priestly benedictions that are almost identical to a priestly benediction in Numbers 6:24–25: "The Lord bless you and keep you; the Lord make his face to shine upon you, and be gracious to you!" The amulets date to the seventh or sixth century BCE and, as the earliest surviving biblical passage attested outside the Bible, they indicate that its contents were already beginning to take shape by this time.

If we did not have the Hebrew Bible itself, however, nothing in the inscriptional record would ever lead us to guess the existence in ancient Judah of a literature as varied and sophisticated as what is preserved there. Who wrote this literature, when, and why? Trying to answer these questions has kept scholars busy for some three centuries, and it is impossible to describe the countless hypotheses they have derived. Still, it is worth noting some points of consensus:

1. *The Hebrew Bible reflects the ancient Near Eastern setting in which its contents were composed.* In the last chapter we noted examples where the contents of the Hebrew Bible parallel other ancient Near Eastern literatures. The flood story in Genesis resembles the flood story incorporated into the *Gilgamesh Epic*, and the birth story of Moses, the birth story of Sargon the Great. In fact, much of the Hebrew Bible has antecedents or parallels in other ancient Near Eastern literature—historical narratives, law codes, ritual texts, prophetic oracles, proverbs, psalms, and lamentations. One more example will help to illustrate how close the similarity can be.

During the nineteenth or eighteenth century BCE, long before any evidence of Israel, a Babylonian king known as Hammurabi promulgated a series of laws in an effort to establish justice in his kingdom. A copy of those laws inscribed on an eight-foot-tall stela was discovered between 1901 and 1902. The stela features a picture of Hammurabi receiving the symbols of justice from the god Shamash, the Mesopotamian god of justice, and a prologue confirms that the laws have divine authorization, though it is the king who inscribes and enforces them. Some of the laws are strikingly similar to laws recorded in the Five Books of Moses. Compare:

When a man strikes the eye of a male or the eye of a female slave, and destroys it, he shall free the person to compensate for the eye. If he knocks out the tooth of a male slave or the tooth of a female slave, he shall free him for the tooth. (Exodus 21:26–27)

If a man of rank has destroyed the eye of a member of the aristocracy, they shall destroy his eye. If he has broken the bone of another man of rank, they shall break his bone. If he has destroyed the eye of a commoner or broken the bone of a commoner, he shall pay one mina of silver. If he has destroyed the eye of another man's slave or broken the bone of a man's slave, he shall pay one-half his value. If a man of rank has knocked out a tooth of a free-man of his own rank, they shall knock out his tooth. If he has knocked out a commoner's tooth, he shall pay one-third mina of silver. (*Code of Hammurabi* 196–201)

The Code of Hammurabi and biblical law are not identical. The Babylonian law makes class divisions that biblical law does not, and the two impose different penalties for the same crime. Still the form and even the content of the Babylonian and biblical laws are strikingly similar—clear evidence for scholars that biblical law is rooted in earlier Near Eastern legal tradition.

The many parallels between biblical literature and ancient Near Eastern literature tell us that the Bible did not come out of a cultural vacuum; its writers employed compositional techniques and drew on intellectual traditions shared with scribes from other Near Eastern cultures. The Bible does exhibit traits without parallel in other ancient literatures, but its distinctiveness only emerges against a backdrop of pervasive similarity, and the more we learn about ancient Near Eastern literature, the more it is clear that biblical literature is basically a variant of this literature (*see box,* How Does the Hebrew Bible Differ from Other Ancient Near Eastern Texts?).

2. *The Hebrew Bible was written by human beings, not one but many living at different points in Israel's history.* A comparative approach to the Bible can help place it in an ancient Near Eastern setting, but it does not tell us who wrote the Bible, or when. Before the onset of the modern age, it scarcely occurred to Jews and Christians to ask this question because they assumed they knew the answer, believing that the Bible was of divine origin, written by Moses and other prophets commissioned by God to write on His behalf. In the seventeenth and eighteenth centuries, however—an age when all kinds of authority, including religious authority, were being questioned in Europe—scholars began to have their doubts about this traditional view. They noticed, for example, that the Five Books of Moses do not actually describe Moses as the author of the entire narrative but, rather, cite particular words that God revealed to him. Moreover, Moses himself is referred to in the third person, and in Deuteronomy 34 the text even describes his death and burial, events that the real Moses should not have been able to write about. If Moses did not write the Five Books of Moses, who did? The text never discloses its author's identity, but judging from clues discovered here and there in the text, he lived long after Moses. A famous example of such a clue appears in Genesis 36:31: "These are the kings who reigned in Edom *before any king reigned over the Israelites.*" The reference to Israelite monarchy places the verse's author not in the days of Moses but later, after the establishment of the monarchy in Israel around 1000 BCE.

The Code of Hammurabi, inscribed on an eight-foot-tall stone pillar.

As they dug deeper, scholars reached an even more surprising conclusion. A close reading of the Five Books of Moses reveals some rather odd features that are hard to explain if the narrative is the work of a single author. In Genesis 6:19, for example, God tells Noah to take two of every kind of animal to store on the ark. Just a few verses later, in 7:2–3, he gives a different version of the same command, instructing Noah to take seven pairs of every clean animal and two of every unclean animal. Why does God seem to repeat the same command twice, and why is it different in the two versions? And why does the text switch names for God from one passage to the next, using the name *Elohim* in 6:22, then

HOW DOES THE HEBREW BIBLE DIFFER FROM OTHER ANCIENT NEAR EASTERN TEXTS?

Although biblical literature resembles the literature of other ancient Near Eastern cultures in many ways, it does have unique characteristics. Part of this distinctiveness is tied to the theological assumptions of the Bible's authors, their belief in Yahweh as the only god that mattered (if not the only god altogether) and their often very subtle understanding of human nature. But it is not just the Bible's theological and psychological presuppositions that distinguish it from other ancient Near Eastern mythologies. If modern literary scholarship of the Bible is correct, its authors developed their own distinctive forms of literary communication, developing news ways to convey psychological and moral complexity. For an introduction to the distinctive artistry of biblical literature, see Robert Alter's *The Art of Biblical Narrative* (New York: Basic Books, 1983) or Meir Sternberg's more challenging *The Poetics of Biblical Narrative* (Bloomington, IN: Indiana University Press, 1987).

    Ultimately, however, what is most distinctive about the Hebrew Bible is its reception history—the role that it played in later Jewish and Christian history. Some ancient Near Eastern texts, such as the *Gilgamesh Epic*, were also transmitted for long periods of time, but no community survived long enough to preserve them beyond antiquity, and it is only in the last two centuries that they have come to light again, retrieved from obscurity through archaeological excavation and the decipherment of such ancient languages as Akkadian and Ugaritic. By contrast, the Bible was never lost—initially preserved by Jews, then by Christians as well—and its continuing significance for these communities makes it a different kind of literature than ancient Mesopotamian, Egyptian, or Ugaritic literature. The Bible is not just an obscure and archaic Near Eastern text but also a sacred literature whose contents remain highly relevant for millions of Jews and Christians.

Yahweh in 7:1? The **Pentateuch** is full of such inconsistencies. It is also full of what biblical scholars refer to as doublets: the same story told twice in slightly varying form—two accounts of how Hagar is driven from Abraham's household (Genesis 16 and 21:9–21), two accounts of how Jacob's name was changed to Israel (Genesis 32:14–33 and Genesis 35:9–10), and so on. If Moses or any individual author wrote the Five Books of Moses, why does the text contain so many factual discrepancies, vary its terminology and style, and tell the same basic story more than once?

    Unable to explain the Pentateuch's idiosyncrasies in this way, scholars came up with another explanation known as the **Documentary Hypothesis.** This theory proposes that the Five Books of Moses are not actually the work of a single author but a composite of preexisting sources. At some point, an editor wove these sources together into a narrative that is coherent but far from seamless. When this editor's sources contradicted one another, he sometimes let the contradiction stand rather than smoothing it out, perhaps because he wanted to reach different audiences with a stake in different versions of the story he was telling. The Documentary Hypothesis remains a hypothesis—the original sources have not been found—but no one has come up with a more plausible explanation for the puzzling way that the Five Books of Moses tell their tale, and it also has the advantage of being consistent with what we know of literary practice elsewhere

in the ancient Near East. For there too, as illustrated by the compositional history of the *Gilgamesh Epic*, texts were often a composite of preexisting material, supplementing earlier documents or weaving together once separate sources.

    The Documentary Hypothesis does not apply to other books in the Bible, but scholarship has reached similar conclusions about how many of them were composed. We have already noted that part of Isaiah, Deutero-Isaiah, was written long after the time of the prophet Isaiah. "First Isaiah," chapters 1–39, seem to come from the Assyrian period, and it is not impossible that it records the words of the prophet himself, but chapters 40 and following reflect conditions in the Persian period, even mentioning King Cyrus by name, as we have noted. Jeremiah and Ezekiel also seem to have grown through a long process of supplementation. So too we have seen that while the Deuteronomistic History may draw on earlier sources for its account, the work as a whole assumed its final form shortly after 586 BCE. It too contains inconsistencies and doublets, including two accounts of how Goliath was defeated, as noted in Chapter 1.

    This approach to the authorship of the Hebrew Bible not only challenges the traditional view of its authorship; it also conflicts with our idea of authorship itself. Like the Five Books of Moses, the Bible's other books were also traditionally ascribed to prophets or divinely inspired kings, such as Solomon. The ability to associate a book with a name suits the modern conception of authorship as a fundamentally individual effort. According to biblical scholarship, however, the Five Books of Moses, 1–2 Samuel, Isaiah, and most other biblical texts in the Hebrew Bible are not that kind of text; they are more akin to the U.S. Constitution, taking shape over a long period of time and incorporating the contributions of multiple and often anonymous writers.

While we cannot prove the Documentary Hypothesis, we do have empirical evidence that other books evolved over a long period of time. In Chapter 3 we will introduce the Dead Sea Scrolls. One reason these texts are so important is that they include the earliest known copies of biblical texts that date from as early as the second century BCE. Many of those manuscripts are different from the Hebrew Bible as it is known today, preserving forms of books such as Samuel and Jeremiah at an earlier stage in their literary development. The Dead Sea Scrolls provide us with before-and-after snapshots of the biblical text as it developed, allowing us to see with our own eyes how it grew and changed over the course of its transmission (*see box,* A Snapshot of the Hebrew Bible in the Making).

3. *The development of biblical literature is tied to the history of the kingdom of Judah.* Once scholars recognized the Bible as a work of human beings, they set about trying to contextualize its composition, to place it within the framework of Israelite history. In doing so, they sought to draw on what they were learning about that history to illumine the making of the Bible, and the result of this effort was a recognition that the composition of biblical literature spans much of the history of the kingdom of Judah in particular, or reflects a distinctively Judahite (as opposed to northern Israelite) point of view.

Consider how much of today's Hebrew Bible comes from Judah. Scholarship eventually identified four distinct authors at work in the Five Books of Moses, known by the initials J, E, P, and D. Two and possibly three of those sources are thought to be the work of Judahite authors (J, P, and probably D; E may come from the north). The historical narratives of Samuel and Kings, focused as they are on the Davidic monarchy, also come from Judah, some material perhaps having arisen in the royal court itself, and the book of Ruth, a story about the Moabite woman who became David's great grandmother, is also Judah focused. Isaiah, Jeremiah, and the majority of other prophetic texts come from Judah as well, or else were written by Judahites in exile (Ezekiel). The book of Psalms contains many hymns probably originally composed for use in the Jerusalem Temple, the sayings gathered in Proverbs probably represent the work of

A SNAPSHOT OF THE HEBREW BIBLE IN THE MAKING

The biblical manuscripts found among the Dead Sea Scrolls demonstrate that the Hebrew Bible used by Jews and Christians today does not always preserve the original form of the text. A dramatic example is what scholars learned about 1 Samuel 11 from a version of that text found among the Dead Sea Scrolls. That version contains a passage (marked in italics below) that does not appear in the present-day Hebrew text of the Bible. While it is possible that the additional material was inserted into the text secondarily, it is more likely that it was part of the original form of the text, and that a scribe accidentally deleted it when he was copying the text, thereby producing the version in use today.

1 Samuel 11:1–2 as the text appears in the Hebrew Bible today: Nahash the Ammonite went up and besieged Jabesh-Gilead. All the men of Jabesh-Gilead said to Nahash, "Make a covenant with us, and we will serve you."

1 Samuel 11 as known from the Dead Sea Scrolls (4Q Samuel A):   *Nahash king of the Ammonites oppressed the Gadites and the Reubenites viciously. He put out the right eye of all of them and brought fear and trembling on Israel. Not one of the Israelites in the region beyond the Jordan remained whose right eye Nahash king of the Ammonites did not put out, except seven thousand men who escaped from the Ammonites and went to Jabesh Gilead.* Then, *after a month,* Nahash the Ammonite went up and besieged Jabesh-gilead. So all the men of Jabesh-Gilead said to Nahash. . . ."

The effort to reconstruct the original form of the Bible involves a kind of scholarship known as *text criticism,* which compares different versions of the Bible in an effort to reconstruct the original form of a text and the history of its scribal transmission. For a translation of the Hebrew Bible in light of what has been discovered about its original textual form from the Dead Sea Scrolls, see Martin Abegg, Peter Flint, and Eugene Ulrich, *The Dead Sea Scrolls Bible* (San Francisco: Harper-Collins, 1999).

Jerusalem intellectuals, and the book of Lamentations preserves the mournful response to Jerusalem's destruction by the Babylonians. Works such as Esther and Ezra–Nehemiah seem to come from Judahites living in exile, or else recently returned to Judah in the Persian period. In short, most of the Hebrew Bible was composed in Judah or by exiled Judahites.

Situating the Bible within Judahite culture explains many things about it. Why does Genesis seem more positively inclined toward Jacob son's Judah, the ancestor of the Judahites, than his older brothers Reuben, Simeon, and Levi? Why do the best and most important kings in biblical history (Hezekiah and Josiah) come from the House of David in Judah, while many of its worst kings (Jeroboam or Ahab) come from the northern kingdom of Israel? Why is the Jerusalem Temple and its priesthood, the descendants of Aaron, the brother of Moses, so central while other temples in ancient Israel are marginalized or condemned? Why does the Bible seem far more interested in the Judahite survivors of Babylonian conquest and their fate than the Israelite survivors of Assyrian conquest? The answers to these and many other questions emerge when one recognizes the Hebrew Bible as the work of authors coming from the kingdom of Judah.

How is it that so much Judahite literature was preserved compared to what survives of the literature from the northern kingdom? The Bible itself suggests an answer. When the kingdom of Israel was destroyed in 722–720 BCE, its inhabitants effectively slipped off the radar screen, deported to other parts of the Assyrian Empire and eventually losing their Israelite identity. If we have some of its literature preserved in the Bible, it is probably because it was incorporated into Judah's literary tradition. The kingdom of Judah was eventually destroyed as well, but its population persisted after 586 BCE, and it was almost certainly this community that preserved the texts now collected in the Hebrew Bible, passing them on to its post-exilic descendants. In fact, a sizeable slice of what became the Jewish biblical canon was actually produced by this community, written by Judahites seeking to make sense of the experience of exile and foreign rule: Lamentations, Ezekiel, Haggai, Zechariah, Malachi, Ecclesiastes, Esther, Daniel, Ezra–Nehemiah, and 1–2 Chronicles, not to mention pre-exilic works expanded in this period, such as Isaiah. Scholars debate whether we can learn anything from the Bible about the early history of the kingdom of Judah, but almost all agree that the end of its history, the period from 600–400 BCE, has left a deep imprint on the formation of biblical literature.

The attempt to reconstruct the origins of biblical literature is an ongoing project, subject to revision in the light of new evidence and theories. What scholars have discovered thus far, however, has done much to explain how this literature came to be. Biblical literature can be exceptionally artful and is arguably revolutionary in some of its religious and ethical claims, but much of it is a variant of the kind of literature produced elsewhere in the ancient Near East in the same historical period, reflecting the same literary practices and cultural interests that shaped Ugaritic, Babylonian, and Egyptian literature. We can only hypothesize about who wrote the Bible, but it is possible to connect much of its composition to known history—not to events that we had a hard time confirming, such as the Exodus, but to demonstrable events, such as Babylonian rule. If we were to try to sum up the results of three hundred years of biblical scholarship in one sentence, we would say that its most important accomplishment is to reinterpret a text seen as supernatural and timeless as the work of humans, like you and me, shaped in what they thought and wrote about by the cultural and political environment in which they lived.

What all this does not explain, however, is how biblical literature became *the Bible,* a literature fundamentally different from any other ancient Near Eastern literature because of its role as a sacred Scripture in later Jewish (not to mention Christian) culture. Scholars are probably right that the book of Genesis combines the work of human authors living between 1000 and 500 BCE, that it is basically a variant of ancient Near Eastern literature, and that its composition was influenced by historical events, but all that only deepens the mystery of how such a text came to be seen as divine revelation. To understand that development, we must return to the history of the post-exilic Judahite community in the Persian period, connecting the emergence of the Bible as a sacred Scripture to cultural and political changes taking place at this time.

Stage II: How Biblical Literature Became a Sacred Text

What distinguishes biblical literature today from other ancient Near Eastern texts is its authority and its sacredness. Whatever its historical origins, biblical literature has long been seen as divine in origins, a communication from God, and it has long been read in that light. Long before the Bible was a book, it was a list—a list of books that Jews categorized as sacred and uniquely authoritative by dint of their divine origins and authority. The listing of that books is what is known as the biblical *canon,* an originally Greek term that is more or less synonymous with the word *catalogue.*

As we have noted, the belief that certain texts had divine authorship and authority does not begin in ancient Israel. In other ancient Near Eastern texts, scribes developed catalogues of books deemed worthy of a collection in a library or for use as a curriculum in teaching their students. It may be that the first efforts to collect and catalogue Judahite literature was an offshoot of such scholarly practices, but their preservation seems to have become even more broadly important in the wake of the Babylonian exile, when those who had survived from Judah were seeking ways to reconstitute their culture.

Judahites living after Bobylonian Exile turned to these texts to fill in the vacuum left by the destruction of other institutions. God himself was believed to be manifest in the Temple, and for this reason people visited the Temple to interact with Him or take refuge in His presence. The Temple's destruction rendered God inaccessible. For hundreds of years, Judah had been ruled by a single family, the descendants of David, providing a sense of political continuity with the distant past. Nebuchadnezzar put an end to this political tradition when he effectively ended the Davidic line. Judahite culture valued tradition: continuity between the present and the past. Babylonian conquest imposed abrupt, violent change, uprooting Judahites from the world in which their ancestors had lived. In these traumatic circumstances, Judahites focused on surviving remnants of their culture that could connect them to the pre-exilic period, objects such as the vessels used in Solomon's Temple that had been deported to Babylon but were potentially retrievable. Texts from ancient Judah were yet another remnant from the pre-exilic past—histories, laws, prophecies, psalms, didactic texts such as Proverbs—and they too took on new significance in the post-exilic age as a resource for restoring all that Judah had lost.

Investing this literature with even more value was the fact that so much of it preserved, or seemed to preserve, the words of God to Israel—God's promise to Abraham and his descendants, the divine revelation at Mount Sinai, and the visions and oracles revealed to later prophets, such as Isaiah and Jeremiah. These divine messages had been addressed to earlier Israelites, but some were also intended for future generations; sometimes, in fact, they seemed to address precisely those dire circumstances in which the Judahites found themselves after the Babylonian conquest:

> When Moses finished writing down in a book the words of this law [Torah] to the very end, he commanded the Levites who carried the ark of the covenant of the Lord, saying, "Take this book of the law [Torah] and put it beside the ark of the covenant of the Lord your God; let it be a witness against you. . . . For I know that after my death you will surely act corruptly, and you will turn aside from the way that I have commanded you. At the

end of days trouble will befall you because you will do what is evil in the sight of the Lord, angering Him with the deeds of your hands." (Deuteronomy 31:24–26, 29)

Judahites struggling to survive in a devastated Judah or languishing in Babylonian exile looked to this and other prophetic passages to find an explanation for their misfortunes. But if exile was their punishment for having done evil in the sight of the Lord, how were they to repair that relationship? Without the Temple, the ritual procedures and atonement sacrifices used to mollify God's anger were no longer operative, nor was there a Davidic king who might restore the cult, as kings had done in pre-exilic Judah. While there were still prophets who spoke for God, they often sent contradictory messages, some, like Jeremiah, urging submission to Babylon even as others encouraged defiance. Biblical interpretation—the searching of texts such as the Five Books of Moses for guidance—emerged during this period as a way to reestablish a relationship with God, a kind of divination through which one could learn why God was angry with Israel, and what it would take for Israel to revive its relationship with him.

Examples of such biblical interpretation can already be found in the Bible itself, in the books of Ezra and Nehemiah. Often treated in biblical manuscripts and by modern scholars as a single composition, Ezra–Nehemiah was probably composed in the fourth century BCE and is one of our major sources for the history of the early post-exilic community. The book of Ezra describes the return from exile, the reconstruction of the Temple, and the mission of Ezra, a Judahite priest and scribe sent to the province of Yehud by the Persian king Artarxerxes to regulate life there according to the law of Ezra's God. Nehemiah was another Judahite in the Persian court, the king's cupbearer, who secured the king's permission to return to Yehud and rebuild Jerusalem—and much of the book of Nehemiah is a first-person memoir of his experiences. Like other biblical books, Ezra–Nehemiah suffers from its share of historical problems, including an extremely confused chronology of events that may put events and people in the wrong historical order. The scribe Ezra is remembered in later Jewish tradition as a pivotal figure in the history of Judaism, an ideal sage second only to Moses himself, but it is not clear that he even existed or, if he did, when he lived or what he did. Still, Ezra–Nehemiah is our only account of this period, and whatever its historical shortcomings, it offers many insights into Persian-period Judahite culture.

Of special relevance to our discussion here is what Ezra–Nehemiah tells us about the emergence of a protobiblical canon in this period. The Five Books of Moses as we know them today may not have existed by this point, but something like them did, a text Ezra–Nehemiah refers to as "the book of the law" or "the law of Moses." If not the actual Five Books of Moses we have today, this law book anticipates many of its characteristics: it contained divine commands that Israel was obligated to obey, it was identified as a "teaching" or "Torah" of Moses, and the public reading of its contents was an important communal experience.

This text was critical to the post-exilic community's efforts to revitalize itself according to Ezra–Nehemiah. In its view of things, the first step was the return from exile and the rebuilding of the Temple, but those steps were not sufficient for a full restoration of the community. When Ezra and Nehemiah reached Yehud, they found that things were still terribly awry: Jerusalem was largely unrestored and vulnerable to its enemies. The people were full of complaints, and—of greatest concern to Ezra and Nehemiah—they were on the verge of assimilating into the local population, intermarrying with foreigners, adopting their ways, even forgetting how to speak their native tongue. The Judahites had returned to the land, but they were still slaves: "Its rich yield goes to the kings whom you have set over us because of our sins; they have power also over our bodies and over our livestock at their pleasure, and we are in great distress" (Nehemiah 9:37). For Ezra–Nehemiah, a full restoration requires the people to recommit to God's law, a process that involves reading and studying Moses' teaching.

From this perspective, the climax of Ezra–Nehemiah occurs in the eighth chapter of Nehemiah when Ezra summons the people to Jerusalem for a public reading of the law, an opportunity for them to remember what it is that God had commanded them to do. But it takes more than reading the law aloud to understand its contents; it must also be studied, interpreted, and implemented, a process that begins on the very next day:

> On the second day the heads of ancestral houses of all the people, the priests and the Levites gathered to the scribe Ezra in order to investigate the words of the law [Torah]. They found written in the Torah, which the Lord had commanded by the hand of Moses, that the people of Israel should live in booths during the festival of the seventh month, and that they should announce and proclaim in all their towns and in Jerusalem, "Go out to the hills and bring branches of olive, wild olive, myrtle, palm, and other leafy trees to make booths, as it is written" [see Leviticus 23:40]. The people went out and brought them, and made booths for themselves, each on his roof, and in their courts and in the courts of the house of God, and in the square at the Gate of Water and in the square at the Gate of Ephraim. All the

community of those who had returned from the captivity made booths and lived in them; for the people of Israel had not made them from the days of Joshua son of Nun to that day. (Nehemiah 8:13–17)

According to Nehemiah, neither the return from exile nor the Temple's reconstruction, were enough to restore Judah's relationship with God. In fact some of God's commands had been forgotten long before the destruction of the Temple, having been neglected since the days of Joshua. It was only by studying the words of the law (or *Torah* in Hebrew, a word that can also be translated as "teaching") that the Judahites were able to fully restore their relationship with God.

We have no way of knowing whether this incident ever happened, but even if it did not, the description of it in Ezra–Nehemiah signals an important shift in Judahite culture: the emergence of a sacred text, the Torah of Moses, as the ultimate source of communal and religious norms in Judahite society. The Judahites of the narrative turn to this text and its laws not only to figure out how to observe religious holidays, but to determine who they are allowed to marry and trade with, how to handle debt, and how to manage the Temple cult—in short, how to conduct themselves as a community. At this time, a good portion of biblical literature may not have existed yet: some books, such as Esther, were only written in the Persian period, perhaps even postdating Ezra–Nehemiah, and many biblical texts would continue to develop for many centuries. What began taking shape in the Persian period was the underlying belief that motivated these later developments, the belief that a certain text, the Torah of Moses, articulated a vision of social and religious organization that Judahites should aspire to realize.

This is not to say that the biblical canon is necessarily the invention of the Persian age. One of the most intriguing episodes for understanding the emergence of a biblical canon appears in 2 Kings 22–23, which describes the discovery of a long lost "Torah of Moses" during the reign of the Judahite king **Josiah** (640–609 BCE). Allegedly rediscovered during repair work on the Temple, the scroll records the commands Israel must follow to keep its covenant with God. The people have been violating those commands, Josiah realizes, and so he initiates a major reform of Judah's religious life, suppressing its idolatrous practices. Modern scholars suspect that the scroll in question was the book of Deuteronomy and that its rediscovery was actually a ruse staged to pass off a newly composed law book as an ancient Mosaic text. If that hypothesis is correct, what we have in 2 Kings 22–23 is a description of how one of the books of the Five Books of Moses came to be published, which suggests in turn that the biblical canon was already developing even before the exile.

Whenever the biblical canon first began to take shape, however, it seems to have been Persian rule that cemented its authority. As part of his efforts to consolidate the organization of the Persian Empire, Darius I apparently tried to codify the local laws of the various communities under his rule, or at least this is the implication of a document from Egypt that indicates that he ordered his satrap to form a committee of Egyptian sages to gather in writing all the old laws of Egypt down to the time of Persia's conquest, a collation of public law, temple law, and private law. Persian rule seems to have undertaken a similar project in the province of Yehud. We may even have the royal decree that authorized this initiative, a letter cited in the book of Ezra:

> This is a copy of the letter that King Artaxerxes gave to the priest Ezra, the scribe, a scholar of the text of the commandments of the Lord and his laws for Israel: "Artaxerxes, king of kings, to the priest Ezra, the scribe of the law of the God of heaven . . . you are sent by the king and his seven counselors to make inquiries about Judah and Jerusalem according to the law of your God . . . appoint magistrates and judges who may judge all the people [in the province] "Beyond the River" who know the laws of your God; and you shall teach those who do not know. All who will not obey the law of your God and the law of the king, let judgment be strictly executed upon them, whether for death or for banishment or for confiscation of their goods or for imprisonment. (Ezra 7:11–12, 14, 25–26)

In this document, the Persian Empire not only recognizes the law of God; it puts its own authority behind that law, ordering it to be taught to those who do not know it and giving Ezra the power to punish those who violate it. Given Darius' known efforts to codify Egyptian law, one wonders whether it was Persian rule that initiated the codification of the Five Books of Moses as well, working through such sages as Ezra to gather the legal traditions of Judah into a single authoritative text. The law of Moses certainly acquired a new status in the Persian period: it became the official law of Yehud, recognized not just by Judahites but by the Persian Empire; measures were taken to teach its contents to the public; and those who violated its prescriptions were subject to punishment.

The Elephantine Papyri (introduced at the beginning of this chapter) may preserve a glimpse into Persia's role in disseminating the law of Moses among Judahites living outside Yehud. One of the Elephantine documents is a letter sent by a certain Hananiah to the Elephantine community and instructing it in how to keep the Passover. The community there does not seem to know about the law of Moses, never citing it

in any of the documents it has left behind, but this letter, dated to 418 BCE, may be an attempt at an introduction:

> Now, this year, the fifth year of King Darius, word was sent from the king to Arsa[mes saying, "Authorize a festival of unleavened bread for the Jew]ish [garrison]." So do you count fou[rteen days of the month of Nisan and] ob[serve the Passover], and from the 15th to the 21st day of [Nisan observe the festival of unleavened bread]. Be (ritually) clean and take heed. [Do n]o work [on the 15th or the 21st day, no]r drink [beer, nor eat] anything [in] which the[re is] leaven [from the 14th at] sundown until the 21st of Nis[an. Br]ing into your closets [anything leavened that you may have on hand] and seal it up between those date[s].

As one can tell from all the words between brackets, the letter is fragmentary and much of its contents must be reconstructed, but what is actually preserved of this document suggests that it was an effort to inform the Elephantine community about how to keep the festival of Passover. Hananiah does not mention the Torah as the source of these laws, but some of his instructions seem to come from it (though not all). What is no less interesting here is that the letter seems to have been commissioned by the Persian government: *"Word was sent from the king."* How did the law of Moses become so authoritative in Judahite culture? This letter, together with the book of Ezra, potentially fills in a part of the answer: recognizing the law of Moses as official Judahite law, Persia recruited Judahite officials, such as Hananiah and Ezra, to promote it among their people.

This effort apparently had an impact, for not too long after the end of Persian rule at the end of the fourth century BCE, about 120 years after Hananiah wrote his letter, Hecateus, a contemporary of Alexander the Great, wrote a description of Judah, and the society he describes is governed by Mosaic law: "The colony was headed by a man named Moses. . . . he established the temple that they hold in chief veneration, instituted their forms of worship and ritual, drew up their laws, and ordered their institutions."

All this only speaks to the emerging authority of the first part of the Hebrew Bible, the Five Books of Moses, the Torah. The Jewish Bible of today now has two other parts: (1) The **Prophets,** the section that includes the historical narratives of Joshua, Judges, 1–2 Samuel, and 1–2 Kings; the large or "major" prophetic texts of Isaiah, Jeremiah, and Ezekiel; and twelve brief or "minor" prophetic books; and (2) the **Writings,** which include Psalms, Proverbs, and Ezra–Nehemiah among other writings. These sections appear to have become a part of the biblical canon after the Five Books of Moses did, but unfortunately we know little about how they became part of the Jewish biblical canon because our evidence trails off around 400 BCE, before this process was complete, and only resumes in the second century BCE, by which time most of these books were already considered part of the canon. What seems to have been key, though, was the perception of these books as divinely inspired and the need for the kind of national literature that other Near Eastern peoples were developing in this same period, a literature that could help define the antiquity and national characteristics of the Judahites, their distinctive customs and beliefs, in contrast to such other peoples as the Greeks, the Babylonians, and the Egyptians, all of whom now had their own national histories.

By the first century CE, the canonization of the Hebrew Bible seems to have been largely completed, by which we mean that the biblical canon was now widely perceived in this period as closed. Earlier scholarship imagined a rabbinic meeting, the "Council of Jamnia," at which a final decision was supposedly made about what books to include in the biblical canon, but this reconstruction has fallen out of favor. Most of the Jewish biblical canon seems to have been firmly in place before the rabbinic age, the product of widespread consensus rather than a specific decision by religious authorities. The era of prophecy was thought to have ended in the Persian period, and so books written after this period could not by definition enjoy the same level of sacredness and authority. It was possible to try to pass off a forgery as an authentic book from this period, to attribute a later composition to a biblical figure such as one of Jacob's twelve sons, Moses, or King Solomon, yielding a strange assortment of texts known as the **Pseudepigrapha** (from the Greek for "falsely inscribed"), but that practice does not seem to have had much success in expanding the Jewish canon as it had taken shape by the first century CE. Most of the books in today's Jewish Bible are in fact from the Persian period or earlier, the one clear exception, the book of Daniel, ostensibly from the period of the Babylonian exile and Persian rule but containing material composed in the second century BCE (*see box,* Bible Stories the Bible Doesn't Tell).

While we cannot fill in all the details of how the early Jewish biblical canon took shape, considerable evidence documents the impact of that canon on Judahite culture after this time. Once the chain of literary evidence picks up again after the second century BCE, signs of the Hebrew Bible's influence are visible everywhere. Philo of Alexandria, a first-century biblical interpreter from Egypt who wrote volumes of commentary on the Pentateuch, claims that parents taught their children the law from a young age, and Jews may have died thinking about the Bible as well, or so it would appear from literary descriptions from this period in which people die with stories of biblical heroes on their lips. Perhaps these sources exaggerate the Bible's centrality, but archaeological evidence of its importance exists. We know, for example, that by Philo's day Jewish men placed biblical passages on their bodies in the form of phylacteries (*tefillin* in Hebrew), small black boxes containing scriptural passages that are fastened by leather straps to the head and arm. Literary evidence for

BIBLICAL STORIES THE BIBLE DOESN'T TELL

Some pseudepigraphical works were found among the Dead Sea Scrolls, but most were known long before then, from translations into languages such as Ethiopic and Armenian, that were preserved by various Christian communities. Thanks to these translations, in fact, we have all kinds of texts attributed to biblical figures but not preserved in the Bible: "apocalypses" that describe the revelation of divine secrets to biblical figures such as Enoch and Baruch (Jeremiah's secretary); "testaments" that preserve the last words of Jacob's twelve sons, Moses, and others; expansions of biblical episodes like the story of how Joseph married his Egyptian bride, Aseneth; and various hymns and prayers attributed to David and Solomon. How do we know these works are not really from the biblical period? Some Jews and Christians believed that they were, but scholarship has come to recognize that they were actually composed by Jews between 200 BCE and 200 CE (several were also probably reworked by later Christians), in some cases because they were written in Greek as used in this period, in others because they reflect ideas and interpretive traditions, including Christian ideas, known to have arisen in this later time. We do not know why these texts did not become a part of Jewish and Christian Bibles, but chances are that they were simply composed too late to be included, most having been written after the Jewish biblical canon was more or less closed. Written centuries after the biblical period, pseudepigraphical literature contains nothing of value for understanding the history and literature of ancient Judah, but it is an extremely useful resource for understanding how the Bible was interpreted in early Jewish culture.

the wearing of *tefillin* goes back to the second century BCE, and remains of *tefillin* have even been discovered among the Dead Sea Scrolls. The scrolls have also yielded the earliest evidence of *mezuzot*, biblical passages affixed to doorposts as a reminder of God's commandments.

The Bible's importance to Jews in this period is also reflected in the rise of a new kind of cultural leader: the biblical interpreter. In the Israelite society described by the Hebrew Bible, the most revered leaders were those with some kind of direct access to God, or the descendants of such people: priests, kings, and prophets. Divinely sanctioned rulers, priests, and even prophets continued to be important in the Second Temple period, but alongside those leaders there arose another kind of authority as well, those who accessed God through the interpretation of sacred texts. As we move forward in Jewish history, that kind of figure—the biblical interpreter—will play an increasingly important role in Jewish life.

You might have noticed that in the last few paragraphs we have begun to use the term *Jewish,* as opposed to *Judahite.* Why the difference? The Jews we are speaking of here saw themselves as the direct descendants of the pre-exilic Judahites, but their use of biblical interpretation to connect themselves to those ancestors was, ironically, an essential difference from them. The culture they developed was a good approximation of pre-exilic Judah as it had existed in biblical times—a culture devoted to a deity named YHWH, centered in Jerusalem, respectful of, if not conversant in, Hebrew, and so forth—but the very fact that this newly reconstituted culture was generated through the reading of the Bible is precisely what distinguishes it from Judahite culture of earlier centuries when much of biblical literature may not have even existed yet. The emergence of the biblical canon, though a process and not a precisely datable event, is such an important turning point that we propose it as the moment Judahite culture becomes Jewish culture.

A Crash Course in the Jewish Bible

Because the Bible became so central to Jewish culture after the Persian period, exerting a shaping influence on Jewish life to this day, it is important to have some sense of its contents. We demonstrate its influence in subsequent chapters and devote the remainder of this one to giving you a kind of crash course in the Jewish Bible: an introduction to its contents and meaning as these emerged in early Jewish culture. Readers who feel they are already familiar with the Bible, or who are eager to push on with the narrative of Jewish history, may want to skip ahead to the next chapter. For those who need more of a sense of what we mean by "the Bible" in this book,

or of how Jewish understandings of the Bible differ from those of other religious communities, the following is an attempt to provide some concise introductory information.

By the term *Bible* we mean the Jewish biblical canon, not a single book but a collection of texts deemed sacred and authoritative by Jewish communities. Other religious communities also venerate the Bible, but they define and understand its contents differently. The early Christian Bible relied on the Septuagint, a Greek translation of the Bible, which included books found in the Hebrew version used by Jews in the Jewish Bible but also books such as Tobit and Judith not found there. This latter set of books, referred to by Catholics as the **deuterocanonical** books, is still part of Scripture in the Roman Catholic and Eastern Orthodox Churches. For their part, Protestants embraced the Jewish definition of the Bible, relabeling the deuterocanonical books as the **Apocrypha** (an originally Greek word that refers to texts of dubious origin) and excluding them from their canon, but of course, their Bible, like all Christian Bibles, also includes the New Testament, which is also not part of the Jewish Bible. Arguably, there are as many conceptions of the Bible as there are religious communities that venerate it (incidentally, biblical figures such as Abraham, Moses, and David are also part of Muslim sacred history, but Muslims believe that God, known in Arabic as *Allah,* also revealed himself to a later prophet, Muhammad, and it is the record of those later revelations, the *Koran,* that constitutes the Muslim scriptural canon) (*see box,* The Jewish, Catholic, and Protestant Biblical Canons).

Our focus is the Bible as defined and understood by Jews, a text now divided into three sections:

1. The core of this Bible is the Five Books of Moses: *Bereshit* (Genesis), *Shemot* (Exodus), *Vayikra* (Leviticus), *Bamidbar* (Numbers), and *Devarim* (Deuteronomy), a section identified with the "Torah of Moses" mentioned by such sources as Ezra–Nehemiah. As used in the Bible, the word *Torah* can mean "law"—and so it was translated by the Septuagint, which renders it with the Greek term *nomos*—but it can also mean "teaching." The Torah was read in both ways by early Jews: as a divine law and also as a divine teaching, a source of religious wisdom and moral guidance.

2. The second section of the Jewish Biblical canon, Prophets, contains two kinds of material: (a) the "Former Prophets," an account of Israelite/Judahite history from the conquest to the Babylonian exile (Joshua, Judges, 1–2 Samuel, and 1–2 Kings)—seen as a work of prophecy because of the central role that prophets like Samuel play in its narrative; (b) the "Latter Prophets," texts that record the words of prophets from the period of Assyrian, Babylonian,

and Persian rule. The first three books in this section, Isaiah, Jeremiah, and Ezekiel, are known as the "Major Prophets" because of their length, while the other twelve books are called the "Minor Prophets" because of their brevity.

3. The third section, the "Writings," includes the Psalms, the Proverbs, the Song of Solomon, Daniel, Ezra–Nehemiah, and other miscellaneous writings. These works were also evidently perceived by early Jews as prophetic, but in contrast to the Torah and the Prophets, which preserve God's efforts to communicate with Israel, several of the books in this section record the human side of the divine–human interaction—words addressed to God in gratitude or need (the Psalms) and observations about how God operates (such as Proverbs and Job). It is not clear why such texts were included in the Jewish biblical canon, but their inclusion may have to do with the fact that many of them were associated with biblical figures deemed to be divinely inspired in their own right, especially David and Solomon (as a matter of fact, one of the Dead Sea Scrolls, the *Psalms Scroll,* claims explicitly that the Psalms were revealed to David by God). The content of this section is more variegated than the Torah and the Prophets, including histories, psalms, a love song, and three "wisdom" texts—Proverbs, Job, and Ecclesiastes—that aim to describe what humans can (and cannot) understand about the workings of God.

This tripartite structure, and much else about the Jewish Bible as it exists today, may not reflect how the Bible was originally organized. We think of the Bible as a text that has been finished—a text written today could not be included in the Hebrew Bible—but for much of the Second Temple period, it was not static in this way: its text was fluid, as were the contents of the biblical canon—what was considered Scripture, and what was not.

One striking piece of evidence for the Bible's fluidity in this period is the contrast between the Bible in use today and the Greek translation used by ancient Greek-speaking Jews and then by Christians. The Jewish Bible in use today is known as the **Masoretic Bible,** named for the group of scribes, the **Masoretes,** who copied this particular version of the biblical text. Active between the sixth century CE and the tenth century CE, the Masoretes not only copied the Bible; they also developed a variety of devices to help Jews read it. In its original form, the Hebrew Bible mainly records the consonants of words, not the vowels (with a few exceptions), and lacks punctuation marks to help readers make sense of the text. Without these guides, the biblical text can be very confusing and ambiguous, hard even to pronounce, much less understand. To facilitate interpretation, the Masoretes developed vowel signs, an accent system that guided how

biblical books were read in liturgical settings, and marginal notations and textual divisions.

The **Septuagint** (a term that originally referred to a Greek translation of the Torah but here is used loosely to describe the Greek translation of the Jewish Bible in its entirety) preserves a form of the biblical canon from a much earlier period than the Masoretic Bible. Not only does this version predate the impact of Masoretic scribal activity; it translates a different form of the biblical text (the Greek version of the story of David and Goliath, for example, is some fifty verses shorter than the Masoretic version). While the Masoretic Bible divides the book into three sections—Torah, Prophets, and Writings—the Septuagint is organized according in a different scheme and includes a number of books not found at all in the Masoretic version—the deuterocanonical texts/apocryphal texts still venerated as Scripture in the Roman Catholic Church. The Septuagint thus preserves another snapshot of the Jewish Bible before its text and ordering were fixed in the form that would eventually become the Masoretic Bible.

Over time, much of this variation was reduced. Most of the textual differences between different manuscripts of the Hebrew Bible were leveled out by the second century CE, at least for Jews, when Jewish religious authorities settled on the particular version of the biblical text, the proto-Masoretic version, that would eventually become the canonical Jewish Bible in use to this day. Perhaps this was because other forms of the Hebrew biblical text had been lost by that time—the Temple may have served as a storehouse for biblical manuscripts in their different forms, and its destruction in 70 CE may have entailed their loss—or perhaps alternative versions were deliberately abandoned for some reason, but we simply do not know. The invention of the printing press, used to publish the Bible, standardized its form and content still more. Today's Jewish Bible is a good approximation of the Jewish Bible of the first century—careful copying preserved its content intact to a remarkable degree, as we can now see by comparing the Masoretic Bible to ancient biblical manuscripts found among the Dead Sea Scrolls—but that same comparison also shows that today's Jewish Bible is still significantly different from ancient Bibles, and much more uniform as well.

The limits of time and space prevent us from summarizing the Bible's contents beyond what we have already done, but some of its most essential claims need to be stressed to understand the development of Jewish culture:

1. *Israel's relationship with God was special, entitling it to a special destiny and also imposing special responsibilities that distinguished it from other peoples.* The Bible begins by

THE JEWISH, CATHOLIC, AND PROTESTANT BIBLICAL CANONS

Jewish Canon	Catholic Canon	Protestant Canon
The Five Books of Moses		
Genesis	Genesis	Genesis
Exodus	Exodus	Exodus
Leviticus	Leviticus	Leviticus
Numbers	Numbers	Numbers
Deuteronomy	Deuteronomy	Deuteronomy
Prophets		
Joshua	Joshua	Joshua
Judges	Judges	Judges
Samuel (1 and 2)	1 Samuel	1 Samuel
	2 Samuel	2 Samuel
Kings (1 and 2)	1 Kings	1 Kings
	2 Kings	2 Kings
Isaiah	Isaiah	Isaiah
Jeremiah	Jeremiah	Jeremiah
Ezekiel	Ezekiel	Ezekiel
Hosea	Hosea	Hosea
Joel	Joel	Joel
Amos	Amos	Amos
Obadiah	Obadiah	Obadiah
Jonah	Jonah	Jonah
Micah	Micah	Micah
Nahum	Nahum	Nahum
Habakkuk	Habakkuk	Habakkuk
Zephaniah	Zephaniah	Zephaniah

portraying God as the creator of all the peoples of the world, but it quickly zeroes in on his relationship with Israel, a people specially favored by God as a "treasured possession" (Exodus 19:5). The central problem that preoccupies the Hebrew Bible is how to sustain this special relationship with God, a relationship that the Pentateuch conceptualizes as a "covenant," a voluntary pact binding God and the people of Israel in a relationship of mutual obligation. The history of this relationship goes back to Noah and Abraham, but most of the Torah focuses on the covenant that God establishes with the Israelites at Mount Sinai after he rescues them from Egyptian bondage. The laws in Exodus, Leviticus, Numbers, and Deuteronomy are the stipulations of the covenant, the terms that Israel must abide by to sustain its relationship

with God (*see box,* The Terms of Israel's Relationship with God).

2. *Israel's relationship with God depends on intermediaries.* Sustaining Israel's relationship required various kinds of intermediaries to keep it going, people specially designated to serve as go-betweens. Moses is the model of the prophetic intermediary. His main role is to convey God's words to the people, demonstrate God's power through the feats and wonders that he performs, and intercede when God is angry with the people. Later prophets play a similar role, though according to one biblical text, they had less direct access to God than Moses, seeing God in visions and dreams rather than speaking to him "face to face" (Numbers 12:6–8). The prophetic section of the Bible, the second section of the Jewish

Jewish Canon	Catholic Canon	Protestant Canon
Haggai	Haggai	Haggai
Zechariah	Zechariah	Zechariah
Malachi	Malachi	Malachi
Writings		
Psalms	Psalms	Psalms
Proverbs	Proverbs	Proverbs
Job	Job	Job
Song of Solomon	Song of Solomon	Song of Solomon
Ruth	Ruth	Ruth
Lamentations	Lamentations	Lamentations
Ecclesiastes	Ecclesiastes	Ecclesiastes
Esther	Esther (with additions)	Esther
Daniel	Daniel (with additions)	Daniel
Ezra–Nehemiah	Ezra	Ezra
	Nehemiah	Nehemiah
Chronicles (1 and 2)	1 Chronicles	1 Chronicles
	2 Chronicles	2 Chronicles
	Tobit	The New Testament
	Judith	
	Wisdom of Solomon	
	1 Maccabees	
	2 Maccabees	
	Sirach	
	Baruch (with Letter of Jeremiah)	
	The New Testament	

What this chart does not make clear is that the different canons also sequence the biblical books differently.

biblical canon, provides a record of what God revealed to such prophets during the period of the monarchy, exile, and Persian rule.

The two other kinds of intermediaries that help sustain Israel's relationship with God are the priest and the king, both defined by their membership in a particular family. Priestly status was a matter of genealogy, of descent from Aaron, the brother of Moses (the larger tribe of Levi from which Aaron came was commissioned to play a supportive role in the sanctuary, a kind of lower class of Temple official who helped guard the sanctuary and maintain its cult). Kingship was a matter of genealogy as well: the only legitimate kings for the Bible are the descendants of David through his son Solomon. The priest presented Israel's offerings before the Lord, protected the holiness of the sanctuary, and delivered messages from God through the Urim and Thummim, mysterious objects worn by the priests. The king led Israel into war on God's behalf, administered justice, and helped keep God accessible to Israel by building and sustaining the Temple.

3. *There are crises in Israel's relationship with God, but they can be overcome.* The Hebrew Bible establishes what it takes for Israel to sustain a relationship with God; it also dramatizes how easily that relationship can go awry. The Israel portrayed in the Bible frequently violates its obligations to God, straying after other gods, mistreating the vulnerable, and committing other sins against God or fellow Israelites. One main role of the prophets was to serve as a warning

The Ten Commandments as they appear on a page from the Masoretic Bible, dating from the ninth century A.D.

THE TERMS OF ISRAEL'S RELATIONSHIP WITH GOD

According to the Hebrew Bible, the Israelites must adhere to the following practices to fulfill their obligations to God:

1. Humans must be fruitful and multiply, an obligation imposed by God on all humanity when the world was first created (Genesis 1:28).

2. Humans cannot take human life and must avoid consuming the blood of animals they kill, an obligation created when God established a covenant with Noah and his descendants (Genesis 9).

3. The descendants of Abraham through Isaac must circumcise male children eight days after birth as a sign of God's covenant with Abraham and his descendants (Genesis 17).

4. The divine commandments given at Mount Sinai and in the wilderness, the terms of the covenant established specifically with Israel, are too numerous to be summarized here, but the best known, listed in no particular order, include the following:

   a. Resting on the Seventh Day

   b. Promoting justice within the Israelite community by following God's instructions for how to treat slaves, strangers, and other vulnerable people; punish crimes and establish the officials and procedures needed to administer the law; and resolve disputes fairly and effectively

   c. Worshipping God in the correct way by avoiding idol worship and other cultic practices used to worship other gods; erecting a sanctuary according to God's specifications and protecting its sanctity; establishing the sanctuary's personnel (priests and Levites) and the ritual procedures they are to follow when drawing near to God; presenting certain sacrifices and other offerings on schedule and in the right way; and observing three annual pilgrimage festivals: Passover, Shavuot, and Sukkot

   d. Conquering the land and distributing its territory according to the laws that God lays out; farming it in a way that respects its status as divine property; and avoiding the kinds of immoral behavior that had so defiled the land when earlier peoples had lived in Canaan that it had ejected them

   e. Adhering to special dietary laws (only eating animals with cleft hooves that also chew the cud—pigs have the first trait but not the latter; only eating sea creatures with fins and scales; avoiding birds of prey, rodents, lizards, and such); and following other practices to maintain the distinction between clean and unclean. Impurity, generated by bleeding, some forms of sexual activity, and death, and easily contracted, was an unavoidable consequence of living in the world, and so God established the rites of the Day of Atonement (*Yom Kippur*) and other rituals through which Israel must rid itself and the sanctuary of impurities that might alienate it from God.

What is Israel to receive in return for following these and other divine commands? A long, prosperous life in Canaan, protection from enemies and other dangers, the esteem of other peoples, and special access to God.

---

system, cautioning Israel against such behaviors, urging it to change its ways.

In the end, according to the Bible, the Israelites failed to abide by their responsibilities, so alienating God that he allows their enemies to destroy the kingdoms of Israel and Judah and to send them into exile. But even in the wake of disaster, biblical literature envisions a future in which Judah and indeed all Israel will be restored. The Bible's description of this future age, frequently referred to in prophetic literature, is vague and inconsistent, and it is not clear when it will occur or what will bring it about. Despite this ambiguity, its very effort to envision such a future generates the possibility of a continued relationship between God and Israel beyond

the loss of the kingship, the Temple's destruction, and Judah's exile from its land.

Early Jewish readers of the Bible believed themselves to be the heirs to the covenant established at Mount Sinai, obligated to keep its laws and hopeful that they could overcome whatever ruptures emerged in their relationship with God. Things were not quite the same in the post-exilic period— many of the tribes were long gone by that time, and Jews could no longer look to a Davidic king to represent them before God—but much of the covenant could nonetheless be sustained in the reality that took shape during the Persian period. Jews had been restored to their land, the Temple had been reestablished, the Aaronid priesthood continued, as did the possibility of prophecy, and Jews were hopeful that what they had lost in the exile might yet be restored if they followed the instructions laid out in the Torah and heeded the warnings of the prophets.

The problem that Jews encountered as they tried to achieve these goals was that it was not always so easy to make sense of biblical texts, which were fraught with informational gaps, ambiguous or obscure language, and occasional inconsistencies. If you were seeking to keep the Ten Commandments as recorded in Exodus 20, for example, consider some of the interpretive problems you would face. There is much at stake in keeping these commands: not only will God punish those who disobey them, God declares, but their descendants will be punished too, while he will show kindness to those who obey them "to the thousandth generation" (Exodus 20:5–6). But to keep these commands, one has to know things that the biblical text simply does not make clear. Does the command not to work on the Sabbath mean that one cannot care for a sick family member on this day? If the person died as a result of your decision to keep the Sabbath, would that not violate the command against killing? And what for that matter is the meaning of "You shall not kill"? Is God prohibiting the killing that happens in war or the execution of a criminal for a capital offense, killing sanctioned by other biblical laws? The Torah does not provide enough information to put these commands into practice.

Yet another problem faced by early interpreters was the difficulty of applying by-then ancient texts to the contemporary reality in which they happened to live. In 2 Samuel 7, God promises David that his descendants will rule forever. What did such a promise mean in a world in which there was no Davidic dynasty and Jews lived under the rule of foreign powers? The prophecies in the book of Isaiah refer to the Assyrians. What did such prophecies mean in a much later age when Jews faced not Assyria but the Greeks and the Romans? Early biblical interpretation is based on the assumption that the Bible is a perpetually relevant text, a text about the past that can also be related to the present, but that assumption stood in tension with the fact that a good portion of the Bible was out of date by the time it was read by ancient interpreters, referring to the kingship and other aspects of Judahite culture that did not pertain to Jewish culture as it later developed.

Early Jewish readers of the Bible solved these problems in a way that often violates our sense of the Bible's intended or literal meaning. They saw meaning in tiny details that seem trivial by our way of reading. From a spare law, such as the command to keep the Sabbath, they derived numerous restrictions and rituals without any basis in the actual biblical text. They read prophecies addressed to the bygone era of biblical times as predictions of *their* future, or even as references to events happening in their own day. Early Jewish readers of the Bible did not play by the same interpretive rules that modern secular scholars do, and their interpretation often seems fanciful or contrived by that standard of how to read the Bible.

An intelligence is at work, however, in how early Jews responded to the Bible. Generally, even the most fanciful interpretations are responding to something in the text, some odd detail or troubling inconsistency that could not be understood without going beyond the information supplied in the Bible. Early Jews assumed that God must have had some reason for implanting these problems in the text, and biblical interpretation was an attempt to figure out that reason, treating the Bible's inconsistencies and gaps as signals that a message, law, or lesson was encrypted in the text that one could detect by resolving the inconsistency or filling in the gap.

Let us return to the Ten Commandments as an illustration. The Bible actually contains two versions of the Ten Commandments: the version cited previously, which comes from Exodus 20, and a second version in Deuteronomy 5. The two versions are nearly identical, with several small differences, including how the Sabbath command is worded: Exodus 20 commands Israel to *remember* the Sabbath day, whereas Deuteronomy 5 bids Israel to *keep* or *guard* the Sabbath. How could God have said "remember" and "keep" at the same time? Modern scholars have certainly noticed this inconsistency, and for them the two versions of the Ten Commandments represent yet another doublet in the Torah, more evidence that it conflates material drawn from different sources. That is a plausible explanation, but it was inconceivable for early Jewish interpreters who instead saw the inconsistency as evidence for something else, not a contradiction but a sign that God was trying to send two distinct messages:

> "Remember" and "Keep"—these two words were said by God in a single word . . . as it is said [in Psalm 62:12]: "One [thing] God has spoken, two have I heard." (*Mekhilta de Rabbi Ishmael*)

As Psalm 62 teaches (in this interpretation of the psalm), the apparent contradiction of "Remember" and "Keep" reflects how we humans experience revelation, not the revelation itself: in a communicative feat impossible for mere mortals, both statements not only come from God but were spoken by him in the same moment. That is, God can communicate in a way that mortals cannot, surpassing the limits of human speech, and therefore his words in the Torah should be read in a different way. Contradictory statements can both be true; words can have more than one meaning; even individual letters, indeed even the forms of letters, can be loaded with significance.

This interpretation is taken from a collection of rabbinic interpretations of the book of Exodus known as *Mekhilta de Rabbi Ishmael.* We will introduce the rabbis in Chapter 5, and we will see there that they practiced a form of biblical interpretation known as *midrash* that was distinctive in many ways, not least because of its assumption that the biblical text could support more than one interpretation. But the rabbis were not alone in their assumption that the difference between "Remember" and "Keep/Guard" was significant. Some early Jews, including the members of the Dead Sea Scroll community, concluded that the command in Deuteronomy 5 to "keep" the Sabbath represented a distinctive commandment, not an inconsistent version of the command in Exodus 20 but a second, separate law revealed at the same time. According to their interpretation, Deuteronomy 5 indicated that Jews had an obligation not simply to observe the Sabbath day itself but to safeguard the Sabbath's observance by stopping work before the Sabbath so as to avoid doing something that might cause one to miss its start time. Though in biblical times the starting point of the Sabbath was already fixed as Friday at sunset, by the first century CE, many Jews were ending work even earlier on Friday, in the late afternoon around 3:00 P.M. What prompted this practice, it seems, was their interpretation of the Torah's command "to guard" the Sabbath.

While this reading might conflict with our modern sense of what the biblical authors intended to communicate, early Jewish interpreters had their reasons for reading it in this way. Nowhere does the Torah indicate when the Sabbath actually begins, an ambiguity that places one in danger of violating it. This reading helps to address that problem by fixing a start point early enough to avoid any possibility of transgressing the command. To our eyes, it may go beyond the text's literal meaning, but early Jews could point to something in that text as the basis for this practice—the discrepancy between "keep" and "remember," which in their view had to have significance since both words came from God. Early biblical interpretation becomes a lot more comprehensible when one remembers that it is not merely an attempt to understand the Bible but also an effort to put it into practice.

This chapter has emphasized that the "Jewish Bible" is not just the biblical text, the words inscribed on a particular collection of scrolls, but the way Jews interact with these words, how they understand and respond to them. Those same words are sacred to other communities as well—Samaritans and Christians—but as read in those communities, the Bible is not a Jewish sacred text but a Samaritan or a Christian one. To understand the *Jewish* Bible, one must understand the meaning of its text in Jewish minds and its role in Jewish lives.

The Bible and the Birth of Jewish Culture

One of the few constants in Jewish culture, persisting from the days of the Second Temple until the modern age, is an engagement with the Bible, the effort to understand its content and to relate it to the present. This is not to say that every Jew has engaged the Bible in the same way—some read it in Hebrew, others in translation, still others depended on other sources for their knowledge of it—but the engagement itself is one of the few threads that runs through all of Jewish history, connecting diverse communities that are otherwise very different from one another. Even today, long after modern scholarship has called the divine authorship of the Bible into question and many Jews have become secularized, the Bible remains central to Jewish life. The history it tells shapes how Jews remember their origins, its laws govern the lives of the religiously observant, and its prophecies and psalms continue to guide and inspire.

In fact, so far as we can tell, Jewish culture and the Bible have been interwoven since the beginning. A case can be made that Jewish culture predates the creation of the Bible. In the Elephantine Papyri, after all, we have evidence of a Persian-period Judahite community, with many of the attributes of later Jewish communities but no sign of the Bible itself—evidence which suggests that Jewish culture was taking shape before the rise of the biblical canon. Alternatively, one can make the case that the Bible predates the Jews, first taking shape in ancient Judah before many of the events that would turn that culture into Jewish culture—for example, the Babylonian exile, the Persian conquest, the missions of Ezra and Nehemiah. Rather than try to solve the chicken-and-egg question of which came first, we embrace what might seem like a paradoxical understanding of their relationship: Jewish culture and the Jewish Bible were born *simultaneously,* with Jewish culture generated through an engagement with the Bible even as it was giving shape to the Bible.

Questions for Reflection

1. Do you think the term *restoration* is the right one to describe what happens to Judahite culture during the Persian period? How is the Judean/Jewish culture that emerges after the exile similar to and different from that of pre-exilic Israelite culture?

2. Why did modern scholars come to question the divine origins of the Bible? What do they view as its actual origins, and how did they reach this conclusion?

3. In what ways is the Hebrew Bible's development tied to the history of Judah?

4. How is the Jewish Bible different from the Bibles of Christians or Samaritans?

5. How does the modern scholarly understanding of the Bible differ from that of early Jews? What assumptions does each approach make about the Bible?

For Further Reading

For an authoritative scholarly history of the Persian Empire, see Pierre Briant, *From Cyrus to Alexander: A History of the Persian Empire* (Winona Lake, IN: Eisenbrauns, 1998). For an accessible introduction to how modern scholarship was able to figure out the authorship of the Torah, see Richard Elliot Friedman, *Who Wrote the Bible?* (San Francisco: HarperSanFrancisco, 1997). To go still further in understanding the Hebrew Bible's composition, try Karel van der Toorn's *Scribal Culture and the Making of the Hebrew Bible* (Cambridge, MA: Harvard University Press, 2006), which uses ancient Near Eastern evidence to illumine how books such as Deuteronomy and Jeremiah were written and canonized. For an introduction to the Bible as read by early Jews, see James Kugel, *The Bible As It Was* (Cambridge, MA: Harvard University Press, 1997), or Kugel's section of a book coauthored with Roland Greer, *Early Biblical Interpretation* (Philadelphia: Westminster, 1986). For a translation of biblical pseudoepigraphia, see James Charlesworth, *The Old Testament Pseudepigrapha*, vols. 1 and 2 (Garden City, NY: Doubleday, 1983–1985).

Chapter 3

Jews and Greeks

Sometime between the third and first centuries BCE, a Jew named Ezekiel composed a work that draws on the Bible as a source yet differs from it in a way that captures how different Jewish culture in this period was from that of ancient Israel: he wrote a Greek tragedy based on the Exodus. The biblical account of the Exodus may not seem particularly "tragic" according to common understanding, but the classical Greek genre of tragedy was defined not by an unhappy ending but by formal traits that Ezekiel's play, known as the *Exagoge,* exhibits in the scant 269 lines that happen to survive. This is clear even from its opening lines, a monologue delivered by Moses that provides the audience with the background it needs to follow the story:

> And when from Canaan Jacob did depart,
> with threescore souls and ten he did go down
> to Egypt's land, and there he did beget
> a host of people: suffering, oppressed,
> ill-treated even to this very day
> by the ruling powers and by wicked men.
> For Pharaoh, seeing how our race increased
> in swarms, devised against us this grand scheme:
> he forced the men to manufacture bricks
> for use in building lofty walls and towers;
> Thus with their toil he made his cities strong.
> he ordered next the Hebrew race to cast
> their infant boys into the river deep.
> At which point, she who bore me from her womb
> did hide me for three months. . . .

The content is taken from Genesis and Exodus, but it is written in Greek, in a poetic meter typical of Greek tragedy. The very idea of beginning a play in this way, with a monologue that provides the audience with a historical overview, is one that Ezekiel probably borrowed from the great tragedian Euripides. Ezekiel borrowed other elements from Greek tragedy too. To

dramatize the parting of the Red Sea, he resorted to a cleverly cost-effective device, using a survivor of Pharaoh's army to describe what happened in retrospect—a trick for dealing with hard-to-stage spectacles pioneered by the Greek playwright Aeschylus.

The *Exagoge* is an example of the early Jewish fascination with the biblical past, but it also illustrates the changes that Jewish culture went through in the wake of **Alexander the Great.** Alexander was born in Macedonia in 356 BCE, and before he was thirty he had managed to conquer the Persian Empire, defeating **Darius III** in 331 BCE. Alexander was not the first Greek to travel in the Near East, and he did not rule this empire for long (he died in 323), but the impact of his conquests transformed the cultures of the ancient Near East for centuries, initiating a period known as the Hellenistic age (from *Hellas,* the Greek word for "Greece") that lasted until the Roman conquest of the Near East and Mediterranean in the first century BCE. Under the rule of Alexander's successors, Greek, or rather a dialect of Greek known as **koine,** became widely used, and Greek-style cities, distinguished by a distinctively Greek notion of citizenship, were established throughout the Near East. The most famous was the city of Alexandria in Egypt, founded by Alexander himself and renowned in antiquity for its architectural wonders and library, and many others were organized in similar ways, including Jerusalem. Greek forms of education and the literature that formed the curriculum for this education—Homer, Plato, and so forth—spread with the Greek city-state, along with Greek artistic and architectural conventions. This is how our author learned the skills he needed to compose the "Tragedy of Moses"—Ezekiel probably lived in Alexandria, receiving an education that included the Bible but also Greek literature.

Not all early Jews were so receptive to Greek influence. In this same period, another Jewish author wrote the

An ancient depiction of the battle between Alexander the Great and the Persian King Darius III.

book of *Jubilees,* a pseudepigraphical text to which we referred in Chapter 2. Like the *Exagoge, Jubilees* is a retelling of the Pentateuch, but it lacks any obvious signs of Greek influence. Whereas the *Exagoge* was written in Greek, for example, *Jubilees,* though now preserved in full only in Ethiopic and Latin translation, was originally written in Hebrew. And it is not just Greek that its author avoids: he seems opposed to any kind of foreign influence on Jewish religious life as well, warning future generations of Israel, for instance, against "walking in the feasts of the gentiles after their errors and after their ignorance" (*Jubilees* 6:35). The phrasing may sound biblical, but *Jubilees* was written in the second century BCE when Greek influence on Jewish culture was becoming acute, and the "gentiles" to which it refers are not the Canaanites of the Bible but probably Hellenized pagans. The *Exagoge* and *Jubilees,* written in the same period, thus illustrate two very different responses to Greek culture: one embracing it, the other distancing itself from it.

Why did some Jews emulate Greek culture while others shunned it? A Jew living in Judea (the name used by the Greeks to refer to the territory of Judah/Yehud) were in a relative backwater compared to other places and may therefore have been more insulated from Greek influence than a Jew living in a cosmopolitan center such as Alexandria, but scholars now realize that the impact of Hellenization transcended the difference between homeland and diaspora. Judea too was subject to Hellenistic influence, and in the same century when *Jubilees* was written, other Judeans were using Greek, studying in Greek educational institutions, and even wearing Greek hats. Whether or not a Jew emulated the Greeks was not just a matter of exposure but also involved decisions about how to survive in a Hellenized world.

Part of what was attractive about Greek culture is that it offered a new range of opportunities not available under earlier rulers. Greek identity as defined in the Hellenistic age was not restricted to people with a particular parentage or birthplace;

in theory at least, it was accessible to any non-Greek willing to adopt the Greek language and follow Greek customs. By speaking, dressing, and acting in a Hellenized fashion, a Jew might gain stature, influence, or even employment from the government. The very accessibility of Greek culture also made it threatening, however, with the adoption of Greek ways potentially displacing the traditions linking Jews to their ancestors. As the culture of those who ruled the Jews, moreover, a Hellenized way of life was linked in the minds of many Jews with the loss of independence, illicit taxation, and other forms of humiliation and exploitation. Thus it was that some Jews, like Ezekiel, saw reason to embrace Greek ways, while others, like the author of *Jubilees,* resisted their influence.

In reality, however, most Jews found ways to mediate between the options of complete resistance to Greek culture and complete assimilation, adjusting to life under Hellenistic rule even as they cultivated a Jewish identity. Our playwright Ezekiel is an example. Though his play is written in Greek in imitation of Greek literary models, Ezekiel probably saw himself as faithful to Jewish tradition, perhaps opting to tell the story he did—the story of an Israelite raised by a foreign princess but nonetheless remaining true to his Hebrew identity—to demonstrate that it was possible to sustain a strong Jewish identity in a foreign setting. We do know of Jews who completely abandon their allegiance to Jewish law, but Ezekiel was not one of them, for while he was clearly influenced by Greek culture, he also seems proud of his Jewish identity.

Our focus in this chapter is this space between resistance and assimilation. We will look at how Jews first encountered Greek culture in the Hellenistic period, and we will consider what people and events were important in shaping their subsequent interaction. During this period, some Jews adjusted their identity as Jews to accommodate Greek culture and rule, while others adapted what they took from Greek culture to preserve their Jewish identity, and still others unconsciously absorbed the influence of Greek culture even as they struggled to preserve intact the native traditions they had inherited from their Israelite ancestors. The Jewish culture that emerges over the course of the Hellenistic period is arguably the product of the interaction with Greek culture, certainly not always reflecting Greek influence in an obvious way, sometimes resisting it, but in one way or another transformed by the process of Hellenization.

First Encounters: The Beginnings of Hellenization Under Ptolemaic Rule

According to some accounts, it did not take long for the Jews and the Greeks to strike a rapport. Clearchus, a Greek disciple of the great philosopher Aristotle, wrote of how his master once met a Jew during one of his visits and found the man to be astonishingly like-minded. The Jew had an exotic background—his people were the descendants of Indian philosophers, Aristotle claimed, and their city had a strange-sounding name: *Hierusaleme*—but he spoke Greek, and indeed, he impressed Aristotle as having the very soul of a Greek. If Clearchus is to be believed, from their very earliest encounter, Jews and Greeks were able to overcome the linguistic and cultural differences dividing them and discovered much that was familiar in the other.

But this story is probably not to be believed—Aristotle himself never mentions such an encounter in his own writings, and the true story of what happened when Jews and Greeks first encountered one another is unknown. Trade contacts between Palestine and the Greek world went back to the Persian period and even earlier, and a Greek military presence can be detected on the coast of Palestine as early as the seventh century BCE. When Alexander the Great conquered Judea, putting an end to Persian rule, certain cultural changes ensued—the Macedonians probably replaced Aramaic with Greek as the language of governance, for example. Still, it may not have been clear to Jews at the time that they were living in a whole new epoch. Judea had been under foreign rule for centuries by that time, and Alexander probably continued Persian administrative practice for the most part, allowing the Jews of Judea to live according to their native laws and institutions as long as they avoided making trouble for him.

Not everyone in Palestine was content to accept Alexander's rule. To the north of Judea, in the territory of the former kingdom of Israel, lived another people who believed in Yahweh; they were not Jews, however, but the ancestors of the people later known as the Samaritans (whom we will introduce more fully in Chapter 4). Some reports state that they rebelled against the Greeks, seizing the official appointed by Alexander to oversee Syria—and burning him alive. Gruesome evidence also points to how the Greeks responded: the discovery in a cave at a site called Wadi Deliyeh of some two hundred skeletons, the remains of refugees who seem to have been hunted down by Alexander's forces in their effort to suppress the revolt (Aramaic papyri found in the cave and dating between 365 and 335 BCE place these unfortunate inhabitants in the period of Alexander's conquest). In Judea, no comparable evidence has been found of a rebellion or repression, and so the historian Josephus may well be right when he reports that the people there willingly submitted to Alexander.

Whatever Alexander's intentions for Judea (if he gave the area any thought at all), he did not live long enough to

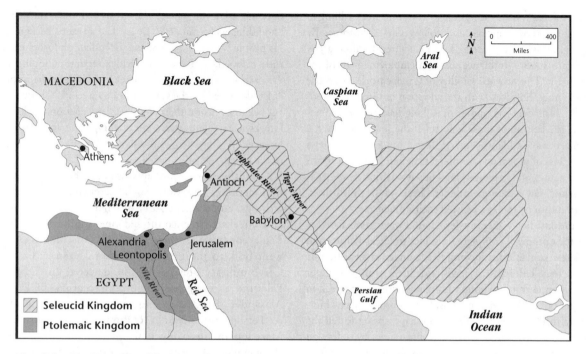

Map 3-1   The Seleucid and Ptolemaic Kingdoms.

implement them himself. When he died in 323 BCE, his generals, known as the *Diadochi* or Successors, fell to fighting over who would control the territory he had conquered, not just in Palestine, but in Greece, Asia Minor, and Egypt. Judea was not of much value itself, but situated between Egypt and Mesopotamia, it found itself in the middle of this conflict. After decades of warfare, Alexander's successors eventually divided his empire into separate kingdoms, two of which are relevant for Jewish history. His general Ptolemy secured control over Egypt, establishing a dynasty that lasted until Egypt was conquered by the Romans in 30 BCE. The **Ptolemaic kingdom** also ruled Judea until 200 BCE, the year Judea was conquered by Antiochus III, ruler of the kingdom established by Alexander's general Seleucus I. Based in Syria, the **Seleucid kingdom** ruled Judea until the first few decades of the first century BCE, when the region came under Roman control (*see* Map 3-1).

The rulers in charge of these kingdoms were Greek, but they were different from those Greeks immortalized by classical literature: Pericles, Socrates, Euripides, and the like. Classical Greek culture was centered in Athens. Alexander and his successors were from Macedonia to the north, a people regarded by the supercilious Athenians as barbarians in their own right. As we have noted, the Ptolemaic and Seleucid kingdoms promoted the establishment of Greek-style cities (the *polis*) whose citizens ran many of their own affairs, but unlike Athens of the classical age, these were not completely independent city-states. Situated within large kingdoms, these cities were granted their status by distant rulers who expected loyalty, taxes, and military support in return.

It is also important to keep in mind that the rulers of the Ptolemaic and Seleucid kingdoms were themselves transformed by their encounters with Near Eastern culture, as "orientalized" as their subjects were "occidentalized." The process began with Alexander himself, who in Egypt offered a sacrifice to the Egyptian god Apis and, when in Persia, wore the clothes of Persian royalty. Best known for her doomed love affair with the Roman Marc Antony, Queen Cleopatra VII (69–30 BCE), the last Ptolemaic ruler of Egypt, provides another memorable example. Cleopatra's ancestry was Macedonian; even her name was Greek (it means "daughter of a famous father"). Why then do we think of her as an Egyptian queen? Because that is how she presented herself: she learned Egyptian, identified with the goddess Isis, and even her suicide by cobra bite was an Egyptianizing touch (the cobra being a symbol on the Egyptian royal crown). *Hellenistic* has come to connote the kind of fusion of Greek with Near Eastern culture that Cleopatra exemplifies: not a one-way process in which the Near East adapted Greek culture, but a mutual adjustment in which Greeks and the peoples of the Near East adapted to one another.

Like the Persians before him, Ptolemy I, founder of the Ptolemaic line, probably allowed Jews in Judea to rule many of their own affairs according to their ancestral laws. At the same time, however, he and his successors introduced organizational changes that tied Judea more closely to the rest of the kingdom. Evidence from this period is hard to come by, but some insights can be gleaned from a cache of letters written by and to a Ptolemaic official named Zenon, an aide to a finance minister of Ptolemy II who went on a fact-finding tour of Palestine in 259–258 BCE. The **Zenon documents** reveal a Palestine that was monitored, controlled, and exploited by the Ptolemaic king. Based in the ancient coastal city renamed for the king, Ptolemais (present-day Akko or Acre), and working through various officials, agents, and informants, Ptolemaic rule involved itself in various aspects of social life, including the affairs of small villages.

Zenon's archive hints at some of the changes that would eventually facilitate the Hellenization of Palestine—increased urbanization and perhaps even the learning of Greek by some locals. Even so, there is not much evidence of Jews adopting Greek ways in the way that Ezekiel does in a later period. Some scholars place the composition of the biblical book of Ecclesiastes in this period, noting parallels between its sage observations about life and certain strains of Greek philosophy, but even assuming they are right about dating the text to the late third century BCE, Ecclesiastes also shows that Greek culture was not yet having the direct impact it would have on later Jewish texts, for it is written not in Greek but in Hebrew (and without the many Greek loanwords that saturate later Hebrew), and the parallels with Greek thought are not precise enough to prove the influence of Greek philosophy. It is not until later in the second century BCE that we find clear evidence of Jews in Judea adopting Greek ways.

As of this point in our history, we can no longer focus exclusively on what was happening in Judea. By this time, Jewish communities had long existed outside the land of Judah in Mesopotamia and Egypt. Hellenistic rule intensified their dispersion throughout the Near East and Mediterranean. Like the Persians before them, the Greeks employed or conscripted Jews as soldiers, settling them and their families in places that they needed to fortify. Thus, for example, according to a Jewish text known as the ***Letter of Aristeas*** (to be discussed in more detail), Ptolemy I brought to Egypt 100,000 captives from Judea, settling 30,000 of them in forts throughout the land. Jews were also drawn to places such as Egypt by the opportunities opened up under Hellenistic rule. Josephus notes that in addition to the Jews taken to Egypt by Ptolemy I as war captives, "not a few of the other Jews came to Egypt of their own accord, for they were attracted by the excellence of the country and Ptolemy's liberality" (Josephus, *Antiquities* 12.9).

Josephus might be projecting the situation of his own day back onto an earlier period, but written evidence from Ptolemaic Egypt confirms that Jews there found a wide range of economic opportunities at this time, owning land, farming it as tenants, or working for the government as soldiers, police, and tax collectors (as nonnative Egyptians themselves, the Ptolemies seem to have relied on Jews precisely because they were fellow outsiders). For many Jews, in other words, Egypt was not a place of exile or servitude but a land of opportunity. This might explain why Artapanus, an Egyptian Jewish historian from this period, does not mention that Joseph was sold into Egypt as a slave but instead reports that he *chose* to go there when he learned of his brothers' conspiracy against him. Similar opportunities elsewhere in the Hellenistic world drew Jews to such places as Syria, Asia Minor, and Greece.

Scholars once believed that Jews in the "diaspora" were more susceptible to Hellenistic influence than the more religiously conservative Jews of Judea. Many scholars now reject the contrast as too simplistic; Jews in Palestine were also subject to Hellenization—they just responded to it in different ways. Still a case can be made that Jews in a place like Alexandria were exposed to Greek culture earlier than the Jews of Palestine if only because, as the seat of Ptolemaic rule, Alexandria was more integrated into the Hellenistic world than Palestine was in the third century BCE; indeed, it was the cultural and intellectual capital of the Hellenistic world. By the time of Ptolemy II, the famous library of Alexandria was in operation, and its treasure-house of 200,000 books drew the best scholars of the day to Alexandria. In the Near East as reorganized by the Macedonians, Judea was an isolated backwater; the Jew of Alexandria lived at the very heart of Hellenistic culture (*see box,* Exile or Dispora?)

Very little literary evidence survives from this period of Jewish history, but enough has been preserved in the citations of later Christian authors to indicate that Jews were active participants in Alexandria's rich intellectual life. Ezekiel was not the only author to recast biblical history in the light of Greek literature; we have examples of Jewish–Greek histories, epics, and philosophy, and most of these works were probably written by Alexandrian Jews. The earliest known Jewish author

EXILE OR DIASPORA?

Different terms are used to describe the Jewish communities that formed outside the land of Israel, and each implies a different understanding of this experience. The Hebrew term *galut* translates as "exile" and is a description that implies that Jews living outside the land are not at home, that their residence abroad is a kind of punishment imposed on them against their will. Many early Jews were indeed settled abroad against their will, exiled there by the Babylonians or taken as war captives during the Hellenistic period, and a number of Jewish sources from the Hellenistic period describe life outside the land as a divine punishment. Other Jews resettled abroad of their own accord, however, moving for economic reasons or to take refuge from political conflicts in Judea, and life outside the land was not an inherently negative experience for many. A first-century Jewish author, Philo of Alexandria, describes Jewish communities outside Palestine not as exiles but as colonists, a description that mirrors the settlement of Greeks throughout the Hellenistic world. And while these Jews revered Jerusalem as their motherland, he continues, they also regarded their new places of residence as a "fatherland," a cherished inheritance in its own right. This is why many scholars of ancient Jewish culture prefer another word to describe Jewish communities outside the land of Israel that does not necessarily imply forced expulsion or divine punishment: *diaspora,* from the Greek for "dispersion." Which term is the more appropriate description depends on the particular history of the community in question, how it came to settle where it did, and how it saw its existence outside the land of Israel.

to write in Greek is a historian named **Demetrius,** probably living at the end of the third century BCE, who tried to solve various chronological problems in his biblical sources in a way that recalls the historiographical methods of the Greeks. Another Jew, **Philo** (not to be confused with the more famous Philo of Alexandria who lived in the first century CE), wrote an epic poem about Jerusalem. The earliest known Jewish philosopher is a Jew named **Aristobolus,** who lived in Alexandria in the second century BCE. His effort to explain the Bible in light of Greek philosophy includes the earliest examples of allegorical biblical interpretation, a technique borrowed from Greek scholars of Homer.

Allegorical biblical interpretation, first developed in Hellenistic Alexandria, is based on the assumption that the Bible has two levels of meaning: (1) the surface or literal meaning and (2) an implicit, allegorical meaning that the biblical interpreter aims to bring out by reading the people and events of the Bible as coded symbols for abstract concepts. On the surface, a text like the Torah appears to be a book of laws, but Jewish interpreters in the tradition of Aristobolus used allegory to show that its details also had a higher significance as a philosophical teaching about the nature of God. To clarify what the Bible means when it refers to God's "hand," for example, Aristobolus explains:

Now "hands" are clearly thought in our own time in a more general way. For when you, being king [Aristobolus is addressing a king named Ptolemy], send out forces, wishing to accomplish something, we say, "The king has a mighty hand," and the hearers are referred to the power which you have. Now Moses indicates this

also in our law when he speaks thus, "God brought you out of Egypt with a mighty hand . . ." it is necessary that the hands be explained as the power of God. For it is possible for people speaking metaphorically to consider that the entire strength of human beings and their active powers are in their hands.

By using this technique, Aristobolus solves a specific question for someone reading the biblical text in a literal fashion: what does the Torah mean when it refers to God's hand? Someone reading the Bible literally might infer from this that God looked like a human being, but that is to miss the true significance of the text according to Aristobolus, a meaning consistent with a more enlightened conception of the divine as an incorporeal being. Beyond explaining a puzzling expression in the Bible, this way of reading helps to turn it into a sophisticated philosophical text comparable to the writings of Plato.

Participating in the cultural life of Alexandria in this and other ways did not mean abandoning a Jewish identity. While authors such as Demetrius, Philo, and Aristobolus (notice that all three names are Greek) tried to accentuate the similarity between Greek and Jewish culture, translating biblical history into a form familiar to Greeks, or finding similarities between the Torah and Plato, they remained strongly connected to Jewish tradition, focusing on the Bible, God, and Jewish history. Aristobolus recognized the value of philosophers, such as Plato, but his point was that Moses was the better philosopher: "It is evident that Plato imitated our legislation," he writes, a remark that makes it legitimate for Jews to read Plato even as it asserts Moses' superiority.

The single most important attempt to reconcile Jewish and Greek culture in Ptolemaic Alexandria was the translation of the Torah into Greek, the translation known as the Septuagint (introduced in Chapter 2). Many Jews in Ptolemaic Egypt probably spoke Greek as their first language, and knowledge of Hebrew may have been relatively rare. One of the roles of the Septuagint was to render the Bible accessible to those Jews, but it may have had another purpose as well: to further integrate Jewish tradition with Greek culture. One can detect the influence of Greek philosophy, law, and even mythology in its translation.

The story of how the Septuagint came to be translated is preserved in the previously mentioned *Letter of Aristeas,* composed in Alexandria in the second or first century BCE. According to this letter, the Septuagint was an initiative of Ptolemy II who commissioned a translation of the laws of the Jews as part of his effort to expand the number of books in the library of Alexandria. To accomplish the task, the king sent a delegation to Judea to ask the high priest in Jerusalem to send six translators from each of the twelve tribes to help in the task. It was these seventy-two translators who inspired the translation's title, the *Septuagint,* which means "seventy" in Latin. A good portion of the *Letter of Aristeas* is a description of the delegates' journey to Jerusalem from the perspective of one of the king's envoys, a Ptolemaic official named Aristeas.

Scholars question the letter's description of the Septuagint's origins, but that debate will not preoccupy us here. What is important is the role that the letter assigns the Septuagint as a bridge between the Jews and the Greeks. As depicted by the letter, the Greeks and Jews of the story share much in common even before the Septuagint brings them closer together. Ptolemy shows great respect for Jewish tradition, making a costly gift to the Temple and showering honor on the translators, while for their part, the Jews in the story exhibit the virtues of cultured Greeks; the narrative goes so far as to claim that the Jews and the Greeks worship the same God, though the latter call him Zeus. Even though the laws of Moses impose behavior that distinguish the Jews from other peoples—for example, special dietary laws—*Aristeas* claims that when the Torah is fully understood, it demonstrates that the Jews share the same underlying commitment to wisdom, goodness, and beauty that characterizes sophisticated Greeks, such as Ptolemy II. By rendering the contents of the Torah accessible to them, the Septuagint could help Greeks to appreciate that the Jews were not barbarians but an enlightened people like themselves.

For all that it does to translate Jewish culture into the philosophical and aesthetic categories of Greek culture, the *Letter of Aristeas* is not seeking to erase the boundary between Jewish and Greek culture. To the contrary! Through the voice of a Jewish high priest in the story, the narrative makes it clear that the very purpose of the law that was being translated was "to prevent [the Jews] from being perverted by contact with others or by mixing with bad influences." What we can glimpse in the Septuagint and other Jewish texts composed in Ptolemaic Egypt is not the abandonment of a distinctive Jewish culture for a Greek way of life but the effort to keep Jewish culture secure, vibrant, and relevant in a Hellenized environment with real-life advantages to thinking, speaking, and acting like the Greek rulers of Alexandria.

We know that Jews in Alexandria and elsewhere in Egypt were able to sustain a distinct cultural identity even as they participated in the larger culture and economy. Many lived in separate, semiautonomous communities bound together by distinctive civic and religious institutions permitted them by their Ptolemaic rulers. By the first century CE, two of Alexandria's five quarters were predominantly Jewish—and the city's Jewish community was allowed its own court system and semiautonomous leader known (at least by the Roman period) as the *ethnarch.* This does not mean that Jews only lived within these communities—one should not imagine these neighborhoods as ghettos to which Jews were confined. Rather, they were harbors within Egypt's multicultural cities where Jews could more easily nurture a culture different from that of the Greeks or native Egyptians, a culture defined by its own customs and laws.

Jews in Egypt also developed distinct ways of worshiping. Many Jews in the Second Temple period regarded the Jerusalem Temple as the only legitimate temple, but we know of two other Jewish temples, both in Egypt. The temple at Elephantine, mentioned in Chapter 2, had been destroyed at the end of the fifth century BCE, and the Jews there were evidently unable to rebuild it, but we know of another Jewish temple in Egypt established sometime in the second century BCE by **Onias,** a Jewish high priest (either Onias III or Onias IV; our only informant, the historian Josephus, is confused on this question), which functioned for several hundred years until it was shut down by the Romans in 74 CE. Having fled Judea, Onias secured the permission of the Ptolemaic king (probably Ptolemy VI) and his queen to build the temple at a place called **Leontopolis,** the site of a ruined Egyptian temple. According to Josephus, the temple he established was modeled on the one in Jerusalem. It is unclear whether Onias intended it to rival the one in Jerusalem or saw it as a complement to it, but either way, Onias believed he was acting at God's behest, claiming the temple fulfilled a prophecy in Isaiah 19:19.

It is also in Ptolemaic Egypt, in the third century CE, that we have our first evidence of the institution later known as the **synagogue.** The fact that our earliest evidence for the synagogue comes from Egypt does not mean that it originated there. One scholar has argued that it arose under the influence of Egyptian temples, which included annexes that served as places of study and writing, but that is conjecture. Other attempts to explain the synagogue's origins suggest that they were a replacement for the city gate in pre-exilic Judah, the place where town elders would assemble to make various communal decisions, or that they were modeled on some part of the Temple itself as an extension of its sanctity. However it originated, the synagogue, like Onias' temple, allowed the Jews of Egypt a way to sustain a collective religious life different from that of Egyptians and Greeks. The Greek word used in Ptolemaic Egypt to describe this institution, *proseuche* from the Greek meaning "prayer," clearly indicates that it was a site for prayer. Some sources describe synagogues as "holy," as if they were temples, but they were not the site of animal sacrifice like the temples of Elephantine and Onias but rather a site for offering *words* to God—prayers or inscriptions. Whether Jews in this period also read and studied Scripture in these prayer houses as their descendants would do in the synagogues of first-century Alexandria is unknown but not inconceivable.

The Jews of Egypt depended on their Ptolemaic rulers to support their distinctive way of life, and that dependence is reflected everywhere in our evidence from this period: in synagogue inscriptions that honor the Ptolemaic king and queen for their support and in literary texts, like the *Letter of Aristeas,* that praise the Ptolemaic king as an enlightened patron. While Ptolemaic rule appears to have been supportive of Alexandria's Jews—welcoming enough that Jews emigrated there from Judea—their situation was not completely secure. The Greek settlers of Egypt were only part of Egypt's population; native Egyptians descended from those who had lived there before Alexander's arrival also lived there, and some were not especially happy about the Jews' presence in their midst, and they did what they could to discredit and displace them. We do not have clear evidence of anti-Jewish riots in the Ptolemaic period of the sort that beset the Jews of Alexandria when it was under Roman rule, but evidence does exist of the anti-Jewish resentment that would eventually boil over into such violence. In fact, the earliest known specimens of anti-Jewish literature come from Ptolemaic Egypt.

An example of this literature is a history of Egypt written by **Manetho,** a Hellenized Egyptian priest. Manetho's account includes a kind of anti-Exodus story that, while it never mentions the Jews directly, was clearly written to ridicule them. In this topsy-turvy version of events, Moses is a renegade Egyptian priest whose commands to his followers are the very antithesis of what a Hellenized sensibility would value:

> He made it a law that they should neither worship the gods nor refrain from any of the animals prescribed as especially sacred in Egypt, but should sacrifice and consume all alike, and that they should have intercourse with none save those of their own confederacy.

One can recognize a grain of truth in Manetho's description—the laws of Moses do prohibit the worship of other gods and certain foods as well, but Manetho has spun Mosaic law into a sacrilegious rejection of Egyptian religion. And who are Moses' followers? In one passage, Manetho identifies them with the Hyksos, cruel invaders deeply resented by native Egyptians; elsewhere he suggests they included polluted lepers whom the king wanted to cleanse from the land. Manetho's accusations anticipate some of the claims of later antisemitism, but his motives were different from those of later Christian or modern antisemites. As an Egyptian, he probably resented the Jews as nonnatives and used the Exodus story to stress how poorly they fit into Egyptian society.

This kind of accusation threatened the Jews of Egypt in two ways. It could incite Egyptians themselves to acts of violence—this happened in Alexandria in the first century CE—and it could also poison the relations between the Jews and the king. As a member of the Ptolemaic court, Manetho was in a position to influence the king, and his Exodus story is probably an attempt to do just that by stressing the Jews' rebelliousness against an earlier king of Egypt. The Ptolemies claimed to embody the Greek value of *philanthropia,* a love of all humanity; as Manetho describes them, the Jews are the mirror image of this virtue, misanthropes whose history and ritual exude a hatred of humanity. Such rhetoric seems to have had little effect in the days of Ptolemy I or Ptolemy II, when Ptolemaic rule seems far more supportive of the Jews than of native Egyptians, but we know that native Egyptians were allowed to play more of a role in the Ptolemaic government by the end of the third century BCE, and as their influence with the Ptolemies grew, the status of Egyptian Jews became all the more precarious.

Much of the Jewish literature that survives from this period can be understood as a response to this pressure, an effort to enhance or safeguard the status of the Jews by aligning them with the Ptolemies or fitting them into Egyptian society. Some works, such as the *Letter of Aristeas,* stress the cultural affinity between the Jews and the Hellenized Ptolemies in both an explicit and implicit way. Aristobolus' philosophical work was dedicated to the Ptolemaic king. Still other works implicitly rebut the accusations of some Egyptian authors by stressing the Jews' positive contributions to Egyptian society. The historical narrative written by a Jew named Artapanus is an example: in its account of the biblical past, Abraham is welcomed into the home of the Egyptian king to whom he teaches astronomy, Joseph is beloved by the Egyptians for organizing the way they farm the land, and Moses is honored by the priests of Egypt as a god. The Jews were not misanthropic foreigners, Artapanus shows through his history; on the contrary, they had been welcome guests and deserve credit for some of Egypt's greatest accomplishments.

Whatever the inherent attractions of Greek culture, such evidence suggests, Egyptian Jews also embraced it for pragmatic reasons: Hellenization was a way to preserve Jewish culture—and the Jewish community—in an environment where Jews were resented by the native population and highly dependent on their Greek rulers. During this period, Egyptian Jews translated the Torah into Greek; recast biblical history in the form of such Greek literary genres as tragedy, history, and epic; and used Greek interpretive techniques, such as allegory, to turn the Bible and its laws into a philosophical text. All these practices helped them to preserve their culture by aligning it with their Ptolemaic rulers.

Hellenization and Its Discontents in Seleucid Palestine

Returning to Judea in the third century BCE, it is hard to detect how exactly life there had been changed by contact with Hellenistic rule and culture. As we have noted, important changes were certainly occurring in this period; it is just that they do not surface in obvious ways in Judean literature composed prior to the reign of Antiochus IV.

One text known as the ***Wisdom of Ben Sira,*** written by a sage named Jesus ben Sira around 200 BCE, offers a rare glimpse into the experience of a Jewish intellectual from this period. The "discovery" of this text is a fascinating story. It was never really lost, having been preserved in the Apocrypha in a Greek translation known as *Ecclesiasticus* (not to be confused with Ecclesiastes), but it was only at the end of the nineteenth century that substantial fragments of the original Hebrew were discovered in a synagogue in Cairo, in a forgotten storage room used in the Middle Ages for the deposit of sacred texts (the number of texts found in this storage room, known as the Cairo Geniza, and their implications for understanding Jewish history dwarf the more famous discovery of the Dead Sea Scrolls, but they mostly pertain to the Middle Ages, not antiquity). If one compares *The Wisdom of Ben Sira* to a work like Ecclesiastes composed a century or two earlier, there are clear differences (*Ben Sira* clearly presupposes

a biblical canon, whereas Ecclesiastes does not), but it is hard to see what difference Hellenization has made. Like Ecclesiastes, *Ben Sira* was originally written in Hebrew, not in Greek, and it never explicitly refers to Greek philosophy in the way that Aristobolus did. If *Ben Sira* is any indication of what sages in Judea were thinking about in 200 BCE, it tells us they were interested in finding wisdom but apparently oblivious to the wisdom of the Greeks.

At about the time that Jesus ben Sira was writing this work, however, something was happening that would soon bring the influence of Hellenistic culture out into the open. In 202–200 BCE, Judea was wrested from the Ptolemaic kingdom by the Seleucid kingdom under **Antiochus III.** Far from trying to change the cultural status quo, Antiochus III seems to have followed the practice of earlier foreign rulers and affirmed the Jews' right to live according to their ancestral customs, a policy that persisted under his successor Seleucus IV. After Seleucus IV, however, **Antiochus IV** came to power, and he adopted a very different and more hostile stance toward Jewish tradition. He looted the Temple, erecting some kind of sacrilegious object within it—an idol or an altar—and later banned religious practices, including circumcision, festival observance, the Sabbath rest, and even the Torah itself. Under the rule of Antiochus IV, which lasted from 175–164 BCE, many Jews in Judea felt so deeply threatened that they considered rebellion against the Seleucids the only option for preserving their tradition.

The Hellenization of Jewish culture was emerging as a threat even before Antiochus tried to impose it on the Jews— at least according to our principal sources for this period, *1 and 2 Maccabees.* The problem began, these sources report, when certain Jews in Jerusalem tried to erase the difference between Israel and other nations by removing the marks of circumcision and introducing various foreign practices into Jerusalem—building a gymnasium (focused not just on exercise but on education), encouraging young men to wear a Greek-style hat, and arranging athletic contests. The leader of these initiatives was a high priest named Jason, who had obtained his office by bribing Antiochus IV, and his goal, it seems, was to reestablish Jerusalem on the model of a Greek city to be renamed Antioch in honor of Antiochus. Jason was soon replaced by another high priest named Menelaus, but he was no better in our sources' estimation.

The involvement of Antiochus IV, however, made the adoption of Greek ways all the more dangerous for Jewish tradition and the Jewish community. In the *2 Maccabees* account, Jason stages a failed attempt to retake Jerusalem from Menelaus, a conflict that Antiochus IV mistakes for an uprising and tries to suppress by conquering Jerusalem. In doing so, he massacres many people and invades the Temple itself

A coin depicting Antiochus Epiphanes (Antiochus IV).

to loot its contents. Antiochus' subsequent actions in 167 BCE were even more lethal: he rededicated the Temple to Zeus, modifying its cult in ways that made it impossible to worship God according to the laws of Moses, and outlawed circumcision, the Sabbath, and the Torah. Antiochus' forces destroyed whatever copies of the Torah they found, executed those found adhering to its laws, and even apparently tried to compel Jews to break the law by torturing them to death, yielding the earliest known accounts of Jewish "martyrdom"—the pious choosing to suffer and die rather than betray God (*see box,* Is Martyrdom a Jewish Invention?).

Antiochus' motives for these measures, the first case of religious persecution in Jewish history, is one of the great unsolvable puzzles of the period. It was one thing to attack a city or loot a temple—these violent acts had plenty of precedent in earlier history; it was quite another to try to abolish an indigenous religious tradition. The norm in the Hellenistic world, established long before the Seleucids, was for the king to show respect to local tradition, as Antiochus III had done by recognizing the authority of Jewish law in Judea and honoring the Temple cult. Antiochus IV not only abandoned that policy but inverted it, actively seeking to abolish Jewish law. To explain his deviation from established practice, some have theorized that Antiochus was simply insane, and they point to his reputation for bizarre behavior (a reputation reflected in a joke at the time that changed his name *Epiphanes* to *Epimanes,* or "Madman"). Others have tried to discern a rational motive for his behavior, arguing that he was motivated by financial, political, or ideological considerations. While such theories have some evidence to support them,

IS MARTYRDOM A JEWISH INVENTION?

A *martyr* is a person who willingly submits to death, allowing others to kill him or her, or even taking his or her own life, out of a sense of commitment to God or religious principle. In recent times, martyrdom is often associated with Islam, but the term itself, from the Greek *martyrein,* "to witness," arose in Christianity where martyrdom was seen as an exemplary way to express one's commitment to God and a way to emulate Jesus' death. In fact, the practice of dying for one's religion is rooted in still earlier Jewish culture. The earliest known accounts of people choosing to die for their religion appear in the 2 Maccabees account of Antiochus' persecution, leading scholars to conclude that what would come to be known as martyrdom originated in this period:

> Eleazar, one of the scribes in high position, a man now advanced in age and of noble presence, was being forced to open his mouth to eat swine's flesh. But he, welcoming death with honor rather than life with pollution, went up to the rack of his own accord, spitting out the flesh, as all ought to go who have the courage to refuse things that it is not right to taste, even for the natural love of life. Those who were in charge of that unlawful sacrifice took the man aside because of their long acquaintance with him, and privately urged him to bring meat of his own providing, proper for him to use, and to pretend that he was eating the flesh of the sacrificial meal that had been commanded by the king, so that by doing this he might be saved from death, and be treated kindly on account of his old friendship with them. But making a high resolve, worthy of his years and the dignity of his old age and the grey hairs that he had reached with distinction and his excellent life even from childhood, and moreover according to the holy God-given law, he declared himself quickly, telling them to send him to Hades. "Such pretence is not worthy of our time of life," he said, "for many of the young might suppose that Eleazar in his ninetieth year had gone over to an alien religion, and through my pretence, for the sake of living a brief moment longer, they would be led astray because of me, while I defile and disgrace my old age. Even if for the present I would avoid the punishment of mortals, yet whether I live or die I will not escape the hands of the Almighty. Therefore, by bravely giving up my life now, I will show myself worthy of my old age and leave to the young a noble example of how to die a good death willingly and nobly for the revered and holy laws." When he had said this, he went at once to the rack. Those who a little before had acted towards him with goodwill now changed to ill will, because the words he had uttered were in their opinion sheer madness. When he was about to die under the blows, he groaned aloud and said: "It is clear to the Lord in his holy knowledge that, though I might have been saved from death, I am enduring terrible sufferings in my body under this beating, but in my soul I am glad to suffer these things because I fear him." So in this way he died, leaving in his death an example of nobility and a memorial of courage, not only to the young but to the great body of his nation. (2 Maccabees 6:18–31)

As depicted here, martyrdom is an act of resistance, a refusal to betray God's laws under any circumstance, but the irony is that Jewish martyrdom may itself be the result of Hellenistic influence. Greek culture had its own martyrs of a sort, people who chose to die rather than betray their principles. The most famous case, and one that was probably known to Jews by the second century BCE, was Socrates, who chose to commit suicide rather than abandon his calling as a philosopher, and it is quite possible that this example exerted an influence on Jewish thinking, introducing a new ideal of what it meant to live a truly committed life. So did Jews invent martyrdom? In a sense, yes, but the Greeks had an important role in its development too.

they are still, in the end, educated guesses. We simply lack the evidence to explain why Antiochus IV acted as he did, which is a good reminder that history sometimes exceeds our reach.

A little easier to understand is why a Jewish leader might collaborate in the Hellenization of Judaism. As we have noted, Hellenistic culture was accessible in a way that the cultures of earlier rulers had not been. In theory at least, one could gain access to it and participate in its educational and civic institutions by learning how to speak and act like a Greek. The more Jerusalem could approximate a Greek city, moreover, the more likely it was to secure the king's respect, which could mean greater autonomy, royal investment in the city's institutions, and even tax breaks. The behavior of a

Jason or Menelaus in Jerusalem may not have been all that different from that of Aristobolus or Ezekiel in Alexandria: this was not an abandonment of Jewish tradition, but a pragmatically minded effort to improve their lot within a Hellenized world.

In Jerusalem, however, these efforts to bridge Jewish and Greek cultures provoked a violent backlash from within the Jewish community. While some embraced the changes taking place, others strongly opposed them. The author of *Jubilees* may have been one such Jew. Scholars detect in his narrative the kind of separatist mentality that would later impel the Dead Sea Scrolls sect to withdraw from Jerusalem into the wilderness, and indeed, *Jubilees* was a popular text within that community, with more than a dozen copies surfacing among the scrolls. But *Jubilees* might also be seen as a precursor to a more violent form of resistance, for its version of biblical history often ascribes to the Patriarchs' acts of violence not mentioned in the original biblical account. Thus *Jubilees* reports that after Abraham failed to persuade his father to give up his idols, he burned down the house in which they were kept (12:12)—a story not found in Genesis. *Jubilees'* version of Genesis 34, where Simeon and Levi avenge the rape of their sister Dinah by slaying the rapist and his townsmen, also diverges from the biblical account when it praises their acts as righteous; in Genesis, Jacob disapproves of his sons' violence (30:17). Looking for ways to preserve the eroding border between Jewish and non-Jewish culture, Jews, like the author of *Jubilees,* found in the Torah an example of how the righteous could deploy violence to defend their religious traditions.

By late 167 or early 166 BCE, in the wake of Antiochus' decrees, some Jews were willing to turn to violence themselves to defend their traditions. According to *1 Maccabees,* Antiochus' officials came to the town of Modi'in not far from Jerusalem to compel the Jews there to offer a sacrifice in accordance with the king's decrees. A priest named **Mattathias** loudly refused, slaying a Jew who had stepped forward to offer the sacrifice, along with a Seleucid officer. He and his sons then took to the hills, beginning a kind of guerilla war against the Seleucids. Mattathias and his sons were not the only ones involved in the ensuing uprising—we know of another group active in the revolt, known as the Hasidim or "The Pious"—but they soon took the lead, first under Mattathias, then, after his death, under his son **Judah.** It is from Judah's nickname, "The Maccabee" or "The Hammer," that the Maccabean Revolt gets its name.

At first, the Maccabean Revolt was probably closer to a civil war than a rebellion against foreign rule, with the Maccabees initially targeting Jewish collaborators rather than the Seleucids themselves. As they gained more of a following, however, the Maccabees began to challenge the Seleucid kingdom more directly, with Judah winning several victories that allowed him to retake Jerusalem and restore the Temple cult—an event Judah commemorated by a festival later known as **Hanukkah.** It may seem remarkable that Judah was able to defeat the much larger armies of the Seleucids, but he seems to have been an effective guerilla commander and a master motivator, converting a small band of followers into a large, highly enthused army. It did not hurt that Antiochus was distracted by what was happening in the eastern part of his kingdom, or that Judah recruited the support of the Romans, whose strength was all too apparent to the Seleucids.

Judah was soon killed in battle, but the fight with the Seleucids continued under his brothers **Jonathan** and **Simon.** It is not clear when to date the end of the Maccabean Revolt: in 161 BCE, Judah defeated Nicanor, a Seleucid general who had threatened to destroy the Temple, and this is where *2 Maccabees* ends its story, but the revolt might have still continued into the 130s, during the reign of Simon's son John Hyrcanus with whom *1 Maccabees* ends. In any case, by 140 BCE, according to *1 Maccabees,* the Maccabees had consolidated their control over Judea, restored the Temple, and driven the non-Jews from the land. Simon was honored for this feat by being declared the high priest and ruler of the Jews "forever," which meant that this position would pass down to his descendants. Known as the Hasmoneans (a name probably inspired by the place where the Maccabean family was from), the successors to the Maccabees controlled Judea until it came under Roman control in 63 BCE.

As our sources depict events, the Maccabees protected Judea from the encroachments of Hellenization, undoing the changes introduced by Antiochus and his Jewish collaborators and restoring the traditions of the Jews. Did they in fact succeed in resisting Hellenistic influence? Some evidence points to a backlash against foreign culture in this period: Hasmonean coins are inscribed in the ancient Hebrew script from the time of the First Temple, and an avoidance of foreign exports in Judea is reflected in the pottery found, or not found, in Judea at the time of the Maccabees, as if a boycott of foreign goods were in effect. On the basis of such evidence, one might think that the Maccabees had undone the effects of Hellenization and even revived the culture that existed in biblical times, but the reality was more complex.

Even in the relative isolation of Judea, it was not easy to escape the influence of Hellenistic culture. In their efforts to find allies, the Maccabees had reached out to the Romans and even to the Spartans, a Greek people known for their military prowess, and that required a knowledge of the Greek language and Hellenistic diplomatic practice. They also took Greek names, such as Alexander, or in the case of the one female Hasmonean ruler, Alexandra, built palaces and tombs modeled on Hellenistic prototypes and minted coins with Greek legends and symbols that emulated Seleucid coinage. One Hasmonean even merited the nickname *Philhellene,* "Lover of the Greeks."

Why did the Maccabees/Hasmoneans resist Hellenized culture so strenuously during the Maccabean Revolt only to behave like typical Hellenized rulers themselves? Did the Hasmoneans' transformation into a successful Hellenistic political elite weaken their identity as zealous defenders of the law? It is tempting to draw such a conclusion, but in the Hasmoneans' defense, it should also be pointed out that they

Jews observing Hanukkah by kindling the lights of a special lamp known in Hebrew as the *menorah*. The practice of lighting a single light for each of the eight nights of Hanukkah is first mentioned in rabbinic literature centuries after the Maccabean Revolt. It is unknown whether this practice goes back to the Maccabees themselves.

may not have seen the inconsistency that we do. It became a cliché in modern European thought to describe the cultures of Judaism and Hellenism as incompatible opposites, or as the famous nineteenth-century culture critic Matthew Arnold put it in his essay "Hebraism and Hellenism," as "rivals dividing the empire of the world between them." The Hasmoneans may not have seen the inherent rivalry that Arnold did two thousand years later, feeling no compunction about acting Greek so long as they did not violate Jewish law.

The Hasmoneans may not have been unique in this regard, for there is evidence that other Jews in this period reconciled Jewish tradition and Hellenization in a similar fashion. A good example is one of the sources we have been relying on for our knowledge of the Maccabean Revolt—*2 Maccabees*—which is actually an abridged account of a longer five-volume work written by a certain Jason of Cyrene that no longer survives. The first known work to use the terms *Judaism* and *Hellenism* is *2 Maccabees,* which uses those

Greek terms to refer to two distinct ways of life. By *Judaism, 2 Maccabees* means the adherence to Jewish law: circumcision, the Sabbath, and the other customs and practices that Antiochus tried to abolish. *Hellenism* refers to participation in the gymnasium and other foreign customs associated with the Greeks. Pitting these ways of life against one another, *2 Maccabees* would seem to support the view of Judaism and Hellenism as incompatible lifestyles, but the work itself actually complicates this distinction because it itself is written in Greek, and emulates Greek literature. If worshipping like a Greek is forbidden, why is writing like a Greek permitted? Because what was opposed in *2 Maccabees* was not the adoption of Greek customs per se but, as its author puts it, "an *extreme* of Hellenization"—adopting Greek practices *that contradicted Jewish law.*

We cannot say for certain that *2 Maccabees* reflects the Hasmoneans' own views on this matter, but it does suggest a way to understand their seemingly inconsistent behavior.

Antiochus had forced Jews to choose between Jewish tradition and foreign practices, a situation that left those committed to Jewish tradition no choice but to rebel or, if rebellion was not possible, to accept death rather than betray the law. In the absence of such compulsion, it was not necessary to choose between cultures. Some Greek practices—sacrificing to gods other than God, eating unclean food—were clearly forbidden by the laws of Moses, but others were not expressly prohibited, and so Jews might engage in those without feeling they had violated their covenant with God.

All this is to address how Jews responded to the Hellenistic influences they could detect, but Hellenization could be unconscious too, affecting Jewish culture in ways that Jews themselves did not realize. In fact, the very conception of Jewish identity itself changed in this period under the influence of Hellenistic culture. The term *Jew*, as it was used in this period, still bears geographical and genealogical significance, tying Jews to the land of Judea or identifying them as descendants of Judah, but it also implies something else—a commitment to a way of life defined by adherence to certain laws and customs. In the biblical period, *Israelite* or *Judahite* was an identity inherited from one's parents. The Bible does record a case where a foreigner, the Moabite Ruth, joins the Israelite community, adopting their worship of God, but she enters the community through marriage, a long recognized method of expanding a family, as the ancient Israelites imagined themselves to be. In the second century CE, birth and marriage certainly continued as the major avenues into the community, but it was also possible to join it by adopting a Jewish way of life. For men, this meant submitting to circumcision and adhering to the laws of Moses. Since the rite of circumcision did not apply to women, their Jewish identity seems to have been fuzzier than that of men, but to the extent their identity was defined, the criterion was the same: adherence to a Jewish way of life.

Some Jewish sources in this period describe this way of life by the Greek term *politeia*, "citizenship," and that might reveal something about the origins of the shift in question. The Hellenistic definition of citizenship, spread through the Near East as the institution of the polis itself spread, was often tied to birthplace and descent, but it also allowed for the possibility of someone not born into a community to become a member of it by adopting its laws. This notion of citizenship colored how Jews defined what it meant to be a Jew, as reflected in Josephus' description of the Jewish community as a *politeia* to which Moses invited "all who desire to come and live under the same laws with us, (the prophet) *holding that it is not family ties alone which constitute membership but agreement in the principles of conduct*" (*Against Apion*, 2.210). The laws that defined this community, the laws of Moses, were not an invention of the Hellenistic age, but their significance as the core of Jewish identity—adherence to these laws making one a Jew whether or not one was born in Judea or to Jews—is something that developed under the influence of the Hellenistic conception of what it meant to be a member of a community.

In our review of the Ptolemaic period, we noted that Jewish embrace of Greek culture did not necessarily entail an abandonment of their identity as Jews. The history of the Maccabees helps to illustrate a related point: even those Jews who were highly resistant to foreign culture and were willing to risk death to protect their ancient tradition against such innovations were transformed by the encounter with Hellenistic culture. Those Jews too were in the orbit of Greek language and social convention, drawing on it when it was in their interest to do so, and, ironically, their effort to battle the Greeks in the Maccabean Revolt only intensified their exposure to Greek culture, bringing them into direct contact with Greek rulers and their ways. Jews could choose the degree to which they emulated the Greeks, deciding not to speak, eat, or worship like them, but the very idea that one had such a choice, that one could become a Jew by acting Jewish or become a Greek by acting Greek, is itself yet another effect of Hellenistic influence. We have used the label "Jewish—Hellenistic" to describe Jews who expressed themselves in Greek, but arguably *all* Jewish culture in this period, at least that culture which has left a literary trace that we can study, was Hellenized to some degree—whether in Ptolemaic Alexandria or Maccabean Jerusalem, whether allied with Hellenistic rule or in open rebellion against it. Even without outward signs of its influence, Hellenization was working in unnoticed ways to transform Jewish identity from within.

The Divergent Trajectories of Jewish Tradition

So far our narrative has focused on *change*, the ways in which Jewish culture was transformed by its encounter with Greek culture, but this focus presents a problem: it obscures what was important to many Jews themselves—the preservation of tradition. As we have noted, Jews in this period were interested in the biblical past because of its relevance to the present. They felt obligated to obey the laws of Moses and looked to figures such as Abraham and David not just as ancestors but as models to be emulated. Tradition was what connected the past to the present, linking present-day Jews to the biblical past through institutions, texts, and patterns of behavior and belief. The changes we have been charting—the imposition of foreign rule, exile, Hellenization—threatened these connections, but the rupture was neither complete nor irreversible, and Jews invested tremendous effort into preserving their tradition, even sacrificing their lives to do so during Antiochus' persecution. At stake was not just their relationship with their ancestors but their relationship with God.

Respect for tradition was widespread among Jews, but serious differences characterized what precisely constituted it. The most important inheritance from the past was the laws of Moses, but Jews differed over how to interpret and apply those commandments. For many Jews, moreover, tradition was more than just the Bible; it might include other sacred texts that purported to record divine revelation, or unwritten traditions transmitted from generation to generation by word of mouth or by example. Also at the center of Jewish tradition was the Temple, but Jews were divided by struggles over who was entitled to be high priest, how to enact sacrificial and purity law, and when to schedule the festivals (this was a point of particular distress for the author of *Jubilees,* who was outraged that the Temple of his day scheduled the festivals according to a lunar calendar of 354 days rather than what *Jubilees* regarded as the correct calendar: a 364-day solar calendar). The priest Onias felt so disgruntled that he left Jerusalem to form a temple of his own in Egypt at Leontopolis, and he may not have been the only defector: the Dead Sea Scrolls sect may have boycotted the Temple as well.

The contents of tradition were probably always matters of dispute among Jews, but differences were particularly fractured in the second century BCE. The Maccabees themselves were the source of much of the controversy. They had had a keen interest in tradition, claiming to have restored it after Antiochus' persecution, but their conception of that tradition was not universally accepted. For centuries, the high priest in Jerusalem had come from the line of David's priest, Zadok. That family lost this position in the time of Antiochus' persecution, and when the high priesthood was eventually claimed by the Maccabees, making them and their Hasmonean successors the ultimate guardians of the Temple cult—this seemed wrong to many Jews. Some challenged their claim to the high priesthood, questioning their lineage; others were critical of their conduct of the Temple cult. One Hasmonean high priest, seeking to perform his duties in the Temple during the festival of Sukkot, found himself the target of an angry mob who pelted him with citrons (a lemon-like fruit used during this festival). The religious unrest and priestly infighting of this period fostered the rise of dissident religious movements, each distinguished from the others largely by how it understood the building blocks of Jewish tradition—the laws of Moses and the Temple cult.

We know of three of these groups by name: the **Pharisees,** the **Sadducees,** and the **Essenes.** Many scholars refer to these groups as *sects,* but whether that label is appropriate or not depends on what one means by *sect.* The definition we prefer here is a small, well-organized group that breaks away from a larger community in the belief that it alone embodies the ideals of that community. By this definition, the Essenes probably qualify as a sect, especially if they are to be identified with the Dead Sea Scrolls community. Josephus reports that they had special rules of admission, and they often lived together in tightly organized communities bound together by the shared ownership of property and ritualized communal meals. The label does not apply quite as well to the group known as the Pharisees. Although their name may have meant "separatist," they do not seem to have separated completely from the larger community and, indeed, exerted significant influence over it. Even the Hasmoneans, who were sometimes at bitter odds with the Pharisees, ultimately felt compelled to align themselves with their perspective.

Perhaps a better label than *sect* is "schools of thought" or "philosophies," the original meaning of the Greek term *haireseis* that Josephus uses to describe these movements. Many of the differences he notes do indeed seem philosophical, reflecting different ideas about the nature of human existence. The Pharisees held that everything is determined by fate but also allowed room for humans to make their own decisions. They also believed that the soul survives the death of the body: the virtuous received a new life while the sinful suffered eternal punishment. The Sadducees denied the immortality of the soul and the governance of fate, believing that humans have free choice between good and evil. Like the Pharisees, the Essenes believed in the immortality of the soul and in divine providence, but they did not make the same allowance for human will, though their lifestyle was aimed at cultivating self-control (*see box,* Immortal Aspirations). Described in this way, these groups do sound like philosophies, resembling Hellenistic philosophical schools, such as the Stoics (in fact, Josephus explicitly likens the Pharisees to the Stoics), but then again, Josephus may exaggerate the resemblance since one of his goals as a writer was to present Judaism in a form that would seem appealingly familiar to a Hellenized audience.

However we label them, the Pharisees, Sadducees, and Essenes all subscribed to different understandings of tradition, of what connected Jews to their past. The Pharisees venerated the laws of Moses but also transmitted what Josephus calls the "tradition of the fathers," laws not written in Scripture that may have been transmitted orally from elders to disciples. The Sadducees, perhaps some kind of priestly group, rejected this tradition, holding "that only those regulations should be considered valid which were written down" (by which Josephus meant, presumably, written down in the laws of Moses). It is not clear what the Essenes thought about the tradition of the fathers, and while Josephus notes that they had an intense interest in the writings of the ancients, we do not know what

IMMORTAL ASPIRATIONS

If the Pharisees, Sadducees, and Essenes are any indication, Jews in the Hellenistic period were acutely interested in what happened to a person after death, many believing that people continued to live in some form. Jewish sources written in the Hellenistic period confirm this interest. An example is the *Wisdom of Solomon,* a work attributed to the biblical king but actually composed between the first century BCE and the first century CE, which describes in a fair amount of detail what happens after death:

> But the souls of the righteous are in the hand of God, and no torment will ever touch them. In the eyes of the foolish they seemed to have died, and their departure was thought to be a disaster, and their going from us to be their destruction; but they are at peace. For though in the sight of others they were punished, their hope is full of immortality. Having been disciplined a little, they will receive great good, because God tested them and found them worthy of himself; like gold in the furnace he tried them, and like a sacrificial burnt-offering he accepted them. In the time of their visitation they will shine forth, and will run like sparks through the stubble. They will govern nations and rule over peoples, and the Lord will reign over them for ever. (*Wisdom of Solomon,* 3:1–8)

The Wisdom of Solomon anticipates the later idea of heaven and hell by envisioning life beyond death—a blissful existence for the righteous and eternal punishment for the wicked. Jews differed in how they imagined this afterlife—some believed that the soul would detach itself from the body (the view of the Essenes), while others believed that the soul would regain a body (a Pharasaic view), and some, like the Sadducees, rejected an afterlife altogether. By the first century CE, however, the basic belief in an afterlife was widespread among Jews, surfacing in a variety of early Jewish texts and shared by movements otherwise at odds with each other, such as the Pharisees and the early Christians.

This interest in the afterlife is much more pronounced in Jewish Hellenistic culture than in Judahite culture during the pre-exilic or Persian periods. Other ancient cultures were interested in what happened after death, and some, like Egypt, developed elaborate conceptions of the afterlife, but the authors of the Hebrew Bible are noticeably disinterested in the topic. Why then did Jewish Hellenistic readers of the Bible take such an interest in the afterlife, and from where did their ideas about it come?

The most widely embraced theory points to the influence of Greek philosophy and especially Plato, who posited an existence for the self beyond the physical world. We know from such Jewish authors as Aristobolus that Jews did in fact read Plato, but even if his writings were the catalyst, that does not explain why Jews found his view of the afterlife so appealing. One possibility is that it fit with a new sense of personal identity that emerges in this period under the influence of Greek culture, a more individualistic orientation that stresses the fate of the individual far more than the more family-centered orientation of ancient Israel did. A political dimension may have applied to this development as well. In contrast to the First Temple period, Jews in the Second Temple period were subject to the control of other peoples, and in that context the possibility of an afterlife took on added appeal as a chance to achieve the power, status, and vindication denied Jews in this world. Notice in the *Wisdom of Solomon,* for example, that the righteous dead are not merely happy; they are also powerful, having dominion over the peoples. What may have fueled Jewish interest in the afterlife in the Hellenistic period, in other words, is not simply the fear of death but the desire for an *empowered* life.

those writings were. They certainly included biblical texts—the Essenes so revered Moses that they allegedly executed anyone who blasphemed his name—and they may have included pseudepigraphical writings as well. Be that as it may, the Essenes were stricter than others in their interpretation of certain laws, even avoiding going to the bathroom on the Sabbath. The way they worshipped God was distinctive too.

One of the reasons the Dead Sea Scrolls are so important—apart from what they reveal about the history of the biblical text—is that they include documents produced by one of these communities. Which community, though, is a matter of recent scholarly controversy. A Roman writer named Pliny placed an Essene settlement between Jericho and the En-Gedi oasis, near where the scrolls were found, and the discovery of a settlement in that area at a site called Qumran may be the remains of that settlement. The community described by the scrolls also resembles the Essenes in many ways: it too had strict initiation procedures, communal ownership of property, overlapping theological beliefs, and even similar toilet habits. Though most scholars identify the Dead Sea Scrolls sect as Essene, the Essene hypothesis is not without its weakness, and some scholars have argued for identifying the sect as a branch of the Sadducean movement (though, they acknowledge, an admittedly Essene-like one). Whoever this community was, the textual remnants it left behind offer us our only chance to view one of these groups from the inside out.

Aerial view of an ancient settlement near the Dead Sea where, according to many scholars, the sect that produced the Dead Sea Scrolls once lived.

Although we cannot be completely confident that the Dead Sea Scrolls sect was Essene, we can learn something of its origins and history from the scrolls themselves. Some time in the first half of the second century, probably after Antiochus' persecution, the sect coalesced around a leader known as the **Teacher of Righteousness.** His identity is unknown, but we think he was a priest who fell into conflict with the Jerusalem authorities, especially a figure known as the "Wicked Priest," who may have been the high priest at the time (the "Wicked Priest" has been identified with one of the Maccabees, Jonathan or Simon, but his identity remains a mystery). For reasons that remain unclear, in 150 BCE or so, the Teacher and his followers withdrew into the Judean wilderness where, many scholars believe, they established the settlement near the Dead Sea uncovered at Qumran, very close to the caves where the scrolls were found.

The community that developed there was a highly organized, disciplined, and hierarchical one that worked hard to keep itself separate from the outside world, avoiding contact with non-Jews, restricting membership, and only using Hebrew in its compositions (though its members could also read Aramaic and Greek). Its members ate, prayed, and studied together, and their behavior was strictly regulated under the supervision of specially appointed officials and teachers. Whatever grievances they nursed against the Jerusalem authorities or the Temple, they expected matters to dramatically improve in the near future and believed themselves to be living at the end of history, just before or at the beginning of an age when God would intervene to defeat his enemies in a final apocalyptic war. So far as we can tell, this community was still waiting for these events to happen when it came to an end during the Jewish Revolt against Rome in 66–70 CE, when its members were wiped out or scattered by the Romans.

That this community was interested in the biblical past is abundantly clear from the content of the scrolls: many of them were biblical manuscripts, and the nonbiblical scrolls include compositions that expand upon the Bible, biblical commentaries, and legal and ritual texts saturated with biblical references. Like other Jews at the time, then, this community was preoccupied with the Bible, but how it related to the Bible was distinctive. Its biblical canon may have been very different from today's Jewish biblical canon, including not just alternative versions of the biblical text but also pseudepigraphical works, like *Jubilees* and the ***Temple Scroll,*** that record alternative accounts of what God revealed to Israel. The sect also developed its own way of reading the Bible, a technique known as ***pesher,*** through which it discovered in the Bible predictions of its own communal history. The term *pesher* may have originally referred to dream interpretation, and as used in the scrolls, it does indeed interpret the Bible as dreams were interpreted in antiquity, detecting within it coded prophecies of the future.

The community also developed its own understanding of biblical law. One of the most important scrolls for understanding the sect's history, known as the ***Halakhic Letter,*** was only published in 1991—and even then it was published in a bootlegged copy, and the scholar whose transcription they had drawn on sued the person who published it (*see box,* Did Someone Conspire to Cover Up the Dead Sea Scrolls?). Written to the priestly authorities in Jerusalem by the leaders of the Dead Sea Scrolls community, the letter gives us a unique glimpse into the legal disputes of the day, enumerating a long list of laws that, in the writers' estimation, were being violated by the Jerusalem establishment: the wrong people were being allowed into the Temple, sacrifices and purification were being mishandled, and the priests were engaging in forbidden sexual unions (the position that the letter

takes on these issues often agrees with Sadducean legal views as known from later rabbinic sources, one of the main reasons that some recent scholars identify the sect as Sadducean rather than Essene). The Dead Sea Scrolls community felt so strongly about these issues that it was willing to challenge the authorities in Jerusalem. It did so diplomatically, by sending a letter, but the refusal of these authorities to reform their behavior according to the sect's views may have provoked a stronger response, for scholars suspect that this legal dispute was the trigger that prompted the sect to give up on Jerusalem and withdraw into the wilderness.

Not only did the sect understand the Bible differently than did other Jews, but it also related to the Temple differently as well. The ***Damascus Document,*** which includes an account of the sect's origins, does not even mention the rebuilding of the Second Temple, as if refusing even to acknowledge its existence, and later sections criticize the handling of sacrifices and other cultic abuses. Other scrolls express or imply similar criticism of the Temple, its priests, and the calendar they used to schedule its festivals (the Dead Sea Scrolls sect followed the solar calendar endorsed by *Jubilees*). Apparently in frustration with the Temple cult, the sect fantasized about a future temple that would be conducted in the right way—the *Temple Scroll* is a kind of blueprint for such a temple—and the sect also developed its own ritual and prayer, based on or inspired by the Bible but adapted to its distinctive beliefs and circumstances. As an alternative to worshipping in the Temple, its members, many of them priests, imagined themselves joining the angels in the heavenly sanctuary. They also organized their community on the model of the Temple as if they themselves were a virtual

DID SOMEONE CONSPIRE TO COVER UP THE DEAD SEA SCROLLS?

By the late 1980s, more than forty years after Arab shepherds discovered the first Dead Sea Scrolls in 1947, many had not yet been published, including important documents, such as the *Halakhic Letter.* The delay was frustrating, but the work of piecing together and deciphering the thousands of fragments involved was painstaking, and many scholars were content to wait for the official team of scholars charged with publishing the scrolls to complete their work. Some were not content, however, and accused the team of being too controlling—or worse, of deliberately suppressing the scrolls for fear that their content would undermine Christianity. Was there a cover-up? The answer, reassuring to some, disappointing to others, is no. Mistakes were made in how the publication was organized—perhaps the team was too small for the kind of work required—and the project lost momentum with time, but its ultimate objective was always to make the scrolls available to scholars and to the public, and moving too quickly might have jeopardized the detailed work needed to reconstruct the scrolls' content. Although the accusations made were hurtful to many individuals, and some of the legal disputes have yet to be resolved, it did have beneficial side effects: the public pressure it created expanded the number of scholars involved in the scrolls' publication and hastened the official publication of such texts as the *Halakhic Letter.* Having learned from the mistakes that that were made, scholars in the field have developed policies to avoid repeating them should anyone be lucky enough to make a similar discovery of ancient texts in the future.

Temple, attending carefully to the purification rituals needed to preserve their sanctity and offering their prayers as a substitute for sacrifice.

The community reflected in the Dead Sea Scrolls was a highly unusual one, at odds with the Jerusalem authorities and conscious of itself as separate from the majority of Israelites. To an onlooker such as Josephus, their way of life—and whether or not the sect was Essene, its lifestyle resembles that of the Essenes as described by Josephus—was admirable but also exceptional. Thanks to the discovery of the scrolls and the excavation of the Qumran settlement, more is known about this community than any other Jewish community in the Hellenistic period, but it occupied an unusual position in that society as a countercultural movement critical of the religious establishment. The picture of Jewish life that one can draw from the scrolls is thus a highly skewed one.

Even if they assumed a highly unusual form, however, many of the impulses at work in the scrolls (the fascination with the Bible, the commitment to keeping its laws, and the need to worship God in accordance with those laws) were not unique to this community. It was precisely this commitment to tradition, shared by many other Jews, that complicated the Jewish encounter with Hellenistic culture, creating a potential predicament that demanded much effort and creativity to negotiate. On the one hand, Jews in this period had many incentives to act like their Greek rulers and faced many disadvantages to not doing so. On the other hand, Jewish identity, rooted in the Bible's description of a special relationship between God and Israel, was premised on a sense of difference, on acting differently from other peoples. How to negotiate between these conflicting pressures, how to participate in the Hellenistic world while preserving Jewish tradition, is *the* question that drives much of the Jewish literature composed in the Hellenistic period.

We have seen that many Jews, including the Maccabees, did find ways to bridge the two cultural orientations, acting Hellenized and preserving Jewish tradition at the same time, and they may not have felt any contradiction in doing so. But another reason that the Dead Sea Scrolls are so important is that they reveal that not all Jews in this period were so eager to integrate into the world around them. For this community at least, the only way to preserve tradition was to escape from the world—to isolate itself from wordly influences. In truth, it was impossible to completely escape from the world, and even the Dead Sea Scrolls, a few in Greek, betray Hellenistic influence, but the sect that produced them did what it could to create a boundary around itself.

This response may have been an extreme one, but the problem the sect was trying to solve, how to preserve Jewish tradition, is one that other texts that we have looked at in this chapter—*Jubilees,* the writing of Alexandrian Jews, *1 and 2 Maccabees,* and others—were engaged with as well. What is *Jewish* about Jewish–Hellenistic culture is precisely this commitment to preserving a traditional Jewish way of life. It may be, as we have noted, that this conception of Jewishness as a chosen way of life was itself a by-product of the encounter with Hellenistic culture, but Jews did not realize that, believing themselves to be doing what their biblical ancestors had done in the days of Abraham and Moses. One cannot understand the development of Jewish Hellenistic culture without taking this belief seriously, for it shaped how Jews responded to Hellenistic culture, guiding what they chose to appropriate from the Greeks and what they felt they had to resist.

The Afterlife of Jewish Hellenistic Culture

The historical period we have been concerned with in this chapter stretched from the fourth century BCE to the first century BCE, but the Hellenization of Jewish culture continued well beyond those years. To illustrate the persistent influence of Greek culture, we conclude this chapter with an example from a later period of Jewish history, a Jewish ritual observance that is both traditional and Hellenized at the same time.

Even as the Israelites were departing from Egypt, the Bible reports, Moses was commanding them to remember the experience, establishing the rites of the Passover festival as a commemoration of the Exodus. Passover as practiced today, reflecting changes that can be traced back to the third century CE, is very different from the biblical festival, however, when the festival was celebrated with a sacrifice of a lamb. Now, the central act of the Passover festival is a banquet structured by a service known in Hebrew as the ***Seder*** that consists of blessings, prayers, stories, questions, and comments as laid out in a kind of scripted recitation of the Exodus story known as the ***Haggadah*** (from the Hebrew for "telling"). One reason for the difference between then and now is the destruction of the Temple, which made it impractical for Jews to offer the Passover sacrifice, but the difference also reflects the impact of Hellenization.

In fact, the Passover meal as structured by the Haggadah shares many traits in common with the customs of the Greek symposium, a ritualized banquet devoted to philosophical discussion. Participants in a symposium would recline for the meal while being served by servants. As they drank wine (the word *symposium* comes from the Greek meaning "to drink together"), they might sing a song in honor of a god or give a speech enumerating the god's special gifts to humankind. When the food was served, its arrival might occasion a question, or one might pick up a piece of food to discuss its origins. All these customs are paralleled in the Haggadah's script for the Passover meal: Jews are to recline at the table and drink four cups of wine. Participants sing songs and recite speeches in praise of God for what He did during the Exodus, and they ask questions about the foods eaten during the meal. The Haggadah even incorporates Greek words taken from the symposium, such as *afikomen*—a special piece of matzoh eaten at the end of the Seder—which comes from a Greek word for the entertainment after the meal.

None of this means that the Haggadah was consciously modeled on the Greek symposium. To the contrary, its authors deliberately avoided the imitation of Greek practices at odds with their own tradition—the invocation of foreign gods or the kind of excessive revelry and drinking at the end of a meal that might lead to an orgy, as happened in some symposia. Participants in the Seder saw themselves as fulfilling an age-old biblical injunction to commemorate the Exodus, and the stories, songs, symbols, and rituals of the Haggadah are mostly modeled on or drawn from the Bible. From the perspective of its participants, in other words, the Passover Seder was a traditional Jewish act. But as we have seen, even when Jews resisted Hellenistic influence or sought to insulate themselves from foreign contact, they were still participants in Hellenistic culture. Its influence can be detected in every aspect of Jewish life, even in how Jewish tradition itself was enacted, as the Haggadah illustrates when it draws on the conventions of the Greek symposium to commemorate the Exodus.

The most obvious signs of Hellenistic influence have been obscured by the accidents of history. At its height, the Jewish community in Alexandria—the most influential Jewish community outside of Judea in the Hellenistic period—probably numbered in the hundreds of thousands, yielding such great intellectuals as Philo of Alexandria, a prolific Jewish philosopher active in the first century CE. That community went into decline in late antiquity, however—overshadowed in its influence on Jewish culture by the Jewish communities that developed in Palestine and Babylonia at this time, communities also influenced by Hellenistic culture but less obviously so. We know of the Septuagint, the writings of Philo, and other accomplishments of the Alexandrian Jewish community only to the extent that its literature was preserved by later Christians.

But the influence of Hellenistic culture transcends the fate of any particular author or community, and its impact on Jewish life was both intensified and broadened by the Romans who were themselves Hellenized by the time they established an empire that encompassed most of the world's Jewish population. A Jew might oppose Hellenistic influence, or be unconscious of that influence, but for Jews living in the Roman Empire, it was not possible to operate completely outside the cultural and social framework that Hellenism had established. Greek language, ideas, laws, and customs would have a major impact on early Christians, such as Paul (yet another Jew who wrote in Greek), and, less obviously but no less importantly, on the sages who would shape rabbinic Judaism—even those who opposed studying Greek and taking Greek names. There was no escaping the influence of Hellenistic culture because Judaism itself was an outgrowth of that culture, inheriting a distinct identity from the Hebrew Bible but reshaping that identity under the influence of—and in response to—Hellenistic culture.

Questions for Reflection

1. Based on what you have read in this chapter, why did Greek culture have such a pervasive and profound impact on the culture of the Near East after Alexander the Great?

2. Given the many advantages of acting Greek in the Hellenized world, why did some Jews resist its influence?

3. The Maccabees were willing to sacrifice their lives rather than betray the traditions of their biblical ancestors, but they and their successor also emulated the Greeks in many ways. How do you account for the apparent inconsistency? Is such behavior truly inconsistent?

4. How did the encounter with Greek culture affect how Jews read the Bible?

5. How do the Pharisees, Sadducees, and Essenes differ in their understanding of Jewish tradition?

6. Based on what you have read in this and Chapter 2, what do the Dead Sea Scrolls tell us about ancient Jewish culture?

For Further Reading

For important, if dated, studies of the Jewish encounter with Greek/Hellenistic culture, see Elias Bickerman, *The Jews in the Greek Age* (Cambridge, MA: Harvard University Press, 1962), or Martin Hengel, *Judaism and Hellenism: Studies in Their Encounter in Palestine During the Early Hellenistic Period* (London/Philadelphia; SCM Press/Fortress Press, 1974). For a more recent survey, see Erich Gruen, *Heritage and Hellenism: The Reinvention of Jewish Tradition* (Berkeley: University of California Press, 1998).

On diasporic Jewish life, see John Barclay, *Jews in the Mediterranean Diaspora: From Alexander to Trajan (323 B.C.E.–117 C.E.)* (Edinburgh: T & T Clark, 1996).

For a concise survey of Jewish literature in this period, see G. Nickelsburg, *Jewish Literature Between the Bible and the Mishnah* (Philadelphia: Fortress, 1981). For a reliable introduction to the Dead Sea Scrolls, see J. Vanderkam, *The Dead Sea Scrolls Today* (Grand Rapids, MI: Eerdmans, 1994). For an accessible translation of Jewish texts from the Hellenistic period, which is also the source of the translation of Ezekiel's tragedy described at the beginning of this chapter, see J. Charlesworth, *Old Testament Pseudepigrapha* (Garden City, NY: Doubleday, 1985), vol. 2, especially 7–34 (*Letter of Aristeas*); 35–142 (*Jubilees*); and 775–919 (Ezekiel's tragedy and other Jewish texts in Greek).

Chapter 4

Between Caesar and God

Not one to miss an opportunity, Judah the Maccabee did not rely on the help of God alone in his war with the Greeks; he also turned to a people known for being a formidable ally: the Romans. The Romans were already so powerful by this time that the mere possibility they might intervene was intimidating, and Judah's efforts to cultivate a "friendship" with them may help to explain why the Seleucids, who had been defeated by the Romans in the past, were willing to come to terms with the Maccabees. In the end, however, it was not the Jews' Greek foes but their opportunistic Roman friends who proved more dangerous when, during the next century, the help that Rome offered the Jews became a pretext for taking over Judea. Roman rule would be devastating not just to the Hasmoneans but also to Jewish culture.

The event that opened the door for the Romans was a feud that broke out between two Hasmoneans, Aristobolus II and Hyrcanus II, over who would succeed their mother, Queen Salome Alexandra, who died in 67 BCE. By then the Roman general Pompey was in the area, having taken over the territory that had belonged to the former Seleucid kingdom, and he used the conflict between Aristobolus and Hyrcanus to insert himself into Judean politics as a kind of impartial arbiter. After hearing the claims of each side, he initially deferred making a decision, but when Aristobolus proved too uncontrollable, he decided to intervene on behalf of Hyrcanus. In 63 BCE, Pompey arrested Aristobolus and marched on Jerusalem to root out what was left of his support.

Pompey scandalized the Jews by entering the Temple, a space forbidden to all but the priests, though according to Josephus he was otherwise highly respectful of Jewish tradition, refraining from looting the Temple's contents and ordering the resumption of its sacrifices. He also seemed to restore self-rule to the Jews, establishing Hyrcanus as ruler of Judea. Even as he did so, however,

Pompey made it clear that he was really in charge now, taking much of the territory the Hasmoneans had ruled and putting it under a Roman governor and reducing Judea to the status of a tribute-paying dependent. Judea was not fully incorporated into the Roman empire for some time, but it was from this moment, as Josephus would later note, that the Jews became subject to Rome.

The ensuing centuries of Roman rule saw many momentous changes in Jewish culture. It was during the Roman period, in the wake of major Jewish revolts in the first and second centuries CE, that Judea lost most of its Jewish population, and the center of Jewish communal life shifted to northern posts of the country and the Diaspora. During this period, Jewish religious life became more diffuse as well. After the destruction of the Temple in 70 CE, Jews developed new ways of worshiping God that were not dependent on the offering of sacrifice, forms of worship tied to institutions that survive until today: the synagogue and the study house. Many of the Jewish groups we encountered in Chapter 3—the Hasmoneans, Pharisees, Sadducees, Essenes/Dead Sea Scrolls sect—disappeared by the second century CE, while new non-Temple-centered movements began to flourish: Christianity, which began as a form of Judaism but developed into a distinct community dominated by non-Jews who did not see themselves as bound by the covenant established at Sinai, and rabbinic Judaism which, while committed to the Sinai covenant, was no less innovative in its interpretation.

Too much happened during the Roman period to fit into a single chapter, and so we have opted to divide our coverage of this period into two. The present chapter covers the early Roman period, from 63 BCE to 135 CE, from Pompey's conquest to the Jewish revolts of the first and second centuries CE. Chapter 5 follows Jewish culture into the seventh century CE, by which time its center of gravity had shifted from a Roman-controlled Palestine to a Persian-controlled Babylonia. Our focus in these chapters is on moments of change: the rise and decline of the Herodian dynasty, Jewish revolts against Rome and their impact, the birth of Christianity and its split from Judaism, and the eventual "rabbinization" of Jewish culture. But we balance our interest in historical change against the fact that Jewish culture in this period was a highly conservative one. Indeed, we cannot understand why it developed as it did without recognizing that even as their culture evolved, Jews were at the same time deeply committed to preserving what they had inherited from the past.

Yielding to Roman Rule

In many ways, the Romans were not that different from the Jews. Like Jewish society in antiquity, Roman society was agrarian based, patriarchal, and highly traditional. The Romans revered their gods and cherished the traditions bequeathed to them by their ancestors. Like Jewish culture, Roman culture too had been transformed by its encounter with the Greeks. By the second century BCE, however, Jewish culture and Roman culture were on sharply divergent paths because, by then, the Romans were operating in the Hellenistic world from a position of much greater power than the Jews. By dint of its military genius and skillful manipulation of alliances, Rome completely reshaped the Hellenistic world, establishing itself as its supreme power by the first century BCE.

How the Romans achieved this position of supremacy is a subject for another book, but a few important turning points bear mentioning. By the fourth century BCE, the Romans had largely consolidated their control over the other peoples of Italy, expanding their reach into the larger Mediterranean. In the western Mediterranean it faced a serious rival, the Phoenician colony of Carthage in North Africa, but by the second century BCE, after three harrowing wars known as the Punic Wars, Rome was able to subdue Carthage once and for all, gaining unchallenged control over Spain and North Africa. In the Eastern Mediterranean and the Near East, it faced the Seleucids and the Ptolemies, among other kingdoms, but it soon overcame their resistance as well. Together with her Roman lover Marc Antony, Cleopatra VII, the last of the Ptolemies, had hoped to reenergize her kingdom, but Cleopatra and Antony's ambition collided with that of Julius Caesar's posthumously adopted son, **Octavian,** who after defeating them in 31 BCE assumed the title of pharaoh of Egypt for himself. Under Octavian, Rome would control a territory that stretched from Spain in the west to the Euphrates in the east (*see* Map 4-1).

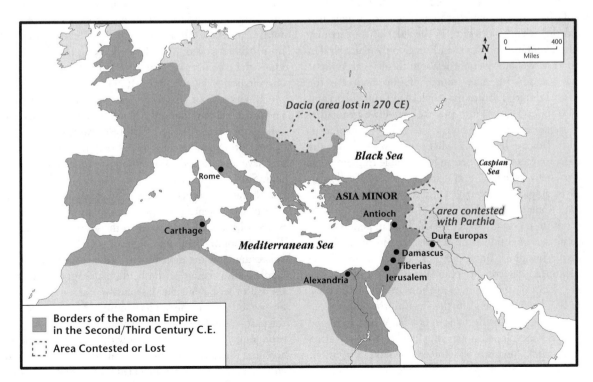

Map 4-1   The Roman Empire in the First Century.

It was also under Octavian that Rome completed its transformation from a republic to an empire. *Republic* in this context was a kind of oligarchy presided over by the Roman Senate, a council of elders (the word *senate* is related to the Latin *senex* for "old man"). The Roman Senate did not pass legislation, as the U.S. Senate does, but made recommendations and appointed various offices. Pompey's conquest of Judea occurred only a few decades before the Republic came to an end in the time of Julius Caesar and Octavian. The latter ostensibly acted to restore the Republic, but he purged Senators he did not like and packed the Senate with those he did, and the result was a compliant body that voted him more and more offices, powers, and titles, including "Commander Imperitor," from which the word *emperor* derives, and "Augustus Caesar," the reason Octavian is also known as **Augustus.** The senate also granted him and his successors supreme authority over all of Rome's legions and provincial governors, making the emperor ruler not just of Rome but of all its considerable territory. On the surface, Octavian had restored the Republic, but it was he who turned it into an empire.

In the course of absorbing the Mediterranean and the Near East into this empire, the Romans also came to control much of the world's Jewish population, not just in Judea and Egypt but throughout North Africa, Asia Minor, Greece, and even Rome. By the first century CE, in fact, the only significant Jewish community outside the Roman Empire was comprised of the Jews in the Parthian kingdom, which had displaced the Seleucid kingdom as the ruler of the territory east of the Euphrates and was then Rome's only major rival in the Near East. We know very little about this Jewish community, however, for our main source of information is the Babylonian Talmud, a source that took shape in the sixth and seventh centuries CE, centuries after the period we are focused on in this chapter (for more on the Talmud, see Chapter 5). Since historians are limited in what they can say about the past by the sources that happen to be available to them, Jewish history between 63 BCE and the age of the Babylonian Talmud is almost completely limited to what happened within the Roman Empire.

Our most important source for the Roman period is one we have already mentioned on several occasions: the historian **Flavius Josephus.** Born in 37 CE to a family of priestly and Hasmonean descent, Josephus was in an excellent position to report on Jewish–Roman relations in the first century CE. He had been a general in the Jewish army during the Jewish Revolt against the Romans in 66 CE. When, in 67, he and his men were pinned down in a cave at Yodefat (often spelled *Jotapata*), Josephus was forced to make a decision: join his men in a suicide pact or surrender to the Romans. Josephus chose both. Under pressure from his men, who

threatened to kill him themselves if he did not agree to take his own life, Josephus assented and proposed a lottery to determine who would kill whom first. Somehow, his lot proved to be one of the last two to be drawn, and it was at that moment that he changed course, he and the other remaining soldier deciding that it was better to surrender to the Romans after all. (Josephus implies that it was divine intervention that saved him, but historians suspect that he manipulated the lots.) Josephus served the Romans as a translator and mediator during their siege of Jerusalem, and after the Romans destroyed Jerusalem in 70 CE, he moved to Rome and began to publish—first an account of the revolt, then an even lengthier "prequel," the *Jewish Antiquities,* which recounts Jewish history from the biblical age to the time just before the Jewish Revolt, along with a work entitled *Against Apion* (a defense of the *Antiquities*) and an autobiography. He died sometime around 100 CE.

Josephus is by no means our only source of information about Jewish history in the Roman period; we have several other textual sources: the copious writings of the Jewish philosopher **Philo of Alexandria,** the Dead Sea Scrolls, pseudepigraphical texts written in this period, references to the Jews in Greek and Roman sources, and the contents of the New Testament, an invaluable source not just for early Christian history but also for early Jewish history. Anyone who has traveled to Israel and seen the excavated portion of the Temple complex in Jerusalem, or wandered among the ruins of Caesarea on the coast north of Tel Aviv, or climbed up to the fortress of Masada overlooking the Dead Sea will know that the Roman period has left behind substantial archaeological evidence. But without Josephus, it would be much harder to fit all this evidence into a larger picture, for he provides us with our only extended narrative of Jewish history in the first 170 years or so of Roman rule.

As dependent as they are on Josephus, however, historians have also learned to be cautious in their use of his writings. Some of Josephus' historical claims have been partially corroborated by other sources or by archaeology: his description of the Essenes corresponds in many ways to the Dead Sea Scrolls sect, the excavation of the southwest corner of the Temple Mount corroborate some of what he says about its architecture, and the discovery of Masada has done much to confirm his account of the battle that happened there after the fall of Jerusalem. But Josephus was an ancient historian, not a modern one: his understanding of how to reconstruct the past was in line with the standards of Greco–Roman historiography of the day, but not with our own standards. He accepted the testimony of earlier sources, without question or corroboration, and often invented speeches and other details to spice up his narrative or make a rhetorical point.

Statue of the Emperor Augustus, first emperor of the Roman Empire.

Also undercutting Josephus' credibility is his skill as a spin doctor who shaded Jewish history to serve both his own interests and those of his Roman patrons. Josephus' ability to publish his works, indeed his very survival in Rome, depended on his ability to curry favor with his Roman patrons, the emperors **Vespasian** and his sons **Titus** and **Domitian,** a new imperial dynasty that owed much of its stature to its victory against the Jews. The fact that Josephus took the first name "Flavius," inspired by the family name of his imperial patrons, reflects his desire to be closely associated with them. He tells us that Titus endorsed his account of the Jewish Revolt, designating it the official account, and it is not hard to see why: it is clearly a work of pro-Roman (and more precisely pro-Flavian) propaganda, glorifying Rome's accomplishment in defeating the Jews, extolling the leadership of Vespasian and Titus, and clearing them of any blame for the Temple's destruction.

But while his pro-Roman bias undermines Josephus' credibility as an historian, it is also revealing in its own right, illustrating one way in which Jews responded to Roman conquest. Unable to resist Roman rule, Josephus and other-like minded Jews decided to submit to it voluntarily, a choice he justified through his writings. The list of peoples subdued by the Romans was long, he notes in his history of the Jewish Revolt, and their submission to Rome was a powerful argument for the Jews to yield as well:

> Look at the Athenians . . . the men who, off the coast of little Salamis, broke the immense might of Asia. Those men today are the servants of the Romans and the city that was queen of Greece is governed by orders from Italy. . . . Look at the Macedonians, who still cherish Philip in their imagination, who with Alexander scattered broadcast for them the seeds of the empire of the world; yet they submit to endure such a reversal of fate and bow before those to whom Fortune has transferred her favors. Myriads of other nations, swelling with greater pride in the assertion of their liberty, have yielded. And will you alone disdain to serve those to whom the universe is subject? (*Jewish War* 2.358–361)

Writing a few decades earlier, the first-century Jewish philosopher Philo, living in a Roman-controlled Alexandria, made a different kind of argument. For him, Roman emperors, at least the good ones like Augustus, were ideal rulers.

Since the Persian period, many Jews, especially among the elite, had been willing to accept the reality of foreign rule and ally themselves with its interests. As is the case with Josephus, such a posture was in their personal self-interest, but those who adopted it may have calculated that it was in the best interests of their society as well. The pro-Roman statements of Philo, Josephus, and rabbinic literature continue that same posture. On the one hand, Roman rule brought many advantages—improved infrastructure, relative peace, a well-developed legal system, along with support and protection for Jewish religious practice and civic rights. On the other hand, resistance was extremely dangerous and probably futile. In their heart of hearts, Jews like Philo and Josephus may have privately detested Roman rule, but whatever secret resentment they nursed, they concluded that outwardly submitting to Rome was the safest course for the Jews.

For its part, Rome had reasons of its own to try to win the goodwill of its Jewish subjects. Like the empires that had preceded it, Rome preferred to build its empire on the existing political structure of the societies it ruled, relying on the local aristocracy to rule on its behalf. At first, it did this in Judea as well, but when the Hasmoneans proved too much trouble, Rome pushed them aside in favor of a more pliant ruler, **Herod,** who ruled Judea from 37 BCE until his death in 4 BCE. Herod worked hard to cultivate a good relationship with the Romans, building Caesarea and other cities in honor of Augustus, and visiting with him and other high-ranking Romans on several occasions. They in turn depended on Herod to keep the peace in Judea, which he was able to do with an army that included Romans, Gauls, and Germans. He kept tight control over the priesthood, appointing a friend to the high priesthood, and also over the **Sanhedrin** (from the Greek for "meeting" or "assembly") of Jerusalem. In exchange for Herod's loyalty, the Romans granted him additional territory and high status within the empire, including the honor of being recognized as a "friend" of the emperor.

Herod is best known for two reasons—his rebuilding of the Temple and the role he plays in the story of Jesus—and both tell us something about the nature of his rule. He was an extremely active builder, initiating the construction of cities like Caesarea, fortresses such as Masada, palaces, theatres, and other kinds of buildings not just in Palestine but as far away as Greece. His expansion of the Temple, a project he undertook in 20 BCE, was his most ambitious project. Employing 10,000 workers and taking years to complete (according to the Gospel of John, 46), the project involved the demolition of the existing temple and the erection of a new one atop a platform big enough to accommodate courts, gates, porticos, a fortress known as the Antonia, and other large buildings. The resulting complex, its massive dimensions now confirmed by excavations of the Temple Mount's support walls, was one of the most awe-inspiring spectacles of the day—so magnificent that, according to Josephus, Titus hesitated to destroy the Temple because he judged it an "ornament" for the empire.

Herod's reconstruction of the Temple creates the impression of a ruler deeply committed to Jewish tradition, and he might have undertaken the project to encourage just that perception. Despite the support of Rome, Herod could not take his legitimacy as a Jewish ruler for granted. From the perspective of Jewish tradition, he had no claim to the kingship or the high priesthood since he was not a descendant of David or Aaron; his very Jewishness was in question since his grandfather was an Idumean convert. He did try to associate himself with the Hasmoneans, taking as his second wife a princess from that family named Mariamne, but their relationship soured, and Herod had her executed. Herod offended his Jewish subjects in other ways as well, introducing various Hellenistic or Roman

One of the Tablets from the *Gilgamesh Epic,* a Mesopotamian text that records a story of a flood similar to the story of Noah's Ark in Genesis 6–9.

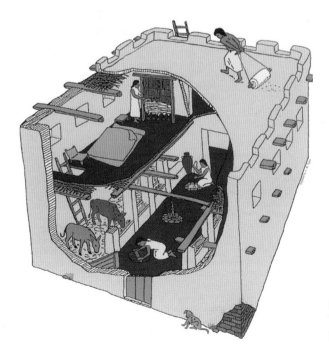

Cross-section of an Israelite House in the Pre-exilic Period. The lower floor probably housed stables, storage, and food processing; the upper floor, space for eating and sleeping.

A Reconstruction of Herod's Temple.

A Silver Scroll, Dated to around 600 BCE and probably used as an amulet, inscribed with phrases known from the priestly benediction found in Numbers 6:24–26. The inscription represents the earliest datable citation of material found in the Bible.

A Contemporary Samaritan Priest from Nablus posing with a Samaritan version of the Five Books of Moses.

Partially Reconstructed Late Antique Synagogue from the Talmudicera village of Qasrin in northern Israel.

A Thirteenth-Century Synagogue in Toledo, Spain, its architecture showing clearly the influence of Islamic art on Jewish material culture. The synagogue was turned into a church after the anti-Jewish pogroms that swept Spain in 1391 and has been known since then as the "Santa María la Blanca" synagogue.

The Miracle of the Desecrated Host was painted by Paulo Uccello between 1465 and 1469 as the platform for the altarpiece in the Church of Corpus Domini in Urbino, Italy. The scene here shows a Christian woman giving the host (the bread used during the Eucharist ceremony) to a Jewish moneylender to pay off a loan, thereby depicting Jews as defilers of Christianity and practitioners of predatory commerce. A subsequent scene (not depicted) shows the host bleeding through the door of a Jewish house as armed men try to break in to rescue it from the Jews.

innovations into Jerusalem, such as athletic games, Greek-style entertainment arenas, and lethal spectacles—"fatal charades" as scholars refer to them, that involved throwing prisoners to wild beasts. His subjects were so suspicious of him that they assumed the theatre he built in Jerusalem had images of men in it that violated Jewish law; he had to take them on a tour of the theatre to assure them this was not the case. Herod's rebuilding of the Temple seems to be another effort to shore up his reputation with the people, casting him as a champion of Jewish piety in the tradition of Solomon.

Another reason Herod is so famous (and infamous) is that he appears in the Gospel accounts in Matthew and Luke of Jesus' birth, and his image there reflects another side of the king. According to the Gospel of Matthew 2:1–18, Herod learned that the king of the Jews had been born in Bethlehem (which, if true, would have undermined his own status as king of the Jews), and unable to find the child, he ordered the death of all the children of Bethlehem. The story, absent from the other Gospel accounts, is probably not historical (it may have been composed to suggest a parallel with the Exodus story, recalling Pharaoh's effort to slay Israel's male babies), but it does capture something genuine about Herod's character. Deeply suspicious of those around him, when Herod sensed that someone was a threat, he did not shirk from killing him or her. Herod's victims included his wife, three of his children, his mother-in-law, John the Baptist, and countless others. Herod's cruelty stood out even by Roman standards. A story told centuries later claimed that when Augustus heard that Herod had slain a number of baby boys, including his own son, he quipped that he would sooner be Herod's pig than his son (since the former was safer than the latter).

Herod's paranoia was not that delusional, actually. He had many rivals, including what was left of the Hasmoneans, and several attempts were made to assassinate him. The consummate survivor, however, he was often able to anticipate his enemies and knew how to protect himself, building fortresses at Masada, and elsewhere, and developing an extensive spy network. Herod managed to rule for more than three decades through a combination of skillful public relations, good intelligence, and sheer ruthlessness.

Herod's successors continued to stay close to Rome, but with the exception of Herod's grandson **Agrippa I** in 37–44 CE, a popular ruler but a short-lived one, they were unable to keep a lid on the tensions within Jewish society. Rome was drawn more directly into Judea's administration as a result. However, the officials sent by Rome, a kind of minor-league governor known first as a prefect and later as a **procurator,** only exacerbated tensions through their cruelty, venality, and disdain for Jewish tradition. Notorious in this regard was **Pontius Pilate,** prefect of Judea between 26–37 CE (or perhaps 19–37 CE, according to some recent scholars). Pilate is remembered today for his role in Jesus' trial but was notorious among Jews at the time, in Philo's words, because of "the briberies, the insults, the robberies, the outrages and wanton injuries, the executions without trial constantly repeated, the ceaseless and supremely grievous cruelty" (*Embassy to Gaius* 302). Pilate's disrespect for Jewish tradition provoked several major confrontations with the Jews, though when he was finally relieved from duty, it was for mismanaging relations with the Samaritans. Other procurators were even worse. For all of Rome's effectiveness in ruling its empire, something was not working in Judea, and by 66 CE its Jewish inhabitants were in revolt.

Resistance and Its Aftermath

The roots of the Jewish Revolt trace back to the early years of the first century, if not earlier. In the year 6, the Romans put Judea under direct Roman rule. In response, a Jew named Judas, a teacher with Pharisaic backing, proclaimed Roman rule a kind of slavery and urged the nation to free itself. No major revolt occurred in this period—Judas evidently died early on and his supporters scattered— but Judas' message resonated for many Jews. His movement, described by Josephus as a **Fourth Philosophy** alongside that of the Pharisees, Sadducees, and Essenes, survived for decades, and served as a precursor to the Sicarii, a leading faction in the Jewish Revolt. Two of the Sicarii leaders of the revolt, Menahem and Eleazar ben Jair, were Judas' descendants.

The Fourth Philosophy was opposed to Roman rule in principle—God alone was their ruler, its adherents claimed, and they would sooner die than call any man master—but a Jew did not have to subscribe to this philosophy to form a hatred of the Romans. First-century Judea was afflicted with periodic famines and widespread unemployment, and Roman rule made economic survival that much more difficult by confiscating land and imposing various kinds of taxes and tolls (according to one estimate, about 30 percent of a typical farmer's income went to paying taxes). Many Jews found themselves landless or in debt as a result, and even sold themselves or their children into slavery out of desperation, or turned to a life of banditry, a rampant problem in Judea during this period. The Romans further inflamed the situation by offending Jewish religious sensibilities. Like earlier rulers, the Romans cast themselves as the defenders of Jewish tradition, intervening to protect Jewish religious tradition. But sometimes their cupidity got the better of them, and they would pilfer the Temple or the donations intended for its use. The Romans were not consistently anti-Jewish—Jews had lived in

THE JEWS IN ROMAN EYES

Following is a sampling of how the Romans saw the Jews, as voiced by some of its leading thinkers and writers. Note the variety of attitudes reflected in these texts, ranging from admiration to hostility to responses that combine a little of both.

Varro (Roman scholar living between 116–27 BCE): "Yet Varro . . . thought the God of the Jews to be the same as Jupiter, thinking that it makes no difference by which name he is called, so long as the same thing is understood."

Cicero (Roman orator and statesman who lived between 106–43 BCE): "Even while Jerusalem was standing and the Jews were at peace with us, the practice of their sacred rites was at variance with the glory of our empire, the dignity of our name, the customs of our ancestors."

Seneca (Roman philosopher who killed himself in 65 CE): "The customs of this accursed race have gained such influence that they are now received throughout all the world. The vanquished have given laws to their victors."

Tacitus (Roman historian living between 56–120 CE): "The Jews are extremely loyal to one another, and always ready to show compassion, but toward every other people they feel only hate and enmity. They sit apart at meals and they sleep apart, and although as a race, they are prone to lust, they abstain from intercourse with foreign women; yet among themselves, nothing is unlawful. They adopted circumcision to distinguish themselves from other peoples by this difference. Those who are converted to their way follow the same practice, and the earliest lesson they receive is to despise the gods, to disown their country, and to regard their parents, children, and brothers as of little account."

Translations are from Menaham Stern, *Greek and Latin Authors on Jews and Judaism*, vols. 1 and 2 (Jerusalem: The Israel Academy of Sciences and Humanities, 1974).

Rome from the second century BCE, and the Jewish community there continued well beyond the Jewish Revolt—but occasionally, it seems, the Jews were seen by the Romans as enough of a threat that it was deemed necessary to expel them from the city of Rome (*see box,* The Jews in Roman Eyes).

In Judea, the Jews were on their home turf, and most Roman administrators seem to have accommodated themselves to their religious practices, but even there, cultural clashes instigated by Roman interference in Jewish religious tradition broke out. Pilate provoked at least two major crises through offensive behavior: first when he tried to install imperial images in Jerusalem in violation of the Jewish ban on images, and again when he appropriated some sacred funds to finance the building of an aqueduct. Even a single action of a single soldier could trigger a major confrontation. According to Josephus, a Roman soldier once sparked a major riot when he turned his back to the Jews and, to put things nicely, emitted a noise that offended them.

For many Jews, the misbehavior of local Roman officials or soldiers acting on their own did not discredit imperial rule in principle. If it was possible to resolve a grievance by appealing to the emperor, the Jewish leadership would often seize on that option, hoping he would make good on his reputation for benevolence. But sometimes the emperor was the problem. One of the worst offenders was the emperor Gaius, better known as **Caligula,** who, angry with the Jews for

refusing to honor him as a god, decided in 40 CE to have a statue of himself as Zeus installed in the Jerusalem Temple. To have done so would have been a catastrophe of immense proportions from a Jewish perspective, and in an effort to prevent it, thousands of Jews came to the Roman governor pleading with him not to implement the order. "If we cannot persuade you," their leaders told the governor, "we give ourselves up for destruction that we may not live to see a calamity worse than death" (*Embassy to Gaius* 233, a treatise written by Philo of Alexandria, who happened to be among the members of a Jewish delegation sent to Caligula to dissuade him from his plans). Caligula's actions might have provoked a major Jewish revolt right then and there were it not for the mediation of the governor, who proved to be sympathetic to the Jews, as well as a personal appeal from Agrippa I, the Herodian leader at the time and a close friend of the emperor. Despite being unable to change Caligula's mind, they stalled him for a time, and his assassination in 41 CE averted the immediate crisis. Caligula's death, however, did not resolve the underlying tensions between the Jews and the Romans—the humiliation of being ruled by another people, the economic hardships, the mutual suspicions, and the cultural and religious differences—and it did not help that Agrippa I's successor, Agrippa II, proved a far less effective mediator.

By 66 CE, many Jews—but not all, by any means—were convinced that it was both necessary and feasible to rebel against Rome and were confident enough that they declared their rebellion in the most public of ways: halting the sacrifices offered in the Temple on behalf of the emperor and the Roman people. As presented by Josephus, the Jewish rebels appear reckless, even irrational, but we have to keep in mind that he was writing in retrospect, after the disastrous outcome of the rebellion was clear, and that his description is shaped by his pro-Roman bias. In reality, the rebels had good reason for thinking they might succeed in a war against Rome. The Jews in Judea were far more numerous than the few thousand Roman troops stationed in Palestine at the time, and they could rely on their knowledge of the terrain and on the formidable defenses of Jerusalem, a city protected by three walls, as well as other Herodian fortresses, such as Masada. The first battle with the Romans would have boosted their confidence even more when, unexpectedly, the rebels were able to rout the enemy. While Rome could have been expected to send a larger force, it had a powerful enemy in the region—the Parthian kingdom—and the rebels seemed to have hoped (in vain) to draw the Parthians into the war with the help of the large Jewish community living in Mesopotamia.

Beyond the Parthians, the rebels counted on another powerful ally, one that had helped their ancestors in many previous battles God. In the decades prior to the revolt, the Romans had had to put down a number of mini-insurrections led by prophetlike figures who had convinced their followers that God was on their side by promising to perform various miracles or to show them divine visions. One such figure, a prophet named Theudas, claimed he could part the Jordan River as if he were Moses or Joshua; another unnamed Egypt prophet led thousands of followers in a failed attempt to take Jerusalem. These movements were inevitably quashed, and their leaders killed, but their failure did not discredit the belief that God himself might one day intervene against the Romans. In fact, just before the revolt, rumors that such intervention was imminent spread like wildfire. Sages discovered in Scripture a prophecy that someone from Judea would rule the world, and people witnessed all kinds of uncanny events that seemed to augur victory: the appearance of a sword-shaped star over Jerusalem, a bright light appearing around the sanctuary during Passover, and armed battalions witnessed hurtling through the clouds. The rebels still believed that God would defend them even at the very end of the war when the Romans had them pinned down in the Temple Mount.

We know in retrospect that their confidence was mislaid. Realizing the threat to his rule, the emperor **Nero** dispatched the general Vespasian to suppress the revolt and, with an army of 60,000 soldiers, he was devastatingly effective. Nero died soon after the start of the war, precipitating a violent struggle over who would succeed him, and in 69 CE Vespasian was declared

emperor. His return to Rome temporarily halted Rome's efforts to suppress the revolt in Judea, but it was resumed under his son Titus who achieved victory within the year. By the time the Romans placed a siege on Jerusalem, internal tensions among the rebels had begun to erupt, with the major rebel factions launching attacks against each other as they vied for control over the Temple Mount. In early August of 70 the Romans destroyed the Temple—an event commemorated on the ninth of the Jewish month of *Ab* in later Jewish tradition, on the same day remembered as the anniversary of the destruction of the First Temple.

By the end of September, the conquest of Jerusalem was complete—the entire city was in flames, and thousands of Jews were massacred on the spot or taken prisoner. It did take a few more years for Rome to quash all the remaining rebels, but quash them it did. At the fortress atop Masada, some 960 rebels withstood a Roman siege until 73 CE, but when they saw that the Romans were about to capture the fortress, they decided to kill themselves rather than become slaves (*see box,* The Mystery of Masada's Final Moments). In Egypt and Cyrene in North Africa, in what is now Libya, the Sicarii tried to stir up rebellion but were betrayed to the Romans by fellow Jews eager to avoid being destroyed themselves.

The aftermath of the Jewish Revolt was terrible. The population of Judea was devastated as was its social structure: Agrippa II lived on, as did many priests, but the institutions of self-government—Herodian rule and the high priesthood—were lost, and Vespasian took the land as his personal possession, distributing some of it to his soldiers. The center of Jewish culture, the Temple, was destroyed, and the Jews were humiliated by a special tax that redirected funds once intended for the Temple to a temple of Jupiter in Rome. Rome stationed an entire legion in Jerusalem to keep matters under control and closed down the temple in Leontopolis lest it become the center of another Jewish rebellion.

Yet all these efforts were not enough to discourage Jews from further acts of rebellion. The second century saw two other major Jewish uprisings: one based in the Diaspora, the other in Judea. We know less about these revolts than we do the first Jewish Revolt because we lack a Josephus to tell us what happened, but they seem to have posed even more of a threat to Roman rule and to have provoked an even greater backlash.

The first of these revolts, known as the **Diaspora Revolt,** was actually a series of interconnected Jewish uprisings that occurred in 115–117 CE during the reign of the emperor Trajan. The foment seems to have started in Libya but quickly spread to Egypt, Cyprus, and elsewhere, fed by long-simmering ethnic tensions. Jews in these places lived alongside large Greek-speaking and native populations, and their tense relationship often became violent. The situation we know best is Alexandria. The Greeks and Egyptians of the city had long resented their Jewish neighbors, and Roman rule only seemed to

THE MYSTERY OF MASADA'S FINAL MOMENTS

One of the most memorable moments in Josephus' description of the Jewish Revolt (though he may have poached it from a source) is his account of the Roman siege of Masada. The episode includes one of the most eloquent speeches in Josephus' narrative, Eleazar ben Yair's impassioned (but reasoned) argument for suicide as the only way for the rebels to preserve their freedom and honor. Then follows one of his narrative's most horrifying moments—a description of how the rebels carried out the act:

> While they caressed and embraced their wives and took their children in their arms, clinging in tears to those parting kisses, at that same instant, as though served by hands other than their own, they accomplished their purpose, having the thought of the ills they would endure under the enemy's hand to console them for their constraint in killing them. . . . Wretched victims of necessity, to whom to slay with their own hands their own wives and children, seemed the lightest of evils! Unable, indeed, any longer to endure their anguish at what they had done, and feeling that they had wronged the slain by surviving them if it were but for a moment, they quickly piled together all the stores and set them on fire; then, having chosen by lot ten of their number to dispatch the rest, they laid themselves down each beside his prostrate wife and children, and flinging their arms around them, offered their throats in readiness for the executants of the melancholy office . . . then, the nine bared their throats, and the last solitary survivor, after surveying the prostrate multitude, to see whether haply amid the shambles there were yet one left who needed his hand, and finding that all were slain, set the palace ablaze, and then collecting his strength drove his sword clean through his body and fell beside his family (*Jewish War* 7.391–397)

The story is so well told, in fact, that one wonders whether it reflects the kind of fictionalizing found elsewhere in Josephus' narratives. On the other hand, we know that this episode was rooted in reality because of corroborating evidence uncovered during the excavation of Masada, including the discovery of eleven pottery pieces, each inscribed with a name or the nickname of a man, that *may* have been the lots used by the rebels to determine who would kill whom (though Josephus claims that only ten lots were drawn).

We can illustrate the difficulty of telling truth from fiction in Josephus' account by asking how it is that he knew about the final moments of a community that destroyed itself. Who told him what Eleazar said to his followers? How did he know that the rebels caressed their wives and children before they killed them? As if he anticipated our questions, Josephus provides the answer at the end of his narrative: "They had died in the belief that they had left not a soul of them alive to fall into Roman hands; *but an old woman and another, a relative of Eleazar, superior in sagacity and training to most of her sex, with five children, escaped by concealing themselves in the subterranean aqueducts*" (7.398–99). There were survivors, Josephus tells us, and it was these, perhaps especially the woman that Josephus praises for her sagacity, who served as informants. But can we be certain that these survivors are not themselves a fiction invented to resolve precisely the kind of doubt we are expressing? We have no way of knowing.

feed their resentment. For their part, the Jews—their status in the city precarious—feared and resented the Greeks. The result was decades of often violent ethnic conflict: in 38 CE, Alexandria erupted in anti-Jewish rioting, in which many Jews were killed and synagogues destroyed; in 41 CE, with the death of Caligula, the Jews struck back in a riot of their own; in 66 CE, the Jews and Greeks fought again in a conflict that ended with a Roman massacre of the Jews. Similar ethnic tensions existed in other cities that also had large Greek and Jewish populations.

The Diaspora Revolt of 115–117 seems to have begun as a similar kind of ethnic riot, but unlike earlier uprisings in Alexandria, the Romans were not able to contain it, and it quickly spread to other parts of the Jewish world—to Cyprus, and perhaps as far as Mesopotamia. The Roman historian Cassius Dio claims that the Jews perpetrated all kinds of atrocities during this war, even eating the flesh of their victims. The cannibalism charge seems to have been concocted—decades before the war, Greco–Egyptian writers such as Apion had been accusing the Jews of kidnapping Greeks to sacrifice and eat them—but Egyptian documents from this period give some sense of the hysteria of the period. The backlash was no less fearsome. To quell the uprising in Mesopotamia, the Romans put thousands to death. In Cyprus, Jews were banned from the island. In Egypt, the great Jewish community of Alexandria was devastated. Jews continued to live there, but for all intents and purposes, the Alexandrian Jewish community—the community that produced the Septuagint, Philo, and much else—comes to an end at that time.

Some fifteen years later, in 132 CE, yet another major Jewish uprising exploded in Judea, the **Bar Kochba Revolt.**

The fortress of Masada.

As for the Diaspora Revolt, we have just enough evidence to sense how important this revolt was but not enough to reconstruct a clear picture. The causes of the revolt are a matter of ongoing and irresolvable debate. The sources—really just a few references in later Roman, Christian, and rabbinic texts—point to at least two possibilities: the revolt might have been triggered by an imperial decree against circumcision or by an attempt to turn Jerusalem into a pagan city, but the evidence for either cause is extremely slim and of questionable reliability, and it is likely that other political factors and grievances fueled the revolt as well.

The goals of the rebellion are also unclear. According to rabbinic literature, the leader of the revolt, Simon bar Kosiba—or Bar Kochba as he was known to his followers—was recognized by the great Rabbi Akiba as the Messiah; indeed, the nickname Bar Kochba or "Son of a Star" refers to a messianic prophecy in Numbers 24:17: "a star shall come out of Jacob." Perhaps then the rebels' goal was not just to assert their independence from Rome but to initiate the messianic age. The evidence we have from the rebels themselves never makes such claims, however, nor does it do much to clarify the motives and goals of the revolt. Coins minted by the rebels refer to Bar Kochba as *nasi,* variously translated as "prince," "patriarch," or "president." The term is used in the book of Ezekiel in a description of a future temple to describe a quasi-royal figure. Does the use of this term on the Bar Kochba coins suggest that Bar Kochba was seen as such a figure? Did the term have messianic resonance? Inscribed on some of these coins is the legend "Freedom of Jerusalem." Does this motto refer to the liberate of Jerusalem? Did the rebels try to rebuild the Temple? We do not know the answers to these questions (*see box,* Letters from a Rebel).

LETTERS FROM A REBEL

The rebel leader Bar Kochba was long shrouded behind a veil of myth. Greek and Roman sources give us some information but few details. Christian and rabbinic literature give a more colorful portrait of Bar Kochba, portraying him as a bandit and a failed Messiah, but their testimony dates from long after the revolt, reflecting an awareness of the revolt's tragic outcome, and the stories they tell incorporate recognizably legendary, polemical, and/or exaggerated elements. So little information can be gleaned from these sources, or even from the thousands of coins left behind by the rebels, that until fairly recently even Bar Kochba's name remained unclear. Was it Bar Kochba, "Son of a Star" as in Christian sources, or Bar Kozeba, "Son of a Liar" as spelled in rabbinic sources?

Beginning in the 1950s, documents from the time of the Bar Kochba Revolt began to come to light and then, in 1961–62, came the most remarkable discovery of all: letters from Bar Kochba himself. These letters do not reveal as much as we would like, but they do tell us some things. His real name, they show, was Shimon Bar Kosiba (Bar Kochba and Bar Kozeba were nicknames, the latter sarcastic), and they reveal something of what he was like as a leader and administrator.

The following two letters show Bar Kochba struggling to sustain the discipline and motivation of his followers:

> From Shimeon bar Kosiba to the men of En-Gedi. To Masabala and to Yehonathan bar Ba'ayan, peace. In comfort you sit, eat and drink from the property of the House of Israel, and care nothing for your brothers.

> From Shimeon ben Kosiba to Yeshua ben Galgoula and to the men of the fort, peace. I take heaven to witness against me that unless you mobilize [destroy?] the Galileans who are with you every man, I will put fetters on your feet as I did to ben Aphlul.

The following passage reflects Bar Kochba's concern with religious observance:

> Shimeon to Yehuda bar Manasheh, to Qiryat Arbayah: "I have sent you two donkeys so that you can send two men with them to Yehonatan bar Ba'ayan and Massabalah so they can pack and send palm branches and citrons to the camp, to you. And you are from your place to send others who will bring you myrtles and willows. See that they are tithed and send them to the camp." [The palm branches, citrons, myrtles and willows were for use during the festival of Sukkot.]

For these translations, and for more about Bar Kochba, see Yigael Yadin, *Bar-Kochba: The Rediscovery of the Legendary Hero of the Last Jewish Revolt Against Imperial Rome* (London: Weidenfeld and Nicolson, 1971), which also describes another great discovery in the cave in which Bar Kochba's letters were found: a bundle of legal documents belonging to a woman named Babata from the period between 93–132 CE.

A coin minted by the Bar Kochba rebels.

What is clear is that, like the Diaspora Revolt, the Bar Kochba Revolt provoked a terrible backlash from a Roman government intent on re-establish its control. The revolt culminated in 135 CE in a final battle a few miles from Jerusalem at the city of Bethar, in which Bar Kochba was slain. Rabbinic sources also depict this period as an age of terrible persecution: the Romans forbade circumcision, the teaching of Torah, and other Jewish religious practices, and they executed in horrifying ways those who defied them by publicly keeping the commandments. The executions of Rabbi Akiba and nine other sages became legendary in later Jewish tradition, their deaths remembered as acts of heroic martyrdom, a "glorifying of God's reputation" (**Kiddush ha-Shem**) as such practice came to be known in rabbinic sources, since the executed were thought to have bravely submitted to torture and death rather than betray their allegiance to God.

Scholars have questioned whether such a persecution ever took place, but this was certainly a very difficult time for Judea, which lost much of its Jewish population during the war. If one believes the Roman historian Cassius Dio, 985 villages were razed to the ground, 580,000 people were slain, and so many people were taken slaves that the price of slaves fell throughout the empire. Any chance of restoring the Temple was lost when the Romans reestablished Jerusalem as a Roman colony named *Aelia Capitolina* (*Aelia* in honor of the emperor Hadrian's family name; *Capitolina* in honor of the god Jupiter Capitolinus). They may even have erected an imperial temple on the site of the Temple Mount, though recent scholars have expressed doubts about that. Jews were forbidden on pain of death from entering Jerusalem except for one day a year, the ninth of Ab, when they were allowed into the city to mourn their temples. Jewish culture survived in other areas—in the Galilee to the north of Judea and in Diaspora settings, such as Babylonia and Rome—but in Judea, it was largely devastated. Indeed, the land of Judea officially lost its Jewish identity when the Romans decided to change the name of the area to *Palestina,* a name derived from the Judeans' age-old enemy, the Philistines.

Writing in the wake of the First Jewish Revolt, Josephus concluded that it was folly to rebel against the Roman Empire, and in a way his narrative of that revolt is an attempt to demonstrate that thesis. The Bar Kochba Revolt led other Jewish intellectuals to rethink rebellion as a tactic of cultural survival. Rabbinic literature, our principal literary source for Jewish culture in the period between 200 and 650 CE, records a range of views about Roman rule. Some sages extolled the benefits of Roman rule, and some collaborated with the Roman government—leading sages, such as Judah the Patriarch, are even said to have enjoyed a close relationship with the emperor—but others criticized its oppressiveness and moral failings. To the extent it is possible to generalize, however, rabbinic literature seems to back away from a posture of open resistance, distancing itself from such rebels as Bar Kochba and greatly narrowing the scenarios in which *Kiddush ha-Shem,* martyrdom, was justified. In fact, in a story that is probably not historical but nonetheless speaks volumes about the rabbinic attitude to Roman rule, rabbinic literature traces the pedigree of rabbinic culture back to Yohanan ben Zakkai, a sage who chose not to join in the Jewish Revolt but rather to escape from Jerusalem by concealing himself in a coffin taken out of the city and to place his personal fate and that of his tradition in the hands of the Romans rather than to die with the rebels.

Recognizing the danger of rebellion, however, did not necessarily mean that one had to willingly embrace Roman rule, and other, less confrontational ways were available to resist it. Many Jews may have adopted a kind of deliberately ambiguous posture toward Roman rule, not challenging it directly but not exactly yielding to it either. A famous example is Jesus' response when asked whether Jews should pay taxes to the Roman Empire (Matthew 22:15–22; Mark 12, 14–17; Luke 20:20–26). Saying yes would seem to endorse Roman rule, but saying no would amount to rebellion, Jesus avoided the peril of either response by finding an answer in between them: "Give to the emperor the things that are the emperor's, and to God the things that are God's." Jesus seems to be saying that Jews should pay their taxes to Rome, but it is also possible to read his remark as saying the opposite: yes, pay Caesar his due, but since God is the only true king (the central tenet of the Fourth Philosophy), nothing is really due Caesar. Then again, if that was Jesus' point, he does not express it in a way that can be pinned down as defiant. This kind of equivocation, also evident in rabbinic literature, allowed Jews to persist under Rome without fully submitting to it.

Yet another way to resist Roman rule without directly challenging it was simply to leave the empire, and many Jews did this as well. The devastation of the Bar Kochba Revolt and its aftermath, along with other economic troubles in third-century Palestine, seems to have prompted even some rabbinic sages to leave the land for Syria, Asia Minor, and Babylonia (which was especially enticing because it was outside the Roman Empire)—a "brain drain" that the sages of Palestine were not able to reverse despite their efforts to restrict migration and extol life in the Holy Land. Compared to Rome, Babylonia was a veritable refuge for Jews—so appealing that one sage explained the Babylonian exile not as divine punishment but as God's effort to save the Jews from the decrees of the Romans (Babylonian Talmud, *Gitin* 16b–17a).

All this is simply to say that the failure of the Bar Kochba Revolt does not mark the end of Jewish resistance to Roman rule; indeed, other Jewish uprisings probably occurred in ensuing centuries, though they appear to have been local insurrections rather than full-scale revolts. But in the wake of the revolts of the first and second centuries, and the severe Roman reprisals that followed, open rebellion was a far less viable option. In the early first century CE, only a few thousand Roman troops were stationed in Palestine; by the second century CE, a whole Roman legion was stationed there, and it knew how to make an example of those who dared to fight it. It is probably not a coincidence that the Galilee, the region north of Judea, fared better than Judea did under the Romans: some Galilean cities were quicker to submit to Roman rule than Jerusalem was. Nor is it likely to be a coincidence that the two most successful movements to emerge out of Jewish culture in the first and second centuries—rabbinic Judaism and Christianity—both came to terms with Rome, each suffering periods of persecution and defiant martyrdom but each resigning itself to Roman rule in the end, and even coming to cooperate with it. Over the long run, those who endured the longest under Roman rule seem to have been those willing to acquiesce to its rule, or else those who relocated themselves beyond its reach.

Ruptures and Revisions in Early Jewish Culture

We again pick up the thread of Jewish political history after the second century CE in Chapter 5, after turning our attention in the rest of this chapter to Jewish social and religious life in the period just before and after the Second Temple's destruction.

Both Philo and Josephus describe the Jews as passionately committed to their laws and institutions and successfully preserving them for hundreds of years. According to Josephus, in fact, Jews would sooner have died than tolerate even the slightest change in the biblical text or its laws. But Jewish culture as it developed in the Roman period was in actuality very different from that of preceding centuries. Our goal in what follows is to introduce some of these changes, focusing on Jewish life in the first century CE. We single out this century because it is relatively well documented—represented by the interpretive treatises of Philo of Alexandria, Josephus, and virtually all of the New Testament, among several other literary and archaeological sources—compared to the first century BCE or the second and third centuries CE. But another reason applies as well: a number of pivotal developments occurred in the first century that continue to shape Jewish (not to mention Christian) culture to this day, including the rise of Christianity, the end of the Temple cult, and the first stirrings of what would become rabbinic Judaism. The first two of these developments—the rise of Christianity and the impact of the Temple's destruction—will occupy us in the rest of this chapter; Chapter 5 will track the rise and development of rabbinic Judaism.

Christianity's Emergence from Jewish Culture

Christianity traces its origins back to an itinerant Jewish teacher and wonder worker put to death in Jerusalem during the administration of Pontius Pilate. In Hebrew, his name seems to have been Yehoshua, or Joshua, but he is better known by the Greek form of this name, **Jesus.** (Christ, the other name by which he is known, did not originate as a personal name but rather as a title, *christos,* a Greek rendering of the Hebrew word "anointed one," applied to Jesus by his followers to signal his status as a royal figure in the line of David.) Today, Jesus is part of Christian belief and history, but he was Jewish, as were his early followers, such as **Paul.** Much can be learned about them, and about Jewish culture in the first century CE, by restoring them to a Jewish context.

Unfortunately, although he is the first century's most famous Jew, Jesus is largely a mystery from a historical point of view. We have no writings from Jesus himself, nor is he mentioned by any contemporary author, and so we must rely on later sources—the letters of Paul and the Gospels of Matthew, Mark, Luke, and John—written thirty to sixty years after his death. Many Christians accept the Gospels as unerringly accurate, but modern secular scholarship is more skeptical because these sources are hard to corroborate, make inconsistent claims, and include many episodes—Herod's attempt to kill the baby Jesus is a good example—that reflect the influence of earlier biblical stories, such as the Exodus, or Greco–Roman literary practice (*see box,* The Quest for Historical Jesus).

We can say a few things about Jesus with relative certainty. He was born between 4 BCE and 6 CE (the Gospels are confusing on this point), reportedly hailing from Bethlehem but known as "Jesus of Nazareth" as if he were from the town of Nazareth in the Galilee. The Gospels associate him with **John the Baptist,** a popular prophet executed by Herod in 28 or 29 CE. We cannot confirm that association, but we have independent testimony from Josephus that John really existed, and really championed baptism, though as Josephus describes it, the significance of this rite is different from that ascribed to it in the New Testament. We also can corroborate the existence of other important figures mentioned in the Gospels: Herod, Pontius Pilate, and even Caiaphas, the high priest at the time of Jesus' death. Scholars have no reason to doubt that Jesus was crucified; this was a sadistic form of execution that the Romans used against outlaws, rebels, and slaves as a warning to those who would consider challenging the order of things. The various Gospels depict his end differently, however, even disagreeing about when it happened. In the Gospel of John, for example, Jesus dies on the fourteenth of the month of Nisan, the day before Passover, and in the other gospels, he dies on the fifteenth, the first day of Passover.

While Jesus is largely beyond the historian's reach, what we know about Jewish culture in the first century can help to explain the rise of the movement he inspired. In Chapter 3, we noted the rise in Judean society of various "philosophies" or sects—the Pharisees, the Sadducees, and the Essenes/Dead Sea Scrolls sect—movements that continued into the first century. The Pharisees appear to have exerted the most influence on the broader population, but no single movement represents the definitive form of Judaism. Rather they should be seen as alternative, even competitive understandings of Jewish culture, offering different accounts of how to understand God, tradition, and the future. Christianity arose as one of these movements, initiated by a Jew and drawing its earliest followers from the Jewish community.

For some Jews, joining such a community was a way to live an ideal lifestyle—to keep the law as it was supposed to be kept, and to avoid the distractions of ordinary life in order to draw closer to God or study his laws. For others, it was something more, a way to prepare for a fundamental change in reality.

Many Jews in the late Second Temple period believed the troubles of the present would soon give way to a different age. Israel was supposed to enjoy God's protection, and yet the lives of Jews were full of suffering and injustice: disease, drought, famine, and oppression at the hand of foreign rulers. Why did God allow the righteous to suffer in this way? Why did God not intervene to save them? As noted in Chapter 1, the prophets of the Hebrew Bible answered these questions by interpreting Israel's troubles as punishment for Israel's sin, a disciplining or chastising that would end one day. Some prophetic passages even refer to a specific time when everything would be set right—a "day of the Lord" or "the end of days" when God would deliver his people. Jews in the Greco–Roman period took even more of an interest in what would happen in that final period of divine judgment, battle, and deliverance—the "eschatological age," as scholars now refer to it (derived from the Greek for "last things"). Some Jews, believing that time to be close at hand, dedicated their lives to preparing for it.

It was widely assumed that God would come to the rescue in the end, delivering Israel from its enemies—but how? Jewish literature from this age reflects various expectations. In some texts, God intervenes directly, or through his angels or other supernatural beings. In others, God works through special humans—either the **Davidic Messiah,** a kingly figure from the line of David, or a **Priestly Messiah,** an alternative savior figure from the line of Aaron. The Dead Sea Scrolls community anticipated those two messiahs working in tandem. Underlying these ideas is the assumption that the present was a transition between an idealized past and an idealized future and that the progress from one to the other had been determined in advance, following a precisely scripted sequence of events. This script was a secret, but God had revealed it to certain righteous humans who had thus come to grasp the true meaning and direction of history: why the righteous suffered, and when and how God would finally make things right (*see box,* A Supernatural Who's Who for Early Jewish Culture).

Among those who believed they knew this eschatological script were the members of the Dead Sea Scrolls sect, and this knowledge was an important rationale for their special lifestyle. The sect seems to have believed that it was living at the beginning of the eschatological age, not yet in the age of final judgment and messianic deliverance but in an initial, difficult period of testing and preparation before that age. Among the Dead Sea Scrolls, a text known as the *War Scroll* describes a final eschatological war between the Sons of Light, who fight with the support of God and his angels, and the Sons of Darkness, an army led by a group of non-Jewish foes known as the *Kittim* (perhaps the Romans). It is possible that the Dead Sea Scrolls sect saw itself as already engaged in this eschatological battle.

The New Testament suggests that the early Jesus movement believed itself to be similarly positioned in time. Like the Teacher of Righteousness, the Jesus of the Gospels knows the plan for the eschatological future, revealing glimpses of it to his followers. Indeed, he has a special role in that plan not just as a herald but as a divine deliverer, the Davidic Messiah long expected by Jews. To the extent that we can recover Jesus' beliefs from our much later sources, he seems to have believed that the eschatological age was imminent, or perhaps already present—another point of similarity with the Dead Sea Scrolls sect, which also saw itself as living near or in the "end of days."

As another way of illustrating the Jewishness of the early Jesus movement, let us consider Jesus' death and how it was understood by his followers. As we have noted, the first century saw the rise of a number of charismatic figures who drew large followings through their prophetic or wonder-working ability or with promises of radical change. Such figures often came to a premature end, as John the Baptist did under Herod, but the death of the leader did not necessarily spell the end of his following, as is the case with the Fourth Philosophy, for example, which survived the death of Judas the

THE QUEST FOR THE HISTORICAL JESUS

The quest to reconstruct what Jesus was really like has been frustrated by the small amount of firsthand evidence. Certainly far more evidence exists for Jesus than for Abraham, Moses, or David, and yet a close examination of this evidence renders Jesus nearly as inaccessible:

1. Writing in the 50s, Paul is the earliest extant source to speak of Jesus. Encountering Jesus only after the latter's death, however, he is not an eyewitness to his life or crucifixion and has little to say about Jesus before his death.

2. The Gospels provide us with four accounts of Jesus' life, and they are the indispensable basis for any biography of Jesus. Their testimony is even later than Paul, however; they are frequently inconsistent in what they report about Jesus; and they report nothing about Jesus that can be directly corroborated by extrabiblical evidence in the way one can confirm some figures, such as Herod. By comparing the Gospels to one another, scholars have come to recognize that each shapes the information it has inherited from earlier sources, sometimes even inventing reported details in the way that Josephus invents details in his historical accounts.

3. Josephus, refers to Jesus in a brief passage in *Antiquities* 18.63–64:

About this time [Pilate's day], there lived Jesus, a wise man, if indeed one ought to call him a man. For he was one who wrought surprising feats and was a teacher of such people as accept truth gladly. He won over many Jews and many Greeks. He was the Messiah. When Pilate, upon hearing him accused by men of the highest standing among us, had condemned him to be crucified, those who had in the first place come to love him did not give up their affection for him. On the third day he appeared to them restored to life, for the prophets of God had prophesied these and countless other marvelous things about him. And the tribe of the Christians, so called after him, has till this day not disappeared.

Here we would seem to have clear-cut corroboration for the existence of Jesus, and it has been cited as such by Christian historians since the fourth century CE. But since the sixteenth century, scholars have suspected that the passage was forged by a later Christian, or at least tampered with, for its implication that Josephus was Christian ("He was the Messiah") seems unlikely given what Josephus says elsewhere about his religious beliefs (not to mention that Josephus' description of Jesus as the Messiah is missing from an Old Arabic version of the *Antiquities*). In any case, Josephus wrote this passage in the 80s or 90s, decades after Jesus, so it does not represent firsthand information either.

4. Supposed archaeological evidence for Jesus' existence has proven bogus as well. In 2002, for example, an artifact was made public that seemed at first to be powerful corroboration: a burial box inscribed in Aramaic with the words "James, son of Joseph, brother of Jesus." For about a year, scholars tried to determine whether the Jesus referred to here was the famous Jesus, but their efforts bore no fruit in the end, because, while the burial box is probably authentic, the inscription written on it has been shown to be a forgery, and the box's owner, an antiquities dealer named Oded Golan, has since been arrested and put on trial.

5. Various noncanonical gospels, including a recently published gospel attributed to Judas Iscariot, have come to light, offering another potential source of information about Jesus. These have proven to be later and less credible than the canonical gospels, however. The Gospel of Thomas might be an exception: depending on who you believe in the debate over when it was written, it might predate some of the canonical gospels. But even if it is early, it does not offer as much help as one might expect, for it is a collection of Jesus' sayings, not a narrative, and while it may reveal something of Jesus' original teachings and beliefs, it does not supply biographical information.

Galilean. The Jesus movement followed this same pattern, persisting beyond Jesus' death because its members understood his execution in light of earlier Jewish understandings of death. One of those ideas was the belief that the righteous dead would be resurrected in the end time, and Jesus' death and his reappearance to his followers seem to fit that model.

Jesus' death seemed to follow an eschatological script in other ways as well. Before God's final deliverance, many apocalyptic texts disclose, the righteous would have to endure a period of tribulation, a time of suffering, and even death. What made this suffering bearable was precisely the knowledge that it was only temporary: the suffering would end, the dead would be restored, evil would be vanquished. The death of the righteous could be instrumental to this happy ending: in a first-century text known as the *Testament of Moses,* the prophet foresees an age of persecution

All this leaves the four canonical Gospels as our only real source of information about the historical Jesus. However skeptical one is inclined to be of their testimony, their authors know too much about Judea in the period between Herod and Pontius Pilate to be discounted in the way many biblical scholars discount Genesis and Exodus. Without other sources against which to check them, they have proven a better gauge of what early Christians believed about Jesus than a source for what Jesus was really like, but for now, their depictions of Jesus are as close as we can come to the historical Jesus.

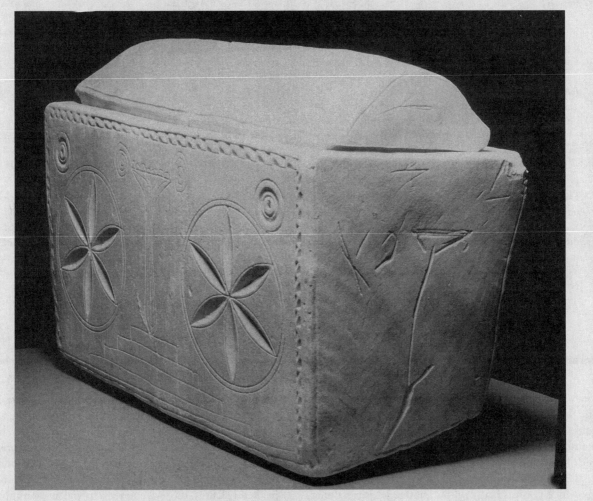

An ossuary (a box where the bones of the dead were gathered) inscribed with the name Caiaphus. An individual named Caiaphus was high priest in Jerusalem at the time of Jesus' trial.

when Jews will be crucified because of their commitment to the law. During this period, the testament continues, a Levite named Taxo will withdraw into a cave, resolving to die so as to trigger God's intervention in history. Early Christians drew on this same pool of ideas to make sense of Jesus' death, interpreting it as a voluntary sacrifice undertaken to save others, and the trigger for the eschatological age.

For the purposes of this brief sketch, we have chosen to accentuate the parallels between the Jesus movement and the Dead Sea Scrolls sect and other eschatologically oriented literature, but we could have easily drawn parallels also with other kinds of Jewish culture. Jesus and another famous teacher from the first century BCE, Hillel, a pharisaic figure important in later rabbinic tradition, share many similarities. Written in Greek and informed by Greco–Roman rhetoric and

A SUPERNATURAL WHO'S WHO FOR EARLY JEWISH CULTURE

Although Jews in the first century were monotheistic, believing in only one God, the world as they conceived it was crowded with other supernatural beings—angels, demons, and other beings connecting the earthly and heavenly realms. Not every Jew necessarily believed in such beings; Acts 23:8 seems to suggest that the Sadducees denied the existence of angels, for example, but most Jews seem to have accepted such beings as a real presence in their lives. Some of these beings functioned as representatives or agents of God and played a benevolent role by offering help and guidance. Others were malicious, and Jews endeavored to ward them off through prayer, singing, the wearing of amulets, and other defensive techniques. Following is a list of some of the supernatural beings appearing in sources from this period; it is not an exhaustive list but enough to suggest the importance and variety of such beings in early Jewish culture.

Angels. The Hebrew word for angel, *mal'akh,* is simply the word for "messenger," which describes the role of angels in much of the Hebrew Bible—they are divine servants sent on various missions. While the Bible was the inspiration for later Jewish belief in angels, the angelology of the Second Temple period is much more elaborate. Angels are mentioned by name—Gabriel, Raphael, Michael, and so on—and angelic life is imagined in more detail, with the angels organized into a ranked hierarchy and given specific roles in heaven or the eschatological age. There is also much more interest in how the angels interact with humans, their role as revealers, guides, teachers, and helpers. Some Jews, including the members of the Dead Sea Scrolls sect, aspired to join the angels or even to become angels.

Demons. The word *demon* is of Greek origin and is only a loose approximation of the kind of malevolent supernatural beings described in Jewish texts from this period, creatures known by various names: "shed," "lilith" (a female demon), "spirits of bastards," and so forth. The history of demons mirrors that of the angels: the Bible was an inspiration, referring to figures such as Satan (although his name derives from the Hebrew for "adversary," the Satan of the Hebrew Bible is not yet the full-blown enemy of God that he becomes in later Jewish and Christian tradition), but the Bible gives little attention to such figures, preferring to emphasize God's complete control over the world, including death and destruction. In Second Temple literature, demons play a much more prominent role. In some texts, they too have a hierarchy, with demonic leaders named Belial, Mastema, or Satan, and they are more directly involved in human life, possessing or colonizing human beings, causing illness, insanity, and death, and also joining in the final eschatological war against God and his forces. The Dead Sea Scrolls illustrate how Jews protected themselves from the demons by preserving spells and songs used to defend against or frighten off the demons.

Stoic philosophy, the letters of Paul share much in common with the writings of Philo of Alexandria, composed a few decades earlier. The more one learns about Jewish culture in the first century CE, the more one can appreciate the extent to which Jesus and his earliest followers were part of this culture.

This insight provokes a question: given its Jewish origins, why isn't Christianity simply another Jewish sect today? How did the Jesus movement evolve into its own religion? Recent scholars stress that the "parting of ways" between Judaism and Christianity was not a simple or immediate development, but the fact is that Christianity today is not a variant of Jewish culture, and the reasons for that go back to the very beginning of Christianity—if not to Jesus, certainly to Paul, his earliest extant interpreter.

Paul was a Jew who identified with the Pharisees before his conversion to Christianity, but the experience he had of Jesus took him, and Christianity, in a very different direction from that being followed by other Jewish followers of Jesus. In a series of letters written between 50 and 60 CE (only some of the Pauline letters in the New Testament are authentic; the others attributed to him were authored by others), Paul helped to organize the Christian communities taking shape in Asia Minor, Greece and Rome. Through those letters, he introduced his understanding of what it meant to be a Christian. In his view, Jesus' death and resurrection had introduced a radical change in the relationship between God and humanity. Before Christ, the Jews enjoyed a special relationship with God by virtue of their participation in the covenant established at Mount Sinai, which through its laws established a way for Jews to overcome sin and achieve salvation not available to non-Jews, but the Sinai covenant was a temporary measure, Paul reveals; God had never given up on the rest of humanity, however sinful it may have been, and had sent Jesus to extend the possibility of salvation beyond the Jews to the rest of the peoples. Now that Christ had been resurrected, Paul claimed, the law, like a teacher whose job was done, was again no longer necessary, for one could overcome sin and achieve salvation by trusting what God had done through Jesus. Along with this change came another one, no less radical: after Jesus' resurrection, it was possible for non-Jews to

Messiah(s). The word *messiah* reflects a Greek form of the Hebrew word for "anointed one" and is used in the Hebrew Bible to refer to people especially commissioned by God— kings and priests. In the wake of Jesus' identification as the Messiah, the term is commonly understood to refer to a figure with divine characteristics sent by God to initiate the eschatological age. It did not necessarily have that connotation in the Second Temple period, but it is then that it develops resonance as a title for a future savior, a king who will defeat Israel's enemies and initiate an age of justice and righteousness, or a high priest in a savior role. (The Jesus of the New Testament combines both traditions. Compare Matthew 21:1–11 and Hebrews 6:19–7:3.) Some of the messianic figures of the first and second century—Bar Kochba is the most famous example—had practical political goals such as ending Roman rule, but such figures were probably not merely political leaders but also divine intermediaries, thought by their followers to have been predicted by Scripture, expected to restore the relationship between Israel and God, and perhaps ascribed supernatural power (as Bar Kochba is in later rabbinic memory). In some texts, the messianic savior is wholly supernatural and otherworldly, a heavenly being known as the "Son of Man" (a term linked to Jesus in such texts as Mark 14:61–62).

Sibyls. Originating in Greek and Roman legend, the sibyls were female prophets—old women who lived for hundreds or thousands of years and were endowed with the power to see the future. Perhaps the title originates from a specific prophetess, but by the Hellenistic period, multiple sibyls were associated with different places, and some lists include a Hebrew sibyl. The Romans took a particular interest in the oracles of the sibyls, collecting them and consulting them in times of crisis, and it seems that some Jews did as well. An extant collection of sibylline oracles includes material added by Jews that predicts various events in Jewish history, including Jerusalem's destruction.

The Stars. Early Jews shared with other ancient peoples an intense interest in the stars—not an astronomical interest but an astrological one premised on the belief that the stars had an influence on the course of a person's life (attend a Jewish wedding and you may hear a vestige of this belief in the stars' influence: the expression *mazal tov* means "good constellation," equivalent to wishing someone a lucky star). In some texts, the stars are under the control of the angels, but in others they are living beings in their own right, sometimes benevolent allies, like the angels, but in a few texts they are malevolent threats.

Wisdom. The biblical book of Proverbs personifies Wisdom as a female being, citing her words as she calls out to men, and that image is developed by Second Temple period texts, such as *The Wisdom of Ben Sira,* which describe how Wisdom found a resting place among the people of Israel, becoming manifest in the Torah (*Ben Sira* 24). The personification of Wisdom as a woman might be a figure of speech, but it is possible that Jews took the language literally, conceiving of Wisdom as an actual being and imagining her on the model of pagan goddesses like the Egyption Isis, a maternal figure involved in the creation of the world.

join in this new relationship with God, a "new covenant." Salvation was no longer a matter of being Jewish or adhering to Mosaic law but of faith in Christ.

Christianity's acceptance of non-Jews did not of itself mark the rupture between Judaism and Christianity. Though some Jews at this time may have looked askance even at converts, not to mention non-Jews, many Jewish communities in this period had room not just for proselytes but even for "God-fearers"—non-Jews who venerated God and adhered to Jewish law but did not convert to Judaism. Early gentile Christians may well have fallen into this latter category, but Paul's theology did much more than welcome non-Jews into the Jewish relationship with God in this way; it allowed them to bypass Judaism and its laws altogether in their pursuit of a relationship with God. To the extent that Jewish religious life in this period was defined by adherence to the laws of Moses, what Paul was advocating was not a Judaism to which non-Jews were welcome but a new relationship with God in which, as Paul famously put it, "There is no longer Jew or Greek" (Letter to the Galatians 3:28).

Paul's theology left open the possibility of a Christianized Judaism—Jews who identify as Jews and adhere to Jewish law but believe in Christ as well—and indeed Paul never seems to have abandoned his own Jewish identity, depicting his embrace of Christ as a transformation *within* a religious tradition rather than as a conversion from one religion to another. But although there continued to be Jewish Christians for some time (a vague category that encompasses born Jews who converted to Christianity and also Christians who felt they should follow Jewish law), Paul's theology provided a compelling rationale for accepting non-Jews into the movement without requiring them to become Jews. By the time the canonical Gospels were written (between 70 and 100 CE), many Christians regarded themselves as something other than Jewish. By the second century, Christians like the soon-to-be-martyred Ignatius were condemning Judaizing Christians for blurring the line between two communities they considered utterly distinct.

Though Christianity soon detached itself from Jewish culture, it was still rooted in Jewish tradition. It laid claim to the Bible, understanding Christians rather than the Jews as the true successors to the tradition established by Abraham and Moses. In this way, early Christians can be compared to a group briefly introduced in previous chapters, the Samaritans. The Samaritans were not Jews—they did not live in Judea, worship in the Jerusalem Temple, or accept the Jewish biblical canon—but they professed an overlapping identity, venerating the Five Books of Moses (but not other biblical books), tracing their descent to the Israelite tribes of Ephraim and Manasseh, and viewing their temple on Mount Gerizim as the cult ordained by Moses. What fueled the antagonism between the Jews and the Samaritans was not just their differences but their similar self-image as descendants of biblical Israel. The Jews faced a similar rival in the Christians, a people with its own way of worshipping God, its own understanding of the Bible (and eventually its own canon), and its own claim to the status of God's people.

It is in the context of this rivalry that one must understand the emergence of a virulent anti-Judaism in early Christian culture, a hostility already evident within the Gospels and coming into sharp relief by the second century. Christians inherited some of the suspicions and prejudices of earlier pagan Judeophobia, which focused on Jewish religious practices as evidence of Jewish malice and barbarism, but Christian antisemitism was not a simple continuation of earlier pagan ideas. Christians did not belittle Jews for rejecting cult statues or worshipping an alien God—Christians behaved similarly, after all. What emerged in place of these motifs was a theological and moral critique of the Jews perhaps best conveyed in the voice of someone who promulgated it— say, the fourth-century theologian Gregory of Nyssa (while perhaps spuriously assigned to Gregory, the passage nonetheless reflects Christian attitudes at that time):

> Murderers of the Lord, murderers of the prophets, rebels and full of hatred against God, they commit outrage against the law, resist God's grace, repudiate the faith of their fathers. They are confederates of the devil, offspring of vipers, scandal-mongers, slanderers, darkened in mind, leaven of the Pharisees, Sanhedrin of demons, utterly vile, quick to abuse, enemies of all that is good. (*In Christi Resurr.* Orat. 5, PG 46, 685)

Concentrated in the preceding passage are some of the main themes of Christian anti-Judaism: (1) the Jews had refused to accept Jesus as the Messiah and son of God, (2) the Jews had murdered God by conspiring to kill Jesus (a view that plays down the fact that Jesus had actually been executed by the Romans), and (3) the Jews were "confederates of the devil," perpetrating various sins under the cloak of piety. In another difference from pagan antisemitism, Christians developed

such views through the interpretation of the Bible, using it to document Jewish sins even as they drew on it to support their own religious claims.

In the first three centuries of the common era, this hostility toward the Jews may have posed no more of a threat than Samaritan hostility did. Despite the legal and economic sanctions that followed the revolts of the first and second centuries, Judaism's legal status remained basically the same: it was recognized by imperial rule as a legitimate religion entitled to protection. Christianity did not enjoy such protection, and in fact suffered through several periods of intense persecution by the Roman government.

However, unlike the Samaritans (who still endure but number only a few hundred today), the Christian community was a rapidly growing and increasingly influential one, and the more influence it gained, the more its anti-Jewish tendencies posed a threat to Jews. Already by the first century, the Christians were making inroads in Syria, Asia Minor, Greece, and even Rome (where Christian missionizing efforts evidently created such a disturbance that the Jews of the city were expelled yet again in the 40s); they had even begun to win African converts. By the second century, Christians were living throughout the empire and beyond—the Christian historian Eusebius places a Christian community as far away as India at this time. It is not clear when Christians became the majority in the empire—they were still facing persecution in the early fourth century—but by this period their influence was such that even the emperor became an adherent. In 312, as he prepared for battle, Emperor **Constantine I** had a vision that inspired him to order his troops to affix a sign of Christ on their equipment. Under his rule and that of almost all his successors, the church had a defender in imperial rule.

Even after its Christianization, the Roman Empire (or empires, after it formally split in 395 into the Western and Eastern, or Western and Byzantine, Roman Empires) never declared Judaism illegal, continuing legal protections for the communities within its domain. But Jewish culture was now vulnerable in its conflict with Christianity in a way that it had not been before. Christian mobs, sometimes instigated by the local Church authorities, attacked synagogues as they did pagan temples, turning some of them into churches. They drove Jews from the communities in which they lived, as happened in Alexandria in 414. Although such violence was not necessarily endorsed by the Roman authorities— indeed, they sometimes intervened to protect the Jews—even the emperor could not always save the Jews. After the burning of a synagogue in the Mesopotamian town of Callinicum in 388 CE, the emperor Theodosius initially tried to intervene to have it rebuilt but then gave up the attempt under pressure from St. Ambrose. The Church did not seek to exterminate the Jews—they were preserved as the Old Testament was preserved—but those Jews living under Christianized Roman rule were now a marginalized minority in a society premised on their purported theological failings.

By this time, Christians are clearly outsiders to Jewish culture, a people who defined themselves, and were seen by many Jews as well, as something other than Jewish. But that is an identity that only crystallized after the first century. For the first few decades of Christian history—in the days of Jesus and his immediate disciples, perhaps still in the time of Paul—the early Christian community was still a part of Jewish culture, one of several competing constructions of Jewish law and tradition. Its belief that Jesus was the Messiah distinguished it from other Jewish sects and movements, but this difference should not obscure the fundamental similarities that linked Jesus and his earliest followers to the Jewish culture of their time: the shared eschatological beliefs, interpretive techniques, patterns of social behavior, and so forth. For as long back as we can trace it, Jewish history has always moved along multiple trajectories, different communities developing in different directions. The earliest Christian movement constitutes one of those trajectories, and in fact many of the very traits that would eventually distinguish Christianity from Jewish culture—its eschatology, its use of such concepts as covenant and sin, the way it read the Bible—are themselves evidence of how rooted it was in the Jewish culture of its day.

Surviving the Temple's Destruction

Although different from ancient Israelite culture in many other respects, first-century Jewish culture continued one important institution established in biblical times: the Jerusalem cult—in fact, one could argue that the Temple had become even more important in this later period than its predecessor was in biblical times. The Bible acknowledges, and archaeology confirms, that pre-exilic Israelites worshipped in a number of locales, including the sanctuaries of Dan and Bethel in the northern kingdom and also other temples and cult sites throughout the land. By the first century, the Jerusalem Temple had few competitors: "We have but one temple for the one God," Josephus claims, "common to all as God is common to all" (*Against Apion* 193). A few exceptions require qualification of this claim—most notably, the Jewish temple built at Leontopolis in Egypt—but the vast majority of Jews, both those in Judea and those abroad, seem to have regarded the Jerusalem Temple as the only legitimate Jewish temple, as reflected in the throngs of pilgrims who flocked to Jerusalem from around the world to celebrate the three major festivals of the year: Passover, Shavuot, and Sukkot.

As the Jerusalem Temple grew more central and important, so too did its priesthood. In the Second Temple period, in the absence of the Davidic dynasty, the priesthood, or at least the priestly families at the upper echelons of the priestly class, emerged as Judea's preeminent social elite—not just as a religious caste but also as a ruling class. Herod and the Romans took great care to control the office of the high priesthood, intervening in appointments and assuming control over the priestly vestments that the high priest needed to perform his duties. The Roman cooptation of the high priesthood undercut its moral standing to some extent, but even so, the priesthood in general retained its authority and status. Josephus cites his priestly pedigree as proof of his noble origins, and the titles *priest* and *priestess* (the latter a title bestowed on the wives and daughters of priests) would continue to function as signs of high status centuries after the Temple's destruction.

The increased centrality of the Temple can be attributed to a number of factors. Since the Persian period, the Temple had figured prominently in the relationship between Jews and their rulers as the focal point of their interaction. To express its benevolence, a foreign ruler would offer to support the Temple in some way, and in turn Jews used the Temple cult to express their gratitude, offering sacrifices on the ruler's behalf. The Temple was also crucial for linking Diaspora Jews to fellow Jews in Judea—and to one another. Philo describes the three major pilgrimage festivals—Passover, Shavuot, and Sukkot—as times when Jews transcended the geographical differences that divided them, feeling themselves part of a larger, like-minded collective:

> Countless multitudes from countless cities come, some over land, others over sea, from east and west and north and south at every feast. . . . Friendships are formed between those who hitherto knew not each other, and the sacrifices and libations are the occasion of reciprocity of feeling and constitute the surest pledge that all are of one mind. (Philo, *Special Laws* 1.69–70)

As this description suggests, the Temple was an important source of Jewish unity, bringing Jews together from all over the world into a shared experience of goodwill and common purpose (in theory at least; in reality the festivals were often marred by violence, much of it targeted against the Romans, but some aimed at fellow Jews). Jews unable to visit the Temple themselves could still express their support for it by sending their payment of an annual half-shekel Temple tax, used to support the daily sacrifice. Jewish culture was dispersed throughout the entire Roman Empire and beyond, divided by geographical, political, linguistic, and economic differences, and it is not an exaggeration to say that among the key links that held it all together, sustaining the sense of shared religious identity, were the symbols and rituals of the Temple cult.

Beyond the political and social roles that it played, the Temple's most fundamental role was religious, as the point of connection between the Jews and God. Following the laws of Moses, Jews understood the rituals of animal sacrifice and the offering of first fruits and other agricultural produce as obligations, a prerequisite for sustaining their covenant with God. Atoning for sin—both individual and collective atonement—was essential to sustaining this relationship as well, and that too required sacrifice, by individual sinners seeking forgiveness and by the high priest on behalf of the whole people on the Day of Atonement. The existence of the Temple allowed God to reside among the Jews, and its cult was essential for sustaining a relationship with him.

All this can help us to understand why the destruction of the Second Temple in 70 CE was such a devastating event: simply put, it ripped out the wiring that connected the Jews with Rome, the Jews of the Diaspora with the Jews of Judea, and the Jews with God. In *2 Baruch,* an apocalypse from this period, life continuing without the Temple can scarcely be imagined:

> Blessed is he who was not born, or he who was born and died. But we, the living, woe to us, because we have seen those afflictions of Zion and that which has befallen Jerusalem. . . . You farmers, sow not again. And you, o earth, why do you give the fruit of your harvest? Keep within you the sweetness of your sustenance. And you, vine, why do you still give your wine? For an offering will not be given again from you in Zion, and the first fruits will not again be offered. And you, bridegrooms, do not enter and do not let the brides adorn themselves. And you, wives, do not pray to bear children, for the barren will rejoice more. And those who have no children will be glad, and those who have children will be sad. For why do they bear in pains only to bury in grief? (*2 Baruch* 10:6–15)

This was not the first time that Jews had faced such a crisis—the Temple had been destroyed before in 586 BCE— and Jews such as the author of *2 Baruch* looked to that event to understand how to survive. But that precedent proved to be of limited relevance, for in contrast to what happened after the destruction of the First Temple, the Second Temple was never restored—all attempts at rebuilding came to naught. Jews found ways to sustain their religious life in the absence of the Temple, however, holding onto the hope that the Temple would be restored someday (a hope still nurtured among some Jews) even as they developed other non-Temple-dependent ways of interacting with God.

To understand how Jewish culture was able to adjust to life without the Temple, we need to take note of how Jewish culture in the year 70 CE differed from that of Judea 500 years earlier, after the First Temple had been destroyed. Three differences are of particular significance:

1. By the first century, some Jews who were alienated from Jerusalem or the Temple had begun to experiment with alternatives to sacrifice, developing practices that could serve in its place. The Dead Sea Scrolls sect seems to have been one such community. Disenchanted with the Temple and its priesthood, it came to view its own community as a virtual temple and its behavior as the equivalent to sacrifice, at least potentially:

> When . . . these men become a foundation of the Holy Spirit in eternal truth, they shall atone for iniquitous guilt and for sinful unfaithfulness, so that [God's] favor for the land (is obtained) without the flesh of burnt offerings and without the fat of sacrifices. The proper offerings of the lips of judgment [is as] righteous sweetness, and the perfect of the Way [are as] a pleasing freewill offering" (*Community Rule* 9.3–5).

Their ability to imagine alternatives to sacrificial worship by the end of the Second Temple period made it easier for Jews to reconceptualize the act of worship after the Temple's destruction in 70 CE, allowing them to transfer the form and function of the Temple to other practices, such as prayer and study, that did not depend on the act of sacrifice and were not tied to a single location, such as Jerusalem.

2. The Jewish community was much larger and more widely dispersed than it was in early post-exilic Judea. While Jews could express their allegiance to the Temple from afar, by this period they had developed other, more localized forms of religious life as well. The best known example is the synagogue. By the first century, synagogues could be found playing a central role at the local level as a communal meeting place, prayer house, and educational institution where the Torah was read and explained on the Sabbath throughout Palestine and the Diaspora (The Acts of the Apostles in the New Testament refers to synagogues in Damascus, Cyprus, Antioch, and Athens, among many other places). It is anachronistic to view the synagogue at this time as a surrogate for the Temple (though in later antiquity Jews would stress their near equivalence by transferring attributes of the Temple's design to the synagogue). In the Temple's absence, however, the synagogue gave Jews others way to stay linked to the Jewish community, worship God, and express their commitment to Jewish law.

3. In contrast to what happened after the destruction of the First Temple, the priesthood did not survive the destruction of the Second Temple, at least not in the position of political and cultural preeminence that it had enjoyed until then. Many priests had died during the revolt, and the high priesthood institution that Josephus traced back to Aaron came to an end in 70 CE. By this time, other kinds of leaders had emerged to fill the leadership vacuum: wonder workers, visionaries, and sages held authority that derived not from their priestly lineage but from their supernatural, intellectual, or interpretive abilities, and they helped to shape the religious response to the Temple's loss. Some of these figures, the anonymous author of *2 Baruch,* for example, envisioned the restoration of the Temple, but others used their religious authority to mitigate the effects of losing the Temple by relocating or substituting for its cultic practices.

Judahite culture had survived the destruction of the First Temple, but at the first opportunity its leadership sought to rebuild it; after the Second Temple's destruction, Jews also wanted to rebuild the Temple, but circumstances prevented them from doing so. Jewish culture survived this change because it had learned to live without the Temple, and that adaptation was rooted in changes that took place even before its destruction.

What occurred in the years immediately following the Second Temple's destruction is largely unknown. The early Christian community quickly learned to live without the Temple, developing alternative ways to worship God, but that was a trajectory that soon led the Christian movement beyond the bounds of Jewish law. The situation for those still committed to Jewish law is less clear because so few texts have survived from the century or two after the Temple's destruction. Josephus simply does not address the question of how Jewish life will continue without the Temple. Apocalyptic texts from this time assume it will be restored one day but do not offer much guidance for what to do in the meantime beyond encouraging their audiences to wait expectantly. Jewish culture did eventually learn to live without the Temple—we know that from Jewish culture as it exists today. Unfortunately, the earliest phase of this transition, the period between 70 and 200 CE, is frustratingly underdocumented.

To complete the story of how Jewish culture evolved beyond the Temple, we need to move beyond 200 CE to Jewish texts produced in Palestine and Babylonia between this date and the seventh century CE. Known collectively as *rabbinic literature,* these texts and the rabbis who produced them are our subject in Chapter 5. They will help us to understand how Jewish culture survived the Temple's demise and, beyond that, the trajectory of Jewish culture after antiquity, how the culture we have been describing in the last few chapters became the Jewish culture that takes shape in the Middle Ages.

Questions for Reflection

1. Why is Josephus an indispensable source for Jewish history? What makes him a questionable source at the same time? What other sources do we have for Jewish culture in the first century CE?

2. Why did so many Jews rebel against Rome in the first and second centuries CE? What impact did these revolts have on the subsequent development of Jewish culture?

3. What was "Jewish" about early Christianity? How and when did it become a distinct religion?

4. What motivated Christian anti-Judaism in antiquity, and how did it differ from earlier pagan anti-Jewish hostility?

5. Why was Jewish culture able to survive the destruction of the Second Temple?

For Further Reading

The Roman period, and especially the first century, has been the focus of extensive scholarship, in part because of its role as background for early Christianity, and in part because of sensational archaeological discoveries, such as those at the Temple Mount and Masada. For more about Jewish history and culture in this period, see Emil Schurer, *The History of the Jewish People in the Age of Jesus Christ,* as updated by Geza Vermes and Fergus Millar (Edinburgh: T & T Clark, 1973); S. Safrai and M. Stern's two-volume *The Jewish People in the First Century* (Assen: Van Gorcum & Co., 1974, 1976); or William Horbury, W. D. Davies, and John Sturdy, *The Cambridge History of Judaism: Volume Three, The Early Roman Period* (Cambridge, England: Cambridge University Press, 1999). Translations used here of both Philo and Josephus can be found in the Loeb Classical Library of Harvard University Press. Translations of Dead Sea Scrolls material is taken from Elisha Qimron and James Charlesworth, in *The Dead Sea Scrolls: Hebrew, Aramaic and Greek Texts with English Translations, Volume 1, Rule of the Community and Related Documents* (Tubingen: J.C.B. Mohr [Paul Siebeck]/Louisville, KY: Westminster John Knox Press, 1994).

Chapter 5

Rabbinic Revelations

In the centuries that followed the destruction of the Second Temple, a community of scholars now known by the title of *rabbi* became central to Jewish culture—so central that Judaism as it exists today is to a large extent Judaism as reshaped by these scholars. Who were these rabbis, and how did they come to exert such an influence on Jewish life? It might have been easier to answer these questions if the rabbis themselves had left us a historical account like the ones that biblical authors produced for ancient Israel or that Josephus wrote for the Second Temple period, but they did not. In lieu of such a narrative, however, one text can serve as a starting point for rabbinic history—it will not help us to pin down the actual origins or development of rabbinic Judaism, but it does tell us something of how the rabbis placed themselves in history.

The work in question, *Pirkei Avot,* or the "Chapters of the Fathers," is included in a larger document known as the Mishnah that we will examine later in this chapter. It is not a history but a kind of anthology that gathers together the maxims and teachings of early rabbinic sages. The name *Avot,* or "Fathers," might refer to the fathers or early authorities in the rabbinic movement or else to the teachings themselves, as the fundamentals of wisdom. Its opening chapter is what is of interest here, as it presents an intellectual genealogy that establishes the credentials of the rabbinic sages by tracing their authority back to the biblical age. Beginning with Moses, *Pirkei Avot* traces the transmission of the Torah from Moses to Joshua, from Joshua to the prophets and elders of the biblical period, and from the prophets and elders to the sage Yohanan ben Zakkai and his students, the scholars who gave shape to what would become rabbinic Judaism after 70 CE. According to this work, in other words, the rabbis were the direct successors to Moses, continuing a tradition that reached all the way back to Sinai.

Pirkei Avot's assertion of continuity is accepted as an accurate depiction of history to this very day among many Jews who embrace the Mishnah as a sacred text. But, in fact, rabbinic Judaism differed from earlier forms of Jewish culture in many ways. Earlier Jews from the Second Temple period, such as the Dead Sea Scrolls sect and Josephus, focused on the priest, a hereditary position whose primary role was not to interpret the Bible or preach to the people but to perform the rituals that allowed Israel to interact with God in the Temple. In rabbinic Judaism, formed in the wake of the Temple's destruction, the priest was eclipsed by the rabbi, whose connection to the biblical past was based on an intellectual rather than familial pedigree and whose religious authority was based not on his role in the rituals of the Temple but on his study and interpretation of Torah.

The focus of this chapter is the rabbinic movement and its transformative impact on Jewish culture in late antiquity. The term **rabbi** was used as a general term of respect in Jewish antiquity, applied to various sages, judges, and teachers, including Jesus and other early Christian teachers. By *rabbi,* we mean not just any teacher, but a sage within a particular social network that took shape after the Second Temple's destruction: the community of sages cited in the Mishnah, the Talmud, and other texts produced by this movement. This group only consisted of a few thousand individuals at most, but we place them at the center of our history because, over time, they completely reshaped Jewish life, transforming how Jews perceived the Torah, how they worshipped God, how their births were celebrated and their deaths mourned. Jewish culture in general is not extensively "rabbinized" until long after the death of these sages, but they were the ones to initiate this transformation, and that is why we make them our focus in this chapter.

Late Antique Jewish Culture Without the Rabbis

Before we introduce the rabbis, it is important to put their movement into a larger context. The idea that the rabbis were the most important religious authorities in late antique Jewish culture (*late antique* describes the period of Near Eastern Mediterranean and European history between roughly 150–750 C.E) is an impression based on rabbinic sources, but recent scholars argue that focusing on the rabbis in this way gives a skewed picture of Jewish life then. Other nonrabbinic sources, such as Jewish inscriptions, pagan and Christian references to the Jews, and the remnants of Jewish tombs and synagogues, give us glimpses of Jewish life beyond the Mishnah and Talmud, and their testimony suggests that rabbinic sources give the rabbis an exaggerated role in Jewish culture of this period, making them more central than they really were.

If we did not have rabbinic sources to consult, what picture would we have of Jewish life in the centuries after the Romans' destruction of the Second Temple? In many respects, and for many communities, it continued as it had before the destruction, but the Jewish Revolt did change things for Jews both in Palestine and abroad, devastating Jewish life in Judea and removing some of the national institutions that had unified a widely scattered Jewish populace. Jews could no longer travel to Jerusalem as pilgrims, nor did a Temple exist to which they could send annual contributions. The trauma of losing the Temple is registered in apocalyptic texts written in the decades following the Jewish Revolt, pseudepigraphical texts such as *2 Baruch* and *4 Ezra,* which couch their response to the destruction of the Second Temple as narratives about the destruction of the First Temple, but what seems to animate such texts is a yearning for continuity, for a restoration of what had been lost. In *2 Baruch,* allegedly recording the experiences of Jeremiah's secretary Baruch, the earth swallows the ark and other cultic objects in anticipation of the day when it will be possible to retrieve them and reestablish the Temple. In *4 Ezra,* God comforts a grieving Ezra by revealing to him that the real Jerusalem, a heavenly city unseen by human eyes, persists undisturbed by what had happened to its earthly copy and waiting to become manifest again in the eschatological future. Unable to practice the Temple cult as they had in the past, some Jews took it underground, using imaginative apocalyptic stories to nurture fantasies of a time when God would defeat their enemies and give back what they had taken away.

Long after the Temple's destruction, an opportunity to restore the Temple did in fact emerge. In 362 CE, an emperor named Julian—known in Christian sources as "the Apostate" because of his hostility to Christianity—undertook to rebuild the Temple as part of his effort to reverse the Christianization of the Roman Empire. It is hard to know what Jews themselves thought about Julian's plans, but some evidence of Jewish support has been identified. An inscription discovered on the "Wailing" Wall in Jerusalem uses a verse from Isaiah 66 to express the sense of rejuvenation some Jews may have felt at the time: "When you see it [i.e., the Temple], your heart will rejoice and your bones will sprout like green grass." Julian died before he finished the project, however, so we will never know how the Temple's restoration might have impacted the course of Jewish history.

What we do know is that despite continuities with the Second Temple period, Jewish culture as it took shape in late antiquity differed from earlier forms of Jewish culture in many ways. By the fourth century, for example, Jewish communities had developed other, more localized settings for religious practice, "institutions that allowed Jews to sustain their religious traditions without a temple." By the first century, synagogues (or structures given other names but serving analogous functions) were established throughout the eastern Mediterranean—surely in Palestine but also in Egypt, Asia Minor, Greece, and Italy. The large number of synagogues in late antiquity (we know of at least eleven in the city of Rome alone, and some scholars suspect the number was higher), their wide distribution around the Mediterranean and Near East, the amount of resources invested in their construction and decoration, and their frequent mention in inscriptions and texts all indicate they were at the very center of Jewish communal life.

The synagogue is often described as a kind of substitute Temple, arising to fill the vacuum created by the Second Temple's destruction. The term *holy ark* or *aron hakodesh,* a sacred object kept in Solomon's Temple, is used to this day to describe the central feature of the synagogue: the chest where the Torah scrolls are kept. The understanding of the synagogue as a substitute Temple may not have arisen until relatively late, however, and in fact, the role that synagogues played (and play) in Jewish worship was very different from that of the Temple. They were not places to make animal sacrifices as the Temple was but centers for study and prayer, and the synagogue's status as a "holy place" derived not from its association with the Temple but from the fact that the Torah, now conceived as a source of holiness in its own right, was stored within it. Synagogues were the setting for many public activities—the administration of justice, communal meals, business transactions, and the manumission of slaves—but their most fundamental role was to connect Jews to the Torah.

In addition to religious changes, we also know of changes in Jewish political life. During the Second Temple period, several forms of national leadership existed that helped to bind the Jewish people to one another and to the Roman Empire, the high priesthood and the Herodian dynasty among them. Both disappeared by the end of the first century, and by the fourth century a new kind of national leader had emerged in their place—the **patriarch,** a kind of

Relief of the Ark of the Covenant on wheels from an ancient synagogue in Caperneum.

ethnic leader without the army and administration accorded to King Herod but as close as Jews had to a national representative to the Roman Empire. Most of what we know about the patriarch comes from rabbinic literature, which portrays him as a rabbi, but the existence of this office is corroborated by Roman legal sources as well.

We do not know of Jewish revolts in this period on the scale of the Jewish Revolt and the Bar Kochba Revolt, but tensions persisted in the relationship between Jews and the Roman Empire, and these were further exacerbated by the empire's Christianization in the fourth century CE. Christians had faced persecution under the Roman Empire, including under the reign of the emperor Diocletian (284–305 CE) when churches were dismantled and Christians executed. Christianity's influence continued to grow throughout this period, however, and a major turning point came during the rule of Constantine the Great (324–337 CE), when Christian pilgrimage to Jerusalem increased and Christian churches and communities were established throughout Palestine. With the exception of the emperor Julian, who tried in vain to revive paganism, Christianity would henceforth have imperial backing in its struggle with Judaism.

The Christianized Roman Empire never sought to abolish Judaism, continuing to recognize it as a legally sanctioned religion. Important in the shaping of this policy of tolerance was the writing of Augustine of Hippo, the great theologian who lived between 354–430. Augustine had sharp religious differences with Judaism, believed the Jews had misunderstood the Bible, and interpreted their suffering and dispersion as divine punishment for their rejection of Christ, but he does not advocate the violent opposition to the Jews characteristic of other Christian thinkers of the day, arguing that they should be permitted to exist, albeit in a miserable state, as living testimony to the veracity of Christian belief. The influence of Augustine's view of the Jews was a major reason they were able to survive under Christian rule through antiquity and the Middle Ages.

Despite this begrudging tolerance, however, proponents of the Church and Christianized Roman rule did act on their hostility to the Jews. Anti-Jewish legislation had the effect of hemming the Jews in, seeking to prevent them from having influence outside the bounds of their community, and occasionally even interfering in internal Jewish matters. By the fourth and fifth centuries, imperial laws prohibited intermarriage among Jews and Christians, Jewish ownership of Christian slaves, and other practices that brought Jews and Christians into close association. As discussed in Chapter 4, Christianity developed a theologically motivated tradition of anti-Judaism, which had grown quite acute in the fourth century. Augustine's relative permissiveness notwithstanding, other Christian leaders could be savage in their denunciation of Jews (and of Christians who adopted Jewish practices), and the attacks were not always merely rhetorical, for Christian mobs sometimes attacked synagogues and Jews in directly violent ways.

Legal segregation and intercommunal violence helped to sharpen the differences between Christianity and Judaism, but that does not mean that Jewish culture developed in isolation from its environment. On the contrary, the boundary between Jewish and non-Jewish culture in late antiquity was not always so clear. An intriguing example is Judaism's relationship with what is known as **Gnosticism,** a movement or movements named for the Greek word for knowledge that focused on the pursuit of a special religious knowledge. Gnostic texts often engage the Hebrew Bible, reflecting interpretive traditions also known from later Jewish mystical literature, and on the basis of such evidence, an earlier generation of scholars argued that Gnosticism actually originated as a form of Judaism. That theory has run into problems: one does not need to be Jewish to take an interest in Adam and Noah, and Gnostic texts can sometimes seem anti-Jewish, as when they demote Yahweh to the position of a second-rate deity animated by envy of a still higher god. Still, it remains possible that Gnosticism developed on the fringes of Jewish culture or through some kind of interaction with it. However we define the relationship between Gnosticism and Judaism, the fact that Gnostic texts (and for that matter the literatures of other late antique religions, such as early Islam) share certain traditions with Judaism cautions us to be careful about imposing artificial and inflexible boundaries between religious communities in this period.

All this relates to Jews living under the jurisdiction of a Christianized Roman Empire. What of Jews living beyond the empire, in places that were dominated by other rulers and other religious traditions, such as Babylonia? In a sense, the Jews of Babylonia were in the same basic situation as Jews living under Rome—they too faced the challenge of sustaining their cultural traditions under foreign rule—but the political and cultural environment in Babylonia was different in important ways. For many centuries, the Jews of Babylonia lived under the same rulers that governed Judea—the Babylonians, the Persians, the Seleucids—but that changed in the first century BCE when they came under the rule of the **Parthian kingdom** based in Iran. When that kingdom fell in the third century CE, the **Sassanian kingdom,** another multiethnic empire based in Persia, took control. In contrast to the Romans, the Parthians and the Sassanians were loosely organized, allowing ethnic/religious minorities, including the Jews, a fair amount of control over their internal organization and communal affairs.

Another difference between Rome and Babylonia was Hellenization. Jews beyond the Euphrates were not beyond the orbit of Hellenization, but their culture also reflects the influence of the indigenous Babylonian or Persian culture. Consider Jewish magical practice as but one measure of this difference. Despite a biblical prohibition of magic, Jews employed for what lack of a better term we can describe as "magic" to protect themselves in a dangerous and unruly world, consulting the stars, expelling demons, and using incantations and amulets to summon supernatural help. We have evidence of late antique magical practice from both Palestine and Babylonia, and it speaks to some of the cultural

A bowl with an Aramaic magical inscription used to protect individuals from evil spirits, including the female demons known as *liliths*.

differences that developed between Jews in these regions. A compilation of Jewish magical recipes known as *Sefer Ha-Razim* ("The Book of Secrets"), composed in Palestine in the fourth or fifth century, is written in Hebrew but contains an invocation of the Greek sun god Helios in a Greek-transcribed-into-Hebrew script. Jews in Babylonia practiced magic too, but much of what we know of their practice, coming from hundreds of Jewish magic bowls discovered in Mesopotamia and Iran, reflects the influence of Babylonian/ Persian culture. The purpose of the bowls was to imprison or repel evil spirits, and the names of some of the demons and angels they invoke are of Mesopotamian or Persian origin, including a class of demon known as *lilith*, a being with deep roots in Mesopotamian folklore. (In later rabbinic legend, the demon Lilith was identified as Adam's first wife

before God created Eve. She was said to have flown away from Adam after a fight and since then has been a danger to newborns.)

How do the rabbis fit into the picture of Jewish life that we have briefly sketched? Not very clearly. Rabbinic literature does reflect many of the cultural characteristics we have described—the rise of the synagogue and the patriarch, the difference between Palestinian and Babylonian Jewish culture—but what is less clear is the impact that rabbis had on the larger community. Nonrabbinic sources do occasionally mention figures identified as rabbis—Jesus is addressed by this title—but scarcely any trace of the celebrated rabbis of the Mishnah and Talmud can be identified outside rabbinic literature. At a large cemetery found next to the town of Beth Shearim in the Galilee, a site where some thirty catacombs were discovered dating from the second to the fourth centuries, the tombs of several rabbis were found, including some known from rabbinic literature (including three successors of the great sage Judah the Patriarch, editor of the Mishnah). But even here the rabbis do not seem to have any special influence or status. If Beth Shearim is any indication, the rabbis were part of Jewish society but not in charge of it.

This only deepens the mystery of rabbinic history. The fact is that the rabbis did eventually redefine what it meant to be Jewish in many communities, giving rise to what would become medieval Jewish culture and continuing to exert a shaping influence on Jewish life until this very day. How did it happen that a small group of sages who in their own day had little discernible impact beyond their own study circles came to transform Jewish culture? The historian's answer to this question spills over into the medieval period, the subject of later chapters, but it begins earlier, in the period between 70 and 650 CE, and it is that part of the story we tell in the rest of this chapter.

Putting the Rabbis into the Picture

Rabbinic literature is vast in its size and scope—the Talmud is described as a "sea" for good reason—and it yields all kinds of information about Jewish life in late antiquity, but it is a very tricky historical source. Rabbinic texts like the Babylonian Talmud, weaving back and forth between Hebrew and Aramaic, are highly technical and opaque, and their argumentation follows a logic only the initiated understand. The stories preserved in this literature can reflect real historical experience, but they appear in texts from a later period; what they say often tells us more about the authors of rabbinic texts and their views than about the people and events that the stories describe.

A much-discussed illustration of the problems involved in reconstructing rabbinic history is a famous story told of one of the founding figures of rabbinic Judaism, the sage **Yohanan ben Zakkai.** Yohanan lived in Jerusalem in the time of the Jewish Revolt, but he was also known for his activities at a place called **Yavneh,** a coastal town, and this story explains how he got from one place to the other. Yohanan had been trapped in Jerusalem by the rebels, who were watching to make sure no Jews defected to the Romans, but he managed to escape by hiding in a coffin that his disciples carried outside the city. Making his way to the Roman general Vespasian, Yohanan predicted that the general would become king, a prophecy that was immediately confirmed by a messenger coming from Rome to announce that Vespasian would now be emperor. A grateful Vespasian allowed Yohanan to make one request, and in one version of

the story, Yohanan asks permission to move to Yavneh with his disciples, thus establishing Yavneh as the first center of rabbinic learning after the Second Temple's destruction.

Is this how the rabbinic movement actually started? While we cannot rule that possibility out, the story as we have it dates from long after the time of Yohanan, and it has been preserved in multiple forms that differ from one another in a number of details. Might the story preserve the memory of real events transmitted orally from Yohanan's disciples to their successors until the time it was written down? Possibly, but many of the story's details seem more legendary than historical. Yohanan's prophecy of Vespasian's kingship, for example, bears a suspicious similarity to a story that Josephus tells about himself in his account of the Jewish Revolt and is probably based on some variant of that story circulated in Palestine after 70. Josephus and other classical authors also told stories of people able to escape a dangerous situation by hiding in a coffin. We know from the existence of multiple versions of the Yohanan story that it was greatly revised over the course of rabbinic literary history, and it is impossible to tell which details were part of the story in its original form or even whether any reflect what really happened.

The story of Yohanan's escape illustrates the challenge of reconstructing rabbinic history: it is hard to know when the sources are describing what really happened and what was invented later. Though scholars have not always been able to overcome this challenge, they have not stopped trying, extracting from rabbinic texts many clues about who the rabbis were and how they came to exert an influence over the larger Jewish community. The following survey, informed by recent scholarship, focuses on three key moments: the emergence of the rabbinic movement after the Second Temple's destruction, the establishment of rabbinic authority in the larger Jewish community, and, finally, the development of (the Babylonian version of) rabbinic Judaism into a worldwide Jewish culture.

The Emergence of Rabbinic Culture

The first stage of rabbinic history, spanning the end of the Second Temple period to 200 CE, is an entirely hypothetical one since we have no rabbinic literature from this period, only traditions found in post-200 rabbinic sources that are questionable as to their historical accuracy. Nevertheless, by putting this testimony together with what we know of Jewish culture at the end of the Second Temple period, it is possible to offer some educated guesses about where the rabbinic movement came from and how its development was shaped by the Jewish Revolt and other events in the first and second centuries CE.

According to *Pirkei Avot,* the rabbis' pedigree goes back to sages living in the period of the Second Temple, figures such as **Hillel** and **Shammai,** who probably lived in the first century BCE. Hillel is an especially important sage in rabbinic memory. The earliest list of rabbinic rules for interpreting the Torah is associated with him, as are many wise sayings, including the famous "If I am not for myself, who will be for me, but if I am for myself alone, what am I?" Both he and Shammai, the latter remembered as the more stringent of the two, founded schools—probably more like the circle of disciples that gathered around Jesus than the institutionalized rabbinic academies of a later era—who transmitted their teachings to later generations. The debates between Hillel and Shammai and their respective schools, covering legal issues ranging from how to recite certain blessings to what it took for a non-Jew to convert to Judaism, loom large in how rabbinic literature recalls the period before the Second Temple's destruction.

Did Hillel and Shammai—and the other sages listed in *Pirkei Avot* for that matter—really do and say the things attributed to them by rabbinic literature? It is impossible to say. A sage named Gamaliel the Elder (the Greek form of the Hebrew name Gamliel), described in rabbinic sources as the grandson of Hillel, appears in the New Testament as a contemporary of Paul, but Hillel and Shammai themselves are never mentioned in Second Temple period literature, at least not by those names. Attempts have been made to link them with two important sages known by other names—a Pharisee named Pollion and his disciple Samais, mentioned by Josephus in his account of Herod's reign—but that is just an educated guess. The images of Hillel and Shammai in later rabbinic texts evolved as rabbinic Judaism evolved, mirroring later understandings of what it meant to be a sage, and it is impossible to reach beyond how they were imagined in later rabbinic sources back to the historical Hillel and Shammai.

While we cannot say much about these particular personages, we do have evidence that this kind of figure was indeed very influential at the end of the Second Temple period. The image of Hillel, Yohanan ben Zakkai, and other Second Temple period sages presented in rabbinic literature overlap to some extent with what we know of the Pharisees from Josephus and the New Testament. One of the distinguishing traits of the Pharisees is their respect for an oral tradition of legal and religious practice transmitted alongside the Hebrew Bible, a tradition that seems to anticipate the central role of oral tradition, or the Oral Torah, in later rabbinic culture. The distinctive beliefs attached to the Pharisees also have parallels in rabbinic sources. According to Josephus, for example, the Pharisees held a view between predestination and free will, believing that human destiny is determined by fate while not depriving humans of the pursuit of what is in their power. Compare this with a teaching attributed to the

famous **Rabbi Akiba** in *Pirkei Avot* 3:19: "Everything is foreseen, yet freedom of choice is granted."

The theory that rabbinic Judaism is an offshoot of Pharisaic Judaism helps us to understand where the rabbis came from, but it should not lead us into simply equating the rabbis with the Pharisees. Although the rabbis exhibited lines of continuity with Pharisaic Judaism, they never actually identified themselves as the Pharisees, or as any other Second Temple period sect. In fact, it has been argued that the rabbis were opposed to sectarianism in general, reshaping Jewish tradition in ways designed to overcome the factionalism that divided Judean society in the Second Temple period.

Whatever its origins, rabbinic Judaism was greatly affected by the destruction of the Second Temple, developing new forms of religious practice that were not centered in the Temple. Rabbinic literature attributes this transformation to Rabbi Yohanan ben Zakkai:

> As Rabban Yohanan ben Zakkai was coming from Jerusalem, Rabbi Joshua (Yohanan's leading student) followed him and beheld the Temple in ruins. "Woe unto us," Rabbi Joshua cried, "that this, the place where Israel atoned for its sins is laid waste." "My son," Yohanan said to him, "Be not grieved; we have another atonement as effective as this. And what is it? It is acts of loving kindness, as it is said [in Scripture], 'For I desire mercy and not sacrifice'" (Hosea 6:6).—*Avot de Rabbi Nathan* 4.18

According to this story, Yohanan recognized a way for Israel to sustain its relationship with God without the Temple, substituting ethical action—*gmilut hasidim*—for the act of sacrifice. Like other rabbinic stories told of Yohanan, this one is probably better classified as legend than history, but the real Yohanan may indeed have worked to revise Jewish tradition in light of the Temple's destruction, albeit in very specific and limited ways. After relocating to Yavneh, he seems to have issued various ordinances (*takkenot*) that modified Temple-centered religious practices in light of Jerusalem's destruction. Before 70 CE, for example, when the shofar was blown on Rosh Hashanah (the Jewish New Year), it was permitted to do so only in the Temple. Yohanan decreed that after the Temple's destruction it could be blown anywhere. The effect of this and Yohanan's other ordinances was to allow the Jews to sustain their religious traditions in the absence of the Temple—this, a major departure from earlier Jewish culture as it had existed in Second Temple times.

Unfortunately, beyond the questionable anecdotes preserved in much later rabbinic sources, we possess no evidence for Yohanan and other rabbinic figures who lived in the period just after the Jewish Revolt and the ensuing decades, making it

WHAT BECAME OF THE PRIESTS AFTER THE TEMPLE'S DESTRUCTION?

The Second Temple period was a time when the priesthood flourished. The high priest was, in effect, the ruler of Judean society, and the upper echelons of the priesthood were at the center of Judea's elite class, enjoying considerable wealth, status, and cultural influence. With the destruction of the Second Temple, the priesthood lost the chief rationale for its existence: the role it played in offering sacrifices and guarding the Temple's sanctity. Still, the priesthood did not disappear or lose its prestige, and it may even have made a partial comeback in late antique Palestine as an influential cultural elite.

One of the most intriguing sources of evidence for a priestly resurgence is comprised of the complex and allusive synagogue poems from this period; they are known in Hebrew as *piyyutim*. Usually written in Hebrew, early *piyyutim* were composed to accompany the public reading of the Torah, in connection with Sabbath, holiday worship, and other public occasions in the life of the synagogue. Some were composed by Galilean priests, including figures with such names as Yohanan the Priest, and others by persons with close social connections to the priestly families who settled in the Galilee after the Temple's destruction. They often incorporate Temple-centered themes, yearning for its reconstruction, or alluding to the twenty-four "priestly orders," the names of the priestly watches that served in rotation in the Temple when it stood. The offering of the Yom Kippur sacrifice, used to atone for the community's sins and sustain God's presence in the Temple, inspired *piyyutim* that glorify the Temple cult and the priest (these poems form the basis of a Yom Kippur service followed to this day in many communities). Priests may also have been the ones to produce *Hekhalot* literature, a late antique offshoot of apocalyptic literature whose descriptions of the heavens and the angelic worship of God practiced there are modeled on the Temple cult (the term *Hekhalot* refers to the chambers of this heavenly Temple).

While priests sustained their interest in the Temple, they were never able to actually restore its cult, much less fully recover their power within Jewish culture. By the time *piyyutim* and *Hekhalot* literature were being composed, the priestly class may already have been largely absorbed into the rabbinic movement (both genres draw heavily on rabbinic literature). To this day in religiously observant communities, priests are granted certain privileges during worship (for example, the right to be called up first in reading the Torah and to recite the priestly benediction), but it is rabbinic law that has determined these privileges, signifying the priesthood's subordination to rabbinic authority.

impossible to know for certain what happened in this important period in the development of rabbinic culture. It is not even certain that we can speak of a rabbinic movement yet, for the rabbis may not yet have had a distinct identity as a group, operating individually or in small circles but without a shared ideology or institutional life. What we are calling "the rabbinic movement" may postdate Yohanan by centuries.

What is it that allowed this movement to develop and flourish in the centuries after the Second Temple's destruction while other Jewish groups did not? This was a time when the central institutions of Jewish life in Jerusalem—the Temple, its priesthood, and the Herodian dynasty—were destroyed or drained of influence. Highly decentralized and widely dispersed in Palestine outside Jerusalem, the rabbis were able to fill in the vacuum of religious authority at least at the local level. The priesthood probably continued in this period, potentially competing with the rabbis for influence, but its authority in society was tied to the now vanished Temple, whereas the rabbis' authority, tied to their role as legal and scriptural experts, was not. In contrast to such Jewish sects as the Dead Sea Scrolls community, the early rabbinic movement seems to have had some tolerance for legal, interpretive,

and ideological difference, and that allowed it to avoid destructive internal divisions and isolation from the rest of society (*see box,* What Became of the Priests after the Temple's Destruction?).

It was probably also crucial to the success of rabbinic Judaism that the early rabbis were willing to live with Roman rule. Some, including the famous sage Rabbi Akiba, were supporters of the Bar Kochba Revolt, but in the wake of its disastrous outcome, the rabbinic movement in general seems to have come to terms with Roman rule—if not actively aligning with it, at least avoiding open rebellion. Rabbinic literature can be extremely critical of Roman rule, but in stories like that of Yohanan ben Zakkai and Vespasian, it distances itself from rebellion, recommending submission, or at least stopping short of public defiance of Rome. It may have been this political posture that spared the rabbinic movement the fate suffered by Jewish movements such as the Zealots and the Bar Kochba rebels, who had both gone extinct by the second century CE.

All this helps to illumine where the rabbinic movement came from and how it managed to secure a footing for itself in Palestine in the first few centuries after the Jewish Revolt, but it does not explain rabbinic influence on the broader Jewish culture. Although he looms large in later rabbinic imaginations, Yohanan may have had little impact on Jewish life in his own lifetime. Rabbinic literature credits Yohanan with moving the Sanhedrin to Yavneh, and some scholars theorize that he derived his influence over Jewish society through his prominent role as the head of this institution. But, increasingly, historians question the very existence of the Sanhedrin, and to the extent that a Jewish court system did exist in Palestine after 70, no real evidence indicates that Yohanan controlled it. Whatever role he played in creating rabbinic Judaism, that movement's emerging influence in Jewish culture probably postdates his death, as well as the deaths of his successors, such as Gamliel II. These leading rabbis may have enjoyed considerable authority within the rabbinic community (to the extent the rabbis were a community at this point) but exerted no clear influence beyond it.

Thus we find that the beginnings of rabbinic history do not answer the question we have posed for ourselves, telling us something about where the rabbis came from but little about how they were able to influence Jewish culture in general. A key turning point seems to have taken place sometime after Yohanan and Gamliel II, when the rabbinic movement came to ally itself with the patriarch, recognized by the Roman Empire as a national Jewish leader. This institution and its impact are our focus in the next section.

Emerging Rabbinic Authority in the Jewish Community

If rabbinic literature is any indication, the rabbis did enjoy some measure of influence in the larger Jewish community from the very beginning. Individuals and even whole communities came to them for legal advice and practical help, treating them with respect and even providing them with food and other kinds of support. But the rabbis were not the only authorities in the Jewish community: Jews were also subject to the influence of nonrabbinic sages, priests, municipal officials, Jewish sectarians, Christians, and perhaps even prophet-like figures who also laid claim to religious or legal authority. Many Jews simply ignored the rabbis—rabbinic literature contains many complaints about Jews who do not act in accordance with the rabbis' rules.

How then did the rabbis come to exert influence on the larger Jewish community? Within the rabbinic community as it is described in rabbinic literature, a teacher could exercise considerable authority over disciples or sages with less academic rank. Rabbis not only taught their students, they provided them with lodging and material support while they studied. In return, it was the student's responsibility not merely to listen to his teacher but to serve him in a personal way. Collectively, certain rabbinic stories suggest, the rabbis sometimes even used coercion to compel compliance, such as excommunicating or threatening to excommunicate sages who refused to submit to communal norms. Within the larger Jewish community, the situation was different. A rabbi could criticize and curse those whose actions he disapproved of, but he could not force them to do what he wanted. If Jews heeded a rabbi, it was not because he represented some official institution or because they were afraid of being punished but because they respected the rabbi's personal abilities—his knowledge of Torah, his wisdom, or his wonder-working ability.

The unofficial and diffuse nature of rabbinic authority changed to some degree when the rabbinic movement in Palestine became associated with the patriarchate, a dynastic office recognized by the Roman government. The Hebrew equivalent to "patriarch" is *nasi* (though the two titles might not be identical in meaning), a title that rabbinic literature bestows on early sages such as Yohanan ben Zakkai. While Yohanan may indeed have played a leadership role in the early rabbinic movement, however, some scholars believe that the description of him as a *nasi* is anachronistic, projecting onto him an office that did not arise until **Judah ha-Nasi** (Judah "the Patriarch"), who was active between 175 and 220 CE. Judah ha-Nasi is known in rabbinic literature simply as "Rabbi" because of his importance in the rabbinic movement, and it was by dint of his authority and that of his successors that the rabbis began to exert significant influence on the larger Jewish community.

Judah's most celebrated innovation was the codification of what would become the first rabbinic text, the work now known as the **Mishnah,** a compilation of rabbinic teaching and law as it had developed by that period. (Although scholarship has yet to prove that he was its editor, we shall assume here that he was.) In terms of its purpose, it is easier to say what the Mishnah is not than to describe what it is. Preserved today as a written text, in the time of Judah it was likely an oral compilation committed to memory by certain sages, hard as it is to imagine remembering so much. The Mishnah is not a work of biblical interpretation—or not chiefly so, rarely citing or referring to Scripture—but rather a presentation of what the sages said, presenting their positions on various legal issues. So far as we can tell, it does not appear to have been a working law code, as it addresses issues such as sacrifice that had no practical application in a post-Temple era, even as it leaves many areas of legal practice completely unaddressed. What the Mishnah does do is gather and organize the oral tradition transmitted by the time of Judah the Patriarch.

What was Judah trying to accomplish by organizing rabbinic tradition in this way? We cannot tell for certain because the Mishnah does not contain any kind of introduction that spells out its aims, but we can offer an educated guess or two. Sherira Gaon, a great tenth-century sage who headed an important Babylonian rabbinic academy, was asked when and how the Mishnah and other rabbinic texts had been compiled. His response, a letter written in 987 CE, represents the first known effort to reconstruct the history of rabbinic literature. According to Sherira, Judah feared that the legal tradition of his predecessors would be lost, and his goal in creating the Mishnah was basically preservative: to conserve and consolidate this tradition, not to create something new. Modern scholars accept the possibility that the Mishnah builds on earlier efforts to organize rabbinic legal tradition, but they also recognize in the Mishnah an effort by Judah to assert his authority over rabbinic tradition. It is not that the Mishnah simply imposes Judah's views—it often cites alternative views without telling us which view is right, and even cites views at odds with the opinion of Judah as attested in other rabbinic sources—but through its editorial activity, it quietly determines who gets to participate in the discussion, whose views should be preserved and taught to students.

The Mishnah thus represents an important step in the consolidation of rabbinic Judaism; indeed its formulation has come to mark a major division in rabbinic history. Those sages who live up until the time of the Mishnah are known as the **Tannaim,** from the Aramaic word *tanna* ("repeater"), referring to one who memorized and repeated legal traditions), and rabbinic literature composed in this period, including the Mishnah as well as a few other early rabbinic collections, is known as *tannaitic literature.* Rabbinic sages living after this period, from 220 to 500 CE or so, are known as the **Amoraim,** from the Aramaic word *amora* ("speaker"), referring to one who repeated the words of a sage aloud and translated biblical verses into Aramaic during public readings of the Torah. The effort to establish the Mishnah as the authoritative codification of rabbinic tradition was apparently successful, and much of subsequent Amoraic activity focused on the study of the rabbinic teachings it recorded. The Palestinian and Babylonian rabbinic communities each developed its own tradition of interpretive responses to the Mishnah. The Palestinian response is preserved in what is known as the

An inscription from a synagogue in Rehov, Israel, from the sixth or seventh century CE, which cites agricultural laws also known from rabbinic texts—evidence for rabbinic literature's growing influence on Jewish culture in late antiquity.

Palestinian or Jerusalem Talmud, completed by the fifth or sixth century CE (not in Jerusalem as the latter name implies, but probably in Tiberias in the Galilee). The Babylonian response is recorded in the even more fully developed Babylonian Talmud, which was probably completed in the sixth or seventh century CE.

The consolidation of rabbinic tradition was not the only accomplishment of Rabbi Judah ha-Nasi (to the extent we can infer anything about the historical Judah). He also appears to have been the first patriarch to actively operate outside the institutional contexts of the school and the rabbinic court. According to rabbinic sources, he sent sages to serve as judges and scribes in local communities and to supervise religious practice there, and he may have expanded the scope of legal issues the sages addressed, thereby increasing their relevance to Jewish communities. By the fourth century, the rabbinic movement in Palestine was more urbanized—and hence less isolated from other Jews and better positioned to influence them—than it seems to have been in earlier centuries, moving into such major cities as Sepphoris, Tiberias, and Caesarea. Historians credit Judah for facilitating the rabbis' entrance into Palestine's population centers by, among other measures, moving the patriarchate to one of these cities, Sepphoris.

Rabbi Judah ha-Nasi also made the vocation of being a sage more accessible to a broader cross-section of Jewish males (*see box,* Female Rabbis in Late Antiquity?). A rabbinic lifestyle was hard to sustain for a number of reasons. The focus of one's life was supposed to be study of the Torah, but everyday life made it difficult to devote one's life to that pursuit. Initially, therefore, the vocation of being a rabbi may have been largely confined to those with sufficient wealth to support themselves without constant labor. Some early sages are, like Akiba, depicted as having had very humble origins, but it has been argued that many early rabbis were prosperous landowners. Rabbi Judah ha-Nasi seems to have made the rabbinic vocation accessible to a broader range of would-be scholars by creating salaried positions for certain sages and by establishing a tithe to support poor disciples—changes that made it easier for the poor to participate in Torah study, and also presumably rendered many sages more dependent on the patriarchate, thus increasing its influence within the rabbinic movement

Beyond these efforts to reach outside rabbinic circles, Judah also seems to have cultivated a political relationship with the Roman Empire that gave his office authority not just in Palestine but in other Jewish communities in the Roman world. With the disruption of the high priestly succession and the disappearance of the Herodian dynasty, Rome was in need of a leader who could serve as an intermediary between its government and the Jews. Rabbi Yohanan ben Zakkai is remembered as having secured the favor of Vespasian, and Gamliel II, Yohanan's successor at Yavneh, may have gained

FEMALE RABBIS IN LATE ANTIQUITY?

Although some rabbinic sources describe Torah study as a duty of all humankind, the rabbis also recognized that not everyone was able to devote their lives to this pursuit, and they excluded one large segment of the Jewish population from their circle altogether: women. This exclusion may not seem surprising given the male-centeredness of Jewish culture in antiquity, but that culture was not completely opposed to female religious leadership and scholarship. Jewish inscriptions from late antiquity ascribe to women titles like "head of the synagogue" that seem to indicate they held leadership positions in local communities. We also know of women esteemed for their intellectual capacities, women praised for being "a good student" or for being "well trained." We even have a report of a female Jewish philosopher in Alexandria of the second century or third century CE: a woman named Maria, famous for her discoveries in the field of alchemy. Such figures were exceptional, but their existence indicates that the idea of a female rabbi in antiquity was not completely beyond the realm of possibility.

In fact, rabbinic literature acknowledges the legal expertise and wisdom of learned women such as Beruriah, the wife of Rabbi Meir. It even imagines Beruriah teaching students. Judging from who is actually cited in rabbinic literature, however, the rabbis of late antiquity did not generally allow women into their circles as teachers or disciples. This does not mean that the rabbis were necessarily bent on repressing women beyond what was the norm in the ancient Mediterranean and Near East—indeed, it has been argued that they sometimes revised earlier Jewish law to give women more control over their fate or to make their situation easier—but their own scholarly community was exclusively male. While recognizing Torah study as a general obligation, the rabbis believed that a woman fulfilled this commandment by supporting her scholar-husband in *his* studies. The question of whether women could be rabbis themselves was not articulated until the nineteenth century, and the first female rabbis in the Reform, Reconstructionist, and Conservative movements were not ordained until the twentieth century.

some kind of recognition from the Roman authorities in Syria, but it was Rabbi Judah ha-Nasi who seems to have cemented the relationship between the patriarchate and imperial rule. In rabbinic literature, he appears as the friend of the Roman ruler Antoninus, perhaps to be identified with the emperor Carracalla. It is hard to believe that Judah enjoyed such a personal relationship with the emperor, but the tradition does seem to accurately register some association between the patriarchate and the Roman government.

This is not to suggest that the patriarch played the same role that the Herodian dynasty did in an earlier period. The patriarchate did not have the benefit of a large army or administration as Herod did nor did it enjoy the same level of official status. It did, however, become a quasiroyal dynasty with authority not just among Jews in Palestine but in the Diaspora as well. Jewish communities saluted the patriarch and prayed for his welfare as they might for a king; the patriarch even acquired a royal pedigree, with rabbinic sources stressing Judah's descent from David. The patriarch was not a full-fledged king in either a biblical or a Roman sense, but in the third century, the Christian biblical interpreter Origen, living in the coastal city of Caesarea and in contact with rabbis, certainly thought he came close, noting in a letter that "we who have experience of [his power] know that he differs in little from a true king" (*Letter to Africanus* 14).

The patriarch does not seem to have depended on the rabbis for his authority, maintaining his position even when they disapproved of him, but he was immersed in the network of rabbinic relationships, and that association elevated the rabbis' status and authority within Jewish society. The patriarch used his authority to appoint certain sages as communal and judicial officials. He took other rabbis on trips with him. He also sent rabbinic envoys to various communities in Palestine and the Diaspora to collect taxes for the patriarchate and to supervise religious practice. More than any other single factor, their alliance with an ascendant patriarchate explains how the rabbis of late antique Palestine were able to extend their authority into the larger Jewish community.

Even as we acknowledge the importance of this alliance, it is also clear in retrospect that the rabbis' emerging influence was not completely tied to the patriarch. Because the patriarch's status depended on imperial recognition, the office's power began to decline in the absence of imperial support in the fifth century CE, and the institution was abolished altogether by 429 CE. The larger rabbinic movement survived long after the patriarchate's demise, in part because it had never completely identified itself with the patriarchate. Even during the time of Judah, the sages were sometimes critical of his behavior, or so rabbinic sources claim, and after his death they asserted their independence by

relocating their main academy from his headquarters in Sepphoris to Tiberias (the patriarchate followed shortly thereafter). Under Judah, the patriarch had been able to ordain rabbis, make appointments, regulate the calendar, and make other decisions on his own authority. Later patriarchs had to share these powers with the rabbis. The rabbis' independence helps to explain how they survived, and even flourished after the demise of the patriarchate in the fifth century CE.

Even without the authority of the patriarchate working on their behalf, rabbinic sages exerted influence in a number of ways. As we have noted, the synagogue was not originally a rabbinic institution. The patriarch may have had some supervisory authority over synagogue practice, but control was mostly in the hands of local communities or wealthy patrons. The rabbis' role as interpreters and judges may have given them a measure of unofficial influence over what happened in the synagogue, or so rabbinic literature suggests (rabbinic influence is nearly impossible to detect in the archaeological evidence for synagogues in this period). Rabbis helped to clarify issues of religious practice, weighed in on how best to pray, criticized practices they deemed offensive, and provided oversight for schooling that happened in synagogues. Some sages may also have exerted influence through their preaching ability, developing the sermon into an elaborately structured and entertaining art form. Most of the sermons identified in rabbinic literature were probably delivered in the study house, to fellow sages, but it is not impossible that rabbis used their homiletic skills to reach a broader audience.

The rabbis provided leadership to the Jews of Palestine after the demise of the patriarchate, using their roles as teachers, judges, and preachers to shape Jewish life. But they were exercising their influence within a community that was in overall decline, at least in terms of demography and status. As a Christian community grew in Palestine, becoming more politically dominant as well, Jewish life persisted: synagogues were built and decorated with beautiful mosaics, scholars continued to operate in Tiberias and other academic centers (including the Masoretes), and Palestinian Jews continued to produce poetry, biblical interpretation, and mystical literature. But by the sixth century, the Jewish community of Palestine was greatly overshadowed by the Christians living there, now the majority. In 614, Jerusalem was conquered by the Persians, briefly kindling the hope among Jews that the Temple would be restored (and also apparently triggering a violent backlash against local Christians), but the Persians soon shifted their support to the Christians as well, ending any chance of a Jewish revival in Palestine. Jewish life certainly continued in Palestine well beyond this, but the center of rabbinic culture had shifted elsewhere, to Babylonia. How the rabbinic movement moved to Babylonia and how the community there came to reshape worldwide Jewish culture provide the subject of the next section.

To Babylonia and Beyond

The origins of the Jewish community in Babylonia go back to the time of the Babylonian exile in 586 BCE, and its history runs throughout the period covered by the four previous chapters, though little is known about that history. After the third century CE, it began to emerge as a major center of rabbinic activity. This shift is reflected in the career of a single sage named Rav Abba, known simply as **Rav** in rabbinic literature. Rav was born in Babylonia, but like other sages from there, he went to Palestine to study, reportedly receiving his ordination from Rabbi Judah ha-Nasi. But then around 219 CE, Rav returned to Babylonia and established a *bet midrash,* or study house, at Sura, which became one of the most important rabbinic academies in Babylonia. For later Babylonian rabbis, Rav's return to Babylonia was a turning point in their relationship with Palestine, long the center of rabbinic authority: "From the time Rav arrived in Babylonia," declared one sage, "we in Babylonia have put ourselves on the same footing as Israel" (Babylonian Talmud, *Bava Kama* 80a).

Like Yohanan ben Zakkai and Judah ha-Nasi, Rav's portrayal in rabbinic literature may not be an accurate depiction, but it does tell us something about how the sages of Babylonia saw themselves: while they never broke from their roots in Palestinian rabbinic Judaism, and held Palestinian figures such as Yohanan ben Zakkai and Judah ha-Nasi in esteem, they saw themselves as having a comparable authority and were willing to act independently in developing their own distinctive brand of rabbinic culture.

Rav was not alone in migrating to Babylonia; many other sages emigrated there as well. Why leave Palestine, a land sanctified by its association with biblical history and the Temple? Probably because Jewish life in Palestine was growing increasingly difficult in this period. Recall that a number of prominent sages had been martyred during the Bar Kochba Revolt and that Judea had become de-Judaized in its wake. The Roman Empire in general and Palestine in particular suffered significant economic turmoil in the third century, adding to the pressures on Palestinian Jews. The Christianization of Palestine, culminating in a Christian majority by the fifth century, made life there religiously inhospitable for Jews as well.

As the rabbinic movement began to coalesce in Babylonia, it began to assert itself vis-à-vis its Palestinian counterpart, emboldened perhaps by the fact that Babylonia happened to fall beyond the jurisdiction of Roman law and hence beyond the patriarch's legal authority and enforcement

powers, whatever those were. Babylonian independence is detectable already in the second century, when a sage named Hananiah, having emigrated to Babylonia after the Bar Kochba Revolt, made an attempt to regulate the calendar from there—a direct challenge to Palestinian legal supremacy. The threat of excommunication was enough to stifle Hananiah's challenge, but the episode was an early sign of the self-confidence that led later Babylonian sages to claim a legal authority equivalent to the sages of Palestine.

The sages of Babylonia could not ignore the centrality of Palestine in Jewish history, but they asserted an almost equivalent status for themselves. They boasted of the fact that their roots in the biblical past as they imagined them predated those of their Palestinian colleagues—after all, as the site of the Garden of Eden and the original home of Abraham, Babylonia was where Jewish history had begun. Yes, Babylonia was also a place of exile, but that had not disrupted their relationship with God who had accompanied the exiles, Babylonian sages insisted, and had taken residence in the synagogues there. Since their arrival in Babylonia, other Babylonian sages claimed, the Jews had jealously preserved their pedigree by avoiding intermarriage, keeping their line purer than did the Jews of Palestine (according to the Babylonian Talmud, in tractate *Qiddushin* 69b, whatever Jews of tainted descent there had been in Babylonia had gone back with Ezra when he moved to Judah). To the extent that authority in the Jewish community derived from the Bible and the biblical past, Babylonian sages saw themselves as in no way inferior to Palestine, despite its status as the Holy Land.

By the ninth century, the Babylonian community was feeling sufficiently confident that one of its sages, Pirkoi ben Baboi, in a letter addressed to the Jewish communities of North Africa, claimed that it was the Babylonian sages, not the Palestinians, who preserved Jewish tradition in its purest form. The Palestinian community, under pressure from a hostile Christian Roman Empire, had forgotten or corrupted Jewish law, he argued, whereas the rabbinic academies of the Babylonian community had not, and so Babylonian legal views should have ultimate authority. In the 920s, the Babylonians and the Palestinians had another dispute over who would set the calendar, long the jealously guarded prerogative of the Palestinian community, but this time the Palestinians were not able to impose their authority on the Babylonians. Some communities followed the Palestinian reckoning for a time, but in the end the Babylonians' calculation—and by implication, Babylonian legal authority—prevailed.

Why did rabbinic Judaism do so well in Babylonia? Pirkoi ben Baboi may have had a point: the sages of Babylonia may have faced less external interference than the sages of Palestine. A large Jewish population had long existed in

Babylonia and Persia, though that is poorly documented in the period between the Bible and the rabbinic period, and its value as a potentially powerful ally in Parthia's struggle with the Roman Empire was incentive for the Parthian king to treat it well. The more decentralized nature of Parthian rule also allowed the Jews a large degree of autonomy. By the third century, an official known as the *exilarch,* the "head of the exile," existed in Babylonia as a state-supported quasiroyal office that, like the patriarchate, claimed descent from King David and enjoyed a large measure of political and legal authority over the Jewish community dwelling within the Parthian and Sassanian kingdoms. In some respects the exilarch's role was like that of the patriarchate but proved far more enduring, surviving in a vestigial form until the fifteenth century CE.

This is not to say that relations with Persian rule were always positive. Tensions manifested, even periods of persecution, especially when the Sassanians, a family of Zoroastrian priests, defeated the Parthians in the third century CE and established a political dynasty that was more religiously activist than the Parthians had been. According to later Geonic sources, during the reign of Yazdagird II and his son Peroz, synagogues were closed and Jewish children were sold to the priests of a Zoroastrian temple. But such oppressiveness was exceptional, and Sassanian policy seems largely to have followed the "live and let live" religious policy practiced by earlier Persian rulers, including Cyrus and the Parthians. In contrast to Christianity, Zoroastrianism made no effort to convert the Jews, nor did it cast the Jews in the role of "god killer." In Babylonian rabbinic literature, relations between the sages and the Sassanian king are often cordial.

The cultural and social autonomy of the Jews living under Parthian and Sassanian rule may explain why Babylonian rabbinic literature seems more insulated from outside cultural influence than Palestinian rabbinic literature. Babylonian rabbinic literature contains far fewer Persian loan words (130 noted so far) than Palestinian rabbinic literature contains Greek and Roman loan words (over 3,000). The Babylonian sages even seem to have distanced themselves from other, nonrabbinic Jews. The rabbis of Palestine, as did philosophers in the Greco–Roman world, taught in public places, such as markets. The more detached academic culture of Babylonia discouraged teaching in such settings, and some sages were even wary of letting outsiders into their academies.

Despite their self-insulating propensities, the sages of Babylonia did find ways to influence the larger community. Their (sometimes tense) alliance with the exilarch gave them real judicial authority in the larger community, and a rabbi's authority may have been enhanced by his wonder-working ability as well. Some of the magical bowls found in Mesopotamia and Persia make reference to an exorcist named Rabbi Joshua ben Perahya, and Babylonian rabbinic literature also makes reference to sages who battle demons. The sages of Babylonia may even have engaged in certain forms of public education. Two months of each year, known as the months of Kallah, were especially busy times for the rabbinic academies of Babylonia—it was then that disciples unable to live in the academy for the entire year arrived for a period of intensive study, during which the sages of Babylonia may have relaxed their self-isolating elitism a bit and included ordinary people in Torah study by means of publicly delivered sermons.

The intellectual vibrancy of the Babylonian rabbinic community has been wonderfully preserved in the **Babylonian Talmud,** a text that is extremely difficult because of its scope, breadth, and intricate argumentation. For Babylonian sages after the tannaitic period, as for Palestinian sages in the same period, the Mishnah had become a canonical document. The Babylonian Talmud preserves a distinctive Babylonian tradition of interpretation and debate about the Mishnah. Its content overlaps with the Palestinian Talmud to some extent, but it is later, more elaborate, and more ingeniously organized, reflecting the contributions of Babylonian Amoraim, who are cited by name in its text alongside Palestinian Amoraim. The successors to the Amoraim in Babylonia are the unnamed sages—known as the Saboraim or, in a term coined by modern scholarship, as the Stammaim—who finalized and edited the Talmud in the period between 550 and 650 CE. Their accomplishment, reflecting the work of generations, is stunning for its massiveness and complexity, a record of carefully structured legal argumentation, biblical interpretation, and storytelling that runs for some 2.5 million words and sixty-three volumes. When Jews today refer to the Talmud, they mean the Babylonian Talmud, reflecting how it came to overshadow the Palestinian rabbinic literature that preceded it (*see box,* Adrift in the Sea of Talmud).

The Babylonian Talmud intermixes Palestinian and Babylonian traditions in a way that makes it appear as if they form one seamless whole. But by comparing Babylonian and Palestinian traditions, scholars have been able to distinguish between the two variants of rabbinic culture. By the time of the final editing of the Babylonian Talmud in the sixth and seventh centuries CE, the sages of Babylonia had developed their own distinctive intellectual culture. They studied in large academies that were more institutionalized, hierarchical, insulated, elitist, and enduring than the informal study circles of earlier generations of Palestinian and Babylonian sages. The more centralized nature of study meant that students had to travel greater distances and spend more time away from home

ADRIFT IN THE SEA OF TALMUD

It may be impossible to learn how to read the Babylonian Talmud without a teacher to initiate one into its secrets. Interweaving Hebrew and Aramaic, saturated with technical terminology, and highly terse and elliptical, the Talmud is extremely difficult to digest no matter how good the translation or extensive the commentary. The Talmud does not contain any kind of opening prologue that explains how to read it, and if you just dive in, you are likely to be misled: the discussion that it records may look like it is meandering, but a sophisticated logic fits all the contradictions, qualifications, and digressions into a structured unit of argumentation known as a *sugya,* which takes time to work through. If it is any consolation, reading the Talmud has always been a challenge, inspiring commentary, and commentary on that commentary, some of which now appears alongside the Talmudic text in printed editions to help the reader. If you can grasp how the twists of its argumentation work, however, the experience can be thrilling.

The legal and ritual issues that inspire Talmudic discussion and debate can seem highly technical and narrow, and that can make it difficult to appreciate what was at stake in the discussion. But what was at stake? The Babylonian Talmud addresses profound theological, ethical, and epistemological issues, serving as a source for some modern philosophers, such as Emmanuel Levinas, but unlike Greek philosophy, it does not attempt to resolve those issues and offers little in the way of definitive insights. This is because the Talmud was rooted in a culture that valued argumentation for its own sake, and its editors were much more interested in reconstructing the process of raising and countering objections than in reaching a final conclusion about this or that issue (indeed, if you follow Talmudic argumentation to its end, you will often find that it does not lead to a clear conclusion). Learning how to swim in the sea of Talmud involves learning to follow this process rather than trying to reach a particular destination, whether that be a definitive understanding of God or a clear-cut decision about how to follow his laws.

In this context, we cannot teach you how to make your way through a Talmudic argument, but we do at least want to introduce you to the text with a brief example from *Pesahim* 116a, a tractate that addresses how to observe Passover (the "a" refers to the front side of a two-sided folio page in the standard printed version). The Talmudic discussion begins by citing an individual unit of mishnaic text, such as the following example drawn from Mishnah Pesachim 10:3, which discusses the ritual Passover meal known as the Seder (see Chapter 3 for more on that ritual). This particular *mishnah* (the word also used for the smallest textual unit of the Mishnah) enumerates a list of special foods that are included in the Seder, including *haroset,* a dip made of fruit and spices:

> They bring before him *matzah,* lettuce, *haroset,* and two cooked dishes, even though *haroset* is not obligatory. Rabbi Eliezer bar Tzadok says: Haroset is obligatory.

Scholars suggest that *haroset* initially became part of the Passover ritual because it was a popular appetizer in ancient Palestine, and perhaps more generally in the Hellenistic world. They theorize that it originally had no religious meaning and was simply a tasty part of any festive meal. The Mishnah reflects the first stage in the rabbinic interpretation of this practice: a difference of opinion between an anonymous voice in the text, claiming belief that this practice is voluntary ("even though *haroset* is not obligatory"), and the voice of Rabbi Eliezer bar Tzadok, who held that *haroset* is a religious obligation in itself—not just a voluntary custom but something one had to eat as part of the scripted performance of the Seder. The text is very brief, however: the Mishnah does not explain the differing viewpoints or the practice's significance. The latter would have been even more of a concern for the sages of Babylonia than those of Palestine because when the Passover customs outlined in the Mishnah traveled to Babylonia, the Babylonian sages had no cultural background for appreciating those parts of the Seder that reflect Palestinian customs. *Haroset* is not a familiar food to them, so it becomes a practice that must be explained. Hence, the discussion in the Babylonian Talmud triggered by this mishnaic passage aims to flesh out the differing points of view and to suggest along the way several possible interpretations of why the *haroset* is eaten. Following is the Talmudic text (words in boldface are citations of the just-discussed mishnah):

than did their predecessors, leading to prolonged absences that placed great stress on marriages. Even if its details are exaggerated, some historical truth does lie behind the Babylonian legend that Rabbi Akiba had a wife willing to wait twenty-four years while he finished his studies. For the sages of Babylonia, the fantasy wife is the woman willing to wait while her husband studies, or else she is the Torah itself, the study of which is sometimes likened to a sexual experience (compare Babylonian Talmud, *Eruvin* 54b).

Life in the academy was governed by a highly developed ethos of argumentation tempered by scholarly etiquette. Sages, often studying together in pairs, debated one another not necessarily to resolve the issue at hand but, rather, for the love of debate and for the respect that one could attain

"Even though *haroset* is not obligatory."

But if eating *haroset* is not obligatory, why is it served?

Rabbi Ami says: Because of the *kappa* [a poisonous worm found in lettuce and other vegetables].

Rabbi Assi says: For the *kappa* of lettuce, take radishes; for the *kappa* of radishes—leeks; for the *kappa* of leeks—hot water; for all kinds of *kappa*—hot water. And in the meanwhile, recite the following: "*Kappa, kappa,* I remember you, your seven daughters and your eight daughters-in-law."

"Rabbi Eliezer bar Tzadok says: Haroset is obligatory."

Why is it a religious obligation?

Rabbi Levi says: In memory of the apple tree.

Rabbi Yohanan says: In memory of the mortar.

Abaye says: Therefore, make it sharp-tasting, and thick—sharp, in memory of the apple tree; and think in memory of the mortar.

As is typical of the Talmud, no attempt is made here to resolve the disagreement but, rather, an attempt is made to explore both sides of the dispute.

If the *haroset* is not a religious obligation, why are we instructed to eat it on Passover? Rabbi Ami proposes that the *haroset* serves medicinal purposes. Since eating lettuce is a religious obligation during the Seder meal, and lettuce sometimes contains the dangerous worms known as *kappa,* the *haroset* comes to neutralize the health dangers.

Rabbi Assi supplements Rabbi Ami's interpretation with other remedies for the *kappa* worm. This is a good example of the breadth of the Talmud's interest; not only religious guidance engaged its editors but also practical wisdom. Some rabbis were particularly celebrated for their accomplishments in medicinal arts. The home remedies and incantation that Rabbi Assi provides might be examples of customs that Babylonian Jews shared with their non-Jewish neighbors.

Having made a credible case for *haroset* as a custom voluntarily observed because of its benefits, the Talmud now turns to the other possibility raised in the Mishnah: that it is eaten to fulfill an obligation. If so, why is it obligatory?

Two possibilities are raised. Rabbi Levi interprets the *haroset* as a remembrance of the "apple tree." (Apples are a key ingredient in *haroset*.) This is an oblique reference to a fanciful legend that is found elsewhere in the Talmud (see Sotah 11b). According to this tradition, the redemption of the Israelites from bondage in Egypt began with miraculous instances of childbirth: when Israelite sons were still under threat of destruction from Pharaoh, the expectant mothers went out to the apple orchards to deliver their babies and were blessed with quiet, painless births. In yet another midrash connected with apple trees, when Israelite men were reluctant to have relations with their wives because of Pharaoh's decrees, the Israelite women seduced their husbands under apple trees so as to ensure that the Israelites would continue to flourish. In other words, one is obliged to eat *haroset* to commemorate the apple tree's role in the Exodus.

Rabbi Yohanan interprets the *haroset* differently. In his view, it is the texture and appearance of *haroset* that are important, serving to remind worshippers of the mortar with which the Israelite slaves built Pharaoh's cities.

The two interpretations of *haroset*'s religious significance point to the overlapping symbolic meanings of the Seder service as a whole: on the one hand, the Seder is meant to celebrate redemption from slavery (here captured by the apple tree), but on the other hand the Seder is designed to bring the memory of slavery to life (here, by putting mortar on the table).

As this section of Talmudic discussion ends with Abaye's comment, both meanings of *haroset* are preserved, so that *haroset* becomes a potent symbol of both bondage and freedom, of suffering and redemption—a powerful example of the Talmudic rabbis' penchant for paradox and their respect for divergent interpretations of the Bible.

This is just the tiniest taste of how a Talmudic discussion unfolds. For a more extended guided tour through a Talmudic passage, see Robert Goldenberg, "Talmud," in *Back to the Sources: Reading the Classic Jewish Texts* (New York: Summit Books, 1984), 129–175.

through intellectual acuity. It is not unusual for a debate in the Babylonian Talmud to lead nowhere: the point was to develop innovative arguments, objections, and responses to objections, not necessarily to reach a clear judgment about the law. A story told in the Babylonian Talmud of a famous rabbinic duo captures this aspect of Babylonian rabbinic culture. After the death of his study partner Resh Lakish, the sages provided Rabbi Yohanan with a new study partner. Unlike Resh Lakish, this colleague was willing to acknowledge when Yohanan was correct. Rather than being consoled, however, Yohanan missed his old partner all the more:

When I made a statement, he [Resh Lakish] would pose twenty-four difficulties, and with twenty-four solutions

I would solve them and thus our discussion expanded. But you [Yohanan's new partner] say, "we learned a teaching that supports you." Of course I know that I am right. [Yohanan] would go out and tear his clothes, crying "Where are you the Son of Lakish, where are you the Son of Lakish?" (Babylonian Talmud, *Bava Metsia* 84a)

What Yohanan yearns for in this story is not to win the dispute but to debate a sharp and aggressive colleague willing to counter his every argument so that the dispute will never end. Here, death puts an end to the debate, but in other Babylonian traditions, the sages expect it to continue forever in a heaven that they imagine as a rabbinic academy.

It was this particular form of rabbinic culture, the one that took shape in Babylonia in the fifth and sixth centuries, that had the greatest impact on later Jewish culture. How it came to exert such influence is a story that takes us beyond the end of late antiquity into the period of Islamic rule, a good portion of it unfolding in the critical but poorly documented period of the **Geonim** (ca. 600–1000 CE). The Geonim were Babylonian sages who headed the two most important rabbinic academies in this period at Sura and Pumbedita. When Babylonia came under Islamic rule, Muslim authorities affirmed the legal authority of the exilarch and the Geonim, and eventually all the Jewish communities in the rapidly expanding Islamic world came under Geonic sway—not just in Babylonia but also in Egypt, North Africa, and Spain. Babylonian rabbis still had to compete with an influential Palestinian community, and they also faced new resistance from dissident Jewish sects, such as the Karaites, who rejected not just the authority of the Babylonian sages but the very legitimacy of rabbinic Judaism in general. With the support of Islamic rule and the intellectual talents of Geonic leaders such as **Saadya ben Yosef** (882–942 CE) working on its behalf, Babylonian rabbinic tradition eventually prevailed over these challenges, however, giving shape to what would become medieval Jewish culture.

The Geonic period falls outside the confines of this chapter, but a point that needs to be stressed here is that, through the influence of the Geonim, rabbinic Judaism, and more precisely, Babylonian rabbinic Judaism, completely reshaped Jewish life. The understanding of Jewish tradition preserved in the Babylonian Talmud—how to study and understand the Bible and the Mishnah, how to serve God and follow His commands—became authoritative for most Jewish communities, shaping their understanding of what it meant to be Jewish. Indeed, during the Geonic period, the Babylonian Talmud became a part of the Jewish canon, transcending its origins as an academic commentary and becoming *the* legal code that Jews looked to as the framework for how to live their lives. From its earliest days, Jewish culture

was a variegated one, developing in different ways in different regions. This diversity continued into the rabbinic period and beyond, but the Talmud-centered culture that developed under Babylonian rabbinic influence came as close as any to establishing itself as a worldwide Jewish culture.

The Rabbinization of Jewish Culture

How is a *rabbinized* Jewish culture different from the Jewish culture that preceded it? The following attempt to answer this question is largely based on the Babylonian Talmud (unless otherwise noted, virtually all the references in what follows are to tractates from the Babylonian Talmud), reflecting a particular and relatively late variant of rabbinic culture. It would be anachronistic to assume that the Talmudic take on rabbinic culture applies to the rabbis of Palestine or even to the rabbinic culture of Babylonia prior to the sixth century CE. But it was the Talmud's take on rabbinic culture that exerted the most influence on *later* Jewish culture, determining how Jews understood rabbinic teaching, and so from here on in this book it will define what we mean by rabbinic culture.

The most fundamental change introduced by rabbinic culture, arguably the root of all the others, was the establishment of the rabbi as the authoritative interpreter of Jewish tradition. Biblical tradition establishes three kinds of intermediaries between God and Israel: the Temple and its priesthood, the king, and the prophet. The rabbis justified their role in Jewish society by aligning themselves with all three figures. While they did not challenge the prerogatives of the priestly class, they usurped its role by presenting Torah study as a substitute for sacrifice. They did not claim to be kings (though figures like Judah claimed Davidic descent), but they identified themselves with kingly tradition by reimagining King David as a sage preoccupied with the study of Torah. As *Pirkei Avot* suggests, rabbinic tradition also cast itself as heir to the prophets, transmitting the Torah revealed to Moses and the other biblical prophets. Sometimes, the Talmud intimates that rabbinic insight into God's will exceeds even that of Moses. In one well-known story, God permits Moses a glimpse of Akiba teaching the Torah to his disciples. After listening to and not comprehending Akiba, the prophet can only express astonishment that God chose to reveal the Torah through him rather than so learned a sage (*Menahot* 29b). Taking over the roles played by other kinds of leader in earlier Jewish society, the rabbi becomes *the* intermediary between God and Israel and the authoritative interpreter of the laws and traditions inherited from the biblical past.

So great was the authority of the sages, in fact, that in some stories their interpretive authority even supersedes that of God. The Babylonian Talmud tells of a legal dispute between Rabbi Eliezer and the other sages. Eliezer commands wondrous acts to support his position: "If the law agrees with me," he tells his colleagues, "let this carob tree prove it," and the carob tree is lifted up and transported a hundred cubits from its place. The other sages do not question the miracle, but it has no effect on their position. And so Eliezer summons another supernatural witness: "If the law agrees with me, let this channel of water prove it." The water in the channel begins to flow backward, but the sages reject this proof too. Finally, an exasperated Eliezer declares, "If the law agrees with me, let it be proved from heaven," at which point a heavenly voice rings out, "Why do you dispute Eliezer with whom the law always agrees?" One might think this would have settled the matter in Eliezer's favor, but the other sages counter, "We do not heed the divine voice because long ago, at Sinai, you wrote in the Torah (Exodus 23:2), 'After the majority you must incline'" (in other words, the resolution to legal disputes such as this should follow the majority view). How does God respond when challenged in this way? He laughs with pleasure, repeating, "My sons have defeated me, my sons have defeated me" (*Bava Metsia* 59b).

This story captures striking elements of Babylonian rabbinic culture. Remember that who wins the debate does not matter all that much in this culture; what does matter is how one debates, and here the sages do so brilliantly, outdoing God by citing His own words as a counterargument, a divine decree in the Torah that trumps any miracle. This is why, rather than taking offense at their challenge, God is delighted to have been outwitted, for like the rabbis themselves he values opponents willing and able to challenge him with a smart objection. The story is also rooted in the delight that the rabbis took in paradox. In what might seem like an act of arrogance, they appear to be placing themselves above God, but it is precisely their commitment to God that leads them to their position. According to the rabbis' interpretation of Scripture, it was God's will that the sages resolve legal disputes according to their own interpretive ability and communal consensus, even when doing so brings them into conflict with God.

As this story illustrates, the source of a rabbi's religious authority was not some prophetic calling but rather his study of Torah, depicted in rabbinic sources as a lifelong commitment of supreme importance. Some sages held that the very reason God created humanity was for it to labor in study (cf. *Sanhedrin* 99b), and the sages debated whether such study took precedence over other supreme commandments, such as the duty to preserve one's own life. Fulfilling this duty to study was not quite like becoming a monk—rabbis got married and worked for a living—but it did require a deferral of worldly pursuits, or existed in tension with them, and rab-

binic literature struggles to reconcile the demands of study with other obligations recognized by the rabbis, such as a man's duty to satisfy his wife's sexual needs.

The rabbis were not the only Jews committed to the Torah, but their understanding of Torah was distinctive in many ways. The rabbis developed their own way of interpreting the Hebrew Bible known as **midrash.** Deriving from a Hebrew root meaning "to seek" or "to investigate," midrash is not an easy term to define. It can refer to a body of literature, collections of rabbinic interpretations of the Bible, but it also describes the mode of interpretation reflected in these collections. Like other early Jews, the rabbis assumed that every detail in the Torah was significant, but midrashic interpretation is even more preoccupied with those details, its commentary triggered by small gaps and redundancies in the text. For the rabbinic interpreter, even small deviations in how a word is spelled hint at a story or message that the rabbi aims to draw out through interpretation.

How midrash explains these details can strike the modern reader as wildly fanciful. It transforms biblical figures—Adam, Jacob, and David, for example—into rabbinic-like sages, draws connections between far-flung biblical verses that seem to have nothing to do with another, and even reverses the literal meaning of biblical texts. (This is what happens in the story about Rabbi Eliezer cited previously in this section. Exodus 23:2, the verse cited by the rabbis in support of the principle of majority rule, actually says the opposite of what they claim: "You shall *not* follow a majority in wrongdoing.") Even so, midrashic interpretation has a logic to it: specific assumptions and reasoning techniques allow for interpretive freedom but also constrain how one draws meaning from the biblical text (*see box,* Cracking the Bible's Code Rabbinically).

One of the most conspicuous characteristics of midrash is that there is no such thing as *the* midrashic reading of the biblical text; rabbinic literature can assign different, even contradictory, meanings to a biblical verse, sometimes presenting different interpretations of the same verse side by side without any indication that one is considered correct and the other wrong. The rabbis believed that God is able to communicate different things to different perspectives simultaneously, and thus it is possible to draw different but equally valid conclusions about the meaning of Torah: "It is taught in the school of Rabbi Ishmael: 'Behold, my word is like fire, declares the Lord, and like a hammer that shatters rock'" (Jeremiah 23:29). As this hammer produces many sparks, so a single verse has many meanings" (*Sanhedrin* 34a). God's "word"—understood in this midrash not as prophecy but as Scripture—is like a fire that can spark different meanings when the text is subject to interpretation.

CRACKING THE BIBLE'S CODE RABBINICALLY

For modern readers of the Bible, midrash appears to be a very strange way of making sense of the text. Often it seems to invent the interpretive problem that it is purportedly solving, and the "solutions" it comes up with do not always fit with a modern sensibility. An example can help to illustrate how midrash differs from how you or I might read the biblical text. A modern reader would probably not be puzzled by the fact that the first letter of the Torah happens to be the Hebrew letter *bet* (in the word *bereshit*, "in the beginning"), but this did puzzle rabbinic interpreters who wondered why God began his Torah with the *second* letter of the alphabet rather than the first (*aleph*):

> Yonah in the name of Rabbi Levi [said]: "Why was the world created with a *bet*? [in other words, what was God teaching by beginning Genesis 1 with the second letter of the alphabet, not the first?]: Just as a *bet* is closed on its side and open from its front, so also you are not permitted to inquire about what is above [in the heavens] and what is below [on the earth]. . . ." Rabbi Judah son of Pazzi explained the Creation according to the words of Bar Qappara: "Why [was the world created] with a *bet*? To make known to you that there are two worlds" [this world and an afterlife, the "twoness" of reality implied by the numerical value of bet, also used as a symbol for the number two]. Another interpretation: "Why [was the world created] with a *bet*? Because [*bet*] is an expression of blessing [the Hebrew word for "blessing" begins with *bet*]. And why not *aleph* [the first letter of the alphabet]? Because it is an expression of curse" [the Hebrew word for "curse" begins with *aleph*].*

Not only does the problem that provokes these responses seem a little contrived, but the sages' solution seems to stray wildly from the Bible's intended meaning as we might reconstruct it, positing that God purposely used the letter *bet* to communicate some message not expressly stated by the text if read literally—to warn against metaphysical speculation, to hint at the existence of an afterlife, or to imply the blessedness of creation. For many modern readers, the first sentence of Genesis, but not the first letter, certainly bears significance. For the rabbinic reader, even the shape of that letter was significant.

But this way of reading the text does not mean that the rabbis were simply making up their interpretations of the Bible without concern for logic or reason. Certain rules govern their interpretation, though the rabbis themselves seem to have disagreed over those rules. One difference had to do with whether the language of the Torah could be understood in the same way that human language is. The view that "The Torah speaks in human language" was associated with Rabbi Ishmael, a second-century sage, who rejected his contemporary Akiba's efforts to find divine meaning in the tiniest elements of the biblical text, including redundant words and even the appearance of individual letters. Such differences notwithstanding, the rabbis shared the belief that scriptural language required special techniques of interpretation—of how to extract meaning from a word or letter, relate it to other parts of Scripture, and resolve apparent contradictions.

In fact, rabbinic literature gave specific labels to these techniques, which it referred to as methods or rules (*middot*). A famous example of such a rule is *gematria*, the calculation of the numerical value of letters (*aleph* = 1; *bet* = 2, etc.) to understand a word's meaning (an interest in the mathematical value of letters is evident in preceding passage, which draws on the fact that *bet* has the value of two to argue that God begins with this letter to teach that *two* worlds exist, this one and the next one). A list of seven such rules was attributed to Hillel, and another of thirteen rules was ascribed to Ishmael. In actuality, midrashic interpretation is not limited to these seven or thirteen interpretive techniques—not even Ishmael always follows the rules ascribed to him—but the formulation of such lists suggests that rabbinic culture was highly self-conscious about how it read Scripture, developing its own criteria for what constituted a plausible interpretation of the Bible.

*Genesis Rabba on Genesis 1:1, adapted from the work of Gary Porton, "Rabbinic Midrash," *A History of Biblical Interpretation, vol. 1,* eds. Alan Hauser and Duane Watson (Grand Rapids, MI: William B. Eerdmans, 2003), 215–216.

In this regard, midrash mirrors the nature of rabbinic culture, which allowed for and even celebrated disagreement and fierce argumentation among the rabbis, debate that could be sharp enough to be described in the Babylonian Talmud as "the war of Torah." In fact, it is the process of argumentation, not the particular legal conclusions that it might lead to, that most interests the editors of the Babylonian Talmud; as we have already noted, much of its argumentation does not lead to a clear decision about the legal issue at stake. Even when rabbinic literature comes down clearly on one side of a legal dispute, it does not discredit the dissenting view. To the contrary, it grants that the losing view has value too, as illustrated by the following story:

> For three years there was a dispute between the school of Shammai and the school of Hillel. One side said, "The

law is according to our views," and the other side said, "the law is according to our views." A divine voice declared, "Both sides are the words of the living God, but the law is according to the school of Hillel." (*Erubin* 13b)

As a practical matter, the law was to be determined according to the views of the school of Hillel, but the views of both schools were thought to reflect the divine will—the reason that even the losing side of a rabbinic dispute is worthy of respectful transmission.

This is not to say that the rabbis liked losing debates. Failure to argue properly, to parry an objection or answer a question, was a source of intense shame for the rabbis, but it was important to avoid shaming an opponent precisely for that reason. Why is it that God preferred the school of Hillel to the school of Shammai, the story asks. "Because they were gracious and modest, and would teach their words and the words of the House of Shammai." As in other stories we have seen, what rabbinic culture valued was not winning the argument but engaging in it in the right way, and that includes showing respect to opponents.

What most distinguishes the rabbinic approach to Torah is not just its interpretive approach but its very understanding of what Torah consists of. By the time of the Babylonian Talmud, rabbinic sages had come to believe that the Torah revealed to Moses had two forms, the **Written Torah** preserved in the Bible and an **Oral Torah** transmitted by the sages. The latter is now preserved in written form—the Mishnah, Talmuds, and other rabbinic sources—but it was originally transmitted orally from rabbis to their disciples through face-to-face instruction. You may recall that the Pharisees venerated an unwritten tradition, and the Oral Torah may represent a later offshoot of that tradition, but for the rabbis of the Talmud, this tradition was more than just an ancestral inheritance: it was Torah itself—part of what God revealed to Moses at Mount Sinai:

> Rabbi Levi son of Chama said in the name of Rabbi Shimon the son of Lakish, "What is the meaning of the verse, 'I will give thee the tablets of stone and the Torah and the commandment which I have written to teach them'?" [Exodus 24:12]. 'Tablets' refers to the Ten Commandments. 'Torah' refers to the Five Books of Moses. 'And the commandment' refers to the Mishnah. 'Which I have written' refers to the Prophets and the Writings. 'To teach them' refers to the Gemara [another word for the Talmud]." [The verse] teaches all of them were given to Moses at Sinai. (*Berakhot* 5a)

In a manner that is typical of midrash, Rabbi Shimon ben Lakish responds to the apparent wordiness of the biblical text, which piles on a long series of phrases in reference to God's commands at Mount Sinai. According to the text, this verse actually contains no redundancy, since each phrase refers to a different aspect of God's revelation to Moses, some referring to the component parts of the Written Torah, and others referring to the components of the Oral Torah—the Mishnah and its Talmudic commentary. According to this and other rabbinic texts, to read the Hebrew Bible is to encounter only a part of what God had revealed to Moses—and, in fact, a very small part. To *fully* understand His Torah, one needs to study the Oral Torah as manifest in the teachings of the rabbis themselves.

The concept of the Oral Torah, like much else in rabbinic culture, is paradoxical. It consists of orally transmitted teachings of the sages themselves: their legal debates and rulings, biblical interpretations, wise sayings of the sort collected in *Pirkei Avot*, and stories of the rabbis' own exploits. This tradition was not fixed like the written biblical canon; it grew over time, becoming larger and more complex through the rabbis' rulings, argumentation, and interpretive activity. It also incorporated within it alternative, even contradictory, views of the meaning of Torah. As illustrated by the story of Rabbi Akiba that we told previously in this chapter, the rabbis knew well that Moses would scarcely have comprehended what Torah had come to encompass in their own day, and yet they also believed that all this innovation was already revealed at Sinai—what later rabbis taught their students, the questions students asked their teachers, the debates held between colleagues: all were part of what was revealed to Moses.

Why wasn't the Written Torah sufficient? Why did God need to reveal himself through the Oral Torah? Jewish scholars would ponder these questions long after the rabbinic age, answering them in different ways, but what their answers share in common is that the two Torahs were interdependent, that Jews needed one to fully understand and enact the other. A story preserved in *Shabbat* 31a illustrates this point by means of a story about the great sage Hillel. A non Jew seeking to convert insists that Hillel teach him only the Written Torah, not the Oral Torah, and Hillel agrees to teach him in a manner that cunningly demonstrates the indispensability of the Oral Torah. In the first lesson, Hillel recites to him the Hebrew alphabet in its conventional order, beginning with *aleph*. On the next day he reverses the order, beginning with the last letter of the alphabet, *tav*. When the convert objects that this was not how things were presented the day before, Hillel makes his point explicit: just as a student relies on his teacher to learn the alphabet, so too must he rely on the guidance of the Oral Torah to understand the Written Torah.

The Oral Torah was necessary in the rabbis' view because the Written Torah was insufficient by itself: it contained too many gaps and interpretive difficulties to enact without supplementation. As noted in Chapter 2, a biblical command—for example, the injunction to keep the Sabbath—is too sparse to put into practice without extensive elaboration. The Oral Torah provided that supplementation, helping to make sense of what could not be understood by reading the biblical text alone. Centuries later, Saadya the Gaon developed this point to counter the Karaites, who rejected the Oral Torah as a rabbinic fraud. Without the Oral Torah, after all, one could not even determine the day of the week of the Sabbath, he argued. But more than helping to explain divine revelation, Oral Torah allowed the rabbis to participate in and reshape the content of revelation. Rabbinic culture was a conservative one, revering what it had inherited from the Bible, but it was also highly creative, valuing legal and interpretive innovation. The concept of Oral Torah helped to resolve the tension between these conservative and creative impulses by allowing the rabbis to understand their own creativity as part of the tradition they were preserving.

Their belief in the Oral Torah helps to explain why the rabbis' understanding of the Bible seems to deviate so sharply from what is in the written text. The rabbinic understanding of the Sabbath is the classic example, including all kinds of prohibitions not found in the Bible. The rabbis identified thirty-nine categories of labor within the Bible's prohibition against work, including activities such as writing two letters or even erasing in order to write two letters. They regulated with great precision what objects could be handled or carried during the Sabbath, how food was to be prepared, even what kind of shoes one could wear (e.g., sandals with nails protruding from the soles were forbidden). Some of these rules could be derived from or connected to specific biblical verses, but many could not. In a famous rabbinic simile recorded in *Hagigah* 10a, the many laws pertaining to the Sabbath are likened to mountains suspended by a hair—that is, they are based on very little scriptural support; in truth, their source was not the Written Torah but, rather, the Oral Torah, the tradition generated through rabbinic teaching and argument.

Many rabbinic sources stress Torah study as an ideal to which all Jews should aspire, but in practice, only a very few sages were able to pursue this ideal. It was very difficult for someone who was poor to leave his family and livelihood for a life of study. In a very real sense, the culture we have been describing here was limited in late antiquity to a small and highly insulated group of intellectuals who seem to have disdained Jews outside their circle, the *am ha'aretz* or "people of the land," defined by their lack of Torah study. But the rabbis also aimed to influence the larger community, and this they achieved as the rabbinic literature that recorded their teachings and deeds, especially the Mishnah and the

Babylonian Talmud, became part of the Jewish canon. This chapter concludes with one example of that influence: how the rabbinization of Jewish culture transformed Jewish worship.

The earliest rabbis, like other Jews, were attached to the Temple, preserving the memory of how the sacrifices and other Temple customs were practiced (entire tractates of the Mishnah are devoted to this topic) in the hope that its restoration would come soon. The Temple remained a model of worship, the rabbis incorporating some of its practices into their post-Temple practice. Believing that Jews should worship God every day, the rabbis tied the timing of their three daily prayers to the timing of the daily sacrifices in the Temple. They also continued liturgical practices taken from the Temple (e.g., the use of "Amen" as a response), showed deference to priests and Levites (though worship was now a communal undertaking, not a duty delegated to Temple officials), and required those engaged in prayer to face in the direction of the Temple.

Eventually, however, rabbinic Judaism developed a distinctly new understanding of worship that reinterpreted Judaism's sacrificial cult in light of the Temple's absence and their own scholarly values. In the rabbinic reformulation of Passover, for example, no Passover sacrifice is made, and the Passover meal, following a fixed "order" (*seder*) of practices, is transformed into a kind of study session. In lieu of the Temple, the rabbis accepted the synagogue as the main setting for communal worship, and they developed various cultic substitutes—study, prayer, deeds of loving-kindness—that allowed Jews to sustain their relationship with God without sacrifice or the priesthood.

While rabbis expressed very precise views about what should happen in the synagogue, however, their discussion seems to have been largely academic, with little discernible impact on the outside community so far as one can tell from synagogue art and other evidence for actual Jewish religious practice in late antiquity. Rabbinic literature acknowledges that synagogue prayer often did not follow the rabbis' prescriptions. Today, rabbis function as religious leaders in the synagogue, but they did not begin to play this role until the Middle Ages. When rabbinic literature was canonized during the Geonic period, however, so too were rabbinic practices. Citing earlier rabbinic tradition as their authority, the Geonic sages developed and canonized the first Jewish prayer book that fixed the wording and sequence of the synagogue prayer service (though much variation in worship practice remained in communities outside the Islamic world, beyond the Geonic orbit). It was in this period that the rabbinic script for commemorating the Exodus during Passover, the Haggadah, was canonized as well. Through Geonic influence, in other words, the rabbinic understanding of how to worship God became the normative Jewish way of worshipping God, establishing the wording of the fixed prayers to be recited three times a day, the blessings recited before and after meals in gratitude to God, the ritualized procedures for the public reading of biblical books in the synagogue, how Jews atone for sin on Yom Kippur, and so on.

We must here be careful not to project rabbinic Judaism as it developed in later periods onto late antiquity. Many practices and beliefs that are now part of rabbinic tradition—for example, the requirement to cover one's head with a *kippah* (a small cap) as a sign of humility before God, the bar mitzvah, and the practice of reciting the Kaddish prayer for the dead—were only developed in the medieval or early modern periods. But the fact that Jews who observe these practices understand them as part of rabbinic tradition, tracing their behavior back to precedents and prescriptions of the Mishnah and Talmud, is itself evidence of this tradition's impact. However little influence they had in their own day, the rabbis of late antiquity, through the legacy of the literature that records their words and deeds, initiated a nearly universal transformation of Jewish culture, radically redefining the contents of Jewish tradition even as they labored to perpetuate it.

TEN USEFUL RABBINIC TERMS

Aggada. Often defined in contrast with *halacha, aggada* describes nonlegal material in rabbinic literature—stories about the biblical past or the rabbis themselves, wise sayings, homilies, and so forth. The term should not be confused with the similar sounding *Haggadah,* the rabbinic liturgical text recited during the Passover meal.

Amora/Amoraim. From an Aramaic word that means "discussers," the term *Amoraim* refers to the rabbinic sages of the post-Mishnaic era whose teachings are gathered in the two Talmuds.

Bet Midrash. The *bet midrash* or study house was the major setting of rabbinic activity. Another term used for such study centers was the Hebrew **yeshiva,** or its Aramaic equivalent *metivta,* originally a term for the rabbinic court but in Babylonia coming to signify a place of study. Early rabbinic "schools" were not like schools or academies in contemporary Western culture—they were not associated with buildings but were based on a personal apprenticelike relationship between the teacher and student. By the post-Talmudic era in Babylonia, however, the rabbinic school had become much more institutionalized, developing fixed curricula and distinctive academic customs.

Halakha. The rabbinic term for the laws that govern Jewish life and the principal focus of the Mishnah and the Talmuds.

Midrash. The Hebrew term used to describe the specifically rabbinic mode of biblical interpretation, Midrash is also used to describe collections of rabbinic interpretation developed in Palestine between, roughly, 200–1200 CE. Following the order in which they are believed to have been composed, these include *Sifra* (a midrashic collection focused on Leviticus), *Mekhilta* (covering parts of Exodus), *Sifre Numbers* and *Sifre Deuteronomy* (covering the Torah's last two books), *Genesis Rabba* (a collection of midrashic explanations of Genesis), *Leviticus Rabbah* (a collection of rabbinic sermons loosely connected to the book of Leviticus), and *Pesiqta deRab Kahana* (organized around the biblical readings for the festivals and special Sabbaths), among other compilations.

Mishnah. The earliest major rabbinic work and the core of the rabbinic canon. (Also used for a paragraph within that larger work.)

Rabbi. Derived from a Hebrew word meaning "great," *rabbi* is the title used for the sages of rabbinic literature. In rabbinic literature, the title is bestowed only on those thought to have been properly ordained. In Talmudic times, such ordination could only take place within the land of Palestine. Hence, the Amoraic sages of the Babylonian title are known by a different title: *rav.*

Talmud. A tradition of commentary and argumentation organized in response to the Mishnah (or in response to earlier responses to the Mishnah). *Talmud* can refer to just this commentary, also known as the Gemara, or to the combination of the Mishnah and the Gemara. Two works are known as the Talmud: the Palestinian or Jerusalem Talmud, which was eclipsed by the later and more elaborate Babylonian Talmud.

Tanna/Tannaim. From an Aramaic word that means "repeater," the term *tannaim* refers to the rabbinic sages whose teachings and rulings are assembled in the Mishnah.

Tosefta. A collection of early rabbinic traditions similar to the Mishnah but containing much material the Mishnah does not include. The Tosefta does not enjoy the religious authority that the Mishnah does.

Questions for Reflection

1. What connects the rabbinic movement to the Pharisees? How were the rabbis different from the Pharisees?

2. When and how did the rabbis begin to exert an impact on the larger Jewish culture?

3. How and why did the center of rabbinic culture shift to Babylonia? How is Babylonian rabbinic culture different from Palestinian rabbinic culture?

4. How is the rabbinic concept of Torah different from that of earlier Jews, such as the members of the Dead Sea Scrolls Sect and Paul?

5. The following photo shows a boy putting on *tefillin* during a bar mitzvah ceremony. What about this boy's religious behavior is pre-rabbinic in origin? What about it postdates the rabbis of the Talmud?

Putting on *tefillin* during a bar mitzvah.

For Further Reading

Because rabbinic literature is so vast, and its usefulness as a historical source so vexed, it is harder to find readable surveys of rabbinic history than for biblical history. Still, good introductions are available. See Shaye Cohen, *From the Maccabees to the Mishnah* (Philadelphia: Westminster, 1987); Lawrence Schiffman, *From Text to Tradition: A History of Second Temple and Rabbinic Judaism* (Hoboken, NJ: Ktav Publishing, 1991); Hershel Shanks, ed., *Christianity and Rabbinic Judaism: a Parallel History of Their*

Origins and Development (Washington, DC: Biblical Archaeology Society, 1992); and for more detail, Steven Katz, *Cambridge History of Judaism, Volume 4, The Late Roman–Rabbinic Period* (Cambridge, England: Cambridge University Press, 2006).

For a sense of the wider religious context, see Peter Brown's classic, *The World of Late Antiquity AD 150–750* (New York: Harcourt Brace Jovanovich, 1971).

Moving from Jewish history to Jewish culture in this period, for the history of the synagogue, see Lee Levine, *The Ancient Synagogue: The First Thousand Years* (New Haven and London: Yale University Press, 2000). For the history of Jewish prayer, see Stephen Reif, *Judaism and Hebrew Prayer: New Perspectives on Jewish Liturgical History* (Cambridge, England: Cambridge University Press, 1993). Rabbinic thought is not easy to summarize, and indeed it is misleading to do so since rabbinic literature is not interested in formulating authoritative theological doctrines. For a synthesis of the evidence, however, see E. Urbach, *The Sages: Their Concepts and Beliefs,* 2 vols., (Jerusalem: Magnes Press, 1965). For an introduction to how to read rabbinic texts, see Barry Holtz, ed., *Back to the Sources: Reading the Classic Jewish Texts* (New York: Simon and Schuster, 1984), 129–211, which includes recommendations for further reading.

Chapter 6

Under the Crescent

Two major historical developments, the collapse of the Roman Empire and the rise of Islam, were especially important for the transition of Jewish history beyond late antiquity and into the Middle Ages.

The fragmentation and reconfiguration of the Roman Empire changed the face of Europe. In 286 CE, the emperor Diocletian divided the empire into western and eastern halves, a division that eventually became permanent. Collapsing under pressure from the "barbarian" invasion of Germanic tribes, Slavs, and other non Greco–Roman peoples, the Western Roman Empire persisted until the fifth century CE, when the last emperor of Rome, Romulus Augustulus, was deposed and exiled in 476 CE.

The fall of the Western Roman Empire is one conventional starting point for the Middle Ages. The Catholic Church and its bishops, preserving a tradition of Latin learning, provided some cultural and administrative coherency, but the economy and political structure of Europe became much less centralized, with various dynasties and kingdoms (some claiming to revive the Christian Roman Empire) arising in the vacuum. Eventually, dynastic kingdoms emerged that would become England, France, and other European nation-states that are known today.

In the Greek-speaking east, the Eastern Roman Empire eventually became what is known as the **Byzantine Empire.** When to date this transformation is a matter of debate, but it is associated with two specific events: the move in 330 CE of the capital of the Roman Empire by the emperor Constantine from Rome to the newly named Constantinople (also known as Byzantium and renamed Istanbul in 1930), and the emergence of Christianity later in that century as the official religion of the empire (the "orthodox" Greek-based Christianity of the Byzantine Empire would develop very differently from the "Catholic" Latin based Christianity of the Roman west). The Byzantine Empire would last in one form or another until the fall of **Constantinople** in 1453 to the Ottoman Turks.

The second major development was the rise of **Islam.** Its founder, **Muhammad,** was born in 570 CE in the Arabian city of Mecca. Muslims believe that Muhammad was a prophet, indeed the last of the prophets, to whom God or Allah revealed a series of revelations now recorded in the **Koran.** Within a few years, Muhammad began to attract large numbers of followers before his death in 632. The leaders who succeeded him, known by the title of **caliph** from the Arabic for "successor," would continue to expand the community, winning over vast numbers of converts and quickly conquering large stretches of territory. Islam soon took over the Arabian peninsula, then defeated the Sassanian kingdom in Persia, pushed up against the Byzantine Empire, and, within a century, successfully expanded into the Near East, North Africa, and even southern Europe. The use of Arabic expanded with Islam, eclipsing localized languages, as well as Aramaic and Greek—the most widely used languages in the Middle East until this time.

The transition from antiquity to the Middle Ages in the broader world of the Mediterranean and the Near East roughly corresponds to major social and cultural changes happening within the Jewish world. As we noted in the Chapter 5, one of the most striking differences from late antique Jewish culture was the impact of rabbinic literature on Jewish life: it had now become central to the Jewish scriptural canon. As interpreted and expanded upon in this period, rabbinic texts and their influence came to reshape Jewish culture, with Jews now looking to the Mishnah and Talmud as a source of juridical, religious, and legal authority. The political and scholarly class most directly associated with this change were the Geonim (sing. Gaon), introduced in Chapter 5. Emerging in the wake of the completion of the Babylonian Talmud, the Geonim presided over Jewish academies in the environs of Baghdad and in Tiberias. They began the project of applying the rabbinic and biblical corpuses to their world; they wrote about, cited, emended, and revitalized the older works in accord with the demands of their times. With the rise of Islam—an event that unified much of the Near East, North Africa, and southern Europe politically, socially, and linguistically—the Geonim were able to extend their influence beyond their academies in Babylonia and Palestine into much of the rest of the Jewish world.

Determining the end point of the Jewish Middle Ages is a more difficult challenge—historical periodization is always artificial to some extent—but here too it roughly corresponds to what was happening in the larger world. A key turning point is 1492, the date of Columbus' famous journey to the Western Hemisphere, for that same year witnessed one of the great catastrophes of Jewish history: the expulsion of the Jews from Spain. While the largest, it was also just the last of a series of expulsions between 1290 and 1492 that drove the Jews from western Europe. Spanish Jewry was dispersed throughout much of the known world, reconfiguring the demography of the Jews in the eastern Mediterranean, and later, eastern Europe, as well as the New World. In the same period, the European world underwent profound political and cultural changes associated with the Renaissance, which also had a transformative impact on Jewish culture in parts of Europe. In Italy, for example, within a quarter century of the expulsion, the concept of the *ghetto* was born, transforming the nature of Jewish urban life.

Defined in this way, the Jewish Middle Ages is a conspicuously long period. What is more, it unfolds over a very broad stage in multiple geographic settings. Jews found themselves dispersed throughout much of the known world—in Europe, Asia, Africa, Persia, and India—and they were divided from one another by both political and religious boundaries. Some lived under Christian rule in Europe and the Byzantine Empire, while others lived under Islamic rule. Some communities used Aramaic; others Arabic; still others, Greek, Persian, Romance languages, and Yiddish. The culture of these widely scattered communities diverged in many ways, and yet we believe it legitimate to think of them all as part of one Jewish culture, if only because, while Jews in this period recognized the differences among themselves and sometimes argued over them quite bitterly, they nevertheless saw themselves as a single community with a shared destiny.

One of the most significant aspects of this shared identity was a deep commitment to the biblical canon and a profound engagement in, if not uniform reverence for, the rabbinic literature of late antiquity: the Mishnah and the Talmud. The preoccupation with the Mishnah and Talmud generated whole new genres of rabbinic literature in the Middle Ages, in fact, all serving in one way or another to explain or develop the contents of the rabbinic canon: (1) **responsa,** or letters written by rabbis in response to specific legal questions posed by constituents;

(2) **codes,** in which ambitious rabbinic thinkers sought to organize, epitomize, and clarify law for daily use; (3) **digests,** compilations of legal positions that were not systematically organized; and **commentaries,** in which scholars interpreted and explained biblical and rabbinic texts. Many of these works enjoyed a vast readership that extended from the Atlantic to the Indian Ocean and, as such, helped generate cohesion among widely scattered Jewish communities.

Another thread connecting diverse Jewish communities to one another was a linguistic one. The Hebrew language enjoyed special distinction as a universal pillar of Jewish life and religion in the Middle Ages. To be sure, many Jewish men knew only rudimentary Hebrew, and for them the language served first and foremost as a language of prayer. In addition, as far as we can tell, very few women knew Hebrew. Nonetheless, Hebrew was not merely a language of worship; it also served as a *lingua franca* (a common language) for Jews from different lands who did not share a common vernacular; a legal language; a business language; a philosophical language; and as a scholarly language by which interpreters decoded the more difficult, ancient Hebrew of the Bible and the Talmud. In all these vital functions, Hebrew (and, to a lesser degree, Aramaic) served to keep far-flung Jews in contact with one another and their predecessors while at the same time distinguishing them from non-Jews. It is also true that Jews by and large adopted the languages of the societies in which they lived, though they tended to Judaize those languages. In Spain, Jews spoke a form of Aragonese, Castilian, or Arabic (depending on the reigning language in a given region) very close to that of the majority culture, while in Germany, and later in eastern Europe, Jews developed a completely independent language, Yiddish, by combining German, Hebrew, and Aramaic. Even in this linguistic diversity, however, one can still discern Hebrew's presence in the culture. Jews introduced Hebrew words or phrases into these dialects and languages, and when they wrote down these languages, they used the Hebrew alphabet.

Yet another common denominator among many Jews was a shared attachment to the Land of Israel (also called Palestine, after the Roman name for the province). Like the Jewish reverence for Hebrew, the sense of attachment to the Land of Israel owed its inspiration to the Bible. But unlike the Hebrew language, which served a practical function, the Land of Israel served more symbolically as a common point of spiritual orientation and eschatological aspiration. Some medieval Jews did travel to the Holy Land, some were buried there, and an important Jewish community persisted there as well, but for most Jews in this period Palestine was a place that existed in their imagination, the focal point of long-held hopes for a return to the Land of Israel in the messianic age. Even so, it functioned as an important unifying factor, its evocation in prayer and poetry reminding Jews around the world of their common geographical and cultural point of origin.

For all these reasons, we can legitimately think of medieval Jewish culture as one that transcended the political and religious boundaries of the Christian and Islamic worlds. Yet at the same time, those boundaries were real, introducing important social, cultural, and linguistic differences between the Jewish communities of each realm. Indeed, as the Christian and Islamic worlds broke into smaller empires or kingdoms, the Jewish community became correspondingly more diffuse and diversified. The major development occurred when the eastern Geonic capitals of Babylonia and Palestine gave way to western centers of learning in Europe and North Africa in the tenth and eleventh centuries. Whereas the primary point of distinction among Jews in the early Middle Ages had either been their relationship to rabbinic tradition (Palestinian, Babylonian, or nonrabbinic) or the political–religious context in which they lived (Christian or Muslim), the diffusion of Jewish communities and growth of local traditions after the tenth century saw a relative proliferation of Jewish identities: Jews defined themselves as Spanish, French, Provençal (southern French), Italian, German, Greek (also called Roman), Egyptian, Palestinian, Iraqi, and so on.

Connected with this greater cultural diversity was a greater assertiveness by local Jewish communities and individual rabbinic scholars. Cities in Islamic North Africa, Spain, and Christian Europe developed into autonomous seats of rabbinic authority, economic activity, and social interaction. Sages from these places—figures such as the famous Jewish philosopher Maimonides, for example—were correspondingly confident and self-directed, willing to act and think independently of the centralized Geonic authorities. We do not want to draw too neat a picture, but it does seem reasonable to observe that the fragmentation of Islamic and Christian rule was mirrored to some extent in a corresponding fragmentation of Jewish communal, religious, and intellectual authority.

What follows is an attempt to trace the overlapping but distinct trajectories of Jewish culture as it developed in the Islamic and Christian realms of the medieval world. The history of each realm intersects with the other at a number of points, with whole regions moving from one realm to the other—including, among others, Palestine, Spain, and Anatolia in present-day Turkey—but they are distinct enough that they justify two discrete narratives. We begin in the present chapter with the history of Jewish life under Islamic rule and then turn our attention in Chapter 7 to Christian Europe.

Jewish History in the Islamic Middle Ages

In the Islamic world (in Arabic, *dar al-Islam*), Jews lived in the vast area from Spain and Morocco in the west, to Persia in the east—and even beyond, into India and China. The language of most of these Jews was Arabic, though a significant population spoke Persian and, to a lesser degree, other local languages. Throughout the Middle Ages, the Jews of Islam represented the great majority of the world's Jewish population—by some estimates up to 90 percent. This balance shifted somewhat only toward the end of the period, as Christian Europe expanded more and more into Spain and other areas under Islamic rule. To understand medieval Jewish history and culture, therefore, requires an understanding of the history of the Islamic world.

Muhammad and the Jews

Islam was founded in the seventh century by the prophet Muhammad. In 622, Muhammad abandoned his hometown Mecca and fled to Medina, where he established the first Muslim community—an event that marks the beginning of the Islamic era. Documents concerning the early prophetic career of Muhammad do not allow historians a clear-cut understanding of the role of Jews in Muhammad's early Muslim society in Medina. It is clear, however, that when Muhammad fled to Medina, he found powerful Jewish clans living there. In the course of a series of negotiations and conflicts with them, Muslims came to understand that they shared monotheistic beliefs with the Jews. The so-called "Constitution of Medina," in which the Muslim community established a treaty with local Jewish tribes, even leaves open the possibility that the Jews might be considered part of the larger Muslim political community. According to this early document, the Muslims ("Believers") promise that "The Jews who follow us get help and equality. . . . The Jews of the Banu 'Auf are one community with the Believers. The Jews have their laws and the Muslims have their laws."

Despite this effort at coexistence, local politics in Medina, probably more than theological issues, pitted some prominent Jewish tribes against Muhammad. When he arrived in the city in 622, a civil war was underway and fragile alliances once formed, were easily broken. Under these conditions, the achievement of a new social order was extremely difficult, and some Jewish tribes, wishing a return to the status quo ante, refused to ally themselves with Muhammad. Some Jewish tribes aligned themselves with non-Jewish forces from both Mecca and Medina to dislodge and even kill Muhammad. Many lost their lives in the battles. Muhammad exiled two of the tribes, the Banu Nadir and the Banu Qaynuqa, while other Jewish clans signed pacts with Muslims and continued to live in peace in Medina long after it became the Muslim capital of Arabia. Another Jewish tribe, the Banu Qurayza, refused to ally itself with Muhammad and, according to Muslim sources, seven hundred of its men were executed—a measure in keeping with contemporary military practice. Reflecting this complicated political reality, the Koran records a kind of ambivalence toward the Jews, sometimes reaching out to them in a conciliatory way, sometimes condemning them (*see box,* The Koran and the Jews). Eventually, as the Muslim community took shape, a balance was reached; Islam recognized the basic right of Jews and other subject groups to live in Muslim society—but only under certain conditions, most especially that they accept their basic subordination to Muslim rule.

The Legal Basis of Jewish Life Under Islam

The rights and obligations of these religions were outlined in a document called the **Pact of Umar,** traditionally attributed to Caliph Umar (r. 633–644), the second caliph, though the earliest extant version of the text we have dates from the tenth century. The pact has the form of a letter from the Christian community to their new Muslim overlords in which the Christians promise "we shall not build in our cities or in their vicinity any new monasteries, churches . . . we shall not hold public religious ceremonies . . . we shall not attempt to resemble the Muslims in any way with regard to their dress . . . we shall not ride on saddles; . . . we will not strike a Muslim" in exchange for living in peace under Islam. After the death of Muhammad, the extraordinary growth of Islam in Syria, Palestine, Iraq, Persia, and Arabia engulfed large Jewish communities, and they too came under the terms of this pact. The non-Muslim parties to this pact, including the Jews, go by the name of ***dhimmi,*** or "protected peoples." Dhimmis may live in security within Islam, but they must obey the restrictions imposed by the Pact of Umar and pay a yearly tribute called the ***jizya,*** which was designed to demonstrate their acknowledgement of Muslim overlordship. Jews were not allowed to hold public office (frequently an ignored stipulation), since this would place them in a position of authority over Muslims, nor were they allowed to build their homes higher than the homes of the Muslims.

The Pact of Umar defined the theoretical and legal foundation of Jewish life under Muslim rule, from the beginnings of the Islamic state through the nineteenth century. It is true, of course, that its stipulations were often enough ignored—synagogues and churches, for example, went up centuries after the Muslim conquests despite the prohibitions spelled out in the Pact of Umar. It is also worth noting that the Pact of Umar may be as remarkable for the restrictions it did not impose as for those it did, for it did not restrict the economic activities or the professions that a Jew or Christian could exercise, nor did it limit their freedom of residence and travel.

On the surface, the status of the *dhimmi* seems similar to the role imposed on Jews in Christian realms: the Jewish community was permitted to exist but only in subjugation. In fact, it is likely that some of the Muslim laws regarding the *dhimmi* were inspired by Byzantine legislation about the Jews, including the prohibition (in principle, though not necessarily in practice) of building new synagogues. However, differences in the status of the Jews within the two religious realms were significant. For the Christians, the subjugation of the Jews, formalized with the passage of the Theodosian Code (438), was partly rooted in frustration with the role of the Jews in the early history of the Christian religion. Jews such as Jesus and Paul figured prominently in the Christian story, but many Jews had resisted their message. Christians blamed the Jews for the death of Jesus and saw their persistence as a counterclaim to Christian belief. By contrast, while Islam also had a stake in the conversion of the Jews, this reflected Islam's attitude toward all peoples; Islam was not rooted in the same kind of theological conflict with Judaism that Christianity was, and Islamic rule did not have the same negative connotation for Jews that Roman rule did. For the Muslims, the Jews belonged to a larger generic category, the *dhimmi,* that included a much bigger and more politically threatening community of Christians, whereas for European Christians, Jews were the most prominent nonchristian other.

Also easing Jewish–Muslim interaction was widespread Jewish adoption of Arabic language and culture. Jews adopted Arabic as their own vernacular and literary language, even developing a Jewish dialect now known as Judeo–Arabic that employed the Hebrew alphabet and loanwords. In the Christian world, while Jews also adapted the local vernacular, they never wrote in Latin, which was the language of religious tradition and intellectual activity

THE KORAN AND THE JEWS

Muhammad, the prophet of Islam, experienced his first revelation when he was around forty years old. The holy Scripture of Islam, the Koran, was not revealed in one single instance but rather in portions throughout the prophet's lifetime, from around 611 until his death in 632. A chapter in the Koran is called a *sura;* when the text of the Koran was standardized, the individual chapters were arranged according to their length, with the second *sura* being the longest one and the shortest chapter appearing at the end (the first chapter, a brief statement of the main Muslim credo in the unity of God, is an exception). Being revealed over two decades, the individual portions of the Koranic text often respond directly to actual historical events, and thus the pronouncements dealing with Jews (and Christians) that one finds in the Koran need to be understood as a response to Muhammad's own encounter with the Jews of Arabia.

In 628, the Muslims of Medina defeated the Jews living in the nearby oasis of Khaybar, a battle that ended with the surrender of the Jews who were granted protection of life and property in exchange for paying an annual tribute to the Muslims. This became an important precedent for the Muslim treatment of Christians and Jews in territories that were conquered by the expanding Islamic empire, and it was duly confirmed in the following Koranic passage revealed after the battle of Khaybar:

> Fight against those to whom the Scriptures were given, who believe not in Allah nor in the Last Day, who forbid not what Allah and his messenger have forbidden, and follow not the true faith, until they pay the tribute out of hand, and are humbled." (Sura 9:29)

This is the classical prooftext in Islamic law establishing the basis for the interaction between Muslims and the so-called "People of the Book," namely Jews and Christians who possessed their own divine revelation (the Torah or the New Testament, respectively) and were thus in a different category than were the pagans. Jews and Christians were expected to pay a special tax (the poll tax, or *jizya*) and recognize the superiority of the new Islamic order in exchange for being granted toleration and protection. In fact, the Koran mandated the political expansion of the Muslim state, but it prohibited the use of force to spread the new religion: "There is no compulsion in religion," as the Koran declares (Sura 2:256).

Some passages in the Koran display a rather positive attitude toward the Jews and Christians and seem to express an early expectation that the Jews of Medina, Muhammad's residence after leaving his native Mecca in 622, may be drawn to the new religion. Consider the following:

> Children of Israel, remember the favor I have bestowed upon you. Keep your covenant, and I will be true to Mine. Dread My power. Have faith in My revelations, which confirm your Scriptures, and do not be the first to deny them. (Sura 2:40–41)

In fact, Jews, Christians, and a somewhat mysterious group referred to as "Sabeans" were reassured in the Koran:

> Believers, Jews, Christians, and Sabeans—whoever believes in God and the Last Day and does what is right—shall be rewarded by their Lord; they have nothing to fear or to regret." (Sura 2:62)

But it soon became clear that the Jews rejected Muhammad's claims as a prophet, and relations in Medina deteriorated quickly. Other passages in the Koran reflect the tensions which emerged at the time:

> O you who believe! Take not the Jews and Christians as friends. They are friends to one another. Whoever of you befriends them is one of them. Allah does not guide the people who do evil." (Sura 5:51)

Another passage singles out the Jews, no doubt because of the political rivalry between the early Muslims and the Jews of Medina and Khaybar who were accused of conspiring against Muhammad with the pagan inhabitants of Mecca:

> You will find that the most implacable of men in their enmity to the faithful are the Jews and the pagans, and that the nearest in affection to them [the Muslims] are those who say: "We are Christians." That is because there are priests and monks among them; and because they are free from pride. (Sura 5:82)

The attitudes toward Jews and Christians in the Koran are thus ambiguous: on the one hand, those traditions were recognized as legitimate religions based on earlier divine revelations; at the same time, the Koran accused Jews and Christians of having tampered with God's word, and political tensions between the groups led to some clearly hostile statements, in particular against the Jews. Overall, however, it was the Koranic mandate for tolerating the "People of the Book" in exchange for payment of the *jizya* and acceptance of an inferior social status that shaped Muslim–Jewish relations throughout the Middle Ages.

in Western Christendom. (The situation was different for the Jews of Byzantium, who did, however, speak and write in Greek.) Arabic, sometimes even more than Hebrew, became the language of Jewish thought, philosophy, and literature for Jews in the Islamic world. For all these reasons, Jewish history under Islamic rule almost inevitably has a more positive cast than it has under Christian rule. Though serious persecutions were conducted under Islamic rule as well, and though the Jews did suffer very real social and political disadvantages, scholars writing about Jewish history under medieval Islam often tend to focus on signs of cultural flourishing in contrast to Jewish experience in Christian Europe.

Jews lived in both the countryside and the cities of the Islamic world, but the city takes center stage in modern understandings of this period, in part because cities were the center of the kind of intellectual, literary, political, and economic activity that leaves a written record. Some cities stand out as especially important for Jewish history. First and foremost, **Baghdad,** the home of the great Talmudic academies, dominated the Jewish world of religion and law from roughly the seventh to the eleventh centuries, under the leadership of the Geonim. Competing for the status as heir to the ancient rabbis, the Land of Israel boasted **Tiberias,** where the Masoretes and the Palestinian Geonate had their academies, and Jerusalem, where the Geonic academy moved and where the Karaites established themselves as a counterweight to Geonic power. In the tenth century, **Cairo** became the capital of the Fatimid caliphate, which extended from Tunisia in the west all the way to Palestine and Syria in the east. We know as much as we do about its community because of the remarkable discovery of the documents hidden in the Cairo Genizah, an unparalleled source for understanding medieval Jewish life (*see box,* The Cairo Genizah). Ultimately, the most significant challenge to the Geonic supremacy of Baghdad, however, did not come from Palestine or Egypt, but from Muslim Spain—specifically from the city of **Cordoba,** which attracted the Jewish world's leading intellectuals. Individually, each of these cities developed its own Jewish intellectual culture, but all were also part of a larger network of personal, economic, and cultural contact, helping to create something of a common Jewish culture across the broad expanse of Islamic rule.

The Umayyad Caliphate and the Expansion of Muslim Rule

Within a very short time following Muhammad's death in 632, Mu'awiyya, the fifth caliph (as a "successor" to Muhammad, the caliph was the religious–political leader of the Muslim community), established the first caliphal dynasty, called the **Umayyad Caliphate,** which lasted from 661 to 750. From their capital in Damascus, Syria, the Umayyad caliphs extended Islam over a vast region from Afghanistan to Spain, almost all of which (with the notable exception of Spain) remains predominantly Muslim to this day. The expansion of Islam under the Umayyads arguably triggered the most fundamental change in Jewish culture since the destruction of the Second Temple in 70 CE, but our picture of Jewish life in this period is very hazy, largely because we know so little about history in general in this formative period of Islamic expansion.

One thing we do know is that, from the outset, Muslim–Christian relations were marked by political rivalry. In the eighth century, the Muslims attempted, unsuccessfully, to capture Constantinople, succeeded in capturing Spain, and were only stopped from reaching farther into Europe by the French monarch, Charles Martel, who at the Battle of Tours in 732 held them south of the Pyrenees. By this point, Muslim and Christian society faced each other as two superpowers, with a dynamic Islam having conquered roughly half of the Roman Empire within less than a century. The Jews under Islamic rule were something of a third party to this standoff, not directly embroiled in the larger political and religious conflict but with much to gain from Islamic rule. Very early on in their conquest, in 634, when the Muslims captured Palestine from the Byzantine Empire, they found there a Jewish population greatly discontented with Roman–Christian rule and willing to deal with the Muslims. In North Africa, also formerly part of the Roman Empire, the Muslims also found Jewish communities beleaguered by religious persecution and ready for a change. In 642, Iraq fell to the Muslims. The rest of the Persian Empire would follow soon, bringing with it a large Jewish population and, with the Babylonian academies, the center of Geonic intellectual and religious authority. Though one can assume that some number of Jews converted to the new faith of Muhammad, large and prosperous Jewish communities throughout the Muslim world were able to sustain their Jewish identity in relatively receptive conditions. In a world where subjugated minorities did not expect equal rights, Islam provided a refuge from the hostility, social barriers, and legal discrimination that Jewish communities had faced under Christian rule.

The Umayyads went on to capture Spain in 711, and there too it is believed they were welcomed by a Jewish population suffering from persecution. In Spain as throughout Europe, Germanic tribes had replaced the Roman government more than two centuries before Islam's arrival, and the Visigoths, the Germanic tribe that occupied most of the

THE CAIRO GENIZAH

The documents found in the Cairo Genizah are the most important source of information for the economic and social lives of the Jews in the Middle Ages. A common feature in Jewish institutions even today, a *genizah* is a document repository that serves a very particular purpose. When Scripture and other sacred writings age to the point of disuse, Jews do not treat them as they would normal trash; rather, such texts are buried in consecrated ground. Since it is inefficient to prepare a hole in the ground for every old document and book, a *genizah* is used as a holding pen. There the documents sit until enough books and writings accumulate, later to be buried all at once.

Such was the case of the *genizah* in the Palestinian synagogue of Old Cairo—with one very important difference: this synagogue boasted a particularly large *genizah,* which had gone for centuries without anyone ever cleaning out the books for burial. In it lay thousands of books and documents from ages past, preserved by the same dry heat that safeguarded Egyptian mummies for millennia.

In the mid-nineteenth century, a scholar named Abraham Firkovitch began to mine the Cairo Genizah (frequently referred to simply as "the Genizah") for books and documents, which he took back with him to his native Russia. There, in St. Petersburg, remains the largest collection from this remarkable cache. Firkovitch did not publicize the provenance of his finds, however, and he left much behind.

Only later in the same century did Solomon Schechter, a Talmud scholar in Cambridge, England (and later president of the Jewish Theological Seminary of America in New York), publicly discover the contents of the Genizah. Two Scottish women had traveled to Egypt and brought back with them the Hebrew text of the apocryphal book Ecclesiasticus (known in Hebrew as Ben Sira) which had been known until then only in Greek. Following the scent of this extraordinary discovery, Schechter found the treasures of the Cairo Genizah and systematically removed them. He brought thousands of pages back to Cambridge, and there he assembled an enormous collection of Judeo–Arabic and Hebrew documents, such as letters, contracts, bills of sale, wills, and literature.

These documents, dating from the tenth to the twelfth centuries, have revolutionized not only medieval Jewish history but also the history of the region in general, by virtue of their astounding wealth of information about daily life, commerce, marriage, and Muslim–Jewish relations, to name only a few topics. Today, historians from many areas of specialization rely on the Cairo Genizah for a window into the Mediterranean world of one thousand years ago.

Iberian Peninsula, beginning in the early seventh century had taken a decidedly hostile approach to the Jews, imposing economic and social restrictions. Perhaps the legends that Spain's Jews gave aid to the Muslim invaders bear some truth. Spain would go on to hold a special place in the history of the Jews, though for some centuries to come it remained very peripheral to a Jewish–Islamic world centered in Baghdad.

In the year 750, the Umayyads fell to the Abbassids, a rival dynasty who, in their bid for power, almost exterminated the Umayyad ruling clan. The new Abbassid rulers removed the caliphate from Damascus to Baghdad, and with that move they realigned the political geography of the Middle East (*see* Map 6-1). From the point of view of Jewish history, this move had the effect of further strengthening the authority of the Geonim in Babylonia/Baghdad. Though the Geonic office predated the Abbassid revolution, it is really only after the caliphate's move to Baghdad that we begin to see individual Geonic leaders exerting far-reaching influence over Jewish life. In that sense, the beginning of the Abbassid period initiates a distinct phase of Jewish history in the Islamic realm.

Abbassid Rule and the Rise and Fall of Geonic Authority

The **Abbassid dynasty** remained the most widely recognized caliphate in Islam (though not the only one) until 1258, when Mongol invaders effectively destroyed it. At the heart of the Jewish world for much of this period were the

An autograph page of Maimonides' *Guide for the Perplexed,* found in the Cairo Genizah.

The Dome of the Rock in Jerusalem, built under the Umayyad caliph Abd al Malik ibn Marwan (r. 685–705) on the site of the Temple. Jerusalem achieved a status of religious significance in Islam and became a major pilgrimage destination for Muslims as much as it was for Jews and Christians.

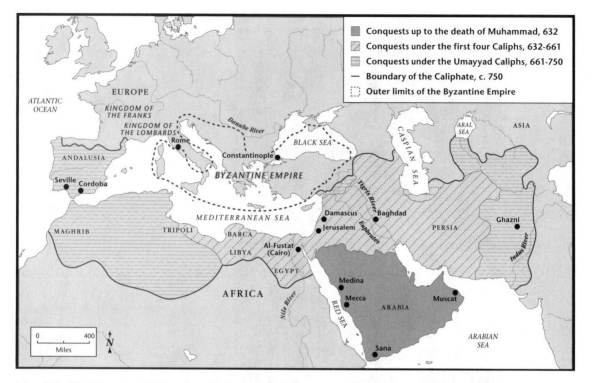

Map 6-1   The Expansion of Islam, from Muhammad to the beginning of the Abbassid caliphate (750).

Geonim of Babylonia, whom we introduced in Chapter 5. In their role as heads of the Talmudic academies in **Sura** and **Pumbedita,** located not far from Baghdad, the Geonim administered the training grounds for the intellectual elite that would dominate Jewish jurisprudence. Twice a year, in late winter and late summer, the academies hosted *kallot* ("gatherings," sing. *kallah*), in which scholars arrived from far and wide, bringing donations from their home communities. At these *kallot,* the Geonim did not necessarily teach all these students directly; rather, their leadership lent prestige to the academies where they studied. The Geonim also spearheaded fund-raising for the schools—an essential function for their maintenance and for the granting of scholarships—and composed influential treatises of case law, by means of which the highly theoretical conversations and disputes of the Talmud took on real-world implications for contemporary life.

The Geonic practice of writing responsa (sing. *responsum*) was perhaps the most important way in which the Gaon exerted his authority across a great geographic expanse. The responsum was a method of justice-by-correspondence, in which a given Gaon wrote out a judicial opinion in response to a specific legal inquiry and thereby established a

legal precedent to which subsequent legal scholars might refer. The responsum has served as an important component of Jewish law ever since, almost always dealing with the daily needs of the Jewish people, such as dietary laws, marriage and divorce, personal injury, and business liability. With the prestige of the Geonim behind them, they provided a kind of practical connection among far-flung Jewish communities, who might use the arguments of these letters to make daily decisions about their prayers, their business practices, or to finalize decisions about divorce, dowries, or inheritances.

The Geonate shared authority with the exilarch, whose authority, which was political in nature and not religious, was rooted in his supposed descent from King David. The Babylonian Geonim, by contrast, derived their authority from their intellectual achievement. In the western part of the Caliphate, particularly that which the Muslims had conquered from the Christian Roman Empire, the Gaon of Palestine also had a position of authority, as both a political and religious leader. The relationship between these authorities was complicated, and sometimes bitter rivalries arose between them. The exilarch had an advantage inasmuch as he represented the Jews before the caliph, but the Geonim had another advantage that proved to have longer-lasting effects: they were in a position to exert their influence broadly through their scholarly and judicial authority. Through the medium of their legal writings, and by training sages in their academies, the Geonim were able to provide a social and religious structure for distant Jewish communities in North Africa and Spain, as well as Iraq and Persia. A clear sign of Geonic authority was this office's power to exact taxes from Jewish communities to subsidize the expenses of the academies it ran—this in addition to the special tax, the *jizya*, that Jews had to pay to Muslim rule.

No figure better personifies the power of the Geonate than **Saadya ben Yosef** (882 or 892–942), who presided as Gaon of the academy of Sura from 928 until his death (hence he is often referred to as Saadya Gaon). An intellectual giant, he wrote many works, including philosophy, linguistic studies, poetry, translations into Arabic, and a very early version of the *siddur,* a standardized compilation of prayers (*see box,* The Geonic Standardization of Jewish Prayer). He had many opponents, and that meant that as a leader his career had its ups and downs (he was deposed as Gaon after a conflict with the exilarch and other opponents but was later reappointed). In terms of early medieval Jewish intellectual history, however, he is the most significant figure in this period, for which reason we will address him again in this chapter.

Saadya's death in 942 was a turning point in the history of the Geonate. Two subsequent Geonim, a father and son, also left their mark. **Sherira** sat as Gaon of Pumbedita from 968–998. He authored the letter that provides most of our information about late antique rabbinic history and the Geonate. At an advanced age, Sherira appointed his son, **Hai,** to replace him. Hai Gaon presided over Pumbedita until 1038, was renowned for his scholarship and legal rulings, and exerted a broad influence on Jewish communities. But Geonic authority seems to have already been in decline by this point—both Sherira and Hai complained about their declining influence as letters went unanswered and financial contributions unpaid. Internal disputes between Sura and Pumbedita, the diffusion of Talmudic studies in new centers of learning, and the rise of independent intellectuals in such places as Egypt and Spain

THE GEONIC STANDARDIZATION OF JEWISH PRAYER

The Bible establishes prayer—praise, petition, confession, and thanksgiving—as an important form of communication with God, but the idea of prayer as a continuous religious obligation, one to be performed by Jews several times a day and following a fixed sequence of prescripted blessings and prayers, seems to have developed over the course of the Second Temple and rabbinic period. The rabbis of late antiquity developed the central communal prayers recited to this day, and even ordered them in a fixed sequence, but that was not the end of the process. It was not until the Geonic period that the first prayer book, the *siddur* (from the Hebrew word for "ordering"), was developed. The earliest systematic ordering of the prayers, compiled by the ninth-century Geonic leader **Amram,** from material in the Talmud and earlier Geonic sources, established that prayers were to be recited throughout the year on weekdays, Sabbaths, the new moon, and special fast days and festivals. Saadya developed another *siddur* about a century later.

The prayer book established by the Geonim has been substantially supplemented throughout the centuries with *piyyutim* and other materials. In addition, the Hebrew poetry of medieval Spain left its impact on Jewish liturgy, as did the Jewish mysticism of the Kabbalah. Regional differences developed over time, with the Ashkenazi, Sephardi, Italian, Yemenite, and other traditions each acquiring their own particular liturgical flavor. In the modern era, the prayer book underwent revisions in the liberal strands of modern Judaism. However, the influence of Geonic efforts is still evident in the basic structure of the prayer service, and indeed in the very existence of the prayer book.

And what is the structure of Jewish communal worship? Jewish males (the obligation of communal prayer was only imposed on males until the rise of the Reform and Conservative Movements) are required to pray at certain hours three times a day in correspondence to the time of communal sacrifice in the Temple. One need not worship in a synagogue, but communal prayer requires a quorum or *minyan* of at least ten adult Jewish males. Prayer follows a precisely scripted sequence of recitations organized around two major components: the *Shema,* a declaration of faith in God derived from the biblical books of Deuteronomy and Numbers, and the *Amida* (from the Hebrew for "standing"), a sequence of nineteen petitionary prayers uttered while standing. The *Kaddish,* a well-known part of the service, is a largely Aramaic recitation uttered at the close of individual sections of the service and at its conclusion; the one at the end, the Mourner's *Kaddish,* is recited by close relatives of the deceased and seems to have become part of the Jewish mourning process in the Middle Ages. The service also includes a public Torah reading on three days of the week, including the Sabbath.

undermined the centrality of the Babylonian Geonate. So too did the surviving remnant of Umayyad rule in Spain, which was only too keen to see its Jewish subjects become independent of authorities located in the Abbassid Empire. Political and religious divides in the Islamic world—the boundaries between Sunnis and Shi'ites, and between the Abbassids, the Fatimids, and the Umayyads—all conspired to dilute the authority of the Geonic center.

One sign of the limits of Geonic authority was the rise of the **Karaites** (from the Hebrew root *qara',* meaning "to read"). While the mainstream of medieval Jewry evolved under the influence of rabbinic Judaism, a dissenting minority within the Jewish people developed in reaction against that influence. This community developed alternative theories of *halakhah,* or legal norms, based, in principle on the Bible alone. The Geonim not only had to vie for authority with one another and the exilarch; they also had to compete for the allegiance of Jewish communities with a sect that contested the very basis of their authority, the Oral Torah.

Historians generally date Karaite beginnings to the eighth century, with the sect reaching its apex in the tenth to twelfth centuries. Even in the eighth century, in fact, it appears that the Karaites were not in fact a single group but rather many different sects who disagreed with each other on many points. More than anyone else from that period, however, **Anan ben David** is identified as the formative figure in the development of Karaite ideology. Rabbinic opponents attributed to Anan the battle cry "Abandon the words of the Mishnah and of the Talmud"—a reflection of the Karaite rejection of Oral Torah and the rabbis in favor of the Written Torah as the sole source of legal authority.

Only in the late ninth and early tenth centuries did Karaism begin to take meaningful shape, especially in the Land of Israel. There, a Karaite population developed a more uniform ideology and permanent institutions. Prospering in Palestine and nearby Egypt, Karaites zealously proselytized within the Jewish community and inspired great resentment among the majority *Rabbanites* (a term used to describe the party of Jews actively aligned with the rabbinic Oral Torah against the Karaites)—so much so, in fact, that the leading rabbinic thinker of the early tenth century, Saadya, felt it necessary to vigorously attack the Karaites in an effort to stem the tide of their growth, going so far as to deny that they were Jewish.

In the eleventh century, the Karaites began to move to the Byzantine Empire (as many Rabbanites were also doing), and there they continued to publish influential works and to populate major cities into the fourteenth century. The Karaite leader of this movement toward the Byzantine Empire was Tobias ben Moses, credited with translating or organizing the translation of classic Karaite texts from Arabic to

Hebrew, for consumption among non-Arabic-speaking Jews. Despite the success of this relocation, the Karaites drew comparatively few members; according to the twelfth-century account of the wide-ranging traveler Benjamin of Tudela, only five hundred Karaites lived in Constantinople. By the time of the Ottoman defeat of the Byzantine Empire in 1453, the Karaites had ceased to publish influential works and their numbers had greatly dwindled. The fact that the Karaite movement was so popular in the earlier tenth to twelfth centuries, however, is more evidence of the declining authority of the Geonate in this period.

Glimpses of Jewish History in Muslim Palestine

By the time the Muslims conquered the Land of Israel in 638 CE, the region had become predominantly Christian. There remained, however, a large and vibrant Jewish community, primarily in the Galilee in the northern part of the Land of Israel. There, Tiberias, the ancient seat of rabbinic authority, continued its role as a scholarly center. As in Baghdad, a Geonate ruled over the region, relying on the Palestinian Talmud in the same manner that the Baghdadi Geonim relied on the Babylonian Talmud. Unfortunately, our sources for the period are very scant, and we only begin to get a clear picture of things in the tenth century. The activity of the Massoretes reach a peak in the tenth century in the work of Aaron ben Moses of the ben Asher family of Tiberias, whose scribal efforts solidified the authority of Massoretic biblical manuscripts, but the Massoretes themselves seem to disappear sometime after his death. Meanwhile, the Karaites, having developed a strong theological tie to the land of Israel, were becoming more populous (in fact, Aaron ben Moses seems to have been a Karaite), retaining a strong presence in Jerusalem in particular until the First Crusade destroyed the Karaite community there.

The Palestinian Gaon, in some ways combining the offices of exilarch and Gaon, held political and juridical power over the Jews of the Fatimid Empire, a Shi'ite dynasty that arose in the tenth century and eventually ruled a region that included the Palestine, Egypt and North Africa. Preserving the authority of the Palestinian Talmud over against that of the Babylonian Talmud, the Palestinian Geonate had control over the remnants of the Jewish community of the Roman Empire now under Islamic control. For a while, the Palestinian Geonate competed for authority with the Babylonian Geonate, but it was eventually overshadowed. By the tenth century, the Palestinian Geonate and its academy had moved from Tiberias to Jerusalem, and then in 1073 to Tyre, situated in modern-day coastal Lebanon. The Palestinian Geonate was further weakened when it split, with secessionists of the Palestinian tradition opening an academy in Egypt.

External events, such as the First Crusade (1095), also played a major role in the demise of the Palestinian Geonate. By the early years of the eleventh century, the Christian invaders had achieved significant success, setting up independent Crusader states, and Jews suffered enormously in the process. The fighting resulted in the deaths of thousands of Jews in and around Palestine—Jerusalem fell to the Crusaders in 1099—and institutions of Jewish learning and community in Palestine seem never to have recovered in the Middle Ages. One rabbi from nearby Aleppo testified to the ravages of the First Crusade: "A haughty arm has struck, it has made way with the brooms of destruction, and has chased away all who unify the Name [i.e., Jews] from every border of the Holy Land." Palestine would not witness significant Jewish cultural vitality for almost five hundred years, when the expulsion from Spain would impel Jews to migrate there.

While the Palestinian Geonate gave way to the Babylonian one, we have noted that it too would soon decline in authority. In fact, both these centers were giving way to the new and newly independent intellectual centers opening up in the west, with the latter favoring the Talmudic tradition of the Babylonian Geonim. Just as western Europe was growing increasingly assertive vis-à-vis the Muslim world, Jewish leaders like Maimonides and the communities they led were growing increasingly assertive vis à vis the traditional Geonic centers based in Palestine and Babylonia.

The Community of the Cairo Genizah

Between the tenth and twelfth centuries, the period documented so richly by the texts found in the Cairo Genizah, the Jewish community of Egypt lived under yet another Islamic empire distinct from both the Umayyads and the Abbassids—the **Fatimid Empire** (969–1171). The Fatimid caliphs were Isma'ilis, a sect within Shi'ite Islam that automatically defined them as rivals to the Abbassid Caliphs in Baghdad who adhered to the antagonistic Sunni stream of Islamic tradition. When the Fatimids moved into Egypt from North Africa in 969, they established themselves by building a new capital called Fustat, sometimes called Old Cairo. This is where the synagogue housing the Cairo Geniza was located. The Fatimids also went on to conquer much of Syria and Palestine, which is a main reason the history of the Jewish community in that region was so closely tied to that of the community in Egypt. Benjamin of Tudela, who visited Cairo in this period, claims 7,000 Jews were there; that may be an overestimation, but the community there was success-

ful and influential, drawing figures such as Maimonides, who resettled in Cairo after fleeing from Spain. Other Jewish communities flourished in Tunisia and Morocco, in a region of North Africa known as the Maghreb, under the rule of the Fatimids or their vassals. The Egyptian Jewish community continued to prosper even when the Fatimids were displaced in 1171 by the dynasty of the great Muslim anti-Crusader, Saladin, but it went into decline under the next Islamic regime, the Mamluks, who ruled Egypt from 1250 to 1517.

The Jewish community of Cairo was initially subject to the religious authority of the Palestinian Gaon, but that changed at the end of the eleventh century when the Palestinian Jewish community was devastated by the Crusades. Egyptian rabbinic authorities eventually displaced the Palestinian Gaon, and the community in which they resided became a robust intellectual center for thinkers, as well as an economic center, through Jewish traders such as Nahrai ben Nissim, who traded from Spain to India, a Jewish community based in Cochin having developed in India.

The Cairo Genizah is such a rich source of evidence for this community that it even allows us glimpses into the lives of Jewish women, almost always obscured in earlier periods of Jewish history. The sources reveal their role in the economy (women often worked in textiles but also as healers and as brokers for products produced by other women); their literacy and their involvement in the education of their children (some Genizah documents are written by women, and women tutored sons in the home and in one case even served as a teaching assistant in a school); even a false messiah in Cairo was female. We will return later in this chapter to the Cairo Genizah and what it tells us about Jewish society under Islamic rule.

The "Golden Age" of Muslim Spain

The period of Islamic rule in Spain (known as *Sepharad* in Hebrew and *al-Andalus* in Arabic) is remembered as a "Golden Age" in Jewish history. This idealized picture obscures a more complex situation: a full understanding of the period must balance high Jewish intellectual and social achievement against periods of persecution, even forced conversion under Islamic rule, tied to the ongoing military conflict between Muslims and Christians for control over the Iberian Peninsula. Still, the description of this age as one of peaceful coexistence, or *convivencia* as it is known in Spanish, a period of stability and prosperity that allowed for the flourishing of scholarship, poetry, and religious innovation, contains much truth.

The story of Muslim Spain picks up where the Umayyad Caliphate leaves off. Overthrown by the Abbassids in 750, the Umayyad dynasty found a new home in the recently conquered region of Spain. Abd al-Rahman I (r. c. 756–788), the surviving Umayyad scion, fled from the Abbassids across North Africa and was able to establish himself as a semiautonomous prince in Spain. Over the course of the next two centuries, his descendants struggled to maintain their rule over Muslim Spain, sometimes managing to rein in independent Spanish princes, and other times failing. When Abd al-Rahman III (r. 912–929) came to power, he found Spain in a particularly fractious state but was able to impose unity, establishing himself as a rival caliph in his capital Cordoba, a vast and sophisticated city that had a population of 100,000 inhabitants in the tenth century and was home to great libraries (including the Caliph's private collection of some 400,000 volumes), observatories, and magnificent mosques.

The Spanish Caliphate lasted until the beginning of the eleventh century, when, once again, various local rulers shook off the central power of Cordoba. Spain descended into civil war, which was resolved unofficially in the year 1013, when the various princes settled into their fiefdoms as independent mini-states, called *taifas*. Their relative disunity emboldened the Spanish Catholic kings, who overcame their own division to unite against their common Muslim enemy. The Christians extended their reach southward over the course of the eleventh century—their most important victory: the capture of Toledo in 1085 (*see* Map 6-2).

In the face of this great loss, the Muslims recognized their failures and called on the Almoravids, a Muslim dynasty from northwest Africa, to defend against the Christian kings of Castile and León, the two Christian kingdoms in northern

Map 6-2   The Christian reconquest (*reconquista*) of Muslim Spain.

Spain. The Almoravids were fueled by religious zeal, not only defending the southern part of Spain from the Christians but imposing a harsh religious order. A brief attempt at conversion of the Jews was averted, but the tone of the relationship between the ruling Muslims and the Jews changed with their reign. The Almoravids were later succeeded by the Almohads, another North African sect defined by an extremely strict interpretation of Muslim law. Supplanting the Almoravids over the course of 1149 to 1157, this new regime directly persecuted the Jews and Christians of Spain with an intensity that neither had experienced until then. It was in this period that the Jewish city of Lucena outside Cordoba was destroyed, an event lamented by Abraham ibn Ezra (c. 1093–1167) as akin to the destruction of Jerusalem in 586 BCE. Note how the following poem evokes the biblical book of Lamentation, composed in the wake of Jerusalem's destruction:

> I weep like an ostrich for Lucena
> Her remnant dwelt, innocent and secure
> Unchanged for a thousand and seventy years
> Then came her day and her people were exiled and she a widow
> Forbidden to study the torah, the prophets and the Mishnah.

In reaction to this attack, many Jews converted to save themselves, while many others fled to southern France, Christian Spain, and North Africa. As a result of the destruction of Lucena and the dispersal of many Spanish Jews, the so-called "Golden Age," which had begun with the caliphate of Abd al-Rahman III, came to an end. In 1212, the Christians would finally gain the military upper hand, at which point the Jews of Spain entered Christian history even though the influence of Arabic culture continued for some time.

Much of the intervening period was an age of prosperity, relative tolerance, and self-government for Jews, however, and it was in that circumstance that Spanish–Jewish culture thrived. It drew great Talmudic scholars such as Isaac al-Fasi (1013–1103) and cultivated new ones such as Joseph ibn Migash (1077–1141) and, of course, **Maimonides** (1135–1204) who made great advances in the study of rabbinic law while, at the same absorbing cutting-edge innovations from Arabic philosophy and literature. When in the twelfth century the Jews of Muslim Spain fell prey to the violence of the Almohad invasion, they realized that a remarkable period had come to a tragic close, as Abraham ibn Ezra's lament so movingly attests.

The Golden Age of Spain had been generated by an internal struggle within Muslim politics; Abd al-Rahman III claimed the caliphate in 912, and in so doing, he trans-formed Spain into a rival to the Abbassid caliphate. Perhaps it is not a coincidence that we find a similar rivalry developing in Jewish culture of the same period. Sometime in the second decade of the tenth century, a Jewish courtier named **Hasdai ibn Shaprut** made his mark in the service of the caliph when he translated a renowned Greek medical textbook known as *Materia Medica*. After rising through the ranks of the court he became a trusted advisor to Abd al-Rahman III, functioning as his leading diplomat, the overseer of the country's customs, and head of the Jewish community. In a remarkable parallel to what Abd al-Rahman III was doing in relation to the Abbassids, Hasdai ibn Shaprut asserted his authority over Jews abroad, acting as representative and defender of communities as far away as Italy, Provence, and the Byzantine Empire while also acting as the leading patron of Jewish culture in Spain. The assertiveness of Hasdai ibn Shaprut helped to establish Spanish Jewry as a rival and competitor to the great rabbinic academies in Babylonia just as the Umayyads were seeking to rival the Abbassids.

Among Hasdai's acts as a cultural patron was his support of two leading scholar-poets of the Hebrew language: Menahem ben Suruq and Dunash ibn Labrat. Both helped to lay the foundations of Hebrew grammar. **Menahem ben Suruq** (c. 920–970) moved from Tortosa, in northeastern Spain, to Cordoba, sometime toward the middle of the tenth century, to become Hasdai's personal secretary. Though also an accomplished poet, Menahem's greatest achievement was the creation of a Hebrew dictionary, the *Mahberet* or *Notebook,* which is notable because of the pioneering way in which it defined biblical words in Hebrew, as opposed to using another language, such as Arabic. Having been written in Hebrew, it had a widespread impact because it served as the chief source of Hebrew philological instruction for Jews who did not know Arabic. It was thus especially important in Christian Europe, where the great sage Rashi and his grandson Jacob Tam, among others, were reliant on the *Mahberet*. From a philological point of view, the book's lasting claim to fame was to establish that Hebrew is a language with cogent, identifiable rules.

The second of these linguists, **Dunash ibn Labrat** (920–990), was a student of Saadya Gaon, and the first to be credited with introducing Arabic meter into Hebrew poetry. He was the first Hebrew grammarian to distinguish between transitive and intransitive verbs and also the first to identify Hebrew verbs as being composed of three-letter roots. He was deeply critical of Menahem's dictionary, claiming its misunderstandings would lead to impiety. Hasdai ibn Shaprut was the patron of both men, but the violent quarrel between the two ultimately led to ibn Labrat usurping ben Suruq's privileged position in the court of Hasdai.

Statue of Maimonides (1135–1204), the eminent medieval scholar of rabbinic law and philosopher, in Córdoba, Spain, where he was born.

A central point of disagreement between Menachem and ibn Labrat turned on the relationship of Hebrew and Arabic poetry. Menaham felt that one could not superimpose standards of Arabic poetry onto Hebrew poetry, while Dunash felt that not only could it be done but it was incumbent to do so. Menaham's position was rooted in his observation that the Hebrew poetry of the Bible has no discernible meter, in contrast to Arabic poetry (how biblical poetry works, and whether it has any kind of meter, continues to puzzle scholars), and it was his belief that biblical poetry should be the model for Hebrew poetry in the present. ibn Labrat, in contrast, concluded from the close linguistic relationship between Hebrew and Arabic, which share grammatical structures and vocabulary, that Arabic poetry could function as a model for Hebrew poetry, and he worked to close the literary gap between them by developing a technique for imitating the quantitative metrics of Arabic poetry in Hebrew.

Beyond the rules of grammar and philology, something far larger was at stake in this dispute—the relation between Jewish and Islamic culture: the question of whether to be open to Arabic influence or not. In the end, the position of Dunash ibn Labrat proved to be more influential, laying the intellectual foundation for the conscious adoption of Arabic models into medieval Spanish Jewish poetry. But even Menaham's position betrays Islamic influence, his esteem for biblical Hebrew mirroring the Muslim esteem for the Arabic of the Koran. Indeed, Menaham's own poetry, though modeled on biblical Hebrew, shows the influence of Arabic language and rhyme.

As golden as the Golden Age of Spain was, we should not exaggerate the extent to which it glittered for all Jews. A good example is found in the contrasting careers of the poet **Samuel ha-Nagid** and his son Joseph. Samuel ha-Nagid was one of the great Hebrew poets of this period; he was also a highly successful courtier in Granada, ultimately becoming a vizier and general of the army. His poems touch not only on the secular themes of friendship and love and pious topics of penitence and devotion, but they also describe, in graphic detail, his military exploits and the grandeur as well as the brutality of war. If the unprecedented success of Samuel illustrates what a court Jew in eleventh-century Spain could achieve, the downfall of his son Joseph in 1066 illustrates the perils of being Jewish in the Islamic Middle Ages. Perhaps through his own fault, Joseph became entangled in the conflicts pitting different ethnic groups in Granada against one another. From Arabic and Jewish sources, it appears that envy at the exalted position of Jews, in particular Samuel and Joseph Ha-Nagid, also led to resentment. An eleventh-century Arabic poem warns its Muslim audience that their chief

. . . has chosen an infidel as his secretary
when he could, had he wished, have chosen a Believer.
Through him, the Jews have become great and proud
and arrogant—they, who were among the most abject
and have gained their desires and attained the utmost
and this happened suddenly, before they even realized it.
And how many a worthy Muslim humbly obeys
the vilest ape [a Jew] among these miscreants.

Abraham ibn Daud, the Spanish Jewish astronomer, historian, and philosopher, noted the fate of Joseph in his chronicle, *Sefer ha-Kabbalah* (Book of Tradition), written sometime after 1161, and offers a reason for his downfall: "Of all the fine qualities which his father possessed, Joseph lacked but one. He was not humble like his father because he grew up in riches, and he never had to bear the yoke [of poverty and discipline] in his youth. Indeed, he grew haughty—to his own destruction. The Berber princes were so jealous of him, that he was killed on the Sabbath, on the 9th of Tevet in the year 4827 [Saturday, December 30, 1066]."

But it was not just Joseph who was murdered. The entire Jewish community of Granada paid the ultimate price in this riot. Ibn Daud recorded that Joseph "and the Community of Granada were murdered." This was one of the very few pogromlike events that we hear about from the medieval Islamic world. The "Golden Age" of Spain was not quite the multicultural paradise that often is portrayed. Jewish communities and their leaders, however successful, were dependent on non-Jewish patrons and subject to their rule. Muslims in Spain and elsewhere were capable of religious persecution of the sort associated with medieval Christians: in one instance in eleventh-century Egypt, Jews were forced to hang on their necks an image of a calf to recall the sin of the Golden Calf; forced conversions of Jews were mandated in places such as Yemen and Spain; and ethnic–religious tensions sometimes resulted in deadly violence, as it did in Granada in 1066.

This said, what Jews accomplished in medieval Islamic Spain cannot be denied as a culturally and intellectually vital moment in Jewish history. It is also a harbinger of future internal Jewish trends. Despite the Muslim persecution that beset Jews living in Spain in the twelfth century and drove individuals, including Maimonides, eastward to Egypt, the flourishing of Jewish culture in Islamic Spain appears in retrospect as part of a larger trend that would ultimately diffuse rabbinic authority and intellectual activity from its Geonic centers, shifting much of it from the Middle East to North Africa and to Europe (*see box,* Ten Significant Dates for Jewish History During the Islamic Middle Ages).

TEN SIGNIFICANT DATES FOR JEWISH HISTORY DURING THE ISLAMIC MIDDLE AGES

622: Migration of Muhammad from Mecca to Medina, where he establishes the first Muslim community. Marks the beginning of the Islamic era.

750: Establishment of the Abbassid Caliphate based in Baghdad. By 750, Islamic rule reaches into central Asia and India in the east; spans the Middle East, Egypt, and North Africa; and extends into southern Europe into such places as Sicily and Spain.

c. 754: First appearance of Anan ben David, a founding figure in the Karaite Movement.

882–942: Saadya the Gaon.

910–1171: Fatimid Empire.

1085: The Christians take the city of Toledo in central Spain, the first major city to be conquered in the centuries-long Christian "reconquest" of Muslim-dominated Spain.

1095: The First Crusade.

1086–1167: The life of the poet Judah ha-Levi.

1135–1204: The life of the philosopher Maimonides.

1492: The Christian Expulsion of Jews from Spain.

Jewish Lives Under Islamic Rule

What was it like to be a Jew in the Islamic Middle Ages? Our knowledge is sharply limited in several respects, but we know far more than one might have expected because of the fortuitous preservation of the documents in the Cairo Genizah, along with previously known sources, such as the responsa of the Geonim, the literature of great Jewish thinkers and writers like Maimonides and Judah ha-Levi, and Muslim references to Jews. The testimony of these sources illumines some corners of Jewish life more clearly than others, revealing more about men than women, more about city life than country life, more about the wealthy than the poor, but it nonetheless allows a much broader and deeper understanding of real-life experience than is attainable for earlier periods.

One change we can see clearly reflected in the sources is the rise of Arabic in place of Hebrew and Aramaic as the language used by many Jews in Babylonia, the Middle East, and North Africa. Most of the documents in the Cairo Genizah are written in Arabic, and Saadya's use of Arabic helped to make it a legitimate scholarly language for Jews, a role it played in the Islamic realm until the sixteenth century. Indeed, Jews developed a dialect of Judeo–Arabic that employed Hebrew letters and vocabulary, graphically registering how successfully Arabic was integrated into Jewish culture.

Another change was increased urbanization. One gets the impression from the Mishnah and the Talmud that most Jews earned their livelihoods from agriculture prior to the rise of Islam. Jews continued to own land and engage in agriculture in the Islamic Middle Ages—to think otherwise is a misconception—but with the rise of Islam, many Jews migrated from the country to town, or from towns to larger cities. Scholars disagree about what drew Jews to cities. Some argue that Jews were drawn to cities by their minority status; there they could congregate in numbers large enough to sustain the civic and religious institutions Jewish law demanded—synagogues, schools, the facilities needed to prepare kosher meat, and so on. Others argue that a relatively high rate of Jewish literacy inclined Jews to seek the kind of employment found in cities, employment that often required and rewarded literacy. Probably no one single factor was at work in increased urbanization; also playing a role were the heavy tax burdens on Jewish farmers relative to Muslim farmers not subject to those taxes, as well as self-imposed Jewish tithes on agricultural produce, plus the decline of irrigation systems in the area of Babylonia.

Jews seem to have integrated well into the economy that developed under Islamic rule. The period saw the emergence of new or intensified trade routes connecting the Mediterranean sea to the Atlantic Ocean, now all under Islamic rule,

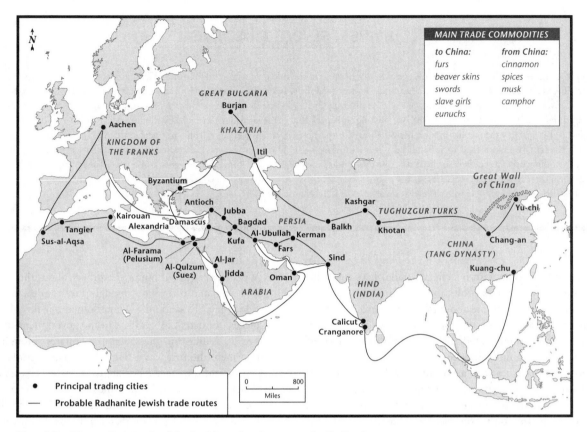

Map 6-3 The trading circuit of the Jewish traders known as the Radhanites.

and Jews were active participants in that trade, along with several other ethnic minorities. One Jewish trading firm deserves special note: the great merchant family of the **Radhanites,** dealers in silk fabrics, slaves, furs, and swords, whose dealings extended from western Europe to China. The sole source on the Radhanites conveys the extent of their business dealings (*see* Map 6-3):

> [T]hese merchants speak Arabic, Persian, Greek, the language of the Franks, Spaniards, and Slavs. They journey from west to east, from east to west, partly on land, partly by sea. They transport from the west eunuchs, female and male slaves, silk, castor, marten, and other furs, and swords. They take ship in the land of the Franks, on the Western Sea, and steer for el-Farama [on the eastern edge of the Nile Delta]. There they load their goods on the backs of camels, and go by land to Kolzum [Suez] in five days' journey over a distance of twenty-five parasangs [93 miles]. They embark in the East Sea [Red Sea] and sail from Kolzum to El-Jar [port of Medina]

and Jeddah [port of Mecca]; then they go to Sind [modern Pakistan], India, and China.

Islamic rule did much to facilitate this kind of wide-ranging trade, introducing new, safer forms of vessels and building additional lighthouses, and the distinctive characteristics of Jewish culture put Jews in a good position to make the most of the new business opportunities that opened up. Personal ties between Jewish communities throughout the Mediterranean—the extended family being an important social unit in Jewish life—made it easier for a merchant to find a trustworthy person with whom to store goods where he could not be himself. A shared legal code provided clarification in the case of legal disputes. And the practice of the ban, or excommunication, proved to be a useful tool for ensuring ethical business practices. "Perhaps you should threaten him that here in Aden we excommunicate anyone who owes us something and does not fulfill his commitments," wrote one Jew in Yemen about someone who had defaulted on a loan (*see box,* Jewish Slave Trading).

JEWISH SLAVE TRADING

One aspect of Jewish trading deserves special notice because of the role it continues to play in antisemitic charges against Jews: slave trading. The charge that Jews ran the slave trade in historical times is a willful distortion of history, but it is true that Jews in the Islamic world did participate in the slave trade, as did Muslims and Christians in the same era, all trading in and owning slaves. If anything was distinctive about Jewish slave owning, it is probably the legal issues generated by the possibility of conversion to Judaism. Biblical law made a distinction between Israelite and non-Israelite slaves, and the former were entitled to certain protections that the latter were not (and incidentally, it is not clear that medieval Jews ever owned fellow Jews as slaves). That gave non-Jewish slaves an incentive to convert to Judaism. It was forbidden for a master to compel the conversion of a slave, but a slave could convert voluntarily, and that, apparently, was a route to manumission for some. The conversion to Judaism of many slaves explains why Christians sought to prohibit Jewish ownership of Christian slaves.

Beyond the economic benefits of trade, Jews may also have been drawn to this profession by the allure of travel. Some Jewish travelers wrote about their adventures, and in so doing provided some of the most important information about the worlds they visited. The itinerary of **Benjamin of Tudela,** by far the most frequently cited and useful of these travelogues, describes an array of Jewish communities throughout the Mediterranean. Benjamin traveled from his home in Tudela, Spain, to the Middle East, during the years 1165 to 1173. In Constantinople, he spoke of the "stir and bustle" among "merchants from Babylon and from Mesopotamia, from Media and Persia, from Egypt and Palestine as well as from Russia, Hungary, Patzinakia, Budia, Lombardy and Spain." In Jerusalem, he counted "200 Jews who live under the Tower of David" and who have a monopoly on the dye works of the city. The existence of such literature suggests that travel held a certain fascination for Jews, as it did for Muslims (think of the legendary voyages of Sinbad the sailor, set in the Abbassid period), and reflects the increased mobility of life in the medieval Mediterranean.

That fascination has to be balanced against the dangers of travel, however, including the risk of being kidnapped by pirates, a serious concern with the rise of maritime trade. Merchants tried to minimize the risk of piracy by arranging for their ships to travel in convoys, but attacks persisted nonetheless, with pirates kidnapping people in the hope of securing a ransom. Fortunately for the kidnapped, they might hope to be redeemed by their family or community, though the ransom could be quite onerous and sometimes proved too burdensome for a community. An eleventh-century letter from the community of Alexandria (a port city and thus all too familiar with this experience) describes how taxing this communal obligation could be:

We inform you, our honored brothers, about the matter of a woman captive. They brought her from the land of Edom [i.e., Byzantium]. We ransomed her for 24 gold pieces [= dinars], in addition to the government tax on her. . . . After this, the sailors [i.e., pirates] brought us two men: the first was a fine young man, a student of Torah, and the other a boy approximately 10 years old. When we saw them in the hands of the Muslims, who were beating them, mistreating and intimidating them before us, we took pity on them, and were deeply moved for them. So we stood as surety for them to their captors . . . but we have stretched our resources to the limits.

To avoid being targeted and gouged by pirates and kidnappers, Jews, like other religious communities, placed a cap on the amount that they would pay. In this, they followed the Talmud, which limited the amount of ransom so that the Jews would not become an overly attractive target. Documents from the Cairo Genizah record the relief that travelers by sea felt when they reached port.

While personal ties and shared behavioral norms eased business between Jews, it should be noted that Cairo Genizah documents and other sources provide ample evidence for trading partnerships across religious lines, not just among Jews but between Jews and Muslims as well. Indeed, Jewish traders and financiers played an important role in the larger economy of the Islamic world before the Crusades, serving in the financial administration, innovating new forms of credit and investment that facilitated trade and capitalism, and making loans to the state in a way that anticipates the role of later "court Jews" in Christian Europe.

Lest one get an exaggerated impression of the role of trade and banking in the Jewish community, it needs to be noted that our impression of economic life is skewed by the evidence that happens to survive: merchants needed to communicate with one another across vast distances, and that required writing the kind of letters found in the Cairo Genizah; we know less about other professions that did not rely on letter writing in the same way. Still, from references here and there, it is clear that Jews were employed in a wide range of professions and manufacturing. One source that lists a number of Jewish occupations included "the tailor and the fuller and the metal and copper and tin and lead smiths and the dyer and weaver, all artisans." Other sources mention Jewish barbers (who doubled as bloodletters), hide tanners, butchers, launderers, coin minters, builders, wine makers, tavern keepers, sugar makers, and jewelers. Astrology and medicine were greatly esteemed in Islamic culture, and Jews were involved in both fields. One of the best-known astrologers in Baghdad in the tenth century was a Jew named Ishaq ben Fulayt, and in some towns in pre-expulsion Spain, Jews made up 50 percent of a town's doctors. As Maimonides' example suggests, Jewish physicians were often appointed to high-ranking leadership positions in the Jewish community and the Islamic court.

Institutions that we think of as personal or religious also played an important economic dimension in this period, including marriage. At the center of family life, the institution of marriage served many purposes, including companionship, and its emotional dimensions are captured in sources from the period, including a letter from an elderly merchant on a trip expressing how much he missed his wife: "[W]hen I stretch out my hand to take something, I think about you, your suffering and your loneliness, and the loneliness of each of us." But marriage was also a business arrangement, a contract between parties, and that side of the relationship is much better documented.

A Jewish marriage in the Middle Ages was formalized in a number of stages. First, parents chose future mates for their children and agreed on the formal terms, to be fulfilled later. When they reached marriageable age, the couple and their families would begin the two official stages of marriage (which were eventually collapsed into one): betrothal and wedding. At the betrothal, the families legally committed to the specific terms of the marriage contract, meaning that the bride and groom had to divorce to break the betrothal (even though the marriage had not truly begun). The wedding ceremony marked the official beginning of the marriage and took place under the *huppah,* or wedding canopy, after which the couple would begin their life together. Marriage thus constituted a promise between two parties, which took the form of the marriage contract called the **ketubbah** (pl. *ketubbot*) and obliged the husband and wife to bear responsibility for one another's well-being. The families of the

bride and the groom contributed money to the marriage to help the young couple to establish their own household and to provide support for the woman in case of divorce or widowhood.

For Jews in the Islamic realm, marriage might involve more than one partner. While monogamy became the norm for Jews in Christian Europe, polygamy—a single husband with multiple wives—continued in the Islamic realm, though it was not necessarily widespread. The internal rivalries that often arose in this kind of marriage made it unappealing for some—many twelfth-century marriage contracts retrieved from the Genizah include a stipulation according to which the husband "took upon himself not to marry another wife and not to keep a slave girl hated by her"—but it was appealing for others, including women themselves, who sometimes encouraged their husbands to take another wife to help out at home.

For their part, although women could not have multiple husbands, they could and often did remarry. Shlomo Dov Goitein, the great scholar of the Cairo Genizah, observed that 45 percent of all women represented in the Genizah documents married more than once (including both widows and divorcées). Jewish law forbade women from initiating divorce themselves—to effect a legal divorce, the husband needed to present his wife with a bill of divorce or, as it is called in Hebrew, a **get.** Some husbands deliberately withheld this document to avoid paying the money specified by the terms of the *ketubbah.* When a husband went missing at sea and his death could not be determined, a woman was in a similar predicament. In such circumstances a Jewish woman was in a very difficult legal situation; known as an **agunah,** she was unable either to receive the money guaranteed her in her marriage contract or to remarry. The Genizah documents suggest the community found ways around this problem, however. For instance, a woman could free herself of her marriage if she declared the following formula before her husband: "I reject this man, my husband; I reject this man, my husband," though she would not be entitled to the economic benefits of a formal divorce. She also could seek recourse in a Muslim court.

As in late antiquity, the synagogue remained a central communal institution, playing both religious and economic roles. Each of the various subcommunities within the larger Jewish community of a given city of sufficient size—Rabbanites and Karaites, those adhering to the Palestinian Talmud and those adhering to the Babylonian Talmud—often had their own synagogues, in fact, helping to distinguish their particular community from that of other Jews. Synagogue construction and upkeep constituted a considerable investment for the community. The basic role of the synagogue, of course, was to serve as a house of prayer and Torah reading but it also served as a kind of public square or community center, a clearinghouse for the collection and distribution of charity (the poor represented a large if largely undocumented percentage of the community), and also a forum where litigants could get a hearing. A person with a grievance was even permitted to interrupt the prayer service to make his case.

Jewish communities enjoyed a large measure of legal and religious autonomy under Islamic rule, with courts that addressed cases according to Jewish laws and Jewish leadership appointed by Jews themselves. An example of this arrangement comes from Egypt, where the Jewish communal leader, the *Nagid* or the *Ra'is al-Yehud,* was not foisted on the community by the Muslim government but appointed by the Palestinian Gaon, and then later by the community. But we should not think of Jews in this period as living in isolation in a ghetto—that was the invention of a later period of European history. Jews and Muslims often lived side by side, and at times even in the same buildings, which could lead to tensions but also to close interaction between members of the different communities.

This account of ordinary life in medieval Jewish society is somewhat misleading because it obscures the importance of what lay beyond ordinary life for Jews in the Islamic Middle Ages. As at the end of the Second Temple period, many Jews in the Middle Ages continued to harbor messianic expectations, often heightened by tumultuous events such as the Crusades, the Mongolian invasion, or the expulsion from Spain. Jewish culture had never developed a single coherent picture of the messianic age, and medieval Jews differed in how they envisioned it. Maimonides counted the Messiah among the essential doctrines of Judaism, stating that God "will send our messiah at the End of Days, to redeem those who await his salvation at the End, and God, in his lovingkindness, will revive the dead," but others like Joseph Albo (c. 1380–1445) in his work entitled *Sefer ha-Ikarim* (*Book of Core Beliefs*) neglect to include messianism as a central Jewish tenet. Some believed that the messianic age would bring political deliverance for the Jews; others saw it as a more cosmic change; some discouraged speculation about the timing of the messianic age; others tried to precisely calculate its arrival. While Jews could differ on these points, messianic belief in a general sense seems to have been widespread.

At particular times in the Middle Ages, particular groups of Jews came to expect the Messiah's arrival in their lifetime—sometimes within a few brief years or even months. We do not know very much about these messianic movements, but in general, they seem to focus on a charismatic individual, usually thought to have been of Davidic descent, who claimed (or who was acclaimed by others) to be the

Messiah. Jewish historians generally call these figures "false messiahs," by virtue of the fact that—judged in retrospect—they did not bring about the messianic redemption. Their following certainly did not believe them to be false, however, and some won many such followers.

One of the earliest false messiahs in the Middle Ages, **Serenus** (or Severus), illustrates the threat such movements sometimes posed to the Jewish community, advocating not only subversive ideas but the suspension of Jewish law as well. It is reported in one source "that many went astray after him and committed heresy—refusing to recite the core prayers, and disregarding the unsuitability of foods." Serenus, who also permitted working on the second day of festivals and abolished the *ketubbah* and certain incest laws, was eventually arrested and brought before the caliph, who handed him over to the Jewish community for execution. Another such figure was **David Alroy,** a messianic leader from twelfth-century Kurdistan, whose followers sent a letter "to all Jews dwelling nearby and far off . . . [that] the time has come in which the Almighty will gather together his people Israel from every country to Jerusalem the holy city." Upsetting the social and political order, militant messianic movements like those led by Serenus and David Alroy could be very dangerous for their adherents. Maimonides tells of one messianic figure in Yemen who said when asked for proof of his claims, "Cut off my head and I will come back to life immediately." His captor complied, and the expected resurrection did not follow, though according to Maimonides, many foolish people were still expecting the fellow to rise from the dead. David Alroy was eventually murdered.

Medieval Jewish messianism can be seen as the mirror image of medieval Jewish everyday life. The Messiah, after all, embodied the hope that Jews would one day be redeemed from the conditions in which they lived in a diasporic present and returned to the land of Israel. Even someone as prosperous as Hasdai ibn Shaprut, living a life of influence and prosperity in Córdoba, was nonetheless discontent enough to want to learn the date of God's promised redemption. The popularity of messianic belief is a reminder that for medieval Jews, life encompassed more than merely earning a living or keeping a home.

Jewish Thought and Imagination During Islamic Rule

Medieval Jews saw themselves as continuing the tradition initiated by the rabbis of the Mishnaic and Talmud period, and, as we have noted, a good portion of medieval Jewish literature and thought was devoted to the explication and application of rabbinic texts. But medieval Jewish thought was at the same time very different from that of late antiquity, and one of the most important reasons for the difference was the influence of Islam. Muslim writers and thinkers were heir to Greek intellectual traditions, most especially Aristotle, whose work in the hands of Muslim interpreters became a model of argumentation and a guide into the various disciplines of philosophical and scientific inquiry: logic, the study of nature, metaphysics, and the analysis of literature, among other fields. Muslim and Arabic culture also cultivated new literary genres, a rich tradition of mysticism, and new techniques of textual interpretation focused on the Koran, and all this had a tremendously stimulating effect on Jewish intellectual and imaginative life—first on Jewish intellectuals under Islamic rule, and then, through their influence, on Jewish scholars in Christian Europe.

Among the ideas that Jewish scholarship absorbed from Islam is an early scientific and philosophic tradition inherited from the Greeks and translated into Arabic, which made appeal to human reason—as opposed to revelation—as the first and foremost source of knowledge about the world. Jews first encountered Greek philosophy in the Hellenistic world, but that tradition, embodied by Philo of Alexandria, was largely lost to Jews of a later age. Islam revived Greek philosophy in a form that made it easier for rabbinicized Jews to absorb it into their thinking, for Islam, like rabbinic Judaism, was based on revelation, was centered on legal practice, and engaged Greek philosophy in the light of its commitment to these traditions. Muslim philosophers did not see Greek philosophy as an alien tradition but as part of their own heritage, believing that the Greeks had learned their wisdom from scriptural sages, such as King Solomon, and they further integrated it into their culture by translating such figures as Plato, Aristotle, and Plotinus into Arabic. (It was from these Arabic translations that Greek philosophy entered the intellectual world of Christian Europeans via translations into Latin and other European languages.)

The two main philosophical schools that had the greatest influence on medieval philosophy were Neo-Platonism and Aristotelianism. **Neo-Platonism** posited a hierarchical structure to the cosmos—an ineffable first principle, the Creator or the One, emanates downward toward the material world through a series of spheres of being. Human beings find themselves at the bottom of this ladder, weighed down by their materiality, but human souls can ascend upward by means of ethical and intellectual activity. The ideas of Aristotle—referred to in Islamic philosophical sources as "The Philosopher"—were even more influential. As understood by Muslims, **Aristotelianism** held that philosophy must proceed independently of supernatural sources of knowledge: one must

reach it by means of empirical observation, reasoned inference, and logical demonstration. Only having conducted this kind of investigation could one ask how conclusions reached rationally related to what one learned through revelation (*see box, On How to Become a Medieval Jewish Philosopher*).

In absorbing the methods and conclusions of Neo-Platonism and Aristotelianism, Muslim thinkers thus had to confront a number of apparent contradictions between philosophy and the tenets of their religion. If God, the cosmos, and the nature of the good could be understood by means of reason, of what use was supernatural revelation as a source of knowledge about the divine? If the highest good in life was philosophical contemplation, of what use was ritual practice? And what of philosophical theories that seemed to contradict the claims of Scripture—Aristotle's idea that the universe was static and eternal versus the scriptural claim that God created the universe at a certain moment? Muslim philosophers worked to resolve such problems in ways that subsequently helped Jewish philosophers navigate similar tensions between philosophy and Jewish belief.

The challenge of how to relate philosophy to religion was central to the work of two of the greatest Jewish philosophers of the Islamic Middle Ages: Saadya and Maimonides. Saadya recognized the danger that stray ideas could pose to religious belief, but he found in the Bible—in the question posed by the prophet Isaiah, "Have you not grasped the origins of the Universe?"—an exhortation to study philosophy. In his own effort to engage in such study, he was influenced by the Islamic theology known as *Kalam,* which is rooted in the assumption that Scripture (in Islam, the Koran) and rationality complement one another. In fact, Maimonides claims that the Geonim, including Saadya, were the first to absorb the influences of Kalam into Jewish thought. Saadya's philosophical writing, in works such as the *Book of Ideas and Opinions,* bears this out, following the structure and style of Kalam. He begins with a discussion of epistemology (how people know what they know and the mistakes to which they are vulnerable), then continues, among other issues he addresses, to provide proofs for how the world was created, to define the nature of God and his attributes, to explain the reasons for divine law, and to reconcile freewill with divine foreknowledge, all as a way of establishing the Written Torah and Oral Torah on rational grounds. And if reason can reveal the truth in this way, why does one need revelation? According to Saadya, revelation imparts the truth to those incapable of rational investigation, and provides guidance for those engaged in philosophical speculation.

Although Maimonides was critical of Saadya's approach, his basic philosophical project is very similar. Maimonides, also known as Rambam (an acronym for **R**abbi **M**oses **b**en

HOW TO BECOME A MEDIEVAL JEWISH PHILOSOPHER

How did medieval Jews acquire the learning necessary to engage in both scriptural interpretation and philosophy? The following text, written in Arabic by a Joseph ben Judah ibn Aknin around 1180, sheds some light on this issue. It lays out a plan of study for a Jewish student until the age of twenty, a plan that begins with traditional Jewish sources and ascends to Greek philosophical and scientific works:

Reading and Writing: The method of instruction must be so arranged that the teacher will begin first with the script, in order that the children may learn their letters, and this is to be kept up until there is no longer any uncertainty among them. . . .

Torah, Mishnah, and Hebrew Grammar: Then he is to teach them the Pentateuch, Prophets and Writings, that is the Bible, with an eye to the vocalization and the modulation in order that they may be able to pronounce the accents correctly. . . . Then he is to have them learn the Mishnah until they have acquired a fluency in it: "Teach thou it to the children of Israel, put it in their mouths" [Deuteronomy 31:19]. The teacher is to continue this until they are ten years of age, for the sages said, "At five years the age is reached for the study of the Scriptures, at ten for the study of the Mishnah." The children are then to be taught the inflections, declensions and conjugations, the regular verbs . . . and other rules of grammar.

Poetry: The teacher is to instruct his pupils in poetry. He should, for the most part, have them recite religious poems and whatever else of beauty is found in the different types of poetry, and is fit to develop in them all good qualities. . . .

Talmud: Then say the wise: "At fifteen the age is reached for the study of the Talmud." Accordingly, when the pupils are fifteen years of age the teacher should give them much practice in Talmud reading until they have acquired fluency in it. Later, when they are eighteen years of age, he should give them the type of instruction in it which lays emphasis on deeper understanding, independent thinking, and investigation. . . .

Philosophic Observations on Religion: When the Talmud is so much a part of them that there is hardly any chance of its being lost, and they are firmly entrenched in the Torah and the practice of its commands, then the teacher is to impart to them the third necessary subject. This is the refutation of the errors of the apostates and heretics and the justification of those views and practices, which the religion prescribes. . . .

Philosophy: These studies are divided into three groups. The first group is normally dependent on matter, but can, however, be separated from matter through concept and imagination. This class comprises mathematical sciences. In the second group, speculation cannot be conceived of apart from the material, either through imagination or conception. To this section belong the natural sciences. The third group has nothing to do with matter and has no material attributes; this group includes in itself metaphysics as such.

Logic: But these sciences are preceded by logic, which serves as a help and instrument. It is through logic that the speculative activities, which the three groups above mentioned include, are made clear. Logic presents the rules, which keep the mental powers in order, and lead man on the path of clarity and truth in all things wherein he may err.

Translation from Jacob Marcus, *The Jew in the Medieval World: A Sourcebook 315–1791,* rev. ed. (Cincinnati, OH: Hebrew Union College Press, 1999), 429–30.

Maimon), was born in Córdoba in 1135 but later fled to Egypt to escape religious persecution under the Almohads. There he served as a communal leader and court physician to the Islamic ruler, somehow managing to write extensively in his spare time before his death in 1204. His writings are voluminous, covering topics ranging from medicine to legal advice. One of the most important is his *Mishneh Torah,* a fourteen-volume code of Jewish law, but for our purposes the most relevant is his *Guide for the Perplexed,* the most important medieval Jewish philosophical text. Counting himself among an intellectual

elite able to discern truth by dint of reason, Maimonides, like Saadya, sought to develop a philosophical understanding of Scripture that would validate and illuminate it by means of logical proofs and argumentation. His work would have a shaping influence on subsequent Jewish philosophy, both as a model for how to bridge revelation and reason and as a foil for those opposed to their reconciliation.

In *The Guide for the Perplexed,* heavily indebted to Aristotelianism, though not always agreeing with it, Maimonides acknowledges the limits of human reason for understanding

God. It is impossible for humans to know anything about God except in a negative way; we can only know what God is not, that God is *not* imperfect, *not* multiple, *not* material, and so forth. In his view, idolatry is an intellectual error, a projection of human attributes onto God, and biblical language that describes God anthropomorphically, in human terms, must be interpreted figuratively. God does not really have an image, does not feel anger or other emotions; biblical language to this effect is an attempt to translate God's attributes into humanly comprehensible terms and is not to be taken as literally true. In contrast to the tenets of Kalam, Maimonides is not committed beforehand to the idea that Scripture and philosophy must always be consistent; he is willing to consider philosophical arguments on their merits even when they might contradict Scripture, though the truth he reaches philosophically is invariably validated by Scripture. Although God is unknowable, divine law offers something of a bridge, a way for humans to improve themselves physically and spiritually. In contrast to Saadya, who divided divine law into two categories—those that were rational and those that could only be understood by means of revelation—Maimonides believed that all the commandments were rational, though some were easier to understand than others. (For example, Maimonides explained Judaism's dietary laws in terms of their salutary effect.) The ultimate good that one can achieve in life is a purely intellectual experience: the afterlife for Maimonides is the intellect living on in contemplation of God.

Maimonides did not resolve the tensions between philosophy and revelation—in fact, his questioning of a literal understanding of Scripture and other views would prove quite controversial in ensuing decades and centuries. As soon as Maimonides died in the year 1204, a fierce debate erupted among Jewish intellectuals in Spain and France about his philosophical and religious positions. What is now known as the **Maimonidean Controversy** provoked increasingly bitter polemic between the supporters and opponents of Maimonides, culminating in a ban placed by the great sages of northern France on his philosophical works. Still, the efforts of Maimonides and of other medieval Jewish philosophers would have a major impact on both Jewish culture and broader European culture. They served a crucial role as intermediaries between Islamic philosophy and Christian European thought as well, stimulating important medieval Christian theologians such as Thomas Aquinas.

Alongside philosophy, another response to Greek rationalism was Jewish mysticism. The study of this literature was long neglected in Jewish studies until the pioneering effort of **Gershom Scholem** (1897–1982) who was able to bring much of its history and intellectual vitality to light. As he and subsequent scholars have shown, medieval Jewish mystical tradition can be traced back to late antiquity—*Hekhalot* literature is an especially important precursor, and Gnosticism may have had some influence as well—but it developed in new directions in the Middle Ages under the influence of Neo-Platonism and the Islamic mystical tradition of Sufism. It is not always easy to draw a clear line between medieval Jewish philosophy and Jewish mysticism—Maimonides' own son, Abraham, openly admired the Sufis and adopted Sufi practices to cultivate a mystical experience of God—but one way to understand Jewish medieval mysticism is to see it as a reaction against the rationalism of such figures as Maimonides.

In Jewish mystical tradition, God can only be known through revelation to those chosen by God, not through the reasoned inferences and proofs of pagan philosophers like Aristotle. Language in the mystical view was not a product of human convention or a barrier between the mind and the divine; it was a direct extension of the divine and a medium of revelation in its own right.

An example of an early medieval Jewish mystical work, arising as early as the third or fourth century CE but exerting an important influence in the Middle Ages, was a composition called the **Sefer Yetzirah** (*Book of Creation*) (Some falsely attributed it to Abraham but its actual author is unknown). One of the contributions of this book was to transform the language of Hebrew into a medium of mystical experience. God had created the world through the combination and recombination of the letters of the alphabet, and, it was asserted, one could draw close to God by understanding the letters of the divine name. Another important term the book introduced was *sefirah* (pl. *sefirot*), though it does not yet carry the meaning it would acquire in later mystical tradition. Here it refers to the ten primordial numbers; as developed by the later mystical text **Sefer ha-Bahir** (*Book of Radiance*), a work that perhaps originated in the twelfth century; though its origins are unclear, the term refers to ten emanations or attributes of God, each of which serves a different function in the universe.

The most famous elaboration of this tradition is the work known as the **Zohar** or *Book of Splendor,* attributed in later tradition to the second-century rabbinic sage Shimon bar Yochai but believed to have been authored largely by a Spanish-Jewish mystic **Moses de Leon**. Living between 1240–1305, Moses hailed from a part of Spain controlled by Christians, and so we might well place the *Zohar* in that context, but he was steeped in the great Jewish works of the Islamic world, including Maimonides, and it is best to think of his work as a product of the cultural intermediate zone between Islam and Christianity that developed in Spain and Provence in southern France in this period.

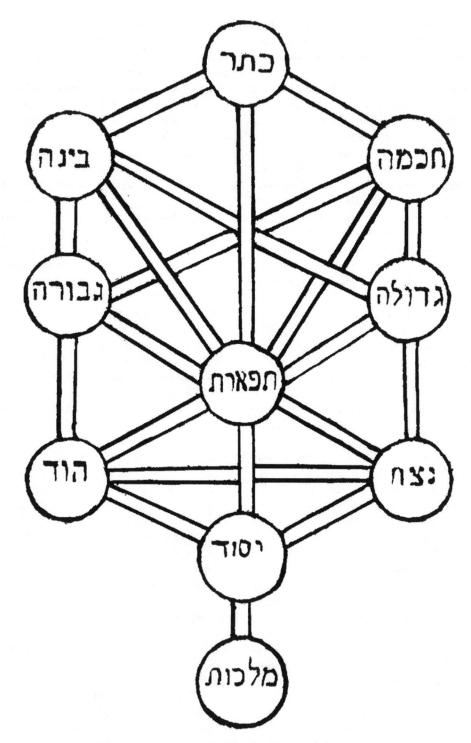

A diagram of the ten *sefirot*, or emanations of God in Kabbalistic tradition, and their relationship to one another. *Keter* is the highest of the *sefirot*, the point beyond which the mind cannot go. The uniting of *Hokhmah* and *Binah*, masculine and feminine aspects of God, produced the lower seven *sefirot*. Jewish mystics believed humans mirrored this structure, their soul originating from within it, and are thus in a position to influence God through their actions, promoting a harmonic and integrated relationship between the different parts of the *sefirotic* system through ethical and ritual practice.

The *Zohar* is more a collection of books than a single book—de Leon did not compose it all himself, and it would not be known in its present form until centuries after de Leon. Written in Aramaic, much of it represents a kind of commentary on the Five Books of Moses and its mysteries as focused through the discussion of Rabbi Shimon bar Yochai and other rabbis from the tannaitic age. Building on the kind of mystical ideas found in the *Book of Bahir*, the *Zohar* treats the Five Books of Moses as a coded story of God, who is unknowable and infinitely mysterious, and his *sefirot*, the emanations by which he is revealed in the world. According to the *Zohar*, to understand the Torah one must understand that when it is talking about a patriarch, or even about Israel, it is deploying a complex system of symbols to refer to the *sefirot*. By decoding its secrets, the reader of the *Zohar* can not only better understand God but can learn to restore the balance between God's different manifestations—justice and mercy, male and female, divine and human—that are out of alignment in the present. The *Zohar* would eventually achieve a kind of canonical status, but that is a later development that must be understood in the context of Christian Europe.

Yet another outlet for medieval Jewish imaginations was poetry, which in the medieval context often overlapped with philosophy and mysticism in its focus. As we noted in Chapter 5, the genre of *piyyut* originated in late antiquity, but it flourished well into the Middle Ages, undergoing changes under the influence of Arabic poetry. Here too Saadya played a pioneering role, using verse to express some of his arguments. The highpoint of medieval Jewish poetry was the period of Islamic rule in Spain. Figures such as Solomon ibn Gabirol and Judah ha-Levi adopted Arabic poetic genres, meter, verse patterns, and figures of speech in their Hebrew poetry. The secularism, bawdy hedonism, and homoeroticism of some of this poetry can surprise people expecting only piety and prudishness from the Middle Ages—some poems are voiced by a male speaking to a male lover in sexualized terms—but it may be that our conceptions of religiosity and gender simply do not fit this period or that modern "liberated" sensibilities cannot fully appreciate the allure of transgressing social norms. The same poets often weave biblical allusions into their poetry, sometimes having composed it for recitation in the synagogue and used it to express spiritual yearning (*see box*, The Role of Poetry in Medieval Jewish Society).

Solomon ibn Gabirol (ca. 1021–1070, though perhaps he died earlier in 1057) was born in Malaga, Spain, and orphaned at an early age. Although he had some important patrons, he spent much of his life as a wanderer, earning a living with great difficulty and suffering a skin condition that seems to have had an isolating effect on him. Some of his poetry is what we would consider secular, mourning his inability to enjoy the pleasures of the world, but some has a mystical orientation, resembling Sufi poetry and revealing a Neo-Platonic cast, as in the following passage from a poem entitled "Keter malkhut" or "Royal Crown," in which he imagines human beings as extensions of the presence of God in the finite world:

> You bestowed upon it the spirit of wisdom
> and called it 'soul' . . .
> And you placed it in the body to serve it and keep it . . .
> because from fire [the body] was created,
> evolving from nothing into something
> when God came to it in fire.

The mystical poetry of ibn Gabirol endows the names of God with mystical significance and describes the upper spheres in great detail. But this is the same author who wrote a philosophical dialogue on metaphysical matters, *Mekor Hayyim* or the *Source of Life*—a reminder not to treat philosophy and mysticism in this period as mutually exclusive pursuits. Originally written in Arabic, *Mekor Hayyim* accepts the Neo-Platonic ideas of emanation, as expounded by Plotinus. But where ibn Gabirol's view of emanation differs is that he sees divine emanation as the result of God's will rather than a natural or mechanical phenomenon. Matter, in the form of emanation, is, therefore, spiritual and flows directly from the Divine; it takes on material form only when far removed from its point of origin.

The poetry of **Judah ha-Levi** (1075–1141), considered to be the greatest of the medieval Jewish poets, also blurs the boundary between philosophy, mysticism, and poetry. Born in Tudela, then under the Muslims, he moved between Christian and Muslim Spain, ultimately leaving Spain altogether for Palestine. He wrote an important philosophical treatise called the *Kuzari*, which describes an imaginary dialogue among a philosopher, a Christian, a Jew, and a Muslim, each of whom attempts to convince the Khazar king that his worldview is the best. The work demonstrates ha-Levi's familiarity with Aristotelianism but is actually a polemic against the use of reason, personified in the dialogue by a philosopher who presents God in intellectual terms and argues that one need not follow any particular law to understand him: "Once you have integrated this philosophy within yourself, you need not concern yourself with which specific dogma, set of rituals and other actions, choice of words or language that you will practice. If you like, you could even fabricate your own religion . . . or you might follow the intellectually stimulating rituals of the philosophers."

THE ROLE OF POETRY IN MEDIEVAL JEWISH SOCIETY

Poetry in medieval Muslim society, and thus also among the Jews of Muslim Spain, played a far more important role than we might imagine today. The Jewish poets writing in Hebrew were patronized by Jews with powerful connections at the Muslim court, just as Muslim rulers supported poets writing in Arabic. Poetry was, of course, an art form—but the recitation of poetry also played an important role as a social pastime (at least for the learned elite); it expressed certain cultural values, and it was a powerful tool of political propaganda.

One poem, by Dunash ibn Labrat, expresses well the secular orientation of a great portion of medieval Hebrew poetry, including the topics of wine and love. But it also, in its second part, raises a more skeptical voice: the voice of the poet as a cultural critic, who is aware of the fragile nature of life and who expresses his unease with the "good life" celebrated in the first part of the text.

There came a voice: "Awake!
Drink wine at morning's break.
'Mid rose and camphor make
A feast of all your hours,

'Mid pomegranate trees
And low anemones,
Where vines extend their leaves
And the palm tree skyward towers,

Where lilting singers hum
To the throbbing of the drum,
Where gentle viols thrum
To the plash of fountains' showers.

On every lofty tree
The fruit hangs gracefully.
And all the birds in glee
Sing among the bowers.

The cooing of the dove
Sounds like a song of love.
Her mate calls from above—
Those trilling, fluting fowls.

We'll drink on garden beds
With roses round our heads.
To banish woes and dreads
We'll frolic and carouse.

The philosopher's argument exposes the threat posed to Judaism by philosophy; if the truth can be apprehended through logic and reason, specific rituals and beliefs have no use in Judaism; one can just as easily invent one's own religion if one likes. Judah ha-Levi countered this view by arguing for the limits of reason. To apprehend God, one needed revelation, an experience limited to Israel. In the *Kuzari,* he wrote:

You have been seduced by false ideas, and you requested to understand that which your Creator never intended for you to comprehend. The physical mind was never given the ability to logically comprehend these things. This ability was granted, however, to a choice group of God's elite, the purest of the pure in all of creation. Such individuals' souls are able to discern the universe in its entirety and are able to see their God and His angels. . . .

Dainty food we'll eat.
We'll drink our liquor neat,
Like giants at their meat,
With appetite aroused.

When morning's first rays shine
I'll slaughter of the kine
Some fatlings; we shall dine
On rams and calves and cows.

Scented with rich perfumes,
Amid thick incense plumes,
Let us await our dooms,
Spending in joy our hours."

I chided him: "Be still!
How can you drink your fill
When lost is Zion hill
To the uncircumcised.

You've spoken like a fool!
Sloth you've made your rule.
In God's last judgment you'll
For folly be chastised.

The Torah, God's delight
Is little in your sight,
While wrecked is Zion's height,
By foxes vandalized.

How can we be carefree
Or raise our cups in glee,
When by all men are we
Rejected and despised

Translation from Raymond Scheindlin, *Wine, Women, and Death* (Philadelphia 1986), 41–2.

We cannot know this kind of knowledge or how to acquire it unless it is brought to us through prophecy.

Some of these same ideas are reflected in ha-Levi's poetry. Approximately eight hundred of his poems are known to us. They often dwell on "secular" topics, such as wine, love, the beauty of boys and women, friendship, and grief. Much of his poetry, however, is religious, as he reflects on the biblical past, expresses personal religious experience, struggles with sin, or expresses his yearning for the redemption of his people and their return to Palestine. The following lines famously express the tension he felt between the material delights of Muslim Spain and the spiritual pull of Zion (he eventually left Spain for Palestine, only to die somewhere on the way):

> My heart is in the East, though I am at the westernmost end
> How can I savor and enjoy my food?
> How can I fulfill my vows and obligations, while
> Zion lies bound by Edom and I by the chains
> of Arabia

As already noted, in the *Kuzari* ha-Levi questions rationality as a source of knowledge about God. Only revelation, and one unique to the Jews, discloses that kind of knowledge. In some of his religious poetry, a similar idea emerges: God reveals himself to the heart but not the mind.

We close this section by noting one other way in which Greek philosophy and science reshaped Jewish intellectual life: biblical interpretation. The Middle Ages saw the rise of the running commentary on the biblical text, and some of those commentaries, reproduced in the margins of the traditional Jewish printed edition of the Bible known as the *Mikra'ot Gedolot* (literally "Big Scriptures"), continue to serve as an important tool for understanding the difficulties of the biblical text in the original Hebrew. Medieval Jewish biblical commentators understood the biblical text in different ways, but two interpretive modes are especially important. **Derash,** related to the word *midrash,* is an attempt to go beyond the explicit meaning of the text and tease out latent meanings or knowledge hinted at in the grammar, word choice, or spelling of the Hebrew text. **Peshat,** often translated as "literal interpretation," "contextual interpretation," or the "plain sense" of the text, sought to understand the biblical text in its historical and linguistic context.

Medieval commentators made great advances in the understanding of the *peshat* of the biblical text with the help of the science of grammar and literary analysis learned from Muslim scholars who developed these fields through the study of the Koran. Based as it was on reasoned analysis, *peshat* interpretation could potentially prove persuasive across linguistic and religious boundaries—its truth value did not depend on the authority of the rabbis or Oral Torah but rather on its correspondence with demonstrable historical or linguistic facts—and for that reason it played an important role in combating rival interpretations of the Bible by Karaites and Christians.

One of the most famous medieval commentators was **Abraham ibn Ezra** (1089–1164), a close associate of Judah ha-Levi, who drew on Arabic grammatical science to rationally derive the contextual meaning of the Bible independent of earlier midrashic understandings. Although he was also a prolific poet and philosopher, mathematician and astronomer, ibn Ezra is best remembered today for his biblical commentary—the first to appear in the Islamic world to be written in Hebrew rather than in Arabic. There he tried to strike a compromise between interpreters who relied on midrash for understanding the Bible and those who tried to understand the Bible independently of rabbinic tradition based on their own reasoning alone, using grammar and his observations of the world to explain the plain-sense meaning of the text while following rabbinic tradition in understanding biblical law. Some of what he suggests, or mysteriously hints at, about the authorship of the Bible—the idea that the second half of the prophet of Isaiah was written after the exile, for example—anticipates the findings of modern biblical scholarship.

The need for commentary demonstrates the peculiar mix of conservatism and innovation that marks the Jewish Middle Ages, innovation fostered by the encounter with Islamic intellectual culture. Both the Bible and the Talmud presented challenges to comprehension—sometimes even on a basic level. Most of the Bible was already over a thousand years old by the onset of the Jewish Middle Ages; even a learned person might not be able to fully understand the text in its entirety; the Talmud was even harder to comprehend, requiring readers to work through highly technical and convoluted argumentation. Through the power of reason, medieval commentators were able to unravel the puzzles posed by these sacred texts. Just as philosophy, science, and mysticism in this period were penetrating the secrets of the universe, biblical commentary of the sort that ibn Ezra exemplifies was revealing the secrets of the biblical text, not in a traditional or mystical sense but in a newly rationalist and scientific one shared with non-Jewish intellectuals. Like medieval Jewish philosophy and poetry, biblical commentary of the day manifests both the religious traditionalism of Jews in this period and their engagement with the past, as well as their openness to new ideas from the outside world.

Afterword: The Reverberations of Jewish–Islamic Culture

The story of the Jews of Islam continues without interruption into the modern period, but its trajectory begins to shift drastically around the thirteenth century. By this time, the Geonate had lost much of its luster with the death of the last great Gaon, Hai ben Sherira, in 1038. The Crusades had a devastating impact on the Jewish community in Palestine, and beyond its effects on the Jews residing there, it marked a tilt in the relationship between Christianity and Islam that would affect Jews throughout the Mediterranean as Christian rule spread into Muslim territory in Spain and the Holy Land. The eastern Islamic world was devastated by the Mongolian invasion in the thirteenth century, which destroyed the Abbassid Empire in 1258 (though Jews continued to live under Mongolian rule, and one even served as the governor of an entire state); Bedouin incursions disrupted life in North Africa; the military order of the Mamluks seemed to stifle Jewish culture in Egypt. Arabic went into a decline as a literary and intellectual language among the Jews of Spain in the twelfth century and was supplanted by Hebrew. It was not until the emergence of a new Muslim state—the empire of the Ottomans who conquered Byzantine Constantinople in 1453 and later defeated the Mamluks of Egypt and Syria in 1517—that the Jews of the Muslim Near East experienced another age of relative tolerance, economic success, and cultural creativity.

But before all those changes set in, Jewish culture as it developed under the influence of Islam began to have effects beyond the borders of Islamic rule. The resettlement of Jewish refugees in other parts of Europe, the translation of Arabic works into Hebrew, and the Christian conquest of Spain and its Jewish inhabitants all facilitated the transfer of Judeo–Arabic ideas and literature into the Christian–European realm where they had a major impact on Jewish and non-Jewish intellectual, religious, and cultural life.

Questions for Reflection

1. Where do the Jewish Middle Ages begin? Where do they end? What is the rationale for dividing Jewish history in this way?

2. What aspects of medieval Jewish culture seem to transcend the differences between Christian and Islamic rule?

3. What political or cultural changes help account for the rising influence of Geonic authority? What explains its eventual decline?

4. Does medieval Judeo–Arabic culture in Islamic Spain qualify as a "Golden Age" in your view? What accounts for the flourishing of Jewish culture in this age? What does the debate between Menahem ben Suruq and Dunash ibn Labrat tell us about how Jews living at this time saw the relationship between Jewish and Arabic culture?

5. What cultural and economic practices allowed Jews to participate in Islamic society? What sustained them as a distinct community?

6. What impact did Arabic–Islamic philosophy have on Jewish thought? In what ways do medieval Jewish mysticism and poetry reflect this influence? In what ways can be they be seen as a reaction against philosophy?

For Further Reading

For Jewish life under Islamic rule, note the classic six-volume work of Shelomo Goitein, *A Mediterranean Society: The Jewish Communities of the Arab World as Portrayed in the Documents of the Cairo Genizah* (Berkeley: University of California Press, 1967–1993), and for a one-volume history, see Bernard Lewis, *The Jews of Islam* (Princeton, NJ: Princeton University Press, 1985). For translations of relevant source material, see Jacob Marcus, *The Jew in the Medieval World: A Sourcebook 315–1791*, rev. ed. (Cincinnati, OH: Hebrew Union College Press, 1999), 429–30; Norman Stillman, *Jews of Arab Lands* (Philadelphia: Jewish Publication Society, 1979).

For the poorly documented Geonic period, see Robert Brody, *The Geonim of Babylonia and the Shaping of Medieval Jewish Culture* (New Haven: Yale University Press, 1998). For the more richly illumined Jewish history of Islamic Spain, see E. Ashtor, *History of the Jews in Muslim Spain* (Philadelphia: Jewish Publication Society, 1973–1984). On majority–minority relations in the medieval period, see Mark Cohen, *Under Crescent and Cross* (Princeton, NJ: Princeton University Press, 1994). On women, see the pertinent material in Judith Baskin, *Jewish Women in Historical Perspective* (Detroit: Wayne State University Press, 1998). For medieval travelogues, see Elkan Nathan Adler, ed., *Jewish Travellers* (New York: Hermon Press, 1966). For Karaite authors, see Leon Nemoy, *Karaite Anthology* (New Haven: Yale University Press, 1952). For more on Jewish communal life and self-rule, see Louis Finkelstein *Jewish Self-Government in the Middle Ages* (New York: P. Feldheim, 1964). For studies of Jewish literature and thought, consult Raymond Scheindlin, *Wine, Women and Death: Medieval Hebrew Poems on the Good Life* (Philadelphia: Jewish Publication Society, 1986) and Dan Pagis, *Hebrew Poetry of the Middle Ages and the Renaissance* (Berkeley: University of California Press, 1991). For studies of medieval Jewish thought, see Colette Sirat, *A History of Jewish Philosophy in the Middle Ages* (Cambridge, England: Cambridge University Press, 1985) and Daniel Frank and Oliver Leaman, *The Cambridge Companion to Medieval Jewish Philosophy* (Cambridge, England: Cambridge University, 2003). For major studies of Jewish mysticism by Gershom Scholem, see his *Major Trends in Jewish Mysticism* (New York: Schocken Books, 1941); *On the Kabbalah and Its Symbolism* (New York: Schocken Books, 1965); and *Origins of the Kabbalah,* trans. A. Arkush (Philadelphia: Jewish Publication Society, 1987).

Chapter 7

Under the Cross

Even before Islam divided the Mediterranean world, the Christian Roman Empire had begun to fracture politically. Germanic tribes and other invaders from the east had occupied most of western Europe, sacking Rome in 475–476, and thereafter its territory came under the rule of a variety of peoples: the Visigoths in Spain, the Franks in most of what became France, and the Lombards throughout much of Italy (gradually expelling the Byzantines from the south). The Byzantine Empire remained intact throughout this period, but its territory was constantly under attack by Muslims, Slavs, and others. Even the efforts of the Frankish king Charles the Great (Charlemagne, r. 768–814) could not unite Europe for long. In the year 800, Charlemagne took for himself the title "Holy Roman Emperor" in an attempt to reestablish the Western Roman Empire, which had ceased to exist almost four hundred years prior, but by the mid-ninth century this empire was already redivided. Within 150 years of Charlemagne's proclamation as emperor, multiple polities and cultures emerged even within France, not to mention the rest of Europe.

In addition to this political fracturing, deep theological issues divided Christians, especially over the nature of Jesus. Gradually, the theological position that came to be known as Orthodoxy dominated Christian Europe and the Byzantine Empire, but another theological viewpoint—Monophysitism, which held that Jesus was completely divine and not human—tended to wield more influence in the eastern Christian world that ultimately fell to Muslims. Orthodoxy, therefore, ended up defining the Christianity of those countries ruled by Christians, whereas those regions ruled by Muslims contained a wider variety of Christian doctrines. Increasing tensions between the two major Orthodox traditions of east and west culminated in the so-called "Great Schism" of 1054. The church of the Byzantine Empire retained the name "Orthodox," while the rival church based in Rome, the Catholic Church, reigned in western and central Europe.

Thus, just as Jews in the Islamic world were divided from one another by the political and religious differences between the Umayyads, the Abbassids, and the Fatimids, so too Jews in the Christian world lived in spheres divided by the religious and political boundaries that separated the Roman Catholic West from the Byzantine Orthodox East. For many centuries, the Jews of the Byzantine Empire, who spoke Greek and boasted a long, continuous history in the empire, outnumbered those in the Catholic west, but that began to change in the eleventh century, the age of the Crusades. Some Jewish communities fell to Catholic conquest in places such as Spain and southern Italy; others immigrated to Catholic regions such as southern France, while still other communities already established in the Catholic realm began to increase in size, along with the noticeable growth in European cities that began in this period. The Jewish community of Italy is a good example of Jewish growth in the Christian Middle Ages: In the year 1300, it hosted an estimated 50,000 Jews out of a total population of 11,000,000. By 1490, two centuries later, the Jewish population numbered 120,000 out of an estimated population of 12,000,000. As Christian Europe began to extend into Islamic realms—and to expand its economic and intellectual influence as well—the Jews under its rule became increasingly important in the larger Jewish world.

In this fractured landscape, Jewish experience varied widely from place to place, but we will nonetheless venture one broad generalization: While Jews prospered in many parts of the Christian realm, it was also in this context that they experienced severe levels of discrimination and violent persecution. In fact, between the expulsion of Jews from England in 1290 and that which took place in Spain in 1492, all of western Europe—with the exception of Italy—partially or completely expelled the Jews. The history of Jews during the Christian Middle Ages therefore begs the question: How do we square the relative cultural and communal prosperity Jews enjoyed under Christian rule with the widespread persecution that they suffered?

The answer to this question is complicated, but we can paint a broad historical picture. Until the thirteenth century, Jews by and large were tolerated by the Christian majority and were even invited to settle in certain areas on the assumption that they would fulfill certain economic functions for the larger community. Pragmatic financial considerations often seem to have overridden feelings of contempt for a group that the Church declared to be deicides. Christian theology fueled antagonism, but it also recognized its kinship to Judaism. The official position of the papacy toward the Jews, one of qualified tolerance shaped by the thinking of Saint Augustine, can be said to have been articulated by **Pope Gregory I** (r. 590–604). Gregory held that Jews were in theological error and enforced restrictions against them, but he also held that they ought not to be forcibly converted or killed. This position eventually became enshrined as official Church policy in a papal bull, ***Sicut Judaeis,*** originally promulgated by Calixtus II (r.1119–1124) and reissued by subsequent popes. It stated that "although in many ways the disbelief of the Jews must be condemned . . . they must not be oppressed grievously by the faithful." *Sicut Judaeis* granted Jews protection and forbade Christians from compelling their conversion. The resulting combination of pragmatism and religious tolerance allowed Jewish communities to exist and even flourish under Christian rule.

Sometimes, especially in times of political, economic, or ecological stress, a more hostile anti-Judaism asserted itself. At such moments, the religious antagonism built into the relationship between Christians and Jews overwhelmed the mutual self-interest that had allowed Jews to settle into a fairly stable symbiotic relationship with larger Christian communities. The resulting antagonism had a major impact on Jewish lives in the Christian realm, leading to the dejudaizing of parts of western Europe altogether while reshaping the legal and economic status of Jews living in other parts of the Christian world. The situation for Jews in western Europe became particularly dire in the twelfth to fifteenth centuries, with four interrelated factors playing an especially catalytic role: the Crusades, the rise of the blood libel and other anti-Jewish accusations, the resentment generated by the role of Jews in the larger economic and political structure of Europe, and a more hostile and interventionist Church. Reacting to an earlier generation of scholarship, historians in the last fifty years have been wary of what Salo Baron famously called the "lachrymose" view of Jewish history that sees the Middle Ages as an era of continuous Jewish misery at the hands of Christians, stressing how sporadic and localized Christian persecutions of the Jews were. The reader should keep that caution in mind when reading the following account, but the fact is that conditions for Jews in western Europe did greatly worsen by the end of the Middle Ages, as measured by the expulsion and migration of Jews from western Europe to other locales. To understand that demographic shift, it is important to have some understanding of the following four developments.

The Crusades

After the year 1000, by which time most Europeans had become Christian, Europe became more aggressively self-confident and went on the march against the Islamic world. In 1095 Pope Urban II called on European Christians to remove the ruling Muslims from the Holy Land, launching the First Crusade. (*Crusade* is a word derived from the crosses appearing on the outer garments of those who responded to the pope's call.) Over the twelfth and thirteenth centuries, other crusades followed. They were ostensibly provoked by Muslim incursions into the Holy Land, but the reports coming back from Jerusalem sometimes depicted the Jews as culprits too, and that drew them into the conflict. Crusaders, impassioned by religious zeal and being part of a violent mob, were thus sometimes deflected from their original mission, attacking instead Jews they came across—the alleged motivation: revenge for the death of Jesus. As one report describes the crusaders' response when they encountered Jews on their way to the Holy Land: "We are going a long way to seek out the profane shrine, and to avenge ourselves on the Ishamelites, when here, in our very midst are the Jews—they whose forefathers murdered and crucified Him for no reason."

During the First Crusade, for example, as the French and German bands of soldiers and stragglers marched eastward toward Jerusalem, the crusaders fell upon the thriving Jewish communities of the Rhineland, in the cities of Speyer, Worms, Trier, and Mainz in what is now the western part of Germany. For their part, the Jews of the area recognized the danger they were in and tried various ways of saving themselves, dispatching letters to sympathetic rulers and offering a large gift to Godfrey of Bouillon, leader of the crusade, but they were unable to stop the violence. In 1096, the crusaders attacked the synagogue in Speyer and killed eleven Jews. One woman took her own life rather than submit to forced conversion, the first instance of Jewish martyrdom during the Crusades. As the crusaders went on the attack, some Jews sought to defend themselves, some fled, others sought the help of local bishops, and some took their own lives rather than accept conversion. When the crusaders finally reached

The statue on the left is a medieval representation of the Church (i.e., Christianity), depicted as a proud and victorious woman. On the right, the synagogue (i.e., Judaism) is depicted as a blindfolded woman bearing a broken scepter. These particular statues are from a thirteenth-century cathedral in Bamberg, Germany, but similar images appeared in many other places in Christian Europe. Their intended message was to show the supremacy of Christianity over Judaism—the latter understood as a blind and impotent faith—and they suggest a theological role for Jews in a Christianized society—to serve as a foil for Christian superiority and as living testimony for what happens to those who reject its tenets.

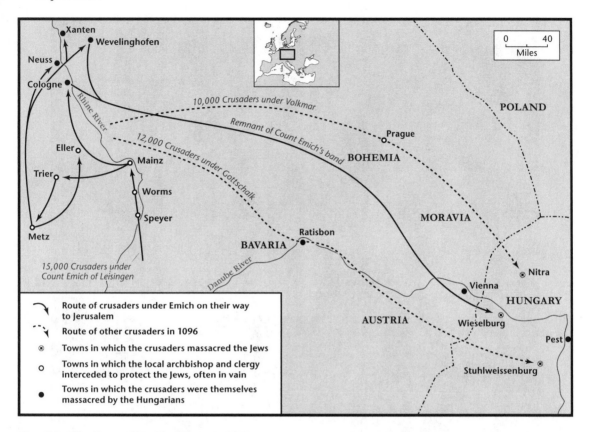

Map 7-1   The Route of the First Crusade, 1096.

Jerusalem in 1099, they killed the Jews there too, along with the Muslims of the city, further weakening the Rabbanite Jewish community of Palestine and essentially destroying the Karaite community (*see* Map 7-1).

When the killing was over, thousands of Jews were dead. Others had been forcibly baptized, and some Jewish children had been kidnapped. But it is, most of all, the stories of suicide and despair that make the chronicles of the First Crusade so unforgettably terrible. The Hebrew sources that we have for the First Crusade describe how Jewish parents, rather than watch their children forcibly baptized, killed them before killing themselves. Christian sources, such as the account of Albert of Aix, corroborate that version of events. Thus, Albert reports:

[The Crusader] Emico and the rest of his band held a council and, after sunrise, attacked the Jews in the hall with arrows and lances. Breaking the bolts and doors, they killed the Jews, about seven hundred in number, who in vain resisted the force and attack of so many thousands. They killed the women, also, and with their swords

pierced tender children of whatever age and sex. The Jews, seeing that their Christian enemies were attacking them and their children, and that they were sparing no age, likewise fell upon one another, brother, children, wives, and sisters, and thus they perished at each other's hands. Horrible to say, mothers cut the throats of nursing children with knives and stabbed others, preferring them to perish thus by their own hands rather than to be killed by the weapons of the uncircumcised.

The Jews who killed themselves in this way came to be seen as martyrs, their deaths perceived as a glorification of God—hence the use of the Hebrew phrase *Kiddush ha-Shem* ("the sanctification of God's name") to describe their act of self-sacrifice. In an effort to endow their death with meaning, Hebrew chronicles compare their death to Abraham's sacrifice of his son Isaac: "Inquire now and look about, was there ever such an abundant sacrifice as this since the days of the primeval Adam? Were there ever eleven hundred offerings on one day, each one of them like the sacrifice of Isaac, the son of Abraham?"

THE FATE OF FORCED CONVERTS

The ideal of *Kiddush ha-Shem*—accepting death or killing oneself to preserve God's honor—was widely embraced as an ideal in medieval Europe, but many Jews nonetheless opted to save their lives and those of their families by accepting conversion to Christianity, and their status posed a difficult legal and social problem: Does a Jew have a greater obligation to preserve his or her own life (with the intent to return to Judaism when it is safe to do so) or to die for the sanctification of God's name? How does coercion affect the status of the person who chooses to convert to save his or her life? And what of forced converts who want to return to Judaism when they are able? Should they be accepted back into the community after having left it for another religion?

Forced converts, though adopting another religion, did not necessarily abandon Judaism in their hearts, and they sustained the family ties and friendships that bound them to the Jewish community. For such reasons, many Jews sought to return to Judaism when it was safe to do so. They were not always welcome, however. As the First Crusade demonstrated, many Jews believed that they had an obligation to sacrifice their lives rather than to betray God. Those who did were treated as heroes, while conversely, those who opted to convert were often deeply resented by fellow Jews.

Seeking to resolve these issues, some medieval authorities tried to strike a balance, acknowledging the ideal of martyrdom while trying to allow room for those choosing conversion over death. Such was the case with Maimonides, for example, who may have briefly converted to Islam under duress. Around 1165, he wrote a letter in which he tried to ease the burden of the Jew who chose to convert under fear of death rather than to die for his faith: "True, it is incumbent upon him to surrender to death, but if he does not, he is not guilty." In fact, he should choose to live, he maintained—to "leave these places (where he was persecuted for his religion) and go to where he can practice religion and fulfill the Law without compulsion or fear." Living under Christian rule, Rabbi Meir of Rothenberg (1215–1293) echoed Maimonides' view. Meir took the position that "although a Jew is required to choose death rather than be forced to worship idols [in this case, to become a Christian], should he violate this law, he would not become disqualified as a witness, though he would be guilty of having committed a sin." In other words, even if forced to submit to baptism, the Jew's core character and faithfulness are not to be doubted by his community, as long as he repents for the sin of idol worship. And Meir goes on to take an even more lenient position for those who clearly converted unwillingly, excusing their action by writing that because "they never actually embraced Christianity, but merely listened without comment to the priest's recitation . . . [so they] never committed a sin." In his mind, it was legitimate to fake conversion to survive: "A Jew is not required to choose death rather than allow the Christians to deceive themselves into believing that they have converted him." Jews who disguised their Judaism under the guise of conversion have come to be known as **crypto-Jews.**

Such views created an alternative to *Kiddush ha-Shem* by allowing for the possibility of a tactical or feigned conversion if that was the only way to preserve one's life. They also justified the reintegration of such Jews when they sought to return to the community. On the other hand, when Christians came to recognize the possible insincerity of Jewish conversion, that intensified their suspicions of both Jewish converts and Jews themselves.

Despite the deep scars that these events left on Jewish psyches, the First Crusade did not significantly derail the growth patterns of German Jewry. In the wake of the Crusades, the Jewish communities of the Rhineland were able to reconstitute themselves with the help of the Holy Roman Emperor Henry IV, who even allowed converted Jews to return to their religion without further penalty. Those who did found themselves in a further difficulty, because, while some Jewish communities embraced them with open arms, others questioned the sincerity of their return. In such cases, rabbis mitigated that problem to some extent by developing legal arguments for their reintegration (see box, The Fate of Forced Converts). The terrible violence of the First Crusade may be what prompted the promulgation of the *Sicut Judaeis,* which institutionalized a more tolerant attitude toward the Jews.

But the First Crusade was not the last. During the Second Crusade (1145–1149), a monk named Rudolf led another violent attack against the Jews of the Rhineland, though efforts by the religious leader Bernard of Clairvaux to prevent such killing mitigated the number of deaths. In England, during the Third Crusade (1189—1192), the one that involved King Richard I (Richard the Lionhearted), Jews were massacred in Lynn, Norwich, Stamford, and Bury St. Edmunds, while the greatest violence against Jews took place in York in 1190 (an incident to which we will return).

The Crusades mark a watershed moment in the history of the Jews in medieval Europe. With the Crusades the nature of anti-Jewish sentiment shifted from being a Mediterranean, ecclesiastical discourse about the Jews' alleged theological error to a northern European explosion of violence perpetrated by soldiers and peasants. The First Crusade marked a shift from a discursive to a physical attack on Jews, the first such significant episode in the history of the Jews of Europe. Even though physical recovery occurred quite quickly for the decimated Jewish communities, the psychological scars created by the First Crusade left a deep impact on European Jewry. Feelings of suspicion, unease, and betrayal shaped Jewish attitudes to the world around them. Special liturgical poems (*piyyutim*) commemorating the events were composed at the time. They reinforced a sense of Jewish vulnerability but also historical memory as the proud example of the Jewish martyrs was recalled, and such poems are included in synagogue services to this day. Further institutionalizing the impact of the Crusades on Jewish memory was the post-Crusades tradition of reciting publicly the deeds of the martyrs on the anniversary of their deaths. Their names and dates were recorded in a *Yizkorbukh,* or memorial book. Following the Crusades, such books were created in most Ashkenazic cities and towns in Europe and added to into the twentieth century.

The Blood Libel and Other Lethal Accusations

From not long after the First Crusade, we have a report of the first known case of **blood libel** against Jews. The term blood libel refers to the accusation that Jews were guilty of various kinds of atrocities, most especially the killing of Christians to use their blood to make the unleavened bread eaten during Passover and for other rituals (despite the fact that Jewish law explicitly prohibits contact with blood).

The association of Jews with blood was further complicated by the claim that Jews used Christian blood as a palliative. Medicine and magic were closely linked, and the Jewish application of Christian blood was said to effect miraculous cures. In the Middle Ages it was said that if a blind Jew were to smear his eyes with the blood of monks, his eyesight would be restored. According to popular wisdom, Constantine was said to have been stricken with leprosy for his persecution of Christians and was advised by his Jewish physician to bathe in the blood of Christian children. The leprotic Richard the Lionhearted was said to have been given similar advice to cure his disease. Other medievals firmly believed that Christian blood applied topically cured Jews of the wound of circumcision. In Hungary it was claimed that once a year Jews strangled a child or virgin with phylacteries, drew blood from the victim, and smeared it on the genitals of their children to ensure fertility. Finally, belief was widespread that Jewish males menstruated, a view articulated by the Italian astrologer Cecco d'Ascoli, who declared that "after the death of Christ all Jewish men, like women, suffer menstruation." This would be a charge repeated with some consistency for centuries to come. Christian blood was said to cure Jewish male menstruation, and thus was it necessary for Jews to procure it.

The blood libel surfaces for the first time in Christian Europe in England in 1144 when the body of a Christian boy named William of the town of Norwich was discovered in the woods and the Jews of the community were accused of having tortured and hanged him in the way their ancestors were believed to have killed Christ. The local sheriff investigating the murder did not act on the charge, but similar accusations would arise on the Continent throughout the twelfth and thirteenth centuries, and these often did result in trials, imprisonment, and violence.

In 1171, for example, a servant in Blois, France, accused a local Jew of murdering a child and dumping his body into the Loire River. According to Ephraim of Bonn, who relates the story, all the Jews of the town (numbering about forty) were imprisoned, and eventually thirty-one were killed. Another terrible instance involved a series of blood libels in Mainz, Munich, and other communities in the 1280s that prompted a mysterious German knight known as **Rindfleisch** to go from town to town urging the massacre of the Jews. This resulted in thousands of deaths in southern and central Germany in 1298 until Emperor Albert I of Austria stopped the killing. One ruler, **Fredrick II of Hohenstaufen** (1194–1250; r. 1212–1250), tried to exonerate the Jews of this kind of accusation and even convened a council of Jewish converts to Christianity, presumed experts in Jewish practice, to refute the blood libel, but it nevertheless persisted.

Another anti-Jewish accusation known as **host desecration** follows a similar trajectory. The precipitant for this kind of accusation was the **Fourth Lateran Council** in 1215, which officially recognized the belief that the wafer used in the Catholic ceremony of the Eucharist, the *host,* actually became the body of Christ during the ceremony, a doctrine known as *transubtantiation.* Some Christians maintained that Jews, believing in this doctrine themselves, stabbed and mutilated the host in a kind of renenactment of the crucifixion of Christ, allegedly causing it to shed blood. Such accusations—the first known case occurred in 1243—often had two consequences: A cult would be established on the site of the desecration, and the community would seek retaliation against the local Jewish community; many Jews were tried and executed for this reason. In 1290, for example, a Jewish moneylender in Paris was accused of host desecration, an event commemorated in a chapel built on the site and probably also the trigger of an expulsion of Jews from France in 1306. Another accusation in 1370 led to the virtual end of the Jewish community in medieval Belgium. The last Jew

BLAMING THE JEWS FOR THE BLACK DEATH

On St. Valentine's Day, February 14, 1349, the Jews of Strasbourg, France, were massacred after the suspicion arose that they had caused the plague by poisoning the wells. The following account, written not long after the events it describes, is from a chronicle written by Jacob von Königshofen (1346–1420). Note the author's recognition of an ulterior motive behind the killing of Jews:

> In the year 1349 there occurred the greatest epidemic that ever happened. Death went from one end of the earth to the other, on that side and this side of the sea, and it was greater among the Saracens (Muslims) than among the Christians. In some lands everyone died so that no one was left. Ships were also found on the sea laden with wares; the crew had all died and no one guided the ship. The bishop of Marseilles and priests and monks and more than half of all the people there died with them. In other kingdoms and cities so many people perished that it would be horrible to describe. The Pope at Avignon stopped all sessions of court, locked himself in a room, allowed no one to approach him and had a fire burning before him all the time. And from what this epidemic came, all wise teachers and physicians could say that it was God's will. And as the plague was not here, so it was in other places, and lasted more than a whole year. This epidemic also came to Strasbourg in the summer of the above mentioned year, and it is estimated that about sixteen thousand people died.
>
> In the matter of this plague the Jews throughout the world were reviled and accused in all lands of having caused it through the poison which they are said to have put in the water and the wells. . . . that is what they were accused of and for this reason the Jews were burnt all the way from the Mediterranean into Germany, but none in Avignon for the pope protected them there. . . .
>
> On Saturday—that was St. Valentine's Day—they burnt the Jews on a wooden platform in their cemetery. There were about two thousand people of them. Those who wanted to baptize themselves were spared. [Some say that about a thousand accepted baptism.] Many small children were taken out of the fire and baptized against the will of their fathers and mothers. And everything that was owed the Jews was cancelled and the Jews had to surrender all pledges and notes that they had taken for debts. The council, however, took the cash that the Jews possessed and divided it among the working-men proportionally. The money was indeed the thing that killed the Jews. If they had been poor and if the feudal lords had not been in debt to them, they would not have been burnt.

Translation from Jacob Marcus, *The Jew in the Medieval World: A Sourcebook 315–1791*, rev. ed. (Cincinnati, OH: Hebrew Union College Press, 1999), 51–53.

killed for the "crime" of host desecration died in the seventeenth century.

Yet another kind of anti-Jewish accusation was triggered by the **Black Death,** an epidemic of bubonic plague and other contagious diseases that swept across Europe between 1347 and 1350. Unable to understand the medical causes of the plague, and with their hostility stoked by the blood libel and host desecration accusations, many Christians came to suspect the Jews of poisoning the wells out of malice and vengeance. Jews were forced to confess and testify against other Jews, and as the accusation spread, more and more were killed, expelled, or martyred. Pope Clement VI, recognizing that Jews too suffered from the plague, tried to protect them as did other rulers, but all such efforts were to little avail (see box, Blaming the Jews for the Black Death).

Economic Tensions

Beyond the prejudices and fears that motivated such violence were political and economic causes as well. The emerging concept of royal (or chamber) serfdom in the twelfth century was an important factor. Jews depended for protection on the temporal leadership—kings, dukes, and barons—and that relationship became formalized as a kind of servitude or serfdom. Jewish communities were entitled to legal protection not because they were citizens of a city or because of privileges granted to them under earlier Roman law but because they were considered part of a ruler's estate.

Royal protection was a major reason that the Jews were able to live in medieval Christian Europe, but royal protection turned out to be something of a protection racket as well. Since Jews were tied to the king as serfs, their freedom of movement was restricted—if they left the realm of their lord, they could in theory be forcibly returned. They were also subject to taxes, penalties, and the ransoms that had to be paid in the case of arrest. Jews were vulnerable to the arbitrary whims and shifting interests of a ruler. He could freely decide to seize for himself the money he was owed, restrict the Jews' ability to charge interest on loans, pressure them to convert, or even expel them from his realm. No less dangerously, their association with the king had the effect of further isolating Jews from the rest of the population, exacerbating their differences, and turning even the benefits of serfdom into a source of resentment. Jews formed vertical alliances with the ruler but few, if any, horizontal alliances with those around them. Heavily protected by the monarch and often regarded as an extension of royal rule, Jews were seen by the local population as a proxy for the king, and thus blood libels and host desecration accusations doubled as a way for the masses to act out against rulers they resented.

Adding to their isolation was the role that some Jews had come to play in the economy of Christian Europe, especially their prominence as moneylenders. A variety of factors promoted moneylending among Jews. While they did own land, they were at a disadvantage because their parcels were smaller than those of Christian landowners, and legal restrictions affected their ability to employ Christian laborers and slaves; they were blocked from various crafts by the existence of closed guilds; they continued to engage in trade but faced increasing competition from Christian merchants; and Christian opposition to Christian usury (the lending of money with an exorbitant interest rate) recommended Jews as a logical alternative source of financing—indeed, in some places Jews were forced to lend money to Christians. Jews became so associated with the profession that Christian lenders were sometimes called "wretched Judaizers" and "baptized Jews." For their part, Jews were drawn to moneylending by the leisure time it afforded for study and communal engagement. Some Jews became quite successful in this way. At the time of his death in 1186, Aaron of Lincoln, one of the richest men in England, was owed 15,000 pounds by 430 people. The financing such figures made available was instrumental in the economic development of many towns and cities, and even the Church came to rely on it—Aaron helped finance the building of Lincoln Cathedral—though it regulated the interest that Jews could charge.

But Jewish moneylending also provoked animosity. Moneylending reversed the expected power relationship between Jews and Christians. Needy Christians resented their dependency and indebtedness to Jews, not necessarily understanding the expenses and risks that might justify the charg-

ing of high interest rates, and could become even more resentful if they had to forfeit the collateral they had pledged to pay off a debt. Moneylending was seen as a kind of blood-sucking. "Money is the vital warmth of a town," observed the fifteenth-century Franciscan monk Bernardino de Siena, "when blood and warmth leave . . . it is a sign of death. The danger is incomparably more imminent when wealth . . . accumulates in the hands of the Jews." Stories of Jewish moneylending could intermix with accusations of host desecration, as in a painting entitled *The Profanation of the Host,* now on display in a palace in Urbino. The villain of the story is a Jewish moneylender who offers to return to a Christian woman the pledge on her loan if she secures a host for him to abuse.

Increased Hostility from the Church

One final source of tension between Christians and Jews was the Church, which became intensely hostile toward Jews, especially in the thirteenth century. The Christianized Roman Empire had passed harsh anti-Jewish legislation already in late antiquity, and many of those restrictions persisted into the Middle Ages, at least in theory, but the thirteenth century can nonetheless be seen as a new era in Jewish–Christian antagonism, of sharpened segregation between Jews and Christians, and of more active intervention by the Church into Jewish affairs.

It was in this period that new or renewed restrictions against Jewish–Christian interaction were imposed. The most important example is the Fourth Lateran Council convened by Pope Innocent III in 1215. Although not primarily concerned with the Jews, the council passed resolutions that restricted the interest rates Jews could charge, barred them from holding office, prevented Jewish converts to Christianity from converting back to Judaism, and required Jews to dress differently from Christians in part to stigmatize them as well as to discourage sexual contact with Christians. The impact of these laws would last for centuries. In some areas, Jews were required to wear a special badge or conical hat. As previously noted, the same council formulated the doctrine of transubstantiation, the trigger for host desecration accusations.

It is important to note that the papacy remained reluctant to act directly against the Jews, respecting the privileges granted by the *Sicut Judaeis* and even reissuing it repeatedly. On many occasions, popes intervened to protect Jews from blood libels and other accusations, although their opposition was often without practical effect. But the Church did sometimes act directly against the Jews. In 1236, a Jewish convert to Christianity submitted a memorandum to Pope Gregory IX, claiming that the Talmud blasphemed Jesus and Mary and expressed hatred of non-Jews. The pope responded by ordering the confiscation and burning of the Talmud and other Jewish books, an act that was repeated by later popes. The use of an inquisition to condemn the Talmud in Paris in 1242, with a special tribunal established to investigate heresy, was an ominous innovation, redirecting a tool developed by the Church to curb Christian heresy against the Jews.

The religious order known as the **Franciscans,** established by Francis of Assisi in 1209, was employed to enforce this order, and together with the religious order known as the **Dominicans** worked to enforce other anti-Jewish decrees of the Church. Working among the poor predisposed the Franciscans against Jewish moneylenders, with Franciscan preachers such as Bernardino de Siena helping to incite expulsions. The last major blood libel of the Middle Ages, in Trent in 1475, resulted in the expulsion of Jews from the city and was instigated by a fanatical Franciscan friar named Bernardino da Feltre. Even as the pope was prepared to defend the Jews,

as he was in this instance, the religious orders of the Church were helping to put the Jews on the defensive.

The increased antagonism between Jews and Christians in this period was reflected in the rise of public disputations between Christian and Jewish theologians in the thirteenth century, the most famous occurring in Paris in 1240 (and culminating in the 1242 burning of the Talmud), in Barcelona in 1263, and in Tortosa in 1414. During these encounters, which took place through the efforts of the Dominicans in the case of the Barcelona disputation, Christian and Jewish representatives openly contested each other's understanding of the Bible and theology. Christians used apostate Jews such as Pablo Christiani with knowledge of the Hebrew Bible and the Talmud to present their case, while Jews relied on rabbinic sages such as Moses ben Nahman, better known as **Nahmanides** (1194–1270), to present the Jewish case. Each side defended its position vigorously and ingeniously. In the Barcelona disputation, Christiani sought not to impugn the Talmud but rather to use it to prove the

A late medieval woodcut illustrating a disputation between Christians and Jews.

claims of Christianity. For his part, Nahmanides was so successful in countering Christiani's arguments that the Spanish king presented him with a gift of three hundred dinars. Still, we should not think the playing field was even. Nahmanides had been coerced into participating and was later tried for abusing Christianity, eventually escaping to Aragon and then Palestine.

The Disputation at Tortosa, led on the Christian side by an apostate named Geronimo de Santa Fé, was an even more fearful experience for Jews; it was not really a debate at all but an opportunity for the Christian representatives to accuse the Jews of betraying their own religion by denying Christ. As the debate dragged on—it lasted for some twenty months—the Jewish side began to despair, but the Jews did manage to develop some effective counterarguments. One rabbi, Astruc ha-Levi, even dared contest the injustice of the proceedings. In the end, though, Geronimo got the last word. Among the results of this disputation for Jews were the imposition of additional anti-Jewish measures, adopted in some communities, the conversion of many Jews to Christianity, and an order that the heretical elements identified by Geronimo in the Talmud be censored.

In addition to such public debates (and the literature that resulted from them), zealous preachers and polemicists, often Jewish converts to Christianity, developed their argument against Judaism in other settings. The preacher Ramon Lull even secured permission from the king of Aragón to preach in synagogues to directly prove to the Jews the superi-ority of Christianity. Such efforts not only further poisoned the atmosphere against Jews (and exacerbated ill feeling toward Christians by Jews), they also intensified the pressure on Jews to convert, and many did so—some out of fear, others out of opportunism, still others out of sincere belief, convinced by Christian arguments against Judaism. Geronimo de Santa Fé, formerly Joshua ha-Lorki, was one of a number of Jews who converted to Christianity after hearing the impassioned sermons of the itinerant Spanish Dominican Vicente Ferrer.

A famous example of the Jewish convert cum Christian missionary from Spain is **Abner of Burgos** (1270–ca. 1348), who attempted to spread his conversionary zeal by means of religious pamphlets, which he published in Hebrew. Abner claimed to have resisted conversion to Christianity for twenty-five years but was ultimately persuaded of its superiority by the degradation of his own people and by the disillusionment he experienced after the appearance of a false prophet. Abner's writing is valuable for the insight it provides into why a Jew in this period might convert; his success also illustrates the existence of at least one theoretical route of entry into Christian society for Jews: conversion. But such converts also added to the pressure on Jews by using their knowledge of the Talmud and other Jewish sources to sharpen the arguments of Christian polemicists. Abner would go on to inform against his former community, and his writings were used by Geronimo de Santa Fé. (*See box, Conversion to Judaism*).

CONVERSION TO JUDAISM

Although less common, examples exist of conversion from Christianity *to* Judaism. Converts to Judaism occasionally appear in the sources, many of whom found their way to Judaism through their training in Scripture as Christian clerics. Bodo, the chaplain to the Holy Roman Emperor Louis the Pious (r. 814–840), converted to Judaism in 838 and adopted the Hebrew name Eliezer before fleeing to Muslim Spain, where he remained for the rest of his life. Proselytes also came to Judaism from other corners of society. As was the case for Christians and Muslims in medieval society, Jewish households could include slaves and servants, and they would sometimes convert to the religion of their masters. In fact, Jewish law encouraged the circumcision and conversion of non-Jewish slaves, and in all probability the bulk of converts to Judaism came from this population. Once converted and eventually freed, these slaves held full standing as formal converts and enjoyed the protection that Jewish law afforded them. The conversion of slaves was deeply troubling to Christian authorities who sought to impede it. The Fourth Council of Toledo in 633 issued a document entitled "On the Keeping of Slaves," in which it was stated, "Jews should not be allowed to have Christian slaves nor to buy Christian slaves, nor to obtain them by the kindness of any one; for it is not right that the members of Christ should serve the ministers of Anti-Christ. But if henceforward Jews presume to have Christian slaves or handmaidens they shall be taken from their domination and shall go free." The boundary between Christianity and Judaism remained as clear as it did not just because Jews sought to defend it but also because Christian authorities patrolled the boundary.

Focusing on the hostility that Jews faced in medieval Christian society presents a considerable historiographical risk that we might paint too dark and tragic a picture of this age. It was not simply one massacre after another. In many regions, and for much of the time, Jews and Christians interacted on a daily basis, engaged in trade, made loans to one another, employed one another for work, and attended one another's celebrations. We even know of a kind of business arrangement known as the *ma'arufia* that allowed Jews to develop exclusive relationships with Christian clients. Jews were invited to live in certain communities; and even when faced with the threat of persecution or expulsion, they often found protection from the cities and towns in which they lived, or from the king to whom they were bound, or from the Church. Recent scholarship has uncovered many ways in which Jewish culture in this period reflects the influence of Christianity. In medieval Germany and France, for example, a Jewish initiation ritual to introduce male children to the study of Hebrew letters developed, in which the child was fed honey cakes inscribed with scriptural verses—the eating of sweet cakes apparently modeled on the Christian rite of the Eucharist. The Jewish practice of wearing costumes on the holiday of Purim is a borrowing of a medieval Christian practice as well: the wearing of costumes on Mardi Gras (which often coincided with the time of Purim). In the German city of Worms, the Jewish ritual bath, the *mikvah,* provided something of an architectural link to the city's cathedral, the Jews having hired the same masons to build the bathhouse.

Even as we acknowledge such coexistence and cultural interchange, however, we must also recognize that the anti-Jewish strain in medieval Christian culture had a marked impact on Jewish culture and demography. For one thing, it stirred in many Jews a deep hatred of Christianity, a sentiment often kept concealed from outsiders but sometimes surfacing in Jewish ritual and literature. Jews developed their own anti-Christian polemical literature, or parodied Christianity in works such as **Toledot Yeshu,** a derogatory history of Jesus that inverts the Christian practice of using Jewish sources against the Jews by using the New Testament against Christians. In the following passage, for example—which depicts Jesus in a disrespectful debate with the rabbis about the Talmud—the narrative uncovers something unusual about Jesus' paternity, not that he was born of God but that he was the fruit of an unlawful and illegitimate sexual union:

One day Yeshu [Jesus] walked in front of the Sages with his head uncovered, showing shameful disrespect. At this, the discussion arose as to whether this behavior did not truly indicate that Yeshu was an illegitimate child and the son of a *niddah* [a menstruant not supposed to

have sex]. Moreover, the story tells that while the rabbis were discussing the [Talmudic] Tractate *Nezikin* [Damages], he gave his own impudent interpretation of the law and in an ensuing debate he held that Moses could not be the greatest of the prophets if he had to receive counsel from Jethro. This led to further inquiry as to the antecedents of Yeshu, and it was discovered through Rabban Shimeon ben Shetah that he was the illegitimate son of Joseph Pandera. Miriam admitted it. After this became known, it was necessary for Yeshu to flee to Upper Galilee.

Christian sources complain of other blasphemous practices, of Jews relieving themselves on Christian symbols or hanging an effigy of Haman during Purim in mock emulation of the Crucifixion. At first, one is tempted to dismiss such reports as akin to the host desecration accusation—trumped-up charges concocted to justify anti-Jewish violence—but recent scholars think they may actually bear some truth. Purim in particular, a raucous, carnivalesque holiday, may have been a time when Jews expressed pent-up resentment of Christianity in a mockingly subversive, if not directly confrontational, way.

Other Jews responded to Christian mistreatment by emigrating. By the end of the fifteenth century, large numbers of Jews migrated from western Europe to the more hospitable environment of central and eastern Europe, the areas of Poland and Hungary. By 1500, the majority of Europe's Jews lived in these areas, and eventually it would become home to the world's largest Jewish population. Add to these migrations the forced conversions and expulsions, and one is left with an immense demographic shift: The populations of French- and German-speaking lands dropped precipitously by 1490; and Jews were completely expelled from England in 1290 and Spain in 1492. In many places Jews and Christians found ways to live together, but in many places they did not, and the result over the long run was a western Europe largely bereft of Jews by 1500 (*see* Map 7-2).

But all this is to describe the history of this period in very general terms. To better understand Jewish history under Christian rule, it is necessary to develop a more nuanced picture by focusing on particular regions, beginning with Spain, a point of intersection between the Christian and Islamic realms.

Medieval Christian Spain

Before they were under Muslim rule, the Jews of the region now known as Spain were subject to the rule of the Visigoths: Christians who had inherited anti-Jewish legislation from

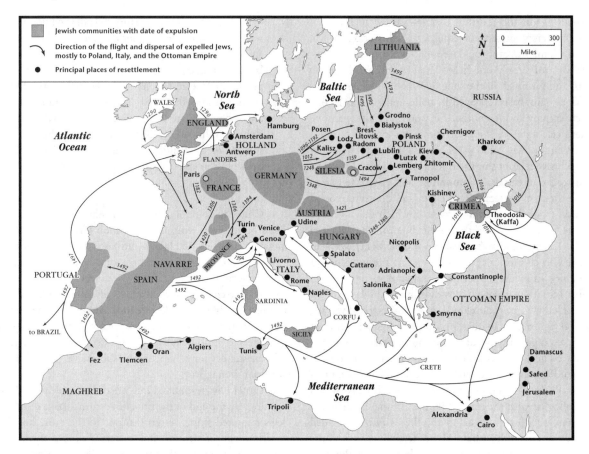

Map 7-2   The Expulsion and Migration of Jews from Western Europe, 1000–1500.

Roman legal tradition. Over the course of the sixth and seventh centuries, Jews faced legal restrictions and even persecutions during and after the reigns of the Visigothic rulers Recared (586–601) and, most of all, Sisebut (612–621). Under Recared, the Third Council of Toledo in 589 ruled that the "Jews may not have Christian wives or concubines. . . . All children born of any such unions must be baptized. . . ."— a law that implies that prior to this period, some degree of intermarriage was occurring in Spain. Sisebut was even more oppressive, ordering the Jews of Spain to either convert to Christianity or leave. Given the oppressive treatment Jews received at the hands of the Visigoths, it is not surprising that they were receptive to the Muslims who conquered Spain in 711 and that few joined the fleeing Christians who sought refuge in the mountains of the north.

Muslim victory did not mean an end to Catholic ambitions to rule Spain, however. The Catholic Reconquest (*Reconquista*) of Spain gained momentum in the eleventh century, as the Catholic kings of northern Spain made headway against the *taifas,* or principalities, that made up Muslim

Spain after the fall of the Umayyad Caliphate. More and more Jews came under Christian rule. At the battle in 1212 of Las Navas de Tolosa, a city in the far south of Spain, the Catholics utterly routed the Muslim forces, and from then on Catholicism prevailed over most of Spain, in the kingdoms of Aragón, Castile, Navarre, and Portugal, which included important centers of Jewish population and culture, among them Barcelona, Toledo, Valencia, Saragossa, and smaller towns such as Tortosa and Tudela.

By this time, Jews had been suffering from Muslim persecution and forced conversion at the hands of the Almoravids, and so they were more receptive to Christian rule than they had been. Though they still clung to Arabic culture for some time, Spanish Jews adopted the vernacular dialects of the Iberian Peninsula, primarily Castilian, Catalan, Aragonese, and Portuguese. Bridging the Muslim–Christian divide, the Jews of Spain represented an important intermediary between the two realms. Judah ha-Levi worked as a diplomat for the emerging Christian kingdoms of the north. From Córdoba, the historian and philosopher **Abraham ibn**

An illuminated Hebrew manuscript of the Jewish prayer book from Spain (ca. 1300). The image depicts knights on horseback, a reflection of a culture celebrating chivalric virtues during this period's Christian "reconquest" of Spain.

Daud (1110–1180), also known as RaBaD, whose work reflects the growing intellectual independence of the western Diaspora, built on the tradition of Islamic Aristotelianism but was also receptive to Christian rule, celebrating the conquest of Toledo by Alfonso VI in 1085. In Barcelona, where Arabic had never struck permanent roots, the legal thinker and rabbi **Solomon ben Aderet** (1235–1310) sponsored a Hebrew translation of part of Maimonides' Arabic *Commentary on the Mishnah* that helped disseminate this work to other parts of Europe. While the Jewish–Catholic relationship was always fraught, Jews did benefit from the fact that they were not Muslims, the true enemy of Spanish Catholicism, and were thus able to find a place under Christian rule as courtiers, government officials, financiers, traders, physicians, and diplomats useful for their ability to communicate with the Muslims in Arabic. It is said that the great eleventh-century hero of the Reconquest, El Cid, had Jews in his employ.

As elsewhere in Europe, the status of Jews depended on their relationship with the local ruler or king: The king protected the Jews as royal serfs, and they owed their loyalty and taxes to him in return. Through negotiations with the king, Jewish communities in Spain were able to secure communal autonomy for themselves in an organized structure known in Hebrew as the *kahal* and in the Arabized vernaculars of Spain as *aljama* or *alhama*. The most important institution within this organization was the court, which applied Jewish law to the conflicts and affairs of the community, though Jews also had recourse to Christian courts. At the head of Spanish Jewish society were Jews who served as courtiers in the royal court—figures such as the members of the **Alconstantini** family active in thirteenth-century Aragón. Such courtiers were an important link to the king but had not been chosen by the Jewish community, and their behavior was sometimes at odds with its religious and legal norms. Nahmanides was extremely critical of the Alconstantinis and was able to persuade the king against appointing members of the family to the position of *dayyan* or judge over all the Jews of the kingdom. The influence of Nahmanides and other distinguished rabbis, such as **Hasdai Crescas** and **Isaac ben Sheshet Perfet,** shows that rabbinic scholars also played an important role in communal leadership. In some places, the larger community began to assert control over the aristocracy by introducing democratic reforms in the structures of leadership.

Despite their successes in Christian Spain, Jews faced economic restrictions and legal discrimination of the sort we have observed elsewhere; in 1250 a blood libel occurred in Saragossa; Spain was host to Jewish–Christian disputations in Barcelona and elsewhere; and when the plague hit Aragón in 1348, Jews were killed in retaliation.

A key turning point in the history of the Jews of Christian Spain came in 1391. In 1378 an archdeacon named Ferrant Martinez began to sermonize against the Jews, calling for the destruction of synagogues, and his efforts eventually triggered a series of riots in which thousands of Jews were murdered or forcibly converted. A great number of Jews fled, heading mostly for North Africa, where well-established Jewish communities were able to absorb the Spanish newcomers. Most Jews, however, stayed in Spain, but with them emerged a difficult problem that eventually led to the expulsion of all Jews in 1492.

The problem was this: thousands of Jews, forcibly baptized, now found themselves legally Christian. Once baptized, they were subject to Catholic legal restrictions. This meant that they could not return to their ancestral religion. Nevertheless, they could not become a different people overnight—they still had family and neighbors that tied them to the Jewish community. Known as *conversos,* some assimilated into the majority culture, but others sustained their Jewish connections and even practiced Judaism in secret. In some cases—the scholar **Profiat Duran** is an intriguing example—the religious identity of a Jew seems fluid and ambiguous. In the wake of 1391, Duran converted to Christianity but later reasserted his ties to Judaism and wrote an anti-Christian polemic entitled *Shame of the Gentiles.* Despite his sharp opposition to Christianity, Duran seems to have sustained a certain sympathy for Jesus, distinguishing him from the religion that developed in his name precisely because, like Duran himself, he allegedly sustained his allegiance to Judaism: "In all that is mentioned in the Gospels, nowhere does it appear that [Jesus] intended to create anything that would diverge from the Holy Torah or that would undermine it."

Jews responded to these cryptic "Judaizers" with varying levels of sympathy; some were welcoming, others critical. For their part, Christians began to distinguish between "Old Christians" and "New Christians" (i.e., recent Jewish converts) and began to discriminate against the later. In 1469, **Isabella,** heir to the throne of Castille, and **Ferdinand,** heir to the throne of Aragón, were married and united their kingdoms just as the Catholic Church was intensifying its efforts to root out new Christians who were secretly adhering to Judaism. Conversos were killed, and where it was deemed impossible to ferret them out, the larger Jewish community was expelled. In 1483, the infamous inquisitor **Tomás de Torquemada** was appointed to his role, and he pressed the Inquisition with a new level of ferocity, but even his efforts were not deemed sufficient. When Isabella and Ferdinand defeated the last vestige of Muslim rule in Spain in 1492, they issued an edict calling for the expulsion of all Jews from Spain, except for those willing to accept Christianity. In response to the edict, some Jews converted and stayed as Christians; large numbers attempted to resettle in nearby Portugal and the kingdom of Navarre, only to be expelled from there by 1498, and the rest left for North Africa or the Ottoman Empire. The total Jewish population affected was about 300,000.

We identified the expulsion from Spain as the end of the Jewish Middle Ages. While it was certainly the end of the medieval Jewish community in Spain, Spanish refugees preserved their cultural and religious traditions in exile and were able to form new communities (and new cultural and religious traditions) in the places where they resettled, including the New World, discovered in the very year of their expulsion.

Medieval Italy

Medieval Italy, a region defined by the Alps in the north and the Mediterranean Sea in the south, was a patchwork of principalities, city-states, kingdoms, and imperial outposts distinguished by different styles of government, histories, and dialects. In Rome, the Jewish presence is well documented, in both Jewish and pagan sources, and reaches far back into imperial times. Pope Gregory I, who sat on the throne of St. Peter from 590 to 604, resisted attempts to forcibly convert the Jews, offering protection to those who lived in Rome, Naples, and elsewhere. When the Byzantine Empire asserted itself in southern Italy in the ninth century, however, it was less tolerant, seeking to compel the conversion of Jews.

Despite an attempt at forced conversion by the Byzantine Emperor Basil I (r. 867–886), Jewish culture, especially Hebrew, would establish roots in southern Italy, measurable in a revival of inscriptional Hebrew and yielding a medieval Hebrew literature exemplified by a work probably written in the tenth century known as **Yossipon,** an anonymous account of the Second Temple period that relies heavily on the histories of Josephus, from whom its name derives. Italy would remain a major center of Hebrew scholarship and literary creativity throughout the Middle Ages.

An important source for our knowledge of Jewish life in Italy comes from the great traveler, Benjamin of Tudela, who departed from Spain around 1160. Among other places, he traveled to southern Italy, and from his account it appears that Italian Jews enjoyed a thriving economy and culture. One Jew, Jehiel Anav, even managed to secure a position as financial supervisor for Pope Alexander III. Jewish fortunes in Italy changed in the thirteenth century, however, when some of the same pressures and problems that beset Jews elsewhere—the campaign against the Talmud, the forcing of Jews to attend missionizing sermons, the blood libel, and forced conversion—came to affect the Jews of Italy as well. The Jewish population of Italy further expanded in this period as Jews fled there from Germany and France, finding a place for themselves in the economy of northern Italy as moneylenders, playing an important economic role as they provided loans to the lower classes. In Venice, Jews were authorized to make small loans to the poor at a reduced interest rate. So identified with moneylending did Venetian Jews become that they would later provide the historical model for Shylock, the fictional Jewish antagonist of Shakespeare's *Merchant of Venice.*

The movement of Jews between Italy and Germany provided an important link between Italian Jewish culture, with its contacts in Spain and the Islamic world—the Jews of Sicily in the Italian south had lived under Islamic rule—and the Ashkenazic Jewish culture taking shape in German-speaking lands. One important family from the city of Lucca in coastal Tuscany stands out as especially important—the **Kalonymus** family, which included many famous scholars, writers, and community leaders. One branch of this family moved to Mainz in Germany in the tenth century; another branch remained in Italy. Members of the German branch were important leaders during the Crusades, and they developed the German mystical pietist movement known as the Hasidei Ashkenaz, to which we will return elsewhere in this chapter.

The Jews of Italy did not suffer the wholesale expulsions that beset the Jews of England, Spain, and other places, but they were certainly not immune from persecution and expulsion. In 1492 Jews were expelled from Sicily and Sardinia under Spanish rule and from Naples in the early sixteenth century, after which no Jewish communities remained south of Rome. In central and northern Italy, however—where Jews benefited from the protection of the pope and the support of important Italian families, such as the Medicis in Florence—Jewish life continued through the end of the Middle Ages, the end of this period marked by the institution of the first ghetto in Venice in 1516.

Medieval France

In the early Middle Ages, just as today, France stretched from the English Channel in the northwest to the Mediterranean Sea in the south. However, the French nation as it exists today did not exist in the Middle Ages. In the tenth century, nobles in the south of the country established their own independent jurisdictions, and this state of affairs continued until the mid-fourteenth century. As a result, distinct Jewish cultures developed in the different political realms of France—the two most important ones bearing names taken from the regions they inhabited: *Tzarfat* and *Provens. Tzarfat,* the Hebrew word for France, referred to the northern part of the country, sometimes meaning the royal domains (called the Île-de-France) but also including surrounding regions such as Champagne and Normandy. *Provens,* in contrast, referred not only to the modern southern regions of Provence, on the Mediterranean Sea, but also to the area known as Languedoc.

The complexity of the situation mirrors the complexity of medieval French political history. The period between 400 and 751 is very murky, but matters become a little clearer during the Carolingian dynasty, founded by Charles Martel (686–741). Under **Charlemagne** (r. 768–814), the greatest king of that dynasty, an important Jewish community thrived under the autonomous leadership of the so-called "king of the Jews." Charlemagne, who was given the title "Emperor" by the pope in the year 800, is also known to have enlisted a Jew named Isaac as an ambassador to the caliph in Baghdad and is said to have brought a Jewish scholar to his realm from Babylonia. Charlemagne initiated the symbiotic relationship between the Jews and the king that would allow Jewish life to thrive in France despite efforts by church officials such as Agobard, Bishop of Lyons, to legislate against the Jews in the ninth century. Jews established themselves as merchants, and in the field of agriculture, they gained a virtual monopoly over the wine trade. An imperial official, the *magister Judaeorum* or "master of the Jews," established by Charlemagne's son Louis II, made sure Jewish privileges were respected.

The Capetian dynasty (987–1328) marks the best-known stage of medieval Jewish history in northern France. At the beginning of this era, French Jews found themselves subject to a weak Crown, a power vacuum filled by local and regional rule. Persecutions took place in the tenth and eleventh centuries, however, and at the close of the eleventh century, French Jews suffered the initial shock waves of the First Crusade. In the twelfth century, French Jewish history follows the pattern observed elsewhere. In 1144, in the first known legal act of a French king preserved in writing, Louis VII expelled from his realm Jews who had converted to Christianity and later returned to Judaism. The Second Crusade (1146–1147) was not as destructive for Jews as the first, but it too was accompanied by local violence. The first blood libel in France was in Blois in 1171, and King Philip Augustus (1180–1223), nursed on such anti-Jewish stories, imprisoned all the wealthy Jews of Paris until he was paid a large ransom. In 1240, the Talmud was put on trial in Paris and was sentenced to be destroyed by fire. In June 1242, twenty-four cartloads of books were consigned to the flames. A contemporary Jewish poet wrote:

I am stunned: how can eating be pleasurable
After I have seen how they gathered your booty?
Gathered it throughout your isolated quarter,
Then burned the holy booty, so that you are unable to
    join your people.
I know not how to find a straight path,
So burdened with the mourning are your paths of
    righteousness.
To brew a cup of tears would be sweeter to me than
    honey;
Oh, that my legs might be chained in your irons.
To draw the waters of my tears would be sweet to
    my eye,
So they might be exhausted for all those who hold fast
    to your cloak.
But those tears dry up as they drop on my cheeks,
For my pity has been aroused by the departure of your
    master.

More destructiveness followed. In 1306, Philip expelled the Jews of royal France, dispersing them among other regions of the country. The thirteenth, fourteenth, and fifteenth centuries saw many other confiscations, persecutions, and expulsions. According to one scholarly estimate, a Jewish population of about 100,000 in 1300 had dwindled to approximately 20,000 by 1490.

Southern France, or Provence, took a different course in the Middle Ages. In the eleventh century, it was the decreasing power of the kingship that left the southern reaches of France, including Languedoc and Provence, under a different regime of local nobility. The result was the distinct Jewish community of southern France, where great schools of Jewish scholarship emerged in the eleventh century, including that established by Rashi (*see box,* Rashi). The Jews of this region straddled the religious boundary between Islam and Christianity, not because they bordered the Islamic world directly but because many Jews had taken refuge there after the Almohad invasion of Spain in 1149. Jewish intellectuals who emerged in this period played an important role as intermediaries between the Jewish cultures of the Islamic and Christian worlds. **Joseph Kimhi** (1105–1170), one such refugee, settled in Narbonne. Entering into the grammatical debate begun in the tenth century between the grammarians Menahem ben Suruq and Dunash ibn Labrat on the side of the latter, he helped to introduce the grammatical insights and interpretive methods of Spanish Jewry into Christian Europe. His son **David Kimhi** (1160–1235), also known as RaDaK, further developed this intellectual tradition and became a highly influential philologist and biblical commentator. Another important scholarly family was the ibn Tibbons. Following in the footsteps of his father, Judah (1120–1190), who fled the Almohads to Lunel and became a translator, **Samuel ibn Tibbon** (1150–1230) translated Maimonides' *Guide for the Perplexed* from Arabic to Hebrew, an act that had a tremendously stimulating and controversial impact on Jewish intellectual life beyond the Islamic sphere.

Languedoc and Provence both fell to the northern French during the Albigensian Crusade (1209–1229), launched to root out the heretical movement of the Cathars, also called the Albigensians. This also put in a difficult position the Jews of Provence and Languedoc, who, while not suffering the expulsion that Jews from the royal domains did, nevertheless suffered terrible violence in 1320, when a band of young men from the north joined what would be called the Shepherds' Crusade. As they moved through the south, the crusaders murdered hundreds of Jews. Thereafter, Jews continued to live in the south of France until 1498 when, on the heels of the Spanish and Portuguese expulsions, the Jews of Provence were also ordered to leave. They did so in 1501.

RASHI

The single most influential medieval Jewish commentator was Solomon ben Isaac of Troyes (1040–1105), better known as Rashi, whose work transformed the nature of Jewish learning. Rashi's biblical commentary, covering most of the books of the Bible, moves back and forth between a midrashic reading of the Bible and a *peshat* approach in an attempt to resolve interpretive problems in the biblical text. For example, Rashi finds a problem at the very beginning of the Torah: If the purpose of the Torah is to present God's commandments as law, why does it delay their presentation with a narrative account of what happened prior to Mount Sinai—the creation of the world and other events narrated in Genesis? Drawing on a midrash, Rashi explains that the purpose was to establish the legitimacy of Israel's conquest of the land of Canaan: By showing that God created the world, the Torah establishes God's right to assign the land to whomever he wishes. Rashi's commentary often focuses on hidden problems and minute ambiguities in the text, drawing on midrash only to the extent that it helps explain the meaning of the text. So influential was Rashi's biblical commentary that it has inspired more than two hundred supercommentaries on its commentary.

An even more impressive intellectual accomplishment was his commentary to the Babylonian Talmud, which has become just as essential to the study of that text in traditional Jewish schools as his biblical commentary is to the study of the Torah. Rashi's commentary has become an indispensable tool for understanding the Babylonian Talmud's terminology and argumentation. His commentary has been included in almost every edition of the Talmud since it was first published in the 1400s.

Medieval England

Coming from northern France, William I "the Conqueror" (r. 1066–1087) captured England in 1066, and most of the Jews who migrated there in the wake of his conquest were also French in origin, language, and culture. They came to serve the needs of the court, specifically to work as financiers. Throughout the Middle Ages, money, in the form of coins, was not necessarily the primary form of currency, but kings found coins extremely useful as a way to pay soldiers, amass treasure, and, when minted with the picture of the king, to disseminate symbols of their personal authority. Bringing with them their expertise at moneylending and enough capital to begin lending immediately, the Jews who migrated to England proved highly useful to William and his successors. Within a century Jews were in London, Lincoln, Oxford, Norwich, and many other cities, though the only Jewish cemetery permitted until 1177 was the one in London.

After William I, Henry I (r. 1100–1135) stands out as the king most active in Jewish affairs. Henry I invoked the principle of the Jews as the king's personal property, apparently granting them certain privileges but also employing them to serve his own commercial interests. He established the Exchequer, or treasury office, which tracked Jewish loans. Henry II (1154–1189), his grandson, continued this policy of encouraging Jewish moneylending, though he also extorted money from Jews, forcibly sent Jewish leaders back to Normandy, and charged the Jews of London a tax of one-fourth the value of their movable property—the aggregate sum of £60,000, almost one-tenth of the estimated wealth of the entire country. The moneylender Aaron of Lincoln illustrates both the benefits and the risks of the financial role that Jews played in England; he died an enormously wealthy man, having used his wealth to finance several monasteries and other buildings, but at his death the king took possession of his entire estate, establishing a special department in the Exchequer to handle it.

Under the reign of the crusader king Richard I (r. 1189–1199), religious zeal against non-Christians and resentment against Jewish creditors resulted in violence in London, York, and other towns. Most notoriously, the massacre of 150 Jews who fled the mob and were hiding in York Castle in 1190 was the greatest slaughter of Jews to take place in England. The attack took place on March 16, around Easter, which became the time that most accusations of ritual murder against Jews were launched. The destruction at York became so notorious that the poet Ephraim of Bonn memorialized the event in a Hebrew chronicle: "There were some that slew themselves for the sake of God's unity, and the number of those slain by others or by themselves was about 150 souls, men and women." William of Newbury, a Christian, describes the motives for the attacks as "not indeed sincere, that is, solely for the sake of faith, but in rivalry for the luck of others or from envy of their good fortune. Bold and greedy men thought that they were doing an act pleasing to God." In fact, it seems that the two motives, greed and faith, were both at play, even though they appear contradictory.

The rioting at York included the burning of the documents recording the debts owed to the Jews, and since that meant in turn a considerable financial loss to the king, Richard established the **Exchequer of the Jews** to make sure copies of every loan contract with a Jew were kept in royal hands. The contracts preserved in this way have survived for centuries and teach us a great deal about the close economic ties and, sometimes, even social relations that Jews and Christians enjoyed in medieval England.

Over the course of the thirteenth century, the kings of England restricted the scope of Jewish moneylending, partially in relation to papal politics, as with the Lateran Council of 1215, which restricted Jewish usury. The Magna Carta, the famous charter established in the same year, originally included a clause that restricted the claims of Jewish moneylenders against those who had died in their debt. The situation of Jews worsened over the next few decades—a new synagogue built in London was confiscated in 1232; blood libel accusations continued, and by the time of the reign of Edward I (r. 1272–1307), the Jews were so financially weakened that they were no longer of use to the Crown, and on July 18, 1290, the king ordered the expulsion of the Jews from England.

What historians know about the Jews of medieval England mostly pertains to their financial dealings with the Crown. For that reason, written testimony speaking to the daily lives of English Jews is all the more precious. Consider, for example, a document written by Gilbert Crispin, the proctor of Westminster Abbey. It records a discussion he had with an unnamed Jew from Mainz. According to Crispin, the two frequently met and argued "in a friendly spirit about the Scriptures." The significance of the work, written before 1096 and entitled *Disputation of a Jew with a Christian About the Christian Faith,* lies in its comparatively friendly tone—evidence that at the beginning of Jewish settlement in England in the early eleventh century, English society had not yet developed the antagonism to Jews that would provoke their expulsion two centuries later.

Though it was small, the medieval English Jewish community did produce several scholars—Benjamin of Cambridge, Moses ben Hanassia of London, the poet Meir of Norwich—but the most famous was a visitor from Spain. In 1158, Abraham ibn Ezra, scholar of science, grammar, and Jewish law, visited England where he published *Yesod Mora,* or the *Foundation of Awe,* under the patronage of Joseph ben Jacob, to whom he dedicated the book. *Yesod Mora* was an effort to plant the intellectual tradition of Spanish Jewry among the Jews of England, but it did not have time to take root before the Jews were expelled a little more than a century later.

Medieval German-Speaking Europe

The origins of the Jews of German lands, called *Ashkenaz* in Hebrew since the twelfth century, are obscure, and we have no real sense of the presence of a German Jewish community or distinct Jewish culture there until the late tenth century. Thereafter, the Jews of the German empire enjoyed a certain degree of protection from the emperors, who recognized their utility in laying the commercial groundwork for cities. In the eleventh century, a clearly defined German Jewish culture began to take shape, with two particular figures occupying center stage. The first figure was Meshullam ben Kalonymus, from a learned family with roots in northern Italy; the family served as a link between the early German communities and the more ancient Italian ones. The second major figure, **Gershom ben Judah Me'or ha-Golah** ("Light of the Exile") (c. 960–1040), established a school of Talmudic studies in Mainz on the Rhine River that would have a major influence on the next three generations of scholarship in France and Germany. Under Gershom's influence, the three major Jewish settlements of the Rhineland—Speyer, Worms, and Mainz—began to assert themselves as independent centers of learning, developing the major institutions of Jewish life. These three towns were the original heartland of Ashkenazic Jewry.

Germany at this time was a composite of city-states loosely connected to one another under the banner of the eastern kingdom of the Holy Roman Empire. Attempting to promote trade and commerce, many of these cities sought to attract Jews by means of charters or municipal contracts that would offer them security in the expectation that they would help the city develop into a trading hub and provide a tax base. The first of these community charters—in fact, the first such charter in all of Christian Europe—was from the city of Speyer. In 1084, to lure Jews there, Rüdiger, the bishop of Speyer, offered them a number of privileges. He promised the Jews "full power to change gold and silver, and to buy and sell what they please, within the district where they dwell, and from that district outside the town as far as the harbor, and within the harbor itself." The same document also suggests a certain level of risk in this arrangement, for even as it grants privileges to the Jews, it also places them "outside the town and some way off from the houses of the rest of the citizens," surrounding them with a wall "lest they should be too easily disturbed by the insolence of the citizens."

The protections afforded Jews as a result of charters were sometimes very specific, and extremely stiff penalties were applied for anyone harming the king's "property." In 1090, Emperor Henry IV issued a charter that sought to guarantee the safety of Jews and laid out specifically the consequences for Christians attempting to rob or harm them:

> No one may dare take from them any of their property. . . . If anyone shall perpetrate violence against them in disregard of this edict, he shall be forced to pay to the treasury of the bishop one pound of gold; also he shall repay doubly the item which he took from them.
>
> They may travel freely and peacefully within the bounds of the kingdom in order to carry on their business and trade, to buy, and sell. No one may exact from them tolls or demand any public or private levy.
>
> If a Christian has a dispute or contention against a Jew concerning any matter or vice versa, each may carry out justice and prove his case according to his law.
>
> No one may force a Jew to judgment by hot irons or boiling water or frigid water or turn them over for whipping or place them in prison.
>
> If anyone shall wound a Jew, but not mortally, he shall pay one pound of gold. . . . If he is unable to pay the prescribed amount . . . his eyes will be put out and his right hand cut off

Based on their usefulness, Jews settled in all the economic centers of the German empire, expanding with immigration from Italy and France (though eventually Jewish communities themselves would restrict immigration in an effort to limit competition). There they developed autonomous communities under the leadership of rabbis and community elders. The aforementioned Gershom ben Judah was one such leader. He operated as a judge deciding matters of civil and religious law and is known for issuing a number of **takkanot** or ordinances that would have a major impact on Jewish legal practice in France and Germany, including a famous ruling attributed to him that enforces the practice of monogamy, the intention being to ensure that traveling businessmen did not resettle abroad and abandon their families in Germany. He is yet another example of the emerging independence of European rabbinic sages, for Gershom rarely cites the Babylonian Geonim in his legal decisions, basing himself directly on the Bible and the Talmud rather than relying on the intervening authority of the Geonim.

Even as these communities were taking shape in the eleventh century, however, religious and class-based violence loomed as a threat. The Jews of Mainz were temporarily expelled sometime at the beginning of the eleventh century, and as we have noted, the First Crusade—just twelve years after the Speyer charter—triggered terrible violence throughout the Rhineland. The Crusades revealed the vulnerability of the Jews and their total dependence on protection from

the authorities—and the inability or unwillingness of local authorities to provide such protection. In the later Middle Ages, Jews came increasingly under the direct control of the emperor (in the German empire) or the kings in other western European countries. Only the central secular authority seemed fit to protect the Jews and had an interest in doing so, not least because Jews were needed and useful as moneylenders. In 1182, the German emperor Frederick I "Barbarossa" declared that all the Jews of the empire were to be considered imperial property, "servants of our chamber." This new arrangement at first proved to be advantageous. During the Third Crusade in 1188, Jews were spared—thanks to imperial protection—most of the persecutions that had marked the First Crusade and (to a lesser degree) the Second Crusade. As Jews were the emperor's legal property, he saw it as his responsibility to protect them; the failure to protect Jews was seen as a sign of imperial powerlessness.

Beyond their political and social effects, the Crusades may also have had an impact on Jewish religious life, inspiring a cult of martyrdom and also a new popular religious movement known as the **Hasidei Ashkenaz,** or German Pietists, that saw in the practice of martyrdom or *Kiddush ha-Shem*, an ethical ideal that it sought to emulate. Arising in German towns such as Regensburg, Speyer, and Mainz over the twelfth and thirteenth centuries, most of the leaders of this movement came from the Kalonymus family. Drawing on earlier mystical works, the movement developed a literature of its own in the thirteenth century: esoteric and moralistic writing that sought to inculcate a life in obedience to the "Will of the Creator," with responsibilities imposed on members beyond what Jewish law explicitly required. These included acts of penitence through bodily self-mortification, such as smearing oneself with honey in summer to attract bee-stings or jumping into icy waters in winter. The most important of these works is **Sefer Hasidim,** an ethical work attributed to the most famous rabbi of the movement, **Judah the Pious** (c. 1140–1217). It advocates self-denial, spiritual focus, decency, and humility. The Crusades—including the martyrs it created and the crusading knights—were a model for the Jewish pietist; if a knight is willing to sacrifice his life for his own honor, argues *Sefer Hasidim,* how much more should the pietist be willing to do so for God's honor? Even as it mirrored Christian ideals, however, this movement also embodied a kind of nonviolent resistance to Christianity, urging members to avoid contact with Christians in situations where the Christians had more power.

While many Jewish communities were able to recover quickly from the First Crusade, they faced new perils in the thirteenth and fourteenth centuries, and the protectors that Jews had relied on in earlier centuries—the Holy Roman

Emperor and the Pope—were weaker in this period and less able to intervene on their behalf. By the end of the fifteenth century, Jews had been expelled from much of the Holy Roman Empire, generally heading east where Austrian, Polish, and Hungarian kings welcomed them in the way that German rulers had done in the eleventh century. Speaking Yiddish, Jews brought with them their trade connections and established in eastern Europe what would become the demographic and cultural heart of Ashkenazic Jewry.

Beyond Catholic Europe

For much of this discussion, we have identified Christianity with the Catholic realms of western Europe, but it is important to keep in mind that Christianity extended beyond the orbit of the Catholic Church, taking a very different form in southeastern Europe and Asia Minor. In what was the divided Roman Empire, the eastern half was known as the Byzantine Empire, though the people who lived in it called themselves Romans and understood their emperor to be the heir to the throne of Caesar. This territory covered roughly the eastern portion of the Mediterranean Sea, until it was halved in size by Muslim conquest into a much smaller empire that included southern Italy, much of the Balkan Peninsula, and Asia Minor. By the end of the eleventh century, the Byzantines had lost their foothold in Italy too, and invading Seljuk Turks captured much of the empire's heartland in Asia Minor in 1071, but a much reduced Byzantine Empire continued until its capital in Constantinople succumbed to the Ottoman Turks in 1453.

The situation for Jews under Byzantine rule was different from that of Jews in Catholic Europe. In a kingdom that understood itself as a continuation of the Roman Empire, Byzantine Jews, like their non-Jewish neighbors, understood themselves to be Romans and did not hesitate to assert the ancient legal status of Judaism as an officially recognized religion as a source of protection. On the other hand, they also faced legal discrimination and persecution under Byzantine rule. On the eve of the Muslim capture of Palestine in 634, Jews found themselves reeling from the persecution imposed on them by Emperor Heraclius (610–641) because they had aided the Persians in their capture of Jerusalem in 614—a major reason, it seems, that Jews were so receptive to Muslim rule in Palestine and other territory that it had captured from the Byzantines. Several later emperors also tried to forcibly convert the Jews, and the Iconoclastic Controversy of the eighth and ninth centuries—a schism over whether Christians should venerate holy images—was a particularly severe period for the Jews, who, because of Judaism's religious prohibition against graven images, were identified with the anti-iconic camp.

These incidents notwithstanding, as one of many different ethnic groups in the empire, Byzantine Jews enjoyed a relatively stable existence as compared to those of Catholic Europe, where the Jews were the only non-Christian minority. According to Benjamin of Tudela, "[T]here is much hatred against them. . . . But the Jews are rich and good men, charitable and religious; they cheerfully bear the burden of the exile." In the eleventh century, conditions were sufficiently welcoming there that Jews immigrated into the Byzantine Empire from elsewhere—Karaites came from Palestine and Rabbanites from Egypt in the wake of Fatimid persecution. Important centers of learning developed in Thebes and Constantinople, and Jewish merchants excelled in the textile trade despite efforts to exclude them from the silk business. Byzantine Rabbanite Judaism did not produce many great scholars of the legal tradition, though many poets and midrashists hailed from the empire. Byzantine Karaite legalists, on the other hand, set the agenda for their entire movement for four centuries. The Rabbanite Tobias ben Eliezer penned a well-known midrashic compilation, *Midrash Leqah Tov*. He also participated in a messianic movement that took the Jews of Greece by storm, as the crusaders made their way eastward from Europe.

We close this survey of the medieval Jewish world with a brief glance at one of the most fascinating Jewish communities from this period, the Jewish kingdom of the **Khazars** in eastern Europe. The Khazars originated as a pagan, seminomadic Turkic people, who came to dominate the area between the Black Sea and the Caspian Sea in the seventh century and played an important role in the relationship between the Byzantine Empire and its Slavic and Turkic rivals. Sometime in the eighth century, the Khazars converted to Judaism, though it is unclear how many people converted beyond the group's leadership. An important source of knowledge about the Khazar conversion to Judaism is the correspondence in the 950s or 960s between the Jewish physician and diplomat Hasdai ibn Shaprut of Córdoba and a Khazar king named Joseph. In his letter, Hasdai describes the Spanish caliphate and his role in it—he was essentially foreign minister—and how he learned of the Khazar kingdom from Jewish travelers. King Joseph's response, written in Hebrew, describes the boundaries and history of his empire before recounting how the Khazars came to convert to Judaism. A dream inspired an earlier king, Bulan, to organize a debate between representatives of Judaism, Christianity, and Islam to determine the true religion, and the ensuing discussion convinced him to embrace the religion of Israel. Stirred by the possibility of living under Jewish sovereignty,

Hasdai said that he would give up all his honor and wealth to witness it (and he may have actually traveled there), and the story of the Khazar king's conversion would later inspire Judah ha-Levi to write the *Kuzari,* a fictionalized account of the debate. Khazaria seems to have collapsed in the tenth or eleventh century in the wake of Russian attacks, though traces of its culture and memory linger in later periods.

Jewish Lives Under Christian Rule

A broad survey of the sort we have been engaged in, focused on moments of crisis and transformation, can obscure what it was like to actually live as a Jew in this environment. We have nothing like the Cairo Geniza to help us reconstruct medieval Jewish life under Christian rule, but we do have many other kinds of evidence—responsa and *takkanot,* rabbinic rulings that tackle the practical concerns of civic and religious life, economic records, chronicles, biblical and Talmudic commentaries, artistic depictions of Jews, and much else that can give us insight into linguistic practice, communal organization, family life, ritual, sexuality and gender, and popular culture.

Divided by political, cultural, and linguistic boundaries, with different relationships to neighbors and the reigning authorities, Jewish culture developed in different directions in different places. One way to gauge this diversity is linguistically. In terms of language, as far as we know, French, Spanish, and English Jews spoke dialects that did not differentiate them markedly from their neighbors (Ladino, a Jewish dialect of Spanish, only comes into view after the expulsion from Spain). Jews in the Byzantine Empire, on the other hand, may have used a distinctive form of Greek, especially in Jewish contexts, and the Karaites too developed a dialect of their own, which survived into the twentieth century. Around the year 1000, Jews in central and eastern Europe began speaking Yiddish, with both regions developing distinct dialects over the centuries. With the majority of the world's Jews coming to live in the Slavic orbit, Yiddish, with its largely German, Hebrew, and Aramaic base, helped create a social, cultural, and psychological boundary between Jews and their neighbors. Against this linguistic diversity, Hebrew functioned as something of a unifying factor—translations and new compositions in Hebrew, such as the commentaries of Rashi, were broadly accessible across Jewish Europe. While the use of Hebrew distinguished Jews from non-Jews, it also served as a bridge to the Christian intellectual elite, as "Christian Hebraists," who would emerge in the early modern period, studied the language so as to facilitate anti-Jewish polemics and penetrate the secrets of ancient Jewish texts.

For much of the Middle Ages, especially in Northern Europe, Jews frequently lived in very small communities, in which all the members knew each other well. In the *Itinerary* of Benjamin of Tudela, only the largest communities were reported to have more than two hundred members, and many appear to have had many fewer than one hundred. Even in larger communities, independent governance and strong cultural bonds kept their members closely knit. Families were correspondingly small and tightly knit as well. While we know of larger extended families that sustained a sense of cohesiveness across a geographical expanse, the typical family seems to have been small—smaller perhaps than neighboring Christian families—a typical household consisting of parents and three or fewer children. Families served the practical, economic role they did in the Islamic world, and evidence points to the emotional bonds that tied people together—the heartbreaking tenderness of parents for their children recorded in accounts of the Crusades-related martyrdoms, or the importance attached to gratifying a wife's sexual desires.

Jews believed strongly in their own theoretical sovereignty. They tolerated the laws of the various kings insofar as those laws did not conflict with Jewish law, subscribing to the legal principle of **dina de-malkhuta dina** ("the law of the land is the law") to justify deference to the authority of the crown, and they relied on the Pope to stick to established precedents and principles that had safeguarded the Jews as a theologically objectionable but protected minority. But while they were dependent on non-Jewish patrons and protectors, Jews valued Jewish self-governance in communal and religious affairs. Jewish life was framed by the community, or **kehillah,** which through scores of *hevrot* (voluntary associations) provided for the religious, educational, medical, social welfare, and judicial needs of Jewish society. Jews were governed by Jewish religious courts, which held jurisdiction in areas dealing with contracts, torts, marriage and divorce law, dietary requirements, ritual purity, and Sabbath and holiday observance, though individuals also had recourse to Christian courts or their rulers.

How were such communities organized and led? Looking to the Talmud for guidance, Jews were guided by a dictum that seemed to invest authority in decisions made by "seven good men of the city" (Megillah 26a), but how to define a good man and who was qualified to play such a role were matters that were left ambiguous. Indeed, in many places, the "good men" of the city often numbered more than seven—in Spain it was sometimes forty men. Where judges in religious courts derived their authority from their intellectual standing, the elevated status of lay leaders was derived from seniority, wealth, family lineage, and connections to Christian rulers. The titles that these lay leaders bore reflect those sources of authority: *parnas* (pl. *parnassim*), meaning "providers" or "funders"; *rabbi,* meaning "sir" (as opposed to *Rav,* meaning "master of the law," referring to the religious or judicial office of the rabbi); and *nasi,* meaning "prince" or "leader." Because of their connections to the world of commerce and government, it was community boards of laypeople—not the Jewish religious courts—who were responsible to Christian rulers when it came to tax collection. In some regions, the king appointed Jewish functionaries to serve as intermediaries with the Jews; in thirteenth-century England, for example, the king developed the office of the *Presbyter Judaeorum,* the head of the Exchequer of the Jews, who supervised the collection of taxes and advised the king on Jewish matters.

One way in which rabbis exerted communal influence was through *takkanot,* or rabbinical ordinances. *Takkanot* recall responsa, but unlike responsa, the power of a given *takkanah* did not grow exclusively out of the authority and prestige of the rabbi who wrote it, nor did the composers of *takkanot* claim to derive authority for their ordinances directly from Talmudic law—though to be sure, any given *takkanah* needed to accord with Talmudic law. Rather, the proponents of *takkanot* relied on communal assent. The vehicle for enforcement of the decree was the *herem,* or ban, according to which every member of the community agreed to excommunicate a person who violated a *takkanah.* Excommunication removed the offender from the community and thus cut him off from the protection, religious participation, and economic sustenance that the community provided.

Takkanot illustrate how local rabbinic leaders could exercise great authority within the Jewish community, eclipsing the role of the Geonim in earlier times. (By the twelfth century, in fact, the title *Gaon* had become very diffuse; originally reserved for the Gaon of the academy at Sura, by the twelfth century Maimonides claimed that all the important sages after the Talmud were Geonim.) Though rabbinic opinions might differ, individual rabbis could combine their powers by meeting in synods with other rabbis and in that way influence a larger region. At the same time, other forces limited rabbinic influence. As the European economy developed, Jewish life in many communities became more competitive and decentralized; *parnassim,* or lay leaders, their status in the community often based on wealth, competed with rabbis for influence and sometimes operated independently of rabbinic courts. The rabbis of medieval Ashkenazic communities had more influence than rabbis in Italy, but even in Germany communal rabbinic leaders had to compete with the rabbinic heads of *yeshivot* and eventually found their powers limited by the *parnassim.* It was out of this situation, in the thirteenth and fourteenth centuries, that the professionalization of the rabbinate began to take shape as rabbis tried to control who could perform rabbinic activities by regulating the ordination of new rabbis.

As noted, anti-Jewish legislation and acts of violence did not prevent Jews and Christians from interacting on a daily basis. Christians and Jews engaged in business together, and Christianity influenced Jewish culture in many ways. The development of Jewish ritual practice offers something of a barometer for this influence. For example, the Jewish rite of circumcision, the ritual by which baby boys are initiated as members of the Jewish community, underwent changes in the medieval period that in some cases seem modeled on the Christian rite of baptism. During the age of Charlemagne, for example, the institution of godparents—adults not related to the infant who participated in the baptism ceremony along with the biological father—was introduced from the Byzantine east into the Catholic west. It is probably not a coincidence that a similar honorific role developed in the medieval Ashkenazic circumcision rite: The *ba'al habrit* or *sandek* is an adult male (women could play a similar role as well) who passes the child to the father and holds the baby during the circumcision.

We have noted that another ritual of childhood, one used to introduce young boys to Torah study, may have been influenced by Christianity. This rite was eventually replaced by the *bar mitzvah* ceremony, and this development also may reflect Christian influence. A *bar mitzvah* is a thirteen-year-old boy considered to have reached the age of legal maturity. Now obliged to keep all the commandments, he marks his change of status by putting on *tefillin* for the first time and being called up to read the Torah publicly in the synagogue (a parallel ceremony for twelve-year-old girls, the *bat mitzvah,* only appears in modern times). Introduced in Germany in the thirteenth century, the *bar mitzvah* ceremony, it has been argued, mirrors a changed conception of childhood in medieval Christianity, one which now required children to be of the age of reasoned consent before they could be pledged to the religious discipline of a monastery or convent.

Even as we take note of commonalities, however, it is also important to emphasize crucial differences between medieval Jewish and Christian cultures. The two communities seem to have had very different sexual norms, for example. Christian culture valued celibacy as an ideal; Jewish culture did not. Jews valued procreation as a sacred obligation and also recognized the importance of satisfying a marriage partner's sexual needs—indeed some authorities allowed for the use of a certain kind of birth control if the intent was not to prevent conception but to enjoy sex. Christian religious life offered alternatives to marriage and sex—the vocations of monks and nuns—while marriage was the ideal for Jews—in the words of spanish robbi, Jacob ben Asher from the fourteenth century: "Whoever lives without a wife lives without well-being, blessing, home, Torah, a protective wall, and

An illustration of the circumcision ritual from Ashkenaz (ca. 1300). Moving from right to left, the scene shows a godmother bringing the child to the synagogue, with the circumcision ceremony itself on the left. The Israel Museum, Jerusalem by David Harris.

indeed without peace." Forbidden in Catholic culture, divorce was permitted in Jewish culture, as was remarriage. The sexual norms of the two communities were so different that medieval Christians considered Jews promiscuous; along with bloodthirstiness and greed, lewdness became yet another characteristic of the Christian stereotype of the Jew.

The lives of women in medieval Jewish life are predictably less documented than those of men, but their roles and life circumstances can be glimpsed in responsa and other sources. Efforts by Gershom ben Judah in Germany to prevent divorce without the consent of the woman, and to block men from traveling abroad for more than eighteen months without the consent of the rabbinic court, suggest the economic vulnerability of women bereft of a husband's support. That it was also necessary to explicitly forbid husbands from beating their wives suggests domestic abuse was a problem. At the same time, a significant number of Jewish households appear to have been headed by a woman—some 22 percent of the families appearing on a martyr list from Mainz were headed by women.

Although in theory women could not own property, they did in fact control property; they could sign contracts, petition courts, engage in moneylending, even travel on business (the *Sefer Hasidim* advises women travelers to dress as nuns to avoid sexual attack). Though confined by the normative values of medieval society, Jewish women were considerably more literate and numerate than Christian women, and thus were more likely to demonstrate greater independence, at least in the domestic sphere and in the marketplace.

While Torah study was a male preserve, some women could also acquire an education, though it helped to be the daughter of a scholar. Rashi allegedly taught his daughters Torah, and in Germany a number of women cantors led prayer services for women and garnered reputations for their beautiful voices. While medieval Jewish women in the Christian world also remained under the control of men, generally moving directly from the father's authority to that of the husband, they do seem to have moved more freely than did their counterparts in the Islamic world.

Jewish Thought and Imagination in the Christian Realm

Jewish thought and imagination in medieval Christian Europe did not develop independently of what was happening in the Islamic world. The translation into Hebrew of the writings of Maimonides and other Jewish, Greek, and Islamic philosophical and scientific works; the wide-ranging travels of scholars, such as Abraham ibn Ezra; and the migration of Jews from Islamic or Christian Spain to southern France all worked to stimulate the rise of philosophy, science, and mysticism in the Christian world of western Europe. But the Jews of the latter realm were not passive recipients of this legacy; they contested elements of it while developing others in bold new directions.

Consider what happened to Jewish–Islamic philosophy in the Jewish intellectual milieu of Christian Europe. The work of Maimonides had a major impact, but it also provoked great division—for example, the Maimonidean Controversy—among rabbis who objected to his philosophical–allegorical understanding of the Bible and believed that Maimonides and his like-minded successors paid too much regard to Greco–Arabic wisdom. The sages of northern France went so far as to pronounce a *herem* on the philosophical works of Maimonides. Nahmanides try to persuade the rabbis to lift their ban, but his efforts at brokering a peace failed. Even in his own commentary on the Torah, Nahmanides developed a more mystical understanding of reality at odds with Maimonidean rationalism. Some rabbinic scholars, notably Solomon ben Adret, sought to restrict the study of Greek philosophy, albeit not going as far in this ban as others were prepared to go (*see box,* Banning Jewish Philosophy). While Levi ben Gershom, or **Gersonides** (1288–1344), from France was a great champion of the Islamic Aristotelian tradition, some of his positions also proved extremely controversial. In addition to what many regarded as his undue regard for astrology, his insistence that philosophy and Torah are compatible led him to make claims that could be considered antithetical to traditional Jewish thought. In his most famous work, *Sefer Milhamot Ha-Shem* (*The Wars of the Lord,* 1329), Gersonides claimed that "if reason causes to affirm doctrines that are incompatible with the literal sense of Scripture, we are not prohibited by the Torah to pronounce the truth on these matters, for reason is not incompatible with the true understanding of the Torah." The issues philosophy raised were crucial to Jewish life both intellectually and socially, with implications for scholarly agendas, Jewish education, and the broader relationship between Jewish and non-Jewish culture, and the controversy they provoked would continue throughout the Middle Ages.

Jewish mystical tradition, developing in Spain and southern France, also moved in new directions. The *Sefer ha-Bahir* (*Book of Radiance*), mentioned in Chapter 6, was an important influence on the Kabbalistic tradition that developed in Spain in the thirteenth century, helping give shape to the production of what would become the *Zohar* in thirteenth-century Spain. That later work would achieve nearly canonical status in the European context by the fifteenth century.

Moving from texts to people, a fascinating and important figure in the development of Jewish mystical tradition in the European setting was **Abraham Abulafia** (ca. 1240–1291). An extensively well-traveled figure, Abulafia was born in Spain, and his life illustrates the interconnectedness of the different parts of the Mediterranean. From Spain, he journeyed to Palestine in search of the mythical river where the Ten Lost Tribes of Israel were expected to be reunited, then made his way through Greece and Italy. In Rome he was sentenced to death after seeking to have the pope take responsibility for Jewish suffering. When the pope died, Abulafia was released and ended up, prior to his death, on an island near Malta. In contrast to the *sefirot*-centered, speculative tradition of the Spanish Kabbalists, Abulafia developed a more practical approach, innovating specialized techniques by which a mystic might achieve ecstatic union with God.

These developments drew on traditions inherited from late antiquity and the Islamic world. *Sefer Yetzirah* as interpreted by Saadya was an important influence on the Hasidei Ashkenaz, for example, but scholars have also tried to explain the development of Jewish mystical traditions in light of Christian influence. The Cathars, a kind of Gnostic Christian sect that flourished in twelfth- and thirteenth-century France, may have shaped the thinking of the Kabbalists there, while the religious movement of the Franciscans might have been a model for the Hasidei Ashkenaz. Whatever the precise effect of Christian culture on the development of Kabbalah, it eventually had an effect on Christian culture, becoming so widely disseminated that Christians such as **Giovanni Pico dela Mirandolla** (1463–1494) would themselves pursue Jewish mysticism as a confirmation of Christian belief and source of esoteric truth. The phenomenon of **Christian Kabbalah** was one of the many scholarly endeavors that helped spawn the Renaissance.

Jews in Christian Europe also introduced important innovations in the field of Talmudic interpretation and legal development. At great remove from the ancient academies of the Geonim, Jewish scholars in Europe seeking to understand the Babylonian Talmud had to develop their own institutions of learning. One of the most important of these *yeshivot* was founded in Mainz in the tenth century by the Kalonymus family and became influential under Rabbi

BANNING JEWISH PHILOSOPHY

Among those with reservations about the study of philosophy was the great Spanish rabbinic scholar Solomom ben Adret (1235–1310). However, Solomon, who was conversant with the work of Maimonides and other philosophers, was not completely opposed to philosophical speculation. The following ban represents something of a compromise, prohibiting the study of philosophy up until the age of twenty-five but not going as far as others who would have banned it altogether while allowing for the study of certain fields, such as medicine.

> Woe to mankind because of the insult to the Torah!
>
> For they have strayed far from it.
>
> Its diadem have they taken away.
>
> Its crown they have removed
>
> Every man with his censer in his hand offers incense
>
> Before the Greeks and Arabs.
>
> Like Zimri [a biblical Israelite who had sex with a Midianite woman, Numbers 25], they publicly consort with the Midianitess
>
> And revel in their own filth!
>
> They do not prefer the older Jewish teachings
>
> But surrender to the newer Greek learning the prerogatives due their Jewish birthright.
>
> Therefore have we decreed and accepted for ourselves and our children, and for all those joining us, that for the next fifty years under the threat of the ban, no man in our community, unless he be twenty-five years old, shall study, either in the original language or in translation, the books which the Greeks have written on religious philosophy and science. . . . We, however, excluded from this our general prohibition the science of medicine, even though it is one of the natural sciences, because the Torah permits the physician to heal.

Jacob Marcus, trans., *The Jew in the Medieval World: A Sourcebook 315–1791,* rev. ed. (Cincinnati, OH: Hebrew Union College Press, 1999), 215–16.

Gershom ben Judah. Among those who studied there was Rashi, who later founded his own school in his home town of Troyes in France. One of Rashi's daughters married Meir ben Samuel, who had also studied at Mainz, and their four sons—Isaac, Samuel, Solomon, and Jacob—all became great scholars and developed a distinctive French school of scholarship. The writings they produced in response to Rashi's commentary on the Talmud, known as "supplements" or **tosafot,** established a new mode of Talmudic study that, along with Rashi's commentary, would become central to rabbinic study.

A page of the printed Talmud as it appears today includes the Talmudic text framed by both Rashi's commentary and the *tosafot.* By minutely dissecting problems in either the Talmudic text or in Rashi's commentary, the Tosafists brought to bear the intellectual legacy of the Geonim, Islamic–Jewish culture, and their own ingenuity, drawing legal inferences and conclusions that spoke to the practical concerns of contemporary Jews in France and Germany. Inspired by projects such as Maimonides' *Mishneh Torah,* the Tosafists also developed legal codes that aimed to categorize and organize Jewish law. The culmination of this tradition was a work known as the *Tur,* produced in the fourteenth century by Jacob ben Asher ben Yehiel. The *Tur* subsequently inspired a commentary in the mid-sixteenth century by Joseph Karo, which in a synopsis form is known as the **Shulhan Arukh** (literally, "The Set Table") —the definitive authority, together with the commentary it inspired, for Jewish *halakhah* to this day. The other major intellectual accomplishment of Rashi's students was in the field of biblical commentary. Especially important was his grandson Samuel ben Meir, also known as **Rashbam** (c. 1080–1174). Whereas Rashi's biblical commentary combined midrashic interpretation with an interest in recovering the *peshat* or plain sense of the text, Rashbam pursued the *peshat* exclusively, and with great intellectual rigor.

Most of what we know about medieval Jewish imaginative life reflects the preoccupations of philosophers, rabbinic sages, and mystics, but it is also worth noting that vestiges of a more popular literature survive, one that seems closely tied to the tastes of non-Jewish popular culture. From thirteenth-century Italy, for example, survives a Hebrew version of the legend of King Arthur, replete with stories about Merlin and Guinevere. Romances of this sort were evidently so popular that Judah the Pious felt it necessary in *Sefer Hasidim* to warn his readers against them. Although the first recorded written Yiddish dates from 1272 and is religious in nature—it is a sentence inserted into a Hebrew prayer book that reads, "May a good day come to him who carries this [*makhzor*] prayer book into the synagogue"—Ashkenazic Jews shared the medieval love of secular, epic, and chivalric poems rendered into Yiddish to suit the tastes and moral sensibilities of the Jewish reading public. Probably spread orally at first, after the invention of the printing press, such stories in Yiddish, with gallant knights and damsels in distress, became the stuff of popular Jewish culture. Whatever their other religious and cultural differences, some medieval Jews and Christians evidently seem to have shared an appreciation for a well-told story.

Afterword

Just as they inherited the cultural legacy of the Geonim and the Jewish–Islamic world, the Jews of medieval Christendom passed on to their successors a remarkable legacy as well. The Jews of France and Germany, particularly Rashi and his school, elevated Jewish learning to new heights, shaping the study of the Bible and Talmud in ways that continue to frame Jewish study of these texts to this day. The Jews of Christian Spain and southern France continued the Spanish tradition of grammatical study and translation and, together with Jews in Ashkenaz, developed the Jewish mystical tradition into its classic form. Beyond their contributions to Jewish culture, the Jews of medieval Christendom also played a catalytic role in larger European history, helping to introduce European intellectuals to the philosophy and science of Greco–Islamic intellectual tradition and playing a facilitative role in Europe's commercial development. The often hostile Christian response to the Jews has also left a negative legacy, consisting of a litany of Jewish stereotypes, discrimination, persecution, and ultimately expulsion, which left western Europe with only very small numbers of Jews by 1500. On the other hand, these expulsions gave rise to the development of eastern European Jewry, which by the early modern period was already the largest concentration of Jews in the world and would contribute to the formation of the heartland of Ashkenazic civilization.

It is impossible to fix a precise end date to the Middle Ages because many of the changes involved were gradual or unfolded at a different pace in different regions. The expulsion from Spain in 1492 is probably the best option because it brought to an end the Spanish Jewry that had acted as such an important conduit between the medieval Islamic and Christian worlds, and it exemplifies in dramatic form the eastward demographic shift underway among Jews at that time, coinciding as it does with Columbus' discovery of a "new world" that soon greatly expanded the horizons of Jewish and European experience. All these reasons also happen to make 1492 a good starting point for the next period of Jewish history, and so we begin there as we follow Jewish history into modernity.

Questions for Reflection

1. What was the nature of the Jews' relationship to the Pope? What was the nature of their relationship to secular rulers? What were the advantages and disadvantages of each relationship for Jewish communities in medieval Christendom?

2. What explains the anti-Jewish hostility and violence that seem so widespread in the Christian Middle Ages? Why does this violence seem to intensify in the thirteenth century?

3. How did Jews come to be associated with moneylending in the Christian Middle Ages? How do the economic activities of Jews help to explain both the vitality and the ultimate demise of many Jewish communities in western Europe?

4. How was Jewish daily life under Christian rule different from under Islamic rule? In what ways was it influenced by Christian culture?

5. How was Jewish life in Catholic Europe similar to and different from that of the Byzantine Empire?

6. How did the position of the rabbi change in a medieval Christian setting?

7. How were the intellectual and literary traditions of the medieval Jewish–Arab world reinterpreted or transformed when relocated in Christian Europe?

For Further Reading

For recent and more detailed overviews, see Kenneth Stow, *Alienated Minority: The Jews of Medieval Latin Europe* (Cambridge, MA: Harvard University Press, 1991), and Robert Chazan, *The Jews of Medieval Western Christendom* (Cambridge, England: Cambridge University Press, 2006). For the history of Jews in particular regions, see Yitzhak Baer, *A History of the Jews of Christian Spain*, 2 vols., L. Scheffman, trans. (Philadelphia: Jewish Publication Society, 1961–1966); Cecil Roth, *The History of the Jews of Italy* (Philadelphia: Jewish Publication Society of America, 1946); Robert Chazan, *Medieval Jewry in Northern France: A Political and Social History* (Baltimore, MD: Johns Hopkins University Press, 1973); Guido Kisch, *The Jews in Medieval Germany* (New York: Ktav, 1970); Kenneth Stow, *The Jewish Family in the Rhineland in the High Middle Ages* (Washington, DC: American Historical Association, 1987); and Andrew Scharf, *Byzantine Jewry* (London: Routledge and Kegan Paul, 1971). On the Crusades and martyrdom, see Robert Chazan, *European Jewry and the First Crusade* (Berkeley: University of California Press, 1989).

On Jewish–Christian relations, see Joshua Trachtenberg, *The Devil and the Jews: The Medieval Conception of the Jew and Its Relation to Modern Anti-Semitism* (Philadelphia: Jewish Publication Society, 1943); Solomon Grayzel, *The Church and the Jews in the XIIIth Century* (New York: Hermon Press, 1966); David Berger, *The Jewish-Christian Debate in the High Middle Ages* (Philadelphia: Jewish Publication Society, 1979); Jeremy Cohen, *The Friars and the Jews* (Ithaca, NY: Cornell University Press, 1982); and Robert Chazan, *Daggers of Faith: Thirteenth-Century Christian Missionizing and Jewish Response* (Berkeley: University of California Press, 1989).

On Jewish communal life, see Louis Finkelstein (ed.), *Jewish Self-Government in the Middle Ages,* reprint (Westport, CT: Greenwood Press, 1972). For Jews and the economy, see Joseph Shatzmiller, *Shylock Reconsidered: Jews, Money-Lending and Medieval Society* (Berkeley: University of California, 1990). On medieval Jewish families, see Elisheva Baumgarten, *Mothers and Children: Jewish Family Life in Medieval Europe* (Princeton, NJ: Princeton University Press, 2004). On medieval Jewish ritual and Christianity's influence on it, see Ivan Marcus, *Rituals of Childhood: Jewish Acculturation in Medieval Europe* (New Haven, CT: Yale University Press, 1996). On medieval Jewish literature, see Susan Einbinder, *Beautiful Death: Jewish Poetry and Martyrdom in Medieval France* (Princeton, NJ: Princeton University Press, 2002). On the Hasidei Ashkenaz, see Ivan Marcus, *Piety and Society: The Jewish Pietists of Medieval Germany* (Leiden, The Netherlands: Brill, 1981).

For an online collection of medieval Jewish sources in translation, see www.fordham.edu/halsall/jewish/jewishbook.html.

Chapter 8

A Jewish Renaissance

The expulsion of the Jews from Spain in 1492 marked in many ways the end of one period in Jewish history and the beginning of another. As we have noted, the expulsion from Spain was the culmination of a long process of a Jewish exodus from western Europe and the decline of Jewish communities that had once defined medieval Jewish culture. England had expelled its Jews as early as 1290; a series of expulsion orders, especially in 1306 and 1394, evicted the Jews from most parts of France. The German lands of central Europe lacked a strong central authority, which is perhaps one reason why a wholesale expulsion of the Jews from medieval Germany never occurred, yet numerous German regions and cities likewise expelled their Jews in the course of the fifteenth century, and a final wave of expulsions in the wake of the Protestant Reformation and the Catholic **Counter-Reformation** ended Jewish life in many of the remaining areas of western and central Europe. By 1570, the only free imperial city in Germany where Jews still lived was Frankfurt, and the remnants of a Jewish presence in western Europe were restricted to a few ecclesiastical states (administered by the Church) in German-speaking lands and some principalities in northern Italy.

But these expulsions also marked a new stage in Jewish history delined by the emergence of two major Jewish centers in the east—in the eastern Mediterranean under the rule of the Ottoman Turks, where many of the Spanish Jews sought refuge, and in the Polish–Lithuanian commonwealth in Eastern Europe, where most of the French and German Jews found a new home. It was the Polish–Lithuanian and the Ottoman Jews who left their imprint on the Jewish culture of the early modern period. These demographic and cultural centers of early modern Jewish life showed a remarkable resilience in the reconstruction of Jewish culture in the generations after the forced mass migrations from the west, but it was also a culture profoundly transformed by its relocation in new east European and Middle Eastern settings. We see in the rise of these new cultural centers the beginning of

modern Jewish history, and so before we turn to their specific histories, we begin this chapter with a broad consideration of the changes that helped transform medieval Jewish culture into early modern Jewish culture.

What was the *early modern* period in Jewish history? Does this term, typically used by historians of Europe to describe the era from the fifteenth to the eighteenth centuries, make any sense when applied to the Jewish historical experience? The *modern* age in Jewish history was a time of revolutionary changes, by the end of which Jewish life, Jewish religion, and Jewish society looked completely different from what they had been before the onslaught of modernity. By contrast, the *early modern* age was one of transition or gradual change. That is to say, profound changes occurred throughout the Jewish world in the two centuries between the Spanish expulsion and the eighteenth century, but Jewish identity and culture remained largely intact. The first fissures appeared in the culture's foundations, but the overall structure of Jewish tradition remained strong.

The main factors in the transformation of Jewish culture in the early modern period were several and came from both outside and inside the Jewish world. The forced migrations themselves played an important role as they led not simply to the relocation of individuals and entire communities but also to encounters between different Jewish traditions. The Spanish Jews "exported" their own cultural heritage to those places where they settled after the expulsion, whether in North Africa or the Ottoman lands in Turkey and the Balkans. After a few generations they had imposed their cultural hegemony over the local Jewish communities, the **Sephardi** tradition deeply transforming and in many cases replacing the traditions of, for example, the Greek-speaking Romaniot Jews of the formerly Byzantine lands.

Both the Spanish Jews and the **Ashkenazi** Jews of France and Germany also took their languages with them, so that Yiddish became the predominant language of the Jews in Eastern Europe and Ladino (or Judeo–Spanish) the dominant language of the Jews in the Ottoman Balkans and Turkey. What was striking in both cases was that now, perhaps for the first time ever, Jews spoke a language that was completely different from the language of their non-Jewish environment. Unlike the situation in medieval Spain and Ashkenaz, the Arabic-speaking lands, or early modern Italy, Jews did not speak their own variety of the local language but rather a different, a "Jewish" language. (This is the significance of **Yiddish,** which means "Jewish.")

Very different was the fate of those Jews who decided to pay the price of conversion to remain in Spain beyond 1492. In 1497, the Jews of Portugal—many of whom were refugees who had left neighboring Spain five years earlier—were all forcibly baptized and converted to Christianity. This mass conversion of Jews, by far outnumbering the forced conversions of the Crusades, created an entire class of people who were nominally Catholics but many of whom retained a sense of Jewishness. Thus, following a first wave of conversions in 1391, after 1492 in Spain, and after 1497 in Portugal, a significant portion of Iberian Jewry lived under the guise of Christianity. Some, perhaps even most, ultimately assimilated into Christian society, but a large number—often called *Marranos,* a derogatory term literally meaning "swine," or *conversos,* the Spanish word for "converts"—adhered to their Jewish identity and some Jewish practices secretly, maintaining an entire subculture of clandestine Judaism. They generated a constant trickle of emigrants who left the Iberian Peninsula in subsequent centuries, settling in various parts of Europe and the Mediterranean, and many returned openly to Judaism when they had an opportunity to do so. For the conversos, assimilation into the surrounding Christian society was a living reality, and they were the first collective of Jews (or former Jews) for whom "Jewishness" held an ethnic rather than a religious meaning, for whom the affirmation of their Jewishness in a religious sense became a matter of choice rather than an accident of birth. This presented an entirely new challenge and anticipated the modern Jewish predicament when Jewish identity could not simply be taken for granted as in traditional society but was increasingly a matter of choice and ambiguous meaning.

Another factor that would transform Jewish culture profoundly, as it did Christian European culture at the same time, was the invention of printing. Print, one of the most important technological innovations of human history, arguably marked the end of the Middle Ages and the beginning of a new era as much as anything else. The new possibilities for communicating knowledge to a growing number of people had a transformative impact on the development of Jewish culture in the early modern age. Different Jewish traditions that had maintained only sporadic contact and did not have much knowledge of each other now began an exchange of knowledge on an unprecedented scale. Ashkenazi Jewry, for example, was exposed more systematically than ever before to the traditions of the Sephardi "Golden Age" in medieval Spain, as well as the new cultural trends to be found among the Spanish Jews living in Ottoman lands after 1492. Printed books not only enabled the spreading of ideas and information across cultural divides but also made information far more accessible to a much broader audience.

The early modern age saw the spread of new ideas generated within Jewish culture, most importantly the unprecedented dissemination of the esoteric teachings of medieval and early modern Jewish mysticism (Kabbalah), knowledge of which had previously been restricted to a small elite in the Middle Ages. Early modern European Jews, like their Christian neighbors, also began to grapple with the impact of the scientific revolution. Medieval Judaism, to be sure, had not necessarily been hostile to "secular" knowledge. Some, like Maimonides, the great philosopher and scholar of medieval Sephardi Jewry, had tried to reconcile Jewish and "secular" learning. Others had been indifferent to what they perceived as "external" knowledge, deeming it to be of little consequence for Jews. In the early modern age, many Jews encountered a whole universe of scientific knowledge that challenged traditional notions: for example, the discovery that Earth was not the center of the cosmos but rotated around the sun and not the other way around, as had been the traditional understanding according to the Bible, classical Greek philosophy, Talmudic Judaism, and medieval Christianity. The fight between the traditional and the Copernican worldviews was the early modern equivalent of the contemporary fight over evolution. Early modern Jews, like non-Jews, had to come to terms with new scientific knowledge that was no longer easily reconcilable with their religious traditions.

An important role in the dissemination of scientific knowledge and its transformative impact on early modern Jewish culture was played by doctors. Beginning in the sixteenth century, Jews from Poland, Tunisia, Germany, and Turkey came to Italy to study medicine at the universities at either Pavia or Padua. This was the first cadre of Jews to be exposed to science in a secular setting, and they returned to their communities after their medical studies as changed Jews.

Political changes in Christian Europe would further transform Jewish life and reverse the trend of expulsion from the west by the end of this period. Partly as a result of the stalemate in the religious war ravaging Europe in the wake of the Protestant Reformation and the Catholic Counter-Reformation, Christian rulers began to give precedence to the political and economic interests of the state over religious considerations.

THE HEBREW PRINTING REVOLUTION

The invention of printing in Europe around the middle of the fifteenth century was perhaps the single most important technological innovation of the early modern period. The cultural consequences of print were numerous and revolutionized the ways in which information was exchanged. The innovation in Europe (printing in China preceded the invention of printing in the West by several centuries) is generally associated with the printing workshop of Johannes Gutenberg of Mainz in southwestern Germany. Gutenberg began to print in the 1440s and produced his famous two-volume printed Bible in 1455. As early as 1444 we already hear of a business contract between a Christian goldsmith and a Jew in Avignon, in southern France, who wanted to engage in the "art of artificial writing" (i.e., print). Nothing came of this first endeavor (only forty-eight movable Hebrew letters had been made), but it is clear that Jews experimented from the very beginning with this new technology and were eager to use it for Hebrew printing.

The first printed Hebrew works that we know of were produced several decades later in Italy: The medieval code of Jewish law known as *Araba'a Turim* was printed in 1475 near Padua, whereas the eleventh-century biblical commentary by Rashi came off the press in Reggio di Calabria in southern Italy. Spanish Jews developed Hebrew printing in the 1480s and then introduced the new technology to the Ottoman Empire after the expulsion from Spain (a Hebrew printing press was opened by Sephardi exiles as early as 1493 in Constantinople). For centuries, Italy—in particular the city of Venice—was the center of Hebrew printing, whereas printing presses proliferated in other parts of the Jewish world—the Ottoman Empire, Cracow and Lublin in Poland, and Prague—in the sixteenth century. In the seventeenth century, successful Hebrew printing houses operated in various German and Polish cities as well, whereas Amsterdam, Holland, and Livorno, Italy, became the new centers of Hebrew print in the seventeenth and eighteenth centuries.

Among the most well-known Jewish printers was the Soncino family, which began its business in 1484 in the Italian city of Soncino (from which the family name is derived). They later expanded and opened printing houses in Salonika and Constantinople in the Ottoman Empire (in the 1520s and 1530s, respectively). It was, however, a Christian printer, Daniel Bomberg, who was responsible for some of the most influential Hebrew printing ventures of the period: Working in Venice, in 1517–1518 he printed a "rabbinic Bible" (i.e., the Hebrew text of the Bible together with its classical Aramaic translation and the most influential commentaries printed on the margins of the page). In the early 1520s, he printed a complete edition of the Talmud. The pagination of every Talmud printed even today still follows the pagination of Bomberg's edition, making it possible to navigate this vast compendium and give precise quotations.

The impact of Bomberg's editions of the Bible and the Talmud are only one example of the profound impact of printing on the development of Jewish culture in the early modern period. First of all, printing greatly expanded the readership of books. The printed book was still an expensive commodity in the sixteenth and seventeenth centuries, to be sure, but it was infinitely more accessible than the hand-copied manuscripts of the Middle Ages. More people had access to more books, and it was precisely this "democratizing" effect that made printing perhaps the most important technological innovation of the period. Literacy rose significantly as printed books became more widely accessible, and knowledge of Jewish texts—from the Bible to the Talmud to the prayer book—became much broader.

Books were not only more widely available; they also were studied differently. Before print, few people had direct access to written texts, so learning was primarily done orally. Thus learning was typically a collective enterprise, involving a teacher and students. Important texts were often memorized, whereas the distinction between the "original" text and its interpretations or commentaries often was blurry when it was studied orally. Printing changed all this as it established an authoritative and widely available text, while it standardized Jewish practices more than before. The unifying impact of print is particularly noticeable in the synagogue liturgy. Differences remained between various traditions, to be sure, but a trend evolved toward unifying practices both in the Sephardi and the Ashkenazi worlds.

Moreover, printing exposed more readers to more ideas by making the exchange of knowledge and information possible across large geographic distances and in less time. Exchange of information no longer had to rely on the personal contact made through travel or letters; rather, wide audiences could be reached in many different places. In Eastern Europe, for example, printing exposed

The new economic politics of mercantilism, each ruler trying to attract as much capital and trade as possible to his own territory, reshaped attitudes toward Jews: The Christian state began to consider potential economic use of Jews as more important than religious status. The expanding financial needs of European states during and after the Thirty Years' War led many Christian sovereigns to regard Jews not as a religious threat but rather as an economic asset. Whether focused on merchants attracted to the port cities of the Atlantic seaboard and Italy or "court Jews" serving as financiers to Christian

Ashkenazim to the cultural production of the Sephardi world, and printing played a major role in the success of works, such as the *Shulhan Arukh* (see Chapter 9).

Also, printing posed a new challenge to the authority of the rabbis. Before, the individual Jew would consult his or her rabbi with all questions relating to correct Jewish practice. Teaching and learning eminently constituted a personal interaction between the rabbi and his students. Print made books more easily available, and individuals could begin to learn by themselves and educate themselves without the guidance of the rabbis. It is true that study in pairs or groups continued to be a typical feature of Jewish learning, but individual reading, for study or for pleasure, was also made possible for the first time by printing.

None of this should be exaggerated. The impact of print did not change Jewish life overnight. Books continued to be a relatively rare commodity, and traditional practices of reading and learning were not dismantled at once. But printing did initiate a process of democratizing Jewish culture, the consequences of which could still be felt centuries later.

The art of printing made books accessible to a much larger audience. Jewish and Christian printers produced editions of the classics of Jewish literature, such as the Talmud or the prayer book. The printed word also contributed to the spreading of new ideas throughout the Jewish world—for example, the new teachings of Kabbalah coming out of sixteenth-century Safed. The image here is from the *Book of Raziel*, printed in Amsterdam in 1701, an anonymous collection of Kabbalistic and magical material that includes this depiction of a protective amulet to be worn by pregnant women.

monarchs, the perception that Jews would be useful to the economic interests of the state transformed significantly the political conditions of Jewish life.

In this chapter, as well as Chapter 9, we explore these issues in greater detail. We ask how the exodus of the Jews from the west and the establishment of new centers of Jewish life in the east changed the contours of Jewish culture in the early modern age. And we explore how early modern Jewish culture developed between the relative cultural isolation of a majority of the Jewish people and the exposure of a minority—for

SEPHARDIM AND ASHKENAZIM

Sephardi. The term *Sephardi* derives from *Sefarad*, a word that appears in the biblical book of Obadiah and has been used in reference to Spain since the Middle Ages. In the strict sense of the word, Sephardi are the Jews of the Iberian Peninsula (Spain and Portugal) and their descendants. After the expulsion of the Jews from Spain in 1492 and the forced conversions in Portugal in 1497, Sephardi Jews established communities in the Ottoman Empire (which they eventually came to dominate culturally and linguistically), in North Africa, in various cities of Italy and northwestern Europe, and in the Americas of the colonial period. The Sephardim of northern Morocco continued to use their Spanish-Jewish dialect, known as *Haketia;* the Ottoman Jews spoke Judeo-Spanish, known as *Ladino;* and the Sephardi Jews of Europe and the Atlantic seaboard continued to use Portuguese and Spanish throughout the early modern period.

Ashkenazi. The name *Ashkenaz* appears in three biblical books (Genesis, Chronicles, and Jeremiah). In the Middle Ages, the term was applied to the Rhineland, and by the early modern period, Ashkenazic included the Yiddish-speaking communities of western, central, and Eastern Europe. If France and Germany were the center of the medieval Ashkenazi world, its demographic and cultural epicenter had moved to Poland and Lithuania by the sixteenth and seventeenth centuries.

The terms *Sephardi* and *Ashkenazi* are also applied to describe the different liturgic and religious–legal traditions that developed in Spain and the Middle East on the one hand and in northern and Eastern Europe on the other. In this broader sense, *Sephardi* would include Jewish communities from the Middle East (Syria, Egypt, or Iraq, for example) who were not of Spanish or Portuguese origin but shared liturgic and religious–legal traditions with the Iberian Jews. In terms of their liturgical practice, it has been suggested that the Sephardi tradition is a continuation of the practice of Babylonia, whereas the Ashkenazi tradition was transmitted from Palestine through Italy to northern Europe. In reality, however, the division is not as clear-cut as this model suggests. In today's usage, the term *Sephardi* is often misleadingly employed to refer to all non-Ashkenazi or all non-European Jews.

Several other groups within early modern Jewry have a historical experience and religious–cultural heritage that set them apart from both the Sephardi and Ashkenazi Jews. These include, in Europe, the Italian Jews who continued to follow their own Italian–Jewish traditions and who lived side by side with the Sephardi and Ashkenazi immigrants who made Italy their home. Outside Europe, these include, for example, the Jews of Yemen, India, Iran, and Muslim central Asia, as well as the Jews of Ethiopia.

example, the conversos and the students at Italy's medical schools—to non-Jewish culture, anticipating many of the challenges of the modern age yet still remaining largely within the confines of the Jewish culture of the Talmud.

Until around 1700, Sephardi and Middle Eastern Jews still represented the majority of the world Jewish population. Throughout the period, however, the demographic growth of the Ashkenazi Jews in Eastern Europe was impressive, and even the widespread massacres afflicting East European Jewry in the mid-seventeenth century turned out to be a temporary setback. Estimates for Polish–Lithuanian Jewry suggest a population growing from around 30000 in 1500 to 100000 (perhaps even more) in 1575. Around the beginning of the eighteenth century, Ashkenazi Jews represented, for the first time in Jewish history, a majority of the Jewish population and Polish–Lithuanian Jewry became the largest Jewish community in the world. (*See box,* Sephardim and Ashkenazim.)

The largest urban Jewish communities in the early modern period were in the cities of the Ottoman Empire, with Salonika (in modern-day Greece) and the imperial capital Istanbul (Constantinople) both having about 20000 Jews in the mid-sixteenth century. Most Jewish communities in Europe, including those in Eastern Europe, were much smaller, with only a few communities—Prague, Vienna, Frankfurt, Cracow, Lvov, Lublin, Mantua, Rome, Venice, and Amsterdam—exceeding 2000 souls before 1650. In the decades after 1650, especially the communities living in important port cities expanded. With its combined Ashkenazi and Sephardi communities, the Jewish population of Amsterdam grew from just over 3000 in 1650 to over 6000 by 1700, while in the Italian port city of Livorno, the Jewish population rose from about 1250 in 1645 to 2500 in the late-seventeenth century. The largest communities in central Europe were Frankfurt, Prague, and, toward the end of the period, the sister communities of Hamburg–Altona–Wandsbeck in northern Germany. In Eastern Europe, the vast expansion of the Jewish population occurred primarily in a large number of small and midsize communities, especially in the eastern part of the Polish–Lithuanian lands.

Iberian Jewry Between Inquisition and Expulsion

The summer of 1391 was a fateful moment for Spanish Jewry. From early June through August, one Jewish community (known as *aljama*) after another was attacked by local Christians. By the end of the widespread violence, many synagogues throughout Spain had been made into churches (such as the two synagogues that can still be seen in the city of Toledo), thousands of Jews had either undergone conversion to escape popular wrath or fled, and many had been killed. Historian Jane Gerber estimates that perhaps one-third of the Jewish community converted, one-third was killed, and one-third survived as Jews. The events of 1391 and the continuing pressure of subsequent years led to a mass conversion of Jews to Christianity, creating an entirely new substratum in medieval Spanish society. Next to the established Christian and Jewish communities (the latter showed a remarkable resilience and regeneration in the remaining century before the expulsion), there was now a third group: the **Marranos,** or conversos. In some places—for example, in the cities of Barcelona and Valencia—no Jewish community remained after 1391 and all the former Jews now lived as conversos.

The attacks on the Jews of Spain had not been the result of an orchestrated push toward mass conversion. In many places, the Crown and its representatives tried, as they had before, to protect the Jews against violence, but incited by lower-ranking clergy and popular preachers, such as **Ferrant Martínez** in Seville, the mob invaded Jewish quarters and made a point of attacking the Jews precisely because they were seen as protégés of the Crown. The new situation would have seemed like a dream fulfilled for Christian Spain: At last, after years of missionary fervor, a large portion of the Jews had undergone baptism, albeit under pressure.

Yet in reality, the mass conversion soon created a whole set of new problems. On the one hand, all the **new Christians** (recent Jewish converts) could not necessarily be expected to fully embrace their new faith. It is true that some were sincere in their embrace of Christianity. The former chief rabbi of Burgos, **Solomon ha-Levi** (1351–1435), converted to Christianity, went to Paris to study theology, and returned to Burgos as the bishop of the city. Under his Christian name, Pablo de Santa María, he penned a historical work, *The Seven Ages of the World,* for the education of the Castilian king, John II. On the other hand, many of the Jewish converts never fully integrated into their new community, never truly embraced the new faith, and continued to think of themselves as Jews. In fact, the conversions of 1391

and the following years created an odd situation that was unprecedented in the medieval period: Often religious differences now divided families, one spouse having converted to Christianity, the other having remained a Jew. Siblings and cousins were divided by religion as well. Further complicating matters, most conversos continued to live in close proximity to their former coreligionists. They continued to inhabit the same houses, to do business with each other, and to socialize with Jewish friends and family members. What is more, those conversos who wished to continue to live secretly as Jews could do so because their Jewish neighbors provided them with books, kosher food, and information about upcoming holidays and religious practice.

At the same time, the "old" Christians (people with no Jewish ancestry) now faced formidable competition in practically all areas of life from "new" Christians. Jews could be, and were, restricted to certain economic and social roles. As Christians, however, the conversos were able to rise high in Christian society, compete with Christians for positions in the state and, as in the case of Solomon ha-Levi, even in the church. Together with the (probably not unjustified) suspicion of the sincerity of their religious convictions, this created a new situation that erupted in 1449 in a violent attack—this time not on the Jews, but on the conversos in the city of Toledo.

In response to these events and given the fact that many conversos continued to exhibit commercial and professional behaviors that were identical to those they displayed when they were Jews, the municipal council of the city—then the seat of the Castilian king—adopted new legal statutes that made a distinction between "old" Christians and conversos. The new laws sought to bar the latter from holding public office. The preamble to these statues stated, "We declare the so-called conversos, offspring of perverse Jewish ancestors, must be held by law to be infamous and ignominious, unfit, and unworthy to hold any public office or any benefice within the city of Toledo . . . or to have any authority over the true Christians of the Holy Catholic Church." This new legislation, known as the statutes of "purity of blood," or *limpieza de sangre,* introduced an entirely new concept that ran counter to established church law and, more generally, against medieval sensibilities. Personal status had been defined by one's religion, and just a century earlier the major law code of Castile, *Las siete partidas* ("The seven chapters"), had explicitly prohibited reminding a Jew or Muslim converting to Christianity of his or her pre-conversion background. Now a racial definition of Jewishness was passed into law for the first time. Initial opposition by the Crown and the church notwithstanding, and though the particular law of 1449 was later revoked, the standard of "purity of blood" was gradually adopted throughout Spain and Portugal over the course of the sixteenth century. Even before the beginning of a new (the early modern) era of Jewish history, medieval Spain witnessed the origins of a new variety of antisemitism, an antisemitism that was racial rather than religious.

The violence of 1391 was followed by an unabated conversionist movement, largely led by Dominican and Franciscan friars. One aspect of the process was the staging of **disputations** between Christians and Jews. One such public "debate," the most important of its kind during the medieval period, took place in **Tortosa** from February 1413 to November 1414. The Christian side, led by a converso to add insult to injury, set out to repudiate Judaism by focusing on the question of whether or not the messiah had yet come. By the disputation's end, the Christian side predictably declared victory over the Jewish representatives, with contemporary reports stating that hundreds of Jews ended up converting to Catholicism. Violence, forced conversions, and endless persuasion had devastating consequences for Spanish Jewry.

Identity of both individuals and groups is often expressed by exclusion: We know who we are and what we have in common as a group primarily by defining who we are *not* and what we do *not* have in common with others. It might be difficult at any given time to clearly pinpoint what it means to be Jewish, for example. The easiest way of defining Jewishness is to identify what it is not. If a basic distinction in medieval Spanish society between "us" and "them" was a religious one, setting Jews apart from Christians and Muslims, the mass conversions of the fifteenth century eroded this situation. The conversos now represented a group that was somewhere in-between, whose status was ambiguous: Christian in name, yet still bearing the stigma of Jewishness.

In 1478, the Catholic monarchs of the recently united Spanish kingdoms of Castile and Aragón decided that it was time to eradicate this problem. They requested authorization from the Pope to establish a national **Inquisition,** which began its work in 1481. The Inquisition was not concerned with Jews, as is often believed, but with Christians. Its task was to root out "heresy," beliefs and practices that were seen as contrary to Church doctrine, and the most important "heresy" that it was set to eliminate was the secret practice of Judaism—**judaizing,** as it came to be called.

Inquisition courts were set up throughout the Iberian Peninsula, and inquisitors established traveling courts, visiting places that lacked a permanent court every year or every other year. When the Inquisition came to town, the process began with a "grace period" of thirty or forty days during which people could come forward, confess their "crime," and be reconciled with the Church. This was still a public and hu-

miliating process, and confession did not necessarily spare one of punishment, except for eluding the death penalty. The inquisitors would also provide the public with a list of practices that were supposed to be indicators of secret judaizing, such as people refraining from eating certain foods, avoiding labor on Saturdays, doing extra shopping before Jewish holidays, slaughtering animals in a certain way, or observing rites of mourning that were seen as Jewish.

Once the inquisition process began, the accused was presumed guilty unless she or he could prove otherwise. The Inquisition tried to get a full, voluntary confession because, although it had recourse to torture, confessions given under torture were of little value and were notoriously unreliable. The records kept by the Inquisition meticulously documented the evidence provided by witnesses and the declarations by the defendants. Today, they represent a fascinating and rich source for historians trying to reconstruct the lives of conversos and other victims of the Inquisition, providing many surprising insights into daily life. One historian has even published a book of recipes based on Inquisition records, for culinary traditions were often identified as signs of judaizing. Refraining from pork might be an obvious example, but a whole converso cuisine developed and was documented by the inquisitors themselves.

In a testimony before the Inquisition court of Ciudad Real, dated December 30, 1483, a certain María Días declared that she had observed the following:

> In the house of the said Pedro de Villarruuia they were keeping the Sabbath and they dressed in clean and festive cloths of linen [in honor of the Sabbath]. And she knows and saw that they were praying on those Saturdays from a book. . . . And they prepared food on Friday for Saturday, and they prepared the entire house on that day, cleaned and washed, and lit new candles. . . . They kept the holidays of the Jews and were fasting on their fast days until the night. And one never saw them eating rabbit or hare or eagle [which are unkosher animals].

The defendants could only prove their innocence by proving that the witnesses were unreliable and motivated by personal revenge and enmity. The problem for the accused, however, was that the identity of the witnesses was not disclosed. If convicted of the "crime" of judaizing heresy, the "guilty" party was handed over to the secular authorities, their property was confiscated, and they were burned at the stake. In fact, the public spectacle, at once restoring the insulted honor of the Church and staging a powerful warning for all other judaizers, was so important that even if someone was found guilty of heresy after he or she had died, the

Maniere de brûler ceux qui ont été condannez par l'INQUISITION.

The Portuguese Inquisition at work: the burning of heretics after an auto-da-fé in Lisbon, as depicted in an eighteenth-century print by Bernard Picart.

Inquisition would have their body exhumed and burned in public and their property confiscated.

When, in January 1492 Catholic Spain conquered the last Muslim stronghold in southern Spain, the emirate of **Granada,** a new political situation had been created on the peninsula. Most of what is modern-day Spain was now under one unified rule, that of the "Catholic kings" Ferdinand and Isabella. In March of that year, the monarchs signed an edict that ended the history of a community that had lived in Spain since Roman times, and it would not be until the late nineteenth century that individual Jews began to "return" to Spain, and not until 1968 that another synagogue would be built there. The edict declared that "we have been informed that in our kingdoms there were some bad Christians who judaized and apostasized against our holy Catholic faith, mainly because of the connection between the Jews and the Christians." The edict then enumerated steps that had been undertaken to solve the "problem," from the segregation of Jews and Christians enforced in 1480 to the establishment of the Inquisition a year later and on to the partial expulsion of Jews from cities in southern Spain in 1483. All this, they concluded, "proved to be insufficient as a complete remedy" and "in order that there should be no further damage to our holy faith, . . . we have decided to remove the main cause for this through the expulsion of the Jews from our kingdoms."

A moving force behind the edict of expulsion was, no doubt, the Inquisition and its chief inquisitor, Tomás de Torquemada. Historians still debate the real purpose of this edict: Did the Catholic monarchs use the religious reasoning as a pretext, did they even mean what they said when ordering all Jews to leave, or did they secretly hope that this would be the last incentive for the remaining Jews to also convert to Christianity, thus removing Judaism as a religion without necessarily removing the Jews? It has been shown that little was gained economically by expelling the Jews while little direct damage resulted to the Spanish economy from the expulsion. The real motivations thus seem to have been religious and political. Whatever the purpose, probably half the Spanish Jews decided to convert and stay; the other half left, most of them for neighboring Portugal, while smaller numbers went to North Africa, Italy, and Ottoman Turkey. Historians disagree about the actual numbers of Jews who left Spain at the time, but probably around 100000 Jews went into exile.

Portugal provided a logical refuge, an exile that could be reached by land since traveling overseas was impractical for many. However, it was only a few years later that the Jews of Portugal faced their own demise. The marriage contract between the Portuguese king Manuel and Isabella, daughter of the Spanish monarchs Ferdinand and Isabella, stipulated that Portugal would have to follow the Spanish example and likewise expel its Jews. On December 5, 1496, the Portuguese king gave all the Jews, many of them Spanish refugees from 1492, ten months to abandon his kingdom. In reality, however, the Portuguese Crown preferred conversion. In early 1497, Jewish children up to fourteen years of age were seized by the state and baptized. Many were sent to the island of São Tomé, a Portuguese possession off the coast of Angola—a part of Portugal's colonial settlement policy that ended, according to contemporary Jewish chronicles, in the death of the children involved. Then in March 1497, the order of expulsion was essentially transformed into a forced mass conversion of *all* Jews, and instead of being expelled, the new conversos were now prohibited from leaving Portugal at all. The Portuguese knew that the transformation of an entire community of former Jews into Christians would take time, and it was not until 1536 that the Inquisition began to operate in Portugal. Certainly many conversos ultimately assimilated

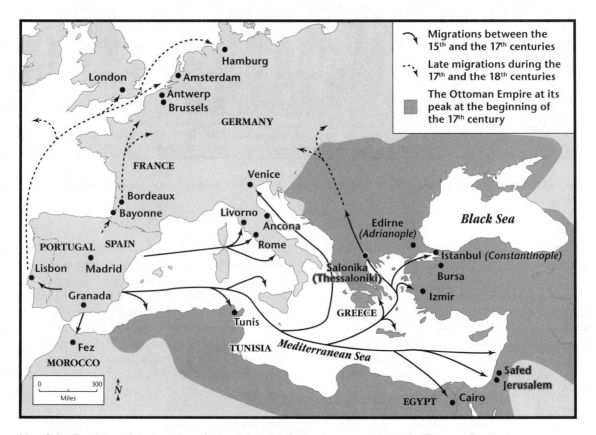

Map 8-1   Expulsion of the Jews from Spain, with major Sephardi communities in the Ottoman Empire.

into Christian society and forgot about their Jewish origins. However, some, especially in Portugal—where the entire community had been forced into conversion—but also in certain places in Spain, maintained a distinct crypto-Jewish converso culture that survived for many generations.

The Inquisition continued its obsessive attempt to root out all judaizing, and its activities were soon expanded to the newly gained Spanish and Portuguese possessions overseas. In 1569, for example, the Spanish Crown established the Inquisition in Lima (Peru) and Mexico City. These efforts notwithstanding, it is striking that still after several generations many conversos had not integrated into Christian society, were still rejecting the Christian religion, and continued to perceive themselves as Jews (as an ethnic group, if not religiously).

When the Portuguese first opened their borders to converso emigration in 1506, a constant trickle of conversos left the country. Many went to join communities established by the Spanish Jewish exiles of 1492—for example, in the Ottoman Empire—whereas others sought opportunities in northern Europe, establishing new communities in the early decades of the seventeenth century in places such as Amsterdam, Hamburg, and London (*see* Map 8-1).

The Sephardi Jews of the Ottoman Empire

The demise of Spanish Jewry coincided with the expansion of the greatest Islamic empire of the early modern period, the **Ottoman Empire,** in the eastern Mediterranean. The origins of the Ottoman state go back to around 1300. Constantly expanding at the cost of other Muslim principalities in Anatolia and of the major Christian power of the east, the Byzantine Empire, the new Ottoman state finally conquered the city of Constantinople in 1453. Later known as Istanbul, Constantinople had once been the capital of Christianity. It then was converted into the capital of an Islamic empire that, at its peak, stretched from Algeria in the west to Iraq in the east, from Hungary in southeastern Europe to Yemen at the southern tip of the Arabian Peninsula. The Ottoman Empire survived until after World War I, though it began losing territory on its European front beginning in the late seventeenth to the early eighteenth century.

It was in this vast empire that many Spanish, or Sephardi, Jews found a new refuge. Some arrived in the major cities of the Ottoman Empire soon after the expulsion from Spain in 1492, whereas others immigrated in the following decades and were later joined by conversos escaping the Inquisition in Portugal and Spain. They established a new and thriving center of Jewish life under the protection of the Ottoman

sultans. Jewish chroniclers of the time went out of their way to praise the hospitality of their new home, and a popular myth developed that the Ottoman sultan **Bayezid II** had actually invited the Spanish Jews to settle in his empire. No document has been found to date that would support this claim, but it is certain that the Ottoman state was a welcoming refuge for the Sephardim and Jews from other countries.

Even before the arrival of the Spanish Jews, the Ottoman lands had absorbed Jewish immigrants from elsewhere in Europe. Rabbi Isaac Zarfati, for example, wrote a letter addressed to his fellow Jews in Germany in which he declared:

> I have heard of the afflictions, more bitter than death, that have befallen our brethren in Germany—of the tyrannical laws, the compulsory baptisms and the banishments, which are of daily occurrence. . . . I proclaim to you that Turkey is a land wherein nothing is lacking, and where, if you will, all shall yet be well with you. The way to the Holy Land lies open to you through Turkey. . . . Here every man may dwell at peace under his own vine and fig-tree.

Zarfati, and many Jewish observers after him, juxtaposed the relative freedom that the Jews encountered under the Ottoman sultans with their dire conditions in much of Christian Europe at the time. It is significant that Zarfati employed biblical language in his praise of the Ottoman Empire, alluding to 1 Kings 4:25: "During Solomon's lifetime, Judah and Israel lived in safety . . ., all of them under their vine and fig trees." The implicit comparison between King Solomon and the Ottoman sultans could hardly escape the readers of Zarfati's missive.

By 1516–1517, the Ottomans had conquered Syria and Palestine and incorporated the Jewish Holy Land into their empire. When the Sephardi exiles and conversos fleeing the Inquisition arrived in the Ottoman Empire, some made their new home in the city of **Safed** in the Galilee where they established a thriving new center of Jewish learning. The main centers of Jewish life under Ottoman rule were, however, the major port cities of the empire: Constantinople (Istanbul), the imperial capital; Salonika (in modern-day Greece: Thessaloniki); and **Edirne** (in the European part of Turkey). The Ottomans were particularly interested in developing their capital city and even resorted to forced transfers of entire population groups to Istanbul in the wake of their conquest of the city in 1453 (a policy known as *sürgün* in Turkish). Among those who were transferred to the capital city were many Jews. It is interesting to note that at about the same time that the Spanish monarchs decided to drive all the Jews out of their dominions, the Ottoman sultans were moving entire Jewish communities into the very center of their empire.

One of the most renowned rabbis of Ottoman Salonika was **Moses Almosnino** (d. ca. 1580), a Sephardi Jew. In the 1560s, Almosnino was part of a Jewish mission from Salonika to the sultan in Istanbul to negotiate more favorable economic conditions for his community. During the lengthy visit to the imperial capital, Almosnino wrote a short history about the Ottoman sultans and a description of the city, all of it in the Judeo–Spanish language of the Sephardi Jews. "The population in Constantinople [Istanbul] and its surrounding areas . . . grew ten times during the reign [of Sultan Suleyman the Magnificent, r. 1520–1566]. One can certainly call this city of Constantinople and its surrounding areas a kingdom and climate unto itself . . . for the immeasurable number of its people." If the tenfold increase of the population was probably an exaggeration, the Jewish population in Istanbul did rise from about 12000 in 1490 to over 20000 in 1688. By that time, more than half of the city's Jewish population was of Sephardi origin. The community of Salonika also grew to an impressive size in the same period. The Sephardim there were by far the most dominant group within the Jewish community, and the Jews represented a significant percentage of the total population of the city. Some 20000 Jews lived in Salonika in the mid-sixteenth century, a number that grew to about 30000, or 50 percent of the total population of the city, in the following century.

Ottoman Jewry throughout the early modern and modern periods was an eminently urban society. The major cities of the Ottoman Empire—in particular port cities such as Istanbul, Salonika, Alexandria (in Egypt), and later Izmir (in Turkey)—were cosmopolitan centers with a population unmatched by most European cities in terms of their religious pluralism and multiethnic makeup.

Ottoman Jewry thrived in the sixteenth century. The Ottoman sultans followed in their treatment of the Jews the most lenient traditions of Islamic practice. Jews and Christians were considered *dhimmis,* non-Muslims protected by the Islamic state who had to abide by certain restrictions and paid a special poll tax (*jizya*). In reality, some restrictions that Islamic law imposed on the non-Muslim population were ignored even in the capital city Istanbul in the sixteenth century. For the most part, the Ottoman authorities were interested in securing the regular payment of taxes and in maintaining the public order. The administration of daily life, economic activities, and the exercise of religious authority all were the prerogative of the Jewish and Christian communities who could otherwise expect little interference in their affairs on the part of the state.

One can learn much about Jewish life under Ottoman rule from the responsa written by the rabbis at the time. One such text, which says a lot about the economic situation of Ottoman Jewry, was the responsum that the Salonikan rabbi **Samuel de Medina** (1505–1589) sent to the Jews of Janina, a city in northern Greece. The question addressed to Rabbi de Medina was as follows:

> The Jews of Janina complain about visiting Jewish merchants who compete with the local shopkeepers. . . . Would it be permissible for the Jews of Janina to use their influence with the local government officials to forbid these non-resident merchants to sell their merchandise in the city?

Samuel de Medina's lengthy and carefully worded responsum started out by declaring:

> [T]he opinions expressed in the Talmud and by the legal scholars of former generations regarding such cases do not apply to our own time . . . [Today,] we [Ottoman] Jews live under one sovereign who imposes no restrictions on travel or on commercial activities on any of his subjects. We see, for instance, that merchandise from Sofia [Bulgaria] is sold in Angora [Turkey] . . . The same is the case regarding the sale of Turkish products in Egypt. . . . And considering the fact that Moslem and Christian merchants are permitted to sell their wares all over the Empire, why should Jews discriminate against Jewish merchants? (English translation from Morris Goodblatt, *Jewish Life in Turkey in the XVIth Century,* New York: Jewish Theological Seminary, 1952, 187–188.)

He therefore declared the exclusion of nonresident Jewish merchants from going about their business in Janina illegal and added, "This is all the more true in the case of the Ottoman Empire where no trade barriers whatsoever are put in the way of foreign merchants. Surely, the Jews of one city cannot legally keep out Jewish merchants of another city or of another kingdom."

Samuel de Medina's responsum is interesting from a variety of perspectives. To begin, it reflects the self-confidence of the Sephardi rabbinate just a few decades after the trauma of the expulsion from Spain. Boldly declaring that certain opinions expressed in the Talmud "do not apply in our own time," Samuel de Medina interprets Jewish law with an eye to the requirements and conditions of his age and feels at liberty to rule against opinions and precedents established by earlier generations of rabbis.

In addition, Rabbi de Medina identifies the Ottoman context as one of essentially unrestricted commercial freedom, as one large economic area under a single political administration without any kind of economic discrimination. If Jews were pushed into certain marginal sectors of the medieval and early modern European economies—for example, moneylending, banking, peddling, and petty trade—no such restrictions existed in the Ottoman Empire. Jews were excluded from many trades and crafts in Christian Europe because, as Jews, they could not become members of one of the guilds that controlled access to most professions. In the Ottoman lands, Jews could form their own guilds, and, perhaps even more surprisingly, guilds with a mixed membership of Muslims, Jews, and Christians were not uncommon.

In the sixteenth century, Salonika and several other cities in the empire, including Safed in northern Palestine, became the major centers of Ottoman manufacture and commerce of textiles. Spanish Jews moving to the Ottoman Empire brought with them new techniques for producing stronger broadcloth at a lower cost. The textile sector emerged as the economic basis of the Sephardi communities in Salonika and Safed and came to be identified so much with the Jews of Salonika that by the mid-sixteenth century the Ottoman government required them to pay their poll tax in cloth to provide for the Janissary corps, a key part of the Ottoman military. As the century progressed, however, the competition of cloth manufactured in England, of both superior quality and at better cost, led to a slow decline in the Ottoman Jewish textile industry. The sector collapsed in Safed, though it held out longer in Salonika. In Europe, the textile and garment trade was also crucial to the Jewish economy, and thus Jewish involvement was, by the early modern period, an international phenomenon.

The trading network that Samuel de Medina alluded to in his responsum was concerned with internal trade within the confines of the empire. The Sephardi Jews, however, also emerged in the sixteenth century as intermediaries between Ottoman lands and Europe. Sephardi Jews living in the Ottoman Empire knew European languages (Spanish/Judeo–Spanish or Portuguese), and they maintained a net of family and business relations throughout the emerging Sephardi Diaspora. Spanish Jews and Portuguese conversos established themselves in port cities throughout the Mediterranean (outside the Ottoman Empire, primarily in Italy in cities such as Venice, Ancona, and Ferrara, as well as in North Africa), and in new communities that emerged in the cities of the Atlantic seaboard (Amsterdam, Hamburg, and London in northwestern Europe, and Bordeaux and Bayonne in southwestern France). These communities formed one of the most impressive **trading diasporas** in the early modern period, spanning various continents and straddling the cultural divide between the Islamic world and the various Christian powers of western Europe.

The Jews of the Ottoman Empire contributed to the economic development of the major Ottoman cities and perhaps the empire more generally, and their fate was tied to the fortunes of this vast Muslim state. Throughout the sixteenth century, the Ottomans moved from one military triumph to another, and even twice laid siege (though unsuccessfully) to the Habsburg capital, Vienna, first in 1529 and again in 1683. This period of Ottoman imperial expansion also was the golden age of Ottoman Jewry, a period of economic well-being and remarkable religious freedom. It was under these circumstances that the Sephardim and former conversos, after settling in the Ottoman Empire, were able to overcome the trauma of expulsion or forced conversion and to generate an unexpected Sephardi renaissance under Ottoman rule.

Living in Spain, the Jews had interacted quite freely with their neighbors and were very much part of the dominant culture—interreligious violence and forced conversions after 1391 notwithstanding. But the Ottoman Empire was a multiethnic and multireligious empire, especially in its provinces in the Balkans and in the major port cities in which the Jews settled. Thus the Sephardim maintained their own traditions and even their own language: Judeo–Spanish, or **Ladino.** In the European provinces of the empire and in Turkey, Ladino eventually became the predominant Jewish language. In places such as Salonika, even non-Jews would speak some Ladino as it soon emerged as a dominant language in the marketplace. Elsewhere—for example, in Istanbul or Janina—Greek-speaking Jewish communities that had lived in the city since late antiquity continued to exist side by side with the more recent Sephardi arrivals. (In the Middle Eastern parts of the empire, on the other hand, the Spanish Jews generally assimilated into the local Jewish culture and adopted Arabic as their primary language.)

The fact that Spanish Jews continued to maintain their original language—which in later centuries became the predominant Jewish language, even among those Jews who had no Sephardi ancestry—does not mean that Jews were completely isolated from their non-Jewish environment. Certainly many Jewish men living in places such as Istanbul or Edirne had at least some knowledge of Turkish or another local language, and many Jewish traditions were clearly influenced by Ottoman culture. Popular culture is a good example of the cultural mix that was generated by the mass immigration of Sephardi Jews into the Ottoman Empire: Bringing with them old traditions from Spain, they continued to sing ballads whose origins were in medieval Spanish culture. But the tunes they used were influenced by Ottoman musical traditions.

A Jewish physician in the Ottoman Empire, sixteenth century, possibly Joseph Hamon, physician at the court of the last Muslim ruler of Granada in southern Spain before the Christian conquest of the city in 1492. Hamon moved to Constantinople, where he became a physician in the service of the Ottoman sultan.

A Jewish woman in Adrianople (Edirne), in the Ottoman Empire, sixteenth century.

A Merchant Iewe.

A Jewish merchant in the Ottoman Empire, sixteenth century.

If some Jews spoke at least some Turkish or other languages outside their homes, within Sephardi families and within the Sephardi communities, Ladino remained the principle idiom. Many women, in fact, probably did not speak any other language. Thus, what emerged in the Ottoman lands of the sixteenth century was a unique Hispano–Jewish culture transplanted, as it were, to the multiethnic empire of the Ottoman sultans. Ladino, like other Jewish languages written in Hebrew characters, borrowed extensively from Hebrew and languages spoken in Ottoman lands, such as Turkish and Greek, but it remained close enough to Spanish that even today a Spanish speaker would be able to understand most of it without major difficulties. It is curious, however, that Ladino remained largely the language of popular culture, whereas rabbinic elite culture continued to be written almost exclusively in Hebrew—in fact, a flourishing Ladino literature did not emerge until the early eighteenth century when, in 1730, the Istanbul rabbi Jacob Huli published the first volume of an encyclopedic commentary on the Bible written in Ladino, the *Me'am Lo'ez.* In the sixteenth century, only relatively few works were written and printed in Ladino, Moses Almosnino of Salonika being the most prominent author.

It was not only Spanish Jews forced to leave Spain in 1492 who arrived in the Ottoman Empire. Throughout the sixteenth century and beyond, a constant trickle of conversos continued to leave Portugal and Spain, often escaping the Inquisition but, at times, simply in search of a better life. These former conversos established a far-flung Diaspora, providing an important link between the Islamic and the Christian worlds, especially in the commercial realm, where, in the early modern period, they undertook the lion's share of trade between these two regions. One outstanding example of the networks established by the former conversos is **Doña Gracia Mendes.** Born into a converso family in Portugal in 1510, her husband had been the owner of one of the most important banking houses in Lisbon and was involved in overseas trade. When he died in 1535, Doña Gracia inherited his large estate. With the establishment of the Portuguese Inquisition a year later, Gracia Mendes decided to leave. She went first to Antwerp (in today's Belgium). The family fortune was so significant that the Holy Roman Emperor Charles V tried to have the estate confiscated, but bribing the emperor and providing him a generous loan, Gracia Mendes was able to save most of her assets and procure a passage of safe conduct from the Venetian government and moved to Venice.

The family later moved to Ferrara and, around 1553, began to live openly as Jews. Soon afterward Doña Gracia left for Istanbul in the Ottoman Empire. It was there that she and her nephew Joseph rose to unprecedented prominence. Joseph was appointed duke of the island of Naxos, which the Ottomans had recently conquered from the Venetians, and controlled a large network of tax farms in the empire. Tax farming involved advancing the tax income for a given region to the government and leasing the right to collect those taxes from the local population. It was a common practice in premodern states and an economic sector in which the Spanish Jews had been active during the medieval period.

In 1555, Joseph and Gracia Mendes demonstrated their international connections when they tried to organize an Ottoman boycott of the Italian port of **Ancona.** Part of the papal states, previous popes had invited Jews and conversos to settle in Ancona to promote trade with the Ottoman Empire. In 1555, however, a new pope, the Counter-Reformation **Pope Paul IV,** came to power and initiated a crackdown on conversos who were secretly practicing Judaism in his lands. When two dozen conversos were burned at the stake in Ancona, Gracia Mendes and her nephew Joseph convinced the Ottoman sultan to formally protest and tried to organize a boycott of the papal port city. The effort ultimately failed, but it illustrates the close connections of the Sephardi converso Diaspora, often based on family and kinship ties, linking the major port cities of the Mediterranean and—increasingly in the seventeenth century—the Atlantic world.

Ottoman Safed in the Sixteenth Century

Palestine, or *Eretz Yisrael* ("the land of Israel"), as it was known to the Jews, came under the rule of the sultans of Constantinople when the Ottomans conquered it, along with Syria and Egypt, from the Mamluks in the early sixteenth century. Soon afterward, the city of Safed (*Tsfat*), in the region known as the Galilee in northern Israel, began to attract a growing number of Jewish immigrants. Former conversos fleeing the Inquisition in Spain and Portugal—along with Jews from other parts of the Ottoman Empire, from the neighboring Arabic-speaking lands, from North Africa and Italy and other parts of Europe—were drawn to Safed and established there what became the leading Jewish community in the Holy Land in the sixteenth century. One reason was the flourishing of Safed's economy in the first century after the Ottoman conquest. Its Jewish population peaked in the late 1560s when it reached perhaps as many as 1800 households, though it declined as the economic situation deteriorated in the following decades.

For many of the rabbis and scholars who moved to Safed at the time, however, it was more than its favorable economic environment that attracted them to the city. Consider this account by an anonymous Jewish traveler from the year

JEWS OF THE *MELLAH*

The largest community of Jews in the Islamic world outside the Ottoman Empire was Moroccan Jewry. Jews had lived in Northern Africa since antiquity and had been closely connected to the Jews of Muslim Spain in the Middle Ages. In the wake of the expulsion of 1492, many Spanish Jews relocated to Morocco where a sense of distinction between the exiles (known as *megorashim*) and the indigenous Moroccan Jews (*toshavim,* also called derogatively *foresteros,* or "strangers," by their Sephardi counterparts) persisted until modern times. Jewish society in Morocco was very diverse, from Spanish-speaking Jews in port cities engaging in overseas trade with Europe to Arabic-speaking Jews in the country's interior, often serving as middlemen between the urban centers and the tribal hinterlands. The Sephardi rabbinic elite (the "sages of Castile") came to dominate the religious life of Moroccan Jewry, but as in the case of the Ottoman lands, a unique blend of the Spanish–Jewish heritage and local conditions developed also among the various communities of Jews in Morocco.

Unlike the Jews of the Ottoman Empire, Jews in early modern Moroccan cities such as Fez or Marrakesh lived in separate quarters, not unlike the Italian ghettos emerging in the same period.

In 1438, the Jews in the Moroccan city of Fez were removed into a special quarter, or *mellah*—a term that denotes the Jewish quarters or ghettos that were established in various cities throughout Morocco in the early modern period. The same Moroccan ruler who moved the Jews from Old Fez into the Jewish *mellah,* Sultan Abd al-Haqq ibn Abi Saʾid (r. 1421–1465) also happened to appoint a Jew, Aaron ben Batash, to the office of vizier (or chief minister) during the last few years of his reign. The decree moving the Jews of Fez out of mixed neighborhoods and into the Jewish *mellah* came as a response to anti-Jewish disturbances. Again in 1465, many of its inhabitants died in the attack of Muslim rebels who rose against the ruling dynasty, partly in protest of the appointment of the Jew Aron ben Batash to the vizierate. These events illustrate the ambiguity of the Jewish experience in early modern Morocco: On the one hand, the Jews of Morocco were subject to rules and practices that were often far more restrictive than those in the Ottoman Empire. The various Moroccan rulers, through to the nineteenth century, took the Koranic imperative of "humiliating" or "humbling" the non-Muslim minorities quite literally, and unlike in the Ottoman lands, the Jews of Morocco lived in separate quarters like some of their European coreligionists did. On the other hand, individual Jews, such as Aron ben Batash, could rise to prominent positions in the royal court, whereas Jews of Spanish and Portuguese origin settling in the cities of Morocco's Atlantic coast established a much needed channel of trade and communication with Europe and provided crucial services to the country.

This ambiguity can also be seen in the daily lives of early modern Moroccan Jews as it was described by European travelers as late as the eighteenth century. One Christian visitor in the late seventeenth century portrays a community marked by discrimination, on the one hand, and cultural integration on the other:

1495, before the Ottoman conquest and the great expansion of the city:

> Safed is built on the slopes of a mountain and is a great city. The houses are small and modest, and when the rain falls it is impossible to walk about on account of the dirt, and also because it is on the hillside. It is also difficult to go out in the markets and the streets even during the summer, for you must always be climbing up or down. However, the land is good and health giving and the waters are quite good. . . . Around Safed there are many caves in which great and pious men have been buried. Most of these are about six miles from the town, and I saw some of them. . . . About six miles from Safed is a certain village called Meron, where very great and pious saints . . . are buried. We entered a certain cave nearby in which twenty-two scholars lie, and they said that these were the disciples of Rabbi Shimon bar Yohai of saintly and blessed memory; and near the spot on the hillside there is an extremely fine monument, which can be seen as far as Safed. (Lawrence Fine, *Physician of the Soul, Healer of the Cosmos: Isaac Luria and His Kabbalistic Fellowship,* Palo Alto, CA: Stanford University Press, 2003, 43–4.)

In Meron, the second-century Rabbi Shimon bar Yohai was believed to be buried, and his grave was an important destination for Jewish pilgrims since the fourteenth century. Bar Yohai was believed to be the author of the *Zohar,* the central work of Jewish mysticism (**Kabbalah**). Actually written in the late thirteenth century by Moses de Leon in Spain, the *Zohar* had become the most authoritative work of Kabbalah and was the basis for the Kabbalistic imagination

> The Jews are very numerous in Barbary, and they are held in no more estimation than elsewhere. . . . They are subject to suffering the blows and injuries of everyone, without daring to say a word even to a child of six who throws stones at them. If they pass before a mosque, no matter what the weather or the season might be, they must remove their shoes, not even daring in the royal cities, such as Fez and Marrakesh, to wear them at all, under pain of five hundred lashes and being put into prison, from which they would be released only upon payment of a heavy fine.
>
> They dress in the Arab fashion, but their cloaks and caps are black in order to be distinguishable. In Fez and Marrakesh, they are separated from the inhabitants, having their quarters apart, surrounded by walls, the gates of which are guarded by men set by the king so that they can conduct their business in peace and sanctify their Sabbath and their other holidays. In the other cities, they are mixed with the Moors [the Muslims]. They traffic in nothing other than merchandising and their trades. There are several of them who are quite rich. (Quoted in Norman Stillman, *The Jews of Arab Lands,* Philadelphia: Jewish Publication Society, 1979, 304.)

Still in the late eighteenth century, another Christian traveler described a community marked simultaneously by social isolation and cultural integration. At the same time, the author reveals his own European bias:

> The Jews in most parts of this empire [Morocco] live entirely separate from the Moors [the Muslims]; and though in other respects oppressed, are allowed the free exercise of their religion. Many of them, however, to avoid the arbitrary treatment which they constantly experience, have become converts to the Mahometan faith [i.e., to Islam]. . . . In most of the sea-port towns, and particularly in Tetuan and Tangier, the Jews have a tolerable smattering of Spanish; but at Morocco [Marrakesh] . . . and all the inland towns, they can only speak Arabic and a little Hebrew. They nearly follow the customs of the Moors [Muslims], except in their religious ceremonies; and in that particular they are by far more superstitious than the European Jews. (Quoted in Norman Stillman, *The Jews of Arab Lands,* Philadelphia: Jewish Publication Society, 1979, 312.)

The image that emerges from these travelogues, however distorted by the prejudices of their authors, is one of a diverse community at once subjected to the humiliating conditions of *dhimmi* (the Jews were the only non-Muslim minority in Morocco) and, at the same time, thoroughly integrated into the fabric of Moroccan society and culture.

of all subsequent generations. Thus, the belief that its presumed author was buried close to Safed along with numerous other holy figures of Jewish history contributed to the reputation of the city as a highly spiritual place.

Many of the scholars attracted to sixteenth-century Safed were Sephardim, often of converso origin, and Moses di Trani later even declared, "In Galilee [i.e., in Safed] people would say: Let us be grateful to the kings of Spain for having expelled our sages and judges, so that they came here and re-established the Torah to all its pristine glory." One of these luminaries of rabbinic learning, born in either Spain or Portugal and making his way to Safed, was **Joseph Karo** (1488–1575). Also a mystic, Karo is now most well known for his compendium of Jewish law, the *Shulhan Arukh* (first printed in Venice in 1565), which, for Orthodox Jews, remains the main Jewish legal code even

today (more on the *Shulhan Arukh* and its impact in Chapter 9).

A second figure leaving his imprint not only on the Judaism of his generation but on Jewish beliefs and practices to this day was **Isaac Luria** (known as *ha-Ari;* 1534–1572). Luria was born to an Ashkenazi father and a Sephardi mother in Jerusalem. When his father died while Luria was still a small child, his mother took him to live in Egypt, where he grew up and resided until emigrating to Safed in 1570. Though he lived in Safed for less than three years before his untimely death at the age of thirty-eight, Luria's teachings and the religious practices ascribed to him and his disciples transformed Jewish religious life in subsequent generations.

Safed had been a center of Kabbalah before Luria's arrival there—presumably this was what attracted him to the city in the first place. Scholars such as Joseph Karo, **Moses**

Cordovero (1522–1570), and others had created a culture of ascetic mystical practice and study. One Safed Kabbalist, Abraham Berukhim, described the common midnight study vigil, noting that "most scholars of Torah, when they rise in the middle of the night in order to study, sit upon the ground, wrap themselves in black, mourn and weep on account of the destruction of the Temple." The community included several individuals—for example, Joseph Karo—who claimed to have mystical visions in which they received secret divine knowledge, preparing for such visions through ascetic practices and self-mortification.

It was in this climate that Luria began to teach his own insights into Jewish mysticism. He did not put any of his highly imaginative teachings into writing, however, and what we know about Lurianic Kabbalah is from the accounts of various of his disciples, in particular **Haim Vital** (1543–1620), who saw himself as Luria's preeminent student.

It is impossible to introduce Luria's elaborate, imaginative, yet unsystematic teachings in the limited space available here. To give a taste of Lurianic Kabbalah—illustrating how influential it was on later Judaism, but also how "foreign" it might seem to modern readers—we present briefly two key concepts of Lurianic mysticism (*tikkun* and *gilgul*) and a religious practice invented by the Safed Kabbalists (*Kabbalat Shabbat*).

Historian Lawrence Fine has described the main theme of Lurianic myth, which is the basis of the idea of **tikkun**, the "restoration" or "mending" of the world:

> Drawing on the basic themes of exile and redemption that permeated Safed even prior to Luria's activities there, he devised a complex and distinctive set of mythological doctrines. At the heart of this mythology stands the . . . notion that sparks of divine light have, in the process of God's self-disclosure or emanation [i.e., in the process of Creation], accidentally and disastrously become embedded in all material things. According to Luria, these sparks of light yearn to be liberated from their imprisoned state and return to their source within the Godhead, thus restoring the original divine unity. The human task in the face of this catastrophic situation is to bring about such liberation through proper devotional means. (Lawrence Fine, *Safed Spirituality: Rules of Mystical Piety, the Beginning of Wisdom*, Mahwah, NJ: Paulist Press, 1984, 62)

This is the process of *tikkun,* or restoration, the purpose of which is not only to disentangle the sacred sparks of divine light trapped in the material world but to restore the original unity of the "male" and "female" aspects of the Godhead—often described in the Kabbalistic sources employing rather explicit sexual metaphors—as it had existed prior to Creation. The ultimate purpose of every religious act—whether it is prayer, a **mitzvah** (the performance of a religious commandment), or the study of the texts of Jewish tradition—if accompanied by the right intention, is to advance the process of *tikkun*. Lurianic Kabbalah provided a powerful rationale for the submission to divine law and the performance of Jewish ritual: Nothing less than the redemption of the world depended on every single religious act as long as it was carried out with the right intention. It thus empowered tremendously both the individual Jew and the Jewish people in general. According to Lurianic teachings, everything (and certainly everything that truly matters) depends on the religious actions of the Jewish people. In a generation facing the uprooting of the once splendid Spanish Jewish community, this empowerment through Kabbalah proved to be attractive. It was a potent answer to the precariousness of Jewish existence.

According to Lurianic Kabbalah, it was not only the sparks of divine light that were trapped in the "shards" of the material world: As a result of Adam's sins (as reported in the famous biblical story), the "sparks" of all future souls also fell into and were trapped by the material world. Therefore, part of the process of *tikkun* is the liberation of these soul-sparks (*nitsotsot ha-neshamot*). In the understanding of the Safed Kabbalah, this happens through the transmigration of the souls, known in Hebrew as **gilgul.** The scattered soul-sparks must be "reassembled" through their various transmigrations until they are reconstituted to their original form and can be reunited with their divine root.

The idea of *gilgul* is not mentioned in the Talmud, nor was it discussed by medieval Jewish philosophers such as Maimonides or Judah ha-Levi; others, including Saadya Gaon and Abraham ibn Daud, rejected the idea. Since the earliest Kabbalah, however, transmigration was taken for granted and can be found, for example, in the twelfth-century *Sefer ha-Bahir.* It was the Safed Kabbalists who developed the idea of *gilgul* further and interpreted events in the Bible, but also the historical experience of the Jewish people or of individual Jews, as a history of transmigrations. The soul, it was taught, would return to a situation similar to the one in an earlier *gilgul* in order to mend the damage done through transgressions in a previous life.

The Lurianic Kabbalists also developed elaborate theories as to the necessary reincarnations for a variety of different transgressions and sins. Eventually, this Kabbalistic idea of *gilgul* proved to be highly influential in both popular and learned Jewish culture in the following centuries. In the early 1700s Rabbi Elijah ha-Kohen of Izmir included a long list of *gilgulim* in his immensely popular work *Shevet Musar,* which was widely read by Jews in the Ottoman Empire and Eastern Europe:

I will give you many examples how the soul of the wicked returns in *gilgul,* so that the person may remember it and will not sin and will thus escape this agony. The *Kavanot ha-Ari* writes that the one who has sexual relations in candle light returns in *gilgul* of a goat. The one who is haughty against other people returns in *gilgul* of a wasp. The one who has killed a person returns in *gilgul* of water, and the proof is "[Only ye shall not eat the blood;] thou shalt pour it out upon the earth as water" [Deuteronomy 12:16]. The one who has illicit sexual relations with a woman who is married or engaged returns in *gilgul* of a water mill, and there both, man and woman, are judged. The one who speaks slander returns in *gilgul* of a stone.

Finally, a ritual developed among the Safed mystics, practiced and developed by Luria himself, is the welcoming of the Sabbath "queen," known in Hebrew as ***Kabbalat Shabbat.*** Described by Luria's disciple Hayim Vital, this practice involved going to the outskirts of the city on the Sabbath eve, turning one's face toward the west as the sun set, and welcoming the "Sabbath Queen." Prior to the regular evening prayer service, one would recite Psalm 29 and then the phrase "Come O Bride, Come O Bride, O Sabbath Queen," followed by Psalms 92 and 93.

Anyone familiar with synagogue services on Friday night—when the Sabbath begins at nightfall—will recognize how this tradition has survived into contemporary Jewish practice throughout all streams and traditions of Judaism, except that the ritual (turning toward the west; the recitation of the Kabbalistic hymn *Lekhah dodi likrat Kallah,* ending with the phrase "Come O Bride . . .") is now performed inside the synagogue rather than in the fields on the outskirts of the city, as was the practice in sixteenth-century Safed. This is by no means the only tradition common among Jews today that goes back to this moment in Jewish history—the custom of studying through the first night of the Shavuot festival is another example. It is a good illustration of how influential Lurianic Kabbalah has been for subsequent generations of Jews, whether or not they knew or cared about some of the more esoteric aspects of Luria's teachings.

Between Ghetto and Renaissance: The Jews of Early Modern Italy

Italy served as a cultural bridge between northern Europe and the Mediterranean world, and it was a crossroads of Jewish cultures. Italy was not a unified state in the early modern period but rather an often confusing mix of different principalities, duchies, republics, kingdoms, and, of course, the Church states with their center in **Rome.** For much of the early modern period the Jews lived only in the parts of Italy north of Rome. Sicily was under Spanish rule and thus expelled its Jews in 1492; when the kingdom of Naples came under Spanish domination, its Jews were expelled in 1541. Rome had a Jewish community the origins of which dated to antiquity. Other centers of Jewish life in sixteenth-century Italy were Mantua, Ferrara, Venice, and the territories of Tuscany and Savoy.

The Venetian government allowed Jews late in the fourteenth century to reside temporarily in **Venice** and engage in moneylending. The charter issued in 1397, however, made a stipulation that Jews could stay in Venice for no longer than fifteen days at a time, and even though many Jews managed to evade the restrictions placed on their residence in the city, they still were not allowed to practice Judaism in public or to open a synagogue. It was only in 1509 that a larger number of Jews flocked into the city as war refugees. Soon after, the Venetian authorities realized that the presence of the Jews would be beneficial to the social and economic interests of the city. As moneylenders they would provide a much needed service to the Christian poor, enabling Christians to avoid violating the Church's prohibition of lending money against interest to their coreligionists. But as in so many other parts of Christian Europe, and clearly distinct from the situation in the lands of Islam, the presence of the Jews was always controversial. As a result—in fact, a compromise between exclusion or expulsion of the Jews and granting them a right of residence—the city of Venice ordered the creation of a strictly segregated Jewish quarter. The area to which the Jews of Venice were confined was known as the *Ghetto Nuovo.* It was the term **ghetto** that came to denote the segregated Jewish quarters that were established in other Italian cities in the sixteenth and seventeenth centuries, as well as outside Italy.

The discussions in the senate of Venice about tolerating the continued presence of Jews in the city was typical for the ways in which various Italian states and cities dealt with Jewish immigration and residence. The most powerful argument in favor of allowing the presence of Jews was one of ***raison d'état,*** or the interest of the state, balancing religious prejudice, popular resentment against Jews, and the fear of competition among the Christian "middle class." A good example of the competing attitudes was the debate in the Venetian Great Council. One Francesco Bragadin argued that "it was necessary to have Jews for the sake of the poor," as there was no other institution in place to provide loans for those in need, and "he cautioned about arguing against the Jews, for even the Pope keeps them in Rome." The next speaker supported his argument, "and he spoke well for an eighty-six year old man, saying that Jews are necessary to assist the poor . . . the statutes must be confirmed . . . and the Jews allowed to lend at interest, because they have no other livelihood."

The continued presence of Jews in Venice also met opposition, however, which was couched in religious and political language: "Next Sier Gabriel Moro . . . got up and spoke out against the Jews, saying that they should not be kept, and that Spain drove them from her lands, then they came to Naples and King Alfonso lost his kingdom . . . and now we are going to do the same thing and stir up the wrath of God against us." However, "many other members of the Consiglio, who were concerned for the well-being of the poor, said that when the Jews were driven out of Spain they brought with them a great quantity of gold. They went to Constantinople, and [the Ottoman sultan] Selim conquered Syria and Egypt." (Quoted from Robert Bonfil, *Jewish Life in Renaissance Italy*, Berkeley: University of California Press, 1994, 39–40.)

The opponents of Jewish settlement, then, resorted to a typical medieval argument: Allowing the Jews to live in their midst would inevitably provoke God's wrath. In the face of early modern considerations of *raison d'état* and a secularization of European politics, this kind of argument had lost some of its persuasiveness. The party supporting continued settlement of the Jews in Venice prevailed, arguing that their services were needed (for example as moneylenders for the Christian poor), and greatly inflating the economic significance of the Sephardi immigration to the Ottoman Empire, which as an Islamic state had never seen the Jewish presence as a problem but simply as a fact of life—and perhaps even as desirable and beneficial to the state.

In March 1516, the first ghetto in Jewish history was established in Venice. The example of Venice was later followed by many other cities throughout the Italian peninsula. In 1555, Pope Paul IV took power in Rome and issued his infamous bull referred to as *Cum nimis absurdum,* after its opening words: "It is profoundly absurd and intolerable that the Jews, who are bound by their guilt to perpetual servitude, should show themselves ungrateful toward Christians; and, with the pretext that Christian piety welcomes them by permitting them to dwell among Christians, they repay this favor with scorn, attempting to dominate the very people whose servants they should be." The bull of this Counter-Reformation pope initiated a new period in the history of relations between the Catholic church and the Jews, not least for the Jews of Rome. The Church increased the pressure on the Jews in Catholic Europe. In August 1553, the Church issued a decree condemning the Talmud as blasphemous and ordered that it be burned—an order widely obeyed throughout Italy. The *Index* of prohibited books issued by Pope Paul IV in 1559 included the Talmud and was later extended to many other Jewish books. Jewish books that were not outright banned would be subject to the censorship of the Church: The *Index expurgatorius* of 1595 listed a total of 420 different Hebrew works that could only be published with certain passages that the Church considered to be offensive to Christians taken out or revised.

Jews had lived in Rome since antiquity and had always been protected by the Roman Catholic Church. In 1555, however, the lives of the approximately 4000 Roman Jews changed significantly when the pope decreed that they move to a small area on the northern bank of the Tiber River to be surrounded, as in the Venetian ghetto, by a wall that was to be closed at nighttime. The Jews were also ordered to wear a distinctive yellow badge (they wore a yellow head covering in Venice). A description of the crowded conditions of the Roman ghetto before it was razed to the ground (nothing of the original ghetto remains today) was provided by a traveler in the middle of the nineteenth century, and probably gives a sense of what the ghetto must have looked like in the sixteenth century:

> [D]irectly ahead are the ghetto houses in a row, tower-like masses of bizarre design, with numerous flower-pots in the windows and countless household utensils hanging on the walls. The rows ascend from the river's edge, and its dismal billows wash against the walls. . . . When I first visited it, the Tiber had overflowed its banks and its yellow flood streamed through the Fiumara, the lowest of the ghetto streets, the foundations of whose houses serve as a quay to hold the river in its course. . . . What melancholy spectacle to see the wretched Jews' quarter sunk in the dreary inundation of the Tiber! Each year Israel [the Jews] in Rome has to undergo a new Deluge, and like Noah's Ark, the ghetto is tossed on the waves with man and beast. . . . Before 1847, a high wall . . . separated the Palace of the Cenci from the Jews' Square. . . . Here was the principal gate of the ghetto. If we now enter the streets of the ghetto itself we find Israel [the Jews] before its booths, buried in restless toil and distress. (Ferdinand Gregorovius, *The Ghetto and the Jews of Rome*, New York: Schocken Books, 1966, 85–90.)

Throughout the sixteenth and seventeenth centuries, most (though not all) Italian cities with a Jewish community

Index of books prohibited by the Catholic Church. In 1559, Pope Paul IV included the Talmud among the books banned by the Church. This title page is from the *Index* published in 1786.

followed the example of Venice and Rome and restricted their Jewish populations to ghettos: Florence and Siena in 1571, Verona in 1602, Padua 1603, Mantua 1612, Ferrara 1624, and Modena 1638, with the ghetto of Correggio established as late as 1779. The irony is that the era of the ghetto in Italian Jewish history was in many ways less violent than other periods: Almost no accusations of ritual murder were made (as had happened in the infamous blood libel of Trent in 1475, which led to the death of the entire Jewish population—some thirty persons—of the city), and in general violence against the Jews or the threat to expel them subsided significantly.

The Jews of Rome created their own pun on the word *ghetto:* They called it their *get,* from the Hebrew word meaning a letter of divorce: In the Roman case, the Jews were resettled in a separate part of a city in which they had lived for centuries. In Venice, the establishment of the ghetto marked the beginning of a permanent presence of the Jews in the city. In both these cases, as in most other Italian cities, the establishment of the ghettos imposed a new set of restrictions on the Jews, while it created a specific space for the Jews in the urban landscape, and thus a specific slot for the Jews within Italian society. It is in this sense that the establishment of the early modern Italian ghetto was experienced with much ambivalence: The wave of expulsions from western Europe, which had begun with the expulsion from England in 1290 and reached its high point with the Spanish expulsion in 1492, was finally coming to an end.

The early modern Christian state, first in Italy and soon elsewhere in western Europe, came to terms with a continued or renewed Jewish presence. It assigned the Jews a separate space, it tried to limit as much as possible and to control the interaction of Jews and Christians, it had the gates of the ghetto locked after nightfall—but in the spirit of *raison d'état,* it also came to recognize the economic utility of the Jews in areas such as moneylending. Commerce began to displace religious considerations that had led to the progressive exclusion of Jews from western European Christendom at the close of the Middle Ages. This led in some instances to granting the Jews a more privileged treatment than the one to which other minorities and immigrants were subject. In Venice, for example, the charter of 1548 allowed the Jews to build synagogues (they previously held their religious services in private homes), whereas the Greek Orthodox Christians were only allowed to build their first church in this Catholic city in 1573, while Protestants received permission to conduct private services but not to have their own church, the first one only being erected in 1657.

What was the impact of the ghetto on the development of Italian Jewish culture? At first one would expect to see a growing isolation, and to a certain degree that was the case when, in the course of the sixteenth and seventeenth centuries Jewish mysticism, or Kabbalah, came to dominate Jewish religious practices. But at the same time, Jews continued to socialize with Christians, meeting in taverns and drinking and gambling together. Jews in Rome shared the culinary taste of their Christian neighbors, their synagogue tunes sounded much like Catholic sacred music, they routinely referred to December 25 as *Natale,* or Christmas, in their rental contracts, and they commonly used Italian names, with their Hebrew names largely employed only in the synagogue.

The autobiography of the seventeenth-century Venetian rabbi **Leone Modena** (1571–1648) provides ample evidence of the cultural proximity of Jews and Christians. With reference to the ancient art of alchemy (considered a serious science until the eighteenth century, a by-product of which was the belief that one could make gold or silver out of lead through chemical processes), Modena writes about his son Mordecai: He "began to engage in the craft of alchemy with the priest Grillo, a very learned man. . . . Finally . . . he arranged a place in the Ghetto Vecchio and with his own hands made all the preparations needed for the craft. There he repeated an experiment that he had learned to do in the house of the priest, which was to make ten ounces of pure silver from nine ounces of lead and one of silver." Even religious events could be shared by Jews and Christians, as the repeated reference in Modena's autobiography to a Christian audience of his sermons in Venice suggests: "At the end of Tevet 5382 [1622], a celebration was held in the Great Synagogue at the conclusion of the study of the talmudic tractate Ketubbot. Eighteen sermons were delivered, and on the last night. . . I gave the sermon before a huge standing crowd, packed in as never before, with many Christians and noblemen among the listeners." (Leon Modena, *The Autobiography of a Seventeenth-Century Venetian Rabbi: Leon Modena's Life of Judah,* trans. Mark Cohen, Princeton, NJ: Princeton University Press, 1988, 108, 117.)

Even though Jews and Christians continued to socialize in this age of the ghetto and continued to partake of a shared culture, the awareness of being different persisted. As one historian of Italian Jewry has remarked, "[A]like did not mean identical." Italian Jewish culture was both Italian *and* Jewish. The subculture of the Italian Jews was in many ways a mirror image of the culture of their Christian neighbors. The culture of Renaissance Italy influenced them—and they adapted it to their own cultural needs—but they also defined their own Jewishness in conscious distinction from their environment. They may have shared the culinary taste of other Italians and eaten pasta—but they were also bound by the Jewish dietary laws, which set them apart from the Christians. They may have used their Italian names—but they also knew that in their synagogues they would step into a Jewish space and be identified by their Hebrew names. Thus, the Italian Jews acculturated, shaping their own culture in relation to the Christian culture that surrounded them, but they never lost their sense of difference, of "otherness." Cultural "assimilation" did not lead, and does not necessarily lead today, to a negation of Jewish identity.

An exceptional but nevertheless telling example that illustrates both inclusion and exclusion of the early modern Italian Jews is the case of **Sara Coppio Sullam,** born to a Venetian Jewish family around 1592. In 1618, she began a correspondence with the Italian monk Ansaldo Cebà of Genoa after reading his verse epic *L'Ester.* The two exchanged letters, pictures, and poems for many years, evidence of the cultural affinity that Jews and Christians could experience. At the same time, Cebà's unconcealed expectation that Sara would eventually convert to Christianity (which she never did) also illustrates the continuing sense of difference that always separated members of the two groups, despite all that they might have in common.

Sara Sullam gathered a salon of learned Christian men—poets, painters, and priests—who met in her home in the Venetian ghetto for intellectual conversation and, often enough, to ask Sara for money. Some of her guests, however, later came to betray her, and one wonders whether the reason was that she was, after all, a Jew, residing in the ghetto, and hence on the margins of Venetian society. One priest and poet who was a regular in Sara's salon accused her in a public treatise of having denied the immortality of the soul—considered a heretical stance by both Catholic and Jewish authorities—to which Sara Sullam responded by publishing a treatise of her own, *Manifesto di Sarra Copia Sulam hebrea,* in which she defended her own views and attacked her opponent. Sara Sullam certainly was an unusual woman, but her example demonstrates the extent to which a Jewish woman (at least one belonging to a prominent and wealthy family), living in the ghetto of Venice, could participate in the culture of Renaissance Italy.

The Jewish communities of Italy were diverse and well connected to Jewish communities both in Europe and the Ottoman world. At least eight different synagogues were operational in the ghetto of Venice, where most Ashkenazi and Italian Jews were engaged in moneylending and secondhand clothes dealing; the more recent Sephardi and converso immigrants (known as Leventini and Ponentini, respectively) were mostly merchants. In the center of the ghetto in Rome, five different synagogues—called the *Cinque Scole*—were housed in the same building, each

representing a different rite (Italian, Sicilian, Ashkenazi, Castilian, Catalan). Each Italian Jewish community had its own flavor, with Ancona and Ferrara dominated by the Sephardi and converso immigrants, Verona having a strong Ashkenazi presence, and the Great Synagogue of Mantua—home to the famous Italian rabbi and philosopher Judah Messer Leon (d. ca. 1526)—following the Italian rite. The Italian communities thus facilitated throughout the period the cultural exchange between Jews of different origin and their diverse traditions, a contribution greatly enhanced by Italy's emergence as the main center of Jewish print in Hebrew, Yiddish, and Ladino. Its communities were much smaller than those of the Ottoman Empire (Rome about 4000, Venice 2500, Mantua over 2300, and other communities numbering in the hundreds). Together, the Italian Jewish communities of the sixteenth century probably did not exceed 30000 souls.

A distinctive feature of Italian Jewish society at the time was the proliferation of confraternities (*hevrot*), voluntary associations that were formed for a variety of purposes. The Gemilut Hasadim confraternity of Ferrara for example, established in 1515, promised in its statutes:

> to attend the sick who are poor and are in need, and to keep vigil over them at night and day, and to serve them for the honor of God until they recover. And to care for the dead when there is need, and after their death to make a coffin for them . . . and to wash their body and carry them to the cemetery and to bury them and to stand vigil over them until their burial. (David Ruderman, "The founding of a 'Gemilut Hasadim' society in Ferrara in 1515," *AJS Review* 1 (1976), 259.)

Other confraternities were established for the study of Torah (*talmud torah*)—for example, in Rome some time before 1540—and for a host of other religious purposes. The establishment of such confraternities goes back to medieval Spain and southern France, where such pious associations are known from the thirteenth century. Imported by the Spanish Jewish émigrés after 1492, these voluntary confraternities became an important venue for socializing in the Jewish communities of early modern Italy and the Ottoman Empire. In Italy, they had their equivalent in Christian society as well: Michel de Montaigne noted during his visit to Rome in 1581, for example, that "they have a hundred brotherhoods and more, and there is hardly a man of quality who is not attached to some one of these."

The rabbis decried any activity that did not involve performing a religious ritual or the study of Torah. They called it *bitul torah,* literally "annulment of Torah." In the rabbinic ideal, Jewish time was guided by the rhythms of religious life—the three daily prayers, the regular study of Torah, the weekly day of rest (Shabbat), the holidays. Jewish space, more clearly delineated in the Italian ghetto than ever before, was to be defined by a religious topography—the synagogue, the study house (*bet midrash*), the school of higher learning (*yeshiva*), and the like. The Jewish confraternities provided a new outlet for Jews to socialize without challenging the rabbinic ideals—and as mutual aid associations they fulfilled an important function in the organization of Jewish society. They provided a setting for individuals to come together and socialize, presumably with a religious purpose (study, charity, and so on), but in reality they provided a place just for spending time together outside the confines of one's family and outside such official community organizations as the synagogue.

A Jewish Renaissance

In the fifteenth century, European scholars coined the term *Middle Ages,* referring to the period between the downfall of the classical world of ancient Greece and Rome and their own times, known as the period of **Renaissance,** which literally means "rebirth." The Renaissance was characterized by a resurging interest in the classical heritage of European civilization. Marked by a conscious break with the "medieval" past, Renaissance thought and art sought to reclaim classical learning, but it was also marked by a plethora of new discoveries: the invention of print and other technological innovations (gunpowder, for example, which made possible the expansion of the Ottoman and Spanish Empires); the discovery of new continents; and scientific discoveries, emblematic of which was the replacement of the old Ptolemaic system of astronomy with the Copernican system, questioning for the first time the centrality of Earth in the known universe. Beginning in the Italian cities of Florence and Rome, the Renaissance also created a new art and architecture. Eventually, the movement spread across Europe, and hardly a European country was not touched by the transformative force of the Renaissance.

All this did not fail to have an impact on Jews and Jewish culture. Jews in Italy were taking an interest in contemporary Italian Renaissance culture, cultivating the arts of rhetoric, music, and dance, whereas the architecture of Jewish synagogues all across Europe betrayed the influence of Renaissance art—evident, for example, in the extensive

rebuilding in the Prague ghetto under the sponsorship of its leader Mordechai Maisel in the late sixteenth century.

At the same time, scientific discoveries presented new challenges to the rabbis. One case in point is Rabbi **Isaac Lampronti** of Ferrara in Italy (1679–1756), author of an encyclopedic work entitled *Pahad Yitshaq,* which shows his interest in Jewish law and in the advances of contemporary science and medicine. A curious example is Lampronti's discussion of whether it is permitted to kill lice on the Sabbath. Traditional Jewish law forbids the killing of an animal on the Jewish day of rest, but earlier rabbis had argued that lice grew out of moisture in the ground and thus cannot be considered living creatures (in contrast to flies, for example). Challenging this ruling, Lampronti cited contemporary scientific studies that suggested lice, like flies, reproduced themselves sexually and thus were to be considered animals, and that there was no such thing as spontaneous generation of creatures from moisture or rotten fruit. "I would say," Lampronti concluded, "that if the sages of Israel might have heard the proofs of the gentile sages, they might have reconsidered and acknowledged [their] opinions." (Quoted in David Ruderman, *Jewish Thought and Scientific Discovery in Early Modern Europe*, Detroit, MI: Wayne State University Press, 2001, p. 261) Even though this conclusion may seem self-evident, others contradicted Lampronti. What was at stake, after all, was to determine what is permitted and what is prohibited on the Sabbath, and it raised the larger question of whether scientific insights could be allowed to challenge the authority of the ancient and medieval rabbis.

Scientific knowledge was spread throughout the Jewish world through a variety of channels. With the invention of print, the exchange of information became much easier and knowledge became more widely accessible. At the same time, a social group responsible for the dissemination of scientific thought was the growing number of Jewish physicians who had obtained a university education and thus had become familiar with European Renaissance thought and science firsthand. Some of these **Jewish physicians** in the early modern period were conversos who had received their education living as Christians in the prestigious universities of Spain and Portugal at the time (Salamanca, Alcalá, Coimbra, for example). Emigrating abroad and living there openly as Jews, these converso physicians played an important role in the dissemination of scientific knowledge and critical thought. At the same time, some Italian universities—first and foremost, the University of Padua—opened their doors to Jewish students of medicine. Providing them with a comprehensive education that included the liberal arts, Latin philology, and natural sciences, in addition to the medical curriculum, Padua attracted a growing number of Jewish students from Italy, Germany, Poland, and the Ottoman Empire. These students, after finishing their studies, likewise served to disseminate secular knowledge—in particular, knowledge of the scientific advances of the time—throughout the Jewish world.

Another example of the impact of Renaissance culture on Jewish literature is the (albeit short-lived) revival of historical writing, mostly among Italian Jews, in the sixteenth century. The writing of history had not been part of the Jewish tradition since Josephus Flavius in the first century CE, and it experienced a revival in the generation after the expulsion from Spain. **Shlomo ibn Verga** was a Spanish Jew living as a Christian in Portugal after the forced conversions of 1497 until he left for Italy nine years later. There he wrote, sometime during the 1520s, his chronicle *Shevet Yehudah,* which has been described as a "proto-sociological" study of recent Jewish history. Most importantly, ibn Verga was interested in finding the "natural causes" for the continuous persecution of the Jews, explaining their sufferings by means of historical analysis rather than through theology. Instead of arguing that the persecution of the Jews past and present was best understood as divine punishment for transgressing God's laws, ibn Verga suggested that social and historical reasons accounted for the violence against Jews. Also, in the sixteenth century **Samuel Usque,** an Iberian Jew, wrote another historical work, *Consolaçam as Tribulaçoens de Israel* ("Consolation for the Tribulations of Israel," in Portuguese and printed in Ferrara, 1553), likewise focusing on the long history of Jewish suffering.

Other historians of the period discovered for the first time an interest in non-Jewish history. **Elijah Capsali of Crete** (d. 1555), for example, had studied in Padua and wrote a history of the Venetian and Ottoman Empires, including an extensive account of the expulsion of the Jews from Spain and their resettlement in Ottoman lands (*Seder Eliyahu Zuta,* written in the 1520s). **Joseph ha-Kohen** (d. 1578) wrote a chronicle of the French and Turkish kingdoms (Sabbioneta, 1554) and prepared a Hebrew translation of Francisco López de Gómara's Spanish *History of New India and Mexico* (1568). Beyond the Italian cultural area, it was **David Gans** (d. 1613), a Westphalian Jew living in Prague, who wrote a remarkable historical work entitled *Tsemah David* (Prague, 1592), which was divided into two parts: One covered general history, the other Jewish history up to the date of the work's publication. The sense of parallel, rather than shared, histories of the Jews and of the world betrays a traditional outlook, to be sure, but Gans' and others'

interest in general history nevertheless indicates the opening of a new horizon of knowledge.

One of the most intriguing figures in this regard, and certainly the one more imbued with the thinking of the European Renaissance than any other, was the Italian Jew **Azariah de' Rossi** (ca. 1513/1514–1578). Born in Mantua, de' Rossi was the most accomplished representative of the Jewish Renaissance, and he was a controversial figure. Other luminaries of the time opposed his work—for example, the celebrated Rabbi Löw ben Betsalel of Prague (known as Maharal), even as he was one of the foremost advocates of a reform of Jewish education and displayed an interest in secular and philosophical studies as long as they could be reconciled with Jewish tradition. De' Rossi's major work, *Me'or Einayim,* was banned by some of the leading rabbis of the time, and it was only with the onset of the Jewish Enlightenment in the eighteenth century that his pioneering study was rediscovered.

The third part of *Me'or Einayim* contains sixty chapters of critical historical studies in which Rossi inquired into the ancient history of the Jews by comparing sources from the Jewish tradition, namely the Talmud, with ancient Jewish and non-Jewish historical sources. His critical approach to the Talmud (though he did not extend it to the study of the Bible) was clearly informed by the new critical studies of the Renaissance period and was nothing short of revolutionary for Jewish literature at the time.

A typical passage from de' Rossi's work, introducing a historical problem, is the following:

> [A]nd let us return to the city of Alexandria. We are confronted with three different accounts. The wicked murderer is identified as Trajan in the Palestinian Talmud, Tarkinus in the Midrash Rabbah texts, and Alexander of Macedon in tractate Sukkah of the Babylonian Talmud, while in tractate Gittin, they change their opinion, and the name of Hadrian is proffered. Now we have undertaken to investigate the truth of all this, although we are not really concerned with the actual event, for whatever happened, happened. Rather, our aim is to ensure that our rabbis are not found to be giving contradictory accounts of well-known events. (Azariah de' Rossi, *The Light of the Eyes,* trans. Joanna Weinberg, New Haven, CT: Yale University Press, 2001, 241.)

De' Rossi acknowledges that the ancient rabbis had not had any interest in historical studies—and it is precisely this fact that serves him as a justification to call their authority on matters other than Jewish law into question. Well known, he suggests, is the following:

> [T]he attitude of our sages toward all occurrences in the world and to events that happen over the course of time to rich and poor alike that have no connection with Torah, but are simply of a general nature and cases about which one would pronounce, 'It makes no difference whichever way one looks at them.' . . . We thought it worthwhile to expatiate on the truth of these [historical] matters. For since the sages of blessed memory were exclusively devoted to and immersed in the study of Torah and did not distract themselves by the conceit of idle talk or read documents about the remote past, it will not come as a surprise to us should they make some mistakes or give a shortened account of any of those stories. (de' Rossi, 386–388)

Echoing the pronouncement by Maimonides but in clear opposition to the dominant opinion of the rabbis of his own time, de' Rossi argued that the rabbis of the Talmud "proceeded on the basis of human wisdom and evaluation which was the scholarly approach prevalent in their time and in those parts of the world." (de' Rossi, 201). To elucidate the historical past, therefore:

> [I]t has been necessary for me to seek the help of many gentile sages for the clarification and elucidation of certain issues. Of course, I would not accept their statements which hint at heresy or make light of our Torah, God forbid. But merely because they are not Jews, they are regarded as aliens whom we do not usually introduce into our community. Consequently, it might occur to some pious individual . . . to contrive against me and make me the target for his attack on the grounds that in Sanhedrin [i.e., Mishnah, tractate Sanhedrin, 10:1], our rabbis of blessed memory forbade the reading of profane literature." (de' Rossi, 86)

Christian Humanism, the Protestant Reformation, and the Jews

Beginning in Italy, Christian scholars of the late fifteenth and sixteenth centuries began to develop an interest in the study of Hebrew. The **humanists,** as the Christian scholars with their renewed interest in historical and philological studies were known, directed their attention to the study of the three classical languages, including Hebrew, the language of the "Old Testament" of the Bible, in addition to Greek and Latin. The humanists emphasized the study of the classical sources in their original language—the slogan *ad fontes* ("to the sources") captures their intellectual program well—and by the middle of the sixteenth century it was common for Hebrew to be taught formally with Greek and Latin in European universities.

Christian scholars, especially in Italy, sought the help of Jews to teach them the Hebrew language but also so they could gain an understanding of rabbinic literature. Some developed a special interest in Kabbalah as they believed that they could prove the truth of Christianity from ancient Jewish traditions and, in particular, from the esoteric lore of Jewish Kabbalah. One Christian scholar, **Giovanni Pico della Mirandola** (d. 1494), for example, was introduced to the Hebrew language by Jewish scholars, including Elijah Delmedigo (d. 1497) and Johanan Alemanno (d. ca. 1504).

Other scholars followed Pico della Mirandola's example. Though outside Italy Christian humanists had much less direct contact with their Jewish counterparts, in Germany humanist scholars also displayed an interest in Hebrew and in Jewish texts. Perhaps the most prominent example was **Johannes Reuchlin** (1455–1522), who developed a deep interest in the Hebrew language, which he considered to be the original language of humanity and the vehicle of communication between God and man. Reuchlin also showed a great curiosity for the Kabbalistic tradition, which he adapted for Christian purposes. Among the books published by Reuchlin figures *De arte cabalistica* (*On the Art of Kabbalah*), published in 1517.

A few years earlier, in 1510, Reuchlin had been involved in a public controversy that came to be known as the "Reuchlin Affair" and was a rallying point for scholars who defended the humanist approach to language and religious knowledge against the opposition of more conservative forces in the Church. The occasion was the anti-Jewish polemic written by a Jewish convert to Christianity, **Johannes Pfefferkorn** (1469–1523), who charged that what kept the Jews from recognizing Christianity was their attachment to rabbinic tradition. Pfefferkorn demanded the wholesale confiscation and destruction of all Hebrew books. The archbishop of Cologne convened a panel of scholars to evaluate Pfefferkorn's suggestion; Reuchlin turned out to be the only dissenting voice to reject the confiscation of Hebrew books. Although the Jewish community was able to bribe imperial officials to stop the confiscations, the public controversy pitting Reuchlin and other humanists against Pfefferkorn and his supporters in the Church continued for several years and preoccupied theologians well beyond Germany. Reuchlin was accused of

"Judaism" by the Inquisition and was eventually fined by the papal court.

Reuchlin's vocal defense of Hebrew literature does not necessarily mean that he was free of anti-Jewish prejudice; his interest was primarily Jewish literature, not the Jewish community living in Germany. Other humanists were in fact openly hostile to Jews and Judaism. **Erasmus of Rotterdam** (ca. 1466–1536), one of the most famous representatives of Christian humanism, was probably the most prominent example of anti-Jewish attitudes within the humanist camp. Having mastered Greek and Latin, Erasmus did not attach much significance to the learning of Hebrew and was critical of Reuchlin's engagement with Jewish thought, in particular Kabbalah. In one of his books, Erasmus even declared, "I would rather, if the New Testament could remain inviolate, see the entire Old Testament done away with than see the peace of Christendom torn to ribbons for the sake of the Jewish scripture."

Humanism, with its focus on the original biblical text and its critique of Church tradition, prepared the ground for the great sixteenth-century revolution in western Christianity, the **Protestant Reformation.** Creating a lasting split between Catholic and Protestant Christendom, the Reformation shattered the certainties of Christian society in western Europe and produced a wide range of cultural, religious, and political transformations in European societies.

Historians have long disagreed on the Reformation's impact on the Jews and have alternatively pointed to the positive and negative ways in which the changes wrought by the Reformation affected the lives of European Jews at the time and in subsequent generations. **Martin Luther** (1483–1546), the German theologian who became the leading figure of the Reformation, stands for what are at first completely irreconcilable opinions: At first he showed a conciliatory attitude toward the Jews that differed starkly from the traditional anti-Judaism of the late medieval Christian Church. Later, however, he adopted an increasingly intolerant and violent stance and actively lobbied for the expulsion of Jews from various German territories.

In a text Luther wrote in 1523, "That Jesus Christ Was Born a Jew," he indicted the Catholic Church for persecuting the Jews, emphasized the Jewish origins of the Christian religion, and called for tolerance toward his Jewish contemporaries. At the same time, however, it is clear from this pamphlet that he nevertheless anticipated the conversion of the Jews and, in fact, this was the ultimate rationale for affording them greater tolerance:

> I will therefore show by means of the Bible the causes which induce me to believe that Christ was a Jew born of a virgin. Perhaps I will attract some of the Jews to the Christian faith. For our fools—the popes, bishops, sophists, and monks—the coarse blockheads, have until this time so treated the Jews that to be a good Christian one would have to become a Jew . . . they have dealt with the Jews as if they were dogs and not human beings. Whenever they converted them, they . . . only subjected them to papistry and monkery. When these Jews saw that Judaism had such strong scriptural basis and that Christianity [i.e., the Catholicism of the Roman Church] was pure nonsense without Biblical support, how could they quiet their hearts and become real, good Christians? (English quotation according to Jacob Rader Marcus, *The Jew in the Medieval World: A Source Book, 315–1791,* Cincinnati: Hebrew Union College Press, 1999, 186.)

However, it soon became clear to Luther and others that the Reformation had little impact on Jewish attitudes toward Christianity. The advance of the Reformation had by no means generated larger numbers of Jewish converts, and, speaking with violent disappointment twenty years later, Luther wrote another text, "Concerning the Jews and Their Lies" (1543), in which he reiterated his goal of Jewish conversion. Now, however, he advocated for increasing the pressure on the Jews as a means to achieve this aim. Moreover, he was increasingly concerned about what he considered to be the Jews' blasphemous rejection of Christianity—and he came to advocate the expulsion of the Jews from Christian territories lest the Christians become complicit in such "blasphemy" committed under their eyes:

> What then shall we Christians do with this damned, rejected race of Jews? Since they live among us and we know about their lying and blasphemy and cursing, we can not tolerate them if we wish not to share in their lies, curses, and blasphemy. . . . First, their synagogues . . . should be set on fire. . . . Secondly, their homes should likewise be broken down and destroyed. . . . Thirdly, they should be deprived of their prayer-books and Talmuds. . . . Fourthly, their rabbis must be forbidden under threat of death to teach any more. . . . Fifthly, passport and traveling privileges should be absolutely forbidden to the Jews. . . . Sixthly, they ought to be stopped from usury. . . . Seventhly, let the young and strong Jews and Jewesses be given the flail, the ax, the hoe, the spade, the distaff, the spindle, and let them earn their bread by the sweat of their noses as is enjoined upon Adam's children. (Marcus, 187–188.)

Despite what appears to be a radical shift in Luther's attitude toward Jews and Judaism, he was consistently hostile to Judaism, which he never considered to be a legitimate religious option. Whether in 1523 or twenty years later, Luther's objective always was the conversion of Jews to Christianity—but as he grew increasingly frustrated with rabbinic interpretations of the Bible, which he saw as a blasphemous rejection of the Christian reading of the same text, his attitude turned more violent. "Judaism" from the outset represented for Luther the opposite of true Christianity, and Jews shared this role of adversary with the papists (the Catholic Church), the Devil, and the Ottoman Turks, all of whom Luther presented as a threat to true Christendom.

Luther's diatribe against the Jews was not just theoretical talk. In 1537, for example, he actively instigated the decision to expel Jews from Saxony. The Jews developed mechanisms to defend themselves and were by no means the passive objects of Christian policy making. Led by **Josel (Joseph) of Rosheim** (d. 1554), the leading representative of German Jewry who used his influence on Emperors Maximilian I (1493–1519) and Charles V (1519–1556) to advocate for the Jews, they fought back and on occasion could even be successful. In 1543, for example, Josel was able to convince the city council of Strasbourg to ban the reprint of Luther's anti-Jewish writings in that city. Another case of Josel's successful lobbying on behalf of the German Jews can be found in his Hebrew memoirs:

In the year [1537] the Elector John Frederick of Saxony was about to outlaw us and not allow the Jewish people even to set foot in his country. This was due to that priest whose name was Martin Luther—may his body and soul be bound up in hell—who wrote and issued many heretical books in which he said that whoever would help the Jews was doomed to perdition . . . With the approval of our rabbis I was given some letters of high recommendation from certain Christian scholars. . . . I did not succeed in presenting the letters until the Elector came to Frankfurt where he met with other rulers, particularly the Margrave of Brandenburg who also intended to expel all his Jews. However, through the course of events and because of disputations which I had in the presence of Christian scholars, I succeeded in convincing the rulers, by means of our holy Torah, not to follow the views of Luther, Bucer [another Protestant reformer], and his gang, with the result that the rulers even confirmed our old privileges. (Marcus, 224–225.)

Through the sixteenth century, and into the seventeenth century, it was the more hostile attitude displayed in Luther's text of 1543 that was more influential, and the wave of expulsions that had affected Jewish communities throughout Germany before the Reformation continued, or even accelerated, in its wake. In the course of the seventeenth century, among Protestant millenarianists (those who were awaiting the imminent "second coming" of Christ) or among the Protestant movement of Pietism, the more tolerant attitude of Luther's earlier text on the Jews was again foregrounded. In seventeenth-century England, for example, a more tolerant attitude toward Jews developed against the exclusionary vision that persisted among Luther's followers in Germany at least until the Enlightenment and contributed to the readmission of the Jews to the country.

Moreover, Protestantism challenged the established authority of the Catholic Church and set out to "demystify" Christian beliefs. One of the central aspects of the Protestant polemic against the established Catholic order was the rejection of what the reformers considered to be superstition and magic. One consequence of this "disenchantment" of the medieval Christian mindset in the wake of the Protestant Reformation was the decline of one of the oldest and vilest antisemitic accusations of the Middle Ages, the blood libel, the false accusation against Jews of committing ritual murder. After the first such blood libel had occurred in England in 1148, it was in the German-speaking lands that the number of ritual murder trials against Jews reached its height in the fifteenth and sixteenth centuries. After 1570, the number of trials declined significantly as a result of imperial protection of the Jews, Jewish self-defense, and the new thinking of the Reformation that called into question many of the old teachings of the Church. However, though ritual murder trials were suppressed from the seventeenth century on by the imperial and theological elites, the popular *belief* in the blood libel persisted well into the nineteenth century (and was revived by Nazi propaganda in the twentieth century).

The impact of humanism and the Reformation on the Jews of central Europe was thus ambiguous. In fact, it was arguably less the Reformation than some of its unintended political consequences that led to a sea change in attitudes toward the Jews and eventually to the return of Jewish life to western Europe: the most important changes being the stalemate that resulted from the prolonged confrontation between Catholic and Protestant forces in the long years of the Thirty Years' War and, in its wake, the emergence of state politics that were now increasingly guided by pragmatic considerations of economic benefit rather than by religious concerns.

Questions for Reflection

1. Why, do you think, 1492 marks a turning point in Jewish history? What was the impact of the events of that year on the subsequent course of Jewish history?
2. Does the experience of the Spanish and Portuguese conversos continue to be part of Jewish history once they embraced Christianity in the period between 1391 and 1497? Why, or why not?
3. Jewish life in the Ottoman Empire has often been described as the "Second Golden Age" of Sephardi Jewry after the expulsion from Spain. What is it that made this a "golden age," and what were the conditions under which it was possible?
4. In Italy, the age of the Renaissance was also the age of the ghetto. Would you describe the Italian Jews as rather integrated or isolated from non-Jewish culture at the time? How do you explain the apparent contradiction between physical separation into ghettos and continued cultural integration?
5. Both internal cultural trends within Judaism (the emergence of Lurianic Kabbalah) and external cultural developments (the scientific discoveries of the period) had a profound influence on early modern Jewish life. What was their impact? Would it be fair to say that both posed a challenge to the traditional, medieval order, and if so, how?

For Further Reading

On the period in general, see Jonathan Israel, *European Jewry in the Age of Mercantilism, 1550–1750,* 3rd ed. (Oxford, England: Littman Library, 1998).

On Spain and the Inquisition, see Jonathan Ray, *The Sephardic Frontier* (Ithaca, NY: Cornell University Press, 2006); Henry Kamen, *The Spanish Inquisition* (New Haven, CT: Yale University Press, 1999); Joseph Perez, *The Spanish Inquisition* (New Haven, CT: Yale University Press, 2006); Haim Beinart, *The Expulsion of the Jews from Spain* (Oxford, England: Littman Library, 2005).

On conversos, see Renée Levine Melammed, *Heretics or Daughters of Israel? The Crypto-Jewish of Castile* (Oxford, England: Oxford University Press, 1999); idem, *A Question of Identity: Iberian Conversos in Historical Perspective* (Oxford, England: Oxford University Press, 2004); David Graizbord, *Souls in Dispute* (Philadelphia: University of Pennsylvania Press, 2003).

On the Ottoman Empire, see Esther Benbassa and Aron Rodrigue, *Sephardi Jewry* (Berkeley: University of California Press, 2000); Avigdor Levy, *The Sephardim in the Ottoman Empire* (Princeton, NJ: Darwin Press, 1993); Minna Rozen, *A History of the Jewish Community in Istanbul: The Formative Years, 1453–1566* (Leiden, The Netherlands: E. J. Brill, 2002).

On Muslim lands in general, see Bernard Lewis, *The Jews of Islam* (Princeton, NJ: Princeton University Press, 1987); Norman Stillman, *The Jews of Arab Lands* (Philadelphia: Jewish Publication Society, 1979).

On Morocco, see Shlomo Deshen, *The Mellah Society* (Chicago: University of Chicago Press, 1989).

On Safed and Lurianic Kabbalah, see Lawrence Fine, *Physician of the Soul, Healer of the Cosmos: Isaac Luria and His Kabbalistic Fellowship* (Palo Alto, CA: Stanford University Press, 2003).

On Italy, see Robert Bonfil, *Jewish Life in Renaissance Italy* (Berkeley: University of California Press, 1994); Kenneth Stow, *Theater of Acculturation: The Roman Ghetto in the Sixteenth Century* (Seattle: University of Washington Press, 2001).

On the scientific revolution, see David Ruderman, *Jewish Thought and Scientific Discovery in Early Modern Europe* (Detroit, MI: Wayne State University Press, 2001).

On the Protestant Reformation, see Dean Bell and Stephen Burnett (eds.), *Jews, Judaism, and the Reformation in Sixteenth-Century Germany* (Leiden, The Netherlands: Brill, 2006).

On blood libel, see R. Po-chia Hsia, *The Myth of Ritual Murder* (New Haven, CT: Yale University Press, 1988).

Chapter 9

New Worlds, East and West

In the Nobles' Republic: Jews in Early Modern Eastern Europe

The early modern period saw the exodus of Sephardi Jews from the Iberian Peninsula eastward into the Ottoman Empire, as well as a parallel migration of Ashkenazi Jews from central Europe to eastern Europe, from Germany into Poland. Like the Ottoman Empire, which became a major center of early modern Sephardi culture in the sixteenth century, **Poland–Lithuania** emerged as the new heartland of Ashkenazi Jewry. Continuous growth throughout the early modern period, despite the disastrous persecutions of the mid-seventeenth century to which we shall return later in this chapter, made Polish–Lithuanian Jewry into the single largest Jewish community in the world by the end of the seventeenth century.

Also not unlike the Jews of the Ottoman Empire, Jews in Poland–Lithuania compared their situation favorably with the conditions of Jewish life in the West. **Moses Isserles** (1520–1572) of Cracow (known by the Hebrew acronym of his name as the ReMA), for example, one of the leading Polish rabbis in the sixteenth century, wrote to a former student, "In this country [Poland] there is no fierce hatred of us [Jews] as in Germany. May it so continue until the advent of the Messiah. . . . You will be better off in this country . . . you have here peace of mind"—a sentiment that also was echoed by several of his contemporaries. Popular imagination created a pun on the Hebrew name for Poland, *polin*. The story is that when a group of exiled Jews arrived in Poland they heard a divine voice declare, *"Poh lin"* ("Dwell here"). This does not mean early modern Poland–Lithuania was without anti-Jewish persecutions: The historian Bernard Weinryb has counted over fifty local persecutions in Poland between the 1530s and the early 1700s, which totals two every three years. However, even the mass murder of Jews during the Chmielnicki massacres of 1648 (see later in this chapter) and the turmoil of the Russian and Swedish invasions of Poland in the following decade, traumatic as they must have been, did not stop the demographic expansion of Polish–Lithuanian Jewry (*see* Map 9-1)

Jews were immigrating from Germanic lands to Poland probably no later than the eleventh century, and this pattern continued in subsequent centuries and accelerated in the sixteenth century. Only in the wake of the massacres of the seventeenth century was this trend somewhat reversed when east European Jews sought refuge in Germany and elsewhere in western Europe, where the political conditions had begun to change and a return of the Jews marked the renewed growth of Jewish communities in the west. Largely thanks to the massive influx of Ashkenazi Jews from Germanic lands, Poland–Lithuania became a flourishing center of Jewish culture in the sixteenth century, sustained by a relatively tolerant legal environment and economic opportunities that grew with the expansion of the Polish–Lithuanian Commonwealth to the east. Exact numbers are, as elsewhere during this period, difficult to establish, and estimates of the Jewish population in Poland–Lithuania vary considerably. It has been suggested that 150000 to 170000 Jews were in Poland–Lithuania in the mid-sixteenth century.

The Polish–Lithuanian Commonwealth created in the **Union of Lublin** of 1569 was a multinational and multi-religious state. One of the largest states in Europe at the time, it bordered the Baltic Sea in the north and the Black Sea in the south, stretching from Pomerania in the northwest to Ukraine in the southeast. In the middle of the seventeenth century, Poles represented only about 40 percent of its population, with ethnic minorities including Ukrainians, Russians, and Lithuanians but also immigrant populations such as Germans, Italians, Scots, and—of course—the Jews. The country was no less diverse religiously, with Catholics representing less than half the population and harboring Orthodox, Protestant,

Map 9-1 Jewish Communities in the Polish–Lithuanian Commonwealth.

Muslim, and Jewish minorities. Thus, at least a degree of religious toleration was no less imperative here than it was in the contemporary Ottoman Empire, and though the Jews hardly enjoyed "equal rights" (a foreign concept in those days), they did enjoy far-reaching religious freedom and autonomy.

Jews benefited from royal charters and the privileges granted to them by nobility and the Polish kings—for example, the privilege of **Casimir III "the Great"** (1310–1370), granted in 1334, which in turn confirmed the earlier privilege granted by Prince Boleslav of Kalisz in 1264 for Great Poland. Such privileges were renewed and at times amended with each new king ascending the throne. But in Poland–Lithuania, Jews were never regarded as *servi camerae,* or royal property, as had been the case in medieval Germany and elsewhere in western Europe. This status had tied the fate of the Jews directly to the interests of the central authorities—which was more often than not, to be sure, to the benefit of the otherwise defenseless Jews.

In the Polish–Lithuanian Commonwealth, in contrast to the Ottoman model, it is impossible to speak of one coherent legal status. Jews were subject to a variety of different authorities and different legal circumstances. A number of Polish cities—namely Warsaw, Cracow, Gdansk, and Lublin—did not admit Jewish settlers, and some royal cities actually extracted a privilege **de non tolerandis Judaeis** from the king, allowing them to exclude Jews from their midst. Warsaw, for example, obtained this privilege in 1527. In some cases, cities tried to restrict the Jewish population to a separate quarter or a nearby suburb, such as **Kazimierz** outside **Cracow,** which had a Jewish population of about 4500 in the first half of the seventeenth century (compared to a general population in Cracow of about 28000).

With the death of the last king of the Jagiellonian dynasty, which had ruled Poland from 1386 to 1572, the country became a **nobles' republic** with the landed gentry electing the king in parliament, the *sejm.* Earlier in the sixteenth century, the constitution of 1505 had severely limited the power of the king as all legislation required the unanimous approval of parliament. The weakness of the monarchy and the ineffectiveness of the *sejm* often blocked in deadlock meant that the central authorities in the Polish–Lithuanian Commonwealth were considerably weakened at a time when other European monarchs began to consolidate their power and enhance the authorities of their central governments. The power of the central government had declined by the seventeenth century so that Poland had come to resemble a federation of territories and private estates.

Especially after 1569, Polish settlement expanded eastward into White Russia (Belarus) and the Ukraine. Magnates and lesser noblemen acquired large estates on which they founded numerous new villages and towns. Vast stretches of territory with thousands of little hamlets and small towns became the private domains of Polish nobility. One magnate was **Jan Zamoyski** who left at his death in 1605 personal property the size of about 2460 square miles, including eleven towns and over two hundred villages. One of the towns owned by Zamoyski was the city of Zamość, to which he invited a number of Sephardi immigrants with the purpose of developing it into a commercial center for trade between Poland and Ottoman lands. Another magnate, Prince Konstanty Wasyl Ostrogski, owned no less than a hundred towns and thirteen hundred villages with an annual profit that equaled the tax revenue of the entire country. The nobles became essentially autonomous rulers over their estates, installing their own courts and maintaining their own private armies.

For the management of properties of this size, spread out geographically throughout the country, the magnates needed intermediaries and agents to oversee the thousands of peasants working for them; to administer the vast estates; to market agricultural produce, lumber, and cattle; and to provide all kinds of goods to the populations in the many villages. It was in this function as intermediaries that many Jews established themselves in ever larger numbers in the eastern parts of the country, managing the Polish nobles' estates, leasing a variety of economic monopolies, and becoming a dominant part of the local urban bourgeoisie in the newly colonized territories in the east. The lease, or ***arenda,*** was an arrangement of particular importance in the relation between Jews and magnates and between Jews and the general population.

A significant portion of Jews in Poland made a living as leaseholders, or *arrendators,* which came to be considered a traditionally "Jewish" economic activity. For magnates the leasing of a **monopoly** on anything from the distillation and sale of alcohol to salt mining to the right to collect tolls and taxes was a convenient way of raising cash and outsourcing the exploitation of the resources in their vast estates. Liquor

production (beer, vodka, and so on) and its distribution in taverns and bars was one of the hallmarks of the *arenda* system, but the *arenda* for a given town or region would likewise include monopolies on mills, salt mines, grain warehouses, tobacco sales, collection of bridge tolls, and more. The general *arrendator*—a wealthy individual or the entire Jewish community—would then subdivide the general *arenda* to individual leaseholders who made a living operating a distillery, running a tavern, or operating a sawmill. The Jewish *arrendator* often found himself in a conflict of interest with other sections of the population, including the peasants and townspeople who might resent high prices, tolls, and taxes being collected by the leaseholder. Anti-Jewish hostility in this context was therefore just as often economically motivated as it was an expression of religious prejudice, and the potential for conflict between the Jewish *arrendators* and their non-Jewish (and Jewish) neighbors was real.

By 1539 King Sigismund I had granted to the nobles authority over the Jews living in the localities they owned. Thus the decision to allow Jewish settlement or even encourage it was entirely up to each individual magnate, as was the treatment of his Jewish subjects. Some magnates, such as the founder of the town of Oleszowo, declared that "the Polish Crown flourishes with people of diverse estates, particularly in regard to their religious allegiance, on the principle that no authority shall exercise power over faith, honor, and conscience." Others took the opposite stance, such as Jan Magier, who declared in 1591, "I exclude from residence Jews, a sordid, cunning, underhanded, and anti-Christian tribe because of the principles of their faith" (Salo Wittmayer Baron, *Social and Religious History of the Jews: Late Middle Ages and Era of European Expansion, 1200–1650; Poland–Lithuania, 1500–1650,* vol. 16, 2nd ed., New York: Columbia University Press, 1976, 127.) This situation led to many inconsistencies in the legal status of Jews in early modern Poland–Lithuania and made them subject to the whims of their noble masters. Jewish literature from the time contains examples of abuse and arbitrary treatment at the hand of Polish landowners. Generally, however, the interests of the Polish nobility and the Jews converged, as the latter performed indispensable services to the magnates and fulfilled a crucial role in the economy of the nobles' estates, and both sides benefited from the contractual relationship between the Jewish leaseholder and land-owning magnate.

A situation that was in many ways similar is described in the autobiography of a young Jew born in Moravia, then part of the Hapsburg Empire, which was, next to the Ottoman Empire and Poland–Lithuania, the third empire in eastern/southeastern Europe with a large Jewish population. The autobiography, written in poor Hebrew and neglecting to give the name of the author, is a good illustration of the economic life of many Jews in eastern Europe in the seventeenth century and their dependence on the goodwill of local notables. "My mother then showed her ability in supporting the family by her own efforts," the author explains, "and [she] started to manufacture brandy out of oats. . . . This was hard labor, but she succeeded. In the meantime my father pursued his studies." Not infrequently did Jewish women play an active role in the economic life of east European Jews of the period, and they were by no means relegated to their homes. In fact, the arrangement described in this early part of the autobiography, a division of labor of sorts that envisioned the men as students of Torah and women as the breadwinners, was probably more an exception in the early modern period when both men and women needed to work; it became a universal ideal only later during the nineteenth century (and still informs the practice of ultra-Orthodox society in Israel today).

The autobiography by this Moravian Jew exemplified that a strict division of spheres—working women and Torah-studying men—was generally not possible to sustain under the circumstances of the early modern period:

> One day a holy man, R. Loeb, the Rabbi of Trebitch . . . came to our town and stayed in our house. When he saw the troubles of my mother, . . . he had pity on her, and gave my father some gold and silver merchandise . . . to get him used to trade. . . . My father was successful and did a good business. Incidentally this brought him the acquaintance of the Count who owned the city. The latter liked him, and turned over to him the distillery in which they were working with seven great kettles, and he gave him servants to do the work and grain to prepare brandy. For this my father paid him at the end of the year a specified amount, in addition to paying a certain percentage of the income in taxes, as was customary.

As in Poland–Lithuania, the brewing and distilling of alcoholic beverages was an important economic activity of Jews elsewhere in eastern Europe.

The autobiography also testifies to the often precarious nature of the economic alliance between Jews and nobles. The author describes how unnamed Jewish enemies, presumably competitors, ruined his father's reputation:

> The latter [the Count] made charges against him in connection with the distillery and other business matters, and put him into prison for two months . . . nothing could be done to save my father, and he had to give up half his wealth in order to be released. On this occasion his enemies wreaked their revenge on him . . . and urged the Count to expel my father . . . from his property. The Count did so. (In Alexander Marx, "A Seventeenth-Century Autobiography," *Jewish Quarterly Review* 8: 288–291.)

Thus, if the Jews fulfilled a crucial function in the magnate-dominated economy of eastern Europe, they also depended on the goodwill of their patrons. In fact, as the example cited here shows, at times rivalries within the Jewish community could actually lead individual Jews themselves to get their Christian overlords involved in internal disputes—a sign of a lack of discipline and coherence within the community that many of its lay and religious leaders were well aware of and tried to contain through ordinances that prohibited taking conflicts to non-Jewish courts.

The Jewish Community in Poland–Lithuania

The semiautonomous governing body of the Jewish community, the *kehillah,* paralleled the Christian municipality in its structure and its functions. As Gershon Hundert, a historian of early modern Polish Jewry, has observed, "what divided Jews from Christians, beyond the psychological distance, was not residence but jurisdiction. . . . Jews were in the town but not of it." Though Jews tended to live in particular streets or sections of a city, they were generally not subject to the jurisdiction of the municipality and instead elected their own leadership, raised their own taxes, provided their own services—from paving streets to providing for the needs of the poor—and maintained their own courts. The leadership of the early modern Polish–Lithuanian *kehillah* was an oligarchic lay leadership that derived its legitimization from both the authority it had been endowed with by the Polish Crown and from Jewish tradition and Talmudic law. The lay leaders of the community, the *tovim,* were elected annually by all tax-paying members. The rabbis were not part of the elected leadership but, rather, employees of the *kehillah.* However, the rabbi's role as representing religious authority, as teacher of rabbinic tradition and judge of the rabbinic courts, was crucial in providing legitimacy to the *kehillah.*

The autonomy of the Jewish community found a clear expression in its right to grant or deny residence rights to Jews from outside the city. The prerogative over **hezqat ha-yishuv,** as the right of residence was known in Hebrew, was a common feature of Jewish autonomy in many Jewish communities in Europe since the Middle Ages (though it had not been used in Spain nor in the Ottoman Empire where, as we have seen, conditions for Jewish settlement were far less stringent and Jews generally enjoyed freedom of movement and residence throughout the empire). In Poland–Lithuania, as in many other European countries, the presence of Jewish outsiders was regulated by each community. In Kazimierz outside Cracow, for example, a nonresident Jew was not allowed to settle or do business, and in general a community's charter, usually limiting the number of residents, and local economic conditions determined whether an individual received the right of residence or not. The purpose of this measure, as of numerous other community ordinances regulating economic and communal life, was to avoid rivalry and competition between Jews, which was seen as ultimately detrimental to the community at large. Outside Poland–Lithuania, in German-speaking lands of central Europe, government restrictions on the permissible number of Jewish settlers applied as well.

One of the most important officials of larger Jewish communities was the **shtadlan,** or intercessor, whose job it was to represent his community—and often the Jews of an entire province—to the various levels of the non-Jewish government. The communities at large were collectively responsible for the tax burden of all Jews and needed to maintain channels of communication with the royal authorities, with the city governments, and with the noble magnates. Legislation could directly or indirectly affect Jewish life in the commonwealth, and the community often had to defend itself against antisemitic accusations, namely accusations of ritual murder and host desecration that continued to haunt Polish–Lithuanian Jewry throughout the early modern period. It fell to the *shtadlan,* always a well-connected individual with diplomatic skills and knowledge of the Polish language and of the ins and outs of politics in the commonwealth, to represent the Jewish community to the outside world.

By the sixteenth century, the desire for coordination of the collective needs of Polish Jewry led to the creation of a central body representing all Jewish communities in Poland and a similar organization in Lithuania. In Poland, the emerging institution was known as the **Council of Four Lands** (*va'ad arba' aratsot*), though in reality its constituent regions fluctuated between three and four until the seventeenth century and exceeded four lands in the eighteenth century. The Lithuanian Council of Provinces was an equivalent institution in that part of the commonwealth, and similar supraregional bodies existed outside Poland–Lithuania as well. Meeting on occasion of the annual commercial fairs of Lublin and other cities, when Jews from all over the region came together, the *va'ad arba' aratsot* and similar institutions did not employ a standing "national" bureaucracy but had, by 1576, established a central court, represented the Jews to the government, oversaw the distribution of taxes among the

various communities, and mediated conflicts that transcended the boundaries between communities and regions. Like individual communities, the central representative bodies of Polish–Lithuanian Jewry employed *shtadlanim* who interceded with the central government and the *sejm.* They watched the legislative process closely to head off any new measures that might be detrimental to the Jews of the realm. In 1623, for example, the Lithuanian Council of Provinces adopted a resolution that "in any period of the *sejmiki* meeting before the Diet the heads of each community are to stand guard and carefully investigate lest any innovation be introduced which might prove to be a harmful thorn to us. The necessary expenditure should be defrayed by each community" (Baron, *Social and Religious History of the Jews,* 135.)

If the community leadership and the Council of Four Lands were dominated by lay leaders, the rabbinate continued to play a central role in the lives of early modern Polish–Lithuanian Jewry. This was a traditional society based on a shared religious tradition and Jewish religious law. Religion was not just one part of life: Rather, religious beliefs and rabbinic law permeated all aspects of the individual and collective existence. The rabbis were the ones responsible for the interpretation and application of religious law in the ever-changing conditions of the rapidly expanding Polish–Lithuanian community. In doing so they had to be mindful of the demands of *halakhah* as it was represented in the Talmud and the growing body of rabbinic–legal literature, while also considering the requirements of social circumstances. An example is the following case described by one of the luminaries of Polish rabbinic culture in the sixteenth century, Rabbi Moses Isserles of Cracow (1520–1572):

> There was a poor man in the land who betrothed his grown daughter to her proper mate. And during the time of her engagement . . . the father died . . . and the daughter was left bereaved. She was without father and only [had] relatives who forsook her and averted their eyes from her, except for one relative . . . who brought her into his home. . . . And when the time for her wedding came . . . there was no dowry or other needs. Yet everyone told her that she should ritually immerse herself and prepare for her wedding because she would have a dowry. And this virgin did as her female neighbors told her. She listened to their voice and they covered her with the veil on Friday as is done to virgins. And when the shadows of the evening became long and the day [the Sabbath] was almost sanctified, when her relatives were to give the dowry, they tightened their hands and did not give as they were supposed to, and there was about a third missing from the dowry. Also, the groom reneged

Image of a Jewish scholar. Woodcut, Strasbourg, 1508.

and did not want to marry her and did not pay attention to all the words of the town leaders who spoke to him saying that he should not embarrass a daughter of Israel because of contemptible money. . . . And the work of Satan succeeded until it was about an hour and one-half into the Sabbath when they reconciled themselves and the groom agreed to enter under the marriage canopy and, in order not to embarrass a worthy daughter of Israel, I arose and performed the marriage at this time. (Quoted from Edward Fram, *Ideals Face Reality: Jewish Law and Life in Poland, 1550–1655*, Cincinnati: Hebrew Union College Press, 1997, 70.)

What is remarkable here is that according to rabbinic law, as codified in the Mishnah, it was prohibited to perform a wedding on the Sabbath, yet Isserles decided to do so nonetheless "in order not to embarrass a worthy daughter of Israel" and taking into account the special circumstances of

the case. One of the things illustrated by this case is the flexibility of legal practice within the confines of traditional Jewish law. Traditional society was not marked by an uncompromising adherence to the letter of the law, as it was later presented by modern Jews. In reality, traditional society retained an unwavering commitment to *halakhah* as divine law, all of which was believed to have been given to Moses at Mount Sinai along with the Ten Commandments and the remainder of the Bible. But traditional rabbis also retained a flexibility, a willingness to interpret and reinterpret the law, and a pragmatic approach that recognized the need to reconcile the demands of the law with the demands of particular social circumstances that could vary from case to case.

In 1648, the existing order was severely disturbed when a wave of violent persecution swept through the Ukraine—the Chmielnicki massacres (or, in Hebrew, the *gezerot tah ve-tat*, after the years in the Jewish calendar), followed by the violence of the subsequent Russian and Swedish invasions that lasted through much of the 1650s. That year, **Bogdan Chmielnicki** (1595–1657), son of a minor noble, led the Cossacks of the Ukraine into a major insurgency against the Polish regime. The Cossacks, as the historian Bernard Weinryb has described them, were "a by-product of the tension between the nomads of the southern Russian steppes and the inhabitants of the settled borderlands." They were independent warriors, at times in the service of the Polish Crown and at times rising in rebellion against it. In 1648, Chmielnicki forged an alliance between his Cossack forces and the Ukrainian peasantry, with which they shared their Greek Orthodox religion, pitting them against the Polish state and landowning nobility; he also ensured the support from the Crimean Tartars. The insurgency led to some of the worst massacres in Jewish history, and thousands of Jews were killed alongside many Catholic Poles.

The worst massacres occurred in the spring and summer of 1648. Many Jews fled the rural areas of the war zone to fortified cities; in many cases it was there that the Cossack forces caught and massacred them in large numbers—for example, in Nemirov where thousands were reported to have been killed. Numerous Jewish chronicles describe the suffering, death, and destruction of those months. One of the most famous is a book called *Yeven Metsulah* (*Abyss of Despair*) by Rabbi **Nathan Neta Hanover** (d. 1683). Here is what he says about some of the earliest massacres committed by Chmielnicki's followers:

> Many communities beyond the Dnieper, and close to the battlefield . . . who were unable to escape, perished for the sanctification of His Name. These persons died cruel and bitter deaths. Some were skinned alive and their flesh was thrown to the dogs; some had their hands and limbs chopped off, and their bodies thrown on the highway only to be trampled by wagons and crushed by horses; some had wounds inflicted upon them, and thrown on the street to die a slow death . . .; others were buried alive. . . . There was no cruel device of murder in the whole world that was not perpetrated by the enemies. . . . Also against the Polish people, these cruelties were perpetrated, especially against the priests and bishops. Thus, westward of the Dnieper several thousand Jewish persons perished and several hundred were forced to change their faith. (Nathan Hanover, *Abyss of Despair*, trans. Abraham Mesch, New Brunswick, NJ: Transaction Publishers, 1983, 43–44.)

Hanover noted here and elsewhere in his chronicle that the Jews were not the only ones attacked and massacred. In fact, modern historians have pointed out the social and polit-ical dimensions of the Chmielnicki revolt against Polish rule in the Ukraine and have suggested that perhaps Jews were not so much singled out as Jews for religious reasons as they were attacked because they were identified with the Polish regime. As we have seen, the Jews in the Ukraine were playing an important role as agents of the Polish landowners and as mediators between the Polish aristocrats, often residing in faraway cities, and the local, enserfed Ukrainian peasant population. Hanover pointed to this fact in his chronicle when he wrote about a certain Jew:

> [He] was the nobleman's tax farmer, as was the customary occupation of most Jews in the kingdom of [Little] Russia [i.e., Ukraine]. For they ruled in every part of [Little] Russia, a condition which aroused the jealousy of the peasants, and which was the cause of the massacres. (Hanover, *Abyss*, 36.)

Modern historians have also significantly revised the estimated number of Jews who were killed at the hands of the rebels. It is now clear that the numbers given in contemporary chronicles are unreliable and often exaggerated. Historian Shaul Stampfer has recently argued on the basis of archival research that perhaps 20000 out of 40000 Jews in the Ukraine were killed in the massacres. Even though this number, both of the total Jewish population and those killed, is significantly lower than had been assumed earlier, it still suggests that half the Jewish population of Ukraine was massacred within just a few months. What is more, Jews continued to suffer, alongside their Catholic Polish neighbors and others, from the continued violence during the Russian and Swedish invasions and the continuing Cossack rebellion in subsequent years. All in all, it is not surprising that these massacres were seen by Ashkenazi Jewry as the "third destruction" (after the destruction of the First and Second Temples in Jerusalem), as Rabbi Shabbatai Horowitz called it.

Perhaps most surprising is the fast recovery of the Jewish communities in Poland–Lithuania from the disaster. Soon after the end of the violence, Jews were back and settling in the towns and cities of Ukraine. Many Jews had fled across the border and came back (though most of those who had fled to cities in Germany and Holland remained there). Others had survived by accepting baptism and returned to Judaism after the massacres; the Polish king authorized them to do so as early as 1649. The Chmielnicki massacres played an important role in Ashkenazi memory, and word of the horror spread throughout the Jewish world—but they were not a turning point in the history of Polish–Lithuanian Jewry, which continued to expand and flourish after the persecution was over.

Early Modern Ashkenazi Culture

A source that is often quoted by historians of Jewish culture in early modern Poland–Lithuania is the last chapter of Rabbi Nathan Neta Hanover's chronicle of the Chmielnicki massacres. In this chapter, Hanover describes the "six pillars" upon which the world rests and all of which could be found among the Jews of Poland–Lithuania: Torah study (to the description of which he dedicated most of his chapter), prayer, charity, justice, truth, and peace. It is obvious that Hanover was drawing an idealized picture of Polish–Lithuanian Jewry, a nostalgic portrait of a world that had come under the assault of widespread violence and destruction. Yet even if we admit that Hanover idealized his community, the description in his *Even Metsulah* nevertheless gives an impression of the centrality of rabbinic learning in early modern Polish–Lithuanian Jewish culture:

> [T]hroughout the dispersions of Israel there was nowhere so much learning as in the Kingdom of Poland. Each community maintained academies, and the head of each academy was given an ample salary so that . . . the study of the Torah might be his sole occupation. . . . Each community maintained young men and provided for them a weekly allowance of money that they might study with the head of the academy. And for each young man they also maintained two boys to study under his guidance. . . . If the community consisted of fifty householders it supported not less than thirty young men and boys. . . . There was scarcely a house in all the Kingdom of Poland where its members did not occupy themselves with the study of Torah. (Hanover, *Abyss,* 110–111.)

Other contemporary sources were more critical of the shortcomings of their generation, to be sure, and admonished the public for not doing enough and for falling short of the ideal described in Hanover's chronicle. But there is other evidence of a growing reach of rabbinic learning at the time, primarily due to the impact of printing.

The first printed edition of the Talmud, this fundamental work of rabbinic Judaism, had been published in Spain in the 1480s, followed by an edition that appeared in Italy between 1484 and 1519. However, with the growing interference of the Catholic Church, through censorship or outright prohibition of the Talmud, Jewish printers ceased to print the Talmud in Italy after the middle of the sixteenth century. In Poland–Lithuania, however, with its more liberal religious climate, editions of the Talmud surpassed the number of all other printed works, including the Bible. Over 100 tractates of the Talmud were printed in Cracow alone in the sixteenth and seventeenth centuries, and 60 in Lublin. One historian estimated that some 48000 to 80000 copies of Talmudic tractates were thus produced in Polish printing houses at the time.

Used in the rabbinic academies throughout the commonwealth, study of the Talmud—now so widely available in print—became the main focus of Jewish learning in Poland–Lithuania and led to the rise of its peculiar method of study known as *pilpul. Pilpul* was a mode of study in which every single apparent inconsistency or contradiction within the Talmud, or between its medieval commentaries, was resolved and reconciled through interpretation. Inconsistencies were to be discovered and reconciled by the avid student of Talmud without regard to either the literal meaning of the texts or the normative legal practice they established. In due course, *pilpul* came under attack from some of the leading rabbis of the period, such as **Rabbi Judah Loew of Prague** (the MaHaRaL; d. 1609) or Rabbi **Yom-Tov Lipmann Heller** (1579–1654). Their critique led eventually to a modernization of rabbinic education in subsequent generations—an educational reform that anticipated the more radical approach of the eighteenth-century Jewish Enlightenment.

In fact, rabbinic culture was by no means uniform and was not without internal tensions. Rather, it was undergoing some very significant and even radical transformations in the early modern period—in Poland–Lithuania as the new center of Ashkenazi culture no less than in other parts of the Jewish world. We have already discussed the emergence of a new school of Jewish mysticism, Lurianic Kabbalah, in the Ottoman city of Safed in the sixteenth century. In Ashkenazi culture, Kabbalah was still one among several areas of study in the sixteenth century and, like all others, was subservient to the study of Talmud. In the seventeenth century, however, it asserted itself as a primary source of reference for Ashkenazi culture and displaced other fields of study, namely philosophy. The major work of Kabbalistic teaching, the *Zohar,* came to occupy a place that was second to none, not even the Talmud, and Rabbi Shabbatai Horowitz went out of his way to declare in 1647 that "surely those persons who decline to study [K]abbalah do not merit a soul."

Another product of the flourishing Jewish culture of sixteenth-century Ottoman Safed had a major impact on early modern Ashkenazi rabbinic culture. The Sephardi rabbi Joseph Karo wrote in the years 1555–1563 a major new code of Jewish law while in Safed. Called *Shulhan Arukh* ("the set table"), the law code was printed for the first time in Venice in 1565. It soon gained wide acceptance and authority throughout the Sephardi Diaspora and beyond, and its growing popularity caused a major debate among the Ashkenazi rabbis of Poland–Lithuania. Eventually the *Shulhan Arukh* became the almost universally accepted digest of Jewish law, and it remains so among Orthodox Jews to this day. At first, however, in the sixteenth and seventeenth centuries, it was highly controversial.

Jewish law had developed over many centuries and in many different places, and though its fundamental set of beliefs and practices were shared, a myriad of more or less significant differences evolved as well. Ashkenazi Jews did not allow the consumption of legumes during the Passover holiday, for example, whereas Sephardi communities did. During Passover, rice was not consumed by Ashkenazim, whereas it was permitted by some Sephardim and prohibited by others, and it actually was a typical Passover food for Syrian Jews. With the printing of a universal code of Jewish law, such differences would be challenged as it would recognize one practice as being correct and all others as wrong.

Karo based his decisions in the *Shulhan Arukh* on three medieval law codes, two of which had been written by Sephardi authors and one by a German rabbi who lived in Spain. Thus even Moses Isserles, an Ashkenazi rabbi sympathetic in principle to the codification of Jewish law in print, could not accept an a priori primacy of Sephardi legal interpretation. What Isserles did in response was to change Ashkenazi Jewry profoundly: In the 1570s he published in Cracow a new edition of Karo's *Shulhan Arukh* with his own comments, in which he clarified the Ashkenazi practice where it differed from Karo's opinion. Given the challenges of a printed code of law to traditional ways of learning, Isserles' version of the *Shulhan Arukh* proved to be controversial, and one rabbi, Hayim of Friedberg, argued—alluding to the title of the *Shulhan Arukh*:

> Just as a person likes only the food that he prepares for himself, in accordance with his own appetite and taste . . . thus he does not like another person's rulings unless he agrees with that person. All the more does he not wish to be dependent upon the books of other authors, just as a person likes only the food he prepares for himself, in accordance with his own appetite and taste, and does not aspire to be a guest at their prepared table [*shulhan arukh*]. (Quoted in Elchanan Reiner, "The Ashkenazi Elite at the Beginning of the Modern Era: Manuscript Versus Printed Book," *Polin* 10: 86.)

In the seventeenth century, individual rabbis were still opposed to the dominance of the *Shulhan Arukh,* but even Rabbi Isaiah Horowitz, who had opposed it before, admitted in 1626, "[Isserles'] coinage has been accepted, and we must follow his opinions and render decisions in accordance with his views. . . . In the Diaspora, in the lands of the Polish Crown, in Bohemia, Moravia, and Germany, the [practice] has spread to render decisions in accordance with his views." (Quoted in Joseph Davis, *Yom-Tov Lipmann Heller: Portrait of a Seventeenth-Century Rabbi,* Oxford, England: Littman Library of Jewish Civilization, 2004, 126.)

This quote testifies not only to the eventual widespread acceptance of the *Shulhan Arukh* with Isserles' glosses in the seventeenth century. It also indicates the development of a sense of an Ashkenazi identity that found its expression here in the geographic scope within which Isserles' ruling was considered to be authoritative. This Ashkenazi cultural area included Poland–Lithuania, the Hapsburg lands of Bohemia and Moravia, and the Jewish communities of Germany.

Apart from adhering to a common rabbinic tradition codified by Moses Isserles, the Ashkenazi world was characterized by its vernacular language: the use of the Yiddish language. Yiddish had developed as the spoken language of the Ashkenazi Jews in northern France and the Rhineland, and like the Spanish Jews took their Judeo–Spanish language with them when they moved eastward to the Ottoman Empire, the Ashkenazi Jews preserved their Yiddish language after they moved to Poland–Lithuania. There, the language underwent significant change, to be sure, and the Western Yiddish of Germany and the Eastern Yiddish of Poland–Lithuania are quite distinct. Perhaps surprisingly, there never emerged a Judeo–Polish language, and YIDDISH—A Jewish language with a Germanic base and Hebrew-Aramaic as well as Slavic elements—remained the common language of the Ashkenazi Jews in eastern Europe.

Early modern Ashkenazi culture thus was not only rabbinic elite culture produced in Hebrew, focusing on the interpretation of the classical texts of Judaism. It also included the production of a rich literature in the vernacular language where rabbinic and popular culture intersected. Doubtless the most popular and most well-known work of this literature was the Yiddish rendering of the Pentateuch (together with the weekly readings from the Prophets and the "five scrolls" read at certain points in the Jewish year), known as **Tsenerene** (from *"tse'enah ure'enah,"* Song of Songs, 3:11) and written toward the end of the sixteenth century by **Jacob ben Isaac Ashkenazi of Yanov** (1550–1624/1625). Though we do not know when it was printed for the first time, the edition of 1622 declared that it had been preceded by three earlier editions that were all already out of print at the time.

Tsenerene presents the weekly portion of the reading from the Pentateuch and the prophetic readings that accompany it during the Sabbath morning service in the synagogue, using Yiddish rather than Hebrew quotations from the original throughout and providing explanations and interpretations interwoven with legends, folktales, and ethical admonishment.

Avoiding philosophical or Kabbalistic teachings and using an accessible language, *Tsenerene* was intended to provide a basic understanding of the tradition to uneducated readers who had no access to Hebrew education.

Tsenerene was often presented as a book for women, just as the terms *vaybertaytsh* (for Yiddish translations) and *vaybershrift* (for the typeface commonly used in Yiddish print; *vayber* means "women") suggested a gendered use of language. In reality, the title page of the earliest extant edition of *Tsenerene* states that "this work is designed to enable *men and women . . .* to understand the word of God in simple language." It is clear that Yiddish literature was not intended exclusively for women, nor was it necessarily read primarily by women. Rather, a distinction was made between those who possessed rabbinic learning and Hebrew literacy and those who did not.

It is true, however, that the traditional educational system provided only boys with a basic training in Hebrew and rabbinic literature in schools, whereas the education for girls was largely informal and done in the vernacular Yiddish. Traditional Jewish society was organized around two separate male and female cultural spheres. Men were expected to participate in public ritual in the synagogue and were, at least in theory, subject to the ideal of perpetual Torah study, whereas women were "exempt" (as rabbinic law called it, or excluded) from many rituals. Their role was, as one historian has called it, as "facilitators" (enabling men to fulfill their religious duties) and as "bystanders." In the course of the early modern period, the rabbinic elite realized that it needed to provide women—and the numerous unlearned men—with a way to absorb the cultural values of the Jewish religion, and this is what led to the development of a growing Yiddish literature during early modern times.

The use of Yiddish also enabled women to develop their own, distinctly female, ways of religious expression: The early modern age saw the proliferation of **tkhines,** prayers written in Yiddish for women (and at times *by* women, though often by male authors for a female audience). Collections of *tkhines* appeared from the late sixteenth century on and, by providing women with the possibility of religious expression independent of the male-dominated ritual of Hebrew synagogue liturgy, invested female ritual (such as lighting the Sabbath candles or the monthly ritual immersion in the *mikvah*) with meaning. One such *tkhine,* said upon lighting the Sabbath candles, read like this:

Master of the Universe, may the mitsvah of my lighting candles be accepted as equivalent to the mitsvah of the High Priest when he lit the candles in the precious Temple. As his observance was accepted so may mine be accepted. . . . May the merit of the beloved Sabbath lights protect me, just as the beloved Sabbath protected Adam and kept him from premature death. So may we merit, by lighting the candles, to protect our children, that they may be enlightened by the study of Torah, and may their planets shine in the heavens so that they may be able to earn a decent living for their wives and children. (Quoted in Moshe Rosman, "Innovative Tradition," in *Cultures of the Jews: A New History*, ed. David Biale, New York: Schocken Books, 2002, 554–555.)

(On Jewish women in early modern Germany, *see box*, Glickl of Hameln and Her *Zikhroynes*.)

The Thirty Years' War (1618–1648), Mercantilism, and the Rise of the "Court Jews"

As we discussed in Chapter 8, the impact of the Protestant Reformation and the Catholic Counter-Reformation was ambiguous in reference to the Jews. No longer were the Jews the only religious minority in the Christian lands of western Europe (eastern Europe had always been more diverse, as we have seen in the case of Poland–Lithuania). The schism between Catholics and the various sects of Protestantism would at times divert attention from the Jews. In England or Holland, and later in colonial North America, the prime targets of religious suspicion by Protestant regimes were Catholics, and the Jews were seen as a lesser evil or even with sympathy. On the other hand, the expulsion of Jews from territories in German-speaking lands continued in the age of Reformation, and Luther's own anti-Jewish pronouncements are notorious. The Counter-Reformation of the Catholic Church beginning in the 1550s, in turn, led to increased antisemitism as well. As we have seen, a campaign against the Talmud began in 1553, and in 1555 Pope Paul IV segregated the Jews of Rome into a ghetto and resumed the persecution of former conversos in the papal port city of Ancona.

Between 1618 and 1648 a cruel war ravaged Central Europe, with the German-speaking lands of the Holy Roman Empire as the main battleground. The battles of the war and the ensuing famines and epidemics devastated entire regions, and the death toll ascended to one-half or two-thirds of the population in certain areas. The **Thirty Years' War** was, in part, a religious war between Catholic and Protestant forces, but it also was a war over political hegemony in Europe, pitching the Hapsburgs of Austria and Spain against France, The Netherlands, Denmark, and Sweden.

GLICKL OF HAMELN AND HER *ZIKHROYNES*

Glickl of Hameln (thus known after her first husband, though she was born in Hamburg in 1646 and lived there with her first husband, Hayim) is mostly known for her unique memoir (*zikhroynes*), which she began to write after her beloved first husband passed away in 1689. Eleven years later she moved to Metz, home of her second husband. She died in 1724. Addressed to her children and written in Yiddish, the memoir was first published in the nineteenth century, providing a rich portrait of Jewish life in seventeenth-century Germany. Writing one's memoirs was in itself a new phenomenon among Jews in the seventeenth century. They suggest yet another feature of Jewish modernity emerging at the time: a sense of self and individuality, a sense that one's own experiences and sensibilities were relevant, even though they continued to be expressed, by Glickl and others, within the confines of Jewish tradition.

The two passages cited here illustrate several aspects of Glickl's world: the constant presence of death; the nature of Jewish–gentile relations, showing how their respective worlds overlapped (in business transactions, for example) but also remained apart (note the role of language); insights into the popular culture of early modern Jews, with a dead person in this story appearing to others in their dreams—something that is simply taken as a fact; and, finally, Glickl running the family business after her husband's death, yet facing the constant fear of what the future might bring:

[My father] was already a widower when he became engaged to my mother. For fifteen years he had been married to . . . Reize, who maintained a large and fine house . . . a previous marriage had blessed her with a daughter, beautiful and virtuous as the day is long. The girl knew French like water. Once this did my father a mighty good turn. My father, it seems, held a pledge against a loan of 500 Reichsthaler he had made to a nobleman. The gentleman appeared at his house one day, with two other nobles, to redeem his pledge. My father gave himself no concern, but went upstairs to fetch it, while his stepchild sat and played at the clavichord to pass away the time for his distinguished customers. The gentlemen stood about and began to confer with one another in French. "When the Jew," they agreed, "comes down with the pledge, we'll take it without paying and slip out." They never suspected, of course, that the girl understood them. However, when my father appeared, she suddenly began to sing aloud in Hebrew, "Oh, not the pledge, my soul— here today and gone tomorrow!" In her haste the poor child could blurb out nothing better. My father now turned to his gentlemen. "Sir," he said, "where is the money?" "Give me the pledge!" cried the customer. But my father said, "First the money and then the pledge." Whereupon our gentlemen spun about to his companions. "Friends," he said, "the game is up—the wench, it seems, knows French"; and hurling threats they ran from the house. . . . My father raised the child as though she were his own. And eventually he married her off. She made an excellent match . . . but she died in her first childbirth. Soon after, her body was robbed and the shroud taken from her. She revealed the outrage to someone in a dream; the body was exhumed and the robbery confirmed." (*The Memoirs of Glückel of Hameln,* trans. Marvin Lowenthal, New York: Schocken Books, 1977, 11–13.)

I was still harassed by a large business, for my credit had not suffered among either Jews or Gentiles, and I never ceased to scrape and scurry. In the heat of the summer and the rain and snow of the winter I betook me to the fairs, and all day long I stood in my store. . . . Despite all my pains and travelling about and running from one end of the city to another, I found I could hold out no longer. For though I had a good business and enjoyed large credit, I stood in constant torment, once let a bale of goods go astray or a debtor fail me, I might fall, God forbid, into complete bankruptcy and be compelled to give my creditors all I had, a shame for my children and my pious husband asleep in the earth. (*Memoirs of Glückel of Hameln,* 225.)

The Jews of the empire generally fared actually better than their Christian neighbors. One Frankfurt rabbi observed the following:

We have seen with our own eyes and heard with our own ears that the living God dwells in our midst, even standing by us in wondrous ways. . . . The soldiers, for years now on march through the towns and villages, have often treated us more kindly than the non-Jews, so that Gentiles have sometimes brought their belongings to Jews for safekeeping. (Quotation in Michael Meyer, ed., *German-Jewish History in Modern Times,* New York: Columbia University Press, 1996, vol. 1, 97.)

After the crushing in 1620 of the rebellion of the Bohemian Protestants—which had triggered the initial

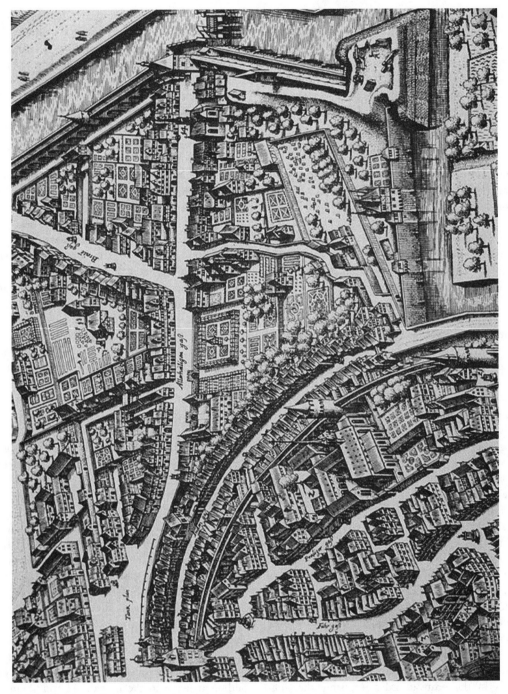

The Jewish ghetto (Judengasse) in Frankfurt. Copper engraving by Matthäus Merian, 1628.

conflagration—the city of Prague was pillaged by imperial troops, with the notable exception of the Jewish ghetto. In fact, houses owned by Protestants adjacent to the ghetto were confiscated and made available for purchase by Jews, finally alleviating the crowded conditions of the Prague Jewish quarter. This preferential treatment of the Prague Jews was no coincidence, of course: **Jacob Bassevi** (d. 1634), one of their leading figures, became one of the most important financiers of the war and thus rendered important services to the Hapsburg war effort.

Throughout the empire, Jewish financiers and provisioners emerged as a crucial factor in the war. Jews actually benefited from their role as outsiders as they were seen as neutral in the religious confrontation between Catholics and Protestants. Most important, they were able to provide exactly the kinds of services (financing and provisioning for the armies fighting the war) that were most needed—a result, to be sure, of the economic roles into which they had been pushed in the course of the Middle Ages, such as moneylending and trade.

With the Swedish invasion of 1630 (the "Swedish war" lasted until 1635), Jews once again were able to provide essential services as financiers and provisioners, this time for the Swedish troops. It seems that the Swedes generally treated the Jews better than others—no doubt because they were relying on their services. Nonetheless, after the defeat of the Swedes the favorable treatment of the Jews at the hands of the Hapsburg emperor continued. A new Jewish elite of financiers and provisioners emerged, working on both sides of the war. Surprising as it may seem, the Jewish population appears to have remained stable, and some communities actually grew during this time.

No decisive victory having been achieved by either side, the Thirty Years' War ended with the Peace of Westphalia in 1648. Recognizing the need for religious tolerance after thirty years of bloodshed and devastation, the new order also benefited the Jews as a religious minority, albeit indirectly. Moreover, the prominent role of individual Jewish financiers and provisioners was not forgotten after the war was over. From the 1650s on, we see the rise to prominence of the so-called **court Jews** (*Hofjuden*, in German), individuals who provided essential services to the rulers of the numerous German states in the postwar order. Arguably the most prominent one was **Samuel Oppenheimer** of Heidelberg (1630–1703), who organized, for example, the Austrian defense against the Ottoman siege of Vienna in 1683.

Still, the situation of European Jewry remained precarious at times. Under pressure from the local burghers, the Austrian emperor decided to expel the Jews from Vienna in 1670 (Samuel Oppenheimer was the first Jew to settle in

Vienna after this last expulsion). A number of wealthy Jewish families from Vienna found a new home in Berlin, where Frederick William of Hohenzollern (1640–1688) invited them to settle. When these Viennese Jews established themselves in Berlin in 1671, they laid the foundations of what became one of the most important Jewish communities in the following two centuries. Frederick William's reasons for inviting the Jews from Vienna were mainly economic and marked a new policy vis-à-vis the Jews guided by pragmatic considerations rather than religious ideology: Recognizing their potential contribution to the reconstruction of his country after the devastation of the Thirty Years' War, the Prussian monarch encouraged the settlement of various religious minorities that would bring much-needed skills to his country. The number of Viennese Jews moving to Berlin—about fifty families—pales, to be sure, in comparison to the 20000 or so Hugenots (French Protestants) who were taken in during the 1680s, but it did mark a new beginning.

In fact, if the previous trend of expulsion and dislocation of the Jews from west to east was reversed in the seventeenth century, it was due primarily to a new primacy of economic considerations in state politics: the rise of **mercantilism.** Thinking in terms of mercantilism, the wealth of a nation depends on the supply of capital and considers trade to be something of a zero-sum game in which the profit of one side means a loss for the other. As European rulers of the early modern period, in particular in the wake of the Thirty Years' War, sought to consolidate their power, the politics of mercantilism went hand in hand with a quest for expanding the role of the state and the emerging primacy of raison d'état, the interest of the state, over other—namely religious—considerations.

An early example of the politics of mercantilism and the new attitude toward Jews could be found in Italy. As we have seen in Chapter 8, the senate of Venice acquiesced to the presence of Jews in the city because of their perceived economic benefit. Also the Grand Duke of Tuscany, Ferdinand I, considered the potential economic benefits of Jews and new Christians if they were to settle in his territory, and in 1593 he granted a charter, known as "La Livornina," which declared that "none shall be able to make any inquisition, inquiry, examination or accusation against you or your families, although living in the past outside our Dominion in the guise of Christians"—a hardly disguised invitation to former conversos to settle in the Tuscan cities of Livorno and Pisa without having to fear the Inquisition. Ferdinand's move proved to be a great success, and by the eighteenth century, Livorno had not only become one of the largest Sephardic communities in western Europe but also the preeminent port city of Italy and a major commercial hub.

The argument of the economic benefits derived from Jewish settlement and immigration was employed rather self-consciously by Jewish leaders as well. Daniel Rodriga, a Jew of Portuguese–converso origin, successfully lobbied the Venetian government in the 1570s and convinced it to actively invite former conversos to come and live openly as Jews in Venice, without having to fear the Inquisition. His argument was that this would help Venetian commerce with the Ottoman Empire. In the following century, **Simone Luzzatto** (ca. 1583–1663)—highly respected by both Christians and Jews in Venice—published in 1638 his influential *Discorso circa il stato de gl'hebrei* ("Discourse on the State of the Jews"), probably the first systematic treatment of the role of the Jews in international trade, wherein he made the case for the economic usefulness of the Jews to the European states.

In central Europe, it was after the religious stalemate and disillusionment of the Thirty Years' War that a class of court Jews rose to prominence and rulers throughout western Europe began to reconsider and reverse their earlier exclusionist policy vis-à-vis the Jews. Monarchs such as Frederick of Prussia encouraged the establishment of Jewish communities in cities throughout Germany, based on the perceived utility of the court Jews and the hope that these Jews, with their international connections and expertise in commerce, would attract trade to their territories. (*See box,* Rich and Poor.)

Questions of Identity: Conversos and the "Port Jews" of the Atlantic World

Balthazar de Orobio, born in Portugal around 1617 to a family of conversos, was apprehended by the Inquisition in 1656. In 1662 he emigrated to the Dutch port city of Amsterdam, where he changed his name to Isaac. He explained his background:

> [In Spain] I presented a Christian appearance, since life is sweet; but I was never very good at it, and so it came out that I was in fact a Jew. If, then, whilst I was there, confronted with the risk of [loss of my] freedom, status, property, and indeed life itself, I was in reality a Jew and a Christian merely in outward appearance, common sense shows that in a domicile where Providence from above affords me a life of freedom, a true Jew is what I shall be. (Quoted in Jane Gerber, *The Jews of Spain: A History of the Sephardic Experience,* New York: The Free Press, 1992, p. 190.)

Orobio was born some 120 years after the forced conversion of the Jews in Portugal, many of them exiles from Spain, in 1497. Like him a large number of these forced converts and their descendants retained a sense of Jewishness in spite of their outward adherence to Christianity. Such a large number of conversos sought to leave Portugal that the Portuguese Crown banned emigration between 1499 and 1507 and again between 1532 and 1538, in the meantime establishing an Inquisition in 1536. The ferocious campaign of the Portuguese Inquisition, which had been established much later than its Spanish counterpart but soon acquired an even worse reputation, proved to be counterproductive. Even more than an attraction to Judaism, it was the persecution at the hands of the Inquisition that pushed an increasing number of Portuguese conversos to leave their country and establish, from the late sixteenth through the end of the seventeenth century, a Diaspora of former conversos.

One of the more unlikely destinations of the Portuguese converso emigration between 1580 (when Spain annexed Portugal) until the 1640s was Spain. There, they still had to live under the guise of Christianity, but they were safe from the Portuguese Inquisition, which had no jurisdiction over them in Spain. Especially under the **Count of Olivares** as head of the Spanish government, Portuguese conversos settling in Madrid assumed a leading role as bankers and tax farmers in Spain, and their connections to Portuguese conversos elsewhere in Spain, Portugal, and their colonies in the New World made them play an important role in trade as well. In the early 1600s, a Spanish official in the province of Guipúzcoa complained that "since these people have entered this region, they have usurped the business and the profits of its natives, in the shipments made to Seville and to the Indies." Historians estimate that some ten thousand Portuguese conversos emigrated to Spain, settling in such places as Madrid, Seville, and Malaga, in those years; others established themselves in the Spanish colonies of Peru and Mexico. However, the downfall of Olivares in 1643 prompted a major backlash against the Portuguese conversos in Spain; Portugal had regained its independence from Spain three years earlier, whereas in Mexico the Inquisition renewed its persecution in the years after 1642.

As the sixteenth century came to a close, the Portuguese conversos discovered new roads of emigration. Some went to establish themselves in southwestern France, where they were tolerated and could even practice Judaism without being disturbed by the Inquisition, but they continued to be regarded officially as Christians until the eighteenth century. In other places, namely in Amsterdam and Hamburg, as well as in the Italian port cities of Venice and Livorno, they found an environment that allowed them to openly return to Judaism and establish their own new Jewish communities. Converso emigration to Hamburg, Amsterdam, and Livorno began in the

RICH AND POOR

The prominence of individual court Jews in Germany or Jewish merchants in Venice and Amsterdam should not lead us to think that most early modern Jews were wealthy: They were not. Like the Christian or Muslim societies around it, Jewish society was stratified and divided into social classes, with the wealthy representing a very small percentage and the vast majority being poor. Though estimates for this period are necessarily imprecise, the image that emerges is rather consistent throughout the Jewish world: Jewish communities most everywhere were impoverished in the course of the sixteenth and seventeenth centuries, leading to social tensions within the communities and conflicts with non-Jewish neighbors. During the fifteenth century, the percentage of under-privileged Jews in German lands rose from 25 percent to over 50 percent; in the mid-1700s, as much as two-thirds of the Jews in Germany were poor. At the end of the eighteenth century in the city of Amsterdam, the largest and one of the wealthiest Jewish communities of western Europe, about 80 percent of the Ashkenazi Jews and 50 percent of the Sephardi Jews received public assistance. The situation was not much different in the Ottoman Empire, where poverty increased in the course of the seventeenth century and the poor made up between one-half and three-quarters of the Jewish communities.

The situation was aggravated by the arrival of large numbers of Jewish refugees from eastern Europe in the wake of the Thirty Years' War and the Chmielnicki massacres of the mid-seventeenth century. The poorest of the poor, known in German as *Betteljuden* ("beggar-Jews"), were forced to move from one town to another and ask for temporary shelter and food. The Christian author Johann Buxtorf noted in his book *Synagoga Judaica* (1603), "Where there is a man who suffers from noticeably great poverty, his rabbis, who know him, give him a begging-letter, in which they document his want and poverty; they demonstrate also that he is pious and of the Jewish faith, etc." Equipped with such a letter of recommendation, the itinerant poor would roam the Jewish communities, which gave out tickets for a limited number of days for lodging and food in the home of a community member, after which the beggar-Jew was expected to move on.

The vagrant poor were often associated in the popular imagination with crime, and indeed Jewish banditry was on the rise in seventeenth-century Germany. There were all-Jewish robber bands—observing the Sabbath rest and traditional dietary laws—as well as associations between Jewish and Christian criminals. In terms of the numbers, where they are available, crime rates among Jews in early modern Germany did not differ much from those of the Christian majority, but from the 1600s on a new anti-Jewish stereotype emerged that identified Jews (namely the poor *Betteljuden*) with crime and gangsterism. The stereotype survived into modern antisemitic prejudice even though, in the age of emancipation, actual crime rates among Jews decreased dramatically until they actually compared favorably with those of the general population.

Traditional Jewish society had long practiced charity to relieve the suffering of its poor. Codes of Jewish law, whether the writings of the medieval philosopher Maimonides or the sixteenth-century *Shulhan Arukh*, included detailed laws concerning the giving of charity (*tsedakah*). In the early modern period, Jewish communities had to deal with growing poverty that led to an expansion of the traditional modes of poor relief: Various charitable societies provided dowries for poor brides, redeemed captives, sent money to the poor communities of the Holy Land, provided medical care to the poor, and buried the dead. Ottoman Jewry in particular developed an elaborate system of poverty relief, funded by the community taxes paid by the wealthy and the middle class. At the same time, Ottoman rabbis perpetuated the traditional belief that poverty was a divinely ordained fate and a necessary feature of human life, and that the community could only try to alleviate the suffering, not change the basic realities of social inequality.

It was first among the Sephardi communities of the west, namely in Amsterdam, that a new—one might say, modern—approach to providing support for the poor developed. In response to the large influx of poor Ashkenazi Jews from Germany and Poland, the Sephardi leadership in Amsterdam grew anxious about the financial burden this imposed on the community—and about the negative consequences of rampant poverty for the image of the Jews in gentile society. A new approach developed there that began to consider poverty as not only an economic problem but as a moral one. This in turn spearheaded the emergence of a modern Jewish philanthropy that sought not just to assist the poor but to eradicate poverty.

1590s. By the end of the seventeenth century, the latter two communities—Amsterdam and Livorno—were the largest communities of Portuguese Jews, each exceeding 3000 souls. Other communities were established by Portuguese Jews, as we shall see, in London, in the Caribbean, and eventually in North America. Between 850 and 1000 Portuguese Jews from Amsterdam were active in Dutch Brazil (in the Recife area, from 1630 until the Portuguese recaptured the region in 1645), and at the end of the seventeenth century some 625 Portuguese Jews lived in Curaçao, 400 in Jamaica, 300 in Barbados, and just 75 in New Amsterdam (later called New York).

Süßkint der Jude von Trimperg. C.

This Early-Fourteenth-Century Illustration captures the special clothes Jews wore that marked them as distinctive from non-Jews in Constantinople. Note especially the tall, pointed hat and the full beard.

Various Learned Women Studying with Men
adorn this page from a late-thirteenth century German
haggadah, the text read during the Passover meal.

**Kazimierz, the Jewish Suburb of Cracow,
Poland,** as depicted in a nineteenth-century
painting.

Jewish Time, Christian Time. The clock tower of the Jewish Town Hall in Prague (built in the sixteenth century). The hands on the Hebrew clock move counterclockwise.

Depiction of the Sacking of the Jewish Ghetto in Frankfurt in 1614 by the guild leader Vincent Fettmilch, who referred to himself as the "New Haman." Many Jews found refuge among compassionate Christians while most were forced into exile. The emperor eventually arrested and executed Fettmilch and his co-conspirators. Jews returned to the city in a festive procession, and the Judengasse (Jews' Street) and synagogue were rebuilt at the city's expense. From this date on, Frankfurt Jewry held an annual commemoration of deliverance with a local Purim celebration preceded by a fast.

A Jewish Marriage Contract *(ketubbah)* from Italy (Casale Monferrato, 1671).

The Magnificent Synagogue of the Portuguese Jews in Amsterdam, which opened in 1675. Painted by the Dutchman Emanuel de Witte (1680), who was best known for painting church interiors.

Georg Emanuel Opiz (1775–1841), *The Poles,* depicting Hasidim attending the Leipzig Fair in the early nineteenth century. Opiz often depicted scenes of different ethnic groups attending the great trade fairs in Leipzig. Jews were a disproportionate presence at the fairs, especially those from Poland. Here, Opiz allows us not only to see the Hasidim as traders at the fair, but we also are given a good sense of the different styles of Hasidic dress. The differentiation in clothing styles and religious customs among Hasidim increased with the rapid spread of Hasidism in the eighteenth century.

The community in Amsterdam is clearly the best studied, in part because of the wealth of the archival material that is available to historians and in part because of the importance of Amsterdam as the foremost center of world trade in the seventeenth century. In fact, it was its economic possibilities as much as the religious freedom it promised that attracted Portuguese conversos to settle in Amsterdam in the first place. Having only recently thrown off Spanish rule, the politics of the newly independent Protestant Netherlands were marked by religious tolerance that extended to the conversos who wished to return to Judaism, and obviously they were at a safe distance from the Catholic Inquisition. But the main reason why conversos were attracted to Amsterdam and similar locations in the Atlantic world, and the reason why the local authorities were willing to accept the influx of this population, was the growing economic role played by the Portuguese Jewish and converso Diaspora in international commerce.

The main circuits of the Portuguese trading Diaspora linked Amsterdam with Portugal and Spain, where the former conversos continued to have extensive contacts, and across the Atlantic, linking Amsterdam, London, and Hamburg with the Spanish colonies and the non-Spanish territories of the Caribbean. When Surinam became the main source of Dutch sugar imports, Portuguese Jews from Amsterdam played a significant role in its colonization. In 1730, 115 of the 400 plantations in Surinam were owned by Jews. In 1639, Jews established the first synagogue of the Western Hemisphere in the township known as Joden Savanne ("Jews' Savannah").

The Amsterdam Jews were not only engaged prominently in the Dutch Atlantic trade and the importation of colonial goods but also in related crafts—for example, operating sugar refineries, tobacco workshops, workshops cutting and polishing diamonds, and chocolate-making facilities. They were also successful as brokers in the Amsterdam stock exchange. In 1657 a full 10 percent of the brokers at the Amsterdam stock exchange, described in colorful detail by a Sephardi author in *Confusión de confusiones* (1688), were Jewish. This book draws a picture of a gambling elite of Portuguese Jews, loving life, pleasure, and luxury—an image perpetuated by many rabbis denouncing the laxity in religious observance among the wealthy Sephardi merchants of Amsterdam and other such communities in the west.

The description of the Amsterdam Jewish quarter by a (non-Jewish) German visitor, Philipp von Zesen, in a book that reads like the early modern version of a travel guide (published in 1664), contrasts with the often bleak image of the crowded Jewish quarters in other European cities and attests to the wealth of the Amsterdam Sephardim in the seventeenth century:

[We get to] the *Breite Gasse* ["wide street"] in which there are living mostly Jews who came here from Portugal, and some from Spain, many years ago because they were persecuted. This street, adorned with beautiful buildings, is wide (as the name suggests) and leads straight to the Anthon watergate. It has two side streets on each side. . . . Between the second side street and the Mont-Albans-graft there the Portuguese Jews have their school and their Temple, or the big Jewish church [i.e., the synagogue], which was created by joining two houses and which has two entrances. . . . One goes up on a wide staircase on both sides up to the church [the synagogue] where there is always light lit in glass lamps and, during the high holidays, in precious silver chandeliers. In the middle [of the synagogue] stand the teachers [i.e., the rabbi and cantor]. . . . Around them sit or stand the other men, with Hebrew books in their hands and with a white cloth over their hat, hanging down their back [i.e., wrapped in the *tallit*, or prayer shawl]. The women are separate from the men, up on the balcony behind a lattice fence. Behind the wooden benches one sees a large wooden wardrobe [i.e., the ark in the front of the synagogue]. . . . In there they keep many precious objects, among others the books of Moses wrapped in artfully designed covers [i.e., the Torah scrolls].

Less then ten years after von Zesen's visit, in 1675, the Portuguese Jews of Amsterdam opened a new, magnificent synagogue, which became a popular tourist destination for both Jewish and non-Jewish visitors and which exists to this day.

In allusion to the setting of these communities of former conversos, historians have called them communities of **port Jews** who were distinguished by their engagement in international commerce, their social integration into the surrounding society, and their nonideological secularism. In fact, the Portuguese "port Jews" of Amsterdam, Hamburg, or London can be seen as "the first modern Jews" ever, as having established a Jewish community and culture that departed from traditional models and ways of life that still went largely unchallenged in the major centers of early modern Jewry in Poland–Lithuania or the Ottoman Empire.

The Amsterdam Sephardim are considered to be "the first modern Jews" for a number of reasons. To begin, this was the first Jewish community ever that had to completely "reinvent" its Jewish tradition. Unlike those Jews and conversos who had joined existing communities in Italy or the Ottoman Empire, the community in Amsterdam was new. When speaking of a "return" to Judaism, we need to remember that the conversos who emigrated to Amsterdam in the course of the seventeenth century had been born into families that had lived as Catholics for generations. They may have had a sense of belonging to the Jewish people and may have been eager to re-embrace Judaism, but they knew little of Jewish traditions and practices and did not, of course, read Hebrew. The ex-conversos in western Europe have therefore been called "the new Jews," as they had to reinvent a tradition that they had lost generations earlier and that the Inquisition had tried to destroy.

Thus, whereas Jews elsewhere in the early modern period absorbed their knowledge of Jewish texts and rituals from their parents and grandparents, the former conversos who emigrated to Amsterdam in the seventeenth century had to learn Judaism from scratch. A rich literature was created by rabbis—many of whom were of converso origin themselves—who addressed their works to an audience of Portuguese Jews who wanted, and needed, to relearn what it meant to live according to rabbinic tradition. In 1609, Moses Altaras published an abridged version of the *Shulhan Arukh* in Spanish, printed in Venice under the title *Libro de mantenimiento de la alma* (*Book of Maintenance of the Soul*). Other such works included Isaac Athias's *Tesoro de preceptos* (*Thesaurus of Precepts*, 1627, in Spanish), *Thesouro dos Dinim* (*Thesaurus of Laws*, 1645–1647, in Portuguese) by **Menasseh ben Israel,** and Abraham Farrar's *Declaração das seiscentas e treze encomendanças da nossa sancta ley* (*Explanation of the 613 Commandments of Our Holy Law*, 1627, also in Portuguese). Knowledge that traditional society imparted to its children in the family home and in schools was now learned from books, often by adult immigrants, and it was learned from books written in European languages printed in Latin characters (as opposed to Yiddish and Ladino, which were written using the Hebrew alphabet). This was much more similar to the modern-day "how to run a Jewish household" type of practical guides than it was to the traditional mode of Jewish learning.

Though Amsterdam failed to produce luminaries of rabbinic learning of the calibre of the communities in eastern Europe, its educational system proved to be very successful and was showered with praise by a visiting Ashkenazi rabbi from Prague, Shabbatai Sheftel Horowitz, who expressed his admiration of the educational institutions established by the Portuguese–Jewish community in Amsterdam in the seventeenth century. Another visitor from eastern Europe, Shabbatai Bass, visited Amsterdam in 1675 and praised the curriculum of its famous academy, *Ets Hayim,* which introduced Jewish children gradually and in a systematic way to the teachings of Jewish tradition. The pupils were divided into six levels:

1. Learning how to read the Hebrew prayers
2. Learning how to recite the weekly portion of the biblical text according to its traditional cantillation
3. Studying of the Pentateuch with its classical commentaries
4. Studying of the Prophets and other biblical writings
5. Study and interpretation of Jewish law (*halakhah*); study of grammar; study of a different law every day, based on the Talmud, and review the laws of any upcoming festival according to the *Shulhan Arukh*
6. Advanced study of Jewish law, including the medieval commentaries on the Talmud and the major law codes of Maimonides and Joseph Karo

Notable is the systematic structure of the curriculum, with each level building upon the foundations of the previous one, as well as the emphasis on Hebrew grammar and the study of practical *halakhah,* rather than the *pilpul* method typical of the east European schools that, as we have seen, was criticized for generating ever new subtleties in the interpretation of the Talmud and its commentaries without regard to the meaning of the text or its practical application. In the Amsterdam model, the influence of European humanism, with its focus on the classical languages (here Hebrew), was combined with the Spanish–Jewish tradition of emphasizing grammatical studies and practical *halakhah.*

In reality, this dedication to the re-creation of a rabbinic tradition for the former conversos of Amsterdam represented only one part of their cultural identity. The Portuguese Sephardim of Amsterdam were eager to provide a Jewish education to their children, but their religious life was focused primarily on the synagogue and the religious calendar of Jewish life. The community tried to ensure that Jewish law—its dietary restrictions, the observance of the Sabbath—was respected and, apparently, was rather successful in its endeavor, but in contrast to other Jewish communities at the time, we find few references in rabbinic writings from Amsterdam that relate to economic life. It seems that Jewish law then was not the all-encompassing point of reference that it was in traditional Jewish societies, but instead was relegated to the synagogue and religious ritual. The western Sephardim in Amsterdam and elsewhere were also the "first modern Jews" because they distinguished between the religious and secular spheres of their individual and collective lives. Their regained Jewish religion was only part of their identity.

Though it might be surprising given the fact that they had mostly fled Portugal and Spain to escape persecution by the Inquisition, it was precisely a continued sense of belonging to the Portuguese and Spanish culture that sustained the western Sephardim as a distinct group within European Judaism. Their Spanish and Portuguese culture was as much a factor in their self-understanding as was their Jewishness.

This can be seen as yet another manifestation of their "modernity": the simultaneous identification with their Jewish origin and religion on the one hand, and general Spanish and Portuguese language, literature, and culture on the other hand.

Thus the Sephardi Jews of Amsterdam and other communities in the west continued to use the Portuguese and Spanish languages as the community was replenished with new arrivals of converso immigrants from Spain and Portugal until the 1720s. Though most were familiar with Dutch, Portuguese remained the spoken language within the community, whereas Spanish was the language of highbrow literature, assuming an almost sacred character as the language of biblical and liturgical translations used by the western Sephardim. What is more, the Sephardi Jews of the west, unlike their Ottoman counterparts, continued to maintain close contact with the Iberian Peninsula and were an eager audience for the literature of the early modern "Golden Age" (*Siglo de Oro*) of Spanish literature, reading the works of Góngora and Quevedo, staging Spanish plays in the Amsterdam theater, and establishing literary academies modeled after the Spanish literary circles of the time (*Academia de los sitibundos* and *Academia de los floridos,* founded in 1676 and 1685, respectively). Many Amsterdam Jews, among them leading rabbis, possessed extensive libraries containing works of European classical and Renaissance literature in the original or in Spanish translation.

Rather than being merely consumers of Spanish and Portuguese culture, Sephardi authors in Amsterdam produced their own literature in the languages of their former homeland. **Miguel de Barrios** (1635–1701), for example, was born in Spain and returned to Judaism in the Italian city of Livorno. Toward the end of 1662, he came to Amsterdam, though he left shortly thereafter and lived for twelve years, once again under the guise of Christianity, as a captain of the Spanish army in Brussels (part of what continued to be the Spanish Netherlands). He maintained his connection to the Jewish community of Amsterdam, however, and eventually returned there. Daniel Levi de Barrios, as he was known after reverting to Judaism, was a prolific poet and playwright. Some of his works provoked the censure of the local rabbinate. One of his supporters, Rabbi **Jacob Sasportas** (d. 1698)—among the leading Sephardi rabbis of the time—noted about de Barrios that he

> wrote poetry in the vernacular and . . . was called a *poeta.* He composed many works of poetry, including a Pentateuch in verse, entitled "Melody of the World," *Harmonia del mundo,* which he had divided into 12 parts each of which he dedicated to a duke, such as the

Duke of Livorno, and to the princes of Holland, Portugal, Spain, and England. All of these promised to reward him and sent him their picture, their banner, their coat of arms. . . . I was among those who supported him to get permission to have the book published, while part of the Mahamad [the governing council of the Sephardi community] and most of the rabbis opposed it saying that the book contained phrases which were not in accordance with our Torah and, also, that he transformed our Torah into gentile, secular literature by copying it in verse form. (Quoted in Daniel Swetschinski, *Reluctant Cosmopolitans: The Portuguese Jews of Seventeenth-Century Amsterdam,* Oxford, England: Littman Library of Jewish Civilization, 2000, 246.)

Sasportas' words testify to how much a former converso intellectual in Amsterdam, like Daniel Levi de Barrios, saw himself both as a Jew and as part of contemporary European culture. It was this closeness to secular European culture and the far-reaching social and cultural integration of the western Sephardim that made them more modern than most of their Jewish contemporaries elsewhere—and it predictably aroused the disapproval of some of their religious leaders. One of them, Rabbi **Saul Levi Morteira** (d. 1660) of Venice who had become a leading rabbi in Amsterdam and a critic of its Sephardi community, admonished his listeners in one of his sermons:

> We must strive to carry out God's will by remaining separate and recognizable and distinct from [the Gentiles] in every respect . . . [so that] whoever sees us will recognize and know and understand the difference between us and the other peoples, since in this land we have no external sign to differentiate us as is the case in all the other lands of our exile. We must therefore establish this differentiation ourselves. We must not imitate the Gentile hairstyle, we must not eat of their foods or drink of their wines. . . . When we travel, we must pray and bring *tefillin* [phylacteries, used during the weekday morning prayers] with us, so that all who see us will recognize us. (English quotation in Marc Saperstein, *Exile in Amsterdam: Saul Levi Morteira's Sermons to a Congregation of "New Jews,"* Cincinnati: Hebrew Union College Press, 2005, 185–186.)

In another sermon he thundered:

> What has enabled the last remnant of "the exile of Jerusalem which is in Sefarad" [Obadiah 20, i.e., Iberian Jewry] to preserve its identity is their refusal to intermarry with the Gentiles of the land. This has preserved

their lineage and their identity, so that they are not lost to the community of the Eternal. Woe to the one who mixes in with them while still in a Gentile state, before conversion, for he destroys his offspring and his future remembrance. (Saperstein, *Exile in Amsterdam*, 198–199.)

Morteira's admonition against sexual relations between Portuguese Jews and Christian women suggests a certain religious laxity among at least some of its members. His insistence on the "pure lineage" preserved by the conversos in the Iberian lands that was then endangered through sexual licentiousness points to another issue: the concern among the western Sephardi Jews with maintaining their Iberian pedigree.

Evidently traditional Judaism did not allow intermarriage (which in any case was impossible in the absence of civil marriage prior to the secularization of European law), but the preoccupation with lineage and nobility of descent was a marginal concept in Jewish law, even while it was of great importance to the Sephardim in the west. In a clear departure from Jewish law, in fact, the Sephardim tried to preserve the identity of their Spanish–Portuguese Jewish "nation," as they called themselves according to the usage of the time (*natie,* in Dutch, or **nação,** in Portuguese) not only against intermarriage with non-Jews but against intermarriage with non-Sephardi Jews, namely Ashkenazim.

This question became more urgent with a growing influx of Ashkenazi immigrants to western Europe, in particular to cities such as Amsterdam, Hamburg, and London, during the Thirty Years' War and in the wake of the Chmielnicki massacres of the mid-seventeenth century. The Ashkenazim of Amsterdam established their first synagogue in 1649 and maintained their own independent congregation. In 1671, the Sephardi community decided that an Ashkenazi Jewish man who married a Spanish–Portuguese girl would not be able to join the Sephardi community; in 1697, they went one step further and declared that a Sephardi man who married a non-Sephardi woman would have to leave the community. Still in 1762, Isaac de Pinto, living in Amsterdam, noted in an open letter to the French philosopher Voltaire that the Portuguese Jews of Western Europe

are scrupulous not to intermingle, not by marriage, nor by covenant, nor by any other means, with the Jews of other nations. . . . The distance between them and their brethren is so great that if a Portuguese Jew dwelling in Holland or England were to marry an Ashkenazic Jewish woman, he would immediately lose all his special privileges: he would no longer be considered as a member of

their synagogue, he would have no part in all sorts of ecclesiastical and lay offices, and he would be completely removed from the Nation. (Quoted in Paul Mendes-Flohr and Jehuda Reinharz, eds., *The Jew in the Modern World: A Documentary History,* 2nd ed., New York: Oxford University Press, 1995, 306.)

Curiously, it was descent more than religion that determined one's belonging to the Spanish–Portuguese Jewish "nation." As Amsterdam Rabbi Menasseh ben Israel noted in his famous address to Oliver Cromwell, Lord Protector of England, when he praised the advantages of the Jewish people in various countries:

[W]e see, that not only the Jewish Nation dwelling in Holland, Italy, traffics [i.e., trades] with their own stocks but also with the riches of many others of their Nation, friends, kinds-men and acquaintance, which notwithstanding live in Spain.

That is to say, the members of the "nation" in Amsterdam continued to maintain contacts with family members who still lived in Spain—who were, thus, still living as Christians and apparently had no intention of abandoning the Iberian Peninsula and returning to Judaism.

At the same time, one of the most well-known and influential charitable organizations maintained by the western Sephardim, the **Dotar societies,** which provided dowries for poor girls and orphans, likewise established an ethnic, rather than religious, definition of who was eligible for their support. The Venetian *Dotar* society provided that the applicants had to be "poor Hebrew girls, Portuguese or Castilian on the father's or the mother's side"—a definition of ethnic descent, even though in Jewish law it was only relevant that one's *mother* be Jewish. The Amsterdam *Dotar* society founded in 1615 went even further and extended its support also to those conversos still living as Christians in Catholic lands but completely excluded non-Sephardim from its membership or as beneficiaries.

Again, what is strikingly "modern" about this is the ambiguity of Jewish identity as it developed in those ex-converso communities in western Europe. The relatively straightforward definition of Jewishness in rabbinic law was now becoming more complicated as cultural–ethnic distinctions irrelevant to Jewish law determined one's being part of the Spanish–Portuguese Jewish "nation," while one's *religious* Jewish identity turned out to be only *part* of being a member of the "nation."

In some cases, people even changed their religious identities according to the circumstances—though, to be sure, this was a practice that was not condoned by the leadership of the community. Daniel Levi de Barrios, as we have seen, reverted to the life of a converso after having returned to Judaism for several years. Other examples are rather picturesque, like the case of a certain Abraham Righetto who acted as a Christian when he was in Antwerp or Florence and as a Jew when he was in Padua or Ferrara. When living in Venice, it was reported that he would walk the streets of the city while alternating the yellow hat of the Jews and a black hat that he kept under his arm, depending on the circumstances.

Some more radical examples of deviation serve as counterpoint to the Jewish tradition otherwise successfully reestablished by the Amsterdam Sephardim. A few intellectuals of *converso* origins began to question rabbinic authority and the validity of rabbinic Judaism—even of revealed religion more generally. **Uriel da Costa** (d. 1640), for example, had been born in Porto and studied theology in the most prestigious Portuguese university at Coimbra. He reverted to Judaism after emigrating to Amsterdam in 1615 and soon after moved to Hamburg. There he wrote a treatise challenging rabbinic law (as opposed to biblical law), and he later explained in an account of his life written shortly before his death:

> Having finished our Voyage, and being arrived at Amsterdam, where we found the Jews professing their Religion with great freedom, as the Law directs them, we immediately fulfilled the Precept concerning Circumcision. I had not been there many Days, before I observed, that the Customs and Ordinances of the modern Jews were very different from those commanded by Moses: Now if the Law was to be strictly observed, according to the Letter, as it expressly declares, it must be very unjustifiable for the Jewish Doctors [i.e., the rabbis] to add to it Inventions of a quite contrary Nature. . . . The modern Jewish Rabbins [rabbis], like their Ancestors, are an obstinate and perverse race of Men. . . . This Situation of Affairs put me upon writing a Treatise in defense of myself, and to prove plainly out of the Law of Moses, the Vanity and Invalidity of the Traditions and Ordinances of the Pharisees [who, he claimed, were the predecessors of the rabbis], and their repugnancy to that Law. . . . Some time after this, as Age and Experience are apt to occasion new discoveries to the Mind of Man . . . I began to question with myself, whether the Law of Moses ought to be accounted the Law of God, seeing there were many Arguments which seemed to persuade, or rather determine the contrary. At last I came to be fully of Opinion, that it was nothing but a human Invention, like many other Systems in the World, and that Moses was not the Writer; for it contained many Things contrary to the Law of Nature. (*The Remarkable Life of Uriel Acosta*, London, 1740, 18–23.)

Da Costa sent his first treatise to Venice from Hamburg, whose rabbis urged the Hamburg community to excommunicate da Costa, which they did in 1618. Five years later, Uriel da Costa returned to Amsterdam and intended to publish a more extensive attack on rabbinic tradition, *Exame das tradições phariseas* ("Inquiry into the Traditions of the Pharisees [i.e., the Rabbis]"). The text opens with a frontal attack on the very foundation of rabbinic Judaism, declaring that "The tradition called the Oral Torah is not a truthful tradition, nor did it originate with the [written] Torah." Da Costa again ridiculed rituals of rabbinic Judaism—the phylacteries, circumcision, the prohibition to consume meat and milk together—and added a lengthy argument denying the immortality of the soul. The book was banned by the Amsterdam community's leadership, and until a copy was found in the Copenhagen royal library in the 1980s it was believed that all traces of da Costa's writing had been successfully destroyed. Excommunicated and socially isolated, da Costa reconciled with the community in a public ceremony in 1633, but seven years later, in 1640, he committed suicide, the exact circumstances of which are unclear.

It is hardly surprising that the Amsterdam community reacted as vigorously as it did to da Costa's challenge: Not only did the rabbis see their authority being challenged openly, but the very foundations of a community established by former conversos was questioned by one of its own members. Da Costa, however, was not the last one to criticize rabbinic tradition. In 1656, the Amsterdam leadership excommunicated **Barukh (Benedict) de Spinoza** (1632–1677) for his heretical views. In 1670, Spinoza published in Latin his famous *Tractatus theologico-politicus,* a pioneering work for modern philosophical and political thought and for modern biblical criticism. What is most relevant in terms of social history, however, is the fact that Spinoza—unlike da Costa—never sought to return to the Jewish community that had expelled him, and he never converted to Christianity either, as other critics of the Jewish tradition had done before him and would do later. Spinoza can be seen as the first ever **secular Jew,** one who rejected the religious teachings of traditional Judaism without embracing another religion. Spinoza thus anticipated a form of Jewish identity that was to become a unique feature of the modern Jewish experience.

What needs to be emphasized, though, is that in spite of the ambiguous religious identity of some conversos, and in spite of individuals challenging the very foundations of

Barukh (Benedict) de Spinoza (1632–1677), the first modern Jewish intellectual—and one of the great philosophers and political thinkers of the seventeenth century.

rabbinic tradition, the Spanish–Portuguese Jews of Amsterdam and elsewhere in western Europe integrated with surprising ease into the culture of rabbinic Judaism. Certain individuals may have been torn and struggled with their identity, but the persistence of traditionalism in these communities established by former conversos is probably more remarkable than the occasional ideological dissent or religious laxity. In fact, though the Amsterdam Jews can be called the "first modern Jews" in the sense that their experience foreshadowed some of the dilemmas faced by modern Jews elsewhere in Europe a century or more later, they did not develop an ideology of reform and religious enlightenment. This would happen in the eighteenth century in Germany. Dissenters could be found among the Amsterdam

THE LOST TRIBES OF ISRAEL

When the Assyrians captured and destroyed the northern kingdom of ancient Israel in 722 BCE, they led the ten tribes making up its population into captivity. For centuries, the Jewish imagination was sparked by speculations over what had become of those "lost tribes." It was already stated in biblical prophecy (namely Ezekiel 37:19–24) that the "return" of the lost tribes was tied to the final redemption of the Jewish people. According to the myth that developed over time, the ten "lost tribes" lived in a mythical Israelite kingdom beyond a river called "Sambation"—a river flowing with rocks and sand that stopped running every Sabbath, and from beyond which the lost tribes would return to join their Jewish brethren in the days of the Messiah.

Throughout the centuries, Jewish and Christian writers and travelers were intrigued by the legend of the lost tribes. In the Middle Ages, the most famous case was the traveler Eldad ha-Dani (ninth century) who claimed that he hailed from the tribe of Dan, now living in Ethiopia, and who told of other tribes living in Africa, Arabia, and Asia.

The fascination with the myth of the ten tribes grew in the early modern age—the era of European discoveries. As Europeans encountered new and unknown lands and peoples to the east and west, and in particular following the European arrival in the Americas in 1492, the legend of the ten tribes became a favorite model to explain hitherto completely unknown cultures and to link foreign peoples to something familiar. The Christian Venetian traveler Marco Polo (d. 1324), for example, reported that Jewish kingdoms existed in the distant Orient. In 1644, Aaron Levi de Montezinos (d. ca. 1650), a converso, returned to Amsterdam from South America and claimed that he had been greeted by a group of natives in Ecuador with the *Shema Israel* prayer. One of the most prominent Sephardi rabbis in Amsterdam at the time, Menasseh ben Israel, published a treatise, first in Spanish and then in Latin and English translations, under the title *The Hope of Israel*. In this book, he reported on Montezinos' findings and argued that these native Americans were descendants of the lost tribes and that their discovery hailed the dawn of messianic times. The age of discovery spawned many such accounts among both Jewish and Christian observers. Exotic lands were identified with the mythical kingdom of the ten tribes and numerous peoples—from the English to native Americans to the Japanese and the Pashtuns of Afghanistan—were at some point believed to be descendants of the lost tribes.

In the middle of the sixteenth century, David Reuveni (d. ca. 1538) aroused messianic hopes when he claimed the he hailed from the kingdom of the lost tribes and that he had been sent to forge an alliance to fight the Ottoman Turks and hasten redemption. Reuveni was received by Pope Clement VII, and his subsequent visit to the king of Portugal (1525–1527) generated much excitement and messianic hopes among the conversos of that country. One of them, Diogo Pires (d. 1532), secretary in the council of the Portuguese king, was so taken with Reuveni's claims that he decided to return to Judaism, circumcised himself, and adopted the name Solomon Molho. He made his way to the Ottoman Empire, where he studied with several renowned Kabbalists and eventually came to believe that he was the Messiah. Even though he was sought by the Inquisition as a renegade converso, Molho went to Italy, where he made a huge impression on the pope who was awed by his prophetic predictions of a flood in Rome and an earthquake in Portugal. Reuveni and Molho met their end when they met up to visit the Holy Roman Emperor Charles V to convince him of their messianic mission and the impending intervention of the ten lost tribes in the final struggle before redemption.

The myth of the lost tribes and the emergence of prophetic–messianic figures such as Reuveni and Molho were signs of the upheavals of the early modern era as an era of discovery and acute messianic expectations among Jews and Christians alike. The myth of the lost tribes helped early modern Jews, and Christians, to understand the changing world around them—to insert the exotic features of a new world into the familiar patterns of biblical history and prophecy.

Jews, but in general their unique fusion of Jewish and Iberian culture was still a rather conservative one.

In certain ways, the new Sephardi–Portuguese communities in England and in the New World were a more radical example of those trends of modernity that we see in Amsterdam. Jews had been expelled from **England** in 1290 by Edward I. In the 1630s, a number of converso merchants established themselves in England, where they continued to live as Christians.

As radical Protestant puritans advocated for a return of Jews to England—believing that England had an important role to play in the conversion of the Jews who would be attracted finally to Christianity in its "purified" Protestant form, as opposed to Catholicism—Menasseh ben Israel, an Amsterdam rabbi, likewise began to labor for a return of Jews to England. He believed that prior to the final redemption the prophecy had to be fulfilled that Jews would be scattered "from one end of the earth to the other" (Deuteronomy 28:64), and it was England that still had no Jewish community and was known in medieval Jewish writings as *katseh ha-arets,* "the end of the earth." (*See box,* The Lost Tribes of Israel.)

In 1655, Menasseh ben Israel headed to London with a pamphlet he had written in praise of Jewish virtues and their beneficial impact on the economy and in refutation of several common antisemitic accusations. He wanted to convince Oliver Cromwell (d. 1658), Lord Protector of the English commonwealth, to readmit the Jews to England. Though Cromwell favored this move, he convened an assembly—known as the Whitehall Conference—of merchants, lawyers, and clergy to discuss the proposal. Due to the opposition of the most conservative clergy and the merchants, fearing a new rival in Jewish commercial networks, the proposal failed. However, as England went to war with Spain in 1655, a number of conversos who were still subjects of the Spanish Crown found it expedient to dissociate themselves from England's wartime foe and commercial rival and began to present themselves in public as refugees from Spanish persecution—and as Jews. Their request for permission to gather privately for Jewish worship and for a Jewish burial place was granted by the government and thus, without much fanfare and without a formal charter allowing the Jews to return to England, the first Jewish community of modern England was born.

This **London** community, which attracted more former conversos and eventually other Jews from abroad, was among the first communities established on an entirely voluntary basis. As such, it lacked the disciplinary authority and the legal autonomy of the traditional Jewish community, which was the basis for Jewish life almost everywhere else at the time. In this sense, as in the relative lack of religious observance and the continuing ambiguity of many of these former conversos vis-à-vis rabbinic tradition, the London community, like the new communities established in the European colonies of the New World, anticipated much of what became a cornerstone of the modern Jewish experience. As historian Todd Endelman has argued, "What bound the community [of London] together in its first half century or so was less an allegiance to Jewish practice than kinship, a shared past, and a common language and cultural outlook" (Todd Endelman, *The Jews of Britain: 1656 to 2000,* Berkeley: University of California Press, 2002, p. 34). At the same time, it was ironic that the failure to adopt a formal charter to readmit the Jews at the Whitehall Conference opened a new and much less torturous path toward emancipation for English Jewry later, as they had never been subject to a formal set of laws defining, and restricting, their legal status.

The first Jews to establish a permanent presence in North America arrived in September 1654 in what was then the Dutch colony of **New Amsterdam**—a city that later, after the English took control in 1664, was renamed **New York.** These twenty-three Jewish immigrants arrived from northern Brazil, where they had settled when the area was a Dutch colony. With the Portuguese defeat of the Dutch in 1654, the Jews—many of whom were former conversos who had returned to Judaism once they were beyond the reach of the Inquisition—had to abandon the colony. Most found a new home elsewhere in the Caribbean or went back to Holland, but a small number ventured farther north.

Most of the new arrivals were Sephardi Jews of Spanish and Portuguese descent, and throughout the seventeenth and eighteenth centuries all American synagogues followed the Sephardi rite and traditions. However, even among the first Jewish immigrants in 1654 were a number of Ashkenazi Jews who were joined, in the course of the following decades, by more Ashkenazi immigrants. They eventually came to represent the majority of American Jewry, yet continued to be integrated into the existing Sephardi congregations. In fact, the establishment of a joint Sephardi–Ashkenazi Jewish community in New York and elsewhere in colonial North America was different from the practice in most European cities, where members of the two major Jewish groups maintained separate synagogues and avoided mingling with each other.

The initial welcome in Dutch New Amsterdam was frosty; the governor, Peter Stuyvesant, tried to have the Jews removed from his colony but had to give in to the Dutch West India Company, which had decided that the Jews were to be tolerated. The trading company did so in part under the influence of the prosperous Jewish community back in Amsterdam, but more so because of merely pragmatic considerations that were to guide both the Dutch and English colonial authorities in their policy toward the Jews: Whatever was good for the colony's wealth trumped traditional religious hostility against the Jews. Seeing as assets the Jews' family and commercial ties that spanned the Atlantic world—especially those of the Sephardim—the English chose to be more tolerant toward the Jews in their colonies than they were in England. The naturalization law for the colonies of 1740 opened naturalization to all Protestants and Jews residing at least seven years in the colonies, creating a legal status for the Jews that they would not enjoy anywhere in Europe until at least fifty years later.

By the eve of the American Revolution, five Jewish communities had been established in North America, all on the Atlantic seaboard and connected in numerous ways with communities in the Caribbean and Europe; In addition to New York, Jews had established communities and synagogues in Philadelphia, Newport, Charleston, and Savannah. The numbers throughout the colonial period remained fairly low (about 100 in New York in 1695, rising to slightly over 240 in 1771), but the Jews had established the basis for what would become in due course the largest Jewish community of the modern world.

Waare afbeeldinge van Sabetha Sebi *den genaemden*
herfteller des Joodtfchen Rijcks.
ij pourtrait de Sabbathai Sevi *qui fe dict Restaura :*
teur du Royaume de Juda & Jfrael.

Shabbatai Zvi (1626–1676), the Messiah of Izmir. Zvi's appearance as the "Messiah" in 1665 generated excitement throughout the Jewish world. The episode effectively ended with his conversion to Islam after the Ottoman authorities grew weary of the phenomenon.

Shabbatai Zvi: A Jewish Messiah Converts to Islam

A startling episode of messianic excitement rocked the Jewish world in the second half of the seventeenth century: In 1665, **Shabbatai Zvi** (1626–1676) of the Turkish port city of Izmir was revealed as the Messiah by a young Jewish mystic, **Nathan of Gaza** (1643–1680). He was not the only false messiah of the early modern age, but his movement was certainly the most successful one, his followers coming from all walks of Jewish society almost everywhere in the Jewish Diaspora.

Shabbatai Zvi, described as manic-depressive by modern scholars, reputedly engaged in a variety of "strange" and "bizarre" acts defying Jewish tradition when he was in Izmir, notably pronouncing the divine name in public (traditionally only the High Priest had been allowed to pronounce the name once a year, on the Day of Atonement, in the holiest part of the Jerusalem Temple). Zvi was married twice, but each time the union had to be annulled because he failed to consummate the marriage. Expelled from Izmir by the community in the early 1650s, he began to wander through Ottoman Greece. During periods of exaltation, Zvi continued to engage in "strange" behavior—for example, when he celebrated the three major festivals of Passover, Shavuot, and Sukkot all in one week. At times, Zvi claimed to be the messiah and announced that the divine commandments had been abolished, introducing the ironic blessing of "Him [God] who permits the forbidden."

In 1662, Zvi settled in Jerusalem, and a year later he was sent by the Jerusalem community on a fund-raising mission to Egypt. There he was married to Sarah, an Ashkenazi girl orphaned during the massacres in the Ukraine in 1648. Raised by Christians, she had returned to Judaism and lived in Amsterdam before the moved to Livorno, Italy. Sarah—whose reputation for promiscuity only added to the scandal—had repeatedly declared that she would marry the Messiah. In 1665, Zvi visited Nathan of Gaza, a Jewish mystic of the Lurianic school, who claimed to have prophetic visions. When Nathan fell into a trance during Shavuot of that year, he publicly declared that Zvi was the Messiah, the latter now reassured in his mission.

Word that Zvi was the Messiah spread like wildfire through the Jewish communities of the Ottoman Empire, the Sephardi communities of western Europe, and throughout Italy, North Africa, and eastern Europe. Though primarily the networks linking the communities of the Sephardi Diaspora disseminated information about the Sabbatian movement, Ashkenazi Jews were likewise drawn into the excitement. Some sources claim that it had been the prophecy of Sarah, predicting her future marriage to the Messiah, that contributed to the spread of Sabbatian beliefs among Ashkenazi Jews.

Glickl of Hameln (1646–1724), in her famous seventeenth-century memoir, describes the response to the news about Shabbatai Zvi in Hamburg:

> About this time people began to talk of Shabbatai Zvi. . . . Our joy, when the letters arrived [bringing news about Shabbatai Zvi] is not to be told. Most of them were addressed to the Sephardim who, as fast as they came, took them to their synagogue and read them aloud; young and old, the German [Jews] too hastened to the Sephardic synagogue. The Sephardic youth came dressed in their best finery and decked in broad green

silk ribbons, the gear of Shabbatai Zvi. "With timbrels and with dances" [Exodus 15:20] they one and all trooped to the synagogue. . . . Many sold their houses and lands and all their possessions, for any day they hoped to be redeemed. My good father-in-law left his home in Hameln, abandoned his house and lands and all his goodly furniture . . . for the old man expected to sail any moment from Hamburg to the Holy Land. (*The Memoirs of Glückel of Hameln,* trans. Marvin Lowenthal, New York: Schocken Books, 1977, 45.)

On December 12, 1665, a memorable Sabbath in his hometown of Izmir, after reciting morning prayers in one synagogue, Zvi marched to the Portuguese synagogue accompanied by a large crowd. After beginning to smash the door with an ax, he was finally admitted. Historian Gershom Scholem describes the remarkable scene that followed:

> Shabbetai Zevi [sic] read the portion of the Torah not from the customary scroll but from a printed copy; ignoring the priests and levites present, he called up to the reading of the Law his brothers and many other men and women [a major innovation, of course, as women were traditionally not actively involved in the public synagogue service], distributing kingdoms to them and demanding that all of them pronounce the Ineffable Name [of God] in their blessings. In a furious speech against the unbelieving rabbis, he compared them to the unclean animals mentioned in the Bible. . . . Then he went up to the ark, took a holy scroll in his arms, and sang an ancient Castilian love song about "Meliselda, the emperor's daughter"; into this song, known as his favorite throughout his life, he read many kabbalistic mysteries. After explaining them to the congregation, he ceremonially proclaimed himself . . . the redeemer of Israel, fixing the date of redemption for the 15th of Sivan 5426 (June 18, 1666). . . . Shabbetai Zevi announced that in a short time he would seize the crown of "the great Turk" [i.e., the Ottoman sultan]. When Hayyim Benveniste, one of the dissenting rabbis present, asked him for proof of his mission, he flew into a rage and excommunicated him, at the same time calling on some of those present to testify to their faith by uttering the Ineffable Name. The dramatic scene amounted to a public messianic announcement and the substitution of a messianic Judaism for the traditional and imperfect one. . . . Besides other innovations in the law, he promised the women that he would set them free from the curse of Eve. Immediately after this Sabbath he dispatched one of his rabbinical followers to Constantinople to make

preparations for his arrival." (Gershom Scholem, "Shabbatai Zevi," in *Encyclopedia Judaica,* ed. Michael Berenbaum and Fred Skolnik, Detroit: Macmillan, 2007, pp. 344–345.)

Zvi was arrested by the Ottoman authorities on his way to the imperial capital, Istanbul, in February 1666. Though imprisoned, he was treated with leniency and transferred to the fortress of Gallipoli, which held important political prisoners. Zvi's detention by no means diminished messianic excitement throughout the Jewish Diaspora. Numerous people from near and far came as pilgrims to visit Zvi. The rabbinate, both in the Ottoman Empire and abroad, continued to be divided between supporters and opponents of the messianic movement, and news about the Messiah continued to be exchanged by both sides with great speed. The excitement reached its height in July and August, but in September the Ottoman authorities grew weary of the messianic agitation and Zvi was brought to Edirne. There, in the presence of the sultan, he was given the choice between facing death or converting to Islam. Throwing his many followers into a profound crisis, Zvi chose to embrace Islam.

Zvi's conversion spelled the end of the Sabbatian movement as a mass phenomenon. Many individuals, including some leading rabbis, however, continued to believe in his messianic mission, interpreting his apostasy as part of the process leading to redemption. Several hundred of his adherents in Salonika even followed his example and converted to Islam, forming a Muslim–Sabbatian sect known as the ***dönme,*** remnants of which exist in Turkey to this very day.

The success of the Sabbatian movement can be explained by a convergence of several trends of early modern Jewish history: the messianism of the former conversos in western Europe; the impact of the Chmielnicki massacres and influx of Jewish refugees from eastern Europe into western European and Ottoman communities, creating a sense of crisis and promoting messianic expectations; the consequences of print, making possible the fast exchange of information on an unprecedented scale; the impact of Lurianic Kabbalah on an elite of rabbis, many of whom supported the false messiah; and a critique of established rabbinic tradition that was pronounced elsewhere as well and found its expression in Shabbatai Zvi's open challenge of traditional rabbinic law.

Questions for Reflection

1. What was the relation between the Jews and the Polish nobility? How did this affect the relations between Jews and their Christian neighbors in Poland–Lithuania?
2. Why have historians described the impact of printing as a revolution? What was the impact of printing on Jewish culture? Would you call these changes revolutionary, and why?
3. What made the Jewish community of Amsterdam unique and different from Jewish communities of earlier times or other places?
4. Who do you think were the most important agents of "modernity" and change in Jewish society during this period, and why?
5. Why do you think Shabbatai Zvi, the false messiah, was so successful at first? What developments of the preceding two centuries would have made Jews receptive to his messianic message?

For Further Reading

On Ashkenazi Jewry of the period, see Jacob Katz, *Tradition and Crisis*, Syracuse: Syracuse University Press, 2000.

On Poland–Lithuania, see Bernard Weinryb, *The Jews of Poland,* Philadelphia: Jewish Publication Society, 1972; Gershon Hundert, *Jews in Poland-Lithuania in the Eighteenth Century*, Berkeley: University of California Press, 2006; Edward Fram, *Ideals Face Reality: Jewish Law and Life in Poland, 1550–1655*, Cincinnati: Hebrew Union College Press, 1997. Look also for the volumes of the series *Polin,* published by the Littman Library of Jewish Civilization.

On early modern Germany, see Michael Meyer, ed., *German-Jewish History in Modern Times*, vol. 1, New York: Columbia University Press, 1996; R. Po-Chia Hsia and Hartmut Lehmann, eds., *In and Out of the Ghetto,* Cambridge, England: Cambridge University Press, 1995.

On Amsterdam and Atlantic World, see Miriam Bodian, *Hebrews of the Portuguese Nation,* Bloomington: Indiana University Press, 1999; Yosef Kaplan, *An Alternative Path to Modernity: The Sephardi Diaspora in Western Europe,* Leiden, The Netherlands: Brill, 2000; Daniel Swetschinski, *Reluctant Cosmopolitans: The Portuguese Jews of Seventeenth-Century Amsterdam,* Oxford, England: Littman, 2004; Mordechai Arbell, *The Jewish Nation of the Caribbean,* Jerusalem: Gefen Publishing, 2002.

On North America, see Eli Faber, *A Time for Planting: The First Migration, 1654–1820,* Baltimore, MD: Johns Hopkins University Press, 1992.

On Shabbatai Zvi, see, Gershom Scholem, *Sabbatai Sevi: The Mystical Messiah,* Princeton, NJ: Princeton University Press, 1973.

Chapter 10

The State of the Jews, The Jews and the State

In traditional Jewish fashion, we begin with a question: When does the modern period in Jewish history begin? The answer would seem to be self-evident: with the onset of modernity, of course. Modernity is something that we can generally define as the state of conscious recognition that the present is unique, original, and meaningfully different from previous eras. Of course, since time immemorial children and young adults have thought of their parents as old fashioned or stuck in their ways and have believed their age to be different from previous eras. But *modernity* is not merely a technical term for the ancient expression of youthful rebellion. While young people have always tended to seek out new fashions and experiment with new trends, the world most people inhabited until the eighteenth century was not too radically different from that which their parents and grandparents knew, even if offspring rebelled against their parents' wishes. While there were many periods of change in the past, including technological advancements and even the emergence of new social classes and the decline of others, social change was nonetheless slow and barely perceptible. The same holds true of the economic circumstances of human existence. Concentrating on Europe, economic historians have concluded that income for almost everyone remained stagnant and at about the same level from at least the year 1000 until the mid-nineteenth century.

Modernity, by contrast saw the rise of entirely new, clearly visible, cultural and intellectual sensibilities that were conditioned by tangible changes in the economic, political, and social environment. The kinds of changes we reference took place in Europe and include monumental historical developments, such as the Enlightenment, the rise of modern science, the decline of the aristocracy and absolute monarchy, and the emergence to political and economic power of the middle classes—

or bourgeoisie. They also include the beginnings of industrialization and the rise of the factory system, as well as large-scale migration from the countryside to the cities and the formation of distinctive urban sensibilities and lifestyles.

In the nineteenth century, both the bourgeois champions of free trade and the working classes that were the productive backbone of the capitalist order became highly politicized. Even the shrinking landed aristocracy emerged from the upheavals as a class with a new self-awareness and demanded and saw to it that it received political representation to protect its interests. To tap into the disparate hopes and frustrations of these groups, mass political parties emerged to represent them. For the first time, the issues that motivated the creation of these new political entities were debated in constitutional assemblies, legislative bodies, and parliaments. These institutions came into being either through revolution, internal reform, or a combination of both. For example, we see such developments in England in 1688 and 1830; the United States in 1776; France in 1789, 1830, 1848, and 1870; and Canada, Australia, and New Zealand in the second half of the nineteenth century. While the various forms of representative democracy still limited participation, excluding, among others, women, blacks, and aboriginal peoples, these developments nonetheless mark the increasing democratization of society.

All these political transformations of the social order were preceded by and to a large extent inspired by the intellectual revolution of the eighteenth century known as the **Enlightenment.** The leading figures of the Enlightenment—men such as the French *philosophes* Montesquieu, Rousseau, and Voltaire; the English economist Adam Smith; and the German philosopher Kant—proposed a refashioning of society based on reason, progress, faith in human ingenuity, and an abiding belief in the capacity of all people for improvement. Inspired by the scientific revolution of the seventeenth century and its inner logic and practice of close observation and experimentation, the *philosophes* rejected all truths based on tradition and religious authority, championing instead a world where individuals, exercising their natural right to liberty, created new economic, political, and social structures for the benefit of both individuals and the greater good. These ideas also gave rise to individualism, the self-conscious recognition that people have personal identities that, while shaped by the larger culture of which they are part, are nonetheless products of personal experience, of individual decisions and opportunities both taken and missed.

The emergence of Enlightenment thought and the liberal political and economic structures that followed in its wake throughout the course of the eighteenth and nineteenth centuries also saw the development of critiques of these rapid changes to traditional modes of existence. In Britain, conservative thinkers such as Edmund Burke advanced a political theory hostile to the French Revolution. In France, monarchists continued to resist the new Republic. Others began to reject the egalitarian ideology at the root of the Enlightenment and the French Revolution by claiming that historical development was determined by the relative superiority and inferiority of certain races. In the political realm, the French Revolution spawned collectivist ideologies, including nationalism, whose disintegrating passions ensured conflict based on ethnic, national, or linguistic identity, thereby again challenging the universalistic tendencies of the Enlightenment. Imperialism and colonialism further exacerbated nationalist chauvinism.

Romanticism, an artistic and intellectual movement that first emerged in the eighteenth century but that increased in appeal following Napoleon's defeat in 1815, further cemented particularism by stressing national difference based on the perception that various ethnic groups possessed certain instincts and drives based on language, history, folk culture, and race. In Germany, Karl Marx advanced a theory of history that predicted the abolition of private property and the bourgeoisie through proletarian revolution, which would eventually lead to the creation of a classless society. In Austria, the psychiatrist Sigmund Freud challenged what he regarded as the hypocrisy of the moralistic bourgeois order by pointing out the effects of irrational impulses and sexual urges that contributed to the formation of individual personalities.

Finally, those wishing the destruction of bourgeois society employed one of the key characteristics of the age—mass politics—to bring about their aims. By the twentieth century, Communism, Fascism, and Nazism had all become revolutionary systems of violence and oppression dedicated to the ruthless destruction of enemies, the decimation of parliamentary democracy, the abolition of freedom of expression, the eradication of individualism, the celebration of violence, and, in the case of Nazism, the promotion of racism. Modernity thus sees mighty historical forces as a tendency and a countertendency.

Modernity has left its trace on all groups, to greater and lesser degrees. For Jews, its impact has been acute. Many of the key markers of the modern age—urbanism, trade, literacy and numeracy, the acquisition of higher education—were developments that Jews pursued with great enthusiasm. Modernity has seen the rise of the professional with expertise in a specialized area of knowledge. In the modern period, in addition to commerce, notable areas of such expertise have been law, medicine, and journalism—known as the "liberal professions." Over the last two hundred years, Jews the world over have produced lawyers, doctors, scientists, journalists, entertainers, and businesspeople in numbers wildly disproportionate to their percentage of the population. Just as the word *doctor* became a term of opprobrium in post-expulsion Spain, for it was used as a euphemism for "Jew," the practice of the free professions in modern Europe likewise became synonymous with the Jews.

Similarly, for those who both celebrated and derided modern arts and entertainment, Jews were in the thick of producing them. From experimental modernist poetry with a small and rarified audience to the Hollywood blockbuster seen by millions, Jews have been central figures in the creation of modern culture. Finally, if the modern world has seen the emergence of groups espousing ideologies wishing to overturn contemporary society and remake it anew, Jews emerged as both expert revolutionaries and victims of revolution par excellence. Often, Jews found themselves at the center of those messianic and maniacal attempts to reinvent the world.

In large measure, the modern period in Jewish history is characterized by the dynamic of successful cultural, economic, and social integration on the one hand, and a backlash against those successes, producing social anxiety and hostility toward Jews, on the other. At the interstices of those opposing developments is an energizing and creative friction that serves as the motor of the modern Jewish experience. Even as Jews could not but bring with them into their encounter with modernity their ancient cultures, collective sentiments, indeed their psychology, their transformation since 1700 has been radical and total. Of course, the entire world has been demonstrably transformed over that same time as well. Mark Twain is reputed to have once remarked, "The Jews are just like everybody else, only more so." How that came to be the case is the story that follows.

Changing Boundaries in the Eighteenth Century

In 1700 the Jews of Europe were easily distinguishable from their non-Jewish neighbors. They dressed differently, ate and drank differently, spoke differently, and read and wrote (and even thought) from right to left. They were still governed by and within the structures of Jewish autonomy, a self-contained world that had begun to crack by the eighteenth century but still continued to serve Jews as it had since Roman times. *Kehillot,* autonomous communities, functioned on the basis of Jewish law and were served by a vast network of Jewish social welfare institutions and fraternities—***hevrot*** (sing. ***hevrah***)—that provided for their members from cradle to grave. The elementary school (*heder*) and the rabbinic academy (*yeshiva*) provided education for men in sacred sources and religious values and ensured the transmission of Jewish culture from one generation to the next. Jewish separateness, however, did not mean cultural insularity, as Jews shared the culture of their surroundings, even if they sometimes modified that culture to suit Jewish tastes and sensibilities. This also means that Jews were highly distinguishable from one another, for their dispersion endowed them with great inner diversity.

The overall feudal order in which such autonomous entities operated saw Jews occupy a place alongside, as opposed to inside, the dominant social order. In return for exorbitant taxes, Jews were accorded residence and occupational rights. Depending on where one lived, these came in the form of charters or letters of protection, and while they ensured Jewish well-being, Jews proved better able to develop vertical partnerships with those who issued them the charters than to make social connections with their immediate neighbors. This tendency often contributed to a further sense of Jewish separateness and vulnerability.

Jews also earned a living in ways that distinguished them from non-Jews, most of whom were peasants engaged in agricultural production. All over Europe, Jews suffered under the yoke of occupational restrictions and myriad taxes. In western Europe, nearly 90 percent were engaged in low-level commerce, generally earning a living from trading, artisanry, and peddling. Ascher Lehmann, who was born in 1769, was rather typical for the age. In his autobiography he tells us of the difficulties he encountered trying to earn a living when he departed from his hometown of Zeckendorf, Germany, to study in Prague, a distance of thirty-six miles. His parents were poor and sent him off with a mere five gulden, knowing that he would be assisted along the way by fellow Jews. Jewish society had developed a system to take care of itinerant travelers

and students. Destitute, Ascher obtained a *blett,* which was a billet or coupon that entitled him to food and lodging from Jews along the way. "I accepted the first *blett,* and it turned out to be as good as the man had said. One has to spend money not only for food, but in every town and borough I had to pay 10, 12, and even 18 kreuzers as a poll tax." It was expensive to be a Jew: Town entrance taxes, poll taxes, Jewish community taxes all cut deeply into meager livelihoods. Arriving at the small town of Eger on a Friday afternoon Ascher went to the synagogue and was in turn invited back to the home of a well-to-do congregant. "And he had a table the likes of which I've never seen again in all my days: a long dining room, in front of every person two large silver candelabra, each with eight branches, for every person two silver plates, for soup and roast, everything made of silver, several forks and spoons. It was the same with the food; there were all kinds of dishes, and on *Schabbes* afternoon, too, there were double portions of *kugel* [pudding] made with *lokschen* [noodles], and with the very best fruit, fruit of every kind." Ascher soon had to leave, and needing to earn a living, he took on a number of odd jobs, tutoring commissions, and eventually turned to peddling which "was not restricted in those days . . . [but] when I came to the acquaintances of my father and offered my wares, with one voice the Catholic peasants, their wives and daughters said: 'Oh, you pretty fellow, what a pity you will go to hell and purgatory. Get yourself baptized!'" When he arrived at a Lutheran town, he wrote, "I couldn't sell a thing. One found villages with some forty to eighty peasants who didn't have a penny's worth of goods bought from a merchant in their houses. They wore nothing but what they had made themselves of wool or linen." The tolerant spirit advocated in Enlightenment tracts had yet to make itself felt in the German countryside. There the Jew, though familiar to all, remained an alien figure (*see box, Friedrich Wilhelm I of Prussia and the Jews*).

There was an important exception to the social marginalization of the Jews in eighteenth-century Central Europe. Among the well-to-do, there was increasing fraternization among Jews and non-Jews. Deep friendships, platonic relationships, and romances characterized a new form of Christian–Jewish contact. Love matches and personal ambition also led to conversions. In the opening decades of the century, the majority of the apostates were to be found among the Sephardic communities of western Europe. By the end of the eighteenth century and into the opening decades of the nineteenth century, the majority of converts were to be found in Germany.

In central Europe, many of these conversions were undertaken out of frustration with continued anti-Jewish discrimination. In Berlin in particular, converts tended to come

FRIEDRICH WILHELM I OF PRUSSIA AND THE JEWS

Friedrich Wilhelm I, who reigned from 1713–1740, was ill disposed toward Jews, especially poor ones. As with his predecessors, he extracted large sums from Jews for the privilege of living in his domains by selling them expensive Letters of Protection. Not long after Friedrich Wilhelm ascended the throne, he sought to limit the number of Jews in his kingdom by charging those with more than one child exorbitant sums for residence permits. A second child cost 1,000 talers and a third child 2,000 talers. Beyond this, he imposed on Jews marriage, birth, death, divorce, travel, and occupational taxes; a special tax for his coronation; and in 1714, a tax to avoid having to carry a red hat while in Berlin. An edict of October 26, 1719, stipulated which gates foreign Jews had to use to enter Berlin, and on November 13, 1719, another edict forbade Jewish beggars from entering Prussia altogether. In 1725, the Berlin Jewish community had to contribute 7,000 talers to the building of a church in nearby Potsdam. An edict of 1727 prohibited Jews from selling goods made of spun wool. In 1728, Jews were required to pay taxes and fees collectively instead of on an individual basis. The cost of Letters of Protection alone was raised to 15,000 talers for all of Prussia. The 1728 tax "reform" edict also prohibited Jews from trading in spices and working in most handicrafts, and it also stipulated that goods taken in by Jewish pawnbrokers could only be sold after a two-year wait. The various prohibitions against Jews increased their general poverty. Reduced to dealing in used clothes and bric-a-brac, as well as begging, the issue of the Jews' so-called "unproductive labor" became a major topic both of the emancipation debates and the Jewish Enlightenment, and even Zionism thereafter. All parties, seeing a link between occupation and character formation, sought to alter the economic and occupational structure of Jewish life to "regenerate" what was widely considered a "degenerate" Jewish existence.

The document pictured here is one of the scores of regularly published edicts in eighteenth-century Prussia that attempted to regulate the movement of Jews. Issued by Friedrich Wilhelm I on January 10, 1724, this edict declares "that all Jews who do not have a letter of passage must leave the country at once."

from among the wealthier Jews. In Germany, about 22,500 people converted throughout the course of the nineteenth century. In Berlin, between 1770 and 1830, nearly 1,600 Jews were baptized (according to the card-file of converted Jews compiled by the Nazis in the 1930s), over 1,200 of them in the first three decades of the nineteenth century. (In truth, at least 400 of Berlin's converted Jews were not Jewish according to halakhah, as their mothers were not Jews at the time they were born.) Many of those baptized were illegitimate children born to mixed Jewish–Christian couples. What is clear is that in the eighteenth century women were more frequently represented than men among Berlin's Jewish converts, which in turn led to a rise in the number of Jewish men who underwent baptism in the early nineteenth century. While the waves of conversions amounted to only about 27 people per year in Berlin, it nevertheless alarmed German Jewish leaders—they referred to it as a "baptism epidemic"—because among the converts were many distinguished names. By contrast, in Russia, where a significant number of conversions took place in the 1840s and 1850s, there was no panic about apostasy because those converting were already socially marginal.

Rahel Levin Varnhagen (1771–1833) was born into a wealthy, observant family in Berlin. A brilliant intellectual, she turned her home, as did a number of other Jewish women in Berlin and Vienna, into a literary salon. There, for the first time in the modern era, Jewish women facilitated a fascinating encounter. Into their homes they invited distinguished poets, authors, artists, philosophers, and political figures, Jews and non-Jews together in a spirit of friendship, religious harmony, and intellectual exchange. She had long lamented the fact that as a woman the gates to formal higher education were locked to her and that her Jewish co-religionists still had to enter cities through a separate Jews' gate. She confronted a double discrimination and described her whole life as a "slow bleeding to death." In 1819, to marry a minor Prussian diplomat, Varnhagen converted to Protestantism. On her deathbed, she confessed her sense of "how painful to have been born a Jewess . . .to which I can ascribe every evil, every misfortune, every vexation that has befallen me."

The sentiments of **Abraham Mendelssohn** (1776–1835), the son of the Berlin philosopher, Moses Mendelssohn, illustrate perfectly the deep anxiety of communal leaders. Abraham and his wife raised their two children as Protestants so that greater social opportunities would be opened to them. The fact that Moses was unable to impart to his son his belief that emancipation was not worth abandoning Judaism for indicates the highly personalized and idiosyncratic accommodation Moses Mendelssohn made with modernity. In a letter Abraham wrote to his daughter upon her confirmation into the Lutheran

church in the summer of 1820, one can detect that he was first and foremost convinced of the efficacy of conversion. The fact that he also viewed Christianity as a religion that preached decency, accorded with his humanitarian spirit: "We have educated you and your brothers and sister in the Christian faith, because it is the creed of most civilized people, and contains nothing that can lead you away from what is good, and much that guides you to love, obedience, tolerance, and resignation." Two years later Abraham and his wife converted to the Lutheran faith. While the majority of Jews remained within the fold, in the era of emancipation, social pressures and seductions led a small but nonetheless influential cohort of upper-class Jews in Germany to abandon Judaism.

In France, prior to the revolution of 1789, about 3,500 Sephardim, mostly merchants, resided in the south and southwest of the country. They were involved in international trade, had a solid and far-flung network of fellow Sephardic merchants with whom they dealt, and operated a guild structure not dissimilar from that of their non-Jewish counterparts in the cities of southwest France. They were also, to a great extent, well acculturated in terms of language, dress, and overall deportment. However, the bulk of the French Jewish population was the approximately 30,000 Ashkenazim who lived in the northeastern region of Alsace-Lorraine. They were wholly unlike the Sephardim of Bordeaux and Bayonne. The chief economic activities of this traditional, Yiddish-speaking community were petty trade and moneylending. With great linguistic, cultural, religious, and economic differences in relation to their peasant neighbors, Alsatian Jews in some way typified the radically distinctive character of a Jewish community on the eve of the French Revolution.

By the middle of the eighteenth century, as many as 8,000 Jews were in England, about 6,000 of them Ashkenazi immigrants who had come to Britain from the Continent to join the previously established Spanish and Portuguese Jews. Between 1750 and 1815, a further 8,000 to 10,000 Jews arrived. These two waves of Ashkenazi settlers, mostly from Germany, Holland, and Poland, formed the basis for the modern Jewish community of Britain. (A modest number of Sephardim fleeing the Inquisition's renewed persecution in Spain and Portugal between 1720 and 1735 also contributed to the growth of the Jewish community.) Once in England, the new immigrants, both Sephardim and Ashkenazim, joined the Jews of London and earned a living from selling a wide array of goods, ranging from oranges and lemons to watches and belt buckles. In particular, Jews became identified with hawking their trade in secondhand items, especially used clothing. Their calling out to prospective customers and aggressively pursuing them—competition was extremely tight—was a common cause of Christian complaint. London alone had hundreds of such Jewish merchants. The sight and sound of Jews, unfamiliar with the English language, calling out to Christian customers and dealing in goods that often came from dubious provenance heightened the perception of Jewish otherness. This same scene played out all over the Continent.

The Jewish urge to emigrate developed because with the exception of the handful of Jewish families in each country that can be classified as having been wealthy, the vast majority of eighteenth-century Jews were impoverished. Germany alone had nearly 10,000 Jews who were classified as *Betteljuden* ("beggar Jews"). In Holland, the material success enjoyed by the Sephardic community in the seventeenth century suffered reverses in the eighteenth with the closing of the United East India Company and the overall decline in Dutch trade. By 1799, the situation had gotten so bad that 54 percent of Dutch Sephardim lived off assistance from the Jewish community. Things were even more dire among the Ashkenazim, the vast majority of whom earned a living as peddlers of secondhand clothes, butchers, cattle dealers, and purveyors of various foodstuffs. None of this was sufficient to provide an adequate means of support, and at the close of the eighteenth century a staggering 80 percent of Ashkenazim in Holland received welfare.

Sephardic Jews in the Ottoman Empire hardly fared any better, and they too experienced significant economic decline by the end of the eighteenth century. Prior to this time, however, fundamental changes in world trade resulted in an increasing share of international shipping going to Dutch, English, and French fleets in the Atlantic. Balkan trade routes and the Jews who were so heavily involved in the commerce that went through them became increasingly marginalized. As Jews were global traders and merchants, a downturn in one area could have a far-flung impact elsewhere. In Greece, the Salonikan textile industry, which was largely in Jewish hands and was a major source of income for Balkan Jews, went into severe decline, impoverishing many of the city's 30,000 Jews and those in communities far from Salonika itself. Arbitrary taxation, epidemics, the competitive rise of Greek and Armenian merchants, the inability of Jewish merchants to adapt and develop new economic strategies, as well as the overall decline of the Ottoman Empire exacerbated the increasing impoverishment of Ottoman Jewish communities.

In Italy too the economic situation of the Jews was perilous. There, Jewish communities such as Venice and Rome saw their Jewish populations shrink by about half throughout the course of the eighteenth century. Between 1700 and 1766, the Jewish community in Venice fell to about 1,700, while that in Rome dwindled to 3,000 by 1800. Other communities such as Mantua, Verona, and Padua merely stagnated. At the same time that Jewish poverty and demographic decline deepened, economic theories of wealth and poverty shifted, from one based on mercantilism, with its emphasis on the accumulation of capital and government protectionism, to one based on physiocracy, the economic idea that national wealth and productivity derived primarily from agriculture. This shift away from trade and toward domestic self-sufficiency would have an important impact on the way European social commentators viewed Jews and their participation in the economy. In the context of the new economic theory, Jewish poverty was seen as symptomatic of deeper moral inadequacies, thus making the physiocratic critique of trade that much more potent.

Aside from religious differences, Jewish poverty and its supposed links to criminality created an impression of the Jews as outside the bounds of respectable society. In his *Discourse on the Diseases of Workers* (1700), the Italian physician Bernadino Ramazzini observed that the Jews, who were involved in tailoring, mattress restoration, and selling old linen and canvas for the manufacture of paper, "are a lazy race, but active in business." He complained that "they do not plough, harrow, or sow" and wryly added "but they always reap." In England, both Jewish and Christian dealers in secondhand goods became infamous for purchasing stolen wares, and Jews became linked to various kinds of criminal activity, such as passing counterfeit coins, pickpocketing, shoplifting, burglary, stealing from carts and warehouses, assault, robbery, and even murder, as was the case in 1771 when nine London Jews broke into a premises in Chelsea with intent to rob and shot dead the servant of the house. And in Germany, where Jews were largely restricted to pawnbroking and trade in secondhand clothes and other used items, they came into contact with members of the underworld and joined them in criminal activity. Some Jews formed bands of highway robbers, holding up stagecoaches in daring armed robberies. Other bands, with names such as the "Long Hoyum" and the "Great Dutch," specialized in commercial and residential burglaries. Jewish bands tended to be almost entirely male (sometimes women could be found among Christian bands) and religiously observant, and the bandits continued to live in Jewish communities. Still other bands were composed of Christians and Jews. Significantly, prior to emancipation (and for quite sometime thereafter) these robber bands were among the first venues outside of relationships in elite circles where religious difference was not a hindrance to genuine Christian–Jewish social interaction.

In the largest Jewish community in the world, that of Poland–Lithuania, the situation was quite different. By the eighteenth century the Jewish population was 750,000 (550,000 in Poland and 200,000 in Lithuania). Since the Middle Ages, Jews had been encouraged to settle and trade there, while others took refuge in Poland in times of distress. After the Jews were expelled from the German city of Braunschweig in 1546, Eliezer Eilburg, a rabbi and medical practitioner, arrived in the Polish city of Poznan and declared it to be a place "where the Jews live in safety, each one under his vine and his fig tree, and there is none to make them fearful." In 1565 a visiting papal diplomat was astonished to observe that Jews "possess land, engage in commerce, and devote themselves to study, especially medicine and astrology. . . .They possess considerable wealth and they are not only among the respectable citizens, but occasionally even dominate them. They wear no special mark to distinguish them from Christians and are even permitted to wear the sword and to go about armed. In general, they enjoy equal rights." While it is unclear what the Vatican's man meant by "equal rights," Jews agreed that their situation was good. The eighteenth-century mystic Pinhas of Korets expressed the widely shared view among Jews that "in Poland exile is less bitter than anywhere else."

Indeed, the kinds of residential and occupational restrictions and humiliating distinctions that were the lot of western European Jews were largely unknown or unenforceable in premodern Poland, particularly in the areas of greatest Jewish settlement. Jews lived all over but especially in the densely Jewish urban centers of the east and south. In those places, Jews lived among Christians and not separate from them, exhibiting a preference, however, for living directly on or very near the market square, a sign of their deep involvement in the economic life of Poland. Up to 75 percent of all Polish–Lithuanian Jews lived in cities, towns, and villages owned by aristocrat–magnates, whose estates were the backbone of the economy. (By contrast, in lands held by the Crown residential and occupational restrictions were in force, while lands owned by the Church sought to exclude Jews altogether. Catholic clergymen often expressed opposition to Jews living in marketplaces because they tended to be where Church processions took place.) Fear that Jews would leave due to mistreatment or in search of better conditions elsewhere meant that the owners of the private towns where most Jews lived encouraged toleration, often in defiance of the wishes of the local Christian residents who resented Jewish competition. Magnates protected the welfare and security of the Jews in return for their managerial and financial skills. Thus, Jews enjoyed an important measure of power and protection from arbitrary abuse.

The central role of Jews in the magnate economy can be measured by the fact that Jews comprised between 80 and 90 percent of merchants in many Polish towns, often making them the only inhabitants involved in commercial activities. Up to 60 percent of all domestic trade was in Jewish hands. In the area of international trade, Jews were likewise prominent. By 1775 the ratio of Polish Jewish merchants to Polish Christian merchants attending the international commercial fairs in Leipzig was 7 to 1. The Jewish merchants exported furs, skins, textiles, and metal goods. (Into the twentieth century, these would remain traditional items of trade among Jews the world over). They worked as jewelers, haberdashers, tailors, butchers, bakers, and bookbinders. At the beginning of the eighteenth century one Christian municipality complained that instead of confining their commerce to their own street, as they were obliged to by law, Jews "brew beer and mead, sell wine, grain, fish, salt, candles, meat, etc., in our marketplace. They even sell pork, which they do not eat." The diversified nature of the Polish Jewish economy stood in marked contrast to that of western European Jews, who tended to earn a living exclusively through petty trade or commerce.

Unlike their co-religionists in western Europe, the Jews of Poland were more closely tied to the rural economy, trading in agricultural goods, between estates and local markets, where they were suppliers to villages and managers of the great estates. While many dealt in luxury goods prized by the nobility, such as gold, silver, gemstones, and furs, the unique feature of the Polish Jewish economy was the *arenda* system. This involved the leasing of large estates by Polish lords to Jews who, in return for paying rent to the nobleman, were granted the monopoly on a host of commodities and means of raising revenue. Jewish lessees earned income from tax and toll collection and sales of grain (often to court Jews in Germany); salt; and grain-based alcohol, one of the most important sources of income for at least one-third of Poland's Jews in the eighteenth century. Vodka became as popular a drink among Polish commoners as beer, with income from sales of vodka on royal estates rising from 6.4 percent in 1661 to 40 percent after 1750.

Although the nobles retained most of the profits, the Jews were the ones most visibly associated with the alcohol trade. The Jewish innkeeper became a prominent figure in the region's social and cultural life. In his novel *The Slave,* the great twentieth-century Yiddish author Isaac Bashevis Singer described the Jewish *arrendar* (leaseholder) and his relation to the serfs, as it existed in Poland following the Chmielnicki massacres (1648–1650):

Josefov by day was a confusion of sounds: chopping, sawing; carts arriving from the villages with grain, vegetables, fire wood, lumber; horses neighing, cows bellowing; children chanting the alphabet, the Pentateuch,

JEWS AND BOXING IN GEORGIAN ENGLAND

The emergence in the eighteenth century of Jewish prizefighters is testimony to the class-character of the Jews in England. The greatest of these boxers was the champion, **Daniel Mendoza** (1763–1836), who proudly fought under the moniker "Mendoza the Jew." His story testifies to the nature of Anglo–Jewish integration and to the extent of Jewish particularism. Mendoza tells us in his memoirs that his parents, who "were by no means in affluent circumstances," sent him "at a very early age to a Jews' school," where he "was instructed in English grammar, writing, arithmetic. . . . I was also instructed in the Hebrew language, in which, before I quitted school, I made considerable progress."

Mendoza was a sports superstar, beloved by Jews and Gentiles alike. No Jew on the Continent could have expected to be embraced in this way by the public at large. In what was perhaps the earliest manifestation of sports merchandising, non-Jewish porcelain and crockery manufacturers produced commemorative pitchers and mugs bearing Mendoza's likeness. That Mendoza was a Jew and openly proud of it seemed to make little difference to the English public and certainly did not prevent him from occupying an important place in the popular culture of Georgian England. Songs were even composed about Mendoza and, in particular, the monumental battles he fought with his principal opponent, Richard Humphreys, whom Mendoza fought three times. One of these songs referred to the challenge Humphrey issued to Mendoza at the latter's boxing school and Mendoza's comprehensive victory when their third and final fight took place at the end of September 1790:

My Dicky he went to the school, that was kept by this Danny Mendoza,

And swore if the Jew would not fight, he would ring his Mosaical nose, Sir,

His friends exclaimed, go-it, my Dicky, my terrible, give him a derry;

You've only to sport your position, and quickly the Levite will sherry.

Elate with false pride and conceit, superciliously prone to his ruin,

He haughtily stalk'd on the spot, which was turf'd for his utter undoing;

While the Jew's humble bow seem'd to please, my Dicky's eyes flash'd vivid fire;

He contemptuously viewed his opponent, as David was viewed by Goliath.

Now Fortune, the whimsical goddess, resolving to open men's eyes;

To draw from their senses the screen, and excite just contempt and surprise,

Produced to their view, this great hero, who promis'd Mendoza to beat,

When he proved but a boasting imposter, his promises all a mere cheat.

the commentaries of Rashi, the Gemara. The same peasants who had helped Chmielnicki's butchers strip the Jewish homes now turned logs into lumber, split shingles, laid floors, built ovens, painted buildings. A Jew had opened a tavern where the peasants came to swill beer and vodka. The gentry, having blotted out the memory of the massacres, again leased their fields, woods, and mills to Jewish contractors. One has to do business with murderers and shake their hands in order to close a deal.

By the last third of the eighteenth century, the economic security of Polish Jewry started to deteriorate as the Polish aristocracy began to respond to calls to limit Jewish involvement in the alcohol trade. These demands often came from the lower (and sometimes impoverished) gentry, who saw themselves as competing with Jews for the favor and leases of the wealthy aristocratic landholders. In 1768, pressure from the Church and lower gentry led the *sejm,* the Polish parliament, to forbid Jews from keeping inns and taverns without the consent of municipal authorities. Though many estate

For Dicky, he stopt with his head,

Was hit through his guard ev'ry round, Sir,

Was fonder of falling than fighting,

And therefore gave out on the ground, Sir.

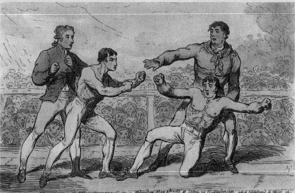

On May 6, 1789, Daniel Mendoza knocked out Richard Humphrey after thirty-five minutes. Mendoza, wanting to give Humphrey a sporting chance, allowed his opponent to rest for half an hour, only to resume the fight and knock him out again. This engraving by an unknown non-Jewish artist, bore the caption "The Christian Pugilist proving himself inferior to the Jewish Hero, as Dr. Priestly when oppos'd to the Rabbi David Levi." Levi had offered the natural philosopher and theologian Joseph Priestly a ringing and learned defense of Judaism. The comparison between Levi and Mendoza sees the boxer become the physical, as opposed to, spiritual defender of his people. In the popular nineteenth-century boxing magazine, *Boxiana*, Pierce Egan wrote in 1812 that Daniel Mendoza, "'though not the Jew that Shakespeare drew' yet he was that Jew, the acknowledged pride of his own particular persuasion."

owners ignored the legislation, Jewish involvement in the alcohol trade slowly began to decline.

In addition to the economic incentive to push Jews out of the liquor trade came the accusation that they deliberately sought to ply peasants with vodka to keep them drunk. This became a staple of eastern European antisemitic discourse, later compounded by expressions of political and national antagonism. Already by the start of the eighteenth century, Polish Jews were being painted as enemies, or at least as not being genuinely Polish because to be Polish was to be Catholic.

The superior economic condition and greater occupational diversity of Polish Jewry found its analogue in the political sphere. After 1550, Polish Jewry enjoyed the most elaborate form of communal autonomy to be found anywhere in Europe. A vast network was in place of voluntary associations to care for community members, artisan guilds to ensure economic welfare, as well as communal, local and regional assemblies. Above it all stood the Council of Four Lands (*Va'ad arba' aratsot*), effectively a Jewish national parliament. Meeting twice annually at the great fairs in Lublin and Jaroslaw, the council was composed of a lay assembly and a council of rabbis. These two bodies formed the two "houses" of parliament, with the lay leadership proposing various plans and measures to tackle particular problems, while the rabbis then formulated the corresponding legislation or edict in strict accordance with the demands of Jewish law. The principal issue that confronted the Council of Four Lands was the apportionment and collection of taxes owed by Jews to the Polish treasury. Generally, the Council calculated a figure and paid the government in one lump sum and then extracted sums from local communities. The nobility long complained that this was to their disadvantage, preferring instead a head tax. In 1764, the crisis of the Polish Crown saw the implementation of fiscal reforms, one of which was the dissolution of the Council of Four Lands.

The social and economic marginalization of central and western European Jewry at the dawn of the modern era should not, however, be mistaken for insularity. While Jews may have had very limited social contact with non-Jews, they were, as Jews had always been, intimately aware of dominant trends. Acculturation into contemporary mores long preceded the lifting of legal disabilities. In England, which had no real Jewish intellectual class to agitate for religious modernization, the process took root early, gradually, in a secular fashion, and perhaps more unself-consciously than in other places. Uniquely in England, the majority of Jews began to adopt the social conventions of the English poor, while on the Continent, Jews tended to imitate the fashions of the middle and upper classes. (*See box,* Jews and Boxing in Georgian England.)

On the periphery of the European Jewish world, English Jewry's modernization took place without open rebellion against communal leadership. Not so on the Continent, where communal authorities attempted to control Jewish participation in non-Jewish public culture. Take the case of the north German communities of Hamburg, Altona, and Wandsbeck. An ordinance issued by the Hamburg *kahal* (community board) in 1726 declared, "Jews of both sexes are prohibited from walking to public houses or inns, or from visiting bowling alleys, fencing schools, or comedies on the Sabbath and holidays. Women under no circumstance should attend the opera." Other ordinances castigated Jews for wearing the latest fashions from Paris, including the application of false beauty spots. Yet another warning sought to regulate the boisterous Jews of Hamburg in synagogue. There, things seem to have gotten out of control: "[It is forbidden] under penalty of 10 Reichsthaler, that on certain holidays, no one is allowed to shoot gunpowder or launch rockets in the synagogue. [They must]

also abstain from hitting and throwing, punishable by a fine of 4 Reichsthaler; therefore, everyone in the community is obligated to warn his children and servants that they should obey this order." Not only does this indicate the rowdiness of Jewish synagogue worship at the time but also that in this, the Baroque Age, where fireworks became a staple of European celebrations, Jews too incorporated them into their own religious festivities in imitation of their Christian neighbors.

The rabbis despaired of these trends, constantly complaining that they were losing their authority over a community that was regularly attending concerts, visiting bars, going to bowling alleys, wearing fashionable clothes, and embracing vernacular culture. In Venice, Rabbi Shmuel Aboab (1610–1694) not only warned against Jews attending the theatre but also against an initiative to open their own "theatres and circuses, establishments which turn kosher Jewish maidens into prostitutes." In Germany, Rabbi Jonathan Eybeschütz (1690–1764), passed a ruling that "The Israelites are to keep away from places of [ill-repute] or other places in which transgressions are a common habit, and more so from places known as Schauspiel [theatre], comedy, opera, and where plays are performed, since Our Sages of Blessed Memory said: sitteth not in the seat of the jesters, these are the houses of theatres, namely those places in which comedians entertain."

Indeed, inspired by their non-Jewish neighbors, Jewish participation in non-Jewish culture was increasingly in evidence prior to emancipation. It becomes all the more intriguing to consider that just as some Jews were clearly becoming more visibly European, eighteenth-century Christian thinkers began to consider the extent to which that process would succeed and even whether such a transformation was fully possible or even desirable.

Jews Through Jewish and Non-Jewish Eyes

When Europeans debated whether to award Jews civic equality and admit them to citizenship, discussions were often couched in ethnological and anthropological descriptions and assessments of Jews and Jewishness. Just who and what were the Jews? Could they become real Europeans? Opinion was mixed.

One of the most vivid descriptions of an eighteenth-century Jewish community comes from the German author Johann Wolfgang von Goethe (1749–1832), who ventured into the Frankfurt ghetto. The Judengasse, or Jews' Street, as the ghetto was called, was home to three thousand inhabitants and was one of the largest, poorest, and most densely packed

Jewish quarters in all of Europe. It was in these humble circumstances that the Rothschild family emerged. **Mayer Amschel Rothschild** (1743–1812), scion of the family, sent his sons to five European cities—Frankfurt, London, Paris, Vienna, and Naples—where they proceeded over the course of the nineteenth century to build the largest private banking house in the world and to amass a vast fortune. The Rothschild name had not yet become synonymous with modern capitalism and fabulous wealth when Goethe visited the Jewish quarter. The majority of Frankfurt's Jews were then simply very poor. In his autobiography, Goethe tells us that

> the confinement, the dirt, the swarm of people, the accents of an unpleasant tongue, all made a disagreeable impression, even when one only looked in when passing outside the gate. It took a long time before I ventured in alone; and I did not return easily after once escaping the obtrusiveness of so many people untiringly intent on haggling, either demanding or offering. . . . And yet, they were also human beings, active, obliging, and even in their obstinacy in sticking to their own customs, one could not deny them respect. One could not question the stubbornness with which they hung on their customs; one could not deny it respect.
>
> Besides this, the girls were pretty, and quite liked it if they encountered a Christian boy on the Fischerfelde on the Shabbat, who proved himself friendly and attentive. I was extremely curious to learn their ceremonies. I did not leave until I had repeatedly visited the school, attended a circumcision, a wedding, and the Laubhuettenfest [sukkot]. Everywhere I was welcomed, well entertained, and invited to return.

Goethe's amazement that the Jews were genuine "human beings" was not mere hyperbole. The accumulated impact of social and economic marginalization born of 1,700 years of Christian teaching—which portrayed the Jews as cruel and inhuman, responsible for the crucifixion of Jesus, doomed to eternal wandering, enjoined to murder Christian children to use their blood to bake matzah, and bent on cheating and extorting Christians—led Europeans, both learned and illiterate alike, to question the very humanity of the Jews and inspired attempts to find out what made them appear to be so fundamentally different from non-Jews.

In the eighteenth century, European expansion and the development of modern branches of science and the arts converged to help shape the way educated Europeans saw Jews. One of the fundamental principles of the Enlightenment was that all people were created equal. This notion, however, came under threat with the increasing contact white Europeans had

with other races as a result of slavery, imperialism, and the great voyages of discovery. The observation that human groups differed physically from one another could be translated into the spurious notion that humans could be lined up on a scale demarking racial superiority and inferiority.

In the eighteenth century, anthropologists and biologists initially concerned themselves with the task of human classification. As an ancient people and Europe's most visible non-Christian minority, Jews were observed by early anthropologists as though they were Europe's own aboriginals—primitive, separate, and threatening—as mere savages. Anthropologists were guided in their assessment of all races by the complex set of aesthetic values concerning human beauty and ugliness that came to the fore at this time. The classical ideal of beauty, as expressed by the ancients in their painting and sculpture, was the measure by which Europeans of the eighteenth and nineteenth centuries determined what was visually pleasing. Idealized images of supposedly "beautiful" races were juxtaposed with stereotypes of races perceived as "ugly." One of the most famous expressions of European aesthetic geography was the description offered by Johann Friedrich Blumenbach (1752–1840) of the Caucasian as the most handsome of all peoples. Blumenbach, a liberal thinker and the recognized founder of modern anthropology, described whites as follows: "I have taken the name of this variety from Mount Caucasus, both because its neighborhood, and especially its southern slope, produces the most beautiful race of men."

In 1795 Blumenbach observed that Jews were somewhat of an exception to the "rules" of nature. He held that differences in human appearance were conditioned by climate, and those qualities were susceptible to alteration when geographic relocation had occurred. "Unless I am mistaken," he wrote, "there are instances of peoples who after they have changed their localities and have migrated elsewhere, in the process of time have changed also their original form of countenance for a new one, peculiar to the new climate." The appearance of the Jews, however, proved exceptional. Their wide geographic dispersion notwithstanding, different environments had been unable to effect a change in Jewish appearance: "Above all, the nation of the Jews who, under every climate, remain the same as far as the fundamental configuration of [the] face goes, [are] remarkable for a racial character almost universal, which can be distinguished at the first glance even by those little skilled in physiognomy, although it is difficult to limit and express by words." Could it be true that all Europeans were subject to change except the Jews?

According to other thinkers, the inalterability of the Jews had to do with their peculiar biology. In 1812, a Dutch anatomist studying of the skull of a thirty-year-old Jewish man noted the peculiarly "large nasal bones," the "square chin," and the specifically Jewish "bony impressions on both sides of the lateral orbits." This, he argued, was due to the fact that "among Jews, the muscles primarily used for talking and laughing are of a kind entirely different from those of Christians." In 1812, the year the Jews were first emancipated in Prussia, the Berlin anthropologist Karl Asmund Rudolphi (1771–1832) remarked on the consistency of Jewish physical features, characteristics that set them apart from the European majority: "Under Julius Caesar [the Jews] were almost as deeply rooted in Rome as they are today in some states of Germany and in Poland, and in a word, have become indigenous. . . . [But] their form has not changed. Their color is here lighter, there darker, but their face, their skulls everywhere have a peculiar character."

It is in the context of these sentiments that we must understand Goethe's astonishment that not only were the Jews "human" but that their women were "pretty" as well. To be sure, behind this latter comment was Goethe's thrill of having entered into the "Oriental" world of the ghetto. Goethe was drawn to the exotic beauty of the Other. But more significant here than Goethe's visual seduction is the fact that his remarks are truly a departure from the norm. Most Christians had never thought about Jews in terms of beauty and humanity. Rather, Jews represented religious enemies and economic rivals. It even took Goethe a few attempts to overcome his reticence and to stay and observe the ghetto, and not run away, repulsed as he was by the sights and sounds of the Judengasse.

Certainly some Christians may have seen fashionably attired Jews at the theatre; some may even have shared the odd joke with them in the vernacular, but the majority of Christians saw Jews, prior to their emancipation, as impoverished, unintelligible, and unappealingly different. The French philosophe, Denis Diderot, spoke for many when he excoriated the Jews as an "angry and brutish people, vile and vulgar men, slaves worthy of the yoke [Talmudism] which [you] bear. . . . Go, take back your books and remove yourselves from me. [The Talmud] taught the Jews to steal the goods of Christians, to regard them as savage beasts, to push them over the precipice . . . to kill them with impunity and to utter every morning the most horrible imprecations against them." While Diderot may have been the most intolerant proponent of the so-called "Age of Toleration," it was his contemporary Voltaire who best summed up the ambiguity of the Enlightenment's attitude toward the Jews: "In short, they are a totally ignorant nation who have combined contemptible miserliness and the most revolting superstition with a violent hatred of all those nations which have tolerated them. Nevertheless, they should not be burned at the stake."

The source of Voltaire's "generosity" was his enlightened belief that all people, including the Jews, had the capacity to improve themselves.

One of the principal arguments concerning the Jews was whether they were capable of becoming productive members of society. For many, their occupations and religious obligations rendered the Jews at best useless and at worst pernicious. Would they remain mired in petty trade and endless study, or would they be able to contribute to the general welfare? Some pointed out that the principal responsibility for the condition of the Jews lay with Christian society. In Germany in 1781, the Prussian bureaucrat **Christian Wilhelm Dohm** (1751–1820) published *On the Civic Improvement of the Jews*. His argument that the Jews be emancipated was intended to make them "happier, better people, more useful members of society." Dohm's remedy was typical of the German solution to the problem: While heartfelt, it was piecemeal. He wished to remove economic restrictions on Jews to encourage them to farm and to pursue arts and science. However, he wished to limit petty trade among them because he considered it corrupting and, finally, he insisted that Jewish access to government service jobs be restricted until such time as they had demonstrated the successful results of "improvement." This approach meant that the Jews were to be placed under constant surveillance and inspected for measurable improvement before they could be emancipated. Other German supporters of Dohm's fundamental position advocated a lengthy period of reeducation for the Jews prior to emancipation. (In Germany, Jewish progress toward emancipation was bound up with the gradual political development of German society. In France, by contrast, as we will see, emancipation was theoretically unconditional as it came as a product of revolution.)

On the Continent, Dohm's tract, which, ushered in the debate and spawned a vast number of publications on the Jewish question, was the first text that advocated the emancipation of the Jews based on the Enlightenment proposition that Jewish difference and deficiency (when he compared them to Christians) was historical rather than innate. In other words, nothing was inherently wrong with the Jews that would prevent them from fulfilling their obligations to the state. If Christians treated them well, then Jews would respond in kind, for after all, Dohm was in fact preceded by the Englishman, **John Toland,** who in his tract of 1714, *Reasons for Naturalizing the Jews in Great Britain and Ireland on the Same Foot with All Nations,* expressed the conviction that "the Jews . . . are both in their origin and progress not otherwise to be regarded than under the common circumstance of nature." Whether in England or on the Continent, such sentiments were relatively novel in that they downplayed

Jewish difference and stressed the common humanity that Jews shared with non-Jews.

Not everyone was convinced. The German Bible scholar, Johann David Michaelis, strenuously objected to Dohm's position. Michaelis questioned both the capacity of Jews to become citizens and the wisdom of those who advocated such a position. For Michaelis, the Jews were simply criminals. He even quantified it, claiming that they were "twenty-five times as harmful or more than the other inhabitants of Germany." Not just their individual behavior but their religion made "citizenship and the full integration of the Jew into other peoples" impossible. For Michaelis, the Jew "will never be a citizen with respect to love for and pride in his country . . . and he will never be reliable in an hour of danger." Michaelis charged that Jews in a Christian army would not eat the rations nor would they fight if the country were attacked on the Sabbath. Now it would seem from this that Michaelis was really advocating changes in Jewish behavior, that if Jews gave up, say, eating kosher food, then they could fit in. But Michaelis remained suspicious of Jewish "hypocrisy," on moral grounds; he claimed that "when I see a Jew eating pork, in order no doubt to offend his religion, then I find it impossible to rely on his word, since I cannot understand his heart." To cement his case against Jewish emancipation, he concluded that "modern warfare requires a specific minimum height for the soldiers . . . [and] very few Jews of the necessary height will be found who will be eligible for the army." Here was a nonbehavioral feature that the Jews could never change. In other words, ultimately their physical nature rather than any cultural differences prevented them from becoming German citizens.

In 1793, the German philosopher Johann Gottlieb Fichte, who admitted the Jews were worthy of human if not political rights, combined a moral argument against the Jews with the proposal for a physical solution to the "problem" that Jews constituted a "state within a state." To eliminate them as a potentially subversive community, he declared, "I see absolutely no way of giving them civic rights; except perhaps, if one night we chop off all of their heads and replace them with new ones, in which there would not be one single Jewish idea." A radical solution, it indicates the extent to which some saw Jews as fundamentally at odds with the creation of a modern non-Jewish society.

Despite the warm reception in some circles that Dohm's ideas received, resistance to full Jewish political emancipation in Prussia prevailed until the last quarter of the nineteenth century. More immediately, however, a major policy change took root in neighboring Austria. There, in 1782, the reform-minded emperor, Joseph II, issued his Edict of Toleration, which sought to "make the Jewish nation useful and serviceable

to the State mainly through better education and enlightenment of its youth. . . ." The edict promised many social benefits to Jews. They would be permitted, even encouraged, to attend non-Jewish primary and secondary schools, learn crafts and new trades, and even train with Christian masters. The edict also repealed the law mandating Jews to wear beards, as well as distinctive and humiliating clothing. It also abolished body and town-entrance taxes and eliminated the prohibition against Jews leaving their homes before noon on Sundays and (Christian) holidays.

To reap the benefits, Jews had to introduce some changes in their own behavior. They were to adopt German surnames and, most invasive of all, they were expressly forbidden to use Yiddish in written business and legal transactions. To facilitate aesthetic and cultural changes prior to their attendance at state schools, Jews were to enroll in German-language Jewish schools. Joseph II hired a Jew from Bohemia, **Herz Homberg** (1749–1841), to be director of these institutions. Homberg encountered stiff opposition from both rabbis and lay leaders, who denounced him to the authorities as a revolutionary and an atheist.

The overall intention of the edict was to wean Jews away from Jewish public culture as part of the empire's goal of Germanizing its subject populations. To that end, the General School Order of 1774 made mass education a goal, while in 1785 the Habsburg monarchy opened German-language Jewish schools in the newly won territory of Galicia. The goal of these schools was to promote Galician Jewry's productiveness and acculturation. The Edict of Toleration was issued under the assumption that Jews were morally and aesthetically defective and required reeducation. Behind its passage lay Joseph II's belief that by fostering educational, occupational, and linguistic change, the Jews could be reformed and turned into worthy and virtuous citizens.

The promotion of policies designed to change Jewish culture came not only from non-Jewish society. Increasing numbers of Jews also sought to effect such changes. In response to the edict, the enlightener, **Naftali Herz Wessely** (1725–1805) published a Hebrew tract, without rabbinic approbation, entitled *Divrei shalom ve-emet* (*Words of Peace and Truth*) (1782). Wessely claimed that two distinct varieties of knowledge existed: *torat ha-adam,* secular knowledge, and *torat ha-elohim,* religious knowledge. He held that familiarity with the former would enhance the capacity of Jews to appreciate better the divine teachings. According to Wessely, secular knowledge "comprised etiquette, the ways of morality and good character, courtesy, proper syntax, and purity of expression." Wessely's work elicited a firestorm of protest. In many places it was literally burned. The Polish rabbi, David ben Nathan Tevele of Lissa, one of the harshest of Wessely's many

Jewish critics, referred to Wessely as "a sycophant, an evil man, a man poor in understanding, the most mediocre of mediocre men" and described *Words of Peace and Truth* as "eight chapters of bootlicking." Reversing Wessely's formulation, Tevele declared that "our children shall study the sciences as an adornment; however, the foundations of their education will be in accordance with the command of our ancient sages of the Talmud." And then the Polish rabbi delivered the coup de grâce: "Wessely, a foolish and wicked man, of coarse spirit, is the one who lacks civility. A carcass is better than he!" The traditional Jewish aesthetic with its own notions of beauty and civility now stood in stark contrast with those of the Christian and, more recent, Jewish bourgeoisie. The battle lines in Jewish society were drawn. For the time being in central Europe the traditionalists won the day, as very little came of Joseph's reforms after the monarch passed away in 1790. But all over Europe, Jewish society and culture were about to change radically—and nowhere more so than in France.

On the eve of the revolution in 1789, the debate over what to do with the Jews also engaged French intellectual circles. In 1785, the primary French advocate of Jewish emancipation, the **Abbé Grégoire** (1750–1831) entered an essay contest sponsored by the Royal Academy of Metz. It posed the question "Are there possibilities of making the Jews more useful and happier in France?" Grégoire, a liberal Jesuit priest, entitled his response, *An Essay on the Physical, Moral, and Political Regeneration of the Jews.* Following a principle already laid down by Dohm, Grégoire declared, "Let us reform their education, to reform their hearts; it has long been observed that they are men as well as we, and they are so before they are Jews." For Grégoire, the reason that Jews stood in need of "regeneration" lay in their mistreatment on the part of Christian government. They differ from their non-Jewish neighbors because "they [had] never been treated as children of the country" in which they live but suffer from "the load of oppressive laws under which they groan." Grégoire counseled the opponents of Jewish emancipation: "You require that they should love their country—first give them one."

Nevertheless, even as staunch a supporter of the Jews as Grégoire was equivocal in his assessment. As a man of the Enlightenment, he pushed for Jewish liberation while conceding at the same time that Jews displayed multiple "marks of degeneration." Many of these were physical. He pointed to uncleanliness, the prevalence of skin disorders, a diet that "is more suited to the climate of Palestine than ours," the endogamy of the Jews, which "causes a race to degenerate, and lessens the beauty of individuals," and the practice of early marriage, a moral failing with physical consequences "preju-

dicial to both sexes, whom it enervates." Some charges were even sexual. Provocatively, Grégoire claimed that Jewish women were nymphomaniacs and Jewish men were chronic masturbators. Still, he believed that an open heart, kind treatment, and French citizenship would lead to the "physical, moral, and political regeneration of the Jews."

Jews and the French Revolution

The historical changes that would facilitate the practical implementation of a program of regeneration were unleashed in the course of the French Revolution. In 1789, the subject of both Protestant and Jewish emancipation came up for debate in the French National Assembly. With the Protestants soon admitted to citizenship alongside the Catholic majority, the question of Jewish eligibility became more urgent. Amid heated opposition, Count Stanislas de Clermont-Tonnerre, the Parisian deputy to the National Assembly and a Freemason, rose in the house on December 23 to declare, "The Jews should be denied everything as a nation, but granted everything as individuals." This justly famous phrase meant that Jews would be granted citizenship at the cost of communal autonomy, something many Jews would object to, even while welcoming the lifting of heavy taxes and other discriminatory impositions. The Jews could not maintain a state within a state, while the revolutionary state guaranteed them their rights as individuals. They would be granted liberty and equality on the condition that they become French and relegate religious practice to the private realm.

Despite the declarations on behalf of the Jews, the debate on Jewish citizenship was postponed because of the vociferous complaints of Alsatian deputies about the unworthiness for citizenship of Jews from their region. The relationship between Jews and non-Jews in Alsace-Lorraine was particularly tense. The peasants were constantly in debt to small Jewish moneylenders while occupational restrictions forced Jews into competition with their Christian neighbors. These factors, combined with the cultural antipathies, led a deputy from Lorraine to ask the chamber, "Must one admit into the family a tribe that is a stranger to oneself, that constantly turns its eye to [another] homeland, that aspires to abandon the land that supports it?"

At this point, the Sephardic community saw that its chances for winning civic emancipation would be improved by disengaging from the Ashkenazim of northeastern France. They turned to the authorities, invoking the letters of patent that they had held since the sixteenth century, guarantees that had effectively extended civil rights to this acculturated community for nearly two hundred years. On January 28,

1790, the French National Assembly declared, "All of the Jews known in France, under the name of Portuguese, Spanish, and Avignonese Jews, shall continue to enjoy the same rights they have hitherto enjoyed, and which have been granted them by letters of patent. In consequence thereof, they shall enjoy the rights of active citizens." The Sephardim of France became the first Jews in Europe to enjoy complete equality.

This situation meant that the Ashkenazim remained unemancipated and politically isolated. However, revolutionary politics aided their cause. The radical Jacobin faction had assumed increasing dominance in Paris, which in turn became decisive in the National Assembly. In January 1791, the Jews of Paris, dressed in their National Guard uniforms, argued their case before the Paris Commune, which in turn informed the assembly that "general will" demanded that the Jews be emancipated. The issue played out a while longer until September 28, 1791, when the Ashkenazim were finally granted citizenship. All the Jews of France had now been emancipated.

Radical revolutionary politics worked to the benefit of Jewish emancipation, as the Jacobins countered their critics by declaring that whosoever was opposed to Jewish emancipation was, in effect, an enemy of the revolution. With the guillotine working overtime, even prior to the onset of what is known as "The Reign of Terror," few risked turning their backs on the revolution. It would be wrong, however, to simply assume that the legislative decision to emancipate the Ashkenazim was motivated by fear of the Jacobins. Rather, the Jews were emancipated in France because of their symbolic significance. Considered degenerate and corrupt, Jews were, for those wishing to test the revolution's ability to transform the "degraded and corrupt" into model revolutionary citizens, the ideal sample group. No class had so far to rise, and no group in Europe would so challenge the Enlightenment's and the revolution's optimistic claims about human nature's capacity for improvement as the Jews. The Jews were thus part of a grand "thought experiment."

Although as elsewhere, the process of Jewish acculturation in France had already begun at least a century before the revolution, in the wake of emancipation Jews rapidly and eagerly adopted French customs and habits. They also took up arms in large numbers in defense of the nation, served in government posts, increasingly sent their children to French schools, and became deeply integrated into the economy of France. They did all this and remained true to Judaism. Jewish emancipation went wherever Napoleon led his armies. Like the Jews of France before them, these Jewish communities would also enter uncharted territory as they sought to synthesize the demands of citizenship and Judaism.

Napoleon's Jewish Policy

As the revolution gave way to empire, Napoleon Bonaparte set about conquering Europe and Jews were emancipated wherever French armies were victorious: Holland in 1796, northern and central Italy in 1796–1798, and the western regions of Germany in 1797. While this was in keeping with the political goals of the revolution, Napoleon, who seized power as the First Consul of France in 1799, also enacted policy that ran counter to the radical ideals of liberty, equality, and fraternity. One area where his conservatism was in evidence was Jewish policy.

The emancipation of French Jewry did not end the debate on the Jewish question. Serious doubts lingered about whether the Jews could be regenerated. As ever, the focus fell on the Jews of Alsace. Tensions between Jews and peasants had always been high in this eastern province, but ironically they increased with the new opportunities both groups came to enjoy as a result of the revolution. When the National Assembly sold off the confiscated lands of émigré nobles, Alsatian peasants were free to make land purchases. Short of funds, they borrowed money from Jewish moneylenders, and quite soon some 400,000 peasants were in deep debt to a few thousand Jews. This situation only got worse when Napoleon changed France's currency, making the money that had been lent to the peasants useless. How would they pay off their loans to their Jewish creditors? They could not. Between 1802 and 1804 Alsatian courts foreclosed on new peasant holdings and passed the aristocratic estates to Jewish lenders. Simmering hatred for Jews erupted into full-scale confrontation.

Seizing on this situation and buoyed by Napoleon's increasingly autocratic and regal pretensions, royalists speaking on behalf of the aggrieved peasantry accused Alsatian Jews of profiteering from the revolution. In this charge lay the origins of a European-wide canard that described Jews as beneficiaries of modernity, conspiring to orchestrate historical developments to their own advantage, while "true nationals" suffered the consequences. For modern antisemites, many of whom had a romantic attachment to the distant collective past, the claim that Jews were responsible for bringing about the destabilizing conditions of modernity became one of the central charges against them. Antisemites celebrated the mythical time prior to Jewish emancipation as an age of alleged perfection, an era to which they wished to return. Everything they loathed and considered rotten about contemporary society could be and was often attributed by them to the emancipation of the Jews, the most immediately visible beneficiaries of the emancipation of European society.

Indeed, Napoleon saw the emancipation of Alsatian Jewry as a failed political experiment. Neither the spirit of the

Enlightenment nor the power of the revolution had been able to effect the regenerative changes. Complaints against Jews did not die out. Inundated with peasant grievances, Napoleon, who had not hitherto given much consideration to Jews and was inherently hostile to commercial culture, now turned to the Jews as the epitome of the socially disruptive effects of trade. In 1806, to assuage the hostility of the Alsatian peasantry, Napoleon suspended all debts owed to Jews for one year. Although he rejected a recommendation that the Jews be expelled and another that emancipation be rescinded, the debt suspension was merely the beginning of Napoleon's reaction. His Jewish policy became part of his larger plans for scaling back the gains of the revolution and the administrative restructuring of France. His goal was to bring both the Catholic and Protestant churches under centralized control. Likewise, the Jewish community would be subject to the discipline of the state.

To effect the integration of Jews into the life of the nation and to assert greater control over them, Napoleon first set out to learn about the Jews, a group about which he knew barely anything. Like earlier Enlightenment-inspired investigations, this attempt was also ethnographic and sociological in nature. On July 29, 1806, Napoleon convened an Assembly of Jewish Notables, a body of 112 distinguished lay and clerical Jewish leaders from France and French-controlled Italy. The emperor put before the delegates a list of twelve questions designed to ascertain the relationship of French Jews to the state and to their fellow citizens. Reflecting the atmosphere of mistrust, Count Molé, a member of the Council of State and an opponent of Jewish emancipation, introduced the questions to the assembly, with a most threatening preamble: "The conduct of many among those of your persuasion has excited complaints, which have found their way to the foot of the throne: These complaints were founded on truth; and nevertheless, His Majesty has been satisfied with stopping the progress of the evil, and he has wished to hear you on the means of providing a remedy." Napoleon's wishes were further clarified by his minister: "Our most ardent wish is to be able to report to the Emperor, that, among individuals of the Jewish persuasion, he can reckon as many faithful subjects, determined to conform in everything to the laws and to the morality, which ought to regulate the conduct of all Frenchmen." Here was the first serious loyalty test administered to the Jews by a modern state. The stakes were enormous.

The questions were as follows: (1) Is it lawful for Jews to marry more than one wife? (2) Is divorce allowed by the Jewish religion? (3) Can Jews and Christians marry? (4) In the eyes of Jews are Frenchmen considered brethren or strangers? (5) What conduct does Jewish law prescribe toward Frenchmen not of their religion? (6) Do Jews born in France, and treated by the law as French citizens, consider France their country, and are they bound to defend it and obey its laws? (7) Who names the rabbis? (8) What kind of police jurisdiction do the rabbis have among the Jews? (9) Are the forms of elections of the rabbis and their police jurisdiction regulated by Jewish law, or are they only sanctioned by custom? (10) Are there professions from which Jews are excluded by their law? (11) Does Jewish law forbid Jews taking usury from their brethren? (12) Does it forbid or allow usury toward strangers?

By August of 1806, the assembly gave its official response. Some of the questions were easy to answer. Insisting that Jews considered Frenchmen their brothers, the Assembly asserted that Jews were loyal to France and its laws and were prepared to defend it. Indeed, Jewish law mandated that non-Jews be treated as equals. True to the spirit of enlightened toleration, the assembly claimed, "[W]e admit of no difference but that of worshipping the Supreme Being, every one in his own way." In a departure from the tradition of communal authority, the assembly averred that rabbinical authority extended only into the spiritual realm. The question concerning intermarriage proved far trickier. The rabbis could not sanction marrying outside the faith, so they gave a subtle and carefully crafted response to avoid giving offense. They replied that Jewish law did not prohibit Jews and Christians marrying and explicitly enjoined against unions only with the seven Canaanite nations, Amon, Moab, and Egypt. With regard to marriage to French men and women, the rabbis noted that Jewish marriages, to be considered valid, required only neutral betrothal religious ceremonies called *kiddushin,* as well as special benedictions. These can only be effected if both bride and groom "consider[ed] these ceremonies as sacred." Without the blessings, the assembly concluded the marriage was civilly but not religiously binding. Shrewdly, the rabbis observed, "Catholic priests themselves would [not] be disposed to sanction unions of this kind"—that is, unions that had no sacramental character.

Of particular interest is the first question, regarding polygamy. While few would have known that polygamy among Ashkenazim was expressly forbidden in a ban issued by Rabbi Gershom ben Yehuda (ca. 960–1028), a towering German Talmud scholar and communal leader, most people, even those as ignorant about Judaism as Napoleon, would have observed that Jewish men took only one wife. Why then would this have been the first question to which he sought an answer? If we bear in mind that the questionnaire was designed to test the ability of the Jews to become Europeans, the interest in Jewish marriage customs reveals the extent to which Judaism was seen as Oriental, its practices exotic and non-Western. With its titillating implications of a harem, few rituals challenged Christian notions of morality to the extent that polygamy did. Aberrant sexuality and racial inferiority are two tropes of a shared discourse. Recall the proemancipationist Abbé Grégoire's claim that Jewish men and women were hypersexualized beings or Goethe's fascination with Jewish beauty. Sexuality became central to the modern discourse on Jews and Judaism. Indeed, the physical character of Jews, perhaps even more than their religious identities, would take the leading role in non-Jewish and Jewish discussions of Jewish status and Jewish fate in the modern period.

Napoleon was satisfied with the answers he received and correctly assumed that the Jews of France constituted a loyal community that wished to serve him and the nation. Not content to leave it at that, Napoleon sought to make the ratification of the assembly's responses a grand affair, one that would confirm his own magnanimity and imperial rule. To this end, he convened a Grand Sanhedrin, named after the supreme religious and judicial body of Jewish antiquity. Its seeming revival after 1,700 years sent a surge of messianic excitement through the Jewish world. Ever the keen strategist, Napoleon called the Sanhedrin not merely to exact the loyalty of Alsatian Jews. By 1807, after defeating the Prussians, the French established the Duchy of Warsaw as a semi-independent Polish commonwealth. With military supplies in great demand, Napoleon turned to eastern European Jewish army contractors who made available to him the military supplies his troops needed. As Napoleon correctly envisioned, in the aftermath of the meeting of the Sanhedrin, eastern European Jewish enlighteners greeted him with enthusiasm as an enemy of Polish backwardness and Russian autocracy. The Grand Sanhedrin confirmed the widespread Jewish belief that Napoleon had been "chosen [by God] as an instrument of His compassion." The Italian representative at the Grand Sanhedrin, Rabbi Salvatore Benedetto Segre (1757–1809), even declared that Napoleon was a greater man than any figure from the Bible. By 1812, when Napoleon failed to bring liberation to the Jews of eastern Europe, they turned against him, and like the majority of Europeans, eastern European Jewry likewise saw Napoleon as a tyrant to be crushed, a symbol of a failed revolution.

Meanwhile, the Sanhedrin, Count Molé claimed, "[would] bring back the Jews to the true meaning of the law, by giving interpretations, which shall set aside the corrupted glosses of commentators; it will teach them to love and to defend the country they inhabit; but will convince them that the land, where, for the first time since their dispersion, they have been able to raise their voice, is entitled to all those sentiments which rendered their ancient country so dear to them." France, in other words, would be the Jews' new Holy Land, and they were to love it and serve it as loyally as they did the original. The seventy-one members of the Grand Sanhedrin concurred

that the Torah was both religious law and political constitution, fully consistent with French law. The former was immutable, but the latter was only in use "for the government of the people of Israel in Palestine when it possessed its own kings, pontiffs and magistrates; . . . these political dispositions are no longer applicable, since Israel no longer forms a nation." Judaism would be reconstructed as a privately held faith, and Jewish identity would be reconstituted to create Frenchmen of the Mosaic persuasion—the self-conception that western European Jews would embrace in the nineteenth century.

Napoleon was not finished yet with the Jews. In 1808, as part of his administrative centralization of France, Napoleon established the Consistory, the formally constituted representative of French Jewry to the national government in Paris. It continues to function to this day as the chief administrative body of French Jewry. At the same time, Napoleon extended the anti-Jewish measures of Alsace. New laws, known among Jews as the **Infamous Decrees,** limited their residence rights and suspended all debts owed to them for ten years. This was a retrograde step that, while not rescinding emancipation, certainly contravened the spirit of the Enlightenment and the revolution.

Following Napoleon's defeat and the restoration of the Bourbon monarchy to the throne, the Infamous Decrees were not renewed, and Judaism was accorded complete equality with Christianity in 1831. The state paid the salaries of Consistory officials, something the revolution had guaranteed for Christian denominations but not for Jews. As far as French Jews were concerned, practice had finally caught up with the egalitarian sentiment that had swept the nation since 1789.

The Anglophone World

While no formal emancipation occurred in the English-speaking world, the story of the attainment of equal rights in England should be seen in the larger context of European Jewish emancipation for it will permit us to see what was unique about the fate of Jewish communities in Britain and the wider Anglophone world. In England, resolution of "the Jewish Question" was bound up with the process of according religious "dissenters" their civic rights. The quest in England focused on the right to hold political office; Jews had been naturalized in British common law since the end of the eighteenth century and had already long enjoyed most freedoms. This also held true for dissenting Protestants and Catholics, but when they each were accorded full rights to hold office in 1829 only the anomalous situation of the Jews remained exceptional. Between 1830 and 1833 emancipation bills that came before Parliament were passed in the House of Commons but rejected in the House of Lords.

Facing few social or legal restrictions, Anglo-Jewry became increasingly anglicized and materially comfortable. However, community elites resented the discrepancy between their anomalous political status and their cultural and economic position. As one of the leaders of the drive for Jewish emancipation put it in 1845, the Jews "desired to be placed on an equality in point of civil privileges with other persons dissenting from the established church not so much on account of the hardship of being excluded from particular stations of trust or honor, as on account of the far greater hardship of having a degrading stigma fastened upon us by the laws of our country." Over time, Jewish legal disabilities were lifted. In 1830, Jews were able to open shops in the City of London; in 1833 they were free to practice as barristers; and in 1845 the Municipal Relief Act permitted Jews to take up all municipal offices. In 1854 and 1856, respectively, Jews were permitted to study at Oxford and Cambridge. Despite the strides made in the third and fourth decades of the century, the one hurdle Jews in England were still unable to straddle was the taking of a seat in Parliament. The issue was put to the test several times by Lionel de Rothschild (1808–1879). He had repeatedly been elected to Parliament by the City of London but steadfastly refused to swear the obligatory Christian oath. Eventually, a compromise was reached whereby each house of Parliament could determine its own oath, and in 1858 Rothschild took a nondenominational oath that allowed him to become England's first Jewish Member of Parliament. The last act in the drawn-out legislative drama came in 1871 when the final barriers against Jews holding fellowships at Oxford and Cambridge were lifted. In all, English Jews were never as vigorous as their Continental co-religionists in demanding the lifting of legal barriers; this came to pass because over the course of the nineteenth century very few Jews felt aggrieved by the remaining disabilities in England. In fact, the majority thrived in its relatively tolerant atmosphere. Compared to the situation on the Continent, the good fortune of Anglo-Jewry was enviable.

Away from Europe in the rest of the English-speaking world, the situation was somewhat different, for official decrees of liberation or emancipatory legislation were neither required nor passed. In 1654, Portugal conquered Dutch Brazil and expelled the small Jewish community of Recife. Some of the exiles went to Surinam, Curaçao and Jamaica, while twenty-three of them made their way to New Amsterdam (later renamed New York)—the first Jews to come to North America. Though opposed to admitting them, Governor Peter Stuyvesant yielded to the directors of the Dutch West India Company, who granted the Jews the same "civil and political liberties" enjoyed by their co-religionists in Holland. Later, under British rule, the Plantation Act of 1740, which granted naturalization to foreign Protestants and Jews throughout the British Empire, saw Jews in the American colonies gain the full array of civil liberties, with the exception of restrictions on holding public office in Maryland and New Hampshire. Those bans were lifted in 1826 and 1877, respectively.

The 2,500 Jews in the United States in 1776 had been guaranteed liberty within the general constitutional context. The security enjoyed by American Jews was enshrined in law in Article VI of the Constitution of 1789, declaring "no religious test shall ever be required as a qualification to any office or public trust under the United States." Of course, unofficial social restrictions against American Jews entering certain venues, institutions, and fields of endeavor prevailed into the twentieth century, but this rarely vitiated Jewish enthusiasm for America. On August 17, 1790, Moses Seixas, the warden of Congregation Kahal Kadosh Yeshuat Israel, better known as the Hebrew Congregation of Newport, Rhode Island, wrote to George Washington, welcoming the newly elected first president of the United States on his visit to that city. Washington responded warmly to the invitation and in so doing took the opportunity to lay out the fundamental American principles of religious freedom and separation of church and state: "May the Children of the Stock of Abraham, who dwell in this land, continue to merit and enjoy the goodwill of the other Inhabitants; while every one shall sit under his own vine and fig tree, and there shall be none to make him afraid." Annually, Newport's Congregation Kahal Kadosh Yeshuat Israel, now known as the Touro Synagogue, re-reads Washington's letter in a public ceremony. (*See box,* An Old Language for a New Society: Judah Monis' Hebrew Grammar)

In Canada, where the first Jewish settlement dates to 1759, Jews mostly settled in Montreal and were engaged in the fur trade. While free to practice their religion and run for office, they were not able to actually hold office until 1832 when legislation was enacted to scrap the mandatory Christian oath for those wishing to take their seat in Parliament.

In Australia, where white settlement dates from 1788, at least eight Jews could be found among the convicts on the First Fleet transported to Botany Bay in Sydney. By 1830 about three hundred Jewish convicts had arrived, and by 1845 that number had swelled to eight hundred. Most were freed after serving short sentences and took their place in the life of the colony without hindrance. The unique feature of the Australian Jewish community in the era of emancipation is that Australia is the only country in the world that had a Jewish population from the very first day of its European settlement. Jews were therefore not seen as immigrants or interlopers. Their right to reside in Australia was never questioned. A pioneer society at great remove from Europe, Australia provided Jews with a level of freedom and acceptance rarely

AN OLD LANGUAGE FOR A NEW SOCIETY: JUDAH MONIS' HEBREW GRAMMAR

The story of the first Hebrew grammar to be published in the United States reflects the deep ambivalence toward Jews in colonial America. Judah Monis (1683–1764) was America's first Hebrew teacher and taught at Harvard College from 1722 to 1760. Born in either Italy or North Africa, into a family of Portuguese conversos, Monis migrated first to New York and then moved to Cambridge, Massachusetts, receiving his M.A. from Harvard in 1720, the first Jew to receive a college degree in the American colonies. At that time, all Harvard upperclassmen were required to study Hebrew. As part of his graduation requirements, Monis wrote a Hebrew grammar, entitled *A Grammar of the Hebrew Tongue,* and in 1720 he submitted a handwritten copy to the Harvard Corporation for its "judicious perusall." On April 30, 1722, the corporation "Voted, That Mr. Judah Monis be approved instructor of the Hebrew Language." The positive attitude of Harvard toward Hebrew was offset by its requirement that all of its faculty be professing Christians. One month before taking up the appointment, Monis converted to Christianity. For this act, he was severely criticized by both Jews and Christians, both parties seeing him as an opportunist. Monis argued for his sincerity with the publication of three books defending the deep faith that lay behind his conversion. Whether true or not, however, he was greeted with great suspicion, and the records of the Cambridge First Church record that he secretly observed the Jewish Sabbath on Saturdays. Both Church and Harvard records refer to Monis as "the converted Jew," "the converted rabbi," and "the Christianized Jew."

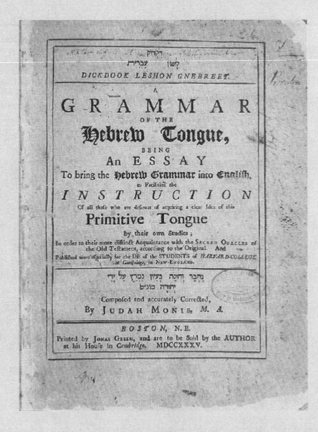

Frontispiece of Judah Monis' "Grammar of the Hebrew Tongue being an Essay to bring the Hebrew Grammar into English, to facilitate the Instruction of all those who are desirous of acquiring a clear Idea of this Primitive Tongue by their own Studies." In 1724, to save his students from the burden of copying, Monis petitioned the Harvard Corporation to publish his grammar. After much procrastination, Hebrew type was shipped from London, and in 1735 one thousand copies of Monis' *Grammar* were published. It was the first Hebrew textbook published in North America.

equaled elsewhere. From the beginning, Jews enjoyed full civil rights, were free to vote and sit in Parliament, and received grants of Crown land for cemeteries and synagogues. As Jacob Levi Saphir, a European rabbi who sojourned in Australia between 1861 and 1863, recorded in his Hebrew travelogue *Even Saphir* (*The Sapphire Stone*): "There is no discrimination between nation and nation. The Jews live in safety, and take their share in all the good things of the country. They also occupy Government positions and administrative posts. In this land [Australia] they [Gentiles] have learnt that the Jews also possess good qualities, and hatred towards them has entirely disappeared here."

In South Africa, Jews too enjoyed religious and civic freedom from the early nineteenth century. Only in the Dutch territories, where being a member of the Reformed Church was a prerequisite for holding office, were Jews (and very often Catholics) summarily and periodically excluded from full participation.

Jewish Emancipation in Southern and Central Europe

An important feature of the emancipation process is the extent to which it differed from place to place. As we have seen, in France and the territories it conquered with its revolutionary armies, emancipation was extended to the Jews as part of the legacy of the French Revolution. In the English-speaking world, emancipation was granted through the passage of discrete pieces of legislation, which followed naturally upon common law or was granted automatically without any formal declaration or legal process (*see* Map 10-1).

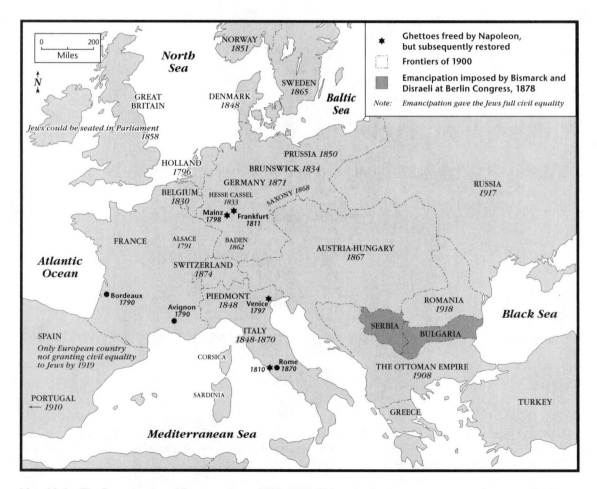

Map 10-1   The Emancipation of European Jewry, 1790–1918. Civic emancipation was a protracted process that began with the French Revolution and continued into the era after World War I. The variety of dates on this map reflects the uneven process of Jewish emancipation.

Italian Jewry experienced yet another kind of emancipatory process, one that was unique to it. When the Jews of Italy were first emancipated in 1797 by Napoleonic forces, they were still a largely traditional community living in ghettos first established in the sixteenth century. However, they quickly embraced the social and economic opportunities that came in the wake of emancipation. This rapidly transformed Italy's 40,000 Jews, making them an integral part of the country's miniscule bourgeoisie. After their newly won freedoms were rescinded in the wake of Napoleon's defeat, Jews were drawn to the Italian liberation movement and many became deeply involved in secret revolutionary societies, or "Carbonari." These groups promoted a liberal agenda of civil rights and an end to clerical and aristocratic rule.

Thus, the revolutionaries seeking to unify Italy—they finally succeeded in 1859—saw Jews as reliable and ideal allies in the struggle against the forces of reaction. During the Risorgimento, the period of national revival extending from 1830 to 1870, when the ideological and military battles for unification were fought, Jews by the thousands actively participated in the struggle, many earning honor and distinction along the way.

Secular and deeply embedded in modern Italian culture, Italian Jews were heavily invested in the nationalization project. The architects of Italian unification, Giuseppe Mazzini (1805–1872), Giuseppe Garibaldi (1807–1882), and Count Camillo Cavour (1810–1861) all recognized the Jewish political, military, and financial contribution. They considered Jews to be central to the foundation of the Italian republic and championed their emancipation, the progress of which followed on the heels of nationalist military victories, with the Jews of Rome the last community to be liberated in 1870. Italian Jews displayed a degree of loyalty and patriotism that set them apart from other Continental Jewries in two ways. First, neither Sephardic nor Ashkenazic, Italian Jews practiced the Apam rite of prayer, so called because the Hebrew initials of four Italian communities—Asti, Fossano, Alessandria, and Moncalvo—form the word *Apam*. Second, Italian Jewry's distinctiveness was reinforced in the political realm; it was only in Italy that the nationalist leadership sided with the Jews. In most of Europe, nationalist forces looked upon Jews with suspicion, if not outright hostility. The acceptance of Jews by Italian nationalists makes the case unique. Italy saw the election of Europe's first Jewish minister of war, Giuseppe Ottolenghi (1838–1904), and was the first nation in Europe to have a Jewish prime minister, Luigi Luzzatti (1841–1927), who served in that role from 1910–1911, after serving for many years in parliament. Already by 1871, eleven Jews had been elected to the Italian parliament, a greater number than in any other country in Europe.

In central Europe Germany presents us with a somewhat different model of Jewish emancipation. The process was shaped by the fact that Germany did not become a unified state until 1871. When in 1782 Dohm launched the emancipation debate with his *On the Civic Improvement of the Jews,* Germany was made up of 324 separate principalities. The progress of emancipation was uneven, with some German Jewish communities being recipients of civic rights thanks to French conquest. This left vast numbers of Jews behind. Even after the Congress of Vienna set about restructuring Europe in the wake of Napoleon's defeat in 1815, Germany was still made up of thirty-eight different principalities. This ensured that disparities in political status would continue to characterize the situation.

The problem confronting proponents of Jewish emancipation in Germany was twofold. First, unlike the situation in France, Holland, and the English-speaking world, emancipation remained conditional. Rather than simply granting emancipation by decree, German authorities sought to micromanage the progress of emancipation with a carrot-and-stick approach. Upon detecting signs of "improvement," authorities exhibited greater inclination to "reward" the Jews. This only served to enhance optimism, frustration, and eventually disappointment. Having instituted cultural, religious, and occupational changes, Jews considered themselves to have done enough to warrant full freedoms. But seeing some improvement, German authorities insisted on more. In this situation, they were able to continually move the metaphorical "finish line," while Jews were forever chasing it. Results-oriented as opposed to ideologically committed, the Germans could not, as the French had done, leave it to the Enlightenment and the liberal political system it spawned to "regenerate" the Jews. Emancipation was thus not considered an inherent right but a reward for a self-regenerative job well done.

The second structural problem that impeded full-scale Jewish emancipation in Germany stemmed from the challenge of emancipating a group within a society that was not yet fully emancipated. The political structures that made for Jewish emancipation in England, the rest of the English-speaking world, and France were absent in Germany. It was not a unified state, a constitutional monarchy, a liberal republic, or a revolutionary nation.

The rocky path of Jewish emancipation in Germany can be divided into three distinct stages:

1. *Between 1781 to 1815,* "the Jewish Question" was debated and certain legislative measures were enacted, such as the

edict of 1812 that made Jews "natives and citizens of the Prussian state" with "the same civic rights and liberties as those enjoyed by Christians."

2. *Between 1815 and 1848,* in the wake of the post-Napoleonic reaction, the emancipation that Jews in formerly French territories in western Germany had enjoyed was annulled. Popular sentiment, informed by a general anti-French, anti-Enlightenment, and reactionary Christian attitude, staunchly opposed Jewish emancipation. This attitude manifested itself most dramatically in 1819 with the **Hep Hep riots.** So called because the rampaging mobs shouted out "Hep Hep, Jud' vereck!" (Hep Hep, Jews drop dead!), violence first erupted in the city of Würzburg among rioting university students, then rapidly spread to southern and western Germany and then north to Hamburg and Copenhagen, and even south to Cracow. Ostensibly a response to the emancipation debate, the riots indicate the passions that the subject evoked. Würzburg, with its tiny Jewish population of thirty families, is a measure of how radically hostile the opposition to the idea of Jewish equality was. Though local governments offered physical protection to Jews, authorities noted that the extension of civil rights to Jews was so inflammatory that withholding emancipation was the most prudent course.

3. *In 1871,* the year Germany became a unified nation the country's 512,000 Jews were finally emancipated, despite the fact that certain positions in the upper bureaucracy and officer corps still remained closed to them until the Weimar years, 1918 to 1933.

While Jewish emancipation in Germany was tied to state building, just as it had been in Italy, the intensity of the debate was far greater in Germany. The respective national liberation movements also viewed Jews differently. German nationalists tended to see Jews as an impediment to the creation of a homogenous Christian nation, while in Italy the nationalists saw Jews as valuable and loyal allies in their struggles.

Jewish emancipation in central Europe was more than a strict change in legal status. It came with the expectation of and desire for acculturation. After 1871, most middle-class Jews in western and central Europe expressed their Jewishness through their voracious consumption of European high culture. Whether through the attainment of a university education or by becoming aficionados and patrons of opera, theatre, and classical music, Jews celebrated and participated in European culture to an extent never seen before. The majority was able to do this while still retaining a sense of Jewish distinctiveness. Acculturation did not mean assimilation or disappearance into the majority. Rather, it meant for many

becoming secular and combining European culture with Jewishness, as opposed to strict Jewish observance. When Sigmund Freud declared himself to be a "godless Jew," he was describing a modern form of Jewish identity, one not derived from religious practice but one steeped in ethnic consciousness and intensely Jewish, just the same.

Status of the Jews Under Ottoman Rule

At the same time that Italian and German Jews were emancipated, the 150,000 Jews in the Ottoman Empire also saw their legal status change. The Jews of the Ottoman Empire lived in a vast area that included Turkey, parts of the Balkans, and cities along the Aegean. As a monotheistic religious minority, Jews (and Christians) living under Islam were regarded as *dhimmi,* protected and tolerated, yet socially and legally inferior to Muslims. Under Ottoman rule, the non-Muslim community was divided into *millets,* administrative units organized on the basis of religion. The four non-Muslim millets were Armenian, Catholic, Jewish, and Greek Orthodox, and each group enjoyed considerable cultural and social autonomy in this arrangement.

As the Ottoman Empire began to slip into decline by the end of the eighteenth century, administrators looked to emulate European forms of state organization and formation to modernize and reassert central control over an increasingly fractious realm. Ottoman elites turned to France, seeing it as a model of a robust, centralized nation-state. Part of the reorganization of the Ottoman state was the recognition that the status of non-Muslim minorities could not remain unchanged. In 1839, the sultan announced the Noble Rescript of the Rose Chamber, a series of reforms (*Tanzimat*) that guaranteed the life, honor, and property of "the people of Islam and other nations." Equality had not been clearly articulated but was implicit in the decree. With the Reform Decree of 1856, equality was explicitly granted to Jews and Christians. This was amended once more in 1869 with the passage of a new citizenship law that defined all Ottoman citizens as subjects of the sultan, irrespective of their religion. The granting of a constitution in 1876 was not really implemented until the Young Turk Revolution of 1908.

Legal and social practice, however, lay far apart. Because Ottoman modernization was uneven and halfheartedly implemented, so too was emancipation. Western ideas and practices did not displace indigenous modes of governing but rather overlapped with them. Without a thoroughgoing process of Ottomanization, characterized by state-sponsored education and linguistic change, Jews never developed the kind of attachment to Turkey and its language that their co-religionists formed vis-à-vis their respective countries, and neither did its other minorities. Further contributing to the alienation, the conservative Muslim establishment succeeded in maintaining the discriminatory *jizya,* or *poll tax,* levied on non-Muslims. The regime also shut Jews and Christians out of the bureaucracy, ensuring an almost complete Muslim monopoly on all bureaucratic positions of importance within the state. Despite the granting of equal rights in 1856, Jews were not subject to compulsory military conscription until 1909. Until that time, attitudes toward *dhimmi* remained unchanged, severely compromising the 1869 law that had granted citizenship and equality.

With the rise of nationalist movements toward the end of the nineteenth century, the disintegration of the Ottoman Empire, and the impact of Western colonialism, massive changes came to the Sephardic Jews of southeastern Europe and Asia Minor. Once imperial subjects, the Sephardic communities now found themselves residing in one of many new nation-states that emerged in the wake of the empire's collapse. Belgrade and Monastir, which had significant Sephardic populations, were now ruled by Serbia, while the Jews of Sarajevo became subjects of the Habsburg Empire. In that same year of 1878, Bulgaria came into existence and extended its authority over most of the Jews of northern Thrace and south of the Danube. Greece, which became independent in 1830, had a small Jewish population, but after it annexed Salonika during the Balkan Wars of 1912–1913, it inherited a large Jewish community. This was the heartland of Sephardic culture and the Ladino language. Like their Ashkenazic co-religionists, who would suffer the loss of collective protection afforded by living in multinational empires, Sephardic Jews in the eastern Levant, had to construct a new relationship to the nation-state and negotiate its homogenizing impulse.

The end of the Ottoman Empire and the advent of modern Turkey in 1923 was a time of increased Jewish marginalization. The genocide of Armenians during the war and the transfer of the Greek population back to Greece in exchange for Turks living in Greece saw the virtual disappearance of the Christian minority, leaving the Jews alone and isolated as the major *dhimmi* population. Intensely nationalistic, the Turkish state embarked on a program of "Turkicization" that intruded on the traditional educational curriculum of Jews. Under Mustafa Kemal Atatürk, the father of modern Turkey, the state rededicated itself to implementing the French model of administration, with a strong central government, but dispensed with intermediary structures such as the millet between state and citizen. Atatürk also brought about the formal separation of mosque and state in 1928, when Islam ceased to be the official religion. Even though these factors could have ensured Jewish integration into the modern Turkish state, they did not. Rather, as with the rise of nation-states in Europe between World War I and World War II, Ottoman Jews merely saw their political and cultural autonomy curtailed, while they experienced official exclusion at the national level.

Russian Jewry and the State

In the nineteenth century, Russia was home to the world's largest Jewish population—approximately five million. By 1871—when most of central, southern, and western European; Ottoman; and Anglo Jewries had been legally emancipated—the vast majority of the world's Jews, those in eastern Europe, remained unemancipated, a condition that would prevail until the Bolshevik Revolution of 1917. The path to emancipation taken by Russian Jewry was longer and more arduous than that of other Jewish communities.

Over the course of the nineteenth century, many of the same issues that animated the emancipation debate in western and central Europe also came to the fore in Russia. But differences, particular to the Russian context, also conditioned government discourse and actions. Unlike states in the rest of Europe, virtually no Jews were in Russia until the eighteenth century. The large-scale Jewish presence there came about with the Polish Partitions of 1772, 1793, and 1795. Over those two decades, Poland was dismantled and divided between Austria, Russia, and Prussia.

The encounter between Polish Jews and the respective empires that came to govern them in the wake of the partitions determined the various paths to modernity taken by eastern European Jewry. Overnight, Polish Jews found themselves accidentally in or deliberately migrated to other parts of Europe, spreading their culture and their sensibilities. By the same token, while the traditional culture of Polish Jews remained intact for quite some time, the exposure to new forms of European culture also began to leave its mark on eastern European Jews.

With the partition of 1772, Russia inherited the lion's share of Polish Jewry, approximately a half million, and thus began the tsarist administration of the Jews. Initially, coming under Russian control did not significantly alter Jewish existence. Jews continued to enjoy considerable social and cultural autonomy and lived as a separate estate among a host of other ethnic minorities in the western borderland regions of Russia. This situation only began to change after the middle of the nineteenth century, when ever more Jews became Russian speakers and official policy underwent a change designed to handle the rising number of Jews.

Russia inherited its Jews so late that it was not until the 1860s, after Russification had begun to make an impact, that the term *Russian Jew* first became popular. Nevertheless, even after this time, the overwhelming majority of Jews in Russia retained their own languages, Yiddish and Hebrew; engaged in their own forms of dress and occupation; and operated a vast network of legal, educational, and charitable institutions, all of which went to ensure a deep sense of religious and ethnic distinctiveness.

Russian policy toward the Jews was dictated by St. Petersburg's need to deal with this large influx of foreigners. Successive tsars enacted policies characterized by a mixture of confusion, contradiction, ineptitude, bigotry, and a genuine desire for reform. We must be cautious before branding Russian policy toward the Jews as driven by antisemitism pure and simple. Sometimes it was, but at other times Jews were treated no differently (even if badly) than other groups in Russian society. Russia was an autocracy and the tsar, who monopolized all political power and decreed all laws, was, in theory, answerable only to God. No one in Russia enjoyed rights either as individuals or as part of a collectivity that were not expressly granted by the sovereign. In the nineteenth-century Russian context, the Jewish situation was not so anomalous, especially when one considers that the majority of the population consisted of serfs and remained so until the abolition of serfdom in 1861.

Russia's first great acquisition of Polish Jews occurred during the reign of Catherine the Great, who ruled from 1762 to 1796. At first amenable to the Jews, she, somewhat like Napoleon, was responsive to complaints about them from various quarters, especially merchants. In 1764, when Catherine issued an invitation to foreigners to settle in Russia, she explicitly excluded Jews. But wishing to promote the growth of towns and cities, in 1786 she decreed that the newly acquired Jews be registered as urban residents, with all the privileges that entailed. No such inclusion of Jews into the estate structure had ever occurred before in Europe. Still, the decree meant little real change, for the *kahals,* the governing boards of Jewish communities, were not disbanded since the government saw them as valuable sources of revenue. So Jewish autonomy remained intact, negating the potential impact of the inclusion of Jews into Russia's estate system. Also, too many Jews lived outside of urban areas to make the decree meaningful. Finally, complaints from Christian merchants about Jewish competition and Catherine's fears of social reform in the wake of the French Revolution led to the passage of a law in 1791 that confined Jews to the newly acquired territories.

The vast area in which Jews were required to reside later became known as the **Pale of Settlement.** Nearly all five million of Russia's Jews lived in the Pale. There they comprised about 12 percent of the area's total population. With a distinct preference for living in towns and cities, they were often the absolute majority of residents in those places. By contrast, Jews were never an absolute majority in any place in western Europe. Overall, by the end of the nineteenth century, Jews were the fifth-largest ethnic group in the Russian Empire, behind Russians, Ukrainians, Poles, and Belorussians. They were the empire's largest non-Slavic non-Christian group. Encompassing much of the western provinces acquired from the Polish Partitions and home to half the world's Jews, the Pale was a vast area covering 386,100 square miles, approximately the size of France, Germany and Austria combined. By way of an American comparison, the size of the Pale was equivalent to the combined area of California, New York State and Florida. The Pale was only abolished with the February Revolution of 1917.

The starting point for an analysis of Russian laws pertaining to Jews must begin with the recognition that the government ruled according to a highly complex legal system in which, by the late eighteenth century, people were divided into numerous groupings, of which some were estate based and some were nationally based, each of which were ruled according to distinct laws. Unlike western Europe, Russia never had a feudal system, so legal emancipation on the French or central European models could never have taken place before 1905, when Russia received a constitution. Before then, Jews could not have been incorporated into any citizenry as equals. Russian governments consistently struggled with the question of how to fit the country's newly acquired Jewish population into this complex legal matrix.

Successive tsarist regimes established commissions designed to provide them with information about and recommendations for the reform of Jews and Jewish life. These reports, some of which were deeply hostile to Jews, were nonetheless often issued in the spirit and language of western European eighteenth-century enlightened opinion. Just such a mixture of liberal intent and harsh application, characterized the **Statute of 1804 Concerning the Organization of the Jews,** the preamble to which noted that "the following regulations are in accord with our concern for the true happiness of the Jews and with the needs of the principal inhabitants of those provinces."

The statute was Russia's first basic law pertaining to Jews, but little in the way of happiness was experienced thanks to this legislation. The goal of the statute was to fit the Jewish population into one of the existing legal categories of either farmer, factory worker and artisan, merchant, or townsman. According to its provisions, Jews were to be admitted to municipal councils and could gain entrance to Russian schools; were required to use either Russian, German, or Polish in commercial or public documents; and were to be granted tax exemptions, land, and loans to establish agricultural colonies. Finally, the statute insisted on elections for Jewish community leadership positions every three years to prevent mini-dictatorships arising. Other provisions, however, made the lot of the Jews worse. In particular, because Jews had been consistently blamed for promoting the drunkenness and exploitation of the Russian peasantry, they were banned from selling alcohol in villages, which until then had been a major source of income for large numbers of Russian Jews. This led to the threat of large-scale expulsion from the countryside. While the departure of many contributed to the process of urbanization, it also created new difficulties as Jews struggled to earn a decent living in the poorly developed urban economies. The government also failed to promote and financially support the occupational change it claimed it wanted to see. Many of the provisions of the 1804 statute were never effectively enforced. In sum, the reforms had little impact, and Jewish society continued to find itself in desperate straits. At the same time, Jews remained a remote and somewhat insignificant foreign population on Russia's western frontier. They did not yet constitute an important group within the minds of the tsar or his ministers.

The Jewish policies of successive tsarist regimes were confused and confusing and ranged from benevolent paternalism that aimed at integration of the Jews to crueler forms of forced assimilation. There were harsh decrees issued to integrate and Russify the Jews and equally harsh decrees designed to drive Jews out of Russia. For Jews (and others) in Russia, beneficent paternalism could have the same devastating impact as cruel autocracy.

The reign of Tsar Nicholas I (1825–1855) exemplified the tension between the integrationist efforts and conversionist agenda of various imperial governments. While Catherine II and Alexander I tried to implement administrative integration, Nicholas promoted official enlightenment, encouraging conversion to Orthodoxy through the use of the military. Nicholas imposed compulsory military service—Russia's vast school of imperial socialization—on many of the groups inhabiting Russia's newly acquired Polish territories in the west of the country. Whereas Jews previously had been exempt from military service upon payment of a tax, in 1827 Nicholas withdrew that option for the majority of them. Now most Jews were subject to conscription for a period of twenty-five years, beginning at age eighteen. But unlike most other groups, a disproportionate number of underage Jewish children were taken, some as young as ten years old—the average age was fourteen—for a preparatory period prior to the beginning of their twenty-five-year service. They were known as **cantonists,** and while the policy of recruitment was in force between 1827 and 1855, about 50,000 Jewish boys found themselves serving as forced recruits in the tsar's army.

The impact of this was devastating on the children in question and their distraught families. Nicholas's ultimate goal of Jewish service in the cantonist battalions was conversion. Unlike non-Jewish cantonists and children of Russian soldiers who were quartered with their families, Jewish cantonists lived in barracks and were likely never to see their families again. The young recruits were subject to physical and psychological pressure. Floggings (applied ecumenically in the Russian army), constant threats, miserable conditions, and forced baptisms were the lot of these young Jewish boys. For those who sought a way out, self-mutilation became an all-too-common tactic; if you shot yourself in the foot (literally), or cut off a few fingers, you were thrown out of the army. Others simply fled into the forests. For the close-knit families, many often lit mourning candles in the expectation that they would never see their sons again. Finally, Jewish communities were fractured by the policy because the tsar left the recruiting up to the Jewish communities. Under pressure from the government, in the last two years of the draft communal authorities sent out **khappers** (Yiddish for "catchers") to apprehend young Jewish boys. According to the Hebrew account of Yehudah Leib Levin, "[O]ne afternoon, a cart pulled by two majestic horses drew up to a house. Six heavy-set men with thick red necks entered the house and soon emerged holding a six-year old boy who was screaming and flailing his arms." As with countless such episodes, it was common for the grieving parents to "thrust into the hands of their sons books of Psalms, sets of tefillin (phylacteries), whatever small religious objects they had in their possession. Stay a Jew! They entreat their boys. Whatever happens, stay a Jew!" Indeed, Jewish conversion rates among draftees were lower than among other sectarian groups. An official government memorandum noted, "Jews do not abandon their religion during army service, in spite of the benefits offered to them for doing so."

The communal administration of the draft bred corruption. Wealthy Jews paid for replacements, while the poor had no resources with which to secure the release of their sons. Resentment, trauma, and class conflict among eastern European Jews exacerbated social divisions created by Hasidism, Mitnagdism, and the *Haskalah,* the Jewish Enlightenment. One popular Yiddish folk song of the era stresses the theme of class conflict as it evokes the bitterness and suffering the children, the families, and the communities experienced:

Tots from school they tear away
And dress them up in soldiers' gray.
And our leaders, and our rabbis,
Do naught but deepen the abyss.
Rich Mr. Rockover has seven sons,
Not a one a uniform dons;
But poor widow Leah has an only child,
And they hunt him down as if he were wild.
It is right to draft the hard-working masses;
Shoemakers or tailors—they're only asses!
But the children of the idle rich
Must carry on, without a hitch.

Communal solidarity was severely compromised, and all over Russia revolts against the *kahal* authorities broke out. When Rabbi Eliyahu Shik stood up to the authorities in the town of Mir, according to one account, "There was a great tumult when he proposed that the community revolt against the kahal leaders, wreak havoc upon their community house and raze it to the ground. Everyone grabbed a hatchet or an ax and followed the rabbi to the kahal building, broke down the doors, cut the bonds of the captives and freed them."

Nicholas I's goal of using the military to promote the integration of ethnic minorities into Russian society was by and large a failure, especially as it pertained to Jews. By law, Jewish and non-Jewish soldiers were distinguished from one another; Jews were barred from joining certain units and were subjected to different criteria for promotion. Because Nicholas had formally established the Pale of Settlement in 1835, which reaffirmed the residence restrictions on Jews established by Catherine, Jewish soldiers were required to return to the Pale upon completion of their military service, even though many had served in Russia's interior. The army as brutal reform school failed to draw the majority of Jews closer to Russian society.

The cantonist experience left deep psychological scars upon Russian Jews and their descendants. In part, this was thanks to the central role the cantonists assumed in Jewish popular culture. Novelists, playwrights, autobiographers, and songwriters all used the motif of the suffering youngsters to portray the heavy yoke that was Jewish life in Russia. Some authors used the cantonist experience to reflect the changing nature of Russian Jewry or their own personal transformation upon leaving Russia. Yehezkel Kotik, who wrote his *Memories* (*Mayne Zikhroynes*) in 1912, recounted how brutal army service led many recruits to undergo radical personality changes. Kotik recalled that a cantonist friend of his, Yosele,

entered his grandfather's house after an absence of many years. He was "barefoot, clad in a large, coarse peasant shirt that reached down to his ankles but without any pants . . . his face was swollen and pale, like that of a corpse. . . . I went up to him and said, 'Yosele, Yosele!' But all my attempts to arouse him were futile—he didn't respond. He had become like a log. . . . They brought him a glass of tea and a sweet roll, but he refused to eat or drink. It was a lost cause." Yosele had been forcibly converted. But no Jew in these accounts emerged from their time in the army unchanged, and their experience in turn impacted other Jews. The memoirist Mary Antin recalled, "There were men in Polotzk [her hometown] whose faces made you old in a minute. They had served Nicholas I, and came back unbaptized." To this very day, many descendants of Russian Jewish immigrants continue to testify that their ancestors may have arrived in New York harbor in 1900 to avoid conscription for a period of twenty-five years—this despite the fact that the policy was abandoned in 1855. It is all the more ironic, then, that after introduction of universal conscription in 1874, Jews enlisted in the Russian army for a regular six-year term out of all proportion to their numbers in the population.

Even while Nicholas I's senior officials were carrying out his policy of military recruitment, the more liberal-minded among them also adopted a different approach that was realized only after the tsar's death in 1855. Under the leadership of P. D. Kisilev, Minister of State Domains and the person responsible for peasant affairs; S. S. Uvarov, Minister for Public Education; and Count A.G. Stroganov, Minister of Internal Affairs under Nicholas, a committee was established in 1840 with the telling title "Committee for the Determination of Measures for the Fundamental Transformation of the Jews in Russia." It determined that the Jews could never be fully integrated into Russia without first undergoing a moral and cultural transformation. Kisilev was influenced by Enlightenment ideas of human malleability and perfectability. He believed that human nature could be transformed through education, noting that "the estrangement of the Jews from the civil order, and their moral vices do not represent some sort of particular or arbitrary deficiency of their character, but rather became firmly established through [their] religious delusions." Kislev was determined to use Jewish schools to eliminate the civic and moral imperfections of Russia's Jews. Seeking to emulate the situation in France with Napoleon's calling of the Sanhedrin in 1807, Kisilev noted, "[T]he Jewish clergy [in France] has been turned into an instrument of the government in the execution of its policies."

As would so often be the case in Russia, Kisilev's committee, which concluded its work in 1863, failed to realize its ambitions. To make effective use of the schools and rabbinate required that the *kahals* be abolished. This happened in 1844. And yet Russian law and Russian social reality were often in conflict, as many *kahals* continued to operate clandestinely. Moreover, the government-sponsored Jewish public schools that were founded failed to attract the anticipated number of Jews and thus, like the army recruitment program, became a failed experiment for the integration of Russia's Jews.

Toward the end of the nineteenth century, during the reigns of the last three tsars—Alexander II (1855–1881), Alexander III (1881–1894), and Nicholas II (1894–1917)—Russian policy toward the Jews changed from the integrationist models of the early tsars, however imperfect they may have been, to exclusionary ones. Despite the fact that Alexander II forbade the conscription of child recruits and allowed Jewish professionals and students to reside outside the Pale, his policies toward the Jews basically continued the failed attempts of his predecessors, as he too was unprepared to entertain any basic restructuring of the social order that would lead to the recognition of individual rights. However, under him the process of Russification intensified along with an increase in the number of Jews attending state-sponsored Jewish schools, Russian gymnasia, and universities. In 1865, a mere 129 Jews (3 percent of the total number of students) were enrolled at Russian universities, whereas two decades later that number had risen to 1,856, or 14.5 percent of all university students. Just prior to World War I, when 80 percent of Russians were illiterate, almost all Jewish boys and most Jewish girls could read and write Yiddish. Tellingly, by 1900 over 30 percent of Jewish men and 16 percent of Jewish women could also read Russian.

A significant feature of the slow but discernible integration of Jews into Russian society, albeit without emancipation, was the emergence of new Jewish communal leaders. The official end of the *kahal* in 1844 and the impact of the drafting of child recruits led to a crisis of communal authority. New leaders arose who bore different credentials from the previous leaders of eastern European Jewry. They were not drawn from the rabbinic elite but were, rather, wealthy young merchants. It is true that the overwhelming majority of Russian Jews were poor (as were the majority of Russians), but it bears emphasis that a substantial merchant class also existed among Jews in Russia. By the middle of the nineteenth century, the 27,000 officially registered Jewish merchants comprised 75 percent of all the merchants in the Pale. When Nicholas I centralized the system of taxation gathering, the principal source of which was alcohol sales, great opportunities opened up for Jews, already heavily involved as they were in the alcohol trade. The wealthiest such Jewish merchants were also permitted to operate in the vast regions outside the Pale, thanks to a decree of 1848. Dealing almost exclusively with non-Jewish merchants and state officials, these Jewish "tax-farmers," as they were called, amassed significant wealth. Influenced by the ideals of the Jewish Enlightenment and their frequent contact with non-Jews, they became Jewish communal leaders of a very different cast from their rabbinic predecessors. While some may have been indifferent to Jewish custom and community, others—such as Evzel Gintsburg—were major philanthropists and promoters of the *Haskalah*. Other merchants, such as Izrail Brodsky, a pioneer of the sugar industry, and Samuil Poliakov, a railroad baron, achieved enormous success and thus influence. The merchants, who were recognized by the state for their services, began to have increasing influence with Russian officialdom, which sometimes sought advice from them in formulating Jewish policy.

As important as this group was, it was unable to substantially alter the economic or political lot of most Jews. Following the assassination of Alexander II in 1881, Alexander III set out to stymie the integration of Jews into Russian society and especially curb Jewish access to higher education and entrance into the professional elite, a development increasingly apparent in the previous reign of Alexander II. While the treatment of Jews up until that time was not exactly anomalous, with harshness characteristic of the treatment suffered by many groups, Alexander III's policies and those of his successor Nicholas II marked a significant and overt attempt to use laws and ordinances to reverse the integration of Jews into Russian society.

The establishment in 1905 of a quasi-constitutional monarchy saw the odd situation arise whereby Jews, granted the electoral franchise and permitted to organize political parties, were elected to the Duma, or parliament. Once there, they joined non-Jewish colleagues in demanding Jewish civic equality. The presence of Jews in the parliament betokened the unusual situation whereby Jewish political rights in Russia were attained before civil rights: the exact opposite of the situation in western Europe. The monarchy and conservative forces, as well as the uncooperative stance adopted by the Left, succeeded in undermining the 1905 revolution and the goal of Jewish emancipation remained unfulfilled.

Despite the reactionary policies of both Alexander III and Nicholas II, Jewish social and cultural integration proceeded apace without the granting of formal emancipation. Finally, it took World War I and revolution to usher in the emancipation of Russian Jewry. On April 2, 1917, the "Decree Abolishing Religious and National Restrictions" proclaimed, "All restrictions on the rights of Russian citizens which had been enacted by existing laws on account of their belonging to any creed, confession, or nationality, shall be abolished."

The fall of the provisional government and the Bolshevik seizure of power did not mean an immediate reversal of recent Jewish fortune. Jewish emancipation was enshrined in law and was reinforced by Lenin's decision to recognize the Jews as a nationality with distinct cultural and political rights. Jewishness became a category recognized in Soviet nationality law. Despite this, as in eighteenth-century France, Soviet Jews would be denied everything as Jews and granted much as Soviet citizens.

Between the French and the Bolshevik Revolutions the political status of world Jewry changed drastically. For over a century the Jewish struggle to attain civic rights was a protracted and complicated one. In central and eastern Europe, in particular, seeming advances were quickly followed by reversals. As such, one cannot speak of Jewish emancipation as a unitary phenomenon. There were different kinds of emancipation, each bearing the mark of specific features, such as country, region, and political conditions. As this chapter has demonstrated, the state of the Jews often determined the state's attitude toward the Jews, as did the state of the state. Over the period that Jewish civic status changed, the political struggle was accompanied by a Jewish cultural revolution, one that profoundly and permanently changed the Jewish people. It is to these developments we now turn.

Questions for Reflection

1. How would you characterize Jewish social and economic life prior to emancipation?
2. What were the particular characteristics of Jewish life in Poland in the eighteenth century that made it unique among Jewish communities in Europe?
3. What were the main arguments put forth by the pro- and anti-emancipationist forces?
4. What are the main differences between the emancipation process in Germany and France?
5. Do Napoleon's policies toward the Jews constitute a continuation or an abandonment of the ideal of the French Revolution?
6. What was the impact of tsarist policy toward Jews?

For Further Reading

On the problem of periodization in modern Jewish history, see Michael Meyer, "When Does the Modern Period in Jewish History Begin?" *Judaism* 24 (1975): 329–338.

For selected general histories of Jews in specific countries or regions, see Todd Endelman, *The Jews of Britain, 1656 to 2000* (Berkeley: University of California Press, 2002); Paula Hyman, *The Jews of Modern France* (Berkeley: University of California Press, 1998); Michael A. Meyer, ed., *German-Jewish History in Modern Times*, 4 vols. (New York: Columbia University Press, 1996); William O. McCagg, *A History of Habsburg Jews, 1670–1918* (Bloomington: Indiana University Press, 1989); Hillel J. Kieval, *Languages of Community: The Jewish Experience in Czech Lands* (Berkeley: University of California Press, 2000); Raphael Patai, *The Jews of Hungary* (Detroit: Wayne State University Press, 1996); Israel Bartal, *The Jews of Eastern Europe, 1772–1881* (Philadelphia: University of Pennsylvania Press, 2002); Zvi Gitelman, *A Century of Ambivalence: The Jews of Russia and the Soviet Union, 1881 to the Present* (New York: Schocken Books, 1988); Esther Benbassa and Aron Rodrigue, *Sephardi Jewry: A History of the Judeo-Spanish Community, 14th–20th Centuries* (Berkeley: University of California Press, 2000); Stanford J. Shaw, *The Jews of the Ottoman Empire and the Turkish Republic* (New York: New York University Press, 1991); André Chouraqui, *Between East and West: A History of the Jews of North Africa* (Philadelphia: Jewish Publication Society of America, 1968); Nissim Rejwan, *The Jews of Iraq* (London: Weidenfeld and Nichloson, 1985); Hasia Diner, *The Jews of the United States, 1654–2000* (Berkeley: University of California Press, 2004); Suzanne D. Rutland, *Edge of the Diaspora: Two Centuries of Jewish Settlement in Australia* (Sydney: Collins, 1988); Judith Elkin, *The Jews of Latin America* (New York: Holmes & Meier, 1998); and Alan Dowty, *The Jewish State: A Century Later* (Berkeley: University of California Press, 1998).

On emancipation, see Pierre Birnbaum and Ira Katznelson., eds, *Paths of Emancipation* (Princeton, NJ: Princeton University Press, 1995); Salo Wittmayer Baron, "Ghetto and Emancipation," *Menorah Journal* 4, 6 (1928): 515–526; Frances Malino, *The Sephardic Jews of Bordeaux: Assimilation and Emancipation in Revolutionary and Napoleonic France* (Tuscaloosa: University of Alabama Press, 1978); Ronald Schechter, *Obstinate Hebrews: Representations of Jews in France, 1715–1815* (Berkeley: University of California Press, 2003); Jacob Katz, *Ghetto and Emancipation: The Social Background of Jewish Emancipation, 1770–1870* (Cambridge: Harvard University Press, 1973); Frances Malino and David Sorkin, eds., *Profiles in Diversity: Jews in a Changing Europe, 1750–1870* (Detroit: Wayne State University Press, 1998); Artur Eisenbach, *The Emancipation of the Jews in Poland* (Oxford: Basil Blackwell, 1991); and Michael C. N. Salbstein, *The Emancipation of the Jews in Britain: The Question of the Admission of the Jews to Parliament, 1828–1860* (Rutherford, NJ: Fairleigh Dickinson University Press, 1981).

On the social and economic conditions in various Jewish communities in the eighteenth and early nineteenth centuries, see Yosef Kaplan, *An Alternative Path to Modernity: The Sephardi Diaspora in Western Europe* (Leiden, The Netherlands: Brill, 2000); Todd Endelman, *The Jews of Georgian England: Tradition and Change in a Liberal Society* (Philadelphia: Jewish Publication Society, 1979); John Klier, *Russia Gathers Her Jews: The Origins of the "Jewish Question" in Russia, 1772–1825* (DeKalb: Northern Illinois University Press, 1986); Gershon Hundert, *The Jews in a Polish Private Town: The Case of Opatów in the Eighteenth Century* (Baltimore, MD: Johns Hopkins University Press, 1992); Gershon Hundert, *Jews in Poland-Lithuania in the Eighteenth Century: A Genealogy of Modernity* (Berkeley: University of California Press, 2004). Murray Jay Rosman, *The Lords' Jews: Magnate-Jewish Relations in the Polish-Lithuanian Commonwealth During the Eighteenth Century* (Cambridge, MA: Harvard University Press, 1990); Mordechai Breuer and Michael Graetz, *German-Jewish History in Modern Times*, vol. 1: *Tradition and Enlightenment, 1600–1780*, ed. Michael A. Meyer (New York: Columbia University Press, 1996); Steven M. Lowenstein, *The Berlin Jewish Community: Enlightenment, Family, and Crisis, 1770–1830* (New York: Oxford University Press, 1994); and J. S. Levi and G. F. J. Bergman, *Australian Genesis: Jewish Convicts and Settlers, 1788–1850* (Melbourne, Australia: Melbourne University Press, 2002).

Chapter 11

Modern Transformations

The Jewish people were energized by their encounter with modernity, stepping forward to meet its challenges by trying to refashion themselves and their faith to suit the demands of changing times. Jewish thinkers, writers, and ordinary people produced a dizzying array of cultural and political options that reflected the prodigious diversity of the Jewish people as they entered the modern period. The relationship of Jews to modernity was not merely reactive. In the process of refashioning themselves, Jews also contributed to the creation of modern sensibilities. What made for the rich variety of responses was the fact that beginning in the early modern period but becoming even more pronounced in the eighteenth century, the Jewish world, particularly in Europe, began to fracture. This was especially the case among Ashkenazim, the majority faction among world Jews. Despite significant differences in *halakhah* (Jewish law) and *minhag* (Jewish custom) between central and eastern European Jews, the pan-Ashkenazic religious culture had been relatively uniform. Beyond this, there was what has been termed a "meta-Ashkenazic interconnecting web of [family and business] relationships." But in the eighteenth century, whatever religious and social cohesion had existed began to further unravel as Ashkenazic communities that extended from England to Russia became increasingly different from one another.

Radically divergent policies across eighteenth-century Europe also left a deep impact on the character of various Jewish communities. In liberal England, the small Jewish population became increasingly English, whereas, at the same time on the Continent, Empress Maria Theresa expelled the Jews of Prague in 1744 as if they constituted a foreign body. What a contrast to the situation in France, where the revolution transformed Jews into French citizens. At the same time, German Jews, while becoming ever more German and middle class, were still denied the full benefits of civic freedoms. Within the Jewish world, moderate and radical Sabbateans fought bitterly with each other, while small but significant numbers left

Judaism altogether, choosing apostasy. Eastern European Jews, while politically disenfranchised, nevertheless expressed great cultural vibrancy with the advent of **Hasidism** and its opposition movement, **Mitnagdism.** Proponents of the **Haskalah** or Jewish Enlightenment further contributed to the splintering of eastern European Jewry. The Ashkenazic world split into a variety of types, courtesy of both historical forces and Jewish attempts to confront, adapt, and often anticipate change. Jews who initiated transformations in Jewish society often did so in reaction to contemporary developments, but it would be inaccurate to claim that Jews were merely playing catch-up. The modern Jewish proponents of the reform or regeneration of Jewish life also acted just as Jews always had, as agents of their own destiny, filled with new ideas born of Jewish needs and experience.

Partitions of Poland

In eastern Europe, Jewish life began to undergo a period of radical change in the last quarter of the eighteenth century. Of the many developments to have an impact on Jews, the **Partitions of Poland** proved to be of utmost significance. Poland, not for the last time in its history, became a battleground for European power struggles and succumbed to economic crisis, political impotence, and war. Austria, Prussia, and Russia partitioned Poland among themselves on three occasions during the eighteenth century: 1772, 1793, and 1795. Having inherited the Jews of the now-defunct Polish state, Russia took in approximately 750,000 Jews, while Austria became home to 260,000 and Prussia, 160,000.

Like the Polish–Lithuanian Commonwealth, Jewish communal life in Poland had already suffered rupture prior to the First Partition. In Poland, a haven for Jews since at least the fourteenth century, Jews had enjoyed a good measure of autonomy under the leadership of the Council of Four Lands (*va'ad arba' aratsot*). Formed in

1580, the council was a supraregional communal body that functioned as a de facto Jewish government. But the crisis of rabbinic authority, often dated to the eighteenth century, had already begun earlier when, across Poland, lay leaders had come to dominate the rabbis, forming a monopoly on power within individual communities. To assert authority, even rabbis came to rely more on their own personal wealth or family connections than on their mastery of rabbinic texts. In the eighteenth century, both groups lost their grip on power as wars and economic difficulties plunged the Council of Four Lands into crisis. Administratively inefficient, incapable of raising revenue, and burdened by debt, the council was dissolved by the Polish parliament in 1764.

As a consequence of the partitions, Polish–Lithuanian Jewry divided along the imperial frontier. In Austria and Prussia, Jewish elites became more Europeanized, learning to speak local vernaculars, such as German, Hungarian, and Czech. Religiously, they embraced liberal forms of Judaism, and culturally, they became increasingly secular, exposed to Western ideas and eventually political emancipation. Cities such as Berlin, Vienna, Prague, and Budapest became major Jewish centers where Jews threw themselves into the hurly-burly of modern culture. The majority of Jews, however, were to be found in eastern Europe, were steeped in traditional Jewish culture, and were overwhelmingly poor. The splitting of Ashkenazic Jewry, occasioned by the partitions and the subsequent cultural and economic relationship between German Jews and their eastern European counterparts, forms a central and fascinating transnational theme in modern Jewish history.

In Russia, which inherited the majority of Poland's Jews, there were barely any liberal trends and no one was emancipated. Economic opportunities were uneven, with a bustling entrepreneurial culture in Ukraine and pockets of deep poverty in the northwest. But even there, great wealth and a small but emerging middle class were to be found. The Jewish encounter with modernity in Russia developed differently from the way the situation unfolded in east-central Europe. While some Jewish elites were deeply attracted to European culture, transformation among the majority of Jews in eastern Europe tended to be more a product of internal processes that first manifested themselves within the context of religious innovation.

Frankism

In the wake of the Sabbatean movement, various new religious experiments emerged among Jews in Poland. One of the most subversive was Frankism, named after its leader, **Jacob Frank** (1726–1791). The term *Frankism* was originally

a slur directed at the descendants of Frank's followers who converted to Roman Catholicism and attempted to conceal their Jewish backgrounds. Claiming to be a reincarnation of both Shabbatai Zvi and King David, Frank engaged in a number of practices and preached certain doctrines that were in deep conflict with Judaism. These included acceptance of the New Testament and a belief in purification through sin, including violations of sexual taboos. In 1759 Frank and five hundred followers converted to Catholicism.

Hasidism

One of the most profound developments in the religious history of the Jewish people took place with the advent of Hasidism in the eighteenth century. Hasidism, which refers to devout piety, originated in the southeastern Polish province of Podolia in the 1750s and was an expression of religious revival based on charismatic leadership, stamped by mystical teachings and practices. The founder of Hasidism was **Israel ben Eliezer,** known as the **Ba'al Shem Tov** (1700–1760). A Ba'al Shem Tov was a wonder worker, especially renowned for his healing talents. Known by his acronym, the BeShT, Israel ben Eliezer was a Kabbalist, a faith healer, a writer of amulets designed to ward off illness, and an exorcist whose earliest followers came from among his patients. (A more recent interpretation has rejected the traditional view that the BeShT was an unlearned but pious man, asserting, rather, that he was a scholar.) The new religious path he trod began with a powerful mystical experience. He reported that on Rosh Hashanah 1746 the Messiah appeared before him and told him that he would return when "your teachings have been revealed in the world and become famous, when the springs of your teachings have spread everywhere." The BeShT marked a shift from esoteric to exoteric mystical speculation.

We know little about the personal life of the BeShT since he did not leave a written record, save for a handful of letters. Most of what we do know comes from the miraculous stories and legends attributed to him by his disciples. The most famous such collection of stories, over two hundred of them, is known as *Shivhei ha-BeShT* (*In Praise of the Baal Shem Tov*), which first appeared in 1815. Ten years later, the collection of Hasidic tales by the BeShT's great-grandson, **Rabbi Nachman of Bratslav** (1772–1811), **was published posthumously.** The BeShT wrote very little, but texts claiming to be his oral teachings proliferated. In fact, *In Praise of the Ba'al Shem Tov* tells us more about his followers and the way they sought to represent their leader than it does about the BeShT. In these tales, supernatural occurrences take place with great frequency, the Ba'al Shem Tov performs miracles, and the world appears not as it is but as it should be. Typical for hagiographies, the hero meets with considerable opposition wherever he goes, but through the power of his message and his personal charisma he begins to win over those who once scorned him.

Of the many themes that appear in the tales, stories that teach the importance of reconciliation, repentance, and economic justice prevail. Hasidism proclaims the need for Jewish unity, and one story stresses the role played by the BeShT in bringing this about. Two disputants arrive at reconciliation after accepting the judgment of the BeShT, his Solomonic wisdom leading the story's editor to say of the litigants, "Both the guilty and the innocent agreed with [the BeShT] because in his great wisdom he appealed directly to their hearts, so that all were satisfied." In a Poland torn apart by Great Power struggles, with a Jewish community that lost its governing body, this message stressing unity and togetherness was met with great receptivity.

Further, the *Shivhei ha-BeShT* elevated storytelling to a high art in Hasidic culture. Many of the masters of modern Yiddish and Hebrew literature came from Hasidic environments, and even as they left those places behind, they took with them the precious legacy of Hasidic storytelling, later adapting it to secular culture. Hasidic music also came to play a role in Jewish musical forms in synagogues, across denominational lines, and in Jewish secular music, particularly klezmer.

In its formative period, Hasidism went through three distinct phases. The first was during the lifetime of the BeShT, when a small clutch of disciples followed the Hasidic path. But it must be stressed that the BeShT neither consciously created a movement nor did he found any institutions. In the second generation, a leading figure was **Rabbi Dov Ber of Mezerich** (d. 1772). This was a vitally important development because Dov Ber's erudition challenged the contemporary critique of Hasidism by its opponents that it neglected Torah study. Dov Ber was widely recognized as an accomplished Talmudist. The advent of Dov Ber did not mean a radical change in the nature of Hasidim. Rather, the ecstatic character of Hasidism was further theoretically refined. For example, he and his followers gave serious consideration to the necessity of mental preparation prior to prayer and the place of song within it. But Dov Ber also expressed disapproval of the more exuberant behavior of some of his students, rebuking Rabbi Avrom of Kalisk, who, together with his circle of Hasidim, had taken to somersaulting during prayer. Dov Ber and his

fellow intellectuals returned Hasidim to the path of Torah study, thus ensuring that it remained within the bounds of normative Jewish tradition, all the while maintaining what was new about Hasidism by remaining true to its popular character.

While Dov Ber was not a man of the people—he was a bedridden intellectual—he succeeded in spreading Hasidism by moving his "court," known in Yiddish as a *hoyf*, from the fairly remote southeastern province of Podolia further north to Volhynia (see Map 11-1). From Volhynia, Hasidism spread rapidly, north to Belorussia and Lithuania and west into Galicia. Hasidism was adopted almost exclusively among Yiddish-speaking Jews. In places where Jews spoke European vernacular languages—Hungarian in Budapest, German or Czech in Prague, and German in Poznan—Hasidism did not take root. Because Russian and Austrian authorities did not regard Hasidism as a separate movement, Hasidim were not required to obtain government permits to open new synagogues and study houses. Ignored by the authorities, Hasidism was free to branch out. With the strategic move of his court to a more central location, Dov Ber dispatched his emissaries to a very wide geographic area, where they preached and won over many new adherents, especially students. The latter then traveled back to Dov Ber's court and from there went out again as foot soldiers of Hasidism in search of new recruits. Because Hasidism was not a movement in the true sense, there was no centralized authority. The Magid of Mezerich had a number of disciples who emerged as leaders even while Dov Ber was still alive. Important Hasidic communities were led by Aron ha-Godol ["the Great"] in Karlin and Menachem Mendel of Vitebsk. The demographic boom experienced by eastern European Jewry in the nineteenth century also proved a great advantage to Hasidism, which created the conditions for the expansion of Hasidism and the formation of Hasidic courts. The formation of different courts made for considerable theoretical diversification within Hasidism. Among leading figures after Dov Ber's death in 1772 were Ya'akov Yosef of Polonoy (d. 1783) and Pinhas Shapiro of Korets (d. 1790).

The missionary aspect of Dov Ber's leadership was augmented by the appearance of the first book that outlined Hasidic teachings, Rabbi Ya'akov Yosef of Polonoy's *Toledot Ya'akov Yosef* (*The Story of Ya'akov Yosef*) (1780). The author's aim was twofold: to put the BeShT's teachings before a broad audience and to explain Hasidism more fully. The book also provided Ya'akov Yosef with the opportunity to launch a stinging critique of the traditional authorities, whom he denounced as arrogant scholars who remained aloof from the people. According to Ya'akov Yosef: "Because

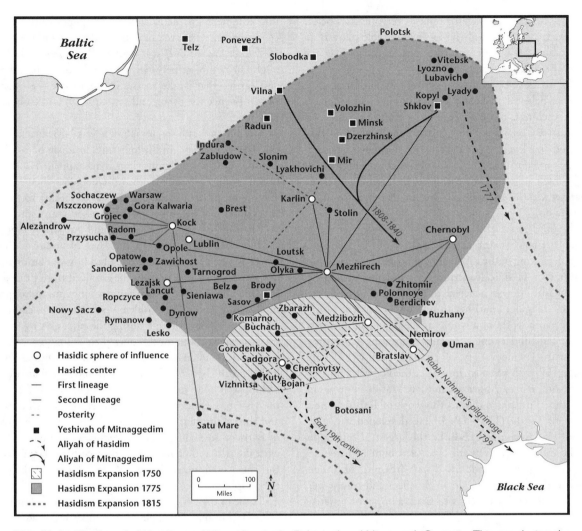

Map 11-1 The Spread of Hasidism and Mitnagdism in the Eighteenth and Nineteenth Centuries. This map depicts the increasing spread of Hasidism: those cities and towns that became major Hasidic centers, as well as Mitnagdic locations, where opposition to Hasidism was strongest.

of their divisiveness they were bereft of Torah. . . . .[because the function of scholars is] to go before the people and light their way with Torah, showing them the proper path to follow, but because of their coarseness of spirit the rabbis disdained to lead them." The author also chastised the uneducated classes for being disdainful toward the rabbis, warning of the dire consequences of such an attitude: "When the people despise the scholars, then the Jews are forced to bend the knee to the unbelievers, and vice versa." Showing respect for the intellectual classes, according to Ya'akov Yosef, also has moral benefits: "[T]he honor that they give to the scholars allows the Jews to transcend [the gentiles]."

Of particular importance was Ya'akov Yosef's formulation of the doctrine of the **tzaddik,** or righteous man. Charismatic leadership became central to Hasidism, at the expense of normative rabbinic authority, derived from one's status as a recognized scholar. The eighteenth-century philosopher **Solomon Maimon** (ca. 1753–1800) was for a brief time a Hasid before he left Poland in search of a secular education in Berlin. Here is his description of the role of the Talmudic scholar in traditional Jewish society: "The study of the Talmud is the chief object of a learned education among our people. . . . Nothing stands higher than the dignity of a good Talmudist. He has the first claim upon all offices and positions of honor in the community. If he enters an assembly—be he of any age or rank—everyone rises before him most respectfully, and the most honorable place is assigned to him. He is director of the conscience, lawgiver and judge of the common man."

The *tzaddik,* by contrast, derives his authority from what were believed to be his divine powers. According to Hasidic teachings, the *tzaddikim* are variously described as "emissaries of God," capable of "sustaining the entire world," of existing on a level that is "higher than the angels," possessing the "power to transform divine judgment into divine mercy." Such is his power that Hasidic teaching declares, "Whatever God does, it is also within the capacity of the *tzaddik* to do."

The third phase of the movement was characterized by decentralization. Between the last quarter of the eighteenth and the beginning of the nineteenth centuries, the pattern of succession for Hasidic leadership was established and became dynastic. It was believed that the *tzaddik* could bequeath his religious charisma to his sons. Characteristic of the Ashkenazic world as a whole in the eighteenth century, Hasidim also underwent a certain splintering (sometimes bitter) with a wide variety of separate groups or courts emerging, all with various ritualistic, theological, and even aesthetic differences. Above all, though, Hasidism grew rapidly in this third phase due to the work of **Rabbi Shneur Zalman of Lyady** (1745–1813). He developed a distinct brand of Hasidism called **HaBaD,** the largest of contemporary Hasidic sects. The word is an acronym of three key concepts: *hokhmah* (wisdom), *binah* (reason), and *da'at* (knowledge). For Shneur Zalman, intellect and reason were considered as legitimate paths to God, along with mystical devotion.

Shneur Zalman developed a systematic theology, which he set down in a book entitled *Likutei Amarim* (*Collected Sayings*). Popularly known as the **Tanya,** the book, which is a guide for Hasidic practice and stresses the need for regular Torah study, first appeared in 1796 and remains a core Hasidic text to this day. In the *Tanya,* Shneur Zalman taught that through a personal relationship with a *tzaddik,* the average person or **beinoni** could achieve **devekut,** a state of "cleaving to God." This is a fundamental teaching of Hasidism and is derived from Lurianic Kabbalah, with its traditions of seeking mystical communion with the divine. One of Hasidism's strengths is that the relationship between the *tzaddik* and his disciples is intimate and mutually necessary. As a mark of this intimacy, Hasidim use the more familiar and warmer sounding word *rebbe* instead of the formal *rabbi* to refer to their *tzaddik.* The *tzaddik* is sometimes referred to as the head or eyes of the body, with the Jewish people as the feet: Only their unity represents cos-

mic completeness, hence Hasidism openly celebrates this co-dependency between rabbinic leadership and the masses. In *Toledot Ya'akov Yosef,* it is written, "I adjure you that there ought to be union between heaven—that is, the rabbis—and earth—that is, the masses of the people—so that one may influence the other, and so that truth and compassion may meet."

While the traditional rabbinate was initially alarmed at the rise of Hasidism, in the long run Hasidism bolstered the waning control of religious elites. This happened in the economic realm, where Hasidism's emergence helped bring about a measure of social harmony and stability to the Jewish economy. When a Jew leased an asset of any sort from a Polish landlord, the price a Jew could pay was firmly fixed by the *kahal,* according to the laws of *hazakah* ("occupancy"). The point was to avoid a bidding war among Jews, keep prices in check, prevent the landlord from price gouging, and ensure some sort of equity of income and opportunity among Jews. The problem was that in the eighteenth century many Jews were ignoring the prices set by the laws of *hazakah* and were outbidding their fellow Jews. Hasidic leaders were adamant that the system of *hazakah* be followed for the benefit of all and, with their charismatic leadership, were able to enjoin Jews to observe the dictates of the system. In so doing, they stabilized the Jewish economy and shored up their own authority by being seen as arbiters of fairness. In reality, Hasidic leaders were often in league with the rich and hence served to exacerbate class divisions. But the overall impression was that they were on the side of the people.

One of the keys to Hasidism's success was that it proved to be a "big tent," capable of encompassing Jews from all walks of life. Learned and uneducated Jews, rich and poor ones, rural inhabitants and those in cities were all to be found among the ranks of followers. Another source of its success was the extent to which it introduced mysticism into everyday religious practice. After the failure of the Sabbatean revolt in the seventeenth century, unfulfilled messianic yearning still prevailed among the Jewish people. Hasidism sought to channel that longing and energy into the psychology of the believer, thereby neutralizing its destructive social impact. While it would not tolerate false messianic claims, neither did it discourage speculation about the coming messianic age. In fact, it openly encouraged people to perform the commandments in the spirit of messianic longing.

Hasidism emphasized mystical prayer as an efficacious way of connecting with God directly and taught that by praying with intense concentration (*kavanah*) one could attain a state of ecstatic joy. As such, Hasidic prayer was (and is) an extremely physical and raucous act, with overt gesticulations, swaying to and fro (known in Yiddish as **shokeling**), hand clapping, foot stamping, singing, and dancing. The earliest Hasidim, as noted, even performed somersaults during prayer. In fact, prayer was sometimes regarded as an erotic act, with one Hasid boldly declaring, "Prayer is copulation with the *Shekhinah* ['Divine Presence']." Another view was expressed by Ya'akov Yitshok of Przysucha. He asked rhetorically, "What is proper prayer?" and responded, "When you are so engrossed that you do not feel a knife when it is thrust into your body."

By stressing the presence of God even in the most mundane circumstances and acts, Hasidism endowed every human action with mystical and deep religious significance. According to **Aryeh Leib Sarahs** (1730–1791), "I did not go to the Maggid of Mezirech to learn interpretations of the Torah from him, but to note his way of tying his shoelaces and taking off his shoes. For of what worth are the meanings given to the Torah, after all? In his actions, in his speech, in his bearing and in his fealty to the Lord, man must make Torah manifest." If God was to be detected in the mundane act of tying one's shoelaces, Hasidic theology held out the hope that even for the common folk it was possible to come into immediate contact with the divine.

Essential to Hasidic teaching was the need to ward off misery, which, it was believed, stood in the way of attaining *devekut*. Hasidism stressed that the way to God was through a joyous demeanor. One of the BeShT's disciples claimed that the master told him "[S]top, for this way is dark and bitter and leads to depression and melancholy. The glory of God does not dwell where there is depression but where the joy in performing His mitzvah prevails."

The belief that God's presence could be encountered in all of life's activities extended even to eating. Foods consumed by Hasidim were chosen for the way they could be interpreted mystically. For example, it became customary on Sabbath to eat a set number of dishes in a fixed order. One of these was a type of noodle, known in Yiddish as *farfel*. Even though the word is actually derived from the Italian form of pasta called *farfalle,* Hasidim ate the delicacy on the Sabbath because the word *farfel* could be linked to the Yiddish word *farfalen,* meaning nullified or forgiven, a reference to the absolved sins of the Sabbath observer. A baked noodle dish called *kugel* (pudding) also became customary because the noodles clung to each other when cooked and hence symbolized unity and peace. One of the most significant and mystically endowed practices of Hasidic food consumption occurred at the rebbe's *tish,* or table. On the Sabbath and festivals, disciples made pilgrimages to the Hasidic court, sat at his table, carefully watched him eat, and when he was finished descended on his

shirayim, or leftovers, in the belief that the rebbe's food had been sanctified. This idea, derived from earlier Kabbalistic traditions, indicates how successfully Hasidism transformed mystical ideas into central elements of the life and practices of individual Jews.

Mitnagdism

Initially, Hasidism met with fierce opposition from learned elites. Early disputes centered precisely on the Hasidic introduction of Kabbalah into the daily life of the masses. Traditional authorities had previously held that such esoteric practices had to be confined to Talmudic masters and mystical adepts. Theological disagreements could also have social and economic consequences. Such was the case in the early dispute that centered on methods of animal slaughter. Hasidim had three principal concerns in this area: (1) that untrained slaughterers were operating in the villages, (2) that some of the slaughterers could be Sabbateans, and (3) that the knives then in use for slaughtering were insufficiently sharp. This latter issue was connected to the widespread belief in reincarnation and concern about the fate of a soul that transmigrated into an animal that had been rendered unkosher (*treyf*) because the knife it had been slaughtered with was not properly honed and had torn, rather than cut, the animal's flesh. If a Jewish soul were to enter into such an animal, then it too would be considered to have been "killed," because the meat would never be eaten by a pious Jew, and the soul would have no chance to reenter a Jewish body. As such, Hasidim were especially strict about the need for the knife blade to be extremely sharp, smooth, and completely free of nicks. The degree of blade sharpness touched off a great dispute. Traditional rabbis maintained that the Hasidic blades were so sharp and thin that they could develop nicks that would tear the animal's flesh, rendering it unkosher. A more important problem arose when the growing numbers of Hasidim refused to eat meat slaughtered under the supervision of the *kahal*. The kosher meat tax was a crucial source of income for the community board, which stood to lose this revenue because large numbers of people were only eating meat slaughtered according to Hasidic standards.

The opponents of the Hasidim crystallized into an identifiable group called *Mitnagdim* ("Opponents"). They deplored the institution of the *tzaddik,* which they saw as a threat to traditionally constituted authority. They were equally appalled by the Hasidim's lack of attention to Torah study, their modes of prayer, and what they considered their lack of decorum. Among other criticisms of the Hasidim were charges of sexual deviancy and immodesty and violations of the times set for communal prayer.

The leading opponent of the Hasidim was the greatest Talmud scholar of his generation, **Rabbi Eliyahu ben Shlomo Zalman** (1720–1797). Known as the **Vilna Gaon** ("Sage of Vilna"), this exceptional man, who never held public office and was said to have cut himself off from the people by studying in seclusion, was a revered figure. He earned a prodigious reputation as a man of deep piety and by the nineteenth century had become an iconic figure among eastern European Jews. He is remembered for many achievements, not the least of which was his astounding memory. He could recite by heart the Torah, both the Babylonian and the more rarely studied Jerusalem Talmuds, as well as the many commentaries. He worked at improving his memory by constantly reviewing legal literature. It is said that once a month for his entire life he went over the Babylonian Talmud. Unlike other scholars of that day who tended to concentrate solely on the *halakhic* or legalistic dimension of rabbinic literature, by studying the various codes of Jewish law, he also mastered the literary component of the corpus in the form of Midrash and Aggadah. He wrote scores of commentaries on a vast array of subjects from Bible to Talmud to Kabbalah to astronomy and algebra. All his treatises, however, represent the tiniest fragment of his accumulated knowledge. His commitment to solitary study was somewhat of an innovation in Judaism—it is a matter of contention to what degree he even attended synagogue, believing that it was primarily a venue for the dissemination of gossip—as was his elevation of Torah study to an end in and of itself. While it would be incorrect to claim that the Gaon was a student of Enlightenment thought—he was most definitely not—he was nonetheless reflective of the age, where emphasis was placed on the individual and his capacity for improvement. Also, in promoting the personality of their father, we can detect in the Gaon's sons the power of a modernizing ethos that celebrates heroic individuality.

Most significantly, the Vilna Gaon led a revolution in the way that Jews studied, initiating a shift away from focus on codes of Jewish law to the Talmud. By endowing Talmud study with primacy over all other forms of Jewish learning, the Vilna Gaon ushered in an institutional and social revolution among Jewish intellectual elites. The change in focus to Talmud study and the advent of the yeshiva bespoke a particular road to modernization among observant circles in eastern Europe that was different from the secularized cast of modernization that would appear among Jews in central Europe

and later among those in eastern Europe, who would seek to throw off what they saw as the burden of tradition.

Even the Vilna Gaon's dogged enemies, the Hasidim, acknowledged and continue to recognize the man's greatness. So large did he come to loom in the culture of eastern European Jewry that Jews from across the political and cultural spectrum—traditionalists, Mitnagdim, and Maskilim (Jewish proponents of the Enlightenment) all tended to see him as their intellectual ancestor. Ironically, for his followers, he played a role somewhat akin to a Hasidic *rebbe* or *tzaddik*.

In terms of communal leadership—and he was rarely involved in matters of the community—the Vilna Gaon led the struggle against the Hasidim. The battle began in 1772 and was inspired by the desire to eradicate Hasidism, which the Gaon and his followers, the Mitnagdim, saw as a deviant and dangerous sect. To achieve their goal, in two communities—Vilna and Brody—the Mitnagdim seized and burned Hasidic texts, had their leaders arrested, and forbade their followers all contact, especially of a religious nature, with the Hasidim.

The battle against the Hasidim was motivated by two principal grievances. The first involved matters of faith. Second, the battle had a political dimension in that the traditional rabbinic elite felt its authority threatened by the increasing popularity of Hasidic rebbes. The rabbis sensed that their grip over the people was losing out to the charismatic power and attraction of the *tzaddik*. We can see how issues of Hasidic separatism and rejection of authority were laid out in the first writ of excommunication (*herem*), delivered by the Vilna Gaon against his Hasidic enemies in 1772:

> [They] meet together in separate groups and deviate in their prayers from the valid text for the whole people. . . . [They] conduct themselves like madmen. . . . The study of Torah is neglected by them entirely. . . . Owing to our many sins they have succeeded in leading astray in many locales the sons of Zion. . . . They consistently mock the angels of the Lord and desecrate the men of greatness in the presence of ignoramuses. . . . When they pray according to falsified texts they raise such a din that the walls quake. . . . and they turn over like wheels [somersaults]. . . . Yet all this is only a little fraction, only a thousandth part of their disgusting practices. . . . Therefore we do declare to our brethren in Israel, to those near and far. . . . All leaders of our people must wear the garment of zealotry, zealotry for the Lord of Hosts, to extirpate, to destroy, to outlaw and excommunicate them. And with God's help we have already uprooted their evil belief from among us, and just as we have uprooted it here, may it be uprooted everywhere.

This document, issued at the conclusion of Passover in 1772, was signed by sixteen leading rabbis of Vilna, including the Vilna Gaon, and circulated throughout many communities. The Gaon followed this up with another letter, detailing other Hasidic practices that he considered transgressive. These included not praying at the appointed times, carelessness with prayers, the insertion of new or mispronounced words, and shouting and bellowing during worship. The second letter included a particularly bitter denunciation of Hasidic attire, such as the *shtrayml,* or fur hat. He also characterized the wearing of white as a blatant attempt to appear saintly. In all, the Gaon saw Hasidic garb as an ostentatious display of piety. He was infuriated by what he thought were excessive expressions of joy, charging Hasidim with frivolousness, made most manifest in their constant smoking of tobacco. Later critics also lambasted the Hasidim for their supposedly excessive alcohol consumption. The Vilna Gaon urged that surrounding communities deal harshly with the Hasidim through ostracism and excommunication.

In Judaism, the *herem*—in its most extreme application—was a kind of social death, where all contact, including speaking with the excommunicated party, was prohibited. For Jews, who lived on the social margins of European society to begin with, the consequences of being driven away from one's own community were dire. However, in the case of the Hasidim, all the writs of excommunication, as well as the bans and the denunciations, issued continually until the first quarter of the nineteenth century, came to naught. The religious revival that was Hasidism continued to blossom; within about three generations of its founding, Hasidism had captured the hearts and minds of nearly two-thirds of eastern European Jewry.

The Volozhin Yeshiva

While the Mitnagdim drew spiritual inspiration from the Vilna Gaon, they followed the practical lead of his most talented student, **Rabbi Hayim of Volozhin** (1749–1821). The Mitnagdim were emboldened in their cause by having behind them Lithuanian Jewry's most prestigious institution, the Volozhin yeshiva, or Talmud academy, established by Hayim in 1803. In fact, the self-supporting yeshiva is a modern institution, appearing for the first time in the nineteenth century. Previously, Torah study generally took place in a *bet midrash,* a study hall adjacent to a synagogue and under the auspices of the local rabbi.

Volozhin became a new type of educational institution, one which reshaped the religious culture of eastern European Jewry. Students came from great distances to study there, and it helped shape a national elite in the same way that Oxford and Cambridge Universities did in England. According to the Hebrew poet and student at the Volozhin yeshiva, **Hayim Nahman Bialik** (1873–1934), Volozhin was the "school where the soul of the nation was formed." A vast array of Jews, from those who remained in the world of Torah Judaism to those who would later make major contributions as writers, philosophers, poets, and Zionists, were educated there.

The yeshiva of Volozhin resembled the great European universities in another way. Its pedagogy offered a Torah-centric version of a liberal arts education. Volozhin did not train young men to become rabbis. Talmud study was undertaken for its own sake (**torah lishma**) and not for the purpose of making legal decisions or in the name of ecstatic and mystical fulfillment, as was the case among the Hasidim. Rather, the goal of Torah study was to arrive at a clear comprehension of the text. This stood in stark contrast to the complicated dialectical method previously common among Torah scholars, *pilpul* (from the Hebrew word for pepper and a reference to the often fiery mode of Talmudic argumentation). Never before in the history of Judaism had such intellectual purism dominated Torah study. Volozhin became the prototype for all the great Talmudic academies of eastern Europe, such as those in the towns of Mir, Brisk, and Telz.

At its peak at the end of the nineteenth century, the Volozhin yeshiva was home to approximately 450 students from all over Europe and the United States. Despite its size, a highly selective admissions process made Volozhin a difficult institution to be accepted into. Life was rigorous for the students, mostly single men aged between eighteen and twenty-five. They were deeply immersed in Torah study, which took place six days a week, with some students beginning their day as early as 3:00 A.M., breaking at 8:00 A.M. for morning prayers, after which students studied until 1:00 P.M. Lunch and a further break would follow until 4:00 P.M., when studies were resumed until 10:00 P.M., with some students even continuing until midnight.

Students lived off stipends granted by the yeshiva, which had raised funds for that purpose. This was a modern innovation that no previous yeshiva had undertaken. Traditionally, the local community supported such institutions and local residents provided for the students' room and board. The financial independence that the young scholars at Volozhin enjoyed thanks to the stipend was very important in their own maturation process. They were no longer infantilized, as young Torah scholars had once been. Students were also encouraged to organize themselves into *va'adim* (councils) for the purpose of raising supplementary funds and exercising a whole host of organizational functions at the yeshiva. This also helped their sense of self-worth to blossom. Another source fed their growing self-confidence: Because students were no longer dependent on handouts from townspeople, the locals adopted a much more respectful tone and manner toward the Volozhin students, for they were fast becoming a new elite.

It was their first time away from home for most of the students at Volozhin, and the diverse origins of the student body gave the yeshiva a very cosmopolitan feel. Moreover, the impact of the separation from family and familiar surroundings and the new forms of community, independence, and male bonding they experienced left a permanent impression on the students. Almost all the students studied together in the Great Hall and, encouraged by the heads of the yeshiva, did so in pairs (*khevruta*). They worked on different texts at the same time. While study was not coordinated, the method of study—with its high-decibel singing, hypnotic chanting, foot stamping, and bodily swaying—lent a uniformity and intensity to the experience that made the participants feel as though they were part of a single great spiritual, social, and intellectual undertaking. Impressions of the study hall at Volozhin remained with students forever. Decades after leaving, Eliezer Isenstadt recalled vividly:

> Imagine a building of large proportion, all of which—barring the large vestibule—is one massive auditorium filled with tables and benches. The tables are covered from corner to corner with oversized and heavy tomes. The benches are occupied by three hundred to three hundred and fifty gyrating young men, swaying back and forth, immersed in Torah study, which they sing. This was not the first time I had ever seen such a phenomenon: in our *bet midrash* on the High Holidays those who prayed would gyrate from side to side and their variegated tunes would echo through the building. But, what I saw [at Volozhin] with my own eyes and with my own ears was beyond anything I could imagine.

The transformative nature of all these new social and cultural arrangements was augmented by new intellectual challenges. At Volozhin, as well as at other similar institutions, there was considerable innovation in the method of Talmud study, with emphasis put on the logic of a Talmudic argument and the linguistic structure of a Talmudic passage. This analytic approach was developed by **Rabbi Chaim Soloveitchik of Brisk** (1853–1918). Ironically, with its stress on abstraction and intellectualism, the Volozhin methodology bred a certain skepticism. Stressing critical analysis above received wisdom, Volozhin fostered the questioning of authority, albeit in the circumscribed and tightly controlled culture of the yeshiva. Chaim of Volozhin even declared that, "[A] disciple is forbidden to accept the statements of his

teacher when he questions them, and sometimes the truth is on the side of the disciple, just as a small tree ignites a large one." In a world dominated by tradition, this encouragement of independent thought marked a significant concession to the age and to the sensibilities of modern culture.

Israel Salanter and the Musar Movement

While pure intellectualism was one of the defining features of the modern yeshiva, increasing laxity of religious practice also began to take root in the Jewish world of nineteenth-century eastern Europe. To counter both of these modernizing trends, **Rabbi Israel Salanter** (1810–1883) formed the ***Musar movement.*** Preaching the goal of ethical self-perfection and self-restraint, something he considered inseparable from Torah study, Salanter hoped to foster a spiritual and ethical revival within Lithuanian Jewry. The *Musar* ("ethics") movement developed its own method of instruction, which eventually came to dominate the world of the Lithuanian yeshiva and competed with the intellectual approach of Volozhin. Students read the ethical literature of Judaism in addition to those passages of Bible and Talmud that taught ethical lessons. Students would read such stories, even singing them to evocative melodies in dim light to heighten the experience. While Salanter did not argue against the ultimate importance of Talmud study, he elevated personal introspection to a level at least equal to, if not above, scholarly achievement. Some rabbis even ordered their students to keep a journal to record their personal failings. Salanter's stress on the cultivation of the individual personality, while owing nothing to the formal teachings of modern psychology, was nevertheless reflective of the modernizing age in which he lived with its emphasis on self-analysis and personal growth.

Despite the vibrant inner life of traditional Jewish elites, increasing secularism was proving attractive to many Jews. One of the earliest creative responses from that camp came from **Rabbi Esriel Hildesheimer** (1820–1899). In 1851 in the Hungarian town of Eisenstadt, he opened the first yeshiva in the modern world, which included the teaching of secular subjects. Hildesheimer encountered considerable hostility and left Hungary in 1869 for the more liberal environment of Berlin. There Hildesheimer became leader of the separatist Orthodox community and in 1873 established the Orthodox Rabbinical Seminary, whose ethos lay in training rabbis equally committed to Orthodox Judaism and the modern methods of critical scholarship.

For some rabbis, the times demanded even greater concessions to non-Jewish culture. In 1905, **Rabbi Isaac Jacob**

Reines (1839–1915) opened eastern Europe's first modern yeshiva in the town of Lida. Fearing that the tide was shifting away from tradition, Reines declared that "soon, the vital and vivid Judaism we still find among the Jews of Russia will suffer a fate like that which befell her in France. A dreadful disaster is imminent!" To prevent such a catastrophe, Reines moved away from the pure intellectualism of Volozhin and the *Musar*-centered yeshivas of Lithuania, offering students practical education in addition to Torah study. Incorporating Hebrew language and grammar, as well as Jewish history, into the curriculum, Reines promised that his "yeshiva will provide its students with a secular education equal to that of the public schools. They will be taught to speak and write Russian fluently, and will study as well Russian and world history, geography of the five continents, arithmetic, geometry, algebra, and some natural sciences." Neither Torah nor ethics—Reines said the students "will be expected to be well behaved and civilized"— were left behind but instead joined with a secular curriculum to produce Jews faithful to both Jewish and Russian culture.

In the early phase of eastern European religious revival, the opposition to Hasidism was as fierce as the loyalty it engendered. By the early nineteenth century, however, the feud between the Hasidim and the Mitnagdim lessened in intensity. With the emergence of such new, secularizing trends as the Jewish Enlightenment, the once bitter enemies found common cause. In defense of religious practice and Torah study, the two most powerful forces of eastern European Judaism formed a unified front to combat what the rabbis and the rebbes saw as the dangers of modernity. In making the self-conscious decision to counter the secularizing trend of the Haskalah, both Hasidim and Mitnagdim came to reject all secular study to an ideological extent that was new in Jewish history. Rabbis in the medieval and early modern period were, to a greater extent than their ultra-Orthodox modern counterparts, open to the acquisition of secular wisdom. Yet, in the self-conscious opposition to modernity, even the new forces of tradition in eastern Europe proved inherently modern movements. In 1892, spurred on by complaints from modernizers within the Jewish community, the Russian authorities sanctioned the Volozhin yeshiva for its refusal to offer more secular subjects by closing the place down. Although it reopened a few years later it never regained its preeminence.

The Haskalah in Western Europe

The principal challenge faced by the Jews of western Europe at the start of the modern period was the claim that Jewish society was stuck in the past, that the Jewish religion was wedded to outmoded traditions and needed to be radically modernized. This was not just an expression of Christian antipathy. Individual Jews too had internalized many of the negative impressions. This was the case among certain Sephardic Jews in western Europe, some of whom were in the vanguard of changing Jewish attitudes to Judaism. In Amsterdam, Uriel da Costa and Baruch Spinoza, both descendants of families forced to convert to Catholicism on the Iberian Peninsula, challenged some of the most fundamental teachings of Judaism, including belief in the immortality of the soul and the divine origin of the Bible. For their skepticism, they were both excommunicated. Da Costa committed suicide after a humiliating public ceremony, which included the public recantation of his opinions, thirty-nine lashes across his bare back, and being forced to lie on the threshold of the synagogue so that all in the congregation could tread on him as they left.

Spinoza embraced a rationalist critique of Judaism, which led to his rejection of all revealed religion; although he abandoned the practice of Judaism, he did not convert to Christianity. He believed that the ceremonial laws of Judaism were the articles of the constitution of a now defunct state: ancient Israel. As such, they no longer applied. Rejecting the authority of the rabbis, Spinoza left Amsterdam after his excommunication and never sought readmission to the faith or the community.

The Sephardic converso experience that led to a radical critique of Judaism differed significantly from the contemporary Ashkenazic experience. While the former constituted the reactions of troubled and disaffected individuals, Ashkenazic intellectuals, first in Germany and later in eastern Europe, formed a loyal opposition, a movement for change, with a clearly articulated ideology. The movement for reform distinguished its efforts from the social transformations of Jewish life that took place in England and Holland.

This reformist project—the Haskalah, or Jewish Enlightenment—is one of the most important developments in the entire history of European Jewry. It began in central Europe in the 1740s, and like the European Enlightenment, which was its inspiration, its followers stressed the primacy of the individual. Seeking to wrest control from the rabbis, who held a monopoly on knowledge and education, the **Maskilim** (proponents of the Haskalah) succeeded in creating the first of what would turn out to be many competing secular ideologies to capture the hearts and minds of modern Jews. The Haskalah served as a "gateway ideology" through which Jews traveled to arrive at liberalism, Jewish nationalism, socialism, Orthodox counterreaction and even, in rare cases, apostasy.

The Haskalah sought to reform Jews and Judaism by harmonizing religious and social life with the ideals of bourgeois culture. Maskilim sought to cultivate those necessary virtues they believed to be absent in the core principles of rabbinic Judaism. Already in the pre-modern era the debate over secular knowledge in the form of philosophy and its compatibility with Torah study became heated. The Haskalah saw the reemergence of this kind of debate but with the focus squarely on the desirability of acquiring a scientific education, European languages, and mores. The Maskilic Jewish project in the west, and then in the east, can be seen as an attempt to transform the aesthetic of the Jews and Judaism: physically, sartorially, linguistically, morally, theologically, liturgically, politically, and occupationally.

Berlin Brahmins

The emergence in Germany of an elite that stood apart from the rabbis was a consequence of the repressive legal code, the Jewry Regulation (*Juden-Reglement*), issued by Frederick II in 1750. Subordinating the authority of the Jewish community to the demands of the centralized state diminished the authority of the *kehillah*. New economic policies led to the emergence of a small band of Jewish entrepreneurs who supported a cadre of Jewish intellectuals. In close contact with Prussian officials whose dedication to cameralist economics and Enlightenment values they shared, the wealthy and the wise of Berlin Jewry rose to lead and sought to promote cultural changes among the Jews, reflective of their own improved status. The Berlin Maskilim constituted a new social group in Jewish society. Despite the concern expressed by some Maskilim that the moneyed elites were thoughtlessly aping Christian culture, both groups saw their respective Europeanization in terms of habits and behavior as not merely a matter of individual choice but an exemplary path for the advancement of the Jews as a whole.

The Berlin Haskalah emerged just at that time when Jews were absorbing secular European culture to a greater extent than ever before, even as Europeans had begun to debate the issue of Jewish emancipation. The Haskalah constituted an elaborate Jewish response to these historical developments; in their self-conscious attempt to create a new Jewish culture, the Maskilim arrogated to themselves the authority previously held by Jewish law (*halakhah*). Prior to the emergence of the Haskalah there had been grumblings about the need to break the monopoly on education, knowledge, and communal authority held by the rabbis. One of the truly innovative features of the Haskalah, however, was that it broadened the demands of a few individuals into a movement that disseminated its demands in German-language periodicals, as well as in Hebrew prose, in Yiddish plays, and in literary salons, forming what one historian has called a new Jewish "republic of letters."

Nevertheless, this challenge to the rabbis did not make the Maskilim enemies of religion. On the contrary, unlike the anti-clerical sentiments of the French philosophes, the Jewish (and non-Jewish) enlighteners in Germany were mostly conservative men respectful of religious belief and religious morality. The Maskilim were dedicated to reforming Jews to better prepare them to assume their place as citizens in a modern state. Their ultimate goal was to change the Jewish character, to create a new kind of Jew—in Hebrew, *ish yehudi shalem,* an ideal of perfected, integral Jewish manhood. The new Jew would be a person who both adhered to Judaism and modern culture.

Moses Mendelssohn

In Germany, the most visible symbol of the possibility of a Jew living in two worlds—the traditional Jewish and the modern secular—was the Berlin philosopher, **Moses Mendelssohn** (1729–1786). The son of a Torah scribe, Mendelssohn had first been exposed to secular wisdom in the form of Maimonidean philosophy by his tutor and intellectual mentor, Rabbi David Hirshl Fränkel of Dessau. When Fränkel moved to Berlin to take up the post of chief rabbi, Mendelssohn, aged fourteen, followed him there. Working as a bookkeeper in a Jewish silk factory by day, Mendelssohn, who had arrived in the capital speaking only Yiddish and knowing only Jewish texts, soon acquired knowledge of Latin, Greek, German, French, and English. He also studied various branches of contemporary and ancient philosophy. Consequently, his reputation soared and he earned the title of the "Jewish Socrates." In 1763, the Berlin Jewish community honored him by absolving him of payment of Jewish communal taxes.

Mendelssohn was a genuine celebrity in Berlin's intellectual world. He was sought out for his character as much as for his intellect. His closest non-Jewish friend, the man who first encouraged him to publish was the playwright, **Gotthold Ephraim Lessing** (1729–1781), whose drama ***The Jews*** (1749) was the first of at least fifty German-language plays between 1750 and 1805 to portray the Jews in a positive light. This was no small thing. According to Mendelssohn, the critics objected to Lessing's main character because "he was much too noble and generous." They claimed that it was an "improbability" that such a Jew could really exist. And as if to prove the point, thirty years later Lessing used Mendelssohn as a model for the character Nathan in his classic play ***Nathan the Wise*** (1779). (Lessing also created Nathan as a counterpoint to Shakespeare's Shylock.) Nathan was a spokesman for the Enlightenment values of universal brotherhood and tolerance. When the publisher and poet Friedrich Nicolai wrote to Lessing, "I am indebted to [Mendelssohn] for the most cheerful hours of the past winter and summer. I never left him, regardless of how long we were together, without becoming either better or more learned," he was expressing a truly revolutionary sentiment. Rarely had a non-Jew spoken so warmly of a Jew. It was, for most non-Jews, inconceivable that one's wisdom or moral character could be improved by friendship with a Jew. This was because the idea that the Jews were degenerate was so deeply a part of the European mind-set that only Jewish improvement could be imagined stemming from intimate Christian–Jewish relations. Few Christians thought that they could morally or intellectually benefit from close contact with Jews.

With his hunchback and unattractive appearance, Mendelssohn was an unlikely cultural icon. For those non-Jews who laid eyes on him for the first time, he evoked the kind of contempt that most Jews had learned to expect. We can see this from the vivid description of a Christian university student who saw Mendelssohn when the philosopher visited the University of Königsberg in 1777. His physical appearance alone, and in a university lecture hall to boot, was enough to incite the crowd. However, people are often judged by the company they keep, and the negative and hostile expressions Mendelssohn aroused soon gave way to feelings of awe when the students realized the purpose of his visit:

> Without paying attention to those present, but nonetheless with anxious, quiet steps, a small, physically deformed Jew with a goatee entered the lecture hall and stood standing not far from the entrance. As to be expected there began sneering and jeering that eventually turned into clicking, whistling and stamping, but to the general astonishment of everyone the stranger stood with an ice-like silence as if tied to his place. . . . Someone approached him, and inquired [why he was there], and he replied succinctly that he wanted to stay in order to make the acquaintance of Kant. Only Kant's appearance could finally quiet the uproar. . . .
>
> At the conclusion of the lecture, the Jew pushed himself forward with an intensity, which starkly contrasted with his previous composure, through the crowd to reach the Professor. The students hardly noticed him, when suddenly there again resounded a scornful laughter, which immediately gave way to wonder as Kant, after briefly looking at the stranger pensively and exchanging with him a few words, heartily shook his hand and then embraced him. Like a brushfire there went through the crowd, Moses Mendelssohn. "It is the Jewish philosopher from Berlin." Deferentially the students made way as the two sages left the lecture hall hand in hand.

Mendelssohn was engrossed by the study of philosophy and, in particular, aesthetics, ethics, and language. His concern, like that of his disciples and so many more modern Jews, involved a linking of these three areas of philosophical speculation with a new Jewish educational curriculum. Mendelssohn, a native Yiddish speaker, came to reject the language, speaking of it disparagingly and in a way that inspired generations of Jews to reject the so-called Jewish "jargon." He detected a cause-and-effect relationship between the lowly status of the Jews and their vernacular: "I fear," he declared, "that this jargon has contributed not a very little to the immorality of the common man and I expect a very good effect from the increasing use of pure German idiom." Indeed, language became central to the Maskilic goal of transforming the Jewish character. Mendelssohn, who remained a traditionally observant Jew his entire life, became a champion of Hebrew and German prose. Similarly, Maskilim in other lands would promote Hebrew and the local vernacular.

Mendelssohn began his publishing career in 1758 with the Hebrew weekly **Kohelet Musar** (The Moralist). In this publication, which shows the influence of philosophers such as Locke, Shaftesbury, and Leibniz, Mendelssohn encouraged his readers to contemplate nature and beauty, to appreciate a higher aesthetic. Both nature, which was God's creation, and poetry and art, the product of man's artistic genius, were to be equally embraced and celebrated.

Early Maskilim had called upon Jews to embrace all forms of knowledge. In his algebra textbook of 1722, the physician Anschel Worms said that he published it in order "to open the gates of understanding to the nation [the Jews] which walks in the dark." All Maskilim, especially physicians, repeatedly lamented Jewish intellectual inferiority and pleaded with their fellow Jews to acquire the rudiments of secular wisdom. Typical was the cry from Moyshe Marcuze, a Jewish doctor from Poland. In his Yiddish *Seyfer Refues* (*Book of Remedies*) (1790), he urged his readers to "take a leaf out of the pages of the Gentiles" and learn science and modern medicine.

In 1778, to assist the transformation of Jewish youth and lead them to an aesthetic awakening, Mendelssohn began the publication of his own German translation of the Bible (in Hebrew characters) with an accompanying Hebrew commentary called the **Bi'ur**. The book's proper name was *Sefer Netivot ha-shalom* (*Book of Paths to Peace*). The text and commentary were both faithful to tradition and employed the exegetical modes of medieval Sephardic rabbis, who focused on the recovery of the authentic text at the expense of elaborate midrash. Originally intended for the use of his son, Joseph, who Mendelssohn said "has all but given up his Hebrew studies," the translation into German became a staple of the Haskalah educational system. Mendelssohn saw it as a vehicle for exposing traditional Jews to modern culture, getting unobservant Jews to return to Judaism, as well as a means of weaning Jews and winning political formula. His oratory, charisma, political skill, and radical agenda proved especially appealing and paradigmatic. Between 1908 and 1913 Adolf Hitler resided in Vienna and saw for himself the power of antisemitic political demagoguery. Both Schönerer and Lueger proved inspirational to him. From both he imbibed the importance of antisemitism and the power of emotional and brutal rhetoric, the necessity of presenting oneself as a savior of the German people, as well as the value of tapping into popular frustration and social discontent.

The other significant source of Viennese antisemitism was a fringe group of occultists led by **Guido von List** (1848–1919) and **Lanz von Liebenfels** (1874–1954). List—who was a major influence on the head of the Nazi SS, Heinrich Himmler—rejected Christianity because of its Jewish roots and urged a return to paganism, especially the religions of ancient Europeans. He was also a proponent of the mystical interpretation of the Runic alphabet, the script of the ancient Germanic tribes. While List's mysticism, paganism, and cult of Odin may seem marginal, when the establishment of a Guido von List Society was proposed in 1905, over fifty prominent Germans and Austrians signed up. By the time the society was officially founded in 1908, many more public figures had joined.

Lanz von Liebenfels a former monk and publisher of the antisemitic *Ostara: Newsletters of the Blond Champions for the Rights of Man,* was one of the most influential Austrian occultists. A pornographic pamphlet widely available at newsstands across Vienna, *Ostara* depicted a struggle between blond Aryans and a race of hairy ape-men. In 1904, Liebenfels published his book *Theozoology,* in which he advocated the sterilization of the "sick" and "lower races" while extolling the virtues of the "Aryan god men." Liebenfels was a major influence on Hitler and represented an extreme secular antisemitism. He extolled racial purity, supported eugenics and selective breeding, and declared Jews to be subhuman, recommending they be castrated.

Antisemitism in France

While much of the social criticism that underlaid German and Austrian antisemitism also appeared in France, other factors informed French antisemitism. Principally, there have been two major sources of antisemitism in modern France: a Right- and a Left-wing tradition. A third source, tied to French imperial politics, emerged less frequently. Political antisemitism is a regular feature of postrevolution French life. Right-wing antisemitism originated in royalist and conservative Roman Catholic or Protestant circles, primarily in the political philosophies of men such as **Count Joseph de Maistre** (1753–1821) and **Viscount Louis de Bonald**

(1754–1840). Hostile to the French Revolution, French reactionaries longed for the restoration of the monarchy, the nobility, and the Church. In particular, they lamented that the revolution had liberated the Jews, whom they deemed as parasites and whose cunning would soon conquer France. Jewish emancipation symbolized everything that seemed wrong and "unnatural" about 1789.

In the late-nineteenth century, the "throne and alter" mantle of conservative antisemitism was assumed by **Edouard Drumont** (1844–1917). A journalist and one-time parliamentary deputy representing Algiers, Drumont penned the scurrilous, thousand-page, two-volume Jewish France (1886). Reissued in over a hundred editions, it was said to be the most widely read book in France and one of the best-selling antisemitic screeds of all time. A mélange of racist, paternalist–socialist and anti-capitalist thinking, *Jewish France* depicts the historic clash between Aryans and Jews. Drumont's Aryans were, of course, from Gaul, chivalrous, idealistic, and brave. Contemporary Frenchmen had inherited these traits. Pitted against them were the Jews, characterized as cunning, avaricious, treasonous criminals with repugnant physical features.

Drumont juxtaposed the dire social and economic conditions of French workers and peasants with the success of Jewish bankers and entrepreneurs. "The Jews," he claimed, "possess half of the capital in the world." The same, he said, was true for France. To solve the problem and redistribute wealth more equitably, Drumont suggested taking a cue from the revolution's expropriation of noble and ecclesiastical riches. He called for the establishment of "The Office of Confiscated Jewish Wealth," justifying the organized theft by claiming that Jewish wealth was "parasitical and usurious [because] it is not the carefully husbanded fruit of the labor of innumerable generations. Rather, it is the result of speculation and fraud." Dispensing with the Jews was central to the counterrevolution against the French republic that Drumont proposed: "With a government scorned by all and falling apart at the seams, five hundred determined men in the suburbs of Paris and a regiment surrounding the Jewish banks would suffice to carry out the most fruitful revolution of modern times. Everything would be over by the end of the day." Here, antisemitism served to rally the people against a postrevolutionary France, unpopular in Rightist circles and unable to redress the grievances of those at the lower end of the social spectrum. Placing special emphasis on the destructive influence of Jews over France after 1870, the year it was defeated by Prussia, Drumont, anticipating the tactic of German reactionaries and Fascists after that country's defeat in the First World War, blamed the Jews for France's decline rather than placing responsibility for the defeat on the nation's military and political elites.

from the general use of Yiddish and their reliance on Yiddish translations of the Bible, two of which had appeared just a few years before the *Bi'ur.* Indeed, this is precisely what **Rabbi Ezekiel Landau** (1713–1793)—chief rabbi of Europe's largest Jewish community, Prague, and one of Mendelssohn's most bitter critics—derided about the translation, claiming that it served to degrade the Torah "into the role of handmaiden to the German language."

Educational Reforms in Berlin

In central Europe, the Haskalah first spread through individual initiative and not through an organized movement. Before the establishment of government schools that offered a dual curriculum, private tutors employed in the homes of the wealthy introduced a new pedagogic agenda, instructing students in secular as well as religious subjects. Then in Berlin in 1778, the first of the new Maskilic schools opened for instruction. Called the **Jewish Free School,** it offered courses in Hebrew, German, French, arithmetic, mechanics, geography, history, and natural science. Jewish school teachers were the first cohort to propound Enlightenment principles beyond their own circles.

Along with tutors and school teachers, physicians constituted the other group advocating changes in Jewish society. Medical doctors were the vanguard of new cultural currents among central European Jews because they were the first aspiring Jewish intellectuals not to attend a yeshiva, choosing to enter medical school instead. As a consequence, Germany acquired a scientifically trained, skeptically inclined Jewish elite that served as role models for future generations of German Jews.

Moses Mendelssohn's *Jerusalem*

Since the 1770s, Mendelssohn had been formulating his position that Judaism constituted the principles of natural religion (belief in the existence of God, in the immortality of the soul, and in Divine Providence) combined with a singular revelation of the law to Jews. In 1783 he laid out the philosophical position of the Haskalah in his book entitled **Jerusalem.** In two separate parts, Mendelssohn presented his vision of the ideal society. In the first section, he declared the state to be pluralistic and tolerant. Only secular authorities could compel action; Mendelssohn rejected all religious instruments of coercion, such as excommunication and censorship. "Let everyone be permitted to speak as he thinks, to invoke God after his own manner." Like his contemporary Thomas Jefferson, who declared in his **Notes on Virginia** (1781), "[I]t does me no injury for my neighbor to say there are twenty gods or no god," Mendelssohn held religious beliefs to be a strictly private matter and advocated freedom of conscience, as well as the separation of church and state.

In the second part of *Jerusalem,* Mendelssohn turned his attention specifically to Judaism, outlining an ideal form of the religion to conform to his image of the ideal state. An ideal Judaism was, like the state, tolerant and rational, and he drew upon the metaphor of the house to illustrate Judaism's relationship to the larger society. On the ground floor resided all of humanity, or at least that large portion that accepted natural religion. In saying that Jews and Christians occupied the same moral ground, Mendelssohn meant that both communities shared fundamental beliefs and were socially compatible. However, also according to him, Jews dwelt on the top floor or in the attic of the metaphorical house. There they performed their ceremonial law derived from revelation, which applied to them alone.

According to Mendelssohn, Judaism did not constitute a revealed religion but revealed legislation. He maintained that adherents of other faiths have their own means of achieving moral goodness; Judaism's path is the way of the Torah. Thus, it is imperative that the commandments be maintained and observed because they have eternal moral value and are "absolutely binding on us as long as God does not revoke them with the same kind of solemn and public declaration with which He once gave them to us." Ceremony, he believed, also provided for communal distinctiveness and the retention of Jewish identity.

In arguing that Judaism was eternally relevant and compatible with philosophical ethics, Mendelssohn expressed the opinion that Judaism was the ideal religion for the secular state because it was free from supernatural dogma, embodying as it did the rationalistic principles of the Enlightenment. *Jerusalem* represents something very new in the history of the Jewish book. It presents Judaism as a religion for readers seeking to learn more about it. Traditional Jewish scholarship engages Torah according to a variety of methodologies—legalistic, mystical, exegetical, to name but three. The rabbis had not, however, produced texts outlining Judaism as though it were a religion that could be explained in a primer. In doing that, Mendelssohn's *Jerusalem* and similar books that followed were distinct inventions of modernity.

While Mendelssohn was a pillar of German Jewry, he was a vocal advocate neither of Jewish emancipation nor of religious reform. While he doubtless would have welcomed it, he was not prepared to compromise Judaism for the sake of emancipation, believing it to be an inherent right, one that must be granted without strings attached. It was not a privilege and thus he declared at the end of *Jerusalem* that if the abandonment of Judaism was the price to pay for emancipation, then the Jews would have to reject the offer.

Literature of the Berlin Haskalah

Mendelssohn's disciples were more active than their master in promoting the cause of the Haskalah. In addition to the new schools that were founded, new publications were dedicated to spreading the Jewish enlightenment. The Hebrew-language journal *Ha-meassef* (The Gatherer), which appeared on and off between 1783 and 1811, was published by the Society of Friends of the Hebrew Language. Written in a highly ornamental biblical Hebrew, reflective of the general Enlightenment's rejection of medieval culture and its preference for antiquity, *Ha-meassef* published poetry, biblical exegesis, and articles on natural science and philology. It also carried biographies of distinguished Jews, book reviews, and news concerning Jewish communities abroad. While the journal played an important role in the secularization of the Hebrew language, it did not last long because, as with the Maskilim's complaint that Yiddish separated Jews from non-Jews, Hebrew did no more to bring them together. After the era of Mendelssohn's immediate disciples, fewer and fewer German Jews could understand the language.

For that reason, in 1806 the language of the Berlin Haskalah changed to German, heralded by the publication of the journal *Sulamith*. Bearing the revealing subtitle *A Periodical for the Promotion of Culture and Humanism Among the Jewish Nation*, *Sulamith* signaled that its goal was to conduct a "civilizing" mission among the Jews. But more than this, the modernization of Judaism and the promotion of secular culture were objectives explicitly tied to the goal of emancipation. In the opening volume of the journal, the editor stated that "Religion is the essential intellectual and moral need of a cultured man. It is the purpose of *Sulamith* to expose this religion to the highest light . . . [and it] wants to point up the truth that the concepts and commands contained in the Jewish religion are in no wise harmful to either the individual or to society" [and] "would never be an obstacle to any political constitution."

Harmonizing Judaism with European culture was the goal of the German Haskalah. And *Sulamith* was committed to the ideals of the Enlightenment. In its second issue, the periodical stated that "Enlightenment teaches us that we must think liberally and act humanely, not offend anyone who thinks differently or worships differently than we." No national group has ever been able to live up to such noble sentiments at all times, but that German Jews adopted them as a code by which to live came to define how they saw themselves and wished to be seen by others.

After Mendelssohn's death in 1786, the leadership of the German Jewish community passed to one of his disciples, a wealthy entrepreneur from Königsberg, **David Friedländer**

(1750–1834). Desiring religious reform, he was not seeking, like Mendelssohn, to forge a harmonious synthesis of traditional Judaism and modern secular culture. A man of wealth and taste, he had to contend with the fact that his political status was not commensurate with his social position. He spoke and wrote German, enjoyed classical literature, and was generally rooted in the European cultural landscape, a feature that would come to characterize German Jewry from that time on.

While Mendelssohn's principal objective was to share a common culture with Germans, for Friedländer and other second-generation Maskilim who had already been reared in German culture, their principal concern was the attainment of political equality. Wealthy, cultured, but politically disenfranchised, these men were concerned with the abolition of humiliating taxes imposed on Jews, their exclusion from state service, and desired the repeal of the law that held well-to-do Jews responsible for paying off the debts of those Jews who had gone bankrupt or who had been found guilty of stealing property. To their dismay, when in 1790 Jewish community leaders approached the Prussian government to abolish this law, the government refused.

While social and political discrepancy shaped their worldview, men such as Friedländer keenly felt the need for internal change. They feared that Jewish religious ceremonies, unless subject to reform, would continue to hinder the quest for civic emancipation. After Jews were emancipated in Prussia in 1812, Friedländer published a pamphlet arguing for religious reform. He called for the abandonment of Hebrew and of the study of the Talmud and demanded that all Kabbalistic references from prayers be excised, along with calls for the restoration of Jerusalem. With these demands Friedländer emerged as a radical. When in 1799 he had offered to convert to Christianity but then reversed himself declaring Christian dogma contrary to reason, few in the Jewish community were perturbed because this was a private affair. But his new proposals split Prussian Jewry because of the consequences that acceptance of his religious reforms would have on the community as a whole. At the 1813 community elections, Friedländer was overwhelmingly defeated. He retreated into private life, becoming even more extreme in his demands. By 1815 he insisted that entirely new prayers for Jewish worship be composed and that Sabbath services be conducted on Sunday instead of Saturday so as to better align Judaism with Christianity. And still he never converted, wishing to remain within the fold. Despite his personal defeats, Friedländer's goal of changing the face of Jewish worship began to take root. Reform rabbis ultimately inherited the mantle of the Maskilim and continued to advocate from the pulpit for their ideal of philosophical, social, and aesthetic synthesis.

The Haskalah led to innovations in Jewish thought and practice. **Saul Ascher** (1767–1822) was a Jewish book dealer from Berlin and a political journalist. A staunch defender of Jewish rights, Ascher challenged Joseph II's right to enlist Jews into the army to fight the Turks in the absence of emancipation. In 1792, Ascher published *Leviathan,* a book that challenged Mendelssohn's synthetic conception of Judaism as a combination of natural religion and revealed legislation. Ascher was also the first to attempt to discern an essence of Judaism in his insistence on dogma.

According to Ascher, Judaism was in possession of unique truths, of which he identified fourteen. Ten, he said, were purely abstract articles of faith, while four were ceremonial practices. The ten abstract principles centered on three basic beliefs: (1) that God revealed himself to the people of Israel at Mount Sinai, (2) that Jews had to uphold their faith in messianic redemption, and (3) that the dead would be resurrected. The four essential ceremonies were circumcision, observance of the Sabbath, observance of holy days, and seeking God's favor through atonement. All these were immutable principles and practices and could not be abandoned. There were, however, 613 commandments in Judaism, while Ascher had identified only four that were indispensable. Ascher claimed that both Jews and non-Jews had reduced Judaism to a cold legalism, with the laws being the end rather than the means to spiritual fulfillment. Arguing against Kant, who had seen Jewish law as the political constitution of a now defunct state, Ascher was the first person to attempt to transform Judaism from a political and national ethos into a purely religious one. Ascher's aim, in keeping with the Enlightenment, was "to present Judaism in such a way that any enlightened man might embrace it, that it might be the religion of any member of society and that it would have principles in common with every religion.

Later nineteenth-century reformers would attempt to attenuate the ethnic dimension of Judaism in the name of pure religion. This was accompanied by changing terminology, such as using the word *temple* rather than *synagogue* because it was a universal word for a house of prayer and called, for example, Jews, Germans, French, and Americans of the Mosaic persuasion.

The Sephardic Haskalah

Mendelssohn's translation project was part of a larger literary trend. The eighteenth century saw a flowering of translations of canonical Hebrew works into vernacular languages. Not only in the Ashkenazic world were the Bible and other texts translated into German and Yiddish, but seminal religious texts were rendered into Ladino in the Sephardic Diaspora.

These Ladino publications were part of a larger global phenomenon. Most Jews knew little or no Hebrew and were increasingly reliant on the vernacular as a means of retaining their allegiance to Judaism and its print culture. In fact, such publishing domesticated Jewish practice by democratizing access to Jewish sources. Just as Yiddish began with Middle High German and added elements of other languages, notably Hebrew, Aramaic, and Slavic words, Ladino began with Spanish as its base and later incorporated Hebrew, Turkish, and Greek, eventually forming a distinct Jewish language. It developed to become the lingua franca of the Jewish communities of the Ottoman Empire, principally those in the Balkans and Asia Minor.

In the era of print, spoken Ladino was augmented by the creation of modern literary texts. This not only heralded Ladino's arrival as a literary language but it also proved central to the modernization of the Sephardic Jews. The most important of these works was Jacob Huli's (1689–1732) *Me-am Loez.* This multivolume compendium of rabbinic lore and Bible commentary began appearing in 1730, and after Huli died in 1732 other authors wrote subsequent volumes. This effort went on well into the nineteenth century. Initially greeted with skepticism by the rabbis, the popular success of the book eventually won it rabbinic approbation. Huli's *Me-am Loez* inspired other Ladino authors. Between 1739 and 1744, Abraham Asa translated the Bible into Ladino, replacing the first such translation of 1547. In 1749, Asa also provided a new translation of important portions of the authoritative Code of Jewish Law, the *Shulhan Arukh.* The translations of such foundational texts provided a spur to other Ladino authors who produced a diverse corpus of literature that included religious poetry, Purim plays, and ethical works. By the nineteenth century, religious treatises in Ladino included the full range of rabbinic literature; works on *halakhah,* however, continued to appear in Hebrew.

In the eighteenth century, Sephardic intellectuals and merchants came into contact with expatriate Italian Jews, known as Francos. They lived in some of the Ottoman Empire's important port cities and the secular ways of these Francos began to have an important impact on Sephardic Jews. In Livorno, David Moses Attias wrote the first book in Ladino that rehearsed the basic themes of the European Haskalah. In his *Guerta de Oro* (*Garden of Gold*) (1778), he encouraged his fellow Sephardim to adopt Western learning and European languages. His book also included an introduction to the Italian language. Attias inspired other authors, and throughout the nineteenth century many textbooks appeared offering Jews instruction in various European languages, Turkish, Hebrew, geography, and mathematics. Just as the Haskalah journal *Ha-meassef* dedicated itself to telling the story of "the great men of our nation," nineteenth-century Ladino authors began to produce biographies of distinguished Jewish personalities from the secular world, such as Moses Montefiore, Adolphe Cremieux, and the Rothschilds. Even the classic authors of contemporary Yiddish literature, such as I. L. Peretz, Sholem Aleichem, and Sholem Asch, were translated into Ladino.

The Haskalah in Eastern Europe

The Haskalah in eastern Europe was both similar to and different from its counterpart in western Europe. Like western European Maskilim, eastern European Maskilim wished to bring about occupational and moral reform through the introduction of secular knowledge into the Jewish school curriculum. Eastern European ideologues similarly displayed a nagging sense of Jewish inferiority. Already in the eighteenth century some individuals sought out knowledge beyond the Pale of Settlement. **Rabbi Baruch Schick of Shklov** (1740–1810), a disciple of the Vilna Gaon, translated Euclidian geometry into Hebrew in accordance with the Gaon's teaching that "if one is ignorant of the secular sciences in this regard, one is a hundredfold more ignorant of the wisdom of Torah, for the two are inseparable." Many eastern European Jewish critics lamented that Jews were ignorant of the sciences, fearing that they were laughingstocks before the Gentile world. The Talmudist turned Maskil, Solomon Maimon, who criticized the traditional education system among eastern European Jews, said that after discovering the world of science he had "found a key to all the secrets of nature, as I now knew the origin of storms, of dew, of rain, and such phenomena. I looked down with pride on all others who did not yet know these things, laughed at their prejudices and superstitions, and proposed to clear up their ideas on these subjects and to enlighten their understanding." Yet these and other like-minded scholars remained lone individuals. They embraced enlightened principles but did not promote a systematic program of curricular and behavioral change. The Haskalah in eastern Europe did not really emerge in full force until the 1820s, but when it did, significant differences from its German predecessor became apparent.

First, there was no substantive and intellectually prominent elite that pushed for greater contacts with non-Jews. Jewish merchants, physicians, and intellectuals who promoted the Haskalah were not part of a social circle that included non-Jews. There were no salons of the variety that existed in Berlin and Vienna, where Jews, especially women, socialized and exchanged ideas with non-Jews. Second, the languages of the Haskalah in eastern Europe would be Hebrew and Yiddish, even though many eastern European Jewish Maskilim knew French, German, Russian, and Polish. Aside from a couple of Yiddish plays and a significant though small number of publications in Hebrew, the Berlin Haskalah soon switched to German. Third, the eastern European Jewish community, compared to the Jewish community in Germany, was more hostile to deviations of traditional behavior. The Haskalah in eastern Europe did not merge with Reform Judaism as it did in Germany; there Maskilim worked in opposition to Jewish tradition. Hasidism posed a particular problem in this regard. Because the Russian Maskilim faced a large and implacably hostile community, they embraced the autocracy in their quest for reform. The Nicholaevan government (1825–1855) advocated the Haskalah among Jews, hoping that it would lead to their integration into Russian society. The alliance between Maskilim and the state served to cast great popular suspicion on the Maskilim and often alienated them from Jewish society.

The Galician Haskalah

After Berlin and Königsberg, the Haskalah spread into the Austrian empire, most crucially into the province of Galicia, an area that lay between Germany and Russia with a Jewish population of around 300,000. In its major cities, such as Brody, Lemberg (Lvov), and Tarnopol, the Haskalah found a home. In all these places, as well as in certain port cities of southern Russia, most notably Odessa, an emerging Jewish commercial class welcomed the winds of Europeanization.

Many of the most prominent Galician Maskilim were from well-to-do families. As in Germany, they were preoccupied with Jewish embourgeoisement. Even though the Maskilim were often derided as radicals by both traditional Jewish leadership and Christian authorities, the Haskalah was in fact a conservative social experiment. All over, tolerance—a hallmark of Enlightenment and Haskalah ideology—was not characterized by an "anything goes" attitude but was tempered by demands for conformity. Bourgeois self-discipline became a substitute for traditional religious and communal discipline.

However, Brody was not Berlin. The particular social and cultural circumstances that prevailed there ensured that the Haskalah in Galicia looked very different from its German forerunner. Socially, for example, a wide gulf separated Maskilim from the Jewish masses. While the bulk of German Jewry became middle class and therefore came to share the social aspirations and cultural inclinations of German Maskilim, most eastern European Jews remained extremely poor throughout the course of the nineteenth century and thus socially distant from the Maskilim in their midst. This feature served to render eastern European Maskilim marginal to Jewish society. None of them, for example, ever attained the paradigmatic status that was accorded Mendelssohn in Germany.

In addition, Galicia was heavily Hasidic and mostly Yiddish speaking. Both would leave their mark on the Haskalah in this region, specifically in the areas of language, genre, and object. Despite Joseph II's reforms and the ban on the use of Yiddish in official documents, the language persisted, thus Maskilim, seeking to have an impact upon the people, used the Jewish vernacular in their writing from the very outset. In Berlin, by contrast, Maskilim first employed Yiddish, then Hebrew, and finally German.

The kinds of genres that marked the literary output of the Galician Haskalah were also new. Here, a secular Jewish national culture in both Yiddish and Hebrew developed in the emergent production of plays, novels, and poetry. In particular, satire assumed great social and artistic importance. By contrast, satire and humor played almost no role in the Berlin Haskalah. The main object of Galician satire was the rabbinate in general and Hasidism in particular. While Moses Mendelssohn indignantly but solemnly attacked the rabbis' power to coerce and excommunicate and David Friedländer questioned the need for ceremony in Judaism, Galician authors drew devastatingly biting and witty portraits of Hasidic life. Their criticism was deeply personal as many of the Maskilim in the Galician and later Russian Haskalah came from Hasidic backgrounds. They shared an internalized anti-clericalism of the sort that eighteenth-century French philosophes, who were mostly from Catholic backgrounds, adopted in their attacks on the Catholic Church. But unlike men such as Voltaire, who became deeply anti-Christian, the Maskilim did not seek to destroy religion. Rather, they sought only to extirpate what they believed were the most obscurantist and superstitious manifestations of contemporary Jewish culture.

The greatest exponent of the early form of Maskilic satire was **Joseph Perl** (1773–1839). Originally from a Hasidic family, Perl became a Maskil and in 1813 established a Jewish school in the Galician city of Tarnopol. The school took as its model Mendelssohn's Jewish Free School in Berlin. Shortly thereafter, Perl, seeking to spread enlightenment among the Jews, began to publish calendars that contained scientific information, interspersed with relevant Talmudic passages. In 1819, Perl published his most significant literary work, *Megaleh Temirin (Revealer of Secrets)*. He wrote two versions of this novel: one Hebrew and one Yiddish; the latter did not appear in print until 1937. Aimed at the Hasidim and written in the form of letters—there are 151 and an epilogue—the book tells the story of Ovadia ben Petachia, a Hasidic hero who, through his magical powers, takes possession of a cache of letters that reveal a number of plots, the most important one being the search for a German-language book that is said to contain all the secrets of Hasidic life. Perl's story, a hilarious comedy of errors, reveals the various intrigues and no-holds-barred tactics

employed by the Hasidim to gain possession of the book and thus keep the secrets of Hasidism from the outside world.

Perl painted such a vivid picture of Hasidic life that most contemporaries took *Revealer of Secrets* as a genuine account rather than satire. One other aspect of Perl's book came to have an unintended consequence: the extent to which he turned the Hasidim into appealing characters. He had them speak Hasidic Hebrew, which, while not grammatically correct, was full of vitality and rang true to Perl's readers. By peppering their language with Yiddish witticisms, Perl created Hasidim who were worldly, wise, and full of humor. Perl's panoramic Jewish comedy set the standard trope for the Jewish literature and theatre that blossomed at the end of the nineteenth century.

In the work of **Nahman Krochmal** (1785–1840), the Galician Haskalah also produced a significant attempt to outline a philosophical approach to Jewish history. Jewish philosophers of note virtually disappeared after Mendelssohn and did not emerge again until the end of the nineteenth century; Krochmal was a singular exception. Born into a merchant family from Brody that maintained traditional values and customs, Krochmal was married off at the age of fourteen and, like Moses Mendelssohn before him, earned a meager living as a bookkeeper while privately studying European languages and philosophy.

In his book *A Guide for the Perplexed of Our Time,* which appeared posthumously in 1851, Krochmal, who borrowed the title from Maimonides' philosophical treatise on Judaism, *A Guide for the Perplexed,* outlined an idealist philosophy of Jewish history. He claimed that the spirit of Judaism differed from that of other religions because it embodied a unique relationship to the Absolute Spirit. Thus the evolution of Jewish history revealed with greater clarity than other cultures the development of the Absolute Spirit of world consciousness, a concept he borrowed from Hegel. Krochmal identified three distinct historical stages of Judaism: (1) Growth—from the time of the Patriarchs to the conquest of Canaan; (2) Maturity—settlement of Israel until the death of King Solomon; and (3) Decline—history of the divided kingdoms of Israel and Judea. But the story does not end with decline and demise since the Jews are an "eternal people." Krochmal posited that following the period of decline, Israel entered into a series of cycles, each marked by rebirth or growth and characterized by an ever more intensified and introspective relationship with the Absolute Spirit. This in turn was followed by a period of maturation and another phase of decline. He concluded that the turn to philosophy and Kabbalistic speculation in the Middle Ages constituted yet another stage of rebirth.

Krochmal was the first modern Jewish thinker to place historical development at the center of a philosophical understanding of Judaism. In so doing, he sought to establish the continuing relevance of a tradition that to many seemed at odds with the modern world. By endowing Judaism with eternal purpose and reason, Krochmal produced a philosophical alternative both to Hasidism and traditional rabbinic culture. Claiming that Judaism remade itself over the course of its history, Krochmal also challenged the contemporary claim of Hegel, who had called Judaism a "fossil religion." For Krochmal and his disciples, Judaism was a vital force whose eternality depended on its capacity to adapt and change.

The Russian Haskalah

From the Galician center of Brody, the Haskalah moved into the Russian Empire. The founding document of the eastern European Haskalah was a book by **Isaac Ber Levinsohn** (1788–1860), entitled *Teudah be-Yisrael* (*Testimony in Israel*). Written in Hebrew and published in 1828, with the support of the tsar, *Testimony in Israel* argues for the relevance of natural sciences and foreign languages to the Jewish school curriculum and urges Jews to change their occupations from commerce to crafts and agriculture.

Levinsohn, in fact, said nothing that other Maskilim had not already said. Rather, the significance of the book lay in the way it reflected the particular nature of the Russian Haskalah and its close ties to the state. In addition to carrying the obligatory approbation of the rabbis, Levinsohn did the unthinkable and dedicated his book to Tsar Nicholas I, an expression of gratitude to the tsar, to whom he had petitioned for a stipend. Levinsohn had received 1,000 rubles.

The impact of *Testimony in Israel* was enormous because its appearance signaled a break between the moderate Haskalah and Talmudic circles in Vilna. Mitnagdic and Maskilic criticism of Jewish culture were similar in the early nineteenth century. Even Levinsohn's demand for secular wisdom was replete with rabbinic justifications for this innovation. Yet, the tsar's patronage contributed to sharpening the battle lines of conflict between opponents and proponents of the Haskalah.

The Haskalah spread throughout eastern Europe thanks to the establishment of modernized state-run Jewish schools. Already during the reign of **Alexander I** (r. 1801–1825) and continuing under **Nicholas I** (r. 1825–1855), it was determined that the authority of the state and Christianity must be strengthened through the school system. To illustrate the point, the ministry of education was merged with the ministry of public worship. Consequently, Jews were fearful of sending their children to Russian schools. In 1840, out of 80,017 children attending elementary and secondary schools in Russia, only forty-eight were Jews. However, Jews who were inclined to provide their children with a secular education could send them to a small number of privately established modern Jewish schools in cities such as Riga and Odessa, or beginning in the 1840s to government-sponsored Jewish schools, established under Nicholas I, by the Ministry of Education. About three thousand children were educated at these institutions, a figure that is proportionately similar to the eighty thousand Russian children receiving elementary and secondary-level schooling. The first cohort of graduates from Nicholas' Jewish schools, as well as from the two modern rabbinical seminaries established in Vilna and Zhitomir, produced the generation that founded modern Russian-Jewish culture and politics. At the same time, the profound opposition of Hasidim to all forms of nontraditional education fueled mass resistance to government schools. Too many Jews remained suspicious that a government-sponsored education had a conversionary bias. In the reign of Alexander II, when the social benefits of secular schooling became evident— a university degree was the passport out of the Pale of Settlement—Jewish students began to seek entry in Russian institutions of higher learning in large numbers for the first time.

As part of his carrot-and-stick program to encourage the social integration of Russian Jewry, Nicholas charged his minister of education, Sergei Uvarov, to sponsor a program of "official enlightenment," which included the creation of a network of reformed Jewish schools, two modern rabbinic seminaries, and the enactment of a set of regulations restricting certain customs, deemed superstitious and a barrier to enlightenment. These included prohibitions on traditional Jewish garb and early marriage. Uvarov cultivated the support of local Maskilim as experts, school teachers, and advisors. An admirer of the integration efforts of German Jewry, he sought out the assistance of the director of the modern Jewish school in the Russian–German city of Riga, Max Lilienthal (1814–1882), to introduce the project to the Russian-Jewish masses. Uvarov dispatched Lilienthal on a tour of the Pale of Settlement to ascertain the attitude of Jewish communities to the government's new educational policies. Almost everywhere he went, Lilienthal, a German-speaking, clean-shaven, short-coated "reformer," was greeted with suspicion and hostility by Jewish communal leaders, who were steeled against both the government and the Maskilim. Only in Odessa, which would later become a center of the Hebrew language revival, did local Jewish enlighteners warmly accept Lilienthal. In search of new economic opportunities, Lilienthal soon left Europe for the United States, where he became a communal leader, first in New York and then most notably in Cincinnati, and was instrumental in the development of Reform Judaism.

Although Nicholas' reform project found nearly universal support among Russian-Jewish enlighteners desirous of using the prodigious resources of the state to implement their own social vision and oust the existing elites (especially the Hasidic rebbes), most Jews associated "official enlightenment" with the conversionary goals of the conscription decree. Indeed, for Nicholas—the proponent of official nationalism, dynastic patriotism, and Orthodox discipline—the line between integration and conversion blurred. In a secret memorandum, the tsar averred that "the purpose of educating the Jews is to bring about their gradual merging with Christian nationalities, and to uproot those superstitions and harmful prejudices which are instilled by the teachings of the Talmud." Under Uvarov, the program took on a life of its own; in fact, the curriculum of the new schools included the teaching of Talmud by enlightened Jewish instructors, charged with teaching all Jewish subjects. Still, most Jews did not appreciate the distinction between "school service" and "military service." Lilienthal admitted that any program of Jewish enlightenment would have to overcome Jewish hostility to government intervention in Jewish affairs—hostility that extended also to the Maskilim—declaring that "an honest Jewish father will never agree to train his child for conversion."

Haskalah and Language

Language formed a key component of the modern Jewish experience. Four essential Maskilic positions reflected a welter of Jewish cultural predispositions, generational and socioeconomic realities, and political inclinations. In both central and eastern Europe, early Maskilim favored the use of Hebrew. In the initial prospectus of the Haskalah journal *Ha-meassef*, the emphasis on Hebrew was made in the following way. Explaining the contents of a section entitled "Essay and Disquisitions," the editors noted:

> At the source will be the words of men who are learned in languages in general and in the wisdom and character of Hebrew in particular. This section will illuminate subjects in Hebrew grammar, clarify problems of phraseology and rhetoric, chart a path in Hebrew poetry, and teach the reader to recognize the meaning of the individual root words.

In the Russian Haskalah, a similar sentiment predominated; what began as a standard Maskilic position later became one of the central planks of Zionism, whose followers became the staunchest advocates of Hebrew culture. In 1868, the Hebrew novelist **Peretz Smolenskin** (1840–1885) founded a journal with the optimistic name *Ha-shahar* (*The Dawn*). More explicitly political than the editors of *Ha-meassef*, Smolenskin declared:

> When people ask what the renewal of the Hebrew language will give us I shall answer: It will give us self-respect and courage. . . . Our language is our national fortress; if it disappears into oblivion the memory of our people will vanish from the face of the earth.

Many doubted the moral appropriateness of using Hebrew for modern, secular culture, while others questioned the project on aesthetic grounds. Did Hebrew have a vocabulary and syntax that could be modernized? The issue of whether it could really be done successfully was answered with the work of the Lithuanian-born **Abraham Mapu** (1808–1867). Regarded as the father of the modern Hebrew novel, he turned explicitly to Israel's past as a source of inspiration for modern Jewish renewal. Influenced by the French Romantic school, Mapu's *Love of Zion* (1853), written in sparse language with evocative descriptions of ancient Israel's terrain, depicts the romance between Amnon and Tamar in the days of King Hezekiah and the prophet Isaiah. The book was extremely popular with Jewish readers.

Yet other modernizers among the Jews of eastern Europe rejected the idea that the language of the Bible could best carry Jews into the modern age and likewise dismissed the idea that Judaism and Jewishness could only be fashioned in Hebrew. Maskilic populists argued that for strategic, political, and cultural reasons, change should be propounded in the dominant language of the people: Yiddish. In the Russian census of 1897, 97 percent of respondents claimed that Yiddish was their mother tongue. Yiddish was the language of millions, indeed the most widely spoken vernacular in Jewish history. The great author **Sholem Yankev Abramovitch** (1836–1917)—known by his popular pseudonym, Mendele Moykher Sforim ("Mendele the Bookseller")—is considered to be *der zeyde* ("the grandfather") of modern Yiddish literature. Abramovitch, the founder of modern Jewish prose in both Hebrew and Yiddish, spoke out against the Hebraists: "Those of our writers who know Hebrew, our Holy Tongue, and continue to write in it, do not care whether or not the people understand it." Despite the dire warnings of his friends, he abandoned Hebrew prose for Yiddish because "my love for the useful defeated false-pride." He went on to publish in the first successful weekly Yiddish newspaper, **Kol Mevasser** (**The Herald**), founded in Odessa in 1863. According to Abramovitch, his novella *The Little Man* (1864), a satire about the backward state of the Jews in the Pale of Settlement, "laid the cornerstone of modern Yiddish literature. From then on, my soul desired only Yiddish." By the turn of the century, Yiddish no longer served only the cause of the Haskalah but also Jewish literary modernism and political expression. By the middle of the nineteenth century, the shtetl had begun to go into economic decline. The emancipation of the serfs in 1861 and the spread of railroads in Russia saw the beginnings of a great flight from the land. Far from train lines and rendered economically marginal, the *shtetlekh* seemed to be left behind by history. The theme of shtetl backwardness was a predominant theme in Haskalah literature and found full expression in the work of Ayzik-Meyer Dik, who in 1868 published his biting satire *The Panic, or the Town of Heres*. Dik also lampooned the rabbis of his day, but not all rabbis. As a moderate Maskil, he celebrated the heroic exploits (real and invented) of rabbis from the distant Ashkenazic past, as if to ask, if we once produced such honorable men, why cannot Russian Jewry do so again?

Hebraists faced stiff competition not only from Yiddish as a language but from Yiddishism, as an ideological movement, which was begun in the 1860s by **Alexander Zederbaum** (1816–1893) with the publication of *Kol Mevasser*. Though Yiddish was already at least eight hundred years old, *Kol Mevasser* marked the emergence of Yiddish as a literary language, for it standardized Yiddish orthography and provided an opportunity for the best young Yiddish writers of the day to publish their works.

By the modern period, Hebrew and Yiddish were engaged in an unfortunate language war. What should never have been an either/or choice saw militants pit one language against the other. Some, like the Zionist author **Micha Yosef Berdichevsky** (1865–1921), did not believe it had to be that way. There was room and indeed necessity for both tongues, something the average eastern European Jew would have instinctively believed. Hebrew was, for Berdichevsky, the language of Jewish tradition and texts, but so too was Yiddish:

> The [Yiddish] language is still so indivisible from the Jew, so thickly rooted in his soul, that all we can say about it is, this is how a Jew talks; . . . You see, anyone can learn Hebrew, provided that he confines himself to his desk for a few years, stuffs himself with the Bible and grammar, and reads some *melitse* books. The mastering of Yiddish, however, is a gift; a faculty one must be born with. I am speaking, of course, of the real thing, of radical, authentic Yiddish.

For Berdichevsky, who wrote mostly but not exclusively in Hebrew, Yiddish was "purely Jewish [for] in it is expressed and revealed the soul of a people." For the Hebrew poet Bialik, Hebrew and Yiddish were a "match made in heaven." Yiddish played a pivotal role in the creation of modern Hebrew, although that is something hardly any of the Hebraists would dare admit. In addition to being a living repository of

Hebrew words and expressions, Yiddish also provided Hebrew with vocabulary, syntax, and intonation, serving to make modern and animate the ancient language. (Modern Hebrew would also borrow liberally from other European languages.) As a vernacular Jewish tongue, Yiddish also served as a model and source of hope for those seeking to turn Hebrew into a daily language for millions of Jews.

The prestige of Yiddish grew immeasurably in the nineteenth century, especially thanks to the creation of a towering literary canon. Due to the dazzling talents of Sholem Yakov Abramovitch, **I. L. Peretz** (1852–1915), and Sholem Rabinowitz, better known as **Sholem Aleichem** (1859–1916), Yiddish was elevated to the status of a great European literature. This gave hope to the ideological proponents of the language while it gave untold pleasure to millions. Yiddish also gained currency as the language of a vibrant newspaper, periodical, musical, theatre, and, later, film culture. (*See box*, Sholem Aleichem.)

The principal theoreticians of Yiddishism were the Jewish nationalist **Nathan Birnbaum** (1864–1937), who also coined the term *Zionism*, and the philosopher, literary critic, political activist, and architect of secular Jewish culture **Chaim Zhitlovsky (1865–1943).** Together, they developed sophisticated theories of Diaspora nationalism and in 1908 organized the First Yiddish Language Conference in Czernowitz, at which Yiddish was declared "a national language of the Jewish people." Though the language was expressive of the Jewish soul, as Berdichevsky said, the great author I. L. Peretz declared at Czernowitz that Yiddish was to be the means by which Jews would draw closer to non-Jews: "We no longer want to be fragmented, and to render to every Moloch nation-state its tribute: There is one people—Jews, and its language is Yiddish. And in this language we want to amass our cultural treasures, create our culture, rouse our spirits and souls, and unite culturally with all countries and all times. . . . If Yiddish is to become a full member in the family of the languages of the world, it must become accessible to the world." It is in such expressions that the universalism of the Yiddishists appeared to clash with the more parochial sentiments of the Hebraists. In truth, however, both languages were so deeply Jewish that neither one became "accessible to the world."

The Orthodox embraced Yiddish. Unlike Jewish politcal revolutionaries or modernists, they used Yiddish to stem the tide of secularization. While they reserved Hebrew for liturgy and Torah study, Yiddish was now the product of self-conscious choice and thus an expression of Orthodoxy's own antagonistic encounter with modernity. For **Rabbi Akiba Joseph Schlesinger** (1837–1922), who officially defined the ideology of ultra-Orthodoxy (*haredi*, in Hebrew), Yiddish

SHOLEM ALEICHEM

Sholem Aleichem (1859–1916) was one of the most gifted of all Jewish writers. Like his equally talented contemporaries, Mendele Moykher Sforim and I. L. Peretz, Sholem Aleichem had begun as a Hebrew writer but switched to Yiddish to speak to his people in their own language. To a greater extent than his fellow Yiddish authors, Sholem Aleichem wrote in such a way as to perfectly capture the nuance and cadence, the rhythms and patterns, of spoken Yiddish. Doing this created an intense intimacy with the reader that few authors in any language have been able to enjoy. Readers heard themselves or their neighbors in Sholem Aleichem's characters.

Sholem Aleichem was a brilliant humorist and created beloved characters, such as Tevye the Dairyman and Menachem Mendl, the latter a ne'er-do-well schemer, into whose mouths he put expressions and aphorisms that were so appealing that they were quickly incorporated into Yiddish. The Tevye character, upon which the Broadway musical *Fiddler on the Roof* was based, was famous for his running monologues with God, arguing with him in a time-honored Jewish tradition. In the story "Tevye Strikes It Rich," we see another characteristic aspect of Sholem Aleichem's style, as Tevye's words flow in a torrent of stream-of-conscious pre-varication: "Well, to make a long story short, it happened early one summer, around Shavuos time. But why should I lie to you? It might have been a week or two before Shavuos too, unless it was several weeks after. What I'm trying to tell you is that it took place exactly a dog's age ago, nine or ten years to the day, if not a bit more or less."

Sholem Aleichem wrote biting (and late in life, rather dark) social commentary. In 1909, he published the short story "Talk about the Riviera," a brilliantly witty satire on the emergence of middle-class values among Jews and, in the process, their adoption of gentile habits. In this case, Jews going on vacation become the object of ridicule and self-parody as the monologist mocks his own plight—being stuck in an expensive European holiday resort:

> Talk about the Riviera?—Thanks but no thanks. . . . Because the Riviera is the kind of place they've got over in Italy that doctors have thought up only to squeeze money out of people. The sky is always blue there. Same old sky as back home. Sun is the same too. Only the sea, that's the worst part! Because all it does is heave and crash about and make a great thundering nuisance of itself—and, by God, you never stop paying for it either. Why pay for it? Oh, no reason. No reason at all. . . . One good thing about the place, though—give credit where credit is due—it's warm there. It's always warm there, the whole blasted year. Both summer and winter. Yes, but what's the point? The point is the sun keeps you warm. Well, yes, but what's the point? Keep a good fire going at home and you won't be cold either. "Air ___ ___," they say. Well, yes, the air isn't too bad as air goes. Doesn't smell too bad either. Got kind of a fragrance to it. Only it's not the air that smells, it's the oranges that smell. Out there, they grow oranges. But I don't know if that's enough reason to be traveling all that way for it. Seems to me there is air all over. And you can buy oranges at home, anyway.

Sholem Aleichem enjoyed international fame and was a genuine hero, read by Jews the world over. As the literary critic Irving Howe put it, "Every Jew who could read Yiddish, whether he was orthodox or secular, conservative or radical, loved Sholem Aleichem, for he heard in his stories the charm and melody of a common *shprakh*, the language that bound all together." When Sholem Aleichem died on May 13, 1916, over 100,000 people lined the streets of New York City to pay their respects. To this day, it remains one of the largest funerals the city has ever seen.

---

was elevated to the status of a sanctified language. In his work of 1864, *The Heart of the Hebrew,* the Hungarian Schlesinger invoked the authority of his teacher, Moses Sofer. "Our sainted ancestors, who were forced not to speak Hebrew, changed the language of the nations into Yiddish. . . . Thus we have to understand Rabbi Sofer's command that we must not change the language (that is, replacing Yiddish with an-other language) since our Yiddish is, from the viewpoint of Jewish law, just like Hebrew." Yiddish was not merely spoken in the Orthodox world but was used in religious scholarship and books in that language constituted about 8 percent of the library holdings of the Volozhin yeshiva. The old canards about Yiddish being the language of Jewish women and unlearned men simply do not comport with social reality.

Yiddish readers in eastern Europe had access to a variety of reading matter, both religious and secular. Yiddish literacy was nearly universal, an astonishing development in light of the fact that on the eve of the Russian Revolution, Russian literacy stood at a mere 20 percent.

Finally, there were those Maskilim who insisted that Jews learn European vernaculars. Even while the Berlin Haskalah sought to revitalize Hebrew, its proponents simultaneously ex-tolled the virtues of learning German. Mendelssohn even claimed that it would be of ethical benefit to the Jews to learn the language, since Yiddish was morally corrupting. After the Ashkenazic Jews of France had been emancipated in 1791, the communal leader and merchant **Berr Isaac Berr** (1744–1828) sent a letter to the Jews of Alsace and Lorraine in which he

שלום עליכם'ס ווערקע

טביה דער מילכיגער

אן

אנדערע ערצעהלונגען

ערסטער באנד

מאדעקלאסטס פרעסס איסנאבעט
ניארק
תרע"ב—1912.

Frontispiece of Sholem Aleichem's three-volume work, *Tevye the Dairyman and Other Stories* (1912).

exhorted his Yiddish-speaking co-religionists: "French ought to be the Jews' mother tongue since they are reared with and among Frenchmen." Wherever the Haskalah began to make an impact, voices were to be heard encouraging Jews to learn the language of the majority. In the first Russian-language Jewish weekly, *Razsvet* (*The Dawn*), the author Osip Rabinovich pointed out that "In other European countries the Jews speak the pure language of their Christian brothers, and that fact does not hinder them from being good Jews." For his own community, he stressed, "The Russian language must serve as the primary force animating the masses, because, apart from divine providence, language is the constitutive factor of humanity. Our homeland is Russia—just as its air is ours, so its language must become ours."

Important though they were, the positions we have outlined were those of cultural ideologues. Other prominent Maskilim counseled Jews to be bearers of more than one culture. In his 1866 poem "Awake My People!" the Russian-Jewish poet Judah Leib Gordon (1830–1892) exhorted his readers: "Be a man abroad and a Jew at home." Generally speaking, most Jews would have concurred. They were not content with monolingualism and often deployed a variety of languages in different social, intellectual, and political settings. (*See box,* Linguistic Border Crossing: The Creation of Esperanto.)

All over Europe and in the Ottoman Empire, Ashkenazim and Sephardim inhabited polyglot worlds where they had facility with three or four languages, at least two of which

LINGUISTIC BORDER CROSSING: THE CREATION OF ESPERANTO

A noteworthy linguistic innovation was the invention of Esperanto by a Polish Jewish ophthalmologist, **Ludwik Lazar Zamenhof** (1859–1917). Raised in Bialystok, Zamenhof was reputedly troubled by the animus that existed between the city's three main ethnic groups: Poles, Belorussians, and Yiddish-speaking Jews. He believed that if they only shared a language much of the hostility they felt toward each other would dissipate. To that end, in 1887 he published the first book in *Esperanto*, a word that means "one who hopes." This was an apt description for Zamenhof, for his utopian goal was to create a language that was easy to learn and would become a universal second language. His ultimate hope was that it would promote peace and international understanding.

were Jewish. Because they could speak several languages, Jews adapted well and quickly to changing economic and political circumstances. This stood them in particularly good stead in the era of mass migration. Combined with vastly superior literacy rates compared to non-Jews, multilingualism also made vast amounts of information accessible to Jews. The acquisition of such knowledge both threatened tradition but also prepared Jews better than most for the demands of modernity.

Wissenschaft des Judentums (Scientific Study of Judaism)

One of the catalysts for the emergence of new Jewish cultural expressions and religious streams within Judaism was the rise of historical consciousness in the nineteenth century. The discipline of history, as we understand it, the desire to grasp the meaning of historical development, to separate myth from reality and record "what really happened," as the historian Leopold von Ranke (1795–1886) said, is a product of modernity. Beginning in the second decade of the nineteenth century in Germany, the first Jewish historians began to appear. Dedicated to casting a reflective and introspective eye on the Jewish past, they sought to apply critical methods of scholarly analysis to those texts that had once principally been the focus of religious devotion and exegesis. Urgency for such a project also came from a violent outburst of antisemitism in Germany. The Hep Hep riots of 1819 (see Chapter 10) inspired a group of largely assimilated German-Jewish university students to join together with some aging Maskilim to defend Jews against a host of charges that surfaced during the riots. They believed that their mightiest weapon in the forthcoming cultural battle was the writing of objective history. To this end, in 1819 they founded the Society for Culture and the Scientific Study of the Jews, thus inaugurating modern Jewish scholarship, known as the Scientific Study of

Judaism or, by its German name, *Wissenschaft des Judentums.*

The old method of Jewish learning was no longer sufficient to satisfy the needs and sensibilities of these young Jewish intellectuals. They had been the first Jews to study anything other than medicine at the university level and armed with the critical academic skills they acquired in the study of history and philology, they sought to define the place of Judaism in a post-emancipation world. The proponents of the academic study of Judaism were motivated by two main impulses. The first was the wish to have it (and by extension the Jewish people) accorded the respect of inclusion in the university curriculum. They believed that only through education could tolerance and bigotry be eliminated. Secular Jewish scholars were of the opinion that civic equality for Jews that was not accompanied by the formal recognition of the cultural value and richness of Judaism would be without value and would, in fact, compromise the legal gains made by individual Jews. Emancipation without respect would ring hollow. Second, prominent figures in the Scientific Study of Judaism movement feared that rapid and increasing social integration meant that not only non-Jews but Jews themselves needed to learn about the magnificence of Jewish religious culture. But they were not optimistic. In his programmatic study *On Rabbinic Literature* (1818), the historian Leopold Zunz declared that in Germany postbiblical Hebrew literature was "being led to the grave," while the bibliographer Moritz Steinschneider declared sarcastically that Judaism needed to be studied "to give it a decent burial."

As **Joel Abraham List** (1780–c. 1848), a Jewish elementary school director and one of the founders of the society, remarked, "Jews one after another are detaching themselves from the community. Jewry is on the verge of complete disintegration." Conversion to Christianity was the most extreme expression of this "disintegration," which, beginning in the

THE NEW ISRAELITE HOSPITAL IN HAMBURG

On the occasion of the laying of the hospital's foundation stone in 1841, the author, Heinrich Heine (1797–1856), nephew of the hospital's patron, Salomon Heine, wrote the following poem, in which he considered the inheritability and indelibility of Jewish identity. Heinrich, who had converted to Protestantism in 1825 because he was unable, as a Jewish law graduate, to gain admission to the bar, never stopped thinking of himself as Jewish:

A hospital for sick and needy Jews,
For those poor mortals who are triply wretched,
With three great evil maladies afflicted:
With poverty and pain and Jewishness.

The worst of these three evils is the last one,
The thousand-year-old family affliction,
The plague they carried from the Nile valley,
The old Egyptian unhealthy faith.

Incurable deep-seated hurt! No treatment
By vapour bath or douche can help to heal it,

No surgery, nor all the medications,
This hospital can offer to its patients.

Will Time, eternal goddess, some day end it,
Root out this dark misfortune that the fathers
Hand down to sons? And some day will the grandson
Be healed and rational and happy?

I do not know! But meanwhile let us honour
The heart that sought so lovingly and wisely
To soften the afflictions one can soften,
By pouring timely balm upon the lesions.

The New Israelite Hospital in Hamburg was founded in 1841 by the Jewish merchant and philanthropist, Salomon Heine (1767–1844), in memory of his wife Betty. Germany had a tradition of establishing Jewish hospitals. The first one was opened in Berlin in 1756 and survived the Nazi era. It remains open today. (Courtesy of Leo Baeck Institute, New York)

eighteenth century, increased dramatically. The poet **Heinrich Heine** (1797–1856), who was a member of the Society for Culture and the Scientific Study of the Jews, converted to Lutheranism in 1825 that he might gain a doctorate or take up a career in the law. His conversion was pragmatic. Heine called his baptismal certificate "the ticket of admission to European culture" and told a friend some years later, "I make no secret of my Judaism, to which I have not returned, because I never left it." (*See box,* The New Israelite Hospital in Hamburg.)

When members of the Mendelssohn family and other famous Jewish personalities began to convert, it bespoke a crisis born of the unfulfilled hopes Jews invested in emancipation. This was the internal motivation for the founders of the Scientific Study of Judaism. The movement's ideology held that in the academic study of Judaism "the bond of science, the bond of pure rationality [and] the bond of truth" would unite Christians and Jews by erasing the differences between the two groups. As **Eduard Gans** (1798–1839), a jurist, historian, and founding member of the Society for Culture and the Scientific Study of the Jews put it in 1822, "[E]verything passes without perishing, and yet persists, although it has long been consigned to the past. That is why neither the Jews will perish nor Judaism dissolve; in the larger movement of the whole they will have seemed to have disappeared, yet they will live on as the river lives on in the ocean." In other words, the Jews would become invisible while Jewishness would persist. Quoting the philosopher Johann Gottfried von Herder, Gans predicted, "There will be a time when no one in Europe will ask any longer, who is a Jew and who is a Christian?"

Nothing in this outlook constituted a program for stemming the tide of Jewish assimilation and conversion. In fact, Gans' own fate confirmed the reality that insurmountable political barriers stymied the progress of talented Jews. Denied an appointment in the law faculty at the University of Berlin because he was Jewish, Gans traveled to Belgium, England, and France seeking a similar appointment. He was unsuccessful. Fed up, he was baptized in Paris in 1825 and returned to Berlin, where he was immediately offered the position for which he had been initially turned down because he was a Jew.

Nonetheless, the Scientific Study of Judaism remained enormously influential in three ways. First, it originated the critical, secular study of Judaism and Jewish history. Second, despite the defection of the founders of the Scientific Study of Judaism, subsequent generations of scholars who remained wedded to the goal of preserving Judaism emerged. And third, later innovations in Judaism, such as Reform, Modern Orthodoxy, and Positive-Historical Judaism, owe their existence to the fact that the leading figures in such developments were imbued with the historical spirit and methodological innovations ushered in by Wissenschaft des Judentums.

The Rise of Modern Jewish Historiography

Leopold Zunz (1794–1886) was a historian of Judaism and one of the founders of the Wissenschaft movement. Typical of a new generation of Jewish scholars, Zunz, who studied philology at the University of Berlin and obtained a doctorate from the University of Halle, studied Jewish texts, employing secular, critical methods. His overriding ambition was to obtain command over the entire corpus of medieval Jewish literature and historically situate each work. Within a few years of founding the Society for Culture and the Scientific Study of the Jews, he became the editor of the important

but short-lived *Journal for the Science of Judaism,* the first publication in the field of Jewish studies. His initial contribution was a biography of the medieval biblical exegete, Rashi. Zunz was ordained as a rabbi and served for two years as preacher in the Reform New Synagogue in Berlin but eventually left because he was too wedded to tradition to accept the innovations of Reform Judaism. This became a feature of his scholarship when, for example, he wrote an essay extolling the high ethical value of wearing *tefillin* (phylacteries). However, his disenchantment with Reform Judaism did not mean any abandonment of Reform's sense of Judaism's historical development over time. Uncovering that process remained for him a noble and necessary goal.

Zunz was a very productive scholar, writing on a vast array of subjects including synagogue liturgy and practice and Jewish religious poetry, as well as an important study of Jewish names. His preeminent scholarly work, *The Sermons of the Jews, Historically Developed* (1832), is a masterful study of the history of Jewish preaching and constitutes one of the first attempts to describe the development of the entire Midrash. Just as the Haskalah was connected to politics, so too was Zunz's scholarship. His *Sermons of the Jews* convinced the German authorities, who were wary of religious innovation—which they felt was but a short step to political rebellion—not to ban Jewish preaching in German. Zunz demonstrated that Jews had preached sermons in the vernacular since the rabbinic period and thus German Jewry's doing so was in a time-honored tradition. Zunz was convinced that Jews had to apply the critical tools of modern scholarship to the examination of Jewish texts in the same manner that Christians were doing for their own sources. It was this, Zunz believed, that would mark the Jews as full participants in German culture because through their use of history they would be treading an intellectual path similar to that of their Christian neighbors.

To a great extent, Zunz was a literary historian. He produced little in the way of a history of the Jews. The first great exponent of that genre was **Isaac Marcus Jost** (1793–1860), a boyhood friend of Zunz. Between 1820–1828, he published his nine-volume *History of the Israelites from the Maccabean Period to Our Own Day.* This was the first modern history of the Jews, one that focused on their relationship to their host societies. Jost had received a traditional Jewish education and also studied history at university. For most of his life he taught in Jewish schools, especially at those institutions that can be considered progressive heirs of Berlin's Jewish Free School. Though little read today, Jost's historical work was a significant achievement for it was the first to apply the methodological principles of modern history writing to the Jewish past. Written in an impartial tone and in a simple, unadorned style, Jost's work was directed to common

Jew and Christian statesman alike. Its principal thrust was to demonstrate the loyalty Jews had displayed to their host societies throughout history. Beyond this, Jost's goal was to show that histories of European states were incomplete if the Jewish dimension to national life was ignored. Though highly learned, Jost's *History of the Israelites* was flat and apologetic and owed more to the rationalism of the Enlightenment than the more vivid nationalist sensibility of the Romantic era in which he actually lived. In later works, however, Jost first raised important questions about the Jewish past that have preoccupied historians ever since. In 1832, he wrote the *General History of the Israelite People,* a two-volume summary of his magnum opus, in which he tracked the uniqueness of the Jewish march through history. If in Jost's day history writing generally focused on high politics and war written by the victors, could one write the history of a group on the margins? As Jost asked, "Can there be a history of a slave?" Today, we might refer to such an attempt as "a history of the subaltern." Being a member of a long-reviled group on the periphery of European society made Jost especially attentive to the special nature of writing the history of the "Other."

Jost initiated a more programmatic approach to the study of the past. He urged fellow Jewish historians to use all available sources to write Jewish history, noting:

> [T]he historical sources are scattered far and wide. . . . One is confronted by an immense number of deeds, speeches, laws, disputes, opinions, stories, poems, legends, and other phenomena affecting the lot of the Israelites. This is to say nothing of the many different places, times, and thinkers. One must consider as well human inclinations, cultural variations, historical setting, and in general the prevailing circumstances of entire nations, districts, and individuals, to say nothing of natural predispositions, emotions, and intellectual movements. All this is necessary to arrive at a certain historical understanding and to derive fruitful results and just evaluations.

While Jost may have pioneered the writing of a comprehensive history of the Jews, that project was continued by **Heinrich Graetz** (1817–1891), the leading Jewish historian of the nineteenth century. Graetz's greatest scholarly achievement was his eleven-volume *History of the Jews,* published between 1853 and 1876. This work differed markedly from that of his predecessor. Where Jost's language was cold and dry, Graetz's was flamboyant and deeply impassioned, and where Jost seemed detached from his subject, Graetz was an advocate of the Jewish people against the prejudice that had followed them throughout history. His passions sometimes got the better of him, and he often lost all semblance of objectivity.

He was merciless toward those he deemed enemies of the Jews: These included entire peoples, such as the Romans, the Christians, and the Germans, as well as individual antagonists, such as Martin Luther and Voltaire. Graetz was nothing if not ecumenical in drawing up his list of enemies, for on it he included Hellenized Jews such as Herod and Josephus, early-modern apostates such as Johannes Pfefferkorn, and contemporary Reformers of Judaism such as Abraham Geiger. Graetz also utterly rejected the historical importance of the mystical tradition in Judaism and was deeply hostile toward eastern European Jewish culture, in particular, Hasidism.

Displaying virtuosic erudition, Graetz wrote Jewish history as no one had before. It has been called "suffering-and-scholarship history" because he focused almost exclusively on the history of anti-Judaism and later antisemitism and the history of rabbinic culture. Writing in a highly emotive style, Graetz observed, "This is the eighteen-hundred-year era of the Diaspora, of unprecedented suffering, of uninterrupted martyrdom without parallel in world history. But it is also a period of spiritual alertness, of restless mental activity, of indefatigable inquiry." In keeping with the way national histories were written in his day, Graetz's magisterial sweep rarely offered a glimpse of the social world of the Jewish people. He concentrated on Jewish intellectual life and the impact on Jews of the host societies' policies. He painted a bleak picture of Jewish life, yet at the same time evoked the grandeur of Jewish tenacity and creativity. Conceptually, Graetz's great innovation was to depict the Jews as a national group. Where previous practitioners of the Scientific Study of Judaism saw the Jews as a religious community, Graetz was a Romantic; he described the Jews as an "ethnic group" and maintained that their history possesses a "national character." In contrast to Jost and Geiger, Graetz characterized the post-Talmudic era as

> by no means the mere history of a religion. . . . Its object is not simply the course of development of an independent people, which, though it possesses no soil, fatherland, geographical boundaries, or state organism, replaced these concrete conditions with spiritual powers. Though scattered over the civilized portions of the earth and attached to the land of their hosts, the members of the Jewish race did not cease to feel themselves a single people in their religious conviction, historical memory, customs, and hopes.

The Rise of Reform Judaism

After some brief French-inspired attempts at transforming the synagogue service in Holland (1796) and in the kingdom of Westphalia (1808), and a private congregation established in

Warsaw in 1802 called *Di Daytshe Shil* ("the German syna-gogue" in Yiddish), the focus of religious reform shifted to Germany. The first synagogue there to introduce aesthetic changes was the private service founded in Westphalia by the man known as the father of Reform Judaism, **Israel Jacobson** (1768–1828). Jacobson's temple not only was met with Jewish opposition but in 1817 was forced by the Prussian government to close. The authorities were of the opinion that the willing-ness to abandon religious tradition might translate into a desire to institute radical political change. Jacobson left Berlin and moved to the more hospitable environment of Hamburg.

There, in 1818, the New Israelite Temple Association founded the Hamburg Temple. The association wished "to re-store public worship to its deserving dignity and importance." As an early defender of the temple stated, "Look at the Gentiles and see how they stand in awe and reverence and with good manners in their house of prayer." Inspired by Jacobson's first efforts at reforming the style of synagogue services, the board of the Hamburg Temple insisted on strict decorum; emphasized the Saturday morning service (at the expense of the normal thrice daily services) and limited it to two hours; allowed for a choir and organ; instituted a confirmation ceremony for boys and girls; mandated weekly sermons in German, time for which was made by eliminating the traditional weekly reading of the prophets; introduced a German-language prayer book, which most significantly eliminated references to the coming of a personal messiah; and removed prayers that called for an end to Jewish exile and a return to Zion.

The rabbinical court of Hamburg immediately pub-lished a volume of responsa that set out its opposition to the temple. Rabbis from across Europe rose up in indignation. The most important opponent of the Hamburg Temple was **Rabbi Moses Sofer** (1762–1839). Popularly known as the Hatam Sofer, in 1806 he was appointed rabbi of Pressburg, at the time the most important Jewish community in Hungary. A renowned Talmudist, his yeshiva was the epicenter of the battle against Reform Judaism. Widely recognized as leading the forces of traditional Jewry, he opposed any changes in Judaism, his battle cry encapsulated in dire warnings such as this:

> May your mind not turn to evil and never engage in cor-ruptible partnership with those fond of innovations. . . . Do not touch the books of Rabbi Moses [Mendelssohn] from Dessau, and your foot will never slip. . . . The daughters may read German books but only those that have been written in our own way, according to the in-terpretations of our teachers. . . . Be warned not to change your Jewish names, speech and clothing—God forbid. . . . Never say: "Times have changed."

Institutionally, it took two generations for Reform Ju-daism to become firmly established in German congregations. After the founding of the Hamburg Temple, Reform houses of worship were not built in significant numbers until the 1830s. Thereafter, Reform Judaism even made itself a palpa-ble presence in rural areas, but it spread slowly. In 1837, the small village of Walldorf had 1,580 inhabitants, 567 of whom were Jewish. Moritz Siegel was born in the village and was the son of a well-to-do textile merchant. His description of Jewish religious life in the German countryside indicates the extent to which religious reform was bound up with other factors, including Jewish contact with non-Jewish society, exposure to general education, and one's social status and class. Essentially, two groups of Jews resided in Walldorf, one poorer and tradi-tional, the other wealthier and religiously progressive:

> In the years of my youth, these two factions also went their own ways socially, so that on holidays, for example, the Festival of Weeks [Shavuot] or the Festival of Booths [Succot], the celebrations were held separately. In our so-cial circle there prevailed a highly proper tone, within the boundaries of the most refined customs and manners, and to be included in our circle was a privilege. Already at the time we celebrated our balls with a gay dinner and lively conversation, with speeches and wine, and although our menus did not conform to the precepts of ritual law, this was no cause for us to enjoy ourselves less. The dietary laws were not strictly observed by the younger generation, most of whom had seen the world and thereby departed from the old customs. I remember quite well, already as a seven- or eight-year-old boy, seeing young grown ups from my family circle or other circles smoking their cigars on Saturday and eating at the inns. This was at the end of the 1840s. To be sure, the fact that many young people had received their training in the outside world con-tributed to this; the growing association with non-Jews and attendance at secondary schools also bore part of the blame; and, in addition, liberal thinking in Christian cir-cles at that time carried over to the Jewish population. What had once been regarded as inadmissible, that is, writing on Saturday, was permitted by Rabbi Hofmann [the Reform rabbi of Walldorf], and was also not objected to by his successors, so that gradually one custom after an-other crumbled away and. . . . Walldorf soon gained a rep-utation for being very liberal among communities that were more hesitant in their reforms.

Most of the new Reform schools and temples that opened in Germany largely in the second half of the nine-teenth century expressed the universalistic sentiments of the

Enlightenment, touting the way such ideals harmonized with Judaism. As Gotthold Salomon, the preacher at the Hamburg Temple put it, "The summons to be an Israelite is the summons to be a human being." But, the most important development that facilitated the growth of Reform theology and practice was the appearance in the 1830s of a new kind of rabbi. University educated, familiar with the secular disciplines of history, philology, philosophy, and classics, the new German rabbi was heir to the Haskalah and often a proponent of Wissenschaft. Neither in eastern Europe nor other parts of western Europe did rabbis with Ph.D. degrees appear on the religious landscape. Of particular significance is the fact that such rabbis appeared among German Orthodox as well as Reform rabbis. This feature made Judaism in Germany distinct, marking it as a unique innovation in Ashkenazic civilization.

The new rabbinical elite brought a new sensibility to the practice and theology of Judaism, one born of their own intellectual encounter with secular studies. Typifying the new outlook was **Abraham Geiger** (1810–1874). The product of a traditional Jewish education, Geiger, who was thoroughly versed in classical Jewish literature, was the spiritual leader of Reform Judaism. After attending the University of Bonn, where he studied Near Eastern languages and philosophy, Geiger spent a lifetime in scholarship, writing the history of Judaism. He employed historical scholarship to demonstrate that instituting reforms was not anathema to Judaism because Jewish culture was constantly in flux, engaged with its surroundings and flexible enough to respond to the demands times.

Geiger's contribution to the writing of Jewish religious history was novel in a number of ways. Methodologically, his approach was truly comparative; he made a genuine attempt to historicize religious origins, seeking to discover the relationship between the three great monotheistic faiths: Judaism, Christianity, and Islam. Moreover, Geiger sought to elevate new textual sources of rabbinic Judaism to their proper place in the development of Christianity and Islam. In Geiger's estimation, both the Gospels and the Koran bore the unmistakable stamp of midrashic and Talmudic wisdom.

Geiger integrated Reform innovations into a coherent ideology and subjected the Jewish religious canon to the dictates of modern textual criticism. In contrast to Graetz, Geiger strenuously denied the national element in Judaism. Only ancient Israel could be characterized as a national entity, but even then, Judaism as an idea did not really require the trappings of nationhood: a common language and national institutions. For Geiger, Judaism's greatness and its survival through the ages lay in the fact that religion transcended national–political externalities. Rather, Judaism was free to grow as a pure expression of faith in God. This formulation

suited Jews who wished to proclaim their loyalty to Germany and remain true to Judaism.

As someone who saw the history of Judaism in evolutionary terms, Geiger divided its development into four conceptual periods: (1) Revelation, a period "which extends to the close of the biblical era, which cannot be said to have ended at the time of Exile, for its outgrowths continued well beyond that date"; (2) Tradition, "the period during which all biblical material was processed, shaped, and molded for life," which stretches from "the completion of the Bible to the completion of the Babylonian Talmud"; (3) Legalism, when "the spiritual heritage was guarded and preserved, but no one felt authorized to reconstruct it or develop it further"—this period extended from the completion of the Babylonian Talmud into the middle of the eighteenth century; and (4) Critical Study, a period of liberation "marked by an effort to loosen the fetters of the previous era by means of the use of reason and historical research." Geiger saw this final period as characterized by the attempt to "revitalize Judaism." In so doing, he endowed his own age with the character of creative vitality akin to the first and second periods of Judaism's initial genius and subsequent growth. Geiger regarded it as scholarship's task to reverse the atrophy of the third period and revitalize Judaism.

Rabbinical Conferences

Despite Geiger's efforts to provide Reform Judaism with a solid intellectual and philosophical grounding, divisions soon began to appear not just between reformers and their opponents but among the reformers themselves, split between lay reformers and rabbis. To heal the fissures and to facilitate the broad acceptance of Reform Judaism, the rabbi and publicist **Ludwig Philippson** (1811–1889) proposed that those dedicated to reform meet to confer about the most pressing issues facing the movement. To that end, rabbinic conferences were held in Germany in 1844, 1845, and 1846. It is noteworthy that similar divisions between traditionalists and reformers also appeared among German Catholics and Protestants in the 1840s. Jewish religious leaders were not alone in seeking to define the role of religion in the modern world.

The first of the conferences took up a variety of issues, some of which produced broad consensus among the participants. For example, all agreed on abolishing the demeaning oath that Jews were still required to swear in courts in certain German states. On the subject of Jewish patriotism, one delegate concluded, "[T]he Jew acknowledges every man as his brother. But he acknowledges his fellow countryman [the Germans] to be one with whom he is connected by a particular bond." The proponent of radical Reform, **Samuel**

Holdheim (1806–1860), seeking to denationalize the links between Jews, likewise declared, "The doctrine of Judaism is thus, first your compatriots then your co-religionists."

At the second conference of 1845 the thirty participants devoted themselves to the question of language and Jewish liturgy. Just as language posed a problem for Maskilim and their opponents, so too did the debate over language concern religious reformers. On one hand, increasing use of German at home left fewer and fewer Jews with a command of Hebrew; on the other, the continued use of what was once the Jews' national language might compromise the conferees' claims to German patriotism. A split emerged between those who supported retaining the centrality of Hebrew prayer and those who felt it both practical and necessary to pray in German. Abraham Geiger declared Hebrew to be his mother tongue but nevertheless declared solemnly, "[A] German prayer strikes a deeper chord than a Hebrew prayer." Ultimately, Geiger held the opinion that Hebrew was dispensable because "anyone who imagines Judaism to be walking on the crutches of a language deeply offends it."

Geiger encountered opposition from **Zacharias Frankel** (1801–1875), the founder of Positive-Historical Judaism. For Frankel, who favored moderate reforms, Hebrew was essential for "it is the language of our Scripture which . . . is a constant reminder of our Covenant with God." Frankel also feared that dispensing with Hebrew meant that it would become the intellectual property of the rabbis alone; this would bring about a breach with the people and thus, as far as Frankel was concerned, could not have been God's intention. In fact, maintaining the centrality of Hebrew was so self-evident to Frankel that he resisted a law to ensure that Hebrew would be the language of liturgy because no one had "ever thought of abandoning the Hebrew language." A narrow majority determined that the retention of Hebrew was a subjective claim by its proponents and that it was probably not necessary. At this point, Frankel walked out of the conference.

Two other issues occupied the attendees at the second conference: Sabbath observance and the place of messianism. The radical Samuel Holdheim found himself almost entirely alone in his recommendation that the Sabbath be shifted from Saturday to Sunday, the day chosen by his congregation in Berlin and later among some classical Reform congregations in the United States. The overwhelming majority insisted on Saturday as the Jewish Sabbath. Messianism was reaffirmed as a central tenet of Judaism but was declared a universal conception, divorced from any projected return of the Jews to the Land of Israel.

The final conference of 1846 was a less charged affair than the previous two but also achieved less. Though it was never put to a vote apparently due to "a lack of time," the assembly heard a report on the status of women in the synagogue, advocating that they should enjoy religious equality, that prayer was as incumbent on them as it was on men, and that they should be counted as part of the *minyan,* the prayer quorum traditionally composed of ten males over the age of thirteen.

In the end, the conferences enjoyed mixed success. The new rabbinate certainly made its presence felt and initiated a serious discussion about Judaism. Over time, some of the assemblies' proposals were instituted in various communities both in Germany and abroad. These included the introduction of the organ, new prayers in lieu of those calling for the restoration of Temple sacrifice, the use of the vernacular in liturgy, and equality for women. We must stress, however, that the aesthetics, ideology, and sensibility of European Reform did not resemble current Reform practices in the United States. Rather, Reform Jewish congregations in nineteenth-century Europe for the most part still had segregated seating; they were not confronted with the issue of widespread intermarriage and the place of non-Jews among the congregants; and they were far more insistent on the denationalization of Judaism. While nineteenth-century Reform and Orthodox Judaism in Europe staunchly opposed Zionism, contemporary Reform congregations are equally staunch supporters of the national idea in Judaism and identify strongly with Israel.

Neo-Orthodoxy

The increasing prominence of the reformers inspired the growth of conservative reaction. The term *Orthodoxy* is itself a product of the modern period and does not appear until 1795. By the nineteenth century it was used as a term to distinguish traditional from Reform Jews. In response to the Reform assemblies, 116 German and Hungarian rabbis circulated a letter of protest, decrying the actions of the reformers. Sensing that Judaism was imperiled, the newly Orthodox not only led a defensive reaction but went on the offensive as well. The leader of what became known as Neo-Orthodoxy was **Samson Raphael Hirsch** (1808–1888) from Hamburg. Though Hirsch's family members voiced opposition to the Hamburg Temple, they were in favor of many aspects of the Haskalah. After receiving a traditional Jewish education, Hirsch went to a non-Jewish high school and then went to the University of Bonn in 1829 where he studied classical languages, history, and philosophy. It was there that he met Abraham Geiger and the two formed a Jewish debating society.

Modern Orthodoxy, of which Samson Raphael Hirsch was the founder, was just as keen to change Judaism's aesthetic as was Reform Judaism. A premium was placed on appearing appropriately attired in a manner befitting someone communing with God. In the mid-nineteenth century, modern rabbis, of whatever denominational stripe, were characterized by their having attended university. In this portrait, note Hirsch's collar and academic gown, which were also typical of contemporary Christian clerical dress. He is also sporting a very closely trimmed beard, and while one can assume Hirsch's head is covered, his skullcap is not visible in this picture.

Between 1830 and 1841, Hirsch served as the rabbi of a principality in north Germany. During this time he began to formulate his response to what he saw as the crisis besetting modern Jews. In 1836 he published his important *Nineteen Letters on Judaism,* following this one year later with *Choreb: Israel's Duties in the Diaspora.* Both of these works sought to establish the essential harmony between traditional Judaism and modernity.

The more famous of the two works, *The Nineteen Letters,* inaugurated a new form of Judaism, a self-consciously modern Orthodoxy that embraced rather than rejected modernity. The book is a passionate defense of traditional Judaism written in the form of an epistolary exchange between two young Jews—Benjamin, the spokesman for the "perplexed" of his generation of Jewish intellectuals whose faith was waning, and Naphtali, the representative of traditional Judaism. Naphtali responds to the skeptical questions of Benjamin in

the form of eighteen answers that explore the relationship of Jewish to secular culture. Hirsch articulates the belief that it is the task of human beings to actualize the infinite good, inherent in the Deity. But the exercise of free will prompts people to confront the choice between good and evil. Here, according to Hirsch, an entire community needs to be dedicated to the mission of teaching humanity to strive for goodness and obedience to God's will. Such a daunting task requires a collectivity with distinctive laws and customs that would illuminate the path for individual Jews, making it possible for them to guide the rest of humanity. The universal applicability of Jewish ethics was a belief shared by all streams of German Judaism. As one of the correspondents writes in the *Nineteen Letters,* "Consider for a moment the image of such an Israel, living freely among the nations, striving for its ideal! Every son of Israel a respected, widely influential priestly exemplar of justice and love, disseminating not Judaism—which is prohibited—but pure humanity among the nations!"

Unlike Mendelssohn, who saw Judaism and secular culture as compatible yet distinctly separate spheres, Hirsch sought to integrate the two in a practical way. He coined the term *Mensch-Jissroeïl,* thereby linking the German words for a human being (*Mensch*) and Israel (*Jissroeïl*) to designate a Jew who fully and with equal gusto celebrated both of these aspects of his personality, the general and the specifically Jewish. The same idea was expressed in a Hebrew concept that he coined, *Torah im derekh erets,* the fulfillment of which was to combine a commitment to Torah with active participation in the life of state and society. It is this aspect that makes Hirsch's brand of Judaism entirely different from the traditional Orthodoxy that preceded it.

Positive-Historical Judaism

The third significant stream of Judaism to emerge in the middle of the nineteenth century was termed Positive-Historical Judaism. Zacharias Frankel was the founding figure of what would later emerge in the United States as Conservative Judaism. He came from a family of distinguished Talmudists but was, like Hirsch, imbued with the values of the Enlightenment. He attended the University of Budapest and received a Ph.D. in the natural sciences, philosophy, and philology. The term *Positive-Historical* refers to Frankel's belief that the essence of Judaism was "positive," divinely revealed, and therefore could not be changed but by rabbinic fiat. But he also recognized that Judaism developed within history, thus its traditions and entire postbiblical development were subject to alteration and continual reinterpretation.

Frankel rejected unbending Orthodoxy as well as radical Reform. Instead, he was in favor of moderate accommodation. As to the question of authority, unlike the Reformers who took it upon themselves to institute changes and the Neo-Orthodox who considered the entire corpus of Jewish law to be inviolable, Frankel considered modifications only if they did not run counter to the sensibilities of the majority of Jews. For Frankel—who saw his brand of Judaism as stemming from Neo-Orthodoxy—religious practice, as established by the people, was a form of divine revelation and thus could not be easily dismissed. But to save Judaism from wholesale rejection by the people, Jewish leadership must "take into consideration the opposition between faith and conditions of the time. True faith, due to its divine nature, is above time . . . but time has a force and might which must be taken account of." Espousing a democratic position, Frankel asserted that change was permissible in Judaism but that it was the people's sensibilities that would determine when

"certain practices [would be allowed to] fall into disuse. . . . Only those practices from which it [the Jewish people] is entirely estranged and which yield it no satisfaction will be abandoned and will thus die of themselves." Frankel's mission was to determine the rate and nature of change in Judaism, his goal being to prove that Jews and Jewish law had been flexible throughout history and that being so in his day was in keeping with the well-established tradition of innovation in Judaism.

In his magnum opus, *Darkhe ha-Mishnah* (*The Paths of the Mishnah*) (1859), Frankel historicized the work of the ancient rabbis, describing the place and time in which they worked, giving them credit for innovative legal thinking and practice. Coincidentally appearing in the same year as Charles Darwin's *On the Origin of Species,* Frankel's work posited a theory of evolution as it applied to *halakhah,* maintaining that Judaism was the product of development and not the result of spontaneous creation. While previous depictions of the rabbis focused on their role as vehicles for transmitting *halakhah,* Frankel represented them as active figures rising to meet the challenges of the present. According to Frankel, the rabbis "instituted ordinances in accordance with the condition of the state and of human society in their days." *Darkhe ha-Mishnah* emerged from the lectures that Frankel gave as head of the Jewish Theological Seminary, founded in Breslau in 1854. Similar to a yeshiva in that it taught traditional Jewish texts, it also included Jewish history in the curriculum, thus combining Positive-Historical Judaism's reverence for tradition with its belief in the power of historical investigation. Both symbolic and representative of this goal was the presence of the historian Heinrich Graetz on the faculty. The Jewish Theological Seminary in Breslau was the precursor to Conservative Judaism's New York institution of the same name established in 1886.

Religious Reforms Beyond Germany

Liberal Judaism spread to other parts of Europe, usually in a far more conservative manner and at a much slower pace than in Germany. One important exception was Hungary. There the pace of change, once it began, was rapid. Prior to 1867, the year Hungary's 542,000 Jews were emancipated, every Jew in Hungary by civil law had to belong to a local congregation, all of which were Orthodox. After Hungary gained autonomy from Habsburg Austria in 1867, the government called all Jewish leaders to meet and form a single nationwide religious organization. This resulted in a schism that led to the emergence of three distinct groups, each organized separately in civil law. The Neologists were Orthodox in practice but were open to some religious and many substantial aesthetic innovations; the radical Orthodox, who were "ultra-religious," were exceptionally scrupulous in their devotion to Jewish law and were opposed to any and all reforms; and a third group represented the status quo ante. These were the Orthodox Jews of the pre-1867 era.

Some of the more significant reforms and aesthetic innovations also took hold among traditional Jews. In England two synagogues broke from the establishment. The West London Synagogue of British Jews was established in 1810. The congregation's most important social innovation was to bring together Ashkenazim and Sephardim as congregants; in the domain of religion, the synagogue took the novel but hardly radical step of abrogating the second day of the four major festivals: Pesach, Sukkot, Shavuot, and Rosh Hashanah. The Manchester Reform Association, composed of many German Jews, began to conduct its own services in 1856. Never as radical as their co-religionists in Germany, the association members used the prayer book of the West London Synagogue but retained the second day of festivals.

In France, reforms were undertaken under the auspices of the central consistory. This meant that, based in law, French Jewish communities retained their hierarchical structure and national cohesion. Still, synagogues that were nominally Orthodox adopted reforms such as confirmation ceremonies, the use of organs and choirs, and rabbis wearing vestments that were nearly identical with those of the Catholic clergy. Synagogue officials even donned uniforms with gold braid, epaulets, and the famous Napoleonic three-cornered hat. In the British Empire, Orthodox rabbis were called "Reverend," and the leading cleric became known as the Chief Rabbi, a position modeled on that of the Anglican Archbishop of Canterbury. In 1844, Nathan Adler became the first such Chief Rabbi and instituted many of the changes in decorum characteristic of Reform Judaism, although in terms of Jewish law, practice remained strictly orthodox.

New Synagogues and the Architecture of Emancipation

Typical of new trends and changing sensibilities were innovations in synagogue architecture. Across the world, Jewish congregations, Orthodox included, were imbued with the spirit of emancipation and religious reform. Increasingly middle class and keen to display residential prominence, as well as to assert their status as citizens with equal rights, Jews began to build monumental synagogues that served as architectural declarations of their residential permanence, as well

as announcements to their neighbors that they were both proud of their Jewish identities and that their Jewishness was completely compatible with being loyal citizens of their nations.

From the mid-nineteenth century to World War I, such synagogues were to be found around the globe. Prior to emancipation, synagogues had generally been small places of worship and study, while the new synagogues, very often recalling the size and grandeur of the Temple in Jerusalem, were enormous structures built in eclectic styles, often modeled on churches and mosques. The "architecture of Emancipation" and the modern aesthetic of the synagogue service that were initiated by Reform Jews spread to other denominations and far beyond the confines of Germany. In Budapest, the Great Synagogue in Dohány Street, also known as the Dohány Synagogue, or the *Tabac-Shul* (the Yiddish translation of *dohány* is *tabac,* or tobacco), was built between 1854 and 1859 by the Neolog Jewish community. One of the largest in the world, the synagogue is grand, with a capacity of 2,964 seats (1,492 for men and 1,472 in the women's galleries). The building is more than 174 feet long and is 87 feet wide. The design of the Dohány Street synagogue is principally Islamic but also features a mixture of Byzantine, Romanesque, and Gothic elements. The western façade boasts arched windows with carved decorations and brickwork in the heraldic colors of the city of Budapest: blue, yellow, and red. Above the main entrance is a stained-glass rose window. The gateway is flanked on both sides by two polygonal towers with long arched windows and crowned by copper domes with golden ornaments. The towers soar to a height of 143 feet each, their decoration featuring carvings of geometric forms and clocks, while atop the façade sit the Ten Commandments. The synagogue's interior is adorned with colored and golden geometric shapes. The Holy Ark is located on the eastern wall, while above it sits the choir-gallery. A gigantic 5,000-pipe organ, exquisite enough to be played by Franz Liszt, bespoke the congregation's commitment to making beautiful music central to the synagogue service. Distinguished cantors from the Great Synagogue in Dohány Street earned worldwide acclaim.

While the Dohány Street synagogue was built by the reformist Neologs (various Reform congregations built similar edifices in other European and American cities), the Orthodox likewise built similar houses of worship. In fact, Orthodox congregations built the majority of such synagogues. Like their Reform-minded co-religionists, Orthodox Jews also strove to present a Judaism to the world that was stately, solemn, and modern.

The names of new synagogues frequently bore the word "Great" or "Grand." This was the case in Paris, Rome, and

Sydney. In 1878, exactly ninety years after the first Jews landed in Australia, the Great Synagogue of Sydney was consecrated. Designed by the distinguished architect Thomas Rowe, it is a glorious structure, a harmonious blend of Byzantine and Gothic styles. The interior is spacious, the height of the synagogue accentuated by cast-iron columns that reach up to plaster decorations, arches, and a paneled and groined ceiling covered with gold leaf stars and other elaborate decorations. Further enhancing the grandeur is the abundance of sunlight that pours through magnificent stained-glass windows. When built, the ninety-foot-high twin sandstone towers made the synagogue the tallest building in the city. Although skyscrapers have now dwarfed the Great Synagogue, the fact that well into the twentieth century a Jewish house of worship was the tallest building in Australia's largest metropolis spoke to the community's confidence in itself and in the nation that it called home. And in apparent fulfillment of Saul Ascher's dream that Judaism, if presented in an enlightened way, "might be the religion of any member of society," a Christian minister from Melbourne reported after a visit to the Great Synagogue in 1896:

The galleries are well filled, so is the amphitheatre like floor space. Facing the ark-alcove, but separated from it by a wide unoccupied space, is the Almemmar, or tribune, a highly ornamented wooden structure with seats for the Rabbis and presiding officials of the synagogue, and a spacious reading stand on which to repose the roll of the Torah, and up to which the successive readers of the lessons advance, supported on either hand by prominent members of the congregation. . . . All the males in the body of the synagogue wear the tallithim [prayer shawls] and have their hats on. As I took my seat the sweet musical voice of the second minister rose clear, plaintive, voicing the heart-cry of the children of the dispersion to their fathers' God to remember Zion and the set time to favour her. The musical Hebrew had a sobbing plaintiveness, indescribably charming, ever and anon the congregation took up the responses. The venerable Chief Rabbi—the Reverend A.B. Davis—now takes his place at the reading stand; the sacred roll is unwound; the aged man, his natural force scarcely abated, in clear, ringing tones, a kind of semi-chant, recites the law of the Lord; the great congregation are on their feet. This is the psychological moment. . . . Rabbi Davis, raising the sacred scroll high in the air, descended from the tribune, and with slow and stately step, marched up the broad steps to the Ark, in which he deposited the Law of the Lord. . . . Then the Chief Rabbi, taking his stand at the top of the flight of steps, in front of the Ark, preached his

sermon; a wonderful effort for an aged man, delivered ore rotundo, with wonderful fire and passion. . . . As I passed into the life of the streets, and nineteenth century feeling again asserted its potency, I felt like one who had been in Dreamland, and had heard things which it is not lawful for a man to speak to the fool multitude.

With the recognition by this Christian clergyman that the Jews engaged in "majestic worship," the elders of Sydney's Great Synagogue might have been well satisfied that the aesthetic changes they rang in were having a positive social and ecumenical impact. In the United States, the Touro Synagogue (1763) in Rhode Island resembled Congregational meetinghouses of the colonial era, while synagogues in the South, such as Beth Elohim (1792) in Charleston, South Carolina, looked very similar to the Georgian churches found in the same city. The latter was rebuilt in Greek Revival style in 1841 after a fire in 1838 destroyed the original building. At the inauguration ceremony for the new Beth Elohim, the Reverend Gustavus Poznanski observed in the fashion typical of Reform Jews of his era, "This synagogue is our Temple, this city our Jerusalem, and this happy land our Palestine."

In Rome, the majestic Great Synagogue was modeled on the Roman- and Byzantine-styled Grand Synagogue of Paris, built between 1867 and 1874. Inaugurated in 1904, the synagogue in the Italian capital was constructed in an eclectic blend of Roman, Greek, Assyro–Babylonian, and Egyptian styles. Its location was of great significance for it was built on the site of the Roman ghetto and thus represented the emancipation of Italian Jews from an enclosed world marked by restrictions and physical confinement. At the inauguration, in the presence of Italy's most important political dignitaries, the Jewish community president, Angelo Sereni, blended republican political hopes and Jewish religious sensibilities (a symbol of the ideal nineteenth-century synthesis), when he declared, "The construction of this Temple is not only a manifestation of the religious feelings of one part of the citizenry who alone may take pleasure in it. It is also an affirmation, a solemn pronouncement that gives cause for rejoicing to all those, with no distinction whatsoever, who harbor high and noble ideals of liberty, equality, and love."

As this chapter has shown, Jews in the nineteenth century responded creatively to the challenges of modernity. In the realms of religious and secular culture, innovation was the order of the day, from Reform Judaism in Germany to Hasidism in Poland to Mitnagdism in Lithuania to Sephardic culture in Italian port cities. Everywhere, Jews were breaking with the past, reconsidering Judaism and their individual Jewish identities in light of the changing times.

Beyond religious and cultural innovations, late-nineteenth-century Jewish life underwent significant change in the social and economic realms. Many of these changes, long advocated by non-Jewish society, nevertheless led to unexpected hostility on the part of non-Jews, which in turn gave rise to innovations in both non-Jewish and Jewish political culture. It is to such developments that we turn in the following chapter.

Questions for Reflection

1. What were some of the main features that accounted for the radical split in eighteenth-century Ashkenazic culture between the Jews of central and eastern Europe?

2. How would you characterize the various modes of religious experience that transformed eastern European Jewry in the eighteenth and nineteenth centuries?

3. What were the distinguishing features of the Haskalah in Germany, Galicia, and Russia?

4. In the nineteenth century, how did German Jewry refashion Judaism to correspond with the demands of emancipation?

5. Why did Jews turn to writing history in the nineteenth century?

6. Why did language choice become a burning question for modern Jews?

For Further Reading

On religious life in Poland, see Gershon Hundert, *Jews in Poland-Lithuania in the Eighteenth Century: A Genealogy of Modernity* (Berkeley: University of California Press, 2004); Gershon Hundert, ed., *Essential Papers on Hasidism: Origins to Present* (New York: New York University Press, 1991); Immanuel Etkes, *The Gaon of Vilna: The Man and His Image* (Berkeley: University of California Press, 2002); Immanuel Etkes, *Rabbi Israel Salanter and the Mussar Movement: Seeking the Torah of Truth* (Philadelphia: Jewish Publication Society, 1993); Ada Rapoport-Albert, ed., *Hasidism Reappraised* (London: Vallentine Mitchell, 1996).

On religious life in Central Europe, see Michael A. Meyer, *Response to Modernity: A History of the Reform Movement in Judaism* (New York: Oxford University Press, 1988); Mordechai Breuer, *Modernity Within Tradition: The Social History of Orthodox Jewry in Imperial Germany* (New York: Columbia University Press, 1992); Jacob Katz, *A House Divided: Orthodoxy and Schism in Nineteenth-Century Central European Jewry* (Hanover, NH: University Press of New England, 1998); and Michael Brenner, Steffi Jersch-Wenzel, and Michael A. Meyer, *German-Jewish History in Modern Times*, vol. 2: *Emancipation and Acculturation, 1780–1871*, ed. Michael A. Meyer, (New York: Columbia University Press, 1996).

On the Haskalah, see David Sorkin, *The Transformation of German Jewry, 1780–1840* (New York: Oxford University Press); Shmuel Feiner and David Sorkin, eds., *New Perspectives on the Haskalah* (Portland, OR: Littman Library of Jewish Civilization, 2001); Shmuel Feiner, *The Jewish Enlightenment* (Philadelphia: University of Pennyslvania Press, 2004); Shmuel Feiner, *Haskalah and History: The Emergence of a Modern Jewish Historical Consciousness* (Portland, OR: Littman Library of Jewish Civilization, 2002); David Fishman, *Russia's First Modern Jews: The Jews of Shklov* (New York: New York University Press, 1995); Michael Stanislawski, *For Whom Do I Toil? Judah Leib Gordon and the Crisis of Russian Jewry* (New York: Oxford University Press, 1988); Shaul Stampfer, "Gender Differentiation and Education of the Jewish Woman in Nineteenth-Century Eastern Europe," in Antony Polonsky, ed., *From Shetl to Socialism: Studies from Polin* (London and Washington: Littman Library of Jewish Civilization, 1993), 187–211; Matthias Lehmann, *Ladino Rabbinic Literature and Ottoman Sephardic Culture* (Bloomington: Indiana University Press, 2005); and Aron Rodrigue, "The Ottoman Diaspora: The Rise and Fall of Ladino Literary Culture," in David Biale, ed., *Cultures of the Jews* (New York: Schocken Books, 2002).

Chapter 12

The Politics of Being Jewish

Among the most salient features of Jewish life in the modern period were the change in residential patterns and the astronomical growth in the Jewish population. By the last decades of the nineteenth century, the village Jew of Alsace, Bavaria, and Bohemia in western and central Europe had largely disappeared. In eastern Europe, the shtetl Jew, though still in evidence until the Holocaust, had become an increasingly less visible figure on the Jewish social landscape. Rather, what typified and conditioned Jewish existence in the modern period was the move to cities. The increase in the sheer number of Jews and in Jewish population density put pressure on local economies. In search of economic and educational opportunities, Jews left their smaller towns for expanding urban areas. Population growth and mobility shaped every aspect of Jewish life, including occupational choice, residential patterns, and emigration, as well as political affiliation and organization. Often, the choices Jews made occasioned a host of responses and reactions among their gentile neighbors that ranged from sympathetic to hostile. The reactions depended on whether one saw Jewish social mobility and increasing prominence in European affairs as a positive or a negative development. Even more so, feelings about Jews proved to be a litmus test for feelings about modernity. Quite often, those disenchanted with it blamed Jews.

Over the course of the nineteenth century, the number of Jews in the world increased dramatically. In 1800, the Jewish population stood at about 2.7 million. That number rose to 8.7 million in 1900 and then just over 12 million by 1910. The population explosion occurred primarily in Europe, where the Jewish rate of growth was greater than that of any other European people. By 1900, approximately 82 percent of all the world's Jews lived in Europe. Nearly 50 percent of those Jews, approximately 5.2 million, lived in the Russian Empire, with a further 20 percent, nearly 2 million, residing in what, after 1867, became the Austro-Hungarian Empire. By the late 1870s just over 10 percent lived in

North America and South America (1 million) and a total of about 7 percent lived in the Middle East and Asia (432,000) and Africa (340,000). Prior to the outbreak of war in 1914, most of the world's Jews were subjects of multiethnic empires: the Russian, Austro-Hungarian, Ottoman, French, or British.

What contributed to Jewish population growth were high birth rates and low death rates. The trend originated in the eighteenth century, though exact numbers are hard to come by for that period. We can be more precise about the period between 1850 and 1880; in eastern Europe, there were 17 more Jewish births than deaths for every 1,000 people. Even in places where the Jewish birth rate remained relatively low, such as in western Europe, the low death rates due to the higher survival rate among Jewish infants ensured a positive Jewish demographic balance. As one Jewish journal article on the subject proudly noted in 1910, "The death rate among Jewish children in the unhealthy, narrow confines of the Frankfurt ghetto is lower than the rate among the city's [Christian] patricians."

Statistics the world over showed the Jews to have been an extraordinarily healthy people. They tended to live longer than non-Jews, had a significantly lower infant mortality rate, had a lower death rate, and seemed to be far less susceptible to the most common diseases of the day, particularly childhood illnesses such as measles, scarlet fever, and diphtheria. Contemporary doctors and social critics offered several explanations for this phenomena. First, they all suggested that the virtual absence of alcoholism among Jews, a disease that ravaged Europeans, especially in eastern Europe, proved to be a great advantage. Second, having fewer offspring meant that Jewish parents could divide their material resources among a smaller number of children. Fewer mouths to feed made for a higher caloric intake per individual and therefore a greater survival rate. Third, contemporary physicians noted that Jewish mothers in both eastern Europe and America breast-fed their children to a

A SHTETL WOMAN

In eastern Europe, Jewish women often worked outside the home and were integral to the Jewish as well as local economy. One gets a vivid sense of the economic role of Jewish women in eastern Europe before World War I in Benjamin Bialostotzky's account of his Lithuanian shtetl, Pumpian. Recalling his grandmother's working life, which he sees as typical for traditional Jewish women, Bialostotzky also recounts how in contrast to their male counterparts, who led more insular lives, Jewish businesswomen forged relationships with non-Jewish women and thus the world outside the shtetl of Pumpian.

My bobeh [grandmother] Chana had traits very characteristic of many Jewish Lithuanian women. My zeyde [grandfather] earned very little from teaching. His main task was waiting for the Messiah, but my bobeh was an *eyshes khayil,* a "woman of valor" [the term is the name of a song based on Proverbs 31:10–31 and is recited by a husband to his wife at the Sabbath table]. She had a garden at home and with her own hands worked and weeded all the plots. From the garden she raised food that was sufficient for months. My bobeh supported zeyde's household, and that was characteristic of many such Jewish women. If not for them, the community's economic situation would have been in shambles. The women made it possible with their labor for their devout husbands to study and to have conversations with the Messiah. These Jewish women kept the stores, went to market, stood at fairs, bought and sold, planted gardens, washed and sewed and spun and wove, and simply sacrificed their lives for the Torah of their husbands!

Thinking about my bobeh Chana, I remember something else that was very characteristic of her and other such Jewish Lithuanian women. She brought together the Jews and the village, the gentile world. She spoke Lithuanian fluently and would go to the village a *verst* [two-thirds of a mile] or two from Pumpian to purchase wheat from the peasants and would also sell them goods from the shtetl. She established a strong connection with many gentile women. When the gentile women came to the shtetl on market days or holidays, before doing anything else they would always come to greet my grandmother. Such Jewish women were the salt of the earth, and there were many of them in my shtetl, just as in the other shtetlakh. My bobeh wove friendships with the gentile Lithuanians who lived in the area.

greater extent, and for a longer period of time, than non-Jewish mothers. Fourth, Jewish mothers, especially in western Europe, tended not to work outside the home after marriage, thus they were on hand to tend to their children. And even in eastern Europe, where Jews were more closely tied to rural economies, the grinding agricultural work done by peasant women was largely unknown among the Jewish population (*see box,* A Shtetl Woman). In 1902, one Viennese physician noted that the excellent health of Jewish children could be attributed in part to "the early exemption of pregnant [Jewish] women from physical labor." Fifth, medical opinion at the turn of the twentieth century unanimously credited Jewish hygiene habits, particularly regular hand washing, with stemming the spread of infectious disease. Sixth, by the late nineteenth century, Jews, especially those in western and central Europe, were better educated, earned more, and, overall, enjoyed higher standards of living than did non-Jews. The vast majority of Jews displayed a host of bourgeois customs and habits that in the areas of hygiene and nourishment worked to minimize infant mortality and improve and extend the life of adults. Of course, most eastern European Jews and immigrants from that part of the world who settled in New York and London were decidedly poor and working class, but they too lived longer and healthier lives than their Slavic, Irish, or Italian neighbors and had a significantly lower incidence of infant mortality. There is no doubt that the modern period produced healthy, vibrant Jewish communities.

By the outbreak of World War I, the Jewish population explosion had begun to run its course. Greater affluence, increased use of birth control, rising levels of assimilation, that in certain instances extended to apostasy, mixed marriage, emigration, and aging all took a significant demographic toll, especially in western Europe. In Germany, for example, the Jewish community was only demographically replenished by the influx of eastern European Jewish immigrants. Jewish birth rates declined not only in western Europe, but also in Russia, Hungary, Poland, and Romania.

The Move to Cities

Despite the decline in the rate of population growth, Jews remained highly visible due to urbanization, a process that began among Jews before it reached the general population.

By 1925, more than a quarter of the world's Jews lived in a mere fourteen large cities, and just prior to the outbreak of World War II half of all Jews lived in cities with populations of over 100,000. This led the distinguished Jewish historian, Salo Baron, to observe: "one may thus speak of the metropolitanization rather than the urbanization of the Jews."

"Metropolitanization" began in earnest toward the end of the nineteenth century, when neighborhoods with significant Jewish populations began to proliferate throughout European capitals. Often, this was the result of eastern European Jewish migration. London's Jewish population rose from 40,000 in 1880 to 200,000 by 1914 thanks to the arrival of Russian Jews. Internal Jewish migration from rural or provincial areas to the capital and major cities also contributed to metropolitanization. Sigmund Freud's Jewish Vienna grew from 72,000 in 1880 to 175,000 in 1910, largely as a result of migration from Galicia. In 1808, the year Napoleon passed his Infamous Decrees, the Jewish population of Paris stood at a mere 8,000. By 1900 the Jewish population of the city had grown to 60,000, largely due to Jews moving to the capital from Alsace. Amsterdam's Jewish community also grew as a result of migration from the Dutch provinces to the capital. While the Jews of Amsterdam totaled 20,000 in 1800, that number had expanded to 90,000 by the turn of the twentieth century. In Germany, when the Second Reich was founded in 1871, its capital city, Berlin, had a Jewish population of 36,000. In a mere forty years, that number had quadrupled, and by 1910 Berlin had 144,000 Jewish residents.

The same pattern was to be seen among Sephardic Jews in the Mediterranean region. In Greece, Salonika became one of Europe's largest Jewish cities, earning it the exalted title *Ir v'em be-Yisrael* ("Metropolis and Mother of Israel"). A haven for Jews after the expulsion from Spain in 1492, Jews continued to come to the city. By 1900, Salonika had a Jewish population of nearly 90,000, a full half of the entire population. With more than fifty synagogues, twenty Jewish schools, the largest Jewish cemetery in Europe, and a full range of Jewish institutions, the city was a vibrant Jewish center. Like cities elsewhere, Salonika's Jewish population increased in the last quarter of the nineteenth century due to the arrival of eastern European Jewish immigrants. The beginnings of decline of Jewish Salonika, however, are not attributed to declining birthrates, as was the case elsewhere, but to the rise of Greek nationalism. In 1917, a massive fire swept through the city, leaving 53,000 Jews homeless. In the aftermath of the devastation, Greek nationalists saw their chance to confiscate substantial tracts of land from the fire-ravaged Jewish quarter and impose a draconian program of Hellenization on Jews and other non-Greek minorities who had displayed allegiance to the imperial rulers of the city, the Ottoman Turks. Many Jews began to leave, and by 1939 the Jewish community of Salonika had shrunk to 56,000.

In eastern Europe, Jews were leaving their small towns (*shtetl,* sing.; *shtetlekh,* pl.) and villages and moving to nearby large cities. The image of Sholem Aleichem's protagonist Tevye the Dairyman as the prototypical Russian Jew corresponded less and less to the social reality of eastern European Jewish life. Between 1897 and 1910 the Jewish urban population of Russia increased by about 1 million, or 38.5 percent. Of the 5.2 million Jews in the Empire, 3.5 million lived in cities. Between 1869 and 1910 the Jewish population of the imperial capital, St. Petersburg, grew from 7,000 to 35,000, while in the Black Sea port city of Odessa—a lively Jewish intellectual and commercial center, home to new Yiddish, Hebrew, and Russian writers—the Jewish population rose dramatically from 55,000 in 1880 to 200,000 in 1912. Over this period, the percentage of Jews among the total population went from 25.2 percent to 32.3 percent. In Warsaw, which would become the largest Jewish city in Europe, a Jewish population of 12,000 in 1804 had, by 1910, climbed to 337,000 or 38 percent of the total population. This increase was the result of mass migration from the Pale of Settlement, which first began in the 1860s and increased substantially over the rest of the nineteenth century; approximately 150,000 Jews from Lithuania, Byelorussia, and Ukraine moved to Warsaw (*see* Map 12-1).

Even in cities where the absolute numbers of Jews was not large, their percentage of the total population stood well above 50 percent. Cities such as Bialystok, Berdichev, Grodno, Pinsk, Lvov, Lodz, Lublin, Cracow, and Vilna all had relatively small Jewish populations as late as 1880, but by 1900, Jewish immigrants, mostly from surrounding areas, had poured into these towns, substantially changing their character. At the turn of the century, Berdichev was 87.5 percent Jewish; Pinsk, 80 percent; Brody, 75 percent; Bialystok, 66 percent; and Vilna, 40 percent. Jews made up between 25 and 50 percent of the total populations in scores of towns and cities in the Russian Empire. Towns like these constituted the provincial heartland of eastern European Jewry.

Outside of Europe, similar trends developed by the start of the twentieth century. New York City soon grew into the largest urban Jewish center in history. A mere 10,000 Jews were in the city in 1846, but by 1917, with mass migration, mostly from Russia and Galicia, 1,503,000 Jews called New York home and comprised a full 26.4 percent of America's largest city. In the Southern Hemisphere, with relatively small Jewish populations, the results of urbanization were perhaps even more striking. By 1900, nearly all Australian Jews were to be found in Sydney, Melbourne, or Adelaide. Nearly half of

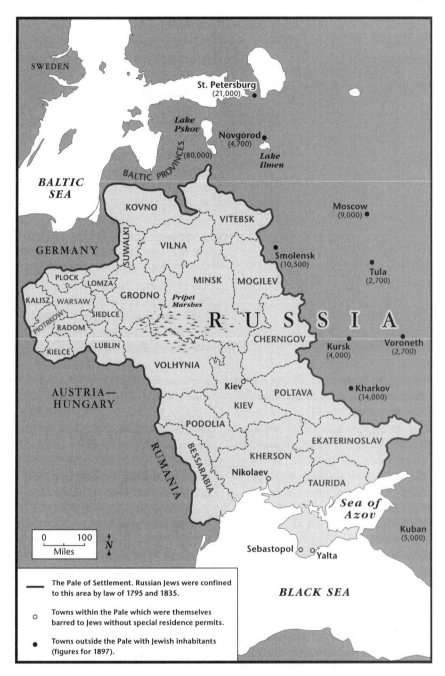

Map 12-1 The Jewish Pale of Settlement, 1835–1917. By 1897, approximately five million Jews lived in the Pale of Settlement, a vast area covering over 386,000 square miles.

Argentina's Jews resided in Buenos Aires. Brazilian Jews were to be found almost exclusively in Rio de Janeiro or São Paulo, while Uruguay's Jews lived mostly in the capital, Montevideo.

In the Muslim world too, where large numbers of Jews lived in small villages in countries such as Morocco and Yemen, the tendency toward urbanization was evident. From across North Africa all the way to Iran, Jews were to be found mostly in cities. Jewish artisans and merchants were highly visible in cities such as Casablanca, Fez, Mogador, Algiers, Constantine, Oran, Tunis, Baghdad, Teheran, and Istanbul.

Living in large cities had a significant impact on Jewish society and culture. The profile of the urban Jew was one of a people alienated from the land. This image shaped the ideas of political ideologues from divergent backgrounds, Jewish and gentile, who latched on to this feature of Jewish life as especially pernicious. Zionists sought to transform Jews by returning them to agricultural work, while enemies of the Jews pointed to their urbanization as a symbol of their divorce from the rural and thus "authentic" heart and soul of the nations in which they lived. City life also had a decided impact on the occupational choices of Jews: They tended to enter industrial, commercial, and professional occupations. Cities also provided Jews with an array of cultural and intellectual offerings, exposing them to ideas and ideologies that would challenge in significant ways both Jewish practices and Jewish beliefs. Making the most of opportunities afforded them by their move to cities, Jews became extremely prominent in all spheres of commercial and intellectual activity. An unforeseen response to Jewish success and cultural integration was the explosive growth across Europe of antisemitism.

Modern Antisemitism

The modern period has seen Jews become heavily involved in politics. This engagement, however, was not always voluntary, for Jews, like other European people, sometimes got caught up in political movements against their wishes. The politics of antisemitism is one such case. Antisemitism, an ideology that sought to attribute contemporary social ills to the Jews, actually led them into politics in the hope of forging responses to the wide variety of accusations directed at them.

Modern antisemitism is characterized by ideological claims and organizational features that make it different from traditional anti-Judaism. Modern antisemitism is mostly secular, although not exclusively so, and grounds its claim in the spurious notion that there exists a Jewish conspiracy to control the world. Organizationally, in nineteenth- and twentieth-century Europe, political parties were founded to oppose Jews, and ideologues and politicians who subscribed to antisemitism often turned hatred of Jews into full-time jobs. The new radical Right, composed of monarchists, clerics, nationalists, university students, and members of the lower-middle classes were especially receptive to antisemitism. On the other hand, while the Left was not immune to Jew hatred, it was more likely to focus on attacking individual Jews, such as the capitalist Rothschilds or commercial occupations that attracted large numbers of Jews, such as banking, the stock market, or even petty trade and peddling. Antisemitism was an ideology that was often able to unite Europeans ordinarily divided along class, religious, and national lines.

The "Jewish Question"

Over the course of the nineteenth century, the movement of central and western European Jews into European culture and out of insular Jewish communities, led to the emergence of a new European-wide discourse about Jews known as the "Jewish Question." The term, which applied to the new problem of the secular Jew, was first used in France in 1833 but was popularized by the German Protestant theologian Bruno Bauer in an 1843 essay of that title. Bauer decried what he saw as the Jews' wish to enter the modern world without surrendering their distinctive culture. The refusal to disappear had been, according to Bauer, the cause of gentile opposition to them. Blaming Jews for the hostility they inspired, Bauer noted, "In history, nothing stands outside the law of causality, least of all the Jews. . . . The will of history is evolution, new forms, progress, change; the Jews want to stay forever what they are, therefore they fight against the first law of history—does this not prove that by pressing against this mighty spring they provoke counter-pressure?" Reversing Christian Wilhelm Dohm's firm contention that "the Jew is more man than Jew," Bauer now declared, "[A]s long as he is a Jew, his Jewishness must be stronger in him than his humanity, and keep him apart from non-Jews. He declares by this segregation that this, his Jewishness, is his true, highest nature, which has to have precedence over his humanity." Nevertheless, Dohm's sentiments still resonated in some quarters in the 1830s. With social disabilities still firmly in place, a German theologian, August Friedrich Gfrörer, declared, "Let us cease treating the Jews as white negroes, then they will no longer hate us as tyrants or deceive us as fools." But such enlightened sentiments were falling out of fashion, and notions of Jewish subversion were beginning to win the day.

Bauer's claim that Jews possess an immutable collective loyalty and essence and plot against the rest of the world lies at the heart of modern antisemitism. But such tropes are themselves of ancient provenance. In classical antiquity, writers such as Tacitus and Juvenal denounced the Jews for being misanthropic. The Catholic Church taught a theological version of these secular claims, decrying Jewish obstinacy for refusing to accept Jesus and fomenting hatred against all Christians. Muslim thinkers said similar things about the Jews' refusal to accept the Prophet Muhammad.

Bauer and his followers drew on ancient and modern, religious and secular prejudices against Jews to create a potent mix of charges that emerged with surprising strength in the closing decades of the nineteenth century. The reason for the popularity of antisemitism rests on the fact that it is not only about Jews and their alleged flaws. While Jews are its principal targets, modern antisemitism also levels a broader critique at the nature of modern society. Antisemites believe in the Jewish presence lurking behind every aspect of modernity that they find objectionable, and since modernity is multifaceted, the Jews can be accused of anything and blamed for everything, including unbridled capitalism, Marxism, Liberalism, Communism, ethnic exclusiveness, cosmopolitan universalism, the uprooting of the peasantry, the demand for workers' rights, the campaign to enfranchise women, the white slave trade in women, the "taking over" of various European cultures, being disloyal to the nation, being excessively patriotic, and, above all, plotting to start a race war against their enemies. As one astute Jewish observer wrote in 1890, "Everywhere this anti-Semitic fury signifies nothing more and nothing less than the beginnings of the social revolution. Let it be clearly understood by all who support anti-Semitism openly or secretly, or who merely tolerate it; it is not a question of the Jews at all, it is a question of subverting the entire order of life, society and the state!" Still, Jews are not merely scapegoats. Genuine antisemites truly believe their accusations against Jews. The belief in Jewish culpability is as real as the antisemites' sense of grievance.

By the 1860s and 1870s, legal emancipation throughout western and central Europe was a fact. European Jews, historically suspicious of their Christian neighbors, were increasingly secure and confident of their place in a secular political order. For many Jews (and for some non-Jews), the "Jewish Question" had been solved. The backlash came, then, as a great shock.

Most central and western European Jews accepted the fundamental premises of the Enlightenment discourse that Jews stood in need of regeneration and that their collective progress would lead to the disappearance of animus. Many Christians, however, were disappointed with the results of emancipation. While Jews, especially those in urban areas, did move closer to European culture, most proved unwilling or unable to erase the communal and psychological characteristics of Jewishness or, more radically, to do what the composer Richard Wagner called on them to do in his paradigmatic antisemitic essay of 1850, *Judaism in Music,* namely, to engage in an act of "self-extinction."

The persistent refusal of the Jews to disappear frustrated many Europeans—both antisemites and philosemites. Jews continued, for the most part, to marry among themselves, to live in Jewish neighborhoods, and to work in largely Jewish sectors of the economy, such as finance, manufacturing, and the liberal professions. The fields of journalism, art, and popular entertainment also proved extremely attractive to Jews. They retained a collective cultural character, one that appeared to observers to be a vestige of their tribal identity. Jewish individuality, combined with remarkable professional success, engendered hatred and envy. Increasing urbanization and industrialization led many Europeans to long romantically for a return to pre-industrial society. Reactionary nationalists, most of whom lived in cities, glorified the peasant and the soil. Antisemites held Jews in contempt for exemplifying the kind of lifestyle typical of increasing numbers of Christians—urban and cosmopolitan. As the prominent German antisemite and "rural romanticist" Otto Glagau declared, "[A]ll Jews and persons of Jewish descent are born opponents of agriculture." Antisemitic nationalists projected their own misgivings about their alienation from the nation's rural roots onto modern Jews.

As the world began to change in the second half of the nineteenth century, European culture was subject to new social tensions. Workers began to demand the expansion of their rights and an improvement in their living and working conditions. The old nobility were anxious about their long-standing privileges, while new commercial elites were protective of their recently won wealth and status. Feeling squeezed between old and new money, the vast petit bourgeoisie made up of state bureaucrats, school teachers, shopkeepers, and artisans often resented the rise of mass culture exemplified by the department store and the factory. On the international plane, military, economic, and colonial competition between England, France, and Germany became more increasingly intense. Aggressive jingoism, nationalism, and racism contributed to the tense atmosphere prior to World War I. In Russia, while the autocratic rule of the tsar remained tenuously intact, radical groups continually sought the destruction of the old order. At the same time, the multinational Austro-Hungarian Empire began to totter under the sway of competing nationalist aspirations. The Catholic Church reacted with hostility and fear at the rising tide of liberalism, modern science, and socialism. Antisemitism proved an important ideological component of the agendas of these countervailing political and social forces.

In central and western Europe, the growth of parliamentary politics added another dimension. Vying for votes and appealing to new interest groups, political parties sought to tap into the anxieties of the age. The advent of anti-Jewish political parties, associations, clubs, and organizations, whether based on economic, religious, or racist principles, is one of the most important distinguishing features of modern antisemitism. Promising a cure for all that ailed the modern world, politicians and cultural critics emerged on both the Right and Left of the political spectrum. While they disagreed about much, they were often able to concur that the Jews were responsible for the uncertain future Europeans were facing. Even if Jews were not charged with responsibility for change, many pointed to the fact that Jews were clear beneficiaries of emancipation, mass politics, parliamentary democracy, the expansion of personal freedoms, and the new economic order. Beginning in the 1870s, antisemites in western Europe dedicated themselves to reversing the gains that Jews had made as a result of their legal emancipation. While the specific charges against Jews were echoed in one country after another, the emergence and varying characteristics of modern antisemitism were driven by local concerns.

Antisemitism in Germany

Germany provided many of the tropes and the organizational structure of the modern antisemitic movement. In the nineteenth century, the major supporters of the German antisemitic parties came from the lower-middle classes and the small farmers; both groups were particularly hard hit by the economic depression of 1873, for which they blamed Jews. Parallel to the increased social and economic vulnerability of the lower-middle classes was the rise of the Jews who, especially after their emancipation in 1871, made extraordinarily rapid social, economic, educational, and cultural strides. Within a very short period of time, most German Jews became solidly middle class, earned more than their non-Jewish neighbors, achieved far higher levels of education than Germans, and played a vital role in the cultural life of the nation. Despite the fact only about 600,000 Jews were in Germany (about 1 percent of the total population), the visibility of individual Jews due to their success inflamed the feeling that Jews had commandeered modern Germany.

Europe's first antisemitic political party—the Christian Social Workers Party—emerged in Berlin in 1878. It was headed by **Adolf Stöcker** (1835–1909), court preacher to the kaiser. Stöcker's initial goal had been to form a political party that would serve to curb the influence of the Social Democrats on workers. His platform stressed Christian ethics and reconciliation between the state and the working class. Stöcker enjoyed very little success (social democracy continued to spread among the German proletariat), but the introduction of antisemitic rhetoric into his speeches produced political traction. In 1879 Stöcker made an inflammatory speech at a party rally that signaled a shift to an openly antisemitic platform. Entitled "What We Demand of Modern Jewry," Stöcker's speech insisted that "Israel must renounce its ambition to rule Germany" and that the "Jewish press become more tolerant." Stöcker declared that Jewish capital should be curbed by the abolition of the "mortgage system in real estate and property should be inalienable and unmortgageable" and that quotas be put in place "to find out the disproportion between Jewish capital and Christian labor." Quotas should likewise be extended to limit the "appointments of Jewish judges in proportion to the size of the population" and to ensure the "removal of Jewish teachers from our grammar schools." Were these steps not

taken, Stöcker offered a bleak prognosis: "Either we succeed in this and Germany will rise again, or the cancer from which we suffer will spread further. In that event our whole future is threatened and the German spirit will become Judaized." Stöcker's slogan was "A return to a Germanic rule in law and business, a return to the Christian faith."

Stöcker was a demagogue, and his powerful oratory attracted a faithful (although small) following. However, after 1879 the larger movement to channel widespread social discontent into antisemitism snowballed and many groups and parties emerged, coalescing into the **Berlin Movement.** Antisemitism had become so widespread that the party of the traditional elites, the Conservative Party, feared that if it did not declare its tacit antisemitism openly, it would lose ground to the radicals. In 1892, the Conservative Party therefore adopted the **Tivoli Program.** In the name of Christianity, monarchy, fatherland, and anti-capitalism, paragraph 1 of the Tivoli Program declared, "We combat the widely obtruding and decomposing Jewish influence on our people. We demand a Christian authority for the Christian people and Christian teachers for Christian pupils."

In their attacks on Jews, the conservatives were joined by associations such as the powerful **Agrarian League,** both a political party and rural lobby group; the nationalist **Pan Germans,** who demanded union with Austria; and the **Reform Clubs,** whose grass-roots members dedicated themselves to the battle against liberalism. It is no accident that antisemites jointly opposed Liberalism; 85 percent of German Jews voted for liberal political parties. These alliances show that antisemitism could mobilize a party representing social elites to work alongside organizations that promised to deliver large numbers of disgruntled lower-middle class voters. Antisemitism proved to be a great political unifier.

German political parties helped make antisemitism acceptable and, in some quarters, even respectable. Everywhere, antisemitic discourse was out in the open. Pamphlets, posters, books, cartoons, and magazines deriding Jews, accusing them of all sorts of conspiracies, caricaturing their physical features, were to be found all over Europe. But Germany, with its highly literate population and its prominent publishing industry produced the lion's share of such material. The German antisemitic movement was extremely well organized, spreading propaganda through clubs, societies, and fraternities, many of which were hardly fringe groups but, rather, respectable organizations central to German society. Many were not specifically antisemitic. They ran the gamut from colonialist organizations with close government connections to a vast array of Right-wing clubs promoting such pursuits as occultism, vegetarianism, nudism, sun worship, and hiking. In all of these, Jews were not welcome. With their emphasis on the perfection of Aryan bodies, often juxtaposed with Jewish ones or their pseudo-pagan practices, often grounded in the celebration of the country's pre-Christian, Germanic roots, Jews were regarded as essentially different, if not the enemy.

While finding a home in the vast political and associational life of Germany, antisemites drew on Germany's intellectual strengths. Science and philosophy combined to produce a new racial antisemitism. Prior to World War I, the idea of race as the chief organizing principle in the battle against Jews received its most elaborate treatment in the work of the economist and philosopher **Karl Eugen Duehring** (1833–1921). One of the principal architects of modern racial antisemitism, Duehring produced an influential polemic entitled *The Jewish Question as a Racial, Moral and Cultural Question* (1881), in which he declared that race and not religion defines the Jews. Even those who had abandoned Judaism and converted to Christianity remained, for Duehring, "racial Jews." In fact, he claimed that it was through conversion and assimilation that Jews entered German society to undermine it from within. Keeping Jews and Germans entirely apart was therefore absolutely necessary for German well-being.

Seeing Jews as racially alien, antisemites went so far as to predict that Jewish–German friction would result in an apocalyptic race war. **Wilhelm Marr** (1819–1904) invented the term *antisemitism*. In his seminal text *The Victory of the Jews over the Germans, Considered from a Non-Religious Point of View* (1879), Marr refrained, as his subtitle suggested, from attacking Judaism the religion, an important departure from previous manifestations of anti-Jewish sentiment. He claimed that it was "idiotic to blame Jews for the crucifixion, a performance staged, as we all know, by the Roman authorities." Marr, in fact, defended the Jews from religious persecution and blamed the medieval Church for relegating Jews to a marginal and despised economic role. Marr praised Jews for being "highly gifted and talented, tough, of admirable endurance and resilience." Presenting a counterimage of the Jews as weak and humiliated, rejected by God, Marr actually claimed that Jews were much stronger than the Germans. The source of their vigor lay in their racial characteristics, which permitted them to "triumphantly resist the western world for 1,800 years. [The Jews then] rose in the nineteenth century to the position of the number one major power in the West." More powerful than Britain or France, not to mention Germany, the Jews, according to Marr, had achieved dominance over the West, since the West was the preeminent power, this meant that Jews were now the most powerful force on Earth.

Marr believed Jewish racial peculiarities made it impossible for non-Jews to live on an equal footing with them. Inevitably, predicted Marr, an apocalyptic race war between Jews and Germans would erupt. He was certain that the Jews would eventually win: "Of tougher and stronger fiber than we, you Jews remained the victor in this people's war which you fought by peaceful means while we burned and massacred you but did not possess the ethical strength to confine you to yourselves and to intercourse among yourselves." For Marr, the problem was no longer the separateness of the Jews but their post-emancipatory integration into German society. This historical process, he believed, ensured Jewish material success. Once granted civic freedom the Jews were able to deploy their superior racial qualities to great advantage. Emancipation, according to Marr, represented the chief ethical weakness at the source of the German problem. Marr's antisemitism was a product of his cultural pessimism. He saw Germans as powerless to defeat the Jews and concluded his book with an anguished cry, "Finis Germaniae!" Germany is finished!

Not all antisemites shared Wilhelm Marr's pessimism. Some were hopeful that emancipation could be scaled back. In 1880–1881, the infamous **Antisemite's Petition** was presented to the German Chancellor, Otto von Bismarck. With a quarter of a million signatures, the petition demanded immigration restrictions; the dismissal of Jews from government jobs, the judiciary, and higher education; and the separate registration of Jews according to religion in all surveys. Bismarck refused to accept it.

Thanks to the organizing power of the German antisemites and the wide appeal of their message, 1882 saw over three hundred people, Adolf Stöcker among them, attend the **First International Antisemites' Congress** in Dresden. Held at a prominent hotel in the center of the city, the congress issued a "manifesto to the governments and peoples of the Christian countries, which are in danger because of Jewry." Like Wilhelm Marr's *The Victory of the Jews over the Germans*, the "Manifesto to the Governments" also lamented the course of modern history and its consequences: "The victorious ideals of the French Revolution—liberty, equality, and fraternity— have torn down the barriers against the Jewish race that had been erected for the protection of the Christian peoples. . . . The emancipation of the Jews . . . which decades ago raised the expectation in Europe that the Jewish clan would assimilate into the Christian nations, has resulted in an absolute disaster. It has merely served to convince any thinking person that it is completely impossible for the European nations to be able to establish a *modus vivendi* with the Jewry living in their midst." Attendees at the convention demanded the establishment of a "universal Christian alliance" to combat Jewish influence. With the threat of violence they concluded that "the Jewish question can only be solved to satisfaction once and for all by following the manner in which the Arab, Tartar, and Turkish questions were solved in the past by the European states under attack." At the Dresden conference, a picture of the alleged victim of the 1881 **Tiszaeszlar** (Hungary) blood libel fraud hung behind the speaker's podium, a striking link between modern antisemitism and medieval anti-Judaism. At the end of the nineteenth century, the medieval charge that Jews ritually killed Christian children and used their blood to bake matzah was resurrected. Between 1891 and 1900, at least seventy-nine such charges were laid against Jews across central and eastern Europe and one in America.

Certain strains of German antisemitism were also endowed with a pseudo-philosophical quality. No one better typified that aspect of German Jew-hatred than **Houston Stewart Chamberlain** (1855–1927). An English Germanophile, Chamberlain was one of Germany's most prominent and well-connected antisemites. His influential *Foundations of the Nineteenth Century* (1899) was Adolf Hitler's bedside reading and Hitler visited Chamberlain when the latter was on his deathbed. Chamberlain was also Richard Wagner's son-in law and a member of the antisemitic circle at Bayreuth, presided over by the composer's wife, Cosima. Together with the Wagners, Chamberlain provided the libretto for racist antisemitism, based in a cultural critique that alleged the Jews were biologically incapable of producing beautiful culture; instead, they mimicked, commodified, and debased art.

Embracing Nietzsche's myth of the superman, Chamberlain championed the theory of Nordic supremacy, depicting history as a cataclysmic struggle between the Aryan and the Semite. He described the former as creative and noble and the latter as destructive and barbaric. As Chamberlain wrote, "Not only the Jew, but also all that is derived from the Jewish mind, corrodes and disintegrates what is best in us." The Jews were, in Chamberlain's view, a powerful threat because "this alien people has become precisely in the course of the nineteenth century a disproportionately important and in many spheres actually dominant constituent of our life." Antisemites repeatedly evoked this dark fantasy—that they were losing control of their nations to the Jews they had emancipated. Chamberlain was a crucial figure in the antisemitic pantheon. The emperor Wilhelm II read Chamberlain aloud to his children; *Foundations of the Nineteenth Century* became standard reading in military officers' schools. Antisemitism became part of the ruling ideology. For emphasizing Teutonic racial and moral superiority, urging Germany to exert itself as a world power, Chamberlain was hailed as a hero and a visionary by German militarists and conservatives. Hitler referred to him as a "Prophet of the Third Reich."

It is important to recall that despite the rampant antisemitic sentiment that swept over Germany, it was not matched by a retraction of the Jews' newly won legal rights nor any diminution in their social and economic gains. At this very same time in America, for example, quotas were in place against Jews attending universities and restrictions prevented them from living in certain neighborhoods, working in various firms, getting medical and legal internships, or even staying at restricted hotels and resorts. In eastern Europe there was violence against Jews. None of this occurred in Germany, where, paradoxically, the blossoming of the antisemitic movement coincided with German Jewry's own flowering. Many Jews were not even fully aware of the antisemitic movement, as they were doing so well. Now, after the Holocaust, we need to be mindful of this question: If things were so bad for Jews in nineteenth-century Germany, how could they be so good? Strangely, what drove antisemitism in Germany was the fact that Jews had done exactly what was demanded of them. They became German, participating fully and eagerly in the cultural and economic life of the nation, but they had done it to such an extent and so successfully that it occasioned an envy-driven backlash.

Antisemitism in Austria

The cradle of Modernism, turn-of-the-century Vienna was an exciting and frantic city. In fields including art, music, psychology, and modern politics, the glittering culture of the Austrian capital broke new ground. Vienna had one other distinction: It was also the most intensely antisemitic city in central Europe, boasting an impressive number of elected openly antisemitic politicians, as well as rabid nationalists, racists, and occultists, all of whom held Jews responsible for the aging Austrian Empire's problems. These ideologues produced a heady brew of hate, their literature and antisemitic cartoons readily available all over Vienna. Their discourse was an important element of the city's background chatter. Young men, including Adolf Hitler, proved especially susceptible to the anti-Jewish sentiment then swirling around the imperial capital.

In 1880 72,500 Jews were in Vienna, but by 1900 that number had swollen to 146,000 and Jews constituted about 8.77 percent of the city's population. With their numerical increase came greater visibility. The Jews of the city were principally of two cultural types. The first was the acculturated German-speaking minority that included famous writers such as Arthur Schnitzler and Stefan Zweig, musicians such as Gustav Mahler and Arnold Schoenberg, and renowned physicians such as Sigmund Freud. The second group, by far the majority, was composed of the Yiddish-speaking Jews who had moved to Vienna from the Austrian hinterland, primarily Galicia. Both groups proved worrisome to the antisemites—the former because they were too much a part of Austrian culture, the latter because they remained too foreign. It is ironic but true to form that despite beings targets of popular venom, Viennese Jewry, like German Jewry, nonetheless continued to prosper and expand. On the other hand, anti-Jewish hostility seemed to increase as Jewish participation in the cultural and economic life of Vienna deepened.

The empire's social problems, rooted in class divisions, rural–urban splits, the discontent of urban workers, the impoverishment of the peasantry, and the rise of aggressive nationalism, both German and Slavic, found expression in Viennese politics. Social divisions pitted Left against Right and German Austria against the various Slavic nationalist movements seeking independence from the multiethnic Austrian Empire. Jews, trusted by neither side, were caught in the middle of this historic struggle. Culturally, they tended to identify with the German elite, while politically, as elsewhere in Europe, they were liberals, an inclination that originated during the revolutions of 1848, when together with industrial workers and students, Jews supported the liberal cause.

In this environment, antisemitism emerged as virulent and all-pervasive, serving to unify a society coming apart at the seams. Politicians and rabble-rousers quickly capitalized on the widespread social discontent to point the finger of blame at Jews, who as a religiously different and professionally successful minority were seen as the cause of Austria's woes. In his newspaper, *The Fatherland,* the conservative Catholic intellectual **Karl von Vogelsang** (1818–1890) summed up the views of many who still resisted the liberating changes ushered in by the French Revolution. Its masthead read, "Our Battle Is Against the Spirit of 1789." Vogelsang held Jews responsible for the exploitation and impoverishment of peasants, artisans, and industrial workers, a position that became widespread in Viennese antisemitic circles.

The Prussian victory over France in 1870 inflamed nationalist passions. At the forefront of the new Pan German movement, which called for the unification of all German speakers, was the radical antisemite **Georg von Schönerer** (1842–1921). Leader of the German Nationalists, von Schönerer's politics rested on two principles. The first was his call for the breakup of the Habsburg monarchy and the push for Austrian union with Bismarck's Germany. The second element of his political agenda was his radical antisemitism. More than any other individual, Schönerer changed the tone and nature of Austrian politics. Debate gave way to verbal abuse and street fighting.

Schönerer unleashed powerfully aggressive antisemitic sentiments. With his massive ego, he portrayed himself as a militant medieval knight come to save the German people from the Jews. He held huge rallies, gave blood-curdling speeches about the "harmful Jewish plutocracy," and attacked Jews for their alleged control of the press. He claimed that "the removal of Jewish influence from all fields of public life is indispensable." Schönerer invited other racists to the podium to recommend higher taxes on Jewish income, marriage, occupational restrictions, and violence. He amassed support from broad elements of the Viennese population, ranging from the lower-middle classes to artisans to student fraternities. Changes to electoral rights in 1884 prompted the enfranchisement of many more artisans and small businessmen. They now came out in large numbers to support Schönerer or other antisemites running for office, one of whom campaigned to have Jews murdered. Schönerer championed the latest racist ideas and was a major proponent of Volkish ideology, his crude slogan being "Let the Jew believe in what he may, racially he is a swine."

Schönerer's political success came to an end in 1888 when he led a violent demonstration against the offices of a liberal daily newspaper. Jailed for four months, he was stripped of his parliamentary seat for five years. While his own career was in tatters, the Austrian antisemitic movement that Schönerer unleashed did not die. His principal political adversary, **Karl Lueger** (1844–1910), immediately sensed an opportunity. Drawing on the same pool of student, artisan, and lower-middle class support as Schönerer, Lueger expanded his electoral base by appealing to school teachers, white-collar workers, state and municipal bureaucrats, and Catholics. Where Schönerer had been a Protestant and dismissed the Church, Lueger sought to empower religious institutions, playing on fears of Catholic decline in the face of increasing secularization. He often held his own antisemitic rallies in churches. When the emperor Franz Josef appealed to Pope Leo XIII to condemn Lueger officially, the Pontiff not only refused but gave Lueger his blessing.

Lueger was enormously successful; his career pointed to the future of modern politics. He developed the politics of the crowd with his demagoguery and spellbinding oratory, while constantly harping on the pernicious role of Jewish plutocrats and financiers. That the bulk of Austrian Jews were extremely poor, especially those in the provinces, seemed to matter little to him or his followers. His principal theme was alleged Jewish power: "Whenever a state has allowed the Jews to become powerful, that state has collapsed." No concrete example was given because to his audience the claim appeared self-evident.

In the municipal election campaign of 1897, Lueger's campaign motto paraphrased a line from Karl Marx's *Communist Manifesto,* when instead of "workers of the world" it called on antisemites to unite. Liberals were outvoted ten to one. After having twice previously refused to appoint Lueger, this time Emperor Franz Josef could no longer resist. Karl Lueger became mayor of Vienna, the first major city in Europe to be ruled by a declared antisemite. With his enormous public support, Lueger made antisemitism a respectable

Election poster for Adolphe-Léon Willette. Willette (1857–1926) was the self-declared "Antisemitic Candidate" for Paris's 9th arrondissement in the legislative elections of 1889. In the picture, a bare-chested Marianne stands above a host of French types, including the stripe-shirted worker and the aging military officer. On the ground at their feet lie the shattered Tablets of the Law, bearing the word *Talmud*. Willette, a staunch supporter of Edouard Drumont, calls upon voters to support his campaign against "Jewish tyranny." The poster declares, "It is not a question of religion. The Jew is of a different race, hostile to ours. Judaism—here is the enemy!" Willette lost his bid for election.

With the popularity of Drumont, antisemitism became central to the republican–radical versus royalist–clerical split in France, sharpened by the Dreyfus Affair, one of the nineteenth century's most dramatic manifestations of antisemitism. In 1894, a Jewish army officer, **Alfred Dreyfus, (1859-1935)** was falsely accused of spying for Germany. The charges were based on forged documents and a massive cover-up in the military. All the while protesting his innocence, Dreyfus was found guilty of treason in a secret court-martial, during which he was denied the right to examine the evidence against him. The army stripped him of his rank in a humiliating public ceremony that included having his epaulets torn off his uniform and his sword broken. He was sentenced to life imprisonment on Devil's Island, a penal colony located off the coast of South America.

The Dreyfus Affair took on even greater significance in 1898 when Emile Zola resurrected the cause of Dreyfus' innocence in his "J'accuse!"—his stunning denunciation of the army, in which he charged it with responsibility for the cover-up. Among doubts as to the justice of the verdict and amid inflamed passions, the army conducted a new trial. Again Dreyfus was found guilty, but this time with "extenuating circumstances." Although returned to Devil's Island in 1899, Dreyfus was granted a presidential pardon when the real identity of the traitor and details of the cover-up emerged. Despite the pardon, public furor forced a delay in his full exoneration until 1906. Restored to his former military rank, Dreyfus was later awarded the Legion of Honor.

For the antisemites, the affair was proof of Jewish treachery. For the defenders of the French Revolution and the Third Republic, Dreyfus was an innocent victim of a terrible conservative conspiracy. The nation was split. While a mob estimated at one hundred thousand took to the streets of Paris in 1898, crying out "Death to the Jews," even members of the intellectual and artistic classes emerged to voice their opinions on Dreyfus. Anti-Dreyfussard intellectuals not only condemned Dreyfus but the Jews in general. For the great French Impressionist painter, Auguste Renoir, Dreyfus was guilty because "[The Jews] come to France to make money, but the moment a fight is on, they hide behind the first tree. There are so many in the army because the Jew likes to parade around in fancy uniforms. Every country chases them out; there is a reason for that, and we must not allow them to occupy such a position in France." Renoir was joined by the radical antisemite Edgar Degas, the master of so many delicate scenes of beautiful ballerinas. His tenderness deserted him, however, when it came to Jews. He was known to launch into violent tirades against them, sometimes bringing himself to tears. He fired a model merely because she expressed doubts about Dreyfus' guilt and on another occasion announced in an art gallery that he was headed for the Paris law courts. An art dealer in attendance was reported to have asked him, "[T]o attend the [Dreyfus] trial?" to which Degas replied, "No, to kill a Jew!" Another luminary among the impressionists, Paul Cézanne, was similarly convinced of Dreyfus' guilt. The affair actually split the Impressionist movement, with painters Lucien Pissarro, Claude Monet, Paul Signac, and others firmly in Dreyfus' camp.

Despite the overt antisemitism behind Dreyfus' ordeal, the event ultimately transcended the fate of Dreyfus or even that of French Jewry. Rather, the Dreyfus Affair tested the strength of revolutionary France. The Third Republic withstood the sway of reactionary forces. Dreyfus' eventual acquittal discredited the military and the Church. Such was the blow to the conservative establishment that in 1905 France officially enacted the separation of Church and state. French antisemites bitterly looked on as French Jews continued to enjoy distinguished careers at the highest levels of the state bureaucracy, in the military, in politics, and in academia. They remained unreconciled to the final verdict and maintained even more strongly that Jews controlled France, particularly the judiciary. Decades later, the remnants of the anti-Dreyfussards merged with the Right-wing and Fascist camp in interwar France and came to include the influential writer Maurice Barres.

From the early nineteenth century, French antisemitism also issued from Left-wing and secular politics. In **Charles Fourier** (1772–1837), **Pierre-Joseph Proudhon** (1809–1865), and **Alphonse Toussenel** (1803–1885), socialism and anarchism found their most strident and influential antisemitic voices. Concerned with identifying the cause of proletarian misery, socialists identified the Jews as the source of the plight of the French underclass, both rural and urban.

For Fourier, Jews epitomized the danger of capitalism and predatory commerce. He lamented their emancipation, an act he decried as "shameful," and claimed that Jews stood poised to dominate France. Only their small numbers prevented the country from becoming "one vast synagogue." Fourier believed the Jews were incapable of change. In contrast to the Enlightenment idea of Jewish "regeneration," Fourier declared: "They will reform, say the philosophers. Not at all: They will pervert our morals without altering theirs. Besides, when will they reform? Will it take a century for them to do so? . . . The Jews, with their commercial morality, are they not the leprosy and perdition of the body politic? . . . Let the Jews remain in France for a century and they . . . will become in France what they are in Poland and end by taking commercial industry away from the nationals who have managed it without the Jews thus far. . . . Wherever they are conspicuous, it is at the expense of the nationals." For the sake of France, the numbers of Jews residing there had to be strictly limited, and their freedom of movement within the nation's borders restricted, so that they would be forced into "productive" labor. Ultimately, Fourier wanted the Jews expelled from France, and he even entertained the fanciful idea of Rothschild resurrecting the Jewish nation under his kingship in the Land of Israel.

Proudhon, the anarchist, famous for his expression "Property is Theft," maintained that Jewish financiers (and Protestant merchants) were bleeding France. But the sins of the Jews extended beyond their contribution to commerce. Echoing the radical secularism of philosophes such as Diderot and Voltaire, Proudhon accused the Jews of being "the first authors of that evil superstition called Catholicism in which the furious, intolerant Jewish element consistently overwhelmed the other Greek, Latin, barbarian, etc. elements and served to torture humankind for so long." But in a contradictory fashion, Proudhon echoed de Bonald and de Maistre by drawing on Christian tropes, saying that Christians were justified in calling the Jews "deicides." And like Fourier, he also wished to be rid of the Jews, a people he described as "unsociable" and "obstinate"; "The Jew is the enemy of humankind. The race must either be sent back to Asia or exterminated. . . . By the sword, by amalgamation, or by expulsion the Jew must be made to disappear. . . . Those whom the peoples of the Middle Ages loathed by instinct, I loathe upon reflection, irrevocably. Hatred of the Jew, as of the Englishman, needs to be an article of our faith."

With Toussenel, a student of Fourier, the link between anti-capitalism and antisemitism was made explicit. He was best known for depicting the modern Jewish financier as a modern version of the medieval usurer. Eliding the distinctions between medieval moneylending and modern capitalism, Toussenel decried that France was gripped by "economic feudalism," of which the Jews were the new nobility. In his seminal book *The Jews: Kings of the Epoch* (1845), Toussenel railed against government corruption and social unrest, blaming the Jews for both. Their "economic feudalism. . . entrenches itself in the soil more deeply each day, pressing with its two feet the throats of the royalty and the people." Toussenel thundered, "The Jew reigns and governs France" and recommended "the king and the people. . . unite in order to rid themselves of the aristocracy of money."

French antisemites on the Left dismissed or at least minimized the achievements of the French Revolution, claiming that true freedom had yet to be attained. With the emancipation of the Jews, new autocrats had emerged to rule France. In place of the economy, Toussenel encouraged his fellow countrymen to recognize that "freed supposedly of the yoke of nobiliar feudalism by the revolution of '89, in fact they had done no more than change masters."

French antisemitism was likewise bound to France's imperial politics, especially in the Near East. The connection was made most clear in the **Damascus Affair** (1840). When a Capuchin monk—Father Thomas—and his servant disappeared, fellow monks and local Christians claimed that the two had been murdered by Jews for ritual purposes. When they petitioned the Muslim leader of the city, Sharif ("Sheriff") Pasha, to investigate, the French consul in Damascus, Count Ratti-Menton, suggested to the sheriff that Jews killed the two men to use their blood for baking matzah. European consuls in the city, representing France, Britain, and Austria, also encouraged the investigation, themselves convinced of the Jews' guilt. (The Austrian consul, Caspar Merlatto, however, soon became a steadfast defender of the Jews against the charges). Mass arrests followed the ransacking of the Jewish quarter. About seventy men and sixty boys, most between the ages of five and twelve, were taken into custody. The city's most notable Jews had their beards set on fire and their teeth pulled out. One of the accused was murdered in custody and another converted to Islam. To bring an end to their suffering, a Jewish barber named Negri confessed. Thereafter, a riot broke out during which a synagogue was ransacked and Torah scrolls desecrated.

The matter soon escalated into an international incident with competing imperial ambitions coming into play. England, in particular, attempted to use the case to undermine French interests in the Near East. The Austrians, on the other hand, took a dim view of the fact that one of the arrested Jews was an Austrian citizen. The story demonstrates the extent to which an antisemitic episode can, in fact, actually have little to do with Jews, although their fate was central to the drama. In fact, the day before his disappearance, Father Thomas had been threatened with death by a Muslim for having blasphemed against the faith. Ratti-Menton had fabricated the story of Jewish guilt because (even if he had sincerely believed the story) blaming anyone in the Muslim community would have upset France's imperial relations with Muhammad Ali, the Egyptian ruler of Syria and ostensibly France's protégé. Father Thomas and his servant effectively went missing on Muhammad Ali's watch, reason enough for the latter to have colluded with Ratti-Menton. Significantly, the ritual murder charge was easily accepted by the Muslim community, even though the accusation was unknown in the Islamic world—it was an import of European imperialism.

Public meetings in support of the Jews were held in London, Paris, New York, and Philadelphia. The lawyer Isaac Crémieux and the Orientalist Solomon Munk, both French Jews, and Sir Moses Montefiore, the leading figure of British Jewry, were sent on a mission to secure the release of the falsely accused Jewish prisoners. After several meetings with

Muhammad Ali, despite his initial obstinance, the delegation secured from him the unconditional release of the men and a full recognition of their innocence. Tragically, the exonerations came too late for many of the accused. The affair had begun in February and it was then August—only nine remained alive of the thirteen originally imprisoned.

Beyond the sphere of international relations, the Damascus Affair was also of great significance within the Jewish world. The affair contributed to the emergence and growth of the popular Jewish press. Written in European languages and therefore open to general scrutiny, itself a marker of increasing cultural literacy and integration, newspapers such as the German *Allgemeine Zeitung des Judenthums,* founded in 1837; the French *Archives Israelite de France,* first published in 1840; and England's *Jewish Chronicle,* established in 1841 (and still in existence), were joined by a host of other Jewish publications across Europe and the United States, all of which helped spread word of the Damascus Affair. The Jewish press transformed a local issue into a modern, international media event.

The advent of a vigorous Jewish press heralded the onset of modern Jewish public opinion and became an important means of discussing the "Jewish Question." Journalism and newspaper publishing also became a common career path for modern Jews. Invariably, in the West wherever Jews owned newspapers, whether for principally Jewish or non-Jewish consumption, such as the *Berliner Tagblatt* or the *New York Times,* they promoted liberal politics. In the early-twentieth-century, mass circulation newspapers—such as the Yiddish dailies from Warsaw, *Der Moment* and *Der Haynt;* New York's *Forverts;* and the biweekly Ladino newspaper from Istanbul, *Il Tiempo*—exposed Jewish readers to world news and politics.

The Damascus Affair had other important consequences. Montefiore and Crémieux, as well as the Rothschilds, represented a handful of Jews with access to seats of power and political influence. While the affair testified to Jewish vulnerability, the presence of strong and well-placed Jewish advocates also reflected the source of Jewish collective vigor. The affair also seems to have altered Jewish sensibilities. Perhaps because the injustice was perpetrated by a representative of France, the liberal nation that most loudly proclaimed the values of liberty, equality, and fraternity, the sense of betrayal Jews felt was much more substantial. The events in Damascus spurred Jews into collective action; they were unwilling to suffer silently; they would now protest injustices with all the means at their disposal. The international dimensions of the affair thus inculcated a new sense of mutual Jewish responsibility. Philanthropy emerged as a major goal of western Jews, prepared more than ever to assist their needy co-religionists in the Middle East and, eventually, in eastern Europe.

Finally, it should be noted, that in France, just as in Germany and Austria, the antisemitic movement did not succeed in disenfranchising the Jews and their integration and embourgeoisement across western Europe continued apace. Nevertheless, there were lasting consequences of the campaign of French antisemites. Toussenel and Drumont provided both postrevolutionary forces on the Right and on the Left with a new language of cultural criticism while both France and her imperial adversaries were inclined to manipulate the fate of a handful of wretched Jews accused of a crime first concocted in the Middle Ages to further their own eminently modern diplomatic agendas. The scope and versatility of antisemitism as a political tool were made abundantly clear with its adoption across the broad spectrum of French politics.

Antisemitism in Italy

In contrast to Germany, Austria, and France, antisemitism was not a constitutive factor of political life in modern Italy. In 1938, when Mussolini imposed race laws, the unprecedented move aroused opposition not only among many ordinary Italians but also among many loyal Fascists. While political antisemitism barely existed in Italy, religious antipathy originated within the Vatican. On one occasion it exploded and had a major impact on political affairs and the formation of the modern Italian state. The **Mortara Affair** (1858) evinces the effects of antisemitism even in the absence of Jews in the struggle between Catholic and secular, nationalist values.

On the evening of June 23, 1858, in the city of Bologna, papal police broke into the home of the Mortara family and snatched six-year-old Edgardo from his distraught and bewildered mother. According to Inquisition authorities in Rome, the family's Catholic housekeeper had had Edgardo secretly baptized when he had fallen very ill at the age of one. The police had the law on their side, for the abduction of Edgardo, the most infamous example of several such cases in nineteenth-century Italy, was sanctioned by canon law, whereby a child once baptized, even involuntarily, had to be removed from his or her Jewish home. Edgardo was taken away in haste, and his Catholicization began immediately. Frantic efforts to have the child released came to naught; his parents were repeatedly told, however, that they could be reunited with their son provided they themselves converted. Despite the storm of international protest, both popular and diplomatic, Pope Pius IX refused to relent and in fact raised Edgardo as his own adopted son. Edgardo Mortara eventually joined the priesthood in 1873. A celebrated preacher, he failed, despite consistent efforts, to induce his parents to convert. He died in a Belgian abbey on March 11, 1940, two months before the Nazis invaded.

Beyond the immediate family tragedy, the event had profound historical repercussions. Count Camillo Cavour, the architect of Italian unification, and Napoleon III of France, both of whom sought to undermine the temporal authority of the Papacy, used the affair to agitate against the rule of Rome. In Britain, Moses Montefiore took up the cause, while in Austria, Emperor Franz Josef appealed in vain to the pope. Protestants across Europe and the United States, where the *New York Times* ran more than twenty editorials demanding Edgardo's release, mobilized against the obscurantism of the Catholic Church. The plight of Edgardo also catalyzed liberal Catholic protest against the conservative papacy of Pius IX.

The Mortara Affair emerged against the backdrop of the Vatican's waning authority in the modern, secular world. While it smacked of medievalism, the kidnapping of Edgardo Mortara and the international responses, characterized by the mobilization of outraged political, public, and editorial opinion, mark it as a distinctly modern episode. While Edgardo was lost to his family and the Jewish community, in the long term the aftermath of the abduction diminished the power of the Papacy, for it galvanized the forces promoting liberalism, nationalism, Italian unification, and anticlericalism. In 1870, Italian troops entered Rome and the temporal power of the popes, which had lasted for a thousand years, came to an end.

Antisemitism in Russia

Although prior to the 1880s many of the harsh decrees of the tsars that pertained to Jews appear to have been driven by antisemitism, very often it was more the desire for reform rather than retribution that drove such policies. However, after 1881 the state purposefully sought to exclude Jews, and their situation among Russia's minorities became anomalous. From that time until the fall of the Romanovs, a series of laws and ordinances, outbreaks of violence, and new forms of accusations constitute a transformed response to Jews, one where Russia joined the ever-rising chorus of antisemitic sentiment heard across Europe but with more dramatic, devastating, and long-lasting consequences.

The greatest threat to Jews in late-nineteenth century Russia came from extremely limited economic opportunity and the imposition of educational and professional quotas. The impact of such anti-Jewish state policies was intensified by the enormous demographic growth and rising population density among Jews, leading many to agitate for revolution and many more to emigrate. For the masses of poor Jews, Alexander III's counter-reaction had a profound impact on the Jewish economy. Forced expulsions from rural areas increased the pace and scope of urbanization, which in turn promoted an intense competition for livelihood among Jews. While historians debate whether some Jews actually benefited from or were victims of Russian industrialization, what cannot be denied is that pauperization among most Jews was spreading and that the impression held by Russian Jews at the time was that their circumstances were desperate and their futures lay either in Russia's bigger cities or outside the country altogether. In 1898, approximately 20 percent of Jews in the Pale applied for Passover charity, while in Odessa 66 percent of Jews were buried at the community's expense. By 1900, as much as 35 percent of Russian Jewry received poor relief of one sort or another. More Jews were driven by poverty and despair, rather than political idealism, to either Zionism or Jewish socialism in the belief that either movement could offer a panacea for the economic plight of Russian Jewry.

Along with the masses, the Jewish intelligentsia also suffered from government policy. Beginning in 1882, the first Jewish quota was introduced at the Military Medical Academy, limiting Jews to just 5 percent of all students. This was followed by the imposition of quotas at various institutions, until in 1887 the Russian Ministry of Education established a formal, Russia-wide *numerus clausus,* or quota: 10 percent within the Pale of Settlement, 5 percent outside it, and 3 percent in both Moscow and St. Petersburg. This led to an exodus of Russian Jewish medical students who went to German universities to study. By 1912, over 2,500 Russian Jews were studying at German universities and technical schools, two-thirds of them attending the universities at Berlin, Königsberg, and Leipzig. Of the Russian Jews at Prussian universities, 85 percent studied medicine, while the figure was 90 percent at non-Prussian institutions. In 1889, the Ministry of Justice ordered that all "non-Christians," meaning Jews, would only be admitted to the bar upon permission granted by the minister. For the next fifteen years, no Jew was registered as a barrister in the Russian court system.

Along with official government policy that targeted Jews, popular sentiment also hardened. Among the Russian masses, the ever-present, theological hatred of Jews was joined by a new development—violence. This marked Russian antisemitism as unusual in the context of late-nineteenth-century antisemitism. Not since the outbreak of the Hep Hep riots in 1819 had Jewish communities been physically attacked on a level comparable to the violence that erupted in 1881, when a series of riots swept through southern Russia. (Two smaller outbreaks of violence against Jews had already occurred in Odessa in 1859 and 1871.) These riots were known by the Russian word **pogrom,** a term that connotes wanton violence, havoc, physical attacks against members of a particular group, and the destruction of property.

The pogroms were one product of the turbulent political situation in late-nineteenth-century Russia. Following the accession to the throne of Alexander II (son of Nicholas I) in 1855, the new tsar charted a somewhat liberalizing course, all the while asserting his autocratic rule. Among his achievements were the emancipation of the serfs (1861) and the institution of far-reaching reforms of military and governmental administration. But the changes he wrought made him too radical for the reactionary forces and too moderate for liberals and the burgeoning revolutionary movement. Unsatisfied with the reforms, radical activities increased among the intelligentsia, which in turn prompted Alexander to respond with heightened repression. When a populist movement (*Narodnichestvo,* "Going to the People," or Narodism) arose in the late 1860s, the government arrested and prosecuted hundreds of students.

Many of the radicals turned to terrorism, and on March 1, 1881, a member of the terrorist group People's Will (*Narodnaya Volya*) assassinated Alexander with a hand-thrown bomb. Among the plotters was Hessia Helfman, a Jewish woman, who, for many Russians on the Right, came to symbolize what they saw as a Jewish plot against Russia. With religious tensions already high because of the convergence of Easter and Passover that year, the assassination furthered the division between those who wept for the fallen tsar and those who did not. The assassination saw the outbreak in mid-April of attacks against Jews in southern Russia, which spread like wildfire and raged until 1883, with approximately two hundred pogroms leaving some forty Jews killed, thousands wounded, homeless, and destitute. There were also some rapes. The pogroms began in the town of Elizavetgrad, where a government report noted, "The city presented an extraordinary sight: streets covered with feathers and obstructed with broken furniture which had been thrown out of residences; houses with broken doors and windows; a raging mob, running about yelling and whistling in all directions and continuing its work of destruction without let or hindrance, and as a finishing touch to this picture, complete indifference displayed by the local non-Jewish inhabitants to the havoc wrought before their eyes." The Jewish memoirist, Mary Antin, reported how the violence began:

> Somebody would start up that lie about murdering Christian children, and the stupid peasants would get mad about it, and fill themselves with vodka, and set out to kill the Jews. They attacked them with knives and clubs and scythes and axes, killed them or tortured them, and burned their houses. This was called a "pogrom." Jews who escaped the pogroms came to Polotzk [her hometown] with wounds on them, and horrible, horrible stories, of little babies torn limb from limb before their mothers' eyes. Only to hear these things made one sob

and sob and choke with pain. People who saw such things never smiled any more, no matter how long they lived; and sometimes their hair turned white in a day, and some people became insane on the spot.

Written after she had emigrated to the United States, Antin's account is most likely exaggerated. The vivid description "of little babies torn limb from limb before their mothers' eyes" echoes motifs drawn from much earlier accounts of anti-Jewish violence. It is also improbable that "people who saw such things never smiled any more." However, her general description of the pogrom as a brutal attack by drunken rioters using deadly weapons against Jews is correct. Antin's compelling account, even if not precise in all of its historical details, is most valuable, however, because it is a genuine reflection of the terror and trauma the pogroms evoked among Jews, perhaps especially among those who were not there. The pogroms did more than any other event to shape Jewish views of Russia thereafter.

Although the government did not orchestrate the pogroms, local authorities rarely intervened, and light sentences were meted out for those perpetrators who were arrested. The new tsar, Alexander III, immediately set out to destroy the revolutionary movement. Jews, who Right-wing agitators identified as conspirators against Mother Russia, were subject to harsh legislation. The **May Laws** (1882), promulgated after the 1881 assassination of Tsar Alexander II, demanded that Jews move into urban areas from villages and rural settlements located outside of cities and towns. In their new locations, they had few prospects for employment and the general economic and social conditions were bleak. Jews could not buy or rent property, other than their own residences, were ineligible for civil service jobs, and were forbidden to trade on Sundays and Christian holidays. Over subsequent years ever more restrictions were added, further degrading the conditions of life for Russia's five million Jews. The tsar's tutor and over-procurator of the Holy Synod, an architect of conservative reaction, Konstantin Pobedonostsev, was said to have remarked that the only way for the "Jewish Question" to be solved in Russia was for one-third to emigrate, one-third to convert to Christianity, and one-third to perish.

When the last tsar, Nicholas II, assumed the throne in 1894, peasants, workers, and students rioted and continued to agitate for change. In 1902, Nicholas appointed a new minister of the interior, Vyacheslav Plehve, to deal with the situation. In a speech given in Odessa in 1903, Plehve stated pointedly and threateningly, "In Western Russia some 90 per cent of the revolutionaries are Jews, and in Russia generally—some 40 per cent. I shall not conceal from you that the revolutionary movement in Russia worries us but you should know that if you do not deter your youth from the revolutionary movement, we shall make your position untenable to such an extent that you will have to leave Russia, to the very last man!"

Incitement continued against Jews, marked by a virulent antisemitic campaign depicting them as menaces to Christianity and the settled social order, culminating in a pogrom that erupted in the town of Kishinev (in present-day Moldova) on April 6, 1903. The **Kishinev pogrom** lasted for three terrifying days. Both Russians and Romanians joined in the riots in a scenario where old prejudices blended with new methods. Just a week prior to the pogrom, a letter was circulated around the teahouses of the city, claiming that Jews performed ritual murder and that with Easter fast approaching the Jews would sacrifice a Christian child again. The rumors were spread by a local journalist, who sought to whip up both his readers and his newspaper sales.

Beginning with the claims of human sacrifice, the circular continued with more modern charges, observing that killing young Christians

is the way of their jeering at us, Russians. And how much harm do they bring to our Mother Russia! They want to take possession of her . . . they publish various proclamations to the people in order to excite it against the authority, even against our Father the Tsar, who knows the mean, cunning, deceitful and greedy nature of this nation, and does not let them enjoy liberties. . . . But if you give liberty to the Zjid [a pejorative term for Jew], he will reign over our holy Russia, take everything in his paws and there will be no more Russia, but Zjidowia.

Russians were dispatched to Kishinev from surrounding towns with students from theological seminaries, high schools, and colleges leading the charge. While some soldiers and police warned Jews of impending pogroms, most issued no warning and offered no assistance. This was true of the garrison of five thousand soldiers stationed in the city. Although they could have easily turned back the mob, they remained in their barracks.

As was the case in 1881, the government did not orchestrate the pogroms, contrary to popular Jewish opinion, but its antisemitic policies and refusal to intervene created the climate wherein pogroms could and did flourish. According to official statistics, 49 Jews were killed, 587 injured, 1,350 houses and 600 businesses and shops were looted and destroyed, and about 2,000 families were left homeless. It was estimated that material losses amounted to 2,500,000 gold rubles—a huge sum in those days and especially for a community that was poverty stricken even before the pogrom.

International protest was immediate, akin to the reaction to the Damascus and Mortara Affairs. A variety of prominent people in Russia, inspired by a host of differing political agendas, protested on behalf of the Jewish victims, even if they offered competing accounts of what had taken place. The famed novelist Leo Tolstoy spoke out, as did the Jewish historian Shimon Dubnov, the Zionist Ahad ha-Am, and the poet Hayim Nahman Bialik, while other Jews founded the Historical Council in Odessa, the purpose of which was to investigate the Kishinev pogrom. Bialik was called upon to collect oral testimonies and other documentary material. Though the report was never published, Bialik's work provided the source material for his epic Hebrew poem, *Be-Ir ha-Haregah* ("In the City of Slaughter"). The poem, which became a catch-cry for the Zionist revolt against the conditions of exile, opened with an anguished summons to the reader to observe for herself what the pogromists had done:

Arise and go now to the city of slaughter;
Into its courtyard wind thy way;
There with thine own hand touch, and with the eyes of
thine head,
Behold on tree, on stone, on fence, on mural clay,
The spattered blood and dried brains of the dead.

Soon, however, Bialik's pain turned to rage when instead of saving his invective for those who perpetrated the atrocities, he blamed the victims for their apparent passivity in the face of the attackers. Challenging Jewish manhood, Bialik "outed" the once-proud Jews, calling them cowards:

Come, now, and I will bring thee to their lairs
The privies, jakes and pigpens where the heirs
Of Hasmoneans lay, with trembling knees,
Concealed and cowering—the sons of the Maccabees!
The seed of saints, the scions of the lions!
Who, crammed by scores in all the sanctuaries of their
shame
So sanctified My name!
It was the flight of mice they fled,
The scurrying of roaches was their flight;
They died like dogs, and they were dead!

The impact of the poem on the nascent Zionist movement was enormous. With translations into Yiddish by Bialik and into Russian by Vladimir Jabotinsky, the poem obtained a wide audience and established Bialik as the national poet.

גְּוִיוֹת סִפְרֵי הַתּוֹרָה הַנִּקְרָעִים

Burying Torah scrolls after the Kishinev pogrom (1903). At the turn of the twentieth century, Jews made up approximately one-third of Kishinev's population of 145,000. An important element in the city's industrial sector, Jews were largely employed in crafts, many as skilled artisans. Agricultural work, especially of the seasonal variety, provided a living for many Jews, as did peddling. Poverty was widespread and increasing and can be measured by the number of families that applied for Passover relief: 1,200 in 1895; 1,142 in 1896; 1,450 in 1897; 1,494 in 1898; 1,505 in 1899; and 2,204 in 1900. Aside from the general poverty of the area, economic restrictions on Jews further exacerbated an already precarious economic situation. An important social welfare network of charity provided assistance to the city's Jews, and in 1898 all such charitable institutions were united under the name of "The Society in Aid of the Poor Jews of Kishinev."

After a period of mounting economic, religious, and political tensions, on April 6, 1903, a pogrom broke out. In addition to the loss of life and destruction of residential and commercial properties, there was also widespread desecration of synagogues. Here, men are posing for the camera with desecrated Torah scrolls, which have been placed on stretchers prior to burial. The custom of burying unusable sacred texts follows from a discussion in the Babylonian Talmud, Tractate Shabbat 115, a–b.

Throughout 1905, Kishinev and some three hundred other towns were again struck by pogroms as the country erupted in revolution. Mainly organized by the monarchist Union of Russian People, and with the cooperation of local government officials, the pogroms left over a thousand people dead and many thousands more wounded. Reactionary forces blamed Jews for the revolution, the constitution that the tsar reluctantly granted in October of 1905, and the general political turbulence then rocking Russia. They openly called for the extermination of the Jews.

While the violence did not have its analogue in the west, the reasons for the pogroms were entirely familiar and identical to the sorts of complaints heard in the west: Jewish economic competition and a totally unfounded but widespread sense that Russia was being taken over by Jews. Here the government did play a role in that it promoted this line of thinking to marshal the people against revolutionary radicalism, in which many Jews were active. The tsar failed to so much as condemn the pogromists, let alone compensate Jews for their losses. All requests for the merest display of compassion were rebuffed. It is little wonder that Jews joined others in feeling abandoned by Mother Russia.

Russia's most lasting contribution to modern anti-semitism is ***The Protocols of the Elders of Zion.*** Concocted by members of the Russian secret police in Paris sometime between 1896 and 1898, *The Protocols* purport to be the minutes of a meeting of Jewish elders plotting world domina-tion. No longer were the accusations limited to this or that particular country. Instead, *The Protocols* portrayed Jews as conspiring on a global scale to foment the most hated forces of modernity: liberalism, parliamentary democracy, capital-ism, Marxism, and anarchism. Both the Russian Revolution of 1917 and Germany's defeat in the First World War turned *The Protocols* from being just another antisemitic text into the "bible" for antisemites the world over. Reactionaries cir-culated *The Protocols* during the Russian Civil War to prove that the overthrow of the tsar was in fact a "Jewish revolu-tion." In postwar Germany, *The Protocols* was used to "prove" that the Jews were promoters of a Judeo–Bolshevik conspir-acy to conquer the nation. The central theme of *The Protocols* of a gigantic Jewish conspiracy against the world continues to resonate with large numbers of people from different cul-tures. After World War I, the book enjoyed wide success in western Europe, was published in the United States by the automobile magnate Henry Ford, was enthusiastically em-braced by the Nazis, and is currently a best seller in the Mus-lim world.

The ritual murder charge against **Mendel Beilis** (1874–1934) in 1911 in Kiev confirmed the continued pres-ence in Russia of older, more familiar forms of anti-Judaism. In February 1911, liberals in the Third Duma (parliament) introduced a proposal to abolish the Pale of Settlement. A tidal wave of Right-wing and monarchist organizations ob-jected strongly. Armed with government subsidies they em-barked on an anti-Jewish campaign. When in March 1911 the body of a young Christian boy was found in Kiev, the tsarist authorities charged Mendel Beilis, the Jewish manager of a Kievan brick kiln, with ritual murder. This occurred de-spite the fact that the authorities already knew the identity of the criminal gang that had killed the boy.

For more than two years, Beilis remained in prison on trumped-up charges while the government built its case, largely through producing forged documents and buying off and threatening witnesses. Entirely novel in this whole episode was the decision of the prosecutor to go beyond Beilis and also put Judaism and world Jewry on trial, calling "expert" witnesses to affirm the reality of the blood libel. Beilis' plight became symbolic of the larger struggle between the regime and opposition forces. The liberal and revolution-ary press exposed the machinations of the minister of justice,

including the fact that throughout the trial he had reported to the tsar, who had kept a close watch on the proceedings. The Beilis case not only drew international attention to the plight of the Jews in Russia, but it also united the conserva-tive Octobrists and the radical Bolsheviks in their opposition to the government. Eventually, to the surprise of the regime and the world, Beilis was acquitted by a jury of illiterate peas-ants. The fate of Judaism was less clear than that of Beilis. The jury failed to deliver a clear-cut verdict on the blood libel, unable to decide whether or not Jews were obliged to practice it.

The Paths Jews Took

The impact of massive Jewish population growth and urban density, desperate economic circumstances in eastern Europe, the rise of organized antisemitism, and the emergence of na-tionalist ideologies and mass political movements influenced Jews in the way they assessed their current situations and imagined their futures. Under the sway of such forces, the Jewish people began to set out in new social and political di-rections. The decisions taken by millions of Jews concerning where they would live, what politics they favored, what lan-guages they would speak, and what, if any, Jewish ritual they would practice began to take shape in the last third of the nineteenth century.

At that time, the bulk of the Jewish people, especially those in eastern Europe, lived, for the most part, in small towns or cities in crippling poverty under a regime that com-bined hostility with callous indifference to the Jews. In the West, material conditions among Jews were sound, indeed getting increasingly better, but the tone and stridency of the antisemitic movement were alarming and confusing precisely because they seemed to grow in tandem with Jewish accultur-ation. The different social, economic, and cultural conditions in various European countries also determined the variety of Jewish responses to the "Jewish Question." There was no uni-tary Jewish response. However, if one general statement can be made, it is that nowhere did Jews sit passively in the face of economic misery and antisemitism. The flowering of na-tionalist sentiment among Jews, which also began to grow in the last two decades of the nineteenth century, was both a re-action to such outside forces as antisemitism but was also the result of internal developments whose origins can be traced to the changing nature of Jewish consciousness that origi-nated with the Haskalah. Many of the developments that his-torians once saw as being a direct response to the events of 1881 actually began long prior to that date—community rupture, the turn to political radicalism, and the less dramatic but powerful process of acculturation can be seen as early as the 1780s.

Yet the pace and nature of Jewish responses to economic and political pressure sped up considerably at the end of the nineteenth century. In the period between 1881 and 1921, from the outbreak of the pogroms until the aftermath of World War I, Jews organized, resisted, accommodated, and adapted themselves to the circumstances in a host of ways.

Essentially, we can identify three major Jewish responses to these events: (1) the rise of modern Jewish politics, basically socialism or nationalism; (2) an activist response among western European Jews characterized by the development of Jewish advocacy and philanthropic organizations; and (3) mass migration out of Europe.

The Rise of Modern Jewish Politics

Toward the end of the nineteenth century, young Jews, energized by frustration and inspired by hope, turned to mass politics. Some sought salvation in socialism, others in nationalism, and still others in a combination of the two. Despite or because of their disenfranchisement and the fact that the Jewish population in the Pale of Settlement increased at a staggering rate of 22 percent from 1881 to 1897, approximately 100,000 per year, Jews in Russia were far more involved and invested in political activity than their emancipated coreligionists in western Europe, although important figures in the West, such as Theodor Herzl, came to have an enormous impact on Jewish political culture.

The burgeoning revolutionary ferment sweeping across Russia in the last decades of the nineteenth century attracted Jewish students to socialism. Many young Jews believed that the "Jewish Question" could only be solved in the context of the larger social question, and that meant getting rid of the old order. Both cruel autocracy and oppressive capitalism would have to be eliminated for both the Jewish and non-Jewish underclasses to be free. Later, preferring not to throw themselves into the general revolutionary movement then raging in the Russian Empire, other Jews articulated a particular Jewish socialism, believing it to be the key to a secure Jewish future.

Others saw no future for the Jews in Europe at all. Jewish nationalists regarded antisemitism as an incurable cancer, poverty an inescapable fact of life, and assimilation a scourge that would lead to the disappearance of the Jews. They held out that the return of the Jews to their ancestral homeland in Palestine was the only solution to the Jewish dilemma. Still others embraced the establishment of Jewish communal autonomy in the Diaspora. Not only did Jews adopt socialism, Zionism, and territorialism, but the boundaries between them were often fluid. What emerged was a syncretistic mixing of ideological positions and political experimentation that proved rich and was reflective of the energy but also the fragmentation and divided nature of modern Jewish culture and society.

Jewish Socialism

Jews first became involved in Left-wing politics in central Europe. Almost all German Jewish socialists came from comfortable middle-class homes and were rarely concerned with specifically Jewish needs. **Ferdinand Lassalle** (1825–1864), who as a fifteen-year old expressed deep dismay at what he characterized as the submissiveness of Jews in the face of the Damascus Affair, never entered the field of Jewish politics but instead became an organizer of German workers and founder in 1863 of the General German Workers' Association, and similarly, the socialist thinker **Eduard Bernstein** (1850–1932) was principally concerned with the lot of impoverished German workers. Whenever such men did consider the "Jewish Question," the response of Bernstein was rather typical: "I believed that the solution would be found in the Socialist International." Writing after the calamity of World War I, Bernstein concluded, "To this belief I still adhere, and it is more important to me that any separatist movement."

What was true in Germany was also true in eastern Europe, where socialists such as **Rosa Luxemburg** (1871–1919), founder of the Social Democratic Party of Poland and Lithuania, claimed in 1916 to have "no room in my heart for Jewish suffering." She felt "equally close to the wretched victims of the rubber plantations in Putamayo, or to the Negroes in Africa with whose bodies the Europeans are playing catch-ball." Leading Bolshevik and commander, **Leon Trotsky** (1879–1940), whose real name was Lev Bronshteyn, was similarly committed to international socialist revolution. He believed it would solve all of humanity's problems, including the plight of the Jews. "The Jews do not interest [me] more than the Bulgarians," he declared in 1903 to a Jewish delegation that had come to him for assistance. And while this was an honest appraisal, his report on the 1905 pogroms entitled "The Tsarist Hosts at Work" bears similarities to Bialik's poem "In the City of Slaughter." Trotsky wrote evocatively of "the crying of the slaughtered infants, the frenzied stabbed mothers, the hoarse groaning of dying old men and wild wailings of despair." If Trotsky only allowed himself occasional expressions of parochial sympathy, the same cannot be said for the bulk of Russian Jewish socialists who were passionately driven by their concern for the needs of Jewish workers in the Pale and elsewhere.

The Bund. Although anarchist and socialist ideas had long proliferated in Jewish immigrant centers in London and

New York, and strike activity and revolutionary agitation had begun among Jewish workers in the Pale of Settlement in the 1890s, the key moment in the history of Jewish socialism occurred in 1897 in Vilna with the founding of the **Bund,** short for Algemayne Bund fun Yidishe Arbeter in Rusland, Poyln un Lite (General Association of Jewish Workers in Russia, Poland and Lithuania). Many of the Bund's early leaders were revolutionaries estranged from their Jewish roots. However, observing the deteriorating Jewish economy, which saw Jews shut out of higher-paying jobs in the industrial sector, confined to sweatshop labor in terrible conditions that included an average workday of between sixteen and eighteen hours, and ongoing discrimination led many to agitate among their people.

Under the leadership of **Aleksandr (Arkadii) Kremer** (1865–1935), the Bund did not officially regard itself as a separate political party but rather as part of the Russian Social Democratic Party. However, there was always ambiguity on this point. Why organize at all if there was not tacit recognition of a specific need to lead Jewish workers? As Kremer declared, "Jewish workers suffer not only as workers but also as Jews, and we must not and cannot remain indifferent at such a time." Despite claims to the contrary, the Bund, by virtue of its very existence, was from its inception a nationalist organization speaking the language of international revolution. Even if the leadership did not see it this way, the Jewish rank and file did. And not only them. The future leader of the Bolshevik Revolution, Vladimir Lenin, correctly characterized the Bund as a national Jewish party with a specifically Jewish character. By 1903, the plight of the Jews in Russia had become clearer to the Bund leadership, and—demanding autonomy—they wanted the Social Democrats to regard them as "the sole representative of the Jewish proletariat." Leading Jewish Social Democrats such as Trotsky opposed this, and the Bund seceded from the party.

The Bund's influence grew quickly among Jewish workers, particularly in the northwest. For most Jews in the Russian Empire, a predilection for Left-wing politics was more than just a matter of individual choice. For many rank-and-file Jewish socialists in eastern Europe, politics were deeply bound up with their own sense that the Jews were a distinct nation and that the "Jewish Question" could not be solved within a larger framework of world revolution. With a mission beyond the purely political, the Bund sought to address a variety of cultural issues that related specifically to the needs of the Jewish worker. Among the Bundists' earliest activities was the organization of Jewish self-defense units during the period of pogroms between 1903 and 1907. By creating a sort of de facto national army, the Bund was the first Jewish political organization to encourage and support the idea that Jews should take up arms to protect Jewish life and property.

While it was a secularist movement, the Bund's rank-and-file membership was more conservative in its approach to religion. Only the most radical of Jews would have been in accord with the feelings expressed by the socialist Yiddish poet, David Edelstadt:

Each era has its new Torah—
Ours is one of freedom and justice . . .
We also have new prophets—
Börne, Lassalle, Karl Marx;
They will deliver us from exile,
But not with fasts and prayers!

By 1905, the Bund had 35,000 members. In command of a powerful constituency, the Bundist leadership attempted to return to the ranks of the Social Democratic Party. Within a few years the partnership began to flounder. Bitter internal debates and constant attacks from within the Russian Social Democratic Party drove the Bund to break openly with the Social Democrats and promote the idea of national—cultural autonomy as part of its continued commitment to socialist revolution. Bundists expected that after the revolution the dictatorship of the proletariat would transfer responsibility for culture, education, and law to democratic institutions elected by the various national minorities. Jewish institutions, the Bund maintained, would conduct their work in the national language of the Jewish masses—Yiddish.

Following the Russian Revolution, political parties other than the Bolsheviks were eventually banned and the Bund was liquidated. Exiled, Bundists moved to the newly independent Poland, where in the interwar period, under the leadership of **Vladimir Medem** (1879–1923), the Bund became the largest and best-supported of all Jewish political parties. During this time the party continued to grow. While it was fiercely anti-Zionist, it could hardly ignore the increasing popularity of the movement, and in response Medem refined what would become a central element of Bundist ideology—***doikayt,*** the Yiddish word for "here-ness." Medem held that the Jewish people could not turn their backs on the places where their history and culture had unfolded. Not only was it important to preserve that past, but he asserted that building upon it "here," by which he meant the Diaspora, was the key to a successful Jewish future. Central to the Jewish cultural patrimony was Yiddish, and the Bund represented itself as the guardians of secular Yiddish culture. The organization portrayed its principal opponents, the Zionists, as unrealistic and irresponsible in wishing to wrench Jews from their homes, move them to Palestine in a risky endeavor, and turn Jews away from Yiddish language and culture.

The Bund's great achievement was to offer working-class Jews a Jewish alternative to radical politics. Bundism tapped into the vast reservoir of *Yiddishkayt* (Yiddish cultural identity) that informed the sensibilities of eastern European Jewry by celebrating all things Yiddish, the language spoken by the majority of Jews well into the twentieth century. In so doing, the Bund fostered Jewish nationalism (while claiming not to). It is little wonder that the non-Jewish Russian Marxist theoretician Georgi Plekhanov quipped that the Bundists "were Zionists with sea sickness."

Jewish Nationalism

Several varieties of Jewish nationalism emerged as political responses to pogroms and poverty in eastern Europe, as well as the rise of political and racial antisemitism and assimilation in western Europe. The issue driving the split between socialists and nationalists turned on the question of "Here or there?" Where would the "Jewish Question" best be solved? One school of thought said "Here" in the Diaspora. Proponents of this idea included the Bund, as well as the short-lived Diaspora nationalist parties, such as the Folkspartey. Led by the distinguished historian Shimon Dubnov and occupying the political center, the Folkspartey platform held that the eastern European Jewish masses needed a home-grown organization to address their needs. Folkists dismissed Zionism as a utopian fantasy incapable of answering the needs of millions of eastern European Jews. Zionists, on the other hand, maintained that only "there" in Palestine, with the establishment of a Hebrew-speaking Jewish homeland, could the problems confronting Jewish society be solved.

The earliest expressions of Jewish nationalism were heavily indebted to the notion of messianic redemption and restoration of the Jewish people to the Holy Land. **Yehuda Alkalai** (1798–1878), a rabbi from Sarajevo and a Prussian rabbi, and **Zvi Hirsch Kalischer** (1795–1874) called upon Jews to return to Palestine to effect the divine salvation of the Jewish people. Kalischer demanded that Jews take history into their own hands rather than wait for redemption. They were to seize the moment, just as Italian, Polish, and Hungarian nationalists had done.

Like some Bundists, the earliest advocates of Jewish nationalism were Jews estranged from their Jewish heritage. In 1862 a one-time socialist and colleague of Karl Marx, **Moses Hess** (1812–1875), published *Rome and Jerusalem,* a reference to the connection between the unification of Italy and the hope that Jerusalem would again rise as the national capital of the Jewish people. Hess broke with the then prevalent view among German Jews that being Jewish was merely a matter of religion. Rather, Hess saw the Jews as a distinct national group and challenged the idea that they could ever or would ever want to be absorbed into the majority, "for though the Jews

have lived among the nations for almost two thousand years, they cannot, after all, become a mere part of the organic whole." Anticipating Zionism, Hess interpreted the "Jewish Question" through the lens of nationality and—typical for his age—race rather than religion. A secular Marxist, he rejected religion, but unlike Marx he no longer considered class essential either. Collective identity and hostility to Jews were the products of deeper national and biological divisions: "The German hates the Jewish religion less than the race; he objects less to the Jews' particular beliefs than to their peculiar noses."

Up until the last two decades of the nineteenth century, Jewish nationalism attracted very few adherents since deeply religious circles rejected the idea of short circuiting the divine plan of Jewish dispersion, while secular Jews in the West anticipated that the current liberal era would soon them see them emancipated. Radical Jews in eastern Europe were mostly drawn to socialism.

In the 1870s, nationalism began to penetrate Jewish intellectual circles. Energized by the pogroms of 1881–1882, a new movement called **Hibbat Tsiyon** ("Love of Zion"; its members were *Hovevei Tsiyon,* "Lovers of Zion") emerged with hundreds of chapters organized into a loose federation in Russia and Romania. Their goal was to see the Land of Israel settled by Hebrew-speaking Jewish farmers and artisans. With their political program short on details and their organization desperately strapped for funds, Hibbat Tsiyon remained a small movement. It was rejected by most Orthodox Jews who opposed its Maskilic leadership, which included the lapsed Orthodox Talmud scholar **Moshe Leib Lilienblum** (1843–1910) and the Russian-speaking doctor, **Leon Pinsker** (1821–1891). Intense disputes broke out between Orthodox Jews and secular members of Hibbat Tsiyon in Palestine at the end of the nineteenth century, often over accepting charity, something many secular pioneers opposed. Most middle-class western European Jews had little time for the movement as they had no intention of leaving Europe and still held out for integration with their host societies, while many poor eastern European Jews pinned their hopes on socialism.

Hibbat Tsiyon was a somewhat sputtering, hamstrung movement, lacking effective organization. In fact its first settlement efforts in Palestine (1881–1904), known as the **First Aliyah** ("First Ascent") can, in practical terms, be regarded as a failure. Nevertheless, the ideology of Hibbat Tsiyon represented the first phase of what became central to later Zionist ideology: the movement of secular Jews to the Land of Israel. Hibbat Tsiyon did not call for the establishment of a Jewish state; that would come later. Rather, it more vaguely promoted the idea of an ingathering and remaking of Jews in the Land of Israel.

Zionism was a revolutionary movement, for it entailed a rejection of traditional religious, family, and social values. In the first instance, Zionism rebelled against the traditional concept of waiting for the messiah to usher in the return of the Jews to Zion. It was a self-conscious effort to realign Jewish history, to stage-manage it by being proactive and not fatalistic. Second, Zionism was also a revolt of youth against their parents. Finally, it meant a rejection of the most fundamental fact of Jewish social life: living in the Diaspora. Like all revolutions, Zionism required the energy and support of the masses, but in all revolutions certain individuals emerge through the force of their ideas or their charismatic personalities to shape those revolutions. In Zionism's formative phase toward the end of the nineteenth century, Leon Pinsker, Theodor Herzl, and Ahad Ha'Am, respectively, provided the movement with a reason, an élan, and a purpose.

Leon Pinsker. Leon Pinsker (1821–1891) was one of Zionism's most important early figures. Although head of Hibbat Tsiyon, his reputation was not built on his leadership qualities. Rather, his fame spread in the wake of his German-language manifesto, *Auto-Emancipation* (1882), which he wrote in response to the pogroms. It was the very first great theoretical work of its kind. Like many educated Russian Jews who were deeply shocked by the pogroms, Pinsker abandoned the idea that Jewish integration was either possible or desirable. The reason was antisemitism. "Though you prove yourselves patriots a thousand times some fine morning you will find yourselves crossing the border and reminded by the mob that you are, after all, nothing but vagrants and parasites, without the protection of the law."

In *Auto-Emancipation* Pinsker offered one of the earliest psychological and sociological analyses of antisemitism. While many had claimed that the pogroms were a display of medieval hatred, Pinsker astutely asserted that they were distinctly modern. Antisemitism, he said, existed because Jews were incapable of being assimilated into the majority. They were terminal strangers. Ethnic tension was exacerbated by economic competition wherein Jews were shut out of local economies and preference was given to members of one's own ethnic group. Pinsker maintained that every society had a saturation point when it came to Jews, and that once there were too many Jews, economic and social discrimination emerged to limit their opportunities. At its most extreme, violence would erupt.

In addition to being a lawyer, Pinsker took a medical degree at the University of Moscow and practiced medicine in Odessa. It is noteworthy that in *Auto-Emancipation* he called antisemitism "Judeophobia," an extreme fear or dread of Jews. Phobia was a word that he would most likely have learned in his medical studies, and he claimed that Judeophobia was a symptom of the chronic homelessness of the Jews. Europeans perceived Jews as disembodied, ghosts, frightening apparitions. "A people without a territory is like a man without a shadow, a thing unnatural, spectral." Judeophobia, claimed Pinsker, was a psychopathology, "an inherited aberration of the human mind" passed through the generations. It was, according to Dr. Pinsker, incurable. The only way to mitigate the effects of the disease was for the Jews to emancipate themselves from Christian society. For Pinsker, the transformation entailed the return of the Jews to a national home of their own; he did not specify where. This process required that the Jews develop a genuine sense of national self-awareness. While emancipation had been a gift bestowed upon western Jews, the changes he was advocating in Jewish self-consciousness could only come from within through an act of "auto-emancipation." Modifying a traditional version of Jewish history, Pinsker concluded his work by saying, "Help yourselves and God will help you."

Pinsker wrote his manifesto in German to appeal to western Jews. For the most part, Jewish society dismissed it. Even in the east, despite translations into Yiddish, Hebrew, and Russian, his ideas gained little popular acceptance. However, among Jewish intellectuals who shared Pinsker's post-pogrom disenchantments, the response was much more enthusiastic.

Theodor Herzl. Jewish nationalism was predicated on two essential points: (1) that all Jews, irrespective of where they lived, were part of a single nation with a common heritage and that they shared the same hopes for a national future built on a shared cultural patrimony and (2) that the Jewish people were to build the institutional framework through which they would develop their goal of an autonomous Jewish homeland. These two principles formed the ideological core of political Zionism, the chief architect of which was **Theodor Herzl** (1860–1904).

Born and raised in Budapest, Herzl and his family moved to Vienna, where he established his career. Although a lawyer by training, he devoted himself to playwriting and journalism. Several of his plays had runs in Vienna theatres, and eventually he became the Paris correspondent for the liberal daily *New Free Press*. Herzl was an unlikely leader of the Zionist movement. Born into an assimilated family that like many others in central Europe celebrated Christmas with greater enthusiasm than they did any of the Jewish holidays, Herzl attended the University of Vienna, where he joined the German nationalist student fraternity, Albia. When, however, that organization began to espouse antisemitism, he quit. His own experience of the increasingly raucous tone of German and

Austrian racism led Herzl to entertain wild fantasies in search of a solution to the "Jewish Problem." In 1893 he envisioned a mass conversion of Jews to Catholicism. He wrote in his diary, "[A]s is my custom, I had thought out the entire plan down to all its minute details," something that would be characteristic of his later choreography of Zionism: "The conversion was to take place in broad daylight, Sundays at noon, in St. Stephen's Cathedral, with festive processions and amidst the pealing of bells. Not in shame, as individuals have converted up to now, but with proud gestures." He portrayed himself as a Moses figure, leading young Jews to the promised land of conversion, one that he did not intend to enter: "I could see myself dealing with the Archbishop of Vienna; in imagination, I stood before the Pope—both of whom were very sorry that I wished to do no more than remain part of the last generation of Jews."

As the level of antisemitism in Vienna increased, Herzl questioned more deeply his previous commitment to assim-

ilation. In 1894, he introduced the subject of antisemitism into one of his plays for the first time. Entitled *The New Ghetto,* the drama was a savage critique of the assimilated Jewish bourgeoisie of Vienna, who had relinquished their Jewish identities without fully becoming Austrians. At the play's conclusion, the hero, Jakob, dies in a duel. For young Jewish men, to participate in a duel was to partake of a particularly seductive aspect of Christian culture, one bound up with honor and machismo, two characteristics the antisemites constantly accused Jews of lacking. By 1896, all forty-four Austrian dueling fraternities had passed resolutions denying Jews the right to duel. According to an official resolution, "[T]here exists between Aryans and Jews such a deep moral and psychic difference [that] no satisfaction is to be given to a Jew with any weapon, as he is unworthy of it." Seeking satisfaction, Herzl's Jakob dies, a consequence of his futile attempt to participate in gentile culture.

Satirical cartoon depicting the process of Jewish assimilation. *The Schlemiel: An Illustrated Jewish Humor Magazine* ran from 1904 to 1923. The magazine was founded in Berlin by Leo Winz, a Jew from Ukraine. With his other publications, such as *Ost und West (East and West),* Winz's declared aim was to "reverse" the process of assimilation and make it acceptable to give public expression to Jewishness in Wilhelmine Germany. In this 1904 cartoon entitled "Darwinism," taken from *The Schlemiel,* which depicts the evolution of a Hannukah menorah into a Christmas tree, the caption reads, "How the menorah of the goatskin dealer named Cohn from Pinne [a Polish city that came under Prussian rule in 1793] developed into the Christmas tree of Kommerzienrat Conrad in Berlin's Tiergartenstrasse." A *Kommerzienrat* was an honorary title conferred on distinguished financiers or industrialists. And "Conrad's" address in Berlin is an exclusive one. The joke depicts the assimilatory process befalling eastern European Jews as they move geographically and socioeconomically from their roots.

In 1894, two episodes in particular led Herzl to a new awareness about the "Jewish Question": the Dreyfus Affair and his deep shock that it took place in France, beacon of liberty, and the election of Karl Lueger as mayor of Vienna, the first major political victory for the antisemites. For Herzl, this signaled an ominous development. During the September mayoral election campaign of 1895, he wrote chillingly in his diary, "I stood outside the polls on the Leopoldstadt on election day to have a close look at some of the hate and anger. Toward evening I went to the Landstrasse district. A silent, tense crowd before the polling station. Suddenly Dr. Lueger appeared in the square. Wild cheering. . . . The police held the people back. A man next to me said with loving fervor, but softly: 'That is our Führer.' More than all the declamations and abuse, these few words told me how deeply antisemitism is rooted in the heart of the people."

More determined than ever, Herzl sought out wealthy philanthropists to support what would be his greatest production: the establishment of a Jewish national homeland. He needed finances and approached the Rothschilds, as well as Baron Maurice de Hirsch, a man already supporting Jewish agricultural colonies in Argentina and Palestine. Neither Hirsch nor the Rothschilds were Zionists and wanted nothing to do with Herzl. Nevertheless, out of notes he prepared for the meetings with the two financiers, Herzl composed the tract that would become his political manifesto, *The Jewish State: Attempt at a Modern Solution of the Jewish Question* (1896).

Three thousand copies were printed and sent to leading figures in the press and politics, and the slender volume was soon translated into several languages. It met with ridicule. As a Jew with unimaginably grandiose plans in Freud's Vienna, it should come as no surprise that (in some quarters) Herzl was considered mentally deranged. His claim that "we are a people, *one* people" upset those western Jews who had placed all their hopes in emancipation and being accepted as citizens of their respective countries. Among the Jews of eastern Europe, however, the impact of Herzl's ideas was immediate and electric, despite the fact that the Russian censor had banned publication of *The Jewish State*. In the east, Herzl was seen as a prodigal son returning to his people and a messianic figure, a persona he did much to cultivate.

Herzl's analysis of modern antisemitism was similar to Pinsker's. Concluding that it was ineradicable, he stated his goal: "Let sovereignty be granted us over a portion of the globe large enough to satisfy the rightful requirements of a nation; the rest we shall manage for ourselves." To this end, Herzl recommended the establishment of two agencies: the "Society of Jews," which "will do the preparatory work in the domains of science and politics" and "will be the nucleus out of which the public institutions of the Jewish State will later on be developed" and the "Jewish Company," which "will be the liquidating agent of the business interests of departing Jews, and will organize trade and commerce in the new country." Before any Jews moved to the new state, Herzl insisted that Jewish sovereignty be "assured to us by international law."

In both *The Jewish State* and then in his utopian novel, *Altneuland* (*Old New Land*), Herzl painted a picture of what the new state would look like. He considered how the land would be purchased, the nature of workers' housing, compensation for labor, the nature of government, "an aristocratic republic," one where both army and priesthood "must not interfere in the administration of the State." Like Switzerland, the Jewish state would be politically neutral and similarly multilingual where "every man can preserve the language in which his thoughts are at home." As for Hebrew, Herzl never imagined it could be resurrected, for "who amongst us has a sufficient acquaintance with Hebrew to ask for a railway ticket in that language?" The inhabitants would speak "the language which proves itself to be of the greatest utility for general intercourse." The people would rally around a flag that would be white, with seven gold stars, white symbolizing "our pure new life; the stars are the seven golden hours of our working-day." Beyond this, a Jewish state would be open to "men of other creeds and different nationalities," with all accorded "honorable protection and equality before the law."

To realize his ambition, Herzl set about assembling a Zionist conference to discuss his ideas. He sought to hold it in Munich, but after the Jewish establishment there, both Reform and Orthodox, formed a united front of opposition, the venue was shifted to Switzerland. The First Zionist Congress opened on August 29, 1897, in Basel. Ever the impresario, Herzl insisted that the two hundred attendees wear formal attire to give the proceedings an air of solemnity. Even the eighty Russian Jews in attendance, not generally accustomed to wearing such finery, agreed to Herzl's demand. He was producer, director, script writer, and star of the Basel conference. Herzl ascended to the podium and gave flight to his soaring oratory, demanding the establishment of a Jewish homeland that would be "openly recognized" by the world and "legally secured" by what were then the Great Powers. Those in attendance were awestruck.

The success of the conference buoyed his already supreme self-confidence. On September 3, he noted in his diary, "Were I to sum up the Basel Congress in a word—it would be this: At Basel I founded the Jewish State. If I said this out loud today I would be answered by universal laughter. Perhaps in five years, and certainly in fifty, everyone will know it." By the Jewish New Year in 1897, within the space of five weeks, the two greatest modern Jewish political movements, Bundism and Zionism, had been born.

Much more work needed to be done, however. Herzl had long believed that Zionism could not be a politically marginal movement but had to have the full backing of the international community to fulfill its aims. He turned to feverish diplomatic activity. Herzl obtained an audience in Constantinople in 1898 with the German emperor, Wilhelm II, hoping that the kaiser would influence the sultan to sign a charter granting permission to Jews to settle in Palestine. The emperor seemed sympathetic and promised to take up the matter when he next met the sultan. Later in the year, Herzl followed the imperial retinue to Palestine and again met with Wilhelm and again was led to believe that the kaiser was amenable to the idea of a Jewish homeland in Palestine. Months passed, nothing happened, and Herzl finally realized he was being strung along. A later meeting with the sultan ended in disappointment; the best the sultan would offer was his government's approval of Jewish settlement throughout the Ottoman Empire, without guarantee of a separate Jewish entity in Palestine. While Herzl's diplomatic missions, which included meetings with both the British colonial and foreign secretaries, all ended in failure, Zionism began to grow. The number of associations increased rapidly from 117 at the time of the Basel Congress to 913 within a year. The congresses became important annual events, passing further resolutions, each one taking nascent state-building steps despite the absence of any ceded territory.

Though still a minority position on the Jewish political landscape, the growing success of Zionism was accompanied by vigorous internal criticism. For all his brilliance and energy, the critics complained, Herzl had neglected one important ingredient: the Jewishness of his imagined state. Russian Zionists expressed profound concern that Herzl's universalist vision took no account of the Jewish character of his proposed homeland. In *Altneuland* Herzl imagined the land crisscrossed with electric trolley cars, dotted with the latest scientific research institutions, and full of people engaging in modern commerce. There would be English boarding schools, French opera houses, and Viennese coffee shops. Everywhere in this pan-European paradise people would chat away in their native tongues. Tel Aviv would be just like any major European capital, only with a sunny climate and an ocean view. Above all, there would be no pogroms. When it was founded in 1909, Tel Aviv did, in many ways, resemble Herzl's vision.

But for eastern European Zionists, creating a Jewish state was always about more than merely finding a place of refuge. For many of them, nationalism involved the creation of a new Jew and a new Jewish culture, expressed in Hebrew.

In Odessa, the Russian Empire's second-largest Jewish city and a center of Maskilic activity, Herzl's un-Jewish vision for a Jewish state met great resistance. The issue turned on whether Herzl wanted to establish a Jewish state or merely a state for Jews. Proponents of a Jewish cultural renaissance grounded in Hebrew—Moses Leib Lilienblum, Hayim Nahman Bialik, and a young ex-Hasid from Ukraine, Asher Ginsberg, better known by his nom de plume, Ahad Ha'am ("One of the People")—imagined something far different from *Altneuland.*

At the 1901 Zionist congress, splits within the movement became apparent, prompting the emergence of the **Democratic Faction.** Inspired by the philosophy of Ahad Ha'am and led by the man who would become the first president of the State of Israel, **Chaim Weizmann** (1874–1952), the group sought to place greater emphasis than Herzl had ever done on Jewish culture. Though they never officially split from Herzl, their cultural mission became central to the Zionist enterprise thereafter.

Through indomitable will and charisma Herzl led the movement in its earliest phase. Though he died prematurely in 1904 at age forty four, Herzl's lasting legacy was the creation of the World Zionist Organization (WZO). The WZO was a democratic and progressive body that housed the nation-building institutions, such as the Jewish Colonial Office and the Jewish National Fund. These were the agencies charged with the purchase and rational management of land in Palestine on behalf of the Jewish people. Questions of Jewish culture, politics, and the work of state building would be taken up by those who followed Herzl.

Ahad Ha'am.   If Herzl was the representative of political Zionism, **Ahad Ha'am** (Asher Ginsberg) (1856–1927) became the great spokesman and theoretician of cultural Zionism. Bitterly opposed to Herzl's diplomatic activities, emphasis on Jewish settlement, and cavalier attitude to Jewish culture, Ahad Ha'am recalled about Basel, "I sat alone among my brothers, a mourner at a wedding banquet."

Where Herzl was concerned to protect the physical safety of the Jews, Ahad Ha'am had been long dedicated to their spiritual welfare. A brilliant Hebrew stylist, steeped in Jewish culture, Ahad Ha'am rejected the state-building efforts of Herzl, insisting that nation building required the establishment of a Hebrew-speaking vanguard who would create a spiritual center in the Land of Israel. According to Ahad Ha'am, the new Hebrew culture would radiate out to the Jewish world to invigorate a moribund and decadent Diaspora Jewry.

Long before Herzl appeared on the world-stage, Ahad Ha'am had been a fierce critic of Jewish settlement efforts in

הקונגרס החמישי של הציונים בבזל תרס"ב

ותחזינה עינינו בשובך לציון ברחמים

Ephraim Moses Lilien (1874–1925) was a Galician illustrator and photographer. A Zionist, he produced many of the movement's most classic and widely disseminated images. In addition to taking the renowned photograph of Theodor Herzl looking out in solitary contemplation from the balcony of his hotel room at the First Zionist Congress in Basel in 1897, Lilien produced many pen-and-ink images in the Art Nouveau style, celebrating Zionism. It was Lilien who was largely responsible for the popularization of symbols such as the menorah, the Star of David, and the olive branch, depicting them as quintessentially Jewish and Zionist. At the Fifth Zionist Congress in Basel in 1901, Lilien organized an exhibition with other Jewish artists, in which Lilien's style represented a new, modernist, Jewish aesthetic.

This striking illustration was one of the most widely reproduced Zionist images. Entitled *From Ghetto to Zion,* it was the semi-official picture of the Fifth Zionist Congress and was used subsequently by the Jewish National Fund, turned into postcards, and issued as a stamp by the Israel Postal Service in 1977. An elderly, religious Jew sits forlorn, enveloped in thorns, a symbol of his diasporic imprisonment. Over his shoulder stands an androgynous angel, with a Star of David on the tunic, pointing the way to Zion, where, in the distance, another religious Jew, rejuvenated by agricultural labor, walks in the sunlight behind a plow and oxen. At the base of the drawing, Lilien has quoted a verse from the *Shemoneh Esreh* prayer: "Our eyes will behold Your return to Zion in mercy."

Palestine. While a member of Hibbat Tsiyon, Ahad Ha'am penned a famous critique of the organization in 1889 entitled "This Is Not the Way." In this essay he expressed his dissatisfaction with settlement efforts. He objected to pioneering that only served the interests of those immediately involved in colonization efforts but failed to move the spirit of all Jews to the Zionist idea. In an oblique reference to Hibbat Tsiyon, Ahad Ha'am wrote, "The demon of egoism—individual or congregational—haunts us in all that we do for our people, and suppresses the rare manifestations of national feeling, being the stronger of the two." Instead of immediately settling in Palestine, "we ought to have made it our first object to bring about a revival—to inspire men with a deeper attachment to the national life, and a more ardent desire for the national well-being." Pessimistic about the disorganized and haphazard nature of Jewish settlement, Ahad Ha'am insisted that "every step needs to be measured and carried out with sober and considered judgment, under the direction of the nation's statesmen and leaders, in order that all actions be directed to one end and that individuals do not, in their private actions, upset the apple-cart." What was needed was "unified and orderly action."

With his emphasis on the rebirth of the Hebrew language and the need to cultivate enthusiasm for the Zionist idea among Diaspora Jews, Ahad Ha'am became the champion of Russian Zionists. Although after the Basel conference the name Hibbat Tsiyon was dropped in favor of the term *Zionism,* Ahad Ha'am saw the advantages of the former. In his 1897 essay " The Jewish State and Jewish Problem," he wrote, "Zionism, therefore, begins its work with political propaganda; Hibbat Tsiyon begins with national culture, because only through the national culture and for its sake can a Jewish State be established in such a way as to correspond with the will and the needs of the Jewish people." Ahad Ha'am was also one of the first Zionists to call attention to the reality of Palestine's Arab population and the real prospect of a confrontation between them and Zionists. In his "Truth from Eretz Yisrael" (1891), a scathing critique of local conditions, he warned against ignoring the Arab population: "If the time comes when the life of our people in Eretz Yisrael develops to the point of encroaching upon the native population, they will not easily yield their place."

When, in 1922, he finally moved to Tel Aviv, the modern world's first Hebrew-speaking Jewish city, he was surrounded by his beloved Odessa circle, which included Bialik and Tel Aviv's first mayor, Meir Dizengoff. Instrumental in advising the latter on the shape the city should take, Ahad Ha'am was the inspiration for Tel Aviv's main academic institution, the Herzliyah Gymnasium. (He also helped found the Hebrew University of Jerusalem.) One of his closest confidants was Moshe Glickson, an editor of Tel Aviv's first daily newspaper, *Ha'aretz* (*The Land*), the official line of which often reflected Ahad Ha'Am's own views.

Ahad Ha'Am's importance lies in the fact that he was both Zionism's chief theoretician and its greatest critic. His sober realism stood in marked contrast to the fantasies and grandiose plans of political Zionists. Whether questioning Herzl's leadership, attempts at Great Power diplomacy, the nature of agricultural produce on Zionist settlements, or the thorny problem of the Jewish character of the state, he provided something essential to the nascent movement: an internal Zionist critique and a cultural vision.

The Uganda Proposal.   The other political development that went directly to the heart of the problem besetting political Zionism and its relation to the question of Jewish culture in any possible Jewish state emerged during the controversy over Uganda. In 1903, the British government offered parts of Uganda to the Zionist movement for the purpose of Jewish autonomous settlement. At the Sixth Zionist Congress of 1903, suggested Uganda as a temporary refuge for Russian Jews, the recent Kishinev pogrom having made the issue all the more urgent. Herzl was still committed to Palestine as the only proper place for a Jewish state, calling Uganda a "night asylum." Nevertheless, his incorrectly named "Uganda proposal" met strenuous opposition, especially from eastern European Jews. Still, he managed to secure a vote of 295–178 in favor of sending an "investigatory commission" to determine the suitability of Uganda. Although the Zionist movement formally rejected the plan in 1905, some members remained committed to finding a place of immediate refuge for Jews under threat and considered many places, including Australia and Canada, both countries in possession of vast and vacant territory. While nothing came of these plans, both nations did eventually become places of refuge for Jews, although mainly after the Holocaust. One project that met with some success at the time of the Uganda proposal was the Galveston project. With financial support from the American Jewish banker Jacob Schiff, some 9,300 Jews settled in Texas between 1907 and 1914.

Varieties of Jewish Nationalism.   Beyond political and cultural Zionism, many other varieties of Jewish nationalism flourished prior to World War I. In 1902, despite religious opposition to Zionism, **Mizrahi** was established as the chief organ of religious nationalism. Seeking to counter the secularism of most Zionist streams, Mizrahi combined strict adherence to tradition and nominal acceptance of Zionism. In 1912 it was transformed into **Agudes Yisroel,** the political arm that represented all branches of Orthodoxy in the Zionist Organization.

One of the most popular variants of Jewish nationalism came in the form of Socialist Zionism. Its leading exponents were **Nahman Syrkin** (1868–1924) and **Ber Borochov** (1881–1917). Syrkin, the founder of labor Zionism, sought to combine utopian or prophetic socialism and Jewish nationalism. As such, he differed from Bundists who believed that the "Jewish Problem" would be solved when the general social revolution took place. Syrkin also maintained that the only viable socialist solution was the establishment of a socialist Jewish state in Palestine. In 1897, he led the Socialist Zionist faction at the First Zionist Congress, and in 1898 he published "The Jewish Question and the Socialist Jewish State," in which he called for the establishment of cooperative settlement of the Jewish masses in Palestine. Syrkin was particularly attentive to the immediate needs of the Diaspora, urging the organization of self-defense among Russian Jews facing pogroms. Like Ahad Ha'am, Syrkin was also a vociferous internal critic of Zionism, attacking virtually every stream, including what he called the "bourgeois and clerical" elements of the World Zionist Organization. He also fell out with Ahad Ha'am over what he regarded as the latter's disregard for antisemitism and the immediate need for mass migration. He was, therefore, amenable to the Uganda proposal, and he regarded Ahad Ha'am's notion of Israel as a "spiritual center" as unrealistic and an unaffordable luxury.

Socialist Zionism also spawned a more radical wing of Marxist Zionists, the great theoretician of which was Ber Borochov. By synthesizing class struggle with nationalism, he attempted to interpret Marxism in accordance with Jewish nationalism. Despite recognizing the growth of antisemitism, Borochov did not regard antisemitism as the impetus for Zionism, nor did he see Zionism as the principal motivation or means for spiritual renewal. Rather, he sought to usher Jews out of the abnormal socioeconomic condition of the Diaspora, which he considered the cause of Jewish economic and political powerlessness. Being a minority meant that the Jews would always lose out to the controlling interests of the ruling majority. Borochov was one of the founders of **Poalei Tsiyon** (The Workers of Zion), formed in 1906 and a forerunner of Israel's Labor Party. Poalei Tsiyon became the first socialist Zionist political party and had branches across eastern and central Europe, Britain, and the United States. (Various local branches of the party had existed as early as 1901.) Addressing the Russian Poalei Tsiyon at its first convention in December 1906, Borochov stated, "The Jewish nation in the Galut [Diaspora] has no material possessions of its own, and it is helpless in the national competition struggle." What was needed was for Jewish life to be made economically productive again, and this could only come about through mass migration to the Land of Israel.

Zionist Culture and the Founding Generation.   As Zionist theoreticians continued to theorize, idealistic pioneers continued to arrive in Palestine prior to the outbreak of World War I. During the **Second Aliyah** (1903–1914), about 35,000 Jews settled in Palestine, taking the total Jewish population to 85,000 or 12 percent of total. The aliyah was not uniform in character. Middle-class Jews tended to live in Tel Aviv, whose population grew to 2,000 by 1914, while pious immigrants went to traditional religious centers. Although many of the immigrants left after a few weeks due to the difficult conditions, a group of about 2,000 to 3,000 Zionists were ideologically committed to the idea of creating the new Hebrew-speaking Jew. Among this group were **David Ben-Gurion** (1886–1973), first prime minister of the state of Israel, **Berl Katznelson** (1887–1944), a leading figure of Labor Zionism, and **Yitzhak ben-Zvi** (1884–1963), scholar of Oriental Jewish communities, a founder of the Jewish defense agency, Ha-Shomer, and second president of the State of Israel.

Two of the more important developments that took place in Palestine in the period before the First World War were the establishment of Jewish agricultural settlements and the revival of the Hebrew language. The first agricultural collective, known as a **kvutza** (group), was set up in Degania in 1910 along the shores of the Sea of Galilee. Ten men and two women formed an autonomous economic undertaking; they rejected private property, capitalism, and urbanism and made decisions on the basis of direct democracy. Later, the expansion of such settlements, where the inhabitants considered themselves an extended family, became known as **kibbutzim** (sing. *kibbutz*). The official Israeli legal definition of a kibbutz is "an organization for settlement which maintains a collective society of members organized on the basis of general ownership of possessions. Its aims are self-labor, equality and cooperation in all areas of production, consumption and education." Eventually, different ideological and cultural goals and even economic practices would come to characterize the varieties of kibbutzim.

After World War I more kibbutzim began to develop, and by the early 1940s the kibbutz population had grown to 25,000 members, approximately 5 percent of the total Jewish population of Palestine. But more important even than the number of people living on kibbutzim was the ideology that informed them and in turn was employed to define the new nation. **Aaron David Gordon** (1856–1903) was the major theoretician of Jewish labor and stressed that the regeneration of the Jews could only come about through Jews working with their own hands. As such, he spoke out sharply against the then practice of employing Arab workers on Jewish agricultural settlements. Jewish self-sufficiency was his catchphrase. Arab opposition to Jewish settlement was apparent from the very beginning, and the existence of kibbutzim saw the need for the establishment of military guard units, such as **Ha-Shomer** in 1909. It was during this time that the agricultural laborer became for Zionism what the cowboy was in American culture: a symbol of attachment to the land, a pioneer spirit, and an authentic representative of the nation.

The Second Aliyah saw the establishment of new political parties, such as Ha-Po'el Ha-Tza'ir ("The Young Worker"), which espoused the ideology of Gordon, and the Marxist–Zionist Poalei Tsiyon. Zionist culture in Palestine at this time was also characterized by a deeply hostile attitude to religious Orthodoxy and especially Yiddish language and culture. Men such as Ben-Gurion made secularism and the bitter rejection of Yiddish central to the culture of the Yishuv (Zionist settlement in Palestine prior to 1948) and then the State of Israel. Many of the most fervent Zionists exchanged their names for new Hebrew ones and were single-minded in their devotion to the Hebrew language. To take the first three prime ministers as examples, David Ben Gurion ("Son of a Lion Cub") had been David Grün ("Green"), Moshe Sharett ("Servant") had previously been Moshe Shertok, while Levi Shkolnik became Levi Eshkol ("Cluster of Grapes"), thereby denoting his link to the Holy Land's soil. Other Zionists took up last names such as Peled ("steel") and Tzur ("rock"). The hebraizing name change was intended to indicate a major transformation from Yiddish-speaking Disapora Jew to the new Hebrew pioneer, tough and fearless. This was not particular to Zionism. Such name changes also took place at the same time in the Soviet Union, where a new man, Homo sovieticus, was also being created. Joseph Dzhugashvili became Joseph Stalin ("steel"), his protégé Vyacheslav Mikhailovich Skryabin became Molotov ("hammer"), while the one-time chairman of the Politburo, Lev Kamenev ("rock") had previously been Lev Rosenfeld.

Although modern Hebrew fiction's origins can be traced to Europe—where authors such as Abraham Mapu explored pastoral themes set in ancient Judea while others explored the spiritual life of the shtetl—it was during the Second Aliyah that the political and literary elite saw to it that Hebrew would become the lingua franca of the new Jew and give rise to a modern Hebrew literature. Writers such as **Micha Yosef Berdichevsky** (1865–1921), **Saul Tchernichovsky** (1875–1943), **Yosef Chaim Brenner,** (1881–1921), and **Shmuel Yosef Agnon** (1884–1970) all arrived in Palestine with the Second Aliyah and wrote in Hebrew. Deeply influenced by the German philosopher Nietzsche, many hard-core Zionists were committed to the "transvaluation of Jewish values." They were revolutionaries who wished to overturn the culture of the Diaspora and create the new Hebrew man and woman. Some made the distinction between Jews and Judaism a point of ideology. According to Berdichevsky, "Our hearts, ardent for life, sense that the resurrection of Israel depends on a revolution—the Jews must come first, before Judaism—the living man, before the legacy of his ancestors." Brenner was harsher, asserting that Jewishness in the absence of religion is possible and natural: "We, the living Jews, whether we are tormented on Yom Kippur and whether we eat meat and milk [together], whether we hold to the conventions of the Bible, and whether we are in our world view students of Epicurus, we do not stop feeling ourselves as Jews. . . . The best of our people here and abroad are fighting, and they don't believe in the Messiah and they have nothing to do with traditional theological Judaism." The most extreme among Hebrew writers and Zionist ideologues promoted an ideology of *shlilat ha-Golah,* "negation of the Diaspora."

Shmuel Agnon, who was the greatest of the authors to arrive in Palestine before World War I, did not share the religious rejectionism of some of his fellow Hebrew writers of the Second Aliyah. Born into a Hasidic family in the Galician town of Buczacz, and remaining personally observant, Agnon often returned to the conflict between tradition and modernity in his works. He wrote evocatively of shtetl life but never in a nostalgic or maudlin way, charting instead its demise, particularly in the wake of World War I, as he did in his 1938 novel *A Guest for the Night,* which was inspired by a return visit to his hometown. Agnon's talents were such that he won the Nobel Prize for literature in 1966, an award he shared that year with the German Jewish poet Nelly Sachs.

The man most associated with the rebirth of Hebrew was **Eliezer ben Yehuda** (1858–1922), who insisted that his family speak only Hebrew after they immigrated to Palestine in 1881, despite the fact that they barely spoke the language. Still he persisted, believing that children held the key to the revival of Hebrew. If they could learn it, then it would flourish. He observed, "The Hebrew language will go from the synagogue to the house of study, and from the house of study to the school, and from the school it will come into the home and . . . become a living language." For it to become a language of the street, it needed a new vocabulary and ben Yehuda toiled away at what would become his seventeen-volume work, *A Complete Dictionary of Ancient and Modern Hebrew.* He invented hundreds of words for a language that was not yet suited to modernity but soon would be. Inspired to give his own young son a Hebrew vocabulary, ben Yehuda invented the Hebrew words for *bicycle, doll, ice-cream,* and *jelly*—the very kind of words that young children needed if they were to live their lives in Hebrew.

The Second Aliyah was far more successful than the First. These pioneers built new political, military, and economic institutions and a Hebrew culture, all of which proved durable. Nevertheless, Jewish settlement in Palestine remained vulnerable. Most of the 85,000 Jews who lived there by 1914 were poor, and the local economy had difficulty sustaining such numbers. Beyond this, the seven hundred thousand Arabs of Palestine were increasingly opposed to Jewish settlement, as were the Ottomans, the region's political overlords. In Europe, however, the aftermath of World War I would see antisemitism intensify and the call of Zionists become ever more urgent.

Philanthropy and Acculturation

The second significant response to the "Jewish Question" entailed a robust assertion of Jewish rights combined with philanthropy and a redoubled commitment to acculturation. Together with the Damascus Blood Libel, the Mortara Affair made Jews aware of the need for a central body to represent their interests, and in 1860 in Paris they founded the **Alliance**

Israélite Universelle. Under the leadership of Adolphe Cremieux, the organization's motto, taken from the Talmud, was "All Israel is responsible for one another." In addition to actively combating discrimination against Jews wherever it occurred, the Alliance also built a vast network of schools throughout the Ottoman Empire to westernize the Jews of the Balkans and the Islamic world and provide them with modern, secular education. At its peak, the Alliance ran 183 schools with 43,700 students across an area stretching from Morocco to Iran. Instruction was in French, while Jewish subjects, taught according to modern pedagogic methods, reflected the cultural sensibilities of Franco-Judaism. An especially important undertaking of the Alliance was its commitment to providing a modern education to Jewish women, who came to enjoy social mobility and increased status, as a result. The Alliance contributed to the breakdown of traditional Jewish communities across north Africa and the Middle East, and as increasing numbers of Jews became acquainted with French, they oriented themselves toward Europe and secular culture. Moreover, the Alliance contributed to the development of a Jewish bourgeoisie and overall increasing prosperity in Jewish communities throughout the Middle East and Asia Minor, particularly in cities such as Istanbul, Salonika, and Izmir.

Philanthropy, in both monetary and educational terms, became a central feature of Jewish communal life in the nineteenth century. In fact, philanthropy became the basis for a Jewish social policy that was administered by experts bearing modern economic and diplomatic skills. Before the advent of the Alliance in 1860, Jewish philanthropy in the form of charity was directed at the poor within one's own community. After this time, however, philanthropy was channeled outward to the needy of other lands. This coincided with two changes: the rise in income levels of western Jews, which enabled them to donate money to Jews in distress, and the rise of mass Jewish immigration due to dire economic circumstances and pogroms in Russia and Rumania, which brought poor, helpless Jews into direct contact with the Jews of western Europe. As such, western European Jews established large organizations to assist and educate their less fortunate co-religionists in eastern Europe and the Near East. After the Alliance was established, it became a model for similar organizations, such as Great Britain's Anglo-Jewish Association (1871), the Israelitische Allianz zu Wien (Israelite Alliance of Vienna) (1872), and in Germany the Hilfsverein der deutschen Juden (Aid Association of German Jews) (1901). All sought to alleviate Jewish poverty at home and abroad and, where possible, to promote educational programs to secularize and westernize Jewish youth.

Philanthropy also supported Jewish agricultural schemes. Through his Jewish Colonization Association, Baron de Hirsch funded Moisesville, a Yiddish-speaking agricultural settlement in Argentina. It began in 1889 with the arrival of 824 Russian Jews. Most of the 81,000 Jews who immigrated to Argentina between 1901 and 1914, however, settled in cities. In Palestine in 1880, out of a total population of 450,000, 25,000 were Jews, two-thirds of whom lived in Jerusalem while the rest resided in Safed, Tiberius, and Hebron, cities with religious significance. Known as the Old Yishuv (settlement), the Jewish population was roughly split evenly between Sephardim and Ashkenazim, the former arriving in the wake of the expulsion from Spain and the latter toward the end of the eighteenth century. Both communities were deeply religious and desperately poor, surviving on charity sent from abroad (*see box*, Bertha Pappenheim and the League of Jewish Women).

Philanthropy also had a decided psychological impact. Those in receipt of aid felt cared for, sensing that they were not being forgotten. The philanthropic communities, on the other hand, derived an important sense that their largesse was deeply meaningful, a fitting testament to the nations where they prospered to the point of being able to offer assistance. This further enhanced their sense of gratitude to those nations where they had been free to succeed. Jewish associations had scores of branches throughout the world, and thus the philanthropic network also created a conscious sense that the Jews were a united people, though globally dispersed, with a mutual responsibility for each other's welfare.

While considerable friction could be found between organizations, antagonisms of a kind that mirrored the larger national tensions between countries, the aid associations worked together for the greater Jewish good, co-sponsoring and jointly funding many projects ranging from schooling to refugee repatriation. Socioeconomically and ideologically, the leaders of these Jewish organizations and the larger communities they represented shared much in common. Economically secure and solidly middle class, their members were unified in their attachment to their respective lands, to emancipation, to acculturation, and to Europe.

Just as philanthropy was an important expression of middle-class Jewish values, so too was the establishment of Jewish self-defense organizations to combat antisemitism. In fact, philanthropic and self-defense activities often engaged the same community leaders. In 1893, the **Central Union of German Citizens of the Jewish Faith** was founded, its goal to safeguard Jewish civil and social equality and combat antisemitism. It did so vigorously, using public relations campaigns, the media, and the court system. It repeatedly sued antisemites for libel and enjoyed great success in the German courts. In the United States,

BERTHA PAPPENHEIM AND THE LEAGUE OF JEWISH WOMEN

In central Europe, Jewish philanthropic efforts were generally directed by men, though middle-class Jewish women were heavily involved in the work. A notable exception was the role played by **Bertha Pappenheim** (1859–1936). From an Orthodox Viennese family, she early on became committed to feminism and social welfare, trying to marry the two to Jewish concerns. More famously known as the patient Anna O. in Josef Breuer and Sigmund Freud's *Studies on Hysteria,* Pappenheim worked as a soup kitchen volunteer, nursery school administrator, and headmistress of a Frankfurt orphanage. In 1902 she founded the "Care for Women Society," whose objective was to place orphans in foster homes, educate mothers in child care, and provide vocational counseling and employment opportunities for women.

Pappenheim's greatest legacy was the League of Jewish Women, which she founded in 1904 and presided over for twenty years. The League had three main objectives: the international campaign against the prostitution and "White Slavery" of young Jewish women from eastern Europe and the Near East; the promotion of the full participation of Jewish women in the political structures of the Jewish communities; and vocational training, so that Jewish women could enjoy financial independence. While seen as a radical by her opponents, Pappenheim was in fact quite conservative. Women were trained in traditional female occupations such as nursing, social work, and housekeeping. Pappenheim also remained committed to religious tradition and made instruction about Jewish family observances central to the training she offered on running a proper Jewish home. Her traditionalism aside, Pappenheim was a maverick, and the league she created was an important vehicle for the self-assertion of Jewish women.

the **Anti-Defamation League** was established in 1913. With a similar mission to its German counterpart, the league's charter states, "The immediate object of the League is to stop, by appeals to reason and conscience and, if necessary, by appeals to law, the defamation of the Jewish people. Its ultimate purpose is to secure justice and fair treatment to all citizens alike and to put an end forever to unjust and unfair discrimination against and ridicule of any sect or body of citizens."

The Pursuit of Happiness: Coming to America

Unlike those Jews in eastern Europe who turned to Jewish politics or those in western Europe who built strong Jewish communities based on bourgeois values, a third path taken by millions of Jews was to leave for the West. In response to economic distress and discrimination, vast numbers left eastern Europe in search of opportunity. Between 1881 and 1924, nearly 2.5 million Jews fled eastern Europe in what was a largely unideological response to persecution and stifling economic conditions. Nearly 85 percent of those Jews went to the United States, or, as the immigrants called it in Yiddish, the *goldene medineh,* the "Golden Land." Demographically speaking, American Jewry's rise was spectacular. In 1800 approximately 10,000 Jews were in the United States. That number had grown to 300,000 by 1870, but by 1880 the number had risen to 1.7 million, and by 1915 America was home to over 3 million Jews.

In the mid-nineteenth century, America underwent a population explosion with the arrival of vast numbers of immigrants from central and northern Europe. Among them were impoverished, young Jewish men from rural Germany. While most came principally in search of economic opportunity, they were further motivated to depart Europe due to a host of antisemitic restrictions, among them limitations on the number of Jewish marriages, laws against opening businesses, and others against the entrance of Jews into various professions. The sense of dismay after the failure of the liberal revolutions of 1848 and the prosecution of Jewish revolutionaries prompted others to leave Germany. Between 1830 and 1860 perhaps as many as 200,000 central European Jews arrived in America. Though, as we will see, there were important distinctions and tensions between the elites of the two Jewish immigrant groups—central and eastern European—and important cultural differences as well, the reasons for the mass of Jews leaving Europe and coming to the United States, their successful integration once there, and the forms of Judaism they came to practice, have much in common. We can see the period of 1820 to 1924 as a century-long time of Jewish immigration out of Europe's poorer regions to the relative abundance of the West.

Uptown Jews: The Rise of the German Jews in America

Moving on quickly from their ports of embarkation, German Jewish emigrants, mostly single men, settled in Midwestern cities such as Cincinnati, St. Louis, and Chicago. Some headed farther west to San Francisco. Most earned a living as they had in Europe, as itinerant peddlers. With astonishing speed, these immigrants soon gave up their carts and packs for small stores and businesses and in some cases, such as that of Lazarus Straus, they turned those little shops into large department stores. From modest beginnings, they created global brands such as Levi's, named after the German Jewish immigrant Levi Straus, who, together with another immigrant, Jacob Davis, took out a patent to manufacture pants with copper-riveted pockets for working men. Still others began as peddlers in the Midwest and the Deep South and became captains of finance in New York. In the 1850s and 1860s they opened businesses that are still in operation today. Among the itinerant salesmen who wandered the American countryside selling such items as shoelaces, fabric, clothes, and pots and pans was Marcus Goldman, the founder of Goldman Sachs; Henry Lehman and his siblings, who formed Lehman Brothers; Joseph, William, and James Seligman, who formed J. and W. Seligman & Co.; and J. S. Bache, whose brokerage house eventually became Prudential Bache. Having made it in America, these families and others, such as the Guggenheims and the Schiffs, formed the backbone of the American Jewish establishment. While these were certainly exceptional success stories, the overall experience of the German Jewish migration

to America was one in which the vast majority became solidly middle-class, productive citizens.

The process of Americanization accompanied the immigrants' movement into the middle class. Their embourgeoisement also provoked renewed interest in their religious life, something that had initially been neglected as the immigrants struggled to make a living in rural America in communities with few Jews and no Jewish leaders. Now they sought to build new Jewish institutions and, in so doing, created a uniquely American Judaism. With considerable hyperbole, the German-born rabbi Adolf Moses of Mobile, Alabama, declared, "From America salvation will go forth; in this land [not in Germany] will the religion of Israel celebrate its greatest triumphs."

One of the first steps in the consolidation of American Judaism was the organization of the scattered frontier communities under a more centralized form of leadership. The most important institution established for this purpose was the **Union of American Hebrew Congregations (UAHC),** founded in 1873. Under the leadership of the Cincinnati rabbi, Isaac Mayer Wise (1819–1900), the Union called for the establishment of institutions that would provide instruction in "the higher branches of Hebrew literature and Jewish theology." To this end, **Hebrew Union College** was established

---

A MEAL TO REMEMBER: "THE TREFA BANQUET"

In July 1883, over two hundred Jews and non-Jews gathered at Cincinnati's exclusive Highland House restaurant to celebrate Hebrew Union College's ordination of its initial graduating class of four American-trained rabbis. The college's founder, Isaac Mayer Wise, a man who strove for unity among American Jews, nonetheless presided over an evening that brought about anything but solidarity. Together with his close friend, the traditionalist Reverend Isaac Leeser, both men sought to emphasize commonalities among American Jews rather than those things that separated them. But there were already deep fissures in the Reform camp. The traditionalists or accommodationists, like Wise, were confronted by radical reformers, men who had attended the mid-century reform rabbinical conferences in Germany and were determined to rid Judaism of what they considered antiquated practices.

The dinner that evening, with its lavish French menu, became immediately infamous. The first course was littleneck clams followed by soft-shell crabs, Salade of Shrimps, meats, ice cream, and cheese. It is unclear whether Wise was responsible for the fiasco or whether some of the radicals, seeking to do mischief, had "gotten" to the caterer, Gus Lindeman. Wise, who kept a kosher home, claimed he knew nothing about it and had, in fact, ordered Lindeman to serve kosher meat. How the shellfish and dairy products came to be served is uncertain. A subsequent investigation by a panel of rabbis from the Union of American Hebrew Congregations (UAHC) cleared Wise of wrongdoing, but the damage was done.

The "Trefa Banquet," as it came to be known, was but one step in the division of the American Reform movement into radical and more traditional camps. In the years after the banquet, a series of debates between radical rabbi Kaufmann Kohler and traditionalist rabbi Alexander Kohut set out the position of both camps. In 1885, the UAHC conference in Pittsburgh, dominated by radicals, adopted the Pittsburgh Platform, which described observance of traditional Jewish laws governing diet and dress as "altogether foreign to our mental and spiritual state" and "apt rather to obstruct than to further modern spiritual elevation."

The various divisions among American Jews were soon institutionalized with a formal split into Reform, Conservative, and Orthodox camps, with many variations within each branch. The "Trefa Banquet" of 1883, while not the cause of such divisions, was profoundly symbolic of them.

in 1875 for the training of Reform rabbis (*see box,* A Meal to Remember: The "Trefa Banquet"). Wise served as President of HUC from its opening until his death in 1900.

The UAHC's initial constitution also called upon the organization to "provide means for the relief of Jews from political oppression and unjust discrimination, and for rendering them aid for their intellectual elevation." To a great extent this became an imperative for those German Jews who had come to America in search of opportunity and had struck it rich. In addition to funding institutions for the benefit of all the residents of cities such as New York, Chicago, St. Louis, and San Francisco, German Jewish notables offered much-needed assistance to Jewish newcomers through a network of charitable and social institutions. Until 1881, the demands on these charities were modest, but with the massive influx of eastern European Jews the situation changed radically, as did the face of American Jewry.

Downtown Jews: Eastern European Jewish Immigrants

While some 15 percent of eastern European Jews went to Germany, France, England, Palestine, South Africa, Canada, Argentina, and Australia, 85 percent went to the United States. More than any other country, moving there was on the minds of potential immigrants. As one of those immigrants, Mary Antin, recalled, "America was in everybody's mouth. Businessmen talked of it over their accounts; the market women made up their quarrels that they might discuss it from stall to stall; people who had relatives in the famous land went around reading their letters for the enlightenment of less fortunate folk . . . children played at emigrating; old folks shook their sage heads over the evening fire, and prophesied no good for those who braved the terrors of the sea and the foreign goal beyond it; all talked of it, but scarcely anyone knew one true fact about this magic land."

Jews scrimped and saved, selling off all their possessions for a ticket in steerage. The conditions were deplorable on a journey that lasted anywhere from ten days to three weeks. The journey, wrote the immigrant George Price, was "a kind of hell that cleanses a man of his sins before coming to the land of Columbus." Having had little to eat once their kosher food quickly ran out, nauseated from seasickness and the open latrines they had endured on board, the immigrants disembarked, mostly in New York, starved, fatigued, fearful, and discombobulated. Numbered and lettered before they disembarked, the immigrants were led into the red-brick buildings of Ellis Island (opened in 1892), where they were subject to medical inspections and a host of intimidating questions, unsure whether their answers would assist or hinder entry. Once admitted, they received assistance from Jewish

charitable organizations such as the **United Hebrew Charities,** founded in 1874, and the **Hebrew Immigrant Aid Society** (HIAS), founded in 1881. Established by Russian Jews and still in operation today, HIAS provided temporary housing to those without relatives, ran soup kitchens, and provided clothing for needy Jews. It has proven to be a lifeline to millions.

Unlike their German Jewish predecessors, between 70 and 90 percent of the eastern European Jews remained in New York. Aside from the fact that they had little money with which to travel beyond the city, New York had industry that required a skilled workforce. After 1900, a greater percentage of Jews were skilled industrial workers than were any other immigrant group, beneficiaries of the process of industrialization that had already begun in eastern Europe. While Jews were only 10 percent of immigrants between 1900 and 1925, they constituted 25 percent of all skilled industrial workers entering the United States in that period.

Cultural reasons compelled many Jewish immigrants to stay in New York. They often had family members who had preceded them to America. Here they found the necessary institutions of Jewish life, such as synagogues, ritual bath houses, and kosher butchers in abundance. They were able to converse with fellow speakers of Yiddish, read a lively Yiddish press, and for entertainment attend the Yiddish theatre, which attracted millions. Between 1890 and 1940, at least a dozen Yiddish theatre companies performed on the Lower East Side, in the Bronx, and in Brooklyn, with another two hundred traveling companies performing all over the United States. Plays often dealt with themes of generational conflict between immigrant parents and their American children and Old World versus New World culture and values. The theatre also produced Yiddish versions of European classics by authors such as Shakespeare, Oscar Wilde, Goethe, and Ibsen, even a much-loved production of Harriet Beecher Stowe's American classic, *Uncle Tom's Cabin.*

The leading light of the Yiddish theatre was **Abraham Goldfaden** (1840–1906). A Hebrew and Yiddish poet and playwright, Goldfaden's revolutionary innovation was to adapt Western popular theatre, an art form that was alien to Judaism, and to transform it in such a way as to make it acceptable and popular among Jews. In single-handedly creating the entire enterprise of Jewish show business, Goldfaden trained Jewish actors and created opportunities for Jewish set and costume designers, makeup people, musicians, librettists, playwrights, and many others. He also helped reconfigure the Jewish economy through its heavy involvement in show business.

The cultural impact of the Jewish theatre under Goldfaden was enormous. According to a recent account, Goldfaden "turned show business into an integral part of Jewish culture, and [thus] contributed tremendously to the secularization and acculturation of Ashkenazi Jews." Though largely unknown today, Goldfaden's importance was recognized by contemporaries, and not just in the world of Yiddish theatre. When he died, the *New York Times* reported on the funeral of "the 'Yiddish Shakespeare' and bard of the Jewish stage":

> Fully 75,000 Jews turned out yesterday morning for the funeral of Abraham Goldfaden, the Yiddish poet, playwright, and Zionist, who died on Wednesday at his home, 318 East Eleventh Street. All the streets through which the funeral procession of 104 coaches passed on its way to Washington Cemetery, in Brooklyn, were thronged with mourners. Even the fire-escapes were crowded.

Eastern European Jewish immigration between 1881 and 1914 differed from contemporary non-Jewish immigration in important ways. Above all, this was to be a permanent settlement. A smaller percentage of Jews returned to Europe than any other immigrant group. Nearly 95 percent of Jews stayed, while the comparable number for non-Jews was 66 percent. Jewish immigration involved families. While the Italians, the Irish, and the German Jews of mid-century came as single males, Jews from Russia came with much larger percentages of women and children. Between 1899 and 1910, 43 percent of Jewish immigrants were women, while 25 percent were children under the age of fourteen. The fact that 70 percent of Jewish immigrants were between the ages of fourteen and forty-four is a measure of the extent to which young Jews anticipated starting entirely new lives in the United States.

The conditions in the tenement flats were deplorable—overcrowded, cockroach infested with fetid air, poor lighting, substandard plumbing, and intensely hot in summer. Where they could, upper-class German Jews, such as the financier Jacob Schiff, who described philanthropy as the "ideal and aim of Judaism," offered assistance. Others made alleviating

Once Jews found work, it was mostly in the garment industry, centered in New York. Many arrived from Europe with knowledge of basic crafts, like tailoring. Jews made up over 50 percent of skilled workers in the clothing trades and a further 40 percent in the production of leather goods. Many Jewish immigrants worked out of their apartments in the densely packed Lower East Side of Manhattan. Dirt and disease and a generally foul atmosphere were the consequences of unprecedented overcrowding. By way of comparison, the heavily Jewish 10th ward of Manhattan had 626 persons per acre, Prague had 485 inhabitants per acre, while Paris only had 125. By 1910, 540,000 Jews lived in the one-and-a-half square miles that constituted the Lower East Side.

the plight of the immigrants their life's work. In 1895, the nurse, **Lillian Wald** (1867–1940), founded the Henry Street Settlement, a meeting place for workers offering them nursing, social, educational, banking, and cultural facilities. A tireless fighter for improvements in public health nursing, housing reform, suffrage, and the rights of women, children, immigrants, and working people, Wald recalled how one of her first visits to a tenement set her on her life's mission: "Over broken asphalt, over dirty mattresses and heaps of refuse we went. . . . There were two rooms and a family of seven not only lived here but shared their quarters with boarders. . . . [I felt] ashamed of being a part of society that permitted such conditions to exist. . . . What I had seen had shown me where my path lay." Pragmatic considerations also played a role in motivating German Jews to assist. As stated in the newspaper the *American Hebrew,* "All of us should be sensible of what we owe not only to these . . . coreligionists, but to ourselves, who will be looked upon by our gentile neighbors as the natural sponsors for these, our brethren."

With no division between workplace and home, hours were crushingly long. Inspectors in 1891 reported that during the slack season clothing workers put in a minimum work week of between sixty-six and seventy-two hours. During the busy season of 1904–1905 it was up to nineteen hours per day, seven days per week. According to Bernard Weinstein, who arrived in America in 1882, "The front room and kitchen were used as workrooms. The whole family would sleep in one dark bedroom. The sewing machines for the operators were near the windows of the front room. The basters would sit on stools near the walls, and in the center of the room, amid the dirt and dust, were heaped in great piles of materials. On top of the sofas several finishers would be working. . . . Old people . . . using gaslight for illumination, would stand and keep the irons hot and press the finished coats, jackets, pants and other clothes on special boards."

Thanks to newly established unions, hours grew somewhat shorter for work done in factories, tellingly called "sweatshops." In 1894, after the cloak-makers' union went on strike, workers were rewarded with a ten-hour day. By 1901 clothing union workers in factories put in a fifty-nine-hour work week. Exploitation was rife and pay was extremely low, around $3.81 per week for men and a miserable $1.04 per week for women. Conditions in the factories were also hazardous, something that became tragically apparent in the massive **Triangle Shirtwaist Fire,** which erupted near closing time on March 25, 1911. With the fire spreading rapidly, an illegally locked door prevented the women workers from escaping down the stairs. Many waited in vain at the windows only to see that the fire department ladders reached just to the fifth floor and the fire hoses likewise proved too short. At that point, many chose to jump out of the ninth floor. An eyewitness, Benjamin Levy, described the harrowing scene:

> I was upstairs in our work-room when one of the employees who happened to be looking out of the window cried that there was a fire around the corner. I rushed downstairs, and when I reached the sidewalk the girls were already jumping from the windows. None of them moved after they struck the sidewalk. Several men ran up with a net, which they got somewhere, and I seized one side of it to help them hold it.
>
> It was about ten feet square and we managed to catch about fifteen girls. I don't believe we saved over one or two however. The fall was so great that they bounced to the sidewalk after striking the net. Bodies were falling all around us, and two or three of the men with me were knocked down. The girls just leaped wildly out of the windows and turned over and over before reaching the sidewalk.
>
> I only saw one man jump. All the rest were girls. They stood on the windowsills tearing their hair out in the handfuls and then they jumped.

In the end, 146 young women workers, mostly Jewish and Italian, lost their lives. Across the political spectrum, the city reeled with righteous indignation. Demands from all corners came for improvement in working conditions, and the governor of New York State appointed a Factory Investigating Commission, which, for the next five years examined working conditions in factories. The result was the passage of important factory-safety legislation. In the Jewish community, the fire redoubled the commitment to trade unionism and progressive politics, more generally.

Even before the fire, agitation against bosses for improved conditions was actually a source of internal Jewish conflict, for of the 241 clothing factories in New York City in the 1880s, 234 were owned by German Jews, including Triangle Shirtwaist Factory. As a trade-union leader observed, "The early class struggles in the modern clothing industry in New York were *Jewish* class struggles; both masters and men were of the Hebrew race." The refusal of working-class eastern European Jews to be exploited extended beyond the garment industry and their relations with German Jewish factory owners. In May 1902, Jewish women organized a successful kosher meat boycott in response to a sudden price hike that saw meat go from twelve cents to eighteen cents per pound. The boycott committee of nineteen women demanded that meat wholesalers reduce their prices, leading as many as twenty thousand protesters on marches and demonstrations through the Lower East Side.

For one month the agitation continued and spread throughout the city, with men joining the women. On June 5 the strike was officially ended when, in a compromise, prices were rolled back to fourteen cents per pound. It is important to recall that most of the eastern European Jews arrived in America already highly politicized, having been participants in the class and cultural struggles that had so gripped and energized them back in Europe.

The "uptown" German Jews and "downtown" eastern European Jews were not just divided along employer–employee lines. There were deep cultural differences as well. The sincere compassion of German Jews often mixed with condescension toward their co-religionists. They were especially ashamed of the immigrants' appearance, dress, language, cultural institutions, and preference for Left-wing, if not Socialist, politics. German Jews also feared that antisemites would see them in the same light as they saw the immigrants, challenging the very Americanness of German Jews. Similar anxiety gripped Jews in Germany who feared that the recent arrival of eastern European Jews compromised them. German Jews sought to civilize the eastern European newcomers by sponsoring English classes, courses on American culture, and vocational training.

For their part, eastern European Jews, though grateful for the assistance, never felt a sense of inferiority and were resentful of the condescension. They did not care much for the ways of their "uptown" co-religionists, especially what many considered the lax religious practices of these overwhelmingly Reform Jews. Especially galling was the fact that many of the eastern European Jews had been distinguished scholars and men revered in their communities prior to emigrating. Now they were reduced to seeking handouts from Jews who did not respect them. As a contemporary observed:

> In the philanthropic institutions of our aristocratic German Jews you see beautiful offices, desks, all decorated, but strict and angry faces. Every poor man is questioned like a criminal, is looked down upon; every unfortunate suffers self-degradation and shivers like a leaf, just as if he were standing before a Russian official. When the same Russian Jew is in an institution of Russian Jews, no matter how poor and small the building, it will seem to him big and comfortable. He feels at home among his own brethren who speak his tongue, understand his thoughts and feel his heart.

As soon as it was possible, eastern European Jews sought to establish self-help organizations and created a network of **lantsmanshaftn,** the Yiddish word for the mutual-aid societies organized around the eastern European city of one's

Description: Dov Ber and Nesha Manischewitz, n.d. The Manischewitz Company symbolizes the harmonious marriage of entrepreneurship and religious observance in America. For most of Jewish history, matzah was made by hand and was produced for local consumption, generally baked in a *kehillah's* communal oven. This tradition was continued in America in the early years of Jewish settlement. But as the Jewish population increased and spread geographically, commercial manufacturers of matzah bakeries sprang up. One such business was owned by Ber Manischewitz, an immigrant from Lithuania. He opened his matzah business in Cincinnati in 1888 and introduced a number of innovations that changed the way commercial matzah was produced. Most important, he introduced modern technology, such as a gas-fired matzah baking oven and the patented "traveling carrier bake-oven," a conveyor belt that served to automate the whole process of matzah baking. The innovations were not immediately accepted by all Jews, the Orthodox rabbinate doubting the halakhic permissibility of Manischewitz's automation process. Rabbi Manischewitz countered that his methods were more sanitary and led to standardized quality. The majority of American Jews had no qualms about consuming Manischewitz products, and as business grew the company shifted operations in 1932 to Jersey City, New Jersey. Today, Manischewitz is the world's largest producer of matzah and kosher food products.

origin. They sprang up as soon as the great wave of migration began, and by 1914 at least 534 of them in New York were providing the immigrants with insurance, sickness benefits, interest-free loans, and coverage of burial costs. The arrivals from eastern Europe also founded a network of Jewish charities, orphanages, hospitals, a school for deaf mutes, and societies to provide for the Jewish blind and crippled. A Passover Relief Committee provided free matzah to the poor. But where poverty was rife, so too was crime, and large numbers of Jewish women were led into prostitution on the Lower East Side. Other Jewish immigrants went into petty crime, and by the last decade of the nineteenth century there were enough Jewish inmates to warrant the establishment in 1893 of a Jewish Prisoners' Aid Society.

Reflective of the many-faceted nature of new Jewish life in America, the Lower East Side was also an intensely religious place. Hundreds of synagogues and, by 1903, at least 307 heders and several yeshivas operated on the Lower East Side, including the Yeshiva Isaac Elchanan, which was opened in 1896 and would later grow into **Yeshiva University,** the premier institution for the training of men for the modern Orthodox rabbinate. Ten years before, in 1886, two Sephardic rabbis had founded the **Jewish Theological Seminary** as an institution to train men for the Conservative rabbinate.

Jewish life was further strengthened by the tight bonds of ethnic solidarity. Intermarriage was almost nonexistent, and in the early years of immigration Jews were even averse to marrying other Jews from different European towns. Still, as time passed, it was difficult for the immigrants to reestablish anything like the all-encompassing religious life they enjoyed in Europe. The distance from centers of tradition, the demands of working seven days a week to make ends meet, the lure of socialism, and the seductions of American life all made adherence to tradition increasingly difficult. With time, the revolt against tradition saw German Jews, eastern European Jews, and even the small Sephardic population begin to put aside their ethnic and cultural differences as they gradually left Europe behind in the process of becoming American. By the outbreak of World War I, there were millions of American Jews where only decades before there had been relatively few. In a mere thirty years America had become home to one of the biggest, most vibrant Jewish communities in the world, and in 1917 New York City became the largest center of Jewish life in history with 1.5 million Jews living there.

Questions for Reflection

1. What was the impact of the Jewish population explosion in the nineteenth century?
2. How does modern antisemitism differ from traditional anti-Judaism, and what are its specific organizational features?
3. How does the turn to politics by Jews reflect the fractured nature of modern Jewish identity?
4. The poet Hayim Nahman Bialik called the relationship between Hebrew and Yiddish a "marriage made in heaven." Why was it also such a stormy relationship?
5. What were some of the features that contributed to the modernization of Sephardic Jewry?

For Further Reading

On modern antisemitism, see Jacob Katz, *From Prejudice to Destruction: Antisemitism, 1700–1933* (Cambridge, MA: Harvard University Press, 1980); Shmuel Almog, *Nationalism & Antisemitism in Europe, 1815–1945* (Oxford and New York: Pergamon Press, 1990); Peter G. J. Pulzer, *The Rise of Political Anti-Semitism in Germany & Austria* (Cambridge, MA: Harvard University Press, 1988); John M. Efron, *Defenders of the Race: Jewish Doctors and Race Science in Fin-de-Siècle Europe* (New Haven, CT: Yale University Press, 1994); John Weiss, *The Politics of Hate: Anti-Semitism, History, and the Holocaust in Modern Europe* (Chicago: Ivan R. Dee, 2003); George L. Mosse, *Toward the Final Solution: A History of European Racism* (Madison: University of Wisconsin Press, 1985); Richard S. Levy, *Antisemitism in the Modern World: An Anthology of Texts* (New York: D.C. Heath, 1991); Edward H. Judge, *Easter in Kishinev: Anatomy of a Pogrom* (New York: New York University Press, 1992).

On politics, see Ezra Mendelsohn, *On Modern Jewish Politics* (New York: Oxford University Press, 1993); David Vital, *A People Apart: A Political History of the Jews in Europe, 1789–1939* (Oxford: Oxford University Press, 1999); Eli Lederhendler, *The Road to Modern Jewish Politics: Political Tradition and Political Reconstruction in the Jewish Community of Tsarist Russia* (New York: Oxford University Press, 1989); Jonathan Frankel, *Prophecy and Politics: Socialism, Nationalism, and the Russian Jews, 1862–1917* (Cambridge, England: Cambridge University Press, 1981); Michael Stanislawski, *Tsar Nicholas I and the Jews: The Transformation of Jewish Society in Russia, 1825–1855* (Philadelphia: Jewish Publication Society of America, 1983); Michael Berkowitz, *Zionist Culture and West European Jewry Before the First World War* (Cambridge, England: Cambridge University Press, 1993); Arthur Hertzberg, *The Zionist Idea: A Historical Analysis and Reader* (Philadelphia: Jewish Publication Society of America, 1959); Michael Brenner, *Zionism: A Brief History* (Princeton, NJ: Markus Wiener, 2003); Steven J. Zipperstein, *Elusive Prophet: Ahad Ha'am and the Origins of Zionism* (Berkeley: University of California Press, 1993); Amos Elon, *Herzl* (New York: Schocken Books, 1975); Jehuda Reinharz, *Fatherland or Promised Land: The Dilemma of the German Jew, 1893–1914* (Ann Arbor: University of Michigan Press, 1975).

On Jewish society and culture in the nineteenth-century, see Steven E. Aschheim, *Brothers and Strangers: The East European Jew in German and German Jewish Consciousness, 1800–1923* (Madison: University of Wisconsin Press, 1999); John M. Efron, *Medicine and the German Jews: A History* (New Haven, CT: Yale University Press, 2001); Derek J. Penslar, *Shylock's Children: Economics and Jewish Identity in Modern Europe* (Berkeley: University of California Press, 2001); Steven Beller, *Vienna and the Jews, 1867–1938: A Cultural History* (Cambridge, England: Cambridge University Press, 1989); Marsha L. Rozenblit, *The Jews of Vienna, 1867–1914: Assimilation and Identity* (Albany: State University of New York Press, 1983); David Feldman, *Englishmen and Jews: Social Relations and Political Culture, 1840–1914* (New Haven: Yale University Press, 1994); Nancy L. Green, ed., *Jewish Workers in the Modern Diaspora* (Berkeley: University of California Press, 1988); Nancy L. Green, *The Pletzl of Paris: Jewish Immigrant Workers in the Belle Epoque* (New York: Holmes & Meier, 1986); Irving Howe, *World of Our Fathers* (New York: Harcourt Brace Jovanovich, 1976); Jeffrey S. Gurock, *When Harlem Was Jewish, 1870–1930* (New York: Columbia University Press, 1979); Benjamin Nathans, *Beyond the Pale: The Jewish Encounter with Late Imperial Russia* (Berkeley: University of California Press, 2002); ChaeRan Y. Freeze, *Jewish Marriage and Divorce in Imperial Russia* (Hanover, NH: University Press of New England, 2002); Olga Litvak, *Conscription and the Search for Modern Russian Jewry* (Bloomington: Indiana University Press, 2006); Hillel J. Kieval, *The Making of Czech Jewry: National Conflict and Jewish Society in Bohemia, 1870–1918* (New York: Oxford University Press, 1988); Benjamin Harshav, *Language in Time of Revolution* (Berkeley: University of California Press, 1993); Robert Alter, *Hebrew and Modernity* (Bloomington: Indiana University Press, 1994); Dan Miron, *A Traveler Disguised: The Rise of Modern Yiddish Fiction in the Nineteenth Century* (Syracuse: Syracuse University Press, 1996); Carole B. Balin, *To Reveal Our Hearts: Jewish Women Writers in Tsarist Russia* (Cincinnati: Hebrew Union College Press, 2000); Marion A. Kaplan, *The Making of the Jewish Middle Class: Women, Family, and Identity in Imperial Germany* (New York: Oxford University Press, 1991); George L. Mosse, *German Jews Beyond Judaism* (Cincinnati: Hebrew Union College Press, 1985); Aron Rodrigue, *Jews and Muslims: Images of Sephardi and Eastern Jewries in Modern Times* (Seattle: University of Washington Press, 2003); Aron Rodrigue, *French Jews, Turkish Jews: The Alliance Israélite Universelle and the Politics of Jewish Schooling in Turkey, 1860–1925* (Bloomington: Indiana University Press, 1990).

Chapter 13

A World Upended

The twentieth century was an age of extremes. Advances in medicine, science, public services, education, labor and safety laws, women's and minority rights improved the lot of millions. At the same time, unprecedented levels of carnage, brutality, and cruelty likewise characterize the era. Across the globe, perpetrators and victims alike came from all racial, ethnic, religious, and class backgrounds.

The twentieth century can be said to have begun with World War I. Up until 1914, the broad patterns of nineteenth-century life—its pace, manners, social hierarchies, and imperial political structures—still prevailed. With the onset of war, however, it soon became apparent that the scale and nature of the conflagration were such that nothing would survive of the Old Order. Along with millions of young men, the old European order died in the trenches.

Jewish society, already transformed by the great nineteenth-century historical processes of secularization, acculturation, politicization, migration, and urbanization, was further shaken to the core by World War I and its aftermath. Jews in eastern Europe suffered violence and communal devastation during the war, while those in central and western Europe experienced initial patriotic euphoria, the camaraderie soon shattered by the intensification of antisemitism as the war began to go badly for the Central Powers. Yet inspired by nationalism and spiritual revival, Jews in the interwar period created vibrant, modern Jewish cultures that bespoke self-confidence and faith in the future. Others participated in the majority cultures as scientists, entrepreneurs, writers, journalists, musicians, actors, and directors. Their work was not Jewish in any definable way, but the disproportionate presence of Jews in these fields of endeavor nevertheless saw them bring to their creative activities the attitude of the marginalized—a willingness to not follow conventions and to create something entirely new. Sigmund Freud, typical of such Jews, declared in a 1926 address to the B'nai B'rith Lodge (of which he was a member) that what he found most appealing about Jews and what he shared with his people was their fierce independence, born of their being outsiders: "As a Jew I was prepared to join the Opposition and to do without agreement with the 'compact majority.'" Indeed, whether as young Zionists rebelling against their father's assimilation, communist revolutionaries trying to remake the world, modernist Hebrew poets rebelling against the canon, or psychoanalysts unearthing the hidden secrets of bourgeois respectability, young Jews in the interwar period very often stood in opposition to the forces of authority, both Jewish and non-Jewish.

World War I

World War I erupted on August 1, 1914, and what all Europeans imagined would be a short war dragged on until November 11, 1918. The Allied Powers—made up of the British Empire, France, Russia, and after 1917 the United States—defeated the Central Powers, composed of the German Empire, the Austro-Hungarian Empire, and the Ottoman Empire. At the conclusion of hostilities, the war had completely transformed the map, culture, politics, mentality, and importance of Europe. Approximately 9 million people were slaughtered, while nearly 22 million were missing or left crippled and mutilated. European economies were left in tatters, and four empires—the Austro-Hungarian, German, Russian, and Ottoman—had collapsed. To many, European civilization appeared to have completely crumbled.

The impact of the war was felt for decades to come. An entire generation was lost, and for winners and losers alike the war was an unmitigated disaster. Due to its massive losses, France sought revenge against Germany and exacted a harsh settlement in the Versailles Treaty. Germany's defeat and subsequent humiliation contributed to the climate of resentment responsible for the rise of Nazism. The war also contributed to National Social-ism's culture of violence and lust for vengeance. Italian Fas-cism too was a product of the war, while in Russia, with a staggering casualty toll of 9 million, the war also provided the opportunity for the Bolshevik victory. Indeed many return-ing soldiers and civilians alike were not only physically dam-aged but also were left brutalized and susceptible to the aggressive messages and exhortations to further violence of radical ideologues such as Lenin, Mussolini, and Hitler.

Also for European Jewry, the war was a disaster. Like their fellow Europeans, Jews flocked to enlist. Approximately 1.5 million Jewish men fought for their respective homelands. Many died, many more were maimed and missing in action. In eastern Europe there were also substantial losses of Jewish property. In fact, the war began to spell the end of European Jewish civilization for it undermined the very existence of Jew-ish life—in different ways in both eastern and western Europe.

Jews on the Eastern Front

On the eastern front, the war raged in the heart of the Pale of Settlement and Galicia, home to almost four million Jews. In these regions, antisemitism was already strong but was exac-erbated by the war as the local population accused Jews of as-sisting the enemy. In addition to being denounced and robbed by Poles and Ruthenian peasants, Jewish civilians were treated brutally by Russian and Cossack troops. Despite the fact that some Jews served as officers in the Russian and Rumanian armed services, they were unable to prevent the violence meted out to Jews by invading Russian forces. Jews suffered pogroms, mass rape, theft, forced labor, and the de-struction of their homes, businesses, synagogues, sacred reli-gious objects, and schools. Shtetlekh and villages were particularly hard hit, especially if the small communities were unable or unwilling to pay protection money to the Russians, who implemented a "scorched-earth" policy. In several towns in the heavily Jewish Kielce province, more than 90 percent of the buildings were destroyed. By the spring of 1915 about 100 Jewish communities in the Kingdom of Poland had been completely destroyed. Decrees were enforced against publish-ing and theatre performance in Yiddish and Hebrew, along with bans on telephone use. Jews were taken hostage and were subject to semijudicial executions, and outright murder, while forced expulsion of Jews occurred on a massive scale. A Jewish soldier with the Austro-Hungarian army reported:

> Whenever the Russians came through, the Christians would put icons in their windows. If there was no icon, the house was therefore Jewish, and the soldiers could de-stroy it without fear of punishment. When our brigade

marched through one village, a soldier spotted a house on a hill, and told our commander that it was probably the home of Jews. The officer allowed him to go and have a look. He returned with the cheerful news that Jews *were* indeed living there. They opened the door and found some twenty Jews half dead with fear. The troops led them out, and the officer gave his order: "Slice them up! Chop them up!" I didn't stay to see what happened next.

Somewhere between 500,000 and 1 million Jews were expelled and moved east behind Russian lines, many given a mere twenty-four to forty-eight hours notice to leave their homes. The Russians took Jewish hostages to ensure that Jewish communities complied with the evacuation order. Forced deportations precipitated a refugee crisis of enormous proportions. In May 1915, over 100,000 homeless Jews poured into Warsaw alone. Other expulsions, such as those from Galicia and Bukovina—both in the Habsburg Empire—saw vast numbers of Jews driven into the capital cities of Vienna and Budapest, where they existed in terrible conditions in refugee camps. Jews were unable to return home because eastern Galicia and Bukovina remained in Russian hands until 1917. Central and western Galicia fared even worse as those areas were so devastated that Jews who fled often had no homes, businesses, or communal institutions to which they could return. The massive international outcry against Russian mistreatment of Jews had the unintended effect of stiffening Russian resolve and increasing the persecution.

The social and material conditions of eastern European Jewry lay in ruins. At least 500,000 Jews served in the Russian army, and about 70,000 men, often the family's sole bread-winner, were killed while many thousands went missing in ac-tion. This left thousands of ***agunot*** (women whose husbands are either unwilling or unable to grant a bill of divorce). *Agunot* became a serious problem for Jewish society, as rab-binical courts refused to accept proof of widowhood, and thus remarriage under Jewish law was impossible. For the Jews of eastern Europe, World War I was a defining moment. It dev-astated economies, fractured families, destroyed the Jewish community, and exposed the vulnerability of eastern Europe's Jews to violence and persecution on a local and state level.

Jews on the Western Front

Unlike Jews in eastern Europe, those in western and central Europe, like their gentile compatriots, greeted the war with great enthusiasm. Everywhere, Jews flocked to enlist. In Germany, 100,000 men or 18 percent of the total Jewish population served; 12,000 of them were killed and 35,000 decorated. In the Austro-Hungarian army, some 275,000 or 11 percent of all Jews fought. On the opposing side, about 41,500 Jews from across the empire fought for Britain; Of 10,000 enlisted as volunteers prior to the institution of conscription in May 1916, 18 percent fought as officers, double the proportion of voluntary recruits-to-officers in the rest of the British army. The highest-ranking Jewish soldier of World War I was **Sir John Monash** (1865–1931), commander of the Australian forces. No other Great Power so lavishly rewarded Jews for their heroic efforts. Jews of the British Empire received 5 Victoria Crosses, 50 Distinguished Service Orders, and 240 Military Crosses. In all, approximately 15 percent of Britain's Jewish population fought in the war, in contrast to the 11.5 percent of the general British population that served. In France, 35,000 Jews or 20 percent of the total Jewish population there joined the army. Jewish women from all over western Europe moved beyond the confines of bourgeois domesticity and volunteered for service, mostly working in clinics, military hospitals, and welfare agencies.

For German Jews, the occasion was especially auspicious because this was their first opportunity since emancipation (1871) to make the ultimate sacrifice for their country. They were swept up in the patriotic frenzy that attended the outbreak of hostilities. On Wednesday, August 5, 1914, German Jews of all denominations heeded the emperor's call for a day of prayer. Throughout Germany and Austria Jews poured into synagogues to celebrate special war services. Over the course of the war, German and Austrian Jewish newspapers of all orientations, stressed their patriotic duty. A Zionist newspaper in Vienna declared, "In these trying days the Jews are the truest of the true. No other Austrian nationality is as willing to sacrifice as the Jews. . . ." Journalists drew on biblical imagery to bolster Jewish morale, with one Austrian Jewish newspaper telling its readers on Rosh Hashanah 1914 that the war was a holy one for Jews, and they should recall the *akedah,* the binding of Isaac by his father Abraham, both because it was the New Year and because the patriarch Abraham and Austrian Jewry alike were called upon to sacrifice their sons. Jewish soldiers were often described as modern Maccabees. In a eulogy for a Berlin rabbi who fell in battle, the speaker said of the dead chaplain, "German courage and Maccabean heroism came together in his worldview." The book of Psalms was also an inspiration. In 1914, an article entitled "The War and the Psalms" appeared in the German-language newspaper *The Truth* and quoted Psalm 144: "Send forth Your hand from on high; redeem me and save me from the mighty waters, from the foreigners' hand, whose mouth speaks falsely, and whose right hand is a right hand of lies." Here, Austrian Jews depicted themselves as biblically sanctioned saviors of Russian Jews. To some extent the notion that the German and Austrian armies were liberators possessed a grain of truth. They certainly posed as such,

even printing posters in Yiddish announcing themselves as liberators. Eastern European Jews, however, were rarely fooled, even when the German general Erich Ludendorff, issued a proclamation in Yiddish entitled "To My Dear Jews in Poland" (*An mayne libe Yidn in Poyln*). In it he promised Jews protection, freedom, and equality after Germany had won the war. The Jews were right to be skeptical. Freedom and equality did not come their way, and after Germany's defeat Ludendorf became a radical antisemite and an early supporter of Hitler.

All German and Austrian Jews spoke of duty and service but perhaps none more enthusiastically than the Orthodox Jew Joseph Wohlgemuth. He drew parallels between Germans and Orthodox Jews, explaining how both were culturally adapted to fighting a patriotic war: "The fact that Germans, more than other nations, have learned how to obey has made it possible for their leaders to prepare for the anticipated victory and carry it out. The adherent of traditional Judaism possesses this inclination toward lawfulness to an even greater degree. His entire life is oriented to subservience to the law. . . . Always loyal to the law, now too he has fought like a hero and died like a hero, just as the law demands."

A small number of prominent Jews spoke out against the war. After initially supporting the cause, the philosopher **Martin Buber** (1878–1965) became an opponent, while the scholar of Jewish mysticism Gershom Scholem (1897–1982) and the psychoanalyst **Sigmund Freud** (1856–1939) were against the war from the start. Scholem's father threw his son out of the house for his pacifism. In a lecture to B'nai B'rith, Freud said that the war was proof that even in the best people, aggressive and egotistical impulses were merely repressed but never entirely absent. The war, he told his audience, truly displayed that even the most cultured Europeans "have not descended as deeply as we fear because they had not risen as high as we believed."

The heady feelings of patriotism experienced by most German Jews soon gave way to disappointment and disillusionment. Just as Jews had drawn on biblical symbolism to justify their efforts and draw closer to their gentile compatriots, non-Jewish Germans drew on Christian symbols to exclude Jews. As the nationalist author Walter Flex observed, "[T]he sacrificial death of the best among our people is but a divinely ordained repetition of the most profound miracle of which the earth knows, the vicarious sufferings of Jesus Christ. The wine of Christ is prepared from German blood."

As the war dragged on and frustration became mixed with German chauvinism, German Jewry, overwhelmingly liberal in sensibility, began to find itself out of touch with prevailing sentiment. Although a young Jew, Ernst Lissauer, wrote one of the war's most popular poems and a personal favorite of the kaiser's, "The Hate Song Against England," the predominately liberal and Anglophile Jewish community rejected it. On the battlefield too, differences between German and Jewish soldiers began to show. In the trenches, one Jewish soldier wrote, "The Jewish comrade suddenly realized that he felt as if he were discovering an unknown world." That world, according to another Jewish soldier was one where "the average German simply does not care for the Jew. I don't want to be anything here but a German soldier—and yet I am given no choice but to believe that it is otherwise."

The increasing sense of distance came to a head with the **Jew Count** (*Judenzählung*) of 1916. As the war ground on and Germans begun to demand explanations for why the quick victory they had been promised had not materialized, accusations came from antisemitic quarters that German military efforts had been compromised because Jews were dodging the draft and shirking service at the front. German Jews were incredulous that they of all people could have their loyalty questioned. The Prussian War Ministry conducted the Jew Count, a census to determine whether the charges of draft dodging were true or not. Noting that Jews were serving at the front in disproportionately large numbers, the war ministry never published the results.

The Jew Count was a critical moment in German Jewish history. It shattered the Jewish illusion that non-Jewish Germans had accepted the process of Jewish acculturation and social integration. The sense of frustration led to greater efforts at Jewish self-assertion. The majority remained patriotic to Germany but many rededicated themselves to their Jewishness as well. For many young German Jews, the process of reclaiming their Jewish identities had already begun to occur with their encounter with eastern European Jews on the Eastern Front. Young German Jews idealized eastern European Jews as authentic representatives of Jewish peoplehood.

A cult of the eastern European Jew developed in the interwar period. For other German Jews, Zionism beckoned in the aftermath of the Jew Count. According to the philosopher **Ernst Simon** (1899–1988), "The dream of commonality was over. The deep abyss, which had never disappeared, opened up once more with terrible force . . .Our vital energy would have drained away completely . . . if Judaism had not spread out its arms to take us back. . . . We had come home; we had once more become Jews. . . . Now we were Zionists, at first without wanting or realizing it."

British Jewry

The war allowed for Anglo-Jewish social tensions to surface. British Jewry was heterogeneous. There was an Anglo-Jewish establishment—middle class, anglicized, and religiously liberal. After 1881, mass immigration from Russia brought about 60,000 working-class, Yiddish-speaking, Orthodox Jews to England. While most settled in London's East End, others went to Manchester, Leeds, Liverpool, and Glasgow.

When war broke out, Jews from the British establishment signed up enthusiastically, identifying themselves with the national cause. The official voice of the community was the world's oldest Jewish newspaper, *The Jewish Chronicle,* founded in 1841. As late as 1914, the paper favored neutrality, but when war was declared the paper changed its stance, declaring on August 7, 1914, "England has been all she could be to Jews, Jews will be all they can be to England."

Still, great discomfort with the cause persisted among Jews. Most members of the native Jewish community had their roots in Germany. Many still had family and business interests there. Some community leaders, such as Lord Rothschild and Lucien Wolf, openly objected to Britain's entente with the hated tsarist regime. Antisemites attacked them and, despite professions of loyalty as well as a rash of name changes to more English- and less German-sounding ones, hostility against Jews was on the rise. When in May 1915, the British ship RMS *Lusitania* was sunk by a German submarine, East Londoners rioted for three days, smashing and looting German- and Austrian-owned shops. Charges of Jewish cowardice and shirking accompanied anti-German hostilities. This tense situation was compounded by the refusal of many immigrant families to volunteer their sons for the army. Few Russian Jewish immigrants wished to risk their sons' lives defending Russia, Britain's ally.

With the imposition of conscription in April 1916, British-born sons of immigrants were called up, but not men of military age (eighteen to forty-one) who had been born in the Russian Empire. Approximately 30,000 Jewish men were thus exempt, classified as friendly aliens. This discrepancy exacerbated tensions between native and immigrant Jews and between Jews and non-Jews. In June 1917, a pogrom took place in Leeds. A mob numbering several thousand destroyed Jewish homes and looted shops in the city's Jewish section. By the Jewish New Year, tensions were so inflamed that in September about **3,000** Jews and gentiles fought each other in the streets with bats and iron bars.

While the war exposed fault lines within the Jewish community and the vulnerability of Jews to popular animosity, the state continued to promote and defend Jews, never countenancing the attitude of the mob. Moreover, a British victory would spell the end of Ottoman dominance in the Middle East. The Zionist movement would be the great beneficiary of these developments as it moved center stage in British–Jewish communal politics.

The Jews of Interwar Europe

After the conclusion of World War I, Zionism, Bundism, and other forms of Jewish nationalism captured the hearts of European and Middle Eastern Jewry. Under grave threat in the new states that emerged in the wake of the war, Jews from Europe to the Middle East were subjected to exclusion, economic boycott, discrimination. and physical violence. They responded in a number of ways including establishing self-defense units, immigration, political activism within a Jewish sphere and also as part of central and eastern European revolutionary movements, promoting Jewish territorial separation, and an intense engagement with Jewish culture conducted at a high level and at a feverish pace. It is one of the great paradoxes of the modern Jewish experience that as Jews were faced with increasing threats, discrimination, economic ruin, and violence in both central and eastern Europe, they were phenomenally productive in the cultural sphere. In particular, secular Jewish culture flourished in Germany, Poland, and the Soviet Union.

After the Paris Peace Conference of 1919 that rearranged the map of Europe, new states emerged from the ruins of the German, Austro-Hungarian, Russian, and Ottoman Empires. Among the new states were Poland, the Soviet Union, Czechoslovakia, Hungary, Lithuania, Latvia, Estonia, Rumania, Greece, and Yugoslavia. Though all were founded on democratic and universalist principles, the majority failed to live up to the ideals enshrined in their written constitutions and by the 1930s had become authoritarian regimes. (The only exception was Czechoslovakia.) Right-wing nationalists preached an integral nationalism that tended to favor the dominant ethnic, religious, and language groups in the country. As a result, Jews were increasingly shut out of the new economies and societies by a systematic process of discrimination. In Russia, the situation was markedly different as the Bolshevik Revolution completely changed the nature of Jewish life, opening up many avenues of opportunity for social and cultural integration and shutting many others in terms of Jewish culture and politics.

Violence against Jews also marked the interwar period. In Poland, over a hundred pogroms occurred by 1919, the biggest in Lvov, where seventy Jews were murdered. Similar outrages occurred in Hungary and Lithuania. The scale of carnage was greatest, however, in Ukraine. Despite the facts that minority rights were guaranteed; that Jews were represented in the central government, or Rada; that they enjoyed considerable autonomy; and that Yiddish was even printed on the Ukrainian currency, the locals everywhere accused Jews of spying for the Bolsheviks. In a time of food shortages, requisitions and fear of the Bolsheviks, Ukrainian peasants, and Cossacks turned on Jews. Looting, rape, and murder took place on an unprecedented scale. Between 1919 and 1921, more than 60,000 Jews were killed, and many thousands more injured. The Ukrainian minister of defense, Semion Petlura, was widely regarded as responsible for the pogroms, for while he never ordered them he never attempted to halt them and even went so far as to justify them. In an act of vengeance, Sholom Shvartsbard, a Jewish refugee from the pogroms in Paris, who had lost fourteen family members in a pogrom, murdered Petlura in the French capital in 1926. Shooting him on the street three times, Shvartsbard exclaimed with each pull of the trigger, "This, for the pogroms; this, for the massacres; this, for the victims." He was tried and acquitted by a French jury, which held that he had committed a "crime of passion."

Everywhere, Jews tasted new freedoms yet, paradoxically, saw antisemitism become dominant. In 1918, the German Empire collapsed, Kaiser Wilhelm fled to Holland, and the Weimar Republic (1919–1933)—Germany's first real experiment in liberal democracy—came into existence. Weimar Germany saw the last vestiges of exclusion lifted, and the nation's 564,000 Jews enjoyed unprecedented access to coveted positions in the state and society. Some Jews placed their hopes in socialist revolution. On November 7, 1918, Kurt Eisner overthrew the Bavarian government and became prime minister. Eisner declared Bavaria a socialist republic but one that, in contrast to what the Bolsheviks had done in Russia, would protect private property. He was assassinated by the nationalist Anton Graf von Arco auf Valley in 1919, while Ernst Toller, who was later found guilty of high treason for assisting Eisner, became one of the most important pacifists, poets, and playwrights of the interwar period. Not long after the Nazis rose to power and Toller fled Germany (he committed suicide in 1933), the propaganda minister, Josef Goebbels, declared, "Two million German soldiers rise from the graves of Flanders and Holland to indict the Jew Toller for having written: 'the ideal of heroism is the stupidest ideal of all.'" The Jewish anarchist Gustav Landauer also preached a new dawn and was assassinated for it. Standing at the center of the political spectrum, the Jewish lawyer Julius Preuss wrote the liberal constitution of the Weimar Republic, which was often referred to by Nazis and other Right-wing parties as the *Judenrepublik* ("Jew Republic"). In 1922, the Jewish industrialist Walter Rathenau became foreign minister, an unprecedented achievement for a Jew. But his assassination by Right-wing extremists that same year also indicates the fragile nature of Jewish life in the public eye. As radicalism took root and Left and Right battled each other for supremacy in the unstable political and economic conditions of postwar Germany, those on the Right were particularly keen to hold Jews responsible for Germany's defeat and postwar suffering. In this environment, antisemitism reached vicious heights.

Interwar Jewry: The Numbers

As a result of the combined impact of mass immigration, the social and economic dislocation caused by the First World War, and the economic warfare waged against Jews in the interwar period, European Jewry declined as a percentage of the European population but, remarkably, increased in sheer numbers. In 1900 82 percent of Jews lived in Europe. By 1925, it was 62 percent, while by 1939 only 57 percent were to be found there. Still, millions of Jews lived in Europe: 8.7 million

in 1900 and 9.3 million by 1925. Nearly everywhere they were a very visible presence in society and the economy. In the fields of law and medicine, Jews were especially prominent. In Budapest, they were 51 percent of the lawyers, 49 percent in Odessa, and about 40 percent in Berlin. Non-Jews in major cities were also quite likely to have had a Jewish doctor. In Vienna and Budapest respectively, 63 percent of all doctors were Jews. Even though interwar Polish Jewry can be classified as having been lower middle class and proletarian, Jewish professionals and intellectuals, perhaps totaling 300,000 people altogether, were important and highly visible. In 1931, of all Poland's physicians, 56 percent were Jews (4,488). In Polish cities the picture is even more startling. In Cracow, Jews constituted 61 percent of physicians, 66 percent in Warsaw, 71 percent in Lvov, 74 percent in Vilna, and 83 percent in Lodz, Poland's second-largest city. Jews constituted 43 percent of Poland's teachers, 33 percent of her lawyers, and 22 percent of her journalists (*see* Map 13-1).

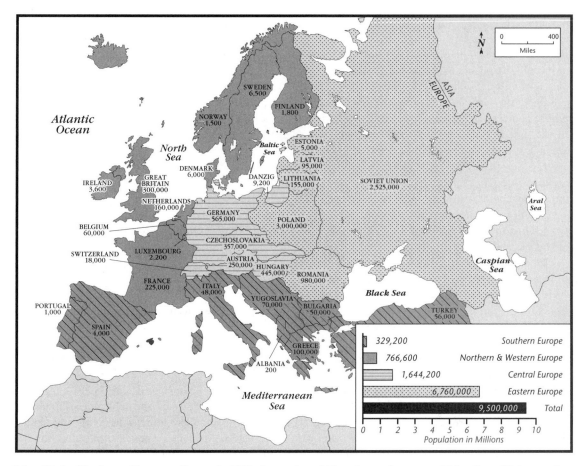

Map 13–1   The Jews of Interwar Europe. In 1933, the total world Jewish population was 15.3 million. Of this number, 60 percent, or 9.5 million, lived in Europe. Of the 9.5 million, about 5.5 million European Jews lived in Poland and Russia.

Across Europe, Jews were also highly visible in the business sector, with 60 percent of all German Jews engaged in commerce, compared to about 16 percent for non-Jews. In interwar east-central Europe, Budapest had the second-largest Jewish population with 215,000 Jews in 1920. (Only Warsaw with 219,000 had a bigger Jewish population, a number that swelled to 352,659 by 1931.) In the Hungarian capital, Jews made up 23 percent of the total population but controlled 60 percent of the city's commerce. Nearly 65 percent of all bankers and executives in the financial sector were Jewish, while 88 percent of the members of the stock exchange were Jewish. Perhaps as much as 90 percent of all Hungarian industry was financed by privately owned Jewish banks. By contrast, while 60 percent of Hungarians were involved in agriculture, only 4 percent of Jews were, and while 44 percent of Jews were involved in trade, only 4 percent of Hungarians were similarly engaged. In Czechoslovakia, Romania, Italy, and Greece, the proportion of Jews involved in commerce was similarly high. In Poland, most Jews who were not members of the professions were employed in the commercial and industrial sectors. In certain areas, such as Galicia, Jews constituted almost the entire commercial class. On the whole, however, none of this served to make the Jews wealthy. Families such as the Rothschilds and the Sassoons were an exception. Rather, the economic activities of Jews made most in western and central Europe comfortable, while the majority in the East and Middle East remained poor. Yet despite economic realities, interwar political and economic conditions across Europe made all Jews objects of envy and hatred by nationalist political groups.

In terms of trade, Jews were to be found concentrated in leather goods, textiles, clothing, and shoe manufacture. One field that seemed to attract Jews was cosmetics. Firms such as Max Factor and Helena Rubenstein, though founded before World War I, all became internationally famous in the interwar period. In Germany, Nivea, the skin cream invented in 1911 by the Jewish scientists Isaac Lifschütz and Paul Unna, was repackaged in 1925 in the now famous blue-and-white container and soon became a household product worldwide. Another commercial phenomenon closely associated with Jewish entrepreneurs was the department store. Consumers in Paris shopped in the Grand Magasin du Louvre and Grands Magasins du Printemps, while in Berlin the department stores of Wertheim, Tietz, and Kaufhaus des Westens attracted new middle-class customers, as did Gerngross and Herzmansky in Vienna. What these professional and commercial characteristics show is that by the interwar period, Jews had made very significant economic strides, especially in western Europe.

In eastern Europe, where, despite the desperate conditions caused by World War I, Jews remained integral to the local interwar economies, and in the Soviet Union they enjoyed a level of occupational freedom that they had not previously known. The 3.3 million Jews of Poland, who comprised about 10 percent of the total population, paid approximately 40 percent of all taxes: little wonder, given the fact that in 1931 in a small city such as Tarnopol, of the 19,667 economically active persons in the city, 92.5 percent were Jews. In the larger city of Bialystok, of the 16,354 people involved in commerce, 84.5 percent were Jewish, while in the capital, Warsaw, 33,910 people were actively involved in commerce, of whom 75 percent were Jews. In Hungary (450,000 Jews), Romania (662,779), Lithuania (157,500), Latvia (95,675), and Estonia (4,500), the Jews of east-central Europe were essentially the productive and commercially active middle class. By contrast, in nearly all these countries, the majority of non-Jews were still tied to rural economies.

Not only did Jews differ from non-Jews occupationally; their patterns of domicile also differed significantly from the majority. By 1930, nearly 30 percent of all Jews were to be found in a mere nineteen world cities. Few ethnic groups were as resolutely urban as the Jewish people. By the 1930s, 90 percent of Latvian, 85 percent of German, 80 percent of Hungarian, 75 percent of Polish, and 70 percent of Rumanian Jews lived in cities. Very often, they were found in capitals: Copenhagen (92 percent), Paris (70 percent), Vienna (67 percent), and London (67 percent). Though not the capital of the United States, New York, which by the interwar period was the largest Jewish city in the world, was 25 percent Jewish. In all, prior to World War II only 1 to 2 percent of all Jews earned a livelihood from agriculture.

Soviet Russia Between the Wars

In November 1917, Vladimir Lenin and Leon Trotsky led the Bolshevik Revolution and tsarist Russia was transformed into the Soviet Union. The revolution was a mixed blessing for Jews. Never before had so much oppression been inflicted alongside the granting of so much liberation, especially in the early phase—the February Revolution—which saw the Jews of Russia finally emancipated and the Pale of Settlement abolished forever. Judaism and secular Jewish culture fared less well than Soviet Jews as individuals, who now enjoyed access to new occupations, professions, and education in a way unimaginable to their forebears in tsarist Russia. They also enjoyed a good measure of physical protection too, as the Red Army sought to save Jews from pogroms. Throughout the 1920s, the Soviet regime actively fought against anti-semitism, which it saw as a primitive by-product of capitalist exploitation.

But political expressions of national Jewish identity were dealt with severely. As was the case with politics in general, all Jewish political activity was crushed as the Bolsheviks grabbed the monopoly on power and shut down the Russian branch of the Bund and various Zionist parties. Further alienation was caused by the Marxist atheism of the Bolshevik Revolution, which led to a direct assault on traditional Judaism. By the early 1920s, the Jewish Section of the Communist Party (**Yevsektsia**) had systematically closed down about 1,000 Hebrew schools and 650 synagogues and religious schools. Jewish religious life was essentially snuffed out or forced underground. In the most radical expression of the goals of the French Revolution, the Jews were to disappear as a religious–ethnic collectivity but enjoy rights as individual Soviet citizens. Despite its zeal and commitment to Communism, the Yevsekstia was always suspect in the eyes of Soviet authorities. It was shut down in 1930, charged with Jewish nationalism, and most of its leaders were eventually imprisoned or executed during the Stalinist purges of 1936–1938. The suffering of Jews and Judaism under the Soviets led many to quip, "[T]he Trotskys make the revolution and the Bronshteyns pay for it," referring to the fact that Trotsky's original name was Bronshteyn.

In the 1920s, the Soviet Union, which believed that language, more than any other characteristic, defined nationhood, poured considerable resources into promoting social, political, and cultural institutions in the languages of its many ethnic groups. The aim was to indoctrinate each minority in the teachings and ways of the new state. While the Soviets dismissed Hebrew and Zionism as expressions of Jewish reaction, Yiddish culture thrived in the interwar period. Admittedly, much of it was of dubious worth as Yiddish writers and journalists produced propaganda, often virulently anti-religious, in the service of the revolution." Yiddish writers and linguists even changed the orthography of Yiddish so as to erase the Hebrew spelling of those words in Yiddish that were derived from the Hebrew language. Still, there was much that was of high quality and the Soviet Union was the only country in the world to have state-sponsored institutions—among them, schools, courts, and publishing houses—of Yiddish culture.

Alongside the pedestrian outpourings of Soviet propaganda in Yiddish, brilliant works of art appeared, especially Expressionist literature and poetry. A thriving Yiddish publishing industry emerged. In 1924, only 76 books and pamphlets appeared. By 1930, that number had increased to 531. Over the same period, the number of Yiddish newspapers increased from 21 to around 40. An important site of Soviet Jewish cultural production was the State Jewish Theater in Moscow. With Jewish actors such as Shlomo Mikhoels, one of the greatest interpreters of *King Lear* in any language, and the celebrated artist Marc Chagall as set designer, the Soviet Jewish Theater produced stunning works while introducing Jewish themes into Soviet culture. In so doing, it promoted a "distinct Jewish identity." Once seen by historians as a mere propaganda tool, the theatre's deployment of "national forms—languages, myths, archetypes, and symbols—were semiotic systems that aroused pre-existing emotions and expectations among [Jewish] audiences familiar with the codes." Because the productions were in Yiddish, Soviet Jews often interpreted them as being more than mere propaganda. They were seen as distinctly and authentically Jewish. Just as the Soviet Union was in the process of creating a new man, *Homo sovieticus,* so too were the interwar producers of Soviet Yiddish culture creating a new form of Jew, the Soviet Jew. In 1926, the leading figure among Soviet Yiddish writers, Dovid Bergelson, declared in his article "Three Centers" that the Soviet Union, in contrast to assimilationist America and decaying Poland, would be the future homeland of Jewish culture.

In the field of Soviet Yiddish literature, Yiddish modernism began in 1917–1918 in Kiev with the group Eygns ("Our Own"). After that time, Yiddish avant-garde groups were to be found in Moscow, Warsaw, and Berlin in writers' circles such as Yung Yidish ("Young Yiddish"), Khalyastre ("The Gang"), and Shtrom ("The Stream") and among those who published journals such as *Oyfgang* ("Ascent or Sunrise") and *Milgroym* ("Pomegranate"). Until 1932, when the Communist Party forced all writers into the Union of Soviet Writers, great artistic and ideological diversity had been the norm among Yiddish writers in the Soviet Union. The demand for conformity compromised what had been an exciting quest for experimentation.

Those Jews who produced Soviet Yiddish culture occupied a particularly delicate role. On the one hand, they were both part of the state apparatus and proponents of the regime. On the other hand, by working in the Yiddish language, Jewish cultural activists played an important role in reaffirming and preserving a distinct form of Jewish identity. As adherents of Soviet language theory, many Yiddishists believed that the language reflected Jewish identity. As Esther Frumkina, a Soviet Yiddish activist observed in 1923, "Whether it is beaming or laughing, serious and harsh or soft and dreamy, dry or damp—[Yiddish] is always a divine work of art, always a picture of the people that created it."

Yet despite state support, Yiddish culture showed signs of decline, as young Soviet Jews displayed a preference for

Russian. Sales of Yiddish newspapers were poor; by the end of the 1920s, total circulation of the three largest dailies was only 28,000. Few people read the works of the prominent Yiddish modernists, the Yiddish-reading public still preferring the classics of Yiddish literature and even Yiddish translations of European classics above the latest avant-garde Yiddish offerings. With the destruction of the religious school system, the only Jewish educational alternative was the secular Yiddish schools, with 366 such institutions in 1924 and 1,100 in 1930. Student enrollment over that period increased from 54,000 to 130,000, but these children tended to be in Ukraine and Belorussia. In the Russian Republic, which had few Jews before the large post-revolution migration, less than 17 percent of Jewish students were enrolled in Yiddish schools. Even religious Jews tended to send their children to non-Jewish schools because there the atheist message denigrated all religions and not especially Judaism, as was the case in Yiddish schools. A prominent slogan displayed in Yiddish schools read, "He who does not work, does not eat," a reference to the "unproductive" Torah scholar. That Yiddish schools only existed at the elementary level further discouraged Jewish parents from sending their children to such institutions. Entrance to secondary schools (and, naturally, university) required Russian. Even though some party cells, courts, and trade unions conducted their affairs in Yiddish, most operated in Russian. Increasingly, Jews considered Russian prestigious while Yiddish was thought of as a cultural remnant from the shtetl. Advancement in all spheres of Soviet society was dependent on mastery of Russian, and that is the cultural route upon which most Jews embarked. It was not just educated Jews who took seriously the message that by abandoning Yiddish and adopting Russian social rewards lay in store. As a Jewish porter remarked at a transport workers union meeting in 1924, "For many years I have carried hundreds of pounds on my back day in and day out. Now I want to learn some Russian and become an office worker." Deepening acculturation among Soviet Jews was another reason that the Yevsektsia was dismantled. There was simply no longer a need for a Yiddish-speaking section of the party.

Until World War II, Jews tended to enjoy more favorable treatment within the context of Soviet nationality policy than other ethnic groups. Like Poles and Germans, Jews were seen as Western. A large intellectual class and a very high literacy rate meant in Soviet eyes that Jews were "advanced." Significant numbers had been convinced socialists even before the Bolshevik Revolution, and thus they were granted greater autonomy than those ethnic minorities the Soviets considered more backward and in greater need of cultural reeducation. One problem for Soviet theoreticians of nationality policy was the landlessness of Jews. Here, they were said to resemble "gypsies" more than Germans. Members of the Yiddish intelligentsia—and here they concurred with their archenemies, the Zionists—also found the Jews' lack of territory problematic. To solve the anomalousness of the Jewish situation, Yiddish intellectuals pushed for the formation of a Jewish territory in the Soviet Union. The regime also saw merit in the idea.

In 1928, Stalin implemented his "Five Year Plan," a program of agricultural collectivization and rapid industrialization, which would quickly modernize Russia. Stalin also sought to encourage socialism among the nationality cultures through a mixture of compulsion and reward. To attract Jews to the agricultural aspect of the scheme, the Soviets decided to create a Jewish territory in the vast, isolated area called **Birobidzhan.** It lay on the Soviet border with China. This region was chosen for four reasons: (1) to redirect recently arrived Jewish farmers away from agricultural settlement in Ukraine, Belarus, and Crimea, where their presence agitated locals; (2) to buffer the Soviet Union from Chinese and Japanese expansionism by creating Soviet settlement in Russia's far east; (3) to exploit the region's natural resources; and (4) to gain international recognition for the Soviets having established the very first Jewish national homeland.

A massive social engineering project, Birobidzhan was elevated in 1934 to the status of a Jewish Autonomous Region (JAR). In addition to those from Russia, Jews from Argentina, Lithuania, and the United States came and settled, desiring to participate in the great experiment. Ultimately, the Communist Party's goal was to establish an autonomous Jewish territory that promoted secular Jewish culture, rooted in both Yiddish and socialist principles. The idea was to provide an alternative to Zionism and settlement in Palestine. Birobidzhan boasted Yiddish schools, newspapers, and cultural institutions. The regional government also printed street signs, railway station signs, and postmarks in both Yiddish and Russian. In 1935, the government decreed that all government documents, including public notices, announcements, posters, and advertisements had to appear in both Yiddish and Russian, and in 1946 the city's main thoroughfare was renamed Sholem Aleichem Street. But the dismal conditions failed to attract large numbers of Jews. (The Jewish population peaked in 1948 at about **30,000,** a quarter of the total population). Land had been neither surveyed nor drained and was mostly unsuitable for farming, and as such less than a quarter of the Jews worked in agriculture by 1939, most having moved into traditional Jewish occupations in the service industries. In the end, Stalin's purges of 1936–1938 destroyed the Jewish experiment, as the JAR's Jewish leaders were arrested for "counterrevolutionary" activities. Even the wife of the region's Jewish Communist Party head, Matvei Khavkin, was imprisoned, accused of spiking her homemade gefilte fish with poison and feeding it to the secretary of the Central Committee of the Communist Party, Lazar Kaganovich, during his visit to the JAR in 1936. From an internal Jewish perspective, the Birobidzhan project was always doomed to failure, as the rapidly assimilating Jewish youth of the Soviet Union were uninterested in returning to what looked to many like a latter-day version of the Pale of Settlement.

Yet with all the opportunity and temptation offered by the Soviet state also came danger. With members of the Russian intelligentsia fleeing in the wake of the revolution, a substantial number of men of Jewish background filled the ranks of revolutionary leadership—such as Leon Trotsky, basically second in command to Vladimir Lenin; Gregory Zinoviev, leading theoretician, head of the Comintern, and one of the most powerful men in the Soviet Union following Lenin's death in 1924; Yakov Sverdlov, head of the All-Russian Executive Committee; and Lev Kamenev, a member and chairman (1923–1924) of the party's five-man ruling Politburo. The apparatus of Stalinist coercion, the Soviet secret police, or NKVD, also had a disproportionate Jewish presence. In January 1937, forty-two of the top NKVD officials were Jews. The NKVD was divided into twenty separate directorates. Twelve of them (60 percent) were run by Jews. Until 1938, the Soviet Foreign Service was almost exclusively Jewish. The reason for the disproportionate Jewish presence in the government and secret police had nothing to do with a particular Jewish penchant or desire to exact revenge on those who had discriminated against their ancestors in the Pale of Settlement. Rather, the prominence of Jews was a result of opportunities for advancement that opened up after the revolution. Despite their origins, Jews in positions of power had next to no regard for Judaism or sympathy for the plight of the Jewish people. Nevertheless, their prominence ensured that the Bolshevik Revolution would be associated with Jews in the minds of the revolution's enemies and antisemites thereafter. The facts that 72 percent of Bolshevik Party members in 1922 were ethnic Russians, and that it was Latvians who provided the highest rate of ethnic overrepresentation, counted for little in terms of Russian and foreign perceptions of the revolution. Everywhere, it was seen as a Jewish plot.

Although the Bolsheviks failed to win the support or sympathy of the Jewish masses, Jews took advantage of the new freedoms and opportunities that came their way, especially in the revolution's early phase. The changed circumstances made for the creation of a new form of radically secular Jewish identity, and a sort of Jewish subculture emerged. Soviet Jews came to occupy a disproportionate presence in the intellectual, scientific, and cultural life of the nation. In this respect, Soviet Jewry, in a strictly sociological sense, came to replicate German or American Jewry, even considering the vast political, social, and economic disparities among these examples.

The changes to Jewish life engendered by the revolution were dramatic and transformed the face of Russian Jewry. Jews were no longer prevented from living in certain areas. By 1939, 40 percent of Jews had left the area that had been the Pale of Settlement. About 1,300,000 Jews lived in parts of Russia that had been off limits to them as recently as 1917. In 1912, Moscow had a Jewish population of 15,300. In 1939 it was about 250,000. On the eve of World War II, 87 percent of all Soviet Jews were urban dwellers, and half of them were to be found in the largest eleven cities. Urbanization was accompanied by economic advancement thanks to the introduction of Lenin's liberalizing New Economic Policy of 1921. Less than 2 percent of the total Soviet population, Jews were 20 percent of all private traders by 1926. They also formed 40 percent of Soviet artisans (mostly tailors). The industrialization of the first Five Year Plan also altered the social profile of Jews, as they left areas of traditional Jewish settlement for the Soviet Union's new industrial cities. Between 1926 and 1935 the number of Jewish salary and wage earners tripled, reaching a high in the latter year of 1.1 million.

More literate than Russians—85 percent compared to 58 percent in 1926—Jews were well prepared to take advantage of the opportunities the revolution afforded. With free access to education and the elimination of the pre-revolutionary elite, the Soviet Union became an intellectual meritocracy for members of the formerly "exploited classes," a category in which many Jews found themselves. By 1939, 26 percent of all Soviet Jews had a high school education compared to 8 percent of the total population. Jews were to be found in the two upper grades of Soviet high schools at a rate of 3.5 times their share of the general population. At universities, even though the proportion of Jewish students declined with the overall opening up of admissions and the implementation of certain programs that gave preference to "indigenous" nationalities in non-Russian republics, Jews continued to disproportionately fill the ranks of university students. Between 1929 and 1939 the number of Jews attending university rose from 22,500 to 98,000, 11 percent of the total or five times their percentage of the total population. Jews were 17 percent of all university students in Moscow and 19 percent in Leningrad. In the Ukrainian capital, Kiev, they were 36 percent of all university students. In 1935, Jews formed 18 percent of the total graduate student population of the Soviet Union.

Where discrimination had kept Jews away from state employment under the tsars, urbanization, education, and loyalty to the Bolshevik regime saw Jews become white-collar state employees after the Soviet Revolution. Considering all bureaucrats who had served the tsarist regime as untrustworthy, highly literate and well-educated Jews were seen as indispensable to the revolution. Lenin observed, "The fact that there were many Jewish intelligentsia members in the Russian cities was of great importance to the revolution. They put an end to the general sabotage that we were confronted with after the October Revolution. . . . It was only thanks to this pool of a rational and literate labor force that we succeeded in taking over the state apparatus." By 1939, 82 percent of all employed Jews in Moscow and 63 percent of those in Leningrad were in state service. In all, there were 364,000 such Jewish workers in the Soviet Union on the eve of World War II. They were mostly bookkeepers, technicians, engineers, teachers and those classified as "cultural and artistic workers."

Soviet Jews also filled the ranks of the professional classes. In percentage terms that exceed those of pre-Nazi Berlin, Vienna, or any major city in the west before the war, by 1939 Moscow and Leningrad Jews comprised about 70 percent of all dentists, nearly 60 percent of pharmacists, 45 percent of defense lawyers, 40 percent of physicians, 31 percent of all writers, journalists, and editors, and just under 20 percent of all scientists and university professors. In the performing arts, nearly 25 percent of all musicians and 12 percent of artists, actors, and directors were Jews. The presence of Jews in the public life and culture of the Soviet Union was unmistakable.

The state's official support of Yiddish culture in the interwar period notwithstanding, the Soviet Union quickly advanced the Russification of the Jews, a process that was already underway toward the end of the nineteenth century. In 1926, only a quarter of the Jews declared Russian as their "native language." By 1939 that number had risen to 55 percent. Urbanization, increased educational opportunities, the atheism of the revolution, and the campaign against antisemitism all contributed to increasing contact between Jews and Russians. This in turn led to a dramatic rise in the intermarriage rate. Between 1924 and 1936 the rate of mixed marriages for Jewish men increased from 2 to 12.6 percent in Belorussia, from 3.7 to 15.3 percent in Ukraine, and from 17.4 to 42 percent in the Russian Republic. Into the period of the Second World War, Russian Jews for the most part were, to varying degrees, literate in both Russian and Jewish culture, the latter in either its secular or religious forms. The Nazi war of annihilation left millions of these Yiddish-speaking Jews dead. Those Russian Jews not immediately caught in the onslaught tended to be the more Russified Jews, those who lived in big cities, deeper inside Russia's interior. This

too sped up the process whereby Soviet Jews became less identifiably Jewish through traditional markers such as language use and religious practice. As in western Europe, however, the intellectual and cultural presence of Soviet Jews was so noticeable that they retained the appearance of a distinct caste.

Soviet Jewish distinctiveness extended to relations with Jews abroad. Throughout the 1920s, contact had been maintained through American aid organizations that assisted Soviet Jews. In the 1930s, as the Great Purge (1934–1939) spread fear and terror through the Soviet Union, Jews found themselves increasingly isolated. Even though the purges were not aimed at Jews per se, and many of those who conducted purges were Jewish (they later became victims themselves), Jews were always particularly vulnerable to charges of "internationalism" and disloyalty. With relatives abroad, they had to be particularly careful about contact with the outside Jewish world. Displaying too great an interest in Jewish culture, which was increasingly dismissed as "petit bourgeois nationalism," was also extremely risky. All Jewish political and cultural expressions were scrutinized for "errors" and "deviations" from orthodox Marxist–Leninist principles. With so many Jews in positions of political and cultural prominence, they were also disproportionately represented among those purged.

Poland Between the Wars

In the new national economies that were formed in Europe after the war, fear of Jewish competition and propaganda about Jewish exploitation led to economic discrimination and the imposition of quotas against Jews. According to the 1931 government census, there were 3.1 million Jews in Poland, the largest European Jewish population outside of Soviet Russia. Economically, the periods 1919–1923 and 1936–1938 were especially bad. Jews were usually the only link between the village producer in Poland and more distant markets. Peasants did try to sell some goods in the nearest towns, but those markets were too small and the peasants had neither the know-how nor the connections to compete in more distant markets. The consequences of the worldwide depression created an economic crisis in western Poland, the country's more industrially developed region. The shrinking economy prompted consumer demand for cheap goods, and Jewish peddlers were well situated to roam the countryside, selling their wares door to door. In the difficult economic circumstances, Jewish merchants and peddlers, with minimum operating costs, were able to survive. This only exacerbated tensions that already existed because of Jewish cultural and religious distinctiveness.

Despite the fact that Jewish merchants barely made enough to survive, a widespread propaganda campaign by Polish nationalists, especially the National Democrats (**Endek Party**), harped on the themes of Jewish exploitation and responsibility for Poland's economic plight. The fact that Jews in interwar Poland were overwhelmingly poor, with about 30 percent of them receiving welfare, seemed to have little impact on those who propagated the myth that Jews were enriching themselves at the expense of "true Poles."

The overall structure of the Polish economy was fragile, and both Jews and Poles struggled to make ends meet. Outright discrimination made the Jewish situation especially precarious. Already in 1919, the parliament had declared Sunday to be an official day of rest, meaning that Jews would not trade on Saturdays and could not trade on Sundays. In retaliation for their presence and as part of the scheme to nationalize industries, Jews were dismissed from government jobs. All but 400 of the 4,000 Jews who worked on the Polish railroads were fired, while all 6,000 employed in the lumber industry likewise lost their jobs. Of 20,000 people employed by the city of Warsaw, whose Jewish population was 30 percent of the city's total, only 50 Jews were employed in government service. The situation was so bad that thousands left, especially to Palestine, Australia, and Latin America, significantly changing the face of Jewish life the world over. In 1934, the chief rabbi of Radzilow, Yehoshuah Gelgor, wrote a desperate letter to Nehemiah Rozenbaum in Australia, who had migrated to the country town of Shepparton, near Melbourne, where in the 1930s there emerged a farming community of Polish Jews. The rabbi's letter to Rozenbaum gives a vivid sense of the terrible circumstances of one family but reflects the larger crisis confronting Polish Jewry:

> I do not know you, seeking your compassion for your nephew Zundel, son of your brother Yitzchak from Grajewo, who is in frightful condition, simply dying from hunger and cold. He is sick and bedridden, unable to earn anything. Our shtetl is very poor because of the crisis prevailing in Poland. Thus we cannot help him, and since I am a neighbor of his, I cannot witness his poverty and destitution and not write it down on paper. It is very upsetting when one enters his home. He is above all a sensitive man; he is embarrassed to talk about his situation. He keeps silent, but as a neighbor I know of his poverty. My conscience dictated that I should ask him for an address of friends abroad and write to them telling how their friend Zundel, son of Yitzchak, Rabbi of Grajewo, is naked and barefoot and hungry and his entire family is starving. He has three nice grown marriageable daughters who all sit at home with nothing to do. They would want to work but there is no work and there are no proposed matches since no one wants to marry a poor girl. Every young man wants a woman with a dowry. These girls don't even have proper clothing, and on top of everything, now is the terrible winter with a great frost and he doesn't even have fuel with which to heat the oven. His situation is very sad. So it is my holy duty to alert and awaken pity for him and his whole family and not allow him and his whole family to die of hunger and cold and be evicted from his residence since he doesn't have money to pay rent. Therefore you must know that if you direct your tzedokeh [charity] to this place, you will simply save people from dying of starvation.

Following the military coup d'état of 1926 by **Marshal Josef Pilsudski** (1867–1935), political conditions improved somewhat for Poland's Jews. He personally opposed antisemitism, as did the Polish Socialist Party (PPS) that he once led, and in 1927 the military government accorded legal status to Jewish communal organizations, the *kehillot,* and these became the channel for funding Jewish institutions and social services. But the death of the marshal in 1935 saw the radicalization of Polish politics, which became increasingly ethno-nationalist. The Endek Party, headed by **Roman Dmowski** (1864–1939), led the antisemitic campaign. For him, the Jews could never be Poles because "in the character of this race so many different values, strange to our moral constitution and harmful to our life, have accumulated that assimilation with a larger number of Jews would destroy us, replacing with decadent elements, those young creative foundations upon which we are building the future." Like other Right-wing Polish nationalists, Dmowski was bitterly opposed to the Treaty of Versailles, in large part because of its Minorities' Treaty, which held that Poland must guarantee "total and complete protection of life and freedom of all people regardless of their birth, nationality, language, race, or religion." He also wished to redraw the border with Germany that he believed had not been placed far enough west. Maintaining that Jews were responsible for the treaty, he claimed it was the product of an "international Jewish conspiracy."

Pilsudski was more accommodating on the issue of Poland's minorities than his bitter rival, Dmowski, who believed that Germans and Jews were threats to Poland and that to be Polish was to speak Polish and be Catholic. In his Poland, there was no room for minorities, especially Jews. But in truth, during the interwar period the political center and the Left came to hold similar views, even if they were not couched in blatantly antisemitic language. Neither Pilsudski nor the

Polish Socialist Party favored the possibility of any form of Jewish national autonomy and were wholly committed to Jewish assimilation. One way this was sought was by not funding the Yiddish or Hebrew school systems, despite the obligation to do so in the Minorities' Treaty. Jews and not the state were responsible for the costs. To make matters worse, the state denied graduates of such institutions admission to Polish universities. This served to guarantee that a national network of Jewish schools would fail and, indeed, it did. The majority of Jewish children attended Polish schools in the interwar period.

In the economic realm after 1936, the nationalists orchestrated an organized campaign of boycotts against Jewish businesses. Jewish businessmen had difficulty obtaining government-backed loans, while Jewish artisans could not get licenses. Official unions of shopkeepers and artisans even promoted a program to resettle Christian merchants and artisans in western and eastern regions with large Jewish populations. While the program was a failure, with probably only 1,000 Catholic shopkeepers and artisans making the move, the plan revealed the extent to which nationalists would go to remove Jews from the Polish economy.

Throughout the interwar period, Jews were increasingly denied admission to universities and enrollment declined dramatically, from about 25 percent in 1921 to just over 8 percent in 1938. In addition to the 1937 imposition of quotas on Jews, antisemitic violence and the constant threat thereof characterized the atmosphere at universities across Poland. Jews were sometimes made to sit on "ghetto benches" at the back of classrooms, and at some universities Jews were attacked and thrown through windows from the upper floors. Violence against Jews was spreading, and between 1935 and 1937 pogroms again swept through Poland, claiming the lives of 79 Jews and leaving about 500 injured. The prevailing atmosphere was summed up by Cardinal Hlond, Primate of Poland, who in a pastoral letter of February 29, 1936, declared, "A Jewish problem exists, and will continue to exist as long as the Jews remain Jews. . . . It is a fact that the Jews fight against the Catholic Church, they are freethinkers, and constitute the vanguard of atheism, and of revolutionary activity. The Jewish influence upon morals is fatal, and the[ir] publishers spread pornographic literature. It is also true that the Jews are committing frauds, practicing usury and dealing in white slavery." In favor of boycotting Jewish businesses but opposed to anti-Jewish violence, Hlond advised Poland's Catholics, "One ought to fence oneself off against the harmful moral influences of Jewry, and to separate oneself against its anti-Christian culture, and especially to boycott the Jewish press. . . . But it is not permissible to assault Jews. . . . When divine mercy enlightens a Jew, and

he accepts sincerely his and our Messiah, let us greet him with joy in the Christian midst."

Romania Between the Wars

Romanian Jewry in the interwar period was extremely diverse, some communities Western in orientation, with a Germanized elite, a majority Yiddish-speaking eastern-European type, a Hungarian-speaking community, and other communities that were variations on these essential types. However, irrespective of such internal differences—and they were significant—they mattered little to Romanians. Jews in Romania faced similar forms of discrimination as those meted out in Poland. Although this new state was formed in 1919, it resisted granting legal equality to Jews until 1923.

In 1930, of 756,930 Jews in Romania, 318,000 earned a living from commerce, and as was the pattern elsewhere in eastern Europe, Romania's overwhelmingly poor Jews were held responsible by nationalist elements for the state of the economy and the suffering of the masses. Parties across the political spectrum promoted a policy of restricting what they called "Jewish capital." Rejecting the nation's obligation under law to protect minorities, a professor at the University of Iasi, Alexandru C. Cuza, head of the violently antisemitic League of National Christian Defense, declared on July 14, 1926, "It is monstrous that the constitution should speak of the rights of the Jews. The solution ought to be to eliminate the Jews by law. The first step ought to be to exclude them from the army. Leases of forests granted to Jews should be canceled. All land held by Jews should be expropriated. Likewise, all town houses owned by Jews should be confiscated. I would introduce a numerus clausus in the schools." Cuza was particularly successful in winning support among university students, who agitated repeatedly during the interwar years for a total ban on admission of Jewish students. In 1922, medical students at a number of universities sought a prohibition against Jews dissecting Christian cadavers. Violent demonstrations at universities were common; the 1926 murder at the University of Cernauti of a Jewish high school student while he inquired about admission was only the most extreme manifestation of the hatred then gripping Romania.

The National Liberal Party, the National Peasant Party, and the National Christian Party were all stridently antisemitic, while the fascist Iron Guard Party, founded in 1927, like the Nazi party in Germany, elevated violent antisemitism to the center of its ideology. Its leader, Corneliu Zelea Codreanu, combined a bloodthirsty antisemitism with fascism and mystical Christianity. By 1938, Codreanu's rivals, the National Christian Party, under the short-lived dual leadership of the poet Octavian Goga and the professor Alexandru

Cuza, imposed antisemitic laws, inspired by Germany's Nuremberg Laws. Even though King Carol crushed the Goga–Cuza government two months after it took power, anti-Jewish measures were not rescinded, and by 1939 at least 270,000 Romanian Jews had lost their citizenship. In 1940, the passage of more antisemitic legislation, which now defined the Jews in racial terms, tightened the noose around Romanian Jewry. Property was confiscated, Jewish institutions were closed down, newspapers were shut, and Jews were by and large excluded from the nation's economy and society. In the late 1930s, despeerate to leave Romania, Jews acticely sought ways to enter Palestine. But British policy and the deteriorating conditions in Romania, including the closure of Zionist organizations that attempted to facilitate the departure of Jews, stymied the plan. In 1935, only 3,616 Romanian Jews emigrated to Palestine, a figure that was significantly reduced in the following years.

Hungary Between the Wars

In Hungary, the loss of the war, which precipitated the demise of the Austro-Hungarian Empire, saw the nation brutalized and dispirited. The country underwent a Communist Revolution in March 1919 under the leadership of **Béla Kun** (1886–1938 or 1939). His disastrous management of the nation and the economy led to widespread suffering. After a failed anti-Communist coup attempt in June 1919, Kun organized a Red Terror campaign with the aid of the secret police and revolutionary tribunals. Hundreds were executed, which in turn increased antisemitic sentiments, as Kun was never permitted to forget the fact that his father had been Jewish. As a result, all Jews in Hungary were held responsible for Kun's actions and Hungary's plight. In retaliation, hundreds of Jews were murdered by Right-wing extremists in a White Terror campaign between 1919 and 1920. The Jews, who had previously been accepted as Hungarians, evidenced by the large numbers that had been ennobled and the high intermarriage rate, were no longer considered truly Hungarian. Antisemitism dominated the political culture until the destruction of Hungarian Jewry in the Holocaust.

In 1920, there were 473,355 Jews in Hungary, approximately 6 percent of the total population, but Jews were to be found disproportionately in all areas of commerce and the professions. Little wonder that Budapest was known derisively as "Judapest." In that same year, the government of Admiral Nicholas Horthy introduced the quota system at the universities, restricting Jewish presence to a maximum of 6 percent of all students enrolled. While outright pogroms ceased because the economy was still dependent on Jewish businessmen, the refugee civil servants from the lost territories, along with the lower-middle classes and the small gentile middle classes, were determined to push Jews out of Hungarian public and commercial life. By 1938 there were 35,000 baptized Jews in Hungary, and when combined with a declining birth rate and emigration spurred on by the government assault on Jews, the overall size of the Jewish population went into decline, sinking to 444,567 or 5 percent of the total population. On May 24, 1938, the Hungarian parliament instituted race laws. Among other provisions, the law limited the employment of Jews in private businesses to 20 percent. A year later, the law was supplemented by further discriminatory measures, which included more stringent application of the numerus clausus, confiscation of Jewish landed property, and denial of citizenship through marriage, naturalization, or adoption.

The Balkans Between the Wars

The principal issue facing the Jews of the Balkans in the wake of the demise of the Ottoman Empire after World War I was poverty and discrimination, the two closely linekd. While the small Ashkenazic communities in the Balkans tended to be comparatively better off than the majority Sephardim, both communities were adversely affected by the overall decline of the Balkan economy, which had been ravished by the war. Social and economic dislocations also resulted in a rightward political drift so that the Jews of the Balkans faced similar difficulties to those encountered by other European Jewish communities in this period. Though Jews had been guaranteed equal rights in places such as Serbia, Bulgaria and Greece, enforcement varied widely and the widespread multi-ethnic tensions of the region saw Jews increasingly marginalized. In these relatively small communities—in the interwar period, Turkey, Greece, Yugoslavia, and Bulgaria were home to about 82,000, 75,000, 68,000, and 48,000 Jews respectively–economic and social pressure from nationalist forces proved a constant problem. Across the region, the creation of peasant cooperatives, government use of specially designated state import-export agencies, and the desire in Turkey to create a Muslim middle class to replace the role previously filled by Jews, Greeks and Armenians all had devastating consequences for Jews. Finally, the impact of the great depression of 1929 did severe damage to the Jewish economy in the Balkans. In the 1920s in Greece, Jews involved in the sugar, rice, coffee and tobacco trades increasingly shut down their businesses or transferred operations abroad. In Salonika, where the 61,000 Jews were one-sixth of the total population, they were responsible for a fifth of all economic activity. Their exclusion from economic life would allow many "true" Greeks to fill the commercial void. Jews organized as best they could. With the assistance of the American Joint Distribution Committee, Jews in Bulgaria formed their own co-operatives, and loan banks called kasas. They were helpful in small measure but the community faced increasing pauperization. By 1940, about 17 percent of the Jews of the Bulgarian capital, Sofia, received financial assistance from the charitable association, *Bikur Holim.* In Greece, two Jewish banks, the Amar Bank and the Union Bank continued to operate in the interwar period and loans to Jews were available but the overall trend in this once thriving community was increasing poverty, as it was across the Balkans.

As elsewhere, the social marginalization of Jews was nonetheless accompanied by increasing westernization and secularization. This is most apparent in the area of language use. In 1895 only 2.79 percent of Serbian Jews claimed to speak Serbo-Croatian. That figure had jumped to 49 percent by 1931. Conversely, over the same period, those who spoke Ladino went from 80.35 percent down to 30 percent. In Bulgaria, a cradle of Ladino culture, nearly 90 percent of Jews claimed the language as its mother tongue in 1926, a figure that declined to just under 40 percent in 1934. Ladino usage had also fallen markedly due to the impact of the ideology and education system of the Alliance Israélite Universelle, which discouraged Jews from speaking the language. (In Bulgaria, by contrast, the slow but steady Bulgarization of the Jews was due in large part to the disappearance of the Alliance schools). Also, the nationalist movements that emerged in these new countries insisted that all citizens speak the national language, and the fact that Ladino had its detractors, even among Jewish journalists and intellectuals who wrote in the language, further compromised its standing. In the 1920s, Atatürk's Latinization of the Turkish alphabet was accompanied by the Latinization of Ladino script. Subsequent to this and the general decline in Ladino usage in Turkey, Ladino publishing was greatly diminished. In Sarajevo, where in 1931 51 percent of Jews still spoke Ladino, Serbo-Croatian was increasingly used in the administration of Jewish community institutions, and even came to replace those newspapers previously published in Ladino. Even in Salonika, the largest Ladino-speaking community, Greek was increasingly used, in large part because of the state's rigorous and uncompromising Hellenization program. All over the Balkans, social and economic advancement required that Jews adopt the dominant languages and relegate Ladino to the domestic sphere. As with Yiddish, the Holocaust destroyed the last remnants of Ladino culture, while those who survived the Nazi genocide and made their way to Israel confronted a burgeoning nation-state that was singularly focused on the promotion of Hebrew, committing few if any resources to maintaining other Jewish languages.

Jewish Cultural Life in Interwar Central Europe

In contrast to the state-sponsored Yiddish culture of the Soviet Union, Jewish cultural activities that took place elsewhere in interwar Europe were private initiatives. Two of the most important centers were Germany, where secular Jewish culture was produced in the German language, and Poland, where Yiddish predominated but was not exclusive. Yiddish and Polish, together with Hebrew, helped form a rich cultural polysystem in Poland, with Jews using all three languages.

Interwar Jewish Culture in Weimar Germany

A combination of the encounter with their brethren on the Eastern Front during World War I, growing antisemitism after the war, and a rejection of the assimilatory path of their parents' generation saw young German Jews turn energetically to Jewish culture trying to reclaim what had been lost in the process of becoming German. But the German Jewish engagement with Jewish culture was not a mere process of reclamation. Instead, an attempt was made to create a specifically modern Jewish culture, one that looked to the past but did not wish to take German Jews back into it. Such a move would be impossible. Rather, the Jewish engagement with Judaism in Weimar Germany would foreshadow most contemporary approaches by Jews to gain access to their own cultural treasures by the "invention" of new traditions.

Prior to World War I certain German Jews, some very detached from Judaism, were already beginning to express an intense interest in their religious and ethnic heritage. Gershom Scholem, who left Germany for Palestine in 1923 and became one of the most formative figures in Jewish intellectual life in the twentieth century, turned to the study of Jewish mystical texts. In Prague, Franz Kafka began attending the Yiddish theatre and studying Hebrew, while Franz Rosenzweig, a man so alienated from Judaism that he was on the brink of conversion, recaptured his faith and became a Jewish philosopher of renown. Together with Martin Buber, Rosenzweig prepared a new translation into German of the Hebrew Bible. Many such figures were in youthful rebellion against what they considered the stultified Judaism of their middle-class parents. Kafka's bitter letter to his father exemplified such revolt:

> But what sort of Judaism was it that I got from you? . . . It was indeed, so far as I could see, a mere nothing, a joke—not even a joke. Four days a year you went to the synagogue, where you were, to say the least, closer to the indifferent than to those who took it seriously, patiently went through the prayers as a formality, sometimes

amazed me by being able to show me in the prayer book the passage that was being said at the moment, and for the rest, so long as I was present in the synagogue (and this was the main thing) I was allowed to hang around wherever I liked. And so I yawned and dozed through the many hours (I don't think I was ever again so bored, except later at dancing lessons) and did my best to enjoy the few little bits of variety there were, as for instance when the Ark of the Covenant was opened, which always reminded me of the shooting galleries where a cupboard door would open in the same way whenever one hit a bull's-eye; except that there something interesting always came out and here it was always just the same old dolls without heads. Incidentally, it was also very frightening for me there, not only, as goes without saying, because of all the people one came into close contact with, but also because you once mentioned in passing that I too might be called to the Torah. That was something I dreaded for years. . . . That's how it was in the synagogue; at home it was, if possible, even poorer, being confined to the first Seder, which more and more developed into a farce, with fits of hysterical laughter, admittedly under the influence of the growing children. (Why did you have to give way to that influence? Because you had brought it about.) . . .

Still later, I did see it again differently and realized why it was possible for you to think that in this respect too I was malevolently betraying you. You really had brought some traces of Judaism with you from the ghetto-like village community; it was not much and it dwindled a little more in the city and during your military service. . . . Basically the faith that ruled your life consisted in your believing in the unconditional rightness of the opinions of a certain class of Jewish society, and hence actually, since these opinions were part and parcel of your own nature, in believing in yourself. Even in this there was still Judaism enough, but it was too little to be handed on to the child; it all dribbled away while you were passing it on.

Most central European Jews were secular, so for those looking to "return" to their Jewish roots, something other than religious practice would have to necessarily constitute their Jewish identity. They became what has been called "post-assimilatory" Jews. Rather than revive and mimic authentic traditions, they sought to construct anew or invent a modern Jewish tradition. In some ways, what Jews were doing after World War I in Germany was similar in to what non-Jews were doing—namely trying to explore and recapture the spirit of cultures that were no more, thanks to the social and economic impact of modernity. Additionally, German Jewry turned increasingly to their Jewish identities in the wake of the Jew Count of 1916 and the increasing antisemitism in the postwar period. For others, the enthusiasm brought about by the political success of Zionism, which had secured the Balfour Declaration, as well as the intense encounter with eastern European Jews, both on the battlefront and with those who came as immigrants to Germany, energized and enthused those German Jews seeking to reject what they considered to be the sterile bourgeois Judaism of their assimilated parents.

The changes that occurred were most dramatic in the area of youth culture. In Imperial Germany, most Jews attended public schools and, where permitted, joined German youth groups. By contrast, in the Weimar period (1919–1933) Jewish schools were established and the Jewish youth movement blossomed. In cities such as Frankfurt, Hamburg, and Cologne, over 50 percent of Jewish children attended a Jewish school. Munich and Nuremberg opened Jewish schools that had been closed for lack of attendance decades earlier. In Weimar Germany, Jews were now mostly excluded from the German youth movements. In response, by the 1920s, a third of Jewish youngsters were members of a broad array of Jewish youth organizations from Zionist to Right-wing German nationalist. Jewish hiking and scouting groups became extremely popular, with even the most secular ones insisting on taking kosher food with them on their trips, more as an act of defiance against their acculturated parents than an expression of faith. Others attempted to play games in Hebrew.

At the center of the "renaissance of Jewish culture," a term coined by the philosopher Martin Buber in 1900, was the **Lehrhaus.** Established in Frankfurt in 1920 by the philosopher **Franz Rosenzweig** (1886–1929), the Lehrhaus was a school of Jewish adult education. Although its name is derived from the Hebrew *bet midrash* ("study house"), the Lehrhaus, characteristically for the larger project of inventing Jewish tradition in Weimar, was not a replica of the traditional *bet midrash* but was modeled on the vast network of contemporary German adult education schools.

The goal of the Lehrhaus was to offer a systematic "reappropriation" of Jewish knowledge through the teaching of classical Jewish texts and traditions. Pedagogically, the most original concept of the Lehrhaus was what Rosenzweig called "learning in reverse order." He sought to offer a kind of instruction that was "a learning, no longer out of the Torah into life, but out of life . . . back into the Torah." By this was meant that the teachers themselves had only recently acquired Jewish knowledge, "returning" to Judaism from having been on its outermost periphery. In 1913, Rosenzweig was about to convert, a promise he had made to his already converted cousins. He had written to his parents, "We are Christians in all things, we live in a Christian state, go to

Christian schools, read Christian books, our whole culture is based on a Christian foundation." Still, he asked for a "time of contemplation" so that he might study more closely that from which he was departing. It was the ten-day period between Rosh Hashanah and Yom Kippur. Attending Yom Kippur services at an Orthodox synagogue in his hometown of Kassel, he is said to have undergone some kind of epiphany or mystical experience, though he never discussed it. He reversed his decision to leave the faith, calling the period his "ten days of return" to Judaism.

At the Lehrhaus, the relationship of teachers to students was more egalitarian than was the hierarchical norm in Germany, and teaching was to be in the form of a dialogue not a monologue, with teachers only one step ahead of the students. The system was a great success. With branches across Germany, the Lehrhaus had enrollments of around 2,000 students per semester in Berlin and about 1,000 per semester in smaller cities. These were higher numbers than the corresponding enrollment figures for non-Jewish adult education schools.

The Lehrhaus was concerned with more than just imparting factual knowledge. A larger philosophical goal lay behind the enterprise. Though the Lehrhaus closed in 1930, three years before the Nazis came to power, one of the teachers, Richard Koch, summed up prophetically the aims of the Lehrhaus: "If our historical suffering should recur one day, then we want to know why we suffer; we do not want to die like animals, but like humans. . . . Often enough others and we ourselves have told us that we are Jews. We have heard it too often. The *Lehrhaus* shall tell us why and for what purpose we are Jews."

As part of the "renaissance" of Jewish culture in the Weimar Republic, the era saw the production of two Jewish encyclopedias, the five-volume *Jüdisches Lexikon* and the ten-volume *Encyclopaedia Judaica,* which covered A through L. (The project had to be abandoned with the rise of the Nazis.) These works covered all fields of the Jewish experience, but as an illustration of the modern and untraditional outlook of the editors, the *Jüdisches Lexikon,* for example, allocated more space to Freud than to one of the greatest of the medieval sages, Nachmanides. The editors were guided by the desire to introduce to German Jews the rich variety of Jewish culture, to reestablish the leading position of German Jewish scholarship—for prior to World War I great multivolume Jewish encyclopedias had appeared in English, Russian, and Hebrew—and to contribute to the creation of a modern Jewish consciousness among German-speaking Jews by presenting Judaism and Jewish history in the distinctly modern form of the reference book. Also, these works deviated from the model of scholarship established by the *Wissenschaft des Judentums* in that they concentrated less on texts and concerned themselves with the social history of the Jewish people. They contained lengthy entries on taxes, workers, Jewish communities, and trades, but there were also entries by the literary critic Walter Benjamin on "Jews in German" Culture and Gershom Scholem's seminal entry on "**Kabbalah,**" a decisive inclusion of a subject studiously avoided by previous generations of German Jewish scholars embarrassed by that tradition in Judaism. The more popular *Jüdisches Lexikon* was a lavish production that covered Jewish sociology, folklore, art, costume, and music and included superb maps, inserts of Jewish sheet music, and facsimiles of letters by famous personalities. Each of its five volumes had a print run of 10,000.

As part of the turn to Jewish culture in Weimar, a number of individuals began to use contemporary Expressionist forms in the production of Jewish art but attempted to claim the new forms as inspired by ancient Jewish culture. For example, composers of Jewish atonal synagogue music claimed they based their compositions on ancient Oriental Jewish musical forms. Others, troubled by the assimilatory trend of German Jewry, turned with appreciation to eastern European Jews, around whom a cult developed. The Jews of eastern Europe were prized as "authentic" Jews. Connected to this, German Jews involved in the reappropriation of Jewishness became enamored of Hebrew and Yiddish. While only a small vanguard made the actual effort to learn the languages, Hebrew once ignored and Yiddish once reviled enjoyed great prestige in this environment. The small number of German Zionists turned to the study of Hebrew, and by 1927 over thirty communities throughout Germany offered evening classes. In addition, the early 1920s saw Berlin become an important center of Hebrew culture. Authors, such as Hayim Nahman Bialik, Micha Yosef Berdichevsky, David Frischmann, Uri Zvi Greenberg, and the nobel laureate Shmuel Yosef Agnon lived there. Bialik even taught at the Lehrhaus, while **YIVO** (the Yiddish acronym for the Yiddish Scientific Institute, the major institution for the study of Yiddish and East European Jewish history and culture) was founded in Berlin in 1925 before making its home in Vilna.

Finally, Weimar Jews flocked to the theatre to watch Yiddish Expressionist productions by the Vilna Troupe and the Moscow State Theatre. Moscow's Hebrew-language theatre, *Habimah,* also drew appreciative audiences. With avant-garde set design and direction, what passed for "authentic" Jewish themes in the minds of German Jews was combined with their predilection for artistic modernism. In eastern Europe, at the time, Jewish audiences viewed such productions quite differently, as simply modern European theatre, something at great and welcome remove from "traditional" Judaism.

The experiment of inventing a secular Jewish culture in interwar Germany was, of course, the product of a minority of Jews but an impassioned one. How broad their impact in Germany might have become, we cannot say, for the storm clouds for German Jewry were fast approaching. But in the period from 1919 to 1933, German Jewry went very far toward creating a viable secular Jewish culture, one that embraced things Jewish in new and modernist forms, and with hindsight they can be said to have produced a model of identifying with Jewish culture that for the majority of Jews who are secular, has become predominant in the Jewish world. (*See box,* Jews in Austrian Culture.)

Interwar Jewish Culture in Poland

Despite the ruinous material conditions that existed for eastern European Jews in the interwar period, they managed to produce a glittering secular Jewish culture, especially in Yiddish, which reached its zenith before being abruptly cut short by the Holocaust. Polish Jewry at this time existed in what has been termed a *polysystem*—namely, a culture that was expressed in three languages: Yiddish, Polish, and Hebrew. One of the major differences between the secular Jewish culture produced in Germany and that to be found in Poland was that politics played a much greater, if not determining role, in Poland. Yiddish and Hebrew culture were generally linked to Jewish nationalist positions; Bundism and Folkism in the case of the former and Zionism in the case of the latter, with some overlap considering that as Zionism grew in strength in the interwar years, some Zionists expressed themselves in Yiddish. Even though they were often bitterly split, the adherents of the two Jewish languages were united in their rejection of the idea that a Jewish culture could be expressed in Polish—another contrast with the potential of a secular Jewish culture in German. That said, while the 1931 census demonstrated that 80 percent of Poland's three million Jews had Yiddish as their mother tongue, with 12 percent claiming Polish and 8 percent claiming Hebrew, increasing numbers (among the Yiddish and Hebrew speakers) were beginning to speak Polish in the interwar period. These figures, however, are not a true reflection of reality because there never were a quarter of a million Hebrew speakers (8 percent) in Poland, nor were there so many that had Polish as their mother tongue. Prior to the census, Zionists encouraged Jews to declare Hebrew as their first language in protest to the ongoing discrimination against Jews. Even the declared figure of 80 percent for Yiddish is subject to debate for there was a protest element within that, as some Polish speakers may have registered as Yiddish speakers. Whatever the true case, the overwhelming majority of Polish Jews spoke Yiddish but were often bilingual and trilingual, and the trend appeared to be in the direction of the increasing Polonization of the Jewish population.

By the mid-1930s, about 500,000 elementary-school-age Jewish children resided in Poland, of whom about 100,000 attended Jewish schools. Despite the increasing secularization of Polish Jewry, approximately 56 percent of all Jewish children were enrolled in religious schools such as Horev and other yeshivot, for boys, and the girls' school system, Beys Yaakov. At these institutions, classical Hebrew texts were studied with Yiddish as the language of instruction. At the Tarbut and Yavneh schools, Hebrew was the language of instruction, with nearly 34 percent of children attending them, while in the small Shul-kult schools, attended by 1.3 percent of Jewish children, a bilingual education in Yiddish and Hebrew was offered. Finally, in the TSYSHO (Central Yiddish School Organization), where 9 percent of children attended, classes were conducted in Yiddish. All these schools also taught Polish. The principal reason the other 400,000 elementary-age Jewish children attended state schools, however, was that state schools were free, unlike Jewish schools, so attendance there was less an ideological expression on the part of parents than it was an economic necessity. Moreover, to gain admission to state-run high schools—the Tarbut and TSYSHO systems also ran high schools—good Polish was required and Jewish schools were not considered strong enough in this area of instruction.

In a variety of areas, such as literature, journalism, scholarship, theatre, cabaret, music, the movie industry, and sports, secular Jewish culture in Poland blossomed. The field of Yiddish literature was especially vast, with genres ranging from cheap pulp fiction for the masses all the way to experimental prose and poetry intended for the intellectual vanguard. The literary group *Yung Vilne* ("Young Vilna") exemplified the diverse nature of Polish Jewish thought. Established in 1929, the group was basically Left-leaning, but of several tendencies, and left a lasting legacy, publishing literary works, anthologies, and periodicals. Among its leaders were the poets Abraham Sutzkever, Chaim Grade, and Leyzer Wolf, who concluded his autobiography with a sentiment that spoke for many in the group, certainly before the Holocaust led to its destruction and the dispersal of surviving members: "My distant ideal is: —a single nation. The world—a single land." But mostly, they considered it crude (and dangerous because of the Polish censors) to write overtly political poetry, preferring more subtle and sophisticated forms of social and artistic expression. The greatest and most famous of the Polish Yiddish authors of interwar Poland were the Nobel laureate **Isaac Bashevis Singer** (1902–1991) and his brother **Israel Joshua Singer** (1983–1944), who rank among the most distinguished names in modern Jewish culture.

Among the jewels in the crown of interwar Yiddish culture in Poland was the theatre. Operating on a shoestring budget, Yiddish theatre was exceptionally popular and a genuine vehicle for national Jewish expression. Comedies, farces, and revues were staged by small theatres such as Azazel and Folks Te'ater (People's Theater); cabarets were performed at Ararat; Khad Gadyo put on avant-garde puppet theatre, and Sambatyon was a theatre grotesquerie founded in 1926 in

JEWS IN AUSTRIAN CULTURE

From the end of the nineteenth century, Jews or people of Jewish descent had been central to the Modernist culture of Vienna. Sigmund Freud, Theodor Herzl, the composer Gustav Mahler, the playwright Arthur Schnitzler, and the writer and aphorist Karl Kraus are only the most well known. In terms of cultural criticism, Jews ran the three most important Viennese cultural journals, while those who sat on the editorial boards of the major liberal dailies were also primarily Jewish. The importance of Jewish involvement in the arts continued into the interwar period. But the political context had changed, and where once there had been a multinational empire there now was a republic, a diminished and fragile nation-state where antisemitism was rampant.

After World War I, some Jewish artists looked to the Catholic Church as a symbol of the multinational Habsburg Empire that had once afforded them stability, protection, and opportunities. In 1920, the Salzburg Festival opened, founded by the part-Jewish Hugo von Hofmannsthal, the Jewish theatre director Max Reinhardt, and the non-Jewish composer Richard Strauss. Under Reinhardt's direction, the festival opened with a performance of Everyman, Hofmannsthal's version of a fifteenth-century English morality play.

Hofmannsthal, who only had one Jewish grandfather, had already been charged with seeking to undermine German culture with his 1906 drama *Oedipus and the Sphinx*, which critics dismissed as having been written in a "Jewish–German way." At Salzburg, *Everyman* contained a Catholic redemptive theme, and Catholic liturgy was central to the play. Hofmannsthal even wrote the first publicity pamphlet for the festival in the form of a catechism. The antisemites reacted harshly, perhaps as much to the perceived Jewishness of Hofmannsthal as to his and Reinhardt's claim that they were merely attempting to draw universal and collective lessons from Catholic Baroque theatre, which, as Hofmannsthal hoped, would infuse the new republic with the spirit of the now defunct Habsburg Empire. In truth, the festival was reactionary but was seen as contrived by the true custodians of reactionary culture, who would not associate Jews with that kind of political or cultural expression. Hofmannsthal drew on Jewish patronage to support the Salzburg Festival, further tainting it in the eyes of critics by reinforcing the sense that Jews were outsiders, come to commandeer Austrian culture.

This was a sentiment that was further enhanced by the deep involvement of interwar Jews in the production of *Heimatoperette,* light operas with nationalist, Alpine themes, meant to emphasize the beautiful natural wonders and traditional values of Austria. The most famous of these was *The White Horse Inn* (1930), where the majesty of the Alpine landscape and nostalgia for the Habsburg Empire are juxtaposed with contemporary social and economic distress. The main composer, Ralph Benatzky, was not Jewish, but it did not matter, for scores of others who worked on the operetta were. For the antisemites, Jews, not being "true" Austrians, did not have the right to extol the virtues of the "real" Austria, the Austria of the Alps. In fact, the Austrian alpine tourist industry in the interwar period was an extremely conservative movement, as these regions attempted to modernize without industrializing. Alpine Austria sought to sell an image of itself to urban dwellers that glorified its stratified, rigid, social structure, its deeply conservative patterns of behavior, and its ethnic and religious homogeneity. Nevertheless, Jewish artists pursued Alpine themes, a further example of this genre being the silent film *Romeo and Juliet in the Snow* (1920) by the German Jewish director Ernst Lubitsch. It is a retelling of Shakespeare's story, but with a happy ending, and is set among the traditional inhabitants of the Alps. Jews were most decidedly not a part of Alpine culture, and thus their writing operettas and novels and making films about it were regarded as unforgivable transgressions.

The more Jews were deeply involved in European cultural life in the interwar period, the more some began to fear a backlash, imagining life in various European cities without Jews. The Austrian author Hugo Bettauer's *Stadt ohne Juden* (*City Without Jews*)

Warsaw. Yiddish theatre performed such Jewish plays as *The Dybbuk,* as well as Shakespeare, Molière, and Eugene O'Neill. A new artform came into its own in the interwar period—Yiddish stand-up comedy, particularly political satire. Performing at clubs such as the Qui Pro Quo and the Morskie Oko, the two greatest exponents of the form, Shimen Dzigan and Yisroel Shumacher, became cult figures, both in Poland and later in Israel after the Holocaust. It is a significant comment on interwar Jewry and its relation to the theatre that just as in the Soviet Union, where Shlomo Mikhoels was the un-

official head of Soviet Jewry, the theatre director Mikhl Weichert played a similar role in Poland. During the war, he would become head of Aleynhilf, the Jewish social self-help organization. Jewish theatre was not confined to Yiddish. Polish-language Jewish theatre was also popular. Attendance at both Yiddish and Polish–Jewish theatre was so high that Jews made up the majority of Polish theatre audiences.

Yiddish scholarship during the interwar period likewise flourished. Thanks in large part to the increasing number of Polish Jews with access to university educations, large numbers of 1922, Artur Lansberger's "tragic satire" *Berlin ohne Juden* (*Berlin Without Jews*) of 1925, and the satirical comedy sketch by the Yiddish comedian Shimen Dzigan, "Der letster Yid fun Poyln" ("The Last Jew of Poland"), performed in Warsaw in 1935, all signaled a world where the antisemites had gotten their fondest wish: the departure of the Jews and the return of culture into non-Jewish hands. These Jewish works all point to how boring and lifeless these cities had become without Jews. Bettauer, a Viennese Jew, sold 250,000 copies of his utopian novel *City Without Jews* in its first year of publication. Written sixteen years before Hitler annexed an approving Austria to Nazi Germany, Bettauer has the Viennese celebrate their triumph in expelling the Jews:

> For Vienna the last day of this year was a holiday unparalleled in the history of that gay and carefree city. By mobilizing all means of transportation, by borrowing locomotives from neighboring countries, and by interrupting all other traffic the authorities had succeeded on that day in sending out the last Jews, in thirty enormous trains. At one o'clock in the afternoon whistles proclaimed that the last trainload of Jews had left Vienna, and at six o'clock in the evening all the church bells rang to announce that there were no more Jews in all Austria. Then Vienna began to celebrate its great festival of emancipation. With his powerful voice, audible even at the opposite end of the square, the Chancellor [Dr. Kurt Schwerfeger] began to speak—briefly, coolly, but all the more effectively: "Fellow citizens, a gigantic task has been completed. Everyone who is not Austrian at heart has left the territory of our small but beautiful country. Now we are alone, a single family. . . . We must show the world that we can live without the Jews. Nay, more—we must show that we will recover because we have removed the foreign element from our organism."
>
> In rapturous delight, the crowd yelled, "We promise. . . . Hail, the liberator of Austria!"

The First World War had exacerbated the widespread and long-held belief that the promotion of cultural modernism by Jews indicated the unbridgeable gulf that existed between them and "real" Austrians. In 1927, the novelist Ludwig Hirschfeld published a humorous travel guide to Vienna and Budapest as part of a series of such guides to cities including London, Rome, Prague, and Cologne. Entitled *What Isn't in Baedeker: Vienna and Budapest,* Hirschfeld's book contained a chapter entitled "Peculiarities that One Must Get Used to in Vienna." One such oddity was the need to play the game "Is He a Jew?" According to Hirschfeld, this was the game that all Viennese played and, depending on the answer, residents of the capital then decided whether they liked the person or not. Since his is a guidebook, Hirschfeld tips his own hand by advising readers not to be "too interesting or original, otherwise you will suddenly, behind your back, become a Jew." Indeed, in Germany, the author Thomas Mann had expressed a similar sentiment: "It is a fact that simply cannot be denied that, in Germany, whatever is enjoyed only by 'genuine Teutons' and aboriginal Ur-Germans, but scorned or rejected by the Jews, will never really amount to anything, culturally."

Although Zionism grew in strength among Austrian Jews, especially among those from eastern Europe, the cultural activity of many Jews in interwar Austria was less specifically Jewish than the contemporary renaissance of Jewish culture in either Germany or Poland and tended to manifest itself more overtly in a liberal, pacifist humanism. Whether the creators were actually Jews—such as the authors Joseph Roth, Friedrich Torberg, and Stefan Zweig; the cabaret performer and composer of famous Wiener Lieder (songs about Vienna), Hermann Leopoldi; converts, such as the café-house wit Hermann Broch; philosophers, such as Ludwig Wittgenstein and Karl Popper, whose parents had already converted to Protestantism before theirs sons were born; or gentiles, such as the author Robert Musil—to the enemies of Modernism, such important distinctions of identity made little difference. They branded everyone whose Modernist culture they opposed as "Jewish," whether they were or were not. It would seem that all that was required, as Hirschfeld had said, was to be "too interesting or original."

of scholars produced historical, linguistic, economic, folkloristic, and ethnographic studies of Polish Jewry. Much of the work was sponsored by YIVO, with its headquarters in Vilna, the city known as the "Jerusalem of Lithuania." Among YIVO's founding supporters were Albert Einstein and Sigmund Freud, while the driving organizational force behind it was its director from 1925 until 1939, **Max Weinreich** (1893–1969), the distinguished linguist and historian of the Yiddish language. Under his guidance, the institute was dedicated to researching the history, language, literature, culture, sociology, and psychology of eastern European Jewry. From humble beginnings, it became one of the Jewish people's great repositories of knowledge. (After the outbreak of war, YIVO moved to New York in 1940, where it remains to this day).

Great impetus for Yiddish culture came from the Bund, the most popular Jewish political party in the interwar period. Dedicated to the preservation and promotion of Yiddish culture, the Bund operated a vast network of cultural activities, aimed in particular at future generations. Among these were two children's organizations, SKIF (The Union of Socialist

Children) and Tsukunft ("The Future"). On the eve of World War II, youth membership in the Bund stood at 12,000. With Jewish life under assault, these associations gave young Jews venues wherein they could express their Jewish identities and develop invaluable leadership skills. Jewish youth culture was extremely well-developed by the interwar period, with all Jewish political parties operating youth movements. In more than a hundred communities, the Bund also supported the Yiddish school network, which ran classes from kindergarten through a teacher's training college. In all, more than 24,000 students attended. The Bund also operated summer camps for impoverished urban youth, providing thousands with wholesome food and a welcome sojourn in the fresh air of Poland's countryside. Other organizations such as the Society for the Protection of Jewish Health (TOZ), funded largely by the **Joint Distribution Committee** in New York, likewise offered summer camps and published health magazines for young readers. Contributing to the deep sense of Jewish nationhood among Poland's Jews was the fact that the country had a vast network of Jewish social services that included, hospitals, sanatoriums, orphanages, welfare offices, and children's summer camps.

Polish Jews were avid newspaper readers, and the interwar period saw the Jewish press flourish. Here again, the Yiddish press outshone both the Hebrew and Polish Jewish press, publishing a wide array of genres from daily newspapers to specialist periodicals such as children's newspapers, health and beauty magazines, and sports papers. In 1936–1937, Warsaw alone boasted eleven Yiddish dailies (there were twenty-five throughout Poland) covering all points on the political and religious spectrum. The sheer number of papers is reflective of the diversity of Polish Jewry. No group of three million people could be homogenous, and Polish Jewry was split along issues of religion, politics, language, and geography. Even among Yiddish speakers, a large linguistic and therefore cultural divide existed between those who spoke Lithuanian Yiddish (Litvish) and those who spoke Polish Yiddish (Poylish). Amid all the secular activity, however, it should not be forgotten that the Jewish community of Poland remained an overwhelmingly traditional society, deeply attached to its religious heritage. Hasidism and Mitnagdism continued to flourish, and Poland remained the center of religious scholarship and publication.

Despite the dramatic growth of Zionism between the wars and in contrast to Yiddish, Hebrew literature and culture actually went into decline in interwar Poland. The reasons for this were a declining readership plus the fact that many of the best authors left Poland for Palestine during the **Third Aliyah** (1919–1923) and **Fourth Aliyah** (1924–1929), turning Palestine into the principal center of secular Hebrew culture. Despite several short-lived attempts, there was not one sustainable Hebrew daily or even weekly newspaper left, no Hebrew theatre, while only 12.6 percent

of Jewish elementary and 6.2 percent of Jewish high school students, respectively, received a Hebrew education. Commentators inside and outside Poland lamented the situation. On the absence of Hebrew literature in Poland, one of the country's last Hebrew writers, Z. Z. Weinberg, declared, "[T]he time has come for grave digging and burial," while an editorial from the newspaper *Ha'aretz* in Palestine asked, "Has the day come when Polish Jewry is fated to live like the other parts of our nation in America, Germany, Russia, etc., — without the ring of a Hebrew word? The idea is a terrible one and difficult to accept." But as a measure of the cultural complexity of Polish Jewry, Hebrew for secular purposes was not entirely abandoned. The relatively small numbers who wished to read Hebrew literature and newspapers now read the material imported from Palestine. In a similar vein, Polish Jews, even if they did not understand Hebrew, flocked to the Hebrew theatre to see performances by visiting troupes from Palestine, such as Habimah and Ohel. Still, Hebrew-language use trailed a distant third behind Yiddish and Polish.

With the establishment of an independent Poland after World War I, Polish was increasingly used as a daily language among Jews. A number of Polish-language Jewish newspapers existed, with the two leading ones in Warsaw having combined daily sales of 100,000. Rather than promote assimilation, most of the Polish Jewish newspapers were Zionist in orientation, published in translation the works of Yiddish and Hebrew authors, and were staunch advocates for Jews, especially in the face of antisemitism. Nevertheless, the Polish–Jewish press faced considerable hostility from the champions of Yiddish and Hebrew, who decried Polish-language Jewish culture as inauthentic and assimilationist.

A central element of interwar Jewish culture in Poland was the existence of a wide array of competing Jewish political parties. While the pattern and culture of Jewish politics was forged in late tsarist Russia, it came into its own in interwar Poland. Covering the entire spectrum of ideologies, Bundists and Poale Tsiyon on the Left, General Zionists and Folkists, represented by the smaller Folkspartey, occupied the center. The Folkspartey was Yiddishist, Disapora-centered, anti-Zionist, and anti-socialist. Jabotinsky's Revisionist Zionists were situated on the right flank as were, to some extent, Agudes Yisroel, the religiously devout, anti-modern, anti-Zionist yet nationalist party led by the charismatic Hasid, the Gerer Rebbe. All these and various small splinter parties vied for the allegiances of the Jewish people. In particular they aimed at winning the allegiances of Polish Jewish youth, who became intensely politicized at this time. As one measure of this phenomenon, over 100,000 young Jews were members of Zionist youth groups.

The central feature of interwar Jewish politics was its divisiveness. Polish politics were also fractious, but the Jewish situation—characterized by questions of "Here or there?"

Youngsters at Jewish summer camp in interwar Poland. TOZ, the Polish acronym for the social welfare organization Society for the Protection of Jewish Health, fought to eradicate the widespread incidence of tuberculosis, diphtheria, and trachoma among Jews in interwar Poland. One of the organization's mottos, "Air-Sun-Water," was intended to promote the benefits of all three. As the economic conditions among Jews deteriorated after World War I, disease became rampant due to the poor living conditions in the Jewish districts of Poland's overcrowded cities. To give children a respite from their dank living conditions, TOZ promoted summer camps across Poland that were attended by tens of thousands of youngsters. Here, before World War II, children at the TOZ summer camp in Pospieszka, just outside Vilna, sit in formation to spell the acronym TOZ.

"Yiddish or Hebrew or Polish?" "Religious or secular?" "Socialist or bourgeois?" and combinations and permutations of all these positions—made Jewish politics intensely complex and fractured. And as with most academic disputes, the intensity and bitterness of the splits was commensurate with the reality of Jewish political powerlessness. Jewish political parties were unable or unwilling to put aside differences or, at least, compromise. Without a unified voice, they were largely rendered weak and ineffective in the context of Polish national politics.

By the mid 1930s the three most powerful political forces in Jewish Poland were the Zionists, the Bundists, and Agudes Yisroel. In an environment of intense nationalism and antisemitism, the Zionist message was especially appealing, although its prestige was severely compromised by the fact that in Palestine the *Yishuv*—the body of Jewish residents in Palestine before the establishment of the State of Israel—had

proven incapable of absorbing large numbers of Jews, with only about 140,000 Polish Jews making it there in the interwar period. And within Poland, Zionism had yet to capture the trade union movement or large religious blocks. Still, Zionism, which had at times in the 1930s as many as thirty delegates in the *Sejm* (the Polish parliament), did benefit from the fact that most Western governments in the interwar period blocked Jewish immigration, leading many Jews to warm to the idea of Jewish self-actualization through Zionism.

A special reason for Zionism's appeal was that it was an umbrella ideology that could make room for socialists, antisocialists, secularists, and the religiously pious. Despite its commitment to Hebrew, there was even room for a Left-wing Yiddish Zionist party, *Linke Poyley Tsiyen* ("Left Workers of Zion"). Zionists were split between two visions: a Palestino- and Hebrew-centric approach dedicated to

MISS JUDEA PAGEANT

While many Yiddish and Hebrew speakers considered those Jews who spoke Polish to be assimilationists, this was not actually the case. One example of the deep involvement in Jewish affairs and the promotion of Jewish popular culture by the Polish-language Jewish press occurred in February 1929. In the midst of economic crisis and intensive antisemitism, the newspaper *Nasz Przeglad* (*Our Review*), which was sympathetic to Zionism, sponsored a beauty contest, the Miss Judea Pageant. Hundreds of Jewish women, aged eighteen to their early twenties, sent in photos of themselves to the editors. Just over 130 pictures were published, and readers were invited to choose the ten they liked best. The finalists were then to attend a gala event at the exclusive Hotel Polonia in Warsaw, where a panel of Jewish journalists would crown the most beautiful Jewish woman in Poland. The Yiddish press was dismissive of the contest, claiming that it mimicked gentile culture, was superficial, assimilationist, and was part of an attempt to destroy "real" Jewish culture—Yiddish culture. Despite such charges, the Jewish public was thrust into feverish excitement by the contest, never once considering it an aping of gentile culture. In fact, the contest generated intense discussions about the notion of "Semitic beauty," with articles in *Nasz Przeglad* about the need to promote it. Most of the contestants, in fact, conformed to stereotypical notions of "Oriental" or "Semitic" beauty. They were dark haired and swarthy, exotic types, diametrically opposed to what passed for "typical" Polish good looks—blond hair, fair complexion, and blue eyes. It is noteworthy that it was this Polish-language Jewish newspaper that touted the "Semitic" ideal of beauty, promoting it as something distinct and superior. This was hardly an expression of assimilationism.

The winner of the Miss Judea Pageant was twenty-year-old Zofia Oldak. In addition to becoming the toast of Jewish Poland, where she met the leading figures in Polish Jewish cultural and political life, Oldak was also the winner of numerous prizes, many of which were donated by some of Jewish Warsaw's premier boutiques. These included a fur coat, couture garments, perfumes, and a record player. But because *Nasz Przeglad* had promoted the winner as a Jewish national icon, the public reacted negatively, claiming that the prizes she won were inappropriate to her heroine status. The paper then promoted a Miss Judea Fund to which readers could contribute for "educational opportunities" for Ms. Oldak.

The positive feelings generated by the beauty contest did not last long. The Miss Judea Pageant soon turned into a political cause célèbre. When Ms. Oldak went to a gala event hosted by the Warsaw Kehillah (a quasi-governmental body comprised of different Jewish political parties), the president of the body, Hershl Farbstein, toasted her by reciting "Song of Songs." Farbstein was a member of the religious Zionist party, Mizrahi. His sworn enemies from the ultra-Orthodox Agudes Yisroel, who were also part of the governing board of the kehillah, attacked him viciously for reciting a sacred text to the winner of a beauty contest. Soon thereafter, upon the death of a leading figure of Agudes, Farbstein, as president of the kehillah, was scheduled to deliver a eulogy at the rabbi's funeral. Trouble broke out at the cemetery when Farbstein took to the podium to speak. His opponents shouted epithets at him while his supporters broke into a chant of "Miss Judea, Miss Judea." The chanting then degenerated into an all-in brawl in the middle of the cemetery. The whole sorry affair became grist for the Jewish humorists' mill as Yiddish satirists and cabaret performers produced stories, cartoons, cabaret sketches, and a musical recalling the whole affair. Because the events took place around Passover, even a parodic Haggadah was produced, with Miss Judea asking the Four Questions.

immediate settlement in Palestine and the more pragmatic approach adopted by the general Zionists, who wished to settle the Land of Israel but also to contribute to Diaspora politics by ensuring that Jewish national rights in Europe were respected. The split was important but not definitive. Sufficient agreement kept the movement intact. The virtue and appeal of Zionism was that it tapped into Jewish national feeling but also provided hope for some kind of eventual escape from existential threat and material want.

As large as the Bund was, its appeal was limited by the fact that its message was only meant for secular and mostly working-class Jews and, like the Zionists, Bundists too were unable to alleviate the plight of the Jewish masses. But the movement nevertheless enjoyed success, especially among the Yiddish intelligentsia and in city elections. However, it never succeeded in getting a single deputy elected to the *Sejm*. Still, as the conditions grew increasingly worse for Polish Jewry, the nationalist dimension of the Bund's activities, which included self-defense units, became increasingly prominent as its internationalist agenda began to diminish. The Bund's great achievement was to offer an alternative to an assimilationist path. It did this by tapping into the vast reservoir of *Yiddishkeyt* (Jewish pride and

ROK VI. Dodatek bezpłatny z dnia 31 marca 1929 r.   DO NR. 84   „NASZEGO PRZEGLADU"   13

NASZ PRZEGLAD
ILUSTROWANY

„MISS JUDEA".

P. ZOFJA OLDAKÓWNA OTRZYMAŁA TYTUŁ „MISS JUDAEI" NA KONKURSIE PIĘK-
NOŚCI ZORGANIZOWANYM PRZEZ „NASZ PRZEGLAD".
P. Oldakówna nosiła suknię ze srebrnej lamy i sortie gronostajowe z firmy M. Apfelbaum (Marszałkowska 125)

Zofia Oldak, Winner of Miss Judea Pageant, 1929.

The event illuminates some of the most important social fault lines of interwar Polish Jewry—the struggle between secular and religious forces, among religious political parties and between the Polish Jewish press and the Yiddish press. Here is "Miss Judea," Zofia Oldak, pictured on the front page of *Nasz Przeglad*, wearing a gown of silver lame and an ermine wrap fashioned by M. Apfelbaum of 125 Marszalkowska Street, Warsaw.

feeling) that informed the sensibilities of eastern European Jewry and did so by celebrating all things Yiddish. In so doing, the Bund was a major force in fostering Jewish nationalism and keeping Jewish culture alive.

Agudes Yisroel was perhaps the most successful of the parties in that it was able to control local *kehillah* politics and it ran the largest of the private Jewish school systems. But the increasing secularization of Polish Jewry, the slow drift to the adoption of Polish language, and the fact that its natural constituency, the Hasidim, remained mired in desperate poverty all meant that Agudes Yisroel was unable to alter the larger cultural trajectory of Polish Jewry or care for the most basic material needs of the Jews it represented.

Zionist Diplomacy Between the Wars

Not long after war erupted in 1914, British Zionists led by Chaim Weizmann approached Whitehall with a proposal. Weizmann sought British government support for the establishment of a Jewish homeland in Palestine, which, in turn, would support British imperial interests in the region. Both the govern-

SPORTING JEWS

One of the most important cultural developments in the modern period, and one that is directly tied to Jewish nationalism, was the participation of Jews in organized sports. Toward the end of the nineteenth century, Jews began to establish sports clubs, the first having been founded in 1895 by German Jews living in Istanbul after they had been expelled from the local German gymnastics club. A second Jewish gymnastics club, Ha-Gibbor (later called Samson), was founded in the Bulgarian city of Plovdiv. In 1897 and thereafter, clubs spread throughout Europe, the Americas, and eventually the Middle East. By the interwar period, sports were one of the most eloquent and ubiquitous expressions of Jewish modernity and secularization. Inspired by **Max Nordau** (1849–1923), the Zionist leader who, in 1898, called for the creation of a "Muscular Judaism," Zionist sports clubs such as Maccabi, Hakoah, and Ha-Gibbor had branches all over Europe. The Zionists' rivals in Poland—the Bund—also promoted sports through its network of sports clubs called Morgnshtern ("Morning Star"). In Hungary, the participation and success of Jews in both table tennis and fencing proved so spectacular that these two sports were identified as "Jewish." In the former, Viktor Barna (1911–1972), who won thirty-two World Championship medals, among them twenty-three gold, six silver, and three bronze, was described by Sir Ivor Montagu, president of the International Table Tennis Federation from 1926 to 1967, as "the greatest table tennis player who ever lived." Fencing, in particular, because of the upper-class milieu from which it sprang, was extremely popular among Hungarian Jews. Many of them were assimilated, raised as Catholics, or were converts. As was often the case, however, the disproportionate presence of Hungarians of Jewish extraction among national and Olympic champions only ensured that that they would be identified and stigmatized as Jews. Hungarian Jews, of course, celebrated their achievements. In the United States, the Detroit Tigers' first baseman and power hitter, Hank Greenberg (1911–1986), who was open about and proud of his Jewish identity, was inspirational to American Jews. Especially in an era of widespread antisemitism, American Jews longed for a muscular sports hero of their own, and that Greenberg played the quintessential American sport at the highest level ensured his iconic status in the Jewish community. His refusal to play on Yom Kippur in 1934 further endeared him to American Jews. Greenberg's principled stance was immortalized by the prolific American poet and writer for the *Detroit Free Press*, Edgar Guest:

> Come Yom Kippur—holy fast day wide-world over to the Jew —
> And Hank Greenberg to his teaching and the old tradition true
> Spent the day among his people and he didn't come to play
> Said Murphy to Mulrooney, "We shall lose the game today!
> We shall miss him in the infield and shall miss him at the bat,
> But he's true to his religion—and I honor him for that!"

In the 1938 season, Greenberg came very close to overtaking Babe Ruth's record of sixty home runs in a single season. With five games remaining, Greenberg had hit fifty-eight. In those last games, several pitchers chose to walk him rather than give him a chance to break Ruth's record. Greenberg never complained, but many observers—and there were non-Jews among them—believed that Major League Baseball did not want a Jew breaking Ruth's record.

In two sports in particular—boxing and soccer—interwar Jewish identity was forged and energized. In Britain and the United States, in particular, the continued existence of a Jewish working class saw many Jews take up boxing. Most of them children of eastern European Jewish immigrants, Jewish boxers adopted colorful names and often fought with a Star of David on their trunks. Men such as Barney Ross, Benny Leonard, Jack "Kid" Berg, Ted "Kid" Lewis (Gershon Mendeloff), "Slapsie" Maxie Rosenbloom, and "Battling" Levinsky were world-class fighters and electrified a Jewish world that was suffering discrimination and violence and was desperately in search of heroes.

In Austria, Hakoah Vienna was an all-Jewish social-athletic club with 5,000 members. It sponsored a vast array of sports but its soccer team was at the heart of the club and achieved the greatest renown. Competing in the Austrian league, the team finished second in the 1921–1922 season but won the Austrian National Championship in 1924–1925. Jewish players from all over the world made up the team, while Jewish fans the world over celebrated their glorious triumph.

ment and the Zionists were certain that the Ottoman Empire would collapse and that Britain would come to dominate much of the Middle East. Intent on controlling the eastern Mediterranean as well as shipping lanes to India, British authorities understood that a foothold in Palestine was necessary to that aim.

To achieve their geopolitical goals, the British concluded deals with various parties, some of which were contradictory and most of which were hazy in their details and obtuse in their language. Deals were struck with the Arabs, the French, and the Zionists. At the start of the war, the British cultivated

(Mirror Photo)

Preparing for Jewish holidays, Jack Kid Berg, who fights Phil McGraw in 10-round St. Nich feature tonight, bought talus (prayer shawl).

Judah Bergman, aka Jack "Kid" Berg, aka "The Whitechapel Windmill" (1909–1991). During the interwar period, when Jews were still predominantly working class and poor, they produced many fine boxers. In England and the United States, Jews were prominent in the sport, and a number of national and world champions were found in the lower weight divisions. Perhaps the greatest of Jewish boxers, Gershon Mendelhoff, aka Ted "Kid" Lewis (1894–1970), born in London's East End and known as the "Aldgate Sphinx," was the winner of nine official world and national titles. What especially endeared these boxers to the working-class Jewish public was that like Daniel Mendoza in an earlier age, interwar Jewish boxers celebrated their Jewishness. They most often wore trunks emblazoned with Stars of David and continued to live in the densely Jewish neighborhoods of London's East End and New York's Lower East Side. In the 1920s and 1930s, when Fascism was on the rise across Europe and antisemitism became increasingly virulent, Jewish boxers became folk heroes, not only for their skills in the ring. Many of London's Jewish boxers associated with criminal gangs, including the notorious "Bessarabians," led by Max Moses, at one time himself an East End boxer. Jewish boxers and gangsters also depicted themselves as (physical) defenders of the Jews, especially against groups like Oswald Mosley's British Union of Fascists. Mindful of their Jewish support, shrewd self-publicists such as England's Jack "Kid" Berg, World Light Welterweight Champion (1930), with a professional record of 157–26–9 (57 by knockout), made sure to invite a newspaper photographer along when he went shopping for a prayer shawl (*tallis*) on the eve of the Jewish New Year in 1929. He not only wore it in synagogue but into the ring as well.

an alliance with anti-Ottoman Arab nationalists through emir Husayn, sharif of Mecca and Medina. The British promised Husayn an independent Arab state, one that Husayn believed would include Palestine, along with much of the Middle East. For his part, Husayn agreed to raise an

Arab force to attack the Ottoman Turks. Led by his son, Feysal, attacks on the Ottoman government began in 1916. In that same year, the secret Sykes-Picot Agreement, named after a British cabinet member and a French diplomat, called for the postwar division of the Middle East between the two imperial powers. This agreement, of course, appeared to run counter to the promises made to Husayn. Meanwhile, some members of the British cabinet were convinced of the necessity of controlling the Suez Canal, the waterway to India, and believed that supporting the Zionists to achieve a foothold in Palestine was the best way of realizing their imperial designs.

For some British officials, however, it was not sympathy for the Zionist cause that led them to this conclusion but, rather, an exaggerated sense that Jews wielded genuine economic and political power in the United States and Russia. They believed that Jews could force America, then still neutral, into the war and that the Jews controlled the Russian government of the February Revolution. Some British feared that Germany, given its alliance with the Ottomans, might make some sort of offer to the Zionists, thus seducing world Jewry to the side of the Triple Alliance.

Weizmann, a supporter both of Ahad Ha-am's cultural Zionism and the political activism of Theodor Herzl, matured as a leader during the war. A chemist of considerable renown at Manchester University, Weizmann was heralded during the Great War due to his advances in the production of acetone, used in explosives production and crucial to the British war effort. As a result, Weizmann saw the doors of power opened to him. Possessed of great personal chemistry, this appealing Anglophile from near Pinsk, who mastered the English language, set about cultivating the British ruling classes.

Like Herzl, Weizmann often acted alone, to the dismay of his Zionist comrades but to the delight of the larger Jewish public, who greatly admired him. Some Zionists believed that Weizmann's success could lead to Ottoman reprisals against a defenseless Yishuv. Like other Russian Jewish expatriates, they were deeply suspicious of the Russian–British alliance. Within British government circles, there was considerable opposition to the Zionist movement, but Weizmann's powers of persuasion paid off. In November 1917, the British War Cabinet issued what would later be called the **Balfour Declaration,** named after Foreign Secretary Arthur James Balfour. It stated, "His Majesty's Government view with favour the establishment in Palestine of a national home for the Jewish people, and will use their best endeavours to facilitate the achievement of this object, it being clearly understood that nothing shall be done which may prejudice the civil and religious rights of existing non-Jewish communities in Palestine, or the rights and political status enjoyed by Jews in any other country." The wording was painstakingly crafted and went through several drafts. In addition to the commitment safeguarding the rights of non-Jews in Palestine, as well as Jews in the Diaspora, most significant are two small words: "a" national home—designed to suggest that Palestine would be just one of many places Jews might live—and "in" Palestine—to indicate that a Jewish national home or state would not take up the entire area of Palestine, just a part of it. This declaration of support for Zionist aims by the world's greatest empire was the first major political achievement of the Zionist movement and a personal triumph for Chaim Weizmann. Despite Weizmann's singular achievement in securing the Balfour Declaration, the Zionist movement faced some of its greatest challenges from within.

Ze'ev (Vladimir) Jabotinsky and Revisionist Zionism

Leadership within the World Zionist Organization (WZO) was held by a group called the General Zionists. After Herzl's death in 1904, this group supplied a string of presidents to the WZO: **David Wolfssohn** (1905–1911), **Otto Warburg** (1911–1920), **Chaim Weizmann** (1920–1931 and 1935–1946), and **Nahum Sokolow** (1931–1935). As its name suggests, General Zionism represented a mainstream element within Zionism, free of stark ideological positions and committed to the primacy of establishing a Jewish state over any class, cultural, party, or personal interests. An opposing group known as the **Revisionists**, led by **Ze'ev (Vladimir) Jabotinsky** (1880–1940), emerged to strike a far more militant pose. Hailing from Odessa, Jabotinsky was an intellectual of considerable force, a respected translator, and a revered orator who captivated crowds in six languages.

Jabotinsky saw himself as heir to Herzl in that he too emphasized politics and diplomacy. And like Weizmann, Jabotinsky aligned himself with the British, helping establish the **Jewish Legion** during the war. The Jewish Legion was composed of three volunteer Jewish combat units who fought for the British. Totaling about 5,000 men, they formed the 38th, 39th, and 40th Battalions of the Royal Fusiliers. All had very different experiences. The 38th Battalion, comprised of veterans from the Zion Mule Corps (created by Jabotinsky and Joseph Trumpeldor in 1915) as well as the British, Russian, and American armies, served as a true combat unit. The 39th Battalion, on the other hand, saw combat during the September 1914 offensive but also spent a great deal of time training in the desert. The 40th Battalion, known as the "Palestinians," included David Ben-Gurion, Levi Eshkol, and Yitzak Ben-Zvi. Ben-Gurion, known to his superiors as a poor and ill-disciplined soldier, even had his rank and pay reduced during his service. In contrast to the 38th Battalion, the 40th spent most of its time training in the desert and being "Anglicized" by British officers, who ordered them to participate in sporting events and educational courses.

Jabotinsky, a courageous commander of the 38th Battalion, was also a combative political figure. He brought his penchant for militarism into his political ideology, dismissing Weizmann's approach as too diplomatic and altogether too soft. He sought to convince the WZO to force Britain to uphold its pledge in the Balfour Declaration, which he took to imply the unrestricted immigration and settlement of Jews in all of Palestine, including the Transjordan. While Labor Zionism was determined to expand Jewish settlement in Palestine, create a Jewish state, and establish a new, Hebrew culture, it spoke the language of internationalism and socialism. It bore few outward traces of militant aggressiveness in its culture or rhetoric. This stood in marked contrast to the tenor of Jabotinsky's politics. Jabotinsky, a deeply cultured and cosmopolitan man, was also an admirer of Mussolini and was openly lured to Fascist symbols and rhetoric. (*See box,* Zionist Culture.)

In 1925, Jabotinsky formed the World Union of Zionist Revisionists, the name of which was intended to indicate the corrective he wished to introduce into Weizmann's centrist Zionism. Revisionism was always more popular in the Diaspora than in the Yishuv, where Labor Zionism held a tight rein on the political culture. Jabotinsky spent most of the interwar period in Europe, as he had been banished from Palestine by the British, who held the Revisionists chiefly responsible for the 1929 riots. He and his followers were convinced that some kind of a catastrophe, particularly economic, was about to befall European Jewry and that only unrestricted immigration to Palestine, coupled with the formation of a militarized Jewish nation, would be an effective response to the plight of the Jews. In Poland and other parts of eastern Europe, which in the 1930s were in the grip of ultra-nationalist and Fascist regimes with openly antisemitic agendas, Jabotinsky's message of aggressive Jewish militarism fell on receptive ears. Even though Revisionists carried out the important service of forming self-defense units against Polish pogromists, the presence of genuine Fascists in eastern Europe tended to moderate the behavior of **Betar** and the Revisionists in Europe.

In Palestine, by contrast, the Revisionists were on the political back foot as Labor Zionism held sway. As such, the Revisionists there regarded themselves as a revolutionary cell. As a radical vanguard, they tended to extremism. In 1932 they formed the *Brit ha-Biryonim* ("League of Thugs"). The league made a virtue of violent protest, its anthem, written by Ya'akov Kahan, proclaiming:

War! War for our country, for freedom, war—
And if freedom dies forever—Long live vengeance!
If there is no justice in the land—the sword shall judge!
The volcanoes will be silent—We shall not be silent.

In blood and fire fell Judea
In blood and fire shall Judea rise!

In 1933, on a Tel Aviv beach, Chaim Arlosoroff, the leader of Israel's main labor party, Mapai, was assassinated. Right-wing assassins were tried for the crime, and radical groups like the Revisionists found themselves severely weakened. In genuine opposition to the conciliatory position of mainstream Zionism toward the British and the Arabs, Jabotinsky led the Revisionists out of the WZO in 1935 after the Zionist Executive rejected Jabotinsky's hard-line political program. He resigned from the Zionist Movement and founded the New Zionist Organization (NZO). Its goal was to undertake political activity independent of the World Zionist Organization, lobby for unrestricted immigration of Jews to Palestine, and establish a Jewish state. Jabotinsky's militarism was not mere rhetoric. It split the Yishuv. In April 1937, during the Arab riots, members of the **Haganah**—the Zionist popular militia established after the Arab riots of 1920 and 1921—defected, with forces loyal to Jabotinsky forming the ***Irgun Tzvai Le'umi*** (The National Military Organization). Known also by its acronym, **ETzeL,** it was the military arm of the Revisionist Movement. In support of Jabotinsky's rejection of the Haganah's policy of "restraint," ETzeL launched armed reprisals against Arabs, actions that served to further alienate the Revisionists from the Jewish Agency, which condemned such behavior. (In 1944 ETzeL would declare war on the British as well.) One of the significant achievements of Jabotinsky's military operations was bringing more than forty boatloads of Jewish refugees from Europe to Palestine.

Zionism and the Arabs

By the end of World War I, various Zionist groups had articulated different positions regarding the Arabs. Herzl took a typically European liberal line, believing that the local Arab population in Palestine would welcome Jews, who would bring economic and agricultural know-how to the land. He imagined Arabs would recognize the advantages to them of Jewish settlement. In fact, Feysal's assurance in 1919 to the American Zionist Felix Frankfurter suggests a similar sentiment among some Arabs. Stressing bonds of kinship, Feysal wrote, "We feel that the Arabs and Jews are cousins in race, having suffered similar oppressions at the hands of powers stronger than themselves, and by a happy coincidence have been able to take the first step towards the attainment of their national ideals together. The Arabs, especially the educated among us, look with the deepest sympathy on the Zionist movement. . . . We

ZIONIST CULTURE

In 1923, Ze'ev Jabotinsky formed a militant youth league, Betar, an acronym for "Brit [Covenant of] Yosef Trumpeldor" ("League of Yosef Trumpeldor"), his goal being to imbue Jewish youth with the same martial values and spirit that typified the fallen hero of Tel Hai. Betar was also the place where the ancient warrior, Bar Kochba, fought his last stand against the Romans. This linkage of ancient and modern symbols of Jewish militancy became central to Zionist culture. It is for that reason that the festival of Hannukah was magnified in importance by the Zionists and transformed from a minor religious holiday recognizing the eight-day divine miracle of the oil into a national holiday celebrating Jewish resistance to oppression. Masada, too, became an important symbol in the Zionist pantheon of sacred places. The ancient hilltop fortress where Jews were believed to have committed suicide rather than fall into Roman hands was venerated as an example of Jewish heroism. Today, in a solemn ceremony held atop Masada, modern Israeli soldiers swear an oath to defend their country.

are working together for a reformed and revived Near East, and our two movements complete one another. The Jewish movement is national and not imperialist. Our movement is national and not imperialist. . . . Indeed, I think that neither can be a real success without the other." Feysal later claimed he did not remember writing the letter, while Arab nationalists claimed it was a Zionist forgery. Most likely it was written by Feysal at the Paris Peace Conference of 1919 to curry favor with the British and, because Palestine was of marginal importance to him, he had set his sights set more squarely on Syria.

In contrast to Herzl's attitude toward the Arabs, Ahad Ha'am was extremely wary and more farsighted, noting as early as 1891 that Arabs were objecting to the presence of Jewish immigrants, particularly to their purchase of land from the Ottomans. Socialist Zionism of varying stripes was riddled with contradictions. Socialists tended to express sympathy for the Arabs, whom they identified as similar to themselves: an economically exploited class. But their desire to lead the class struggle that would unite Jews and Arabs, pitting them against two empires—tsarist Russia and Ottoman Turkey—meant that Jews would dominate and lead Arabs rather than form an egalitarian union with them. Many Labor Zionists were convinced that only Jewish democracy would provide Arabs with an environment free of imperial oppression. Above all, the Labor Zionist belief in "conquest by labor" meant that their position would lead them into conflict with indigenous Arabs, including the displacement of many through the Jewish attempt to own and control the land. Ben-Gurion's constant recourse to the historic claims of the Jewish people to the land was typical of this contradiction.

The position of Jabotinsky and the Revisionists differed starkly from the more accommodationist approaches of the General Zionist and Socialist Zionist camps. Political maximalists, they sought to create a Jewish state on both sides of

the Jordan. In their vision, if Arabs were prepared to live under Jewish sovereignty, they were free to stay. If not, they were free to move to neighboring Arab lands. Jabotinsky believed that given Jewish political and military weakness, it was crucial to redress the power imbalance between Arabs and Jews. Only from a position of strength would Jews be able to fairly negotiate with Arabs. Jabotinsky expressed sympathy for Arab nationalist claims but believed in light of the threats facing Jews in Europe that Zionist aspirations were morally compelling. Testifying before the Peel Commission in 1937, Jabotinsky observed, "[I]t is quite understandable that the Arabs of Palestine would also prefer Palestine to be the Arab State No. 4, No. 5, or No. 6—that I quite understand; but when the Arab claim is confronted with our Jewish demand to be saved, it is like the claims of appetite versus the claims of starvation."

Mandate Palestine Between the Wars

In 1917, Britain invaded Palestine to defeat the Turks, and by September 1918 they were in complete control of the land. Palestine remained under British military administration until 1920. At the San Remo Conference, the Allied Powers divided up the former Ottoman Empire. Lebanon and Syria went to France, while Britain took control of Palestine and Iraq. British dependencies were called mandates, and according to President Woodrow Wilson's notions of national self-determination, the mandate governments were to lead their charges toward democracy.

By international agreement and in accordance with the terms of the Balfour Declaration, Britain was to facilitate Jewish immigration to Palestine. Eventually, the vague language of the declaration gave way to the evasive and obstructionist policies of the British mandatory government. From the perspective of Zionist leadership, the period of 1917–1920 was a period of growth. Britain dispatched Sir Herbert

Samuel, a Jewish former cabinet minister, to be High Commissioner of Palestine. With deep sympathy for Zionism, Samuel was permitted to deal with the Jewish Agency, the de facto Jewish government of the Yishuv. Jewish immigration to Palestine increased from 1,800 in 1919 to 8,000 in 1920–1921. In May 1921, Haj Amin el Husseini, a leading figure in Palestinian politics in the mandate period and a man appointed by Sir Herbert Samuel to the position of Grand Mufti of Jerusalem, instigated Arab riots in Jaffa and Petah Tikvah, which claimed the lives of forty-three Jews. As a result, in 1922 the attitude of Whitehall to Jewish immigration changed. Winston Churchill, in his capacity as colonial secretary, declared in a White Paper, "We do not intend for Palestine to become as Jewish as England is English." Britain then intended to limit Jewish immigration to a level commensurate with the ostensible economic capacity of the country to absorb immigrants. The Zionists were content to place a limit on Jewish immigration, for they too agreed that the local economy could not support an infinite number of newcomers. They came to favor a policy of selective immigration. The Arabs, on the other hand, were bitterly disappointed that the Balfour Declaration was not rescinded altogether and refused to countenance any form of Jewish settlement whatsoever. In 1925, there were 121,000 Jews in Palestine, a mere 14 percent of the total population, but by 1930 the number had risen to 175,000 Jews, or 17 percent of the total. The lower birth rate of Jews was offset by their lower death rate in comparison to the Arab population and the steady, though relatively small, influx of immigrants. During the mandate period, Arabs also immigrated to Palestine from surrounding countries.

In the immediate postwar period, the Zionist movement was beset by certain structural problems. The leadership of the movement was in Germany, while London occupied an increasingly important place. The majority of the Zionist rank and file, however, lived in eastern Europe, while the most important economic benefactors were to be found in the United States. But in the early 1920s, the funds and donations that the Zionist movement anticipated, especially from American Jewry, the largest financial supporter of Zionism, were not forthcoming. Beyond this, the number of immigrants, about 10,000 per year, was lower than expected, and Weizmann's leadership came under attack from various quarters—from Jabotinsky who believed Weizmann was too accommodating to the British and from far away in the United States. There, the leader of American Zionism was the distinguished lawyer, **Louis Brandeis** (1856–1931), who headed the Federation of American Zionists from 1914 to 1916, when his appointment to the U.S. Supreme Court forced him to give up that position of leadership. Nevertheless,

he retained a lifelong attachment to the cause. Brandeis was imbued with American pragmatism and had little patience for the ideological schisms within the Zionist movement. Because of his intellectual and moral authority, Weizmann saw Brandeis as a competitor. Their falling out was more than a failed relationship between two men but exemplified the fractured and weakened nature of the Zionist movement in the early 1920s. Brandeis, inspired by the political Zionism of Herzl, believed that the Balfour Declaration officially recognized Zionist aspirations and that attention now had to be placed on the construction of a sound economy in Palestine. Weizmann, by contrast, felt that the political work of Zionism was just beginning. He regarded the Zionist Organization as a provisional government and the Keren Hayesod (Foundation Fund), the name of the fund-raising campaign he launched in the United States in 1920, as the basis of a national treasury. Indeed, the workers' movement in the Yishuv drew funds from *Keren Hayesod* for salaries, agricultural settlements, public works, and industrial projects. Brandeis objected to this use of public funds. Although he supported trade unions and expected big business to act in a morally responsible manner, Brandeis saw the American Zionist organization as a business, obliged to seek out private investment, using public funds only for nonprofit initiatives such as medical care and education.

In 1920, matters came to a head at the Zionist conference in London. Weizmann publicly confronted Brandeis, telling him, "I do not agree with your philosophy of Zionism. . . . We are different, absolutely different. There is no bridge between Washington and Pinsk." In many respects, Weizmann was correct: Brandeis and the eastern European Zionists were utterly different. Brandeis had no time for Zionist theorizing, preferring to concentrate on rational organizing: "Members! Money! Discipline!" That is what Zionism needed. What further separated Brandeis from the eastern European Zionists was that he was not overly concerned with the Jewish character of a future homeland and instead regarded the American ideals of Wilsonian national self-determination, cultural pluralism, and democracy to be at one with the needs of a Jewish state. For Brandeis, Zionism and Americanism were fully compatible. As he said in 1915, "Every American Jew who aids in advancing the Jewish settlement in Palestine, though he feels that neither he nor his descendants will ever live there, will likewise be a better man and a better American for having done so."

Under the British Mandate, the various institutions and political culture of a future Jewish state were established. Western-educated and fluent in English, Zionist leaders in Palestine were able to develop close working relations with the British high commissioners. Since Palestinian Arab leaders refused to sit on a joint Jewish–Palestinian Legislative Council, Zionists were free to develop the structures and experience required for self-government alone. Driven by military needs, the ruling British authority built Palestine's road, rail, telephone, and telegraph systems, as well as the port of Haifa. When the Jewish state was eventually established, it inherited a modern infrastructure and its leadership had honed the administrative skills to run that state.

Still, despite permitting Jewish immigration, fostering Jewish political autonomy, and incorporating the weak economy of the Yishuv into that of the British Empire, British efforts were the fruit of self-interest. They did little to assist the Zionist Organization directly. Zionist settlement in Palestine remained tenuous and to succeed required massive financial assistance from world Jewry, as well as a steady supply of immigrant labor. In contrast to other modern nationalist movements, all of which had an indigenous peasantry, whose labor formed the backbone of a local economy, Jews needed to import a labor force to create a national economy that could support an independent Jewish state. This was extremely difficult. Although an agricultural economy carried out on collective farms, such as the *moshav* or *kibbutz,* became mainstays of the Jewish economy in the 1920s, Jewish immigrants to Palestine remained an overwhelmingly urban people. By 1938, only about 15,000 people lived on 68 collective agricultural settlements. Still, the ideal of the Jewish agricultural laborer captured the imaginations of Palestinian and world Jewry alike.

The **Third Aliyah,** (1919–1923) which brought about 35,000 Jews to Palestine, mostly from Ukraine and Russia, fostered a pioneer ethos that stressed themes of sacrifice, national rebirth, the anguish involved in preparing the soil, clearing malarial swamps, and defending the land. Central to the literature and music of the period was *halutziut* ("pioneering"), and the *halutz* ("pioneer") became a revered figure in Israeli culture. The sentiments of this group were articulated by **Uri Zvi Greenberg** (1896–1981), a Yiddish and then later Hebrew poet, whose uncompromising and sometimes violent imagery reflected the passions of those who made up the Third Aliyah. Building the land and defending it to the death were recurrent themes in Greenberg's lyrics and in the subsequent culture he helped create. As he wrote in "With My God, The Blacksmith":

And over me stands my God, the blacksmith, hammering
    mightily.
Every wound that Time has cut in me, opens its gash and
    spits forth the pent-up fire in the sparks of moments.
This is my fate, my daily lot, until evening falls.
And when I return to fling my beaten mass upon the
    bed, my mouth is a gaping wound.

Then, naked, I speak to God: "You have worked so
    hard. Now night has come; let us both rest."

The Third Aliyah was similar to the second in that at its core were young Jews with deep Zionist as well as socialist convictions. Their lasting achievements were to build some of the most important institutions of the Yishuv and what would become the State of Israel. In 1920, this generation of leaders founded the **Histadrut,** the major labor union. It built roads, housing, and expanded agricultural settlements. Beyond this, the Histadrut was also an all-encompassing cultural and social institution sponsoring sporting activities, a newspaper, book publishing, and medical insurance for Jewish workers.

The health care facilities of the Histadrut were supplemented by the work of **Hadassah,** the largest Zionist women's organization. Established in 1912 by the American Jewish activist, Henrietta Szold, Hadassah grew quickly and had over 40,000 American members by 1927. The large and energetic membership specialized in providing health care to both Jews and non-Jews in Palestine, and by 1930 Hadassah had opened four hospitals, a nurses' training school, and fifty clinics. With medical research laboratories, pharmacies, and prenatal and infant health centers, Hadassah was able to exert an enormous influence on the development of the Yishuv. It helped to drastically reduce the incidence of tuberculosis, malaria, trachoma, and typhoid. As a result the Jewish mortality rate fell from 12.6 per 1,000 in 1924 to 9.6 per 1,000 in 1930. Jewish infant mortality in the Yishuv also declined sharply over that same period from 105 per 1,000 to 69 per 1,000.

Among the most important developments in the 1920s was the political triumph of Labor Zionism. Under the leadership of Ben-Gurion and **Chaim Arlosoroff** (1899–1933), the Left abandoned its doctrinaire Marxism and made peace with the Yishuv's bourgeois elements. By 1930, the various streams of the left coalesced into **Mapai,** an acronym for *Mifleget Poalei Eretz Yisrael* ("Land of Israel Workers' Party"). Rather than shun private capital, Mapai recognized it as essential to the welfare of the Yishuv. Though Brandeis had been defeated by Weizmann, the American's belief in the need for private enterprise and sound financial accounting found a footing in the policies of Ben-Gurion.

The **Jewish Agency,** founded in 1923, was responsible for facilitating Jewish immigration into Palestine, purchasing land from Arab owners, and formulating Zionist policy. It was largely controlled by Mapai and the Histadrut. After 1929, the Jewish Agency also took control of the Haganah. This effectively meant that Mapai, led by Ben-Gurion, who had become a de facto prime minister during the British Mandate period, now enjoyed the allegiance of most workers, had built a de facto government, and had a military force under its control. Ben-Gurion's special achievement lay in centralizing the political, economic, and military structures in Palestine, placing them under the control of his own party. All such institutions could now be put in the service of the Zionist revolution, and for Ben-Gurion the goals of that revolution were nothing less than overturning 2,000 years of Jewish history, or at least his tendentious reading of it: "Galut [Diaspora existence] means dependence—material, political, spiritual, cultural and intellectual dependence—because we are aliens, a minority, bereft of a homeland, rootless and separated from the soil, from labor, and from basic industry. Our task is to break radically with this dependence and to become masters of our own fate—in a word, to achieve independence."

In its early stages, Zionism was a movement driven by secular Jews. By the 1920s, however, the voices of religious Jews in Palestine added an important dimension to Zionist ideology. Most crucial in this development was **Avraham Yitzhak Kook** (1865–1935), who in 1921 was appointed the first Ashkenazic Chief Rabbi of Palestine. Kook forged an important alliance between Orthodox Jews traditionally hostile to Zionism and secular leaders of the movement. Kook, who in his youth had personally opposed Zionism and all forms of secular Jewish nationalism began to see Zionism as part of a cosmic plan for divine redemption. Although he interpreted the work of Labor Zionists in ways they personally rejected— he saw them as unwitting servants of the Lord—both factions made accommodation for each other. Thereafter, secular and Orthodox Jews in Palestine and then Israel have reached a general consensus, deeply strained to be sure, but thus far workable, about how to live together. With the necessity that coalition governments be formed out of unions between secular and religious parties, both sides regularly abandon core principles for the sake of maintaining power.

The **Fourth Aliyah** (1924–1929) was of a different character than its predecessors. Restrictions on departure from the Soviet Union reduced the number of Russian Jewish immigrants to a trickle. At least half of the 67,000 Jews who came to Palestine in the mid- to late-1920s were middle-class shopkeepers and artisans from Poland. Fleeing the economic crisis that gripped Poland and the campaign to push them out of the national economy, they were not pioneering souls like Jews who made up previous waves of immigration. Rather, they were urbanites, who settled in cities, principally Tel Aviv, and expanded the economy of the Yishuv by introducing the commerce of leisure in the form of cafés, hotels, and restaurants, as well as new industries, particularly in the field of construction.

The development of urban culture (and economy) was reflected in changes that took place within Hebrew literary culture in the 1920s and 1930s. Writers struggled to modernize the language by making it less ornate, having it reflect as well as energize the language of the street. A distinctly hardedged urban poetry emerged that took account of modern life and its capacity to alienate. In his poem written after the State of Israel was established, "Said John Doe of His Neighborhood," **Avraham Shlonksy** (1900–1973) expressed the modernist poets' themes of fear, grief, agony, and boredom:

> The house I live in is 5 floors high,
> and all its windows yawn at their opposites,
> like faces of those standing before a mirror.
> There are 70 bus routes in my city,
> all chock-full, stifling with the stench of bodies;
> traveling, traveling, traveling, deep into the heart of the
>   city, as if one couldn't die of boredom right here, in
>   my own neighborhood. . . .
> The house I live in is 5 floors high—
> that woman who jumped from the window opposite
>   only needed 3.

Here was modern, Hebrew poetry that was neither biblical in its imagery, overly formal in its language, or idealistically romantic in its subject matter. It constitutes a complete rejection of social, critical realism and the pseudo-folk culture of much of the Hebrew culture that came before it.

While some may have felt psychologically estranged in their new land, the majority of those who faced difficulties were mostly victims of the economic crisis that hit Palestine in the mid 1920s. At least half of the 13,000 who arrived in 1926 left the country, while in 1927 more than 5,000 people departed, more than double the number that had arrived. Immigration stagnated in 1928 when only about 2,000 people arrived, with about the same number leaving. The Fourth Aliyah is generally considered to have ended in 1929, when Arab riots in Jerusalem erupted in protest against Jewish immigration.

More than 250,000 Jews came to Palestine in the **Fifth Aliyah** (1929–1939), the majority coming from Germany and Austria, after Hitler's rise to power in 1933. Most settled in urban areas; over half went to Tel Aviv, which grew from 4,000 Jewish residents in 1921 to 135,000 in 1935. German and Austrian immigrants expanded the commercial and light industrial sector of the economy. Most noticeably, this aliyah included many professionals, particularly physicians, lawyers, accountants, scientists, and scholars, all of whom greatly enhanced the intellectual life of the Yishuv.

Building Zionist Culture

Early Zionists sought to establish national cultural institutions, the most important of which opened in the interwar period. In 1903, Boris Shatz, a founder of the Royal Academy of Art in Sofia, Bulgaria, proposed to Theodor Herzl that a school of arts and crafts be established in the Land of Israel. In 1905, delegates to the Seventh Zionist Congress in Basel decided to establish the Bezalel School of Art, and a year later the Bezalel Academy of Art and Design opened in Jerusalem. From its inception, Bezalel was intended to be a national academy of art, its goal being the creation of a new, national Jewish style that would be achieved by blending Middle Eastern and European forms. The Bezalel School artists used Art Nouveau to portray both biblical and Zionist subjects. Besides the attempt to create a new style, what further enhanced the concept of a national school of art were the diverse origins of artists at Bezalel. European and Middle Eastern Jews worked together at the academy. Particularly influential in creating a national style of decorative art were Yemenite Jews, who possessed a long tradition of jewelry making, silversmithing, and elaborate costume design. World War I cut Bezalel off from its executive committee in Berlin, as well as from its patrons and supporters across Europe. Due to lack of funds, the academy closed in 1929, but under the directorship of the Berlin print artist Josef Budko, Bezalel reopened in 1935 as the New Bezalel School for Arts and Crafts, counting among its artists many refugees from Nazi Germany who introduced a new element into the design agenda of Bezalel: Bauhaus. Budko influenced a shift in Bezalel's emphasis to typography and graphic arts—particularly important in the public visual culture of the Yishuv, with its growing need for posters, signage, and graphics that were expressive of national development.

The arrival of numerous Jewish architects from Germany in the interwar years resulted in Tel Aviv becoming a center of Bauhaus architecture. Founded on sand dunes in 1909, Tel Aviv experienced significant growth in the interwar period. This coincided with the highpoint of modernist architecture's Bauhaus movement. Most of the architects working in Tel Aviv at this time were refugees from Europe and implemented Bauhaus designs, or what became known as the International Style. At least seventeen of the city's architects had been students at the Bauhaus school in Dessau, Germany, which the Nazis closed on April 11, 1933. Championing function over form, volume over mass, repetition over symmetry, Bauhaus architecture focused on the social dimension of building design and was especially preoccupied with creating a new form of social housing for workers. Some of the key design elements that were adapted for the climate in Palestine were the installation of small, horizontal strip windows, called "thermometer windows," to balance the need for light and for keeping out the strong sun, balconies to take advantage of the moderate climate, placing buildings on stilt-type columns, which raised them off street level thereby creating room for a garden area and providing for greater airflow, and finally, a flat, as opposed to the traditional, European steepled roof. The buildings are usually between two and four floors, built as a single building and covered with a shade of white plaster. In all, the style is characterized by asymmetry, functionality and simplicity. The modernist style of the architecture helped establish Tel Aviv as the first Hebrew City. It was not beholden to historic styles, but, rather, to the new, the modern, the avant-garde. The style was an apt expression of Zionism's social and cultural goals—the emphasis on practicality over decorativeness, collective well-being and simplicity.

During the interwar period the foundations of a national Hebrew theatre were also erected. *Habimah* ("The Stage") was the world's first Hebrew theatre company and was founded in Moscow in 1917. Out of the revolutionary and messianic atmosphere, which then had Russia in its grip, the country became a laboratory of both political and cultural experimentation. One such experiment was Hebrew theatre, and its use of the ancient, sacred tongue, for modern, secular culture. The language of the prophets also fit the language of revolution. David Ben-Gurion, who visited Moscow in 1923, was astonished. Knowing the opposition to Hebrew of the regime, and especially the Jewish Section of the Communist Party, Ben-Gurion asked rhetorically, "Does all this exist in the Moscow of 1923, where the state library does not allow Hebrew newspapers, and conceals many of its Hebrew books, where study of the Hebrew language is not permitted? . . . A sense of miracle grips me, a feeling of wonder, of rebellion against the laws of reality." Bialik, who had also visited the theatre in Moscow, was struck by how incongruous it was for there to be a Hebrew theatre in the Soviet Union: "Perhaps under the strange circumstances of the Revolution in Moscow, . . . Habimah, too, drank from the intoxicating cup affecting others. I do not know if the masters of Habimah will be privileged to enjoy again such months and days." What Ben-Gurion and Bialik saw was actually a multicultural event. Habimah performed in Hebrew the Yiddish play by Ansky, *The Dybbuk,* under the direction of the Armenian director Eugene Vakhtangov. Bialik was the Hebrew translator of *The Dybbuk.*

Led by Nahum Zemah, Habimah performed in Moscow for nearly eight years until it left on a world tour in 1926 to perform the classic *The Dybbuk.* The company never returned to the Soviet Union. While in the United States in 1927, Habimah split. Some, including Zemah, stayed in America while the others went to Palestine in 1928. Although many accomplished Hebrew prose stylists and poets were working in Palestine at this time, few playwrights were. The earliest plays staged by Habimah were the historical dramas *B'layil Zeh* (*On This Night,* 1934), which depicted the destruction of the Temple in Jerusalem, and *Yerushalayim ve-Romi* (*Jerusalem and Rome,* 1939) about the ancient Roman Jew Josephus. By 1930, three professional Hebrew theatre companies were active in the Yishuv, but it was Habimah, which later developed into the National Theater of Israel.

As far back as 1884, Hibbat Tsiyon had proposed the establishment of a university where instruction would take place in Hebrew. This remained a goal of many within the Zionist movement, but funding and staffing such an institution took time. While the cornerstone of the Hebrew University in Jerusalem was laid in 1918, it was not until 1925 that the institution finally opened its doors. The faculty comprised almost exclusively academics from German-speaking Europe who had come in the Fifth Aliyah. The Technion in Haifa, dedicated to research and instruction in the sciences, was opened in 1924 by the German Jewish foundation Ezrah. In the twelve years between the laying of the cornerstone in 1912 and the beginning of classes, a bitter debate over the language of instruction took place. Ezrah, which had managed to open twenty other schools between 1912 and 1913, demanded that German be used at the Technion, for it was the preeminent language of science. The organization challenged the partisans of Hebrew, claiming that the ideas and practice of modern science could not be expressed in the ancient language. After Germany's defeat in World War I, instruction in Hebrew became the norm throughout Palestine. Both the Hebrew University and the Technion were more than places of higher learning: They were national institutions, established to educate leaders of a new, modern nation by providing them with a secular education in Hebrew. During the interwar period, the revolutionary and youthful leadership of the Yishuv were successful in building the institutions and essential characteristics of Zionist culture, one that was felt in all fields of the arts, scholarship, and public sector service. This new Jewish culture was vital, as it was informed by both European and Jewish elements fused in an entirely novel and experimental way.

Tensions with the Palestinian Arabs

At first, European Zionist aspirations were animated by the myth that the Land of Israel was empty of inhabitants. But those Jews who migrated there soon found out that this was far from the case. About 700,000 non-Jews were living in Palestine in 1914, a number that increased to nearly 1 million by 1939. Rather than the benign, cooperative relationship between Jews and Arabs that Herzl and many later Labor Zionists imagined, the encounter was marked by hostility and a recurring cycle of violence. From the beginning of Zionist settlement, neither side has been willing to see the merits in the other party's claims. From the Zionist perspective, the young immigrant Jews harbored utopian and peaceful visions of a Hebrew future on the land; for Palestinian Arabs, predatory colonialists from Europe had come to dispossess them. Jews assumed that Arabs would welcome their technological and scientific know-how and were

convinced that Arabs would appreciate the material benefits of modern, productive land management.

So long as the size of the Jewish population was negligible, so too was Arab protest against the Jewish presence. This changed during the interwar period as the Jewish population of Palestine grew from about 85,000 in 1914, or 12 percent of the total population, to 475,000, or approximately 31 percent of the total population on the eve of World War II. Growing Arab nationalism, hatred of the British mandatory authorities, and genuine fear of displacement due to the growing stream of Jewish immigrants—most of them refugees fleeing Europe, and to a lesser extent, a host of countries in the Middle East— led to increasing Arab frustration and anti-Jewish violence. In 1920, Arabs attacked the Jewish settlement in the Upper Galilee at Tel Hai and killed eight Jews, among them the Zionist leader and veteran of the Russo-Japanese war, **Yosef Trumpeldor** (1880–1920). His last words were purported to be "Never mind, it is good to die for our country." Revered by the political Right as an example of the muscular Jew who fought back and by the political Left as a defender of socialist agricultural settlements, Trumpeldor's death became an inspiration and a milestone in Zionist collective memory.

On September 24, 1928, a minor incident at Jerusalem's Wailing Wall, which was under Muslim jurisdiction, led to rioting and substantial loss of life. Orthodox Jews erected a screen to separate Jewish male and female worshippers. Arabs considered this a provocative first step to a Jewish takeover of the Al-Aqsa Mosque on al-Haram al-Sharif, or the Temple Mount. Protests and counterprotests ensued. For nearly a year tensions simmered, until August 23, 1929, when bands of armed Arabs marched on Jerusalem and attacked the Jewish quarter of the Old City. The rioting soon spread to Haifa, Jaffa, and Tel Aviv. For five days the bloodletting continued. The result was 133 Jews killed, 60 of them massacred in Hebron. In repelling the rioters, the British killed 116 Arabs.

One of the most significant Zionist responses to increasing Arab militancy was the formation of the **Haganah** defense organization. Originally a popular militia, established after the riots of 1920 and 1921 for the purposes of protecting agricultural settlements, the Haganah lacked a strong central authority, was poorly equipped, and lacked proper training. Thereafter, and particularly in response to the Arab Revolt of 1929, the Haganah was transformed into a better-trained and more effective armed force. By 1936, the Haganah had 10,000 men under arms and about 40,000 reservists. Soldiers were now equipped with arms purchased from overseas and with light weapons they manufactured themselves.

The British response to the riots made it clear to the Yishuv that they were losing the confidence of Whitehall. The colonial secretary, Lord Passfield, issued a White Paper in 1930, recommending that Jewish land purchases and

"White City" in Tel Aviv (1930s). A district where the buildings are covered with a shade of white plaster, hence the name of the area. The buildings were mostly residential, but many commercial structures were also built in this style, including the building that housed a pharmacy in the right foreground of this photograph. This image of Ben-Yehuda Street gives a sense of the extent to which white Bauhaus buildings predominate Tel Aviv's architectural landscape, giving it the greatest collection of Bauhaus architecture in the world. In "White City," about 4,000 such buildings were constructed between the 1930s and 1948. An intense period of building coincided with the arrival of refugees from Nazi Germany, when 2,700 buildings were constructed in this style between 1931 and 1937. Lack of funds, the harsh beach weather, and a neglect of the buildings when the style fell out of fashion means that today many of the buildings are in a state of disrepair. Approximately 1,100 of these International Style buildings are slated for preservation. White City is considered such an architectural gem that in July 2003 UNESCO, the United Nations Educational, Scientific and Cultural Organization, proclaimed "The White City" of Tel Aviv–Jaffa a World Cultural Heritage site.

immigration levels be restricted. Although the British prime minister, Ramsay MacDonald, essentially overturned the White Paper in 1931, it was clear to Chaim Weizmann that doors, which had once been open to him, were now closing. Even Jewish deaths at the hands of the Arabs failed to arouse British sympathy. Beatrice Webb, Lord Passfield's wife, commented callously, "I can't understand why the Jews make such a fuss over a few dozen of their people killed in Palestine. As many are killed every week in London in traffic accidents, and no one pays any attention." At the official level, the British were beginning to realize that they could not adhere to the terms of the

Balfour Declaration and accommodate Arab demands at the same time.

The increasingly precarious plight of Jews in Poland and Germany encouraged Jewish immigration to Palestine throughout the 1930s. This in turn exacerbated Arab opposition and led to increasingly organized protests, the most significant of which was the Arab Revolt of 1936–1939. In 1936, a loose coalition of Arab political parties, known as the Arab Higher Committee (AHC), was created. Led by the Grand Mufti Haj Amin al-Husayni, it declared a national strike in April 1936, a boycott of all Jewish and British products, and a tax revolt in support of three basic demands: the cessation of Jewish immigration, an end to all further land sales to the Jews, and the establishment of an Arab national government. The protests soon turned violent, with attacks directed at both the Jews and the British. With the aid of their regional Arab allies, the British were able to mediate a ceasefire, which fell apart in 1937. Between 1937 and 1939 Palestine was drenched in blood. With the aid of Syria, Iraq, and Egypt, Palestinian resistance to Zionism took on the character of a pan-Arab nationalist uprising. (Nazi and Italian Fascist agents also offered encouragement and assistance.) Arab demands and expectations grew as the uprising became intertwined with a peasant revolt. Internecine feuds also erupted. Poverty-stricken *fellahin* attacked Palestinian landowners, British authorities, and Jews. The British responded with brutal force. By 1939, nearly 5,000 Arabs and 415 Jews had been killed, and thousands were wounded and imprisoned. The AHC was dissolved, and Amin al-Husayni fled to avoid capture by the British.

In the midst of the Arab Revolt, the British **Peel Commission** (1937), issued its recommendation for the partition of Palestine into Jewish and Arab states. The Arab state, the larger of the two, was to be united with Transjordan and would consist of what is today the West Bank, the Gaza Strip, and the Negev. The Jewish state was to consist of the Mediterranean coastal plain and the Galilee. The zone between Jaffa and Jerusalem, including both of those cities, would remain under British control.

The Arabs rejected the partition plan; the Zionist leadership, while opposed to the proposed size of the Jewish state, nonetheless grudgingly accepted it. However, important Zionist factions rejected the partition, the most significant being the Revisionists led by Ze'ev Jabotinsky. A smaller group of religious Zionists also rejected partition, believing that God had promised the Land of Israel in its entirety to the Jewish people.

As the 1930s passed, it became increasingly clear to Britain that war with Nazi Germany was a distinct possibility. England needed allies in the Near East. Just as Jabotinsky had been drawn to the Fascism of Mussolini, so too were many Arab nationalists attracted to Hitler's message, especially his antisemitism. Yet Britain could not chance alienating the Arabs by accommodating Zionist ambitions, and it could ill afford to jeopardize its access to oil, a resource that it would desperately need should the nation find itself at war. The British White Paper of 1939 reflected a change in attitude to Zionism and fears for the health of the British Empire in the face of Nazi belligerence and Italian designs on North Africa and the Mediterranean. The British then renounced the idea of partition, declaring that Arab Palestine would become an independent state within ten years and that Jewish immigration would be limited to a further 75,000 people over the next five years.

The Jews of the Eastern Levant and Muslim Lands

Around 1914, while nearly 90 percent of the world's Jews were of Ashkenazic origin, approximately 1 million Jews of Sephardic and Middle Eastern descent were still living in the Balkans and in Muslim lands, stretching from Morocco to Afghanistan. These communities were highly differentiated from one another culturally and socioeconomically, living under a variety of political regimes. The massive changes that affected the Muslim world in the nineteenth and into the twentieth centuries are manifold. Internal and external causes were both driving political, social, and economic transformations, with the impact of European dominance in the area among the most important. Certainly for Jews of the region, European, especially French, hegemony played a decisive role in changing the character of Sephardic and Middle Eastern communities. This historical influence was highly uneven, with communities such as those in Istanbul, Baghdad, and Tehran far more receptive to westernization than Jewish communities in, say, Kurdistan, Afghanistan, and the interior of Yemen.

Language is an important marker of difference among these Jews. The Sephardic communities of western Europe retained Spanish and Portuguese into the eighteenth century. Neither was ever written in Hebrew script and can make no claim to being Jewish languages. Thereafter, descendants of European Sephardim adopted the local vernacular. By contrast, Sephardic Jewry in the Ottoman Empire, especially in the Balkans and in Turkey, developed Ladino into the Jewish vernacular. The Ottomanization of Balkan Jewry came at the expense of the indigenous, Greek-speaking Romaniot Jews, who largely disappeared, demographically swamped by the large Sephardic influx beginning in the sixteenth century. In the Balkans, Ladino retained Spanish as the core language but liberally incorporated Hebrew, Turkish, and Greek. Unlike other Jewish languages, it was written in Rashi script, originally a fifteenth-century form of cursive script used by Spanish Jews. Eastern Sephardim have used numerous names for their language in addition to Ladino: *Espaniol* (Spanish), *muestro Espaniol* ("our Spanish"), and *djudezmo*.

Ironically, Ladino culture flourished where French, thanks to the Alliance Israélite Universelle, made its greatest inroads. French became the language of high culture, but Ladino remained the language of the Jewish masses and catered to their tastes with scores of newspapers, novels, plays, and translations. At the same time, the number of religious texts appearing in Ladino went into marked decline, as Jews increasingly wanted their Ladino literature to reflect their secular sensibilities.

Across North Africa, the Sephardic population never exceeded that of the indigenous Jewish communities. Spanish soon died out, and Sephardim, like native-born Jews, began to speak Judeo-Arabic. (A few small communities in northern Morocco, such as Tangier and Tetuán, spoke a form of Judeo-Spanish called Haketia, which remained in use until the twentieth century.) In other Arab lands, such as Iraq, Syria, and Lebanon, Jews spoke Arabic. A neglected yet significant number of Arabic-speaking Jewish intellectuals emerged in the late-nineteenth and early-twentieth centuries, and their contributions mark a distinctly Middle Eastern Jewish encounter with modernity. Arabic writers such as Esther Azhari Moyal in Beirut and later Jaffa, who was an outspoken feminist and supporter of Arab women's rights, as well as a passionate defender of Jews, and the Egyptian nationalist playwright and journalist Ya'qub Sanu' (Jacob Sanua) characterize an engagement between Jews and Arab culture that further illuminates the vast cultural differences that existed among Jews in the Muslim world. In Iran, Jews spoke Judeo-Persian until the twentieth century, at which time they shifted to Farsi. By contrast, a large proportion of Sephardic and Middle Eastern Jews became French speakers, a result of the vast educational network established by the Alliance Israélite Universelle. All these language differences indicate the great diversity and varying levels of cultural integration and openness of the various Jewish communities to their host nations or the extent to which they sometimes felt a greater affinity for European culture and colonial authority.

In North Africa, Jews in Libya, Tunisia, Algeria, and Morocco comprised the only non-Muslim minority in the Maghreb, the area of Africa north of the Sahara Desert and west of the Nile River. Until the arrival of the European powers in the nineteenth century, Jews lived as *dhimmis,* second-class but protected subjects of the sultan. They paid an annual *jizya* and lived under the strictures of the Pact of Omar, an eighth-century legal code intended to ensure Jewish subservience to the Muslim majority. At certain times, it was imposed more stringently than at others, depending on many variables, including who was in power and which Muslim religious forces were in the ascendancy. Jewish status was changed when the French took control of North Africa and extended French citizenship to Jews. The first beneficiaries were the 15,000 Jews of Algeria in 1830, thanks to the tireless efforts of **Adolphe Crémieux** (1794–1880), leading statesman, founder of the Alliance and from 1834 until his death vice president of the Consistory. Tunisia's 25,000 Jews won citizenship in 1881, the 100,000 Jews of Morocco in 1912. Finally, in 1916 the 16,000-strong Jewish population of Libya (an Italian colony) was emancipated.

The majority of North African Jews were desperately poor, though for a significant number, socioeconomic conditions improved with the opportunities that came in the wake of European colonization. Christians, who were also *dhimmi,* benefited equally from European rule. By the twentieth century, like their Ashkenazic co-religionists, North African Jews tended to concentrate in urban centers or in port cities. Many engaged in commerce, while the majority were artisans and tradesmen. The officially constituted Jewish communities in Morocco were called *mellahs,* while in other parts of North Africa they were called *haras.*

Across North Africa, violence and discrimination had plagued Jewish communities for centuries. A non-Jewish account of Jewish life in Tunisia shortly before the coming of the French painted a miserable picture:

> [The Jews] had to live in a certain quarter, and were not allowed to appear in the streets after sunset. If they were compelled to go out at night they had to provide themselves with a cat-o'-nine-tails . . . which served as a kind of passport to the patrols going around at night. If it was a dark night, they were not allowed to carry a lantern like the Moors and Turks, but a candle, which the wind extinguished every minute. They were neither allowed to ride on horseback nor on a mule, and even to ride on a donkey was forbidden them except outside the town; they had then to dismount at the gates, and walk in the middle of the streets, so as not to be in the way of Arabs. If they had to pass the "Kasba," they had first to fall on their knees as a sign of submission, and then to walk on with lowered head; before coming to a mosque they were obliged to take the slippers off their feet, and had to pass the holy edifice without looking at it. As Tunis possesses no less than five hundred mosques, it will be seen that Jews did not wear out many shoes at that time.

Muslim humiliation and discrimination against Jews diminished significantly with the arrival of European rule. Economic and educational opportunities became available thanks to the French presence, and even the health of Jews improved with the introduction of new systems of sanitation. By 1900 the lifespan of Algerian Jews was significantly higher than that of their Muslim neighbors, a feature in keeping with the rest of the Jewish world.

The largest Jewish community in North Africa lived in Morocco, a highly fragmented society whose Jewish population followed suit. There were Jewish city dwellers, village Jews in the Atlas Mountains, and Jewish Berbers, all making for a highly diverse population. According to the Moroccan census of 1936, three-quarters of Morocco's 161,000 Jews were bilingual in Berber and Arabic, and another 25,000 were exclusively Berber speakers. There were also Spanish-speaking Jews in the north of the country, which, for a while, was under

Spanish control. As in other parts of North Africa, the Jewish population was also divided into what were known in Hebrew as *megorashim* (descendants of those expelled from the Iberian Peninsula) and *toshavim* (native-born Jews).

In Tunisia, the Jews were divided between an Arabic-speaking majority and an Italian-speaking minority. Where possible, they sought to remain separate. They attended different synagogues, were buried apart from each other, and turned to parallel community institutions. Little intermarriage occurred between the two groups. In certain circumstances, however, the lines between the two communities blurred, especially when a wealthier or more westernized Arabic-speaking Jew returned from Europe and sought access to the Italophone community. Community size also played a factor. Where a *haras* was especially small, separate institutions made little sense and could, in fact, endanger the existence of the community. In those circumstances, there was a much greater degree of fraternization.

In Algeria, the Jewish population had grown considerably in the interwar period, from 74,000 in 1921 to 99,000 in 1936. The Crémieux Decree of 1870, which bestowed French citizenship on Algerian Jews, was a source of Muslim and Christian envy and hostility. The access to French education provided opportunities for Algerian Jews to improve their lives, and their social and economic situation soon outstripped that of any other Jewish community in the Maghreb and tended to exceed that of their Muslim neighbors. By 1941, although they constituted only 2 percent of the total population, Jews were 37 percent of all Algerian medical students and 24 percent of all law students. Organized into the consistory system—in Algiers, Constantine, and Oran, Algerian Jews were linked directly to the central consistory in Paris and to the French administration in Algiers. The level of Jewish acculturation was extremely high, as the Jews rapidly became French speakers and often sent their children to Paris for study and work. By the interwar period, about 90 percent of the Jews were evenly divided among artisans, merchants, and salaried employees of the French state.

Libya was under Ottoman control from 1835 until 1911 and then was ruled as a colony by the Italians from 1911 until 1943, at which point the British captured it. In Libya, with a relatively small Jewish population of about 25,000 in the interwar period, Jews were nevertheless a notable presence. The 15,300 Jews who lived in Tripoli in 1931 formed about 20 percent of the capital city's total population. In the late 1930s the situation of the Jews began to markedly deteriorate when Mussolini's Fascist government extended its antisemitic laws to Libyan Jews.

By the 1930s the existence of the ancient Jewish communities found throughout the Middle East became increasingly precarious. In most cases Arab nationalism and Muslim fundamentalism played their part in the decline. But even in Turkey, with the more favorable conditions under the rule of Atatürk, the Jewish population declined in the twentieth century, a process that began in earnest in the 1920s. In 1927, half of the 81,500 Turkish Jews lived in Istanbul. They were mostly Sephardim, but there were Ashkenazic communities as well. Over the course of the next decade, significant numbers began to leave for the Americas and Palestine.

Iraq, where the Jews, mindful of their long tenure in that country, referred to themselves in Hebrew as Babylonian Jews, came under Ottoman control in 1638. Iraqi Jews were essentially divided into two main groups: the mountain Jews of Kurdistan, numbering up to 20,000 in the twentieth century, and the highly Arabized communities of the lowland regions, principally Baghdad. Originally one community, sometime in the fifteenth century the Jews split into these two distinct communities. Principally poor artisans, traders, and agriculturalists, Kurdish Jews were subject to the oppressive rule of local Kurdish chieftains, called *agas*. They spoke Judeo-Kurdish, an Aramaic dialect known as "Targum" by its speakers, and had their spiritual center in Mosul. The harsh conditions of Jewish life in Kurdistan became worse in the 1930s and 1940s, when riots against Jews in the south of the country began to move northward. In response many Kurdish Jews emigrated to Palestine.

Most Iraqi Jews, however, lived in Baghdad, a center of both Jewish religious and secular culture. Baghdad was home to one of the leading rabbinic authorities of the nineteenth century, **Joseph Hayyim** (1834–1909), a revered scholar, renowned for his *halakhic* flexibility and his receptivity to modernization. By 1927, Baghdad also had five Alliance schools, which Rabbi Hayyim publicly opposed, believing that they would lead not merely to Jewish modernization, something he deemed important, but to Jewish secularization. His fears were not unfounded. Iraqi Jewry was faced with some of the same competing ideological trends that were readily apparent in other Jewish communities and its Western-educated elite likewise dominated communal affairs.

Like other Iraqis, the Jewish community was deeply affected by British rule. When the British captured the southern Iraqi city of Basra in November 1914, the governing Ottomans panicked and their rule became arbitrary and often brutal, characterized by executions and extortion of Jews, Christians, and their fellow Muslims. Under these circumstances, many Jews fled. When the British occupied Baghdad in March 1917, the Jews of the city declared it a "Day of Miracle." Jewish communities in Mosul and Kirkuk did likewise. When the British took control of Iraq, Jews were granted civil rights and made equal to Muslims before the law.

When the British arrived in 1917, Baghdad was a noticeably "Jewish city." Jews were the single largest ethnic group in the capital. Of a total population of 202,000, 80,000 were Jews. Sunnis, Shi'ites, and Turks totaled 101,000; Christians, 12,000; Kurds, 8,000; and Persians, 800. The Jews were a significant presence in nearly all walks of life. In 1926, when the Baghdad Chamber of Commerce was established, of the fifteen members, five represented Jewish merchants, four Muslim merchants, three British-owned businesses, one each for Christian and Persian merchants, and one for the banks. Baghdadi Jewish importance went beyond numerical superiority. Part of the strength of the Jewish merchant class, with the Sassoon and Kadoorie families most prominent, derived from its vast international trading networks, extending in one direction to London and in the other to India and on to the Far East.

Throughout the mandate period, 1922 to 1932, the Jews of Iraq continued to enjoy economic vitality and participated in government and national affairs. A rising chorus of Muslims, echoing the language of European Fascists, began decrying Jewish "control" of the Iraqi economy and the disproportionate Jewish presence in the country's administration. As Baghdad became a gathering point for Arab nationalists from Syria and Palestine, implacable hostility to Zionism further contributed to the increasingly delicate position of Iraq's Jews.

When Iraq gained full independence in 1932, Jews became Iraqi citizens. This did not, however, protect them from Arab hostility as much as they thought it would. In 1936, rising Arab nationalism broke out in violence against the Jews of Iraq. Three people were shot and killed around the Jewish New Year. The next day, which had been declared Palestine Day, was marked by violent protests, as anti-Jewish sermons rang out from mosques. As was the case elsewhere, when the loyalty of Iraqi Jews was questioned, the response was a ringing assertion of Jewish patriotism, a swipe at Europe, and a dissociation from Zionism. In 1936, the Jewish school principal, scholar, and writer Ezra Haddad proclaimed, "The Arab Jew, when he makes his attitude to the Zionist question clear, feels in his innermost being that he does that of his own free will and motivated by considerations of justice, conscience and . . . well established facts. And when he speaks of the Arab lands, he speaks of homelands which from time immemorial surrounded him with generosity and affluence—homelands which he considered and continues to consider as oases in the midst of a veritable desert of injustices and oppressions which were the Jews' lot in many of the countries which boast of culture and civilization." Not long before he published this piece, Haddad published

another with the title "We Were Arabs Before We Became Jews."

Haddad's declarations on behalf of Jewish Arabization reflected general community sentiment. The Jews of Iraq were among the most Arabized of all communities in the region. Their level of cultural integration and modernization was enhanced by the Alliance education they received and, according to a report sent from the British consul-general's office in Baghdad to the foreign office in London in 1910, contributed to further the process of secularization: "In contradistinction to past days, the clergy enjoy no influence over their co-religionists, and this may confidently be ascribed to the effect of education diffused among the classes of the community."

The secularization of the Jewish middle classes rapidly advanced among all Sephardic and Middle Eastern Jewries. Even poor Jews were not immune. Nothing so clearly illustrates the results of this process as the formal critique lodged in 1929 by an Alliance teacher, Monsieur L. Loubaton. He feared a complete "de-judaization" among the Jews of Tunisia: "Hebrew instruction for children, which was highly valued in the time preceding the arrival of the Alliance, can be said to be non-existent. . . . The children are ignorant of all that represents the beauty and uniqueness of our doctrine; they have no notion of biblical history or Jewish history; they are totally unaware that a modern Jewish literature exists." At the synagogues, Loubaton saw only impiety: "I myself go out to the terrace for a moment. It is like entering a public meeting place. Everyone has closed his book, circles of people have formed, and there is chatting, yawning, jesting, laughing. In the evening, more than three-fifths of those attending services are gathered on the terrace." In the city of Sousse, the situation was the same: "Let us consider the cafés on a Saturday. They are literally invaded by Jews. With few exceptions, all are smoking, gambling—often for large sums of money—at cards or at backgammon, or discussing business." Loubaton also observed that "already, mixed marriages are becoming common." The only remedy that Loubaton envisioned was the "founding of yeshivot and for the encouragement of theological studies [and] the creat[ion] of a rabbinical corps." This needed to be undertaken by the Alliance, for "the very preservation of Tunisian Jewry, which now shows so many signs of degeneration, depends on this undertaking."

What Loubaton identified as a local, Tunisian Jewish problem was, in fact, part of a general historical process that existed in modern Jewish communities, whether in Europe, the Middle East, or the Americas. The decline of traditional observance went hand in hand with rising educational and socioeconomic levels and the emergence of new, vibrant secular cultures.

Questions for Reflection

1. Why was World War I a watershed in Jewish history?
2. What accounts for what has been called a "renaissance of Jewish culture in the Weimar Republic"?
3. In what ways can Jewish life in interwar Poland and the Soviet Union be said to have been a mixed blessing for Jews?
4. What were the main tasks that confronted the Zionist movement in the interwar period?
5. What are the various factors that contributed to a deterioration of Jewish–Arab relations in the Yishuv?
6. How did the encounter with modernity change the character of Sephardi and Middle Eastern Jews by the 1930s?

For Further Reading

On World War I, see George L. Mosse, "The Jews and the German War Experience, 1914–1918" (New York: Leo Baeck Institute, 1977); David Rechter, *The Jews of Vienna and the First Word War* (London and Portland, OR: Littman Library of Jewish Civilization, 2001); Mark Levene, *War, Jews, and the New Europe: The Diplomacy of Lucien Wolf, 1914–1919* (Oxford, England: Oxford University Press, 1992)

On Jewish politics and culture in the interwar period, see Michael Brenner and Gideon Reuveni, eds., *Emancipation Through Muscles: Jews and Sports in Europe* (Lincoln: University of Nebraska Press, 2006); Michael Brenner, *The Renaissance of Jewish Culture in Weimar Germany* (New Haven, CT: Yale University Press, 1996); Steven Beller, *Vienna and the Jews, 1867–1938: A Cultural History* (Cambridge, England: Cambridge University Press, 1986); David Shneer, *Yiddish and the Creation of Soviet Jewish Culture, 1918–1930* (Cambridge, England: Cambridge University Press, 2004); Jeffrey Veidlinger, *The Moscow State Yiddish Theater: Jewish Culture on the Soviet Stage* (Bloomington: Indiana University Press, 2000); Michael Steinlauf and Antony Polonsky, eds., *Polin* 16 (2003); Zvi Gitelman, ed., *The Emergence of Modern Jewish Politics: Bundism and Zionism in Eastern Europe* (Pittsburgh, PA: University of Pittsburgh Press, 2003); Ezra Mendelsohn, *The Jews of East Central Europe Between the World Wars* (Bloomington: Indiana University Press, 1983); Yuri Slezkine, *The Jewish Century* (Princeton, NJ: Princeton University Press, 2004); David N. Myers, *Re-inventing the Jewish Past: European Jewish Intellectuals and the Zionist Return to History* (New York: Oxford University Press, 1995); Tom Segev, *One Palestine Complete: Jews and Arabs Under the British Mandate* (New York: Owl Books, 2001).

Chapter 14

The Holocaust

The greatest catastrophe to befall the Jewish people in its long history occurred between 1933 and 1945. Due to the actions of the Nazis and their accomplices across Europe, Jews were robbed of their rights, dispossessed of their property, and slaughtered without pity. At the war's end at least six million were dead and both the Ashkenazic and Sephardic civilizations that had flowered on European soil over the previous millennium had been utterly destroyed.

The assault on European Jewry began with World War I. The war, which devastated Europe, took the lives of a generation of young men and left societies and economies in ruins. The violence and loss were translated by many returning veterans into a vicious political ideology bent on destruction and vengeance. Across the Continent in the interwar period, Fascists either came to power or left their mark on Europe's political culture, preaching the virtues of integral nationalism, anti-Communism, militarism, violence, and antisemitism. (The only exception to the latter was Italian Fascism, which had Jews as party members until 1938.) After the war, Jews across Europe confronted virulent antisemitic rhetoric, economic boycotts, the imposition of quotas, and outbreaks of violence.

In Fascism's most extreme variant, Nazism, antisemitism was elevated to holy writ. Even if a majority of those who voted for Hitler did not do so because of the Nazi Party's antisemitism, the majority of Germans were indifferent to the endless harangues against Jews. While all too many applauded Hitler's threats to exact retribution against the Jews for Germany's defeat and humiliation in World War I, most dismissed them as bluster or paid no heed. While the destruction of European Jewry by the Nazis was not inevitable and was not even foreseeable when they came to power, their radical antisemitism was apparent from the start. Jews were central to Hitler's political worldview, and in his war of world conquest he saw them as Germany's principal enemy.

The Jews in Hitler's World View

The state-sponsored attack on German Jewry began when Adolf Hitler became chancellor of Germany on January 30, 1933. Upon taking office, Hitler unleashed a political program characterized by his pathological antisemitism, his hatred of all groups he considered inferior, an unquenchable desire to avenge Germany's defeat in World War I, and a passionate craving for world conquest. All these aspects of Hitler's political and cultural ideology were intimately linked.

Jews occupied the center of Hitler's world view. Seeking to dehumanize them, in his speeches and in his political testament *Mein Kampf* (1925), Hitler repeatedly called Jews "parasites," "maggots," "cockroaches," "bacilli," and "cancer." These descriptors were not Hitler's invention. He borrowed them from the language and ideas of antisemites who had preceded him, especially those drawn from the circles of occult-racists in Vienna, not one of whom had held the reins of political power. Hitler was determined to practice a "biological politics," using the nation's intellectual, economic, and military resources to forge a new world order. Once in office, Hitler had the means to implement a program predicated on the idea that Germans were biologically and morally superior to all other groups. Nazi ideology held Germans to be *Übermenschen* ("supermen"), while Jews were categorized as inferior *Untermenschen* ("subhumans") disguised in human form, though they were, in fact, held to be inhuman. "In the course of centuries, their exteriors had become Europeanized and human looking," Hitler once confided to an early supporter. "The Jew is the counter Man, the Anti-Man. The Jew is the creation of a different God. He must have grown from a different root of the human tribe. If I put the Aryan next to the Jew and call the former a man, then I have to call the other by another name. They are as far apart as the animal is from the human. Not that I want to call the Jew an animal. He is farther removed from the animal than the Aryan. He is a being foreign to nature and removed from nature."

Hitler confessed to having an adverse physical reaction to Jews, claiming that they nauseated him: "The odor of these caftan wearers often sickened me," he wrote. But he judged their morality as being even more offensive to him. And it was with this that Hitler and the Nazis came to hold Jews responsible for all the ills of humanity: "Was there any kind of filth or brazenness, particularly in cultural life, in which there was not at least one Jew participating? As soon as you cautiously cut into such an abscess, you would find, like a maggot in a rotting body, blinded by the sudden light, a little Yid!" Hitler set himself a political goal with a religious-like mission: to create a purified world ruled according to the laws of racist biology, wherein he played the role of high priest. Such an expansionist agenda, one that demanded war be waged on a global scale, was justified because, according to Hitler, "all occurrences in world history are only the expression of the races' instinct of self-preservation, in the good or bad sense." By starting and winning a preemptive war, the Nazis sought to defeat their eternal enemies and then remake the world anew.

Essential to the creation of this pristine universe was the removal of the Jews because they were regarded as a menace to all peoples. Hitler believed that the Nazis were performing a service for all humanity by destroying the Jews, who, he said, were bent on "world domination." Hitler claimed that "if . . . the Jew is victorious over the other peoples of the world, his crown will be the funeral wreath of humanity and this planet will . . . move through the ether devoid of men." Hitler thus imagined his battle against the Jews—and Bolsheviks, categories he elided—to be an apocalyptic struggle on a global scale. It had to be a worldwide war because the Jews lived everywhere. According to the historian Saul Friedländer, Hitler preached "redemptive anti-Semitism." Assuming for himself the role of crusader in a quasi-religious mission, Hitler observed, "I believe that by defending myself against the Jew, I am fighting for the work of the Lord."

Nazi ideology was also centered on seeking vengeance for Germany's defeat in World War I and subsequent humiliation at Versailles. Because the Nazis regarded the loss as the fault of the Jews, revenge would come through world conquest and the assertion of German hegemony. "Justice" would be delivered in the form of the destruction of the Jews. The Holocaust, then, was not a separate or discrete aspect of World War II but lay at the center of Nazi war aims.

For a long time, historians have debated just when Hitler took the fateful decision to exterminate European Jewry. One group of historians, referred to as "intentionalists," maintain that it was always Hitler's intention to embark

on mass murder, a goal he had set himself sometime toward the end of World War I. An opposing view is held by historians, referred to as "functionalists." They maintain that the decision to murder European Jewry evolved during World War II. The majority of historians believe the decision was taken sometime in 1941. Most likely a written order was never given but, rather, Hitler gave an oral directive to the head of the SS, **Heinrich Himmler** (1900–1945). Opinions within each camp also differ significantly. It would seem that a "moderate intentionalism" best describes the process. This position recognizes the centrality of antisemitism to Nazism and Hitler's determination to rid Germany of Jews while it acknowledges that "removing" Jews did not originally mean murder but most likely dispossession and expulsion. In other words, Hitler's aim at first was to throw the Jews out of Germany and the territories she occupied, and only later was a policy change instituted that had genocide on a European-wide scale as its goal. As such, the history of the Holocaust can be divided into two periods: 1933–1939 and 1939–1945. The first phase sees the exclusion of Jews from the economic, social, and cultural life of Germany and Austria, while the second coincides with the war and the systematic plunder and extermination of European Jewry.

Phase I: The Jews in Nazi Germany (1933–1939)

Although Hitler's assault on Jews began upon his taking office, he had thought about it long before 1933. His promise to push the Jews out of German public life was a central plank of the Nazi Party's **Twenty-Five Point Program** (1920). Point 4 noted, "Only a member of the race can be a citizen. A member of the race can only be one who is of German blood, without consideration of creed. Consequently no Jew can be a member of the race." The implementation of this program was made possible by Hitler's rise to power and the increasing centralization of the Nazi state. Through a combination of intimidation, violence, weak opposition, and his personal popularity, Hitler gained control of the most important organs of state: the armed forces, the judiciary, the state treasury, and the press.

At the heart of the system of repression were the concentration camps. At first, only four specific groups were targeted for incarceration: political enemies, inferior races, criminals, and "asocial elements." The camps were places where Himmler encouraged the commandants to terrorize the inmates. The first concentration camp, Dachau, was opened in March 1933, and Jews were among the earliest inmates. In the early phase of the Nazi regime, Jews were taken

"Exodus of the Chosen People out of Kassel." Soon after the Nazis came to power in 1933, the persecution of Jews became ritualized and even a form of public entertainment and celebration. In this undated photo, a swim club on the Fulda River won first prize in a People's Fair (*Volksfest*) for this exhibit. It shows members of the team dressed as ragtag Jewish refugees, replete with false beards, odd hats, and big noses, sitting amid their luggage and hanging clothes onboard a boat. The sign above them, referring to the pauperization of German Jews and the ordinances that forbade them from engaging in public activities such as being members of clubs and associations, is written in Hessian dialect: "Dr. Isak, Dr. Isidor Levi and Chana have gone bankrupt. They may no longer go swimming [in the Fulda] and have been packed off to Palestine."

to camps, frequently because they were socialists, not because they were Jews, and on signing a statement declaring that they had been well treated, they were often released. Other Jews, however, were killed outright in the camp. Over the course of the Third Reich the camp system grew enormously large and was composed of a variety of different kinds of camps.

At first, anti-Jewish policy proceeded along two tracks. For one, stormtroopers from the SA, also called "brown-shirts," and other party activists physically attacked Jews and their property at random. Decisions on when and where to do this were taken at a regional and local level. More conservative government officials sought likewise to persecute Jews but wished to do so in a way that was less obvious and was not poised to harm Germany's international reputation and

economic recovery. Thus, after Hitler's purge of the SA in 1934, the anti-Jewish campaign was directed from Berlin, although local initiatives were still encouraged, provided they were in keeping with the government's goals. Whether regionally or centrally directed, the persecution of the Jews became an ongoing ritual within Nazi Germany.

The Nazi goal to remove the Jews from German public life and effectively rescind their emancipation by stripping them of their citizenship began in dramatic fashion. On April 1, 1933, the Nazis led a boycott of Jewish-owned stores and businesses. The propaganda minister, Joseph Goebbels, declared on that day, "The year 1789 is hereby eradicated from history." Indeed, the Nazis set out to eliminate the French Revolution, with its ideology of liberty, equality, and fraternity. The revolution had also emancipated the Jews—for the

Nazis, an historic error in need of correction. Each day brought with it new laws and intensified discrimination. On April 4, the German Boxing Association excluded all Jewish boxers. There were not many such young men, but the action signifies the extent of Nazi determination to remove the Jews from all areas of public life. And although not many Jews were employed in the Civil Service, on April 7 the passage of the "Law for the Re-Establishment of the Professional Civil Service" resulted in the dismissal of all civil servants who were not of "Aryan descent." (On April 11, *non-Aryan* was defined as "anyone descended from non-Aryan, particularly Jewish, parents or grandparents. It suffices if one grandparent is non-Aryan."). The definition of *non-Aryan* formed the foundation for all subsequent persecution of the Jews.

Jewish lawyers and doctors were prominent in Germany: 16 percent of all lawyers and 11 percent of all doctors. After the passage of the Civil Service law on April 7, Jewish lawyers and judges were beaten up and even dragged from court in the middle of proceedings. Initially, Jewish lawyers could continue to practice if they were World War I veterans or if they had been in practice for a long time. They were, however, removed from the national registry of lawyers and put on a special list.

Hitler was cautious when it came to Jewish doctors, especially since Jews made up as much as 50 percent of all physicians in Berlin. To have dismissed them at once, when so many German patients depended on them, risked a backlash. The program of Nazi discrimination against Jewish doctors occurred in three stages. In the first phase, beginning in 1933, Jewish physicians were expelled from the national insurance scheme and were replaced with "Aryan" doctors who had long sought a way into the system. Persecution paid off. By 1934 the annual taxable income of "Aryan" doctors had increased by 25 percent. When the financial windfall resulting from the persecution of Jewish doctors is combined with the fact that Nazi Germany organized itself along racial lines and that primacy was given to biology (with doctors serving as arbiters of life and death), it is little wonder that the German Medical Association was the most easily and eagerly Nazified of any professional group: Over 50 percent of German doctors were members of the Nazi Party.

The second phase, which began in the summer of 1938, saw the decertification of all Jewish physicians. Jews could no longer treat Germans and could only refer to themselves by the degrading term "sick-treaters," rather than physicians. Due to emigration, forced retirement, incarceration, suicide, death, and murder, the number of Jewish physicians remaining in Germany by early 1939 was a mere 285. In the final phase, which covered the war years, health care for Jews was confined to the few remaining Jewish hospitals the Nazis permitted to remain open. Eventually, even these institutions, with the exception of the Jewish Hospital in Berlin, were closed down and the staffs, together with their patients, were deported to ghettos and death camps in the east. There, until their own deaths, Jewish doctors and nurses continued to administer treatment to the sick and dying Jews as best they could.

In April 1933, the systematic dismissal of Jewish faculty and teaching assistants at the universities began. Even at this early stage, with no inkling of what the future held, fear gripped German Jews. The philologist and professor of Romance languages at Dresden's Technical University, Victor Klemperer, who remained in hiding with his non-Jewish spouse in Dresden throughout the war, recorded in his diary on April 12, 1933, "For the moment I am safe. But as someone on the gallows, who has the rope around his neck, is safe. At any moment a new 'law' can kick away the steps on which I am standing and then I'm hanging." And new laws kept coming. On April 19, Jewish cattle dealers in the state of Baden were forbidden to speak Yiddish. On April 21, kosher slaughtering of animals was outlawed, while on April 25 the "Law Against the Overcrowding of German Schools and Universities" was passed. Jews were not to exceed 5 percent of enrollments.

Jews experienced rapid and abrupt ostracism from German society. Children were especially affected and confused by how quickly their world collapsed. Playmates with gentiles one day, Jewish children were shunned the next. Hilma Geffen Ludomer, a Jewish girl from Berlin recalled, "Suddenly, I didn't have any friends. I had no more girlfriends, and many of the neighbors were afraid to talk to us." Martha Appel from Dortmund remembered, "[T]he children had been advised not to come to school on April 1, 1933, the day of the boycott. Even the principal of the school thought Jewish children's lives were in danger. . . . My heart was broken when I saw tears in my younger child's eyes when she had been sent home from school while all others had been taken to a show or some other pleasure. . . . Almost every lesson began to be a torture for Jewish children. There was not one subject anymore, which was not used to bring up the Jewish question. And in the presence of Jewish children the teachers denounced all the Jews, without exception, as scoundrels and as the most destructive force in the country where they were living. My children were not permitted to leave the room during such a talk; they were compelled to stay and to listen; they had to feel all the other children's eyes looking and staring at them, the examples of an outcast race." As the situation grew worse, she noted, "[W]ith each day of the Nazi regime, the abyss between us and our fellow citizens grew larger. . . . Of course we were different . . . since we were hunted like deer." Henny Brenner, in Dresden, recalled how fearful her teachers made her. Her biology teacher taught Nazi racial theory to the children and came into the class looking the part, with "her hair in braids and a big round swastika brooch on her blouse." The teacher, who was new to the school, did not know the students and mistakenly called on Henny, who was blond-haired and blue-eyed, to stand before the class and pronounced, "Here is a [perfect] example of Aryan womanhood." As the students were smirking, Henny, who was not amused, said "I am Jewish." From that time on, she said, "all hell broke loose." Her math teacher, who also "looked like a prototypical Nazi, big and blond," always wore his SS uniform to class, complete with a "Death's Head" insignia.

On May 10, 1933, at universities across Germany, the public burning of books by Jewish and anti-Nazi authors took place. Increasingly pessimistic Jews recalled the words of the nineteenth-century German Jewish poet, Heinrich Heine, who, in his play *Almansor*, said of book burning, "That was only a prelude; where they burn books they will, in the end, burn human beings too." On July 14, celebrated as Bastille Day in France, the Nazis outlawed all other political parties. On that same day they also passed "The Law for the Prevention of Genetically Diseased Offspring." It permitted the sterilization of anyone suffering from a host of diseases, including "feeble-mindedness, schizophrenia, manic depression and severe alcoholism." Many who later were involved in the murder of Jews "trained" in the sterilization and euthanasia programs. Over the years, hundreds of laws, decrees, and local ordinances were added, vitiating any form of normal life whatsoever. From job dismissal to laws against Jews using public parks, mass transit, and swimming pools; attending movies, theatre, opera, and musical concerts; growing private vegetable gardens; possessing electrical appliances, cigars, cigarettes, and even house pets, German Jews felt the noose growing ever tighter.

Responses of German Jews

In their overall persecution of Jews, the Nazis were especially insistent that Jews play no part in the enjoyment or performance of German culture. On June 16, 1933, the Nazis forced the formation of the **Kulturbund** (German Jewish Cultural Association). Shut out of the cultural life of the nation, Jews active in the Kulturbund were forbidden to perform medieval and Romantic-era works, the classics of German theatre such as Schiller and Goethe, while foreign works such as Shakespeare's *Hamlet* were permitted but not the "To be or not to be" soliloquy. With time, Jewish musicians were forbidden to play the likes of Beethoven or Mozart. Altogether,

Jews were forced to configure their cultural activities in a sphere completely separate from that of Germans. It was a cultural ghetto that anticipated the physical ghettos into which Jews would later be herded.

The Kulturbund's significance lies in the fact that it not only provided a venue for Jews to continue their engagement with culture, a necessary tonic in such bitter circumstances, but it also supplied desperately needed work for actors, directors, musicians, singers, costumers, set designers, and makeup artists. The Kulturbund's existence even sparked heated debates about what constituted Jewish culture. Throughout the country, the Kulturbund sponsored three theatre companies, two philharmonic orchestras, one opera, one cabaret, one theatre school, and several choirs and also hosted many lecture series. About 2,500 people earned a modest but desperately needed living as employees of the Kulturbund. It was telling that the very first production of the Kulturbund was Gotthold Ephraim Lessing's play *Nathan the Wise*. The choice was bold and controversial among Jews and was staunchly defended by **Kurt Singer** (1885–1944), one of the founders of the Kulturbund. This physician and Weimar-era conductor of the Berlin Opera wrote to a Zionist newspaper in 1933, "There can be no doubt that *Nathan* should be the very first play to produce, precisely because it is a modern, combative work. Its language, its dramatic qualities . . . and its purely human, timeless spiritual nature are all chords that resonate in harmonic unity."

In September 1933, the Nazis established a new central organization for German Jewry, the *Reichsvertretung der deutschen Juden* ("Reich Representation of German Jews"). It was led by **Rabbi Leo Baeck** (1873–1956) of Berlin. An ecumenical body, the Reichsvertretung represented all streams of German Jewry and was the single organization permitted to speak for the Jewish community to the Nazi government. Its principal activities were to provide vocational training, especially to those preparing to emigrate, cater to the educational needs of young and old alike, and make available extensive welfare services and economic assistance in the form of labor exchange and small loans. Given the large number who had already lost their livelihoods, the Reichsvertretung provided invaluable material aid and spiritual encouragement to the increasingly desperate Jews of Germany.

The principal Jewish response to Nazi persecution was to leave Germany, though departure did not take place in a mad rush but, rather, in a steady exodus. Psychological, economic, and demographic factors helped fashion Jewish decision making when it came to emigration. When the Nazis came to power in 1933, 525,000 Jews were in Germany. Only 37,000 left that year because none of them knew what

Welding instruction for prospective Jewish emigrants (1936). The trauma of forced emigration from Nazi Germany was often accompanied by the need for occupational retraining. These men from Berlin are learning the trade of welding. Their activity was sponsored by the *Hilfsverein der Juden in Deutschland*, the Relief Organization of Jews in Germany. Pursuant to their policy of forcing Jews to the leave the country, the Nazis charged the Hilfsverein with facilitating the emigration of Jews, who began fleeing Nazi Germany as soon as Hitler took power. Between 1933 and 1938, about one-quarter of Germany's 525,000 Jews left the country. Most went to neighboring countries, where they were later captured by the Nazis after their conquest of western Europe in 1940. Between 1933 and 1939, approximately 60,000 Jews made their way to Palestine.

we know now. None of them could predict the future. Across the political and cultural spectrum, German Jewry expressed similar sentiments of dismay but certainty that the situation would improve. In June 1933, the liberal Central Union of German Jews, representing the majority of German Jews, declared, "[T]he great majority of German Jews remains firmly rooted in the soil of its homeland, despite everything." The Orthodox Jewish community wrote to Hitler in October 1933: "The position of German Jewry today, as it has been shaped by the German people, is wholly intolerable . . . [their economic and social position] means that German Jews have been sentenced to a slow but certain death by starvation. . . . [But] even if some individuals harbor such an intention, *we do not believe it has the approval of the Führer and the Government of Germany.*" Even the Zionists cautioned against

wholesale departure for Palestine, believing that the sight of a mass flight of Jews from Germany would encourage other nations to step up discrimination against Jews to hasten their departure. Even Zionists still imagined a future for Jews in Germany, albeit on an entirely new political footing. On May 30, 1933, an article appeared in a Zionist newspaper stating the following:

> Only a fraction of the half million German Jews can emigrate; an even smaller percentage have the prospect of settling in Palestine and thus returning to agriculture on their ancestral soil. Undoubtedly one cannot let the Jews of Germany starve, hence German Jewry can make a virtue of necessity—if the State gave them the opportunity. . . . The first step toward integrating the Jews into

the new State should be domestic colonisation. Jewish farming villages in Germany are no less possible than in Argentina or Soviet-Russia. One can assume that the Jewish farmer in Germany will develop certain capabilities peculiar to him, which, without negating his own nature, will be of value to the life of the German Volk.

On the occasion of the April 1 boycott, the Zionist leader, Robert Welsch, encouraged German Jews to turn the circumstances to their advantage, declaring, "The Yellow Badge, Wear It with Pride!" Welsch was not referring to the wearing of a yellow badge as a distinguishing marker for Jews under Nazi rule. (That decree was first implemented on November 23, 1939, against Polish Jews over ten years of age and for German Jews on September 1, 1941.) Rather, Welsch was speaking about the daubing of Jewish businesses with the Star of David by Nazi hooligans.

At the time, these sentiments were neither naïve nor delusional. Jewish history and psychology made Jews keen observers of political storm clouds on the horizon. Though deeply distressed, most did not panic. Hitler was not the first antisemite in history, and he would not be the last. The historical record showed that the Jewish people had survived all previous antisemitic regimes. Why should this be different? As the German Jewish historian Ismar Elbogen wrote in a Jewish newspaper in 1933: "Think of the history of our forefathers; repeatedly they experienced such catastrophes, yet did not surrender their will to live!" The elitism of German political culture also made it difficult for anyone to believe that an ill-educated, loutish Austrian corporal could take control of Germany for a sustained period of time. If recent politics were any guide, the average lifespan of a Weimar government was nine months. Most reasonable people (including European statesmen and diplomats) expected the Nazis to fall sooner rather than later.

German Public Opinion

Germans voiced barely a word of opposition to the persecution of the Jews. Not all, but most either approved or simply did not care. Widespread enthusiasm for the regime led many to a conviction that the Jews were a problem, if not a "misfortune," for Germany. Often left unarticulated, the widespread feeling was that "something" had to be done about the Jews. Such sentiments cut across gender, class, religious, and educational lines. Lydia Gottschewski was a leader of the Nazi Women's League and implored her sisters to be merciless: "Often, much too often, one hears . . . 'I find the fight against the Jews too severe.' . . . Sentimental gush that the other person is also a human being and feels and senses like

ourselves. . . . The Jew . . . is a subtle poison since he destroys what is necessary to our life. If we are to be healed as a people . . . and conquer a place in the world that is our due, then we must free ourselves ruthlessly from that parasite."

No university professors spoke out when books were burned and their 1,200 Jewish colleagues were dismissed in 1933. University students were even more openly antisemitic than their teachers and celebrated the exclusion of Jewish students. As early as January 1933, before the dismissal of Jewish professors, students harassed fellow German students who attended classes taught by Jews. At the Technical University of Berlin, students brought cameras into classrooms to photograph the German students enrolled in such classes. No support of Jewish professors came from the intellectual classes. In the business world, Jews were dismissed from their positions on corporate boards, with the vacancies filled by eager German executives. In some instances, positions were found for Jews overseas, but the majority had no such good fortune. The companies they served did little for their Jewish employees. As the Hamburg banker Alwin Muenchmeyer admitted in a rare moment of self-criticism: "We did nothing and we didn't think anything of it."

Jews also waited in vain for the representatives of the Protestant and Catholic Churches to speak out. On April 4, 1933, when taking a public stand was at least possible, Bishop Otto Dibelius, the leading Protestant clergyman in Germany, showed his support for the regime by declaring, "I have always considered myself an antisemite." In September 1933, the Vatican signed a Concordat with the Nazis, in consequence of which Rome did not raise a voice of protest against the persecution of the Jews. Occasionally, both churches expressed concern about the mistreatment of Jewish converts to Christianity. For the most part, although they were not as viciously antisemitic as the Nazis, the clerical and intellectual elites of Germany were enthusiastic about the Nazi revolution. Like the great majority of Germans, they were indifferent to the fate of the Jews. Moreover, no one was able to claim with any sincerity that he or she did not know what was going on because measures against Jews were widely reported in the press and high-ranking Nazis publicly boasted about their campaign to remove the Jews from German life.

The year 1934 lulled some Jews into a false sense of security. The anti-Jewish agenda seemed to recede in importance as the regime was principally concerned with consolidating its power and rooting out opposition. But from the Jewish perspective the suffering continued. Widening exclusion, public humiliation, and physical terror were experienced everywhere. Poverty also began to grip this once comfortable middle-class community. At least 20 percent of German Jewry had by now lost their livelihood.

A new phase in Hitler's assault on the Jews occurred with the passage of the **Nuremberg Laws** (September 1935), which revoked the German citizenship of Jews and forbade intermarriage between Jews and Germans, and in fact, all sexual contact. In practical terms, the laws did not change the lives of German Jews. Rather, they ratified the discrimination they were already suffering. The point was to exacerbate the divide between Jews and Germans and to isolate Jews from the public life of the nation. As Hitler told one of his adjutants, "Out of all the professions, into a ghetto, enclosed in a territory where they can behave as becomes their nature, while the German people look on as one looks at wild animals."

When one year passed into the next and it became certain that the Nazis were not going to disappear, an air of desperation began to swirl around German Jews. On October 27, 1937, Victor Klemperer confided to his diary, "The thought that it makes no difference how I am going to spend the rest of my life is constantly on my mind: I no longer believe there will be any political change. Furthermore, I don't believe a change will help me in any way in my circumstances or in my feelings. Feelings of scorn, disgust and deep distrust towards Germany will never leave me. And until 1933 I was so convinced of my being German."

The Nazis fed the German people a steady diet of propaganda to convince them that the Jews were their sworn enemies. As early as 1928, Joseph Goebbels published an article in his newspaper, *Der Angriff* ("The Attack"), entitled "Why Are We Enemies of the Jews?" He listed several reasons: "The Jew was the cause and beneficiary of our enslavement," he was "the real cause for the loss of the Great War," and "it is because of the Jew that we are pariahs in the world." In short, "the Jews had triumphed over us and our future . . . he is the eternal enemy of our national honor and our national freedom." The Jew as enemy was the Nazi's most consistent doctrinal theme. On November 18, 1942, in the midst of the slaughter of European Jewry, the Reich Propaganda Directorate of the Nazi Party issued its "Word of the Day": "Who Bears the Guilt for the War? Roosevelt, Churchill, and Stalin Bear Responsibility for the War in the Eyes of History. Behind Them, However, Stands the Jew." Another directive issued that same month bore a picture of Roosevelt with a number of smiling men identified as Jews. Ominously, the caption read: "They Will Stop Laughing!!!" The charges and threats never varied and were publicly known from beginning to end.

The Economics of Persecution

When Hitler came to power, about 100,000 Jewish-owned enterprises were operational in Germany. Business quickly turned sour. Even though the April 1, 1933, boycott was called off after a couple of days, an unofficial boycott remained in place. Companies refused to deliver goods to Jewish businesses, stormtroopers stood a threatening vigil outside Jewish shops, windows were repeatedly smashed, welfare recipients were not permitted to use their food stamps in Jewish grocery stores, local newspapers were forbidden to publish advertisements of Jewish businesses, and campaigns discouraging Germans buying products from Jewish-owned enterprises continued unabated. One widespread claim declared, "Whoever buys Nivea articles is helping to support a Jewish company." The economic stranglehold on German Jewry ensured that by 1938 between 60 and 70 percent of German Jewish businesses had shut down.

Businesses that did not close their doors completely were most likely to have been stolen through the provisions of the campaign known as **Aryanization,** referring to the transfer (under pressure) of Jewish-owned businesses to "Aryan" owners in two stages: a "voluntary" period from 1933 to 1938 and then a period of compulsory forced transfer after November 1938. Aryanization measures were coordinated by economic advisors to local Nazi leaders, local chambers of commerce and industry, and regional and central tax authorities. Duplicity, threats, intimidation, and violence went hand in hand with the "orderly" mechanics of business transfer, which eventually evolved into a systematic, transcontinental robbing and trafficking in stolen goods of the Jewish people. In 1935, the head of the program, Herbert Göring, brother of Hermann Göring, outlined one of the strategies for taking over a Jewish-owned firm: "One method is apparently [for us] to approach Jewish firms with an offer to help them as Party members by joining their board of directors, administrative board, Executive Board or in some other 'advisory' capacity, naturally in return for a fee. . . . Once the ties to the Jewish firm have been firmly established and people have managed in some way to 'get inside,' then difficulties of a personal or political nature are soon created for the Jewish owner." On March 26, 1938, a German official wrote with undisguised glee to Hermann Göring regarding the situation in Vienna (recently annexed to the Reich): "[It] can be anticipated that the Jews will be ready to sell their stores and companies at the cheapest prices. I think it will be possible, in this way, to bring a large part of Jewish property into Aryan hands under the most favourable economic terms." After the *Kristallnacht* of November 1938, all pretense of voluntary ownership-transfer was dropped and the outright theft of Jewish property and businesses became the order of the day. Jewish enterprises that had remained in Jewish hands until that point were put under a government-appointed trustee, whose task was to "Aryanize" them. The frenzy to rob Jews led to internecine Nazi envy, evident in the remarks of the

Nazi Party Chief of Finance of South Westphalia in November 1938: "As we all know, as of 1 January 1939, no Jew is to be owner of an enterprise any longer. This means that Aryanization will have to be conducted at an extreme[ly] high pace. . . . people who only recently joined the Party and who in the past were on the other side of the fence, are now taking over Jewish businesses for ridiculous prices. People now talk of Aryanization profiteering—just as they talked in the past about the profiteers from inflation." The widespread enthusiasm for the Nazis lay in large part with the fact that Germans became material beneficiaries of Nazism. By first securing loyalty through extremely generous social programs, such largesse was supplemented by theft, first from German Jews, then from foreign Jews and the very nations the Nazis conquered when they exacted tribute and hauled off the booty. Billions of reichsmarks in stolen property were directed into Germany's genocidal war of conquest, alleviating Germans of the cost of the war they instigated. According to historian Götz Aly, "By exploiting material wealth confiscated and plundered in a racial war, Hitler's National Socialism achieved an unprecedented level of economic equality and created vast new opportunities for upward mobility for the German people. That made the regime both popular and criminal."

Theft was accompanied by wholesale defamation. A relentless stream of antisemitic propaganda permeated all aspects of daily life and would continue to do so until the end of the war. Germany was dotted with antisemitic billboards and posters, exhibiting vile images of Jews, often bearing captions such as "The Jewish Conspiracy," "The Wire Pullers: They Are Only Jews," and "The Jews Wanted the War." Hate-filled radio programs, plays, and movies entertained the masses while the reading public was offered a steady diet of antisemitic newspapers, magazines, and "scholarly journals." The teaching of hate began in childhood. Books for young readers, such as *The Poisonous Toadstool,* carried images of Jews intended to frighten and "educate" them. In July 1937, the **Degenerate Art** exhibition opened in Munich, displaying art by Jews and other artists disapproved of by the regime. The Nazis heaped scorn on all elements of modern art, the "degeneracy" of which they blamed on Jews. On November 8, 1937, the German Museum in Munich showed a huge exhibit entitled "The Eternal Jew." Through the use of inflammatory pictures and captions, the Nazis sought to depict Jews as thoroughly repellent, and in fact admitted as much. At the conclusion of a film shown at the exhibition, the chief ideologue of the Nazi Party, Alfred Rosenberg, appeared on the screen and said to the audience, "You are horrified by this film. Yes, it is particularly bad, but it is precisely the one we wanted to show you."

In 1935 Hitler declared that Germany would be ready to go to war in four years. To do so, however, he believed it imperative to remove Jews from German society so that they could not, in his mind, stab Germany in the back as he had claimed they had done in World War I. It is for this reason that Hitler's assault on the Jews was intensified as war approached. The year 1938 marks a drastic downturn in the perilous condition of German Jewry. At the start of the year, German Jews had to turn in their passports, with new ones going only to those intending to emigrate. On March 12, 1938, Hitler annexed Austria, the act known as the **Anschluss.** As he rode into Vienna amid the adoring throng, a further 190,000 Jews fell under Nazi rule. The antisemitic frenzy that ensued in Austria surpassed anything like that which had occurred in Germany. Antisemitism was key to the popular support the Nazis enjoyed in Austria, something that distinguished it somewhat from Germany. Beatings and outright theft began immediately, as did public humiliation. Jews were forced to scrub the capital's cobblestone streets. By contrast, the city's most famous Jewish resident, Sigmund Freud, did not have to get down on all fours. His celebrity saved him from that. He was, however, under surveillance, was interrogated, had his apartment broken into, and was robbed by stormtroopers. The Nazis even placed a swastika over the entrance to his apartment building. On June 4, 1938, together with his wife, Martha, and his daughter, Anna, he was allowed to leave Austria, but not before Princess Marie Bonaparte paid his hefty ransom, his emigration tax had been paid, and he had signed a declaration stating that he had not been mistreated. He added a sarcastic comment to his signature, addressed, perhaps, to the Austrians themselves: "I can most highly recommend the Gestapo to everyone." While Freud was able to spend the last year of his life in London, his three sisters were less fortunate. Denied exit visas by the Nazis, they all perished in concentration camps.

The local attacks on Jews were so outrageous that the head of the Security Service, the SD, **Reinhard Heydrich** (1904–1942), the man who would come to have operational responsibility for the "Final Solution," told the head of the Austrian Nazis to better control the mobs who had attacked Jews "in a totally undisciplined way." If he did not, the Gestapo would arrest them all. Even this threat did not work. The violence continued, as did the theft. Shortly after the Anschluss, the Nazis established the Property Transfer Office. Five hundred bureaucrats worked efficiently and within eighteen months were able to report to Himmler that they "had practically completed the task of de-Judaizing the Ostmark [Austrian] economy." Nearly all Jewish-owned businesses had been stolen. Prominent Jewish executives were murdered, and the majority of Jews were rendered penniless.

It is a measure of the Austrian zeal for theft that of the 33,000 Jewish-owned businesses in Austria, 7,000 were stolen even before the Property Transfer Office had been established in May 1938. In what would be typical of the process of ghettoization once the war began, the Nazis also stole apartments. By the end of 1938, of the 70,000 apartments owned by Jews in Vienna, 44,000 had been taken over by gentile owners. As Jews moved in with one another, often up to six families per apartment, the overcrowding plunged the persecuted into further distress. On August 20, 1938, Berlin authorized the establishment of a Central Office for Jewish Emigration. One of its two heads was **Adolf Eichmann** (1906–1962), who helped to run the operation that robbed wealthier Jews to fund the forced emigration of the poorer majority. Later, his job would involve working out the logistics of the mass murder of European Jewry.

As the situation in Germany and Austria grew increasingly worse and many Jews were attempting to leave, Franklin Roosevelt, president of the United States, called for an international forum to discuss the ensuing refugee crisis. The **Evian Conference** (July 6–13, 1938) was convened with thirty-two nations in attendance. Part of the invitation read, "[N]o country would be expected to receive a greater number of emigrants than is permitted by its existing legislation." No special efforts to assist Jewish refugees were expected. Even before the conference began, deals were brokered to ensure that nations would do even less than what they were capable of doing. In this regard, Britain insisted that the possibility of Palestine as a place of refuge not be publicly discussed, while the United States requested that no mention be made of the fact that American immigration quotas went unfilled year after year. Sometimes outrageously disingenuous claims were made to avoid providing a haven for Jews. The Australian delegate to the conference, the cabinet minister Thomas Walter White, declared, "[A]s we have no real racial problem, we are not desirous of importing one," a claim that would have come as a great surprise to Australia's aboriginal population. In fact, the most unequivocal Australian support for Jews in distress came from aboriginals. On December 6, 1938, William Cooper led a deputation from the Australian Aborigines' League to the German Consulate in Melbourne. He brought with him a firmly worded resolution, attempting to present "on behalf of the aborigines of Australia, a strong protest at the cruel persecution of the Jewish people by the Nazi Government of Germany." The consul-general, Dr. R. W. Drechsler, refused the delegation admittance. Nonetheless, a group that was itself suffering from genocidal policies stood up for the Jews of the Third Reich. It was a bold and heroic gesture, and even if without effect, it signaled an attempt to intervene in a way that few nation states did.

After 1921, Canada began to close its doors to immigrants and in 1931 effectively bolted them. From that time forward, an extremely strict quota system was maintained in place, largely designed to keep out Jewish refugees. Only 15,800 were granted entry into Canada between 1921 and 1931. As in many countries, especially those hard hit by the Depression, Canadians were largely opposed to allowing in foreigners during the interwar period. The prime minister, Mackenzie King—who supported British appeasement policies toward the Nazis and met with Hitler, describing him as "a reasonable and caring man . . . who might be thought of as one of the saviors of the world"—shared the common prejudices of his day. In 1939, ignoring pleas from the Jewish community to admit Jews and their promises that they would financially support the stranded passengers of the S.S. *St. Louis*, King refused to grant them asylum. The prime minister's attitudes were echoed by the director of the Immigration Branch of the Department of Mines and Resources, Frederick Charles Blair. In 1938, he wrote to King, boasting that "Pressure by Jewish people to get into Canada has never been greater than it is now, and I am glad to be able to add that after 35 years of experience here, that it has never been so carefully controlled." The following year, when asked how many Jewish immigrants Canada would accept after World War II, Blair replied, "[N]one is too many." Groups that were willing to help could not, and those that were in a position to do so would not. Chaim Weizmann summed up the international mood aptly when he observed, "The world was divided into two camps: those that wanted to get rid of the Jews and those that refused to take them in."

Jews wishing to leave Germany under the Third Reich faced many obstacles. The entry permits that various nations demanded had to demonstrate the capacity of immigrants to sustain themselves. However, after they had paid the Nazis the exorbitant flight tax, valued at about 25 percent of one's property value, and exchanged their reichsmarks for foreign currency at terrible exchange rates, little was left over that would prove "sustenance capacity." Another fact that militated against German Jewry leaving en masse was that the Jewish population had twice as many people over the age of sixty than the rest of the German population. It was simply harder for such people to leave, learn a new language, and start life afresh in a foreign land. In addition, the chief obstacle to leaving was that there was barely anywhere to go. Still, even though most countries refused to accept Jewish refugees, by the outbreak of World War II about half of the German Jewish population had managed to leave.

One means by which many escaped was through the **Ha'avara Agreement** (1933–1939). The German Ministry of the Economy and Zionist representatives in Germany concluded a deal on August 27, 1933, that permitted the transfer of Jewish assets to Palestine in exchange for the export of German goods to Palestine. About 100 million reichsmarks were transferred, and about 60,000 German Jews emigrated to Palestine between 1933 and 1939. Neither side trusted the other. The Zionists were under no illusions that the Nazis were being altruistic, and the Nazis were always ambivalent about Zionism, enticed by the idea that it was a means of ridding themselves of Jews but also fearful that an independent Jewish homeland would be a bridgehead in the so-called "world Jewish conspiracy."

After Evian, the Jewish situation deteriorated in other countries. Evian made evident that Jewish fate would not become an international cause. Other governments could follow the Nazi lead and pursue antisemitic policies without fear of world censure. In 1938, both Italy and Hungary joined Germany in instituting antisemitic race laws, while other states in eastern Europe continued to discriminate against Jews both legally and socially. The refusal of the world's nations to take in Jewish refugees merely emboldened Hitler, leading him to believe that most countries were in agreement with his policies. An internal SD report on the Evian Conference stated, "[T]he many speeches and discussions show that with the exception of a few countries that can still admit Jewish emigrants, there is an extensive aversion to a significant flow of emigrants either out of social considerations or out of an unexpressed racial abhorrence against Jewish emigrants." The headline of a Nazi newspaper was more blunt, screaming, "Nobody wants them!"

On August 17, 1938, all Jews were forced to adopt the additional names of Israel for a man and Sara for a woman, while on October 5, Heinrich Rothmund, head of the Swiss Alien Police, recommended that passports of Jews be stamped with a letter J. The Nazis passed the measure into law. The territory of the Third Reich, which had been expanded with the annexation of Austria was further enlarged when, pursuing a policy of appeasement, the Western powers ceded the Sudetenland to Hitler on October 1, 1938. Hitler, who had been initially greeted with considerable skepticism in Germany's elite military circles, was increasingly celebrated as a great conqueror. He had rearmed Germany, brought it international recognition (hosting the Olympic Games in 1936), disenfranchised and robbed the Jews in the absence of meaningful international protest, and expanded the country's territory, all without firing a shot. With his regime consolidated, his personal appeal at record levels, and his justified sense that the world was indifferent to the fate of the Jews, he launched his most massive assault yet.

On October 28, 1938, Germany expelled some 17,000 Polish Jews from its territory, dumping them in a no-man's land across the border. In Paris on November 6, Hershel Grynszpan, the distraught son of two deported Jews, entered the German Embassy and shot the third secretary, Ernst vom Rath. In retaliation for vom Rath's death, Hitler authorized a proposal by Goebbels to unleash "spontaneous" demonstrations. On the night of November 9–10, SA, party functionaries, and fanatical citizens carried out a series of pogroms throughout the Reich known as the ***Kristallnacht***, or **Night of Broken Glass.** Scores of Jewish homes and 7,500 Jewish-owned shops and businesses were destroyed, and over 1,000 synagogues were looted and ransacked, with about 300 put to flames. Ninety-one Jews were killed, and about 26,000 were rounded up and placed in concentration camps. Goebbels, who was in Munich, exalted in his diary: "I see a blood-red [glow] in the sky. The synagogue burns. . . . From all over the Reich information is now flowing in: 50, then 70 synagogues are burning. . . . As I am driven to my hotel, windowpanes shatter. Bravo! Bravo! The synagogues burn like big old cabins." The police and fire brigades were ordered by Hitler not to interfere except when German life and property was in danger.

For five years, discrimination, robbery, and defamation met with popular indifference or approval. The widespread violence and property damage of Kristallnacht, however, was not popular, a Nazi report declaring that "in viewing the ruins and attendant measures employed, all of the local crowds observed were obviously benumbed over what had happened and aghast over the unprecedented fury of Nazi acts that had been or were taking place with bewildering rapidity." Still, there was barely any protest, which by now had little chance of success anyway. To allay any doubts among the populace about the legal basis of Nazi persecution and to help Germans justify the orgy of destruction to themselves, the Nazis broadcast a radio version of Shakespeare's *Merchant of Venice* not long after the Night of Broken Glass. The message was that Shylock, who stood for all Jews, got his comeuppance just as did the Jews of the Third Reich on Kristallnacht. The November pogrom would be the last time that such a violent outburst against the Jews would take place in full view of the German public.

The violence and damage inflicted on Jews that night left the authorities with the problem of insurance compensation. The property that was insured entitled policy holders to make their claims, and major insurance companies, such as Allianz, could not default on claims without risking their international reputations and business. Göring called a meeting of Germany's major insurance executives for November 12, and, with Goebbels also in attendance, announced that after the insurance companies had paid out to Jewish property owners, the government would then impound the money as

Burned out interior of Berlin's Fasanenstrasse Synagogue after Kristallnacht. As the Jewish population of Berlin's western suburbs grew rapidly from less than 5,000 in 1885 to over 23,000 by 1910, it became necessary to build a new synagogue. The Fasanenstrasse Synagogue, one of the largest in Berlin was built between 1910 and 1912 and sat 1,720 worshippers. The total cost for the purchase of the land and construction was 1.7 million gold marks. The monumental synagogue was predominantly of Romanesque design, with some Byzantine elements. It was home to a liberal congregation headed by Berlin's last chief rabbi, Leo Baeck. The Nazis closed the synagogue in 1936, and it was destroyed on Kristallnacht, November 9, 1938, one of over 1,000 synagogues destroyed on that night. Joseph Goebbels, Minister of Propaganda, personally gave the order to burn down the synagogue.

part of a one billion reichsmarks fine, called an "atonement penalty," for the murder of vom Rath. It was also determined that the Jews were to pay for the cleanup. Having devised this scheme to further cripple the Jewish economy, Göring took the opportunity to accelerate and complete the process of Aryanization by forcing what remained of Jewish property into the state's coffers. The state paid the Jewish owner the bare minimum and in turn sold the property to Aryan owners at its real value, thereby pocketing the sizeable difference. Finally, Göring declared that effective January 1, 1939, the Jews were to be totally excluded from the German economy. This last stipulation meant that Jews would have to sell their businesses as well as works of art and jewelry. Göring concluded the meeting by saying, "Incidentally, I'd like to say again that I would not like to be a Jew in Germany."

Most Jews agreed with Göring's statement, and about 120,000 left in the winter of 1938–1939. For some, leaving turned out to provide only the illusion of relief. On May 13, 1939, a German passenger ship, the S.S. *St. Louis,* left Hamburg bound for Cuba with 900 Jews aboard. Most were headed for the United States. Cuba had charged each one $150 for an entrance visa, but one week before the ship departed Cuba declared the visas invalid. And still the *St. Louis* sailed. Upon arrival in Havana the passengers were denied entrance into the port. The German press, which had fanned the flames of antisemitism in Cuba to orchestrate precisely this response, was ecstatic. Here was further confirmation that no one wanted the Jews. On June 2, the ship set off for Miami, amid protracted negotiations with the Cuban government. A Jewish welfare agency had provided sustenance to the Jews while they were in Cuba, and still the government would not yield. The U.S. government also refused to admit the *St. Louis*. The ship then had no choice but to return to Europe. Belgium, Holland, Great Britain, and France offered to take the Jews until the United States would admit them. The process took too long for those who landed in Belgium, Holland, and France. Trapped during the German invasion, the passengers of the *St. Louis* were deported and murdered in the death camps.

Immediately after Kristallnacht, more decrees and laws followed. On November 15, all Jewish children still attending German schools were expelled. A November 23 police ordinance prevented Jews from entering certain areas and determined the times that Jews could appear in public. On November 29, it became illegal for Jews to keep carrier pigeons, a stunningly petty decree in light of the major assault on Jewish life. On December 3, Jews were forbidden to own automobiles and motorbikes and had to turn in their drivers' licenses.

At the November 12 meeting, Göring still harbored a desire to "kick the Jew out of Germany." The ultimate goal at this stage remained forced emigration. The idea of shipping Jews off to the French island of Madagascar, a plan first entertained in the 1930s in both France and Poland, was seriously considered by the Nazi government. At the start of the war, the Nazis toyed with the Nisko Plan, or the Lublin Plan, with the idea of shipping Jews off to a "reservation" near the city of Radom, some eighty kilometers south of Warsaw. Like the idea of Madagascar, it was shelved as impractical, despite the fact that by January 1940 about 70,000 Jews from Vienna, Czechoslovakia, Germany, and western Poland had already been relocated there.

Hitler was concerned about uninhibited private profiteering from the Aryanization of Jewish businesses and property. On December 6, 1938, Göring warned regional Nazi party heads that all profits from Aryanization belonged to the Reich and were to be deposited with the finance ministry. Göring offered a most revealing reason for this demand: "[I]t is only thus that the Führer's rearmament program can be accomplished." The forthcoming world war would be partly financed by robbing Jews.

Kristallnacht and its immediate aftermath essentially brought to an end the millennial existence of German and Austrian Jewry. As Hitler's foreign policy became more bellicose, so too did his threats against Jews become increasingly blunt. On January 21, 1939, he told the Czech foreign minister, Frantisek Chvalkovsky, "[W]e are going to destroy the Jews. They are not going to get away with what they did on November 9, 1918. The day of reckoning has come." And then on January 30, 1939, on the sixth anniversary of his accession to power, Hitler told the German parliament, the

Reichstag, "Today I will once more be a prophet: if the international Jewish financiers in and outside Europe should succeed in plunging the nations once more into a world war, then the result will not be the Bolshevization of the earth, and thus the victory of Jewry, but the annihilation of the Jewish race in Europe!"

Phase II: The Destruction of European Jewry (1939–1945)

World War II broke out on September 1, 1939, when Germany invaded Poland. One week before, on August 23, 1939, Germany and the Soviet Union signed a nonaggression treaty known as the Molotov-Ribbentrop Pact, named after the foreign ministers of the two countries. The pact included a secret protocol, in which the independent countries of Finland, Estonia, Latvia, Lithuania, Poland, and Romania came under "spheres of influence" of the two nations. The pact ensured Hitler that he would not have to fight a war on two fronts, and Stalin benefited by acquiring vastly expanded territory. After the German invasion of Poland (the Soviets invaded from the east on September 17), the country fell after three weeks and was partitioned, for the fourth time since the eighteenth century, according to the terms of the Molotov-Ribbentrop Pact.

The Ghettos

At the start of the war, the Jewish community of Poland numbered 3.3 million. The assault on them began with the German invasion as the Nazi aerial bombardment campaign specifically targeted Jewish neighborhoods in Warsaw. The defeat of Poland also meant its division. As prearranged by the two conquerors, 1.2 million Jews in the east of the country came under Soviet rule and more than 2 million Jews came under direct German control. Not long after invading Poland, the Germans froze all Jewish bank accounts, safety deposit boxes, and securities. All these assets were then to be deposited in one bank, and for deposits over 2,000 zlotys, account holders were prohibited from withdrawing more than 250 zlotys per week to cover living costs. Policies that had been implemented against German Jews after Hitler came to power were then imposed on Polish Jews. An order of December 16, 1939, decreed that Polish Jews in the General Government no longer had any claims on disability pensions, unemployment insurance, and sickness benefits. Hospitalization for Jews was only permitted in exceptional circumstances, and as of March 6, 1940, Jewish doctors, dentists, and midwives were only permitted to treat Jewish patients, thus severely limiting their ability to earn a living.

Plunder and dispossession, though a matter of policy, differed from place to place according to whim and local conditions, but the situation in Lvov was rather typical. In August 1941, the Nazis imposed a fine of twenty million rubles on the Jews of the city. The "justification" given was that Lvov had been severely damaged in the war and, because the war was the fault of the Jews, they had the responsibility of paying for the damage. People stood in long queues at the offices of the Jewish Council, paying a lot or just a little. Giving eighteen rubles (the figure numerically equivalent to the word "chai," Hebrew for life) was quite common, but the Judenrat accepted payment in all forms. Jews handed over gold and silver items, watches, brooches, candelabras, and wedding rings. The silverware alone amounted to over 1,400 kilos. To ensure payment, the Germans with their Ukrainian collaborators took Jewish hostages. By August 8, the "contribution," as it was called by the Nazis, had been paid.

Everywhere, German soldiers, policemen, officials, and even civilians felt entitled to take anything they wanted. In Warsaw and Lodz, military and police forces confiscated the contents of textile and grocery warehouses. In Lodz, the robberies were so brazen and on such a huge scale that senior Nazi officials complained about the "wild confiscations." In February 1940 in the small town of Kutno, ethnic Germans (*Volksdeutsche*) robbed Jews of such household items as bedding and furniture. Nearly every Jewish home was plundered. Sometimes the extortions were for private use by German officials and very specific. In Warsaw a demand was issued to the chairman of the Judenrat on July 22, 1941, on behalf of Brigita Frank, wife of Hans Frank, governor-general of occupied Poland. She insisted on being given "a coffee-maker to brew Turkish coffee, one lady's traveling kit, and leather boxes large enough to serve four or six people on a picnic."

With the German conquest, arbitrary terror was immediately inflicted on Poland's Jews. Beatings, shootings, and public humiliation characterized daily life. Shaye Chaskiel recalled:

I was 10 years old and had only 4 years of schooling when World War II broke out in Poland in 1939. In January 1940, the Gestapo decided to hang 10 Jewish people in the city square in the town [Chenstochova] that I lived with my family. Amongst the 10 was my father's uncle Manus.

The Jewish police chose my father as one of the people to go out and hang them. My father refused and fought with the police. One of the Gestapo came into our home and tried again to force my dad to hang these people—again he refused. The Gestapo came back, took my father out and shot him.

My sister and I carried our father to a cart and we wheeled him to the cemetery. At the age of 11, I had to dig a hole and bury my father.

Shaye Chaskiel's horror occurred outside of the two main institutions created by the Nazis to destroy the Jews—the ghettos and the camps. But the randomness of the terror he experienced outside those settings that day—he later wound up in the Lodz ghetto, Auschwitz, and Buchenwald—remained a constant feature of Jewish life under the German occupation of Poland until the end of the war. The establishment of ghettos and camps facilitated the practice of terror on a far larger, more systematic scale.

On September 21, 1939, just after Poland's collapse, Heydrich ordered the ghettoization of Polish Jewry, which took place between October 1939, and April 1941. All Jewish communities of fewer than 500 persons were dissolved, and the inhabitants were herded into nearby ghettos, most of which, according to Heydrich, were "to be located along railroad lines." The goal was the immediate concentration of Jews for the purposes of exploiting them for the German war effort and, as Heydrich said, for a "final aim" yet to be determined but one "which will require an extended period of time."

Heydrich's order also carried the stipulation that each ghetto was to be administered by a "Council of Jewish Elders," a *Judenrat*. Each Jewish Council was composed of twenty-four members drawn from the prewar secular and religious elites. The Jewish Councils led a desperate struggle to provide welfare to Jews—they were responsible for housing, medical care, food distribution, and education, and the latter provision was only permitted in some ghettos—but their principal obligation remained the "exact and punctual execution" of Nazi orders. Their tasks included providing the Nazis with maps of the ghettos, accurate lists of Jews and their professions, slave labor, confiscated Jewish property, valuables and "contributions." Worst of all, the Jewish Councils were later made responsible for selecting which ghetto inhabitants were to be sent to the gas chambers at extermination camps. The Nazis made Jews complicit in their own destruction.

The word *ghetto* is a misnomer, for the ghettos established by the Nazis bore no resemblance to the original ghetto established in Venice in 1516. Though intended to separate Jews from the rest of the population, the early modern ghetto never prevented contact between Jews and gentiles and, in fact, never inhibited Jewish life. In short, ghetto gates were locked from the inside at sundown and then opened at sunrise, permitting Jews to exit and non-Jews to enter. The Nazi ghettos, by contrast, were prisons, locked from the outside by German guards. Surrounded by a fence or a wall, Nazi ghettos were constructed in the poorest sections of towns. The non-Jewish population was moved out and Jews were transferred in.

There were hundreds of ghettos, and each varied significantly based on when and where it had been built, the nature of the local economy, the occupational structure, demographic, and cultural makeup of the Jewish community, and the topography of the surrounding area. It was in the ghettos that the physical destruction of the Jewish people began in earnest, as Jews suffered from overcrowding, epidemics, starvation, terror, and isolation from the outside world.

Theft was the handmaiden of murder. In November 1939, the Nazis established the Trust Office of the General Government of Poland. Its purpose was to secure confiscated Polish national assets, Jewish assets, and property now deemed ownerless because of the war. In Warsaw alone, Jewish real estate assets amounted to approximately 50,000 properties, valued at two billion zlotys. With those confiscations, not only did the owners lose out, but the building superintendents and tradesmen who maintained them—plumbers, carpenters, electricians, and handymen—all lost their livelihoods. Literally tens of thousands of small, medium, and large businesses owned by Jews were stolen by the Trust, which in turn dismissed the Jewish employees of these enterprises. With so much booty to process, a sub-branch of the Trust was established to sell off the property, clothes, and household items of Jews deported from their communities into the ghettos.

The brutality of the Nazis took Polish Jewry, accustomed as it was to antisemitism, by surprise. On March 10, 1940, a Hebrew diarist in the Warsaw ghetto, Chaim Kaplan, observed defiantly:

The gigantic catastrophe which has descended on Polish Jewry has no parallel, even in the darkest periods of Jewish history. First, in the depth of the hatred. This is not just hatred whose source is a party platform. . . . It is a hatred of emotion, whose source is some psychopathic malady. In its outward manifestations it functions as physiological hatred, which imagines the object of hatred to be unclean in body, a leper who has no place within the camp. . . . It is our good fortune that the conquerors have failed to consider the nature and strength of Polish Jewry, and this has kept us alive. . . . But we do not conform to the laws of nature. A certain invisible power is embedded in us and it is this secret which keeps us alive and preserves us in spite of all the laws of nature. . . . The Jews of Poland . . . love life, and they do not wish to disappear from the earth before their time. The fact that we have hardly any suicides is worthy of special emphasis. We have been left naked but as long as that secret power is concealed within us, we shall not yield to despair. The strength of this

power lies in the very nature of the Polish Jew, which is rooted in our eternal tradition that commands us to live.

When Kaplan wrote these lines, the Nazi death machine was still not operating at full capacity. The situation would only get worse. In the beginning, aid was made available to those incarcerated in ghettos through the **Joint Distribution Committee** ("the Joint"), an American organization founded in 1914 to offer material assistance to Jewish communities abroad. The Joint was permitted to send in food parcels and other necessities to ghettos located in the General Government (those parts of Poland occupied by the Germany military), which it did through the Jewish Social Self-Help (JSS or, in Yiddish, *Aleynhilf*), an organization that was headquartered in Cracow under the leadership of theatre director Dr. Michael Veychert. In turn, the JSS distributed the items inside the ghetto directly to individuals or through other mutual aid societies such as TOZ, a health care agency; CENTOS, an association that cared for orphans; and ORT, a vocational training organization.

In Warsaw, the JSS was known as ZETOS and was headed by the distinguished historian **Emanuel Ringelblum** (1900–1944). Under his creative and energetic leadership, ZETOS became a vast organization operating departments that dealt with refugee affairs, housing, clothing, culture, and public kitchens. Where the JSS often acted in concert with the Jewish Councils, in Warsaw ZETOS was continually opposed to the Judenrat. Because of this and due to the assistance it was able to dole out, ZETOS won the trust of the people and was seen by them as the leading Jewish force in the ghetto. Operating on a budget of about $20,000 per month, the JSS distributed money through "house committees," established in the courtyards of apartment buildings in the ghetto. The committees, which did not exist in other ghettos, attempted to provide for the starving inhabitants' material and spiritual needs by running kitchens and organizing recreational activities, makeshift schools, and religious services. Tenants paid dues that were determined at a public meeting, and means testing saw to it that the wealthier were taxed at a higher rate than the poor. Taxes were supplemented by ongoing fund-raising campaigns. In 1940, 788 house committees were serving the needs of 7,500 people, and by 1942 the number of committees had increased to 1,108. The task was overwhelming, and it meant that despite its best efforts ZETOS was unable to provide sufficient food and other forms of welfare for Jews in the ghetto. In Warsaw, at least 75 percent of the 100,000 Jewish children under the age of fifteen required welfare assistance of some kind.

The Joint's relief activities ended when Nazi Germany officially declared war on the United States in December 1941.

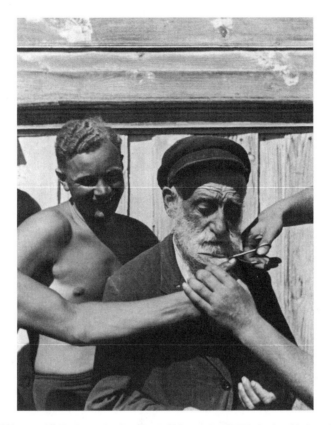

Persecution of orthodox Jew in Warsaw, 1941. An orthodox Jew in Warsaw in 1941 is having his beard cut off by two soldiers while a third looks on laughing. Just as in Nazi Germany before the war, the persecution of Jews in Poland (and elsewhere) after the war began was characterized by humiliation and an attempt to shame. It was also a source of "entertainment" for German soldiers, as can be seen in this photograph. Religious Jews, in particular, were singled out for such treatment.

After that, conditions in the ghettos quickly deteriorated. The first to succumb were the refugees brought into the ghettos from surrounding towns. They had no local contacts and were entirely dependent on a welfare system, unable to provide even for the native Jews of the city, let alone newcomers. Piotrkow's Jewish population went from 8,000 to 12,000, while in Cracow the prewar Jewish population of 56,000 increased to 68,000 thanks to the arrival of Jewish refugees from neighboring small towns. Warsaw took in as many as 150,000 refugees from at least 700 locales. Overcrowding was a constant problem. The ghettos were large, with the biggest in Warsaw, whose population at its peak was about 450,000, an extraordinary number given that the prewar Jewish population of the city was 337,000. A German official in Warsaw reported in January 1941, "The Jewish quarter extends over about 1,016 acres. . . . Occupancy therefore works out at 15.1 persons per apartment and 6 to 7 persons per room." In Vilna, a Jew wrote, "About 25,000 persons live in our ghetto in 72 buildings on 5 street sections. This comes to one-and-a-half to two meters per person. Narrow as the grave." Similar conditions prevailed in the Lodz ghetto (which held about 200,000 Jews) and Lvov (about 120,000), the second- and third-largest ghettos.

Overcrowding spread disease, as plumbing soon broke and toilets overflowed. Little heat was had in winter, and water became extremely scarce. Of the 31,271 apartments in the Lodz ghetto, only 725 had running water. Parents were often faced with the insoluble dilemma of whether to use precious water for cooking or for washing lice out of a child's hair. In such conditions, typhus, tuberculosis, and dysentery ran rampant. People were caked in lice. A typhus epidemic that broke out in the Warsaw ghetto in late 1940 claimed 43,239 victims. Starvation became not just a by-product of ghetto life but a deliberate policy of the Nazis. In Lodz, the starving young diarist, Dawid Sierakowiak, recorded on December 28, 1942, "The ration for the first ten days of January has been issued. There are no potatoes at all in it, only 5 kilos of vegetables and a bit of marmalade. . . . the prospect of cold and hunger fills me with indescribable terror. . . . Today we went to bed without supper because [my sister] Nadzia portioned out our remaining potato scraps for tomorrow and the day after tomorrow." Dawid was eighteen years old when he died on August 8, 1943, of what was known as "ghetto disease," a combination of tuberculosis, starvation, and exhaustion. For Sara Plagier, a fourteen-year-old girl also in the Lodz ghetto, food even determined time itself: "In the ghetto we had no need for a calendar. Our lives were divided into periods based on the distribution of food: bread every eighth day, the ration once a month. Each day fell into two parts: before and after we received our soup. In this way the time passed."

The daily bread ration in Warsaw was less than a hundred grams (3.5 ounces). The bread was often made with sand or sawdust. In January 1941, the official total daily caloric intake granted Jews was 220. By August 1941, it was reduced to 177. Moreover, it had become increasingly unaffordable. A kilogram of bread cost four zlotys in 1940, rose to fourteen zlotys in May 1942, and was fetching forty-five zlotys by summer. The meager amount and poor quality of the bread coupled with the rising prices had the desired effect for the Nazis. In January 1941, 818 people starved to death in the Warsaw ghetto. Month after month the number rose. In August 5,560 perished from hunger. The situation was so bad that the Jewish ghetto hospital was able to conduct some of the first clinical studies of the effects of hunger on the human body. By January 4, 1942, Chaim Kaplan's tone had changed as he described the hunger, disease, and misery that surrounded him: "It is not at all uncommon on a cold winter morning to see the bodies of those who have died on the sidewalks of cold and starvation during the night. . . . In the gutters, among the refuse, one can see almost naked and barefoot little children wailing pitifully. These are children who were orphaned when both parents died either in their wanderings or in the typhus epidemic." Only smuggling prevented even more people from dying, and it was often organized by the prewar Jewish criminal class and executed by children small enough to pass through gaps where walls failed to touch the streets or through holes in fences. The young smugglers risked their lives to sneak vegetables past the Jewish police and Nazi guards. They became memorialized in popular song:

> Over the wall, through holes, and past the guard,
> Through the wires, ruins, and fences,
> Plucky, hungry, and determined,
> I sneak through, dart like a cat

Smuggling, soup kitchens, and rudimentary medical care, as crucial as they were, could not prevent 500,000 Jews from dying of starvation and disease in the ghettos before the mass killings of 1941 even began.

Early on, Nazi ranks were divided about the purpose of the ghettos. There were two groups, the productionists, who thought ghettos could be effectively exploited for the Nazi war effort, battled attritionists, who were of the opinion that the sole purpose for the ghettos was to destroy the inhabitants. In truth, both policies were pursued, but the attritionists always had the upper hand—and the final say. In fact, the Nazis invoked the unsanitary conditions in the ghettos as justification for murdering the inhabitants. As the Nazi Party ideologist Alfred Rosenberg said after visiting the Warsaw ghetto, "[S]eeing this race en masse, which is decaying, decomposing, and rotten to the core, will banish any sentimental humanitarianism." Propaganda Minister Joseph Goebbels, expressed similar sentiments even more bluntly after visiting the Vilna ghetto: "The Jews are the lice of civilized humanity. One has to exterminate them somehow, otherwise they will continue to play their tortuous and annoying role." Cynically, Nazi doctors and party officials embarked on a deliberate policy of spreading disease, then claimed that exterminating the ghetto inhabitants would prevent the spread of contagion.

In the ghettos, terror was everywhere. Selection for murder accompanied daily humiliation. Orthodox Jews were force-fed pork and made to urinate and defecate on Torah scrolls. Jewish men were made to pay to have their beards shaved, and very often beards were burned off or cut off so brutally that lumps of flesh came away from the face.

A prevailing characteristic of ghetto life all over Poland was the sense of isolation. Jews were cut off from the outside world. As Jurek Becker, who was in the Lodz ghetto, wrote in his novel *Jacob the Liar:* "Well . . . it is evening. Don't ask me what time it is. Only the Germans know that." In all ghettos, rules were arbitrary yet designed to isolate and stigmatize Jews. On August 2, 1941, a Nazi decree forbade Jews in the Vilna ghetto "to use sidewalks" and compelled them to "use only the right hand verges of roadway and walk in single file." In all ghettos Nazis confiscated radios, telephones, and newspapers. The use of such items was punishable by death. Mail service barely functioned.

Jewish suffering brought forth a new artistic genre— Holocaust music. The subject matter of the songs was grim and blunt: beatings, shootings, starvation, torture, and the loss of family and home. The songs capture the multiple moods of the doomed. Some were defiant. In Kovno, Jewish slave-labor brigades sang:

> We don't weep or grieve
> Even when you beat and lash us,
> But never for a moment believe
> That you will discourage and dash us.

Other songs reflected despair tinged with the faintest hope of emerging alive. Workers led from the Radom ghetto used to sing:

Work, brothers, work fast,
If you don't, they'll lash your hide.
Not many of us will manage to last—
Before long we'll all have died.

After his wife's death in 1943, Vilna songwriter and resistance fighter Shmerke Kaczerginski wrote the following Yiddish love song, *Friling* (*Springtime*):

I walk through the Ghetto alone and forsaken,
There's no-one to care for me now.
And how can you live when your love has been taken,
Will somebody please show me how?
I know that it's springtime, and birdsong, and sunshine,
All nature seems happy and free,
But locked in the Ghetto I stand like a beggar,
I beg for some sunshine for me.

After the defeat of Poland, the Nazi war machine swept through western Europe, ensnaring more Jews in its grip. Between April and June 1940, the Nazis conquered Denmark (Jewish pop. 8,000), Norway (Jewish pop. 2,000), France (Jewish pop. 350,000), Belgium (Jewish pop. 65,000), Luxembourg (Jewish pop. 3,500), and Holland (Jewish pop. 140,000). In southeastern Europe in April 1941, the communities of Serbia (Jewish pop. 75,000) and Greece (Jewish pop. 77,000) came under Nazi control. Occupation brought roundups of Jews, passage of anti-Jewish laws and ordinances, confiscation of property, and pressing of Jews into forced labor. Antisemitic legislation was also adopted in countries allied with Nazi Germany, either before the war began or thereafter: Slovakia (Jewish pop. 135,000), Vichy France (Jewish pop. 350,000), Italy (Jewish pop. 57,000), Romania (Jewish pop. 757,000), Hungary (Jewish pop. 650,000), Bulgaria (Jewish pop. 50,000), and Croatia (Jewish pop. 30,000).

In Germany, the myriad antisemitic decrees continued to mount. On the first day of the war, Jews were forbidden to leave their homes after eight o'clock in the evening. The rationale was that they "used the blackout to harass Aryan women." Special orders for when and where Jews could shop were issued. In Württemberg at the turn of the year 1939–1940, the minister of food and agriculture forbad Jews from purchasing cocoa and gingerbread. Increasingly during the war, Jews were moved into "Jews' Houses," separate apartment buildings for them alone. Those Germans writing Ph.D. dissertations were instructed to quote Jewish authors

when it is "unavoidable on scientific grounds." Jewish authors were to be listed in a separate bibliography.

In June 1940, as the Nazis conquered western Europe, the Soviet Union gained control over the Baltic states: Lithuania, Latvia, and Estonia. In addition, the Soviets, through military victories and the terms of the Molotov-Ribbentrop Pact, gained control over Volhynia and eastern Galicia (annexed from Poland in September 1939) and from northern Bukovina and Bessarabia (annexed from Romania in 1940). These additional territories were home to about 2 million Jews, and thus the Soviet Union's Jewish population went from 3 million in 1939 to 5 million by 1940. These annexed Jewish communities, which had displayed remarkable cultural vibrancy in the interwar period, alarmed the Soviet authorities, who feared that they had inherited millions of Jewish nationalists rather than Soviet patriots. Concerned about their attachment to the various forms of Jewish secular and religious culture, Moscow immediately set about suppressing Jewish cultural and religious institutions. Yiddish newspapers, synagogues, and schools were shut down. Some Zionist and Bundist leaders, as well as religious functionaries, merchants, businessmen, and industrialists were killed, but most were exiled to Siberia. Altogether, the Soviets inadvertently saved a quarter of a million Jews from certain death at the hands of the Nazis by deporting these Jews to the Soviet interior. Whatever ill will the Soviet assault on Jewish life generated among Jews, however, soon subsided with the Nazi attack on the Soviet Union.

Mass Shootings in the Soviet Union

On June 22, 1941, Hitler launched **Operation Barbarossa,** the invasion of the Soviet Union. The war with Stalin's Russia was to be the great apocalyptic struggle with Communism, one that Hitler called a *Vernichtungskrieg* (a "war of annihilation"). Given his linking of Jews and Bolshevism, this was to be the race war that antisemites had been predicting since the nineteenth century. Despite the Soviet Union's assault on Jewish life, Jews were under no illusions. Their destiny lay with Soviet victory. Jews in the territories annexed by the Soviet Union looked upon the Soviets as liberators and were especially buoyed by the sight of Jewish Red Army officers. Non-Jews in these same areas tended to see the Soviets as their oppressors and Germans as liberators. This divergence of opinion would manifest itself in widespread local complicity with the Nazis in the murder of Jews. Among Soviet Jews, the war also sparked a great awakening. For those Jews who had their Jewish identity attenuated, if not obliterated by the Russian Revolution, the war against the Nazis rekindled a sense of their origins. The Jewish writer Ilya Ehrenburg delivered a speech in August 1941 in which he gave voice to a new sentiment: "I grew up in a Russian city. My native language is

Russian. I am a Russian writer. Now, like all Russians, I am defending my homeland. But the Nazis have reminded me of something else: my mother's name was Hannah. I am a Jew. I say this with pride. Hitler hates us more than anyone else. And that does us credit."

Hitler appears to have decided upon the mass murder of Soviet Jewry at some point during the planning phase of the invasion of the Soviet Union. Then, sometime in the last three months of 1941, this was extended to European Jewry as a whole. The exact timing of the order is a point of conjecture because no written and signed document has ever been discovered. It probably never existed. Rather, the decision to destroy the Jews was most likely conveyed orally from Hitler to Himmler. By this time, Hitler no longer really distinguished between the Allies and the Jews. They were one and the same, and both were the enemy. This was an ideological race war, one to finally rid the world of Jews. For Hitler, it would be history's most decisive moment. The destruction of the Jews was part of a policy designed to "clean up" the east in preparation for a massive program of German colonization. The area to be settled by Germans was called *Lebensraum* ("living space"). With the German invasion of the Soviet Union, several thousand Jews from the Baltic states joined the Red Army, while as many as 900,000 more were able to flee eastward into Soviet territory. In all, as many as 500,000 Jews served in the Red Army during the war; about 180,000 fell in battle. Millions of Jews, however, were unable to escape the invading Nazis.

Close on the heels of the 3 million German troops that attacked the Soviet Union, were four mobile death squads, the *Einsatzgruppen.* Each killing unit, made up of between 500 and 900 men, was further divided into smaller commando squads. Made up of SS, police battalions, regular German army units, and local collaborators, the Einsatzgruppen fanned out in search of civilians from the Baltic states in the north to the Black Sea region in the south. The perpetrators came from all walks of life. Of the first four commanders of the death squads, three held doctorates. Among other leaders were a physician and pastor and even an opera singer. Troops would arrive in a town in the early hours of the morning, take their victims by surprise, march them to an anti-tank ditch, or force them to dig their own graves. Robbed and made to strip, the naked Jews were then machine-gunned. Killings generally went on from dawn to dusk, the killers more often than not drunk as they shot their victims without mercy or let-up.

At first Einsatzgruppen mostly targeted Jewish men, but later women and children were included in the shootings. They also murdered Soviet political commissars, partisan fighters, Roma (Gypsies), the sick, and the disabled. The victims were either shot directly into or were dumped into mass graves. The numbers killed in this manner were staggering.

In the Baltic states and in Belorussia between July 23 and October 15, 1941, Einsatzgruppe A killed 135,567 Jews. Under the command of Franz Walter Stahlecker, the killing took place on a frantic scale. In two periods of just two days each, November 29–30, 1941, and December 8–9, 1941, 25,000 Latvian Jews from Riga were shot. Einsatzgruppe B, operating in White Russia under the command of Arthur Nebe, killed 45,467 Jews by mid-November 1941. In addition to shooting, Nebe used dynamite and then introduced gas vans to murder mental patients. In one of the most notorious mass killings on the Eastern Front, 33,371 Jews from Kiev were shot by Einsatzgruppe C at a ravine named **Babi Yar** in a two-day slaughter that took place on September 29 and 30, 1941. According to Nazi documents, the belongings of the Jews were sent to the National-Socialist Welfare Association and distributed to needy Germans. In retaliation for partisans having blown up a Nazi military post in southern Ukraine on October 22, 1941, Einsatzgruppe D rounded up 19,000 Jews and shot them. Immediately afterward, Romanian collaborators, without German participation, shot another 40,000 Jews in anti-tank ditches. Sometimes smaller Jewish communities were wiped out in a single day. On December 13, 1941, Einsatzgruppe D killed all 9,600 Jews of the Black Sea town of Simferopol. With assistance from Lithuanian, Latvian, Estonian, Ukrainian, Romanian, and Hungarian "militia units," the Einsatzgruppen had murdered over 1.4 million Jews by the spring of 1943.

Rivka Yoselevska was at the site of a mass shooting on August 22, 1941, just outside her hometown of Powost. In May 1961 she delivered her eyewitness testimony at the trial of Adolf Eichmann in Jerusalem. Speaking in Yiddish, she told the courtroom that on the day in question Germans and Belorussians entered the ghetto and a truck moved in:

> Those who were strong enough climbed up by themselves, but the weak ones were thrown in. They were piled into the truck like cattle. . . . The rest they made run after the truck. . . . I was holding my little girl and running after the truck, too. Many mothers had two or three children. All the way we had to run. When somebody fell down, they wouldn't let him get up; they shot him on the spot. All my family was there.
>
> We arrived at the place. Those who had been on the truck had already got down, undressed and stood in a row. . . . It was about three kilometres away from our town. There was a hill and a little below it they had dug something like a ditch. They made us walk up to the hill, in rows of four, and . . . shot each one of us separately. . . . They were SS men. They carried several guns with plenty of ammunition pouches. . . .

[My six-year old daughter, Markele and I] stood there facing the ditch. I turned my head. He asked, "Whom do I shoot first?" I didn't answer. He tore the child away from me. I heard her last cry and he shot her. Then he got ready to kill me, grabbed my hair and turned my head about. I remained standing and heard a shot but I didn't move. He turned me around, loaded his pistol, so that I could see what he was doing. Then he again turned me around and shot me. I fell down. . . .

I felt nothing. At that moment I felt that something was weighing me down. I thought that I was dead, but that I could feel something even though I was dead. I couldn't believe that I was alive. I felt I was suffocating, bodies had fallen on me. . . . I pulled myself up with the last bit of strength. When I reached the top I looked around but I couldn't recognize the place. Corpses strewn all over, there was no end to the bodies. You could hear people moaning in their death agony. . . . The Germans were not there. No one was there.

When he shot me I was wounded in the head. I still have a big scar on my head, where I was wounded by the Germans.

When I saw they were gone I dragged myself over to the grave and wanted to jump in. I thought the grave would open up and let me fall inside alive. I envied everyone for whom it was already over, while I was still alive. Where should I go? What should I do? Blood was spouting. Nowadays, when I pass a water fountain I can still see the blood spouting from the grave. The earth rose and heaved. I sat there on the grave and tried to dig my way in with my hands. I continued digging as hard as I could. The earth didn't open up. I shouted to Mother and Father, why I was left alive. What did I do to deserve this? Where shall I go? To whom can I turn? I have nobody. I saw everything; I saw everybody killed. No one answered. I remained sprawled on the grave three days and three nights.

Hermann Graebe was a German engineer and manager of a German construction firm in the Ukraine. Traveling around recruiting construction workers, he had occasion to witness the mass murders of Jews. Determined to do what he could to prevent such killings, Graebe, like Oskar Schindler, sought to use his position to save as many Jews as possible by providing them with work. On one occasion in July 1942, hearing that a massacre was about to take place, he obtained a "writ of protection" from the deputy district commissioner and hastily went to Rovno. Brandishing a gun, and the writ, he managed to secure the release of 150 Jews just before they were to be shot. On October 5, 1942, he accidentally came upon an execution squad killing Jews from the small Ukrainian town of Dubno. After the war at the Nuremberg trials, Graebe was the only German to testify for the prosecution and gave the following eyewitness testimony of the slaughter of 5,000 Jews (which elicited such hostility that he left Germany in 1948 and emigrated to San Francisco):

My foreman and I went directly to the pits. Nobody bothered us. Now I heard rifle shots in quick succession from behind one of the earth mounds. The people who had got off the trucks—men, women and children of all ages—had to undress upon the order of an SS man who carried a riding or dog whip. They had to put down their clothes in fixed places, sorted according to shoes, top clothing and undergarments. I saw heaps of shoes of about 800 to 1000 pairs, great piles of under-linen and clothing.

Without screaming or weeping these people undressed, stood around in family groups, kissed each other, said farewells, and waited for a sign from another SS man, who stood near the pit, also with a whip in his hand. During the fifteen minutes I stood near, I heard no complaint or plea for mercy. I watched a family of about eight persons, a man and a woman both of about fifty, with their children of about twenty to twenty-four, and two grown-up daughters about twenty-eight or twenty-nine. An old woman with snow white hair was holding a one year old child in her arms and singing to it and tickling it. The child was cooing with delight. The parents were looking on with tears in their eyes. The father was holding the hand of a boy about ten years old and speaking to him softly; the boy was fighting his tears. The father pointed to the sky, stroked his head and seemed to explain something to him.

At that moment the SS man at the pit started shouting something to his comrade. The latter counted off about twenty persons and instructed them to go behind the earth mound. Among them was the family I have just mentioned. I well remember a girl, slim with black hair, who, as she passed me, pointed to herself and said, "twenty-three years old." I walked around the mound and found myself confronted by a tremendous grave. People were closely wedged together and lying on top of each other so that only their heads were visible. Nearly all had blood running over their shoulders from their heads. Some of the people shot were still moving. Some were lifting their arms and turning their heads to show that they were still alive.

The pit was nearly two-thirds full. I estimated that it already contained about a thousand people. I looked for the man who did the shooting. He was an SS man, who sat at the edge of the narrow end of the pit, his feet dangling into the pit. He had a tommy-gun on his knees and was smoking a cigarette. The people, completely naked, went down some steps, which were cut in the clay wall of the pit and clambered over the heads of the people lying there to the place to which the SS man directed them. They lay down in front of the dead or wounded people; some caressed those who were still alive and spoke to them in a low voice. Then I heard a series of shots. I looked into the pit and saw that the bodies were twitching or the heads lying already motionless on top of the bodies that lay beneath them. Blood was running from their necks. The next batch was approaching already. They went down into the pit, lined themselves up against the previous victims and were shot.

Despite the vast numbers of Jews murdered by the Einsatzgruppen, the Nazis considered the process laborious, inefficient, and too dependent on valuable manpower. It also proved too emotionally difficult for the Germans to carry out. On November 29, even as the death squads were functioning at full capacity, Heydrich invited representatives of government, Nazi Party, and police agencies to a meeting to be held "followed by luncheon" to discuss "the remaining work connected with this final solution." The meeting eventually took place on January 20, 1942, and is known as the **Wannsee Conference,** after the suburb of Berlin in which it was held. Fifteen men attended. Heydrich first asserted the authority of Himmler (and by extension himself) over what emerged as the "Final Solution" and then summarized the various methods used against German Jewry thus far, indicating that they were insufficient to deal with the eleven million Jews slated for annihilation. Operations on a grander scale were to be employed. As he told the participants, "In the course of the practical execution of the final solution, Europe will be combed through from West to East."

The registration, deportation, expropriation, and murder of so many Jews required expert planning and, above all, the cooperation and coordination of all branches of the Nazi government. Heydrich assured those at the meeting that the decision had been taken at the very highest authority and that there was no turning back. The ninety-minute Wannsee Conference was the moment when every major minister or senior bureaucrat of the Nazi government became an accomplice, fully complicit in what would come to be known as the Holocaust.

The Extermination Camps

By the time of the Wannsee Conference, the Nazis had already decided to murder all the Jews of Europe. To realize this goal required a change in strategy. For the mass shootings

of the Einsatzgruppen, the murderers went after the Jews by hunting them down. The death camps, by contrast, transported Jews to fixed killing installations. Hitler, who took a keen interest in the "progress" of the Einsatzgruppen, was concerned that the extermination of Europe's Jews could not be carried out expeditiously by shooting. Gassing would become the preferred method of murdering Jews. While hundreds of Nazi concentration and labor camps were spread across Europe, there were only six extermination camps. All six were located in Poland because of its large Jewish population and the country's central location: **Chelmno, Belzec, Sobibor, Treblinka, Lublin-Majdanek,** and **Auschwitz.** The first gassing of Jews began at Chelmno on December 8, 1941. The Jewish and Roma (Gypsy) prisoners were gassed by being driven around in vans, with a hose attached to the exhaust pipe redirected into the passenger compartment. Though deadly, this method proved inefficient for the Nazis. The first camp to use gas chambers was Belzec, which became operational in March 1942. Two more death factories were created soon thereafter: Sobibor and Treblinka. In these three extermination camps, approximately 1.7 million Jews had been gassed by October 1943. A mere 120 people survived these three camps.

Auschwitz and Majdanek were composite camps with an extermination center and slave labor operations. The largest extermination camp was **Auschwitz-Birkenau** in southern Poland, fifty kilometers west of Cracow. Over a million Jews and tens of thousands of Roma, Poles, and Soviet prisoners-of-war were gassed there by November 1944 in four gas chambers using the deadly cyanide-based insecticide, **Zyklon B.** At the height of the deportations, up to 7,000 Jews were gassed each day at Auschwitz-Birkenau.

The camps at Belzec, Sobibor, and Treblinka were administered and in part designed by Christian Wirth, one of history's greatest mass murderers. These were pure killing centers that existed for no other purpose than killing as many Jews as possible as quickly as possible. These facilities were manned and operated by about a hundred people who, like Wirth, had gained experience in institutional mass murder in the "euthanasia" or **T-4 program** operated in Germany between 1939 and 1941 in an attempt to reengineer the biological or racial character of society by eliminating the sick and the "inferior" from the gene pool. Categorized as "life not worthy of life," about 100,000 mentally and physically disabled children and adults went to their deaths in six killing facilities in Germany and Austria. Most were gassed with carbon monoxide, a method personally recommended by Hitler. The T-4 operations were not confined to Germany. Early in the war, the SS rounded up and shot at least 17,000 Poles in various hospitals and asylums as part of the program. The link between the euthanasia program and the Holocaust lies in the shared personnel, similar killing methods, and ideological justification of eliminating lives deemed worthless or harmful.

The height of the killing in the death camps occurred in 1942 as the Germans began liquidating the ghettos. Between March 1942 and October 1943, the following ghettos were destroyed: Lublin, Warsaw, Lvov, Cracow, Chenstochova, Bialystok. In addition, Jewish residents in hundreds of small towns were murdered. The number killed was over 2 million in this period alone. Deporitng Jews to extermination camps was known euphemistically as "resettlement" or "evacuation," and the Nazis used collaborating locals—Ukrainians, Belorussians, Romanians, and those from the Baltic states to assist them. (see Map 14-1).

Between July 22 and September 21, 1942, mass deportations began from the Warsaw ghetto. In that fifty-two-day period, about 300,000 people were taken and gassed at Treblinka. Of the 450,000 people crammed into the ghetto at its peak, only about 55,000 Jews now remained alive. They were spared because they were either working in German factories within the ghetto or living in hiding. A small remnant would form the core of the resistance that would break out in April 1943. In all the ghettos, the liquidation process was similar. The Nazis would demand of the Judenrat a specified number of Jews, generally to be delivered the next day. In Warsaw, on July 22, 1942, the quota was set at a minimum of 6,000 per day. The responsibility for this fell on the head of the Judenrat, **Adam**

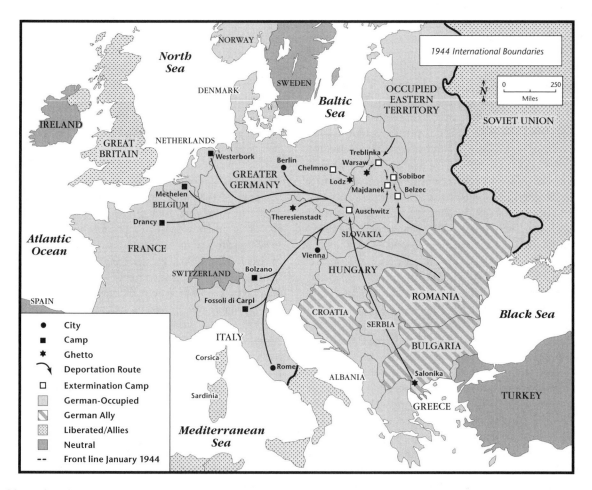

Map 14-1 Deportation Routes to Death Camps, 1942–1944. Of the approximately 6 million Jews who perished in the Holocaust, around 2.75 million were murdered in the six extermination camps that operated in Poland. Trains from all over Europe arrived at the camps on a daily basis. Most Jews were sent to their deaths immediately upon arrival. This was the fate of about 875,000 of Auschwitz's 1 million Jewish victims. At Treblinka, the second-largest death camp, situated eighty kilometers northeast of Warsaw, between 25 and 35 SS men and police and an auxiliary guard unit of between 90 and 150 non-Germans murdered as many as 925,000 Jews between July 1942 and November 1943.

Czerniakow (1880–1942), the Germans having threatened him that his wife would be shot on the spot if he did not comply. He negotiated for exemptions, in particular for orphans. His requests were turned down and he refused to sign the "resettlement" order. Consumed by despair, the next day he committed suicide. He left two suicide notes, one to his wife and the other to his fellow members of the Judenrat, in which he stated bluntly, "I am powerless. My heart trembles in sorrow and compassion. I can no longer bear all this. My act will prove to everyone what is the right thing to do."

Lodz, the second-largest ghetto, was located in a major industrial city where the incarcerated Jews worked in factories for the German war effort. The ghetto leader was **Chaim Rumkowski** (1877–1944). He constantly assured the ghetto inhabitants (and himself) that they would be spared if they kept working and were seen as productive. This led him to make decisions few other ghetto leaders made. On September 4, 1942, he spoke to the entire ghetto:

> The ghetto has been struck a hard blow. They demand what is most dear to it—children and old people. I was not privileged to have a child of my own and therefore devoted my best years to children. I lived and breathed together with children. I never imagined that my own hands would be forced to make this sacrifice on the altar. In my old age I am forced to stretch out my hands and to beg: "Brothers and sisters, give them to me!—Fathers and mothers, give me your children. . . ." (Bitter weeping shakes the assembled public). . . . Yesterday, in the course of the day, I was given the order to send away more than 20,000 Jews from the ghetto, and if I did not—"we will do it ourselves." The question arose: "Should we have accepted this and carried it out ourselves, or left it to others?" But as we were guided not by the thought: "how many will be lost?: but "how many can be saved?" we arrived at the conclusion—those closest to me at work, that is, and myself—that however difficult it was going to be, we must take upon ourselves the carrying out of this decree. I must carry out this difficult and bloody operation. I must cut off limbs in order to save the body! I must take away children, and if I do not, others too will be taken, God forbid. . . . (terrible wailing).
>
> I cannot give you comfort today. Nor did I come to calm you today, but to reveal all your pain and all your sorrow. I have come like a robber, to take from you what is dearest to your heart. I tried everything I knew to get the bitter sentence cancelled. When it could not be cancelled, I tried to lessen the sentence. Only yesterday I ordered the registration of nine-year-old children. I wanted to save at least one year—children from nine to ten. But they would not yield. I succeeded in one thing—to save the children over ten. Let that be our consolation in our great sorrow.
>
> There are many people in this ghetto who suffer from tuberculosis, whose days or perhaps weeks are numbered. I do not know, perhaps this is a satanic plan, and perhaps not, but I cannot stop myself from proposing it: "Give me these sick people, and perhaps it will be possible to save the healthy in their place." I know how precious each one of the sick is in his home, and particularly among Jews. But at a time of such decrees one must weigh up and measure who should be saved, who can be saved and who may be saved.
>
> Common sense requires us to know that those must be saved who can be saved and who have a chance of being saved and not those whom there is no chance to save in any case.

Rumkowski remains a controversial figure. His personal manner and his administration of the ghetto were unnecessarily cruel—he rode around the ghetto imperiously in a horse-drawn carriage and had his picture printed on ghetto currency. He was widely reviled by Jews of the ghetto. Yet Lodz remained the last ghetto to be liquidated, perhaps because Rumkowski had made Jewish workers useful to the Germans. They were not, however, indispensable. In August 1944, the Nazis began transporting Jews out of the Lodz ghetto to Auschwitz. At the same time, the Red Army was closing in on Lodz, but it stopped its advance, decamping a mere seventy-five miles from the city. Still remaining in the ghetto were 70,000 Jews. Had the Soviets continued their march, liberation could have been at hand and perhaps Rumkowski's theory may have proven correct. Instead, he and his family were placed on one of the last trains to leave the city. It is said that Rumkowski was murdered in Auschwitz by some of his fellow deportees from Lodz.

The summer of 1942 was the most deadly in Jewish history. In addition to the destruction of Polish and Slovakian Jewry, the Nazis began the wholesale deportation to the gas chambers of Jews from western Europe, beginning with the Jews of Holland, France, and Belgium. Although the number of Jews in the west was far smaller than in eastern Europe, the fact that they had not been corralled into ghettos made their rounding up more complicated. The job was done, however, by collaborationist regimes and local Nazi sympathizers. A report sent to Himmler on September 24, 1942, read, "The new Dutch police squadrons are performing splendidly as regards the Jewish question and are arresting Jews in the hundreds, day and night." In two years of deportations, 1942 to 1944, 107,000 Dutch Jews were gassed in Auschwitz and Sobibor.

In France, with the biggest Jewish population in western Europe—350,000—the Vichy government instituted antisemitic race laws. The impact on the French Jewish economy was devastating, as confiscations, dismissal from jobs, and the institution of quotas severely restricted the lives of Jews. Of the Jewish population, only 150,000 were French born. The rest were stateless Jews, mostly from Poland who had come as refugees in the interwar period. When the deportations began, they were taken first. The roundups were almost exclusively conducted by French gendarmes and, by the end of 1942, 42,500 Jews had been deported to Auschwitz from France. By the time of the last deportations in 1944, over 77,000 Jews from France had been murdered in Nazi camps. Over 14 percent of those deported were under the age of eighteen.

The situation in Belgium differed from that in Holland and France. Despite the fact that over 90 percent of Belgium's 70,000 Jews were foreign born, Belgians were less compliant with Nazi demands. Large numbers of "ordinary" people helped rescue Jews, while over 25,000 Jews went into hiding, assisted by the Belgian Resistance, which, heavily influenced by Communists, was sympathetic to Jews. Consequently, German military police carried out the deportations between 1942 and 1944. Nearly 25,000 Jews from Belgium were sent to their deaths in Auschwitz.

In all, approximately 60 percent of Holocaust victims were murdered in the six death camps. The killing in the death camps was conducted according to assembly-line methods. It was, says historian, Omer Bartov, "industrial murder." To make it efficient, the Nazis constantly refined and experimented with varying methods. An army of specialists, among them architects, builders, engineers, accountants, and economists, brought their expertise to bear on the process of killing men, women, and children. Not all the killers were brutal thugs. The huge death toll and the efficiency of slaughter in the camps were the efforts of respectable, educated people. Unlike the killing centers of the T-4 program, the extermination camps were not hospitals, nor were they disguised as such. Rather, they looked like military encampments with soldiers in uniform, barbed-wire fences, guard towers, barracks, and twice-daily roll calls that lasted for hours, irrespective of the weather.

Jews from the four corners of Europe were packed into sealed cattle cars without food, water, or toilets and shipped to one of the six extermination camps. Sometimes, in the case of the Jews from Greece, the trip to Auschwitz took as long as four days. Many were dead upon arrival. Those still living were ordered off the train, where they were confronted by SS doctors, guards, and snarling dogs. At Auschwitz, the notorious Nazi doctor Josef Mengele awaited the transports. Victims were then directed by him to either the left or the right—instant death or a temporary reprieve. Up to the final moment, the lying and deception continued. Gas chambers were often disguised as showers, and an orchestra comprised of fellow Jews serenaded victims on their way to be gassed. At Auschwitz, up to 2,000 people were crammed into each gas chamber, dying an agonizing death in about twenty minutes as people desperately attempted to climb over each other to escape. Being permitted to live condemned the person to slave labor or to becoming objects of ghastly medical experiments. At other times, survival was the arbitrary result of congestion at the gas chambers and crematoria. For those who survived the initial selection, fear, starvation, terror, and a deliberate process of dehumanization began. With shaven heads, striped prison clothes, and a number tattooed on the forearm, inmates were stripped of their individual identities. People were then subject to the camp social hierarchy, which mirrored Nazi racial categories. German political and "asocial" prisoners were on top, then Slavs, and then Jews on the bottom rung.

The killing process was intended to be self-financing. In 1942, Göring declared, "The war must sustain the war!" In the eastern territories, which encompassed the Baltic states, eastern Poland, western Belarus, Ukraine, and Russia, Göring's statement was put into practice with the announcement of October 24, 1942, that Jewish property "regardless of its worth and usefulness" was to be expropriated. So deeply ingrained was the German belief in the "right" to spoliation of the Jews that directives such as that of October 24 were often superfluous or out of date. Already in August 1942, the Jews of Kovno had been robbed of all possessions and the ghetto had been made to function as a "cashless economy."

Among their many larcenous calculations, Nazi bureaucrats in the Food Ministry took account of the extra food that would be available to Germans with the extermination of the Jews. It was theft that sustained the German war machine. In the camps, those slated for gassing were stripped of their clothes and possessions, including jewelry, watches, eyeglasses, and other items. Work details of prisoners picked through the belongings. Women's hair was shaved off and sent to Germany to make carpet underlay, while clothes and shoes were sent to needy Germans on the home front. Gold teeth were extracted from corpses. These robberies were officially recorded as "general administrative revenues" in the annual budget of the Third Reich, thus hiding the reality, which was that the systematic robbery of the Jewish people (and others) supported the creation of Germany's racist welfare state. During the destruction of Hungarian Jewry in the summer of 1944, around 7,000 Hungarian Jews were being gassed and cremated each day. So frantic was the pace of murder that nearly one-third of the total number killed at Auschwitz were gassed in a two-month period that summer. To speed up and reduce the costs of the burning process, Nazi engineers designed a means whereby human fat oozing from the burning bodies was channeled back to fuel the flames of the crematoria. In this way, the theft continued even after the Jews were dead.

In the last year of the war, as the Nazis faced total defeat, Hitler was determined to at least be victorious in his war against the Jews. The Nazis, even at the expense of the war effort, dedicated themselves with great energy to the destruction of those Jews still alive. When the Allied armies began closing in on the Reich in the winter of 1944–1945, the Nazis began to empty the camps of prisoners, sending them by train and on foot back to Germany. They did not want prisoners to fall into the hands of the Allies and provide evidence of Nazi atrocities. The forced marches were brutal, and anyone unable to keep up the hectic pace was simply shot on the spot. Approximately 250,000 Jews and non-Jews died on these death marches. Survivors found themselves interned in concentration camps in Germany, such as Bergen-Belsen, Dachau, and Buchenwald. Between April and May 1945, these camps were liberated by British and American forces.

Jewish Resistance

All over Europe, Jews did not passively accept their fate at the hands of the Nazis and their collaborators but resisted in a variety of ways. These ranged from emigration when possible, as was the case for about half the Jews in Germany and Austria before the war, to various forms of spiritual resistance and outright armed struggle. In western and eastern Europe, Jews tried to save their children by sending them away to be cared for by non-Jews. About 10,000 Jewish children from the Reich were sent to England on what were called **Kindertransport.** When the war began, many parents entrusted their children to convents, where they were saved and raised as Catholics.

In Poland, Emanuel Ringelblum undertook one of the most significant acts of resistance by organizing a secret operation code-named **Oyneg Shabbes** ("Sabbath Delight"), the goal of which, Ringelblum said, was to gather "materials and documents relating to the martyrology of the Jews of Poland." Documenting ghetto life in as much detail as possible, Ringelblum enlisted the help of dozens of writers, journalists, teachers, rabbis, social scientists, and historians. They wrote reports, collected documents and photographs, commissioned papers and even essays from schoolchildren, and conducted interviews with ghetto dwellers from all walks of life. One worker considered his job "a sacred task," while another, David Gerber, only nineteen years old, wrote in his will, "What we could not cry out to the world, we buried in the ground. May this treasure be delivered into good hands, may it live to see better times, so that it can alert the world to what happened in the twentieth

century." Just prior to the liquidation of the Warsaw ghetto in the spring of 1943, the archive, consisting of thousands of documents, was placed in three milk cans and ten metal boxes and buried in the cellars of several Warsaw buildings. (In 1946, two of the milk cans were unearthed; in 1950, the boxes.)

Much of what we know about ghetto life, particularly in Warsaw comes from Ringelblum's material. Among other things, the Oyneg Shabbes archive revealed the extent of Jewish resistance to the Nazis. We learn that the death rate from hunger would have been even higher were it not for the extensive smuggling activities of children. Cultural programs existed in all ghettos. Poets, painters, writers, and even musicians did their best to carry on their work. Although religious services were banned in most places, including Warsaw, Ringelblum reported the existence of 600 clandestine synagogues. In most ghettos—Lodz was a notable exception—the Nazis forbade Jewish education. In fact they systematically destroyed libraries and shut down Jewish newspapers and all forms of intellectual life. Still, an illegal Jewish high school functioned in the Warsaw ghetto between 1940 and 1942. Vocational courses, as well as those in pharmacology and technical drawing, were offered. Several university-level courses were available, some in the field of medicine. One of the riskiest activities was organized political activity, which was completely banned. Zionist and Bundist youth nevertheless continued to print newspapers and offer spiritual and intellectual comfort to the ghetto inhabitants. When word of mass murders began to spread in the ghettos and the full understanding of the word *deportation* became clear, political youth groups changed tactics and began to concentrate on mounting armed resistance.

For several reasons, armed resistance, though also widespread, was not a viable option for most Jews. Starvation, disease, and terror in the ghettos and the rapidity of Einsatzgruppen executions destroyed the fabric of Jewish existence. Jews had no government-in-exile, as did the Poles, and thus there was no access to information or weapons. The isolation of the ghettos meant Jews had no one upon whom they could rely, nor could they gain the military intelligence necessary to mount armed operations against the Germans. The exclusion of Jews from the civic life of central and eastern European nations before the war meant that there was no formally trained Jewish military officer corps. As such, Jewish access to arms depots was impossible. Many Jews in the ghettos also had difficulty believing the reality of the mass shootings and death camps. In addition, Jewish family life was intensely strong, so many felt great reticence about abandoning family members to go off and join an underground ghetto organization or escape and hook up with partisan groups, many of which were antisemitic. (See box, Resistance in the Vilna Ghetto.)

Given the fact that the Jewish population was composed largely of starving civilians, children, and elderly and that many had been killed over time, the amount of physical resistance is remarkable. Of 5.7 million Soviet prisoners of war, all battled-hardened young men, 3.3 million died at the hands of the Nazis, with barely any resistance mounted at all. Even the leader of the Polish Home Army, General Stefan Rowecki, said on Feb 5, 1941: "Active warfare against the Nazis can take place in our country, only when the German people will be broken by military defeats, hunger and propaganda. . . . Any attempt by us to take action while the German army is at full strength, regardless of their numbers. . . will be drowned in a terrible bloodshed."

Jews, who had less to lose, did not wait for the collapse of the German army. Acts of resistance occurred in as many as a hundred ghettos and extermination camps, such as Sobibor, Treblinka, and Birkenau. As many as 30,000 Jews formed their own partisan units or joined up with Soviet partisans operating in forests in the east. Jews also joined with French partisans in western Europe and with Italian, Yugoslav, and Greek units in south and southeastern Europe. In ghettos where chances of survival were negligible, Jewish Councils were more likely to cooperate with underground groups. In Bialystok, Judenrat leader Efraim Barash provided money and work passes for members of the underground. In Minsk, the fourth-largest ghetto, with 84,000 Jews, about 10,000 fled to the forests with the assistance of the Judenrat. Most of them were killed fighting the Germans, and in the autumn of 1943 the Nazis destroyed the ghetto. In ghettos where Jewish Council members believed that their ghettos might survive, such as in Lodz, there was no cooperation with resistance groups.

The **Warsaw Ghetto Uprising** (April 1943) represents the most well-known case of Jewish armed resistance to the Nazis. After the end of the mass deportations from the Warsaw ghetto in September 1942, only about 6,000 Jews were left alive. No one over age eighty survived; only 45 people between the ages of seventy and seventy-nine were alive; and of the 31,458 children under age ten still living, only 498 survived. Feelings of guilt and a burning desire for revenge swept the ghetto.

About 1,000 young people, members of Zionist or Bundist youth movements formed the Jewish Fighting Organization under the command of **Mordechai Anielewicz** (1919–1943). As the Germans entered the ghetto to liquidate it on the eve of Passover, April 19, 1943, Jewish resistance fighters were lying in wait. Armed with pistols and Molotov cocktails, they fought pitched battles with the Germans, who were eventually forced to bring in reinforcements and heavy artillery. For three weeks street battles between Nazi soldiers and Jewish ghetto fighters raged until Anielewicz was killed,

Jewish hideouts were discovered, and many arrests were made. On May 16, 1943, SS General Jürgen Stroop reported that Warsaw was completely liquidated. As a mark of his victory, he blew up Warsaw's Great Synagogue.

In the end, whether or not a Judenrat cooperated with a resistance movement made no difference. Even the fact of resistance made no difference to the final outcome. The rationale behind armed resistance among Jews was different than it was for non-Jews. For the latter, all resistance activity was part of the larger war effort to secure victory against the Nazis. For the Jews, who had lost everything, taking up arms against the Nazis was not part of an overall strategy for military victory. It was about revenge and self-respect. In his last letter, Mordechai Anielewicz wrote, "[T]he fact that we are remembered beyond ghetto walls encourages us in our struggle. . . . Jewish armed resistance and revenge are facts. I have been witness to the magnificent, heroic fighting of Jewish men in battle."

So different was the Jewish situation that even survival was considered with ambiguity, for it brought with it the stark realization that all was lost. What did survival even mean in such circumstances? In the Vilna ghetto, the great Yiddish poet and partisan fighter **Avrom Sutzkever** (b. 1913) darkly pondered what it meant for a Jew to emerge from Hitler's inferno. On February 14, 1943, amid the ruins and remnants, Sutzkever wrote the poem "How?"

> How will you fill your goblet
> on the day of liberation? And with what?
> Are you prepared, in your joy, to feel
> the dark shrieking of your past
> where shards of days lie congealed
> in a bottomless pit?
>
> You will search for a key to fit your old jammed locks.
>   You will bite
> into the street like bread,
> thinking: It used to be better.
> And time will quietly gnaw at you
> like a cricket caught in a fist.
>
> Then your memory will resemble
> an ancient buried town.
> And your gaze will burrow down
> like a mole, like a mole . . .

Awareness of Genocide and Rescue Attempts

A particularly contentious historical debate involves the issue of contemporary awareness about the Holocaust. What did people know, when did they know it, and in the case of the Allies, what did they do with the information they had? In the

RESISTANCE IN THE VILNA GHETTO

Beginning on July 4, 1941, the Nazis began shooting Vilna's Jews in massive pits at the nearby forest of Ponary. Employing a rationale used by Chaim Rumkowski in Lodz, the head of the Vilna Judenrat, Jacob Gens, had turned over Jews to the Nazis in the hope that he would be able to save a remnant. Gens believed he too could save Jews through a "life-for-work" plan. Addressing the ghetto, he defended his action: "With hundreds I save thousands; with the thousand that I deliver, I save ten thousand. . . . That there be some remnant, I myself had to lead Jews to their death. And in order for some people to come out of this with a clean conscience I had to put my hands into filth, and trade without conscience."

For those convinced that the goal of the Nazis was to exterminate all Jews, strategies such as Gens' were pointless. On January 1, 1942, with over 30,000 of Vilna's 57,000 Jews already shot, the Hebrew poet and ghetto fighter **Abba Kovner** (1918–1987) read a declaration to a gathering of youth movement members encouraging resistance:

> Since our last meeting . . . our nearest and dearest have been torn from us and led to death with masses of other Jews. . . . The truth says that we must not believe that those who have been taken from us are still alive, that they have been merely deported. Everything that has befallen us to this point means . . . death. Yet even this is not the whole truth. . . . The destruction of thousands is only a harbinger of the annihilation of millions. Their death is our total ruin. It is difficult for me to explain why Vilna is bleeding while Bialystok is peaceful and calm . . . But one thing is clear to me: Vilna is not just Vilna. [The shootings at] Ponary are not just an episode. The yellow patch is not the invention of the local SS commander. This is a total system. We are facing a well-planned system that is hidden from us at the moment.
>
> Is there any escape from it? No. If we are dealing with a consistent system, fleeing from one place to another is nothing but an illusion. . . . Is there a chance that we might be rescued? Cruel as the answer may be, we must reply: no, there is no rescue! . . . Maybe for dozens or hundreds; but for the . . . millions of Jews under the yoke of German occupation there is no rescue.
>
> Is there a way out? Yes. There is a way out: rebellion and resistance.

Within weeks of this speech, Zionist youth leaders and Communists within the ghetto formed the United Partisans Organization (Fareynikte Partizaner-Organizatsye) (UPO). Led by the Communist, Itsik Wittenberg and Abba Kovner, the UPO sought to unite the various resistance groups in the ghetto, carry out acts of sabotage, and encourage widespread resistance. They succeeded in blowing up a German military train, smuggling arms into the ghetto, setting up an illegal printing press outside of the ghetto, and establishing links with nearby Soviet partisans. The UPO also sent couriers to the Warsaw and Bialystok ghettos to warn Jews about the mass killings of Jews in the occupied Soviet Union. In the numerous songs they sang, Vilna partisans gave expression to their deepest hopes. In the Rudnicki forest, the UPO fighters gathered each morning for reveille and sang their official song in Yiddish, a march entitled "Never Say" (*Zog Nit Keyn Mol*):

prewar phase, Nazi policy toward Jews was public knowledge. This was, after all, happening to neighbors. Once the war and the subsequent slaughter of European Jewry began, most preferred not to know the details, and the German use of euphemisms helped camouflage reality. But news of the killings was difficult to keep secret. German soldiers and civilians in Poland took pictures of suffering and humiliated Jews, went to the ghettos, and in Warsaw even filmed what they saw. Pictures and artifacts brought back were shared, providing graphic evidence of what was happening. At official levels, the Nazis published pictures of filthy, lice-ridden ghetto inhabitants to justify German claims that the Jews were subhuman. Still, with the nation at war, Germans focused on their own losses, ignoring the fate of a people cast as their mortal enemy.

In the West, definitive news of Hitler's war against the Jews was made known in London and Washington thanks to a letter of August 8, 1942, from Gerhard Riegner, a representative of the World Jewish Congress in Geneva. He spoke about "a plan to exterminate all Jews from Germany and German-controlled areas in Europe." In the autumn of 1942, a Polish underground courier, Jan Karski, snuck into the Warsaw ghetto to learn firsthand what was happening. On December 1, 1942, he informed the Polish government-in-exile in London of the extermination of Polish Jewry. Karski's report was then relayed to the Allies. Throughout 1942, the Allies repeatedly threatened the Nazi leadership with severe retribution for its crimes. The leaders of Germany's allies, including Mussolini in Italy, Admiral Horthy of Hungary,

Never say that you are walking your final path;
Leaden skies conceal blue days!
The hour we have longed for is so near,
Our step will beat out like a drum. We are here!

From the green land of palms to the
Land of white snow;
We arrive with our pain, with our hurt.
And wherever a spurt of our blood has fallen
Our might and courage will sprout.

The morning sun will gild our today
And yesterday will vanish with the enemy,
But if the sun and the dawn are late in coming,
May this song go from generation to generation like a password.

This song is written with blood and not
With pencil-lead
It's no song of a free-flying bird,
A people among collapsing walls
Sang this song with pistols in their hands.

Never say that you are walking your final path;
Leaden skies conceal blue days!
The hour we have longed for is so near,
Our step will beat out like a drum. We are here!

When the Nazi secret police, the Gestapo, infiltrated the local Communist underground in July 1943, it learned that Wittenberg was the leader of the UPO. It demanded that the Judenrat turn him over. After an agonizing debate within the resistance organization, Wittenberg surrendered. He committed suicide with cyanide given him by Jacob Gens.

Gens' attitude to resistance was mixed. Initially, he maintained close connections with the UPO but later concluded that the organization's activities placed the whole ghetto at risk, so he sought to extract concessions from the Germans by turning over Jews for forced labor in Estonia. The ghetto inhabitants were also opposed to the resistance organization, believing that their best hope for survival lay with deportation to Estonian labor camps. Gens was shot by the Gestapo on September 14, 1943, during the final liquidation of the ghetto.

Marshal Antonescu of Romania, and President Tiso of Slovakia, were all aware that Jews were being deported to their deaths, as did the collaborationist regime of Vichy France under Marshal Petain and Pierre Laval. On December 17, 1942, a declaration was made in the British parliament. The Germans "are now carrying into effect Hitler's oft-repeated intention to exterminate the Jewish people in Europe." In April 1944, an eyewitness report came from Auschwitz, with the stunning escape of two Jewish inmates, Rudolf Vrba and Alfred Wetzler. Making it to Slovakia, they then dictated to Jewish officials a highly detailed thirty-two-page account of Auschwitz-Birkenau and the preparations then being made for the arrival and impending destruction of Hungarian Jewry. Little came of this revelation. Fearing that Hungary might make a separate peace with the Allies, Germany occupied Hungary in March 1944. The SS were now in charge of the country, and Adolf Eichmann was dispatched to Budapest to organize the deportation of the Jews. He worked with great haste. Between May 15 and July 7, 1944, 437,000 Hungarian Jews were murdered in Auschwitz. Nearly all were gassed upon arrival.

Though Jews sought assistance from the West as soon as the war began, Jewish leaders had difficulty coming to terms with the Nazi program of genocide. Many found it difficult to believe, and thus their incomplete knowledge hindered their actions. Jews were, the world over, a politically impotent minority. In the United States they had very little access to power and, given the extent of antisemitism, Jewish leaders

THE MODEL CONCENTRATION CAMP: THERESIENSTADT

On November 24, 1941, the Germans established a "model ghetto"—in reality, a concentration camp—in the Czechoslovakian town of Terezin. It was known by its German name, Theresienstadt, until its liberation on May 8, 1945. Most of the acculturated Jews imprisoned there were German, Czech, Dutch, and Danish. Among them were elderly and prominent Jews and Jewish veterans of World War I.

The Nazis used Theresienstadt for propaganda purposes. They called it a "spa town" and claimed that elderly German Jews had been brought there so that they could "retire" in safety. By 1942, conditions in the ghetto were so bad that thousands perished of starvation and disease. The Nazis built a crematorium there to dispose of 200 bodies a day. Still, the Nazis persisted with their deception and in June 1944 permitted the International Red Cross, which wanted to investigate rumors of extermination camps, to visit and see conditions for themselves. In preparation, the ghetto was "beautified." Large numbers of Jews were shipped to Auschwitz to avoid the appearance of overcrowding. Gardens were planted, buildings were renovated, and cultural events were staged for the visitors. Theresienstadt had a Judenrat, and the Red Cross delegation was even introduced to the camp's Jewish "mayor," Paul Eppstein. The investigators left satisfied that Jews were being well treated. A propaganda film was made about the "excellent" conditions for Jews in Theresienstadt, the Nazis having coerced the Jewish prisoner and director Kurt Gerron to film it. After finishing the film, most of the cast, along with Gerron, who years before had starred alongside Marlene Dietrich in *The Blue Angel,* was deported to Auschwitz, where they were murdered.

Due to the high number of prominent artists interned at Theresienstadt, the Nazis, as part of their elaborate hoax, permitted cultural activities. Painters, writers, academics, musicians, and actors taught classes and put on exhibitions, readings, lectures, concerts, and theatre performances. Jewish themes were emphasized. The ghetto even maintained a lending library of 60,000 volumes. The Viennese artist **Friedl Dicker-Brandeis** (1898–1944), gave art classes and lectures to children, offering them a sophisticated form of art therapy that was designed to allow them to cope with the stress of their situation. Just before she was deported to Auschwitz in September 1944, she filled two suitcases with 4,500 drawings, and left them hidden at Theresienstadt. Approximately 140,000 Jews were sent to Theresienstadt. About 33,000 died there. Approximately 90,000 were deported to Auschwitz, Treblinka, other extermination camps, and ghettos farther east and murdered in those places.

Jewish money from Theresienstadt. Known as *Judengeld,* or "Jews' money," this 50-kroner banknote was used in the Theresienstadt ghetto (January 1943).

were loath to plead the Jewish cause when the national war effort was at stake. In the 1940s, few American parents would have wanted their sons to die saving the lives of European Jews. In Palestine too, despite family ties to eastern Europe, even the Yishuv did not completely comprehend the events. Beyond this, the Yishuv was weak and had nothing to offer European Jewry in terms of rescue. Nongovernmental agencies such as the Red Cross sought to maintain neutrality and turned a blind eye to the extermination process, even after delegations visited the Theresienstadt ghetto and Auschwitz (*see box,* The Model Concentration Camp: Theresienstadt). Despite being in possession of a steady stream of information concerning the destruction of European Jewry, Pope Pius XII, a man who was deeply hostile to Jews—believing, among other things, that they were behind a Bolshevik plot to destroy Christianity—steadfastly refused to issue any kind of unambiguous condemnation about the murder of European Jewry. Even in quarters where more sympathy could have been expected, such as in the French Resistance, none was forthcoming. In June 1942, a statement in *Cahiers,* the official organ of the French underground observed, "Antisemitism in its moderate form was quasi universal, even in the most liberal societies. This indicates that its foundation is not imaginary."

Across Europe, civilian populations were generally indifferent, if not enthusiastic, about the removal of Jews from their respective societies. That said, thousands of Jews were saved by the brave actions of individuals. Raoul Wallenberg, a Swedish diplomat in Budapest, provided 30,000 Jews with Swedish passports, set up "safe houses" for them, and distributed food and medical supplies. In Lithuania, the temporary Japanese consul, Chiune Sugihara, saved thousands of Jews. In the summer of 1940, Polish Jewish refugees in Kovno learned that two Dutch colonial islands, Curacao and Dutch Guiana (Suriname), did not require formal entrance visas. The honorary Dutch consul in Kovno, Jan Zwartendijk, told the refugees that he could stamp their passports with entrance permits to the islands. But to get to them, the refugees would have to pass through the Soviet Union. The Soviet consul was prepared to let them pass on one condition: that in addition to the Dutch entrance permit, they would also have to show a transit visa from the Japanese because getting to the Dutch islands required that they transit through Japan. Sugihara requested the transit visas, but the foreign ministry in Tokyo flatly refused. In defiance, from July 31 to August 28, 1940, Sugihara and his wife worked feverishly to write out over 6,000 visas by hand. In France, Pastor Andre Trocme and Daniel Trocme in the Huguenot village of Le Chambon-sur-Lignon, France, hid and saved 5,000 Jews. In Holland, a combination of widespread complicity with the Nazis and flat, open terrain, which meant there were neither mountain nor forest hideouts, led to a huge death toll. Of 140,000 Jews in The Netherlands in 1939, 105,000 were exterminated. But at least 25,000 of the survivors owe their lives to their Dutch compatriots who hid them. (*See box,* Anne Frank.)

Throughout Poland too, thousands of individuals hid Jews at great personal risk. There was no promise of reward and only the guarantee of death if caught. A Polish aid organization, **Zegota** (The Council for Aid to Jews), was set up in 1942 by Left-wing political parties that received funds from the Polish government-in-exile. The most dramatic mass rescue of Jews during the Holocaust occurred in occupied Denmark. On the night of October 1, 1943, the Germans began rounding up Jews but found very few because, due to Danish resistance that formed quickly in the previous weeks, the police, the churches, the Danish royal family, and various social organizations had found hiding places for the country's 7,500 Jews. From their hideouts, Jews were shuttled to the coast, where they boarded fishing boats that ferried them to neutral Sweden. Over the course of a month, about 7,200 Jews and 700 of their non-Jewish relatives made it to safety in Sweden. Across Europe, tens of thousands of individuals blessed with courage and conscience saved Jewish neighbors and strangers. Their heroic actions, however, were not enough to stop the genocide.

Another contentious issue among historians has been the assessment of Allied behavior—in particular, whether Britain and the United States should have bombed the death camps to stop or at least impede the slaughter. In June 1944, the U.S. War Department said it could not be done, even though it never investigated the possibility of bombing the camps. A variety of excuses were offered. Such an undertaking, according to Assistant Secretary of War John J. McCloy, "could only be executed by the diversion of considerable air support essential to the success of our forces now engaged in decisive operations and would in any case be of such doubtful efficacy that it would not amount to a practical project." Even though requests to bomb the train lines leading to Auschwitz-Birkenau were dismissed as logistically unfeasible, the Americans were bombing factories at and around the extermination camp between August 20 and September 13, 1944. Ironically, it was also claimed that innocent people in the camps would have been killed. It is true that millions of Jews had already been murdered by this time, so bombing the camps would not have prevented the Holocaust. The real value in mounting a sustained campaign to destroy the death factories would have been a symbolic act but an important one.

On January 13, 1943, outraged by their government's refusal to act decisively to rescue European Jewry, members

ANNE FRANK

Anne Frank was born to Otto and Edith Frank on June 12, 1929, in Frankfurt, Germany. After the Nazis seized power in 1933, the Franks fled to Amsterdam. Anne, who had remained behind in the care of her grandparents, joined the family in Holland in February 1934.

The Germans occupied Amsterdam in May 1940, and the SS installed a civil administration, appointing Arthur Seyss-Inquart as Reich commissar. In January 1941, the German occupation authorities demanded that all Jews be registered. This amounted to a total of 159,806 persons, including 19,561 persons born of mixed marriages. Among the total number of registered Jews were approximately 25,000 Jewish refugees from the German Reich. The Frank family was among this group.

The arrest and deportation of Jews led to a protest strike by Dutch workers in February 1941. This show of support notwithstanding, there was widespread collaboration in Holland with the Nazis. In July 1942, Dutch sympathizers helped round up Jews and concentrate them in Amsterdam while they sent foreign and stateless Jews to the Westerbork transit camp. From there, Jews were deported to Auschwitz and Sobibor.

During the first week in July of 1942, Anne Frank and her family went into hiding—four other Dutch Jews were in the same house as the Franks. For two years they lived in a secret attic apartment at 263 Prinsengracht Street. They were hidden and given food and clothing by friends of Otto Frank. Thanks to a tip from an anonymous Dutchman, the Gestapo uncovered the hiding place on August 4, 1944, and the Franks were arrested and sent to Westerbork on August 8. One month later, the Franks and the other Jews who had been hiding with them were deported to Auschwitz. Because they were young and eligible for forced labor, Anne and her sister, Margot, were transferred to the concentration camp Bergen-Belsen in late October 1944. Both of them died of typhus in March 1945, only weeks before the British liberated the camp on April 15, 1945. The only family member to survive the war was Otto Frank.

Anne wished to become a writer, and in addition to her diary, for which she is most famous, she wrote short stories, fairy tales, essays, and the beginnings of a novel. Anne was between thirteen and fifteen years of age during her two years in hiding; she was enormously productive during that time, filling five notebooks and writing more than three hundred loose, handwritten pages. Her diary, which was published posthumously in 1947 and has been translated into about seventy languages, covers an astonishing array of subjects from the personal to the political. She was an astute observer, capable of mixing hard-bitten realism with an optimism that bespeaks her profound humanity. Her diary entry for June 20, 1942, clearly gives a sense of the noose tightening around Jewish life, and yet her resilience shines through: "Anti-Jewish decrees followed each other in quick succession. Jews must wear a yellow star, Jews must hand in their bicycles, Jews are banned from trams and are forbidden to drive, Jews are only allowed to do their shopping between three and five o'clock. . . . Jews must be indoors by eight o'clock. . . . Jews are forbidden to visit theaters. . . . Jews may not visit Christians. Jews must go to Jewish schools, and many more restrictions of a similar kind. So we could not do this and were forbidden to do that. But life went on in spite of it all." On April 17, 1944, Anne wrote what turned out to be her final entry. "I see the world gradually being turned into a wilderness, I hear the ever approaching thunder, which will destroy us too, I can feel the sufferings of millions and yet, if I look up into the heavens, I think that it will all come right, that this cruelty too will end, and that peace and tranquility will return again. In the meantime, I must uphold my ideals, for perhaps the time will come when I shall be able to carry them out."

Anne Frank was one of the more than one million Jewish children murdered by the Nazis and their collaborators.

of the U.S. Treasury Department released a damning document entitled "Report to the Secretary on the Acquiescence of This Government in the Murder of the Jews." On January 17, 1944, the report was submitted to President Roosevelt, who responded by establishing the **War Refugee Board.** It was mandated to negotiate with foreign governments, even enemy ones, to rescue Jews. The whole government was put at the War Refugee Board's disposal, but its efforts were stymied at nearly every turn. The board received little government funding, and President Roosevelt took hardly any personal interest in it. And yet, the War Refugee Board was able to save 200,000 Jews, a significant number. A concerted effort, if undertaken earlier, and with more serious support, could have saved even more Jews. In the end, all that stopped the slaughter was Allied victory over Nazi Germany, in particular the Red Army's conquests of the killing fields of eastern Europe. For 6,000,000 Jews, however, victory came too late.

Questions for Reflection

1. What political, social, and cultural factors do you think account for the Holocaust?
2. In the period from 1933 to 1939, how did German Jews cope under Nazi rule? What survival strategies did they employ?
3. What were the various forms that Jewish resistance took?
4. What role did the Allies and churches play in saving European Jews from the Nazis?

For Further Reading

On the Holocaust, see Deborah Dwork and Robert Jan van Pelt, *Holocaust: A History* (New York: W.W. Norton, 2002); Saul Friedländer, *Nazi Germany and the Jews: The Years of Persecution, 1933–1939* (New York: Harper Collins, 1997); Saul Friedländer, *Nazi Germany and the Jews: The Years of Extermination, 1939–1945* (New York: Harper Collins, 2007); Lucy Dawidowicz, *The War Against the Jews, 1933–1945* (New York: Holt, Rinehart and Winston, 1975); Michael Berenbaum and Abraham J. Peck, *The Holocaust and History* (Bloomington: Indiana University Press, 1998); Susan Zuccotti, *Under His Very Windows: The Vatican and the Holocaust in Italy* (New Haven, CT: Yale University Press, 2000); Gulie Ne'eman Arad, *America, Its Jews, and the Rise of Nazism* (Bloomington: Indiana University Press, 2000); Abraham I. Katsh, *Scroll of Agony: The Warsaw Diary of Chaim A. Kaplan* (Bloomington: Indiana University Press, 1999); Alan Adelson, *The Diary of Dawid Sierakowiak: Five Notebooks from the Lodz Ghetto* (Oxford, England: Oxford University Press, 1998); Primo Levi, *Survival in Auschwitz* (New York: Touchstone Books, 1996).

Chapter 15

Into the Present

Most Holocaust survivors eventually made their way to countries far from Europe. In Israel, the United States, Australia, Canada, and Latin America, Jewish refugees set about the quietly heroic task of rebuilding their shattered lives. Having escaped their would-be killers, the response of survivors to the nightmare of the Holocaust was to get married, raise a family, and provide for their children. That this is what the overwhelming majority of Jews were able to achieve, irrespective of where they ended up, is one of the great success stories in Jewish history.

The dissolution of Jewish life in Arab lands also quickened in the postwar world. While some Jewish communities in North Africa were directly touched by the Holocaust, with the Nazis incarcerating thousands of Jews in concentration camps they established there, the majority of Middle Eastern Jewish communities effectively came to an end by 1950 due to local politics. Arab nationalism, antisemitism, and anti-Zionism had been on the rise prior to World War II. In Iraq, occupational and educational discrimination, as well as physical attacks, including murder, became the lot of Iraqi Jews after the country achieved independence in 1932. Such developments culminated in the *Farhud,* a pogrom that occurred on June 1 and 2, 1941. Demobilized Iraqi soldiers joined by tribesmen and ordinary Baghdadis went on a rampage and looting spree against the capital's Jews. When it was over, 180 Jews had been killed and hundreds more had been wounded. Significant numbers of Muslims who came to the aid of their Jewish neighbors were also killed by the mob. With the emergence of the State of Israel in 1948, levels of suspicion and outright persecution increased to such an extent that emigration was the only option. Most chose to go to Israel. The continued existence of Jewish communities elsewhere in Muslim lands—the exceptions were Morocco and Iran (until the Islamic Revolution of 1979)—also became untenable.

Even before the establishment of the State of Israel, Jews all over the Arab world were considered potential traitors and branded as Zionist agents. Life for them had become increasingly untenable. In November 1945, a pogrom in Libya resulted in the murder of 140 Jews and the destruction of five synagogues. In June 1948, amid protests against the new Jewish state, rioters murdered 12 Jews and destroyed 280 Jewish homes. Although emigration was illegal, more than 3,000 Jews left for Israel. When the British legalized emigration in 1949, and in the years immediately preceding Libyan independence in 1951, further riots promoted the departure of some 30,000 Jews. Over time and according to Libyan law, Jewish assets were seized and transferred to state ownership. As late as July 1970, the innocuously worded "Law Relative to the Resolution of Certain Assets to the State" held that a state-appointed General Custodian would administer the liquid funds of the property of Jews as well as the companies and the company shares belonging to Jews.

The situation was similar in Syria in 1943 for approximately 30,000 Jews. The 1947 pogrom in Aleppo caused 7,000 of the town's 10,000 Jews to flee. In 1949, banks were instructed to freeze the accounts of Jews, and all their assets were expropriated. Nearly all Jewish civil servants were dismissed from their jobs, freedom of movement within Syria for Jews was severely curtailed, and frontier posts were established to control the movement of Jews out of the country. In all, approximately 800,000 Jews from Arab lands were displaced and dispossessed after the establishment of the State of Israel.

With the demise of European Jewry and the displacement of Jews from Arab lands, the geographical centers of Jewish settlement shifted. By the middle of the twentieth century, the ancient Jewish civilizations, in both Christian Europe and the Muslim Middle East, had come to an end through a mixture of voluntary immigration, forced expulsions, and mass murder. After the war, the Soviet Union, Israel, and the United States emerged as the three countries with the largest Jewish communities in the world. By the end of the twentieth century, the demise of the Soviet Union resulted in a massive exodus of Jews. A century after the first great wave of migration out of eastern Europe,

Into the Present   407

Jewish dispersion from Russia after 1990 again significantly changed the face of Jewish communities across the world.

The emergence of Israel a mere three years after the Holocaust was greeted with unrestrained joy by world Jewry. Even avowedly secular Jews saw Israel as a miracle. Emotionally, the Jewish people had experienced a wild mood swing in a very short period of time from deep despair to euphoric hope. It was a reversal of national fate that knew no parallels in Jewish historical experience. For individual survivors, however, the postwar experience proved far more complex. Refugees who went to western Europe or the Americas were mostly welcomed by local communities. Often, they married local Jews but also maintained wide networks of friends among Holocaust survivors. They formed official Holocaust survivor organizations, as well as more informal groups, that provided material aid, comfort, and the opportunity to share stories. One such group still meets regularly in Melbourne, Australia. They call themselves the "Buchenwald Boys" due to the fact that when the Buchenwald concentration camp was liberated in April 1945, 60 out of the more than 900 young prisoners made their way to Australia. Mostly orphans, they landed in Melbourne, and with financial and emotional support from the local community they went about rebuilding their shattered lives. For Jack Unikowski, one of the survivors, "After all we had been through, we came to realize that we had arrived in a paradise, too good a life for many Europeans to imagine." Each year, on the anniversary of their liberation, the Buchenwald Boys celebrate their survival by hosting the Buchenwald Ball. Across the world, the dwindling numbers of survivors continue to meet in groups dedicated to the preservation of the memory of the Holocaust.

In addition to the impact of the Shoah, the Cold War, decolonization and wars in the Middle East, the collapse of Communism, and the impact of global capitalism are just some of the phenomena that in reshaping the world have transformed the Jewish people yet again. Since 1945, the rise of new Jewish centers, the growth of ultra-Orthodoxy, declining birthrates among secular Jews, ongoing assimilation in many quarters and, conversely, Jewish revival in others, all characterize a people still feeling the effects of their encounter with modernity.

In the Aftermath of the Holocaust

Between 1945 and 1952, approximately 250,000 Jews, 80 percent of whom were from Poland, ended up in displaced persons (DP) camps administered by the Allies and the United Nations in Germany, Austria, and Italy. The last DP camp closed in 1957. By 1946, 185,000 displaced persons were, much to their dismay and horror, in Germany, living "among the murderers." The ultimate goal of the DPs was to leave Europe but, as was the case before the war, few countries were enthusiastic about opening their doors to refugees. Britain was especially determined that Jews should not reach Palestine and turned many away from there. Nevertheless, from 1945 to 1948, the *Brihah* ("Flight") organization managed to smuggle more than 100,000 Jews into Palestine.

In the DP camps, Jews immediately tried to reestablish a semblance of normality. In the first place, this meant having children. The Nazis left very few Jewish children alive. The birthrate was tremendously high among Jewish DPs. In 1945, the birthrate among non-Jews in Bavaria (the state where most DP camps were located) was 5 births per 1,000 persons. Among Jews in 1946 it was 14.1. Very soon, kindergartens and schools were opened, with teachers coming from Palestine and the United States. Religious services were held and yeshivot were founded. In 1946, a new edition of the Talmud was published in Munich, the frontispiece showing the camps surrounded with barbed wire and the Jews walking beneath the rays of the sun into the Land of Israel. Denied the practice of religion for so long, Jews in the DP camps created lively religious centers. The DP camps in the American zone of occupation in 1946 were home to 4 yeshivot, 18 rabbis, 16 kosher slaughterers, and significantly 4 *mohelim* (circumcisers).

The DP camps were also sites of vibrant, secular culture. Starved for news throughout the war, the DPs were voracious consumers of news and literature. Over 170 publications appeared in the camps. Theatre and musical troupes toured the camps, while 169 sports clubs from the camps played against each other. In addition to soccer, boxing—perhaps not surprisingly—proved especially popular. The DP camps were, of course, only temporary refuges. The majority of survivors wished to leave Europe and start new lives far away from the killing fields.

The Rise of the State of Israel

Despite its bitterness over the 1939 **White Paper,** the leadership of the Yishuv realized that it had no choice but to fight alongside Britain against Germany. Further impetus came from the fact that the Grand Mufti, an unabashed antisemite, lived in Berlin during the war, had an audience with Hitler on November 30, 1941, was on close personal terms with Heinrich Himmler, and frequently broadcast Arabic-language messages of support for the Nazi campaign against European Jewry, over the radio on Nazi Germany's Oriental Service. Moreover, as the Germans advanced into Egypt under the command of General Erwin Rommel, the Yishuv had reason to fear that the Holocaust would come to them. Since the summer of 1942 an SS Einsatzgruppen unit had

EXODUS 1947

In July 1947, the *Exodus* left France for Palestine with over 4,500 Holocaust survivors on board. British destroyers surrounded the ship outside of Palestine's territorial waters and then boarded, transferring the passengers onto British navy ships and sent them back to France. There they refused to disembark, and the French authorities would not force them to do so. Passengers went on a hunger strike. To avoid adverse publicity, the British then misguidedly took the passengers on to Hamburg, where they were sent to Displaced Persons camps. The public outcry was immense, as was the embarrassment and humiliation for Britain. In the end, the affair served to garner worldwide sympathy for the Holocaust survivors and Zionism.

been on standby in Athens, ready to move on Palestine in advance of Rommel's anticipated victory, and then begin exterminating the Jews. In May 1942, 600 Zionists gathered in New York's Biltmore Hotel and issued what became known as the **Biltmore Program.** The document addressed the refugee problem-in-the-making that would follow the end of the war. The delegates officially rejected the White Paper on behalf of the Zionist movement, as well as plans for partition, demanding immediate Jewish sovereignty in all of Palestine.

In the 1940s, the combined impact of the Holocaust and Britain's obstructionism, which continued to prevent Jewish refugees from getting to Palestine, radicalized certain elements in the Yishuv. By early 1946, the British had interned 26,000 illegal Jewish immigrants to Palestine on Cyprus, where they were held in camps surrounded by barbed-wire fences. Still, 70,000 Jews managed to enter Palestine between 1945 and 1948. (*See box,* Exodus 1947.)

The Irgun, 2,000 strong and led by **Menachem Begin** (1913–1992), a future prime minister of Israel, called for a revolt against the British in Palestine. They launched military operations against British installations and an even more extreme terror group, the **Stern Gang,** named after its leader **Avraham Stern** (1907–1942), repeatedly attacked the British, funding itself through criminal activity, including robbing the Histadrut Workers' Bank. After Stern was killed by the British in 1942, some of his followers formed *Lehi,* an acronym for *Lohamei Herut Yisrael,* or Warriors for the Freedom of Israel. Its leader was **Yitzhak Shamir** (b. 1915), another future prime minister of Israel. Committed to extremist acts, Lehi was responsible for the 1944 assassination of Britain's Minister of State for the Middle East, Lord Moyne, and the 1948 assassination of the United Nations representative in the Middle East, Count Folke Bernadotte. In 1945, the Haganah, the Irgun, and Lehi joined forces to attack the British, who had 100,000 soldiers in Palestine. The British cracked down with a violent operation known as "Black Sabbath." They imposed a curfew on Tel Aviv and Jerusalem, arrested 3,000 Jews, tortured many, and deported some to Africa. One month later,

the Jewish response was fierce. In July 1946, the Irgun blew up the King David Hotel in Jerusalem, which served as British military and administrative headquarters. Ninety-one people were killed, most of them British personnel.

By 1947, Britain was no longer an imperial power. "Rule or quit," cried one English newspaper headline. Severely weakened, Britain no longer had the capacity or the will to rule. It was time to leave Palestine. In February, recognizing that it had lost control of the situation, Britain turned the jurisdiction of Palestine over to the United Nations. Pressure for British departure also came from the Arab side. After the war, the Arab Higher Committee was reconstituted, expressed vehement opposition to any partition plan, demanded the cessation of Jewish immigration, and called for immediate Palestinian Arab independence. The United Nations (UN) Special Committee on Palestine reiterated the Peel Commission plan for partition. In a tactical concession, Ben-Gurion accepted the recommendation that there be an Arab state and a Jewish state, and he agreed to the placement of Jerusalem under international trusteeship. Arab states remained opposed. On November 29, 1947, the UN General Assembly put the matter to a vote and received the necessary two-thirds majority: 33 to 13. As the mandatory power, Britain had abstained; the Soviet Union, which saw in the Yishuv a potential socialist ally, voted yes, most likely to curb British influence in the Middle East; the United States supported partition, as did Latin American nations, who, with no geopolitical considerations at stake, were deeply moved by the plight of the Jews. The resolution was due to take effect in May 1948. Although the partition plan gave the Zionists far less than what they wanted, the vote was a great diplomatic victory, the greatest since the Balfour Declaration of 1917.

The problem was that the vote of November 29 came from a body without the power to enforce it. Diplomacy quickly turned to military struggle between Jews and Arabs. War broke out in two stages between November 1947 and May 1948, initially between Jews and Arabs in Palestine. In the first few weeks more than 80 Jews and 90 Arabs were killed. Arabs attacked Jewish stores and exploded bombs in city centers while the Haganah attacked Arab villages. Palestinian militia groups killed hundreds of Jews. Jewish Jerusalem was under siege, and some neighborhoods were on the verge of starvation. Palestinian Arabs were soon joined by forces from armies throughout the Arab world. The Yishuv was outnumbered two to one. Violent opposition to the partition plan was not confined to Palestine. In Aleppo, Syria, 300 Jewish homes and 11 synagogues were burned to the ground, and 2,000 fled. In Aden, 76 Jews were murdered. In Baghdad, mobs ran riot in Jewish areas and Chief Rabbi Sassoon Kadoori was forced to issue a statement condemning Zionism. By April 1948, mass demonstrations in the Iraqi capital brought chants of "Death to the Jews!"

The second phase of fighting in Palestine carried into 1948. In March, the Jewish leadership, in an attempt to secure the borders of a future Jewish state, drove Palestinian guerillas out of the villages from where they were launching attacks. To achieve what was known as Plan D, in many cases the Jewish authorities sanctioned the expulsion of Arab villagers. One hundred thousand Arabs were forced from their homes with the Israeli conquest of Lydda and Ramle, but these expulsions were not part of a systematic policy. According to the available evidence, Israeli objectives were centered on conquest and not depopulation. There were also massacres, the most notorious of which occurred on April 9, 1948, in the Palestinian village of **Deir Yassin,** near Jerusalem. There, the Irgun killed approximately 120 Arabs, many of whom were unarmed civilians. The fighting left between 600,000 and 750,000 Palestinian refugees. The majority fled either to the West Bank or the Gaza Strip.

The military victories buoyed Ben-Gurion and his comrades and led them to the conclusion that the time was ripe to declare independence, in full expectation of a multinational Arab invasion. At 4:00 P.M. on May 14, 1948, just hours after the Union Jack was lowered over Palestine, signaling the British departure, Ben-Gurion read the Declaration of Independence from the Tel Aviv Museum. Declaring the establishment of the State of Israel, Ben-Gurion recounted the history of Zionism and the series of international agreements, including the Balfour Declaration and the UN vote; stressed the Jewish people's unbroken attachment to the Land of Israel; noted their struggle, in defiance of international restrictions, to get there; and, of course, addressed the impact of the Holocaust. Solemnly, he proclaimed, "By virtue of our natural and historic right and on the strength of the resolution of the United Nations General Assembly, [we] hereby declare the establishment of a Jewish state in Eretz-Israel, to be known as the State of Israel." That night, the new state was recognized by the United States and three days later by the Soviet Union. Ben-Gurion was named prime minister, and Chaim Weizmann became the first president after the honor had been declined by Albert Einstein.

The next day, Arab armies attacked, beginning what would be called the **War of Independence.** Though poorly coordinated, the Arab forces inflicted a heavy toll on the Yishuv. A UN-brokered truce in June made it possible for Israel to regroup and resupply its army. When the Arabs recommenced hostilities in July, Israel fought and won decisively, capturing the western Galilee, territory that was to have gone to the Palestinian Arabs in the partition plan. Israel also took control of the Negev. The new territories enlarged the new state by 20 percent more than the partition plan initially allowed. A Palestinian state did not come into being and, instead, Egypt and Transjordan (later renamed Jordan) seized control of those parts of Palestine they conquered in the war. Jerusalem was partitioned by the UN between Israel and Jordan, with the latter controlling the most important of Jewish holy sites, the Western Wall.

Only fifty years separated Ben-Gurion's proclamation and Theodor Herzl's entry in his diary at the First Zionist Congress in Basel in 1897, when he wrote, "Today I created the Jewish state!" Sadly, Herzl's vision of a Jewish state at peace with its neighbors has not been realized. After the war, Ben-Gurion declared, "We extend our hand to all neighbouring states and their peoples in an offer of peace and good neighbourliness. . . . The State of Israel is prepared to do its share in a common effort for the advancement of the entire Middle East." These intentions have not translated into peaceful coexistence.

In the State of Israel

The war of 1948 gave birth to the modern Israeli, endowing the combatants with mythic proportions. They represented the new Hebrew warrior. For all of Ben-Gurion's efforts to link the State of Israel with the long, historical experience of the Jewish people, there developed in the 1940s an influential aspect of Israeli culture that sought to establish a clear demarcation between the notion of Israeli and Jewish identity.

The Canaanites

Although it only had about two dozen registered members, a new group that called itself the Canaanites fostered the contrast between the healthy, sun-tanned native-born Israeli, or Sabra, and the weak, downtrodden Jew of the Diaspora. The Canaanite activists included poets, authors, journalists, sculptors, and educators. Their ideology of "negation of the Diaspora" contributed significantly to the creation of modern Israeli culture.

Led by the poet Yonatan Ratosh and the sculptors Binyamin Tammuz and Yitzhak Danziger, the Canaanites rejected Judaism and longed for a return to a Middle Eastern identity that predated both Judaism and Islam. They claimed that large parts of the Middle East, which they named the Land of Kedem (*kedem,* meaning east or antiquity), constituted an ancient, Hebrew-speaking civilization. They aspired to a Hebrew renaissance that would liberate Jews from Judaism and Arabs from Islam. Both religions, they believed, consigned their adherents to medieval superstition, keeping at bay the advances of secular modernity.

Influenced by Fascist culture, the Canaanites were radicals who rejected any links to Judaism and Jewish history, preaching instead a Hebrew universalism. Before and during the 1948 war, they objected to the expulsion of Arabs, believing that this only constituted a population transfer from one part of the Land of Kedem to another. Most Jews rejected Canaanite ideology, but its glorification of the new Hebrew man and woman and the uncompromising rejection of the Diaspora proved appealing to intellectual circles. But the sharp distinction between Israelis and Disapora Jews was keenly felt at all levels of Israeli society and helped shape an important element of Israeli culture in the state's formative period.

The new, fragile state of some 600,000 people not only required the financial and political support of the international community but desperately needed Jewish immigrants, although some high-ranking officials complained that Israel could not take in any and all Jews. The minister of finance, Eliezer Kaplan, stated, "We need workers and fighters." Others were concerned about the cultural level of some immigrants, others about their political affiliations. Some government officials objected to immigrants based on their countries of origin while some preferred to make admission contingent upon occupation. Those who came as refugees, without ideological commitment to the Zionist cause, were, in theory, especially unwelcome. But in reality, the new state could not pick and choose which Jews to accept, and so, to facilitate mass immigration, on July 5, 1950, the government promulgated the **Law of Return,** which endowed "Every Jew [with] the right to immigrate to the country." Over the next four years, some 700,000 people arrived. The two largest groups included Holocaust survivors from Europe and Jewish refugees from Arab lands. Adjustment for both was difficult.

Approximately 350,000 *Shoah* (Holocaust) survivors had made their way to Israel by 1949. There they took comfort among each other, with a wide network of groups offering support, and, as in the Diaspora, the survivors did a remarkable job of doing the unremarkable—rebuilding family life. Survivors immediately participated in the task of defending and building up the fledgling state, but their political and cultural integration proved very difficult under the circumstances. Many survivors felt that they were the last Jews alive and believed they had an obligation to share their experiences. But the mood and the culture of the country meant that few people wanted to listen to such tales of sorrow. The heroic ethos of the new Hebrew warrior promoted social antipathy toward survivors, in so far as the latter physically embodied the weakness Zionist ideology claimed was characteristic of Diaspora Jewry. David Ben-Gurion contemptuously referred to Holocaust survivors as "human dust." Others were equally callous. A Mapai (Labor Party) leader said of the survivors, "They must learn love of the homeland, a work ethic, and human morals." However, a more complex rationale informed the official encouragement of silence and the shunning of Holocaust survivors. The presence of survivors evoked the painful realization that contrary to Zionist claims of power, the Yishuv had proven unable to rescue large numbers of Jews, let alone prevent or even put a stop to the Holocaust.

By 1949, one out of every three Israelis was a survivor. Nearly all those who had come to Palestine prior to the war lost family members in the Holocaust. Many people were wracked with guilt about their escaping in time. For their part, some survivors seethed with anger at the leaders of the Yishuv. Yosef Rosensaft, a leader among the Jewish displaced persons at Bergen-Belsen declared, "You danced the *hora* while we were being burned in the crematoriums." Relations between survivors and the Yishuv were tense. Yet Israel provided Holocaust survivors what few other places could—an environment free of antisemitism, the security of being surrounded by fellow Jews, and the chance to be reunited with family members thought to have perished during the war. Thousands of Jews could relate to the experience of Rita Waxman, a recently arrived survivor, in the winter of 1949. While shopping in Haifa one day, Waxman caught a glimpse of a soldier queuing up to buy a movie ticket. She stopped dead in her tracks. "Haim?" she called out. As he turned, they stared at each other. They embraced—mother and son. Haim was now twenty-one. Separated in Poland when Haim was fourteen, each presumed the other to have been killed. In addition to chance encounters such as this, thousands of Jews were reunited thanks to newspaper advertisements and radio call-in shows.

By the 1950s, Arab nationalism effectively put an end to Jewish life in Arab lands. Most Middle Eastern Jews emigrated to Israel. The largest number—230,000 Jews—arrived from Morocco between 1948 and 1978. They were mostly poor. The wealthier Moroccans and Tunisians went to France and Canada. Almost all Algerian Jews immigrated to France. In Israel, the Ashkenazi establishment looked with disdain upon

Emile Pierre Joseph de Cauwer's Depiction (1865) of the Oranienburger Straße Synagogue. In 1856, Berlin's Jewish population stood at about 26,000. The one large synagogue in existence was increasingly unable to cater to the needs of the growing Jewish population and following an open competition, the community commissioned the architect, Eduard Knoblauch, to build what would be known as the New Synagogue. Before its completion, Knoblauch fell ill and his place was taken by August Stuehler. The design was a striking addition to Berlin. Situated on Oranienburger Strasse, the New Synagogue is a fine example of the Orientalist tradition in nineteenth-century synagogue architecture. At a time when large public buildings were being constructed in a neo-Gothic style that romanticized the Christian Middle Ages, Jews had little interest in commemorating in stone (and at great expense) a period that most thought of as one of endless Jewish suffering. Instead, in both Europe and the United States in the middle of the nineteenth century, Jews opted for monumental synagogues that blended styles, often giving preference to Moorish design elements.

With the final cost of construction 750,000 taler, a steep increase from the original estimate of 125,000 taler, Berlin's New Synagogue was inaugurated in 1866 and had seating for more than 3,000 worshipers. Ornately decorated inside and out, the massive building's most prominent feature was the 50-meter high golden-ribbed dome atop the synagogue. It immediately became one of Berlin's most visible architectural features, but opinion within the Jewish community was bitterly divided. Although the majority approved of the synagogue, some found the building too ostentatious, while others baulked at the Moorish style, believing it hindered integration by reaffirming the "oriental" identity of Jews. Still others objected to the use of an organ and Reform liturgy.

During the Kristallnacht, November 9, 1938, the synagogue escaped damage because a courageous police officer, Wilhelm Krützfeld, who stood up to members of the S.A., who were attempting to burn down the synagogue. Services took place at the New Synagogue until 1940 when the German army then began using the building as a repository for military uniforms. In November 1943, Allied bombing heavily damaged the building and in 1958 it was demolished. All that remained was the front facade and entrance, which were retained as a memorial. Restoration on this front section began in 1988, and in May 1995, the building was opened as a museum, exhibiting the history of the synagogue.

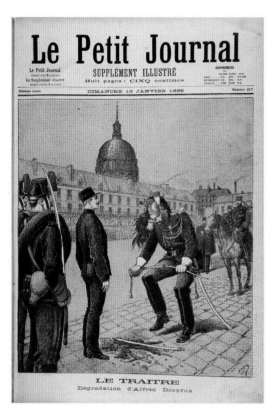

LE TRAITRE
Dégradation d'Alfred Dreyfus

The Degradation Ceremony of Alfred Dreyfus. In October 1894, Captain Alfred Dreyfus, a French Army General Staff trainee of the 14th Artillery, was accused of high treason and subsequently sentenced to life imprisonment on Devil's Island. On January 5, 1895, in the courtyard of the Military School in Paris, Dreyfus was subjected to the official degradation ceremony, as depicted in this front-page illustration of the newspaper *Le Petit Figaro*. As Dreyfus recalled some years later in his autobiography:

> The degradation took place Saturday January 5 [1895]. I submitted to this horrible torture without weakness. . . . Between four men and a non-commissioned officer I was led to the center of the square. Nine o'clock sounded. General Darras, commanding the execution parade, had the arms brought. I suffered the martyrdom, I stiffened myself in order to concentrate all my force; in order to support myself I evoked the memory of my wife and children.
>
> After the reading of the judgment I cried out, addressing myself to the troops: "Soldiers, they are degrading an innocent man! Soldiers, they are dishonoring an innocent man! "Long live France! Long live the army!"
>
> An adjutant of the Garde *Républicain* approached me. Rapidly, he tore off my buttons, the bands on my pants, the insignias on my kepi and sleeves, and then he broke my saber. I saw fall to my feet all these scraps of honor. And then, despite the horrible jarring of my entire being, my body upright, my head high, I called out again to the assembled soldiers and people: "I am innocent!"
>
> The ceremony continued. I had to make a circuit of the square. I heard the cries of an abused crowd, I felt the shivering that made them vibrate, for they had had presented to them a man condemned for treason, and I attempted to make pass over to them another shiver, that of my innocence.

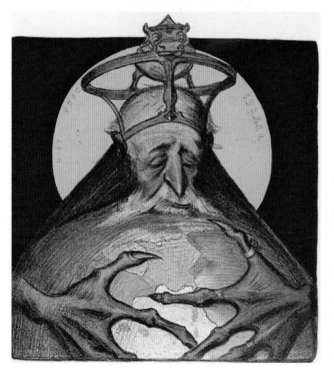

From *Die Juden in der Karikatur* (1921) by Eduard Fuchs. This ghastly and antisemitic depiction of Rothschild by the French artist Charles Léandre was first published in 1898. In that year the forces of French antisemitism were ascendant, as the frenzied passions surrounding the Dreyfus Affair led to enormous street demonstrations in Paris, with as many as 100,000 people shouting "Death to the Jews!" While antisemites rallied and railed against Dreyfus, their almost permanent symbol of Jewish perfidy was Rothschild. Antisemites on both the Left and Right hated Rothschild as a symbol of predatory capitalism and Jewish wealth. In this picture, Rothschild, wearing a crown, hugs a globe with his clawed hands. The image represents the antisemitic trope of world Jewish conspiracy.

OZE Breastfeeding Poster. OSE (Russian acronym) TOZ (Polish acronym) was established in St. Petersburg in 1912. Its mission was the prevention, early detection, and cure of diseases among Jewish people. It also sought to promote improved living conditions, focusing in its public outreach on the physical and mental development of Jewish youth. After World War I and the pogroms that followed, demands on the organization were monumental. It rose to the challenge and grew accordingly. Thirty-four branches of OSE operated in the Russian territories. The organization maintained 12 hospitals, 125 nurseries, 60 dispensaries, 40 feeding centers for school children, 13 summer camps, 4 sanatoria for tuberculosis patients, and scores of other medical, dental, psychiatric, and child-care facilities. Branches opened in the newly established states of Poland, Lithuania, Latvia, and Romania, as well as other countries in central and western Europe. The OSE budget was around $2 million per annum. Seventy-five percent of its funds came from membership fees and fund drives. The remaining 25 percent of its budget came from contributions from Jewish communities all over the world and the American Jewish Joint Distribution Committee. This poster is part of the special programs OSE ran to promote infant welfare through breastfeeding and shows a woman rejecting cow's milk to feed her baby. The Yiddish reads: "For health and long life, a mother's milk." This striking Art Deco public health poster was issued by OSE and the American Jewish Joint Distribution Committee in Berlin in 1926.

"A Call to Arms Against the White Paper and for the Immigration, Settlement and Defense [of Erets Yisrael]." Without homes, families, or communities to return to, the majority of Holocaust survivors in the displaced persons (DP) camps wanted to go to Palestine and regularly protested British immigration policy. Zionism was the dominant political position among survivors in the DP camps, and about 60 percent of the 250,000 inmates, the majority of whom were Polish Jews, eventually made their way to Palestine. Pictured here is a Poalei Tsiyon (Zionist Workers' Party) poster issued in a German DP camp after 1945. It urges Jews to join in opposing British policy that restricted the entrance of Jewish refugees to Palestine.

This "Hanucah Entertainment" program (1907) from a Philadelphia religious school in 1907 captures one way that American Jews have sought to balance Jewish tradition with participation in a larger Christian culture: a Hanukkah remodeled on but also serving as an alternative to the gift giving, plays, and holiday cards of Christmas.

"Let My People Go" poster created for the Union of Councils for Soviet Jews by the graphic artist and Academy Award–winning film director Saul Bass.

the new arrivals. In 1949, an official of the Jewish Agency said of Sephardic newcomers, "[We] need to teach them the most elementary things—how to eat, how to sleep, how to wash." The view that they were primitive was widespread. Also in 1949, an incendiary editorial in the newspaper *Ha'aretz* declared, "[The North African Jews]. . . . have almost no education at all, and what is worse is their inability to comprehend anything intellectual. . . . In the . . . [immigrant absorption] camps you find filth, gambling, drunkenness and prostitution. . . . [There is also] robbery and theft. Nothing is safe from this anti-social element, no lock is strong enough." The Left-wing author of this piece, Arye Gelblum, then took a swipe at the future Right-wing prime minister Menachem Begin and his political party: "Perhaps it is not surprising that Mr. Begin and Herut are so eager to bring all these hundreds of thousands at once—they know that ignorant, primitive and poverty-stricken masses are the best raw material for them, and could eventually put them in power."

Like their European predecessors, most immigrants from Arab lands had been highly urbanized, but when they arrived in Israel they were sent to semirural development towns or poor farming districts. Others lived in poverty amid urban blight. The Jewish Agency warned that the immigrant slums were becoming "quarters in which poverty, idleness, crime and violence breed—a new Carthage." Social discontent about inadequate housing and unemployment became widespread. Alienation was mounting and, in the 1950s, turned to rioting. The most infamous episode occurred in the Haifa neighborhood of Wadi Salib, when on July 9–10, 1959, demonstrations erupted, led by North African Jewish immigrants against ethnic discrimination and the ruling Labor Party. On July 11, similar riots broke out in Tiberias and Beersheva.

Aside from the perception that they were culturally and socially primitive—similar things were being said about European Shoah survivors—Middle Eastern Jews suffered from economic privation. Most arrived completely destitute. Ashkenazic refugees were likewise without independent means upon arrival, but many received assistance from family who had migrated to Palestine years before; Jews from the Middle East rarely had such sources of support. Moreover, the reparation payments from the German government that many Ashkenazim later received served to further widen the economic gap between the two groups of newcomers to Israel. Yosef Amoyal, a North African Jewish cobbler living in Jaffa, expressed the sentiments of many poor Sephardim in a letter he wrote to Prime Minister Ben-Gurion: "I seem to be a stepson to the Israeli people."

The absorption of immigrants was a huge and expensive undertaking. In 1949, it was estimated that to provide 230,000 immigrants with housing and employment would cost as much as $700 million. In addition to receiving foreign assistance, the government resorted to inflationary measures and printed money to pay for government services. It also instituted an austerity program, with strict price controls and rationing of food, raw materials, and foreign currency. Modeled on British wartime rationing, the program was intended to ensure a minimum standard of living both for veteran Israelis and newcomers.

While the goal of providing a minimum standard of living was achieved, the program was extremely unpopular. Women, in particular, bore the brunt of its impact. It was mostly they who waited in long lines to purchase staples. After waiting for hours, women often went home empty handed because the food had run out. Oftentimes, certain foodstuffs were declared suddenly available and women had to go through the routine of returning daily to stores. The situation was worse in summer. Few people owned refrigerators, so food could only be bought in small quantities lest it spoil. The program bred widespread anger, frustration, and uncertainty. The system also bred corruption as the government determined which shops would sell what and which suppliers would have the right to provide certain items. Still, some supporters of the plan were drawn to it for ideological reasons. The poet Uri Zvi Greenberg, then a member of the Knesset, was so enamored of the austerity program that he wanted it to become Israel's "life-long constitution." His was a Zionist celebration of privation and anti-consumerism. Others were more pragmatic. The architects of the plan were certain that given the challenges facing the country, there was no other way. As Ben-Gurion declared in the Knesset, without the austerity program it was all but impossible to carry out the country's three great tasks: "defense, immigration absorption and the maintenance of an acceptable living standard."

Large numbers of immigrants kept arriving; 35,000 from Yemen between May 1948 and December 1949. In the next few years, they were joined by a further 14,000. All 49,000 Yemenite Jews arrived in the country on a total of 450 airline flights in what was known as **Operation Magic Carpet.** Not all politicians were enthusiastic about the arrivals from Yemen. The Knesset member Yitzhak Greenbaum declared, "By bringing Yemenites, 70 percent of whom are sick, we are doing no good to anybody. We are harming them by bringing them into an alien environment where they will degenerate. Can we withstand an immigration of which 70 percent are sick?" Others had a very different response, welcoming the Yemenite Jews by romanticizing that they are "a fabulous tribe, the most poetic of the tribes of Israel. Their features bear the ancient Hebrew grace, their hearts are filled with innocent faith and a fervent love of the Holy Land."

Ben-Gurion exhibited both tendencies. In November 1950, he wrote of the Yemenite Jews to chief of staff, and later famous archaeologist, Yigal Yadin: "This tribe is in some ways more easily absorbed, both culturally and economically, than any other. It is hardworking, it is not attracted by city life, it has—or at least, the male part has—a good grounding in Hebrew and the Jewish heritage. Yet in other ways it may be the most problematic of all. It is two thousand years behind us, perhaps even more. It lacks the most basic and primary concepts of civilization (as distinct from culture)." The following year, Ben-Gurion told the Knesset that the government's goal was to inculcate the Yemenite immigrant in the ways of Israel to the extent that he forgets where he came from, just "as I have forgotten that I am Polish." (*See* Map 15-1.)

One of the largest waves of migration to Israel was called **Operation Ezra and Nehemia** (1950–1951), an airlift of 100,000 Jews from Iraq. Although Zionism was never very strong among Iraqi Jews, when the Iraqi government stopped making distinctions between Jews and Zionists after the establishment of the State of Israel, emigration became imperative. When Iraq froze the assets of departing Jews, effectively stealing their property, the Israeli government—which had been directed by the United States and Britain in 1948 to compensate Palestinian refugees—linked the two events, effectively neutralizing both claims. Iraqi Jewish refugees, expecting Israel to compensate them for their losses, were told by Jerusalem to lodge claims with the government of Iraq, the very entity that had robbed them. By the 1970s discontent among Middle Eastern Jews ran so high that a protest movement called the **Black Panthers,** named after its American counterpart, was formed. They succeeded in calling attention to economic, educational, and social disparities between mizrahim (Middle Eastern Jews) and Ashkenazim.

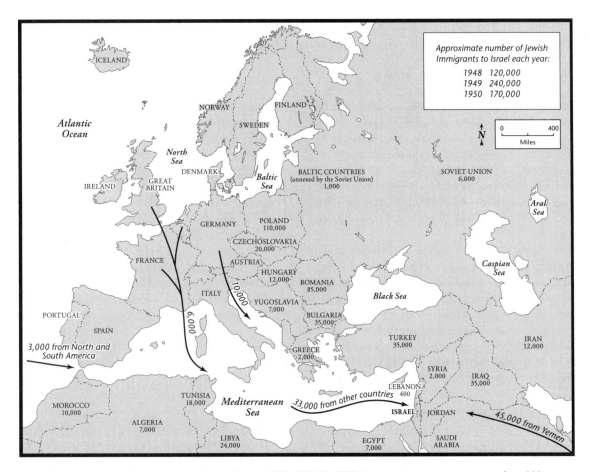

Map 15-1   Jewish Immigration to the State of Israel, 1948–1950. By 1950, the two most ancient centers of world Jewry—Europe and the Middle East—had been decimated by mass murder and forced emigration. For Holocaust survivors in Europe and Jewish refugees from Muslim lands, the newly created State of Israel proved the most favored destination.

Camp trunks. For the most part, Jewish refugees to Israel in the late 1940s and early 1950s were first placed in refugee transit camps prior to their integration into society at large. Here, Iraqi Jews sit with their possessions, contained in the mountains of suitcases and trunks.

Serious social problems notwithstanding, Israel has been enormously successful in integrating so many people, from so many different cultures, with a wide variety of religious and political sensibilities. The divisions among modern Jews that we have charted in this book have not disappeared. Jews remain split between secular and religious, Left and Right, those of Ashkenazic background and those who are not. And among Israelis, as in any nation, there are haves and have-nots. Out of the vast differences, however, a nation was forged.

Above all, it was government that provided the solid institutional framework for the new Jewish state. Jewish sovereignty, depicted with national flag and anthem, also provided people with a rallying point and sense of belonging and purpose. Organizationally, Israel had long prepared for national independence. With the declaration of statehood in May 1948, government ministries were immediately formed out of the various departments and bureaus that comprised the National Council and the Jewish Agency. While national governance was new, administering individual departments

was not. Newly created government ministries—such as health, religious affairs, politics, culture, education, finance, immigration, labor, trade, industry, commerce, and foreign affairs—all had fairly experienced leaders from the outset. This is not to say that efficiency was the handmaiden of experience. Assuredly, it was not, for the cabinet ministers presided over a notoriously cumbersome bureaucracy. To make matters worse, the pay and conditions of civil service jobs were abysmal and failed to attract Israel's best and brightest. Yet the necessary infrastructure for successful governance was in place.

Initially, Israel was run by a provisional government. It enjoyed the loyalty of the majority, and its authority to establish a supreme court, issue the nation's currency and postage stamps, and collect taxes went unquestioned. While dissatisfaction accompanied the austerity program, the government's right to install it was also broadly accepted. What was needed was the installation of a permanent government, always intended but postponed due to the War of Independence.

Adhering to the principle of universal suffrage, the election of a new government was set for January 25, 1949. Elections continued to employ the long-established system of proportional representation. This had been the case in both Zionist Congresses and in the Yishuv's National Assembly. The Constituent Assembly, which later became the Knesset, was to have 120 members. They were to be elected by voters, irrespective of race, creed, or sex, so long as they were at least eighteen years of age. The provisional government, led by Ben-Gurion (Labor), won the first election. Thereafter, the Labor Party held onto the reins of power until 1977.

Elections were and remain based on the system of proportional representation, in which small parties are crucial for the formation of government. In this arrangement, majority and minority parties, often with starkly conflicting worldviews, are dependent on each other, and small parties pledge allegiance to the party with the highest number of seats, usually in return for legislative favors. A reflection of the radical and often irreconcilable diversity of modern Jews, this system, with its myriad parties and narrow agendas, while functioning, has also proven to be highly unstable.

The formation of a government and military was an enormous task, and while foreign aid and donations from world Jewry were crucial, it is what Israelis energetically and creatively did with the assistance that made for the successful absorption of the immigrants and their transformation into modern Israelis. Most notably, through the use of Hebrew as the national language and the integrative impact of compulsory military service, the modern Israeli was formed out of a shared culture and experience. Moreover, Israel achieved statehood and cultivated Israeli identity under the particularly difficult circumstances of near-constant war and economic vulnerability. This further tightened the social and cultural bonds among Israelis.

Israel's Wars

The difficulties of building a state, with meager resources and a highly diverse population, would have been difficult enough in a peaceful environment. That Israel did so in a near-constant state of war is a remarkable achievement. After the 1948 War of Independence, Israel fought six wars against Arab nation-states. In the summer of 1949, Israel signed armistice agreements with Egypt, Jordan, Lebanon, and Syria, but belligerence took other forms, and in August 1949 Egypt closed the Suez Canal to Israeli shipping. In response to a 1951 UN resolution calling on Egypt to open the shipping lanes, the Egyptian government relaxed its prohibition only to reimpose the ban in 1952. Border skirmishes also took place, and verbal hostility continued to mount. The

Egyptian foreign minister, Muhammad Salah al-Din, declared in 1954, "The Arab people will not be embarrassed to declare: We shall not be satisfied except by the final obliteration of Israel from the map of the Middle East." In the **Sinai Campaign** (1956), Israel fought its second war against the Arabs. In October, with the support of France and Britain, Israel captured the Sinai Peninsula. The U.S. government, unaware of the scheme, was furious and publicly rebuked Britain and France. Thereafter, European states would become minor players in Middle Eastern affairs, shadows of their former imperial selves. The United States, by contrast, became the dominant party in brokering Arab–Israeli relations. The United States forced Israel to surrender the Sinai (a UN force moved in, ensuring Israel's shipping access through the Straits of Tiran), and Israel emerged from the Sinai Campaign with its regional and global reputation enhanced while Muhammad Salah al-Din's boast appeared to be an empty threat.

Under the powerful Egyptian ruler Gamal Abdul Nasser, plans were again made to launch war against Israel. The **Six-Day War** (1967) was Israel's third war against the Arab world. In May, Nasser decided to provoke hostilities by closing the Straits of Tiran to Israeli shipping. He ordered the UN force in the Sinai to leave, and a war of words occupied the world for two tense weeks. The blood-curdling rhetoric about Israel's imminent obliteration that came from Arab capitals filled Israel's citizens with dread. Following the Eichmann trial, whatever feelings of superiority Israelis may have once felt toward Holocaust survivors had dissipated (*see box,* The Eichmann Trial). The crisis Israelis were now facing made them identify with the Holocaust more than ever. The possibility of their own defeat and the sense of impending doom were so great that rabbis sanctified public parks in the expectation that the death toll would climb into the hundreds of thousands.

On June 5, sensing that it could wait no longer, the Israeli air force bombed the airfields of Egypt, Jordan, Syria, and Iraq, destroying their fleets. With lightning speed, Israel moved into Gaza and Sinai, took the Golan Heights from Syria, occupied the whole west bank of the Jordan River, and captured Jordanian-controlled East Jerusalem. Israel was now 28,000 square miles larger. Although the country had lost 759 soldiers and sustained about 2,500 casualties, the entire Jewish world was electrified by the Israeli victory, especially the sight of Israeli soldiers at the Western Wall. Even the staunch secularist, General **Moshe Dayan** (1915–1981), entered Jerusalem's Old City, proclaiming, "We have returned to all that is holy in our land. We have returned never to be parted from it again." Amid the euphoria, few gave much thought to the one million Palestinians now under Israeli occupation.

THE EICHMANN TRIAL

An important change in Israeli attitudes toward Holocaust survivors took place with the Eichmann trial, which was held in Jerusalem from April 11 to August 16, 1961. Adolf Eichmann, a member of the Nazi SS, was a leading figure in organizing the deportation of Jews to extermination camps. He had escaped from American custody after the war and wandered around Germany until 1950 when, with the help of a Catholic organization dedicated to ferrying ex-Nazis out of Europe, he fled to Argentina. There he lived under the alias Ricardo Klement until 1960, when agents of the Israeli Security Service (Mossad) abducted Eichmann and brought him to Israel to stand trial. He was indicted on fifteen criminal charges, including crimes against humanity, crimes against the Jewish people, and membership in a criminal organization. Three judges presided over the trial while Eichmann sat in a specially constructed bulletproof glass booth in the dock.

The prosecution presented more than 1,500 incriminating documents and a hundred witnesses (ninety of whom were Nazi concentration and extermination camp survivors). On December 11, 1961, the judges announced their verdict: Eichmann was convicted on all counts. He was hanged at midnight between May 31/June 1, 1962. His remains were cremated and his ashes scattered in the sea beyond Israeli territorial waters.

The trial was given wide international coverage, and in Israel dramatic survivor testimonies, most heard for the very first time, alerted Israelis to the detailed horrors of the Holocaust. A changed attitude and consciousness emerged as empathy for the victims and memory of the event became increasingly central to Israeli culture and sense of self.

One who did was the now celebrated author, Amos Oz, who in a 1967 article "Land of Our Forefathers," warned, "Even unavoidable occupation is a corrupting occupation." One of the most dire assessments came from the philosopher Yeshayahu Leibowitz, who urged that Israel not hold on to the territories. His advice went unheeded, and he declared, "Israel won the war in six days and lost it on the seventh." Eight Arab nations convened in Khartoum at the end of August 1967, vowing to carry on the struggle against Israel and declared the following three principles: no peace with Israel; no negotiations with Israel; no recognition of Israel.

Victory in the Six-Day War proved a turning point in the character and nature of Israel as its domestic life and foreign policy changed. The state began to pursue an agenda of territorial expansion and settlement building on Palestinian land. That policy has split Israeli society and Jewish public opinion abroad.

Israel's fourth war is known as the **War of Attrition** (1968–1970). It was a conflict of low but constant intensity in which Egypt sought to eject Israel from Sinai. The Soviet Union supported Egypt, with Russian pilots flying sorties in Egyptian planes. The war proved inconclusive, and a truce was signed in 1970. Attempts to sign a formal peace treaty failed as the Israeli government refused to meet Arab demands for withdrawal from the occupied territories. Terrorist activity of the Palestine Liberation Organization (PLO, founded in 1964) stiffened Israel's resolve not to negotiate a deal. The most infamous terrorist attack was the seizure of Israeli athletes at the 1972 Munich Olympic Games, perpe-trated by the Palestinian group Black September, which had close ties to Yasser Arafat. After a protracted standoff and a botched rescue operation by German paramilitary troops, eleven of the athletes were killed. The murders of Jews at an event organized to express international goodwill and fellowship, and in Germany of all countries, proved especially shocking.

The fifth Arab–Israeli war was called the **Yom Kippur War** (1973). After making friendly overtures to Israel, which were greeted with suspicion, Anwar Sadat, Nasser's successor, planned to attack Israel. Egypt would cross the Suez and its ally Syria would descend on the Golan Heights. The attack began at 2:00 p.m. on October 6, 1973. With many Israelis at synagogue observing Yom Kippur, the country was caught completely by surprise. The attack on the Day of Atonement was only part of the reason for this. Buoyed by the events of 1967, an overconfident Israeli military and intelligence establishment ignored repeated public threats by Sadat and detailed warnings by King Hussein of Jordan and the U.S. Central Intelligence Agency (CIA). The 1973 war presented a far graver threat than any previous war. Although Israel ultimately prevailed, the losses were enormous: over 2,500 dead, 5,500 wounded, and 294 taken prisoner. The myth of Israeli military invincibility was shattered. Politically and culturally, the country became increasingly factionalized between Right and Left. In the course of this crisis of morale, the fragile political consensus disintegrated. For their part in the Yom Kippur failure, Prime Minister **Golda Meir** (1898–1978) and Defense Minister Moshe Dayan were forced to resign.

In the international arena, Israel grew increasingly isolated. OPEC, the Arab-led cartel of oil-producing nations, used its control of oil production as a weapon against the West. Tripling the price of petroleum, Arab states applied pressure to Third World countries to break off relations with Israel. The plight of the Palestinians likewise engaged world opinion against the Israeli occupation, especially in western European Left-wing circles. In 1974, the head of the Palestine Liberation Organization, Yasser Arafat, took the podium at the United Nations with an olive branch in one hand and a gun in his holster to make the case to the General Assembly for Palestinian independence. In November 1975, the General Assembly passed a resolution condemning Zionism "as a form of racism," with a vote of 75 for, 35 against, and 32 abstentions.

In Israel, geopolitical tensions brought dramatic political change. In 1977, Menachem Begin, head of the Right-wing Likud party, was swept into office thanks to the support of Jews from Arab lands, dissatisfied with their treatment at the hands of the Ashkenazic establishment, and those alienated by Labor's secularism and its disdain for religious Orthodoxy. This was the Labor Party's first electoral defeat since the founding of the state in 1948. The triumph of the Right was of historic proportions. Begin was a man of intense political passions, given to demagoguery and histrionics. He repeatedly invoked the legacy of the Holocaust to denounce his political enemies and to justify his policies and personal actions. In addition to his former membership in the Stern Gang and his violent opposition in the early 1950s to Ben-Gurion's willingness to accept financial compensation from the German government for the Holocaust, Begin is also to be remembered for pursuing both peace and Israeli territorial expansion at one and the same time.

When President Anwar Sadat concluded that peace with Israel was possible and desirable, he made the historically monumental decision to come to Israel and meet with Begin. In November 1977, an ecstatic Israeli public welcomed President Sadat to an historic meeting with Prime Minister Begin. The Knesset also gave Sadat an enthusiastic reception as he addressed the chamber. The next year, at Camp David, Anwar Sadat, Menachem Begin, and U.S. President Jimmy Carter negotiated a peace treaty, which was signed in 1979. Sadat's decision proved to be a fatal one. Viewed as a traitor for his overture to Israel, Sadat was assassinated by Muslim fundamentalists in 1981. Although his successor, Hosni Mubarak, has continued to pursue peace with Israel, official circles in Egypt and other Arab countries have done next to nothing to change popular sentiment toward Israel and Jews. In the press throughout the Muslim world, the state-controlled media regularly publish hostile articles about Israel, and antisemitic caricatures of Jews are standard fare.

Begin's 1977 victory led to the promotion of a "Greater Israel" program, intended to expand the territory of the state through the establishment of Jewish settlements all over the Land of Israel. (It was a policy that Left-wing governments also pursued.) Begin stuck to this policy even while signing a peace treaty with Egypt. During Begin's tenure as prime minister, Israel formally annexed the Golan Heights. The deep fissures in Israel's political culture, particularly in response to expansionist policies, began to emerge more fully under Begin's rule. The distinguished Hebrew University political historian, Jacob Talmon, wrote to the Prime Minister in October 1980, "Mr. Prime Minister. . . . [T]he desire at the end of the twentieth century, to dominate and govern a hostile foreign population. . . is like an attempt to revive feudalism. . . The idea is simply not feasible . . . as France learned in Algeria." A host of military, labor, and business leaders expressed similar sentiments. Begin and an increasingly strident Right wing ignored their warnings. The continued occupation of the Palestinians, the building of new settlements in the West Bank, the impact of the oil embargo, the increasing potency of Arab voices in world affairs, Israel's formal annexation of East Jerusalem in 1980, and even its spectacular bombing of Osiraq (the Iraqi nuclear reactor) in 1981 all further eroded Israel's international status. The universal admiration Israel briefly enjoyed in 1976, after the audacious raid to free hostages at the Entebbe airport, has long receded.

Begin and his minister of defense, **Ariel Sharon** (b. 1928) launched Israel's sixth Arab–Israeli war, **Operation Peace in Galilee** (1982). Sharon led Israeli troops into Lebanon to drive the deeply entrenched Palestine Liberation Organization from the country. The ground war resulted in large numbers of casualties, approximately 600 Israelis and 20,000 Lebanese killed. Over objections from members of the Israeli military, Sharon recklessly disregarded the original plan to move no farther than twenty-five miles into Lebanese territory. Instead, he led his troops to the outskirts of Beirut and cut off the city's food, electricity, and water supplies. Deep dismay gripped regular soldiers who formed a movement named "Soldiers Against Silence." Former foreign minister Abba Eban wrote in a newspaper that "these six weeks have been a dark page in the moral history of the Jewish people." It was about to get worse. In seeking to oust Palestinian guerillas from the city and drive the PLO from Lebanon altogether, the Israeli army was assisted by Lebanese Christian forces. Taking advantage of the Israeli presence, Lebanese militia entered the Sabra and Shatila refugee camps where, on September 16 to 18, 1982, they massacred as many as 2,300 innocent civilians.

Around the world, the reaction was one of outrage, mostly directed at Israel but also toward Jews in the Diaspora.

Airport workers in Italy boycotted the Israeli national airline El Al and synagogues in Rome and Milan were bombed. The Rome bombing caused the death of a two-year-old. The link between Israel's treatment of the Palestinians and Nazi treatment of Jews became a common element of anti-Zionist propaganda. But the massacres in Lebanon sparked fury in Israel too. On September 25, 1983, 300,000 Israelis demonstrated in Tel Aviv, demanding to know what role their government had played in the slaughter. Public opinion condemned Sharon and his troops for failing to intervene to stop the killing. An Israeli judicial commission found that while the Israeli army did not participate in the murders, it should have stopped them. The commission held that Sharon "bears personal responsibility." The so-called Kahan Commission concluded that Sharon should not hold public office again. (He later became prime minister.) Begin stayed in office until 1983 and left broken and in disgrace. Even though for a short while the objective of driving the PLO from Lebanon and stopping cross-border shelling into northern Israel had been achieved, the Lebanon war had irreparably damaged the domestic credibility of the government as well as Israel's international standing.

With a weakened political system, Israelis opted for a Labor–Likud coalition government with a rotating premiership. Yitzhak Shamir of Likud first took office as prime minister for a two-year term. Shamir, a hard-liner who had voted against the peace treaty with Egypt, remained committed to staying in Lebanon despite the continued hemorrhage of Israeli troops. He also pursued the expansionist settlement policies of his predecessor. True to his own background, Shamir condoned the vigilantism of various West Bank settler groups. The unprecedented phenomenon of conscientious objection to military service increased under his administration while the fragility of the national economy contributed to social unrest. The Lebanon war, the building of settlements, and the implementation of expensive social programs designed to buy support were unsustainable. Inflation hit 400 percent per year. Panic selling on the Tel Aviv stock exchange followed, as did a run on banks, with people withdrawing increasingly worthless shekels from savings accounts to buy durable goods.

The government crisis reached its peak in the summer of 1984. New elections were called. The results revealed the weakness of the two major parties, Likud and Labor, and demonstrated that they were powerless to form a government without the assistance of smaller, primarily religious parties. To win support, both major parties lavished the smaller parties with all sorts of rewards, out of all proportion to electoral strength. The stalemate at the polls promoted Shimon Peres (b. 1923) to the post of prime minister. Peres was a veteran of Labor Zionism, a close ally of Ben-Gurion, and an accomplished technocrat.

Committed to getting the troops out, Peres ended the Israeli occupation of southern Lebanon in 1985. Only about 200 Israeli soldiers remained in the southern "security zone." Between 1985 and 1988, many of them were killed as Palestinian militants returned to the area, supported by Hezbollah, a new military and political group. With support from Iran, Hezbollah has proven to be an implacable enemy of Israel.

As the years passed, the Israeli occupation of Palestinian territory became more deeply entrenched and institutionalized. In 1987, Palestinians in the occupied territories rebelled, launching the **intifada,** an Arabic word for "shaking off." The intifada took the form of civil unrest, store closings, tax strikes, mounting barricades, and throwing stones at Israeli soldiers. The minister of defense, **Yitzhak Rabin,** responded with brutal force but to little effect in terms of being able to quell Palestinian rage and discontent. More broadly, Israel's political standing has never matched its military power, and the country has often been stymied in dealing with enemies. In the first Gulf War (1990), Iraq fired Scud missiles on Tel Aviv. Fearful that the warheads were tipped with chemical or biological weapons, Israelis donned gas masks and hid in underground shelters for nearly two weeks. Prevented by U.S. pressure from retaliating, nothing pointed to increasing Israeli impotence—conjuring up Holocaust images—as starkly as the sight of Jews waiting in fear of being gassed.

The early 1990s brought events that proved to be a catalyst for peace. The defeat of Iraq in the Gulf War and the fall of the Soviet Union, both in 1991, and the 1992 Israeli elections that gave Left-wing parties 60 out of 120 seats provided Prime Minister Yitzhak Rabin with a diplomatic and political mandate. His government conducted secret talks with the PLO that ultimately led to the Oslo Accords in 1993. Breakthroughs in the mid-1990s promised much but delivered precious little. Peace accords were signed with Jordan in 1994 and the Palestinians in 1995, but the assassination of Yitzhak Rabin by an Israeli Right-wing extremist, Yigal Amir, set the peace process back immeasurably. Rabin's suppression of the first intifada had failed, and a second intifada erupted in 2000. The Israeli armed forces were pressed into serving the politics of the occupation. Once engaged with armies of enemy states, they were now reduced to quashing a popular uprising.

The site of well-armed Israeli soldiers attacking Palestinians, many of them stone-throwing children, has only worsened the image of Israel in world public opinion. As early as 1984, Alexander Haig, former secretary of state under U.S. President Ronald Reagan and a staunch supporter of Israel, warned, "The sympathy of world opinion which had always before largely belonged to Israel, was in considerable measure transferred to the Palestinian Arabs. Acts of terrorism against Jews . . . aroused less indignation that

Israeli acts of reprisal." Haig's analysis has been correct, despite the specter of Palestinian suicide bombings targeting Israeli civilians. Suicide bombings over the next decades engendered widespread revulsion among understandably terrified Israelis, including the most vocal critics of the occupation. In response, in June 2002, the Sharon government began construction of a wall to separate Palestinian and Israeli populations in the West Bank. The respective names for the wall indicate how deep the divide is between the two peoples. Israelis refer to it as a "security fence" while Palestinians call it the "Apartheid Wall." Ironically, Israel's settlement policy and the rejectionist Arab stance have produced both a real and a metaphysical reduction of territory under conflict. Palestinians remain stateless while most Israelis do not venture into Palestinian areas nominally under their government's control. The unresolved condition of the Palestinians remains the greatest moral and political challenge facing the State of Israel.

The great geopolitical issues confronting Israel parallel the domestic tensions that beset Israeli society. The unstable political system, with its reliance on small parties designed to cater to specific interest groups, reflects the cultural fracturing of the Jewish people in the modern period. Should the state be a religious one? If so, what kind of Judaism ought to reign? Orthodox, perhaps? One would be immediately entitled to ask, what kind of Orthodoxy? Modern Orthodox? Hasidic? Mitnagdic? Something based on the spiritual lives of Jews from Arab lands? The divisions and subdivisions defy easy solutions and blight political compromise. Secular sensibilities and practices, reflective of a free democratic society, such as flying the national carrier, El Al, on the Sabbath, elicit a backlash from increasingly vocal, observant voters. The positions appear to be irreconcilable. How does a liberal state cater to the demands of those who in 2006 fought to host a gay pride march in Jerusalem without alienating those for whom such a thing is religiously offensive, or how does the state protect the rights of those Jews rejected merely because they have undergone non-Orthodox conversions? Admittedly, this is less a problem of the state but, rather, the unwillingness or inability—given the hamstrung nature of party politics—of secular political parties to stand up to the religious parties, who, in electoral terms, represent only a minority of Israeli Jews.

Debates over the character of the State of Israel reflect the multiple worldviews formed by Jews in the wake of emancipation, acculturation, and the Holocaust. Zionism's call for an ingathering of Jews put Israel to the test with the large influx of Ethiopian and Russian Jewish immigrants that came to the country in the 1980 and 1990s. An intransigent rabbinic establishment was loath to believe that all the immigrants were indeed Jewish, or at least Jewish in a way that satisfied Israeli rabbis. In the end, these newcomers have been integrated into Israeli society, and in the case of the nearly one million Jews from the former Soviet Union, they have noticeably changed the cultural and political landscape of Israel.

Social fissures run deep in Israel, just as they do in all countries. While religion plays an overt role in public life, the population is overwhelmingly secular. One of the most scientifically advanced societies in the world, Israel remains awash in superstition, which has, of late, crept into the political culture. Opposed to Ariel Sharon's intention to withdraw from Gaza, a group of Right-wing zealots performed the elaborate curse of *Pulsa Dinura,* an Aramaic term for "whip of fire." During the ceremony participants called upon angels of destruction to punish Sharon for his transgressions and called down biblical curses to bring about his death.

Zionism has come to mean different things to different Israelis; from liberal conceptions that envision a secular Jewish state living alongside a Palestinian one to the apocalyptic nationalism of the settlers who believe that building the settlements could hasten the Messianic Age. Many Israelis even believe that the word *Zionism* is an anachronism and should be abandoned now that Zionism has moved into a "postzionist" stage after having achieved its ultimate goal of establishing a Jewish state. Others suggest that the word and ideology behind it still retain their value given that antisemitism can still threaten Diaspora communities and that Israel remains far from secure and still requires the allegiance of all Jews, wherever they may live.

An immigrant society, Israel has only known radical social change. In its first fifty years of existence, Israel's population has increased from 600,000 to 6,000,000. The pioneering ethos has given way to the reality of life in an industrial, largely urban modern welfare state. The farmer and writer Moshe Smilansky (1874–1953), who believed passionately in the redeeming quality of agricultural work in the national Jewish revival, decried Tel Aviv's "shopkeeping mentality," which, he said, would lead the residents to "hucksterism, assimilation and apostasy." Earning an honest living in an urban center never led to apostasy in the Diaspora. It is ironic that he only predicted it for Israel. Smilansky was wrong, of course. Tel Aviv has been transformed into the world's biggest and liveliest Jewish city. The country as a whole has followed the global trend of urbanization. In the mid-1950s, 16 percent of Israelis worked in agriculture. By 1995 that figure stood at only 3 percent.

When the state was born, the majority of its Jewish citizens were Ashkenazic Jews from Europe. At the beginning of the twenty-first century, at least 60 percent of Israeli citizens are of Middle Eastern origin. Whether refugees or motivated

Zionists, nearly all Jews who came to build a new life in Israel had turned their backs on their countries of origin. But by the 1970s and 1980s, the impact of multiculturalism and ethnic revival prompted Jews from Morocco to celebrate festivals rooted in their North African heritage, while Hasidic Jews began to make devout pilgrimages back to eastern Europe. The nearly one million secular Jews from the former Soviet Union who had come to Israel as of the year 2000 have their own political parties and Russian-language media. A burgeoning Israeli prose literature is written in Russian; movies often feature foreign languages alongside Hebrew. With its largely Georgian script, Dover Koshashvili's "Late Marriage," relates the culture clash experienced by Georgian immigrants, as they encounter modern, secular Israeli mores, while English, Arabic, and some Hebrew form the dialogue in Eran Kolirin's film, "The Band's Visit," the touching and thoughtful story of an Egyptian Police orchestra's trip to Israel. The multilingual approach also holds true for popular music where contemporary Israeli groups such as the Ethiopian hip-hop ensemble, Kafeh Shahor hazar (Strong Black Coffee), sing in Hebrew and Amharic, as does the Idan Raichel Project. Raichel, of Eastern European Jewish heritage, uses music a means of reinvigorating Ethiopian identity in Israel, observing: "I noticed that immigrants from the Ethiopian community changed their names when they got to Israel. They try to assimilate into Western culture and don't keep their roots." He has urged the youth of that community to "remember that they like hip-hop but they are not from Harlem, they like reggae but they are not Bob Marley. The Ethiopians have a great culture that should be cherished." These diverse expressions of creativity, sometimes rooted in an artist's ethnic pride in Diaspora roots have become important to the changing nature of Israeli identity and are helping redefine Israeli culture, which, in its transformation, is becoming a multilingual polysystem, reminiscent of but in no way identical to the experimental culture of interwar Jewish Poland.

In addition, many citizens and residents of Israel are not Jewish at all and are not acculturated into Zionism. A good number are foreign guest workers, and about 20 percent of Israel's total population is of Arab origin. Many are in solidarity with the Palestinians, frustrated that the equality guaranteed them by law does not always translate into social parity. About 25 percent of Jewish Israelis consider themselves religious, and within that group is a sizeable ultra-Orthodox non-Zionist camp. How does Israel go about inculcating Zionist (and Jewish) values into an increasingly heterogeneous, and in some sectors non-Zionist and non-Jewish, population? One of the greatest challenges confronting Israel is reconciling its Jewish character and Theodor Herzl's ideal of a "tolerant modern civil state."

At Home in America

After 1945, the United States emerged as home to the world's largest and most influential Jewish community. In the past, Jewish communities enjoyed preeminence based upon antiquity of settlement or the intellectual prestige of its rabbinate. By contrast, the American Jewish community derived its strength from a combination of demography and economic power. From a class of poor immigrants, American Jews rose rapidly after World War II to become middle- and upper-middle-class professionals and businesspeople. By the 1930s the proportion of Jews working in industry had fallen to 20 percent, while the percentage engaged in commerce and public sector employment had risen to 60 percent. During the interwar period, the percentage of Jews engaged in the liberal professions rose from 3 to 15 percent. The economic advantages from such a rise up the ladder of success have come as a blessing but also at considerable social and cultural cost.

After World War I Jews (and other immigrants) who had poured into the United States since 1881 were still newcomers. Many still had relatives in Europe and maintained strong ties to the older centers of Jewish life. Still, the work of building an "American Jewry" was well underway. The great pressure on second-generation American Jews was to enter into the American mainstream. Many Jews in the interwar period sought to rid themselves of many of the markers that most clearly identified them as Jews. Yiddish was the most visible sign of Jewish difference. The 1930 U.S. census indicated that about 1,750,000 Yiddish speakers lived in the United States. The language was as vibrant as the Jewish community itself. But many Jews began to consider that they had to abandon the language to become American. Public school authorities agreed and were even amenable to the demands of Zionist activists who succeeded in 1931 in having Hebrew become an elective in New York City's public high schools. Ironically, Hebrew language instruction accompanied Jewish acculturation.

While the public school was the great vehicle for the integration of immigrants into American life, powerful forces were deeply hostile to Jews (and other minority groups). Antisemitism was widespread throughout America in the first half of the twentieth century and was to be found not just in the ideological baggage of hate groups like the Ku Klux Klan but in "respectable" society as well. Clubs and hotels such as the Hilton chain refused admission to Jews, and discrimination was evident in employment and housing. Educational institutions were also restricted. After the rush of Jews into the universities in the 1920s, a backlash followed the disproportionate presence of Jewish students on campus, and quotas against Jews were put in place. In the Ivy League, these quotas were not removed until the early 1960s. In the 1920s many of the most stridently antisemitic voices were those of prominent and revered Americans. The most famous was the automobile magnate, Henry Ford, whose newspaper *The Dearborn Independent* published *The Protocols of the Elders of Zion.* Ford repeatedly spoke of a "Jewish menace," as did another antisemite from Detroit, an infamous Catholic priest, Father Coughlin, who spewed invective against Jews via his Saturday afternoon radio program that went out to fifteen million listeners per week. Into the 1930s a slew of nativist associations, such as the Daughters of the American Revolution, the American Coalition of Patriotic Societies, the Veterans of Foreign Wars, the American Legion, and in the 1940s the America First Party, all promoted American isolationism, rejection of the New Deal, anti-Communism, and antisemitism. They also lobbied vigorously for immigration quotas on Jews to remain in force. And they had the political power to do so. By the early 1940s the American Legion had 1.2 million members, of which 28 were senators and 150 were congressmen. The overall atmosphere was such that it was still possible in that age for a Democratic congressman from Mississippi, John Rankin, to make antisemitic speeches in the House of Representatives and use the word *kike.*

It is a curious fact of American life that individuals who were beyond the pale of respectable Jewish society stepped into the fight against antisemitism and became, on this one issue, admired heroes. Notorious Jewish gangsters such as Meyer Lansky and David Berman broke up Nazi rallies in New York and Minneapolis in the 1930s, while the official Jewish establishment preferred to remain quiet, despite repeated requests from rabbis to get such events closed down. While no legal means could prevent such rallies, on one occasion New York State Judge Nathan Perlman personally asked Meyer Lansky to break up a German-American Bund rally. His only stipulation was that no one would be killed. Years later, Lansky recalled, "I was a Jew and felt for those Jews in Europe who were suffering. They were my brothers." In Minneapolis, David Berman, who controlled the city's illicit gambling, attacked Nazis at a Silver Shirt Legion rally. At an appointed time, Berman and his men burst into the meeting room and beat up the Nazis. Covered in blood, Berman took the microphone and announced, "This is a warning. Anybody who says anything against Jews gets the same treatment. Only next time it will be worse." Berman and his men did the same thing on two more occasions, after which no more Silver Shirt rallies were held in Minneapolis.

A different Jewish response to Fascism and the intolerance that permeated the political culture in the interwar years led to one of the most remarkable contributions of Jews to American—indeed to world—culture. In 1934, two impoverished Jewish boys in Cleveland, Jerry Siegel and Joe Schuster, brought to life the fictional, comic-book character Superman. Siegel imagined the discovery of a young child in the Midwest, born on a distant planet and possessing extraordinary strength. Superman represents a Jewish assimilationist fantasy. Clark Kent, Superman's alter ego, represents the bespectacled nerd. Thoughtful, shy, and "mild-mannered," he was, despite his all-American demeanor, the weak Jew of common stereotype. But for Siegel and Schuster, he had another side—that of the fearless, invincible Superman, the Man of Steel, who fought for "truth, justice, and the American way." Siegel and Schuster worked on their character for four years before Superman made his initial appearance in the fateful year of 1938, when the Nazi menace increasingly threatened Jews and the rest of the free world alike.

Superman was a patently Jewish creation. On the planet Krypton, from which he hails, Superman was known as Kal-El, Hebrew for "Vessel of God." He shared much with the biblical Moses, who also emerged from obscure origins, was discovered as a child, and rose to defeat injustice in the form of Pharaoh, becoming a fighter for truth, justice, and the Jewish way. Siegel and Schuster may also have drawn from Jewish folklore to create their hero by reworking the tale of the Golem, the mythical figure of sixteenth-century Prague who protected the beleaguered Jews of the ghetto. Prior to World War II, this ancient figure of Jewish folklore was widely popularized in books, plays, and films, and Superman's protective instincts and great strength recall certain attributes of the Golem.

In World War II, 550,000 American Jews served, 10,500 were killed, 24,000 were wounded, and 36,000 were decorated for bravery. After the war, American Jewry experienced significant changes in its relationship to America. Like other returning veterans, American Jews were beneficiaries of the GI Bill, as opportunities to pursue higher education increased. But more specifically, victory over the Nazis and American awareness of the Holocaust began to make overt antisemitic sentiments disreputable. With few exceptions, the social barriers faced by American Jews in the 1920s and 1930s began to disappear and Jews ascended the socioeconomic ladder. In the course of the process, Jews also began to enter into the American religious consensus. Antisemitism did not entirely disappear but increasingly took political form, which further contributed to the Jewish embrace of American values. In the aftermath of the espionage trial of Ethel and Julius Rosenberg, executed for treason in 1953, John Rankin, alluding to Jews, said in the House of Representatives, "[C]ommunism is racial. A racial minority seized control in Russia and in all her satellite countries, such as Poland, Czechoslovakia, and many other countries I could name. They have been run out of practically every country in Europe in the years gone by, and if they keep stirring race trouble in this country and trying to force their communistic program on the Christian people of America, there is no telling what will happen to them here."

American Jews reaffirmed their loyalties to America and to Jewish values and asserted the compatibility of the two. One of the great themes that animates the postwar American Jewish experience is the compatibility of secular, bourgeois identity and the assertion of ethnic identity. While the majority of American Jews were no longer religiously observant, they remained identifiably Jewish. They explored a host of cultural possibilities and modes of political expression in the English language that allowed for intense expressions of Jewishness.

Three great historical factors made for the increasingly open and celebrated expression of Jewish identity: the Holocaust, the rise of the State of Israel, and the decline of antisemitism. The period between 1948 and 1967 represents a distinct era in the history of the American Jewish experience. During that time, prosperity and suburbanization fostered the creation of a distinctly American Jewish religiosity. In the 1950s, most Jews, especially those in large cities, continued to live in densely populated Jewish neighborhoods. In New York in particular, Jews in parts of the Bronx and Brooklyn felt as though they were living in a majority Jewish world. For the most part, Jews socialized among themselves and lived in neighborhoods that provided all the amenities required for Jewish life: kosher butcher shops, bakeries, and delis, as well as bookstores, libraries, synagogues, nursing homes, and welfare agencies.

Increasing prosperity, the racial realignment of cities, and a postwar housing shortage encouraged Jews to leave urban areas and move to the suburbs. Some towns had "gentlemen's agreements," legal covenants or deed restrictions between developers and town officials that contained "no Jews" clauses; as a result, Jews tended to congregate in certain neighborhoods where they were welcome. In these new residential areas they built elaborate synagogues, marking both their success and their intention to stay. Lacking the density of urban life, these new suburban communities did not offer the vast array of secular goods and services previously available to Jews in cities. Instead, the synagogue became the center of communal life. (*See box*, Rebelling Against American Jewish Suburbia.)

Like suburban churches, the new synagogues were hardly places of traditional devotion. American Jews remained secular and confined worship to life-cycle and holiday occasions. Synagogue pews sat empty on most days, despite the fact that over half of American Jews held congregational membership. Most people joined the suburban synagogues for the educational and even recreational programs they offered. Religious practice had little to do with their choice to join. According to the American sociologist, Herbert Gans, the synagogues represented "not a return to the observance of traditional Judaism, but a manifestation in the main of a new symbolic Judaism." American "symbolic Judaism" was fully consistent with a genuine commitment to American civil religion. Amer-

ican Jews wholeheartedly supported the activities of the American Civil Liberties Union and joined the fight to maintain separation of Church and State and to keep religion out of public schools. In so doing, they considered what was good for them also was good for America.

In the aftermath of the Holocaust, American Jews dedicated themselves to eradicating radical discrimination, particularly that faced by African Americans. Most saw in the fight a direct link to Jewish experience. **Abraham Joshua Heschel** (1907–1972), in a classic essay wrote, "At the first conference on religion and race, the main participants were Pharaoh and Moses. Moses' words were: 'Thus says the Lord, the God of Israel, let My people go that they may celebrate a feast to me.' While Pharaoh retorted: 'Who is the Lord, that I should heed his voice and let Israel go? I do not know the Lord, and moreover I will not let Israel go.' The outcome of that summit meeting has not come to an end. Pharaoh is not ready to capitulate. The exodus began, but it is far from having been completed. In fact, it was easier for the children of Israel to cross the Red Sea than for a Negro to cross certain university campuses. Let us dodge no issues. Let us yield no inch to bigotry, let us make no compromise with callousness." (*See box,* The Jews and The Blues.)

It was not just the vicissitudes of ancient Israel that provided inspiration. The Holocaust was of direct significance in forming Jewish responses to the struggle for civil rights. Rabbi Joachim Prinz, a refugee from Nazism, was one of the official representatives of the Jewish community to the march on Washington in 1963. In his address to the crowd, he said, "When I was the rabbi of the Jewish community in Berlin under the Hitler regime, I learned many things. The most important thing that I learned under those tragic circumstances was that bigotry and hatred are not the most urgent problem. The most urgent, the most disgraceful, the most shameful and the most tragic problem is silence." Sometimes those who refused to remain silent paid a terrible price. Andrew Goodman and Michael Schwerner, two Jewish men from New York, together with African American James Chaney, were murdered in 1964 in Mississippi while investigating the bombing of black churches. Although Goodman and Schwerner never invoked a connection between being Jewish and their civil rights work, American Jews saw them as symbols of a Jewish commitment to social justice and revered them as heroes and martyrs.

But despite Jewish participation in the civil rights struggle, black–Jewish relations began to falter toward the end of the 1960s over issues related to education. Jewish groups opposed segregation but feared the consequences of social engineering involved in busing. Most Jewish organizations refused to participate in the 1964 boycott of New York City schools by the civil rights movement, which was calling for action to address racial inequalities in education.

REBELLING AGAINST AMERICAN JEWISH SUBURBIA

In the late 1950s and early 1960s, a rebellion of sorts against the materialism and perceived shallowness of American Jewish suburban culture began. In particular, writers such as Philip Roth, Saul Bellow, and Bernard Malamud wrote of the immigrant Jewish experience with a certain admiration and then more scathingly examined the next step in the transformation of American Jews, which took place in the suburbs. They lamented the cultural loss that such a process entailed.

While Jews were prevalent in every aspect of the entertainment industry, as performers they were especially drawn to stand-up comedy, and the growing revolt against postwar authority and tradition provided grist for the Jewish comedian's mill. Many got their starts in the Jewish holiday resorts of the Catskills in upstate New York. There, the humor was deeply and openly Jewish. Later, television and Hollywood beckoned, and although Jewish themes were not always or predominantly part of the material of Jewish comedians, biting social criticism and parody became hallmarks of artists such as Mel Brooks, Larry Gelbart, Carl Reiner, Neil Simon, Woody Allen, and Lenny Bruce. The critical, comedic voice that paid particular attention to language, deploying it in the service of "observational humor," was indelibly associated with Jews.

Lenny Bruce (1925–1966) one of the most important Jewish comedic voices, was born Leonard Alfred Schneider. Early in his career, he was found guilty on obscenity charges but refused to censor his act, wanting to shock and offend with words the America that he held to be prudish and hypocritical. Bruce was, for example, unsparing in his criticism of politics, religion, and the justice system. He also reflected on ethnicity and Jewish assimilation in America by blurring lines of difference. In one of his most beloved sketches, he praised aspects of gentile culture that he found to be Jewish and was dismissive of Jews he identified as having strayed too far from their roots. In so doing, he both celebrated and ridiculed American and postwar Jewish culture:

> Now I neologize Jewish and goyish.
> Dig: I'm Jewish. Count Basie's Jewish. Ray Charles is Jewish. Eddie Cantor's goyish.
> B'nai B'rith is goyish; Hadassah, Jewish. Marine corps—heavy goyim, dangerous.
> Kool-Aid is goyish. All Drake's cakes are goyish. Pumpernickel is Jewish, and, as you know, white bread is very goyish.
> Instant potatoes—goyish.
> Black cherry soda's very Jewish. Macaroons are very Jewish—very Jewish cake. Fruit salad is Jewish. Lime jello is goyish.
> Lime soda is very goyish.

Of course not everyone has sought to issue such devastating critiques but, rather, in silent recognition of what Lenny Bruce what was driving at, some have attempted to reinvigorate American Jewish life and impart it with a meaningfulness that they believed was lost with the process of suburbanization. This takes many forms—day schools, summer camps, "Birthright" trips to Israel, learning Hebrew, a vast Jewish internet presence, new journals of Jewish opinion, the growth of ultra-Orthodoxy, and the Jewish Renewal Movement, among them. One of the most interesting developments has been the creation of what the cultural critic, Jeffrey Shandler has called "postvernacular language and culture," by which he refers to the multifarious ways Yiddish continues to provide meaning and purpose even to people who do not have command of the language. He observes that Yiddish serves as "a language of study, as an inspiration for performers and their audiences, as a literature increasingly accessible through translation, as a selective vocabulary sprinkled through the speech of Jews and non-Jews, and as an object of affection." What may have once been an ideological commitment to the language in the immediate postwar years has been transformed into a more positive and creative application of Yiddish, intended to recapture some of what was lost by a mixture of violence, acculturation and suburbanization. But it constitutes more than an attempt to keep alive that which can never be fully resuscitated. Instead "postvernacular Yiddish" is a vehicle for entirely new explorations and experimentation in Jewish culture.

The urban riots in the summer of 1965 drove another wedge between the communities. Looting and burning of stores in cities, including New York, Philadelphia, and Los Angeles, resulted in the destruction of Jewish property. In Philadelphia, Jews owned 80 percent of the damaged stores. In the Los Angeles neighborhood of Watts, Jews owned 80 percent of the furniture stores, 54 percent of the liquor stores, and 60 percent of the food outlets that were damaged. The owners themselves were not affluent people but small shopkeepers besieged by the mob. Jewish organizations were careful to avoid charges of antisemitism, interpreting the riots as a symptom of the larger racial animosities playing themselves out at the time. Embattled Jewish store owners did not always see it that way.

As early as 1965, black nationalist leader Stokely Carmichael told whites, and perhaps especially Jews, given their heavy participation in the civil rights movement, that they were to "get off the bandwagon," for they had no role to play in the

Exterior of Beth Shalom Congregation, Philadelphia. Across the United States after World War II, Jews began to leave the deteriorating inner cities for the suburbs. By 1957, approximately 50,000 of Philadelphia's Jews, one-fifth of the total Jewish community, had moved to the northern suburbs. Many of the city's major Jewish institutions were also relocating, among them the Home for the Jewish Aged, the Einstein Medical Center, and Gratz College. By 1965 ten Reform and Conservative congregations were established in and around the suburb of Elkins Park. One of the synagogues to relocate to this area was Temple Beth Sholom, a congregation originally founded in 1919.

In 1954, the congregation's rabbi, Mortimer J. Cohen, commissioned the distinguished architect Frank Lloyd Wright to build a new synagogue. Cohen wrote to Wright, "Our hope is to make Beth Sholom (House of Peace) a symbol for generations to come of the American and the Jewish spirit, a House of Prayer in which all may come to know themselves better as children of the living God." The complicated design—Cohen wanted a sunken *bimah* (reader's platform), recalling the passage from Psalms 130, "Out of the depths I cry to Thee, O Lord!" while Wright wanted the building to soar to 100 feet (zoning laws only permitted a thrust of 65 feet). The grand conceptions meant delays and spiraling costs. The only synagogue ever designed by Wright, Beth Sholom finally opened in 1959. While it was an exceptional example of modernist, ecclesiastical architecture, the temple also typified the large, postwar suburban synagogues whose designs owed very little to history and promised a new beginning for postwar Jewish communities. Beth Sholom's main sanctuary seats 1,020, while the Sisterhood Sanctuary located downstairs replicates the main sanctuary on a smaller scale and seats 242. The building's structure is pyramid shaped, with three steel tripod girders supporting steeply inclined walls. The design allows for complete freedom from internal support columns and thus an entirely open space. The lattice walls of the sanctuary are composed of translucent layers of wire, glass, and plastic. In daylight hours, the glass walls allow natural sunlight to fill the sanctuary, while at night artificial lighting permits the entire building to glow from within. Wright, who passed away just before the building was completed, described Beth Sholom as a "luminous Mount Sinai."

struggle of African Americans. In the 1970s, official Jewish opposition to racial quotas in university admissions and hiring also further soured relations between the two groups. Later, public expressions of hostility from two prominent African Americans set off a firestorm. In 1984 Jesse Jackson referred to New York as "Hymietown," while Nation of Islam leader Louis Farrakhan called Judaism a "gutter religion." In 1991 the incident in which an African American child, Daren Cato, was accidentally hit and killed by a car driven by a Hasid in Brooklyn led to a full-scale riot (Jews called it a pogrom) in which Yankel Rosenbaum, a visiting yeshiva student from Australia, was stabbed and killed. A widening socioeconomic gap between blacks and Jews drove them further apart. While both groups continued to publicly voice a similar commitment to ethnic self-assertion and shared aspirations to "social justice," they tended to pursue these goals more separately than together.

After the Eichmann trial, not only did American Jews begin to invoke the Holocaust on behalf of the civil rights

THE JEWS AND THE BLUES

A tradition of cultural affinity between Jews and African-American culture long predated the advent of the Civil Rights era. Cultural icons, such as the Russian immigrant Irving Berlin (1888–1989), were especially drawn to ragtime music, even though they did not fully understand the great Scott Joplin's syncopated rhythms. Berlin even wrote songs for black performers. Al Jolson (1886–1950), who appeared in the first talking picture, *The Jazz Singer* (1927) and performed in blackface, played the son of a cantor caught between his father's wish that he follow in his pious musical footsteps and his own wish to sing black music.

George Gershwin (1898–1938) was deeply influenced by the blues and in 1924 penned the classic *Rhapsody in Blue.* He followed this with a string of spirituals, rags, and blues, including the American original "I Got Rhythm." The year 1935 saw the premiere of his play *Porgy and Bess,* and Gershwin so perfectly captured the feel and cadence of black life and music in that production that the *New York Herald-Tribune* review of the play called it "a piquant but highly unsavory stirring-up together of Israel [and] Africa."

Jews also played prominent roles as managers of black artists, when hardly any white promoters dared to cross color lines. Ella Fitzgerald, John Coltrane, Miles Davis, Louis Armstrong, and B.B. King all had Jewish managers. A most significant development took place in the late 1950s when two Jewish immigrant brothers from Poland, Leonard and Phil Chess, founded Chess records in Chicago. At this hallowed institution they recorded blues giants such as John Lee Hooker, Elmore James, Bo Diddley, Willie Dixon, Buddy Guy, Howlin' Wolf, and Muddy Waters. Chuck Berry also recorded for Chess in 1950. Many of these performers had no record contracts at the time that the Chess brothers signed them and were poor and little known outside Chicago's south and westside club scene. The Chess brothers not only recorded music that suited black tastes but introduced the most authentic modern American musical tradition to white audiences and performers the world over. What in large measure allowed for the British invasion of the 1960s, spearheaded by the Beatles, the Rolling Stones, and virtuosos such as Eric Clapton, came courtesy of the precious Chess recordings that made their way to England, allowing the young Englishmen to learn from their idols.

In the 1960s, Jewish performers such as Bob Dylan were deeply influenced by the blues, again helping introduce an American art form to white American audiences. Jewish musical promoters were also in the forefront of breaking down racial barriers in the 1960s. Bill Graham at the famed Fillmore West in San Francisco and Fillmore East in New York invited performers including Jimi Hendrix, Albert King, and B.B. King to take the stage with white performers at a time when most venues in America were still segregated.

crusade, but Holocaust memory also began to play a major role within Jewish self-understanding. Poems and prayers of remembrance for European Jewry were incorporated into liturgy across the Jewish denominational divide. A Haggadah published in New York in 1950 included a picture of Auschwitz and another of Treblinka in the "Pour Out Your Wrath" section of the service. Public monuments to the recent European tragedy were erected as well. Thanks to the Synagogue Council of America, new synagogues that opened in the suburbs throughout the 1950s received ritual objects salvaged from Europe. New communities thus expressed a direct link to ancient communities that no longer existed. Warsaw ghetto memorial events were held all over America, and Jewish summer camps chose the midsummer fast of Tisha Ba'Av, which commemorates the destruction of the two Temples in Jerusalem, to teach children about the recent horrors in Europe.

As American Jews asserted their commitment to civil rights, they discovered another civil rights issue that needed addressing—the plight of Soviet Jewry. With a nagging sense that America and American Jews had perhaps not done all they could have done for European Jewry during the war, they now refused to sit idly while another European Jewish community appeared to be in distress. The

"Free Soviet Jewry" movement became a rallying cry for American Jews, both at the individual and institutional level. By supporting the desire of many Soviet Jews to emigrate, the campaign also demonstrated the community's loyalties in the Cold War, especially important given the extent to which American Jews identified with the political Left. Despite their increased affluence and great security, American Jews continued to vote Democratic, with percentages varying between 75 and 85 percent.

After 1967, American Jews overwhelmingly defined their Jewishness through support for the State of Israel. At the time, significant numbers of American Jews actively opposed the war in Vietnam and were disproportionately represented in radical student politics. Like others on the Left, they voiced their opposition in terms of their disavowal of "American imperialism." Generally supportive of countries engaged in the post-colonial struggle, American Jews admired Israel as a small, heroic bastion of democracy. Israel was seen as a David to its neighboring Goliaths and not just by Jews but by most people on the political Left. But in the summer of 1967, the rise of Holocaust consciousness, especially in the aftermath of the Eichmann trial, produced support for Israel as a specifically Jewish cause. M. Jay Rosenberg, a Left-wing radical who had only the most marginal identification with Jewish culture, recalled the impact of the Six-Day War: "On Monday June fifth [1967], I awoke to the news that Israel was at war. . . . I knew that my concern was not as a leftist or even, at that moment, as an American. I did not fear for Israel because she was 'the only democracy in the Middle East' or because she was a 'socialist enclave' surrounded by 'feudal sheikdoms.' I cared because Israel was the Jewish state and I was a Jew. Her anguish was mine, the anguish of my people. I would not forget that."

Rosenberg's view reflected those of many other American Jews. People felt an intimate bond with the fate and future of Israel. This intensified after the Yom Kippur War of 1973, when Israel became increasingly dependent on U.S. aid. American Jewish political groups began to calculate their interests in terms of the impact of certain American policies on Israel and lobbied accordingly. Consensus stifled debate within the American Jewish community regarding Israel's policies, and Israel's embattled status was repeatedly invoked to inhibit critical Jewish voices and dissent. Groups such as *Breira* ("Option" or "Choice"), its successor New Jewish Agenda, and American Friends of Peace Now were hounded and decried from within the Jewish world.

The 1982 Lebanon war was a watershed in the way Israelis began to reassess aspects of state policy. It exercised a similar impact on American Jews. Just as Israelis spoke out against their government, American Jews voiced similar opinions publicly. Young Jews, especially on university campuses, split from the Jewish establishment's uncritical support for Israel. Out of deep and abiding concern, increasing numbers of American Jews expressed objections to the occupation and to the settler movement. That many of the settlers, including some of the most radical, were American, added another level of intensity to the protest. American Jewry split over Israel, even more bitterly, after the Oslo Accords of 1993. While the majority waxed enthusiastic about the prospects for peace, symbolized by the famous handshake between Yitzhak Rabin and Yasser Arafat on the White House lawn, others could not accept the necessary diplomatic accommodations.

American Jews often feel alienated from Israel's religious politics. The most divisive issue concerns the Israeli rabbinate's refusal to recognize only Orthodox marriages, burials, and conversions to Judaism as valid. The rabbinate rejects Reform Judaism, the denomination of most American Jews. The rejection extends to Israeli political circles. In 2006, the president of Israel, Moshe Katsav, welcomed a delegation of American Jewish clergy to Israel but refused to address Eric Yoffie, the leader of the Reform Conference of American Rabbis, as "Rabbi Yoffie." The Israeli rabbinate rejects liberal positions on the ordination of women, patrilineal descent, and any accommodation for gay and lesbian congregants. Disagreement over Israeli policies toward the Palestinians and official attitudes toward non-Orthodox Jews has translated into decreased personal commitments of American Jews to Israel. The impact is quantifiable as smaller numbers of Jews visit the country and the level of philanthropic giving to Israel has declined.

Great differences among Jews regarding a whole host of issues have further polarized American Jewry. Sharp political divisions have been exacerbated by the process of suburbanization. Jews of different backgrounds and beliefs once lived in close geographical proximity to each other. Today, increasingly integrated into suburbia, they often live at greater remove from other Jews. In the early years of the twenty-first century, most Jews grow up and live among Jews exactly like themselves without much appreciation for or even awareness of the full scope of Jewish diversity.

American Jewish Cultures

Beginning in the 1960s, the prominence of American Jews in fields such as politics, journalism, entertainment, business, and academia has been so disproportionate that it has become commonplace. Prohibitions or inhibitions against Jews occupying important positions in the public life of the nation are no longer an issue. Senator Joseph Lieberman's run for the office of vice president in 2000 was testament to that. The culture or religion of American Jews no longer constitutes a barrier to integration. Film, television, and theatre address Jewish themes with such regularity that non-Jewish audiences can see them as universal or even uniquely American. The Jewish aspect of cultural creations does not hinder their massive appeal. High-school students across America read Elie Wiesel's Holocaust memoir, *Night,* while the American public warmly received television programs such as *Seinfeld,* with several identifiably Jewish characters. NBC initially hesitated to pick up *Seinfeld* for fear that it might be "too Jewish," and then it was delighted to have been proven wrong by the extent to which "Middle America" loved the program.

In the 1980s, as the remaining victims of the Holocaust were rapidly beginning to pass away, survivors—Eli Wiesel among them—began to express fears that the memory of the Holocaust would fade away with the eyewitnesses. This has proven to be incorrect. The Six-Day War invigorated Jewish self-consciousness by making American Jews aware of the precariousness of Israel's existence. Its vulnerability occasioned public reflection on the extermination of European Jewry and inspired the ongoing work of commemoration. The aging of the survivors and the multicultural environment of the 1970s and 1980s that celebrated group difference contributed to propelling the Holocaust to a central place in American Jewish culture. After the fall of Communism, visits by Jewish groups, especially of young people to the liberated death camps in Poland, have intensified the public culture of Holocaust awareness among American Jews.

In the immediate postwar period, Holocaust memorialization was conducted by and for Jews. More recently, however, Holocaust awareness has emerged into American culture. As American Jews became integrated into public life, often holding elected office, their fellow non-Jewish politicians began to attend Holocaust memorial events. The widely watched 1978 NBC miniseries, *Holocaust,* further intensified American public interest in the event, as did Steven Spielberg's 1993 film, *Schindler's List.* The diary of Anne Frank is as well known to American schoolchildren as any diary by an American citizen. Classes on the Holocaust in high schools and universities are commonplace throughout the United States, as is the phenomenon of Holocaust survivors publicly recounting their experiences. Thanks to these transformations, Holocaust memory has taken on an American cast, exemplified by the opening on the Washington Mall of the United States Holocaust Memorial Museum in 1993. What the Americanization of the Shoah will mean for the way the Holocaust is remembered remains to be seen.

Secular Jewish culture, from nineteenth-century Yiddish theatre to Hollywood films, has outpaced religious innovation on American soil. Institutionally, the three denominations of Judaism—Reform, Conservative, and Orthodox—predominate. While all three have undergone significant changes in America, all trace their aesthetic and doctrinal origins to Europe. Reconstructionism represents one of the few attempts to develop a new form of distinctively American Judaism. Its founder, **Mordecai Kaplan** (1881–1983), emigrated from Vilna to the United States with his family in 1889. An observant Jew and a graduate of the Jewish Theological Seminary, Kaplan grew increasingly disenchanted with Orthodoxy. He articulated his critique of American Judaism in a work entitled *Judaism as a Civilization* (1934). Kaplan rejected the notion of supernatural revelation as a fundamental basis for Judaism and argued instead that Jewishness was a civilization. While he identified beliefs and practices as important to Judaism, Kaplan assigned great significance to language, culture, literature, ethics, art, history, social organization, symbols, and customs. Kaplan's anthropological approach dovetailed

with the needs of second- or third-generation American Jews, moving toward "symbolic Judaism." Kaplan's effort to "reconstruct" or revive Judaism along ethnic lines proved remarkably prescient. Although Reconstructionism failed to win the sympathies of American Jewry to any appreciable extent, perhaps because its stress on Jewish ethnicity alienated American Jews who were seeking acceptance as Americans, Kaplan's idea of the synagogue as a social and cultural center, offering a variety of cultural and educational programs, has won wide acceptance among all streams of Judaism. Kaplan, an egalitarian, also instituted the *bat mitzvah* ceremony for girls. His daughter Judith was the first celebrant in 1922. This innovation entered Jewish practice the world over.

Kaplan's concerns for the future of Jews and Judaism were grounded in the secularization of Jewish social experience in the United States. As early as 1920, he saw American Judaism as stagnant and claimed that its creative developments were initiatives of eastern European Jewish immigrants. "Judaism in America," he wrote, "has not given the least sign of being able to perpetuate itself." While such dire predictions have not come true, American Jewish leaders, especially since the 1960s, have continually expressed their concerns and fears that "assimilation" is ravaging the Jewish community. They point to Jewish religious and cultural illiteracy, the very small numbers of children attending Jewish day schools, the fact that perhaps half of America's Jews have never been to Israel, the decline in giving to Jewish charities, and, above all, to the 50 percent intermarriage rate in 2004, up from about 9 percent in 1964.

The scholarship on intermarriage takes an ambivalent view of the numbers. There are pessimists and optimists as regards the historical significance of such trends. Intermarriage is a sign of the decline of suspicion and hostility on both sides of the religious divide, hence the ambivalence. Where once religious belief and communal attitudes led parents to object to intermarriage and even perform the ritual of sitting *shivah* (the custom of mourning the dead), parental interest is now principally concerned with the individual happiness of children. The personal shame and communal stigma that once accompanied intermarriages no longer arise. Mutual acceptance in the most intimate sense has broken down traditional borders on both sides of the religious divide.

Jewish religious leaders have met the challenges of intermarriage in various ways. The Reform movement has taken the most proactive stance in mounting "outreach" programs to intermarried couples and by easing conversion. Some Reform rabbis have even performed wedding ceremonies in tandem with Christian clergy to satisfy the needs of both parties to the marriage. This has elicited cries of "assimilation" and "betrayal" from Conservative and Orthodox circles, and even those within Reform have been split over the issue. In 1983, in response to the increasing number of children from mixed marriages, the leaders of the Reform movement undertook to accept as Jewish anyone who had had a Jewish education and had at least one Jewish parent, mother or father. They also permitted non-Jewish spouses to become synagogue members and to participate in the life of the congregation. In making these changes, American Reform rabbis have made repeated reference to both the social reality of contemporary American Jewish life and the continued impact of the Holocaust. The Jewish people, they argued, are not in a demographic position to turn anyone away. Reconstructionists typically sided with the Reform movement on this issue. Orthodox Jews have held to the ancient prohibitions against intermarriage. Conservative Jews, as often happens, found themselves somewhere in the middle, not condoning intermarriage but recognizing that it does not necessarily manifest the desire to reject Judaism. Rather, it is a consequence of an open society in which there are no barriers to dating people of a different or of no faith. Indeed, people can often fall in love for reasons that do not reflect a larger cultural or philosophical position. The Conservative movement thus neither officially promotes nor rejects intermarriage. Some congregations have adopted a policy of *kiruv,* drawing intermarried couples nearer without explicitly endorsing such unions. Conversions to Judaism have also changed the nature of American Jewish life and have risen together with the rise of intermarriages. In 1954 about 3,000 non-Jews converted to Judaism. At the end of the 1970s the rate of conversion was about 10,000 per year.

Between 1967 and 2000, American Jewry entered a new period of its postwar history. In the last thirty years of the twentieth century, American Jews tended toward two opposing poles in terms of their Jewish identities. Many developed intense commitments to Jewish culture and engaged in the search for continuity. Many others became more secular and drew further away from organized Jewish life. The latter development has given rise to expressions of great alarm within the Jewish community about the future of American Jewry. Fears about biological continuity have been a feature of the modern Jewish experience. Before World War I, Jewish leaders and demographers in western and central Europe repeatedly expressed fears that assimilation was leading to the demise of Jewish communities. Recent American Jewish expressions of this phenomenon fit into these long-held concerns.

While religious practice among most American Jews remains relatively weak, the Jewish community possesses great reserves of institutional strength and cultural creativity. Unrivaled anywhere else in the Diaspora is the commitment to secular Jewish studies at the highest educational levels.

Universities all over America are fulfilling the dreams of the nineteenth-century founders of Wissenschaft des Judentums as they produce cutting-edge research and teach about Jewish civilization in all its forms to packed classrooms of students from a dizzying array of backgrounds. Secular education is also found in bastions of modern Orthodoxy. Yeshiva University in New York maintains a commitment to observant Jewish practice that is perfectly compatible with secular education.

While synagogue membership and attendance at Reform and Conservative congregations may be on the decline—ultra-Orthodoxy, by contrast, is experiencing a revival that began after World War II. Ultra-Orthodox Jewish communities were especially devastated during the war, given that their inability to pass as non-Jews and their lack of close contacts among neighboring gentiles meant that most were unable to be hidden. After the war, the remnants of Hasidic communities began to rebuild life in Israel, Britain, Canada, France, Belgium, Australia, and especially the United States. The postwar story of American Hasidism runs counter to the standard narrative of Jewish acculturation and suburbanization. Instead, Hasidic communities dedicated themselves to rebuilding their numbers and remaining apart from American culture through communal insularity and scrupulous observance of religious ritual to an extent rarely seen before the war.

The postwar growth of American ultra-Orthodoxy was led by the heads of the three major Hasidic courts: the Satmar Rebbe, **Joel Teitelbaum** (1887–1979); the Lubavitcher Rebbe, **Menachem Mendel Schneerson** (1902–1994); and the Bobover Rebbe, **Shlomo Halberstam** (1907–2000). Under their leadership—and that of smaller sects such as Belzer, Vishnitzer, Gerer, Skverer, and Bratslaver—the number of American Hasidim has increased significantly. Only a few thousand made their way to the United States after the war. Out of about 3,000 Bobover in 1939, only about 300 survived the Holocaust. By the year 2000, between 7 to 9 percent of American Jews were Orthodox, and probably half of them, about 350,000 were Hasidim. This constitutes about half the world's estimated 700,000 Hasidim. The growth rate of American Hasidim is approximately 5 percent per year, far in excess of secular Jews, which means a doubling of their population every fifteen years. One estimate has it that between 8 million and 10 million Hasidim will reside in America by the year 2075.

The Hasidic communities in postwar America avoided assimilation by retaining Yiddish for daily speech, maintaining traditional dress—one group can be distinguished from another by such markers as hats, pants, and even shoe style and sock color—and living in densely packed communities such as Borough Park, Crown Heights, and Williamsburg in Brooklyn, New York, and in Monsey and New Square in Rockland

County, New York. In those communities, a vast network of schools, social service agencies, and voluntary associations provide for community members from cradle to grave.

Beyond agreeing upon the need to avoid American culture, Hasidic communities have differed in terms of their relations with the outside world. While most have been extremely insular, especially when it came to contacts with the rest of American Jewry, Lubavitch or Chabad Hasidism, under the leadership of Menachem Mendel Schneerson, vigorously promoted its form of Judaism among secular Jews. The community sent emissaries out to the wider world, approaching Jewish men on the street to lay tefillin and women to light Shabbat candles; driving around in "mitzvah-mobiles" and beckoning to Jews via megaphones; and instituting Hannukah lighting ceremonies in public squares and even the White House. Especially active among young Jews, by the 1990s Lubavitch had established more than 900 so-called "Chabad Houses" on college campuses and had a network of such activities operating in seventy different countries. (Even Reform Judaism's late-twentieth-century outreach program to unaffiliated Jews owes some measure of inspiration to the success of such programs run by Chabad.) Chabad has also been extremely effective in establishing a vast publishing industry, with Yiddish newspapers, textbooks, and novels, and a communications network, with radio, television, movies, and Internet sites.

In part due to Chabad's success, many among the Lubavitcher Rebbe's followers genuinely believed that he was the Messiah. For many critics, this was idolatry, some going so far as to claim that Chabad Judaism is christological in nature. The claims and counterclaims about the Lubavitcher Rebbe, as well as difficulties of leadership succession among both Satmar and Bobover Hasidim, have fostered deep divisions and intense acrimony within ultra-Orthodoxy. In part, this is a consequence of the growth and success of Hasidism in the United States, where communities now in the tens of thousands are far more difficult to manage and control than their small predecessors and where the economic success of various Hasidic communities, such as Chabad, add a further dimension to various power struggles. In some measure, centralized leadership is giving way to centrifugal forces.

Elsewhere, independent prayer and study groups, new synagogues, and secular Jewish cultural activities have found grassroots support across the United States. Some of them are syncretistic, combining eastern traditions such as meditation and chanting with Judaism, or incorporating Hasidic singing into otherwise secular services. A well-established alternative synagogue in Berkeley, California, called the Aquarian Minyan, was established in 1974. For the High Holidays it offers "services [that] are co-created and led by members and friends of the Aquarian Minyan community [and]. . .will combine innovative and traditional approaches, including participatory liturgy, music, chanting, meditation, and movement."

The sexual politics of the 1960s also ushered in challenges to American Judaism. Jewish women, an important constituency of Second Wave feminism, demanded equal religious rights, an innovation that was embraced in Reconstructionism in 1968; followed by Reform Judaism's first ordination of a woman rabbi, Sally Priesand, in 1972; followed by Amy Eilberg, who in 1985 became the first woman to graduate with rabbinical ordination from the Conservative movement's Jewish Theological Seminary. At an informal level, many new changes and innovations were appearing thanks to feminism. New Jewish rituals were developed, specifically tied to life-cycle events such as giving birth to daughters or menstruation. In some quarters Rosh Chodesh (New Moon) was adopted as a special time for women to study texts and perform Jewish rituals particular to them. Many of the demands put forth by Jewish feminists appeared in the pages of *Lilith,* a Jewish feminist magazine founded in 1973. Even Orthodox communities have felt the impact of such changes, and women's study groups and access to higher education have become commonplace. Reflecting a greater willingness to finally make their voices heard, gay Jews, who long felt shut out of communal life, began to establish separate synagogues in the 1980s. A perfect microcosm of the broader Jewish community, these congregations ranged from liberal to the liturgically conservative. The place of gay Jews in the ritual life of synagogues remains a controversial issue in Conservative congregations, is accepted in Reform temples, and is anathema in Orthodox circles.

An extremist politics born in the 1960s also found echoes in the Jewish world. As American Jews became more solidly middle class, thousands of poor Jews who did not have the means to move to the suburbs remained in the inner cities. Inspired by militant black nationalists and protective of what he called the "little Jews" stranded in hostile neighborhoods, Rabbi **Meir Kahane** (1932–1990) founded the **Jewish Defense League** in 1968—its motto "Never Again," a reference to the Holocaust. An aggressive alarmist, Kahane castigated the major American Jewish organizations for not doing all they could to protect American Jews from "another Holocaust." Kahane's vigilantes patrolled the streets with baseball bats and lead pipes, threatening and sometimes carrying out violent acts against those they thought threatened Jews. In response to the JDL, American Jewish welfare agencies began to take notice of the "little Jews" and engaged in a concerted effort to financially assist Jews left out of the "American dream." The JDL also demonstrated outside the United Nations, Soviet consulates,

Logo of Justice for Jews from Arab Countries (JJAC). As was the case in Europe in the interwar period, the rise of Arab nationalism and Muslim fundamentalism in the 1930s and 1940s led to increasing hostility toward Jews. This was exacerbated with the founding of the State of Israel in 1948. At this point, Jewish life became all but impossible in Arab lands and approximately 800,000 Jews from across the Middle East were displaced and dispossessed. The JJAC, founded in 2002, is a coalition of major American Jewish communal organizations. Its mandate is "To ensure that justice for Jews from Arab countries assumes its rightful place on the international political agenda and that their rights be secured as a matter of law and equity." To that end, the JJAC seeks to educate the public on the historic plight of Jews who were displaced from Arab countries and to advocate for redress.

and Russian artistic performances on behalf of Soviet Jewry. Its activities presented a model of Jewish political militancy that was novel in the American setting. In 1990, an Egyptian militant assassinated Kahane in New York.

Immigration continues to transform American Jewry. In the period between 1967 and 2000 new Jewish immigrants arrived from Russia, Syria, Morocco, and, after 1979, Iran. Native Jews regarded it as their responsibility to integrate the new arrivals and provided considerable community resources for their absorption. While not all the new immigrants wanted to be incorporated into Jewish communities, the presence of so many newcomers has added great diversity to religious and neighborhood life. Brighton Beach in Brooklyn became "Little Odessa," while the Pico-Robertson section of Los Angeles, a densely populated enclave of Persian Jews, has acquired all the markings of an authentic, urban Jewish neighborhood.

At the beginning of the twenty-first century, most American Jews are no longer bound to Judaism or Jewishness by social or communal discipline but out of a conscious

choice. Large numbers, perhaps as many as 2 million out of America's 5 million Jews, remain unaffiliated. But there is a vast reservoir of talent, creativity, and energy propelling American Jewry in novel directions.

Eastern Europe After the Shoah

Soviet Union

The war and the Holocaust exacted a terrible toll on Soviet Jewry. The prewar Jewish population stood at around 3 million. Around half that number were murdered in the Holocaust, and untold numbers of Jews died in combat. In 1945, the total Jewish population of the Soviet Union had been reduced to about 1.5 million. Altogether, Jewish losses during the war were proportionately higher than they were for any other Soviet nationality. Still, with the large number of Jews deported and evacuated, as well as the overall Allied victory, the Soviet Union emerged after the war with the largest Jewish population in Europe.

In 1942, the Soviet government permitted the formation of the **Jewish Anti-Fascist Committee** (JAFC). The goal was to marshal political and financial support for the Soviet war effort from Jewish communities in the West. In 1943, Shlomo Mikhoels, the renowned actor, and the Yiddish poet Itsik Fefer traveled to the United States, Canada, and Mexico to garner moral and financial support for the Soviet Union. Ilya Ehrenburg, a prominent Soviet Jewish journalist, writer, and leading member of the JAFC, stayed behind but reminded American Jews, "There is no ocean behind which you can hide. . . . Your peaceful sleep will be disturbed by the cries of Leah from Ukraine, Rachel from Minsk, Sarah from Bialystok—they are weeping over their slaughtered children." The delegation not only met with celebrities such as Albert Einstein, Charlie Chaplin, Eddie Cantor, and Yehudi Menuhin but also addressed large rallies, including one at New York's Polo Grounds, attended by 50,000 people. During the war, Jewish organizations from abroad, mostly in the United States, provided about $45 million in aid to the Soviet war effort. With its own newspaper and through the offer of support to Yiddish artists and writers, Russian and Polish, Romanian and Baltic, the JAFC was the only official Jewish institution operating in the Soviet Union. It therefore became a focal point of Jewish cultural activities, and for many, a promoter of Jewish nationalism. As such, the JAFC came under suspicion.

Joseph Stalin, increasingly paranoid and psychotic, began an antisemitic campaign against "rootless cosmopolitans," a code word for Jews allegedly harboring "anti-patriotic views." Between 1948 and 1953, the Soviet authorities initiated a

Itsik Fefer, Solomon Mikhoels, and Albert Einstein (1943). During their trip to the United States in 1943 on behalf of the Jewish Anti-Fascist Committee (JAFC), Fefer and Mikhoels met with a number of celebrities, including Charlie Chaplin and Albert Einstein. The JAFC trip was a huge success, in that it raised large sums of money and garnered much moral support for the Soviet war effort. At the moment that Soviet Jewry was faced with extinction by the Nazi invasion, the JAFC was also a rallying point for Jewish national identity in the Soviet Union. The trip to the United States by Mikhoels and Fefer also helped American and Russian Jews reconnect with each other. Out of the contacts came a decision to publish simultaneously in the United States and the Soviet Union a black book documenting the anti-Jewish crimes of the Nazis. In 1944, the writer Ilya Ehrenburg sent a collection of letters, diaries, photos, and eyewitness accounts to the United States to be used in the book. The *Black Book* was published in New York in 1946, with a preface written by Albert Einstein. No Russian edition appeared.

deliberate campaign to liquidate what remained of Jewish culture. Prior to his own arrest, the celebrated Yiddish author Peretz Markish remarked to a friend, "Hitler wanted to destroy us physically. Stalin wants to do it spiritually." The most well-known of Stalin's victims was the Yiddish actor and de facto head of Soviet Jewry, Solomon Mikhoels. On January 13, 1948, he was murdered by the secret police. They then ran over him with a truck to make it look like an automobile accident. As part of the sham, Mikhoels was even honored with a large state funeral. Not long afterward, Markish went to Mikhoels' dressing room and wrote the opening stanzas of his poem "Sh. Mikhoels—A Memorial Flame at Your Coffin." Courageously declaring that Mikhoels had been

murdered, Markish has the anguished voice of Mikhoels state bluntly that he (and the Jewish people) were murder victims:

> I want eternity to come before your violated threshold
> With murder-marks and blasphemy on my face,
> The way my people roam five-sixths of the earth—
> Marked by axe and hate—for you to know them by.

With Mikhoel's murder, a campaign was initiated against Jewish culture that saw Jewish libraries, publishing houses, research institutes, theatres, and at the end of 1948 the JAFC shut down. Such closings were immediate and without warning. Ester Markish, wife of Peretz Markish, recalled the closure of the Soviet Union's last Yiddish publishing house: "[T]rucks filled with State Security agents pulled up in front of the house. Soldiers in civilian clothes burst into the printing plant and disconnected the machines. Everything came to a standstill; all was silence. 'Your publishing house is closed down!' one of the pogromists bellowed." Hundreds of Yiddish writers, journalists, editors, actors, performers, artists, and musicians were arrested, their state subsidies withdrawn. Many were sentenced to years of hard labor in the Gulag, the Soviet prison system. Others, such as the distinguished Yiddish authors Itsik Fefer (1900–1948), Dovid Bergelson (1884–1948), and Peretz Markish (1895–1949), were publicly tried, found guilty of attempting to establish a Zionist state in Crimea, and executed.

When Jews were arrested, the press began to print the original Jewish name of the accused in parentheses after his or her assumed Russified name, thus "exposing" or "outing" those Jews charged with being "anti-patriotic." Descriptions of the charges often carried editorial comment that drew on a nineteenth-century antisemitic trope, namely, that being Jewish precluded fully comprehending the national culture. As a question posed in the official party organ, *Pravda,* asked, "What kind of an idea can Gurvich have of the national character of Soviet Russian man?"

The campaign against "Zionist cosmopolitans" in positions of leadership in the Communist Party culminated in November 1952 in the Prague show trials of Rudolf Slánský and his comrades. "During the investigation," it was announced, "we discovered how treason and espionage infiltrate the ranks of the Communist Party. This channel is Zionism." One of the charges brought against Slánský was that he used Jewish doctors to assassinate his enemies. On December 1, Stalin announced to the Politburo, "Every Jewish nationalist is the agent of the American intelligence service. Jewish nationalists think that their nation was saved by the USA (there you can become rich, bourgeois, etc.). They think they're indebted to the Americans. Among doctors, there are many Jewish nationalists." On December 3, thirteen former Communist leaders of Czechoslovakia, eleven of whom were Jews, were executed.

On January 13, 1953, Stalin, who saw counterplots everywhere, turned on Soviet Jewish physicians, accusing them of a plot to poison him and members of the Communist Party leadership. That day in *Pravda,* the headline read, "Vicious Spies and Killers Under the Mask of Academic Physicians." The article informed the Soviet public that "The majority of the participants of the terrorist group . . . were . . . recruited by a branch-office of American

intelligence—the international Jewish bourgeois-nationalist organization called 'Joint' (American Joint Distribution Committee). The filthy face of this Zionist spy organization, covering up their vicious actions under the mask of kindness, is now completely revealed. . . . Unmasking the gang of poisoner-doctors [has] struck a blow against the international Jewish Zionist organization." Initially, nine people were arrested, suspected of taking part in the "Doctors' Plot." In the period from 1948 to 1953, the charges against Jews multiplied, as they were accused of corruption, speculation, and other economic crimes against the state. Retribution was demonstrable. The percentage of Jews in the Central Committee of the Communist Party declined from ten in 1939 to two in 1952. In the Soviet Republics, Jews were removed almost entirely from positions of authority in the party. In addition, Jews were systematically dismissed from leading positions in the armed forces, the press, the universities, and the legal system. To ethnically cleanse the state apparatus of Jews, the Soviets engaged in a massive exercise of "investigative genealogy," studying the backgrounds of leading figures to see if they were of Jewish descent and, thus, enemies of the state.

One month after Stalin's death on March 5, 1953, *Pravda* declared that the Doctor's Plot had been a fraud, and the accused were released from prison. A thaw in relations set in, and the repression eased. Among Jews, many got their jobs back, but this was easier in scientific fields, whereas ideologically sensitive positions in the humanities, as well as in the security apparatus and foreign affairs, remained off limits. Even though many of those Jews murdered or imprisoned were officially "rehabilitated" when Stalin's successor, Nikita Khrushchev, denounced Stalin in 1956, he never mentioned the campaign against Jews. While Jews gained back some measure of their individual rights, Jewish cultural institutions were never restored and antisemitism was not officially denounced, as it had been in the 1920s. Some Jews were pleased that the worst excesses of the system were being corrected and attempted to make the best of the situation. Others were less satisfied.

The war had indeed fostered the emergence of Jewish nationalism among many Soviet Jews, and that sentiment intensified during the postwar period, with its assault on Jewish culture. The establishment of the State of Israel in 1948, which was initially supported by the Soviet Union, also encouraged—as the Soviets had feared—Zionist sympathy among Soviet Jews. When Golda Meir, Israel's first ambassador to the Soviet Union, arrived in 1948, large demonstrations in support of Israel greeted her at every public appearance. On October 4, Rosh Hashanah, she attended synagogue and the assembled crowd began shouting "Shalom!" At Yom Kippur services ten days later, a crowd gathered outside the Metropole Hotel to serenade the delegation of Israeli diplomats with the chant "Next Year in Jerusalem!"

The only officially sanctioned and state supported expression of Jewish culture was the Yiddish newspaper *Sovietish heymland* (*Soviet Homeland*), launched in 1961. But in the more relaxed post-Stalin period, the authorities granted permission for the existence of a large number of unofficial clubs, societies, and organizations dedicated to Jewish culture. Religious life, though severely circumscribed by the Bolshevik Revolution, was never entirely eliminated. Although their numbers were greatly reduced by the mid-1930s, select synagogues continued to function throughout the Soviet period, and committed Jews continued to celebrate Jewish holidays, often in secret. In some cases, the meanings of holidays were reinterpreted in light of current realities. Passover seders, for instance, could commemorate the oppression of ancient Jews under Egyptian slavery while simultaneously acknowledging the current oppression under which Soviet Jews were living. Religious practice was not necessarily an expression of faith among Jews in the Soviet Union. Rather, it was just as likely an expression of ethnic solidarity.

The brief period of liberalization under Khrushchev, which saw the opening of a Moscow yeshiva and the publication of a *siddur* (prayer book), came to an end in 1957. For the next seven years a widespread campaign against all religions struck with particular ferocity against Judaism because, unlike the similar program in the 1920s, this one went beyond a critique of religion and was plainly antisemitic. The post-revolutionary attack on Judaism was largely conducted in Yiddish because it was meant for internal consumption. During the campaign in the 1950s and 1960s, publications were presented in the major languages of the Soviet Union and were thus accessible to non-Jews. Very often, the attacks were anti-Zionist tirades, with accusations that Jews, especially Zionists, actually collaborated with Nazis during the war. Synagogues were closed, and in 1960 the baking of matzah for Passover was banned. The latter decree was repealed in 1964 in the face of widespread international protest.

Loss of jobs and status, trials against Jews for having committed "economic crimes" in the early 1960s that resulted in a disproportionate number of Jews executed, general economic stagnation, Cold War tensions, and the euphoria aroused by Israel's victory in the Six-Day War led to an increase in the number of Jews wishing to emigrate to Israel. Jews were overrepresented among Soviet dissidents and were increasingly seen as intellectual agitators against the regime. The accusation was not far from the truth. A favorite joke among Soviet Jews revealed where they stood in relation to

Communism, and even in relation to their parents, who had often been true believers:

> A political instructor asks Rabinovich:
> "Who is your father?"
> "The Soviet Union."
> "Good. And who is your mother?"
> "The Communist Party."
> "Excellent. And what is your fondest wish?"
> "To become an orphan."

Soviet Jews felt like orphans and were treated as such. Discrimination in education and employment increased, but rather than back down, Jews requested exit visas in even greater numbers. Moscow soon began to believe that getting rid of troublesome Jews was preferable to forcing them to remain in the Soviet Union. American political pressure also played an important role in the Kremlin's change of policy. In the early 1970s, the regime began to permit Jews who wished to leave to do so. Not everyone who applied to leave could go, but nearly a quarter of a million went to Israel, the United States, Australia, and Canada. In 1974, the Soviets reversed policy after the U.S. Congress passed the Jackson-Vanick Act, which denied Most Favored Nation status to the Soviet Union unless it liberalized its emigration policies. Rather than capitulate, the Soviet Union hardened its stance, barely permitting any Jews to leave the country between 1980 and 1986.

American Jewish organizations such as the American Jewish Conference on Soviet Jewry and the Anti-Defamation League have tended to credit themselves with bringing about the liberalization of Soviet immigration policy, without fully recognizing the role played by Soviet Jews themselves. While the collective efforts of the "Let My People Go" campaign were far from negligible, increasingly vocal dissent by Soviet Jews, including the attempted hijacking of a plane from Leningrad to Israel in 1970, and the subsequent trial in which the defendants openly expressed Zionist sentiments, probably led to the relaxation of Soviet emigration restrictions in 1971–1972. Many Jews were inspired by the accused's actions. As one Soviet Jew, Dov Goldstein, later recalled of the hijackers, "[H]ere are Jews who don't simply talk about Israel, don't just dream, but they do something, and are not afraid of the danger and the punishment." The Soviet Union seems to have concluded that it was mutually beneficial to simply have Jews leave rather than turn these "Prisoners of Zion," as they were known, into martyrs.

Most important for the massive exodus of Jews from the Soviet Union were the liberalizing reforms of President Mikhail Gorbachev and then the state's collapse in 1991. Between 1988 and 1994, 776,867 legal emigrants left the

Soviet Union. About 200,000 Jews settled in the United States, as many as 100,000 went to Germany, and nearly 500,000 settled in Israel, joining the more than 200,000 Jews who had gone to Israel in the two decades prior to 1988. In total nearly 1.3 million Jews fled the Soviet Union between 1968 and 1994. Despite significant growth in communal institutions, such as a network of schools, synagogues, and community centers, the Jewish population is shrinking and though for different reasons—principally immigration and aging—reflects the general demographic decline of Russia. In 2006, the total number of Jews in the areas contained in the former Soviet Union (Russia, Ukraine, Belorussia, the Baltic states, Moldavia, Transcaucasia, and Central Asia) was about 345,000. Of this number, 228,000 live in the Russian Federation.

Poland

After the war about 250,000 Jews remained in Poland. When attempting to return to their homes, stunned survivors were greeted with hostility and violence. Jewish leaders were convinced that the Church had it in its power to effect a transformation in the public's negative attitude toward Jews. In May 1945, the Central Committee of the Jews in Poland wrote to the then highest-ranking official of the Catholic Church in Poland, Adam Sapieha, the archbishop of Cracow, requesting that he intercede:

> For a long time we have been receiving alarming and frightening reports from various cities and towns about bestial murders committed by armed bands on the defenseless remnants of the Jewish population. We are even more concerned since sporadic incidents have been recently transformed into systematic and organized action, the goal of which is to annihilate the survivors. . . . We are turning to your Eminence, as to one of the leading representatives of the noble Polish humanitarianism, and we appeal to you to speak in public about the matter.

The Central Committee was right to be fearful. About 1,500 Jews were killed in pogroms that swept through Poland in the postwar period. The largest of these occurred in the town of Kielce on July 4, 1946, in the wake of an accusation that Jews had ritually murdered a Polish child. About fifty Jews were shot or beaten to death with iron bars by the mob, which included policemen and soldiers sent to restore order. Any hope that the Church, which saw itself as the authentic custodian of Polish national interests, might offer solace to the victims came to naught. Cardinal Hlond, Primate of Poland, explained away the pogrom as a consequence of Jewish participation in the Communist government: "The

fact that this condition [anti-Jewish violence] is deteriorating, is to a great degree due to Jews who today occupy leading positions in Poland's Government and endeavor to introduce a governmental structure which the majority of the people do not desire. This is a harmful game, as it creates dangerous tensions. In the fatal battle of weapons . . . it is to be regretted that some Jews lose their lives, but a disproportionately large number of Poles also lose their lives."

At various points thereafter, antisemitism entered into political discourse, either as a vestige of Polish Catholicism or for the purposes of discrediting political opponents. In 1968, Communist hard-liners resorted to an antisemitic campaign and rounded up Jewish party functionaries. About 20,000 Jews emigrated, mostly to Israel, between 1968 and 1970. By the late 1970s, only about 5,000, mostly elderly, assimilated Jews were still in Poland, caught in a cultural no-man's land. Not seen as sufficiently Polish by Poles, they also had no place in the Jewish community.

The second half of the 1970s was an era of political liberalization, during which it became possible to raise the subject of Jewish identity in Poland. Jewish "Culture Weeks" were organized by dissident Catholic intellectuals, and among Jews an institution known as the **Warsaw Jewish Flying University** opened as a forum for young Jews. The university did not put out a call for collective Jewish action or promote the idea of reinvigorating Jewish life in Poland. It was aware that was impossible. It was, however, a valuable and meaningful experience for the participants on an individual level. Some of them began to learn Yiddish, others lectured on Jewish subjects to gentile audiences, some considered immigration to Israel, though they never left, while others became religious. When it disbanded in 1981, the university had about sixty members, all of whom developed strong attachments to Jewish identity.

After 1989, American Jewish organizations began to provide various forms of assistance to Jews in Poland. As a result of American encouragement, large numbers of Jewish youth began to attend Jewish events. Jewish newspapers and an important journal of Jewish opinion, *Midrasz,* began to appear. Each summer the Cracow Jewish Festival takes place in the old Jewish quarter of the town, the largest Jewish festival of its kind in Europe. A smaller Jewish cultural festival also takes place each year in Wroclaw. The Center for Jewish Culture in Cracow is an extremely active institution, sponsoring lectures, exhibitions, concerts, and summer school programs, with courses in Polish, English, and German on Jewish history and culture. In Cracow, an independent Jewish youth society, *Czulent* (Cholent), is dedicated to the integration of young Jewish people from Cracow and its surrounding region. The organization especially caters to the significant number of people in Poland who only find out later in life about their Jewish roots. Czulent sets itself the task of reintegrating such people into Jewish life, teaching them Jewish traditions, customs, history, and culture. It also seeks to promote community development and Poland's Jewish heritage and to strengthen Polish–Jewish relations.

In 1994, the first Jewish school in Warsaw since 1949 opened. In 2007, the Lauder–Morasha School had an enrollment of 240 students, ranging in age from three to sixteen years old. The school is a secular Jewish institution; students are taught Hebrew and Jewish tradition and culture, alongside a standard Polish curriculum. The school has a sister school—Lauder Etz Chaim—in the western Polish city of Wroclaw. These schools are part of a larger network of 36 Lauder schools and kindergartens in sixteen central and eastern European countries. There is now a boom in Jewish tourism to Poland, and the post-Communist government retains very close and open ties to Israel.

Elsewhere in the Eastern Bloc, what remained of Jewish life after the Shoah lay in tatters. The security of Jews was compromised by the presence of Jews in the Communist leadership in the various client states of the Soviet Union. Most of these countries permitted Jewish emigration, and those Jews who could leave did so. Predictably, the elderly and infirmed stayed. The largest postwar Jewish populations in Communist Europe were to be found in Romania and Hungary.

Romania

In Romania, 400,000 Jews survived out of a prewar total of 700,000. After the Soviet Union, this was the largest Jewish population in postwar Europe. With the abolition of the Romanian monarchy in 1947, a crackdown on Jewish economic, political, and institutional life followed. Over 40 percent of Jews were engaged in commerce; their economic ruin was assured with the nationalization of the economy. Many Jews were rounded up for forced labor. The political inclinations of Romanian Jews both before and after the war were decidedly Zionist. There were 100,000 members of the Zionist movement, which was banned in 1948 because, according to a government denunciation, "[Zionism] in all its manifestations, is a reactionary nationalist movement of the Jewish bourgeoisie, supported by American imperialism, that attempts to isolate the masses of Jewish workers from the people among whom they live." The Jewish Democratic Committee, an arm of the Romanian Communist party that had assisted with the suppression was also eliminated.

After 1948, all Jewish communal needs and activities were supplied and coordinated by the Federation of Romanian Jewish Communities. Though the government closed down many communal institutions, the federation was permitted to maintain synagogues and cemeteries, run a yeshiva, ritual bathhouses, kosher slaughterhouses, and kosher bakeries. The federation also published a Romanian, Yiddish, and Hebrew newspaper. Beginning in 1964, the chief rabbi served as the chairman of the federation. In the early 1960s, about 100,000 Jews were still in Romania. While all schools were nationalized in 1948 and Jewish schools were closed down, an exception was made for a few Jewish schools with instruction in Yiddish, which remained in operation until 1961. Another exception to the closure of many Jewish institutions in 1948 were the State Jewish Theaters in Bucharest and Iasi. They had no connection with the community but performed in Yiddish until 1968.

Beginning in 1953, with Stalin's death, Romania began to skillfully carve out greater independence from Moscow, not by rebelling but by displaying loyalty and exploiting matters of mutual interest. In 1958, Moscow, convinced of Romania's reliability, withdrew Soviet troops, allowing Bucharest greater freedom of movement. It sought closer ties to the West, and the regime, suffering under antisemitic misapprehension, believed that this was to be achieved by currying favor with Jews. Following the Six-Day War, Romania refused to follow Moscow and sign a statement denouncing "Israeli aggression." It also refused to break off diplomatic relations. In fact, in 1969 Romania and Israel elevated the status of their respective diplomatic missions to the rank of embassies.

Despite certain positive tendencies in foreign and domestic policy with regard to Israel and Jews, the social life of Romanian Jewry continued to disintegrate as a result of aging, emigration, and poverty. Many Holocaust survivors were elderly, and today over half of Romania's Jews are between the ages of sixty and eighty. However, the biggest factor in the decline of the community was the departure of the Jews. Between late 1949 and the end of 1989, close to 300,000 Romanian Jews were sold to Israel to raise hard currency. Under the reign of Nicolae Ceausescu (1965–1989) in particular, these sales for thousands of dollars each were made a priority. A key figure in the postwar life of Romanian Jewry was the talented chief rabbi, Moses Rosen. Through skillful maneuvering, he convinced the regime of what it wanted to hear, namely, that it would be to their material advantage to treat Jews well. Knowingly, he observed, "I succeeded in convincing the Romanian Government that, by doing good to the Jews, by meting out justice to them, it could obtain advantages in matters of favourable public opinion, trade relations, political sympathies." Some have seen Rosen as a willing tool of the regime and an apologist for it. Many Romanian Jews, however, were able to exit the country thanks to his intercession with the authorities. Only around 10,000

Jews are left in Romania, and for the most part they are poor and elderly, their pensions rendered nearly worthless after the fall of Communism. The community is funded almost entirely by the American Joint Distribution Committee.

Hungary

After World War II, about 80,000 Jews were in Hungary, organized into about 250 Jewish communities. Many of the smaller rural communities were not viable, and those Jews soon moved to Budapest or emigrated. The Hungarian government abolished anti-Jewish legislation and tried and punished those involved in the Hungarian Holocaust. While isolated pogroms broke out in 1946, the government officially recognized the Jewish community in 1948, offering it financial assistance and guaranteeing freedom of religious practice. Between 1948 and 1952, substantial aid also arrived from the American Jewish Joint Distribution Committee. Zionism was a powerful movement and ran schools and youth groups. In 1948, the Hungarian government established formal diplomatic relations with Israel.

The situation changed drastically after the communists came to power in 1949. Accused by enemies of being a "Jewish government"—at least nine out of twenty-five politburo members were Jews, with many more occupying positions of authority at the party's lower levels—the Communists in power meted out particularly harsh treatment toward Jews to allay suspicions of a Jewish–Communist conspiracy against Hungary. Many Jewish institutions were closed, religious observance was banned, Jewish activists were arrested, Zionism was outlawed, and emigration was prohibited. Hardship was increased in the wake of a series of expulsions of "capitalists" and "unproductive elements" in 1951, wherein about 20,000 Jews, mostly from Budapest, were driven from cities to the provinces. After spending time interned in labor camps, exiled Jews were permitted to return to the capital in 1953. In the wake of the 1956 Hungarian Revolution and its suppression by the Soviets, it is estimated that another 20,000 Jews fled Hungary. After 1956, the more liberal regime of Janos Kadar relaxed restrictions on the economy and loosened censorship. After the 1960s, Jews were disproportionately represented among doctors, lawyers, academics, journalists, politicians, and cultural circles. With limited private ownership permitted, Jews, like other Hungarians, opened small businesses.

Jewish communal life was supported with government money, and a broad network of institutions was established, including dozens of synagogues, a hospital, old age homes, and secular and religious schools. With the collapse of the Communist government in 1989, finances, in large part from abroad, were used to rebuild communal institutions and provide for the needs of east-central Europe's largest Jewish community of 100,000 people.

Ironically, Jewish life in cities such as Cracow, Budapest, and Prague (Jewish population 1,600) gives the impression of being very lively, thanks to tourists visiting Jewish sites. Each summer throngs of people stand in line to visit Europe's oldest functioning synagogue, the medieval Altneuschul in Prague or the magnificently ornate Tabakshul in Budapest. In Poland, the majority of the attendees at Europe's largest Jewish summer event, the Cracow Festival, are non-Jews, as are the owners of the "Jewish" shops in the Old Jewish Quarter, Kazimiersz. In Poland, statues and pictures of dancing Hasidim are emblazoned on everything from refrigerator magnets to vodka bottles. Jewish kitsch is to be seen everywhere. East-central Europe has become the site of "virtual Judaism."

Western Europe After the Shoah

France

French Jewry suffered terribly during the war at the hands of the collaborationist Vichy regime. A deep sense of trauma and betrayal gripped French Jews. They wondered how, in the nation that first emancipated the Jews and that was seen by so many as a beacon of liberty, the Holocaust could have occurred with such widespread French complicity. Between the end of the war and the 1970s, the issue was avoided altogether in French public discourse, but between the 1970s and the 1990s avoidance slowly turned to acceptance of responsibility. In 1995, the government of President Jacques Chirac officially admitted French culpability for the way Jews were treated under Vichy.

Despite having lost one-quarter of its Jewish population during the war, French Jewry began to grow in the postwar period thanks to the arrival of Jews from North Africa. With over 500,000 Jews—over 50 percent in Paris—France is home to the third-largest Jewish community in the world. In the 1950s, Jews came from Tunisia and Morocco, and then in 1962 almost the entire Jewish community of Algeria migrated to France. Many of the 220,000 North African Jews who came to France in the 1960s arrived as French citizens. As such, they, like other immigrants with French citizenship, were entitled to generous government loans, as well as housing and employment assistance. A Jewish social welfare agency, the Fonds Social Juif Unifié (FSJU), founded in 1949, also offered material assistance and advice to the immigrants.

The Jews who migrated to France tended to be wealthier and spoke French, while the poorer North African Jews generally settled in Israel. Like eastern European Jews who migrated to New York and London at the end of the nineteenth century, North African Jews transformed the existing French Jewish communities and became the dominant force in communal, cultural and religious life. New synagogues, community centers, and schools sprouted. In the 1950s only ten consistorially supervised kosher butchers could be found in the Paris region. By 1977, that number had increased to ninety-seven. In the postwar period, most of the rabbis trained in France were Sephardim of North African origin, as have been the last two grand rabbis, René Sirat and Jacques Sitruk.

There are significant differences in religious attitudes among North African Jews in France. According to one important sociological study that examined the first generation of such immigrants, the Tunisians were the most observant, and the Algerians the least observant, with the Moroccans falling somewhere in between. Despite institutional growth, North African immigrants tended not to participate heavily in the activities of the organized community, preferring to conduct their religious and cultural lives in the home. As elsewhere in the contemporary Jewish world, Lubavitch Hasidism is a vibrant presence in France, with significant numbers of adherents in Paris and Strasbourg.

Among the postwar North African newcomers, just under 30 percent were working class, about the same percentage were employees and professionals, and 15 percent were small merchants and artisans. The pattern of upward socioeconomic ascent followed the general pattern among Diaspora Jews. With a rapid reduction of the fertility of North African Jewish immigrants—a 50 percent decline between the years 1957–1961 and 1967–1971—their economic status improved, making it possible for them to provide their children with education. In the postwar period, a greater proportion of Jews in France—Sephardim and Ashkenazim—than non-Jews attend institutions of higher learning.

Jewish immigrants from North Africa introduced a new expression of Jewishness into the French public sphere. Like Jewish elites in Britain, those in France preferred "quiet diplomacy" to vigorous protest. By contrast, North African Jews were more assertive than the Ashkenazic establishment in France. Politically, North African Jewish immigrants expressed a combative style, reminiscent of the interwar Jewish immigrants from eastern Europe, whose ranks and political culture had been decimated by the Holocaust. Still, a more demonstrative style of French Jewish political culture that cuts across the Sephardic–Ashkenazic divide emerged in the late 1960s. It can be attributed to the impact of the Six-Day War, the 1967 slur of Charles de Gaulle that the Jews were "an elite people, sure of themselves, and domineering," his implication of Jewish disloyalty to France, the subsequent

realignment of French foreign policy against Israel in favor of the Arabs, and the student revolt of May 1968, which included many Jewish intellectuals who became more militantly expressive of their Jewishness.

A rise in the number of antisemitic incidents, including cemetery and synagogue desecrations and beatings of Jews, most often perpetrated by Muslim immigrants, and the emergence of the political far Right under Jean-Marie Le Pen in the 1980s, continue to stoke the fears of French Jews. Most significant in the changing political culture of French Jewry is the extent to which Zionism, repudiated by Jewish organizations before World War II, was warmly embraced after it. Zionism was not the only political or cultural form of Jewish expression to emerge. In 1967, the Gaston Crémieux Circle, a Diasporist movement, was inaugurated by Jews of eastern European origin. It celebrated Yiddish culture not in the hope of reviving the language but as a model for French Jews to articulate a new form of French Jewish identity. Their slogan, *le droit à la différence* ("the right to be different") was a repudiation of the French Revolution's ideal of the homogenizing impact of national citizenship. Arguing for the right of minority cultures to exist in France, the circle's leader, Richard Marienstras, formed alliances with other national minority groups such as Bretons and Armenians. Although France did not adopt a presidential committee's report that recommended official state recognition of national minority cultures, the circle was instrumental in leading the French debate on the nature of French identity. In the 1970s and 1980s both Left- and Right-wing governments publicly endorsed the right of France's national minorities "to be different."

In 1980, Alain Finkielkraut, a Jewish intellectual whose refugee parents had arrived in France from Poland in the 1930s, articulated another vision for Jewish identity, one that was based neither on Sephardic or Ashkenazic nostalgia nor on Zionism or Yiddishism. Finkielkraut wished for Jews of his generation to develop forms of identity that were not dependent on the trauma of the Holocaust. He found such an identity to be inauthentic because, as he put it, "I inherited a suffering that I had not undergone." Deeply sensitive to Jewish history and memory and the centrality of the Shoah, he nonetheless called for a personal, rather than collective, engagement with Jewishness. In addition to Marienstras and Finkielkraut, many other French Jewish intellectuals openly propose reconfigurations of Jewish identity, whether in the form of religious Orthodoxy, Sephardic militancy, or a return to medieval Jewish philosophical traditions in lieu of the perils (to Jews) inherent in Western thought and nationalism. (*See box,* French Jews and the Invention of Post-Modernism.)

JEWS AND THE INVENTION OF POST-MODERNISM IN POSTWAR FRANCE

The intellectual life that has taken shape in France since World War II has had a major impact on contemporary academic life in Europe and the United States, and some of its most seminal thinkers have been French or French-speaking Jews. The famous philosopher and literary theorist **Jacques Derrida** was born in 1930 to a Jewish family in Algeria and later moved to Paris to continue his studies. Derrida, who died in 2004, is famous for introducing an interpretive method known as *deconstructionism* that aimed to challenge prevailing assumptions about textual meaning, otherness, religion, and the ethics of interpretation. Though Derrida claimed to know little about Judaism, subsequent interpreters have discerned a deep engagement in Jewish themes and an analogy between his negatively constructed Jewishness and the deconstructive project. Among those who stressed the Jewishness of Derrida's thinking was his associate **Hélène Cixous** (b. 1937), also an Algerian-born Jew, who has been enormously influential in her own right as a feminist writer. One of the other major French Jewish thinkers to exert a far-reaching intellectual impact, including upon Derrida, was **Emmanuel Levinas** (1906–1995), who was born in Lithuania and moved to France in 1923. Seeking to overcome the limits of German phenomenology, Levinas sought to place otherness and a responsibility to the other, rather than the self, at the center of his philosophical and ethical system. Among his writings are his readings of Talmudic texts, in which he aimed to enlist them in his rethinking of rationality and ethics. Beyond their general influence on academic life, such thinkers have had a major impact on the field of Jewish Studies, influencing scholars to apply a host of critical categories to Jewish texts and experience such as post-modernism, feminism, queer theory, and contemporary ethical thought.

Germany

In Germany, postwar Jewish life can be divided into two postwar phases: (1) 1945–1951, the era of the displaced persons (DPs) camps and (2) 1951 to the early twenty-first century. Most of the DPs had left Germany by the early 1950s, taking their deep knowledge of Judaism and strong Jewish identities with them. Many people stayed behind for a variety of reasons. Some were too old and sick to move or psychologically shattered by recent events. Others felt they simply had nowhere else to go. Some Jews had quickly established businesses and were committed to providing for their families (some had German spouses) and were fearful of another rupture and starting over again. Others, who wanted to leave, stayed because they felt a deep-seated obligation to help those who could not or would not leave.

After the DP camps closed in the 1950s, about 30,000 Jews were in Germany, living in over a hundred different communities. About 12,500 of them had left Germany between 1933 and 1938 and returned after the war. About half the Jews in Germany were of eastern European origin, the other half were German born, but this breakdown differed considerably according to region. In Bavaria, over 90 percent of the Jews were from eastern Europe, whereas German Jews made up 70 percent of the community in Berlin. Officially constituted communities also differed greatly in size. Some had only 6 or 7 people, while Berlin had 8,000 and Munich, 3,300.

Deep disagreements often divided community members. In some towns, German Jews refused to accept eastern European Jews as full members of their respective communities. The nature of religious observance also changed, thanks to the encounter between eastern European and native German Jews. Eastern European Orthodoxy held sway over the Liberal Judaism of German Jews. Different tunes, different customs, different forms of Hebrew pronunciation brought forth old frictions between German and Polish Jews in many towns. Disagreements were even greater over the future of the communities. Generally speaking, eastern European Jews saw their presence in Germany as a temporary stop on their way to Palestine, while many German Jews felt a historic obligation to stay and rebuild Jewish life.

The choice to stay was not easy, and certainly most Polish Jews would have preferred to leave. A spate of ritual murder charges in Bavaria in 1948, the more than one hundred Jewish cemetery desecrations that had occurred throughout Germany by 1949, and the daubing of swastikas and antisemitic graffiti on buildings exacerbated Jewish antipathy to being in Germany. Those who remained in Germany often felt like history's remnant, their sense of aloneness worsened, as one scholar has noted, by being "shunned and despised by Jews outside Germany." In July 1948, the World Jewish Congress warned that Jews should never again settle on "blood-soaked German soil." Major Jewish organizations even blocked membership of Jews from Germany into the 1960s.

Many who stayed had difficulty explaining to their children why, if the majority of DPs had managed to leave Germany, they remained behind. Children felt as though they unfairly bore the stigma of their parents' wrong decision. While the parents were "suspicious of and ambivalent toward all things German," children often resented being placed in the position of being raised in Germany. There are even problems of categorization for those born in Germany. Who were they? They were not German Jews, for that would suggest a continuation of prewar German Jewry, but rather are "Jews in Germany," an ambivalent term of self-description that is still in official use, as the community's governing body, founded in 1950, is named the Central Council of Jews in Germany.

After 1989 and the collapse of the Soviet Union, Germany again became a land of Jewish immigration with the eventual arrival of about 100,000 Jews from Russia. These immigrants provided a demographic boost to the preexisting Jewish population in Germany of about 30,000 and soon began to take up prominent positions within the communities. In fact, for several years community business was conducted in Russian and then translated into German. The 130,000 Jews of Germany form the fastest-growing Jewish community in Europe.

While Jewish life in Germany is fraught with the impact of the past, a younger generation of German Jews has its eyes on the future. Increasingly, discussions concerning issues of Jewish identity take place in the public sphere. As a consequence, an exciting new German Jewish culture is in the making. There is a small but growing literary, theatre, and film scene that tackles the theme of being a Jew in Germany. Universities too contribute to the Jewish discourse. In Munich and Berlin significant numbers of students, most of them not Jewish, pursue Jewish Studies and produce original scholarly research. In both cities, new museums of Jewish history attract large numbers of visitors. Aside from organized Jewish life, informal networks—Jewish study groups, choral societies, the *Tarbut* (Hebrew for "culture") adult education conference, which attracts round 300 participants annually—are evidence of an increasingly vibrant Jewish cultural life in Germany.

Other Western European Countries

Elsewhere in western Europe, Jewish populations have never been able to recover from the Holocaust, natural demographic decline, emigration, and assimilation. In 1939 the Jewish population of Holland stood at 140,000. In 2005 it was 30,000. Belgium was home to 90,000 Jews on the eve of the war and now has 31,000 Jews. Italy's Jewish population has decreased from 57,000 in 1939 to 28,000 in 2005. In all these countries, basic issues of finding Jewish spouses—

less of a problem in Belgium with its significant Hasidic population—and the absence of Jewish cultural life have resulted in a steady exodus of young Jews to England, the United States, and Israel.

Even in England, beyond the Holocaust's reach, the Jewish population shrank from over 400,000 in the 1950s to under 300,000 by the 1990s. The main reason for the decline is a very low birthrate and high death rate. Middle class and relatively affluent, with a plethora of communal institutions, British Jewry has enjoyed material success. For a brief period in the 1970s and 1980s, five Jews served as cabinet ministers in Margaret Thatcher's government. But events in the Middle East plague British Jewry and raise public concern. Groups within the radical Left, such as the British Association of University Teachers, which in 2006 called for an academic boycott of Israeli universities and mainstream liberal institutions such as *The New Statesman,* the *Guardian,* and the BBC, have at various times given expression to virulent anti-Israel sentiments, sometimes indistinguishable from anti-semitism. On January 14, 2002, the *New Statesman* ran a story on "excessive" Jewish influence and power and carried a front-page illustration of the Union Jack being pierced with a Star of David with the caption "A Kosher Conspiracy?" Although Jews are not under any threat in England, younger more dynamic voices have urged the ordinarily quiescent leadership, the Board of Deputies, to be more aggressive in its representation of the community. This faction felt particularly frustrated and abandoned by traditional leaders at the time of the proposed boycott of Israeli academic institutions. The board's traditional approach of "quiet diplomacy" was, according to Jewish critics, a remnant of an earlier, more insecure time, and what was called for now was a more combative mode of self-defense. The divide over this issue may spill over into other areas of Anglo-Jewish life and prove a force for creative and more vocal expressions of Jewish identity.

The Jews of the Southern Hemisphere

In the eighteenth and nineteenth centuries, Jewish immigrants began to make their way to Latin America, South Africa, and Australia. Stable and settled, these communities were far from centers of tradition and authority. Latin America is home to approximately 500,000 Jews, with the biggest communities in Argentina and Brazil.

In Argentina, Jews have had a very mixed experience since World War II. In 1946 Juan Perón, a Nazi sympathizer and Catholic authoritarian, came to power. While he put an end to Jewish emigration and allowed the country to be a haven for Nazis on the run (Adolf Eichmann was captured there in 1960 by Israeli agents), he also established diplomatic relations with Israel in 1949. During the military dictatorship of 1976 to 1983, Jews were accused of Left-wing and sometimes Zionist sympathies and were prominent targets of the junta and secret police. They were kidnapped, tortured, and numbered among the *desaparecidos,* or "the disappeared." During this period, Jews lived in fear and many emigrated to Israel.

When the junta fell in 1983, antisemitic attacks also declined. The Jewish community welcomed the democratically elected government of Raul Alfonsin. But antisemitism had not disappeared, and tragedy struck the community in 1994 when the central Jewish communal offices in Buenos Aires were blown up by terrorists in the pay of the Iranian government. Right-wing Argentine circles also appear to have been involved, their presence in the government helping to explain the deliberate foot dragging of the investigation. In 2005, the Argentine investigator declared the bombing to have been the work of a Lebanese suicide bomber from Hezbollah. No one has yet been brought to justice. Eighty-seven people were murdered in the attack, and over a hundred more were injured.

About 185,000 Jews remain in Argentina. As elsewhere, they are overwhelmingly secular, middle class, and concentrated in commerce. Once a thriving center of spoken Yiddish culture and publishing, the community is almost entirely Spanish speaking now, though Yiddish theatre is still performed. There is also a wide of array of Jewish cultural, sporting, and educational institutions. But the community is anything but secure. The collapse of the community's cooperative banking system in the 1960s still continues to be felt, and the most recent economic crisis produced an increase in poverty rates, so relatively large numbers of Jews have chosen to emigrate to Spain, whose Jewish community has enjoyed something of a boost. In the context of economic and possibly political uncertainty, Argentinean Jews fear the resurgence of antisemitism.

In the interwar period, neighboring Brazil took in approximately 30,000 Jewish immigrants, and about 42,000 Jews were living there when the Nazis came to power in 1933, after which time Brazil tightened its restrictions on Jews seeking to enter the country. For twenty years after World War II, postwar immigration and natural growth saw the community grow to around 120,000, though some estimates put it at 150,000 Jews. Mostly centered in São Paulo and Rio de Janeiro, the communities came to boast an array of day schools, community centers, museums, and Jewish newspapers. Deeply integrated into the economic and cultural life of the country, Jews also came to hold important political offices at state and federal levels. In contrast to Argentina, in Brazil antisemitism in the postwar period has been negligible. As in many other countries, deep pockets of assimilation and an intermarriage rate perhaps as high as 60 percent reflect the high level of Jewish integration into the dominant society.

Since World War II, in lands of the British Commonwealth, Canada, South Africa, and Australia, Jews have enjoyed levels of social acceptance barely matched anywhere else. In Canada, when antisemitism has flared, it has largely been confined to Quebec, linked with Francophone hostility to the Anglo-Protestants. Following World War II, Canada reversed its strict anti-immigration policies. Between 1946 and 1960, 46,000 Jewish immigrants were admitted into Canada, a combination of Holocaust survivors and Jews who fled Hungary after the 1956 uprising. The Jewish population reached 200,000 by 1950.

By 2005, 372,000 Jews were in Canada, making it the fourth-largest Jewish community in the world. Most Jews are settled in the urban centers of Montreal, Toronto, and Winnipeg. Well integrated into Canadian society, Canadian Jewry, more conservative than its American counterpart, has exhibited a greater degree of insularity (a trait shared by other ethnic groups in Canada) and a much stronger degree of commitment to Jewish traditions than American Jews. Zionism, continuing use of Yiddish after the 1950s, less geographical dispersion, and greater contact with refugees and Holocaust survivors—by 1990, between 30 and 40 percent of Canadian Jews were descendants of Holocaust survivors compared to 8 percent of the U.S. Jewish population—has made for a tightly knit Jewish community in touch with older traditions.

Jewish life in South Africa thrived both before and in the decades after the war despite considerable difficulties. In 1948, the country adopted apartheid and South African Jewry had to walk a thin line between protest and acquiescence. The ruling Afrikaner elite was also antisemitic and South African Jewry was constantly on trial. Not too many Jews expressed their disgust with the system, preferring to keep a low profile while accepting its social benefits. However two of the most outspoken white critics of apartheid were Jews—**Helen Suzman** (b. 1917) and **Joe Slovo** (1926–1995). Suzman, an economist, was a member of the liberal Progressive Party and spent thirty-six years in parliament as a dogged English-speaking opponent of apartheid in a political chamber full of male Afrikaner Calvinists. Slovo, an immigrant from Lithuania, was head of the South African Communist Party and one of the few white members of the African National Congress. By the 1980s, a host of Jewish groups were working with black Africans to bring an end to apartheid. In 1985, Jews for Justice, located in Cape Town, and Jews for Social Justice, centered in Johannesburg, joined forces to reform South African society and attempt to bring the white and black communities together.

While Afrikaner rule never pursued antisemitism as a matter of policy, Jews nonetheless felt insecure. Some started leaving as early as 1960 in the aftermath of the Sharpeville Massacre, in which 69 black Africans were killed and at least 200 were injured when police opened fire on demonstrators protesting against the pass laws dictating where, when, and for how long a person could remain in "white" areas. In the 1970s and 1980s, as racial tensions rose and political conflict seemed unavoidable, many Jews began to leave in fear of violence. Some, especially university students, left to avoid military service on behalf of a regime they disliked and an ideology they loathed. Between 1970 and 1992, more than 39,000 Jews left South Africa for Britain, the United States, and Australia. As of 2005, about 72,000 Jews remained.

One of the few postwar communities that continues to grow is Australian Jewry. With 103,000 Jews, Australia is the tenth-largest Jewish community in the world. It has benefited from a very tolerant atmosphere, a strong economy, and since the 1970s waves of migration from South Africa, Russia, and Israel. As of 2001, 12.5 percent of all Jews in Australia were South African. The two largest communities live in Melbourne and Sydney, both exhibiting different characteristics thanks to the fact that Jewish immigrants to Melbourne, beginning in the 1930s, tended to be Yiddish-speaking Jews from eastern Europe, Poland in particular, while more acculturated German, Austrian, and Hungarian Jews gravitated to Sydney. In 1933, some 23,000 Jews were living in Australia. Between 1938 and 1961, the arrival of refugees, Holocaust survivors, and Hungarian Jews fleeing the political turmoil of 1956 resulted in a total Jewish population increase to 61,000.

Australian Jewry is deeply committed to Jewish tradition, Zionism, and a particular form of Jewishness best described as *yiddishkayt,* the legacy of Yiddish language, culture, and history. The community takes its particular cast from interwar refugees and postwar Holocaust survivors. After the war, survivors and refugees were intensely concerned with the Jewish future. Given that postwar governments admitted Jews but felt that it was the responsibility of the existing Jewish community to assist the newcomers, an elaborate communal welfare system was established to assist with the integration of survivors. Representatives of the welfare agencies met incoming boatloads of Jews at the ports, organized housing and employment, and provided interest-free business loans. The task of caring for the refugees was a great burden for the small, local Jewish community, which in turn requested and received help from American aid agencies such as the Joint Distribution Committee, the Hebrew Immigrant Aid Society, and the Refugee Economic Corporation. Given the high number of Holocaust survivors in Australia, between 1952 and 1965 significant funding was obtained from the Conference on Jewish Material Claims Against Germany. With its higher percentage of Polish Jews who came to Australia bearing a strong philanthropic and social service tradition, Melbourne Jewry was extremely energetic and proactive in assisting the immigrants. As such, this tended to attract an even greater percentage of Holocaust survivors, 60 percent of whom settled in Melbourne.

The impact of such a high percentage of Jews who either fled or survived the Nazis came to have a decisive impact on Australian Jewish culture. Seeking to rebuild Jewish life after the devastation of the Holocaust, the community focused attention on its children, pouring its resources and energy into building up what would become the largest and most successful network of Jewish day schools in the Disapora. By 1943, a German Jewish refugee in Sydney, Elchanan Blumenthal, had already established the North Bondi Jewish Kindergarten and Day School. A newspaper report in the *Hebrew Standard of Australasia* reported on the official opening of the institution, revealing the founders' raison d'être: "Let us sadly remember them, all those who over there on the other side are experiencing the full brunt of mysterious Jewish suffering and all the centres of Jewish learning are lying in ruins." The focal point of the Australian day school system is in Melbourne, home to the world's largest such school, Mount Scopus Memorial College, founded in 1949. In the 1980s, the school had over 3,000 students spread over several campuses. The immediate success of Mount Scopus served as inspiration to open other Jewish day schools. Such institutions cater to a gamut of modern Jewish ideologies from ultra-Orthodox, to Zionist schools, to a Bundist-inspired Yiddish day school. This school system has fostered a tightly knit community, which has openly expressed in word and deed its vehement opposition to assimilation. Jewish day schools exist in all major cities in Australia, and it is estimated that approximately 70 percent of Australian Jewish children are educated in these institutions. Despite the overwhelmingly secular character of Australian Jewry, the intermarriage rate as of 1996 was 15 percent, a figure that, while on the rise, remains extremely low in comparison to other Disapora communities, and some sociologists have attributed it to the high proportion of Jews attending day schools.

What constitutes an unusual model of modern Jewish identity in Australia is the extent to which Jews have been able to remain insular while being, for the most part, secular. A 1992 survey or attitudes toward religion found that 6 percent of respondents identified themselves as "strictly Orthodox," 33 percent were "traditional religious" (not necessarily observant but when they do attend synagogue, even if infrequently, they choose an Orthodox one), 15 percent were "Liberal/Reform," 43 percent were "Jewish but not religious," and 3 percent were either opposed to religion or identified as something else. The popularity of Chabad Judaism among otherwise secular Jews is further testament to a kind of Jewish diversity rarely seen elsewhere and one that reflects an ecumenical spirit among Australia's secular Jews.

The Road to the Future

At the beginning of the twenty-first century, the overwhelming majority of Jews live in countries free of official antisemitism. Nowhere in the West or in the countries of the old Soviet bloc are restrictions in place against Jews. Even religious anti-Judaism is on the wane, in the case of the Catholic Church's Nostra Aetate (1965), which not only recognizes that the Church received the wisdom of the Old Testament from the Jews but admits, "True, the Jewish authorities and those who followed their lead pressed for the death of Christ; still, what happened in His passion cannot be charged against all the Jews, without distinction, then alive, nor against the Jews of today. The Catholic Church is the new people of God, the Jews should not be presented as rejected or accursed by God." The Church has attempted to build bridges between Catholics and Jews and has sought to come to terms with the disastrous impact of its millennial, anti-Jewish teachings. In 1979 Pope John Paul II went to Auschwitz and paid homage to Jewish Holocaust victims. In 1986, he was the first modern pontiff to visit the Rome synagogue.

Less encouraging are the gains of the far Right in western Europe. But there is no real sense that Jean-Marie Le Pen's National Front in France, Jorg Haider's Freedom Party in Austria, or Alessandra Mussolini's Italian neo-Fascist Alternativa Sociale constitute a real threat to Jews. While such groups do harbor antisemitic views, their principal targets are Muslim immigrants and mainstream politicians disavow their language and sentiments.

On the far Left of the political spectrum, the enthusiastic support for Israel that was once widespread has now dissipated, often replaced with legitimate criticism of Israel's policies vis à vis the Palestinians. Increasingly, however, those criticisms morph into questions about or outright opposition to the legitimacy of Israel's existence. Such sentiments, which are often patently antisemitic, frequently entail a critique of Jews and or Jewish institutions, charging them with conspiratorial actions, and are very often found in the print and electronic media, at universities, and at "the dinner parties of the chattering classes. A further characteristic of contemporary European antisemitism is its "status as an epiphenomenon of anti-Americanism," something referred to by the sociologist Andrei Markovits as "twin brothers." Such views have become increasingly prevalent among educated groups that identify themselves as "liberal" or "on the Left." Only in the Muslim world are antisemitic stereotypes, rhetoric, and Holocaust denial deployed with regularity and condoned or promoted by the government-controlled press and education ministries. But aside from the 20,000 Jews who remain in Iran, few Jews are directly affected by the prevailing Islamic sentiment.

Historians are not in a position or expected to make predictions about the future. It would be foolhardy to do so. No one writing a history of the Jewish people in 1939 could have imagined that within six years two-thirds of European Jewry would be murdered or that within nine years there would be a Jewish state in Israel. Nor could anyone have predicted that the bulk of the Jewish people would no longer practice the rituals of Judaism and be unfamiliar with many of its fundamental practices and teachings. Secularization and social acceptance have created unimaginable opportunities as well as unforeseen problems. Just as one can be killed by hate, one can be loved to death as well. What we can say with certainty is that the Jews of today bear little resemblance to those Jews with whom we began our long story.

For the overwhelming majority, in a mere three hundred years, the places where Jews lived, the languages they spoke, the jobs they performed, the clothes they wore, and even the foods they permitted themselves to eat have all changed. This has happened as a result of their complex encounter with the modern world, both its blessings and its horrors. In their engagement with modernity, Jews fashioned a set of responses that allowed them to transform general culture and Jewishness. How these will serve the needs of the Jewish people in the future should be left to succeeding generations of historians to ponder.

Questions for Reflection

1. What was the impact on world Jewry of Israel's victory in the 1967 Six-Day War?
2. What have been some of the consequences of Israel's settlement policies?
3. What has been the impact of suburbanization on American Jewry?
4. What factors have animated Jewish life in Europe after World War II?

For Further Reading

On the survivors in postwar Europe, see Yehuda Bauer, *Flight and Rescue: Brichah* (New York: Random House, 1970); Michael Brenner, *After the Holocaust: Rebuilding Jewish Lives in Postwar Germany* (Princeton, NJ: Princeton University Press, 1997); Lucy S. Dawidowicz, *From that Place and Time: A Memoir, 1938–1947* (New York: W.W. Norton, 1989); Jan T. Gross, *Fear: Anti-Semitism in Poland After Auschwitz* (New York: Random House, 2006).

On Israel, see Howard M. Sachar, *A History of Israel: From the Rise of Zionism to Our Time* (New York: Knopf, 2001); Tom Segev, *1949: The First Israelis* (New York: Free Press, 1986); *Tom Segev, The Seventh Million: The Israelis and the Holocaust* (New York: Owl Books, 1991); Benny Morris, *The Birth of the Palestinian Refugee Problem, 1947–1949* (Cambridge, England: Cambridge University Press, 1987); Yael Zerubavel, *Recovered Roots: Collective Memory and the Making of Israeli National Tradition* (Chicago: University of Chicago Press, 1995); Derek J, Penslar, *Israel in History: The Jewish State in Comparative Perspective* (London and New York: Routledge, 2007). Eli Lederhendler, *The Six-Day War and World Jewry* (Bethesda, Md.,: University Press of Maryland, 2000); Alvin Z. Rubinstein, ed., The Arab-Israeli Conflict: Perspectives (New York: HarperCollins, 1991); Alan Dowty, *Israel/Palestine* (Cambridge, England: Polity, 2005); Alan Dowty, *The Jewish State: A Century Later* (Berkeley: University of California Press, 1998); Benny Morris, ed., *Making Israel* (Ann Arbor: University of Michigan Press, 2007).

On postwar American Jewry, see Arthur A. Goren, *The Politics and Public Culture of American Jews* (Bloomington: Indiana University Press, 1999); Eli Lederhendler, *New York Jews and the Decline of Urban Ethnicity, 1950–1970* (Syracuse: Syracuse University Press, 2001); Robert M. Seltzer and Norman J. Cohen, eds., *The Americanization of the Jews* (New York: New York University Press, 1995); Marc Dollinger, *Quest for Inclusion: Jews and Liberalism in Modern America* (Princeton, NJ: Princeton University Press, 2000); Hasia Diner, *The Jews of the United States: 1654 to 2000* (Berkeley: University of California Press, 2006).

On Soviet Jewry, see Salo W. Baron, *The Russian Jews Under Tsar and Soviets* (New York: Schocken, 1987); Jeffrey Veidlinger, *The Moscow State Yiddish Theater: Jewish Culture on the Soviet Stage* (Bloomington: Indiana University Press, 2000); Zvi Gitelman, *A Century of Ambivalence: The Jews of Russia and the Soviet Union, 1881 to the Present* (Bloomington: Indiana University Press, 2001); Zvi Gitelman, ed., et al., *Jewish Life After the USSR* (Bloomington: Indiana University Press, 2003); Yuri Slezkine, *The Jewish Century* (Princeton, NJ: Princeton University Press, 2004). Anna Shternshis, *Soviet and Kosher: Jewish Popular Culture in the Soviet Union, 1923–1939* (Bloomington: Indiana University Press, 2006).

On Jews in contemporary Europe, see Eliezer Ben-Rafael, Yosef Gorny, and Yaacov Ro'I, eds., *Contemporary Jewries: Convergence and Divergence* (Leiden, The Netherlands, and Boston: Brill, 2003); Zvi Gitelman, Barry Kosmin, and András Kovács, eds., *New Jewish Identities: Contemporary Europe and Beyond* (Budapest and New York: Central European University Press, 2003); Bernard Wasserstein, *Vanishing Diaspora: The Jews in Europe Since 1945* (Cambridge, MA: Harvard University Press, 1996). Sander L. Gilman and Karen Remmler , eds., *Reemerging Jewish Culture in Germany: Life and Literature since 1989* (New York: New York University Press, 1994).

On Jews of the southern hemisphere see, Kristin Ruggiero, ed., *The Jewish Diaspora in Latin America and the Caribbean: Fragments of Memory* (Brighton, England, and Portland, OR: Sussex Academic Press, 2005); Gideon Shimoni, *Community and Conscience: The Jews in Apartheid South Africa* (Hanover, NH: University Press of New England, 2003); Suzanne D. Rutland, *Edge of the Diaspora: Two Centuries of Jewish Settlement in Australia* (New York and London: Holmes and Meier, 1997).

Timeline of Jewish History

Ancient Israelite/Biblical History (Chapters 1–2)

Accurate dating of events in the biblical narrative is notoriously difficult; not all scholars agree on the historicity of various events in the Bible, such as the exodus from Egypt or the conquest of Canaan by the Israelites. Others believe that while these events did take place, they cannot be accurately dated. Dating historical events from other ancient cultures like that of Egypt can also be complicated, with the same event dated in different ways by different scholars.

2334–2279 BCE	Life of Sargon I ("the Great"), founder of one of the earliest centralized empires in Mesopotamia
19th or 18th century BCE	Babylonian king Hammurabi promulgates his code of laws
16th century BCE	Expulsion of Hyksos by native Egyptians
1500–1100 BCE	Semi-nomads from Canaan called "Shasu" appear in Egypt
1482 or 1457 BCE	Thutmoses III victorious at Megiddo in Canaan, begins Egyptian control over Canaan
14th–13th century BCE	High point of Syrian city-state of Ugarit
1377–1361 or 1350–1334 BCE	Amenhotep IV rules in Egypt, renames himself Akhnaten
1213–1203 BCE	Merneptah rules in Egypt
1207 BCE	People of Israel appear to live in Canaan by this point (*see* Merneptah Stele *in Glossary*)
1153 BCE	Death of Egyptian king Rameses III and end of Egyptian control of Canaan
1200–1000 BCE	Alleged period of the Judges
1180 BCE	Philistines arrive on Canaanite coast around this time
1000 BCE	Around this time, David rules as king over Israelite
c. 930 BCE	Death of Solomon
c. 925 BCE	King Shishak of Egypt invades Canaan
9th century BCE	Kingdoms of Israel and Judah exist by this point
9th–8th centuries BCE	Assyrian Empire expands from Mesopotamia into Syria and Canaan
853 BCE	Ahab, king of Israel, participates in a battle against the Assyrians
722–20 BCE	Assyria's conquest and destruction of the northern kingdom of Israel
701 BCE	Assyrians conquer most of Judah
598/597 BCE	Babylonians capture Jerusalem
587/6 BCE	Destruction of First Temple by the Babylonian king Nebuchadnezzar II
539 BCE	Edict of the Persian king Cyrus II allowing Babylonian exiles to return to the province of Yehud and rebuild the Temple
522–486 BCE	Reign of Persian king Darius I, who permits the completion of the Temple
5th century BCE	Judahite (or Jewish) community on the Egyptian island of Elephantine

Jews and Greeks (Chapter 3)

356 BCE	Birth of Alexander the Great
331 BCE	Alexander the Great invades Asia, soon defeating Darius III and conquering the Persian Empire, including Judea
323 BCE	Alexander dies; Egypt and Judea pass to the control of the Ptolemaic kingdom

283–246 BCE	Reign of Ptolemy II; Zenon's archive and the Septuagint date to this period
200 BCE	*Wisdom of Ben Sira* composed
202–200 BCE	The Seleucid king Antiochus III conquers Palestine from the Ptolemies, beginning Seleucid rule in Judea
175–164 BCE	Rule of Antiochus IV
167 BCE	Antiochus IV rededicates Jewish Temple to Zeus, and outlaws circumcision, Sabbath observance, and Torah study
167/166 BCE	Mattathias and his sons, including Judah the Maccabee, begin guerrilla war against Seleucid rule
164 BCE	Recaptured by Judah the Maccabee, the Temple is purified and rededicated to God
C. 150 BCE	"Teacher of Righteousness" and his followers withdraw into the Judean desert
140 BCE	Judah's brother Simon is recognized as high priest and ruler of the Jews, a position passed down to his descendants the Hasmoneans; during Maccabean/Hasmonean rule in Judea, both the Dead Sea Scroll community and other Jewish sects arise

Between Caesar and God (Chapter 4)

1st century BCE	Activity of Hillel and Shammai
76 BCE	Death of Alexander Jannaeus, an important Hasmonean king
67 BCE	Hasmonean Queen Salome Alexandra dies, setting off succession struggle between her sons, Aristobolus II and Hyrcanus II
63 BCE	Pompey intervenes on behalf of Hyrcanus II, arresting Aristobolus II and conquering Jerusalem; Hyrcanus II appointed ruler of Judea, but a Roman governor controls much of the territory that the Hasmoneans once ruled
63 BCE–14 CE	Life of Augustus, first Roman emperor
44 BCE	Julius Caesar assassinated the last Herodian ruler
37 BCE	With Roman help, Herod conquers Jerusalem from a briefly revived Hasmonean dynasty and begins his rule over Judea around this time
30 BCE	Rome conquers Egypt, ending Ptolemaic rule there
20 BCE	Herod begins massive expansion of the Temple
4 BCE	Herod dies
4 BCE to 6 CE	Birth of Jesus
6 CE	Judea is put under direct Roman rule
26–37 CE	Pontius Pilate is prefect of Judea; recent scholarship argues that he was prefect from 19–37 CE
28 or 29 CE	John the Baptist executed by Herod
37 CE	Gaius Caligula becomes emperor and Flavius Josephus is born
37–44 CE	Agrippa I, grandson of Herod, rules Judea; he is succeeded by Agrippa II
38–41 CE	Ethnic violence between Greeks and Jews of Alexandria
40 CE	Caligula decides to have statue of himself as Zeus installed in Jerusalem Temple; delegation of Jews sent to Rome to petition Caligula; the emperor's assassination in 41 ends crisis
50–60 CE	Paul writes a series of letters introducing his understanding of what it means to be a Christian
66–70 CE	Jewish Revolt against Rome
70 CE	Romans destroy the Temple and lay waste to Jerusalem
73 CE	Jewish rebels holed up in Masada fortress commit suicide before imminent Roman capture
ca. 80 CE	Josephus published his account of the Jewish Revolt around this time; his *Antiquities of the Jews,* an account of Jewish history from the biblical period to Roman times, published a decade or so later
115–117 CE	The "Diaspora Revolt," a series of interconnected uprisings during the reign of Trajan spreads from Libya, to Egypt, Cyprus, and even Mesopotamia; it is brutally suppressed by the Romans
132 CE	Bar Kochba Revolt erupts in Judea
135 CE	Bar Kochba Revolt culminates in final battle at Bethar, in which Bar Kochba himself is killed

Rabbinic Revelations (Chapter 5)

175–220	Judah ha-Nasi ("the Patriarch") active
c. 200	Mishnah redacted by Judah ha-Nasi
219	After study in the Land of Israel, Rav Abba ("Rav") returns to Babylonia and establishes what would become a major rabbinic academy at Sura

226	Fall of Parthian kingdom and rise of the Sassanian dynasty
286	Diocletian divides the administration of the Roman Empire into eastern and western Roman halves
312	Constantine affixes the sign of Christ on his troops' equipment after a vision before the Battle of the Milvian Bridge
330	Constantine makes Constantinople capital of the Roman Empire
362/3	Roman emperor Julian "the Apostate," as part of effort to reverse the empire's Christianization, plans to rebuild the Jewish Temple but dies before finishing the project
395	Roman empire splits into Western and Eastern (or Byzantine) Empires
414	Christian mobs drive Jews out of Alexandria
354–430	Augustine of Hippo writes *Tractatus Adversus Judaeos* (*Treatise Against the Jews*), which despite a sharp critique of Judaism argues that the Jews should be permitted to exist, though in a state of misery, as living testimony to the truth of Christianity
429	Office of patriarch abolished by this time
476	The last emperor of Rome, Romulus Augustulus, is deposed, marking the end of the Western Roman Empire

Under the Crescent (Chapter 6)

c. 570	Birth of Muhammad in Mecca
622	Muhammad flees Mecca for Medina, where he establishes a community of followers
628	Muslims of Medina defeat Jews of nearby Khaybar; Jews are granted protection in exchange for annual tribute paid to Muslims–a precedent for the *jizya*
c. 632	Death of Muhammad
634	Muslims conquer Palestine from the Byzantine Empire
634–44	Rule of Umar I
642	Muslims conquer Iraq
661	Mu'awiyya establishes the Umayyad Caliphate, ruled from Damascus; it lasts until 750
711	Umayyads capture Spain
c. 754–775	Appearance of Anan ben David, regarded by the Karaites as the founder of the sect
732	French monarch Charles Martel holds Muslim armies to the area south of the Pyrenees at the Battle of Tours
750	Umayyad dynasty falls to Abbasids
750–1258	Abbasid dynasty rules from its new capital, Baghdad
756	Abd al-Rahman I, the Umayyad scion, flees from the Abbasids and establishes princedom in Spain; he rules until 788
912	Abd al-Rahman III comes to power and consolidates power in Spain, establishing a rival caliphate based in Cordoba; he rules until 961; his reign marks the beginning of a "Golden Age" in Jewish culture in Andalusia (Muslim Spain)
928	Saadya (882–942) becomes Gaon of the academy of Sura; he holds the post until his death
968–998	Sherira presides as Gaon of Pumbedita
969	Fatimids establish dynasty with capital in Fustat (near present-day Cairo); it lasts until 1171
c. 970	Death of Hasdai ibn Shaprut, distinguished Jewish courtier of Abd-al-Rahman III; Death of Menahem ben Suruq, Hasdai ibn Shaprut's personal secretary and the creator of a Hebrew dictionary called the *Mahberet*
c. 990	Death of Dunash ben Labrat, Hebrew grammarian
998–1038	Hai presides as Gaon of Pumbedita
1013	Period of the *Taifas,* independent mini-states ruled by princes, begins in Muslim Spain
1056	Death of Samuel ha-Nagid, Hebrew poet and successful courtier, who rose to become a vizier and general in the Muslim kingdom of Granada
1057	Death of Solomon ibn Gabirol, Hebrew poet
1066	Joseph ha-Nagid, courtier in Granada and son of Samuel ha-Nagid, is killed after becoming entangled in the conflicts between rival Muslim factions in Granada; riots target the Jewish community of Granada
1085	Spanish Christian forces capture Toledo from Muslims
1086	Princes from Muslim Spain call in support from the Berber Almoravid dynasty in northwestern Africa The Almoravids take control of the local princedoms and attempt, unsuccessfully, to forcibly convert the Jews; their dynasty lasts until 1147

1099	Jerusalem falls to the Crusaders and Jewish institutions of learning there are ravaged
1141	Death of Judah ha-Levi
1047–1212	The Almohads, North African followers of an extremely strict interpretation of Islam, rule in Spain and persecute Jews and Christians
1165–1173	Benjamin of Tudela travels from Spain to the Middle East
1164	Death of Abraham ibn Ezra, biblical commentator, philosopher, scientist and poet
1171	Fatimids displaced from Egypt by Saladin
1204	Death of Maimonides
1250	Mamluks begin their rule of Egypt; it lasts until 1517, when they are defeated by the Ottomans
1258	Mongolian invasion of Abbasid empire
1290s	Moses de Leon composes the *Zohar* in Spain

Medieval Christian Europe (Chapter 7)

590–604	Gregory I is Pope; he insists that Jews ought not to be forcibly converted or killed even though they are in religious error
612–621	Under the reign of the Christian Visigothic king Sisebut in Spain, Jews face restrictions and oppressive policies, including forcible conversion
633	Fourth Council of Toledo reaffirms a prohibition on the ownership of Christian slaves by Jews
711	Muslims conquer Spain, as many Christians flee to the mountains in the north; most Jews stay put
800	Charlemagne, King of the Franks, takes title "Holy Roman Emperor"; he initiates a symbiotic relationship between the Jews and the king that allows Jewish life to thrive
838	Bodo, the chaplain to the Holy Roman Emperor Louis the Pious (r. 814–840), converts to Judaism, adopting the Hebrew name Eliezer; he flees to Muslim Spain
950s/960s	Correspondence between Hasdai ibn Shaprut of Cordoba and a Khazar king named Joseph, who recounts the story of the Khazars' conversion to Judaism
960–1040	Life of Gershom ben Judah, "Light of the Exile," who established a school of Talmudic studies in Mainz
1040–1105	Life of Rashi
1066	William the Conqueror (r. 1066–1087), the Duke of Normandy, captures England and brings with him Jews of French origin, language, and culture
1071	Seljuk Turks capture much of the Byzantine Empire's heartland in Asia Minor
1084	In the Rhineland, Bishop Rüdiger of Speyer issues a community charter that grants the Jews economic privileges and protections, while also confining them to residence "some way off from the houses of the rest of the citizens"
1090	King of Germany and Holy Roman Emperor Henry IV issues charter guaranteeing Jews protection
1056–1105	Reign of Henry IV, king of Germany and Holy Roman Emperor, who safeguards and supports Jews living in his realm
1095	Pope Urban II calls for removal of Muslims from Holy Land, launching First Crusade
1096	Crusaders attack Jewish communities of Rhineland in Speyer, Worms, Trier, and Mainz
1099	Crusaders kill Muslims and Jews upon reaching Jerusalem
1110–1180	Life of Abraham ibn Daud, Spanish, historian and philosopher
1120	Calixtus II promulgates *Sicut Judaeis* papal bull, which grants Jews protection and forbids Christians from forcibly converting them
c. 1140–1217	Life of Judah the Pious, founding figure of Rhineland community known as Hasidei Ashkenaz
1144	The first blood libel in Christian Europe surfaces in the English town of Norwich
	The Capetian king Louis VII of France expels from his realm Jews who had converted to Christianity and returned to Judaism
c. 1150–1230	Life of Samuel Tibbon, who translated Maimonides' *Guide for the Perplexed* from Arabic to Hebrew
1158	Visiting England, Abraham ibn Ezra publishes Yesod Mora(The Foundation of Awe)
c. 1160–1235	Life of David Kimhi, Hebrew grammarian and biblical commentator, son of Joseph, also an important grammarian.
1171	Blood libel in the town of Blois in France
1182	German emperor Frederick I ("Barbarossa") declares that all the Jews of the empire are imperial property
1189–1192	During the Third Crusade, Jews are massacred in several English cities

1190	150 Jews are massacred at York Castle
1194–1270	Life of Nahmanides
1212	Catholics defeat Muslim forces at Las Navas de Tolosa in the far south of Spain, placing many centers of Jewish population and culture, such as Barcelona, Toledo, Valencia, Saragossa, Tortosa, and Tudela, under Christian rule
1215	Fourth Lateran Council officially asserts that the wafer (the "host") and wine used in the Catholic ritual of the Eucharist actually becomes the body and blood of Christ during the ceremony (the doctrine is known as transubstantiation). Council also imposes upon Jews the requirement to wear distinguishing marks (badges) or items of clothing
1209–1229	Albigensian Crusade targets the heretical movement of the Cathars in southern France
1232	Maimonidean Controversy
1240	Public disputation between Jews and Christians is held in Paris; it culminates in the burning of the Talmud two years later
1240–1291	Life of Abraham Abulafia, itinerant mystic
1242	The Talmud is condemned by an inquisition; forty cartloads are burned
1263	Public disputation between Jews and Christians held in Barcelona
1280s	Series of blood libels in Mainz, Munich, and other German towns
1290	Edward I (r. 1272–1307) orders the expulsion of the Jews from England
1298	Rindfleisch massacres of Jews in southern and central Germany lead to thousands of deaths
1306	Jews expelled from France by Phillip IV
1320	During the Shepherds' Crusade, northern French crusaders moving through the south of the country kill hundreds of Jews
1349	Jews of Strasbourg are massacred on St. Valentine's Day after an accusation of well poisoning
1378	A Spanish archdeacon named Ferrant Martinez begins preaching against the Jews, calling for the destruction of synagogues
1391	A series of anti-Jewish riots sweep through the Iberian Peninsula; many Jews are killed or forcibly converted
1413–1414	Public disputation between Jews and Christians held in Tortosa
1438	Jews in the Moroccan city of Fez are moved into a separate quarter (*mellah*)
1453	Ottoman Turks capture Constantinople, putting an end to the Byzantine Empire and placing its large Jewish population under Muslim rule
1463–1494	Life of Giovanni Pico dela Mirandolla, Christian Kabbalah scholar
1469	Isabella, heir to the throne of Castille, and Ferdinand, heir to the throne of Aragon, are married and unite their kingdoms
1475	Last major blood-libel accusation of the Middle Ages surfaces in Trent, Italy
1483	Tomás de Torquemada appointed as inquisitor
1492	Ferdinand and Isabella defeat kingdom of Granada, last Muslim stronghold in Iberia; they call for the expulsion of all Jews from Spain except for those willing to convert
1496	Portugal orders expulsion of Jews unless they convert
1497	Jews of Portugal forcibly converted en masse
1498	Jews of Provence expelled
1516	First ghetto established in Venice

A Jewish Renaissance (Chapter 8)

1442 and 1450	Expulsions of Jews from Bavaria
1449	Mob attacks converso population in Toledo
1455	Gutenberg prints famous two-volume *Gutenberg Bible*
1455–1522	Life of Johannes Reuchlin, German humanist
1475	The law code *Arab'a Turim* by the Spanish rabbi Yaakov ben Asher (d. 1340) is printed in Padua, as one of the first Hebrew books that appeared in print
1478	Ferdinand and Isabella ask pope to authorize Spanish Inquisition to investigate the secret practice of Judaism by Jews who had converted to Christianity
1481	Spanish Inquisition begins its work
1483	Partial expulsion of Jews from cities in southern Spain

1484	The Soncino family opens its printing house in the Italian city of Soncino; they later open printing houses in Salonika (1520s) and Constantinople (1530s)
1492	On March 31, Ferdinand of Aragon and Isabella of Castile decree expulsion of all Jews from their realms
1496	On December 5, after his marriage to Isabella, the daughter of Ferdinand and Isabella, King Manuel of Portugal orders all Jews to leave his kingdom within ten months
1497	In March, all Jews in Portugal are forcibly baptized and converted to Christianity
1506	Following anti-converso riots in Lisbon, Portugal temporarily opens its borders to allow conversos to emigrate; many join Spanish exiles in the Ottoman Empire and Italy, while others later establish new communities in Amsterdam, Hamburg, and London
1510	Expulsion of Jews from Electorate of Brandenburg, including its capital Berlin
1516	Ghetto established in Venice
1516–1517	Ottomans conquer the Holy Land and incorporate it into their empire
1517	Jewish immigrants, including many former conversos, flock to the city of Safed in the Galilee
	Martin Luther said to have posted his *95 Theses* on the door of the Castle Church of Wittemberg; with this, Luther challenged the Catholic Church's teachings on penance, its sale of indulgences, and even the authority of the pope
1517–1518	In Venice, the Christian printer Daniel Bomberg prints a "rabbinic Bible" (the Hebrew text together with its classical Aramaic translation and the most influential rabbinic commentaries on the page margins)
1519–1556	Reign of Holy Roman Emperor Charles V
1520	The Christian printer Daniel Bomberg produces the first complete, printed edition of the Talmud
1520s	Shlomo ibn Verga writes his chronicle *Shevet Yehudah*
1523	Martin Luther writes "That Jesus Christ Was Born a Jew"
1529	Ottomans besiege Vienna but fail to capture it
1534–1572	Life of Isaac Luria, known as *ha-Ari*
1536	Portuguese Inquisition established
1541	Jews expelled from Naples after it comes under Spanish domination
1543	Martin Luther writes "Concerning the Jews and Their Lies"
1553	Samuel Usque publishes his "Consolation for the Tribulations of Israel" in Ferrara
1555	Joseph and Gracia Mendes, former conversos, at this point living openly as Jews in Istanbul, try to organize an Ottoman boycott of the Italian port of Ancona in response to the persecution of conversos
	Pope Paul IV issues a bull called *Cum nimis absurdum*, which marks a worsening in relations between the Church and the Jews
	Ghetto established in Rome
	The Church issues a decree condemning the Talmud as blasphemous
1565	*Shulhan Arukh* first printed in Venice
1569	Spanish crown establishes inquisition in Lima and Mexico City
1570	Death of Safed kabbalist Moses Cordovero
1571	Jewish populations of Florence and Siena restricted to ghettos
1578	Death of Azariah de' Rossi, author of *Me'or Einayim*
1592	David Gans publishes *Tsemah David* in Prague
1618	Correspondence of Sara Coppio Sullam of Venice with the Italian monk Ansaldo Cebà of Genoa
1648	Death of Venetian rabbi Leone de Modena
1683	Ottomans besiege Vienna but are repulsed

New Worlds, East and West (Chapter 9)

1334	Charter by the Polish king Casmir the Great grants residential and economic rights to Jews
1386–1572	Jagiellonian dynasty rules in Poland
1525–1527	David Reuveni, claiming to hail from the kingdom of the lost tribes of Israel, is received by Pope Clement VII and the king of Portugal
1527	Warsaw obtains privilege *de non tolerandis Judaeis* from the king of Poland, allowing the city to bar Jews from living in its borders
1539	King Sigismund I grants to the nobles authority over the Jews living in their localities
1569	Creation of the Polish–Lithuanian Commonwealth with the Union of Lublin

1572	Death of Moses Isserles of Cracow ("Rema")
Mid-16th century to 1764	Council of Four Lands (*va'ad arba' aratsot*) exists as a central institution of Jewish self-government in Poland
1570s	Moses Isserles publishes edition of Joseph Karo's *Shulhan Arukh* with glosses for Ashkenazi customs, in Cracow
1593	Grand Duke of Tuscany, Ferdinand I, grants charter that in effect allows former conversos to settle in Livorno and Pisa
Late-16th century	Jacob ben Isaac Ashkenazi of Yanov writes Yiddish rendering of the Pentateuch, called *Tsenerene*
1609	Moses Altaras publishes abridged Spanish-language version of the *Shulhan Arukh,* entitled *Libro de mantenimiento de la alma* (*Maintenance of the Soul*), in Venice
1618	Uriel da Costa is excommunicated by the Hamburg Jewish community
1618–1648	Thirty Years' War ravages Central Europe, ending with Peace of Westphalia
1620	The Bohemian Protestants' rebellion is crushed and Prague, with the exception of the Jewish quarter, is pillaged by imperial troops
1639	Synagogue established in township of Joden Savanne ("Jews' Savannah") in Surinam
1648	Chmielnicki massacres sweep through Ukraine
1649	Ashkenazim of Amsterdam establish their first synagogue in the city
1650s onward	Rise to prominence of "court Jews" (*Hofjuden*)
1654	First Jews to establish a permanent presence in North America arrive in the Dutch colony of New Amsterdam (later New York)
1655	Menasseh ben Israel publishes pamphlet to persuade Oliver Cromwell to readmit the Jews to England
1656	The Amsterdam Jewish community excommunicates Spinoza
1665	Shabbatai Zvi (1626–1676) of Izmir is declared to be the messiah by Nathan of Gaza, a young Jewish mystic
1666	Shabbatai Zvi converts to Islam
1670	Expulsion of Jews from Vienna; many move to Berlin
	Spinoza publishes his Tractatus theologico-politicus
1675	An eastern European Jew, Shabbatai Bass, visits Amsterdam and praises the curriculum of the Ets Hayim academy established by the Portuguese Jewish community
1683	Death of Nathan Neta Hanover, chronicler of Chmielnicki massacres
	Simone Luzzatto publishes "Discourse on the State of the Jews" in Venice
1689	Glickl of Hameln begins writing her memoir

The Age of Emanciportion (Chapter 10)

1714	John Toland publishes the earliest call for Jewish emancipation, a tract called "Reasons for Naturalizing the Jews in Great Britain and Ireland on the Same Foot with All Nations"
1740	The Plantation Act grants naturalization to foreign Protestants and Jews throughout the British Empire; Jews living in the American colonies gain full array of civil liberties—except in Maryland and New Hampshire, where bans on holding public office persist until 1826 and 1877, respectively
1759	Jews first settle in Canada
1768	Pressure from the Church and lower gentry leads the Polish parliament to forbid Jews from keeping inns and taverns without the consent of municipal authorities
1772	First Polish Partition
1781	Christian Wilhelm Dohm, a Prussian bureaucrat, publishes *On the Civic Improvement of the Jews*
1782	Austrian Emperor Joseph II issues Edict of Toleration
	Naftali Herz Wessely published *Divrei shalom ve-emet* (*Words of Peace and Truth*)
1785	Abbé Grégoire publishes "An Essay on the Physical, Moral, and Political Regeneration of the Jews"
1788	Jews first settle in Australia; at least eight in number, they are among the first group of convicts shipped to Botany Bay (Sydney)
1789	French Revolution begins
1790	On January 28, the French National Assembly emancipates the Sephardim
1791	On September 28, the French National Assembly emancipates the Ashkenazim
1793	Second Polish Partition
1795	Third Polish Partition
1797	Italian Jews are first emancipated by Napoleonic forces
1799	Napoleon seizes power as First Consul of France

1804	The first basic law concerning Jews in Russia is introduced in the form of a "Statute Concerning the Organization of the Jews"
1806	On July 29, Napoleon convenes Assembly of Jewish Notables and addresses series of questions to it
1807	Napoleon convenes "Grand Sanhedrin" in Paris
1808	Napoleon establishes Consistory, to represent Jews to the central government in Paris
	Napoleon issues "Infamous Decrees" in Alsace, limiting Jews' residence rights there and suspending for ten years payment of debts owed to them
1812	Jews are declared "natives and citizens of the Prussian state," but their emancipation is rescinded in 1815
1815	Congress of Vienna
1819	Rahel Levin converts to Protestantism in order to marry Karl August Varnhagen, a minor Prussian diplomat
	Anti-Jewish "Hep Hep" riots sweep across Germany
1822	Abraham Mendelssohn, son of Moses Mendelssohn, and his wife convert to Lutheranism
1827	Tsar Nicholas I introduces conscription policy under which a disproportionate number of underage Jewish child recruits (called "cantonists") are pressed into military service; the policy lasts until 1855
1830	Bill seeking to grant Jews the right to hold office is passed by the English House of Commons but rejected by the House of Lords
1831	Judaism accorded complete equality with Christianity in France, following the restoration of the Bourbon monarchy to the throne
1832	Jews in Canada allowed to take seats in parliament
1833	A second bill seeking to grant Jews the right to hold office is passed by the English House of Commons but rejected by the House of Lords
	Jews are allowed to practice as barristers in England
1835	Tsar Nicholas I formally establishes the Pale of Settlement, reaffirming residence restrictions on Jews established by Catherine
1839	*Tanzimat* ("reforms") in the Ottoman Empire imply equality for religious minorities
1845	The Municipal Relief Act allows Jews to take up municipal offices
1854	Jews permitted to study at Oxford
1856	Jews permitted to study at Cambridge
	Reform Decree explicitly grants equality to Jews and Christians in the Ottoman Empire
1858	After being allowed to take a nondenominational oath, Lionel de Rothschild becomes England's first Jewish member of parliament
1869	New citizenship law defines Ottoman citizens as all subjects of the sultan, irrespective of religion
1871	Following the unification of Germany, Jews are emancipated, although positions in the upper bureaucracy and officer corps remain closed to them until the Weimar Republic
1881	After the assassination of Tsar Alexander II, Alexander III sets out to thwart the integration of Jews into Russian society, especially limiting their entry into higher education and the professional elite
1902	In Italy, Giuseppe Ottolenghi becomes the first Jew to serve as minister of war in a European country
1910	In Italy, Luigi Luzzatti becomes the first Jew to serve as prime minister of a European country
1917	On April 2, the provisional government removes all laws discriminating against Jews and other religious or national minorities in Russia

Innovations in Modern Jewish Culture (Chapter 11)

1700–1760	Life of Israel ben Eliezer, the Ba'al Shem Tov
1720–1797	Life of Rabbi Eliyahu ben Shlomo Zalman, the Gaon of Vilna
1730	In Istanbul, Jacob Huli publishes the first volume of a biblical commentary written in Ladino, *Me'am Lo'ez*
1739–1744	Abraham Asa translates the Bible into Ladino
1740–1810	Life of Rabbi Baruch Schick of Shklov
1745–1813	Life of Rabbi Shneur Zalman of Lyady
1753–1800	Life of Solomon Maimon
1758	Moses Mendelssohn begins his publishing career with the Hebrew weekly *Kohelet Musar* (*The Moralist*)
1759	Jacob Frank and 500 of his followers convert to Catholicism in Poland
1772	Vilna Gaon delivers writ of excommunication (*herem*) against Hasidim
1772–1811	Life of Rabbi Nachman of Bratslav
1772	Death of Dov Ber of Mezerich

1778	Moses Mendelssohn begins the publication of a German translation of the Bible (in Hebrew characters), as well as an accompanying Hebrew commentary
	David Moses Attias publishes Guerta de Oro (Garden of Gold), one of the first pieces of Ladino Haskalah literature
	Jewish Free School opens in Berlin
1779	Gotthold Ephraim Lessing publishes his play *Nathan the Wise*
1780	First book outlining Hasidic teachings, Rabbi Ya'akov Yosef of Polonoy's *Toledot Ya'akov Yosef* (*The Story of Ya'acov Yosef*) appears
1783	Death of Ya'akov Yosef of Polonoy
	Moses Mendelssohn publishes *Jerusalem*
1784–1811	The Hebrew-language Haskalah journal *Ha-meassef* (*The Gatherer*) appears sporadically
1791	Berr Isaac Berr exhorts Alsatian Jews to learn French
1792	Saul Ascher publishes *Leviathan*
1796	Shneur Zalman of Lyady publishes *Likutei Amarim* (*Collected Sayings*). Popularly known as the *Tanya*, it is a systematic theology and guide to Hasidic belief and practice
1797–1856	Life of Heinrich Heine
1803	Rabbi Hayim of Volozhin establishes Volozhin yeshiva
1806	First issue of *Sulamith* appears in Berlin
1810–1883	Life of Rabbi Israel Salanter, founder of the *Musar* movement
1812	David Friedländer publishes pamphlet calling for Jewish religious reform
1815	*Shivhei ha-BeShT* (*In Praise of the Ba'al Shem Tov*) published
1817	Israel Jacobsen's Reform Temple is forced to close by the Prussian government
1818	The New Israelite Temple Association founds the Hamburg Temple; Rabbi Moses Sofer (the "Hatam Sofer") spearheads a campaign against it
1819	Joseph Perl publishes a Haskalah satire, *Megaleh Temirin* (*Revealer of Secrets*), aimed at the Hasidim
	Society for Culture and the Scientific Study of Judaism founded in Berlin
1820	Isaac Marcus Jost (1793–1860) publishes the first of his nine-volume *History of the Israelites from the Maccabean Period to Our Own Day*
1828	Isaac Ber Levinsohn publishes Teudah be-Yisrael (Testimony in Israel)
1832	Leopold Zunz publishes *Sermons of the Jews*
1836	Samson Raphael Hirsch publishes *Nineteen Letters on Judaism*
1845	At the rabbinic conference, Abraham Geiger, affiliated with Reform, is opposed by Zacharias Frankel, the founder of Positive-Historical Judaism
1851	In Eisenstadt, Hungary, Rabbi Esriel Hildesheimer opens the first yeshiva in the modern world that includes the teaching of secular subjects
	Nahman Kochmal's *Guide for the Perplexed of Our Time* published
1853	Abraham Mapu publishes first Hebrew novel, *Love of Zion*
1853–1876	Heinrich Graetz publishes eleven-volume *History of the Jews*
1854	Jewish Theological Seminary founded in Breslau
1859	Zacharias Frankel publishes *Darkhe ha-Mishnah* (*The Paths of the Mishnah*)
1859–1916	Life of Sholem Rabinowitz, better known as Sholem Aleichem
1863	Sholem Yankev Abramovitch, better known as Mendele Moykher Sforim (Mendele the Bookseller), founds the first successful Yiddish weekly, *Kol Mevasser* (*The Herald*) in Odessa
1864	Rabbi Akiba Joseph Schlesinger publishes *Lev ha-ivri* (*The Heart of the Hebrew*)
1866	Judah Leib Gordon publishes "Awake My People!"
1868	Peretz Smolenskin founds the journal *Ha-shahar* (*The Dawn*)
1887	Ludwik Lazar Zamenhof, a Bialystok Jew, publishes first book in Esperanto, a language invented by him
1897	In the Russian census, 97 percent of Jewish respondents claim Yiddish as their mother tongue
1905	Rabbi Isaac Jacob Reines opens eastern Europe's first modern yeshiva in the town of Lida

Jews and Politics (Chapter 12)

1833	The phrase "Jewish Question" first appears in public discourse in France
1837	*Allgemeine Zeitung des Judenthums* (*Universal Newspaper for Judaism*) founded in Germany

1840	Damascus Affair
	Archives Israelite de France first published in France
1841	*Jewish Chronicle* founded in England
1842–1921	Life of the radical Austrian antisemite George von Schönerer
1843	Bruno Bauer publishes an essay on "The Jewish Question," popularizing the term
1845	Alphonse Toussenel publishes *The Jews: Kings of the Epoch*
1850	Richard Wagner publishes *Judaism in Music*
1856–1927	Life of Ahad Ha'am
1858	Mortara Affair
1860	Alliance Israélite Universelle founded
1860–1904	Life of Theodor Herzl
1861	Tsar Alexander II emancipates the serfs
1862	Moses Hess publishes *Rome and Jerusalem*
1863	Ferdinand Lassalle, a German Jew, founds the General German Workers Association
1870–1871	Franco-Prussian War ends in Prussian victory and the creation of the German Empire
1870	Crémieux Decree bestows French citizenship on Algerian Jews
1873	Economic depression in Germany after stock market crash
1874	United Hebrew Charities founded in the United States
1878	The Christian Social Workers Party, headed by Adolf Stöcker, emerges in Berlin as Europe's first antisemitic political party
1879	A large number of antisemitic groups coalesce into the Berlin Movement
	Wilhelm Marr publishes *The Victory of the Jews Over the Germans, Considered from a Non-Religious Point of View*
1880–1881	Antisemite's Petition is presented to German Chancellor Bismarck
1881	Karl Eugen Duehring publishes *The Jewish Question as a Racial, Moral and Cultural Question*
	Hebrew Immigrant Aid Society founded in the United States
	On March 1, Tsar Alexander II is assassinated by the terrorist group People's Will; among the plotters is a Jewish woman
1881–1883	Beginning in mid-April, anti-Jewish riots (pogroms) sweep through southern Russia
1881–1882	*Hibbat Tsiyon* (*Love of Zion*) movement founded
1882	First International Antisemites' Congress held in Berlin
1886	Edouard Drumont publishes *Jewish France*
1892	The Conservative Party in the German Empire adopts the antisemitic Tivoli Program
1893	Central Union of German Citizens of the Jewish Faith founded
1894	A Jewish captain in the French army, Alfred Dreyfus, is falsely accused of spying for Germany
1896	Theodor Herzl publishes *The Jewish State: Attempt at a Modern Solution of the Jewish Question*
1896–1898	The Russian secret police in Paris concocts an antisemitic forgery entitled *The Protocols of the Elders of Zion*
1897	After being elected for a third time as mayor of Vienna, the antisemite Karl Lueger takes office; his accession to mayor had twice been vetoed by Emperor Franz Josef
	First Zionist Congress takes place in Basel
	The Bund (General Association of Jewish Workers in Russia, Poland, and Lithuania) is founded in Vilna
1898	Emile Zola publishes "J'accuse!" charging the French army with a cover-up in the wrongful conviction of Alfred Dreyfus
1899	Houston Stewart Chamberlain publishes Foundations of the Nineteenth Century
	Alfred Dreyfus is given a presidential pardon when the real identity of the traitor is revealed; due to public anger Dreyfus is not fully exonerated until 1906
1902	Religious Zionist party, Mizrahi, founded
1903	Kishinev pogrom
	Uganda Proposal
1904	The occultist and racist Lanz von Liebenfels publishes *Theozoology,* which advocates sterilization of the "sick" and "lower races"
1905	France officially enacts the separation of church and state
	Another wave of pogroms in Russia, including in Kishinev
1906	Alfred Dreyfus is fully exonerated of the charge of treason and restored to his former military rank

1908–1913	Adolf Hitler lives in Vienna, where it is thought he is deeply influenced by the prevailing antisemitic political culture
1908	Antisemitic and occultist Guido von List Society founded in Vienna
1910	First Jewish agricultural collective founded in Degania
1911	Ritual murder charge against Mendel Beilis in Kiev
	Triangle Shirtwaist Factory fire in New York
1913	Anti-Defamation League established in the United States

World War I and its Aftermath (Chapter 13)

1914	World War I erupts on August 1
1916	Prussian War Ministry conducts "Jew Count"
1917	Russian Revolution
	Balfour Declaration
1917–1921	As many as 60,000 Jews killed in anti-Jewish violence in Ukraine
1918	World War I ends on November 11
	On November 7, Kurt Eisner declares Bavaria a socialist republic
1919	Béla Kun leads Communist Revolution in Hungary
1919–1920	"White Terror" campaign in Hungary targets Jews; Admiral Nicholas Horthy comes to power
1920	Lehrhaus established by Franz Rosenzweig in Frankfurt
	Histadrut founded
1921	*Haganah* founded in Palestine after Arab riots
1922	German Jewish industrialist Walter Rathenau becomes foreign minister of the Weimar Republic
1923	Jewish Agency founded
1925	YIVO (Institute for Jewish Research) founded in Vilna
	Ze'ev Jabotinsky forms the World Union of Zionist Revisionists
1926	Shlomo Shvartsbard, a pogrom refugee, assassinates Ukrainian minister of defense, Semion Petlura in Paris
	Military coup d'état by Marshal Josef Pilsudski in Poland
1927	The fascist and antisemitic Iron Guard party is founded in Romania
1928	Stalin implements "Five Year Plan" in the Soviet Union
1929	In August, Arab riots target Jews in Jerusalem, Haifa, Jaffa, Tel Aviv, and Hebron; overall, 133 are killed; the British army kills 116 Arabs in its suppression of the riots
1930	White Paper by English Colonial Secretary Lord Passfield recommends curtailing Jewish immigration and land purchases in Palestine
1934	Birobidzhan is declared a Jewish Autonomous Region
1934–1939	Great Purge in the Soviet Union
1936–1939	Arab Revolt in Palestine
1937	*Irgun Tzvai Le'umi* (The National Military Organization) founded in Palestine
	British Peel Commission recommends a partition of Palestine into Jewish and Arab states; it is accepted by the Zionists and rejected by the Palestinian Arab leadership

The Holocaust (Chapter 14)

1920	Nazi Party's Twenty-Five Point Program makes removal of Jews from German public life a central plank of its platform
1925	Hitler publishes *Mein Kampf*
1933	January 30: Adolf Hitler, as head of the single largest party in the Reichstag is appointed chancellor
	March 21: First concentration camp is established at Dachau
	April 1: Boycott of Jewish shops announced
	April 7: "Law for the Reestablishment of the Professional Civil Service" bars Jews from employment
	Jews banned from most professions
	Medical schools closed to Jews (but only in 1938 are doctors thrown out completely)
	April 25: Laws against the "overcrowding" of German schools and universities cap Jewish attendance at 5 percent
	May 10: Nazis organize book burnings

	June 16: *Kulturbund* established
	July 14: Law against creation of new political parties is passed
	August: Jews are banned from public swimming pools
	September: Nazis set up *Reichsvertretung der deutschen Juden* (Reich Representation of German Jews) to represent German Jewry to the government
	September: Nazis sign Concordat with Vatican
1934	June 30: Purge of Nazi storm troopers (SA), known as the Night of the Long Knives
1935	September and November: Nuremberg Laws
1934–1938	Stalin stages show trials, executes victims of political purges, and sends many to slave labor camps in the Soviet Union
1935–1937	"Aryanization" of Jewish property in Germany
1936–1939	Spanish Civil War
1936	March 7: Wehrmacht marches into Rhineland
1937	July: "Degenerate Art" exhibition opens in Munich
1938	March 12: Germany annexes Austria (Anschluss)
	July 6–13: Evian Conference
	August: Jews forced to adopt "Israel" and "Sarah" as middle names
	September 27: In the Munich Crisis, the Western powers capitulate to Hitler's demands on Czechoslovakia
	October: Germany gets the Sudetenland
	A red letter "J" is stamped into German Jews' passports (at the suggestion of Swiss border police)
	November 7: Hershel Grynszpan, whose parents had been expelled from Germany, assassinates German diplomat Ernst vom Rath
	November 9–10: Kristallnacht throughout the Reich
	Near total exclusion of Jews from Germany economy and society
1939	January 30: Hitler makes speech in Reichstag threatening the destruction of Jewry
	March 15: Wehrmacht enters Prague
	August 23: Molotov-Ribbentrop Pact of non-aggression between the Soviet Union and Germany
	September 1: Germans invade Poland
	September 3: France and Britain declare war on Germany
1940	Nazis set up "ghettos" in Eastern European cities
	April–June: Nazis conquer Denmark, Norway, France, Belgium, Luxembourg, and Holland
1941	Nazis conquer Yugoslavia and Greece
	Mass murder of European Jewry commences
1941	June 22: Beginning of German campaign against the Soviet Union (Operation Barbarossa)
1941–1942	Einsatzgruppen kill as many as 1.4 million Jews in the occupied USSR
	December 7: Pearl Harbor
	December 11: Germany declares war on United States
1942	January 20: Wannsee Conference
1942–1944	Chelmno, Auschwitz, Belzec, Sobibor, Majdanek, Treblinka in full operation
1943	April–May: Warsaw ghetto uprising
	October: Danish resistance smuggles Jews of Denmark to Sweden
1944	June 6: D-Day: Normandy Invasion
1945	May 9: End of WWII in Europe

The Jews After 1945 (Chapter 15)

1941	June 1–2: An anti-Jewish pogrom (*Farhud*) sweeps through Baghdad
1944	Militant Zionist group, Lehi, assassinates Britain's Minister of State for the Middle East, Lord Moyne
1945	November: Anti-Jewish pogroms in Libya
1945–1948	The *Brihah* ("Flight") organization smuggles more than 100,000 Jews from displaced persons (DP) camps to Palestine
1946	June–July: British carry out Operation Black Sabbath against Jewish militias in Palestine
	July: The Irgun blows up the King David Hotel, British military and administrative headquarters, killing 91
	July 4: Anti-Jewish pogrom in Kielce, Poland

1947	February: Britain hands over jurisdiction of Palestine to the United Nations (UN)
	Pogrom in Aleppo, Syria
	November 29: The UN General Assembly approves the Peel Commission plan for partition
1948	May 14: Ben Gurion declares the independence and establishment of the State of Israel
	May 15: Syrian, Lebanese, Egyptian, Transjordanian, and Iraqi troops invade the newly established country
	June 11–July 8: A UN-brokered truce between Israel and the Arab states holds until it is broken by an Egyptian attack
	July: Israeli offensives aim to secure communication between Tel Aviv and Jerusalem; Lydda (today, Lod) and Ramle are captured and their Arab populations expelled
	July 18–October 15: Second UN-brokered truce is observed
1948–1949	May 1948–December 1949: Operation Magic Carpet brings 49,000 Yemenite Jews to Israel
	October 15–July 1949: Israel launches several successful military operations to drive out Arab armies and secure the borders of the state
1949	Wave of Jewish cemetery desecrations in Germany
	Israel signs armistice agreements with Egypt, Transjordan (later Jordan), Syria, and Lebanon; resulting borders give Israel an area 20 percent larger than the one proposed in the Partition Plan
	January 25: The Labor Party wins the first elections held in Israel
	In Syria, banks are instructed to freeze Jewish assets and nearly all Jewish civil servants are dismissed from their jobs
	August: Egypt closes the Suez Canal to Israeli shipping
1950–1951	Operation Ezra and Nehemia airlifts 100,000 Jews from Iraq to Israel
1952	Antisemitic show trials of Rudolf Slánský and others in Czechoslovakia
1953	In the United States, Ethel and Julius Rosenberg are executed for espionage on behalf of the Soviet Union
	Stalin accuses Soviet Jewish physicians of trying to poison him, claiming to have uncovered a "Doctors' Plot"
1956	Sinai Campaign
1957	Foehrenwald, southwest of Munich, is the last DP camp to close
1961	Trial of Adolf Eichmann begins
1964	Palestine Liberation Organization (PLO) founded
	Andrew Goodman and Michael Schwerner, two Jewish men from New York, together with James Chaney, an African American, are murdered in Mississippi while investigating the bombing of black churches
1967	June: Israel's victory in the Six-Day War leaves it in control of the West Bank, Gaza Strip, Golan Heights, and Sinai Peninsula
	August: At Khartoum, eight Arab nations declare that there will be "no peace with Israel; no negotiations with Israel; no recognition of Israel"
1968	Jewish party functionaries are rounded up in Poland
1968–1970	War of Attrition between Egypt and Israel
1972	Eleven Israeli athletes are murdered at the Munich Olympic Games by Palestinian terrorists
1973	Yom Kippur War
1975	UN General Assembly passes a resolution condemning Zionism as "a form of racism"
1976	Israel frees hostages taken by Palestinian and German hijackers at Entebbe airport in Uganda
1977	Menahem Begin, head of the Right-wing Likud Party, wins the elections in Israel
1979	A peace treaty is signed between Egypt and Israel
1980	Israel formally annexes East Jerusalem
1981	Israeli air force destroys Iraqi nuclear reactor Osiraq
1982	Israeli Prime Minister Menahem Begin and Minister of Defense Ariel Sharon launch Operation Peace in Galilee, attacking PLO bases in Lebanon
	September 16–18: Christian Lebanese militia kill as many as 2,300 civilians in the Palestinian refugee camps at Sabra and Shatila
1985	Amy Eilberg becomes the first woman to graduate with rabbinical ordination from the Conservative movement's Jewish Theological Seminary
1987	*Intifada* breaks out in the occupied territories
1989	Fall of the Berlin Wall and end of Communist rule in eastern Europe
1990	As a result of the Soviet Union's collapse, thousands of Soviet Jews immigrate to Israel, North America, Europe, Australia, and other parts of the world
	Iraqi Scud missiles hit Tel Aviv during the first Gulf War

1993	Israel signs Oslo Accords with the PLO
1994	Israel signs peace accord with Jordan
	Israeli Prime Minister Yitzhak Rabin, Israeli Foreign Minister Shimon Peres, and PLO Chairman Yasser Arafat share the Nobel Peace Prize "for their efforts to create peace in the Middle East"
	The building of the Asociación Mutual Israelita Argentina (Argentine Jewish Mutual Association, or AMIA) in Buenos Aires is bombed by Hezbollah terrorists, killing 85 people
	Lauder–Morasha Jewish Day School opens in Warsaw
1995	Prime Minister Yitzhak Rabin is assassinated by an Israeli Right-wing extremist, Yigal Amir
2000	On May 24, Israel withdraws its last troops from southern Lebanon under Prime Minister Ehud Barak
	In late September, the second *intifada* erupts
2005	Israel evacuates its settlements and outposts in the Gaza Strip under Prime Minister Ariel Sharon's "Disengagement Plan"
2006	In early January, Israeli Prime Minister Ariel Sharon suffers a stroke that renders him comatose; he is succeeded by Ehud Olmert
	Second Lebanon War, fought mainly between Israel and Hezbollah from July 12 until August 14
	On November 9, the new Ohel Jakob synagogue and a Jewish community center open in Munich on the site of the original Ohel Jakob synagogue destroyed on Kristallnacht in 1938

Glossary

Abbassid dynasty: Based in Baghdad, replaced the Umayyad dynasty as rulers of an increasingly fragmented Islamic world, persisting until 1258.

Abbé Grégoire (1750–1831): Henri Grégoire, French Catholic bishop who became a revolutionary leader. Before the revolution, he penned "An Essay on the Physical, Moral, and Political Regeneration of the Jews" (*see entry*).

Abner of Burgos (1270–c. 1348): Jewish convert to Christianity who became an active missionary in Spain.

Abraham: According to the Bible, an important ancestor of the Israelites, whose life story is narrated in Genesis 11:29–25:8, and who began a covenantal relationship with the God of the Bible after following His command to move from Mesopotamia to Canaan. Jews, Christians, and Muslims all claim Abraham as their patriarch.

Abraham ibn Daud (1110–1180): Also known by the Hebrew acronym of his name, RaBaD I, a Spanish Jewish philosopher and historian.

Abraham ibn Ezra (1089–1164): Author of the first biblical commentary in the Islamic world to be written in Hebrew rather than in Arabic; he tried to derive the contextual meaning of the Bible independent of earlier midrashic understandings (*see* Midrash).

Abramovitch, Sholem Yakov (1836–1917): Yiddish author, known by his popular pseudonym, Mendele Moykher Sforim (Yiddish/Hebrew for "Mendele the Bookseller").

Abulafia, Abraham (c. 1240–1291): A wandering mystic who traveled from Spain to Palestine to Greece and Italy. Sentenced to death in Rome for charging the Pope with responsibility for Jewish suffering, he escaped with his life when the Pope subsequently died. Abulafia developed a more practical Kabbalah (*see entry*) than the speculative tradition of the Spanish mystics, focusing on mystical techniques that would allow the individual to achieve ecstatic union with God.

Achaemenid dynasty: Dynasty that lasted from 559 to 330 BCE and ruled the Persian Empire that controlled much of the Middle East and Central Asia at its height. It was founded by Cyrus II (*see entry*), who permitted the Jewish exiles to return to Judah and begin the restoration of the destroyed Temple.

Agnon, Shmuel Yosef (1884–1970): Hebrew author and 1966 Nobel Laureate.

Agrarian League: A late-nineteenth-century German antisemitic political party and lobby group advocating on behalf of agrarian interest.

Agrippa I: Grandson of Herod (*see entry*) and popular but short-lived ruler of Judea from 37–44 CE.

Agudes Yisroel: Political arm that represented all branches of Orthodoxy in the Zionist Organization, founded in 1912.

Agunah: (pl. *agunot*) Literally, an "anchored" or "chained" woman. In Jewish law, a wife who is tied to her marriage and unable to remarry because her husband has not given her a *get* (*see entry*)—either because he is deliberately trying to avoid paying the sum specified in the *ketubbah* (*see entry*) or because he went missing without his death having been verified.

Ahad Ha'am (1856–1927): Hebrew for "One of the People." Pseudonym of the cultural Zionist Asher Ginsberg.

Ahasueres: In the Book of Esther, the Persian king who is almost deceived by his courtier, Haman, into destroying the Jewish people.

Akiba, Rabbi (ca. 50–ca.135 AD): One of the most important rabbinic sages from the tannaitic period, martyred in the period of the Bar Kochba Revolt.

Al-Aqsa Masjid: Arabic for "the farthest mosque." The mosque with the silver-colored dome located on the Temple Mount, or *Haram al-Sharif* ("Noble Sanctuary," the term used by Muslims).

Alconstantini: Family of Jewish courtiers active in Aragón during the thirteenth century.

Alexander I: Tsar of Russia from 1801–1825.

Alexander the Great: Greek ruler, born 356 BCE, who conquered the Persian Empire and through his conquests of the Near East initiated the Hellenistic age, which lasted until Rome rose to dominance in the first century BCE. Alexander died in 323 BCE.

Aliyah: Hebrew for "ascent." Term used to denote immigration to the Land of Israel. **First Aliyah** (1881–1904): First settlement efforts by *Hibbat Tsiyon* in Palestine. **Second Aliyah** (1903–1914): Immigration of about 35,000 Jews to Palestine between 1903 and 1914. **Third Aliyah** (1919–1923): Immigration of about 35,000 Jews to

Palestine, mostly from Ukraine and Russia. Known for its pioneer ethos. **Fourth Aliyah (1924–1929):** Immigration of about 67,000 Jews to Palestine. Most were middle-class shopkeepers and artisans fleeing the interwar economic crisis and discrimination in Poland. **Fifth Aliyah (1929–1939):** Immigration of about 250,000 Jews to Palestine. Most of them were Jews fleeing Germany and Austria after Hitler's rise to power; over half went to Tel Aviv.

Aljama: See Kahal.

Alkalai, Yehuda (1798–1878): Rabbi from Sarajevo who called on Jews to return to the Land of Israel in order to bring about the divine salvation of the Jewish people.

Alliance Israélite Universelle: International organization founded by French Jews in 1860 to represent Jewish interests and concerns among Middle Eastern and Balkan Jews.

Almosnino, Moses: Renowned rabbi of Ottoman Salonika (d. ca. 1580) who took part in a mission to the Sultan to negotiate better economic conditions for the Jews of his city.

Alphabet: The new kind of writing system invented in the Middle Bronze Age (2000–1500 BCE), perhaps in Canaan. Named after the system's first two letters, *aleph* and *bet,* it expressed the basic sounds of a language using a small number of characters.

Amarna Letters: Collection of Egyptian documents, discovered at el-Amarna in 1887, which provide a glimpse into the difficulties that the Egyptians had ruling Canaan's city states. They refer, among other things, to a people called "Habiru" (*see separate entry*).

Amenhotep IV: Pharaoh of Egypt (1352–1336 BCE) who, departing from traditional Egyptian religion, declared the sun god Aten the only true god and renamed himself Akhnaten in his honor. His religious innovation is seen by some scholars as an antecedent to Israelite monotheism.

Amida: From the Hebrew for "standing." A sequence of nineteen petitionary prayers uttered while standing, which makes up the heart of every prayer service.

Amoraim: Generations of rabbinic sages who lived in the period after the redaction of the Mishnah and whose views are recorded in the Talmud.

Amorites: A Mesopotamian people named in ancient Near Eastern sources, once thought by scholars to be connected to Abraham's origins.

Amram (d. 875): A Gaonic leader and head of the Talmudic academy at Sura. Author of many responsa (*see entry*) and of the first *siddur* (*see entry*).

Anan ben David: A formative figure in the development of Karaite ideology, to whom his rabbinic opponents attributed the battle cry "Abandon the words of the Mishnah and of the Talmud"—a reflection of the Karaite rejection of Oral Torah and the rabbis in favor of the Written Torah as the sole source of legal authority. Most of Anan's polemical activity took place in the second half of the eighth century.

Ancona: An Adriatic port city in Italy that was the target of an attempted boycott by Joseph and Gracia Mendes (*see* Doña Gracia Mendes) in 1555, when the Counter-Reformation Pope Paul IV (*see entry*) initiated a crackdown on *conversos* (*see entry*) secretly practicing Judaism in his lands. Their effort failed.

An Essay on the Physical, Moral, and Political Regeneration of the Jews: Essay by Abbé Grégoire (*see entry*), published in 1785, for a contest by the Royal Academy of Metz soliciting responses to the question "Are there possibilities of making the Jews more useful and happier in France?"

Anielewicz, Mordechai (1919–1943): Commander of the Jewish Fighting Organization, consisting of about 1,000 Zionist and Bundist youth movement members, who fought in the Warsaw Ghetto Uprising (*see entry*).

Anschluss **(German, "union"):** The annexation of Austria by Nazi Germany in 1938.

Anti-Defamation League: American organization established in 1913 to protect Jewish civil and social equality and to fight antisemitism.

Antiochus III "the Great": Seleucid ruler (r. 223–187 BCE) who conquered Judea from the Ptolemaic kingdom in 202–200 BCE. He followed the policy of earlier rulers in allowing the Jews to live according to their ancestral customs.

Antiochus IV Epiphanes: Seleucid ruler (r. 175–164 BCE) who adopted a hostile stance toward the Jewish religion, looting and desecrating the Temple and, later, banning circumcision, Sabbath and Festival observance, and the Torah itself. The rule of Antiochus IV caused many Jews in Judea to see rebellion against the empire as the only way to preserve their way of life.

Antisemite's Petition: A petition presented to the German Chancellor, Otto von Bismarck, in 1880–1881, which demanded the dismissal of Jews from positions in government, the judiciary, and higher education, as well as myriad other discriminatory measures. It was signed by a quarter of a million people, but Bismarck refused to accept it.

Apocrypha: Of Greek origin, the term used to refer to Jewish texts from the Second Temple period not included in the Jewish or Protestant biblical canons but which are included in the Catholic biblical canon, in which context they are referred to as the deuterocanonical texts. Examples include Tobit and Judith.

Aramaic: A Semitic language group whose dialects were widely spoken and written in the Middle East from the twelfth century BCE until the seventh century CE, when Arabic began to replace it. Large parts of the books of Ezra and Daniel were written in Aramaic, as was much of the Talmud. Today, different dialects of Aramaic are still spoken by small Christian, Mandaean, and Jewish minority populations.

Arenda: "lease" or "rent." The *arenda* system involved the leasing of large estates by Polish lords to a Jewish lessee (*arendator*) who, in return for paying rent to the nobleman, was granted the monopoly (*see entry*) on a host of commodities and means of raising revenue.

Aristobulus: Earliest-known Jewish philosopher, who lived in Alexandria in the second century BCE. His explanations of the Bible using Greek philosophy included the earliest examples of allegorical biblical interpretation, a technique borrowed from Greek Homer scholars.

Aristotelianism: One of the great currents in medieval thought, it held that philosophy must proceed independently of supernatural sources of knowledge. In this system of thought, one must reach the truth by means of empirical observation, reasoned inference, and logical demonstration.

Ark of the Covenant: A wooden receptacle in which the tablets of the covenant were thought to have been kept during biblical times. The Ark of the Covenant has been understood as a kind of divine footstool or chariot that signaled God's presence among the Israelites.

Arlosoroff, Chaim (1899–1933): Labor Zionist who, together with David Ben-Gurion (*see entry*), made peace with the bourgeois Zionist parties.

Aryanization: Word used to refer to the transfer (under pressure) of Jewish-owned businesses to "Aryan" owners during the Third Reich; the peak period of such activity was 1935–1937.

Ascher, Saul (1767–1822): Jewish book dealer and political journalist from Berlin. Author of *Leviathan* (1792), which tried to discern an essence of Judaism by identifying what he believed were its dogmas.

Asherah: A Canaanite goddess known from Ugaritic literature, who was the female companion of El and the mother of the gods.

Ashkenazi (*or* Ashkenazic): From the Hebrew word used to describe the area of the Rhineland in Germany (*Ashkenaz*). The term initially referred to the Jews in Germany and northern France in the Middle Ages. With the migrations of Jews from the German lands eastward to Poland in the early modern period, the term came to encompass all of Yiddish-speaking Jewry and its descendants.

Assyrian Empire: The Mesopotamian Empire that began its westward expansion into Syria and Canaan in the ninth century BCE, crushing the kingdom of Israel in 722–720 BCE under Shalmaneser and his successor, Sargon II.

Augustus: The name by which Octavian became known after assuming the title of Augustus Caesar in 27 BCE (*see* Octavian).

Auschwitz: Nazi extermination camp complex located 50 kilometers west of Cracow. Three main camps were housed there: Auschwitz I (administrative offices, prisoner incarceration, medical experiments on inmates, and killing); Birkenau (death camp); and Monowitz (slave labor camp). In addition, dozens of satellite camps formed a ring around Auschwitz.

Auschwitz-Birkenau: The Nazi death camp in Auschwitz (*see entry*). Approximately one million Jews were murdered there, mostly in the gas chambers by means of Zyklon B (*see entry*).

Azariah de' Rossi (ca. 1513/1514–1578): Mantua-born physician and scholar, whose erudite work *Me'or Einayim* showcased the historical critical spirit of his time.

Baal: A Canaanite warrior god associated with fertility.

Baal Shem Tov: *See* Israel ben Eliezer.

Babi Yar: Site of the shooting on September 29–30, 1941, of 33,371 Jews from Kiev by Einsatzgruppe C (*see* Einsatzgruppen).

Babylonian Talmud: Finalized and edited between 550 and 650 CE by the Saboraim or (in a term coined by scholars) Stammaim in Babylonia, successors to the Amoraim (*see entry*), this massive work of carefully structured legal debate, biblical interpretation, and storytelling that takes the Mishnah (*see entry*) as its starting point runs more than 2.5 million words in sixty-three volumes. (Talmud *for information on the Palestinian Talmud.*)

Baeck, Rabbi Leo (1873–1956): Berlin rabbi who led the *Reichsvertretung der deutschen Juden* ("Reich Representation of German Jews"), set up by the Nazis in September 1933 as the political organization of German Jewry.

Baghdad: In addition to being the capital of the Islamic world, the city also dominated the Jewish world under the Abbassid caliphate from roughly the seventh to the eleventh centuries, when it was home to the great Talmudic academies.

Bahir: *See Sefer ha-Bahir.*

Balfour Declaration: November 1917 declaration by the British War Cabinet, which expressed support for the establishment of a national home for the Jewish people in Palestine. Named after Foreign Secretary Arthur James Balfour.

Bar Kochba Revolt: Jewish revolt that broke out in Judea in 132, led by Simon bar Kosiba, who became known as Bar Kochba ("Son of a Star") to his followers. The nickname was a reference to the messianic prophecy in Numbers 24:17: "a star shall come out of Jacob." The revolt was crushed by the Romans in a last battle at Bethar in 135, close to Jerusalem. Bar Kochba was later dubbed "Bar Koziba," from the word *kazav,* meaning "lie."

Barrios, Miguel de (1635–1701): Poet and playwright writing in Spanish, born as a converso in Spain and later active in Amsterdam.

Bassevi, Jacob (d. 1634): Important financier for the Habsburgs of the Thirty Years' War.

Bayezid II (r. 1481–1512): Sultan under whose rule many Muslims and Jews fleeing Spain came to the Ottoman Empire. Though no document has been found to support the legend that Bayezid invited Spanish Jews to settle in the sultanate, the Ottoman state was no doubt a welcoming refuge for them.

Begin, Menahem (1913–1992): Leader of the *Irgun* (*see entry*), a 2,000-strong militia in Palestine, advocating open revolt against the British in the post-WWII period. Served as prime minister of Israel, 1977–1983.

Beilis, Mendel (1874–1934): A Jewish man accused of ritual murder in Kiev in 1911.

Beinoni (Hebrew, "average"): An ordinary person, described in the *Tanya* (*see entry*) as being able to achieve union with God (*see* Devekut) through the mediation of the *tzaddik* (*see entry*).

Belzec: Nazi death camp in the Lublin district in Poland.

Ben-Gurion, David (1886–1973): First prime minister of the State of Israel.

Ben Zvi, Yitzhak (1884–1963): Scholar of Oriental Jewish communities, founder of the Jewish defense agency, Ha-Shomer, and second president of Israel.

Berdichevsky, Micha Yosef (1865–1921): Hebrew author.

Berlin Movement: A coalescence of antisemitic parties and interest groups in Berlin that came together in 1879.

Bernstein, Eduard (1850–1932): German Jewish socialist thinker.

Berr, Berr Isaac (1744–1828): Alsatian Jewish communal leader.

BeShT: *See* Israel ben Eliezer.

Betar: Militant youth league founded by Ze'ev Jabotinsky (*see entry*) in 1923. An acronym for "Brit [Covenant of] Yosef Trumpeldor" (*see entry*) and the site of a heroic last stand by Bar Kochba (*see entry*).

Bethel: Site of a sanctuary constructed by Jeroboam I in the south of the kingdom of Israel, not far from Jerusalem.

Bet midrash: Hebrew for "study house"; the central institution of rabbinic learning.

Bialik, Hayyim Nahman (1873–1934): Hebrew poet.

Biltmore Program: Statement issued at a May 1942 conference by American Zionists about the refugee problem that would follow the end of the war. The delegates officially rejected the White Paper of 1939 (*see entry*), as well as plans for partition, demanding immediate Jewish sovereignty in all of Palestine.

Birnbaum, Nathan (1864–1937): Principal ideologist of Yiddishism. He also coined the term *Zionism.*

Birobidzhan: Yiddish-speaking territory created by the Soviets on the eastern border with China. In 1934 it was officially designated as a Jewish Autonomous Region (JAR).

Bi'ur: Moses Mendelssohn's (*see entry*) commentary to the Bible published in 1778. Its proper name was *Sefer Netivot ha-shalom* (*Book of Paths to Peace*).

Black Death: An epidemic of bubonic plague and other contagious diseases that swept across Europe between 1347 and 1350. Unable to understand the medical causes of the plague, and with their hostility stoked by blood libel and host desecration accusations, many Christians came to suspect the Jews of poisoning wells out of malice and vengeance.

Black Panthers: Protest movement formed in the 1970s by *mizrahi* (*see entry*) Jews in Israel, named after the American group of the same name.

Blood libel: Medieval accusation that Jews killed Christians to use their blood to make the unleavened bread eaten during Passover and for other rituals (despite the fact that Jewish law explicitly prohibits the consumption of blood).

Bonald, Viscount Louis de (1754–1840): French counter-revolutionary philosopher and politician, who saw the French Revolution's emancipation of the Jews as a historical error, one that would result in free Jews conquering France.

Borochov, Ber (1881–1917): Yiddish linguist and theoretician of Marxist Zionism.

Brandeis, Louis (1856–1931): Distinguished American lawyer and leader of the Federation of American Zionists from 1914 to 1916, when he was appointed to the U.S. Supreme Court and dropped his formal affiliation, though not sympathy, with the organization.

Brenner, Yosef Chaim (1881–1921): Hebrew author.

Buber, Martin (1878–1965): German Jewish philosopher and Zionist.

Bund: Short for *Algemayne Bund fun Yidishe Arbeter in Rusland, Poyln un Lite* (General Association of Jewish Workers in Russia, Poland and Lithuania), founded in Vilna in 1897.

Byzantine Empire: The name given to the eastern half of the Roman Empire, beginning in 330, when Constantine moved his capital to the newly named Constantinople (*formerly* Byzantium; *today* Istanbul). The empire's "orthodox" Greek-based Christianity developed quite differently from the "Catholic" Latin-based Christianity of the Roman west. The Byzantine Empire lasted until 1453, when it was conquered by the Ottoman Turks.

Cairo: Capital of the Fatimid caliphate, which ran from Tunisia in the west to Palestine and Syria in the east. Home of the Cairo Geniza (*see entry*).

Cairo Geniza: This *geniza* (repository of sacred texts) in a Cairo synagogue became famous after its discovery at the end of the nineteenth century. It contained approximately 200,000 medieval manuscripts and fragments in Hebrew, Arabic, Judeo–Arabic and Judeo–Greek and has proved of great importance to historians and Judaic studies scholars.

Caligula: Roman emperor (r. 37–41) who, angry with the Jews for refusing to honor him as a god, decided in 40 CE to have a statue of himself as Zeus installed in the Jerusalem Temple. A Jewish delegation that included Philo of Alexandria (*see entry*) vigorously protested the plan. Caligula's assassination in 41 averted a major crisis.

Caliph: Arabic for "successor," these leaders followed Muhammad and continued to expand the community of Muslim believers.

Cambyses: Son and successor of Cyrus II (*see entry*) who conquered Egypt for the Achaemenid Empire.

Canaan: An ancient term for the region that encompasses parts of modern-day Israel, Lebanon, Syria, the West Bank, and the Gaza Strip. In the Bible, God allots the Land of Canaan to the Israelite tribes as an "inheritance" (Numbers 34:2), and their descendants settle there in the time of Joshua.

Canaanites: The peoples who inhabited the Land of Canaan before the Israelites.

Cantonists: Underage Jewish recruits taken from their families between 1827 and 1855, on average at the age of fourteen, for a preparatory period before their twenty-five-year service in the Russian army. Fifty thousand Jewish boys were forcibly recruited in this way.

Casimir III "the Great" (1310–1370): (Kazimierz III Wielki, in Polish) Polish monarch who granted a charter to the Jews.

Central Union of German Citizens of the Jewish Faith: Association founded in 1893 to safeguard Jewish civil and social equality and combat antisemitism.

Chabad: *See* HaBaD.

Chamberlain, Houston Stewart (1855–1927): English Germanophile, who became one of Germany's most prominent and well-connected antisemites. Author of a foundational antisemitic work, *Foundations of the Nineteenth Century* (1899).

Chanukah: *See* Hannukah.

Charlemagne (r. 768–814): King of the Franks from 768 until his death, Carolus Magnus ("Charles the Great") acquired the title of emperor from the Pope in 800, borrowing from the past glory of the Western Roman Empire. He initiated the symbiotic relationship between the Jews and the king that would allow Jewish life to thrive in France despite efforts by some Church officials.

Chelmno: Site of a Nazi death camp, seventy kilometers from Lódz in Poland.

Chmielnicki massacres: The slaughter of thousands of Jews during the course of a Cossack uprising against the Polish regime in the Ukraine in 1648. Wave of violent attacks are referred to in Hebrew as the *gezerot tah ve-tat* ("evil decrees of [the years] [5]408 and [5]409"). They were led by Bogdan Chmielnicki (c. 1595–1657).

Christian Kabbalah: The pursuit by some Renaissance Christian scholars, such as Giovanni Pico della Mirandola (*see entry*) of the study of Jewish mystical texts, often in the belief that they would yield esoteric truths confirming Christian belief. (*See* Kabbalah.)

Cixous, Hélène (b. 1937): Algerian-born Jewish feminist theorist.

Codes: Rabbinical works that sought to organize, epitomize, and clarify law for daily use.

Commentaries: Works in which scholars interpreted and explained biblical and rabbinic texts.

Constantine I: Roman emperor (r. 306–337) who, after a vision that he had before a battle in 312, announced the toleration of Christians in the empire in 313, in the Edict of Milan. He later converted to Christianity.

Constantinople: The capital of the Eastern Roman Empire, later called the Byzantine Empire, built by Constantine on the site of the older city of Byzantium in 330. The city fell to the Ottomans in 1453. It was officially renamed Istanbul in 1930.

Conversos: Spanish for "convert." Jews who had converted to Catholicism in Spain and Portugal, specifically during the fourteenth and fifteenth centuries, some of whom assimilated into the majority society while others secretly continued practicing Judaism.

Cordoba: Important city in Muslim Spain, which attracted some of the Jewish world's leading intellectuals.

Cordovero, Moses (1522–1570): Known as RaMaK, Cordovero was an important Kabbalah (*see entry*) scholar who built a circle of followers in Safed (*see entry*).

Costa, Uriel da (d. 1640): Portuguese *converso* (*see entry*) who reverted to Judaism after emigrating to Amsterdam. He published two critiques of rabbinic law, both of which earned him excommunication. Although he reconciled with the Jewish community, his officially sanctioned public humiliation by the community eventually led him to commit suicide.

Council of Four Lands (*va'ad arba' aratsot*, in Hebrew): A central body that represented all the Jewish communities in Poland, first formed in 1580 and lasting until 1764, when it was dissolved by the Polish parliament, the *sejm* (*see entry*). A similar body existed in Lithuania.

Counter-Reformation: The revival in the Catholic Church, also known as the "Catholic Reformation," that began in the mid-sixteenth century. (Reformation.)

Court Jews (German, *Hofjuden*): Beginning in the 1650s, wealthy Jewish individuals who provided essential services and goods to the rulers of the numerous German states.

Cracow (Kraków, in Polish): City in southern Poland. In the Middle Ages, Cracow lay on a commercial route between Germany and Prague. German Jewish merchants began to settle in Cracow in the late thirteenth century. As its prestige grew in the fifteenth and sixteenth centuries, Cracow continued to attract Jews, who helped the city develop into a thriving commercial hub and one of the greatest centers of rabbinic scholarship. By the twentieth century, Cracow had become an important site of secular Jewish culture and political activity. In 1939, Cracow's 60,000 Jews made up a quarter of the city's total population.

Crémieux, Adolphe (1794–1880): Leading statesman and founder of the Alliance Israélite Universelle (*see entry*).

Crypto-Jews: Jews who disguised their Judaism under the guise of conversion.

Cuneiform: A complex writing system developed in Mesopotamia.

Cyrus II: Persian king (r. 559–530 BCE) who defeated the Neo-Babylonian Empire in 539 BCE and allowed the exiles in Babylonia to return to Judah and restore the Temple. Known as "the Great," Cyrus founded the Achaemenid dynasty (*see entry*).

Czerniakow, Adam (1880–1942): Head of the Warsaw *Judenrat* (*see entry*). He committed suicide during the great deportations of Warsaw Jewry to the Treblinka death camp.

Damascus Affair (1840): Blood libel in the Syrian capital of Damascus, where the local Jewish community was accused of having killed a Capuchin monk and his servant.

Damascus Document: A Dead Sea Scrolls (*see entry*) community document that includes an account of the group's origins. It does not mention the rebuilding of the Second Temple or acknowledge its existence.

Dan: Site of a large sanctuary constructed by Jeroboam in the north of the kingdom of Israel.

Darius I ("the Great"): Achaemenid king (r. 522–486 BCE) who consolidated the Persian Empire. Darius allowed the completion of the restoration of the Jewish Temple in the province of Yehud (Judah), which had begun under Cyrus II.

Darius III: Last king of the Achaemenid dynasty and ruler of the Persian Empire (r. 336–330 BCE). Defeated by Alexander the Great in 331 BCE.

David: Second king of Israel, who defeated the Philistines and secured the kingdom's borders.

Davidic messiah: Developed especially in first-century Jewish eschatology, the Davidic Messiah was represented as a kingly figure from the line of David, who would deliver Israel from its enemies. (Messiah *and* Priestly messiah.)

Dayan, Moshe (1915–1981): Israeli general, politician, and government minister.

Dead Sea Scrolls: An assortment of some 800 to 900 manuscripts, dating from the final centuries of the Second Temple period, discovered in a series of caves located close to the Dead Sea. The scrolls include the earliest known manuscripts of the Hebrew Bible; Hebrew and Aramaic compositions such as *Jubilees,* 1 Enoch, and Tobit, previously known only in translation; and still other compositions from a sectarian community, possibly Essenes, who may have lived at the nearby site of Qumran.

Degenerate Art exhibit: Staged in Munich in July 1937, an exhibition of modern art by Jewish and non-Jewish artists, whose work the Nazis declared to be "degenerate."

Deir Yassin: Palestinian village that was the site of a massacre by the Irgun (*see entry*) on April 9, 1948. The group killed 120 Arabs, many of whom were unarmed civilians.

Demetrius: Earliest known Jewish author to write in Greek. Lived at the end of the third century BCE and tried to solve chronological problems in biblical sources in a manner reminiscent of Greek historiographical methods.

Democratic Faction: A Zionist group in the Ahad Ha'am (*see entry*) camp that emerged after 1901 and sought to place greater emphasis than had Theodor Herzl (*see entry*) on Jewish culture.

De non tolerandis Judaeis: A privilege granted by the crown to a number of Polish cities in the early modern period that allowed them not to admit Jews.

Derash: A mode of interpretation that attempts to go beyond the explicit meaning of the biblical text, trying to discern latent meanings or knowledge hinted at in the grammar, word choice, or spelling of the Hebrew text. (contrast Peshat).

Derrida, Jacques (1930–2004): Outstanding literary theorist who coined the term *deconstructionism* and became one of the representative faces of poststructuralism. Born to a Jewish family in Algeria, he arrived in France in the late 1940s.

Deuterocanonical: Term used by the Catholic and Eastern Orthodox Churches to describe books such as Tobit and Judith, which were not part of the Hebrew Bible but were included in the Greek translation of the Bible (the Septuagint). For the Catholic and Eastern Orthodox Churches, these books are part of the scriptures, while Protestants see them as the Apocrypha (*see entry*).

Deutero-Isaiah: Greek for "Second Isaiah," in reference to Chapters 40–55 of the book of Isaiah, which seem to have been added to its original core by a later author. This section makes explicit reference to Cyrus II (*see entry*).

Deuteronomistic History: The hypothetical work assumed by biblical scholars to be the basis of the great historical narratives in the Hebrew Bible (i.e., the books of Deuteronomy, Joshua, Judges, 1–2 Samuel, and 1–2 Kings). While some of its stories may go back to the beginnings of Israelite history, Bible scholars believe that their compilation dates to the period of the Babylonian exile in the sixth century BCE. One of its goals was to explain why God permitted the catastrophe of the destruction of the Temple in 587–586 BCE, conquest of Judah, and exile of its population.

Devekut **(Hebrew, "cleaving"):** State of "cleaving with God" described in the *Tanya* (*see entry*).

Dhimmi: A non Muslim (but monotheistic) person party to the Pact Of Umar which offered protection in exchange for loyalty to the Muslim state.

Diaspora: From the Greek for "to scatter" or "disperse." With the translation of the Hebrew Bible into Greek (*see* Septuagint) the term came to be used to refer to the exile of the Jews after the destruction of the Temple by the Babylonians in 587/6 BCE, and thereafter to the population of Jews living outside the Land of Israel. It is used more generally to mean a group's state of exile or dispersion from a homeland. The term also refers to ethnic or religious groups scattered across countries but maintaining ties with each other across imperial, national, or city boundaries.

Diaspora Revolt: Series of unconnected Jewish uprisings in the Roman Empire from 115–117, during the reign of Trajan (r. 98–117). The first revolts took place in Libya, spread to Egypt, and then to Cyprus.

Dicker-Brandeis, Friedl (1898–1944): Viennese artist interned at Theresienstadt.

Digests: Compilations of legal positions that were not systematically organized.

Dina de-malkhuta dina: Aramaic term denoting the legal principle of "the law of the land is the law," according to which Jews were to follow the law of the state as long as it did not conflict with Jewish law.

Disputations: Publicly staged debates between Christians and Jews that took on new importance in fourteenth-century Spain, after the violent riots against Jews in 1391. (*See* Tortosa.)

Dmowski, Roman (1864–1939): Polish politician and founder of the chauvinistic National-Democratic Party (*see* Endek Party).

Documentary Hypothesis: A theory developed by biblical scholars to account for idiosyncrasies in the Pentateuch, such as factual discrepancies and contradictions. It proposes that the Torah was not written by a single author, such as Moses, but compiled from preexisting sources.

Dohm, Christian Wilhelm (1751–1820): Prussian bureaucrat who published an essay *On the Civic Improvement of the Jews,* in 1781, arguing for the removal of restrictions on Jewish participation in political and economic life.

Doikayt: The Yiddish word for "hereness," and a central element of Bundist ideology, developed by Vladimir Medem (*see entry*), that stressed the need to work for an improvement in the conditions under which Jews lived in the Diaspora.

Dominicans: A religious order of mendicant friars established by Dominic in 1214, known for its obedience to the church and involvement with the Holy Inquisition.

Domitian: Son of Vespasian, brother of Titus (*see entries*), and Roman emperor who ruled from 81 to 96.

Dönme: A sect of followers of Shabbatai Zvi, who converted to Islam in the second half of the seventeenth century, as did Zvi. Remnants of them live to this day in Turkey.

Dotar **societies:** Organizations maintained by western Sephardi communities that provided dowries for poor girls and orphans.

Dov Ber of Mezerich, Rabbi (d. 1772): A respected Talmudist and follower of the Baal Shem Tov (*see entry*), who was instrumental in disseminating the BeShT's message. He steered Hasidism to stay within the bounds of the normative Jewish tradition. Dov Ber succeeded in spreading Hasidism partly by moving his *hoyf* (Yiddish for "court") northward to Volhynia from the relatively remote southeastern province of Podolia.

Drumont, Edouard (1844–1917): A journalist and leading French antisemite; author of a two-volume diatribe entitled *Jewish France* (1886).

Duehring, Karl Eugen (1833–1921): German economist and philosopher. A key ideologist of modern racial antisemitism, who published a work in 1881 called *The Jewish Question as a Racial, Moral and Cultural Question.*

Dunash ibn Labrat (920–990): A student of Saadya Gaon, the first to be credited with introducing Arabic meter into Hebrew poetry.

Edirne: Formerly Adrianople (in English), this city in Thrace, the European part of Turkey, became a major Jewish center after the 1492 Expulsion of the Jews from Spain, along with the cities of Salonika and Constantinople (*see entries*).

Egypt: The ancient civilization based around the Nile basin that exerted considerable influence on the history of early Israel. The modern state of Egypt was in conflict with the State of Israel until the peace treaty of 1979.

Eichmann, Adolf (1906–1962): SS bureaucrat who worked out the logistics of the mass murder of European Jewry.

Einsatzgruppen: German for "task forces." The four mobile death squads that followed three million regular German army (Wehrmacht) troops during the invasion of the Soviet Union (*see* Operation Barbarossa) in June 1941. Composed of between 500 and 900 men each, including *Schutzstaffel* (SS), police battalions, regular German army units, and local collaborators, the squads systematically shot and killed approximately 1.4 million Jews in the region from the Baltic states in the north to the Black Sea in the south.

El: The supreme creator deity in the Canaanite pantheon. The Bible refers to God using the same name and titles, such as *El Elyon* ("El, the Most High").

Elephantine: An island situated in the middle of the Nile River in southern Egypt that in the fifth century BCE was home to a garrison of Judahite soldiers and their families, deployed there by the Persian Empire. A set of documents from the island, the Elephantine Papyri, have yielded invaluable data to scholars.

Eliezer ben Yehuda (1858–1922): Staunch advocate of Hebrew, who immigrated to Palestine in 1881. Author of the seventeen-volume *Complete Dictionary of Ancient and Modern Hebrew.*

Elijah Capsali of Crete (d. 1555): Graduate of Padua University and author of a history of the Venetian and Ottoman Empires, including an extensive account of the expulsion of the Jews from Spain and their resettlement in Ottoman lands (*Seder Eliyahu Zuta*, written in the 1520s).

Eliyahu ben Shlomo Zalman Gaon, Rabbi (1720–1797): Eliyahu of Vilna, the Vilna Gaon, or GRA. Greatest Talmud scholar of his generation and the leading opponent of Hasidism.

Endek Party: Polish short form for the anti-Jewish, xenophobic National-Democratic Party founded by Roman Dmowski (*see entry*) in 1897.

England: The Jews of England were expelled in 1290 by Edward I. In the 1630s, a number of *converso* merchants established themselves in England, where they continued to live as Christians. When war broke out with Spain in 1655, a number of them began to identify as Jews, marking the beginning of the Jewish community's reconstitution.

Enlightenment: The intellectual revolution of the eighteenth century

Erasmus of Rotterdam (ca. 1466–1536): Most famous representative of Christian humanism. Critical of the engagement of such humanists as Johannes Reuchlin (*see entry*) with Jewish texts.

Eretz Yisrael **(Hebrew for "The Land of Israel"):** The term used by Jews for the area roughly equivalent to that comprised today by the State of Israel and the Palestinian territories of the West Bank and the Gaza Strip.

Eschatology: Religious thought concerned with the end of the world.

Essenes: A religious sect that emerged in the second century BCE. As described by Josephus, its members believed in the immortality of the soul and in divine providence, but they did not make the same allowance for human will that the Pharisees (*see entry*) did. Their lifestyle was ascetic, cultivating self-control. Many scholars identify the Dead Sea Scroll sect as an Essene community.

Esther: Biblical book, set in the Persian Empire, which features the rescue of the empire's Jews from imminent destruction due to the intrigues of an evil courtier. The deliverance of the Jews takes place as a result of the interventions of Esther, a Jewish woman selected to marry the king of Persia, and her guardian Mordechai. Probably written in the fourth century BCE. (*See* Ahasueres, Haman, and Purim.)

Ets Hayim: Academy established by the Portuguese–Jewish community of Amsterdam in the late seventeenth century, acclaimed for its systematic curriculum.

ETzeL: Acronym for *Irgun Tzvai Le'umi* (*see entry*).

Evian Conference: Conference convened by U.S. President Franklin Roosevelt on July 6–13, 1938, to address the refugee crisis caused by Nazi rule in Germany and Austria.

Exchequer of the Jews: Office established under Richard I ("the Lionheart") of England (r. 1189–1199), which kept copies of every loan contract with a Jew in royal hands. Richard I set up this post after episodes of rioting at York in 1190 that led to the burning of documents recording the debts owed to the Jews, which in turn led to a considerable financial loss to the king (who taxed the Jews' profits).

Ezra ("the scribe"): Leader of the Judahite community during the Persian period for whom the biblical book of Ezra is named.

Farhud: Anti-Jewish pogrom in Baghdad that occurred on June 1–2, 1941.

Fatimid Empire: A Shiite Muslim dynasty that ruled Egypt from 969 to 1171 and also controlled other parts of North Africa and Palestine during this period.

Ferdinand II of Aragón and V of Castile: Ferdinand "the Catholic" (1452–1516; r. with Isabella over Castile 1474–1504; r. over Aragón 1479–1516) married Isabella I of Castile in 1469 (*see* Isabella).

First International Antisemites' Congress: Convened in Dresden in 1882, it demanded the formation of a "universal Christian alliance" against Jewish influence.

Flavius Josephus: Born (b. 37 CE, d. ca. 100 CE) to a priestly and Hasmonean family, served as a general in the Jewish army leading the Jewish Revolt against Rome in 66 CE. In 67, he surrendered to the Romans and worked for them as a translator and mediatory. In 70, with Jerusalem destroyed, he moved to Rome and began writing his first history, the *Jewish War,* followed by the *Jewish Antiquities,* and a polemical work entitled *Against Apion,* defending the *Antiquities.*

Fourier, Charles (1772–1837): French antisemite, utopian socialist, and philosopher.

Fourth Lateran Council: The Lateran Councils were ecclesiastical synods held at the Lateran Palace in Rome. The Fourth Lateran Council, held in 1215, officially recognized the belief that the wafer used in the Catholic ceremony of the Eucharist, the *host,* actually became the body of Christ during the ceremony, a doctrine known as *transubstantiation.* Charges of host desecration against Jews (*see entry*) soon followed. The Council also prescribed identifying clothes that Jews were required to wear, such as badges and conical hats for men.

Fourth Philosophy: The name given by Flavius Josephus to a movement begun in 6 CE by a teacher named Judas, with the backing of the Pharisees (*see entry*). Judas proclaimed Roman rule a kind of slavery and urged the nation to free itself. While no major revolt occurred in this period, the movement was a precursor to the Sicarii, a leading faction in the Jewish Revolt.

Frankel, Zacharias (1801–1875): Dresden rabbi who founded Positive-Historical Judaism (*see entry*).

Franciscans: A religious order established by Francis of Assisi in 1209 whose members were active in anti-Jewish agitation.

Frank, Jacob (1726–1791): The leader of a messianic religious movement in Poland who claimed to be a reincarnation of Shabbatai Zvi, as well as King David. He advocated acceptance of the New Testament and a belief in purification through sin, including violations of sexual taboos. In 1795, he and five hundred adherents converted to Catholicism.

Fredrick II of Hohenstaufen (1194–1250; r. 1212–1250): Holy Roman Emperor (from 1220) who tried to exonerate the Jews of the blood libel, convening a council of Jewish converts to Christianity, presumed experts in Jewish practice, to refute it. (The efforts proved unsuccessful).

Freud, Sigmund (1856–1939): Viennese Jew and father of psychoanalysis.

Friedländer, David (1750–1834): Wealthy German Jewish entrepreneur from Königsberg, who argued for religious reform within the Jewish community, calling for the abandonment of Hebrew and of the study of the Talmud.

Gans, David (1541–1613): Author of *Tsemah David* (Prague, 1592), a history divided into two parts: one covered general history, the other Jewish history up to the date of the work's publication.

Gans, Eduard (1798–1839): Jurist, historian, and founding member of the Society for Culture and the Scientific Study of the Jews.

Gaon: *See* Geonim.

Geiger, Abraham (1810–1874): Frankfurt-born philologist and historian who became the spiritual leader of Reform Judaism.

Geonim (plural of *Gaon*): Literally, "pride" or "splendor"; a title equivalent to "His Excellency," an honorific used for the heads of the two most important Babylonian rabbinic academies at Sura

and Pumbedita, active between 600 and 1000 CE. When Babylonia came under Islamic rule, Muslim authorities affirmed their legal authority, and eventually all the Jewish communities in the rapidly expanding Islamic world came under their sway.

Gershom ben Judah (c. 960–1040): Known as the "Me'or ha-Golah" or "Light of the Exile," a major Central European rabbi of the Middle Ages who established a Talmudic academy in Mainz. He is most famous for a *takkanah* (*see* Takkanot) enforcing the practice of monogamy.

Gersonides (1288–1344): Levi ben Gershom of France, a philosopher who championed the Islamic Aristotelian tradition.

Get: A bill of divorce delivered by the husband to his wife.

Ghetto: In response to the growing influx of Jews into Venice, the authorities ordered in 1516 the strict confinement of the Jews to a part of the city called the "Ghetto Nuovo." The term *ghetto,* a Venetian word meaning "foundry," came to denote segregated Jewish quarters established in other European cities in the sixteenth and seventeenth centuries.

***Gilgul* (pl. *gilgulim*):** (Hebrew for "revolution") Mystical term from the Safed Kabbalah for the transmigration of souls.

Ginsberg, Asher: *See* Ahad Ha'am.

Giovanni Pico della Mirandola (1463–1494): A Christian scholar who pursued Jewish mysticism, seeing it as a confirmation of Christian belief and a source of esoteric truth.

Glickl of Hameln (1646–1724): Glikl bas Yehuda Leib, a Jewish businesswoman known through her famous seventeenth-century Yiddish memoir.

Gnosticism: Named for the Greek word for knowledge (*gnosis*), a movement or movements that focused on the pursuit of a special religious knowledge.

Goldfaden, Abraham (1840–1906): Yiddish poet, playwright, and theatre impresario who adapted Western popular theatre to make it acceptable among American Jews.

Gordon, Aaron David (1856–1903): Theoretician of Jewish labor who spoke out against the practice of employing Arab labor on Jewish agricultural settlements, arguing for Jewish self-sufficiency.

Graetz, Heinrich (1817–1891): Leading Jewish historian of the nineteenth century, who, between 1853 and 1876, published an eleven-volume *History of the Jews.*

Granada: Site of the last Muslim stronghold in Iberia; conquered by the Christian monarchs Isabella and Ferdinand (*see entries*) in 1492.

Greenberg, Uri Zvi (1896–1981): Israeli poet and politician who began writing in Yiddish but switched almost exclusively to Hebrew after moving to Eretz Yisrael in 1924.

Grégoire, Henri: *See* Abbé Grégoire.

Ha'avara Agreement (1933–1939): Deal between the German Ministry of the Economy and Zionist representatives concluded on August 27, 1933, which permitted the transfer of Jewish assets to Palestine in exchange for the export of German goods to Palestine.

HaBaD: Also commonly spelled "Chabad." Hebrew acronym for the words *hokhmah* (wisdom), *binah* (reason), and *da'at* (knowledge).

The name of the brand of Hasidism developed by Rabbi Shneur Zalman of Lyady (*see entry*) and the largest of contemporary Hasidic groups.

Habiru (*also* Hapiru): A term found in the Amarna Letters, which refers to a socially marginal class composed of rebels, runaways, mercenaries, and outcasts living outside the Canaanite city-states. The term's linguistic similarity to the word *Hebrew* suggests some kind of connection between the Habiru and the Israelites.

Hadassah: Established in 1912, a Zionist women's organization, whose large and energetic membership began by providing health care in Palestine to both Jews and non-Jews and by 1930 had opened four hospitals, a nurses' training school, and fifty clinics.

Haganah: Hebrew for "defense." The Zionist popular militia established after the Arab riots of 1920 and 1921 in Palestine.

Haggadah: The recitation of the Exodus story read at the *Seder* (*see entry*) on the festival of Passover.

Hai: Son of Sherira (*see entry*), served as Gaon of Pumbedita until 1038.

Halakhah: Jewish religious law. Like its Islamic equivalent, *shari'ah,* it encompasses both civil and religious commandments and prohibitions.

Halakhic Letter: One of the most important scrolls for understanding the history of the Dead Sea Scrolls sect. It is a letter by the Dead Sea Scrolls (*see entry*) community to the priestly authorities in Jerusalem and lists the laws that were being violated in Jerusalem in the eyes of the community.

Haman: The evildoer in the Book of Esther, who plots to have the Persian Empire's Jews killed but is finally struck down himself by the king.

Hannukah: A festival created to commemorate the restoration of the Temple cult in Jerusalem following the victories of Judah the Maccabee and his insurgency against the Seleucid ruler in 165 BCE

Hanover, Nathan Neta (d. 1683): Author of a chronicle about the Chmielnicki massacres (*see entry*) called *Yeven Metsulah* (*Abyss of Despair*).

Hasdai Crescas (c. 1340–1410 or 1411): Jewish philosopher and legal scholar in Christian Spain.

Hasdai ibn Shaprut (915–970 or 990): A Jewish courtier who became one of the most trusted officials of the caliph Abd al-Rahman III. Abd al-Rahman had claimed the caliphate in 929, presenting a challenge from Spain to the Abbassid caliphate based in Baghdad. Hasdai became a leading diplomat, the overseer of the caliphate's customs, and the head of its Jewish community.

Ha-Shomer: A Jewish guard unit founded in 1909 by Yitzhak ben-Zvi (*see entry*).

Hasidei Ashkenaz ("The Pious of Ashkenaz"): A mystical pietist movement of the thirteenth century, which in its esoteric and moralistic writing sought to inculcate a life in obedience to God's will with responsibilities imposed on members beyond what Jewish law explicitly required, including acts of penitence through bodily self-mortification.

Hasidism: From the Hebrew term *hasid* ("pious man," pl. *hasidim*), used generally to designate especially scrupulous observers of the law, as well as ascetics. Hasidism was the movement of religious revival based on charismatic leadership and stamped by mystical teachings and practices that originated in the southeastern Polish province of Podolia in the 1750s. In contrast to earlier generations of *hasidim,* the followers of what we call "Hasidism" today did not promote ascetic practices.

Haskalah: A movement that began in Berlin in the 1740s, with the intention of promoting among Jews Enlightenment values, including philosophical rationalism, religious modernization, and the introduction of secular subject matter into the Jewish school curriculum. Following its German phase, the Haskalah evolved in a different direction taking after it took root in Galicia and Russia. The overall impact of the Haskalah was to transform the Jewish people as it led down a path toward increased secularism and greater participation of Jews in European culture and involvement in politics, informing those who crafted Jewish political responses to the social condition of European Jews.

Hayim of Volozhin, Rabbi (1749–1821): Leading figure of Mitnagdism (*see entry*). Founder of the prestigious Volozhin yeshiva (in 1803).

Hayyim, Joseph (1834–1909): Baghdad rabbi and community leader.

Hebrew Immigrant Aid Society: Founded by Russian Jews in 1881 to aid Jewish immigrants to New York.

Hebrew Union College: Seminary established in Cincinnati in 1875 for the training of Reform rabbis.

Hebrew: A member of the Semitic language family closely related to other dialects of Canaanite used by Judahites and Israelites in the period described by the Hebrew Bible. The language in which most of the Hebrew Bible is composed, along with later Jewish sacred texts from the Second Temple period, Late Antiquity, and the Middle Ages. Revived as a spoken vernacular in the twentieth century and used today as the national language of the State of Israel.

Heine, Heinrich (1797–1856): Acclaimed German-Jewish poet who converted to Lutheranism in 1825.

Hep Hep riots: Anti-Jewish disturbances that began in Würzburg and spread from southern and western Germany northward to Hamburg and Copenhagen, and even south to Cracow. They seem to have broken out in response to debates about Jewish emancipation. Rioters shouted out "Hep Hep, Jud' vereck!" (Hep Hep, Jews drop dead!).

Herod: King of Judea from 37 BCE until his death in 4 BCE; a pliant Roman ally who replaced the more troublesome Hasmonean rulers. Best known for his rebuilding of the Temple and his role in the story of Jesus, he managed to rule for more than three decades, despite repeated assassination attempts and challenges to the legitimacy of his rule.

Herzl, Theodor (1860–1904): Chief architect of political Zionism.

Heschel, Abraham Joshua (1907–1972): Born in Warsaw, Heschel became one of American Jewry's most significant theologians. Rising to prominence during the civil rights movement, he linked the Jewish experience to the struggle of African-Americans against racial discrimination.

Hess, Moses (1812–1875): A socialist who became a Jewish nationalist, publishing in 1862 a work entitled *Rome and Jerusalem,* which linked the recent unification of Italy to his hopes for the restoration of Jerusalem as the capital of the Jewish people.

***Hevrah* (pl. *hevrot*):** Jewish social welfare institution or fraternity that provided for members from cradle to grave.

Heydrich, Reinhard (1904–1942): Head of the Nazi *Sicherheitsdienst* (SD, or Security Service), with operational responsibility for the "Final Solution."

Hezekiah: King of Judah from the late eighth until the early seventh century BCE, who became a vassal of the Assyrian king Sennacherib.

Hezqat ha-yishuv: Right of residence. The Jewish *kehillah* (*see entry*) strictly controlled the residence rights of Jews who came from outside the city in order to ensure that local resources were not strained by the presence of outsiders.

***Hibbat Tsiyon* ("Love of Zion"):** A movement with the goal of settling the Land of Israel with Hebrew-speaking farmers and artisans, which emerged in the 1880s with hundreds of chapters in Russia and Romania. Its adherents were called *Hovevei Tsiyon* ("Lovers of Zion").

Hildesheimer, Rabbi Esriel (1820–1899): Founder of the first modern yeshiva that included the teaching of secular subjects (in Eisenstadt, Hungary, in 1851). In 1873, he established the Orthodox Rabbinical Seminary in Berlin.

Hillel: An important sage in rabbinic memory who probably lived in the first century BCE. Many wise sayings in *Pirkei Avot* (Chapters of the Fathers) are associated with him, as is the earliest list of rabbinic rules for interpreting the Torah. He and his disciples are known for their disagreements with Shammai (*see entry*) and his followers.

Himmler, Heinrich (1900–1945): Commander of the *Schutzstaffel* ("Protective Squadron" or SS).

Hirsch, Samson Raphael (1808–1888): German rabbi born in Hamburg who founded modern Orthodoxy (Neo-Orthodoxy).

Histadrut: Major Zionist labor union founded in Palestine in 1920.

Holdheim, Samuel (1806–1860): Proponent of radical reform who sought to de-nationalize the links between Jews living in different countries.

Homberg, Herz (1749–1841): Bohemian Jew commissioned by the Habsburg Emperor Joseph II to direct state-run, German-language schools for the empire's Jewish population.

Host desecration: The charge that Jews stabbed and mutilated the host (used in the Catholic ceremony of the Eucharist) in a kind of reenactment of the crucifixion of Christ, allegedly causing it to shed blood. The first known accusation was made in Berlitz, near Berlin, in 1243. Consequently, the Jews of Berlitz were burned, and the place of their deaths was renamed *Judenberg,* "Jews' Mountain."

Humanists: Classical scholars of the late fifteenth and sixteenth centuries who emphasized the study of ancient sources in their original languages.

Huppah: Wedding canopy under which the Jewish wedding ceremony takes place.

Hyksos: Asiatic rulers, perhaps from Canaan, who gained control over part of Egypt in the seventeenth century BCE. The term derives from the Greek transliteration of the Egyptian *heqaw khasut,* "rulers of foreign lands." Some scholars have identified the Hyksos as the people from whom the Israelites descended, but the evidence is inconclusive.

Index: List of prohibited books issued by the Church. In 1559, Pope Paul IV (*see entry*) added the Talmud to it.

Infamous Decrees: Anti-Jewish measures passed by Napoleon in 1808, targeting the Jews of Alsace. The decrees limited Alsatian Jews' residence rights and suspended all debts owed to them for ten years.

Inquisition: The Inquisition was originally established by the papacy in the 1230s in response to heretical movements in Europe, such as the Cathars in southern France. This "Papal Inquisition" was controlled by the Church and focused on rooting out heresy among Christians. The Spanish Inquisition was established and administered by Isabella and Ferdinand (*see respective entries*), with authorization from the Pope, in 1481. Unlike the earlier Papal Inquisition, it was concerned with seeking out a particular kind of heresy—the secret practice of Judaism—"judaizing"—by *conversos* (*see entry*). A Portuguese Inquisition was established by King João III in 1536.

***Intifada* (Arabic for "shaking off"):** The wave of protests by the Palestinians of the occupied territories in the West Bank and Gaza, which began in 1987. The Second *Intifada* (also referred to as *al-Aqsa Masjid Intifada*), which began in September 2000, was more violent than the first and included suicide bombings and other attacks against Israeli civilians and soldiers. (*See* al-Aqsa Masjid.)

***Irgun Tzvai Le'umi* (abbreviated by the Hebrew acronym *ETzeL*):** "The National Military Organization"; a militia that broke off from the main Zionist fighting force in pre-state Palestine, the Haganah, during the Arab riots of April 1937. It was loyal to Ze'ev Jabotinsky (*see entry*) and rejected the Haganah's policy of restraint.

Isaac ben Sheshet Perfet (1326–1408): Distinguished Spanish Talmudist.

Isabella I of Castile (1451–1504; r. 1474–1504): Isabella "the Catholic," with her marriage to Ferdinand II of Aragón (*see entry*) in 1469, presided over the increasing unification and centralization of Christian Spain. Named "the Catholic monarchs," she and Ferdinand were permitted to establish the Spanish Inquisition (*see* Inquisition). In 1492, the Christian monarchs defeated the last Muslim stronghold in Iberia, the kingdom of Granada and in the wake of this conquest issued an edict of expulsion of all the Jews in Spain, except for those willing to convert to Christianity.

Islam: The monotheistic world religion founded by Muhammad in the seventh century. *Islam* in Arabic means "submission."

Israel: The name bestowed upon Jacob by a mysterious stranger (Genesis 32:29), with whom he struggles an entire night (Genesis 32:25). The Hebrew etymology of the name given in the Bible is "one who has struggled with God." Israel also becomes the collective designation of the twelve tribes whose descent the

Bible traces to the sons of Jacob; later, it becomes the name for the Jewish people.

Israel ben Eliezer (1700–1760): Born in Podolia in present-day Ukraine, and the founding figure of Hasidism (*see entry*). Known as the Baal Shem Tov or BeShT, Israel ben Eliezer was, as his Hebrew name indicates, a "Master of the Good Name," meaning someone who could use the esoteric names of God for practical, magical effects such as healing or exorcism. His transformation into the founder of an incipient religious revival seems to date to Rosh Hashanah (the Jewish New Year) of 1746, when he had a vision of the Messiah.

Isserles, Moses (1520–1572): Leading Polish rabbi born in Cracow and known by his Hebrew acronym as ReMA. He composed the work *ha-Mapah* (*The Table-Cloth*), a commentary on the *Shulhan Arukh* (*see entry*).

Jabotinsky, Ze'ev (Vladimir) (1880–1940): Respected translator and talented orator from Odessa who founded the Right-wing Revisionist Movement, after breaking with the General Zionists.

Jacob: The son of Isaac and Rebecca, and the grandson of Abraham and Sarah. Jacob fathered Reuben, Simeon, Levi, Judah, Issachar, Zebulun, and Dinah from his wife Leah; Gad and Asher from her maidservant Zilpah; Dan and Naftali from the maid of his wife Rachel; and Joseph and Benjamin from Rachel herself.

Jacobson, Israel (1768–1828): Father of Reform Judaism who in 1817 founded a private synagogue in Westphalia with a reformed service.

Jeroboam: A leader who organized a rebellion of ten of the twelve tribes against the rule of Rehoboam, son of Solomon. Jeroboam became the first king of the northern kingdom of Israel.

Jerusalem: The political and religious center of the kingdom of Judah, where, according to the Bible, Solomon constructed the Temple.

***Jerusalem* (1783):** Work of political theory and Jewish theology by Moses Mendelssohn.

Jesus: Born between 4 BCE and 6 CE. Central to Christian belief and history as the Christ (Greek for the Hebrew phrase "anointed one"). An itinerant Jewish teacher and wonder worker whose Hebrew name seems to have been Yehoshua (Joshua). He was put to death in Jerusalem under the administration of the Roman prefect, Pontius Pilate.

Jew Count: The *Judenzählung* was a census conducted by the Prussian War Ministry in 1916, during World War I, to determine whether Jews were avoiding frontline service. Noting that Jews were serving at the front in disproportionately large numbers, the war ministry never published the results.

Jewish Agency: Organization founded in 1923, which was responsible for facilitating Jewish immigration into Palestine, purchasing land from Arab owners, and formulating Zionist policy.

Jewish Anti-Fascist Committee (JAFC): Organization set up in 1942 with the permission of the Soviet Union to raise support for the Soviet war effort in western Jewish communities.

Jewish Defense League (JDL): Founded in 1968 by Meir Kahane (*see entry*), the JDL's motto was "Never Again," a reference to the Holocaust. It organized vigilante groups to protect Jews living in crime-ridden areas American cities.

Jewish Free School: School modeled on the ideals of the Haskalah (*see entry*), opened in Berlin in 1778.

Jewish Legion: A force of three volunteer Jewish combat units who fought for the British during World War I. About five thousand men in total, they made up the 38th, 39th, and 40th battalions of the Royal Fusiliers.

Jewish physicians: One of the main channels responsible for the dissemination of scientific thought in Jewish society. In the early modern period, many of them were *conversos* who had studied at Christian universities in Spain and Portugal and begun living openly as Jews when they left the Iberian Peninsula. Others had graduated from such universities as Padua in Italy, which opened its doors to Jews in the same time period. In eighteenth-century Germany, physicians were the first Jewish intellectuals in the Ashkenazi world who did not attend a yeshiva and instead sought an entirely secular education, thus bringing to an end the traditional figure of the physician-rabbi.

Jewish Theological Seminary: The New York institution founded by two Sephardi rabbis in 1886 to train Conservative rabbis. A Jewish Theological Seminary (*Jüdisch-Theologisches Seminar*) was founded in Breslau in 1854 to train those in the tenets of Positive-Historical Judaism; it was later shut down by the Nazis.

Jewry Regulation: *Juden-Reglement*," in German. Law code issued by Frederick II in 1750; it subordinated the authority of the Jewish community to the demands of the centralizing Prussian state.

Jizya: Yearly tribute that *dhimmis* (*see entry*) had to render to their Muslim overlords.

John the Baptist: A popular prophet executed by Herod in 28 or 29 CE, whom the Gospels associate with Jesus of Nazareth.

Joint Distribution Committee: American Jewish organization founded in 1914 to offer material assistance to Jews abroad.

Jonathan: Brother of Judah the Maccabee (*see entry*).

Josel (Joseph) of Rosheim (d. 1554): Leading representative of German Jewry who used his influence on Emperors Maximilian I (1493–1519) and Charles V (1519–1556) to advocate for the Jews. Among his victories was persuading the Strasbourg city council to ban the anti-Jewish writings of Martin Luther (*see entry*).

Joseph: The second-youngest and beloved son of Jacob, born to him by Rachel, who was sold into slavery by his older brothers but ended up as a successful minister in the Egyptian court. His dramatic life story is narrated in Genesis 30:22–50:26.

Joseph ha-Kohen (1496–1578): Born in Avignon, France. Wrote a chronicle of the French and Turkish kingdoms and translated a Spanish history into Hebrew.

Josephus: *see* Flavius Josephus.

Josiah: Judahite king (r. 640–609 BCE) believed responsible for a major religious reform, which he apparently legitimated by the staged discovery of a scroll of laws (probably the book of Deuteronomy) during repairs of the Temple.

Jost, Isaac Marcus (1793–1860): German Jewish historian and author of the nine-volume *History of the Israelites from the Maccabean Period to Our Own Day.*

Judah "The Maccabee" ("The Hammer"):: The son of Mattathias (*see entry*), who after his father's death became the leader of the Maccabean Revolt, which targeted Jewish collaborators of the Seleucids and later the empire itself.

Judah ha-Levi (ca. 1075–1114):: Medieval Jewish poet, whose most famous work, the *Kuzari,* describes an imaginary dialogue among a philosopher, Jew, Christian, and Muslim, each trying to persuade a Khazar king that his view is the best. Born in Tudela, then under Muslim rule, but moved to Christian Spain thereafter; at the end of his life, he embarked on a journey to the Land of Israel.

Judah ha-Nasi (Judah "the Patriarch"):: Active between 175 and 220 CE. His most important contribution to rabbinic Judaism was his compilation of the Mishnah (*see entry*).

Judah the Pious (c. 1140–1217):: Important figure in the Hasidei Ashkenaz movement (*see entry*).

Judaizing:: The secret practice of Judaism or observance of Jewish laws and rituals by *conversos* (*see entry*).

Judenrat **(German for "Jewish Council")::** According to an order by Reinhard Heydrich (*see entry*), each ghetto established by the Nazis was to be administered by a Jewish Council of twenty-four members who were forced to implement Nazi orders.

Juden-Reglement: See Jewry Regulation.

Kabbalah: (Hebrew for "receiving") The Jewish mystical tradition that began to take shape in France and Spain in the Middle Ages. (*See* Zohar *and* Sefer ha-Bahir.)

Kabbalat Shabbat **(Hebrew for "Receiving of the Sabbath [Queen]")::** Today a common feature of Friday night synagogue services, which involves the recitation of a number of psalms and a hymn welcoming the "Sabbath Queen." Pioneered by the circle of mystics in early sixteenth-century Safed (*see entry*).

Kaddish **(Aramaic for "holy")::** A largely Aramaic recitation uttered at the close of individual sections of the prayer service and at its conclusion; the one at the end, the Mourner's *Kaddish*, is recited by close relatives of the deceased and seems to have become part of the Jewish mourning process in the Middle Ages.

Kahal: The organized governing structure of many medieval, early modern, and modern Jewish communities. In medieval Spain it was also known as the *aljama* or *alhama.*

Kahane, Meir (1932–1990):: Extremist rabbi who espoused a racist, chauvinistic form of Judaism. In addition to founding the Jewish Defense League in the United States (*see entry*), in the early 1970s, Kahane, who had immigrated to Israel in 1969, founded a new political party, Kach. In 1984, the party won a single seat in the Knesset, with Kahane as the sitting member. In 1986, Kach was declared a racist party by the Israeli government and banned from the Knesset. In 1994, the party was banned altogether. In 1990, Kahane was assassinated after a speech he delivered in New York. One branch of Kahane's supporters formed a small group, known as the Kahane Movement, which is listed on the United States' list of terrorist organizations.

Kalischer, Zvi Hirsch (1795–1874):: Prussian rabbi who called on Jews to return to the Land of Israel to bring about the divine salvation of the Jewish people.

Kalonymus:: Important family of rabbis and community leaders with an Italian branch in the Tuscan city of Lucca and another branch in the German city of Mainz. Members of the German branch became community leaders during the Crusades and members of the mystical pietist movement known as the Hasidei Ashkenaz (*see entry*).

Kaplan, Mordecai (1881–1983):: Founder of Reconstructionism, a new form of distinctively American Judaism.

Karaites (*qara'im,* in Hebrew):: Related to the Hebrew verb "to read" and possibly signifying "readers of scripture." A dissident Jewish sect that emerged during the Gaonic period in Baghdad. The Karaites rejected the "oral law"—that is, the Talmud and other rabbinic writings that formed the basis of rabbinic Judaism.

Karo, Joseph ben Ephraim (1488–1575):: A mystic as well as a legal scholar, Karo is renowned for his compendium of Jewish law, the *Shulhan Arukh* (*see entry*), first printed in Venice in 1565. Born in Spain or Portugal, he settled in the town of Safed (*see entry*). The *Shulhan Arukh* was a digest of the much larger *Beit Yosef.*

Katznelson, Berl (1887–1944):: Founding figure of Labor Zionism.

Kazimierz (*Kuzmir,* in Yiddish):: Suburb of Cracow to which Jews were confined in the fourteenth century and which thereafter became the heart of the city's Jewish community; named after Casimir III "the Great" (*see entry*).

Kazimierz III Wielki:: *See* Casimir III.

Kehillah **(pl. *kehillot*)::** Semiautonomous body governing the Jewish community.

Kehillot: See Kehillah.

Ketubbah **(pl. *ketubbot*)::** Jewish marriage contract. It commits the husband and wife to provide for each other's well-being and obliges the husband to pay the wife an amount specified by him in case of divorce.

Khappers **(Yiddish for "catchers")::** Men sent out by Jewish communal authorities, pressured by the state, to apprehend young Jewish boys for forcible recruitment into the Russian army.

Kibbutz **(pl., *kibbutzim*)::** Agricultural cooperative.

Kiddush ha-Shem: Hebrew for "sanctification of God's name"; describes acts of self-sacrifice, especially those that occurred during the First Crusade of 1096, seen as a glorification of God.

Kimhi, David (1160–1235):: Also known as RaDaK, Kimhi further developed the intellectual traditions wrought by his father, Joseph Kimhi (*see entry*), becoming a highly influential philologist and biblical commentator.

Kimhi, Joseph (1105–1170):: Grammarian who fled the Almohad invasion of Spain in 1149 and settled in the French city of Narbonne, where he introduced the grammatical methods and interpretive techniques of Spanish Jewry living under Islam to the Jews of Christian Europe. Father of David Kimhi.

Kindertransport: Refers to the 10,000 Jewish children from the Third Reich who were sent by their parents to England to be raised by non-Jews there.

Kishinev pogrom:: Three-day riot against the Jews of the Russian city of Kishinev (today, Chişinău in Moldova) in April 1903.

Kohelet Musar (*The Moralist*): Hebrew weekly published by Moses Mendelssohn (*see entry*) in 1758, which dealt mainly with philosophical themes, influenced by Locke, Shaftesbury, and Leibniz.

Koine: Dialect of Greek that became widely used in the Mediterranean and Near East during the Hellenistic age following Alexander's conquests.

Kol Mevasser (*The Herald*): First successful weekly Yiddish newspaper, founded in Odessa in 1863 by Sholem Yankev Abramovitch (*see entry*).

Kook, Avraham Yitzhak (1865–1935): Religious supporter of Zionism, who sought to build an alliance between Orthodox Jews and the secular leaders of the movement. He was appointed the first Ashkenazi Chief Rabbi of Palestine in 1921.

Koran: Also transliterated as Quran. Islam's central religious text, which records the divine message revealed by God to Muhammad.

Kovner, Abba (1918–1987): Hebrew poet and World War II ghetto fighter.

Kremer, Aleksandr (Arkadii) (1865–1935): Leader of the Bund (*see entry*) in Vilna.

Kristallnacht (German for "Crystal Night"; also known as "Night of Broken Glass"): A countrywide pogrom targeting Jewish homes, businesses, synagogues, and persons, carried out by SA members, Nazi party functionaries, and zealous citizens on November 9–10, 1938.

Krochmal, Nahman (1785–1840): Galician Maskil (*see entry*) who produced an idealist philosophy of history.

Kulturbund: The "Cultural Association" that the Nazis forced Jewish performers to form on June 16, 1933, after excluding them from enjoying or performing German culture.

Kun, Béla (1886–1938 or 1939): Hungarian Communist of Jewish origin who seized power in 1919. His disastrous management of foreign policy and the economy, as well his brutal treatment of the opposition, soon led to a counter-revolutionary coup in which hundreds of Jews were killed between 1919 and 1920 in "retaliation" for the fact that Kun's father was Jewish.

Kvutza: (Hebrew for "group") First Jewish agricultural collective in Palestine, set up in 1910 in Degania near the Sea of Galilee.

Ladino: Also, Judeo–Spanish, Judezmo, or Spanyol. The language of Sephardi Jews, especially in the Ottoman Empire. Based on Old Castilian Spanish, with a significant lexicon of Hebrew words, as well as Portuguese, French, Turkish, Greek, and some South Slavic influences.

Lampronti, Isaac (1679–1756): Rabbi and author of an encyclopedic work, *Pahad Yitzhaq*, which shows his interest in Jewish law and in the advances of contemporary science and medicine.

Landau, Rabbi Ezekiel (1713–1793): Chief rabbi of Europe's largest Jewish community, Prague, and one of Moses Mendelssohn's (*see entry*) most bitter critics.

Lantsmanshaftn: Yiddish word for mutual-aid societies organized around the eastern European city of one's origin that sprang up in New York and other immigrant destinations.

Lassalle, Ferdinand (1825–1864): German Jew who founded the General German Workers' Association in 1863.

Law of Return: Legislation enacted by the State of Israel on July 5, 1950, which gave "Every Jew the right to immigrate to the country."

Leah: Laban's elder daughter, whom Jacob, as a result of a ruse on Laban's part, accidentally takes as his first wife. Jacob had intended to marry her younger sister, Rachel (Genesis 29:16–25).

Lebensraum: German for "living space." In Nazi plans, the area in eastern Europe to be settled by ethnic Germans once it had been "cleansed" of undesirable elements.

Lehi: Hebrew acronym for *Lohamei Herut Yisrael* (Warriors for the Freedom of Israel), a splinter group formed by members of the Stern Gang (*see entry*) after Avraham Stern's (*see entry*) death in 1942. The group carried out the 1944 assassination of Britain's Minister of State for the Middle East, Lord Moyne, and the 1948 assassination of the United Nations representative in the Middle East, Count Folke Bernadotte.

Lehrhaus: Jewish adult education school established in Frankfurt in 1920 by Franz Rosenzweig (*see entry*).

Leontopolis: Site of a Jewish temple in Egypt, built by the high priest Onias (*see entry*) in the second century BCE and modeled after the one in Jerusalem; earlier, the location of a ruined Egyptian temple.

Lessing, Gotthold Ephraim (1729–1781): German playwright who developed a close friendship with Moses Mendelssohn (*see entry*).

Letter of Aristeas: Believed to have been composed in Alexandria in the first or second century BCE, this text narrates the story of the Septuagint's (*see entry*) creation. According to the *Letter,* the Greek translation of the Hebrew Bible was commissioned by Ptolemy II, who summoned seventy-two translators from Judea, six from each of the twelve tribes, for the task. *Septuaginta* is Latin for "seventy," the closest round number to seventy-two.

Levinas, Emmanuel (1906–1995): Lithuanian-born Jew who moved to France in 1923, and became a renowned philosopher and Talmudic commentator.

Levinsohn, Isaac Ber (1788–1860): Russian Maskil (*see entry*) who in 1828 published a book, *Teudah be-Yisrael* (*Testimony in Israel*), arguing for the introduction of natural sciences and foreign languages into the Jewish school curriculum. The book was endorsed by and dedicated to Tsar Nicholas I, thus discrediting it in the eyes of most Russian Jews.

Liebenfels, Lanz von (1874–1954): Austrian, former monk, and publisher of the antisemitic *Ostara: Newsletters of the Blond Champions for the Rights of Man.*

Lilienblum, Moshe Leib (1843–1910): Lapsed Orthodox Talmud scholar who was one of the leaders of the *Hibbat Tsiyon* (*see entry*) movement.

Limpieza de sangre ("purity of blood"): Legislation enacted in Toledo in 1449, which barred *conversos* (*see entry*) from holding public office or testifying in court cases. By racializing the pre-conversion Jewishness of "new Christians," these statutes introduced an entirely new concept that ran counter to established Church law and, more generally, against medieval sensibilities.

Lipmann Heller, Yom-Tov (1579–1654): Scholar and poet. Author of a commentary on the Mishnah (*see entry*).

List, Joel Abraham (1780–c. 1848): One of the founders of the Society for Culture and the Scientific Study of the Jews, established in Berlin in 1819.

Livorno ("Leghorn" in archaic English usage): Important port to the Tyrrhenian Sea in the north of Italy's western coast, where many Sephardic Jews settled beginning in the sixteenth century.

London: The London Jewish community was reconstituted in the seventeenth century by former *conversos* and eventually other Jews from abroad. It was among the first communities established on an entirely voluntary basis.

Loew of Prague, Rabbi Judah (d. 1609): Renowned rabbi, mystic, philosopher, and commentator, known as the MaHaRaL (*Moreinu ha-Gadol Rabbi Loew,* "Our Great Teacher"). Legend attributes the creation of a Golem (an automaton made of clay) to him as part of an effort he made to defend the Jews of Prague from attacks.

Lublin-Majdanek: Nazi death camp located four kilometers from the Polish city of Lublin.

Lueger, Karl (1844–1910): Populist mayor of Vienna who rose to power by exploiting anti-Jewish sentiment.

Luria, Isaac (known as *ha-Ari;* 1534–1572): Born to an Ashkenazi father and Sephardi mother, Luria grew up in Egypt. He moved to Safed (*see entry*) in 1570, where his mystical teachings developed, and the religious practices ascribed to him and his disciples greatly transformed Jewish religious life in subsequent generations.

Luther, Martin (1483–1546): German theologian who became the leading figure of the Protestant Reformation (*see entry*). He veered from a conciliatory attitude toward the Jews to an increasingly violent stance.

Luxemburg, Rosa (1871–1919): Jewish revolutionary and socialist theorist who founded the Social Democratic Party of Poland and Lithuania; later a key figure in the German revolutionary Spartacist League. She was killed by a Right-wing paramilitary unit in Berlin.

Luzzatto, Simone (ca. 1583–1663): Venetian Jewish author who published a *Discorso circa il stato de gl'hebrei* ("Discourse on the State of the Jews") in 1638, where he argued for the economic utility of the Jews to the European states.

Maimon, Solomon (1753–1800): Eighteenth-century philosopher, born in Poland into a Hasidic milieu and later departed for Berlin, where under the influence of the German Enlightenment he explored the philosophical teachings of Kant. His autobiography charts his departure from Poland to Germany and the change in worldview such a journey entailed.

Maimonidean Controversy: Bitter polemic between the supporters and opponents of Maimonides, over a vast array of subjects such as attempts to synthesize Judaism and Aristotelian philosophy, anthropomorphism, resurrection of the body, the authority

of the Geonim, and the very structure of Maimonides' *Mishneh Torah.* The dispute culminated in a ban placed by the rabbis of northern France on his philosophical works.

Maimonides (1135–1204): Rabbi Moses ben Maimon, the greatest Jewish philosopher of the Middle Ages. Born in Cordoba, he fled to Egypt to escape persecution under the zealous Almohads. In Cairo, he served as a Jewish communal leader and physician to the Islamic ruler, while also writing extensively on medicine, Jewish law, and philosophy. His most important works are the *Mishneh Torah* and *The Guide for the Perplexed.*

Maistre, Count Joseph de (1753–1821): French philosopher who advocated a counter-revolutionary and authoritarian conservatism that identified Jews as being responsible for France's woes.

Manetho: Hellenized Egyptian priest from the Ptolemaic period who wrote an anti-Exodus story meant to ridicule the Jewish account of the Israelites' deliverance from Egypt through Moses. Manetho's work is one of the earliest examples of anti-Jewish literature.

Mapai: Hebrew acronym for Land of Israel Workers' Party (*Mifleget Poalei Eretz Yisrael*), which absorbed various streams of the Zionist Left in the 1930s.

Mapu, Abraham (1808–1867): Author of the first Hebrew novel, *Love of Zion* (1853).

Marr, Wilhelm (1819–1904): Inventor of the term *antisemitism,* probably in the late 1870s, and author of a pamphlet entitled *The Victory of the Jews Over the Germans, Considered from a Non-Religious Point of View* (1879).

Marranos: A derogatory term used for *conversos* (*see entry*) in Spain and Portugal. Literally, "pig" in Spanish.

Martínez, Ferrant: A popular preacher who incited violence against the Jews in Seville in 1391.

Maskilim (sing., Maskil): Jewish enlighteners, adherents of the Haskalah (*see entry*).

Masoretes: The group of scribes who between the sixth and eighth centuries CE copied the Bible and, developed vowel signs to the biblical text, a system of accents for public reading, marginal notations, and textual divisions.

Masoretic Bible: The particular text used as the Jewish Bible today, named after the Masoretes.

Mattathias: The father of Judah the Maccabee and a priest, who refused to offer a sacrifice ordered by Antiochus IV in the town of Modi'in. After killing a Jew who did follow the order, as well as a Seleucid officer, Mattathias and his sons fled to the hills and began an insurgency against the Seleucids.

May Laws (1882): Russian decrees promulgated after the 1881 assassination of Tsar Alexander II, which ordered Jews to move into urban areas from villages and rural settlements located outside of cities and towns.

Me'am Lo'ez **(Hebrew, "From a People of a Strange Language"):** An encyclopedic commentary on the Bible written in Ladino and published by the Istanbul rabbi Jacob Huli in 1730. The title is taken from Psalms 114:1.

Medem, Vladimir (1879–1923): Leader of the Bund (*see entry*) after it moved to Poland during the interwar period.

Mein Kampf (**German, "My Struggle"**): Adolf Hitler's political testament, published in 1924.

Meir, Golda (1898–1978): Fourth prime minister of Israel (1969–1974). Forced to resign after the Yom Kippur War.

Menahem ben Saruq (c. 920–970): An accomplished poet, one of his greatest achievements was the creation of a Hebrew dictionary, the *Machberet Notebook*.

Menasseh ben Israel (1604–1657): Portuguese Jewish rabbi and author who spent most of his life in Amsterdam but is best known for his advocacy on behalf of the readmission of the Jews to England. In 1655 he issued his *Humble Addresses to the Lord Protector*. After a bitter response by the Puritan polemicist William Prynne, who was opposed to readmitting the Jews, Menasseh published his ringing apologia, *Vindiciae judaeorum* (1656).

Mendelssohn, Abraham (1776–1835): Son of the philosopher Moses Mendelssohn; unlike his father, who remained committed to Judaism, Abraham raised his two children as Protestants.

Mendelssohn, Moses (1729–1786): Leading German and Jewish luminary in eighteenth-century Berlin. A philosopher as well as biblical commentator, who became an icon of the Haskalah (*see entry*).

Mendes, Doña Gracia (1510–1569): A Portuguese *conversa* (*see* Conversos) who, upon her husband's death, inherited his estate, which included one of Lisbon's largest banking houses. Fleeing the inquisition established in Portugal in 1536 (*see* Inquisition), she moved first to Antwerp, then to Venice, and finally to Istanbul, where she and her family began living openly as Jews.

Mendoza, Daniel (1764–1836): Champion Anglo–Jewish pugilist, who proudly boxed under the name "Mendoza the Jew."

Mercantilism: Economic theory that rose to prominence in the seventeenth century, in which the wealth of a nation is seen as depending on the supply of capital (how much gold and silver it has, for example), which should be increased by maintaining a positive balance of trade. Mercantilists thus favored exports and sought to discourage imports, often through tariffs.

Mesopotamia: A word of Greek origin meaning "land between the rivers," that is, between the Tigris and Euphrates in present-day Iraq.

Messiah: From the Hebrew *mashiah*, "anointed one," used first to refer to kings and priests who were anointed with oil upon assuming their positions. By the first century, the term had come to refer to a king or priest who would deliver Israel from its tribulations. Davidic messiah *and* Priestly messiah (*see entry*).

Midrash: Deriving from a Hebrew root meaning "to seek" or "to investigate," *midrash* can refer to a body of literature, collections of rabbinic interpretations of the Bible, but it also describes the mode of interpretation reflected in these collections.

Minyan: A quorum of at least ten adult Jewish males—at least until the rise of the Conservative and Reform Movements, which count women as part of the quorum—required for the recitation of certain prayers, public reading of the Torah, and other liturgical practices.

Mishnah: The codification of rabbinic teaching and law completed around 200 CE. It is a presentation of what various sages said.

Although probably not a working law code, it gathered the oral tradition transmitted by the rabbis until then.

Mitnagdism: From the Hebrew *mitnaged* ("opponent"). A movement of direct opposition to Hasidism (*see entry*). It stressed the importance of Torah study and sought to uphold traditional bases of rabbinic and thus communal authority.

Mitzvah (**pl.,** *mitzvot*): Often translated as a "good deed," a *mitzvah* is actually a commandment prescribed in the Torah, which contains 613 such *mitzvot* according to Jewish tradition.

Mizrahi: (Hebrew for "eastern") The term used to describe the Jews of or descended from North African, Middle Eastern, Caucasian, Central Asian, and Indian communities.

Modena, Leone (1571–1648): Venetian rabbi whose autobiography paints a vivid picture of Jewish life in seventeenth-century Venice.

Monash, Sir John (1865–1931): Highest-ranking Jewish soldier of World War I; he commanded the Australian forces. Monash University in Melbourne is named for him.

Monotheism: The belief that there is only one god. In Jewish tradition, that deity is identified as the God of the Hebrew Bible.

Mortara Affair (1858): The abduction of a six-year-old (Edgardo Mortara) Italian Jewish boy from his family by the papal police. Inquisition authorities claimed that the boy had been secretly baptized by his Catholic housekeeper; as a Christian child he had to be removed from his Jewish home, according to canon law. He was never returned to his parents and died a priest.

Morteira, Saul Levi (d. 1660): A Venetian who became the leading rabbi of Amsterdam, where his sermons admonished the Sephardi community for its religious laxity.

Moses: Israelite prophet to whom God revealed the contents of the covenant with Israel at Mount Sinai, and according to Jewish tradition, the author of the Torah.

Moses ben Nahman: *See* Nahmanides.

Moses de Leon: The Spanish Jewish mystic (1240–1305) credited with composing the core of what would become the *Zohar*.

Muhammad (570–632): Born in the Arabian city of Mecca and believed by Muslims to be God's last prophet. Muhammad attracted large numbers of adherents to follow the law revealed to him by God and eventually recorded in the Koran. By the time of his death, he had converted almost all of Arabia to his cause.

Murashu archives: Babylonian records of a banking firm from the fifth century BCE, which refer by name to some eighty Judahite individuals, testifying to the integral involvement of Judahites in the Babylonian economy and society.

Musar **movement:** From the Hebrew for "ethics," the nineteenth-century *Musar* movement preached ethical self-perfection and self-restraint, linked with Torah study.

Nação: (Portuguese for "nation") Term used by the Spanish–Portuguese Jews to describe themselves.

Nachman of Bratslav, Rabbi (1772–1811): Also, Nahman of Breslov, or of Uman. Great grandson of the BeShT (*see entry*). Founder of the Bratslav or Breslov Hasidic dynasty.

Nahmanides (1194–1270): Moses ben Nahman, a Spanish rabbinic sage coerced into participating in the 1263 Barcelona disputation. In Barcelona, Nahmanides had to debate a Jewish convert to Christianity, Pablo Christiani, who sought to use the Talmud to prove the claims of Christianity. Famed for his biblical commentary and mystical and legal writing.

Nathan of Gaza (1643–1680): Young Jewish mystic who became the prophet of Shabbatai Zvi (*see entry*), promoting him as the messiah.

***Nathan the Wise* (1779):** Play by Gotthold Ephraim Lessing (*see entry*), whose protagonist, a Jew of noble bearing named Nathan, was said to have been based on Moses Mendelssohn (*see entry*). Critics felt the character was not believable.

Nebuchadnezzar II: Babylonian king who decimated the kingdom of Judah in 586 BCE, destroying the Temple and exiling a large part of Judah's population to Babylon.

Neo-Platonism: A philosophical school that together with Aristotelianism (*see entry*) had the greatest influence on medieval philosophy. It posited a hierarchical structure to the cosmos, with the Creator as a first principle emanating downward toward the material world through spheres of being. Humans are at the bottom of this ladder, weighed down by their materiality, but human souls can ascend upward by means of ethical and intellectual activity.

Nero: Roman emperor (r. 54–68) who fought a successful war against the Parthians, suppressed the revolt led by Queen Boudica in the British Isles, and dispatched Vespasian to crush the Jewish revolt in 67.

New Amsterdam (later New York): The Dutch colony where Jews first established a permanent presence in North America, having arrived in September 1654.

New Christians: Jews or Muslims (and their descendants) who had converted to Christianity in the wake of the violence and coercion of the late-fourteenth century.

New York: During the twentieth century, New York City was home to the largest Jewish population in the world. By 1950, Jews comprised just under 30 percent of the city's total population.

Nicholas I: Tsar of Russia from 1825–1855.

Night of Broken Glass: *See* Kristallnacht.

Nobles' republic: System of rule in Poland–Lithuania after the death of the last Jagiellonian king in 1572. Henceforth, the landed gentry of the country elected their king in parliament.

Nordau, Max (1849–1923): Zionist leader and writer who in 1898 called for the creation of a "Muscular Judaism."

Nuremberg Laws (*Nürnberger Gesetze* in German): Passed in September and October 1935, this legislation revoked the German citizenship of Jews, forbade intermarriage (and all sexual contact) between Jews and Germans, defining them as distinct racial groups.

Octavian: Born in 63 BCE, Caesar's posthumously adopted son who defeated Marc Antony and Cleopatra VII in 31 BCE in the Battle of Actium to assume the title of pharaoh. Subsequently, in 27 BCE Octavian assumed the title of Commander Imperator and Augustus Caesar, restoring the Roman republic in name but beginning its formal organization as an empire. Octavian became known as Augustus and ruled Rome as its first emperor until his death in 14 CE.

Olivares, Count of (1587–1645): Gaspar de Guzmán y Pimentel, Count of Olivares and Duke of Sanlúcar, Spanish minister who directed the government's foreign policy. Lenient toward Portuguese *conversos* (*see entry*) settling in Madrid in the period following Spain's annexation of Portugal in 1580.

Onias (either Onias III or Onias IV): Jewish high priest who established a Jewish temple at Leontopolis (*see entry*) in Egypt, sometime in the second century BCE, with permission of the Ptolemaic king (probably Ptolemy VI).

Operation Barbarossa: Hitler's invasion of the Soviet Union, launched on June 22, 1941.

Operation Ezra and Nehemia (1950–1951): Airlift of 100,000 Iraqi Jews to Israel.

Operation Magic Carpet: Airlift of 49,000 Yemenite Jews to Israel in December 1949.

Operation Peace in Galilee (1982): Sixth Arab–Israeli war, launched by Ariel Sharon (*see entry*) against the Palestine Liberation Organization entrenched in Lebanon. The ground war resulted in large numbers of casualties, approximately 600 Israelis and 20,000 Lebanese killed.

Oppenheimer, Samuel (1630–1703): Born in Heidelberg; Court Jew (*see entry*) who provisioned the Austrian defense against the Ottoman siege of Vienna in 1683.

Oral Torah: According to the rabbinic sages, the traditions and interpretations of law transmitted orally, alongside the Written Torah (*see entry*) of the Bible. The Oral Torah was recorded in written form in the Mishnah and the Talmud.

Ottoman Empire: The empire established in the late thirteenth century, when a Turkish Anatolian emir, Osman I (from whom we have the word "Ottoman"), declared himself sovereign from the Seljuk Sultanate, then in decline. Having expanded at the expense of the other Muslim emirates in Anatolia, Osman and his descendants turned west to the major Christian power of the eastern Mediterranean, the Byzantine Empire. In 1453, the new Ottoman state finally conquered the Byzantine capital of Constantinople, today's Istanbul.

Pact of Umar: Traditionally attributed to the Caliph Umar (r. 633–644), the second caliph, though the earliest extant version of the text we have dates from the tenth century. The pact has the form of an epistle sent by the Christian community to their new Muslim rulers. In the letter, the Christians promise to obey certain restrictions in exchange for living in peace under Islam.

Pale of Settlement (*cherta osedlosti,* in Russian; *tekhum,* in Yiddish and Hebrew): The western border region of imperial Russia to which the state, beginning with Catherine the Great in 1791, tried to confine Jews. By the end of the nineteenth century, it was home to more than five million Jews and covered 386,100 square miles. The Pale was abolished with the February Revolution of 1917.

Pan Germans: Late-nineteenth-century German nationalists advocating a union in one country of all German speakers in Germany, the Habsburg monarchy, and elsewhere in Europe.

Pappenheim, Bertha (1859–1936): Daughter of an orthodox Jewish family who became committed to feminism and social welfare and is more famously known as the patient Anna O. in Josef Breuer and Sigmund Freud's *Studies on Hysteria.*

Parthian kingdom: A kingdom based in Persia that controlled Mesopotamia after defeating the Seleucids at the end of the third century BCE. The Parthians fell to the Sassanians in the third century CE.

Partitions of Poland: In the second half of the eighteenth century, the Polish–Lithuanian Commonwealth (*see* Poland–Lithuania) was truncated three times by Russia, Prussia, and Austria: in 1772, 1793, and 1795. The last "partition" placed all of Poland under foreign control. The partitions divided the Jewish population of Poland–Lithuania, creating different Jewish societies with particular cultural and economic characteristics in each of the three states.

Patriarch: A translation of the Hebrew word *nasi,* the title of a leading Jewish communal representative in the late Roman/ Byzantine Empire.

Paul: Known as Saul before becoming a disciple of Jesus, Paul was Jesus' most influential follower. As part of his effort to reach out to various Christian communities, he composed letters now preserved in the New Testament that interpret Jesus' life and death in a way that rendered adherence to the laws of Moses unnecessary for a relationship with God and thus gave non-Jews a much greater role in the Christian community. Dying sometime between 64 and 67 CE, Paul and his writings had a major impact on the development of Christian belief and biblical interpretation.

Paul of Burgos: *See* Solomon ha-Levi.

Peel Commission: A British commission that recommended, in the midst of the Arab Revolt in 1937, that Palestine be partitioned into Arab and Jewish states.

Pentateuch: The Five Books of Moses.

Peretz, I. L. (Isaac Leib) (1852–1915): Yiddish author.

Perl, Joseph (1773–1839): Galician Maskil (*see entry*) who founded a Jewish school in Tarnopol. He published a satire of Hasidism in 1819 entitled *Megaleh Temirin* (*Revealer of Secrets*).

Peshat: A mode of contextual interpretation, concerned with the "plain sense" of the biblical text, which sought to understand it in its historical and linguistic context. (Contrast Derash.)

Pesher: A technique used by the Dead Sea Scrolls (*see entry*) community to interpret the Bible as containing coded prophecies of the future. The word may have originally referred to dream interpretation.

Pfefferkorn, Johannes (1469–1523): A Jewish convert to Christianity. He wrote an anti-Jewish polemic charging that rabbinic tradition kept the Jews from accepting Christianity and that all Hebrew books ought therefore to be destroyed.

Pharisees: A Judean religious movement or school of thought that emerged in the second century BCE. Most often contrasted with the Sadducees (*see entry*), the Pharisees believed in the laws of Moses but also in ancestral traditions not written in scripture that had been transmitted orally from elders to disciples. In this, they are the predecessors of the rabbis who emerged in the next centuries.

Philippson, Ludwig (1811–1889): German rabbi and publicist associated with the Reform Movement.

Philistines: A people from the Aegean that arrived on the coast of Canaan in the early twelfth century BCE as part of the migration of "Sea peoples."

Philo: Author of an epic poem about Jerusalem, who probably lived in the second century BCE. Not to be confused with Philo of Alexandria, who lived in the first century CE.

Philo of Alexandria: Philo (20 BCE–50 CE) practiced allegorical interpretations of the Bible to harmonize Greek philosophy and Judaism.

Philosophes: The deistic or materialistic writers and thinkers of the eighteenth-century French Enlightenment.

Pilpul: Mode of study that seeks to reconcile every inconsistency or contradiction in a Talmudic passage by using interpretation. It came to dominate rabbinic learning in Poland–Lithuania in the sixteenth century.

Pilsudski, Marshal Josef (1867–1935): Military commander and Polish statesman during the interwar period.

Pinsker, Leon (1821–1891): Physician and founder of *Hibbat Tsiyon* (*see entry*). Author of a pamphlet called "Auto-Emancipation" and the inventor of the word "Judeophobia."

Poalei Tsiyon: (Hebrew for "The Workers of Zion") Marxist Zionist party founded in 1906.

Pogrom: From the Russian *pogromit,* meaning "to break" or "destroy" or "to conquer." In the nineteenth century, the term *pogrom* came to mean a riot, especially a violent attack targeting a particular group and involving the destruction of property. After the anti-Jewish rampages of 1881–1882, the term came to be used especially to refer to mob attacks against Jews.

Poland–Lithuania: The Polish–Lithuanian Commonwealth, which lasted from 1569 to 1795, was a multireligious, multiethnic empire that covered a vast area. Its possessions included, in addition to the lands comprised by modern-day Poland and Lithuania, large parts of Ukraine and Estonia, the entire territory of Belarus and Latvia, and parts of what is today western Russia. Beginning in the sixteenth century, it became the demographic heartland of Ashkenazi (*see entry*) Jewry.

Pontius Pilate: Roman prefect of Judea (r. 26–37 CE, or perhaps 19–37 CE), notorious for his role in the trial of Jesus; also despised by Jews of the time for his corruption, cruelty, and contempt for Jewish traditions.

Pope Gregory I (r. 590–604): Held that Jews were in theological error, enforced restrictions against them, but also held that they ought not to be forcibly converted or killed.

Pope Paul IV (1476–1559; r. from 1555): Counter-Reformation pope who issued an infamous bull that began, "It is profoundly absurd and intolerable that the Jews, who are bound by their guilt to perpetual servitude, should show themselves ungrateful toward Christians." This initiated a new phase in Jewish–Catholic relations, which led to increased pressure on European Jews and included their ghettoization, first in Venice in 1516.

Port Jews: Former *converso* (*see entry*) Jews who settled in important port communities and engaged in international commerce, most notably, the Portuguese Jews of Amsterdam, Hamburg, and London. Some scholars have called them "the first modern Jews," as in establishing new communities they often had to "reinvent" traditions, especially since they had only recently returned to Judaism.

Positive-Historical Judaism: Stream of Judaism today identified with the Conservative Movement in the United States, founded by the German rabbi Zacharias Frankel (*see entry*). It assumed a position between Reform and Neo-Orthodoxy, Frankel arguing that Judaism developed within history, but that its essence was "positive" or divinely revealed.

Prefect: *See* Procurator.

Priestly messiah: In Jewish eschatological texts from the first century, a priestly figure who would deliver Israel from its trials. Messiah *and* Davidic messiah.

Procurator: Type of Roman official sent to Judea to rule as a lower-ranked governor (earlier called *prefect*) in the first century CE. Known for cruelty, venality, and contempt for Jewish traditions, procurators sharpened tensions in the province.

Profiat Duran (ca. 1350–1415): A Spanish Jewish scholar who converted to Christianity after the violence and forcible conversions of 1391 but later returned to Judaism and wrote an anti-Christian polemic entitled *Shame of the Gentiles.*

Prophets: The section of the Jewish Bible that contains the historical narratives of Joshua, Judges, 1–2 Samuel, and 1–2 Kings; the large or "major" prophetic texts of Isaiah, Jeremiah, and Ezekiel; and twelve brief or "minor" prophetic books.

Protestant Reformation: The religious revolution that broke out in sixteenth-century Europe with the writing and public activity of Martin Luther (*see entry*) in 1517. It led to a permanent split in western Christianity, between the Catholic Church and different Protestant denominations. Jews were initially hopeful that Protestantism would adopt a friendlier attitude toward them, both because of its break with Catholicism and with the appearance of Luther's *That Jesus Christ Was Born a Jew* (1523), in which he decried the maltreatment the Catholic Church had meted out to the Jews. But the subsequent refusal of Jews to accept the Protestant faith saw Luther become increasingly frustrated, and in 1543 he published his violent polemic *On the Jews and Their Lies.*

Protocols of the Elders of Zion, The: A fictional account of a meeting by Jews plotting world domination, concocted by the Russian secret police in Paris sometime between 1896 and 1898. A canonical work in antisemitic literature unto the present day, with translations in many languages.

Proudhon, Pierre-Joseph (1809–1865): French antisemite, anarchist, and socialist theorist.

Pseudepigrapha: From the Greek for "falsely inscribed," the term refers to texts from the late Second Temple period and the following centuries attributed to biblical figures such as the sons of Jacob, Moses, and King Solomon. Although preserved by various Christian communities, many pseudepigraphical texts were either originally composed by Jewish authors or draw on Jewish sources.

Ptolemaic kingdom: Named after one of Alexander the Great's generals, Ptolemy, who, following Alexander's death established a dynasty in Egypt that lasted until the Roman conquest in 30 BCE. The Ptolemies also ruled over Judea until 200 BCE, when the province was conquered by the Seleucids (*see entry*).

Pumbedita: Town outside of Baghdad that was home to one of the great Talmudic academies of the Gaonic age.

Purim: A festival that commemorates the deliverance of the Jews described in the Book of Esther. From the Hebrew *pur* ("lot"), which Haman cast to decide when the Jews were to be killed.

Quran: *See* Koran.

Rabbi: A general term of respect in Jewish antiquity, applied to various sages, judges, and teachers, including Jesus. More specifically, a sage within the particular social network that emerged after the destruction of the Second Temple, and produced the Mishnah and the Palestinian and Babylonian Talmuds. The title "rabbi" is also used today to refer to religious authorities trained and ordained in the legal tradition established by these earlier texts.

Rabin, Yitzhak (1922–1995): Israeli general and prime minister, who won the Nobel Peace Prize in 1994 and was assassinated by a Jewish extremist, Yigal Amir.

Rabinowitz, Sholem (1859–1916): The Yiddish author better known as Sholem Aleichem.

Rachel: Leah's sister and Laban's younger daughter, whom Jacob finally marries after fourteen years of service (Genesis 29:20–27).

Radhanites: An important medieval Jewish merchant family whose dealings extended from western Europe to China.

Raison d'état: (French for "reason of state") A philosophy of following the "interests of the state" (often fiscal) rather than religious or other ideological factors in making policy. In the early modern period, *raison d'état* became a powerful argument in favor of allowing Jews to reside in certain cities and countries.

Rashbam (c. 1080–1174): Samuel ben Meir, biblical commentator who pursued the *peshat* (*see entry*) exclusively.

Rashi (1040–1105): Solomon ben Isaac of Troyes, single most influential medieval Jewish commentator, whose work transformed the nature of Jewish learning. Rashi's biblical commentaries move back and forth between a midrashic reading of the Bible and a *peshat* approach in an attempt to resolve interpretive problems in the biblical text. An even more impressive intellectual accomplishment was his commentary to the Babylonian Talmud (*see entry*), which has become essential to the study of that text.

Rav: The name by which Rav Abba is known in rabbinic literature. Born in Babylonia, he went to Palestine to study like many others from Babylonia, purportedly receiving his ordination from Rabbi Judah ha-Nasi (*see entry*). But then around 219 CE, Rav returned to Babylonia and established a *bet midrash* (*see entry*) at Sura, which became one of the most important rabbinic academies in Babylonia.

Reform Clubs: Associations dedicated to the battle against liberalism in late-nineteenth-century Germany.

Rehoboam: Son of Solomon, under whose reign Jeroboam seceded from the Davidic kingdom and established the northern kingdom of Israel. Rehoboam reigned over a much-reduced kingdom in the territory of the tribe of Judah in the south.

Reines, Rabbi Isaac Jacob (1839–1915): Founder of eastern Europe's first modern yeshiva, in the town of Lida, in 1905.

Renaissance: The cultural revival ("renascence") that began in Italy and spread northward roughly between the fourteenth and seventeenth centuries. It was marked by a revival of classical learning, advances in the visual arts, and a plethora of new inventions.

Responsa: Letters written by rabbis in response to specific legal questions posed by Jews.

Reuchlin, Johannes (1455–1522): German scholar who developed a deep interest in the Hebrew language and published the book *De arte cabalistica* (*On the Art of Kabbalah*) in 1517. He became embroiled in a controversy with the Jewish convert to Christianity, Johannes Pfefferkorn (*see entry*), in which Reuchlin spoke out against the proposed confiscation and destruction of Hebrew books.

Revisionists: Zionist faction opposed to the General Zionists; embraced a more militant, nationalist line. Founded by Ze'ev Jabotinsky (*see entry*).

Rindfleisch: German knight who, after a series of blood libels (*see entry*) in the 1280s in Munich, Mainz, and other communities, began traveling from town to town to urge the massacre of the Jews. His agitation led to the deaths of many Jews in southern and central Germany in 1298.

Ringelblum, Emanuel (1900–1944): Distinguished Polish Jewish historian who founded ZETOS, a Jewish Social Self-Help organization, which provided crucial help to the inhabitants of the Warsaw ghetto. Ringelblum also ran a secret documentation project called *Oyneg Shabbes* ("Sabbath Pleasure").

Rome: Ancient capital of the Roman Empire and the seat of power for the Church over most of the Middle Ages and early modern period. Capital of the modern Italian republic. Home of a Jewish community that went back to the early days of the Roman Empire.

Rosenzweig, Franz (1886–1929): Important existential Jewish philosopher. Author of the *Star of Redemption*.

Rothschild, Mayer Amschel (1743–1812): Founder and patriarch of the Rothschild banking empire. Born on Frankfurt's Judengasse ("Jews' Alley"), he sent his sons to London, Paris, Vienna, Naples, and Frankfurt, where in the nineteenth century they built the largest private banking house in the world.

Rumkowski, Chaim (1877–1944): Highly controversial, autocratic leader of the Lodz ghetto's *Judenrat*.

Saadya ben Yosef (882 or 892–942 CE): Also known as Saadya Gaon, the outstanding figure of the Gaonic period (*see* Geonim), whose philosophical and exegetical works gave shape to what would become medieval Jewish culture. Saadya played an important role in the struggle against the Karaites, a dissident Jewish sect. An intellectual giant, he wrote many works, ranging from philosophy to mysticism, as well as linguistic studies, poetry, translations into Arabic, and a very early version of the *siddur*, a standardized compilation of prayers.

Sadducees: The Sadducees were probably a priestly group that crystallized in the second century BCE, amid widespread political and religious dissatisfaction in Judea. Unlike the Pharisees (*see entry*), they denied the immortality of the soul and rejected the governance of fate. From Josephus' account it seems that they also believed strictly in the written law, against the Pharisees' adherence to orally transmitted traditions.

Safed (Hebrew, *Tsfat*): City in the Galilee where a number of learned Sephardi (*see entry*) exiles and *conversos* (*see entry*) fleeing the Inquisition settled and established a thriving center of Jewish scholarship, especially of Kabbalah (*see entry*).

Salanter, Rabbi Israel (1810–1883): Lithuanian rabbi who founded the *Musar* movement (*see entry*).

Salonika: Important Ottoman port city that became a major center of Jewish life. Today, it is the Greek city of Thessaloniki.

Samaritans: A people that, until the present day, claims descent from the northern tribes of Ephraim and Manasseh. Jews in antiquity regarded them as non-Jews who feigned a Jewish identity after settling in the territory of the former Northern Kingdom of Israel.

Samuel ben Meir: *See* Rashbam.

Samuel de Medina (1505–1589): Sephardi rabbi from Salonika, also known as RaShDaM.

Samuel ibn Tibbon (1150–1230): Translator of Maimonides' *Guide for the Perplexed* (*see entry*) from Arabic to Hebrew.

Samuel the Nagid (993–1055): Statesman, military commander, scholar, and poet who reached the highest level achieved by a Jew in medieval Muslim Spain, serving as vizier of Granada and leading a Muslim army into battle.

Sanhedrin: From a Greek term for "meeting" or "assembly," the sanhedrin of Jerusalem, probably one of many sanhedrins in Palestine during the Roman period, has been understood as a kind of supreme legislative council/court comprised of priests and/or other traditional leaders.

Sarah: The first matriarch of the Israelites, who married Abraham and begat him a son, Isaac, in their old age (Genesis 21:2).

Sarahs, Aryeh Leib (1730–1791): Disciple of the Baal Shem Tov (*see entry*).

Sasportas, Jacob (d. 1698): Leading Sephardi rabbi of his time who supported the poetry of Miguel de Barrios (*see entry*), written in the vernacular (i.e., in Spanish).

Sassanian kingdom: A multiethnic empire based in Persia that took control over the Parthian kingdom in the third century CE. It was home to a large Jewish population in Babylonia, which was given a fair amount of control over internal organization.

Saul: First king of the Israelites, who began the process of establishing permanent, centralized rule but lost his kingship to David.

Schick of Shklov, Rabbi Baruch (1740–1810): A disciple of the Vilna Gaon, who translated Euclidian geometry into Hebrew.

Schlesinger, Rabbi Akiba Joseph (1837–1922): Hungarian rabbi who officially defined the ideology of ultra-Orthodoxy.

Schneerson, Menachem Mendel (1902–1994): Known as "The Rebbe," Schneerson was the leader of the Hasidic Chabad (*see entry*) movement in America.

Scholem, Gershom (1897–1982): Pioneering scholar of Jewish mysticism.

Schönerer, Georg von (1842–1921): Austrian Pan-German nationalist and radical antisemite.

Seder: The central act of the Passover festival as reinterpreted in rabbinic tradition. A banquet structured by an order of blessings, prayers, stories, questions, and comments as laid out in a kind of scripted recitation of the Exodus story known as the Haggadah.

Sefer ha-Bahir (*Book of Brightness*): A mystical book first published in southern France in the twelfth century, which had an important influence on the Kabbalistic tradition that developed in Spain in the thirteenth century.

Sefer Hasidim (*Book of the Pious*): An ethical work of the Hasidei Ashkenaz (*see entry*) attributed to Judah the Pious (c. 1140–1217) (*see entry*). It advocates self-denial, spiritual focus, decency, and humility.

Sefer Yetzirah (*Book of Creation*): An early mystical work that might date to the first centuries CE, which has God creating the world through manipulation of the letters of the alphabet. It is the first mystical text to use the term *sefirot,* which comes to refer to the emanations or spheres through which God becomes manifest in the world.

Sejm: The Polish parliament.

Seleucid kingdom: Dynasty founded by one of Alexander's generals, Seleucus I, after the former's death. Based in Syria, the Seleucids conquered Judea in 200 BCE under Antiochus III and ruled it until it came under Roman control in the first century BCE.

Sephardi: From the Hebrew word for "Spanish" (*sefaradi*). Initially, Iberian Jews and their descendants. Following the 1492 expulsion, Sephardi Jews brought their religious and cultural traditions to their new homes in western Europe, north Africa, and the Ottoman Empire, sometimes displacing local traditions—this was especially true in Turkey and the Balkans. The term came to describe, somewhat inaccurately, all Middle Eastern Jewish communities who followed the Sephardi liturgy. Strictly speaking, however, the Jews of places such as Iraq, Syria, and Persia are not Sephardi; today, the more accurate term used to describe them is *mizrahi* (*see entry*).

Septuagint: Originally a Greek translation of the Torah by Alexandrian Jews. The name derives from the Greek for "seventy," after the number of translators who worked on it (*see* Letter of Aristeas); scholars often refer to it as "LXX," Roman numerals for "seventy." The term is used loosely to describe the Greek translation of the Jewish Bible in its entirety, done between the third and first centuries BCE. The Septuagint contained a biblical canon from a much earlier period than the Masoretic Bible, and it was a translation of a different text than what became the Masoretic one (*see* Masoretes).

Shabbatai Zvi (1626–1676): Most popular messianic figure of the early modern period. Born in the Turkish port of Izmir, Shabbatai Zvi attracted followers from across the Jewish world, who believed him to be the messiah.

Shamir, Yitzhak (b. 1915): Leader of Lehi (*see entry*) and, later, a prime minister of Israel.

Shammai: A sage from the first century BCE known especially for his disagreements with Hillel (*see entry*). In many of these, he is represented as taking the more stringent and (usually) losing view.

Sharon, Ariel (b. 1928): Israeli general, politician, and prime minister from 2001 to 2005.

Shasu: A term used in Egyptian documents from 1500 to 1100 BCE referring to seminomadic tribes from the area of Palestine, from whom the Israelites may have originated (though evidence is inconclusive).

Shema: A declaration of faith in God, recited twice daily, which is composed of the verses in Deuteronomy 6:4–9, 11:13–21, and Numbers 15:37–41. The name is taken from the first verse of the passage, which begins *"Shema Yisrael"* ("Hear, O Israel") and continues "the Lord our God, the Lord is one."

Sherira: Gaon of Pumbedita from 968–998 after Saadya (*see entry*). He authored the letter that provides most of our information about late antique rabbinic history and the Geonate itself. Succeeded by his son Hai (*see entry*).

Shirayim (Hebrew and Yiddish for "leftovers"): Remains of a Hasidic rebbe's food, eaten by his disciples in the belief that it has been sanctified.

Shlomo ibn Verga: Spanish Jew living as a Christian in Portugal after the forced conversions of 1497, until he left for Italy nine years later. Published a "proto-sociological" study of recent Jewish history, *Shevet Yehudah,* in the 1520s.

Shlonksy, Avraham (1900–1973): Modernist Hebrew poet.

Shneur Zalman of Lyady, Rabbi (1745–1813): Founder of HaBaD (*also* Chabad) Hasidism, for whom intellect and reason were considered as legitimate paths to God along with mystical devotion. He was crucial to the growth of Hasidism.

Shokeling: Yiddish word meaning "swaying to and fro." Refers to the bodily movements in the Hasidic manner of praying.

Sholem Aleichem: *See* Rabinowitz, Sholem.

Shtadlan: An intercessor who represented the Jewish community and even the Jews of an entire province to the non-Jewish government.

Shulhan Arukh ("The Set Table"): The definitive compilation of Jewish law (*halakhah; see entry*) in use to this day, written by Joseph Karo (*see entry*) in the mid-sixteenth century. It was a digest based on Karo's earlier compendium, the *Beit Yosef.*

Sicut Judaeis: Papal bull that became official Church policy, which stated that "although in many ways the disbelief of the Jews must be condemned . . . they must not be oppressed grievously by the faithful." It was originally promulgated by Calixtus II (1119–1124) and reissued by subsequent popes.

Siddur: From the Hebrew for "ordering," originally used to refer to the first systematic arrangement of the prayers, compiled by the ninth-century Geonic leader Amram (*see* Gaon and Geonim). Saadya developed another *siddur* about a century later. Now *siddur* is the Hebrew word for a Jewish prayerbook.

Simon: Brother of Judah the Maccabee (*see entry*), who led the rebellion against the Seleucids together with his brother Jonathan after Judah's death. By 140 BCE, he had consolidated control in Judea, restored the Temple, and driven non-Jews from the land. Simon was declared high priest and ruler of the Jews "forever," turning both positions into hereditary ones.

Simon, Ernst (1899–1988): German Jewish philosopher and Zionist.

Sinai: Mountain in the desert region between Egypt and Canaan where God established a covenant with the Israelites.

Sinai Campaign (1956): Israel's second war against Arab armies, in which, with the support of Britain and France, it captured the Sinai Peninsula. The U.S. government, left in the dark, publicly rebuked the scheme, and it had to be aborted.

Singer, Isaac Bashevis (1902–1991): Yiddish author and Nobel laureate. Brother of Yiddish author Israel Joshua Singer (*see entry*).

Singer, Israel Joshua (1983–1944): Yiddish author. Brother of Isaac Bashevis Singer (*see entry*).

Singer, Kurt (1885–1944): Leader of the *Kulturbund* (*see entry*). Physician and conductor.

Six-Day War (1967): Israel's third war against the Arab world, which many Israelis and Jews in the Diaspora experienced as a miraculous rescue in the face of extermination. It led to the conquest and occupation of the Golan Heights (from Syria), the West Bank (from Jordan), and the Sinai and the Gaza Strip (from Egypt).

Slovo, Joe (1926–1995): A Lithuanian Jewish immigrant who became the head of the South African Communist Party and one of the few white members of the African National Congress.

Smolenskin, Peretz (1840–1885): Russian Maskil (*see entry*) who founded the journal *Ha-shahar* (*The Dawn*).

Sobibor: Nazi death camp established in a remote, underpopulated part of the Lublin district in Poland.

Sofer, Rabbi Moses (1762–1839): Popularly known as the Hatam Sofer. Fierce opponent of the Jewish Reform movement.

Sokolow, Nahum (1859–1936): Hebrew journalist and leader of the World Zionist Organization from 1931–1935.

Solomon: Son and successor of David who according to the Bible ruled an expanded kingdom of Israel, built the Temple in Jerusalem, and was renowned for his wisdom. After his death, his kingdom split into the northern kingdom of Israel and the southern kingdom of Judah.

Solomon ben Aderet (1235–1310): Widely known as the Rashba, a medieval Talmudist born in Barcelona. He defended Maimonides (*see entry*) during the Maimonidean Controversy (*see entry*) and encouraged the translation of the former's Arabic *Commentary on the Mishnah.* However, he sought to restrict the study of Greek philosophy.

Solomon ben Isaac of Troyes: *See* Rashi.

Solomon ha-Levi (1351–1435): The former chief rabbi of Burgos who converted to Christianity in 1390 or 1391, studied theology in Paris, and returned to Burgos as the city's bishop. He became a sincere Catholic, assuming the name Pablo de Santa María (or Paul of Burgos) and wrote a historical work, *The Seven Ages of the World,* for the education of King John II of Castile.

Solomon ibn Gabirol (1020–1057): A mystical Hebrew poet and Neo-Platonist philosopher of the Spanish Golden Age.

Soloveitchik of Brisk, Rabbi Hayyim (1853–1918): Influential scholar who developed the analytic Brisker or Volozhin methodology of Talmud study, which emphasized the logic of a Talmudic argument and the linguistic structure of a Talmudic passage.

Spinoza, Baruch (Benedict) (1632–1677): Towering philosopher of the seventeenth century, who grew up in a Portuguese converso (*see entry*) family who had returned to Judaism in Amsterdam. He was excommunicated for his critique of rabbinic law in 1656 and never sought a return to the Jewish community (though he also never converted to Christianity).

Stern Gang: A Jewish terrorist group that repeatedly attacked the British in Mandate Palestine, funding itself through criminal activity.

Stern, Avraham (1907–1942): Leader of the Stern Gang (*see entry*) until his death at the hands of the British.

Stöcker, Adolf (1835–1909): Court preacher to the kaiser and the head of Europe's first antisemitic political party, the Christian Social Workers Party, founded in Berlin in 1878.

Sullam, Sara Coppio (ca. 1592–1641): Italian Jewish poet. Born into a prominent Venetian Jewish family, known for her correspondence, which included a long exchange of sonnets and letters with an Italian monk, Ansaldo Cebà.

Sura: Town outside of Baghdad that was home to one of the great Talmudic academies of the Geonic age (*see* Geonim).

Sürgün: A Turkish word for the policy of forced population transfers practiced by the Ottomans, often to colonize newly conquered cities with an economically desirable group.

Sutzkever, Avrom (b. 1913): Yiddish poet and partisan fighter who escaped from the Vilna ghetto in 1943.

Suzman, Helen (b. 1917): A South African Jewish economist and member of the liberal Progressive Party in South Africa, who was one of the country's most outspoken white critics of apartheid.

Synagogue: Jewish house of worship. Originating in the third century BCE, the synagogue is a site for communal prayer and Torah reading and plays many other communal functions as well.

Syrkin, Nahman (1868–1924): Exponent of Socialist Zionism.

T-4 program: Nazi euthanasia program. Named after its headquarters located on Tiergartenstrasse 4 in Berlin, the program consisted of six killing facilities in Germany and Austria, created to "euthanize" 100,000 mentally and physically disabled children and adults using carbon monoxide gassing. T-4 was part of the Nazi attempt to reengineer the biological character of society by eliminating the "inferior."

Takkanot (sing. takkanah): Decrees in matters of civil and religious law issued by a rabbinic court. Unlike responsa (*see entry*), the power of a given *takkanah* did not derive from the authority of the rabbi who wrote it, nor was it derived directly from Talmudic law. Instead, *takkanot* relied on communal assent and were enforced using the *herem,* or ban, according to which every member of the community agreed to excommunicate a person who violated a *takkanah.*

Talmud: When Jews today refer simply to the Talmud, they mean the Babylonian Talmud (*see entry*). Another Talmud exists—the Palestinian Talmud—which was compiled earlier and is shorter and often more laconic than the massive Babylonian Talmud.

Tannaim: The earliest generations of rabbinic sages from the end of the Second Temple period until the redaction (ca. 200 CE) of the Mishnah (*see entry*), a record of their sayings and rulings.

Tanya: Work by Shneur Zalman of Lyady (*see entry*), first published in 1796. Core Hasidic text to this day.

Tchernichovsky, Saul (1875–1943): Hebrew author.

Teacher of Righteousness: A figure identified in the scrolls of the Dead Sea sect around whom the members coalesced sometime in the first half of the second century BCE. He and his followers may have withdrawn into the Judean wilderness to found the Dead Sea Scrolls (*see entry*) sect because of a conflict with the high priest in Jerusalem at the time.

Temple Mount (*har ha-bayit* in Hebrew): Located in Jerusalem, it is Judaism's holiest site on which the innermost sanctuaries of the First and Second Temples once stood. Muslims refer to the area as the *Haram al-Sharif* (Noble Sanctuary), and it houses two mosques today, the golden Dome of the Rock and the silver-domed *al-Aqsa* mosque (*see* al-Aqsa Masjid).

Temple Scroll: A Dead Sea Scroll that recorded an alternative account of what God revealed to Israel during the time of Moses, including laws bearing on the Temple and its cult unknown from the Torah.

The Jews (1749): Written by Gotthold Ephraim Lessing (*see entry*), and one of the first European plays to portray Jews in a positive light.

Thirty Years' War (1618–1648): War fought mainly between Catholic and Protestant forces in German lands. It pitted the Habsburgs of Austria and Spain against France, The Netherlands, Denmark, and Sweden. It left a swath of destruction, especially in Germany.

Tiberias: The most important center of learning in the Land of Israel, home to the Masoretes (*see entry*) and the Palestinian Geonim (*see entry*).

Tikkun: (Hebrew for "repair") The main theme of Lurianic Kabbalah (*see* Kabbalah *and* Luria), which is focused on the mystical mending of the world.

Tiszaeszlar: Town in Hungary that was the site of a blood libel (*see entry*) accusation in 1881.

Titus: The eldest son of Vespasian (*see entry*) who ruled as emperor from 79–81. As a military commander under his father, he helped to defeat the Jewish army in the First Jewish-Roman War (69–70). In 70, he subjugated the Jewish revolt, laying siege to Jerusalem and destroying the Temple. His victory was commemorated in the Arch of Titus in Rome. He was succeeded by his younger brother Domitian (*see entry*).

Tivoli Program: Platform adopted by the German Conservative Party in 1892, which in its first paragraph declared its opposition to the "Jewish influence" on the German people.

Tkhines: Prayers written in Yiddish for women. They proliferated in the early modern period.

Toland, John: His tract of 1714, *Reasons for Naturalizing the Jews in Great Britain and Ireland on the Same Foot with All Nations,* was the earliest call for Jewish emancipation.

Toledot Yeshu (*The History of Jesus*): A derogatory history of Jesus from the Middle Ages that uses the New Testament against Christians.

Tomás de Torquemada (1420–1498): A Dominican friar who was the confessor of Isabella I of Castile (*see entry*) and became the head of the Spanish Inquisition in 1483. He is known for his zealous pursuit of suspected *converso* (*see entry*) "Judaizers" (people who continued to practice Judaism secretly).

Torah lishma: "Torah for its own sake."

Tortosa: Site of an important disputation (*see entry*) from February 1413 to November 1414, in which Spanish Jews were forced to debate against a Jewish convert to Christianity, who set out to repudiate Judaism by focusing on the question of whether or not the messiah had yet come. Contemporary reports state that when the Christian side declared victory over the Jewish representatives, hundreds of Jews ended up converting to Catholicism.

Tosafot (Hebrew for "supplements"): Responses and discussions stimulated by the commentary of Rashi (*see entry*) on the Talmud, which began to be composed by his grandsons—Isaac, Samuel, Solomon, and Jacob (known as the *Tosafists*)—in the twelfth century. They were continued by their pupils and eventually printed in most editions of the Talmud on the outer margins of the folio (Rashi's commentary being on its inner margins).

Toussenel, Alphonse (1803–1885): Antisemitic French writer and journalist who was a student of Charles Fourier (*see entry*).

Trading diasporas: A *diaspora* refers to a people scattered or dispersed across countries, often as a result of forced expulsion from their homeland. Merchants scattered across continents or in port cities located in different polities, such as the Sephardi Jews after the expulsion of 1492, constitute trading diasporas. The exiles, who settled in western European cities and in the Ottoman Empire, could draw on the Mediterranean and the Atlantic diasporas of Sephardi Jews to facilitate transactions.

Treblinka: Nazi death camp located a hundred kilometers northeast of Warsaw.

Triangle Shirtwaist Fire: A blaze that erupted at a garment factory in New York on March 25, 1911, in which 146 young women workers, mostly Jews and Italians, lost their lives because the doors had been illegally locked. The tragedy drew attention to the appalling conditions in the clothing industry.

Trotsky, Leon (1879–1940): Leading Bolshevik and Red Army commander, born Lev Davidovitch Bronshteyn.

Trumpeldor, Yosef (1880–1920): Zionist leader and veteran of the Russo-Japanese war, killed in an Arab attack on the Tel Hai settlement in the Upper Galilee in 1920.

Tsenerene: (from *"tse'enah ure'enah,"* Song of Songs 3:11) Yiddish rendering of the Pentateuch (together with the weekly readings from the Prophets and the "five scrolls" read at certain points in the Jewish year), composed near the end of the sixteenth century by Jacob ben Isaac Ashkenazi of Yanov (1550–1624/25).

Twenty-Five Point Program: The Nazi Party's program promulgated in 1920, which, among other things, promised to push the Jews out of German life.

Tzaddik (Hebrew, "righteous man"): A term that appeared frequently in Jewish literature before the rise of Hasidism (*see entry*) to denote pious ascetics. Under Hasidism, the authority of the charismatic *tzaddik* replaced that of normative rabbinic leaders.

Ugarit: An ancient Syrian city-state that flowered in the fourteenth and thirteenth centuries BCE. Extant Ugaritic literature contains stories about various Canaanite gods, such as El, Asherah, and Baal.

Ummayad Caliphate: With its capital in Damascus, this dynasty established the first Islamic empire, which lasted from 661–750. A remnant of the dynasty ruled Spain until the eleventh century.

Union of American Hebrew Congregations (UAHC): Founded in 1873 by Rabbi Isaac Mayer Wise (1819–1900) of Cincinnati to provide a central coordinating body for Jewish religious and communal institutions.

Union of Lublin: Treaty that created the Polish–Lithuanian Commonwealth (*see* Poland–Lithuania) in 1569.

United Hebrew Charities: Philanthropic association founded in New York in 1874.

Usque, Samuel: Iberian Jewish author of a historical work, "Consolation for the Tribulations of Israel" (in Portuguese), published at Ferrara in 1553.

Varnhagen, Rahel Levin (1771–1833): German Jewish intellectual who operated a salon at her home in Berlin, where Christian and Jewish poets, authors, philosophers, and political figures met.

Venice: Northern Italian city on the Adriatic. A dominant maritime power, which controlled much of the Mediterranean trade, from the Renaissance until the seventeenth century. The Venetian republic allowed Jews to settle in the city temporarily to engage in moneylending in the fourteenth century. Sephardi and other Jews arrived in larger numbers in the sixteenth century; in 1516, the first "ghetto" was established in Venice.

Vespasian: Born in 9 CE, Vespasian was a senator and successful military commander who subjugated Judea during the Jewish rebellion of 66. He ruled as emperor from 69 until his death in 79, having seized control from Vitellius in the "Year of the Four Emperors" that followed Nero's suicide. He was succeeded by his eldest son, Titus (*see entry*).

Vilna Gaon: *See* Rabbi Eliyahu ben Shlomo Zalman.

Vital, Haim (1543–1620): A member of the circle of Isaac Luria (*see entry*) in Safed (*see entry*), Vital is our main source of knowledge about the former's teachings. He regarded himself as Luria's preeminent student.

Vogelsang, Karl von (1818–1890): Austrian Catholic intellectual who held Jews responsible for the exploitation and impoverishment of peasants, artisans, and industrial workers.

Wald, Lillian (1867–1940): Jewish nurse who fought for improvements in public health, nursing, housing reform, suffrage, and the rights of women, children, immigrants, and working people.

Wannsee Conference: A ninety-minute meeting held on January 20, 1942, during which Reinhard Heydrich (*see entry*) informed representatives of the German government, Nazi Party, and police officials of the plans for a "Final Solution" to the "Jewish problem." Heydrich declared that in the course of the "practical execution of the final solution," Europe would be "combed through from west to east," in search of the continent's eleven million Jews.

Warburg, Otto (1859–1938): Botanist, industrial agriculture expert, and leader of the World Zionist Organization from 1911–1920.

War of Attrition (1968–1970): Israel's fourth war, a low-intensity conflict in which Egypt attempted to expel Israel from the Sinai.

War of Independence: The war that broke out with the attack of the Arab armies one day after David Ben-Gurion and the Zionist leadership declared the independence of the State of Israel on May 14, 1948.

War Refugee Board: An organization set up by President Roosevelt in 1944 to negotiate with foreign governments, even enemy ones, to rescue Jews. In reality, its efforts were thwarted at every turn, and yet the board was able to save some 200,000 Jews.

Warsaw Ghetto Uprising (April 1943): Uprising by Jews that took place as the Germans entered to liquidate the Warsaw ghetto on Passover, April 19, 1943. It was organized in the wake of the September 1942 mass deportations, which had depopulated the ghetto and eliminated hope for most.

Warsaw Jewish Flying University: A cultural and social institution opened by Jewish dissidents in Poland in the second half of the 1970s.

Weinreich, Max (1893–1969): Distinguished linguist, historian of the Yiddish language, and one of the founders of YIVO (*see entry*).

Weizmann, Chaim (1874–1952): Leader of the Democratic Faction (*see entry*) among early Zionists and later the first president of the State of Israel.

Wessely, Naftali Herz (1725–1805): A Maskil or Jewish enlightener known for his 1782 Hebrew tract, *Divrei shalom ve-emet* (*Words of Peace and Truth*), which was published without rabbinic approbation and elicited fiery protests from many rabbis, who believed its promotion of secular education was a call to assimilation.

White Paper of 1939: Policy paper issued by the British government that rejected the idea of partitioning the British Mandate in Palestine, instead advocating the creation of an independent Palestine governed by Arabs and Jews according to their share of the population. It set a limit of 75,000 Jewish immigrants for the period from 1940 to 1944.

Wisdom of Ben Sira: Also known in Greek as Ecclesiasticus, text by a sage named Jesus ben Sira written around 200 BCE.

Wolfssohn, David (1856–1914): Leader of the World Zionist Organization from 1905–1911. Member of the General Zionists faction.

Writings: The section of the Jewish Bible that includes Psalms, Proverbs, and Ezra–Nehemiah among other writings.

Written Torah: The rabbinic sages had come to believe that the Torah revealed to Moses had two forms; the written one was preserved in the Bible, while the Oral Torah (*see entry*) was transmitted by the sages.

Yavneh: The coastal town in Judea where Rabbi Yohanan ben Zakkai established the first center of rabbinic learning after the destruction of the Second Temple.

Yeshiva (pl. yeshivot): Rabbinic academy.

Yeshiva University: Premier institution for the training of men for the modern Orthodox rabbinate; it began as the Yeshiva Isaac Elchanan in 1896, on the Lower East Side in New York.

Yevsektsia: The Jewish Section of the Russian Communist Party, which by the 1920s had systematically closed down about 1,000 Hebrew schools and 650 synagogues and religious schools.

YHWH: The tetragrammaton (four-letter word), regarded as unpronounceable by many religious believers today, that denotes the name of God in the Bible (alongside other designations, such as *El* and *Elohim*) and in rabbinic literature.

Yiddish: Emerging around the year 1000, it was first the spoken language of the Ashkenazi Jews in northern France and the Rhineland. Like the Spanish Jews who took their Judeo–Spanish language with them when they moved to the Ottoman Empire, the Ashkenazi Jews preserved their Yiddish language after they had moved to Poland–Lithuania, although it underwent significant changes. By the twentieth century, Yiddish had become the most widely spoken Jewish language in history. On the eve of World War II there were between eleven and thirteen million Yiddish speakers worldwide.

YIVO: The Yiddish acronym for the Yiddish Scientific Institute, the major institution for the study of Yiddish and East European Jewish history and culture. Officially founded in Berlin in 1925 but headquartered in Vilna.

Yohanan ben Zakkai: Founding figure of rabbinic Judaism renowned for his escape from Jerusalem, then besieged by the rebels, inside a coffin carried by his disciples. Yohanan predicted that Vespasian, then a general, would become emperor.

Yom Kippur War (1973): The fifth Arab–Israeli war, which began on Yom Kippur (October 6) at 2:00 P.M. and caught the country completely by surprise. Though Israel eventually prevailed against Egypt and Syria, it suffered enormous losses with over 2,500 dead, 5,500 wounded, and 294 taken prisoner.

Yossipon: An anonymous account of the Second Temple period that relies heavily on the histories of Josephus, from whom its name derives.

Yung Vilne ("Young Vilna"): Yiddish literary group founded in 1929 in Vilna (today's Vilnius, capital of Lithuania), then part of Poland. Its leaders were the poets Abraham Sutzkever, Chaim Grade, and Leyzer Wolf.

Zamenhof, Ludwik Lazar (1859–1917): Jewish dentist from Bialystok who created Esperanto, a language that was easy to learn and designed to become a universal second language. Zamenhof's ultimate hope was that Esperanto would promote peace and international understanding.

Zamoyski, Jan (1542–1605): Polish magnate and lessor of estates to Jews. He owned eleven towns and more than two hundred villages.

Zederbaum, Alexander (1816–1893): Founder of the ideological movement of Yiddishism, in Russia in the 1860s.

Zegota: The Council for Aid to Jews set up by Left-wing, Polish political parties in 1942, which received help from the Polish government-in-exile.

Zenon documents: Collection of letters written by a Ptolemaic official named Zenon, an aide to a finance minister of Ptolemy II, who toured Palestine in 259–258 BCE. The documents provide a picture of the Ptolemaic king's control over the province.

Zhitlovsky, Chaim (1865–1943): Philosopher, literary critic, political activist, and architect of secular Yiddish culture.

Zion: The mountain where Yahweh's temple in Jerusalem was located.

Zionism: A modern international movement that began in the nineteenth century and advocated for the establishment of a national homeland in Palestine for the Jewish people and later refers to support for the state of Israel.

Zohar (*The Book of Splendor*): The central work of Jewish mysticism or Kabbalah, attributed to the second-century rabbinic sage Shimon bar Yochai, but probably composed by the thirteenth-century Spanish–Jewish mystic Moses de Leon (*see entry*). It treats the Five Books of Moses as a coded story of God, who is Himself unknowable and infinitely mysterious, and his *sefirot,* the emanations by which He is revealed in the world.

Zunz, Leopold (1794–1886): German Jewish historian and philologist, a founder of the Society for Culture and the Scientific Study of the Jews, editor of the *Journal for the Science of Judaism,* whose preeminent scholarly work was *Sermons of the Jews* (1832).

Zyklon B: The deadly cyanide-based insecticide used in the gas chambers of the Nazi death camps.

Text Credits

Photo Credits

Chapter 1
Page 8, ANCIENT ART & ARCHITECTURE / DanitaDelimont.com; **Page 13,** © Z. Radovan, Jerusalem; **Page 18,** Zev Radovan; **Page 21** (left), © Z. Radovan, Jerusalem; **Page 21** (right), North Wind Picture Archives.

Chapter 2
Page 29, ANCIENT ART & ARCHITECTURE / DanitaDelimont.com; **Page 32,** The Code of Hammurabi, 1792-1750 BCE Engraved black basalt stele. 1st Babylonian dynasty, 1st half of 18th BCE. Originally from Babylon, found in Susa. Location: Louvre, Paris, France. Erich Lessing / Art Resource, NY; **Page 44,** Zev Radovan.

Chapter 3
Page 50, Dagli Orti (A)/ Picture Desk, Inc./Kobal Collection; **Page 58,** © Z. Radovan, Jerusalem; **Page 61,** PHOTOMONDO/ Getty Images, Inc. – Taxi; **Page 65,** © Z. Radovan, Jerusalem.

Chapter 4
Page 73, Foto Vasari/ Index Ricerca Iconografica; **Page 79,** Israel Ministry of Tourism, North America; **Page 80,** © The Trustees of the British Museum; **Page 85,** © Z. Radovan, Jerusalem.

Chapter 5
Page 94, ANCIENT ART & ARCHITECTURE / DanitaDelimont.com; **Page 96,** © The Trustees of the British Museum; **Page 101,** © Z. Radovan, Jerusalem; **Page 114,** Paul Chesley/Getty Images Inc. - Stone Allstock.

Chapter 6
Page 8 (top), Maimonides' Guide of the Perplexed (Dalalat al-ha'irin), T-S 10 K A 4.1 recto. Reproduced by kind permission of the Syndics of Cambridge University Library; **Page 8** (bottom), Erich Lessing/Art Resource, N.Y; **Page 130,** Linda Whitwam © Dorling Kindersley; **Page 140,** John Efron - Steve Weitzman.

Chapter 7
Page 149, Knud Petersen/Art Resource/Bildarchiv Preussischer Kulturbesitz; **Page 155,** Art Resource/Bildarchiv Preussischer Kulturbesitz; **Page 159,** Ruth Schact/Art Resource/Bildarchiv Preussischer Kulturbesitz; **Page 169,** Israel Museum Jerusalem.

Chapter 8
Page 177, National Archives of Canada; **Page 181,** Getty Images/De Agostini Editore Picture Library; **Page 186,** Rabbi Abraham Levy/Lebrecht Music & Arts Photo Library; **Page 187,** Rabbi Abraham Levy/Lebrecht Music & Arts Photo Library; **Page 188,** Rabbi Abraham Levy/Lebrecht Music & Arts Photo Library; **Page 195,** Bibliotheque Nationale, Paris, France/The Bridgeman Art Library.

Chapter 9
Page 209, Art Resource/Bildarchiv Preussischer Kulturbesitz; **Page 215,** Wikemedia Commons; **Page 224,** Getty Images Inc. - Hulton Archive Photos; **Page 227,** The Library of The Jewish Theological Seminary.

Map Credits

Map 4-1: Adapted from www.thejournal.org/studylibrary/maps/greatest-extent-of-roman-empire.htlm

Map 8-1: Adapted from "Sephardim," in *Encyclopedia Judaica,* vol. 18, 2nd ed., ed. Michael Berenbaum and Fred Skolnik. (Detroit: Macmillan Reference USA, 2007), p. 293.

Maps 6-1, 6-2, 6-3, 7-1, 7-2, 8-1, 10-1, 12-1: Adapted from "Martin Gilbert," in *The Routledge Atlas of Jewish History.* (Routledge, 2006).

Map 11-1: Adapted from "Eli Barnavi," in *A Historical Atlas of the Jewish People : From the Time of the Patriarchs to the Present.* (New York : Knopf ; Distributed by Random House, 1992).

Maps 13-1, 14-1, and 15-1: Adapted from www.ushmm.org.

Index